LAW FOR BUSINESS

EIGHTH EDITION

LAW FOR BUSINESS

A. JAMES BARNES, J.D.

TERRY MOREHEAD DWORKIN, J.D.

ERIC L. RICHARDS, J.D.

All of Indiana University

McGraw-Hill Irwin

Boston   Burr Ridge, IL   Dubuque, IA   Madison, WI   New York   San Francisco   St. Louis
Bangkok   Bogotá   Caracas   Kuala Lumpur   Lisbon   London   Madrid   Mexico City
Milan   Montreal   New Delhi   Santiago   Seoul   Singapore   Sydney   Taipei   Toronto

McGraw-Hill

A Division of The McGraw·Hill Companies

LAW FOR BUSINESS
Published by McGraw-Hill/Irwin, a business unit of The McGraw-Hill Companies, Inc., 1221 Avenue of the Americas, New York, NY, 10020.
Copyright © 2003, 2000, 1997, 1994, 1991, 1987, 1983, 1980 by The McGraw-Hill Companies, Inc. All rights reserved. No part of this
publication may be reproduced or distributed in any form or by any means, or stored in a database or retrieval system, without the prior
written consent of The McGraw-Hill Companies, Inc., including, but not limited to, in any network or other electronic storage or
transmission, or broadcast for distance learning.
Some ancillaries, including electronic and print components, may not be available to customers outside the United States.

This book is printed on acid-free paper.

1 2 3 4 5 6 7 8 9 0 DOW/D0W 0 9 8 7 6 5 4 3 2

ISBN 0-07-248826-3

Publisher: *John E. Biernat*
Senior sponsoring editor: *Andy Winston*
Editorial coordinator: *Sara E. Ramos*
Marketing manager: *Lisa Nicks*
Producer, Media technology: *Jennifer Becka*
Project manager: *Catherine R. Schultz*
Senior production supervisor: *Michael R. McCormick*
Coordinator freelance design: *Mary L. Christianson*
Supplement producer: *Joyce J Chappetto*
Cover and display pages photograph: © *Jules Frazier/Getty Images, Inc.*
Typeface: *10/12 Cheltenham Light*
Compositor: *GAC/Indianapolis*
Printer: *R. R. Donnelley & Sons Company*

Library of Congress Cataloging-in-Publication Data

Barnes, A. James.
    Law for business / A. James Barnes, Terry Morehead Dworkin, Eric L. Richards.—8th ed.
        p.   cm
    Includes index.
    ISBN 0-07-248826-3 (alk. paper)
    1. Commercial law—United States. 2. Trade regulation—United States. 3. Business
law—United States. I. Dworkin, Terry Morehead. II. Richards, Eric L. III. Title.
KF889.B28 2003
346.7307—dc21   2002067168

www.mhhe.com

PREFACE

For more than 20 years, *Law for Business* has set the standard as an easy-to-read textbook that provides students the tools for understanding the legal environment of business. The text goes well beyond merely identifying the current legal rules and regulations affecting business by offering insights into new developments and trends that will greatly affect the future of business. The result is a comprehensive yet concise treatment of the legal issues of fundamental importance to business students and the business profession.

We have been very pleased with the number of institutions—and instructors—representing a wide range of programs in business that continue to adopt *Law for Business*. The feedback from faculty and students alike confirms that they particularly like the clear exposition, the careful selection and editing of high-interest cases, and the attractive and readable design.

In preparing the eighth edition of *Law for Business*, we have tried to maintain the strengths of past editions while updating the material and cases and slightly reducing its length. The most significant change in content is in the Secured Transactions chapter (Chapter 41), which incorporates Revised Article 9 now that it has been adopted in each state.

Other features—maintained from previous editions—that keep *Law for Business* on the cutting edge of business law/legal environment textbooks include the following:

PEDAGOGY

To assist students in their comprehension and critical analysis of the sometimes complex topics discussed in any business law course, we have employed a number of proven pedagogical devices.

Case Videos—Adopters of the eighth edition can obtain Irwin's case videos to supplement classroom instruction. The videos (20 segments in all) portray common business law issues. Portions of the case videos are integrated into the problem cases in many of the chapters.

Business Law and the Marketplace—Also available is a set of documentary-style segments (real-world situations) featuring real companies and situations involving torts, contracts, employment law, and many other important business law topics.

Chapter Openers—Most chapters begin with the issues related to a high-interest case and a list of questions or issues introducing the reader to the concepts presented in the chapter.

Concept Summaries—These outlines, figures, or drawings are presented throughout each chapter to reinforce important or difficult concepts.

Visual Illustrations—Flowcharts and other visual illustrations have been inserted in each chapter to facilitate student understanding of key topics.

Icons in the margins—These allow students to quickly identify material that relates to international business and computer law.

CASES

The textual material is supplemented by current, high-interest cases decided by state and federal courts. The cases have been selected to demonstrate a practical application of the important legal concepts introduced in the chapter. While the cases are brief, they provide enough facts and analysis to clearly illustrate the law in action. To reduce confusion, each case is placed immediately after the textual point it discusses. Multi-issue cases are sometimes presented in several sections to permit the isolation of issues to simplify analysis.

INTERNET LAW

Chapter 48, renamed Internet Law, enables students to better understand the current rules governing the Internet and provides insights so they can more accurately identify future regulatory efforts and consider the implications for business. As noted above, icons throughout the book provide easy identification of cases and material concerning the Internet.

ETHICS

We assist student understanding of the ethical issues confronting business managers through the inclusion of brief "Ethical Implications" throughout the book. These comments, questions, and cases permit students to more fully appreciate the complex and pervasive nature of the ethical issues they will encounter in the business world.

INTERNATIONAL FOCUS

Chapter 47 of the text exclusively concerns the legal issues confronting businesses that venture into the international environment. This global approach is supplemented by separate International Business Perspective features in the other chapters (indicated by the globe icon) that introduces concepts with international implications.

SUPPLEMENTS PACKAGE

Instructor's Manual.   The authors have prepared an instructor's manual providing insights into the major topics introduced in each chapter. Every case is briefly summarized and accompanied by a "Points for Discussion" section that poses ideas for classroom discussion. This manual also includes the answers to all of the Questions and Problem Cases that appear in text, as well as references to appropriate places within the chapter to discuss particular end-of-chapter cases.

Test Bank.   The Test Bank has been enhanced. It contains true-false, multiple choice, and short essay questions with answers and a difficulty rating.

Computest.   A computerized version of the test bank also is available. It allows you to generate random tests and add your own questions.

Online Learning Center at www.mhhe.com/barnes8e.   The website also includes resources for both instructors and students, such as PowerPoint slides, flashcards, and links to websites where students who want to explore topics in more detail can readily do so.

PowerPoint Electronic Acetates.   More than 200 PowerPoint slides have been created for use in classroom lectures. These slides refer back to figures and concept summaries from the text and provide original material not found anywhere else.

Student Study Guide.   The print Student Study Guide features significantly enhanced content that gives students additional practice reviewing the major concepts in each chapter and preparing for exams. It includes learning objectives, learning hints, and true-false, multiple choice, and short essay questions.

ACKNOWLEDGMENTS

We wish to thank the many adopters of our prior editions; we have greatly profited from their suggestions. Of course, we have had to use our judgment in determining which ones to follow. Accordingly, responsibility for any shortcomings in this edition remains ours. We do solicit the comments and criticism of instructors and students who use this edition.

The following reviewers provided ideas and insights for this edition. We appreciate their contributions.

Laurence C. Aaronson, Community College of Baltimore County

Theodore M. Dinges, Longview Community College

Edward C. Goldberg, West Virginia State College

Howard R. Hunnius, John Tyler Community College

Jacqueline Middleton, Montgomery College

Scott E. Miller, Gannon University

We also acknowledge the assistance of the following individuals at Indiana University who facilitated the preparation of the manuscript: Sarah Jane Hughes, Marlys Shields, Lori Kale, and Thomas Snider.

A. James Barnes
Terry Morehead Dworkin
Eric L. Richards

ABOUT THE AUTHORS

A. James Barnes, J.D., is Professor of Public and Environmental Affairs and Adjunct Professor of Law at Indiana University in Bloomington. He previously served as Dean of the School of Public and Environmental Affairs (SPEA). His teaching interests include environmental law, alternative dispute resolution, law and public policy, and ethics and the public official. He has written, testified, and spoken extensively on environmental issues and has considerable international experience dealing with environmental officials in other countries. He currently consults on a variety of environmental matters.

From 1985 to 1988, Professor Barnes served as the deputy administrator of the U.S. Environmental Protection Agency. As the agency's number two official, he gained extensive experience in environmental policy making and administration. From 1983 to 1985, he was the EPA General Counsel, and in the early 1970s participated in the formation of EPA and served as the chief of staff to its first administrator, William D. Ruckelshaus.

Professor Barnes also served as a trial attorney for the U.S. Department of Justice and as general counsel of the U.S. Department of Agriculture from 1981 to 1983, where he dealt with a wide variety of public policy issues, including environmental issues involving the Forest Service, Soil and Conservation Service, and federal agriculture programs. For six years, from 1975 to 1981, he had a commercial and environmental law practice with the firm of Beveridge and Diamond in Washington, D.C.

Terry Morehead Dworkin, J.D., is the Jack R. Wentworth Professor and codirector of the Center for International Business Education and Research (CIBER) at Indiana University in Bloomington. She was the Resident Director for the Program in European Studies at the Center for European Studies, Rijksuniversiteit Limburg in Maastricht, The Netherlands.

Professor Dworkin's primary research interests focus on employment issues, particularly discrimination, whistleblowing, and privacy. She is an author of numerous articles on employment law, corporate compliance, and product liability law and of two books on business law. Several of her publications have an international focus.

Professor Dworkin has had significant international experience in the last few years including presenting a workshop on harassment at the UN/NGO Forum on Women in Beijing; spending a semester at the Institute for Advanced Legal Studies in London, followed by six weeks in Kiel, Germany; and presenting papers in Austria, the Czech Republic, England, and Germany. She has given several invited lectures on issues of international ethics and management.

Eric L. Richards, J. D., is Associate Professor of Business Law at Indiana University. Professor Richards has taught a wide variety of law courses at both the graduate and undergraduate levels including personal law, international law, the legal environment of business, and commercial law. His research interests have resulted in scholarly publications exploring antitrust law, the first amendment, international trade law, and environmental issues. For the past 20 years he has been on the faculty of the Kelley School of Business at Indiana University. Prior to that he was an Assistant Professor at Kansas University for two years.

During his academic career, Professor Richards has been awarded numerous university and national awards for both his teaching and his research. He also has owned and operated his own business—a martial arts school—for more than 20 years.

CONTENTS IN BRIEF

TABLE OF CONTENTS

CHAPTER 25
Formation and Termination of Corporations 432

CHAPTER 26
Management of the Corporate Business 457

CHAPTER 48
Internet Law   959

APPENDIXES   985

CASE LIST

*Cases ending with asterisks were in last edition but were not included in Case List. They are *not* "new" cases.

LAW FOR BUSINESS

PART I

Introduction to the Law

CHAPTER 1

Law and Its Sources

In an attempt to clean up its red-light district, New York City passed a law designed to banish strip clubs and sex shops from most of its neighborhoods. However, a lawyer for a topless nightclub discovered that the ordinance specifically targeted "adult" establishments. Accordingly, the nightclub opened its doors to minors. A state supreme court justice ruled that the nightclub is not violating the law, saying the club "cannot be defined as an adult eating and drinking establishment if it does not exclude minors." Calling the decision "one of the jerkiest rulings I've ever seen," New York's mayor accused the judge of ignoring the intent of the law, which prohibits sex-oriented theaters, bookstores, and clubs from operating within 500 feet of homes, daycare centers, and schools. The city's lawyers explained that the "adults-only" language was included in the law so it would not interfere with legitimate theatrical performances.[1]

- *What are the basic functions of the law?*
- *Which of those functions was this ordinance designed to promote?*
- *How do judges determine whether behavior violates a law?*
- *What options are available to the city now that the judge has ruled that the nightclub has not violated the ordinance?*

---

[1] "New York Strip Club Admits Children," *Bloomington Herald-Times*, Nov. 7, 1998, p. A5.

.... *INTRODUCTION* ....

When you think of law, what images come to mind? Some people think of police officers, while others see courts or lawyers. Many people view law as a regulation or some other command from the government. Each of these perceptions is at least partially accurate because each is part of our legal system.

Law is an important component of our culture. Like language, it reflects the values, history, and current problems shaping society. A true understanding of our society requires a basic comprehension of the nature and function of our legal system. In recent years, the need to understand the legal system has grown in importance. This is reflected in the tremendous increase in the use of lawyers and the corresponding growth in the number of lawyers.

LAW IN BUSINESS

Effective managers and employees must develop a knowledge of both law and business because people involved in business also are involved in, and greatly affected by, the law concerning business. With each passing day this link between law and business grows even stronger.

CHAPTER OVERVIEW

This introductory chapter begins by investigating the essential features of law and our legal system. Then, after considering several fundamental classifications of law, we turn our attention to the constitutional underpinnings of the American legal system. This discussion is followed by an introduction to the primary sources of law and a look at how courts decide cases. We then examine how law promotes orderly change. A brief survey of the predominant schools of legal philosophy in existence today follows. The chapter closes by introducing students to the importance of practicing preventive law.

.... *THE NATURE OF LAW* ....

We cannot fully understand the role of law in our lives without first identifying its fundamental nature. This requires a recognition that law is both a process and a product. This section introduces the process notion by considering what is meant by a legal system. It also examines the product idea with the formulation of a definition for the term "law." The section ends with an introduction to the basic functions served by law.

THE LEGAL SYSTEM

Legal philosophers and scholars do not agree on a single definition of "the law." The term is sometimes applied to a **legal system,** as when we speak of "the rule of law." Here we are referring to a political system in which all people within the system, including the most powerful leaders, are required to follow the rules called "the law." Furthermore, they are all answerable to the system of courts that applies that body of law. In the United States, the Constitution is the foundation of the legal system.

Our legal system involves processes for social control. It provides institutions such as legislatures and government agencies for the creation of rules of behavior. It also establishes police forces and courts to enforce the rules and resolve disputes.

LAW AS RULES

More commonly, when people speak of "law" they refer to the rules themselves. "The law says that you must . . ." is a phrase you often hear. This is the sense in which "the law" generally is used in this book. Accordingly, the following definition may be useful:

The law is a set of principles, rules, and standards of conduct that:

1. Have general application in a society.
2. Were developed by a legitimate authority for that society.
3. Trigger penalties when they are violated.

Law is seen in all societies. However, in some primitive societies where there is little change over time, the rules of behavior may not be consciously developed by the leaders or representatives of the society. Instead, they may be handed down as custom from earlier generations. But they apply to all of the society, or at least to all of a certain class of people within the society. And various penalties are meted out to those who break the rules.

Some people give the term "a law" a more limited meaning. They use it to describe the rules (statutes) enacted by legislatures. However, as we shall see, legislatures are only one source of law. There are numerous other ways in which law is created.

FUNCTIONS OF LAW

The basic functions of law are:

1. Keeping the peace.
2. Enforcing standards of conduct and maintaining order.
3. Facilitating planning.
4. Promoting social justice.

Several years ago, the state of Texas outlawed desecration of the flag for two reasons. First, it argued that flag-burning incidents are likely to provoke anger and disruptive behavior in the audience. Second, it wished to preserve the flag as a symbol of nationhood and national unity. These rationales seem to invoke the peacekeeping and maintenance-of-order functions. The city ordinance in the chapter opener was designed to enforce certain standards of moral conduct.

The first two functions—*keeping the peace* and *enforcing standards of conduct and maintaining order*—help further another function of law that is especially important: *facilitating planning.* Contract law is an example of this function. In making the courts available to enforce contracts, the legal system ensures that parties to contracts either carry out their promises or pay for the damages they cause. For example, through contracts, a manufacturing company can count on either receiving the raw materials and machinery it has ordered or else getting money from the contracting supplier to cover the extra expense of buying substitutes.

While all societies use law to keep peace and maintain order, societies such as ours also use the law to achieve additional goals. The tax laws, for example, seek not only to raise revenue for government expenditure but also to redistribute wealth by imposing higher inheritance and income taxes on wealthy people. The antitrust laws seek to prevent certain practices that might reduce competition and thus increase prices.

CONCEPT SUMMARY	The Nature of Law
Definition	**Functions of Law**
A set of principles, rules, and standards of conduct that:	Keeping the peace
1. Have general application in the society	Enforcing standards of conduct and maintaining order
2. Have been developed by an authority for that society	Facilitating planning
3. Have an associated penalty imposed upon violations	Promoting social justice

Consumer laws have a wide range of purposes from prohibiting the sale of unsafe products to providing more information to shoppers.

The function of these statutes is to *promote social justice* by protecting the disadvantaged. Courts, in applying the law, also seem to be seeking to balance the scales to benefit the "little guy" in dealing with big business, big labor, and big government. Helping the ordinary citizen to deal with a very complex and quite impersonal economy also is the objective of the federal legislation establishing social security, welfare, housing, and medical programs.

. . . . **CLASSIFICATIONS OF LAW** . . . .

There are many ways to subdivide the law. One is to distinguish between substantive law and procedural law. Another important distinction is between criminal and civil law. This section examines these legal classifications.

SUBSTANTIVE VERSUS PROCEDURAL LAW

Substantive law sets out the rights and duties governing people as they act in society. *Duties* tend to take the form of a command: "Do this!" or "Don't do that!" An example is the Civil Rights Act of 1964. It tells employers that they must not discriminate among people in hiring and employment on the basis of race, color, religion, sex, or national origin.

Substantive law also establishes *rights and privileges.* An example is the freedom of speech granted by the U.S. Constitution. Another is the right you have to defend yourself if physically attacked—the so-called right of self-defense. A slightly different example is the privilege of receiving food stamps if you meet the qualifications set up by Congress.

Procedural law establishes the rules under which the substantive rules of law are enforced. Rules as to what cases a court can decide, how a trial is conducted, and how a judgment by a court is to be enforced are all part of procedural law. Consider the following case, which illustrates the overlap between substantive and procedural law. Be certain to identify when the court is dealing with substantive law and when it is examining procedural law. Simultaneously, consider how the growth of the Internet has brought about clashes between the substantive and legal rules of differing nations.

YAHOO! V. LA LIGUE CONTRE LE RACISME ET L'ANTISEMITISME
169 F.Supp.3d 1181 (N.D. Cal. 2001)

C O M P U T E R *law*   INTERNATIONAL
                                          business

FACTS

Yahoo! is a U.S. corporation and an Internet service provider that operates various Internet websites and services that any computer user can access. Yahoo! subsidiary corporations operate regional Yahoo! sites and services in 20 other nations, including France. Yahoo!'s regional sites use the local region's primary language, target the local citizenry, and operate under local laws. Yahoo!'s auction site allows anyone to post an item for sale and solicit bids from any computer user from around the globe. Yahoo! is never a party to a transaction, and the buyer and seller are responsible for arranging privately for payment and shipment of goods. Yahoo! informs auction sellers that they may not offer items to buyers in jurisdictions in which the sale of such an item violates the jurisdiction's applicable laws. However, Yahoo! does not actively regulate the content of each posting, and individuals have in fact posted highly offensive matter, including Nazi-related propaganda and Third Reich memorabilia, on Yahoo!'s auction sites. La Ligue Contre Le Racisme Et l'Antisemitisme (LICRA), a French nonprofit organization dedicated to eliminating anti-Semitism, asked a French court to issue a cease and desist order against Yahoo! because it discovered the sale of Nazi and Third Reich related goods through Yahoo!'s auction sites in violation of French law. The French court ordered Yahoo! to render impossible any access via Yahoo.com to Nazi auction services or any site or service that may be construed as an apology for Nazism or a contesting of Nazi crimes to French citizens. The order subjected the company to a penalty of 100,000 Euros for each day that it failed to comply. Yahoo! claims that because it lacks the technology to block French citizens from accessing its auction site to view materials that violate the French order, it cannot comply with the French order without banning Nazi-related material from Yahoo.com altogether. It contends that, because such a ban would infringe impermissibly upon its First Amendment right to speak under the U.S. Constitution, the U.S. district court should issue a declaratory judgment holding that the French court's order is not enforceable under the laws of the United States.

ISSUE

Will the U.S. court issue a declaratory judgment holding the French order unenforceable in the United States?

DECISION

Yes. This case presents novel and important issues arising from the global reach of the Internet. Indeed, the specific facts implicate issues of policy, politics, and culture that are beyond the purview of one nation's judiciary. Thus, it is critical that the court define at the outset what is and is not at stake in the present proceeding. This case is *not* about the moral acceptability of promoting the symbols or propaganda of Nazism. Nor is this case about the right of France or any other nation to determine its own law and social policies. France clearly has the right to enact and enforce laws such as the French order at issue here. What *is* at issue here is whether it is consistent with the Constitution and laws of the United States for another nation to regulate speech by a U.S. resident within the United States on the basis that such speech can be accessed by Internet users in that nation. In a world in which ideas and information transcend borders and the Internet in particular renders the physical distance between speaker and audience virtually meaningless, the implications of this question go far beyond the facts of this case. The modern world is home to widely varied cultures with radically divergent value systems. There is little doubt that Internet users in the United States routinely engage in speech that violates, for example, China's laws against religious expression or the laws of various nations against advocacy of gender equality. If the government or another party in one of these sovereign nations were to seek enforcement of such laws against Yahoo! or another U.S.-based Internet service provider, what principles should guide the court's analysis? This court must and will decide this case in accordance with the Constitution and laws of the United States. It recognizes that in so doing, it necessarily adopts certain value judgments embedded in those enactments, including the fundamental judgment expressed in the First Amendment that it is preferable to permit the nonviolent expression of offensive viewpoints rather than to impose viewpoint-based governmental regulation upon speech. The government and people of France have made a different judgment based upon their own experience. In undertaking its inquiry as to the proper application of the laws of the United States, the Court intends no disrespect for that judgment or for the

(continued)

YAHOO! V. LA LIGUE CONTRE LE RACISME ET L'ANTISEMITISME
(concluded)

experience that has informed it. A declaratory judgment protects potential defendants from multiple actions by providing a means in which a court declares in one action the rights and obligations of the litigants. Declaratory judgment actions are justiciable only if there is a substantial controversy between parties having adverse legal interests of sufficient immediacy and reality to warrant the issuance of a declaratory judgment. The French order is valid under the laws of France, it may be enforced with retroactive penalties, and the ongoing possibility of its enforcement in the United States chills Yahoo!'s First Amendment rights. Thus, Yahoo! has shown that an actual controversy exists and that the threat to its constitutional rights is real and immediate. Accordingly, a declaratory judgment precluding enforcement of the French order in this country is warranted.

Ethical Implications	Can you think of an example of a duty imposed by substantive law that might violate some moral or ethical belief of an individual? How should such conflicts be resolved? Consider the following case. Two clinics operated in Fargo, North Dakota. One performed abortions while the other provided only pregnancy tests and antiabortion counseling services. However, the antiabortion clinic used a name similar to that of the abortion clinic in order to confuse the public into mistakenly contacting the wrong clinic. Further, it misled the public into believing that it performed abortions, and then, when women seeking abortions arrived, they were given antiabortion materials. After the antiabortion clinic started these tactics, there was a considerable decline in the abortion clinic's business. The jury found that the antiabortion clinic violated the state's false advertising statute.[2]

CRIMINAL VERSUS CIVIL LAW

Criminal law defines breaches of duty to society at large. It is society, through government employees called *prosecutors* (such as district attorneys), that brings court action against violators. If you are found guilty of a crime such as theft, you will be punished by imprisonment or a fine. When a fine is paid, the money generally goes to the state, not to the victim of the crime.

Private duties owed by one person (including corporations) to another are established by **civil law.** For example, we have a duty to carry out our contractual promises. Tort law defines a host of duties people owe to each other. One of the most common is a duty to exercise reasonable care with regard to others. Failure to do so is the tort of negligence.

Suit for the breach of a civil duty must be brought by the person wronged. Generally, the court does not seek to punish the wrongdoer but rather to make the wronged party whole through a money award called *damages.* For example, if someone carelessly runs a car into yours, that person has committed the civil wrong (tort) of negligence. If you have suffered a broken leg, you will be able to recover damages from the driver (or his or her insurance company). The damages will be an amount of money sufficient to repair your auto, to pay your medical bills, to pay for wages you have lost, and to give you something for any permanent disability such as a limp. Damages for "pain and suffering" also may be awarded.

Although the civil law generally does not aim to punish, there is an exception. If the behavior of someone who commits a tort is outrageous, that person can be made to

---

[2]Fargo Women's Health Organization v. FM Women's Help and Caring Connection, 444 N.W.2d 683 (N.D. Sup. Ct. 1989).

pay *punitive* damages (also called *exemplary damages*). Unlike a fine paid in a criminal case, punitive damages go to the injured party.

Sometimes, the same behavior can violate both the civil law and the criminal law. For instance, a person whose drunken driving causes the death of another may face both a criminal prosecution by the state and a civil suit for damages by the survivors of the victim. If both suits are successful, the driver would pay back society for the harm done with a criminal fine and/or prison sentence, and compensate the survivors with the payment of money damages.

See Table 1–1 for a general comparison of criminal and civil law cases.

TABLE 1–1   Criminal versus Civil Law

	Criminal Case	**Civil Case**
Elements	Intentional violation of a statute	Harm to another person or property (tort) or breach of a contract
Actors	Prosecutor v. Defendant (government) (accused)	Plaintiff v. Defendant (wronged party) (wrong party)
Punishment	Fines, imprisonment, execution	Defendant may have to pay the plaintiff compensatory and punitive damages

NEW YORK STATE NATIONAL ORGANIZATION FOR WOMEN V. TERRY
159 F. 3d 86 (2d Cir. 1998)

FACTS

A group of women's organizations, health care clinics, and abortion providers sought an injunction to restrain Randall Terry and Operation Rescue from blocking access to medical facilities that provided abortions. One day after the court issued a temporary restraining order (TRO) enjoining the defendants from trespassing on, or blocking access to, facilities that perform abortions, Terry violated the order during a demonstration outside an abortion clinic. The court then issued a new TRO that included coercive sanctions of $25,000 for each day defendants violated the order and required that they notify the city of New York in advance of the location of any future demonstrations. After defendants violated this order, the court adjudged Terry and Operation Rescue in civil contempt and held them jointly and severally liable for a $50,000 fine. In response to Terry's publicized plan to carry out more protests, the court converted the TRO into a preliminary injunction. When defendants threatened to block access again, the judge issued a permanent injunction that included a schedule of protective coercive sanctions for future violations. They would subject a violator to civil damages of $25,000 per day for the first vio-

lation. Each successive violation of the order subjected the violator to a civil contempt fine double that of the previous fine. In subsequent civil contempt proceedings, the court found that the defendants had violated the TRO, preliminary injunction, and permanent injunction on four separate dates. It fined Terry and Operation Rescue, jointly and severally, $100,000 payable to the United States, subject to a "purge provision" under which defendants could avoid both the contempt holding and the penalties if they obeyed the injunction and published an affirmation of intent to abide by its terms. Terry challenged the ruling on the ground that the contempt fines were criminal in nature and, therefore, could be imposed only with criminal procedural protections (i.e., a criminal jury trial).

ISSUE

Were the contempt fines criminal in nature?

DECISION

No. Whether a contempt is criminal or civil turns on the character and purpose of the sanction. Civil contempt

(continued)

NEW YORK STATE NATIONAL ORGANIZATION FOR WOMEN V. TERRY
(concluded)

fines seek one of two objectives. One is coercion—to force the violators to conform their conduct to the court's order. The second is compensation. Where the conduct has caused injury to the beneficiary of the court's order, a civil fine may be imposed on the violator to compensate the victim for the loss or harm caused by the unlawful conduct. Criminal fines, by contrast, are intended primarily to punish the wrongdoer and vindicate the authority of the court. A purge provision permits the violator to escape a fine by conforming his conduct to the court's order or by declaring an intention to do so. The absence of a purge provision means that the fine will be imposed regardless of reform and commitment to obey. A fine without a purge provision therefore suggests an intention to punish past misconduct rather than to ensure future lawfulness. The consideration of these factors in the context of this case leads to the conclusion that these fines are civil in nature, because their purpose is coercion. The court's contempt order includes a purge provision that excuses defendants from paying contempt fines. As for the size of the fines, while they are large enough to warrant concern with the adjudication process, they are nonetheless fully consistent with the court's coercive objective. Their size does not compel the conclusion that they are punitive and criminal in the face of the strong indications that the fines are designed to coerce compliance with the court's order, and may be escaped by the defendants if they conform their conduct.

.... *CONSTITUTIONAL FOUNDATIONS* ....

Although law is made and enforced by government, it also defines and organizes the government. To understand the American legal system, you need to be familiar with the constitutional foundation of American government. A very brief review is presented here.

CHECKS AND BALANCES

The original 13 colonies became sovereign (independent) nations after they won independence from England. Although people in each state were fearful their state might be dominated by other states with different interests, they came to realize the federal government needed more power than had been given to the Continental Congress. So, the founders set up a system of **checks and balances** between the powers of the states and those of the federal government. However, they also wrote the *supremacy clause* into the Constitution. It declares that where state laws conflict with legitimate federal laws, federal law shall prevail.

The founders also devised a system of checks and balances within the federal government. They established three equal branches of government—the legislative, executive, and judicial branches—which have different but complementary functions. As a check on the passage of statutes that might be ill advised, proposals will not become law unless the president and both houses of Congress approve them. A two-thirds majority is required in each house to override a veto by the president. Furthermore, Congress itself cannot enforce a statute; that is left to the executive and judicial branches. The initiative for enforcement must be taken by the executive branch—originally the attorney general.

Today, regulatory agencies take the lead in enforcing certain statutes. However, the executive must go to the judicial branch to punish violations of a statute. Also, it is this branch—the judicial—that interprets statutes and other sources of law.

CONSTITUTIONAL POWERS

Under the Constitution, laws enacted by Congress are invalid if the Constitution does not give Congress the power to pass that kind of legislation, or if the Constitution prohibits such a law. These restraints are also a part of the system of checks and balances.

Most federal regulations are based on power given to Congress under the Constitution's **commerce clause,** which permits Congress to regulate interstate and foreign commerce. Supreme Court decisions since the 1930s generally have interpreted that power very broadly. For example, the Civil Rights Acts were passed under the commerce clause power; so was the Clean Air Act.

The federal **taxing power** has been used to regulate business activities. For example, high import duties can be used to shut off the importation of certain foreign goods. In addition, the income tax laws (the Internal Revenue Code) are used to regulate behavior. When the government wishes to encourage certain kinds of investments, it offers tax credits.

CONSTITUTIONAL LIMITATIONS

Many prohibitions against government regulation are contained in the **Bill of Rights** (the first 10 amendments to the Constitution). These amendments guarantee certain rights to the people, including the familiar rights of free speech, freedom of religion, and the privilege against unreasonable search and seizure.

Judicial interpretations of the protections offered by the Constitution have varied throughout history. At one time the **due process clause** of the Fourteenth Amendment was construed to prohibit many types of business regulation by state governments. Its statement that a person's liberty shall not be taken without due process was interpreted to be a guaranty of almost total freedom of contract. Under this approach, judges regularly held state and federal regulations unconstitutional. Interpretations of the law change over time, however, and today few statutes regulating business activity are found to violate the due process clause.

FEDERALISM

Under the notion of **federalism** the United States is composed of 51 different legal systems. The Constitution established a federal government with limited powers rather than a national government. This variety of legal systems is part of the concept of checks and balances. There is a federal legal system, and each state has its own system. However, as noted earlier, when there is conflict between the two systems, the federal rules prevail. This, of course, assumes the federal government is acting under one of the powers granted to it by the Constitution (see Table 1–2).

SOURCES OF LAW

There are numerous sources of law within each of the 51 systems. The primary sources are:

1. Constitutions
2. Treaties
3. Statutes
4. Administrative rules and decisions
5. Executive orders
6. Court decisions
7. Private law

CONSTITUTIONS

The U.S. Constitution is the highest source of law in the United States. Every other form of law must be consistent with the Constitution or it will be struck down by the courts. Each state also has a constitution that is similar to the U.S. Constitution in the design of the government it provides. However, many of them are much more specific and

TABLE 1-2   The Constitution

An instrument of power	Congress can exercise powers only granted by the Constitution	Sources of regulatory power: Commerce Clause Taxing power
A symbol of restraint	Government power is restricted by the individual rights safeguarded by the Constitution	Sources of restraint: Various amendments (freedom of speech, freedom of religion, privilege against unreasonable search and seizure)

detailed. As a result, they are not as adaptable to changing conditions as the U.S. Constitution, and many have been completely rewritten one or more times. The U.S. Constitution, on the other hand, has had only 17 additional amendments in the more than 200 years since the adoption of the Bill of Rights.

Although state constitutions are subordinate to the U.S. Constitution, they are superior to law derived from other sources within the state. The importance of this will become clearer when the power of judicial review is discussed later in this chapter.

TREATIES

The Constitution declares that treaties made by the president with foreign governments, and ratified by at least two-thirds of the Senate, are "the supreme law of the land." They therefore may override acts of Congress or state legislatures and other laws that are inconsistent. However, conflicts of this sort seldom arise since the states may not make treaties with foreign countries.

STATUTES

Within each legal system, federal or state, statutes stand next in the hierarchy. A statute is the product of the lawmaking of a legislature. Statutes may add details to the government framework by establishing a regulatory agency or an agency to provide a public service. Or statutes may establish rules that govern certain kinds of activities, such as the use of automobiles on highways. The entire criminal law, the law applicable to sales of goods, and almost all law limiting or regulating business activities is **statutory law.**

Both Congress and the state legislatures enact a large number of statutes at every session. People tend to turn to Congress and/or the state legislatures to urge the passage of "a law" (statute) whenever they recognize a problem. This seems to be true whether it is primarily an economic problem (such as the dwindling availability of petroleum), a moral problem (such as sexual practices), or a health problem (such as misuse of drugs). Because there are 50 state legislatures, statutory law varies from state to state. There is a trend, however, to pass uniform laws in areas such as business where uniformity is seen as particularly important. The Uniform Commercial Code (UCC), which regulates a wide variety of commercial transactions, is the most widely adopted uniform law. The legislatures of all 50 states have enacted the Code in some form.

Governmental units within the states, such as cities and counties, also have the power to legislate. Their enactments are called **ordinances.** Local legislation regulating zoning and noise levels are examples of ordinances.

ADMINISTRATIVE RULES AND DECISIONS

Congress and the state legislatures can delegate some of their lawmaking power to a government agency. During the twentieth century many administrative agencies were established to regulate particular areas of activity. Businesses are heavily regulated in this manner. While states also establish agencies, our discussion focuses on the federal regulatory agencies.

Independent Agencies

The first federal regulatory agency was the Interstate Commerce Commission (ICC), which was organized by a statute passed in 1887. Congress has followed this model often in establishing other agencies. These are called **independent agencies** because they are not really part of the executive branch of the government under the control of the president. Rather, they are headed by a board or commission. Although the members are nominated by the president, approximately half of them must be from each major political party, and their appointment is confirmed by the Senate for fixed terms.

This type of regulatory agency is given authority by Congress both to make rules and to enforce them. Congress grants rule-making power to the agency instead of establishing detailed rules in statutes. It was believed that the agency members and staff would have greater expertise than Congress and would develop it further through regulatory experience. In addition, it was hoped that continuous regulatory supervision by the agency would be more adaptive to specific needs than reliance on legislation. An example of an agency that relies primarily on rule-making is the Securities and Exchange Commission, which issues rules and may go to the federal courts to enforce them.

Constitutionality of Agency Rules

To make its delegation of power constitutional, Congress must provide adequate standards or guidelines in the statute creating the agency. However, the Supreme Court has upheld some very broad delegations of rule-making power that contained extremely vague guidelines. If adequate guidelines are provided, rules issued by an agency have the same force as statutes passed by Congress.

Judicial Functions

A number of agencies also make law by deciding cases. Some of them regulate primarily on a case-by-case basis through their decisions. Here, the agency performs a quasi-judicial function. It is also, in effect, the prosecutor, since the agency staff decides whether or not to begin an enforcement action. If the agency enforces one of its own rules, it also is performing an executive function. This concentration of functions in a single agency was much criticized until passage of the Administrative Procedure Act of 1946, which requires a separation of the functions within the agency. Now, independent administrative law judges (ALJs) hear the evidence and make preliminary decisions. The agency board or commission then issues a final order. Such orders are appealable to, and enforced by, the federal courts. (See Table 1–3 for a summary of independent agencies.)

EXECUTIVE ORDERS

Congress or a state legislature also may delegate rule-making power to the president or a governor. Again, guidelines must be furnished. An example of an important **executive order** was President Franklin D. Roosevelt's 1943 order requiring all contracts for war supplies to include a clause prohibiting race discrimination. Like agency rules, executive orders have the force of law if they are within the authority granted by statute.

TABLE 1-3   Independent Agencies

Creation	Congress passes enabling legislation specifying the powers of the agency
Features	Headed by a board or commission Members nominated by president Appointments confirmed by Senate Appointees drawn from the two major political parties
Powers	Investigative Rule making Adjudicatory

COURT DECISIONS

Courts make law in three ways:

1. *Interpretation*—they determine the meaning of statutes, administrative rules, executive orders, and even treaties and constitutions.
2. *Common law*—They "find" or determine the law in settling disputes where none of the other sources of law appears to supply an applicable rule.
3. *Judicial review*—they review the constitutionality of the acts of the legislative and judicial branches.

Interpretation

Both federal and state courts make law by the first process—**interpretation.** The courts have the last word on what a legislature has said in a statute. Since many statutes are written in very broad and general language, the "power to interpret" is an important one. Of course, a court cannot say the legislature meant to establish a 65-mile-per-hour speed limit when the statute says 55. However, courts can decide if a statute applies to a specific case. This is especially important where the case involves a situation the legislature did not foresee when it passed the law. Through such interpretation courts can broaden or narrow the reach of a law.

In interpreting a statute, courts generally:

1. Look to the **plain meaning** of the statute's language.
2. Examine the **legislative history** of the statute.
3. Consider the **purpose** to be achieved by the statute.
4. Try to accommodate **public policy.**

Where a statute has been interpreted by a government agency, the courts traditionally defer to that interpretation if it seems reasonable. Think about the factors that influenced the court's interpretation of the city ordinance in the chapter opener.

COMPUTER

IN RE REALNETWORKS
2000 U.S. Dist. LEXIS 6584 (N.D. Ill. 2000)

FACTS

RealNetworks offers free basic versions of two products, RealPlayer and RealJukebox, for users to download from RealNetworks' site on the World Wide Web. These products allow users to see and hear audio and video available on the Internet and to download, record, and play music. Before a user can install either of these software packages, he or she must accept the terms of RealNetworks' End User Licence Agreement, which specifically requires that any unresolved disputes arising from the agreement must be submitted to arbitration in the

(continued)

In re RealNetworks

(concluded)

state of Washington. After using RealNetworks' products and consenting to the terms of the License Agreement, Michael Lieschke read a *New York Times* article, which stated that RealNetworks' products collected personal information about users' listening habits and places they had visited on the World Wide Web and sent the information to RealNetworks via the Internet. Lieschke then filed a lawsuit in Illinois against RealNetworks for trespass to property and privacy, alleging that the company's products allowed it to access and intercept his electronic communications and stored information without his knowledge or consent. RealNetworks asserted that the court lacked jurisdiction to decide the case because the License Agreement required the dispute to be arbitrated in Washington. However, Lieschke argued that the arbitration clause was not binding because federal law requires that agreements to arbitrate be written in order to be enforced. According to Lieschke, the License Agreement is an electronic agreement and electronic agreements do not satisfy the "written" agreements provisions of the Federal Arbitration Act.

Issue

Does the electronic License Agreement constitute a writing?

Decision

Yes. Both parties agree that Congress intended the Federal Arbitration Act to apply only to written contracts. Because the terms in the statute must be given their plain meaning and do not explicitly allow for an "electronic" agreement, Lieschke reasons that an electronic communication cannot satisfy the writing requirement. Although contract terms must be given their plain and ordinary meaning, the Court is unconvinced that the plain and ordinary meaning of "writing" or "written" necessarily cannot include any electronic writings. Courts frequently look to dictionaries in order to determine the plain meaning of words and particularly examine how a word was defined at the time the statute was drafted and

enacted. Webster's Dictionary defined "writing" as: *1. The act or art of forming letters or characters on paper, wood, stone, or other material, for the purpose of recording the ideas which characters and words express, or of communicating them to others by visible signs. 2. Anything written or printed; anything expressed in characters or letters.* Webster's defined "written" as the participle of write, which it defined as: *1. To set down, as legible characters; to form the conveyance of meaning; to inscribe on any material by a suitable instrument; as, to write the characters called letters; to write figures.* Thus, although the definition of a writing included a traditional paper document, it did not exclude representations of language on other media. It would seem that the plain meaning of the word "written" does not exclude all electronic communications. Of course, that does not mean that all electronic communications may be considered "written." However, those that are easily printable and storable should be. Although any computer use can be intimidating, the process of saving, retrieving, or printing this License Agreement is no more difficult or esoteric than many other basic computer functions. Lieschke's argument that Congress' present day discussions about electronic communications show that the Federal Arbitration Act's writing requirement cannot be satisfied by electronic communications is not correct for two reasons. First, modern congressional discussions do not serve as evidence of Congress' intent when it enacted the arbitration statute in 1925. Second, it seems that the License Agreement would constitute a writing, even for purposes of Congress' discussions today, because the License Agreement may be printed and stored. Finally, national policy encourages arbitration of disputes. While submission to arbitration is consensual, not coercive, ambiguities in agreements to arbitrate are resolved in favor of arbitration. A claim will be deemed to be arbitrable if an arbitration clause is capable of any interpretation that a claim is covered.

Common Law

The second manner in which courts make law is by "declaring" the law. This "decisional law" arises because courts generally must decide any dispute properly brought before them. If there is no statute or other type of law providing a rule the court can use to resolve a dispute, it is not excused from making a decision. Instead, the court must declare the rule of law for that dispute. Such court-created law is called **common law.**

The term "common law" comes from English origins. The Normans conquered England in 1066, and one of the principal devices William the Conqueror and his successors used to unite the country was to send royal judges around to hold court in the various cities. In this manner the varying customs and law of each locality were replaced by a uniform or "common" system. The common law developed as the judges resolved the disputes brought to them. If the facts were similar to those of an earlier case, they tended to follow the earlier decision. In this way the rule of *precedent* (or the doctrine of *stare decisis*) was developed. (*Stare decisis* is more fully discussed later in this chapter.) Over centuries during which thousands of disputes were settled, a large body of law came into being. This body of law was adopted by the American colonies when they won their freedom from England.

Another important source of decisional law is **equity.** The early English common law courts could determine title to land and could award money damages in settling disputes. However, when someone wanted some other remedy, such as an order to the defendant not to do something, that person's only recourse was to petition the king through the chancellor. Eventually a new court, the court of chancery, took form. It provided remedies different from those of the common law courts, most notably the *injunction.* An injunction is a court order forbidding a party to do some act, or ordering the party to do something. Equity also differed from common law because its procedures were much less rigid. It sought fairness between the individual parties more than blind adherence to past precedents. Almost all states have now abolished a separate court of chancery, but the remedies and the approach of the equity courts continue to be applicable in the kinds of disputes those courts were accustomed to handling.

Judicial Review

The third way in which courts make law—**judicial review**—derives from their power to interpret a constitution. A court has the power to declare that a decision of a lower court is inconsistent with a state or U.S. Constitution. In addition, courts have the power to declare statutes passed by the legislature, as well as acts of the executive branch, unconstitutional. In the case that follows, a federal court held that a state constitutional provision did not violate the U.S. Constitution.

COALITION FOR ECONOMIC EQUITY V. WILSON
110 F.3d 1431 (9th Cir. 1997)

FACTS

California voters adopted an initiative that amended their state constitution. The amendment provides: "The state shall not discriminate against, or grant preferential treatment to, any individual or group on the basis of race, sex, color, ethnicity, or national origin in the operation of public employment, public education, or public con-

tracting." This amendment was challenged as imposing an unequal political structure that denies women and minorities a right to seek preferential treatment from the state and local governments. This was claimed to violate the Fourteenth Amendment to the U.S. Constitution, which prohibits race and gender discrimination.

(continued)

COALITION FOR ECONOMIC EQUITY V. WILSON
(concluded)

ISSUE

Does the state constitutional provision violate the U.S. Constitution?

DECISION

No. The U.S. Supreme Court recently reminded federal judges that we should not even undertake a review of the constitutionality of state law without first asking: "Is this conflict really necessary?" Warnings against premature adjudication of constitutional questions bear heightened attention when a federal court is asked to invalidate a state's law, for the federal tribunal risks friction generating error when it endeavors to construe a novel state Act not yet reviewed by the state's highest court. However, we are satisfied that "yes, this conflict really is necessary." Under the U.S. Constitution any governmental action that classifies individuals by race or gender is presumptively unconstitutional and subject to the most exacting judicial scrutiny. However, this amendment to the California constitution prohibits the state from classifying individuals by race or gender. A law that prohibits the state from classifying individuals by race or gender does not violate the U.S. Constitution.

PRIVATE LAW

The sources of law discussed above owe their existence to public institutions. However, private individuals also can create law through their power to contract. When two or more individuals enter into a valid *contract,* the courts will enforce the terms of their agreement. Unlike the other sources of law, contracts are **private law.** As such, only the parties to the agreement are required to comply with the contractual obligations. (Contracts are discussed more fully in Chapters 6–15.)

LAW AND ORDERLY CHANGE

People cannot comply with the law unless they know and understand its requirements. This means it must be predictable. On the other hand, in a society in which technological and social change is rapid, law must adapt to changing conditions. This is especially true when basic values are shifting. A fundamental dilemma faced by any legal system is the need to promote certainty and stability while simultaneously accommodating flexibility and change. In short, if a legal system is to stand the test of time, it must have some method of permitting *orderly change.*

PROCEDURAL SAFEGUARDS

There are several procedural requirements imposed by law on legislatures that help to make statutes knowable to the people. For example, all bills that are introduced are published so citizens as well as legislators can become aware of them. A bill is assigned to a committee, which may hold a public hearing on it. If reported out of the committee, the bill is discussed on the floor of the house that originated it. Amendments are likely both in committee and on the floor. The same process is then followed in the other house. If signed by the chief executive, the bill becomes law. It is then published in its final form.

The Constitution prohibits ***ex post facto*** **laws.** This means a new statute applies only to actions taken after it becomes effective. Since one cannot adjust one's conduct to a statute not yet passed, this requirement is essential to justice.

TABLE 1-4   Methods of Ensuring Predictability in the Law

Statutes	Public hearings Publication of enacted statutes No ex post facto laws
Administrative rules	Notice of intent to issue rules Public hearings Publication of final rules
Court decisions	*Stare decisis* (following past precedent)

The Administrative Procedure Act requires federal rule-making agencies to publish notices of intent to issue regulations and the text of final ones in the Federal Register. It also requires agencies to hold hearings or consider comments from interested parties about the proposed rules. The new rules then are printed in the Code of Federal Regulations (CFR), where all administrative rules are published.

STARE DECISIS

The feature of decisional law that is more important in permitting orderly change is the doctrine of ***stare decisis.*** (The Latin phrase *stare decisis* means "let the decision stand.") This doctrine says that a court, in making a decision, must follow the rulings of prior cases that have similar facts (*precedents*). Three steps are involved in applying *stare decisis:*

1. Finding an earlier case or cases in the same jurisdiction that has similar facts.
2. Deriving from the decision(s) a rule of law.
3. Applying that rule to the case presently before the court.

Stare Decisis and Predictability

Stare decisis lends predictability to decisional law. This is because, by relying on prior decisions, the doctrine is backward looking. Within any jurisdiction, people generally can count on a degree of consistency among judicial decisions.

Of course, there are some limits to this certainty. State court decisions that serve as precedent are binding only within the same state. Although all states adopted the English common law, over time the judges decided cases differently. Hence, the common law differs from state to state. A court in California may follow a precedent established by a court in Arizona. However, it is no more bound to do so than to follow a precedent of a Canadian or New Zealand court. (See Table 1–4 for a summary of methods of ensuring predictability in the law.)

Stare Decisis and Adaptability

Although *stare decisis* is backward looking, it does not render law rigid and unchanging. To understand how flexibility in the common law is possible, one must understand more about the operation of stare decisis.

The judge, or a lawyer seeking to influence the judge's thinking, has considerable freedom in picking precedent cases. Seldom are all of the facts in a case exactly the same as in an earlier case. Therefore, the judge or lawyer can choose, within limits, which facts to emphasize and which to disregard in seeking precedent cases. Certainly a lawyer for the plaintiff (the party bringing the lawsuit) will choose as

TABLE 1–5   How Stare Decisis Permits Change

1.	Courts have broad discretion in selecting appropriate precedent.
2.	Courts may choose which facts to stress and which to ignore in selecting precedent.
3.	The rule of law from the precedent case may be interpreted broadly or narrowly.
4.	Courts may distinguish the precedent case.
5.	Appellate courts may overrule a precedent case.

precedent those cases in which the decision favors the plaintiff's position. He seeks to persuade the judge they are the precedents that should be followed. The defendant likewise argues for precedents favorable to her position.

There also is flexibility at the second step; the lawyer or judge can state the rule to be applied from the precedent cases broadly or narrowly. A difference of a few words in the way the rule is phrased may either include or exclude the case in dispute. The third step—application—follows the first two almost automatically. If the analysis appears acceptable in the first step and the description of the rule seems reasonable in the second step, the third step is convincing.

Furthermore, the highest appeals court in a jurisdiction can **overrule** a precedent case. This does not occur frequently; more commonly a court will **distinguish** the case before it from the precedent by finding differences in facts between the current case and the precedent cases. The constitutional prohibition of ex post facto laws does not apply to common or decisional law. Therefore, precedent determined to be in error or out-of-date may be overruled without prior notice, and the new rule may be applied to the current case.

Finally, a legislature may override *stare decisis* and change a common law rule by enacting a statute. The rule established by the statute applies thereafter. There is a trend toward increasing *codification* (enactment into statute) of the common law. Much of this codification is through the passage of uniform laws. See Table 1–5.

As you read the following case, note the court's use of previous decisions to formulate its opinion. Simultaneously, notice how it deals with the earlier case that seemingly contradicts the present court's position.

SHERBROOKE TURF V. MINNESOTA DEPARTMENT OF TRANSPORTATION
2001 U.S. Dist. LEXIS 19565 (D .Minn. 2001)

FACTS

Sherbrooke Turf provides landscaping services in Minnesota for land adjacent to highways. In order to be selected as a highway subcontractor, it submits bids on federal funded highway construction projects in the state. Sherbrooke claims that because it is owned and operated by Caucasian males, it suffers injury when bidding on Minnesota's federally funded road construction projects because of the Disadvantaged Business Enterprise (DBE) provisions of the Transportation Equity Act for the 21st Century (TEA-21). That statute is the latest in a series of

federal highway funding acts first enacted in 1982. The first law required that at least 10 percent of appropriated federal funds be expended on small businesses (called DBEs) that were owned and controlled by socially and economically disadvantaged individuals. It presumed that Black Americans, Hispanic Americans, Native Americans, and Asian Pacific Americans were socially and economically disadvantaged. In 1987, a new statute included women in this list of DBEs because they were presumed to be socially and economically disadvantaged as

(continued)

SHERBROOKE TURF V. MINNESOTA DEPARTMENT OF TRANSPORTATION
(continued)

well. A third statute with the same 10 percent set aside for DBEs was enacted in 1991; however, it was declared unconstitutional by this court. In 1998, Congress enacted TEA-21, which again called upon states to expend not less than 10 percent of their federal highway funds on DBE-provided services. Under the U.S. Department of Transportation (USDOT) regulations implementing TEA-21, a recipient-state's receipt of federal highway funds are conditioned on the state establishing a DBE program. However, they make clear that the 10 percent figure is an aspirational goal rather than a requirement. These regulations further specify that if a state's annual projected goal can be achieved through race-neutral means, the state must implement its contract without including goals during that year. They encourage states to meet their DBE goals through race-neutral measures and indicate that, as long as a state implements its DBE program in good faith, no penalty will be imposed for failure to meet the aspirational goal. Pursuant to the regulations, Minnesota considers the number and types of certified DBEs in the state as well as their readiness and ability to bid on construction contracts. It set an 11.6 percent overall goal for DBE participation and determined that it could meet 2.6 percent of its participation goal using race and gender-neutral means, including selecting DBEs based on the lowest bid. The remaining 9 percent of the state's goal was to be met through contract goals. To implement these highway contracting goals, Minnesota requires each prime contract-bidder to provide evidence showing it either subcontracts to DBEs in order to meet the contract goal, or engages in a good faith effort to meet it. Sherbrooke submitted the lowest bid for landscaping on a federally assisted highway project; however, the contract was awarded to a DBE. As a result, Sherbrooke asked the court to rule that the DBE program is unconstitutional because it discriminates on the basis of race, sex, or national origin.

ISSUE

Is the DBE program unconstitutional?

DECISION

No. In *Adarand Constructors v. Pena*, the U.S. Supreme Court applied a "strict scrutiny" test to race-conscious remedial legislation. However, it also noted that the unhappy persistence of both the practice and the lingering effects of racial discrimination against minority groups in

this country is an unfortunate reality and that the government is not disqualified from acting in response to it. Specifically, the *Aderand* Court found that federal race-conscious preference programs, as well as state and locally enacted affirmative action programs, will be upheld if they serve a compelling interest and are narrowly tailored to further that interest. The 10th Circuit Court of Appeals, in *Adarand Constructors v. Slater*, held that the government has a compelling interest in not perpetuating the effects of past discrimination in its own distribution of federal funds and in remediating the effects of past discrimination in the government contracting markets created by its own disbursements. However, in *City of Richmond v. J. A. Croson*, the Supreme Court made clear that Congress may not merely express concern about such issues; it must make findings describing the problem's existence and the specific cure it prescribes. In the case of TEA-21, Congress has complied with these requirements. Before adopting the Act, Congress considered evidence detailing the barriers faced by minority-owned construction firms and the specific nature of discrimination within the construction and subcontracting industry. Congress also reviewed evidence describing a significant statistical disparity in DBE and minority subcontracting in markets in the absence of affirmative action programs. Sherbrooke argues that the Supreme Court's decision in *Kimel v. Florida Bd. of Regents* mandates an independent judicial assessment of the data Congress reviewed prior to enacting TEA-21. However, Sherbrooke is wrong. *Kimel* is a case which questioned whether Congress had compiled sufficient findings to pierce a state's 11th Amendment sovereign immunity. This is not such a case. Congress's attempts to address race and gender issues–invoking Commerce Clause and 14th Amendment powers–are readily distinguishable from actions which might abrogate sovereign immunity. The Supreme Court emphasized this point in *City of Boerne v. Flores*, when it said "it is for Congress in the first instance to determine whether and what legislation is needed to secure the guarantees of the 14th Amendment and its conclusions are entitled to much deference." *Adarand* also requires that a race-conscious program be narrowly tailored to serve the compelling interest. According to *Croson*, part of this narrow tailoring requirement asks whether there was any consideration of the

(continued)

SHERBROOKE TURF V. MINNESOTA DEPARTMENT OF TRANSPORTATION
(concluded)

use of race-neutral means to increase minority business participation in government contracting. TEA-21's implementing regulation, unlike the earlier statutes, reveals a heightened commitment to incorporating race-neutral elements in the DBE program. The program also meets *Croson's* mandate that it be appropriately limited such that it will not last longer than the discriminatory effects it is designed to eliminate. Ultimately, while the Supreme Court has expressed grave concerns about programs which afford random or blanket benefits to minority groups without connecting these benefits to a specific history of discrimination, that is not the case here. The government has shown a factual and logical connection between the race-conscious measures included in TEA-21 and the ongoing effects of discrimination in the highway construction industry.

JURISPRUDENCE

Our examination of the nature and function of law has revealed law as much more than a set of rules. Instead, it is a vibrant institution that reflects the past and the present, while simultaneously shaping the form and substance of the future. This living nature is attributable largely to the legal philosophies of the key decision makers (judges and jurors) who resolve the numerous cases and controversies that arise on a daily basis. The chapter next examines four schools of **jurisprudence** (legal philosophy) that are predominant today: legal positivism; natural law; sociological jurisprudence; and legal realism.

LEGAL POSITIVISM

Some people view law as something separate and distinct from morality. They see it as the command of legitimate political institutions and, as such, believe it must be enforced to the letter. **Legal positivists** are unlikely to consider public policy and their own sense of morality when enforcing the law. Instead, they look to the plain meaning of the words in order to strictly follow the will of the lawmakers. While legal positivism often creates harsh results by refusing to recognize equitable exceptions, it provides a great sense of predictability to the enforcement of legal rules.

NATURAL LAW

Natural law thinkers disagree with the idea that law and morality are separate. They recognize a higher set of rules that override the legitimacy of laws promulgated by political institutions. Natural law judges consider their own sense of morality when applying the law and often overturn statutes they believe are unjust. A major criticism of natural law jurisprudence is that it does not provide the level of predictability attained by legal positivism because each judge's sense of morality may differ.

Ethical Implications	Ernesto Cordero and Henry Lagarto were found guilty of raping, torturing, and murdering a 7-year-old girl by a court in the Philippines. Under that country's laws the death penalty is mandatory in rape cases in which the victim is killed. However, the judge, citing his Christian beliefs, refused to follow the law and sentenced the two men to life in prison. The girl's family is outraged, congressmen want the judge fired, and communist rebels have threatened to kill him. What would you do if your legal duty conflicted with your moral beliefs?

SOCIOLOGICAL JURISPRUDENCE

Under **sociological jurisprudence** each case and legal decision is viewed as a piece of a much bigger, and more important, puzzle. Legal sociologists have a vision for where society is going or should be going and make decisions that promote this social agenda. Thus, when interpreting statutes they look beyond the plain meaning of the words and fully consider the legislative intent as well as the prevailing social policies. Unlike legal positivists, legal sociologists stress the need for law to change and keep pace with the evolution of society.

LEGAL REALISM

Legal realism stresses that law must be considered in light of its day-to-day application. It focuses on *law in action* rather than on the theoretical rules themselves. The idea behind legal realism is that decisions often are more attributable to the biases and moods of decision makers than they are to the formal legal rules that are supposed to determine the outcome. Legal realists suggest that decision makers often mask the true basis for their decisions behind the rhetoric of the law.

PREVENTIVE LAW

In the past quarter century there has been a qualitative as well as a quantitative change in the concern of business managers with law. In earlier times, business managers generally employed lawyers only in emergencies. A lawyer might be hired if a business was sued, if a debt could not be collected, or if a supplier's goods were defective and no settlement could be reached. Today, business managers also retain lawyers to help them plan to avoid such emergencies and to comply with the rapidly growing mass of legal rules imposed on business operations by government bodies. This use of lawyers by businesspeople is called **preventive law.**

OBJECTIVES OF PREVENTIVE LAW

The objectives of preventive law are to arrange business plans and methods to increase profits by (1) avoiding losses through fines and damage judgments and (2) reaching business goals through enforceable contracts while avoiding government prohibitions. By involving a lawyer in the business-planning process, a desired business objective can be reached with less legal risk. Preventive law further aims to minimize the possibility of failure if the business has to go to court to enforce its rights.

ROLES OF LAWYERS AND CLIENTS

Almost every business activity involves legal risks and consequences. To avoid costly judgments and to get that to which they are legally entitled, businesspeople generally need to be familiar with the law applicable to their activities. Studying this book will aid in this, but it will not prepare you to be your own lawyer. Consider an analogy from the field of medicine. While there are times when you need a doctor, you still need a good knowledge of first aid to deal with the most common problems. Such knowledge also will help you to know when you should call a doctor—or in this case, a lawyer.

The practice of preventive law requires a knowledgeable client as well as a knowledgeable lawyer. The client needs to understand the legal system and the applicable law well enough to be able to communicate with the lawyer. (See Figure 1–1.)

FIGURE 1–1   Preventive Law

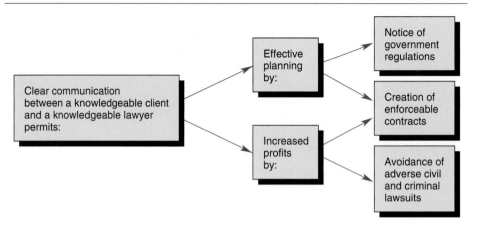

The client needs to know what information is relevant and necessary to the lawyer's opinion. Too often clients get into trouble because they have not fully informed their lawyers. A legal opinion is no better than the information on which it is based. Problems also arise when clients apply legal advice to situations not contemplated by the lawyer. This can lead to a lawsuit, or it may discourage the client from doing something that is clearly legal.

QUESTIONS AND PROBLEM CASES

1. What are the primary functions of law?
2. Describe the various ways in which the courts *make* law.
3. What is the relationship between state statutes and the state or federal constitutions?
4. Why are predictability and adaptability both desirable in a body of law?
5. How does criminal law differ from civil law?
6. The *Line Item Veto Act* gave the president the power to "cancel in whole" three types of provisions that have been signed into law: (1) any dollar amount of discretionary budget authority; (2) any item of new direct spending; or (3) any limited tax benefit. The Act required the president to adhere to precise procedures whenever he exercised his cancellation authority. In identifying items for cancellation he was required to consider the legislative history, the purposes, and any other relevant information about the items. He needed to determine, with respect to each cancellation, that it would (i) reduce the federal budget deficit; (ii) not impair any essential government functions; and (iii) not harm the national interest. Moreover, he was required to transmit a special message to Congress notifying it of each cancellation within five calendar days after the enactment of the canceled provision. It is undisputed that in his use of the line item veto, President Clinton meticulously followed these procedures. A cancellation took effect upon receipt by Congress of the special message from the president. If, however, a "disapproval bill" pertaining to a special message was enacted into law, the cancellations set forth in that message became null and void. A majority vote of both Houses of Congress was sufficient to enact a disapproval bill. The Act did not grant the president the authority to cancel a disapproval bill, but he did retain his constitutional authority to veto such a bill. The effect of cancellation prevented an item of new direct spending or limited tax benefits from having legal force or effect. Is the *Line Item Veto Act* constitutional?

7. One wheel on an automobile manufactured by Buick Motor Company was defectively made. Buick would have discovered the defective condition if it had made a reasonable inspection of the wheel. Buick sold the car

to an automobile dealer who in turn sold it to MacPherson. MacPherson was injured when the wheel collapsed. MacPherson sued Buick for negligent failure to inspect the wheel. Buick's main defense was that it had not dealt directly with MacPherson and thus owed him no duty. The general rule governing such suits at the time of this action was that a buyer could not sue a manufacturer for negligence unless there was a contract between the buyer and the manufacturer. However, there had been a previous case, *Thomas v. Winchester*, where a manufacturer falsely labeled a poison that was sold to a druggist, who in turn sold it to a customer. The customer was able to recover against the manufacturer. Further, in *Devlin v. Smith*, a contractor was held liable when he improperly built a scaffold for a painter and the painter's employees were injured when it collapsed. Based on this information, explain how the court could permit MacPherson to recover from Buick.

8. Alan Howard is a subscriber of America Online (AOL), an Internet service provider that provides Internet access, electronic mail, and numerous other services to its users. Howard filed a lawsuit against AOL, alleging that the company violated the Communication Act by making unreasonable charges, practices, classifications or regulations; by unreasonably prejudicing some subscribers by favoring others; and by failing to protect subscriber privacy. AOL defended on the grounds that the Communications Act regulates only common carriers and, since it was not a common carrier, it was not governed by that statute. Carefully explain the process by which the court will determine if AOL is a common carrier.

9. As a part of its collective bargaining agreement with the United Steelworkers of America, the Kaiser Aluminum and Chemical Company established a new on-the-job craft training program at one of its plants. The selection of trainees for the program was based on seniority, but at least 50 percent of the new trainees had to be black until the percentage of black skilled craft workers in the plant approximated the percentage of blacks in the local labor force. Brian Weber, a rejected white applicant, would have qualified for the program if the racial preference had not existed. Weber argued that Kaiser's affirmative action program violated federal laws prohibiting discrimination on the basis of race. Is Kaiser's affirmative action program legal? Explain.

10. In the previous question, the Supreme Court, in deciding the case, stated that: "*A thing may be within the letter of a statute and yet not within the statute because it is not within its spirit.*" In the context of what you have read in Chapter 1, carefully explain what the court is saying.

CHAPTER 2

Dispute Settlement

Plastix shipped five cases of decorative boxes to Trendco, Inc., for which Trendco had agreed to pay $10,000. Trendco sent Plastix a check for $8,000, claiming that the boxes in one of the cases were defective. Plastix has strict quality control procedures and is sure the boxes were not defective when they left its plant. Plastix wants the $2,000 but is concerned about maintaining good relations with Trendco, which has been a valued customer for several years.

- *What alternative does Plastix have to pursuing a lawsuit for the additional $2,000?*
- *If Plastix decides to sue, where must it file its lawsuit?*
- *If Plastix decides to sue, what procedures will be followed in the suit?*

.... **MEANS OF DISPUTE SETTLEMENT** ....

NEGOTIATION

Disputes arise in business for many reasons: goods may be defective; customers may not carry out their promises; government regulators may be unreasonable. The courts are the most visible and familiar vehicle for dispute settlement but most disputes are, and should be, settled by negotiation.

In an earlier day, most businesspeople shunned lawyers and the courts. Typically, a lawsuit was filed only as a last resort after the parties had decided not to do business with each other again. Avoidance of lawyers and the courts is certainly not the rule today. Indeed, we are now a more litigious society. Many of us are quick to go to court. There are many more lawyers, and, as indicated in the preceding chapter, business-people call on them frequently.

The cost of bringing or defending a lawsuit has been increasing rapidly. The fees of lawyers have increased; however, the big increases in costs have come because discovery procedures (discussed later in this chapter) and the trials themselves have become much more time consuming, involving the time of both businesspeople and lawyers.

Settlement of disputes through negotiation is, therefore, even more attractive than it was earlier. If this can be done by the businesspeople themselves, good! However, many attorneys are skilled negotiators, and having a competent advocate speak as an intermediary is often more effective than speaking for oneself. If negotiations fail, there are many ways to pursue a resolution.

ALTERNATIVE DISPUTE RESOLUTION

Because of the time, money, and personal resources that get tied up in litigation, businesses and individuals are increasingly turning to alternatives to trials to settle disputes. Courts, also, often require parties involved in certain kinds of disputes to try alternatives in an effort to get the parties to settle before trial. These **alternative dispute resolution (ADR)** mechanisms share many advantages over trials: They are generally quicker, cheaper, less complicated procedurally, and receive less publicity. In addition, because they are not as adversarial, they facilitate a continuation of business between the parties after settlement of the dispute. Finally, unlike at trial where there must be a winner and a loser, ADR more readily adapts to compromise solutions.

Mediation

A voluntary process that is sometimes used when negotiation seems to be failing is **mediation.** The parties to the dispute choose a third party to assist them in settling it. This **mediator** often tries first to communicate the positions of the parties to each other. Frequently, the areas of serious disagreement are narrower than the parties think. The mediator then usually proposes a basis or several bases for settlement. A mediator merely facilitates negotiation; no award or opinion on the merits of the dispute is given by the mediator. If the mediation is successful, it can result in a *mediation agreement.*

The Federal Mediation and Conciliation Service makes experienced mediators available to serve in labor disputes. When the president declares a "cooling off" period after finding that a strike endangers the national safety or health, the Service is called in. It is available in other cases as well at the request of the union or the employer. Either arbitration or court action may follow unsuccessful mediation.

Mediation is especially useful in situations in which the parties have some continuing relationship because it allows them to compromise and to reach a solution themselves. As a result, they are more likely to be able to constructively work within the agreement. Thus, mediation would be a good method for Plastix and Trendco to use to settle their dispute. Mediation is increasingly being used in interpersonal disputes such as divorce, where child custody arrangements will require the parents to deal with each other for several years. Court-annexed mediation is often provided or compelled in these cases.

Arbitration

Arbitration is another widely used alternative to settling disputes in court. Arbitration differs from mediation in that the third party to whom the dispute is submitted decides the outcome. Contracts involving securities and commodity trading, casualty insurance, and other kinds of commercial contracts often contain arbitration clauses. Most union–management contracts and many employment contracts also have them. The *Circuit City Stores* case illustrates the strong support of the Supreme Court for arbitration. It has also led to a large number of employers requiring employees to sign arbitration agreements.

CIRCUIT CITY STORES, INC. V. SAINT CLAIR ADAMS
121 S. Ct. 1302 (2001)

FACTS

When Saint Clair Adams applied for a job at Circuit City Stores, he signed an application that contained this language, "I agree that I will settle any and all previously unasserted claims, disputes or controversies arising out of or relating to my application or candidacy for employment, employment and/or cessation of employment with Circuit City, exclusively by final and binding arbitration before a neutral Arbitrator." Two years after he was hired as a sales counselor, Adams filed suit against Circuit City based on discrimination and tort claims. Circuit City challenged the suit and sought to have the claims submitted to binding arbitration.

ISSUE

Does the Federal Arbitration Act (FAA) include private employee contracts?

DECISION

Yes. The FAA was passed in 1925 to overcome court hostility to enforcing arbitration agreements. It compels courts to enforce a wide range of written arbitration agreements. The FAA excludes from its coverage "contracts of employment of seamen, railroad employees, or any other class of workers engaged in foreign or interstate

commerce." All Courts of Appeals except the Ninth Circuit have interpreted this clause to exclude only the contracts of transportation workers. The Ninth Circuit, where Adams' claim is brought, construed it to exclude all employment contracts. The other circuits' interpretation is the better one. It is consistent with the purpose of the FAA to broadly enforce arbitration agreements and is consistent with canons of construction which state that when general words are followed by specific words, the general words are construed to embrace only objects similar in nature. *Transportation workers* is similar to *seamen* and *railroad employees*.

In *Gilmer v. Interstate/Johnson Lane Corp.*, we held that the FAA required arbitration of age discrimination claims based on an agreement in a securities registration application. As noted in that case, there are real benefits to arbitration. It avoids the costs of litigation, which may be of particular importance in the employment context because smaller sums of money are often involved than the amounts in commercial contracts. It also avoids other problems like choice of law issues. One does not forgo statutory rights by this interpretation; it merely submits the resolution of the issue to an arbitral rather than a judicial forum.

A particular advantage of arbitration is that an arbitrator who is familiar with the technical or social setting of the dispute may be chosen. This may be particularly important in an international trade dispute or a labor dispute. While arbitration is often provided for in a contract, parties who have not so provided can also choose to have their dispute arbitrated after it has arisen. Many consumer-related disputes now go to arbitration. Additionally, many courts now order or provide court-annexed arbitration for certain kinds of cases such as those with limited dollar amounts in dispute.

Usually there is only one arbitrator. The parties may select the arbitrator in any way they desire. They may ask the American Arbitration Association to provide a list of available arbitrators. The parties can then alternate in eliminating names from that list until a single name remains. Sometimes a board of three arbitrators is chosen by having each party choose one person; the two chosen arbitrators then select the third.

Most states have passed the Uniform Arbitration Act, which makes both the agreement of parties to arbitrate and the arbitration award enforceable in court. A court will not review the wisdom of the decision of an arbitrator. It may, however, hold that the dispute was not arbitrable under the agreement of the parties, or that the arbitrator exceeded his or her authority, or acted arbitrarily, capriciously, or in a discriminatory manner. The parties may or may not require an opinion (reasons for the award) from the arbitrator. Arbitration awards are usually not published, although many labor dispute awards have been.

The increasing volume of international trade, coupled with the complex nature of many of these relationships, has led to increasing reliance on arbitration to resolve contractual disputes. In addition, the arbitration can occur in a neutral location. The growing attractiveness of arbitration has resulted in the establishment of arbitration centers in world capitals such as London, Paris, Cairo, Hong Kong, and Stockholm, and major cities such as Geneva and New York. Recognition and enforcement of international arbitration agreements and awards is generally controlled through multilateral treaties.

Minitrial and Summary Jury Trial

The **minitrial** is designed to refocus the dispute as a business problem. Executives of the disputing companies, who have settlement authority, hear a shortened presentation of the case by the lawyers for each side. The executives, who now have a better understanding of the strengths and weaknesses of their case, and know how a settlement would fit in with their business objectives, meet with the lawyers to negotiate a settlement. The minitrial often involves a neutral third-party advisor. If a settlement is not reached, she or he will render a nonbinding opinion regarding how the dispute is likely to be resolved if it goes to trial, and how the court is likely to rule on factual and evidentiary issues. After this, the parties again try to negotiate a settlement.

A **summary jury trial** has many similarities to the minitrial. However, it is conducted under court guidance, while the minitrial is voluntarily conducted by the parties themselves. In the summary jury trial, a six-member mock jury empaneled by the court hears a shortened presentation of the case by the lawyers for each side, and renders an advisory verdict. The presiding court official, who is either a judge or a magistrate, then meets with the parties to help them reach a settlement. Because summary jury trials have been effective in encouraging settlement, and court dockets are so clogged, some courts, such as the U.S. Court of Claims, routinely use the procedure in appropriate cases.

CONCEPT SUMMARY	Alternative Dispute Resolution*		
Form	**Decision Maker**	**Advantages**	**Conductor**
Arbitration	Arbitrator	Arbitrator often has expertise in area of dispute.	Arbitrator
Mediation	Disputants	Parties can better work within jointly reached solution.	Mediator
Minitrial	Executives of disputing companies	Companies are more likely to settle.	Neutral third party
Summary Jury Trial	Six-member mock jury	Disputants are more likely to settle.	Judge or magistrate
Private Judge	Hired judge	Circumstances are like a trial, but without a waiting period.	Hired judge

*All these forms of ADR are usually quicker, cheaper, and more private than formal trial litigation. Other advantages are listed within.

Private Judging

Some parties are able to avoid trial while engaging in a process similar to a formal court proceeding by hiring their own judge to settle their dispute. In this **private judging,** or "rent-a-judge" method of dispute resolution, the hired judge (who is often a retired judge) renders a binding opinion after hearing the proofs and arguments of the parties. Many states, such as Ohio, have adopted rules for the handling of these cases.

Other Dispute Resolution Mechanisms

While the ADR systems discussed above are the most commonly used alternatives to trial, especially in business disputes, there are many others. These range from an **ombudsperson,** who is an individual appointed within an organization to settle disputes, to private panels, to small claims court (discussed later in the chapter). **Med/arb** (a combination of mediation and arbitration where the third party first serves as a mediator, then as an arbitrator) and early neutral evaluation (a court-annexed procedure where a neutral private attorney with expertise in the area of the dispute objectively evaluates the case) are emerging ADR approaches. It is fortunate that disputants are increasingly trying to settle disagreements through alternative means, for our court system is incapable of handling the large number of disputes that occur. However, there is a price to be paid for the speed, economy, informality, and other benefits gained from these alternatives. The most important trade-off involves the traditional procedural safeguards used during litigation to guarantee that every person has his or her "fair day in court." These procedural safeguards are discussed in the following section.

THE COURTS

The dispute resolution mechanism of last resort (short of the use of force) is the courts. Either party to a dispute can bring the lawsuit. If the party brings it to the proper court, the court must decide it. The court cannot wait for the legislature to pass a statute or suggest that the parties go to a different or higher court. However, there are some general kinds of cases that American courts do not consider. Courts do not decide a case if the issue has become **moot.** A case is moot when events occurring after the filing of the lawsuit have made a decision beside the point. An example was a case brought by a white applicant to a law school.[1] At first he was not admitted and claimed reverse racial discrimination; however, he was later admitted before his case

---

[1]DeFunis v. Odegard, 416 U.S. 312 (1974).

had been decided on appeal to the U.S. Supreme Court. The Court refused to rule on the case because it was moot, even though other similar cases were being brought.

Federal courts and most state courts hear only real controversies—concrete disputes between actual parties. *They do not give advisory opinions, nor do they make rulings on hypothetical cases.* This saves the time of judges and avoids the danger that the arguments for one side might not be vigorously pressed because no one as yet has been truly hurt.

JURISDICTION

As we said above, a court must decide a case if it is brought to the proper court. A court can only hear a case over which it has **jurisdiction.** Jurisdiction is the authority of a court to hear and determine disputes. Jurisdiction can be limited in several ways. Some courts are limited by subject matter jurisdiction. They can hear only cases involving certain types of controversies, such as tax disputes, or juvenile matters. Other courts are limited by the amount of damages being sought or the penalty to be assessed. The small claims courts discussed later in this chapter are limited by such jurisdiction. The jurisdiction of all courts is limited geographically. The "borderless" Internet has created new problems in determining jurisdiction. This issue is discussed in Chapter 48. The jurisdiction of a particular court will be pointed out when that court is discussed.

Venue concerns where within a jurisdiction a suit must be heard. Venue rules are established by the states. These rules tell the county where plaintiff must file suit. For example, a criminal case must usually be filed in the county where the crime took place. Parties who feel they cannot get a fair trial in the designated area can ask the court for a **change of venue.**

STATE COURTS

The names of the various courts and the way jurisdiction is divided between them vary from state to state. We will use the courts of California as an example: They are typical of most states (see Figure 2–1). In general, the state courts have jurisdiction to

FIGURE 2–1   The California Court System

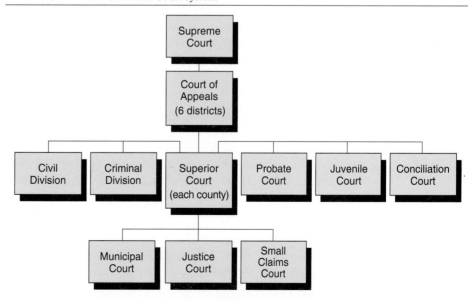

hear almost any sort of dispute except those involving certain federal laws and issues. Most disputes between citizens of the state and disputes arising from events occurring within the state, such as automobile accidents, are tried in state courts.

INFERIOR COURTS

Most minor criminal violations and civil disputes involving small amounts of money are handled by courts that keep no record (transcript) of the testimony or proceedings. They are, therefore, not **courts of record.** Without a record there can be no appeal. Usually a dissatisfied party claiming error in such a court may have a new trial (a **trial *de novo***) in a court of record. Inferior courts may be called **municipal courts** in urban areas and **justice of the peace** courts in rural areas. In many states, as in California, justice of the peace courts have been replaced by minor courts such as the justice courts, which operate in less populated counties.

Many cities also have **small claims courts.** These courts handle civil matters involving a limited amount of money. In these courts, the procedures are informal, the parties may argue their own cases, and the judicial officer, who may not be a lawyer, determines both the facts and the law, and renders a decision. These courts, therefore, offer a quick, inexpensive, and easily accessible forum for the settlement of minor disputes.

TRIAL COURTS

Trial courts, like inferior courts, perform the same basic functions: finding the relevant facts, identifying the appropriate rule of law, and combining the facts and the law to reach a decision in settlement of the dispute. Trial courts differ from inferior courts in that the trial courts are courts of general jurisdiction; they are not limited by the amount of civil damages that can be awarded or the criminal penalties that can be imposed. Their geographic jurisdiction is often a county. They also differ in that the judge must be a lawyer, and juries are provided for. The juries decide the facts, and, under instructions from the judge about the applicable law, reach a verdict. In addition, trial courts are courts of record. Thus, an appeal can be taken from a trial court decision.

The name of the trial courts that have general jurisdiction varies greatly among states. These courts may be called circuit, district, county, or, as in California, superior courts. Trial courts may be divided into those that hear criminal cases and those that hear only civil cases. Where there is a large population, specialized courts may be established. For example, there may be domestic relations courts (called conciliation courts in California) to hear divorce and child custody cases, probate courts to handle estates of deceased persons, and juvenile courts.

APPEALS COURTS

As the name implies, state appeals courts hear cases that have been appealed from trial court decisions or state administrative agency rulings. Generally, appellate courts do not hear witnesses or determine facts. Their job is to review the proceedings in the trial court and correct legal errors made by the trial judge. Appellate courts must accept the trial court's findings of fact unless it goes against all the evidence.

Some states have only one court of appeals, usually called the supreme court. The majority, however, have two levels of appellate courts. The intermediate court is frequently called the court of appeals.[2] Some states allow certain types of cases, such

---

[2]In New York and Maryland the highest court is called the court of appeals. New York's intermediate court is called the supreme court.

as those in which the death penalty has been imposed, to be appealed directly to the highest court. California and several other states permit the supreme court to select the cases it wants to hear and to assign others to the court of appeals.

.... FEDERAL COURTS

Cases heard in the federal courts fall into one of two classes: They are either cases involving a federal question or cases in which there is diversity of citizenship between the parties. Federal questions include cases in which a federal statute is involved, such as a violation of a federal criminal law, or a violation of a right granted by the Constitution. Federal courts have exclusive jurisdiction over patents, copyrights, bankruptcy, crimes defined by federal statutes, and a few other matters. One of these areas involved maritime cases, which are decided under admiralty law. See Figure 2–2 for a diagram of the types of courts in the federal court system.

Diversity cases are those in which the parties to the dispute are citizens of different states. If the parties are from different states, and the amount involved in the dispute is $75,000 or more, the plaintiff may choose to bring suit in either state or federal court. If the plaintiff chooses to bring suit in state court, the defendant may petition to **remove** the case to federal court. Federal judges tend to have more prestige, so the federal courts attract, on the average, more competent judges. Another common reason for choosing a federal court is to obtain certain procedural advantages that may be available. This may make it easier to get jurisdiction over the defendant and force witnesses to testify. Lack of local bias is also more certain in federal court.

The federal courts generally apply state law in diversity cases. Where a state court has not developed a rule, the federal court will guess, based on past decisions in similar cases, how the highest court of that state would decide the case. There is a body of procedural law called **conflict of laws** that provides rules for a court to follow in deciding which state's law to apply.

FIGURE 2–2   The Federal Court System

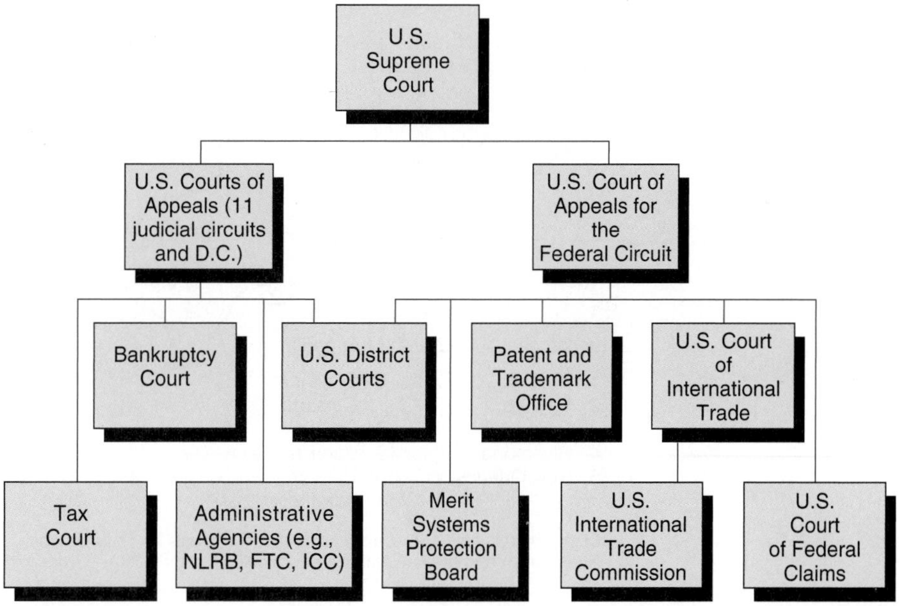

DISTRICT COURT

With few exceptions, lawsuits brought in federal courts must be started in district courts. These are the federal trial courts. Like state trial courts, they have both fact-finding (by the judge or jury) and law-finding (by the judge) functions. There is at least one U.S. district court in each state. Most states have two districts; some have more. The number of judges assigned to a district depends on the caseload; some districts have only one judge. Almost all cases are heard by a single judge.

SPECIAL COURTS

As Figure 2–2 shows, there are several specialized courts in the federal court system. Although the district courts may also hear such cases, contract claims against the United States may be brought in a special U.S. Claims Court. A U.S. Court of International Trade hears disputes over duties imposed on imported goods. The Tax Court hears appeals from decisions of the Internal Revenue Service, and bankruptcy cases are heard by the U.S. Bankruptcy Court, which is divided into the same districts as the district courts. Chapter 46 discusses in greater detail the work of the bankruptcy court.

COURT OF APPEALS

An appeal from a district court is taken to a U.S. court of appeals. The appeal is ordinarily taken to the court of appeals for the region in which the district court is located (see Figure 2–3). Like state intermediate appellate courts, the U.S. courts of appeals generally do not have a fact-finding function. They only review the legal conclusions

FIGURE 2–3   The Federal Judicial Circuits

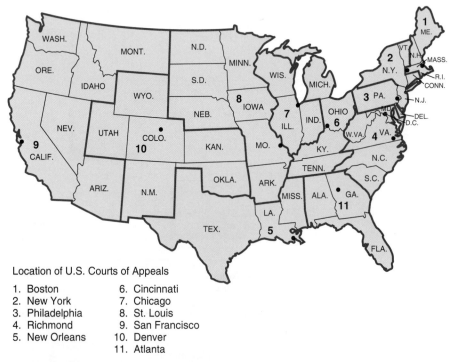

Location of U.S. Courts of Appeals

1. Boston	6. Cincinnati
2. New York	7. Chicago
3. Philadelphia	8. St. Louis
4. Richmond	9. San Francisco
5. New Orleans	10. Denver
	11. Atlanta

District of Columbia: D.C. Circuit and Court of Appeals for Federal Circuit.
Note: Hawaii and Alaska are in the 9th Circuit.

reached by lower federal courts. The courts of appeal also hear appeals from many federal administrative agency decisions.

There are 13 U.S. courts of appeal. Twelve of the circuit courts have general federal appellate jurisdiction. One of these serves the District of Columbia alone because so many appeals involving the federal regulatory agencies arise there. The other 11, as shown on the map, cover several states. Usually a case is heard by a panel of three judges, but some cases may be heard **en banc,** that is, by all the judges of that circuit. The 13th circuit, the U.S. Court of Appeals for the Federal Circuit, hears a wide variety of specialized appeals, including patent, copyright, and trademark matters; Claims Court decisions; and decisions by the Court of International Trade.

THE SUPREME COURT

As the name implies, the U.S. Supreme Court is the highest court of the land. It has final responsibility for interpretation of the Constitution and federal statutes. However, the idea that a party who is dissatisfied with the decision of a lower court can always "take it all the way to the Supreme Court" is erroneous.

The primary way a case can be appealed to the Supreme Court is through **writ of certiorari (cert.).** Hearing such cases is entirely discretionary with the Court. The Court may grant *cert.* where there have been conflicting decisions in similar cases by different courts of appeals. It may also grant *cert.* in a case from the highest court of a state where a right is claimed under the Constitution or where the validity of a federal statute is in question.

Because most appeals to the Court involve its *certiorari* jurisdiction, and relatively few of these are heard, the Court decides only a small percentage of the cases appealed to it. If the Court does hear a case, a long opinion is usually published. In most cases the justices do not all agree. Then there may be a **concurring opinion,** which states the reasoning of those who agree with the result but not the rationale of the majority, and/or a **dissenting** (minority) **opinion.** These opinions do not have the force of the law and cannot be cited as precedent.

THE ADVERSARY SYSTEM

American courts, following the British practice, operate on the **adversary system—** trial through a battle of words between two lawyers. The adversary system represents the idea that truth is best discovered through the presentation of competing ideas. Each lawyer acts as the advocate of his or her client. It is the lawyer's job to present the client's view of the facts to the judge, or to the jury if one is used. The lawyer tries to persuade them not only that the client's version is correct, but also that the other party's view of the facts, to the extent that it is inconsistent, is in error. The lawyer also seeks to persuade the judge that the law favors the party he or she represents. Trickery or dishonesty by the lawyer in carrying out the advocacy role is improper and may result in disbarment of the wrongdoing lawyer.

THE FUNCTION OF THE JUDGE

The judge's role, under the adversary system, is viewed as not only unbiased but also essentially passive. The trial judge is to keep order in the court and, when a jury is present, to see that the lawyers do not use improper methods to influence the jury. In essence, a trial judge acts as a referee. Generally, the judge stops questions from lawyers or orders witnesses to change their behavior only when asked to do so by one of the lawyers. He or she need not be totally passive, however. The judge is responsible for the correct application of the law to the facts of the case and instructs the jury regarding the law.

This differs from the judge's role in most European countries and other jurisdictions that originally derived their law from the Roman Code. In these systems, judges have a duty to direct the search for truth rather than expecting it to emerge from the efforts of the lawyers for the parties. Therefore, they assume a much more active role in directing proceedings in the court, in requesting certain evidence, and in questioning witnesses.

Advantages and Disadvantages

Advocates of the adversary system believe that truth is most effectively determined as a result of each lawyer presenting his or her client's "case" through witnesses, and that deception and misperception are best exposed through cross-examination. In addition, the system makes it more difficult for a dishonest or biased judge to control the outcome of a case. Critics argue that honest witnesses can be confused by hostile questioning. They say that the system does not work when the opposing lawyers are of unequal skill. This gives an advantage to the wealthy, who can hire better lawyers. Furthermore, the competition to win encourages suppression of unfavorable facts and overstatement, if not misstatement, of the truth.

PROCEDURE

The Functions of Procedure

Procedural law is the body of legal rules governing the conduct of a case. Rules of procedure are complex and technical. The basic purpose of procedure is fairness. The nonlawyer needs to know only enough of this body of law to be able to understand the progress of a case through the courts. The procedure in criminal cases differs somewhat from that in civil cases. Here we will focus on civil procedure.

Pleadings

The complaint, answer, and reply, each of which is discussed below, are known as the **pleadings.** These are the first documents filed with the court, and they start and define the lawsuit. They serve two major functions: They inform the parties of each other's claims and they form the basis for a trial. Only those matters that are disputed in the pleadings are tried in court. If a fact material to the case has been omitted from the pleadings, a court may permit a party to amend the pleading. A growing number of courts allow the documents to be filed electronically.

The Complaint

The first step in starting a lawsuit is the filing of a **complaint** with the court. Information about the claim of the plaintiff and the remedy requested, usually damages of a certain amount, are listed in numbered paragraphs (see Figure 2–4). The complaint must contain sufficient facts to show that the plaintiff is entitled to some legal relief and to give the defendant reasonable notice of the nature of the plaintiff's claim. No evidence will be permitted to be given at a trial that is not related to a material fact stated in the complaint.

FIGURE 2–4   Complaint

UNITED STATES DISTRICT COURT
SOUTHERN DISTRICT OF INDIANA
INDIANAPOLIS DIVISION

JOHN SMITH	)	
	)	
Plaintiff	)	
	)	
v.	)	CIVIL ACTION NO. IP 79-53-C
	)	
WORLD PRESS, INC.,	)	
and HERBERT MILLER	)	
	)	
Defendants	)	

PLAINTIFF'S COMPLAINT

Plaintiff, for his complaint, states:

1. Plaintiff is a citizen of the State of Indiana. Defendant World Press, Inc., is a Delaware corporation incorporated under the laws of the State of Delaware having its principal place of business in New York, N.Y. Defendant Herbert Miller is the author of the book *40 Seconds and Death* and is a citizen of the State of New York. The matter in controversy exceeds, exclusive of interests and costs, Seventy-Five Thousand Dollars ($75,000.00). Jurisdiction is based upon diversity of citizenship.

2. Defendant World Press, Inc., owns, operates, and publishes books under the name of World Press.

3. During 1998, defendant World Press, Inc., published without plaintiff's prior knowledge or consent, and expressly against plaintiff's permission, in excess of one million copies of the book *40 Seconds and Death*, authored by defendant, Herbert Miller, which contained within Chapter Four (4) a section entitled "Weekend Tryst." This book unnecessarily exposed to the public the private affairs of the plaintiff, John Smith. A copy of said chapter is attached hereto as Exhibit One (1).

4. Said chapter disclosed private facts that would be offensive to a reasonable person and were not of legitimate public interest or concern. Defendant World Press, Inc., and defendant Herbert Miller knew that the plaintiff did not want the matters contained in the chapter to be exposed to the general public and published said chapter over the expressed warnings of the plaintiff.

5. Defendant Herbert Miller was personally told by the plaintiff that he did not want to be quoted by defendant Herbert Miller nor did plaintiff want any reference to plaintiff's family or relatives to appear in any publication. The matters published were culled from a private conversation and amount to an unwarranted intrusion into the plaintiff's private life.

6. Defendant Herbert Miller misled the plaintiff to his detriment by publishing matters of a personal nature without securing the plaintiff's consent. The article exposed private matters concerning plaintiff's marital difficulties and his intimate relationships with family members.

7. The identity of the plaintiff was altered in the book, but the name used in the publication made the plaintiff's true identity readily apparent to neighbors, friends, relatives, business associates, and other members of the community who read the book.

8. As a direct and proximate result of the publication of said book the plaintiff has suffered great mental anguish and humiliation. Relatives of the plaintiff who had been purposely kept unaware of the marital difficulties existent between plaintiff and his wife were notified of same upon reading the book. The plaintiff has become the subject of public curiosity and gossip in his community, and his business affairs have been adversely affected. The plaintiff is a reasonable person of ordinary sensibilities who has been justifiably aggrieved by virtue of having his private life exposed by this publication in a manner constituting an actionable invasion of privacy.

(continued)

FIGURE 2–4   *(concluded)*

9. Defendant World Press, Inc., and defendant Herbert Miller maliciously intended to injure and aggrieve the plaintiff by thrusting on him unwarranted and undesirable publicity and notoriety, knowing that the plaintiff did not wish the matters contained in the chapter to be published. The plaintiff seeks punitive damages of Five Hundred Thousand Dollars ($500,000.00).

   WHEREFORE, plaintiff prays for judgment against the defendant World Press, Inc., and Herbert Miller as follows:
1. General damages of One Million Dollars ($1,000,000.00);
2. Special damages as may hereafter be ascertained;
3. Punitive damages of Five Hundred Thousand Dollars ($500,000.00);
4. Costs of this action;
5. Compensation for reasonable attorney's fees;
6. Such other and further relief as the Court may deem proper in the premises.

QUIK & BONO

Quick and Bono

By:
Attorneys for Plaintiff,
John Smith

Summons

The serving of a **summons** on the defendant gives notice to the defendant of the suit, informs him or her who the plaintiff is, and states the time within which the defendant must make an **appearance** (see Figure 2–5). In most states the complaint must be served with the summons.

The rules regarding the service of the summons vary widely. Generally, it is served by the sheriff or other appropriate public official, and only within the geographic limits of the court's jurisdiction. In state courts this is normally a county. In some types of cases, service by mail or by leaving the summons at the defendant's residence or place of business is allowed.

The defendant usually makes an appearance by filing an **answer** to the complaint. This is ordinarily done by defendant's attorney. If the defendant fails to appear, the plaintiff is entitled to a **default judgment.** This has the same effect as if the plaintiff had won in court everything requested in the complaint.

The Answer

The answer generally responds to the complaint paragraph by paragraph. Each **allegation** (statement) of the complaint is admitted or denied, or the defendant may disclaim knowledge and leave the plaintiff to prove the allegations made (see Figure 2–6 on pages 38 and 39).

The answer may also state an **affirmative defense.** An affirmative defense is a rule of law enabling defendant to win even if all of plaintiff's allegations are true. For example, the plaintiff may allege that defendant breached their contract. The defendant might respond by admitting that the contract had been breached but that he or she

FIGURE 2–5   Summons

UNITED STATES DISTRICT COURT
SOUTHERN DISTRICT OF INDIANA
INDIANAPOLIS DIVISION

JOHN SMITH   )
)
            Plaintiff   )
)
      v.   )   CIVIL ACTION NO. IP 79-53-C
)
)
WORLD PRESS, INC.,   )
and HERBERT MILLER   )
)
      Defendants   )

SUMMONS

To Above Named Defendants _____

You have been sued by the person(s) named "plaintiff" in the court stated above.

The nature of the suit against you is stated in the complaint which is attached to this document. It also states the demand which the plaintiff has made and wants from you.

You must answer the complaint in writing, by you or your attorney, within twenty (20) days, commencing the day after you receive this summons, or judgment will be entered against you for what the plaintiff has demanded. You have twenty-three (23) days to answer if this summons was received by mail. Such Answer Must Be Made in Court.

If you have a claim for relief against the plaintiff arising from the same transaction or occurrence, you must assert it in your written answer.

Date_____November 12, 1998_____   *Oliver M. Jones*
                                            Clerk (Seal)

Quirk and Bono
Attorneys for Plaintiff
430 S. Walnut St.
Bloomington, IN 47401
Telephone _____812-336-0000_____

should not be held liable because the contract had been induced by plaintiff's fraudulent misrepresentations. The defendant's affirmative defense must be supported by facts presented in the same manner as in a complaint.

FIGURE 2–6   Answer

UNITED STATES DISTRICT COURT
SOUTHERN DISTRICT OF INDIANA
INDIANAPOLIS DIVISION

JOHN SMITH   )
)
              Plaintiff   )
)
         v.   )   CIVIL ACTION NO. IP 79-53-C
)
WORLD PRESS, INC.,   )
and HERBERT MILLER   )
)
              Defendants   )

DEFENDANTS' ANSWER

Defendants World Press, Inc., and Herbert Miller make the following answer to Complaint of plaintiff John Smith.

First Defense

1. They admit the allegations of paragraph 1, except deny that Herbert Miller is a citizen of New York. He is a citizen of Maine.
2. They admit that World Press, Inc., publishes books under the name World Press. They deny all other allegations of paragraph 2.
3. They admit that during 1998 World Press, Inc., published a book entitled *40 Seconds and Death* authored by Herbert Miller and that the book contained in its Chapter 4 a section entitled "Weekend Tryst." They admit that Exhibit One (attached to plaintiff's Complaint) is a copy of that section of the book. They deny all other allegations of paragraph 3.
4, 5, 6. They deny the allegations of paragraphs 4, 5, and 6.
7. They admit that plaintiff's real name was not used in the book. They are without knowledge or information sufficient to form a belief as to the truth of the remaining allegations of paragraph 7.
8, 9. They deny the allegations of paragraphs 8 and 9.

Second Defense

Plaintiff John Smith consented to the publication of the information complained of.

Third Defense

The information published by defendants relates to an event and topic of general and public interest. Defendants' publication of the information complained of was privileged by the First and Fourteenth Amendments to the United States Constitution and by Article I, Section 9, of the Indiana Constitution.

(continued)

The defendant can also **counterclaim** for damages. A counterclaim is a new claim stating that plaintiff owes defendant damages because of harm resulting from the

FIGURE 2-6   *(concluded)*

Fourth Defense

The information published by defendants is true or substantially true in all relevant respects.

WHEREFORE, defendants World Press, Inc., and Herbert Miller pray that plaintiff John Smith take nothing by his complaint, for their costs, and for all other proper relief.

Roger P. Rogers

Roger P. Rogers
Attorney for Defendants
World Press, Inc., and Herbert Miller

---

incident alleged in the complaint. In the above example, defendant might claim that plaintiff's fraud caused several hundred dollars' worth of damages for which the plaintiff should be liable.

The defendant may make a **motion to dismiss** the case rather than give an answer. If it is clear that the plaintiff has no case, it would be wasteful for the case to continue, and the motion would be granted. The ground for such a motion might be that the facts given in the plaintiff's complaint are not legally sufficient to "state a cause of action"—that is, even if the facts alleged can be proved, the law does not give a remedy for the type of injury alleged. For example, Bill sues the local school system because it gave him a high school diploma but taught him to read only at a fifth-grade level. Even if this is true, the law does not allow suits for educational malpractice, so the case would be dismissed.

Reply

In some jurisdictions plaintiff is allowed or required to **reply** to defendant's affirmative defense or counterclaim. The reply answers paragraph by paragraph the affirmative defense or counterclaim of the defendant.

DISCOVERY

The **discovery** phase of a lawsuit is the time during which the parties gather the evidence they will use at trial to prove or disprove the allegations made in the pleadings. Modern rules of discovery are designed to ensure that both parties have equal access to the facts so that the case can be judged on its merits. Thus, an attorney can request a copy of almost any relevant document, photograph, or other type of evidence that the opposite party might rely on or that, if available, would help the lawyer's case. The limits of discovery are set by the trial judge according to the procedural rules of the jurisdiction.

There are many kinds of discovery. For example, in a claim for physical or emotional injuries, the plaintiff can be required to undergo physical or mental examinations. A party may also take depositions from the opposite party and key witnesses. A *deposition* is an examination under oath, much like the questioning at a trial, in the presence of the attorney for the other party. Or a party may be required to answer written questions called *interrogatories,* which are answered in writing, under oath.

Pretrial Conference

A procedural device that is designed to narrow issues to be proved at trial, or to facilitate a settlement, is the **pretrial conference.** It was created to help deal with the increasing congestion in most civil courts. The conference is held in the judge's chambers. The parties themselves and their witnesses are not present because the conference is likely to go better if the parties are represented by intermediaries.

At the conference the judge tries to get the parties' attorneys to **stipulate to** (agree to) as many of the material facts as possible. The judge may find that, in spite of the appearance of the pleadings, there is no true disagreement on some important facts. For example, in an automobile accident case there may be no real issue as to whether the defendant was negligent; the only real question may be whether the plaintiff has suffered permanent disability and what value should be put on it. It saves much court time if the parties stipulate to the facts about the collision.

The judge may also try to persuade the parties to settle the case before trial. By suggesting the difficulty of proving some of the facts alleged in the pleadings and the uncertainty of what decision the jury will render, the judge may get the parties to conclude that they would rather settle than fight in court.

THE TRIAL

Setting the Case for Trial

Once the pleadings are complete, the case is set for trial on the court calendar. Because of congestion, there may be a delay of several months or even years before the trial occurs. Fortunately, most cases are settled before trial, or the congestion would be much worse. Frequently, cases have to be **continued** (postponed) and another date set for any one of several reasons. For example, it may be that another trial has lasted longer than expected or a necessary witness is unavailable.

If a jury is requested, arrangements must be made to have prospective jurors present at the time the trial is scheduled to begin. The jury list is drawn by chance from a list of eligible citizens. Judges differ as to their willingness to accept excuses from prospective jurors who desire to avoid this duty of citizenship. If neither party requests a jury, the judge will hear the case, making separate findings of fact and law in reaching a judgment.

Opening the Case

After the jury, if any, is selected and sworn, the attorneys make **opening statements,** with plaintiff's attorney going first. The attorneys explain the nature of the case and what they intend to prove. The opening statements are more elaborate and probably more dramatically presented when a jury is present than if the case is tried before only a judge.

Presentation of Testimony

The plaintiff's attorney then presents the plaintiff's evidence through witnesses and exhibits. Each witness is sworn and then examined by the plaintiff's attorney; this is called **direct examination.** The defendant's attorney may **cross-examine** each witness, trying to raise doubts as to the person's credibility or trustworthiness. The plaintiff's attorney may then conduct a **redirect examination** to clarify the plaintiff's view of the facts and perhaps to minimize whatever negative effect was created in the cross-examination.

During a witness's testimony, the opposing attorney may object to the presentation of certain evidence. The judge then decides whether the evidence is admissible under the rules of evidence. These rules are designed to ensure that evidence is accurate, nonprejudicial, and legally relevant.

Following the end of testimony by witnesses for the plaintiff, the defendant's lawyer frequently makes a motion for a **directed verdict.** The judge grants the motion only if plaintiff's evidence is clearly insufficient to support his or her allegations. If the motion is granted, the trial ends. Usually the motion is denied, however, and the trial continues. There is then direct examination of the defendant's witnesses by the defendant's attorney, followed by cross-examination. This is again usually followed by a motion for a directed verdict.

Closing the Case

The attorneys then make closing arguments that sum up the case. Normally the defendant's attorney goes first. This give the plaintiff, who has the **burden of proof,** the last word. The burden of proof for a criminal case is different from that for a civil case. In a criminal case the state, as plaintiff, must convince the fact finder—jury or judge—**beyond a reasonable doubt** of the defendant's guilt. In a civil case the plaintiff need only have the **preponderance of the evidence** on his or her side. This means that the plaintiff must have shown that it is more likely than not that what was alleged is true.

If there is a jury, the judge instructs it on the law applicable to the case. The attorneys for the parties suggest instructions, tailoring them to the facts as they hope the jury will find them. The judge need not use the proposed instructions since giving proper instructions is her or his responsibility. In many states standard instructions have been developed for common types of cases.

After being instructed, the jury goes to the jury room, where it discusses the case, determines the facts, and applies the law to these facts as instructed by the judge. Ballots are taken until a verdict is reached. In important criminal cases involving much public interest and discussion, the jury may be **sequestered.** This means that jurors are not permitted to leave the supervision of the court, day or night, until excused. This is to keep outside influences away. Once there is unanimous agreement (or whatever majority is required by law) on a verdict, the jury foreperson reports this to the judge. If the jury cannot come to a verdict, there is a **hung jury.** Then a decision must be made by the plaintiff (or the prosecutor in a criminal case) whether to bring the case to trial again.

Whichever way the jury finds, the losing party in a civil case can make a motion for **judgment notwithstanding the verdict (judgment n.o.v.).** This is a claim that no reasonable jury could come to that verdict on the basis of the evidence presented at the trial. Such a motion is very rarely granted. The state cannot make such a motion if the defendant is acquitted in a criminal case.

Enforcing the Judgment

At the conclusion of the trial (or after the appeal, if one is taken), the party who wins a remedy is entitled to receive it. In a civil case, this is usually an award of money damages. If the loser does not pay the judgment, the winner can get the court's help to enforce it through the issuance of a writ of execution or a writ of garnishment. A **writ of execution** orders the sheriff to seize and sell enough of the defendant's property to satisfy the judgment. All states have *exemption laws* that exempt certain classes and amounts of a debtor's property from execution. A **writ of garnishment** is designed to reach things belonging to the debtor that are in the hands of third parties, such as wages, bank accounts, and accounts receivable. Garnishment proceedings, like execution sales, are highly regulated by statute. When the property needed to satisfy the judgment is in another state, the plaintiff will have to use the garnishment or execution procedures of that state. Under the U.S. Constitution, the second state is required to give "full faith and credit" to the judgment of the state in which the trial occurred.

Where the court has awarded an equitable remedy such as an injunction, the losing party may be found in **contempt of court** and subjected to a fine or imprisonment if he or she fails to obey the court's orders.

APPELLATE PROCEDURE

Basis for Appeal

Being dissatisfied with the judgment of the court is not a sufficient ground for an appeal. To be able to appeal, a party must claim that the court made an *error of law* or that the evidence in the trial did not support the trial court's decision. For example, if an attorney objects to a question asked of a witness by the other attorney, the judge must rule on it. This ruling can serve as a basis for appeal by the party against whom the ruling was made. Or the losing party might claim the judge misstated the law in the instructions to the jury. In order to serve as a basis for appeal, the attorney must have *objected* to the judge's action at the time the alleged error was made. This is to give the trial judge a chance to correct the error and avoid the possible expense of a new trial.

THE APPEAL

To appeal, the party must file an appeal with the proper appellate court within the period of time established by statute. A **transcript** of the entire trial proceeding, including the testimony of all the witnesses and any discussions between the judge and the attorneys, must be prepared and forwarded to the appeals court. The attorneys for each party also submit a **brief,** or written argument supporting their claims. *Citations* (references) are made to precedent cases and perhaps to *treatises* (textbooks) or articles written by legal scholars. When people or groups other than the parties involved are interested in the outcome of a certain appeal, they may request to be permitted to file *amicus curiae* (friend of the court) briefs.

The appellate process is essentially based on written documents. The appellate courts hear no witnesses and gather no new evidence. Although attorneys for the parties often ask to make oral arguments to supplement the written briefs, permission is not always granted. If the court allows the attorneys to argue orally, they are given

CONCEPT SUMMARY	**Stages of a Lawsuit**		
Pleading Stage	**Discovery Stage**	**Trial Stage**	**Appellate Stage**
Complaint	Types of discovery:	Selection of jury	Filing of appeal
Answer	Deposition	Opening statements	Transcript and briefs filed
Reply	Request for admissions	Cases in chief	Oral argument if permitted
	Written interrogatories	Closing arguments	Opinion rendered
	Production of documents	Instructions to jury	
	Request for physical examination	Verdict	
	Request for mental examination	Judgment	
	Pretrial conference		

only a limited amount of time in which to do so, and the judges frequently interrupt to ask questions. The facts as found by the jury (or judge) at the trial are accepted as true. An exception occurs when it is claimed that there was no competent evidence at the trial to support a finding of fact or the granting or refusal of a motion by the court. For example, an appellate court would have to review the evidence presented at the trial when the error by the trial judge is alleged to be a failure to grant a motion for a directed verdict. The transcript of the trial is used for this purpose. If there is doubt, it is assumed that the trial judge who heard the witnesses made the correct assessment.

RESULTS OF APPEAL

In order to successfully appeal, the party must show that the errors that were made were **material,** that is, important enough to possibly change the trial outcome. The large majority of appeals are not successful. This is primarily because most errors made at trial are not material; the result would have been the same even if the error had not been made.

Decisions of the appellate courts are based on majority rule. Once a decision is reached, the judges generally write an opinion explaining their legal reasoning. These opinions are published and form the basis of our legal system of precedent. The appeals court may **affirm** (uphold) the judgment of the trial court, or it may **reverse** it. Sometimes a court may reverse and **remand.** This sends the case back to the trial court for further proceedings, and a new trial is then required. It may be remanded on a very narrow question of fact, or it may be a complete retrial of the case. Frequently the parties settle their controversy at this point rather than going through another trial.

COURT PROBLEMS AND PROPOSED SOLUTIONS

SOME CRITICISMS

Like most institutions, the courts are the subject of much criticism. As mentioned earlier, one of the greatest problems is delay. It is often said, "Justice delayed is justice denied." Despite the recent addition of more judges, especially in the federal courts, delay in the courts remains a major problem. A victim of an automobile collision who cannot get a trial on his or her claim for damages for two, three, or five years may be financially ruined before the losses can be recovered.

Another major criticism is that today courts are trying to deal with cases that they are ill equipped to handle. Examples are cases that involve solving social problems such as racial discrimination in the public schools and inhumane conditions in state prisons or mental institutions. A lawsuit is filed because a person claims his constitutional or other legal rights have been invaded. However, many people question whether the adversary process is the best way of dealing with these complicated problems. Should judges serve as school superintendents? Not in an ideal world; but what if the school board fails or refuses to end the discrimination? A traditional role of the courts is to prevent violence by providing an alternative, peaceful, and more just means of resolving disputes. Critics may well be asked how else or better the interests of the weak and powerless, whether minorities, prisoners, or others, can be protected.

PROPOSALS

There are not sufficient resources to solve the problems of congestion and delay through the addition of judges. Other proposals include removing whole classes of cases from courts. A large proportion of court time is taken by automobile accident cases. Product liability cases (involving injuries and losses caused by defective products) and malpractice claims against doctors and other professionals are rapidly growing in number. Often the cost of bringing suit, including attorneys' fees, eats up more than half the damage award in these kinds of cases. It has been suggested that these cases could be handled as well or better by administrative agencies, much as workers' compensation cases now are. It has also been proposed (and implemented in many states) that noncontested divorces and distributions of the property of deceased persons be handled administratively.

Other devices have been developed to speed trials and make courts more efficient. These range from computerizing the court to severely limiting postponements and/or discovery to limits on expert witnesses. Class actions (where the harms of several people are litigated in a single lawsuit) are increasingly used, especially in product liability and mass-disaster cases, to resolve many disputes in one case. These devices have some beneficial effects, but cannot solve the basic problem as long as our society continues to be so litigious and inadequate resources are allocated to the courts. One thing seems certain—people will increasingly resort to the use of alternatives to the courts as long as litigation remains so slow and expensive.

QUESTIONS AND PROBLEM CASES

1. Explain two types of ADR and why these mechanisms are increasingly being used.
2. Explain *venue* and why a judge would grant a motion for a change of venue.
3. Explain why an appeal can be taken only from a court of record.
4. Explain the differences between the judge's role in the adversary system and the role in a code system common in Europe.
5. What is *discovery* and when does it occur in the litigation process?
6. What is the burden of proof in a civil suit, and how does it differ from the burden of proof in a criminal suit?
7. Explain diversity jurisdiction.
8. When Gilmer was hired as a broker he was required to sign a NYSE registration form under which he agreed to "arbitrate any dispute, claim or controversy" arising between him and his employer. When his employment was terminated six years later (when Gilmer was 62), he sued for age discrimination under the Age Discrimination in Employment Act. His employer argued that the dispute had to be arbitrated. Will Gilmer have to arbitrate his arbitration claim?
9. Connie, a resident of Michigan, was visiting her grandmother in California. While dining at a restaurant, a light fixture fell and severely cut Connie's arm. Connie required surgery and several months of physical therapy before she was able to use her arm properly, and she still has residual damage. She sues the restaurant, asking for $500,000 to reimburse medical expenses, lost wages, and the permanent damage, and $500,000 for pain and suffering. Where can the lawsuit be heard, and why?

CHAPTER 3

Crimes

Hartley was accused of conspiring to defraud the U.S. government by supplying breaded shrimp that did not conform to military specifications, of committing mail fraud by sending the government invoices through the mail seeking payment for the shrimp, and of interstate transportation of money obtained by fraud by obtaining treasury checks for the invoices for the shrimp. He and his company were also charged with violating the Racketeer Influenced and Corrupt Organizations Act (RICO) because these crimes allegedly established a pattern of racketeering.

- *What constitutional protections does Hartley have as one who has been accused of a crime?*
- *What are the essentials of a crime that the government must show in order to obtain a conviction?*
- *Can these related acts flowing from one incident committed by a legitimate business establish a pattern of racketeering activity?*

.... *THE NATURE OF CRIMES* ....

Crimes are **public wrongs**—acts prohibited by the *state* or *federal government*. Criminal prosecutions are brought by the prosecutor in the name of the government. Those who are convicted of committing criminal acts are subject to punishment established by the state or federal government in the form of fines, imprisonment, or execution.

Crimes are usually classed as felonies or misdemeanors, depending on the seriousness of the offense. **Felonies** are serious offenses such as murder, rape, and arson that are generally punishable by confinement in a penitentiary for substantial periods of time. Conviction of a felony may, in some cases, also result in **disenfranchisement** (loss of the right to vote) and bar a person from practicing certain professions such as law or medicine. **Misdemeanors** are lesser crimes such as traffic offenses or disorderly conduct that are punishable by fines or confinement in a city or county jail. Those convicted of crimes must also bear the **stigma** or social condemnation that accompanies a criminal conviction.

Whether a given act is classified as criminal or not is a social question. Our definitions of criminal conduct change with time. Behavior that was once considered criminal (e.g., blasphemy) is no longer treated as such. Today, we see many proposals to decriminalize certain kinds of behavior such as gambling, prostitution, and consensual sex. Those who argue for decriminalization maintain that attempts to treat such "victimless crimes" criminally are ineffective, cause corruption, overburden the courts and police, and cause a loss of respect for the law. We also see calls for increased criminal penalties as a way to control corporate behavior. Deciding how to treat unwanted behavior is one of the more difficult problems facing society today.

THE ESSENTIALS OF CRIME

In order for a person to be convicted of criminal behavior, the state must (1) demonstrate a prior statutory prohibition of the act, (2) prove beyond a reasonable doubt that the defendant committed every element of the criminal offense prohibited by the statute, and (3) prove that the defendant had the capacity to form a criminal intent. Figure 3–1 gives an overview of these steps.

Prior Statutory Prohibition

Before behavior can be treated as criminal, the legislature must have passed a statute making it criminal. Both Congress and the state legislatures can make an act a crime, and individuals are subject to the criminal laws of both systems. The Constitution protects against ***ex post facto laws***—statutes that would punish someone for an act that was not considered criminal when the act was committed. Only those who commit the prohibited act *after* the effective date of the statute may be prosecuted.

The power of Congress and the state legislatures to make behavior criminal is constitutionally limited in other ways. Congress and state legislatures cannot make behavior criminal that is protected by the U.S. Constitution. For example, they would be prohibited from enforcing laws that unreasonably restrict the First Amendment right to freedom of speech and expression. Criminal statutes must also define the prohibited behavior clearly, so that an ordinary person would understand what behavior is prohibited. This requirement comes from the Due Process Clauses in the Fifth and Fourteenth Amendments to the U.S. Constitution. These limits are illustrated by the *Morales* case.

FIGURE 3–1   A Criminal Case

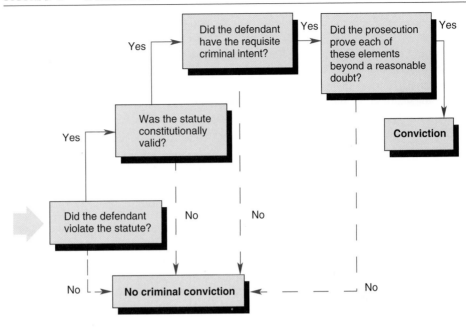

CHICAGO V. MORALES
527 U.S. 41 (U.S. Sup. Ct. 1999)

FACTS

Chicago passed a loitering ordinance after hearings which determined that criminal street-gang activity was largely responsible for the increasing murder rate and that gang members established control over "their" territory by loitering and intimidating others from entering that area. The ordinance provided: "Whenever a police officer observes a person whom he reasonably believes to be a criminal street gang member loitering in any public place with one or more other persons, he shall order all such persons to disperse and remove themselves from the area. Any person who does not promptly obey such an order is in violation of this [ordinance]." " 'Loiter' means to remain in any one place with no apparent purpose." The police adopted a policy of arresting anyone who did not promptly obey the order. Morales and other youths were observed loitering and were arrested when they failed to promptly disperse. They challenged their arrest, arguing the statute was unconstitutional.

ISSUES

Is the loitering ordinance unconstitutionally vague?

DECISION

Yes. The fact that the ordinance applies only to persons who are stationary and allows arrests only after an order to disperse has been ignored does not provide police any guidance in deciding whether to issue the dispersal order. Additionally, the "no apparent purpose" standard is inherently subjective because its application depends on whether some purpose is apparent to the officer on the scene. The police are not required to inquire about a possible purpose. They don't know or inquire whether the reason that a gang member and his father, for example, might loiter near Wrigley Field is to rob an unsuspecting fan or just to get a glimpse of Sammy Sosa leaving the ballpark. It also does not give sufficient notice to the public of what conduct is prohibited. It is difficult to imagine

(continued)

CHICAGO V. MORALES
(concluded)

how any citizen of Chicago standing in a public place with a group of people would know if he or she had an "apparent purpose." Engaging in idle conversation or simply enjoying a cool breeze on a warm evening may not show an "apparent purpose." The limitation that the officer reasonably believes that one member of the group is a gang member is also insufficient. However, a similar statute may be constitutional. If the ordinance applied only to loitering with an apparently harmful purpose or effect, it would be constitutional, and it may be constitutional if it covered only suspected gang members.

Proof beyond a Reasonable Doubt

In view of the fact that in criminal cases we are dealing with the life and liberty of the accused person, as well as the stigma accompanying conviction, the legal system places strong limits on the power of the state to convict a person of a crime. Criminal defendants are *presumed innocent.* The state must overcome this presumption of innocence by proving every element of the offense charged against the defendant **beyond a reasonable doubt** to the satisfaction of all the jurors. This requirement is the primary way our system minimizes the risk of convicting an innocent person.

The state must prove its case within a framework of procedural safeguards, discussed later in this chapter, that are designed to protect the accused. The state's failure to prove any material element of its case results in the accused being acquitted or found not guilty, even though he or she may actually have committed the crime charged.

The Defendant's Capacity

Mens rea (criminal intent) is an element of most serious crimes. The basic idea behind requiring intent is that the criminal law generally seeks to punish *conscious* wrongdoers. Criminal intent may be inferred from the nature of the defendant's acts, but the defendant must be capable of forming the required criminal intent. Generally, a person can be incapable of forming the required intent due to intoxication, infancy, or insanity.

Voluntary intoxication is generally not a complete defense to criminal liability. It can, in some cases, diminish the extent of a defendant's liability if it prevents the formation of a specific criminal intent. For example, many first-degree murder statutes require proof of **premeditation,** a conscious decision to kill. A highly intoxicated defendant may not be capable of premeditation and may therefore be convicted of only second-degree murder, which does not generally require premeditation.

In common law, children under the age of 7 were incapable of forming a criminal intent, children between the ages of 7 and 14 were presumed incapable, and children between the ages of 14 and 21 were presumed capable. This is the concept of **infancy.** The **presumptions** relating to **capacity** were **rebuttable** by specific evidence about the intellectual and moral development of the accused. Today, most states have statutes that treat defendants below a stated age (usually 16 or 17) differently from adult offenders. The focus of these laws is rehabilitation rather than capacity, and they provide for special juvenile court systems and separate detention facilities. Repeat offenders, or those charged with very serious offenses, may be treated as adults.

The Supreme Court even upheld imposition of the death penalty for a 16-year-old murderer.[1]

Insanity on the part of a criminal defendant can affect a criminal trial in three ways. If the accused is incapable of assisting in the defense of the case, trial may be delayed until the accused regains sanity. An accused who becomes insane after trial but before sentencing is not sentenced until sanity has been regained. Insanity at the time the criminal act was committed absolves the defendant of criminal liability.

The states have adopted various insanity tests for criminal responsibility. These tests are not medical tests. They are legal tests designed to punish conscious, willful wrong-doers. A person may have been medically insane at the time of the criminal act but still legally responsible. Until recently, the trend was to broaden the legal definition of insanity by using such tests as the **irresistible impulse** rule or the test proposed by the American Law Institute, which says that defendants are not criminally responsible if, due to a mental disease or defect, they lack the substantial capacity to appreciate the wrongfulness of the act or to conform their conduct to the requirements of the law. Recent well-publicized cases have caused some jurisdictions to return to a narrower standard. For example, the standard adopted for federal criminal cases absolves only those defendants who cannot understand the nature and wrongfulness of their acts. In addition, some states have instituted a "guilty, but mentally ill" verdict as an alternative to the traditional "not guilty by reason of insanity" verdict. This alternative allows jurors to convict rather than acquit mentally ill defendants, with the assurance that they will be given treatment after conviction.

A criminal defendant is presumed to be sane. The defendant must introduce evidence that creates a reasonable doubt as to his or her sanity. Juries are often hostile toward insanity pleas, fearing that defendants are only trying to avoid punishment. Recent legislative changes in some jurisdictions have made it more difficult to successfully raise the insanity defense by requiring defendants to prove their insanity beyond a reasonable doubt.

CRIMINAL PROCEDURE

In addition to the presumption of innocence, our legal system has several other built-in safeguards to protect the accused. These safeguards are designed to prevent innocent people from being convicted of crimes they did not commit. They also represent an ideal of the proper role of government in a democracy. As Justice Oliver Wendell Holmes once said, "I think it less evil that some criminals should escape than that the government should play an ignoble part."

Table 3–1 on page 51 illustrates some of the safeguards enjoyed by criminal defendants in our legal system.

Many of these safeguards are based on the Fourth and Fifth Amendments to the U.S. Constitution. The Fourth Amendment safeguards are designed to protect individuals from arbitrary and unreasonable governmental intrusion on their right to privacy. The Fifth Amendment safeguards protect against compulsory self-incrimination and multiple prosecutions for the same offense. None of these protections is absolute. For example, while people cannot be compelled to testify against themselves, **nontestimonial** evidence such as fingerprints, hair samples, and bodily fluids can be obtained through compulsion.

---

[1]Standford v. Kentucky, 109 S. Ct. 2926 (1989).

In determining whether a governmental action has unconstitutionally infringed on an individual's right, the court must balance the governmental need to do the action against the intrusion on the individual's rights. In the *Kyllo* case, the balance is struck in favor of the individual.

KYLLO V. UNITED STATES
121 S. Ct. 2038 (U.S. Sup. Ct. 2001)

FACTS

Federal law enforcement officers suspected Kyllo of drug violations. They scanned his home with a thermal imager and got evidence of unusually high levels of heat coming from the home. They concluded this heat "signature" indicated the use of high-intensity lights used to grow marijuana. Based on this and other information, they obtained a warrant to search his home. The search uncovered an indoor marijuana-growing operation, weapons, and drug paraphernalia. When indicted, Kyllo sought to exclude the evidence from the search, arguing that the scanning was itself a search which needed a warrant. Since the warrant the officers obtained was based on the illegally obtained imaging evidence, the subsequent evidence was barred under the exclusionary rule.

ISSUES

Is scanning a home with a thermal imaging device a search which requires a warrant?

DECISION

Yes. In most instances, a warrantless search of a home is not reasonable and is therefore unconstitutional. How-ever, what is a "search" for Fourth Amendment purposes is sometimes a hard question. A search does not occur—even when its object is a house explicitly protected by the Fourth Amendment—unless the individual shows a subjective expectation of privacy that society recognizes as reasonable. It is assumed that it is reasonable to expect privacy within one's home. To withdraw protection of this minimum expectation would be to permit police technology to erode the privacy guaranteed by the Fourth Amendment. Thus, obtaining any information regarding the home's interior by sense-enhancing technology that could not otherwise have been obtained without physically entering the home, is a search, at least when the technology used is not in general public use. We reject the argument that the search was constitutional because it did not detect intimate details. In the sanctity of the home, *all* details are intimate details. This holding assures the preservation of that degree of privacy against government that existed when the Fourth Amendment was adopted.

Many of the safeguards discussed in Table 3–1, such as the exclusionary rule, the *Miranda* warning, and the places where one can reasonably expect to be protected from unreasonable warrantless searches, are being narrowed through recent Supreme Court interpretations. In times of rising crime rates, we frequently hear the argument that the incidence of crime is somehow related to our treatment of criminal defendants. While it is no doubt true that criminal safeguards allow some guilty persons to go free, attacking the root causes of criminal behavior is likely to do more to reduce crime than any reformation of the constitutional mandates.

Some of the protections discussed in Table 3–1 have been eroded for people suspected of being terrorists. This results from the attacks of September 11. The Supreme Court has not yet ruled on these changes.

TABLE 3–1   Criminal Procedural Protection

Description	Common Identification	Amendment
1. Illegally gained evidence (evidence resulting from "unreasonable searches and seizures" prohibited by the Fourth Amendment) cannot be used in criminal prosecutions.	Exclusionary rule	Fourth Amendment
2. A warrant for a search or arrest cannot be issued without probable cause.	Probable cause requirement	Fourth Amendment
3. Acquitted defendants can't be tried twice for the same crime.	Prohibition against double jeopardy	Fifth Amendment
4. Defendants in criminal cases have the right to remain silent and can't be compelled to testify against themselves.	Part of the *Miranda* warning	Fifth Amendment
5. When persons are taken into custody, the police must inform them of the right to remain silent, the right to counsel (which will be provided it they can't pay), and that anything they say can be used against them in court. Confessions made without these warnings cannot be used to convict a person.	*Miranda* warning	Fifth Amendment
6. Persons charged with crimes have a right to be represented by effective counsel if imprisonment can result from conviction.	Part of the *Miranda* warning	Sixth Amendment
7. Accused persons have a right to a speedy, public trial by a jury of their peers.	Trial by jury	Sixth Amendment
8. Persons accused of crimes have the right to confront and cross-examine their accusers.	Right of confrontation	Sixth Amendment
9. Excessive bail or fines, and cruel and unusual punishment are prohibited.	No cruel and unusual punishment	Eighth Amendment

CRIME AND PEOPLE IN BUSINESS

People in business today are more likely than ever before to have some unpleasant contact with the criminal justice system. There is a trend today to get tough with white-collar crime. *White-collar* crime is the term used to describe various nonviolent criminal offenses committed by businesspersons and organizations. The focus of this trend is on business-related acts that primarily harm people outside the corporation. Such crime costs the public billions of dollars a year. A part of this trend is to make violations of regulatory statutes criminal offenses punishable by fines and/or imprisonment.

Many prosecutors and judges are demonstrating a "get tough" attitude about white-collar crimes that have often been treated leniently in the past. As the *Sabine* case illustrates, corporate officials are even being tried for homicide and related crimes under state criminal law because prosecutors feel that the officials' actions (or lack thereof) are responsible for the deaths and serious injuries of employees or consumers and that federal laws are not sufficiently tough or enforced. It is argued that personal liability for corporate executives is necessary to **deter** corporations from violating laws and from viewing any fines imposed on the corporation as merely a cost of doing business.

Sabine v. Texas
806 S. W. 2d 553 (Tex. Crim. App. 1991)

Facts

Sabine Consolidated Inc., and its president, Joseph Tantillo, were charged with criminally negligent homicide for the deaths of two workers killed when the walls of the excavating trench in which they were working collapsed. The walls were not properly supported or sloped as required by Occupational Safety and Health Administration (OSHA) regulations. Tantillo's conviction was challenged on the ground that OSHA, a federal regulatory scheme, *preempted* state enforcement of workplace safety through the use of general criminal laws.

Issue

Can an individual be prosecuted under state criminal law when federal regulations cover the same behavior, and the federal penalties are much less?

Decision

Yes. The doctrine of *preemption* is based on the Supremacy Clause of the U.S. Constitution. It invalidates state laws that interfere with, or are contrary to, federal law. OSHA is designed to be preventative and focuses only on workplace safety. The criminal law is reactive and retributive, and covers a broad range of criminal conduct. Simply because a state criminal law may incidentally concern an area controlled by federal law does not automatically make the state law impermissible. Applying state criminal laws to conduct in the workplace does not present an obstacle to OSHA's goals of assuring employees safe and healthful working conditions. If anything, it supports the OSHA duty and standards. Several states now allow prosecution under state criminal law for deaths and injuries from unsafe working conditions.

Problems with Individual Liabilities

The get-tough attitude on the part of law enforcement officials is probably the result of several factors. There has been a long-standing public outcry against the lenient treatment of white-collar crime. This has been aggravated by statistics indicating the tremendous cost of such crime and by the post-Watergate atmosphere of public hostility toward people in positions of power and authority.

Imposing individual criminal responsibility on persons in business poses difficult problems for prosecutors, however. The criminal law was developed with individual wrongdoers in mind. Corporate decisions are often the product of the inputs of numerous individuals. "Bad news" about corporate activities may not reach upper-level managers. As a result, it is often difficult to prove criminal intent on the part of individual managers. One legislative response to this problem of difficulty of proof has been the creation of regulatory statutes that impose liability without proof of the level of intent or knowledge traditionally required for criminal liability. As *Dean* illustrates, courts have also become more lenient in interpreting the intent or knowledge requirements.

United States v. Dean
969 F. 2d 187 (6th Cir. 1992)

Facts

Dean, the production manager of a metal stamping, plating, and painting facility, oversaw an operation that disposed of liquid hazardous chemicals in an earthen lagoon outside the facility, and buried solid waste in barrels in a pit behind the facility. Dean knew the chemicals were hazardous because of information provided him by the chemical manufacturers. This information also stated the chemicals were subject to state and federal pollution control laws. Dean was also familiar with the company's disposal methods. The facility did not have a permit for

(continued)

UNITED STATES V. DEAN
(concluded)

treating, storing, and disposing of hazardous waste as required by the Resource Conservation and Recovery Act (RCRA). When Dean was convicted of violating the act, he challenged the conviction on the ground that the government did not prove that he knew of the permit requirement.

ISSUE

Is proof that defendant knew he needed a permit necessary for conviction under the act?

DECISION

No. Knowledge of the permit requirement is not an element of the crime. The statute penalizes anyone who "knowingly treats, stores, or disposes of hazardous waste . . . without a permit." The word "knowingly" requires knowing that one is treating hazardous waste. The statute requires proof that the treatment was done without a permit. It does not require the person charged to have known that a permit was required. Persons involved in hazardous waste handling have every reason to be aware that their activities are regulated by law. Here the documentation provided by the manufacturers of the chemicals abundantly illustrates one means by which knowledge of hazardous waste laws is communicated.

Sentencing Guidelines

Another illustration of the get-tough attitude is contained in the *Federal Sentencing Guidelines* designed to establish consistent sentences for federal crimes. The guidelines require judges to use a formula based on issues such as the seriousness of the crime, the defendant's criminal record, and the circumstances of the crime to arrive at the sentence. They specifically mandate stiffer penalties for white-collar crime. For example, crimes such as price fixing, bid rigging, and insider trading carry a minimum two-month prison term, and the likelihood of a prison term for tax fraud is more than doubled.

In addition to individual penalties, the *Corporate Sentencing Guidelines* establish penalties for organizations, including *corporate probation.* Under corporate probation, federal courts can monitor convicted companies and force them to establish programs to prevent and deter wrongdoing. The Guidelines also provide that corporations can reduce penalties by cooperating with investigations, making good faith efforts to self-police, and self-reporting wrongdoing.

RICO

Numerous crimes are encompassed within the term *white-collar* crime from bribery to fraud to price fixing to regulatory violations such as the environmental pollution involved in *United States v. Dean.* A statute increasingly being used to prosecute white-collar crime is the Racketeer Influenced and Corrupt Organizations Act (RICO).[2] Much of the current activity and controversy in the area of criminal laws affecting business surrounds this act.

RICO was passed by Congress as part of the Organized Crime Control Act of 1970 and, as the name suggests, was designed to stop the entry of organized crime into legitimate business enterprises. The broad language of the RICO statute, however, has resulted in its application to legitimate businesses in cases involving white-collar crimes such as securities fraud, mail fraud, and wire fraud. This development has made RICO one of the most controversial pieces of legislation affecting business in

---

[2]18 U.S.C. Secs. 1961–1968 (1976).

our legal history. Supporters of RICO argue that the law is not abused when it is used against those not involved in organized crime because the conduct prohibited by the statute is harmful no matter who engages in it. These supporters view RICO as an effective and much-needed weapon against unethical business practices. Critics of RICO, on the other hand, assert that it is an overbroad statute that has needlessly hurt business reputations and that it ought to be amended by Congress so that it cannot be used against legitimate businesses. The Supreme Court has generally refused to narrow the reach of RICO. Thus, change in this controversial legislation will likely come from Congress.

RICO prohibits (1) using income derived from "a pattern of racketeering activity" to acquire an interest in an enterprise, (2) acquiring or maintaining an interest in an enterprise through a pattern of racketeering activity, (3) conducting or participating in the affairs of an enterprise through a pattern of racketeering activity, or (4) conspiring to do the preceding. *Racketeering activity* includes the commission of any of over 30 federal or state crimes that include bribery; mail, wire, and securities fraud; and extortion. To show a pattern of activity, the prosecution must prove, at a minimum, the commission of two offenses within a 10-year period.

As the *King* case illustrates, companies also face civil liability under RICO. The government can seek civil penalties, and individuals injured by RICO violations can recover treble damages (three times their actual loss) plus attorneys' fees. The treble damages provision has caused a growing number of individuals to bring RICO claims and has contributed to the controversy surrounding the act.

CEDRIC KUSHNER PROMOTIONS, LTD. V. DON KING
121 S. Ct. 2087 (U.S. Sup. Ct. 2001)

FACTS

Cedric Kushner Promotions, a promoter of boxing matches, sued Don King, the president and sole shareholder of Don King Productions, a competitor, claiming that King had conducted the boxing-related affairs of the organization in violation of RICO through a "pattern" of at least two offenses of mail and wire fraud, and bribery. King argued that he could not be sued under RICO because the law requires two separate entities, a person and an enterprise through which the person improperly conducts business. In this instance, he is both.

ISSUE

Is King sufficiently legally distinct from the organization to be sued under RICO?

DECISION

Yes. RICO makes it unlawful "for any person employed by or associated with any enterprise . . . to conduct or participate . . . in the conduct of such enterprise's affairs through a pattern of racketeering activity." Thus, it requires two separate entities. In this case the corporate owner/employee, a natural person, is distinct from the corporation itself, a legally different entity with different rights and responsibilities due to its different legal status. Even where the employee is the corporation's sole owner they are distinct; after all, incorporation's basic purpose is to create a distinct legal entity. This interpretation is consistent with the statute's basic purposes to protect a legitimate enterprise from those who would use unlawful acts to victimize it, and protect the public from those who would unlawfully use an enterprise as a vehicle through which unlawful activity is committed.

In addition to growing criminal liability, businesses are increasingly being asked to help fight crime. This is evident in money-laundering rules. The USA Patriot Act, passed in the wake of the September 11, 2001, attacks, broadened the types of businesses involved in the fight against money-laundering well beyond the banks that

CONCEPT SUMMARY	RICO		
Prohibited Acts	1. To use income from racketeering activity to purchase an interest in an enterprise 2. To acquire or maintain an interest in an enterprise through racketeering activity 3. To conduct or participate in the affairs of an enterprise through racketeering activity 4. To conspire to do 1–3		
Requirements	1. Two listed offenses within a 10-year period 2. Threat of continued criminal activity (pattern of racketeering activity)		
Common Business Violations	Mail fraud Securities fraud Wire fraud Bribery		
Penalties	**Criminal**	**Civil**	
	Fine up to $25,000 Imprisonment up to 20 years Forfeiture	In government suit: Divestiture Dissolution Other forfeiture	In private suit: Treble damages Attorneys' fees

were traditionally involved. The new law includes organizations such as securities and commodities brokers; travel agencies; dealers in precious metals or jewels; car, boat, and airplane dealers; casinos; and those involved in real estate closings and settlements. Among other things, these businesses must report suspicious activity including large cash transactions.

Because of the increased liability faced by businesses and businesspeople in recent years, knowledge of the criminal law is an essential element of a contemporary business education.

QUESTIONS AND PROBLEM CASES

1. What is the burden of proof in a criminal case, and why is it set so high?

2. What is an *ex post facto* law?

3. Name three procedural safeguards and describe what protection they give.

4. An ordinance of Alexandria, Virginia, made it a misdemeanor to loiter with the intent unlawfully to possess or traffic in drugs. The ordinance spelled out specific circumstances that would show such intent, including being in the same general location for at least 15 minutes during which the person has two or more face-to-face encounters that last no more than two minutes with other individuals, while engaging in actions or movements consistent with exchanging money or other small objects and attempts to conceal an object. The ordinance was challenged as being unconstitutional because it restricted constitutionally protected activities. Does it?

5. The Michigan state police established a sobriety checkpoint program following an advisory committee's guidelines. During the first 75-minute check, 126 cars were stopped. The average delay was 25 seconds while officers briefly examined drivers for signs of intoxication. Two drivers were detained for field sobriety tests, and one of them was arrested for driving under the influence (DUI). A third driver who did not stop was apprehended and arrested for DUI. Sitz, a Michigan driver, sought an injunction preventing the police from conducting the sobriety checkpoints because he said they unconstitutionally invade a driver's right to privacy. Is he correct?

6. John R. Park, the president of Acme, a large national supermarket chain, was charged with violating the Federal Food, Drug, and Cosmetic Act by receiving and storing food in a warehouse where it was accessible to and

contaminated by rodents. In 1970 and 1971, federal investigators notified Park of unsanitary conditions in Acme's warehouses. Park conferred with his vice president for legal affairs, who said that corrective action would be taken. A 1972 follow-up investigation showed some improvement, but there was still rodent contamination and Park was charged. Park argued that he had delegated authority to his subordinates and that the government had to show some "wrongful action" on his part before he could be convicted. Do these facts justify Park's conviction?

7. Dow Chemical Company ran a 2,000-acre facility at Midland, Michigan, consisting of several covered buildings with equipment and piping between the buildings. It had elaborate security around the facility to prevent ground-level public views, and investigated any low-level flights over the facility. It did not protect all equipment from aerial views, however, because that was too expensive. The Environmental Protection Agency hired a commercial aerial photographer to photograph the facility from various heights. When Dow discovered this, it sued to prevent copying or release of the pictures and further photography. Were the governmentally ordered pictures an unconstitutional invasion of the company's privacy?

8. The car Houghton was riding in was stopped by an officer for speeding and driving with a faulty brake light. The officer noticed that the driver had a hypodermic syringe in his pocket and asked him about it. The driver said he used it to take drugs. The officer then searched the car for contraband, and during the search found Houghton's purse on the back seat. Inside the purse was a wallet and a pouch, and inside each was drug paraphernalia and illegal drugs. Houghton, who was charged with a felony drug offense, argued the warrantless search of her purse violated her Fourth Amendment rights. Is she correct?

9. Fitzgerald filed a consumer class action suit for fraud under RICO. It alleged that Chrysler Corp. committed wire and mail fraud through an "enterprise" consisting of the corporation, its franchised dealers, and subsidiaries engaged in various facets of production, financing, and marketing of Chrysler cars. Chrysler argued that these entities do not constitute an "enterprise." Do they?

10. Johnson & Towers, Inc., and two of its employees, a foreman and a trucking service manager, were indicted for violating the Resource Conservation and Recovery Act (RCRA) by knowingly dumping hazardous waste into a Delaware River tributary without a permit. The employees challenged the indictment, arguing that the government must prove that the employees knew they were dumping hazardous waste, and knew they were doing it without a permit. Must the government prove defendants knowingly violated the statute in order to obtain a conviction?

CHAPTER 4

Intentional Torts

Stevens was leaving a local department store when an armed security guard grabbed her arm and asked her to accompany him to an office in the back of the store. Once there, she was accused of shoplifting, and security personnel searched her, her purse, and the contents of a bag she was carrying. They found nothing incriminating. The store personnel kept her there for over two hours, badgering her to sign a release admitting her guilt in exchange for an agreement by the store not to prosecute her.

- *What intentional torts has the store committed against Stevens?*
- *What elements would Stevens have to show in order to prove these torts?*
- *Is Stevens likely to get punitive damages?*

.... *INTENTIONAL TORTS* ....

Torts are private (civil) wrongs against persons or property. Persons who are injured by the tortious act of another may file a civil suit for actual (**compensatory**) damages to compensate them for their injuries. Injury in tort can include much more than physical injury (and resulting direct injuries such as loss of pay and medical benefits). It also encompasses such intangible harms as loss of privacy, emotional distress, and injury to reputation. In some cases, **punitive damages** in excess of the plaintiff's actual injuries may be recovered. Punitive damages are used to punish the defendant and deter the defendant and others from repeating behavior that is particularly offensive. Defendant's actions in the *Jacque* case, described later in this chapter, are an example of the kind that could lead to the imposition of punitive damages.

The same behavior may give rise to both civil (tort) and criminal liability. For example, a rapist is criminally liable for the crime of rape and is also civilly liable for the torts of assault, battery, false imprisonment, and intentional infliction of emotional distress. The reason more victims of crimes do not file civil lawsuits against their attackers is simply that most criminal defendants are financially unable to pay a damage award. Some of the important differences between torts and crimes are shown in Table 4–1.

The plaintiff's burden of proof in a tort case is proof by a **preponderance of the evidence.** This simply means that when both sides have presented their evidence, the greater weight of the believable evidence must be on the plaintiff's side. This standard of proof is applied in all civil cases, in which only money is at stake, in contrast to criminal cases, in which the defendant's life or liberty may be at stake.

In tort law, society is engaged in a constant balancing act between individual rights and duties. What kinds of behavior should a person have to tolerate in his or her fellow citizens, and what kinds of behavior should be considered intolerable? Historically, our legal system seems to be expanding the grounds for tort liability. Torts are generally classified according to the level of fault exhibited by the wrongdoer's behavior. This chapter deals with **intentional torts:** types of behavior that indicate either the wrongdoer's conscious desire to cause harm or the wrongdoer's knowledge that such harm was substantially certain to result. **Negligence** and **strict liability** torts will be discussed in Chapter 5.

TABLE 4–1   Crimes versus Intentional Torts

	Crimes	**Intentional Torts**
Nature	Criminal	Civil
Elements	(1) Violation of a statute (2) Intent	(1) Harm to another person or property (2) Intent
Actors	Government prosecutor v. defendant	Plaintiff v. defendant (victim) (tortfeasor)
Burden of Proof	Prosecutor must establish defendant's guilt beyond a reasonable doubt.	Plaintiff must establish defendant's liability by a preponderance of the evidence.
Punishment	Fines, imprisonment, execution	Defendant may have to pay the plaintiff compensatory and punitive damages.

INTERFERENCE WITH PERSONAL RIGHTS

Battery

The basic personal interest that any legal system can protect is a person's right to be free from injurious or unpleasant physical contact with others. Battery, an intentional, unconsented-to touching that is harmful or offensive, protects that interest. The least touching can be a battery if it produces injury or would be considered offensive to a *person of ordinary sensibilities.*

The defendant need not actually touch the plaintiff's body to be liable for battery. It is sufficient to touch anything connected to the plaintiff's body. For example, if Bob snatches Mary's purse off her shoulder, or kicks her dog while she is walking it on a leash, he is liable for battery even though he has not touched her body. In addition, a battery can be committed by setting something in motion that touches the plaintiff. The cigar smoke in the following case is an example.

LEICHTMAN V. WLW JACOR COMMUNICATIONS, INC.
634 N.E. 2d. 697 (Ct. App. Ohio 1994)

FACTS

Leichtman, a nationally known antismoking advocate, was invited to appear on the WLW Bill Cunningham radio talk show to discuss the harmful effects of smoking and breathing secondary smoke. Cunningham, known for his "blowtorch rhetoric," allegedly encouraged Furman, another WLW talk-show host, to light a cigar and repeatedly blow smoke in Leichtman's face. Leichtman sued for battery, claiming the smoke caused him discomfort, humiliation, and distress. Defendant argued that the smoke was too trivial and insubstantial to be a battery.

ISSUE

Is blowing smoke at someone a sufficiently offensive touching to be a battery?

DECISION

Yes. A defendant is liable for battery if he acts intentionally to cause a harmful or offensive contact, either directly or indirectly, with the person of another. A touch-

ing is offensive if it is disagreeable or nauseating or painful because it is an outrage to taste or sensibilities or is insulting. Tobacco smoke has the physical properties capable of making contact. When Furman blew cigar smoke in Leichtman's face, he committed a battery. No matter how trivial the incident, a battery is actionable, even if damages are only one dollar. As Pound said, "In civilized society, men must be able to assume that others will do them no intentional injury—that others will commit no intentional aggression against them."

Arguably, trivial cases are responsible for an avalanche of lawsuits that can delay important cases and deny justice for those who must wait for their day in court. However, Ohio's constitution states, "All courts shall be open and any person for an injury done him . . . shall have a remedy by due course of law. . . ." This case emphasizes the need for some form of alternative dispute resolution operating outside the court system. Until such a forum is created, Leichtman's case can proceed to trial.

Consent must be freely and intelligently given to be a defense to battery. Consent may in some cases be inferred from a person's voluntary participation in an activity. For example, a boxer could hardly complain about normal injuries suffered in a fight. However, a quarterback who is knifed on the 50-yard line clearly has a battery claim. What about a hockey player who is hit by a hockey stick in a fight that erupts during a game? Should his claim be barred on account of his voluntary participation in an admittedly violent sport? Such cases raise difficult issues about the scope of consent; there are no easy answers.

Assault

The tort of assault is designed to protect people from threats of battery. **Assault** is putting another in apprehension of an imminent (immediate) threat to his or her physical safety. No contact is necessary. Assault focuses on the well-grounded apprehension in the mind of the plaintiff.

Would an ordinary person in the plaintiff's situation have thought that battery was imminent? Most courts say that "mere words are not enough" for assault and require some affirmative act, like a threatening gesture by the defendant. Threats of battery in the future ("I'll get you next week") or attempts at battery that the plaintiff is not aware of at the time, like a bullet fired from a great distance that misses the plaintiff, are not grounds for a civil assault suit.

False Imprisonment

The tort of false imprisonment protects both physical (freedom of movement) and mental (freedom from knowledge of confinement) interests. **False imprisonment** is the intentional confinement of a person for an appreciable time (a few minutes is enough) without the person's consent. *Confinement* occurs when a person substantially restricts another person's freedom of movement. A partial obstruction of a person's progress is not false imprisonment. Two examples of partial obstruction are standing in a person's path and locking the front door of a building a person is in without locking the back door.

If escape from confinement is possible but involves an unreasonable risk of harm or affront to the person's dignity, false imprisonment has occurred. Traditionally, a person must know that he or she is confined, and any consent to confinement must be freely given. Consent given in the face of an implied or actual threat of force by the confiner or an assertion of legal authority by the confiner is not freely given.

Most false imprisonment cases today probably involve shoplifting. Under common law, the store owner who stopped a suspected shoplifter was liable for any torts committed in the process if the plaintiff was innocent of any wrongdoing. Today, many states have passed statutes giving store owners a **conditional privilege** to stop persons they reasonably believe are shoplifting, as long as the owner acts in a reasonable manner and detains the suspect only for a reasonable length of time. The store in the example at the beginning of the chapter probably exceeded its statutory privilege because it kept Stevens for over two hours after determining that she did not have any stolen items, and it badgered her to sign a release. Thus, Stevens could sue the store for false imprisonment, as well as other torts such as battery and intentional infliction of emotional distress. The store may also be liable for punitive damages.

Intentional Infliction of Mental Distress

The courts have traditionally been reluctant to grant recovery for purely mental injuries for fear of opening the door to fictitious claims. Developments in modern medicine have, however, made such injuries more provable. As a result, most courts have moved away from the traditional "impact" rule, which allowed recovery for mental injuries only if a battery had occurred, and are allowing recovery solely for severe emotional distress. Some courts still require physical manifestation of the emotional distress, such as a tic or an ulcer, before they allow a suit to be brought. All courts require that the defendant's conduct be **outrageous**—that is, substantially certain to produce severe emotional distress in a person of ordinary sensibilities.

ROACH V. STERN
675 N.Y. S. 2d 133 (N.Y. App. Div. 1998)

FACTS

Deborah Roach, who used the name Debbie Tay, was a tattooed topless dancer who often was a guest on Howard Stern's show. Stern labeled her "Space Lesbian" because of her stories of sexual encounters with female aliens. After Roach died, she was cremated and her sister gave a portion of the remains to Hayden, Tay's close friend. Stern encouraged Hayden to appear on his show and bring Tay's remains; Tay's brother told the station he objected to this. When Hayden appeared on the show, Stern, Hayden, and other participants made comments about the remains while handling various bone fragments. Among other things, Stern encouraged a participant to taste some of the remains and say what it tasted like, encouraged Hayden to wear some of the remains around his neck, speculated about what various parts were, and said, "wow, she was a piece of ash." Roach's brother sued Stern, Hayden, and the broadcasting company for intentional infliction of emotional distress.

ISSUE

Were Stern's actions sufficiently outrageous to allow a claim for intentional infliction of emotional distress?

DECISION

Yes. The element of outrageous conduct is "rigorous and difficult to satisfy." Its purpose is to filter out trivial complaints and assure that the claim of severe emotional distress is genuine. Although the defendants contend that the conduct was not particularly shocking, in light of Stern's reputation for vulgar humor and Tay's actions during her guest appearances on his program, a jury might reasonably conclude that the manner in which Tay's remains were handled, for entertainment purposes and against the express wishes of her family, went beyond the bounds of decent behavior.

Defamation

Since injury to a person's reputation can cause that person considerable anguish and harm, the torts of **libel** (written defamation) and **slander** (oral defamation) were designed to protect against such injury. The basis of both torts is the publication of an untrue statement that injures a person's reputation or character. *Publication* in this context means communication of the statement to at least one person other than the defamed party. If that statement exposes a person to hatred, contempt, or ridicule, it is defamatory. It is usually up to the jury to decide if a given statement is defamatory.

Because it is the *individual's* reputation that is being protected, the defamatory statement must be "of and concerning" the plaintiff to be actionable. Thus, the plaintiff could not sue for defamation when slanderous statements such as ethnic slurs are made about a group, even though she is a member of that group. As the *Levinsky's* case illustrates, courts recognize a limited right of corporations and other business entities to protect their reputations. They can bring claims for defamatory statements that harm them in conducting their business or that deter others from dealing with them. False statements about the quality of a company's products or services may give rise to a cause of action for **disparagement,** which is discussed later in this chapter.

LEVINSKY'S INC. V. WAL-MART
127 F. 3d 122 (1st Cir. 1997)

FACTS

A reporter interviewed the manager of a Wal-Mart store in a suburb of Portland, Maine, about a tongue-in-cheek ad campaign the local retailer Levinsky's ran comparing its operation to Wal-Mart's. Among other things, the manager said that Levinsky's puts callers "on hold for 20 minutes" or never answers at all, and that it is a "trashy" store. Levinsky's sued Wal-Mart after the remarks appeared in a Portland business magazine.

ISSUE

Were the manager's statements defamatory?

DECISION

Partially. Statements usually are not actionable unless they include objectively verifiable assertions. Opinions, "imaginative expression" and "rhetorical hyperbole" are not actionable. Describing Levinsky's operation as "trashy" is this type of language, and is therefore not actionable. The word is "loose language" that is susceptible to numerous connotations. As such, it belongs to the category of protected opinion. The statement about callers being put on hold for 20 minutes or not answering is a statement capable of being verified and therefore can be treated as fact-based defamation.

Damages are presumed in libel cases, unless the written statement is not defamatory on its face. For example, an announcement in the newspaper that Bob married Sue is not defamatory on its face even though Bob was married to Mary at the time, because the average reader would not think there was anything wrong with Bob marrying Sue. Because slander is oral, and therefore considered less damaging, a person may not recover for it without proving actual damages, unless the nature of the defamatory statement is so serious that the law has classified it as *slander per se*. Classic forms of slander per se are statements that a person has a "loathsome" disease, has committed a serious crime, is professionally incompetent or guilty of professional improprieties, or is guilty of serious sexual misconduct. Broadcast defamation, which involves both oral and visual impressions, is generally considered to be libel. For a discussion of defamation on the Internet, see Chapter 48.

Truth is a complete defense to a defamation suit. No matter how embarrassing or terrible the statement, if it is true, the person who communicated it cannot be held liable. False statements may also not be the basis for a successful defamation suit if they are communicated in a privileged situation. The law recognizes that in certain kinds of situations, the necessity to speak without fear of liability is more important than protecting reputation or character. The greater the necessity, the broader the privilege. Therefore, statements communicated in some situations are granted **absolute privilege**—they can never serve as a basis for a successful defamation suit. Statements by members of Congress on the floor of Congress, statements by participants in judicial proceedings, and private statements between spouses are absolutely privileged. Other statements are only **conditionally privileged**—they can serve as a basis for a successful suit if the person publishing the statement abuses the privilege. Statements made in the furtherance of legitimate business interests, such as providing employee references or credit reports, are often conditionally privileged.

The U.S. Supreme Court has given the media an almost absolute privilege when discussing public officials by requiring that the official prove **actual malice** when suing for false and defamatory statements. This means that the official must prove that the statement was made with knowledge of falsity, or with reckless disregard for the truth, which is usually very difficult to do. The Court felt that the public interest in the "free and unfettered debate" of important social issues justified this limitation on a public official's rights.[1] **Public figures** (private persons who are famous or have involved themselves in some public controversy) face a similar burden of proof for similar reasons.[2] The courts have also recognized a conditional privilege protecting fair and accurate media reporting of public proceedings.

Invasion of Privacy

The recognition of a **right of privacy** is a relatively recent development in tort law. This area is still undergoing considerable development and has currently expanded to include several kinds of behavior that infringe on a person's "right to be let alone." Intrusion on a person's solitude or seclusion is a widely recognized form of invasion of privacy. Phone harassment of debtors by creditors, illegal searches of a person or a person's property, and obscene phone calls are examples of this form of invasion of privacy.

Publishing true but private facts about a person can also be an invasion of privacy. Acts like putting an ad in the paper saying that a person does not pay his or her bills, publishing embarrassing details of a person's illnesses, or publishing pictures of a parent's deformed child are examples of this form of invasion of privacy. Putting a person in a false light in the public eye by signing his or her name to a public letter or telegram, or using a person's photo to illustrate an article with which that person has no real connection, have also been held to be invasions of privacy. These forms of invasion of privacy are based on **publicity.** Therefore, some widespread dissemination of the information is necessary for liability. It should also be noted that truth is not a defense to "publication of private facts." Publication of matters of public record, or of newsworthy items (items of legitimate public interest), cannot be the basis of a successful suit for invasion of privacy, as the *Felsher* case illustrates. Likewise, public figures cannot complain about publicity that is reasonably related to their public activities. Since the right of privacy is a personal right, corporations cannot rely on it as is illustrated by the following case.

C O M P U T E R *law*

FELSHER V. UNIVERSITY OF EVANSVILLE
755 N.E.2d 589 (Ind. Sup. Ct. 2001)

FACTS

Felsher, a professor of French at the University of Evansville, was fired in 1991. In 1997 he created websites and electronic mail accounts containing the names of University officials and the initials UE, a common abbreviation for the University of Evansville. He posted articles on the websites that alleged wrongdoing by the officials. Using the e-mail accounts, he nominated the officials for jobs at other universities and directed the reader to his website for references. The officials and the University sued Felsher for putting them in a false light and for

misappropriating their identities. Among other claims, Felsher asserted that an organization does not have a right to privacy in tort law.

ISSUE

Can a corporation sue for invasion of privacy?

DECISION

No. We live in an age when technology pushes us quickly ahead, and the law struggles to keep up. In this case we

(continued)

---

[1] New York Times v. Sullivan, 376 U.S. 254 (1964).
[2] Curtis Publishing Co. v. Butts, 388 U.S. 130 (1967).

FELSHER V. UNIVERSITY OF EVANSVILLE
(concluded)

address for the first time the unauthorized and retaliatory use of private or personal names on the Internet. A number of existing statutes and common law precepts seem to serve surprisingly well in this dramatic new environment. It is frequently feasible to pour new wine into old legal bottles. Nearly anyone can create a website or an e-mail address with readily available software. People purchase websites, register domain names, and establish e-mail addresses to efficiently and effectively market and promote products, services, and ideas to the literal "world" of the WWW. The ease of doing this also tempts the interests of wrongdoers, particularly in the context of domain name registration involving "cybersquatters" and "copycats." Copycats register a domain name and use the address to operate a website that intentionally misleads users into believing they are interacting with someone else. Flesher's actions fall within this category. He created the imposter websites and e-mail addresses for the sole

purpose of harming the reputation of the University and its officials.

Traditional invasion of privacy encompasses four distinct torts: Intrusion upon seclusion, appropriation of name or likeness, public disclosure of private facts, and false-light publicity. These are tenuously related by their common focus on the right to be left alone. Felsher was previously held liable for placing the officials in a false light before the public. The question before us now is whether a corporation can sue for invasion of privacy. The tort right to privacy is a personal right; thus, the corporation cannot sue under it. This does not mean that organizations do not have other claims they could use under these circumstances. The University would likely have a cause of action for tortuous interference with business relations, and under trademark and unfair competition laws. However, they only sought relief under privacy laws in this case.

A final form of invasion of privacy involves using a person's name or likeness for commercial purposes without that person's consent. For example, using a person's name or image in an ad to imply that he or she endorses the product or service, if done without permission, would be an invasion of privacy. This form of privacy protects a property interest one has in oneself. This is a developing area of privacy, and exactly what is protected, how long it is protected, and whether the right is inheritable varies greatly from state to state. The *White* case expands what is protected under this cause of action.

WHITE V. SAMSUNG ELECTRONICS AMERICA, INC.
971 F. 2d 1395 (9th Cir. 1992)

FACTS

Samsung Electronics advertised current products by showing them still in use in the 21st century. One ad, which was designed to be humorous, had a robot dressed in a wig, gown, and jewelry designed to look like Vanna White, hostess of the TV game show "Wheel of Fortune." The robot, in a stance similar to one for which Vanna is famous, was posed next to a game board like that used on "Wheel of Fortune." The ad's caption read, "Longest-running game show. 2012 AD." Both Samsung and the ad's designer referred to the ad as the "Vanna

White ad." Vanna sued for violation of her right to publicity/privacy.

ISSUE

Did the use of the robot appropriate Vanna's name or likeness without her consent?

DECISION

Yes. Several cases have held that a person's right of publicity can be invaded by other than direct use of the

(continued)

White v. Samsung Electronics America, Inc.
(concluded)

person's image. For example, in one case a photo of the plaintiff's race car was used in a commercial, and in *Carson v. Here's Johnny Portable Toilets, Inc.*, the defendant marketed his toilets by using Johnny Carson's signature "Tonight Show" introduction. The right of publicity has developed to protect the commercial interest of celebrities in their identities. If the celebrity's identity is commercially exploited, there has been an invasion of that right. The identities of the most popular celebrities are not only the most attractive for advertisers, but also the easiest to evoke without resorting to obvious means such as name, likeness, or voice. The individual aspects of the ad in this case, when viewed together, leave little doubt about the celebrity the ad is meant to depict. Indeed, defendants themselves referred to their ad as the "Vanna White ad." They appropriated her identity.

Misuse of Legal Proceedings

Malicious prosecution, wrongful use of civil proceedings, and abuse of process are three tort theories that protect people from harms resulting from wrongfully brought lawsuits. **Malicious prosecution** gives a remedy for the financial, emotional, and reputational harm that can result when criminal proceedings are wrongfully brought. An action for **wrongful use of civil proceedings** compensates for similar damages arising from wrongfully brought civil suits. In both instances, the plaintiff must show that the wrongfully brought suit *terminated in his favor,* that the suit was brought *without probable cause* to believe the suit was justified, and that it was brought *for an improper purpose.*

Brennan v. Tremco Inc.
20 P.3d 1086 (Cal. Sup. Ct. 2001)

Facts

Tremco Inc. sued its former employee, Brennan, under several theories when he went to work for a competitor. After Brennan obtained summary judgment on some of the claims, the parties agreed to binding arbitration of the remaining claims. As part of this agreement, they waived any right to a trial de novo or an appeal. The arbitrator found in favor of Brennan. Brennan then filed suit against Tremco and its attorneys for malicious prosecution. Tremco argued that they could not be sued under this theory because it requires a court judgment in the plaintiff's favor, and cannot be based on an arbitrator's decision.

Issue

Can an arbitrator's decision supply the requirement of a successful outcome for malicious prosecution purposes?

Decision

No. In order to establish a cause of action for civil or criminal misuse of the legal system a plaintiff must show that the prior suit was commenced by the defendant and pursued to a legal termination in plaintiff's favor, that the suit was brought without probable cause, and that it was initiated with malice. There is a trend to allow parties to voluntarily choose to resolve disputes by binding arbitration. When parties choose arbitration, they typically expect their dispute will be resolved without necessity for any contact with the courts. To avoid an unending roundelay of litigation, we have held that malicious prosecution should not be expanded. The arbitrator's decision should be the end, not the beginning of the dispute. If there has been abuse, the arbitrator can impose sanctions.

Table 4–2   Misuse of Legal Proceedings

Type	Requirements			
	Malice	**Wrongful Suit Ended in Plaintiff's Favor**	**No Probable Cause**	**Wrongful Motive**
1. Malicious prosecution	yes	yes	yes	yes
2. Wrongful use of civil proceedings	yes	yes	yes	yes
3. Abuse of process	no	no	no	yes

Abuse of process does not require that the suit terminate in the defendant's favor or that there be no probable cause in order for the person wrongfully sued to win. What is required is proof that the suit was brought for a primary purpose other than the one for which such proceedings are designed. This often involves situations in which the person bringing the suit is trying to force the defendant to take an action unrelated to the subject of the suit. For example, assume Craig wants to buy Andrew's business but Andrew refuses to sell. If Craig then brings a **nuisance** suit against the business in order to force the sale, Craig may be liable to Andrew for abuse of process. See Table 4–2 for a summary of the misuse of legal proceedings.

Interference with Property Rights

Property rights have traditionally occupied an important position in our legal system. Suits for tortious interference with property rights are generally brought by the party with the right to *possess* the property rather than its owner. However, the owner of land that has been leased to another may bring a suit if the interference also results in lasting damage to the property. Trespass to land, trespass to personal property, and conversion are the traditionally recognized torts against property.

Trespass to Land

Any entry by a person onto land in the possession of another is a **trespass,** unless the entry is done with the possessor's permission or is privileged. The same is true for causing anything to enter the land in the possession of another. A person who remains on the land of another, as in the case of a tenant who stays after the lease has expired, or who allows anything to remain on another's property, is trespassing. No actual harm to the property is necessary for trespass. However, if no actual losses result, the plaintiff usually will recover only nominal damages.

Jacque v. Steenberg Homes, Inc.
563 N.W. 2d 154 (Wisc. Sup. Ct. 1997)

Facts

Steenberg Homes had a mobile home to deliver. The easiest route of delivery was across the Jacques' land. Each time the elderly couple was asked if delivery could be made across their land, they refused. On the morning of the planned move, the Jacques called some neighbors and the town chairman, and they met with Steenberg's manager. The manager asked how much it would take to allow them to deliver across the land. Mr. Jacque replied

(continued)

JACQUE V. STEENBERG HOMES, INC.
(concluded)

it was not a question of money; he just did not want them to cross his land. After the meeting, the manager ordered the delivery anyway and had the town road blocked so that no one could see what they were doing. Steenberg employees plowed a path through Jacques' snow-covered field and delivered the home. The Jacques sued and were awarded $1.00 in nominal damages, and $100,000 in punitive damages. Steenberg challenged the award of punitive damages as excessive and not justified because only nominal damages were awarded.

ISSUE

Can punitive damages be awarded in a trespass case in which the damages were only nominal?

DECISION

Yes. In some trespass cases, the actual harm is not in the damage done to the land, but in the loss of the individual's right to exclude others from the property, which is one of the most essential rights accompanying possession of property. Both the Jacques and society have a significant interest in deterring intentional trespass to land. A right is hollow if the legal system provides insufficient means to protect it. Private landowners should feel confident that wrongdoers will be appropriately punished; when they do, they are less likely to resort to "self-help" remedies. It is easy to imagine a frustrated landowner taking the law into his or her own hands when faced with a brazen trespasser like Steenberg. Punitive damages have the effect of bringing to punishment types of conduct that, though oppressive and hurtful, almost invariably go unpunished by the public prosecutor. If punitive damages are not allowed in a situation like this, what punishment will prevent intentional trespass to land? Intentional trespass may be punished by a large damage award despite the lack of measurable harm.

Trespass to Personal Property

Intentional interference with personal property in the possession of another is a trespass if it (1) harms the property or (2) deprives the possessor of its use for an appreciable time. Consent and privilege are defenses to trespass to personal property.

Conversion

Conversion is the unlawful taking of or exercise of control over the personal property of another person. The essence of conversion is the wrongful deprivation of a person's personal property rights. One who unlawfully takes goods from the possession of another is liable for conversion even though the taker mistakenly believes he or she is entitled to possession. The same is true of those who wrongfully sell, mortgage, lease, or use the goods of another. Plaintiff's remedy for conversion is the reasonable value of the property. Some courts reduce the plaintiff's damages when the property can be returned unharmed and the defendant's conversion was the result of an honest mistake.

The difference between conversion and trespass to personal property is based on the degree of interference with another's property rights. Courts consider such factors as the extent of the harm to the property, the extent and duration of the interference with the other's right to control the property, and whether the defendant acted in good faith. The greater the interference and lack of good faith, the more likely the act will be considered to be conversion, for which the defendant must pay the reasonable value of the property.

INTERFERENCE WITH ECONOMIC RELATIONS

The tort law protecting persons against unreasonable interference with their economic relations with others is a more recent development than the previously discussed areas. Three classic torts in this area are disparagement, interference with contract, and interference with economic expectations.

Disparagement

False statements about the personal behavior of persons in business are covered by the tort of defamation. False statements about the quality of a seller's product or services, or the seller's ownership of goods offered for sale, may give rise to the tort of **disparagement.** Proof of actual damage (e.g., lost sales or other opportunities) is necessary for a successful disparagement action.

Interference with Contract

One who intentionally induces a person to breach a contract with another, or who prevents performance of another's contract, may be liable in damages to the party deprived of the benefits of the contract. This tort, **interference with contract,** seeks to protect the sanctity of private contractual relationships. Some courts do not hold a person liable whose conduct merely caused a breach of contract (as opposed to actively inducing the breach). Inducing a breach of contract may be justifiable in some cases.

Interference with Economic Expectations

Early examples of this tort, **interference with economic expectations,** involved the use of force to drive away a person's customers or employees. Today, liability has been broadened to include nonviolent forms of intentional interference as well.

CONCEPT SUMMARY　　　**Intentional Torts**

	Type	Main Elements	Common Defense
Interference with Personal Rights	Battery	Unconsented-to harmful or offensive touching	Consent
	Assault	Putting in immediate apprehension for physical safety	
	False imprisonment	Unconsented-to confinement for appreciable time	Privilege
	Infliction of mental distress	Outrageous conduct	
		Emotional distress	
	Defamation	Publications of untrue statements injurious to reputation or character	Truth
	Invasion of privacy	Unwarranted publicity; commercial use of identity; intrusion; false light	Newsworthy
	Malicious prosecution; wrongful use of civil proceedings	Malice; no probable cause; plaintiff's success in wrongful suit	Probable cause
	Abuse of process	Wrongful motive	
Interference with Property Rights	Trespass to land	Entry on other's land without permission	Privilege
	Trespass to personal property	Interference with another's personal property	
	Conversion	Unlawful dominion over other's property	
Interference with Economic Relations	Disparagement	False, harmful statements about products or services	Truth
	Interference with contract	Inducing breach or preventing performance of another's contract	Privilege
	Interference with economic expectations	Unreasonable interference with another's business	

QUESTIONS AND PROBLEM CASES

1. Explain the elements required to prove false imprisonment.
2. Explain the four types of invasion of privacy.
3. Explain the difference between defamation and disparagement.
4. Robert B. represented to Kathleen K. that he was free from venereal disease when he knew or should have known he had herpes. Relying on this representation, Kathleen K. had sexual intercourse with him and contracted the disease. She sued him, in part basing her case on battery. Her suit was dismissed because the trial court found that there was not a cause of action for this type of private sexual conduct. On appeal, can Kathleen K. show the elements of battery?
5. In 1979 the *Courrier Times* published a series of three articles about boarding homes used to house mentally ill and disabled people. A regulatory body, in an effort to supervise these homes, had established standards of disapproval. One ground for disapproval was a criminal conviction for a sex crime in the past ten years. Jenkins, who operated a home, had been convicted of a sex crime in 1973. The articles discussed the fact that Jenkins had been convicted of sex crimes in 1942, 1960, and 1973, and had been committed to the state hospital. Jenkins sued the paper for invasion of privacy, arguing that the first two convictions and the commitment were irrelevant for the public to know because the disapproval standards did not apply to them. Is he correct?
6. Starr, the general manager of a Pearle Vision store in Tulsa, met with three Pearle employees to discuss a $4,000 deficit in the petty cash account. Starr was fired for refusing to cooperate with the investigation. Statements about Starr's situation were made to two other employees who were also being investigated. Later, Starr's successor as store manager told Starr's friend, who was not a Pearle employee, that Starr "is no longer here" and "is in big trouble." Starr sued Pearle for defamation. Will she be successful?
7. Jerry Falwell, a nationally known minister and commentator on politics and public affairs, sued *Hustler* magazine for libel and intentional infliction of emotional distress over a parody of a Campari ad campaign. The real Campari ads

had celebrities describing their "first time" drinking its liquor. The parody had Falwell, in a fabricated interview, describing his "first time" as a drunken sexual encounter with his mother in an outhouse. His libel claim was denied because the jury found that the parody could not reasonably be understood to describe actual events and therefore it did not harm his reputation or character. He was awarded $200,000 on his emotional distress claim, though, and the magazine appealed. Should the *malice* standard required of public figures in libel cases be extended to suits for intentional infliction of emotional distress brought by public figures for defamatory publications?

8. The Wilsons moved into their home in 1955 and built a fence around their yard in 1957. The fence encroached on the lot next door. Through the legal doctrine of adverse possession, the Wilsons gained ownership of the encroached property in 1977. In 1980 the Pearces bought the house next door and asked the Wilsons to move their fence even though the Pearces had no legal right to demand it. When the Wilsons did not, the Pearces began a campaign of harassment that included cursing and threatening the Wilsons, making obscene gestures and comments to them and their children, reporting them for alleged violations of city laws, and throwing things and shooting into their yard. They had Mr. Wilson arrested for criminal trespass while he was mowing his lawn inside his fence but on the property claimed by the Pearces. Wilson, who the Pearces knew had a heart condition, had to take nitroglycerin pills and shook uncontrollably after the arrest. Do the Wilsons have a claim for intentional infliction of mental distress?

9. Toyota and its American distributors were concerned that when the Lexus was introduced in the United States, a resale market for the cars might develop in Japan. Thus, sales were barred in Japan after the U.S. roll-out, and U.S. dealers were required to have a "no export" clause in their contract saying they could sell only to U.S. customers. Despite this, a Japanese Lexus market began to develop. Toyota reminded its dealers of the clause, and compiled an "offenders" list, which it distributed to the

dealers. They were warned that doing business with those on the list would lead to sanctions from Toyota. Della Pena, an auto wholesaler, was on the list. During 1988 and 1989 he bought Lexus cars in the United States and resold them in Japan. After the list was distributed, his supply of cars dried up. He sued Toyota for antitrust violations and intentional interference with economic relations. Will Della Penna have to prove that Toyota committed a wrongful act other than the interference itself in order to prove interference with economic relations?

10. The Bradleys, who lived on Vashon Island, sued American Smelting for trespass because microscopic, airborne particles of heavy metals from its copper smelter at Ruston, Washington, four miles away, had, when the wind was right, been deposited on the Bradley's property. The smelter's emissions met all federal, state, and regional regulations, and had caused no actual damage. Is the knowing deposit of microscopic particles on a person's property, without damage, a trespass?

11. Bridges was abducted from work at gunpoint by her estranged husband. He took her to their former apartment, where he forced her to disrobe in order to prevent her escape. On hearing a gunshot, the police stormed the apartment, rescued Bridges, who was clad only in a dishtowel, and escorted her to a police car. Cape Publications published a picture of her rescue. The picture revealed little more than could be seen had she been wearing a bikini. Other, more revealing photographs were not used. Bridges sued the paper for invasion of privacy. Did the publication invade her privacy?

12. Mr. and Mrs. Bhattal checked into the Grand Hyatt in New York, sent their luggage to their room, and, after stopping briefly at their room, locked the door and went to lunch. When they returned, their luggage was gone. Due to a computer error, the hotel had shipped their luggage to the airport along with the luggage of a Saudi Arabian flight crew who had previously occupied the Bhattal's room. The Bhattals filed a conversion suit against the hotel. Will they recover from the hotel?

CHAPTER 5

Negligence and Strict Liability

Mr. Property Management owned the Chalmette Apartments. Over a two-year period police investigated numerous serious crimes committed at the apartment complex. Soon thereafter, a man abducted a 10-year-old girl from the sidewalk in front of her house, dragged her across the street to a vacant apartment in the complex, and raped her. The apartment's front door was off its hinges, the windows were broken, and the apartment was filthy and full of debris. A city ordinance required property owners to keep the doors and windows of vacant structures securely closed to prevent unauthorized entry.

- *Could the owner of the apartments foresee that a crime of this type was likely to happen and therefore should have taken steps to protect against it?*
- *Does the statutory requirement establish the standard of conduct that the owner must follow in order not to be negligent?*
- *Can the owner be held liable for acts of violence that are committed by others?*

.... *NEGLIGENCE* ....

The Industrial Revolution, which began in the early part of the nineteenth century, created serious problems for the law of torts. Railroads, machinery, and newly developed tools were contributing to a growing number of injuries to people and property that simply did not fit within the framework of intentional torts since most of these injuries were unintended. The legal system was forced to develop a new set of rules to deal with these situations, and the result was the law of negligence, which requires people to take reasonable care to avoid injuring others.

Basically, **negligence** is an unintentional breach of duty by the defendant that results in harm to another. A plaintiff in a negligence suit must prove several things to recover (see Table 5–1):

1.   That the defendant had a duty not to injure the plaintiff.
2.   That the defendant breached that duty.
3.   That the defendant's breach of duty was the actual and legal (proximate) cause of the plaintiff's injuries.

To be successful, the plaintiff must also overcome any defenses to negligence liability raised by the defendant.

TABLE 5–1   Requirements for a Negligence Case

Duty	Breach of duty	Injury	Cause in fact
			Proximate cause

DUTY

The basic idea of negligence is that every member of society has a duty to conduct his or her affairs in a way that avoids injury to others. The law of negligence holds our behavior up to an **objective** standard of conduct: We must conduct ourselves like a "reasonable person of ordinary prudence in similar circumstances." This standard is *flexible,* since it allows consideration of all circumstances surrounding a particular accident, but it is still objective, since the "reasonable person" is a hypothetical being who is always thoughtful and careful never to endanger others unreasonably.

Whether a person owes a particular duty to another person is determined by the court. Often the court will look at the *relationship* of the parties. For example, a contractual relationship can give rise to duties that would not otherwise exist. Likewise, common carriers, innkeepers, and today even landlords have special duties to protect those who use their facilities from harm.

DIGGS V. ARIZONA CARDIOLOGISTS, LTD.
8 P.3d 396 (Ct. App. Ariz. 2000)

FACTS

Diggs was stricken with severe chest pain and paramedics took her to the emergency room of St. Luke's. Dr. Johnson took her history, examined her, and ordered an electrocardiogram (EKG) and an echocardiogram. Johnson thought she was suffering from pericarditis, not a myocardial infarction, but he was untrained in reading

(continued)

DIGGS V. ARIZONA CARDIOLOGISTS, LTD.
(concluded)

echocardiograms and therefore could not make a differential diagnosis. Also, the computer interpretation of the EKG conflicted with Johnson's diagnosis. Johnson saw Dr. Valdez, a cardiologist, visiting another patient, and asked for Valdez's opinion. Valdez agreed with Johnson's diagnosis of pericarditis and that Diggs should be treated for that and discharged. Diggs died three hours after discharge as a result of acute myocardial infarction. Diggs' estate sued several defendants for negligence including Dr. Valdez. Valdez argued that he owed no duty to Diggs because they had no contractual relationship.

ISSUE

Does a consulting physician owe a duty of care to the patient?

DECISION

Yes. Although a contractual physician-patient relationship clearly gives rise to a duty to the patient, the absence of such a relationship does not necessarily exclude a duty. We must determine whether there was a sufficient relationship that, as a matter of policy, Valdez owed Diggs a duty of reasonable care. Duty is, after all, merely an expression of the sum total of those considerations of policy which lead the law to say that the plaintiff is entitled to protection. One reason to impose a duty is to prevent future harm. Valdez was in a unique position to prevent future harm to Diggs. Valdez was the head of St. Luke's cardiology department, and Johnson approached him because Johnson was not fully qualified to interpret the readings. Dr. Valdez was in the best position to correct any error in Dr. Johnson's diagnosis. One who undertakes to render services to another which he should recognize as necessary for the protection of a third person is subject to liability for failure to exercise reasonable care. Dr. Valdez knew that the computer analysis indicated myocardial infarction, that Johnson did not have expertise in the area, and admitted that if Diggs were his patient, he would have ordered an enzyme test to rule out an infarction.

Statutes can also establish duties. Generally, people who do not do what a statute requires are considered to be **negligent per se** because they are not acting as the "reasonable person" would. If the actions cause injury of the kind the statute was designed to protect against, and if the person who is injured is within the group of people the statute was designed to protect, then the defendant is presumed negligent.

The ordinance in the Mr. Property Management summary at the beginning of this chapter set a standard from which the apartment owner deviated. The statute was designed to deter criminal activity by removing conspicuous and easily accessible opportunities for criminal conduct. It was designed to protect the general public. Since the rape victim is within this class of people, and the harm she suffered was the type the statute was designed to prevent, she can rely on the doctrine of negligence per se. See Table 5–2. The plaintiffs in the Oklahoma City bombing case which follows cannot use the doctrine, however, because they do not come within the statute.

TABLE 5–2   Negligence Per Se: The Elements

Statute prohibits or requires action.	Defendant's actions violate statute.	Plaintiff's injuries are the kind the statute was designed to protect against.	Plaintiff is within the group the statute was designed to protect.

GAINES-TABB V. ICI EXPLOSIVES USA INC.
1988 U.S. App. Lexis 28228 (10th Cir. 1998)

FACTS

On April 19, 1995, a bomb made with ammonium nitrate (AN) fertilizer destroyed the Alfred P. Murrah Federal Building in Oklahoma City. People injured in the bombing filed suit against the manufacturers of ammonium nitrate alleging liability under a variety of theories including negligence per se. They alleged the defendants violated laws and regulations regarding the sale of explosives.

ISSUE

Does the doctrine of negligence per se apply in this case?

DECISION

No. In a negligence action, the defendant's conduct is measured against the "reasonably prudent person" acting in similar circumstances. When conduct is governed by statute or regulation, the requirements of those laws can set the negligence standard. To establish negligence per se, plaintiff must show that: (1) the injury was caused by the violation; (2) the injury was the type to be prevented by the statute; and (3) the injured party was of the class meant to be protected by the statute. The statute which defendants allegedly violated makes it a violation to fail to register the sale of explosives. "Explosives" is defined as "any chemical compound, mixture, or device, of which the primary purpose is to function by explosion, and includes but is not limited to dynamite and other high explosives. . . ." AN comes in either "explosive" or "fertilizer" grade. AN sold as fertilizer, which is what the bombers bought, does not come within the statutory definition. Additionally, even if it did, plaintiffs cannot show that the failure to register the sale caused the injuries suffered. Plaintiffs cannot rely on negligence per se.

BREACH

A person is guilty of breach of duty if he or she exposes another person to a foreseeable, unreasonable risk of harm, something the "reasonable person" would never do. The courts ask whether the defendant did something the reasonable person would not have done, or failed to do something the reasonable person would have done. If the defendant guarded against all foreseeable harms and exercised reasonable care, he or she is not liable even though the plaintiff may be injured. So, if Bob is carefully driving his car within the speed limit and a child darts into his path and is hit, Bob is not liable for the child's injuries. In deciding the "reasonableness" of a given risk, the courts ordinarily consider several factors. What is the likelihood that harm will result from a person's actions, and how serious is the potential harm? On the other hand, does the actor's conduct have any social utility? If so, how easy would it be for the actor to avoid or minimize the risk of harm associated with that conduct?

CAUSATION

Even if the defendant has breached a duty owed to the plaintiff, he or she will not be liable unless the breach actually caused the plaintiff's injury. For example, Bob is speeding down the street, breaching his duty to those in the area, and Frank falls down the front steps of his house and breaks his leg. Bob was negligent but since there is no causal connection between his breach of duty and Frank's injury, he is not liable for it.

In some cases, a person's act may be the **cause in fact**—the actual or direct cause—of an incredible series of losses to numerous people. In intentional tort cases the courts have traditionally held people liable for all the consequences that directly result from their intentional wrongdoing, however bizarre and unforeseeable they may be. With the creation of liability for negligence, the courts began to recognize that negligent wrongdoers (who were less at fault than intentional wrongdoers) should not necessarily be liable for every direct result of their negligence. This idea of placing a legal limit on the extent of a negligent person's liability came to be called **proximate cause.** So, a negligent person is liable for only the *proximate* results of his or her negligence.

The courts have not, however, reached agreement on the test that should be used for proximate cause. The proximate cause question is really one of social policy. In deciding which test to adopt, a court must weigh the possibility that negligent persons will be bankrupted by tremendous liability against the fact that some innocent victims may go uncompensated.

Some courts hold defendants liable only for the reasonably foreseeable results of their negligence. Others hold defendants liable only for injuries to plaintiffs who are within *the scope of* the foreseeable risk. If the defendant could not have reasonably foreseen some injury to the plaintiff, then the defendant is not liable for any injury to the plaintiff that in fact results from his or her negligence. The *Restatement (Second) of Torts,* recognizing the "after the fact" nature of proximate cause determinations, suggests that negligent defendants should not be liable for injuries that, looking backward after the accident, appear to be "highly extraordinary."

In the Mr. Property Management case at the beginning of this chapter, the court must decide if the apartment owner should have foreseen the risk that someone might use the empty, easily accessible apartment to commit a crime, or whether the rape that occurred there was "highly extraordinary." The fact that there had been many serious crimes in the apartment complex in the past two years would help lead to a finding that the lack of maintenance was a proximate cause of the injury. A similar analysis is involved in the following *Coles* case.

Ethical Implications	Assume that Mr. Property Management is operating its apartment complex in a city without an ordinance requiring the sealing of vacant structures. Does it have an ethical duty to securely close vacant structures in urban, high-crime areas?

Courts also consider whether an intervening force, which happens after defendant's negligent act and contributes to plaintiff's injury, should excuse defendant from liability. For example, suppose Deborah leaves her keys in the car while she runs into the store, and Mary Beth steals the car. While driving recklessly, Mary Beth hits Angela, severely injuring her. Should Deborah be liable for Angela's injuries? Usually, the courts say that if the intervening force was **foreseeable,** it will not excuse the defendant from liability. If it was foreseeable that someone might steal a car with keys left in it, and drive recklessly, then Deborah would be liable for Angela's injuries.

COLES V. JENKINS
34 F. Supp. 2d 381 (D. W. Va. 1998)

FACTS

Donald and Emily Egan of Chicago took a bike tour with Vermont Bicycle Touring (VBT) of Virginia's horse and wine country. VBT planned the route, rented the bikes, supplied tour guides, and provided a van for people who wanted to ride in it for part of the tour. They warned riders that traffic on part of the ride might be heavy and that the shoulder was narrow, and they could opt to ride in the van. After the Eagans had ridden almost a mile on

(continued)

COLES V. JENKINS
(concluded)

the part warned about, they were hit by a driver, Jenkins, who was legally blind, incompetent, and whose license had been confiscated by his guardian. Donald died and Emily was seriously injured. VBT defended against the Egan's negligence suit by arguing that they were not the proximate cause of the accident.

ISSUE

Was Jenkins a sufficient superseding cause of the injuries so that VBT should be held not to be the proximate cause of the injuries?

DECISION

No. When the intervening act of a third party is sufficiently extraordinary and unforeseeable, it can supersede any prior acts of negligence. The questions here are whether the harm caused was different in kind from that which would have occurred from defendants negligently choosing a dangerous route, and whether the intervening act was foreseeable. The result one could reasonably expect from selecting an unduly dangerous road for a bike tour is that a motorist might get hit. Jenkins' driving while legally blind and unauthorized to drive is unusual, but it has the same consequences as would a more ordinary act of reckless driving such as driving drunk or a distracted driver hitting a bicyclist due to inattention. While Jenkins would have been a danger on any road, on a safer road something might have been done to prevent the accident. Defendant's negligence can be a proximate cause even if the precise injury that happened could not have been foreseen. The jury should decide whether VBT should be liable for the Egan's injuries.

GENERAL CAUSATION RULES

Regardless of what test for proximate cause the courts adopt, they generally agree on certain basic principles of causation. One such basic rule is that negligent defendants "take their victims as they find them." This means that if some physical peculiarity of a person aggravates his or her injuries, the defendant is liable for the full extent of the injuries. For example, Jim's head strikes the windshield of his car when Mike's negligently driven truck runs into him. Due to the fact that Jim's skull was abnormally thin (an "eggshell skull"), he dies from the blow, which would have only slightly injured a normal person. Mike is liable for Jim's death. Likewise, negligent persons are generally held liable for diseases their victims contract while weakened by their injuries, and jointly liable (along with the negligent physician) for negligent medical care their victims receive for their injuries.

JENSON V. EVELETH TACONITE CO.
130 F.3d 1287 (8th Cir. 1997)

FACTS

Jenson was the named plaintiff in a class action suit against Eveleth Taconite Co. for sex discrimination and harassment. The court found that Eveleth Mines maintained a work environment sexually hostile to women and one that condoned pervasive sexual harassment. After the decision, the master appointed to determine damages awarded limited damages because he found that the "eggshell skull" rule only applied to pre-existing *physical* conditions. Plaintiffs appealed.

ISSUE

Does the "eggshell skull" doctrine apply to emotional as well as physical injuries?

DECISION

Yes. It is a universal doctrine of tort law that people who commit torts take their victims as they find them. While

(continued)

JENSON V. EVELETH TACONITE CO.
(concluded)

the doctrine has traditionally been applied in cases of physical injury such as "eggshell skull" cases, tortfeasors are liable for all of the natural and proximate consequences of their actions. This includes damages for harm caused to a plaintiff who happens to have a fragile psyche. The callous pattern and practice of harassment by the defendant inevitably destroyed the self-esteem of the plaintiffs. The emotional harm resulting from this record of human indecency sought to destroy the human psyche as well as the human spirit of the plaintiffs. They deserve money damages for these injuries.

Negligent persons are also generally liable for injuries sustained by those who are injured while making reasonable attempts to avoid being injured by the negligent person's acts. So, if Jamie dives out of the path of Howard's negligently driven car and breaks her arm in the process, Howard is liable for her injury. It is also commonly said that "negligence invites rescue," and that negligent persons should be liable to those who are injured while making a reasonable attempt to rescue someone endangered by the negligent person's act.

RES IPSA LOQUITUR

In some cases negligence may be difficult to prove because the defendant has superior knowledge of the circumstances surrounding plaintiff's injury. If the defendant was in fact negligent, he or she will be understandably reluctant to disclose facts that prove liability. If the defendant had exclusive control of the thing that caused the injury, and the injury that occurred would not ordinarily happen in the absence of negligence, the doctrine of **res ipsa loquitur** ("the thing speaks for itself") creates an inference of negligence. This puts the burden on the defendant to show that the injury was not caused by his or her negligence. If the defendant fails to do so, he or she may be found liable. *Res ipsa* has been used frequently in plane crash and product liability cases in which the cause of the injury may be difficult to prove because important evidence was destroyed in the accident.

NEGLIGENT INFLICTION OF EMOTIONAL DISTRESS

In Chapter 4, we discussed the reluctance of the courts to allow recovery for purely mental injuries produced by intentional acts. The courts have been even more reluctant to allow such suits when the emotional injury is the product of negligent behavior. Fearing spurious claims and "opening the floodgates of litigation," courts initially required some "impact" (contact with the plaintiff's person) before recovery would be allowed. As scientific proof of emotional injury became more available, many courts dropped the impact rule but still insisted that plaintiffs show some physical injury or symptoms resulting from their mental distress before allowing recovery. Recently, a growing number of courts have allowed recovery without proof of physical injury if plaintiff suffered serious emotional distress as a foreseeable result of defendant's conduct.

Courts are also increasingly allowing *third parties* to recover for emotional distress resulting from witnessing harm caused to another person by defendant's negligent acts. For example, a mother is watching her child get off the school bus when he is hit by a negligently driven car. In the past, the mother would have been denied recovery unless she suffered some impact as a result of the negligence or was within the "zone of danger" created by the negligent act. Today, an increasing number of courts would allow the mother to recover. Generally, these courts require that the person actually

TABLE 5–3　Negligent Infliction of Emotional Distress on Third Parties

Defendant's negligence causes injury to victim.	Witness suffers serious emotional distress.	Witness is a close relative.	Witness saw or in some way perceived the injury when it occurred.	Physical symptoms resulting from emotional distress required by some states.

witness the injury, that it be to a close relative, and that he or she suffer serious emotional distress as a result. Many courts also require that this emotional distress result in physical symptoms or injury. See Table 5–3. The court in *Dunphy* expands the category of people who can sue for this injury.

DUNPHY V. GREGOR
642 A.2d 372 (Sup. Ct. N.J. 1994)

FACTS

Dunphy saw her fiancé, Burwell, with whom she had been living for two years, hit by a car while changing a flat tire. He was dragged or thrown 240 feet, and she tried to help him when she reached him. She accompanied him to the hospital, where he died several hours later. Dunphy, who received psychiatric treatment as a result of the experience, sued for the emotional trauma.

ISSUE

Can a nonrelative who witnesses the negligent injury of a loved one sue for negligent infliction of emotional distress?

DECISION

Yes. In prior cases we have required four things to be proved by a bystander–witness in order to recover: (1) the death or serious injury of another caused by defendant's negligence; (2) a marital or intimate familial relationship between the plaintiff and the injured person; (3) observation of the death or injury at the scene of the accident; and (4) resulting severe emotional distress. Regarding (2), it was the presence of "deep, intimate, famil-

ial ties between the plaintiff and the physically injured person" that made the harm to emotional tranquility so serious and compelling. It is foreseeable that people who enjoy an intimate familial relationship with one another will be especially vulnerable to emotional injury from a tragedy happening to one of them. If a relationship is deep, lasting, and genuinely intimate, severe emotional injury is foreseeable. It is foreseeable that persons engaged to be married and living together would suffer such injury. While other courts have refused to expand the category beyond the family in order to keep liability of negligent actors within reasonable bounds, we do not believe we need this "bright line" in New Jersey. A jury can determine if a relationship is sufficiently significant, stable, and intimate. Factors to be considered are the duration of the relationship, the degree of mutual dependence, the extent of common contributions to a life together, the extent and quality of their shared experience and their day-to-day relationship, whether they were of the same household, their emotional reliance on each other, and the way they related to each other in attending to life's mundane requirements.

DEFENSES TO NEGLIGENCE

The two traditional defenses to negligence are **contributory negligence** and **assumption of risk.** These defenses are based on the idea that everyone has a duty to exercise reasonable care for his or her own safety. Persons who fail to exercise such care should not be able to recover because their own behavior helped cause their injuries. So, if Craig steps into the path of Andy's speeding car without checking to see whether any cars are coming, his contributory negligence would prevent him from receiving damages for his injuries from Andy.

Contributory negligence, however, can produce harsh results. Slightly negligent persons might not recover anything for very serious injuries caused by defendants' greater negligence. To ease the harshness of this result, a number of courts adopted the doctrine of **last clear chance.** This doctrine holds that even though plaintiff was negligent, he or she can still recover if it can be shown that the defendant had the "last clear chance" to avoid the harm. Thus, if Craig is crossing the street not realizing the light has changed, and Andy is speeding down the street, if Andy could have stopped in time to avoid the accident but failed to do so, Craig can still recover for his injuries.

Recently, most states have abandoned contributory negligence and last clear chance and adopted a **comparative negligence** system. This is seen as fairer because it distributes the cost of the accident according to the degree of both plaintiff's and defendant's fault. While comparative negligence systems differ in their details, most states have adopted a "pure" comparative negligence system. This system allows plaintiffs to recover the portion of their losses not attributable to their fault. For example, in the situation above, assume that the jury determined that Craig was 33 percent at fault for his injuries, and Andy was 67 percent at fault, and that Craig suffered $27,000 in damages. Under a pure comparative fault system, Craig could recover $18,000 from Andy. A few states have adopted a "mixed" comparative fault system. Under this system, plaintiffs are barred from recovery if they are as much or more at fault for their injuries as defendant. Thus, if Craig were found to be 55 percent at fault for his injuries, he would not be able to recover anything under a mixed system.

There are some cases in which plaintiffs in negligence suits have voluntarily exposed themselves to a known danger created by another's negligence. For example, Liz voluntarily goes for a ride with Jim, who is obviously drunk. Such plaintiffs have **assumed the risk** of injury and are barred from recovery. The plaintiff must fully understand the nature and extent of the risk to be held to have assumed it. Some of the states that have adopted comparative negligence have also done away with the assumption of risk defense, treating all forms of contributory fault under their comparative negligence scheme.

COLES V. JENKINS
34 F. Supp. 2d 381 (D. W. Va. 1998)

FACTS

This is the same case that appeared earlier in the chapter. Another defense asserted by VBT was that the Egans has assumed the risk of injury.

ISSUE

Did the Egans assume the risk of injury by riding on the road?

DECISION

A plaintiff cannot recover for injuries suffered from a risk which he assumed. A finding of assumption of the risk requires two things: that plaintiff fully understood the nature and extent of the risk, and the risk must have been voluntarily assumed. VBT stresses that written and oral warnings about the heavy traffic and narrow shoulder of the route were given on the day of the ride, the option of taking the van was stressed, and the nature of the road was immediately apparent to the Egans when they got on it, yet they continued to ride for almost a mile rather than take the van. There is substantial evidence for a jury to find assumption of the risk.

RECKLESSNESS

When a defendant's behavior indicates a "conscious disregard for a known high degree of probable harm to another," the defendant is guilty of **recklessness.** Like negligence, recklessness involves posing a foreseeable risk of harm to others. However, that risk of harm must be significantly greater than the degree of risk that would make an act negligent. For example, Bob bets his friends he can drive down a crowded street blindfolded, and he strikes Tom. Recklessness is more morally objectionable than negligence (i.e., than if Bob had been merely speeding) but less objectionable than intentional wrongdoing (i.e., if Bob had driven up on the curb after Tom). Therefore, contributory negligence is not a good defense to recklessness but assumption of risk is a good defense. So, the fact that Tom did not look before stepping into Bob's path would not defeat his recovery, but evidence that Tom had bet Bob's friends he could run in front of Bob without being hit would bar any recovery by Tom. Since recklessness involves a high degree of fault, plaintiff stands a good chance of recovering punitive damages in recklessness cases.

STRICT LIABILITY

The third kind of tort, in addition to negligence and intentional torts, is **strict liability.** Strict liability means that a person who participates in certain kinds of activities is held responsible for any resulting harm to others, despite the use of the utmost care and caution. For this reason, strict liability is commonly described as "liability without fault." The basic idea behind strict liability is that the risks associated with certain activities should be borne by the person whose actions created the risk and caused the loss, rather than by an innocent person who has suffered the loss. Traditionally, strict liability was imposed for those activities that were considered abnormally dangerous or *ultrahazardous*. Thus, people who kept animals that were "naturally dangerous" and people who did blasting were subject to strict liability when their activities injured someone, regardless of the precautions they took to avoid injuring others. Generally speaking, assumption of risk is a good defense to strict liability suits.

The most recent major application of strict liability is to the manufacturers of defective products that are "unreasonably dangerous"—that is, defective in a way that endangers life or property and is not readily apparent to buyers. This important topic is discussed in greater detail in Chapter 17.

CURRENT ISSUES

In the last few years, virtually all states have passed tort reform measures. The impetus behind this is the assumed "crisis" in the liability insurance area characterized by dramatically higher premiums, reductions in coverage, and sometimes refusal to cover certain activities. While there is heated debate about whether a crisis actually exists, business and insurance lobbying groups have persuaded legislatures to pass reform bills. Common reform measures include limits on the amount of noneconomic damages (such as damages for pain and suffering and emotional distress) that can be recovered in a torts suit, and limits on punitive damage amounts and the way they are awarded. Certain defendants such as doctors, the skiing industry, and municipalities have gained limits on their liability and restrictions on the way a case against them can be handled. Sometimes these reform measures are combined with regulation of

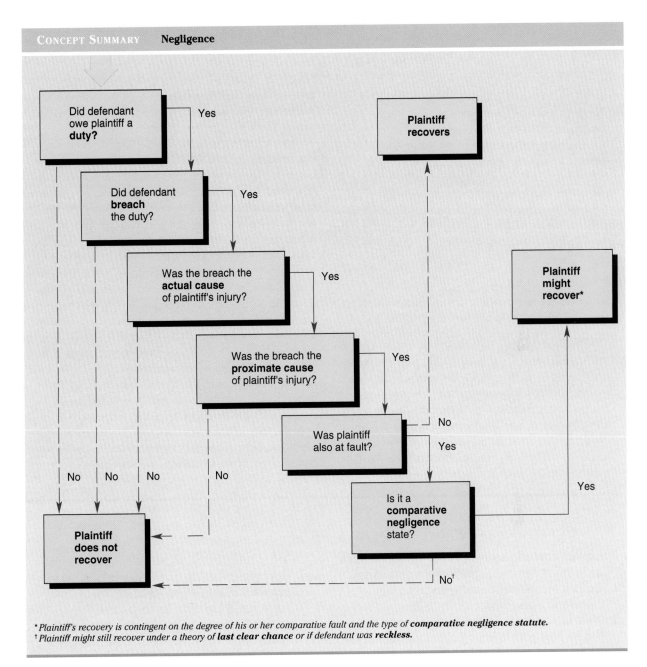

CONCEPT SUMMARY   Negligence

* *Plaintiff's recovery is contingent on the degree of his or her comparative fault and the type of **comparative negligence statute**.*
† *Plaintiff might still recover under a theory of **last clear chance** or if defendant was **reckless**.*

insurers to help control or reduce premium increases and policy cancellations. In some states the courts have held the reform measures to be unconstitutional under the state constitution because they unfairly limit plaintiffs' right to seek redress in the courts for their injuries. The debate about the need to reform tort law is unlikely to end soon, and legislatures can be expected to continue to be active on the insurance and tort reform front.

KLEIN V. PYRODYNE CORPORATION
810 P. 2d 917 (Sup. Ct. Wash. 1991)

FACTS

Pyrodyne, a pyrotechnic company, was hired to conduct the Fourth of July fireworks display in Puyallup, Washington. During the display one of the five-inch mortars was knocked into a horizontal position and when ignited flew 500 feet parallel to the ground and exploded near the spectators, injuring several of them. Danny Klein, one of the spectators, was severely burned and sued Pyrodyne under a theory of strict liability. Pyrodyne argued that strict liability should not be applied to authorized fireworks displays.

ISSUE

Is conducting fireworks displays an abnormally dangerous activity that should be subject to strict liability?

DECISION

Yes. The *Restatement (Second) of Torts* provides that one who carries on an abnormally dangerous activity is subject to liability for harm resulting from the activity although he has exercised the utmost care to prevent the harm. In determining whether an activity is abnormally dangerous, the court should consider if there was a high degree of risk of harm, the likelihood that the harm that results would be great, the inability to eliminate the risk

by reasonable care, the extent to which the activity is not a matter of common usage, the inappropriateness of the activity to the place where it is carried on, and whether its value to the community is outweighed by its dangerous attributes. Igniting aerial rockets to explode in the air carries a high risk of serious personal injury. No matter how much care is exercised, that risk cannot be entirely eliminated when setting them off near crowds. The dangerousness is shown by the fact that pyrotechnics is highly regulated, technicians must be licensed, and insurance must be obtained before each show. Few persons engage in public fireworks displays. Thus, the first four considerations are met. While the show was conducted in an appropriate place, and having fireworks on the day celebrating our national independence and unity outweighs the risks, it is not necessary that all considerations be met. Conducting public fireworks displays is an abnormally dangerous activity, similar to detonating dynamite, that justifies imposing strict liability. In addition, public policy considerations state that the professional pyrotechnicians, as opposed to the innocent victims, bear the loss. In ultrahazardous cases in which all evidence has been destroyed in the accident, it would not be fair to require the victim to prove negligence.

.... QUESTIONS AND PROBLEM CASES ....

1. Explain duty and some of the things the courts consider in determining whether a duty exists.
2. Explain the difference between proximate cause and cause in fact.
3. What factors must be present for a successful suit for negligent infliction of emotional distress on third parties?
4. What factors do the courts consider in deciding whether to treat an activity as one deserving strict liability?
5. McLauglin injured his back while working as a lumberjack. He became addicted to pain killers during treatment for the injury. He was then treated for the addiction three times, but he never stopped using the drug. When he moved to Indiana, he sought treatment for his back injury and obtained a prescription for the pain

killer. He filled the prescription much faster than prescribed. In one 60-day period he received 24 refills, getting tablets that should have lasted 138 days. In one month the prescription was filled 12 times, meaning that McLaughlin or his wife was at the pharmacy every two to three days. When his doctor discovered the misuse, he refused to prescribe more. McLauglin became depressed as a result of withdrawal and attempted suicide. He sued the pharmacy, claiming it had a duty to stop filling the prescription because the pharmacist knew or should have known that McLauglin was consuming the drug so quickly that it was a threat to his health. Is he correct?

6. Ford was seriously injured when his head struck a tree limb as he was waterskiing backward and

barefooted. Ford sued Gouin, the driver of the boat that was towing him, for causing him to go too close to the riverbank and hit the overhanging limb. A law stated that "No person shall operate . . . any vessel, towrope, or other device by which the direction or location of water skis . . . may be affected or controlled so as to cause [them] or any person thereon, to collide with, or strike against any object or person." Ford argued that the doctrine of negligence per se should apply. Is he correct?

7. About six weeks after Clark was diagnosed as pregnant, her doctor, Norris, determined the fetus was dead and that a minor surgical procedure, a D&C (dilatation and curettage), was necessary to remove it. During the D&C, Norris perforated Clark's uterine wall and damaged her intestine. As a result, she required additional surgery and suffers from chronic diarrhea. Clark was not allowed to use *res ipsa loquitur* to help prove her malpractice case against Norris, and when she lost, she appealed. Should *res ipsa loquitur* apply to this case?

8. Rockwell, after ordering food at Whataburger, sat down in a booth to wait for it. He looked around and saw a group of three young men eating at another booth. One of these men yelled at him, asking him if he had "a f___ing problem." Rockwell replied, "No, but apparently you do." The verbal harassment escalated until each side threatened the other. The restaurant manager told them to "take it outside" if they were going to fight. Rockwell asked the manager several times to call the police but she did not do so until they were outside. When outside, one of the men hit Rockwell in the head with a brick, seriously injuring him. Was Whataburger the proximate cause of Rockwell's injuries?

9. A robber grabbed a customer at Kentucky Fried Chicken (KFC), held a gun to her back, and ordered the cashier to open the register. When she said she needed a key to do so, the robber threatened to shoot the customer. The customer yelled at the cashier to open it, which she eventually did. Did the restaurant breach a duty to the customer by failing to quickly follow the robber's orders?

10. Quesada died on December 9, 1979, and his body was to be taken to the Oak Hill Memorial Park after an autopsy. When the body was delivered to Oak Hill, it contained a toe tag identifying it as someone else. When the family went to view the body, they were shown the body of a stranger. They informed the cemetery that this was not Quesada's body but Oak Hill refused to believe them, and ridiculed and mocked them. It conducted the burial ceremony with the stranger's body. Five days later, the mix-up was admitted, the stranger was exhumed, and Quesada was buried in his stead. Quesada's sister and niece sued for negligent infliction of emotional distress. Will they be successful?

11. Cheong and Antablin, longtime friends and experienced skiers, went skiing. Antablin felt he was going too fast for existing conditions and turned right in an effort to slow down and regain control. In so doing, he collided with Cheong, injuring him. Should assumption of the risk be a defense to Cheong's suit?

12. Waterson was driving her car when it went out of control and hit a telephone pole due to a defective axle. Waterson was not wearing a seat belt, and she was severely injured. She sued General Motors for her injuries. Should Waterson's failure to wear her seatbelt be used to reduce the award?

PART II

Contracts

CHAPTER 6

The Nature and Origins of Contracts

The outline in Figure 6–1 gives you an overview of what you will be studying in the next 10 chapters, in Part II of this book, "Contracts." The outline presents an approach you can use in organizing the material you learn about contract law and in analyzing contract problems. The material is presented in the context of four broad questions. After studying the chapters, you should be able to determine the answers to these questions in the context of specific fact situations. For example, after studying Chapters 7, 8, and 9, you will know how to determine if there was the good offer, acceptance, and consideration necessary for a contract. The four basic organizational questions are:

- *Is there a contract?*
- *Is the contract enforceable?*
- *Who can enforce the contract?*
- *Was the contract breached and what are the remedies?*

FIGURE 6–1   Contracts

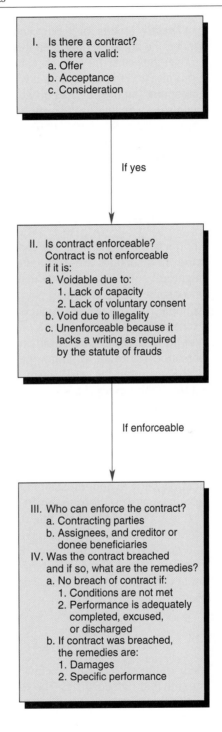

.... **WHAT IS A CONTRACT?** ....

A **contract** is a *legally enforceable promise* or set of promises. However, not all promises are contracts. If Bill promises to take Mary to the movies on Saturday night but takes Judy instead, can Mary successfully sue Bill for breaking his promise? No. If Bill buys a car from Friendly Motors and promises to pay for it in monthly installments, can Friendly Motors force Bill to honor his promise if he stops making payments? Yes. What is the difference between these two promises?

Over the years, the common law courts developed a number of requirements that a promise had to meet before it would be considered a contract. A contract is (1) an agreement (an *offer* and an *acceptance* of the offer) (2) supported by consideration (with some exceptions) (3) voluntarily entered into (4) by parties having capacity to contract (5) to do a legal act or acts. In addition to these elements, *written* evidence of some kinds of contracts is required.

Chapters 7–13 will discuss each of these elements. When you fully understand each element, you will be able to differentiate a contract from an unenforceable promise.

WHY HAVE CONTRACTS?

Contracts are probably a necessary device in any kind of market economy where goods and services are exchanged by people acting in their own interest. People might not enter into agreements that call for some future performance unless they know some means (the law) exist to force other people to honor their promises. For example, a small business might be afraid to supply its goods to a large corporation in exchange for the corporation's promise to pay for them next month unless the business knows it could have outside help to force the corporation to pay. Similarly, a weak person might not be willing to pay a strong person today for goods to be delivered next week unless the weak person knows there is outside help available to enforce the return of the money if the goods are not delivered, or if the goods delivered are not what was agreed to.

It is also true that it would probably be impossible to have an industrialized, market economy without contracts. A manufacturer would be unable to do the kind of planning necessary to run a business if it could not rely on agreements with suppliers to furnish the raw materials needed to make its products. Similarly, a manufacturer might not be willing to commit itself to buy raw materials or hire employees if it could not rely on buyers' promises to buy its products.

It is not surprising, then, that the contract was accepted as the basis for business transactions at a very early point in history. Egyptians and Mesopotamians recognized and enforced contracts thousands of years before Christ. By 1603 the common law courts of England recognized the enforceability of simple contracts. To fully understand why our contract law took its present shape, we must look briefly at its historical roots.

HOW HAS CONTRACT LAW DEVELOPED?

Many of the rules of contract law you will study in later chapters were developed in the 18th and 19th centuries. The social conditions existing at that time played a strong role in shaping contract law.

Most contracts people entered into in the 18th and 19th centuries fit a typical mold. People dealt with each other on a face-to-face basis; the parties often knew each other personally, or at least knew each other's reputation for fair dealing. The kinds of things people bought and sold were relatively simple, and the odds were that the buyer knew enough about the purchase to make an intelligent choice.

The 19th century also saw *laissez-faire* (free market) economic theories treated as a highly important part of public policy. The courts were unwilling to interfere with people's private agreements or to do anything that might interfere with the country's growing industrialization. "Freedom of contract" was the rule of the day. This "hands-off" policy made contracts an ideal device for business. People in business were able to do the kinds of economic planning that increasing industrialization required. They were also able to limit or shift many of their economic risks by placing clauses in their contracts that they could be sure the courts would enforce. For example, manufacturers were commonly allowed to *disclaim* (avoid responsibility for) any liability for injuries caused by their products.

The result of these factors was what may appear to you to be a hard-nosed attitude on the part of the courts. As long as a person voluntarily entered into a contract (within the broad limits discussed in Chapter 12), the courts would generally enforce it even if the results were grossly unfair. It was not uncommon for courts to say things such as, "It is not the business of the courts to relieve fools of the consequences of their folly." The courts were also generally unwilling to consider the argument that a party did not freely enter a contract because the other party had superior bargaining power and used that power to force the weaker party to accept "unfair" contract terms.

The Industrial Revolution that modernized America also changed many of the basic assumptions underlying contract law. The things people bought and sold became more and more complex. Buyers often had little or no knowledge about the goods they bought. People were buying products manufactured hundreds of miles from their homes, from sellers they often did not know.

An increasingly large percentage of agreements were based on *form contracts*. Frequently, people did not sit down and bargain about the terms of their agreement; instead, they used a printed contract form created before their agreement, often doing little more than filling in the blanks. Any student who has signed a lease or taken out a loan has had experience with form contracts. Some people argued that many parts of our economy in fact had imperfect or monopolistic competition and that free-market theories were no longer the correct basis for public policy in modern society.

The legal system began to respond to these changes in our way of life, changing contract law in the process. Many important contractual relationships that had earlier been left to private bargaining began to be controlled to some degree by legislation. Think for a minute about all the state and federal laws that govern employment contracts: minimum wages, maximum hours, workers' compensation, unemployment benefits, nondiscrimination, and so on. The legislatures have also, for example, passed statutes that make manufacturers more responsible for the products they produce. Often, this public interference in private contracts is justified as an attempt to protect those who lack the power to protect themselves by bargaining for fair contract terms.

Many courts also began to shift their emphasis from protecting business and promoting industrialization to protecting consumers and workers. Courts today are generally willing to consider defenses based on inequality of bargaining power between the parties, and they may refuse to enforce or may even rewrite contracts to avoid injustice. Most modern courts also, for example, tend to view with great suspicion attempts by manufacturers to limit their responsibility for their products by contract. This is particularly so when the buyer is a consumer. It is probably safe to say that the trend toward more judicial and legislative input into private contracts will continue for some time to come. Despite this trend, however, the idea that a contract is an agreement freely entered into by the parties is still the basis for enforcing most private contracts today.

Contract law continues to change to meet new challenges and conditions. On-line commerce is causing many contract rules to be reexamined. Contracting in cyberspace is discussed in Chapter 48.

######## *THE UNIFORM COMMERCIAL CODE* ....

The biggest reform of contract law has resulted from the adoption of the Uniform Commercial Code (UCC) by all the states (except Louisiana, which has adopted only part of the Code). The Uniform Commercial Code was created by the American Law Institute and the National Conference of Commissioners on Uniform State Laws. The drafters had several purposes in mind including promoting fair dealing and higher standards of behavior in the marketplace. The most obvious purpose was to establish a uniform law to govern commercial transactions that often take place across state lines.

Despite the intentions of the drafters, complete uniformity has not been achieved. This is so for several reasons. Some sections of the Code were drafted with alternatives, giving adopting states two or three versions of a section to choose from. Some states later amended various sections of the Code, and some sections of the Code have been interpreted differently by different state courts. However, much greater uniformity exists now than existed previously. Work is currently under way to revise many of the Code sections to reflect changes that have occurred since the Code was drafted. Some of these include the transition from a goods to a service economy, changes in what creates commercial value, and the increasing use of computers.

The Code is divided into 9 articles that deal with many of the problems that might ordinarily arise in a commercial transaction. Most of these articles are discussed in Parts III, VII, and VIII of this book. Article 2, the article that applies to contracts for the sale of goods, is discussed in the following contract chapters as well as in Part III.

######## *ARTICLE 2* ....

Article 2 applies to all contracts for the **sale of goods** (2-102).[1] Although the Code contains a somewhat complicated definition of *goods* (2-105), the most important thing to understand is that the term *goods* means *tangible personal property*. This means that contracts for the sale of things such as motor vehicles, books, appliances, and clothing are covered by Article 2. Article 2 does not apply to contracts for the sale of real estate or stocks and bonds and other intangibles.

Article 2 also does not apply to service contracts. This can cause confusion because, while contracts for employment or other services are clearly not covered, many contracts involve elements of both goods and services. The test the courts most frequently use to determine whether Article 2 applies to a particular contract is to ask which element—goods or services—*predominates* in the contract. Basically, this means that any agreement calling for services that involve significant elements of personal skill and judgment is probably not governed by Article 2. For example, Lucy suffers an injury due to impurities in a permanent solution for hair. Can she sue for breach of warranty under the Code, or must she sue on some other theory? If Lucy bought the solution ("goods") at a drugstore and applied it herself, the Code applies. If, however, the solution was applied at a beauty shop (the application by a trained

[1]The numbers in parentheses refer to specific Uniform Commercial Code sections. The sections appear in the website for this book. Article 2A applies to *leases*.

professional is a substantial service element), a court would probably not apply the Code. Construction contracts, remodeling contracts, and auto repair contracts are other examples of mixed goods and services contracts that may be considered outside the scope of the Code.

The first question you should ask when faced with a contracts problem is: *Is this a contract for the sale of goods?* If it is not, apply the principles of common law contracts. If it is, apply the Code rule, *if there is one.* The Code has modified only some of the basic rules of contract law. If there is no specific Code rule governing the problem, apply the relevant common law rule. See Figure 6–2.

CREATION OF PRACTICAL CONTRACT RULES

Article 2 reflects an attitude about contracts that is fundamentally different from that of the common law. The Code is more concerned with rewarding people's legitimate expectations than with technical rules, so it is generally more *flexible* than traditional contract law. A court that applies the Code is more likely to find the parties had a contract than a court that applies contract law (2-204). In some cases, the Code gives less weight to technical requirements such as consideration (discussed in Chapter 9) than is the case in contract law (2-205 and 2-209).

The drafters of the Code sought to create practical rules to deal with what people actually do in today's marketplace. We live in the day of the form contract, so some of the Code rules try to deal fairly with that fact (Sections 2-205, 2-207, 2-209, and 2-302). Throughout the Code, the words *reasonable, commercially reasonable,* and *seasonably* (within a reasonable time) are found. This reasonableness standard is different from the hypothetical "reasonable person" standard used in tort law. A court that tries to

FIGURE 6–2   Choice of Law: Goods vs. Services

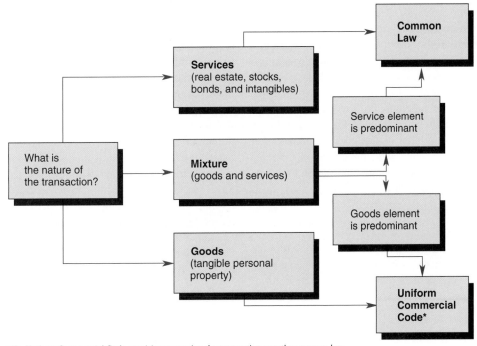

If there is no specific Uniform Commercial Code provision governing the transaction, use the common law.

decide what is "reasonable" under the Code is more likely to be concerned with what people really do in the marketplace than with what a nonexistent "reasonable person" would do.

GOOD FAITH AND FAIR DEALING

The drafters of the Code also tried to promote fair dealing and higher standards of behavior in the marketplace. They attempted to do this in several ways in Article 2. The Code imposes a duty on everyone making agreements under the Code to act in *good faith* (1-203). It expressly recognizes the concept of an *unconscionable* contract (2-302)—one that is grossly unfair or one-sided—and gives the courts broad powers to remedy such unfairness. Further, the Code imposes certain standards of quality on sellers of goods as a matter of law. These are called *implied warranties* (2-314 and 2-315) (discussed in Chapter 17). Sellers' power to contractually deny (disclaim) responsibility for their goods is also limited (2-316 and 2-302).

SONS OF THUNDER, INC. V. BORDEN, INC.
690 A.2d 575 (N.J. Sup. Ct. 1997)

FACTS

Borden, Inc., had a contract to purchase the clams that Sons of Thunder's (SOT) vessels caught. The contract allowed either party to cancel the contract by giving prior notice in writing 90 days prior to the effective date of cancellation. In reliance on Borden's representation that SOT had a five-year contract with it, the bank gave SOT a loan to buy another boat. For most weeks, Borden did not purchase the contractually required number of clams. Borden came under new management, acquired a seafood company and its fishing boats, and brought in a new manager who refused to purchase clams from SOT unless kickbacks were paid. When SOT attempted to sell the clams to other suppliers, Borden charged a fee for shucking equipment it had asked SOT to put on its boats. Borden then sent a letter cancelling the contract after 90 days. SOT eventually sued for breach of contract and alleged, among other things, that Borden breached its covenant of good faith and fair dealing through its cancellation.

ISSUE

Was Borden's cancellation in bad faith, and therefore in breach of the duty of good faith and fair dealing, even though it was not in breach of a specific contract term?

DECISION

Yes. Article 2 of the Uniform Commercial Code, which New Jersey has adopted, governs this contract because it involves the sale of goods. The Code imposes an obligation of good faith and fair dealing on every contract governed by it. This includes the requirement that neither party shall do anything that will have the effect of destroying or injuring the right of the other party to receive the fruits of the contract. This obligation is included in contracts that contain express and unambiguous provisions permitting either party to terminate the contract without cause. A party to a contract may breach the implied covenant of good faith and fair dealing without violating an express term of a contract. Such a violation will allow a party to sue for breach of contract even though no violation of the express terms of the contract has occurred. Borden knew that SOT depended on the income from its contract with Borden to pay back the loan, yet Borden continuously refused to buy the required number of clams, stated that it would not honor the contract, failed to fulfill other obligations, and charged a fee for the shucking equipment. There is sufficient evidence to find that Borden was not honest in fact as required by the U.C.C. and that it acted in bad faith.

Some sections of the Code (Sections 2-201[2], 2-205, 2-207[2], and 2-314), *in some cases,* impose a higher standard of behavior on "merchants" than on nonmerchants in recognition of the fact that buyers tend to place more reliance on professional sellers and that professionals are generally more knowledgeable and better able to protect themselves than nonprofessionals. The Code defines **merchant** (2-104[1]) on a case-by-case basis. If a person *regularly deals in the kind of goods being sold,* or pretends to have some special knowledge about the goods, or employs an agent in the sale who fits either of these two descriptions, that person is a *merchant* for the purposes of the contract in question. So, if you buy a used car from a used-car dealer, the dealer is a merchant for the purposes of your contract. But if you buy a refrigerator from a used-car dealer, the dealer is probably not considered to be a merchant for purposes of that sale.

Because Article 2 exhibits the basic tendencies of contract law discussed earlier in the chapter, many courts apply Code concepts to cases not specifically covered by the Code. In addition, many courts have broadly interpreted the Code to apply to contracts for things one would not normally classify as "goods." The Code concepts of good-faith dealing and unconscionability have also enjoyed wide application. Thus, contract law under the Code and the common law are growing more similar.

CONTRACTS FOR THE INTERNATIONAL SALE OF GOODS

In 1980 a group of nations adopted a uniform law governing contracts for the international sale of goods, the **U.N. Convention on the International Sale of Goods** (CISG). It was designed to provide a uniform code for international contracts in the same way the Uniform Commercial Code provides uniformity for transactions among contracting parties from different states in the United States. It applies to contracts between signatories (countries that have agreed to be bound by the treaty) and is very similar to the Uniform Commercial Code. The United States ratified the convention in 1986, and it became effective for U.S. companies in 1988. Companies can choose not to have CISG apply to their contracts, but that must be stated in the agreement. The Convention will be discussed in greater detail in Chapter 49.

TYPES OF CONTRACTS

Several terms are used to describe the different kinds of contracts our legal system recognizes. These terms will be used throughout the following chapters.

VALID, UNENFORCEABLE, VOIDABLE, AND VOID CONTRACTS

A **valid contract** is one that meets all the legal requirements for a contract. Valid contracts are therefore enforceable in court.

An **unenforceable contract** is one that meets the basic legal requirements for a contract but will not be enforced due to some other legal rule. For example, in Chapter 13, we will see that the law says some kinds of contracts must be in writing to be enforceable. Contracts for the sale of real estate are one example of a contract required to be in writing. So, Bob may agree to sell his house to Mary and every basic requirement for a contract may be present (a voluntary agreement to do a legal act by parties with the capacity to contract, supported by consideration), but if the agreement is not in writing, the contract will not be enforced by the court.

A **voidable contract** is one that may be canceled by one or both of the parties. It is enforceable against both parties unless a party with the right to cancel the contract has done so. For example, in Chapter 10, we will see that minors have the legal right to cancel their contracts. So, if Frank buys a used car from Honest Bob's Used Cars and Frank is a minor, the parties have a voidable contract. It is binding and enforceable against both parties unless Frank decides to cancel the contract.

The **void contract** lacks one or more of the basic requirements for a contract. Such an agreement has no legal force or effect. An example is an agreement to steal a car. One of the basic requirements for a valid contract is that the thing the parties have agreed to do is legal. Stealing a car is illegal; therefore, such an agreement would be considered void.

UNILATERAL AND BILATERAL CONTRACTS

Contracts are called either unilateral or bilateral depending on whether one or both of the parties made a promise. In a **unilateral contract,** only one of the parties makes a promise. The other party performs an act in exchange for that promise. For example, Mary runs an ad in the paper offering a $5 reward for the return of her lost dog, Sparky. Mary has made a promise to pay the person who performs the act of returning Sparky.

In a **bilateral contract,** both parties make a promise. For example, Sue Smith, the owner of Hi-Fi Heaven, orders 100 stereo receivers from Steve Jones, a salesman for Slick Sound Manufacturing Company. Sue has made a promise to pay for the receivers in exchange for Slick Sound's promise to deliver them. In the next chapter, you will learn that unilateral contracts create some special problems in the areas of offer and acceptance. This fact causes the courts to treat a contract as bilateral whenever it is possible to do so.

CONCEPT SUMMARY	Types of Contracts by Enforceability
Valid	Contains all elements needed to be enforceable
Unenforceable	Contains basic elements required for a contract but the courts will not enforce it due to a legal rule (such as the statute of frauds)
Voidable	One of the contracting parties can avoid the contract
Void	Lacks basic element(s) necessary for a contract

EXECUTED AND EXECUTORY CONTRACTS

A contract is **executed** when all the parties have fully performed their duties under the contract. A contract is **executory** as long as it has not been fully performed. A contract is partially executory when one person has performed his promise under the contract but the other person has not performed hers.

EXPRESS AND IMPLIED CONTRACTS

A contract is **express** when the parties have directly stated its terms at the time the contract was formed. They may have done this orally or in writing. So, when Bill tells Joe, "I'll sell you my 1988 truck for $10,000," and Joe replies, "You've got a deal," an express contract has been created.

There are many cases, however, in which the parties have clearly reached an agreement, even though they have not expressly stated its terms. When the surrounding facts and circumstances indicate that an agreement has in fact been reached, an **im-**

plied contract is created. Suppose you go to your dentist for treatment. Ordinarily you would not expressly state the terms of your mutual agreement beforehand, although it is clear that you do, in fact, have an agreement. A court would infer a promise on the part of your dentist to use reasonable care in treating you and a promise on your part to pay a reasonable fee for the dentist's services.

VARNI BROS. CORP. V. WINE WORLD, INC.
41 Cal Rptr. 2d 740 (Ct. App. Cal. 1995)

FACTS

Wine World, Inc., a producer and supplier of wines such as Beringer, Napa Ridge, and Chateau Souverain, distributed its wines through independent distributors including Varni Bros. Varni maintained warehouses, a fleet of trucks, and trained salespeople and provided other services to its suppliers, including Wine World. Varni started distributing Wine World wines in 1975 on the basis of a handshake. Written contracts were rare in the business; everyone "understood" what a "distributorship" involved. There was no discussion regarding how long the arrangement would last. In 1989 Wine World consolidated its distribution network and terminated its arrangement with Varni on 60 days' written notice. Varni sued, arguing that an implied term of their contract, supplied by industry custom, was that they could be terminated only for good cause.

ISSUE

Can industry custom supply a term of an implied contract?

DECISION

Yes. An implied contract's existence and terms are manifested by conduct. The parties in an implied contract have manifested assent but the agreement and promises have not been expressed in words. Varni's and Wine World's conduct showed they had a distribution contract. Because no terms were expressed or discussed, the terms of the contract must be determined by their conduct. Usage and custom of trade can be used to supply terms of a contract that were not expressed so long as they are not inconsistent with the conduct. Because there was no agreement regarding duration, the contract here was of indefinite duration, terminable at the will of either party. While there may have been an industry custom that distributor arrangements were only terminable for cause, this did not continue past 1985. Thus, it was not in effect in 1989, and Wine World was free to terminate the implied contract with Varni.

It is possible to describe any contract by using one or more of the terms discussed earlier in this chapter. Consider this contract: Martha's Beauty Salon sends Hair Affair Manufacturing Company an order for 10 cases of hair spray at $75 a case. Hair Affair sends Martha's an acknowledgment form accepting the order. The parties have a *valid, express, bilateral contract.* The contract is *executory* until Hair Affair has delivered the goods and Martha's has paid for them.

.... QUASI CONTRACT ....

As you saw in Chapter 1, the common law as it initially developed was a fairly rigid, inflexible way of dealing with many problems. One aspect of this rigidity was that the courts insisted that all the elements of a contract be present before the courts would find a legally binding agreement between the parties. This attitude caused an injustice in some cases. Sometimes a person might have done something that benefited another person but there were no facts from which a court could infer an agreement between the parties. In such a case, the party who received the benefit could be *unjustly enriched* at the expense of the other party. This unfair result could be avoided if a court created or implied a promise by the benefited party to pay the reasonable value of the benefit.

A **quasi contract** is a legal fiction created by the court to avoid injustice in such cases. It requires the defendant to act as if he had promised to pay for the benefit he voluntarily received. Since there is no factual basis for implying a promise to pay, as we have in an implied contract case, the courts, in effect, create the promise. This promise imposed by law is applied in a wide variety of cases. It is impossible to list all the kinds of cases that may create a liability based on quasi contract. The basic idea is that quasi contract applies where one of the parties *voluntarily receives a benefit* from the other party under circumstances that make it *unfair* to keep the benefit without paying for it. Generally, the person is required to pay the *reasonable value* of the benefit received. A person is not held liable under quasi contract for benefits he or she received unknowingly, or for benefits he or she reasonably believed were given as a gift.

For example, Fred's Painting Company has a contract to paint Walter's house at 525 East Third Street. Fred's painters arrive by mistake at Bob's house at 325 East Third Street and begin painting. Bob sees Fred's painters but does not say anything because his house needs painting. Bob later refuses to pay for the paint job, arguing that the parties have no contract.

There are clearly no facts here to justify implying an agreement between Fred's and Bob. However, the courts would probably hold Bob liable to Fred's on a quasi contract basis. On the other hand, if Bob had come home from vacation to find his home mistakenly painted, he would not be liable to Fred's since he did not knowingly accept the paint job.

BREWER v. NEW YORK
672 N.Y.S.2d 650 (N.Y. Ct. Claims 1998)

FACTS

Value-Added Communications, Inc. (VAC) contracted with the New York State Department of Corrections Services (DOCS) to provide telephone services to inmates as part of the Inmate Call Home Program. VAC was required to pay DOCS commissions on the gross revenues generated by collect calls plus a penalty for late payment. VAC later filed for Chapter 11 bankruptcy, and Brewer was appointed bankruptcy trustee. Within 90 days before the bankruptcy filing, VAC sent three checks to DOCS totaling $58,303.45. After the filing, it made three payments totaling $488,548.52. Normally, such payments are recoverable under bankruptcy law. Brewer was not allowed to seek recovery of the money in bankruptcy court due to consti-

tutional problems. Brewer then sought to recover the money for the bankrupt estate under a theory of quasi contract.

ISSUE

Should DOCS be required to return the money in order to avoid unjust enrichment?

DECISION

Yes. Under bankruptcy law, DOCS had no right to the payments. It knowingly received money belonging to the estate the trustee is administering. It should not be allowed to keep the money to the detriment of all of VAC's other general creditors. The requirements of quasi contract are present.

········· *PROMISSORY ESTOPPEL* ·········

Another important idea that the courts developed to deal with the unfairness that sometimes results from the strict application of contract rules is the doctrine of

CONCEPT SUMMARY	Types of Contracts
Unilateral	An act exchanged for a promise
Bilateral	A promise exchanged for a promise
Executory	A contract that has not been fully performed
Executed	A contract that has been fully performed
Express	Terms are stated orally or in writing
Implied	Terms are indicated by facts and circumstances
Quasi Contract (Implied-in-Law)	Contractlike duties imposed by the court to prevent unjust enrichment

promissory estoppel. Traditional contract law is basically designed to protect *bargains* that people make and that satisfy all the legal requirements for a binding contract. Around the turn of this century, however, the courts were confronted with cases in which persons relied on promises made by others that did not amount to contracts because they lacked some element required for a contract. Allowing the person who made such a promise (the promisor) to argue that no contract was created could, in some cases, work an injustice on the person who relied on the promise (the promisee).

In cases where denying enforcement would produce a serious injustice, some courts began to protect promisees by saying that the promisors were *estopped* (prevented) from raising any legal defense they might have to the enforcement of the promise. For example, John's parents told him that they would give the family farm to him when they died. Relying on this promise, John stayed at home and worked on the farm for several years. When they died, John's parents left the farm to his sister Martha. Should Martha and the parents' estate be allowed to defeat John's claim to the farm by arguing that the parents' promise was unenforceable because John gave no consideration for the promise (since the parents did not request that John stay home and work on the farm in exchange for their promise)? Many courts began to say that Martha and the parents' estate were estopped from raising this defense because of the unfairness to John that would result. Out of such cases grew the doctrine of promissory estoppel.

The *Restatement (Second) of Contracts,* an authoritative work on the common law of contracts that is often relied on by the courts, says:

> A promise which the promisor should reasonably expect to induce action or forbearance on the part of the promisee or a third person and which does induce such action or forbearance is binding if injustice can be avoided only by enforcement of the promise. The remedy granted for breach may be limited as justice requires. [Section 90]

While the *Restatement* does not have the force of law, most courts follow the requirements for promissory estoppel stated in it. Thus, they require a *promise* that the promisor should foresee is likely to induce reliance; significant *reliance* on the promise by the promisee; and *injustice* as a result of reliance. Promissory estoppel is fundamentally different from traditional contract theory since it protects *reliance,* not bargains. In the following chapters, you will see promissory estoppel being used to enforce promises that are not supported by consideration, and oral promises that would ordinarily be required to be in writing. The growth of this new theory for enforcing promises is one of the most important developments in contract law in this century.

GOFF-HAMEL V. OBSTETRICIANS & GYNECOLOGISTS, P.C.
588 N.W. 2d 798 (Neb. 1999)

FACTS

Goff-Hamel, an employee of Hastings Family planning for 11 years, was approached by Dr. Adams, a part-owner of Obstetricians, to come and work for it. Initially she refused, but after meeting with him and hearing the details of the offer, she accepted. It was agreed she would start work two months later. Before the starting date, Goff-Hamel went to Obstetricians office and was fitted with uniforms, which were included in the offer. She also gave notice at Hastings that she was quitting. The day before she was to start at Obstetricians, she was notified not to come to work because one of the part-owner's wives objected to her hiring. Goff-Hamel sued for promissory estoppel, among other theories.

ISSUE

Can Goff-Hamel use the theory of promissory estoppel to enforce a promise of employment at will?

DECISION

Yes. People hired for an indefinite period of time are employees at will and can be fired at any time for any reason. Therefore, Goff-Hamel cannot sue for breach of contract even though Obstetricians offered her a job and she accepted. She argues, however, that she should be able to recover because of her detrimental reliance on Obstetricians promise. In promissory estoppel, damages are based on what justice requires as opposed to being based on the benefit of the contract bargain, and will be awarded if the plaintiff reasonably relies on a promise that the promisor could reasonably foresee would induce reliance, and it would be unjust not to enforce it. Some jurisdictions hold that prospective employees cannot recover under these circumstances because it is unreasonable to rely on a promise of employment at will. Prospective employees should know they can be terminated at any time. We believe, however, that in our state she should be able to recover. Here Obstetricians' offer to Goff-Hamel was very specific as to terms and conditions. She gave up a very good position and benefits that she would have kept except for their promise.

Figure 6–3 summarizes the requirements for promissory estoppel.

FIGURE 6–3   Requirements for Promissory Estoppel

A promise is made that the promisor should know is likely to induce reliance. → There is significant reliance on the promise by the promisee. → An injustice will occur if the promise is not enforced.

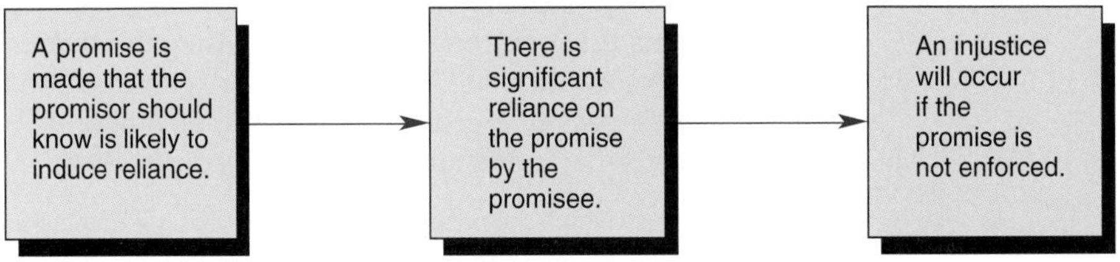

.... **QUESTIONS AND PROBLEM CASES** ....

1. Explain the difference between an express and an implied contract, and give an example of each.
2. Explain some major changes in contract law in the 20th century.
3. What conditions must be present before the court will use the doctrine of quasi contract?

4. Explain how the court will determine whether a contract involving goods and services should be decided under the Code or the common law.
5. Michelle Triola Marvin lived with actor Lee Marvin for almost six years. When the couple separated, she claimed that she was entitled to

half the property he acquired during their relationship in exchange for her giving up a singing career to provide him with homemaking services and companionship. Did Michelle have any contractual right to half of Lee Marvin's property?

6. The Abelmans hired Capital Termite and Pest Control Company to treat their home. Velsicol manufactured the chemical used on the Abelmans' home. It sold the chemical to a distributor, who sold it to Capitol. Capitol used one 55-gallon drum to treat several homes. It was later discovered that the chemical contained chlordane and heptachlor, which were shown to cause cancer in laboratory animals, and Velsicol suspended sales until a safer application method could be devised. The Abelmans abandoned their home because of the chemical residue and sued Capitol and Velsicol for breach of the warranties provided by the U.C.C. Capitol and Velsicol challenged the suit on the ground that there had been no sale of goods, and therefore no warranties were created. Are they correct?

7. Darling, an inventor of an erosion protection system, gave samples of his invention to oil companies that were exploring for oil from an artificial island they had constructed. He told them that a patent was pending on his design. Darling hoped to get a contract from them. He did not get the patent or the contract. He later sought compensation under a theory of quasi contract, claiming the companies appropriated his design without paying for it. Should the oil companies be ordered to pay Darling?

8. Cummins, an Elvis Presley impersonator who performed under the name Elvis Wade, met Brodie, a movie and record entrepreneur who was interested in promoting Cummins's career. After several conversations, Cummins and Brodie signed a "letter of intent" mentioning a movie, a television show, an album, and a weekly salary for Cummins, and proposing the formation of a corporation to produce these and other products. Cummins also signed an exclusive employment agreement with the proposed corporation, which was signed and accepted by Brodie. Brodie arranged for Cummins to cut an album, and advised him to cancel his current bookings to make himself available for more profitable engagements. Cummins canceled between 30 and 40 bookings. Brodie made some effort to promote Cummins's album, and rejected offers for Cummins to do a commercial and perform at a Las Vegas hotel because he thought they would not be professionally advantageous. The corporation was never formed, and no other bookings were secured. Cummins sued Brodie for breach of contract, alleging failure to secure replacement bookings. Was there an implied contract requiring Brodie to secure replacement bookings for Cummins?

9. Dreifus, an author writing a story on therapist-patient sexual abuse, interviewed Ruzicka. Ruzicka agreed to the interview on the condition that she not be identified or made identifiable in the article, and Dreifus agreed. When the article, "Sex with Shrinks," appeared in *Glamour* magazine, it contained sufficient details that Ruzicka could be identified. Does Ruzicka have a claim under promissory estoppel?

CHAPTER 7

Creating a Contract: Offers

Cagle went to Roy Buckner Chevrolet to discuss buying a 1978 Limited Edition Corvette CP (the "Indy Vette"). The salesman agreed to sell one to Cagle, and signed his name in the middle of the company's form after putting "list price" as the price to be paid. The form was left partially uncompleted. Cagle signed the form and left a deposit of $500. Buckner later refused to deliver the car to Cagle, claiming the agreement was too indefinite to be a good offer.

- *How specific must an offer be to form the basis of a contract?*
- *What do the courts look at to determine whether the offeror intended to make a binding offer?*
- *What does the court do to fill in missing terms?*

FIGURE 7–1   Offers

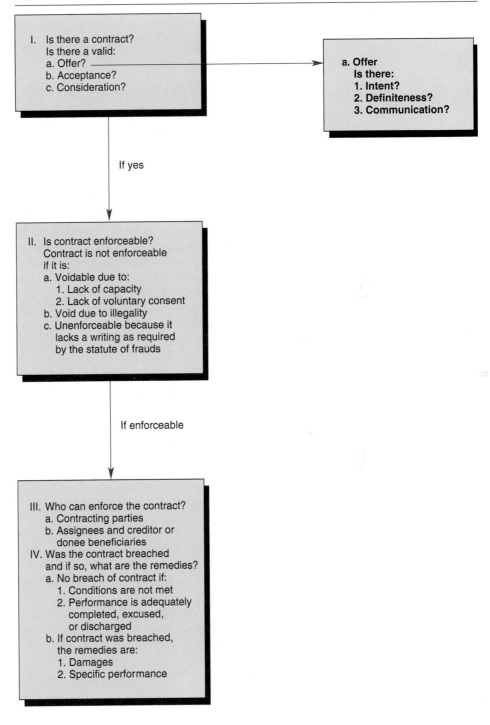

.... INTRODUCTION ....

When a dispute arises between the parties to a contract, there are two basic questions the court often has to answer: Did the parties in fact have a contract? If they did, what are its terms? The manner in which the court answers these questions is very important in shaping its decision.

The main thing a court looks for in deciding whether the parties entered into a contract is an **agreement,** or a "meeting of the minds" between the parties. This is so because the whole of traditional contract law is based on the idea of enforcing agreements that the parties made freely. At a very early point in the development of contract law, the courts created the basic formula for a contract:

$$\text{Offer} + \text{Acceptance} = \text{Agreement}$$

Did one of the parties indicate to the other party that he or she was willing to enter into an agreement on certain terms and conditions? Did the other party indicate that he or she was willing to agree to those terms and conditions? If so, then the parties have indicated the mutual assent necessary for a contract.

There are two things that you should bear in mind while studying contracts. The first is that the courts do not rely on what the parties say they *actually* (subjectively) intended. This can never be known, and, after a dispute has arisen, such statements are often unreliable. Instead, the courts look at the intent of the parties *objectively*. Would a reasonable person who knew all the circumstances surrounding the agreement believe that the parties intended to enter into a contract?

The second thing you should bear in mind is that when courts use the words **offer** and **acceptance,** they are using them in their technical, legal sense. This can cause confusion in two ways. *Offer* and *accept* have everyday meanings that are not necessarily the same as their legal meanings. Also, the parties to a dispute may have used these words in their everyday sense, being unaware of their legal meaning. This can lead to the potentially confusing situation where a party says "I accept" but the courts find that he or she, in fact, made an "offer." Therefore, it is very important that you understand the legal meaning of offer and acceptance.

.... WHAT IS AN OFFER? ....

An *offer* is the manifestation of a willingness to enter into a contract if the other person agrees to the terms. The question of what amounts to an offer is important for several reasons. If there is no offer, there is nothing to accept and a contract cannot be created. A person who has made an offer (the **offeror**) has given the party to whom he or she has made the offer (the **offeree**) the power to create a binding contract by accepting. It is also important to know what is included in the terms of the offer, since the offer often contains all the terms of the contract. This is so because in most cases all the offeree does is indicate acceptance of the offer.

INTENT

The basic thing the courts require for the creation of an offer is a **present intent to contract** on the part of the offeror. When all the circumstances surrounding the parties' dealings are considered, did the offeror ever, in effect, say: "This is it—agree and we have a contract on these terms"? As the *Mears* case illustrates, this is objectively determined.

The two main things a court looks for in answering this question are how **definite** the supposed offer is and whether the offeror has **communicated** it to the offeree.

MEARS V. NATIONWIDE MUTUAL INS. CO.
91 F 3d 1118 (8th Cir. 1996)

FACTS

Nationwide Mutual Insurance Company (Nationwide) planned to hold a regional convention to boost morale and recognize employee achievements. A planning committee decided to have a contest to determine a theme for the convention and ran an announcement that included the following:

Here's what you could win:

His and Hers Mercedes
An all-expense-paid trip for two around the world
Additional prize to be announced . . .
(All prizes subject to availability)
Only two rules apply:
1. The slogan is limited to not more than eight words.
2. All entries must be submitted . . . by August 1, 1993.

Mears, a claims adjuster for Nationwide, submitted several themes and, several months later, left Nationwide. In October, 1993, Mears was notified that his theme had been chosen for the convention. In January, Mears inquired about his Mercedes. He was told he might not get them for three reasons: (1) Nationwide might change the theme, (2) Mears was no longer an employee, and (3) the contest was a joke. His theme was used for the convention. Afterwards, Mears was informed that Nationwide never intended to award the Mercedes and offered him a restaurant gift certificate instead. Mears sued for breach of contract.

ISSUE

Was there sufficient evidence of intent to form a binding contract?

DECISION

Yes. Nationwide's contest offered several prizes, including two Mercedes. At trial both Mears and Nationwide's representative, Peterson, testified that Peterson told Mears he had won the Mercedes. Peterson testified she said it in a facetious tone and that, in reality, there was no intent to award the cars. Mears, however, believed her, as did others around Mears. There was sufficient objective evidence that Mears had won the Mercedes.

.... *DEFINITENESS* ....

Did the offeror specifically indicate what he was willing to do and what he wanted the offeree to do or agree to do in return? If not, his behavior will probably be classed as an "invitation to offer" or an "invitation to negotiate," and will have no legal effect. If the offeror said, "If we're going to trade cars, you'll have to give me some money in addition to your car," this clearly was not an offer. The parties are still negotiating and may never reach a mutually satisfactory agreement. On the other hand, if the offeror said, "I'll trade you my car for your car and $500," this looks like an offer. If the offeree accepts, both parties are bound to a contract. This is what happened in the *Cagle* case at the beginning of this chapter. The court found that offering to sell a specific car at list price was sufficiently specific to constitute a valid offer.

The more specific the proposal, the more likely the court is to call it an offer. Courts have traditionally said they are contract enforcers, not makers. They did not want to force parties to do something they had not agreed to do. While courts today still will not make contracts for parties, the trend is to tolerate more indefiniteness and, consequently, more open and missing terms. Both the Code and the *Restatement*, through doctrines such as good faith and commercial reasonableness, provide ways to fill in the gaps. At a minimum, the terms of the offer, which can be express or implied from the circumstances, must be sufficiently clear so that what was promised can be determined. Without that, the courts could not decide whether the contract was breached, or what the remedy should be in case of breach.

Mears v. Nationwide Mutual Ins. Co.
91 F. 3d 1118 (8th Cir. 1996)

FACTS

In this case, discussed earlier in the chapter, the district court reversed a jury verdict for Mears because it held that the terms of the contract were not sufficiently definite and that there was not a reasonably certain basis to award an appropriate remedy.

ISSUE

Were the terms of the contest offer sufficiently definite to form the basis of a contract?

DECISION

Yes. The law does not favor the destruction of contracts because of uncertainty. A contract is sufficiently certain if it provides a basis for determining the existence of a breach and for giving an appropriate remedy. The contest offered several prizes and did not indicate which would be awarded. However, a contract that is facially ambiguous can be made certain by the subsequent actions or declarations of the parties. Mears was told he had won the Mercedes, and this was within the language of the offer. The only remaining uncertainty was in the type of Mercedes to be awarded; there is a wide range of prices depending on the model and year. This uncertainty is not fatal. Contract terms are interpreted with strong consideration for what is reasonable. It is reasonable to expect the cars to be new. Mears can insist on two of the least expensive new models as his prize.

No part of Article 2 is a better indication of the Code's desire to dispense with technicalities and protect people's expectations than its general rules governing the creation of sales contracts (2-204). A sales contract can be created "in any manner sufficient to show agreement, including conduct by both parties which recognizes the existence of a contract" (2-204[1]). So, if the parties are *acting as though they have a contract* (by delivering or accepting goods or payment, for example), this is enough to create a binding agreement, even if it is impossible to point to a particular moment in time when the contract was created (2-204[2]). The fact that the parties did not expressly agree on all the terms of their contract does not prevent its creation. A sales contract does not fail due to "indefiniteness" if the court finds that the parties *intended* to make a contract and that their agreement is complete enough to allow the court to reach a fair settlement of their dispute ("a reasonably certain basis for giving an appropriate remedy" 2-204[3]).

The Code contains several gap filling rules to fill in the blanks the parties left in their agreement regarding price (2-305), quantity (2-306), delivery (2-307, 2-308, and 2-309), and time for payment (2-310) (these are further discussed in Chapter 16). Of course, if the facts indicate that a term was left out because the parties were unable to reach an agreement about it, this would probably mean that the intent to contract is absent, and no contract was created.

········ ### COMMUNICATION TO THE OFFEREE ········

An important factor in determining whether an offeror had the required intent to contract is whether she communicated her offer to the offeree. The act of communicating the offer indicates that the offeror is willing to be bound by its terms. On the other hand, an uncommunicated offer may be evidence that the offeror has not yet decided to enter into a binding agreement. For example, Bill has been discussing the possibility of selling his house to Joan. Bill tells Frank, a mutual friend, that he intends to offer the house to Joan for $35,000. Frank calls Joan and tells her of his conversation with Bill. Joan then calls Bill and says, "I accept your offer." Is this a contract? No; since Bill had not communicated his proposal to Joan, there was no offer for Joan to accept.

PROCD, INC. V. ZEIDENBERG
86 F.3d 1447 (7th Cir. 1996)

FACTS

ProCD compiled information from more than 3,000 telephone directories into a computer database which had many potential uses from manufacturers compiling lists of potential customers to callers avoiding long distance information charges or looking up lost friends. ProCD charged a lower price to the general public for the database and a higher price to commercial users. In order to protect this pricing scheme, it printed on the box that the software came with restrictions stated in an enclosed license. The license limited use of the general public database to noncommercial use. Zeidenberg bought a consumer package but decided to ignore the license. He formed a company to resell the information and offered it on the Internet for a price less than ProCD's. ProCD sued for breach of contract.

ISSUE

Are contract terms that appear on the inside of a software box adequately communicated?

DECISION

Yes. These licenses are ordinary contracts accompanying the sale of products; therefore they are governed by the U.C.C. Placing the package of software on the shelf is an "offer" which the customer "accepts" by paying the asking price. A contract includes only the terms on which the parties have agreed. One cannot agree to hidden terms. Vendors can put the entire terms of a contract on the outside of a box only by using microscopic type, removing other information that buyers might find more useful, or both. Transactions in which the exchange of money precedes the communication of detailed terms are common. One example is buying an airline ticket. The traveler calls an agent, gets a price, reserves a seat, pays, and gets a ticket. The ticket contains elaborate terms, which the traveler can reject by canceling the reservation. Just so with a ticket to a concert. Drugs come with a list of ingredients on the outside and an elaborate package insert on the inside. Under U.C.C. §2-204, ProCD proposed a contract that a buyer would accept by *using* the software after having an opportunity to read the license at leisure. If he was unsatisfied after reading the license terms, he could return it. Shrinkwrap licenses are enforceable unless their terms are objectionable on grounds applicable to contracts in general, such as whether they violate a rule of positive law, or whether they are unconscionable.

.... SPECIAL PROBLEMS WITH OFFERS ....

There are several common problems for students when they attempt to determine whether an offer exists. These problems involve situations in which the courts have applied special rules to certain types of behavior, or in which there are difficult problems of interpretation.

.... ADVERTISEMENTS ....

The courts have generally held that ads for the sale of goods at a specified price are not offers; instead, they are treated as invitations to negotiate or to make an offer. The same rule is generally applied to catalogs, price lists, price quotations, and goods displayed in stores. This rule probably fairly reflects the intent of the sellers involved, since they probably have only a limited number of items to sell and do not intend to give everyone who sees their ad the power to bind them to a contract. It can cause problems for would be buyers, however, who may believe they have a legal right to the advertised goods they attempt to buy. In reality, such a buyer is making an offer to purchase the goods on the advertised terms, which the seller (as offeree) is free to accept or reject.

Under certain circumstances, however, courts have held that specific ads were offers. These cases generally involve ads that are highly specific about the goods that are offered and what is requested in return. Still, specific terms, standing alone, are probably not enough to make an ad an offer. Most of the ads that have been treated as offers require the buyer to do something extraordinary to accept. The great potential for unfairness to the offeree in such cases is probably the true basis for the courts' holdings that ads of this sort are offers. For example, Friendly Ford runs the following ad in the newspaper: "We're bananas about the new Mustangs! The first person to bring us five tons of bananas will receive a brand new 1999 Mustang fully equipped with every available option." Mary reads the ad and buys five tons of bananas and presents them to Friendly. Most courts would probably hold that Mary is entitled to the car.

LEONARD V. PEPSICO, INC.
210 F.3d 88 (2nd Cir. 2000)

FACTS

Pepsico ran a contest for "Pepsi Stuff" featuring different items of merchandise that could be obtained with Pepsi "points" a consumer got by buying Pepsi Cola. One ad featured a teenager gloating over items he had purchased, and ended with the teenager arriving at high school in a Harrier Jet he had purchased with 7 million points. A Harrier Jet is a Marine Corps fighter aircraft. Leonard described himself as "typical of the Pepsi Generation . . . young, with an adventurous spirit," and the notion of acquiring the jet was very appealing to him. He consulted the Pepsi Stuff Catalogue which pictured youths enjoying the available items, and an order form. Neither showed the jet. Undeterred, Leonard acquired points plus $700,000 from acquaintances to buy enough points for the jet. He filled out the order form, writing in at the bottom, "1 Harrier Jet" and enclosed the check and points. Several weeks later he was told the jet was unavailable and that its use in the commercial was "fanciful and [was] simply included to create a humorous and entertaining ad." Leonard sued for delivery.

ISSUE

Was the ad an offer that Leonard accepted by tendering the 7 million points?

DECISION

No. The general rule is that an advertisement does not constitute an offer. Advertisements to the general public are understood to be mere requests to consider and examine and negotiate. It is possible to make an offer by advertisement under unusual circumstances, but it usually requires an invitation to take action without further communication. An ad is not transformed into an enforceable offer merely by a potential offeree's expression of willingness to accept by, among other things, filling out an order form. The exception to this general rule is created when the ad is clear, definite, explicit, and leaves nothing open for negotiation. This case is distinguishable from the exception because the commercial specifically reserved details of the offer to a separate writing, the Catalogue. The commercial did not tell the steps a potential offeree would have to take to accept the alleged offer of a Harrier Jet. It also stated that the offer was not available in all areas and told viewers to see details on specially marked packages. Additionally, no objectively reasonable person could have considered the ad to offer a Harrier Jet.

Advertisements are regulated outside of contract law by the Federal Trade Commission and consumer protection laws. These outlaw such things as false advertising and "bait and switch" tactics. Discussion of such regulation is contained in Chapter 47.

REWARDS

Ads for rewards for the return of lost property, for information, or for the capture of criminals are generally held to be offers for unilateral contracts. The offeree must perform the requested act to accept—that is, return the lost property, supply the requested information, or capture the wanted criminal.

AUCTIONS

Sellers at auctions are generally held to be making an invitation to offer. Bidders at such auctions are treated as offerors, making offers the seller is free to accept or reject. Therefore, an item can be withdrawn from sale at any time prior to acceptance. Acceptance occurs when the auctioneer declares the goods sold. Only when the auction is advertised as being "without reserve" is the seller required to accept the final offer—the highest bid. Section 2-328 of the Uniform Commercial Code contains the rules of law that govern an auction of goods.

BIDS

The bidding process in construction work is a source of many legal disputes. People who advertise for such bids (the owner of the project or a general contractor who wants to farm out a portion of a large job to a subcontractor, for example) are generally held to have made an invitation to offer. Those who submit bids are treated as offerors. This causes particular problems in disputes between general contractors and subcontractors.

A general contractor may rely on a subcontractor's bid by using the subcontractor's figures in arriving at the total amount of its bid. Later, the subcontractor may find that the price of the materials or labor needed to do the job has risen, and may wish to revoke the bid. Unfortunately, the subcontractor may find that revocation will not be allowed (see the section on estoppel later in this chapter). The subcontractor may then be especially disturbed to find that when the general contractor's bid is accepted, the general contractor does not have to award the subcontractor the job. This is because the courts usually hold that the general contractor's use of the subcontractor's bid in computing its own is not an acceptance of that bid.

CONCEPT SUMMARY	Solicitations of Offers	
Ads	**Auctions**	**Bids**
1. Solicitations: general ads, price lists, goods displayed in stores.	1. Solicitations: offering the item at auction.	1. Solicitations: advertising for bids.
2. Construed as an offer if specific acts are required of offeree and unfairness would result if not enforced.	2. Becomes an offer if advertised as "without reserve."	2. Even though a subcontractor's bid is an offer, it generally cannot be withdrawn if the general contractor has relied on it.

This treatment of subcontractors is probably not so unfair as it seems at first glance. A general contractor whose bid is accepted is bound by contract to do the job at the bid price. If the subcontractor is allowed to revoke, the general contractor may not be able to get anyone else to do the subcontractor's job for the price of the subcontractor's bid. The general contractor's profit on the job will then be reduced, and it may even have to do the job at a loss. On the other hand, the subcontractor who does not get the job generally has lost only the cost of computing the bid, a normal business expense.

WHAT TERMS ARE INCLUDED
IN OFFERS?

Once a court decides that an offer existed, it must then decide what terms were included in the offer so that it can determine the terms of the parties' agreement. Another way of asking this question is to ask what the offeree agreed to. Is a person going to a show bound by the fine print on the ticket? How about fine print or clauses on the back of a contract?

There are no easy answers to these problems. The courts have generally held that if the offeree actually reads the terms, or if a reasonable person should have been on notice of them, the offeree is bound by them. However, as you saw in the last chapter, judges are increasingly refusing to enforce clauses they think are unconscionable because the offeree did not reasonably know of their existence, they place unfair burdens on the offeree, or they are worded in such a way that the offeree could not reasonably be expected to understand their meaning. Nonetheless, it is still fair to say that people are expected to live up to the agreements they make.

Ethical *Implications*	Is it ethical for a business to use misleading headings, small print, complex language, or language on the reverse side of the contract to hide terms? Would your answer differ if the other party to the contract were another business instead of a consumer?

ARONSON V. UNIVERSITY OF MISSISSIPPI
201 Miss. App. LEXIS 385 (Oct. 2, 2001)

FACTS

Aronson, a high school senior in Georgia, researched colleges on the Internet. One of his and his family's primary considerations was cost and the nature and types of financial aid. The University of Mississippi's (UM) website had information on a John Waddell Scholarship, which provided $1,000 per year and a waiver of out-of-state tuition. Based on this information, Aronson requested an application package. When he received it in October 1997, it contained the 1997 catalog. The catalog further described the scholarship, including that it was offered to students who score 26–27 on the ACT test and have a GPA of 90 percent or higher. Priority consideration was given to those admitted to UM by April 1, 1997. To keep the scholarship while at UM, the student had to maintain a 3.0 GPA. Based on this information, Aronson sent in the admission application and was admitted on November 6, 1997. Aronson sent a check dated April 6, 1998, for orientation fees and a room deposit. Before orientation, Aronson's stepfather called UM to ensure that Aronson met the scholarship requirements. He was told he did, and that it was for $1,000 per year and waiver of out-of-state tuition. At orientation, the stepfather was informed that the criteria had changed, that Aronson did not qualify for the

out-of-state tuition waiver, and that the scholarship had been reduced to $2,000. When the University refused to give him the $4,000 plus the waiver, Aronson sued.

ISSUE

Did Aronson and MU have a contract based on the terms in the catalog?

DECISION

Yes. Many courts have held that a contractual relationship exists between a student and a university based on terms that may be in a student handbook, catalog, or other statement of university policy. Here Aronson initiated the process of contract negotiation by submitting his application. He was conditionally offered enrollment based on successfully completing high school and getting measles and rubella shots. He accepted the conditional offer by paying his orientation fees and room deposit in April 1998. The terms of the contract are those MU had placed in the public domain at the time Aronson accepted the offer. At that time it was the information in the 1998 catalog. The scholarship amount had been reduced to $2,000, but out-of-state tuition was still waived. Thus, Aronson should get that amount.

.... *How Long Do Offers Last?* ....

Once you know that an offer existed and what its terms were, you must then decide how long the offer was in effect. This is important because if an offer has been terminated for some reason, the offeree no longer has the power to create a contract by accepting. In fact, an offeree who attempts to accept after an offer has terminated is himself making an offer because he is indicating a present intent to contract on the terms of the original offer. The original offeror is free to accept or reject this new offer.

TERMS OF THE OFFER

The offer itself may include terms that limit its life. These may be specific terms such as "this offer good for 10 days" or "you must accept by October 4, 2004," or more general terms such as "by return mail," or "immediate acceptance." Obviously, the more general terms can cause difficult problems for courts in trying to decide whether an offeree accepted in time. This is also true of more specific terms such as "this offer good for 10 days" if the offer does not specify whether the 10 day period begins when the offer is sent or when the offeree receives it. The courts do not agree on this point. It should be clear that wise offerors will protect themselves by being as specific as possible in stating when their offers end.

LAPSE OF TIME

If the offer does not state a time for acceptance, it is valid for a "reasonable time," which depends on the circumstances surrounding the offer.

If the offer covers items that have rapidly changing prices, such as stocks and bonds or commodities, a reasonable time may be measured in minutes. If the offer covers goods that may spoil, such as produce, a reasonable time for acceptance is also fairly short. On the other hand, a reasonable time for the acceptance of an offer to sell real estate may be several days.

If the parties have dealt with each other on a regular basis, the timing of their prior dealings is highly relevant in measuring a reasonable time for acceptance. Also, the nature of the negotiations, whether by letter or telephone, for example, can also influence the reasonable length of an offer.

REVOCATION

Offerors generally have the power to revoke their offers at any time prior to acceptance even if they have promised not to revoke for a stated period of time. However, there are several exceptions to the general rule that can take away an offeror's power to revoke.

FIRM OFFERS

The drafters of the Code knew that offerors often promise to hold their offers open and that those who receive such offers are often ignorant of the law and believe them to be irrevocable. So, the Code protects the expectations of offerees in the **firm offer** rule. A firm offer is irrevocable even though the offeree has given no consideration to support the offeror's promise to hold the offer open. For an offer to sell goods to be a firm offer, it must meet three basic requirements:

1.   It must have been made in a *signed writing* (no oral firm offers).
2.   The offeror must be a *merchant.*
3.   It must contain *assurances* that it will be held open (some indication that it will not be revoked).

If any one of these requirements is missing, the common law applies, allowing the offeror to revoke at any time prior to acceptance. Firm offers are irrevocable for the period of time stated in the offer. If none is stated, they are irrevocable for a reasonable time, as determined by the circumstances of the case. The outer limit on the period of irrevocability for firm offers is three months, whatever the terms of the offer may say. So, the offeror who makes a firm offer and promises to hold it open for six months could revoke after three, assuming the offeree has not accepted.

OPTIONS

If the offeree gives the offeror something of value in exchange for a promise not to revoke the offer for a stated period of time, an option contract has been created. An **option** is a separate contract for the limited purpose of holding the offer open. The offeree, as with any other offer, is free to accept or reject the offer; he or she has simply purchased the right to accept or reject within the stated period. (See Figure 7–2.)

Ethical Implications	Under the common law an offer can be revoked any time prior to acceptance even if the offeror has promised to hold it open longer, unless the offeree has purchased an option. Is it unethical to renege on a gratuitous promise to hold an offer open?

FIGURE 7–2   Creating an Option

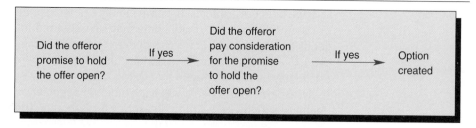

ESTOPPEL

In some cases, the doctrine of promissory estoppel, which was discussed in Chapter 6, can operate to prevent offerors from revoking their offers before acceptance. If the offeror makes her offer in such a way that the offeree might reasonably expect her not to revoke it, and if the offeree in fact does reasonably rely on the offer in such a way that he will suffer some significant loss if she is allowed to revoke it, a court may say she is *estopped* from revoking. This means that the court will deny the offeror the power to revoke in order to avoid unjustly injuring the offeree. As you will recall, promissory estoppel requires a *promise* that the promisor should foresee is likely to induce reliance, *significant reliance* on the promise by the promisee, and *injustice* as a result of reliance. If any one of these three elements is missing, estoppel does not apply.

Consider the subcontractor–contractor dispute discussed earlier in this chapter. Estoppel is frequently applied to such cases. Smith Electrical Supply (a subcontractor) submits a bid of $100,000 to Evans Construction Company (a general contractor) for the electrical work in the new Acme Building. Smith's bid is the lowest Evans receives, and Evans knows Smith to be a reliable firm, so Evans uses Smith's $100,000 figure in computing its bid for the total job. Due to rising costs of electric wiring and conduit,

Smith decides it cannot profitably do the job and tries to revoke. Evans is awarded the contract and cannot get anyone to do the electrical work for less than $120,000. Smith will be estopped from revoking. Smith knew Evans was likely to rely on its bid (in fact, it hoped Evans would). Evans relied on Smith's bid by making an offer to perform based, in part, on Smith's price. Evans will lose $20,000 if Smith is allowed to revoke.

What if Evans could get Walters Electric to do the job for $100,000? In this case, estoppel would not apply since no injustice would result to Evans if Smith were allowed to revoke.

REVOCATION OF OFFERS FOR UNILATERAL CONTRACTS

The concept of promissory estoppel is often used to prevent unfairness in unilateral contract offer withdrawals. The general rule that the offeror can revoke at any time prior to acceptance causes special problems when the offer is for a unilateral contract. The common law traditionally held that the offeree must fully perform the requested act to accept an offer for a unilateral contract. What if the offeree intends to accept and starts to perform but the offeror revokes before the performance is complete?

If the offeror benefited from the offeree's attempted performance, some courts may allow the offeror to revoke but require him or her to pay the offeree the reasonable value of the performance under a quasi contract theory. Suppose Bob says to Frank, "I'll give you $800 to plow my 40 acres," and Frank begins to plow, intending to accept. After Frank has plowed 15 acres, Bob says, "I've changed my mind; I revoke." Bob is allowed to revoke but is liable to Frank for the reasonable value of plowing 15 acres.

If the offeror did not benefit from the offeree's attempted performance, most courts hold that the offeree has a reasonable time to complete the performance and that the offeror cannot revoke for that reasonable time. So, if Betty offered Frank a commission for finding her a $10,000 loan at a 10 percent annual rate and Frank has begun to contact lenders about the loan, Frank will have a reasonable time to get a loan commitment. During this time, Betty is not allowed to revoke. This rule prevents unfairness to Frank but may result in unfairness to Betty. If Frank's attempted performance is half-hearted or ineffective, Betty must wait for a reasonable period before making her offer to someone else.

To avoid these kinds of problems, many courts hold a contract to be bilateral whenever possible. This is similar to a view the *Restatement* takes. It holds that once the offeree has begun performance, the offer cannot be withdrawn because the beginning of performance is interpreted to be the offeree's promise to render complete performance. This promise makes the contract bilateral.

THE EFFECTIVENESS OF REVOCATIONS

Difficult problems of timing can result when an offeror is trying to revoke and an offeree is attempting to accept. The general rule is that a revocation is not effective until it is *actually received* by the offeree. So, if the offeree accepts before he or she has received a mailed revocation, a contract results. This rule recognizes the possibility that offerees who are unaware of a revocation may act in reliance on their belief that the offer is still open. A few states hold that a revocation is effective when it is sent, however.

A major exception to the general rule involves offers made to the general public in newspapers and on radio and television. Since it would be impossible in most cases to reach every offeree with a revocation, the courts have held that a revocation made in the same manner as the offer is effective when published, without proof of communication to the offeree.

REJECTION

An offer is terminated when it is rejected by the offeree. An offeree may *expressly reject* an offer by stating that he will not accept it or by giving some other indication that he does not intend to accept the offer.

An offeree may *impliedly* reject an offer by making a **counteroffer.** Any attempt by the offeree to change the *material* terms of the offer or to add significant new terms to the offer is treated as a counteroffer. This is so because the offeree is showing her unwillingness to accept the offeror's terms. If an offeree merely asks about the terms of the offer without indicating a rejection of it (*an inquiry regarding terms*), spells out *terms implied* in the offer, or accepts but complains about the terms (*a grumbling acceptance*), a rejection is not implied. Determining whether an offeree has made a counteroffer, an inquiry regarding terms, a grumbling acceptance, or is merely expressing implied terms is sometimes a difficult matter, to be decided on the facts of each case.

The general rule on effectiveness of rejections is that rejections, like revocations, must be actually received by the offeror to be effective. This means that an offeree who has mailed a rejection can change her mind and accept if she communicates her acceptance to the offeror before the rejection arrives.

ESTATE OF CHOSNYKA v. MEYER
585 N.E.2d 204 (Ct. App. Ill. 1992)

FACTS

Meyer, after seeing a sign on Chosnyka's land reading, "FOR SALE 95 ACRES," and running a title search, sent Chosnyka an offer to buy the land as described by its legal description. The offer required acceptance by returning a signed copy within 10 days. Chosnyka signed and returned the copy the next day, along with a paper stating that he accepted with the following conditions: (1) that the closing date be within 60 days and (2) that the land's legal description was accurate but the acreage stated in it was only an estimate. The next day Meyer went to the property and discovered an underground pressurized gas line on it. Because of this and the lack of a warranty that the property was exactly 95 acres, he refused to buy the property for the amount stated in the offer. Chosnyka insisted on that price, and when Meyer refused to pay, sold the property for less to someone else. He then sued Meyer for breach of contract.

ISSUE

Was Chosnyka's acceptance with conditions really a counteroffer?

DECISION

No. In order to accept, an offeree must strictly comply with the terms of the offer, including the mode of acceptance dictated therein. Here, the buyer signed the copy and delivered it to the stated address within 10 days, as required in the offer. The offer was to buy the property contained in a legal description. Therefore the fact that Chosnyka stated that the legal description was not a guarantee that the property was exactly 95 acres is irrelevant. A contract was formed when the signed copy was delivered.

DEATH OR INSANITY OF EITHER PARTY

The death or insanity of either party to an offer automatically (without notice) terminates the offer. This is so because no "meeting of the minds" is possible when one of the parties has died or become insane.

DESTRUCTION OF SUBJECT MATTER

If the subject matter of a proposed contract is destroyed without the knowledge or fault of either party after the making of an offer but before its acceptance, the offer is terminated. So, if Joan offers to sell Ralph a boat but a storm destroys the boat before Ralph accepts, the offer is terminated when the boat is destroyed.

INTERVENING ILLEGALITY

If the performance of a proposed contract becomes illegal after the offer is made but before it is accepted, the offer is terminated. So, if Johnson Farms has offered to sell its wheat crop to a buyer for Iraq but two days later, before Johnson's offer has been accepted, Congress places an embargo on all grain sales to Iraq, the offer is terminated by the embargo.

CONCEPT SUMMARY   Offer

I. There is a valid offer if there is:

   a. Intent—
     Objectively determined.
   b. Definiteness—
     Sufficiently clear so that what was promised can be determined.
   c. Communication—
     Terms that are not adequately communicated (such as those in fine print) are not part of the offer.

II. The offer is still valid if it has not:
   a. Been terminated by its own time limit.
   b. Lapsed.
   c. Been revoked.
   d. Been rejected.
   e. Been terminated by operation of law due to:
     1. Death or insanity of either party.
     2. Destruction of the subject matter.
     3. Intervening illegality.

.... *QUESTIONS AND PROBLEM CASES* ....

1. Explain how the intent of an offeror is determined.
2. Explain why ads are not considered offers.
3. Explain why a subcontractor's bid is treated as an offer.
4. Explain three things that can cause an offer to lapse.
5. Monsanto manufactured S-54 AstroTurf used on playing fields. It often had annual remnants of 100,000–300,000 square feet, which it sold to others. The Major Mat (MM) company was formed to make golf tee mats out of it. When MM placed several orders, Monsanto called to find out what the company was doing. MM refused to say, but did inquire whether Monsanto would enter into a contract for the purchase of all of its remnants. MM was told it would have an unending supply. MM said that it hoped Monsanto would not make its own mats; Monsanto said not to worry, that it was a supplier of products, not a fabricator. Three years later Monsanto formed a subsidiary which produced artificial turf products including golf tee mats. Monsanto greatly increased the price of the turf to MM, so that Monsanto's mats would be much cheaper. MM sued Monsanto for breach of contract. Was there a contract?

6. Kiley had an interest bearing, no service fee checking account with Baltimore Federal (BF) that required no minimum balance. When First National Bank acquired BF, it sent a letter to customers stating, "We're excited about having

you as a First National customer and want to assure you that any change to your accounts will be to your benefit." In 1990 First National sought to impose a $15 monthly service fee on Kiley's account. When he complained, it was dropped. In 1992, First National announced it was imposing a service fee and minimum balance on all accounts. When Kiley objected, the bank suggested Kiley close his account if he was not satisfied with the terms. Can Kiley successfully sue for breach of contract?

7. Saunder was a friend and employee of Baryshnikov, helping him to adjust to his new life after defecting from the U.S.S.R. and becoming premier dancer, choreographer, and artistic director of the American Ballet Theatre. She translated for him; handled his correspondence, appointments, and dinners; oversaw his interior decorations; hired help; and made travel arrangements. She became a signatory on his checking account. Baryshnikov was generous in his gratitude, giving her interest- free loans (many of which were never repaid) and cars, taking her on several foreign dance tours, and paying a large portion of her living expenses. After six years, she was put on an annual salary of $20,000. Later the arrangement fell through, and Saunder sued for $1 million, claiming Baryshnikov had promised to take care of her and her financial needs for life in exchange for the substantial services she had performed for him. Is the promise Saunder alleges too vague to be enforced?

8. Blaine–Hays Construction Company submitted a bid to build a motel for the Marriott Corporation. In preparing its bid it received a bid from Efficient Electric Company (Efficient) to do the electrical work for $259,000. When Blaine–Hays was awarded the contract, it sent a letter to Efficient accepting Efficient's bid. It subsequently sent a subcontract agreement to Efficient, but it was never signed by Efficient. Efficient worked on the motel for three months, and then notified Blaine–Hays it would not continue, stating it did not have a contract and was not required to finish the job. Is this correct?

9. Saltarelli worked for Future Ford and had his health insurance under its group plan. He then went to work at a Bob Baker dealership and signed up for its insurance. However, because Baker's policy had a three-month waiting period, this coverage did not start until April 8. Saltarelli therefore continued his coverage with Future through April. On May 4 Saltarelli was diagnosed with stomach cancer, and he died on May 29. When his estate tried to collect for his medical bills, Baker refused to pay, citing a statement in the definitions section of a 43-page booklet describing the plan that excluded preexisting conditions such as cancer. Was the term effectively and fairly communicated?

10. Jackson read an ad in the *Miami Herald* stating that the jackpot for picking the six winners in the dog races on the last night of the season was $825,000. Jackson went that night and correctly picked the winners. Investment Corp., the track owners, refused to pay more than $25,000 because they had intended the ad to be for that amount. When they submitted the ad to the paper it read, "Guaranteed Jackpot $25,000 must go tonight." The newspaper employee who prepared the ad misread the dollar sign with one line as an "8." Can Jackson collect the $825,000?

11. Schiff, a self styled tax protestor who made a career out of his tax protest activities, appeared live on the CBS "Nightwatch" program. During the program, which had a viewer participation format, he stated, "There is nothing in the Internal Revenue Code which says anyone is legally required to pay the tax." He later said, "If anybody calls this show and cites any section of this Code that says an individual is required to file a tax return, I will pay them $100,000." Newman, an attorney, did not see "Nightwatch" but did see a segment of the show repeated several hours later on the "CBS Morning News." Newman called and wrote to CBS citing Code provisions that require people to pay federal income tax. When Schiff refused to pay the reward on the ground that Newman had not properly accepted the offer, Newman sued. Did Schiff properly accept Newman's offer?

12. McCarthy listed some real estate for sale with her broker. When the price had been reduced to $125,000, Madaio made an offer of $100,000. McCarthy counteroffered $110,000, and they agreed to a sale at $105,000. The contract was to

be effective when Madaio returned a signed formal contract. On January 12, McCarthy signed a formal contract prepared by her agent, and it was delivered to Madaio on the same day. Madaio signed it the next day but did not mail it back to McCarthy until January 18. On January 16, McCarthy called Madaio and said she was withdrawing the offer. Madaio said he had already signed the contract, and intended to go ahead with the offer. He sued for specific performance of the contract. Did Madaio effectively accept the offer before McCarthy withdrew it?

CHAPTER 8

Creating a Contract: Acceptances

Stephens sent Horwitz an offer to sell her his house and adjoining orchard for $300,000. Horwitz, after thinking about the offer for a few days, wrote Stephens a letter accepting his offer and asking if he intended to leave his farming equipment with the property. The next day, before Horwitz's letter arrived, Stephens phoned Horwitz and told her he had decided to sell his property to someone else who had offered him $320,000.

- *Was Horwitz's letter an effective acceptance or a counteroffer?*
- *When does acceptance through the mail become effective?*
- *Was Stephens's phone call an effective revocation?*

FIGURE 8–1   Acceptance

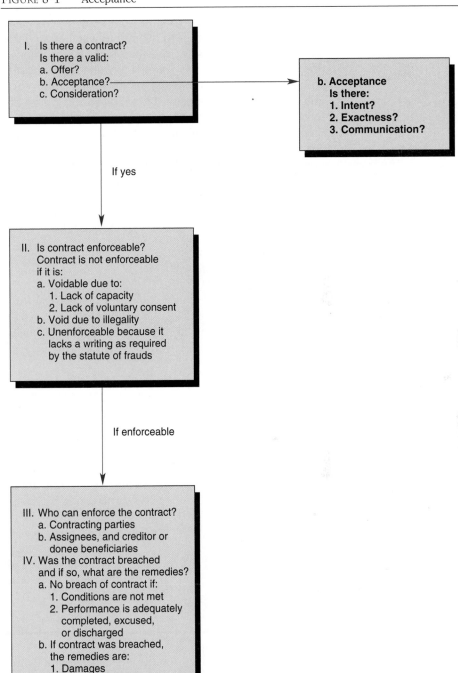

.... *WHAT IS AN ACCEPTANCE?* ....

Once the court has found that one of the parties to a dispute made an *offer,* the next thing it looks for in order to determine whether a contract resulted is whether the offeree **accepted** the offer. The court looks for the same *present intent* to contract on the part of the offeree that it earlier looked for on the part of the offeror. When all the circumstances surrounding the parties' dealings with each other are considered, did the offeree ever, in effect, say: "I'm willing to enter into a binding contract on the terms of your offer?" If so, the offer has been accepted. The offeree may indicate assent expressly or impliedly. The offeree must, however, accept the offer on the offeror's terms.

WORKMON V. PUBLISHERS CLEARING HOUSE
118 F. 3d 457 (6th Cir. 1997)

FACTS

Workmon received a mailing from Publishers Clearing House (PCH) designed to solicit magazine subscriptions. The front of the envelope said, "ACT NOW FOR ANOTHER CHANCE TO WIN TEN MILLION DOLLARS." The back read, "You may already hold the winning number that will make you rich for life." When Workmon opened the envelope, the certificate read:

> Personal I.D. No.
> 09 0067 9696 U
> has been reserved exclusively for
> RAYMOND J. WORKMON
> If said number is returned by
> January 6, 1989
> RAYMOND J. WORKMON
> wins our
> **TEN MILLION DOLLAR
> SUPERPRIZE**

The certificate front also stated other things such as that Workmon could enter the sweepstakes, extend his current *Time* magazine subscription, and receive a free 35 MM camera. The back stated:

> The unique Personal Superprize number . . . has been registered in your name alone. If you return your entry

by the deadline and your entry matches the preselected winning number for SuperPrize IX, you will win $10 million.

Workmon concluded he had won $10 million. He returned his form and renewed his *Time* subscription. After receiving confirmation of his renewal, he contacted PCH to inquire about the $10 million. After being told he had not won, Workmon sued.

ISSUE

Can Workmon accept only part of the offer and reject the rest?

DECISION

No. In order for Workmon to win the prize, he had to meet all the conditions for acceptance. Workmon argues that the two sentences about his being a winner apply specifically to him, but that the rules, the rest of the certificate, and the envelope's language were of general application. This is not correct. The offer must be construed as a whole. Workmon sought to ignore the conditional language in the material he received. No reasonable person in Workmon's position would assume that he had successfully accepted and won the prize merely by mailing in his form and the subscription renewal.

As the preceding chapter indicated, any attempt by the offeree to materially alter the terms of the offer is treated as a counteroffer and terminates the offer. In the introductory problem to this chapter, Horwitz's letter was an acceptance since she was merely inquiring about Stephens's intentions regarding the machinery. If she had said she accepted on the condition that he include the farm machinery, however, it would have been a counteroffer.

THE BATTLE OF THE FORMS

The Uniform Commercial Code has created an exception to this "mirror image" rule in cases where contracts for the sale of goods are made by exchanging forms (2-207).

Since the majority of contracts are form contracts, this rule has wide impact. The seller of goods and the buyer send each other forms that have terms beneficial to their individual interests. Seldom do these forms agree in their entirety, and the parties seldom read the other's form in its entirety. Yet the parties usually assume, and proceed as if there is, a contract. Applying the mirror image rule to such cases would often frustrate the parties' original intent. If a dispute arose before the parties started to perform, a court applying the mirror image rule would hold that the parties did not have a contract. If a dispute arose after the parties started to perform, the court would probably hold that the offeror had impliedly accepted the offeree's counteroffer and was bound by its terms. Neither of these results was very satisfactory.

The Code changes the common law rule by saying that a timely *expression of acceptance* creates a contract even if it includes terms that are *different* from those stated in the offer or states *additional* terms on points the offer did not address (2-207[1]). This controversial rule is known as the "Battle of the Forms." The only exception to this rule occurs when the attempted acceptance is *expressly conditional* on the offeror's agreement to the terms of the acceptance (2-207[1]). In that case, no contract is created.

What are the terms of a contract created by the exchange of nonconforming forms? The Code says that if the parties are both *merchants*, the *additional* terms in the offeree's form are included in the agreement unless:

1. The offer *expressly limited acceptance* to its own terms.
2. The new terms would *materially alter* the offer.
3. Or the offeror gives *notice of objection* to the new terms within a reasonable time after receiving the acceptance (2-207[2]).

If one or both parties are nonmerchants, the additional terms are treated as "proposals for addition to the contract."

When the acceptance is made expressly conditional on agreement to the new terms, or when the offeree clearly is making a counteroffer by expressly rejecting the offer, no contract is created. However, the Code (2-207[3]) says that if the parties begin performance (or do something else that "recognizes the existence of a contract"), a contract is created. The terms of this contract are those on which the writings of the parties *agree*, supplemented by appropriate gap-filling provisions of the Code (discussed in Chapter 16). Remember that the "Battle of the Forms" rules apply only when both parties have forms.

JOM, INC. V. ADELL PLASTICS, INC.
193 F.3d 47 (1st Cir. 1999)

FACTS

JOM makes casino gaming chips from palletized polyester resin. From 1986 to 1994 it purchased the resin from General Electric. However, in 1994 it started buying its resin from Adell because Adell asserted the resin was of equal or superior quality, but sold it for less. The purchase orders that JOM sent to Adell contained no language regarding warranties or remedies in the event of a breach.

The forms that Adell sent to JOM with each shipment did contain such terms including a damages limitation clause. This clause stated that no claim of any kind could be greater in amount than the purchase price of the materials. JOM's casino customers began to complain that the chips were less attractive and durable, and that it had to replace more than one million chips. When JOM sued,

(continued)

JOM, INC. V. ADELL PLASTICS, INC.
(concluded)

Adell argued that JOM could not sue for more than the purchase price.

ISSUE

Is the clause on the back of Adell's form an effective limitation of damages?

DECISION

No. This claim rests on an interpretation of UCC section 2-207. It was drafted because of "the sad fact that many [modern] sales contracts are not fully bargained, not carefully drafted, and not understandingly signed by both parties." Thus, contracting parties commonly exchange "canned" forms. Typically, the prospective buyer forwards a purchase order to a prospective seller after filling in the quantity and price. Then the seller delivers the goods to the buyer along with an invoice. It is not uncommon for the order and invoice to have different conditions of sale, normally as prompted by the perceived self-interest of the sender of the form. Under the common law "mirror image" rule, an invoice from the seller with materially different terms would be considered a mere counteroffer rather than an acceptance. Section 2-207 is designed to foster contract formation despite differing terms. Under this section, the invoice is an acceptance and, between merchants, the additional terms become part of the contract unless (a) the offer is expressly limited to its terms, (b) the terms make a material alteration, or (c) notice of objection is given within a reasonable time. A term makes a material alteration if it would result in unreasonable surprise or hardship. JOM can prove that the damages limitation clause makes a material alteration.

CONCEPT SUMMARY   Accepting the Exact Offer

Common Law Rule (for sale of real estate and services, primarily)	Acceptance cannot materially vary from the offer.	If it does, it is a rejection of the offer and a counteroffer.
UCC Rule (2-207) (for sale of goods)—when contract made by exchange of forms	Acceptance form can have terms additional to or different from the offer.	A contract can result, but the differing terms may not be part of the contract (see Chapter 14).
UCC Rule—when forms not exchanged	Acceptance cannot materially vary from the offer.	If it does, it is a rejection of the offer and a counteroffer.

ACCEPTING AN OFFER FOR A UNILATERAL CONTRACT

As you saw in Chapter 6, in a unilateral contract a promise is exchanged for an act. To accept an offer to enter into such a contract, the offeree must perform the requested act or make the requested promise. So, if Mary tells Sue, "I'll give you $100 (the promise) if you find my lost dog Sparky (the requested act)," Sue must find the dog to accept Mary's offer.

ACCEPTING AN OFFER FOR A BILATERAL CONTRACT

The courts, if possible, interpret an offer as proposing a bilateral contract. A bilateral contract is a promise for a promise, and the offeree must make the promise requested in the offer. So, if Tom hands Betty a detailed offer for the purchase of Betty's house and Betty signs the offer without changing any of its terms, both parties are bound on the terms of the offer. Betty has promised to deliver a deed on the agreed-on closing date in exchange for Tom's promise to pay the agreed-on price on that date.

An offeree may expressly accept the offer, as Betty did in the preceding example, or may impliedly accept by doing something that objectively indicates agreement. For example, James, a farmer, leaves three bushels of tomatoes with Roger, the owner of a grocery store. James says, "Look these over. If you want them, they're $3 a bushel." Roger sells the tomatoes to his customers. By treating them as if he owned them, he has impliedly accepted James's offer.

SILENCE AS ACCEPTANCE

Since the basis of contract law is the voluntary agreement of the parties, the law generally requires some affirmative indication of assent from offerees before it binds them to the terms of an offer. This generally means that an offeror is not allowed to word his or her offer so that the offeree must act to avoid being bound to a contract. An offer that said: "If you do not object within 10 days, we have a contract" imposes no legal duty on the offeree to respond. It also means that mere silence on the part of the offeree is generally not acceptance.

On the other hand, always bear in mind that the ultimate question of the courts in acceptance cases is: Did the offeree objectively indicate an intent to be bound by the terms of the offer? Sometimes the circumstances of the case impose on the offeree a duty to reject an offer or be bound by it. In such a case, the offeree's silence constitutes an acceptance and a contract is created. If the parties have dealt with each other before and silence signaled acceptance in their prior dealings, the offeree who remains silent in the face of an offer may be held to have accepted.

Return to the example of the farmer and the grocer. Assume that for the last two years, James has regularly sent Roger certain produce items and Roger has always promptly returned those items he did not want. James sends Roger 10 bushels of green beans, and Roger does not return them. At the end of the month, as is his usual practice, James bills Roger for the beans. Roger sends back the bill, saying, "I don't want the beans; come to the store and pick them up." Was there a contract? Most courts would say that, due to the prior dealings between the parties, Roger accepted the beans by failing to reject them. A similar situation could arise due to trade usage, where the parties are both members of a trade in which failure to reject promptly customarily indicates acceptance. An offeree's silence can also operate as acceptance if the offeree has indicated that it will ("If you don't hear from me in five days, I accept.") or if the offeree allows the offeror to perform the offered services without objection.

Ethical Implications	In most circumstances, silence is not acceptance. What ethical problems would arise if silence generally was presumed to constitute acceptance?

WHO CAN ACCEPT AN OFFER?

The only person with the legal power to accept an offer and create a contract is the original offeree (or his or her agent). An attempt to accept by anyone other than the offeree is, therefore, treated as a legal offer, since the party attempting to accept is indicating a willingness to contract on terms of the original offer. The original offeror is free to accept or reject this new offer. For example, Mary offers to sell her business to Jane. Jane tells Mike about the offer, and Mike sends Mary a letter attempting to accept her offer. No contract is created. Since Mike is not the offeree, he has merely made an offer that Mary is free to accept or reject.

ACCEPTANCE WHEN A WRITING IS ANTICIPATED

Often the parties who are negotiating a contract prepare a written draft of the agreement for both parties to sign. This is a good idea because then there is written evidence of the terms of their agreement if a dispute arises at a later date. If a dispute arises before the writing is signed, however, there may be a question about when or whether the parties in fact reached agreement. One of the parties may want to back out and argue that the parties did not intend a contract to result until the writing was signed. The other party may argue that a contract was created before the writing was signed and that the writing was merely intended to record on paper the agreement the parties had already reached.

The courts determine the intent of the parties on this point by applying the objective test of what a reasonable person familiar with the circumstances would be justified in believing the parties intended. If it appears that the parties concluded their negotiations and reached agreement on all the material aspects of the transaction, the courts will probably conclude that a contract resulted at the time when agreement was reached. The failure of the parties to sign the writing is therefore unimportant. If, on the other hand, it appears that the parties were still in the process of negotiation at the time the dispute arose, the courts will probably find that no contract was created. The same would be true when the parties have clearly indicated an intent not to be bound until both sign the writing.

SHANN V. DUNK
84 F.3d 73 (2d Cir. 1996)

FACTS

Dunk, who owned a controlling interest in an explosives company, wanted to retire. He proposed to sell his shares to Shann, a British citizen who manufactured and sold explosives for mining. Early negotiations fell through due to financing problems. On November 24, 1992, Dunk proposed that he finance the sale, Shann's solicitor agreed, and an agreement was drawn up and faxed to Shann for his signature. The agreement, which Shann signed on November 25, was in rough preliminary form and contemplated memorialization in a more formal contract. Shann and Dunk hired attorneys to draw up the final stock purchase agreement. Soon thereafter a dispute arose about specifics in the final document, and each side proposed a writing different from the November 24 agreement. Shann eventually agreed to sign a document like the November 24 agreement, but Dunk refused. Dunk and Shann then sued each other.

ISSUE

Was the November 24 agreement a contract or an agreement to negotiate further?

DECISION

Ordinarily, preliminary manifestations of assent that require further negotiation do not create binding obligations. However, if a preliminary agreement clearly manifests such intention, it can create binding obligations. Where all essential terms have been agreed upon in the preliminary contract, no disputed issues are perceived to remain, and a further contract is envisioned primarily to satisfy formalities, a binding contract has been formed. Here, notwithstanding their intention to sign a more elaborate and formal contract, the parties viewed themselves as having reached a complete agreement on all significant terms on November 25 and intended to be bound. Although the parties recognized that the final contract would include additional "boilerplate," they foresaw no disputes relating to the boilerplate.

COMMUNICATION OF ACCEPTANCE

To accept an offer for a unilateral contract, where a promise is exchanged for an act, the offeree must perform the act requested by the offeror. When the act is completed, the contract is created. Notice of this type of acceptance is not necessary for the creation of the contract unless the offer specifically requires notice. In order to accept all other offers, however, the offeree must make the requested promise. The general rule is that such promises must be *communicated* in order to be effective and create a contract.

MANNER OF COMMUNICATION

The offeror may specify (**stipulate**) in the offer the time, place, or method of communicating acceptance. In such a case, the offeree must comply fully with the offeror's stipulations. Any material deviation makes the attempt to accept ineffective. If the offer merely suggests a method or place of communication, or is silent on these points, the offeree may accept within a reasonable time by any reasonable means of communication.

FARAGO ADVERTISING, INC. v. HOLLINGER INTERNATIONAL, INC.
157 F.Supp. 2d 252 (S.D. N.Y. 2001)

FACTS

In June 1999 Farago Advertising started work on an advertising project for Hollinger under an oral agreement. The only term at that time was for monthly payment for work performed. Farago asserted that advertising contracts customarily included a 90-day termination clause because an agency needs to reassign or discharge staff for a new client. As Farago worked on the campaign, it negotiated about a written contract with Hollinger. A central issue in the negotiation was a notice of termination clause. In October 1999, Farago's attorney proposed a 60-day termination period to Hollinger's attorney, who did not have authority to enter into a binding agreement for Hollinger. The next day Farago e-mailed Hollinger that the proposed language be inserted into the written contract, and copies be sent out for signatures. Hollinger did so and sent the master document back unsigned along with a note that said, "Please have your client execute both copies of the Agreement and return them to me in the enclosed pre-addressed, pre-paid Federal Express envelope. I will then have them signed, and return one . . . to you. . . ." Farago signed the contract and returned it to Hollinger, who never signed it. Soon thereafter Hollinger paid Farago for the work done from June 1999 to October, and paid $42,000 per month for two additional months. Hollinger notified Farago on December 20 that it would not be executing the agreement letter. Farago sued for $84,000 for two months termination payment plus fees and expenses.

ISSUE

Was there an effective acceptance?

DECISION

No. An offeror can dictate the manner of acceptance. For example, he can require that the document be in a writing signed by both parties. There is no doubt that the proposal contained an exclusive mode of acceptance. The parties had been negotiating for weeks about the termination clause. Farago's e-mail message was an offer on the terms in the written document. When Farago signed and returned the written document, it was the offer and stipulated how it must be accepted, which was that it must be signed by both parties to be effective. If Farago did not like that term, it could have changed the document. There is no doubt that Hollinger intended to be bound only by a signed agreement.

WHEN IS ACCEPTANCE COMMUNICATED?

When acceptance is effective can be critically important. In most instances, the offeror has the power to revoke the offer at any time before acceptance. The offeror may be seeking to revoke an offer at the same time the offeree is trying to accept it. A mailed or telegraphed acceptance may get lost and never be actually received by the offeror. The time limit for accepting the offer may be rapidly approaching. Was the offer accepted before a revocation was received or before the offer expired? Does a lost acceptance create a contract when it is dispatched, or is it totally ineffective?

If the parties are dealing face to face or the offeree is accepting by telephone, these problems are minimized. As soon as the offeree has said, "I accept," or words to that effect, a contract is created (assuming the offer is still in existence). For example, Mary offered to sell Chuck her 1965 Mustang for $500. While talking on the phone to Bruce, she mentions her offer. Bruce tells her that old Mustangs are in big demand and her car is worth at least $2,500. When she hangs up the phone she sees Chuck walking up her driveway. She opens the window and yells, "I take back my offer!" The startled Chuck then yells, "You can't. I accept!" Is there a contract? Clearly not, since Mary revoked her offer before Chuck accepted.

Problems with the timing of acceptances multiply when the offeree is using a means of communication that creates a time lag between dispatching the acceptance and its actual receipt by the offeror. The offeror can minimize these problems since he or she has the power to control the conditions under which the offer can be accepted. The offeror need only state in the offer that he or she must *actually receive* the acceptance for it to be effective. This is clearly the best thing for an offeror to do since it affords the offeror the maximum amount of protection. It gives the offeror the most time to revoke and ensures that he or she will never be bound to a contract by an acceptance that is not received.

The offeror who does not use the power to require actual receipt of the acceptance will find that the law has developed rules that make some acceptances effective at the moment they are dispatched, regardless of whether the offeror ever actually receives them. These rules generally apply when the offeror has made the offer under circumstances that might reasonably lead the offeree to believe that acceptance by some means other than telephone or face-to-face communication is acceptable.

AUTHORIZED MEANS OF COMMUNICATION

As a general rule, an acceptance is effective *when dispatched* (delivered to the communicating agency) if the offeree uses an **authorized means** of communication. The offeror can expressly or impliedly indicate the authorized means. He or she can expressly authorize a particular means of communication by saying, in effect, "You may accept by mail (telegram, etc.)." In such a case, a contract is created at the moment the acceptance was mailed, even if it was lost and the offeror never received it. Any attempt by the offeror to revoke after the letter was mailed would be ineffective. Likewise, an offer sent by a **stipulated means** is effective when dispatched.

Under traditional contract principles, a given means of communication may also be impliedly authorized in one of two ways. First, if the offer or circumstances do not indicate otherwise, the means the offeror used to communicate the offer is the impliedly authorized means for accepting. So, mailed offers impliedly authorize mailed acceptances, telegraphed offers impliedly authorize telegraphed acceptances, and so on. In the problem case described at the beginning of the chapter, Horwitz used an impliedly authorized means of acceptance. Thus, her acceptance was good when mailed, and a contract was created at that time. Stephens's attempted revocation was therefore ineffective.

Trade usage may also impliedly authorize a given means of acceptance. If both the parties are members of a trade in which acceptances are customarily made by a particular means of communication, the courts assume the offeree is impliedly authorized to accept by that means unless the offer indicates to the contrary. Many courts today are following the lead of the Uniform Commercial Code and the *Restatement Second* by saying that the offeror who remains silent impliedly authorizes the offeree to accept by any **reasonable** means of communication.

ACCEPTANCE BY SHIPMENT

Stating that the offeror impliedly authorizes acceptance in any reasonable manner means that in cases in which it is unclear whether the offer calls for acceptance by a return promise or by performance, either manner of acceptance, if reasonable, will be effective to create a contract. So, in some cases a seller may accept a buyer's offer by *shipping* the goods or by *promising* to ship them. Sellers who accept by performing, however, must notify the buyer of their acceptance within a reasonable time. Buyers who have not received such notice may treat the offer as having "lapsed" before acceptance and may contract with another seller (2-206 [2]).

The Code specifically says that an order requesting "prompt" or "current" shipment of goods impliedly invites acceptance by either a prompt promise to ship or a prompt shipment of the goods (2-206 [1] [b]). For example, Mary's Office Supply sends Bob's Business Machines an order for 25 Compaq personal computers, to be shipped "as soon as possible." The day Bob receives Mary's order, he ships the computers. Later that day Mary phones Bob and tries to revoke her offer. She cannot revoke, since a contract was created when Bob shipped the computers.

What if Bob did not have 25 Compaqs in stock and shipped 15 Compaqs and 10 IBM personal computers? The Code says that the seller who ships "nonconforming goods" (something different from what was ordered) has *accepted and breached* the contract, unless the seller reasonably notifies the buyer that such a shipment is intended as an "accommodation" to the buyer. In such a case, shipment is in effect a counteroffer that the buyer is free to accept or reject (2-206 [1] [b]). This provision is designed to protect buyers against the so-called unilateral contract trick. A dishonest seller who has received a "rush" order may send the wrong goods, hoping that the buyer's necessity will force him to accept. Under common law rules, the seller was making a counteroffer. If the buyer took the goods, she had accepted the seller's counteroffer. If she rejected them, the seller had no liability for sending nonconforming goods. The Code rule forces the seller to give the buyer timely notice of his inability to fill the order, which allows the buyer to accept or the time to seek other goods.

If an authorized means of acceptance is expressly or impliedly present, any attempt by the offeree to accept by a **nonauthorized means** is not effective until the acceptance is actually *received* by the offeror. The following example illustrates these principles: On May 1, 2002, Bob received a telegram from Ralph offering to build Bob a resort cottage for $200,000. On May 5, 2002, at 10 AM, Ralph sends Bob a telegram attempting to revoke the offer. At 11 AM on the same day, Bob mails Ralph a letter attempting to accept the offer. At 11:30 AM, Bob receives Ralph's revocation. Do the parties have a contract? The answer depends on several factors:

1. Assume Ralph's telegraphed offer said: "Acceptance by mail is advisable." If so, the parties have a contract because Ralph expressly authorized acceptance by mail. Therefore, Bob's mailed acceptance would be effective when dispatched at 11 AM and a contract would be created at that time. Ralph's revocation would be ineffective, since it was not actually received (as revocations must be) before the contract was created.

2. Assume Ralph's offer was silent on the question of what means Bob could use to accept. If so, under traditional contract principles, the parties would not

have a contract because the impliedly authorized means of communication in this instance was telegram (the means Ralph used to communicate the offer). Bob attempted to accept by a nonauthorized means (mail), so his acceptance would not be effective until Ralph actually received it. Ralph effectively revoked the offer before receiving Bob's acceptance. However, in a state that holds that the offeror impliedly authorizes acceptance by any reasonable means, the parties may have a contract if the court concludes that mail was a reasonable way for Bob to accept Ralph's offer.

3. Assume Bob and Ralph are both construction contractors and the custom in the construction business is to offer by telegram and accept by mail. In this instance, the parties would have a contract because Bob used the means of communication impliedly authorized by trade usage. His acceptance would be effective when mailed, creating a contract before Ralph's revocation was received.

CANTU V. CENTRAL EDUCATION AGENCY
884 S.W.2d 565 (Ct. App. Tex. 1994)

FACTS

Cantu was hired for the 1990–1991 school year as a special education teacher. On August 18, shortly before classes started, she hand delivered her resignation, effective August 17, 1990, to her supervisor. In her letter she requested that her last paycheck for the previous year be sent to an address 50 miles from the school district. The superintendent received the resignation August 20. The same day he wrote a letter accepting the resignation and mailed it at 5:15 PM. About 8:00 the next morning, August 21, Cantu hand-delivered a letter to the superintendent's office withdrawing her resignation. In response, he hand-delivered a copy of the letter sent the previous day accepting her resignation. When she was not allowed to withdraw her resignation, Cantu sued, arguing that the superintendent used an unauthorized means to accept her offer of resignation.

ISSUE

Was the superintendent's letter ineffective because it was sent by an unauthorized means?

DECISION

No. Offerors, as "masters of their offers," can impose conditions or specify the manner of acceptance. Usually, though, an offeror does not expressly authorize a particular means of acceptance. In such cases, courts have adopted the mailbox rule, which makes acceptance effective on dispatch. The modern common law adopts the approach that acceptance by any means reasonable under the circumstances is effective on dispatch absent a contrary indication in the offer. Acceptance by mail is impliedly authorized in two cases: (1) where the offer was communicated by mail and (2) where the circumstances are such that it must have been within the contemplation of the parties that the mails might be used to communicate the acceptance. It was reasonable for the superintendent to use the mail for acceptance. Cantu tendered her resignation shortly before the start of the school year—a time when both parties could not fail to appreciate the need for immediate action to find a replacement. Also, Cantu's request that her final check be sent to an address 50 miles away indicated she could no longer be reached in town.

There is one major exception to the rule that acceptances by the authorized means of communication are effective on dispatch. If the offeree has dispatched inconsistent responses to the offer by sending both a rejection and an acceptance, whichever response reaches the offeror first will determine whether a contract is created. So, if Marty sends Frank a letter offering to sell him a condominium in Florida for $150,000

CONCEPT SUMMARY	Communication of Acceptance	
Stipulated Means of Communication	Time, place, or method of communication spelled out in offer.	Full compliance required for effective acceptance.
Authorized Means of Communication	Spelled out in offer, implied by way offer communicated, or implied by trade usage.	Acceptance effective when dispatched.
Reasonable Means of Communication (rule of UCC and some courts)	Any means deemed reasonable by the court in light of the circumstances.	Acceptance effective when dispatched.
Unauthorized Means of Communication	Generally, a means slower than the way the offer was communicated.	Acceptance not effective until received.

and Frank sends Marty a letter offering $135,000 (a counteroffer), but later changes his mind and sends a letter accepting the original offer for $150,000, no contract will result if Marty receives the counteroffer before he receives the acceptance. This exception is designed to protect offerors like Marty who receive rejections and may rely on them by selling to someone else, being unaware of the fact that the offeree has also sent an acceptance.

CONCEPT SUMMARY	Acceptance
	There is a valid acceptance if there is
	1. Intent
	Objectively manifested.
	2. Exactness
	No material changes from the offer.
	3. Communication
	a. In the stipulated manner as spelled out in the offer.
	b. By an expressly or impliedly authorized means (effective when dispatched).
	c. By a nonauthorized means (effective when received).

QUESTIONS AND PROBLEM CASES

1. Explain the three main requirements for an effective acceptance.
2. What are the three exceptions to 2-207's general rule that in forms exchanged between merchants, the offeree's additional terms become part of the contract.
3. Explain a *stipulation* and the effect it has on an acceptance.
4. Explain when an acceptance sent by nonauthorized means is effective.
5. Jerry Falwell, on his "Old Time Gospel Hour" show number 595, preached about the second coming of Christ. As part of this sermon, he talked about God's wrath that would be poured

out on false religions. He cited the Metropolitan Community Church, a gay church founded by Jerry Sloan, his former roommate from his seminary days, as one of these false religions, a "vile and satanic system [that] will one day be utterly annihilated and there will be a celebration in heaven." He also spoke of them as immoral and "brute beasts." Falwell later appeared on a TV talk show in California. Sloan, who was in the audience, asked Falwell why he said these things, and Falwell denied ever saying them. When Sloan said he had a tape of the show, Falwell again made a denial and offered to pay $5,000 if the tape could be produced. Sloan, who had the tape at home, later gave it to Falwell and demanded the $5,000. Did Sloan effectively accept Falwell's offer?

6. The Hills ordered a computer over the phone, using their credit card. The Gateway 2000 computer arrived in a box that contained a list of terms. One of those terms required that disputes arising under the contract be arbitrated. It also stated that if the computer were kept over 30 days, the terms were accepted. The Hills kept the computer over 30 days before complaining about its components and performance. When the Hills sued Gateway 2000, Gateway insisted the dispute must be arbitrated. Is it correct?

7. First Texas Savings & Loan Association (First) ran a "$5,000 Scoreboard Challenge" contest. Contestants who filled out entry forms and deposited them with First had a chance to win an $80 savings account with First plus four tickets to a Dallas Mavericks basketball game if their form was drawn. In addition, if the Mavericks held their opponents to 89 points or less, they would also win a $5,000 money market certificate. Drawings were held monthly. In October, Jergins filled out a form and deposited it with First. On November 1, First attempted to amend the contest by posting notices at its branches that the Mavericks would have to hold their opponents to 85 points or less in order to win the $5,000. In late December, Jergins's form was drawn, and she was notified she had won the $80 account and four tickets to the January 23 Mavericks game. At that game, the Jazz scored 88 points. When Jergins tried to claim the $5,000 certificate, First refused to give it because the Jazz had scored more than 85 points. Did Jergins accept First's offer for a unilateral contract when she filled out the form and deposited it?

8. Pearsall and Alexander, friends for over 20 years, met twice a week after work at a liquor store. There they bought what they called a "package"—a half-pint of vodka, orange juice, two cups and two lottery tickets. They then went to Alexander's home to scratch the tickets, drink, and watch TV. When they won, they bought more tickets. One day Pearsall bought a package, and when he returned to the car, asked Alexander regarding the lottery, "Are you in on it?" Alexander said, "Yes." When Pearsall asked him for half the price, Alexander said he had no money. At his home, Alexander worried that Pearsall might lose the tickets, grabbed them, and scratched them. They were losers. Later Alexander bought another package. This time Pearsall snatched the tickets and he scratched one and Alexander the other. Alexander's won $20,000. He refused to split the money with Pearsall. Does Pearsall have a right to half the winnings?

9. Penzoil Co. made a public tender offer to buy 16 million shares of Getty Oil Co. It contacted Gordon Getty, who owned 40.2 percent of the outstanding shares of Getty Oil, and the J. Paul Getty Museum, which owned 11.8 percent, and they drafted and signed a Memorandum of Agreement, subject to approval of Getty Co.'s board, whereby Penzoil would become an owner of Getty Oil. On January 2, the board rejected the offer. On January 3, the board received a higher offer from Penzoil, which it voted to accept if Penzoil would raise the "stub" price. Penzoil accepted the board's offer later that day. On January 4, Getty Oil and Penzoil issued identical press releases announcing an agreement in principle on the basis of the Memorandum, and Penzoil's attorneys began drawing up a formal agreement. On January 5, Texaco offered to buy Getty stock for a higher price, and the museum and Gordon Getty agreed to sell their stock to them. On January 6, Getty Co.'s board voted to withdraw its counteroffer to Penzoil and accept Texaco's offer. Penzoil sued Texaco for tortious interference with its contract, and Texaco defended by arguing there was no contract. Was Texaco correct?

10. Reddick had a life insurance policy on her son from Globe Life effective December 1, 1987, to December 1, 1988. The policy provided a 31-day grace period after the due date for payment of a premium, during which time the policy remained in effect. If the payment was not made by the end of the grace period, the policy lapsed. When Reddick did not pay the premium due in December, the policy lapsed January 5. On that date Globe sent Reddick a letter offering to continue the policy if the premium

was received by January 20. Reddick's son died on January 17; on January 20 Reddick called Globe and notified it of his death. The company told her the policy had lapsed. She then sent the premium, which it did not receive until after the 20th. Was the mailing of the check on the 20th an effective renewal?

11. Western Title, Inc., had a lease with Skredes that was due to expire on April 30, 1978. The lease was renewable for five years if Western notified Skredes of its intent to renew at least 30 days before April 30. It also stated that the notice would be effective only when it was deposited in a U.S. Post Office by registered or certified mail. Western's attorney sent a notice of renewal by ordinary mail, which arrived after April 1. On April 5, the attorney discovered his mistake and sent another notice by certified mail. On April 14 Skredes notified Western the lease was canceled. Had Western effectively accepted before the cancellation?

12. John Soldau was discharged by Organon. He received a letter from Organon offering to pay him double the usual severance pay if he signed an enclosed release of all claims he might have against Organon. Soldau signed and dated the release and put it in a mailbox outside the post office. When he returned home, he found he had received a check from Organon in the same amount as was offered in the letter. He then returned to the post office, persuaded a postal employee to open the mailbox, and retrieved the release. He cashed the check and then filed suit against Organon alleging violation of the Age Discrimination in Employment Act and state law. Was a contract formed when Soldau put the release in the mailbox?

CHAPTER 9

Consideration

The Carrocias contracted to have Todd build them a log home. Todd used inadequate construction techniques that resulted in structural problems. After a windstorm brought the inadequacies to light, the Carrocias hired Todd to replace tie-rods in the walls to correct the structural problems. They did not pay him for the tie-rod work.

- *Was the Carrocias' promise to pay for the tie-rod work enforceable?*
- *Did Todd give any legally valuable consideration in return for the Carrocias' promise to pay?*
- *Can Todd recover for the work done under an equitable theory?*

FIGURE 9–1   Consideration

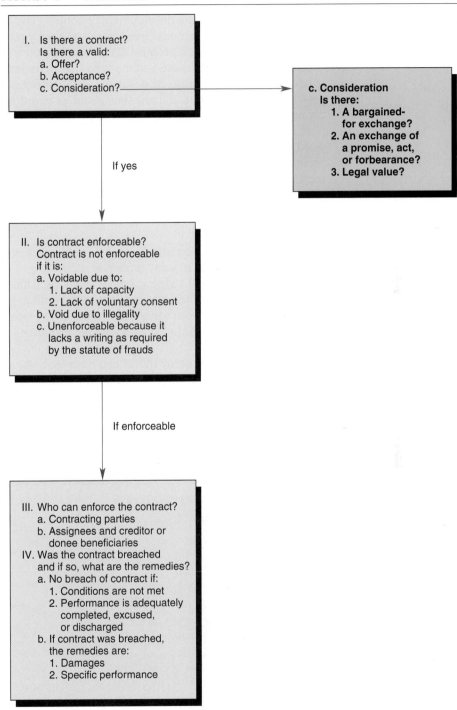

I. Is there a contract?
    Is there a valid:
    a. Offer?
    b. Acceptance?
    c. Consideration?

c. Consideration
   Is there:
   1. A bargained-
      for exchange?
   2. An exchange of
      a promise, act,
      or forbearance?
   3. Legal value?

If yes

II. Is contract enforceable?
     Contract is not enforceable
     if it is:
     a. Voidable due to:
        1. Lack of capacity
        2. Lack of voluntary consent
     b. Void due to illegality
     c. Unenforceable because it
        lacks a writing as required
        by the statute of frauds

If enforceable

III. Who can enforce the contract?
     a. Contracting parties
     b. Assignees and creditor or
        donee beneficiaries
IV. Was the contract breached
     and if so, what are the remedies?
     a. No breach of contract if:
        1. Conditions are not met
        2. Performance is adequately
           completed, excused,
           or discharged
     b. If contract was breached,
        the remedies are:
        1. Damages
        2. Specific performance

········· *THE IDEA OF CONSIDERATION* ·········

At a fairly early point in the development of contract law, the common law courts decided not to enforce gratuitous (free) promises. Simply put, this means that the courts generally do not enforce a promise against the person who made it (the **promisor**) unless the person the promise was made to (the **promisee**) has given up something in exchange for the promise. In effect, the requirement of **consideration** requires a promisee to pay the "price" the promisor asked for in order to gain the right to enforce the promisor's promise. This idea is consistent with the common law idea that the purpose of contract law was to enforce *bargains*. So, if Mary (the promisor) promises to give Bob (the promisee) a diamond ring and Bob has done nothing in return for her promise, Bob will not be able to enforce Mary's promise against her, since it was *not supported by consideration*. A useful definition of *consideration* is *legal value, bargained for and given in exchange for an act or promise*.

LEGAL VALUE

A promisee's consideration may be an *act* (in the case of some unilateral contracts) or a *promise* (in the case of some unilateral contracts and all bilateral contracts). Consideration can have **legal value** in one of two ways. If the promisee does or agrees to do something he or she had no prior legal duty to do in exchange for the promisor's promise, that provides legal value. If the promisee agrees not to do something he or she has a legal right to do in exchange for the promisor's promise, that also provides legal value.

Under this definition many things can have *legal* value without having *monetary* (economic) value. So, if Frank's grandmother promises to pay Frank $500 if he will quit smoking for one year and Frank quits, he can enforce her promise against her. He has given legal value (by not doing something he had a right to do) in exchange for her promise, despite the fact that his quitting smoking has no everyday value in dollars and cents.

BERGEN V. WOOD
18 Cal. Rptr. 2d 75 (Ct. App. Cal. 1993)

FACTS

Duane Wood, a former president of Lockheed and a widower, met Brigit Bergen, a German actress, in Monte Carlo when he was 65 and she was 45. They developed an intimate relationship, but never cohabited. Bergen kept her apartment in Munich, and when she was in California, where Wood lived, she kept a room at a Beverly Hills hotel. Bergen traveled with Wood and accompanied him to social events. He paid for her travel expenses and hotels, and gave her money. The relationship ended after seven years, in 1988. Bergen sued Wood for breach of contract, alleging that in 1982 Wood agreed to provide her financial support in accordance with her needs and his ability to pay in exchange for her promise to be his companion, confidant, and homemaker, and to assist with his business affairs by acting as a social hostess. When the trial court awarded Bergen $3,500 for 48 months, Wood appealed on the ground that sexual services do not constitute legal value, and therefore the agreement lacked consideration.

ISSUE

Did the agreement lack consideration?

DECISION

Yes. Unmarried adults who live together and engage in sexual relations can contract regarding their earnings and property rights as long as the agreement does not rest upon illicit sexual activities. Cohabitation normally is a necessary condition of these property agreements because from cohabitation flows the rendition of domestic

(continued)

BERGEN V. WOOD
(concluded)

services, which services amount to lawful consideration for a contract between the parties. Further, if cohabitation were not a prerequisite to recovery, every dating relationship would have the potential for giving rise to claims such as this. Bergen and Wood did not cohabit and therefore no consideration was given by Bergen severable from their sexual relationship. While Bergen did act as Wood's social companion and hostess, these activities are not normally compensated and are inextricably intertwined with the sexual relationship. Bergen cannot enforce the agreement.

ADEQUACY OF CONSIDERATION

Legal value has nothing to do with *adequacy* of consideration. As long as the consideration given by the parties to an agreement has legal value, the courts generally do not concern themselves with whether parties to a contract received any actual value in exchange for their promises, or whether the promises or performances exchanged were of relatively equal value. Freedom of contract is the freedom to make bad bargains as well as good ones, so promisors' promises are enforceable if they "got what they asked for" in exchange for making their promises, even if "what they asked for" is not nearly so valuable in worldly terms as what they promised in return.

Several qualifications must be made to this general rule. First, if the inadequacy of consideration is apparent *on the face of the agreement,* most courts would not enforce the agreement because they would assume it was a gift disguised to look like a contract. Thus, an agreement by Martha to pay her brother $500 in exchange for $100, with no other terms or conditions, is unenforceable.

Agreements that recite "$1" or "$1 and other valuable consideration" as the consideration for a promise are similarly treated. This **nominal consideration** is generally not recognized by the courts unless it was in fact *truly* bargained for. If it wasn't bargained for, the promise is a disguised gift and unenforceable.

Gross inadequacy of consideration may also give rise to an inference of fraud, duress, lack of capacity, and so on. In addition, gross inadequacy may lead to a finding of unconscionability under the Uniform Commercial Code. Inadequacy of consideration standing alone, however, is not enough to prove lack of reality of consent or capacity.

Courts may refuse to grant **equitable remedies** to those who seek to enforce grossly inadequate bargains on the grounds that such persons are not entitled to the special treatment equity affords. So, if Bob agrees to sell Mary his house (worth $155,000) for $125,000, Mary can probably recover damages for breach of contract if Bob refuses to perform, but she probably will not be able to get an order for the specific performance of Bob's promise (ordering Bob to give Mary a deed to his house).

Ethical Implications	Is it ethical to insist on a strict enforcement of a contract when you have paid nominal or inadequate consideration?

EARL v. ST. LOUIS UNIVERSITY
875 S.W.2d 234 (Ct. App. Mo. 1994)

FACTS

Earl was the St. Louis University Hospital's chief financial officer for six years. Due to restructuring, his position was not re-funded. Since he had overseen earlier terminations, he was told to write his termination package on the basis of earlier agreements, which he did. The vice president of the medical center, after reviewing the document with legal counsel, signed it, as did Earl. In the agreement Earl agreed to release the University from all claims arising from his termination, to waive his statutory right to a service letter, to cooperate in completing projects, and to continue working until a specific date or until he found other employment. In exchange, he received 8 months' severance pay, an incentive bonus payment, and the right to buy the car the University had provided him at its depreciated value. When the president of the university saw the signed agreement, he said it was unacceptable. When Earl sued to enforce the agreement, the University challenged its enforceability on the ground that it lacked adequate consideration because Earl's promises caused him no detriment. He had no legitimate claims against the University over his termination and agreed to keep working only until he found another job or a date certain.

ISSUE

Was what Earl promised adequate consideration to support the hospital's promise to pay?

DECISION

Yes. Consideration, which is a necessary element for a contract, can consist of either a detriment to the promisee or a benefit to the promisor. The detriment can be doing anything one is not legally bound to do or refraining from doing something one has a legal right to do. There is no need to decide whether the waiver of any claims Earl might have against the University was adequate, because the waiver of the service letter and the promise to continue working were legally sufficient to support the agreement. Earl gave up his legal right to the letter. He was an employee at will and gave up his right to quit at any time. While the University may not value these, it is well settled that disparity in value is not a defense. This rests on the policy of letting parties weigh the benefits pro and con, and make whatever contract between themselves that they please. Disparity in value between the detriment to Earl and the benefit he received, in the absence of fraud, does not affect the enforceability of the agreement.

BARGAINED FOR AND GIVEN IN EXCHANGE

Saying consideration must be bargained for means that, in addition to having legal value, the consideration given by the promisee must be the consideration the promisor *requested in exchange for making his or her promise.* The courts are saying, in effect: "If you [the promisor] got your price for making your promise, we will enforce your promise against you."

See Figure 9–2 for a summary of the concept of consideration.

.... SOLVING CONSIDERATION PROBLEMS ....

Students often have difficulty with the concept of consideration. One reason is that most disputes about consideration involve *bilateral contracts* (a promise for a promise). This causes confusion in two ways. First, since bilateral contracts by definition include two promises, each party is both a promisor (on the promise he or she made to the other party) and a promisee (on the promise the other party made in

FIGURE 9–2   The Concept of Consideration

A legally valuable promise, act, forbearance	Bargained for and given in exchange for	A legally valuable promise, act, forbearance

return). Second, students often forget that *merely making the requested promise* is enough for consideration in bilateral contracts cases.

Here is a simple problem-solving method to help you in determining whether consideration has been given in a case. Ask yourself:

1. *Which promise is at issue?* This ordinarily is the promise that a court is trying to decide whether to enforce.
2. *Who is the promisee of that promise?* This is the party seeking to enforce the promise.
3. *Has the promisee given consideration?* If so, and if the other elements of a binding contract are present, the promise is enforceable.

If you understand the definition of consideration and use this method, you will be able to work out most consideration problems with ease. Take a simple bilateral contract situation and see how this problem-solving method works.

FACTS

On May 15, 1999, Mary enters into an agreement with Apex Painting Company to have Apex paint her house before June 15, 1999, for the sum of $3,000.

Alternative Case A

On May 20, 1999, Mary calls Apex and tells it the deal is off, since Ralph's Painting Company has agreed to paint her house for $2,500. Apex sues Mary, and she argues lack of consideration as a defense.

1. The promise at issue is Mary's promise to pay Apex for painting her house.
2. The promisee on this promise is Apex.
3. Apex has given consideration. Apex agreed to do something it had no prior duty to do—paint Mary's house—in exchange for her promise. Apex can enforce Mary's promise against her.

Alternative Case B

On May 15, 1999, Apex calls Mary and tells her it will not be able to paint her house because it just got a very profitable job painting a new apartment complex. Mary sues Apex, and it argues lack of consideration as a defense.

1. The promise at issue is Apex's promise to paint Mary's house.
2. Mary is the promisee on this promise.
3. Mary has given consideration. She agreed to do something she had no prior duty to do—hire and pay Apex for painting her house—in exchange for Apex's promise. She can enforce Apex's promise against it.

Now that you understand the meaning of consideration and have a method to help you solve consideration problems, you are ready to learn some of the traditional rules about consideration. These are mostly statements about how the requirement of consideration works in various kinds of situations.

. . . . *RULES OF CONSIDERATION* . . . .

PREEXISTING DUTIES

As a general rule, performing or agreeing to perform a preexisting duty is not consideration. This makes sense when you remember the definition of consideration. In order to have given *legal value,* the promisor must either have done (or agreed to do) something he had no duty to do or have agreed not to do something he had a right to do. If the promisor already had a duty to do what he has done or promised to do, the promisor has not given legal value. The same is clearly true if the promisor agreed not to do something he had no right to do. Several examples of this rule follow.

Promises Not to Commit Crimes or Torts

Every member of society has a duty to obey the law and not commit crimes or torts. Therefore, a promisor's promise not to commit such an act can never be consideration. For example, Bill promises to pay Mike, the school bully, $2 a week for "protection" in exchange for Mike's promise not to beat Bill up. Bill refuses to pay. Bill's promise is unenforceable because it is not supported by consideration.

Promises by Public Officials to Perform Official Duties

Public officials obviously are bound to perform their official duties, so promises by public officials to perform these duties are not consideration. For example, Harry owns a liquor store that has been robbed several times. He promises to pay Fran, a police officer whose beat includes Harry's store, $50 a week to "keep an eye on the store" while walking her beat. Harry's promise is unenforceable, since it was not supported by consideration.

Promises to Perform Preexisting Contractual Duties

By far the greatest number of preexisting duty cases involve **contractual** duties. These cases usually occur when the parties attempt to modify an existing contract but no new consideration is furnished to support the agreement to modify.

For example, Capucine enters into a contract with Toptex Construction Company to build a new house for her for $175,000. When the construction is partially completed, Jones, the owner of Toptex, calls Capucine and says that due to the rising cost of building materials, Toptex will have to stop work unless she pays an extra $5,000. Capucine agrees but later refuses to pay more than the $175,000 originally agreed on. Toptex sues for $5,000. The promise at issue is Capucine's promise to pay the extra $5,000. Toptex cannot enforce that promise because Toptex has not given consideration. All Toptex has done is build the house, something it already had a legal duty to do under the parties' original contract. Similarly Todd, the builder in the introductory problem, cannot collect for the tie-rods. He was under a duty to construct the house in a workmanlike manner. Providing tie-rods to supplement his defective construction is merely a continuation of that preexisting duty.

M. GOLD & SON INC. v. A. J. ECKERT INC.
667 N.Y.S.2d 460 (N.Y. S. Ct. App. Div. 1998)

FACTS

Adirondack Community College had a contract to have heating and air conditioning systems in many of the buildings on its campus replaced. Gold was a subcontractor for part of the work. Due to the unavailability of the basic thermostats which were specified in the original plans, Gold substituted more complicated and expensive thermostats. This resulted in additional work and expense for which it sought to recover.

ISSUE

Can Gold collect for the more expensive materials it used to complete its contract?

(continued)

M. GOLD & SON INC. v. A. J. ECKERT INC.
(concluded)

DECISION

No. In order to be held liable, the contracting party must have assented to the change. There is no evidence that

they approved any change or specifically consented to any work performed by Gold beyond that set forth in the original specifications.

Of course, if *new consideration* is provided to support a modification, it is enforceable. So, if Capucine had asked Toptex to add a room that was not called for in the original plans and promised to pay an extra $5,000 for the new room, her promise to pay more would be enforceable. Toptex, in this case, would have done something it had no legal duty to do in exchange for Capucine's promise.

Ethical Implications	Is it ethical to promise to pay a person more to complete a job and then to renege on the promise because the other party had a preexisting obligation to complete the task at the original price?

The parties to a contract can always terminate their old contract and enter into a new one by mutual agreement (called a *novation*) even if the obligations of one party remain the same while the obligations of the other party are increased. The courts, however, are very suspicious of these situations, asking, in effect: Who would voluntarily agree to pay more for what they have a right to for less? Therefore, the courts require clear and convincing evidence that the termination of the old contract and the creation of the new one are free of any elements of coercion or fraud.

The consideration requirement is often criticized as being too formalistic; mechanical application of the rule can lead to significant injustice. Therefore, the modern trend is to relax the requirement by expanding exceptions to the rule and providing substitutes for it. This is the case with some preexisting contractual duties.

Unforeseeable Difficulties

Generally speaking, a court will enforce a modification that is not supported by new consideration if a contracting party has run into **unforeseeable difficulties** that make his or her performance impossible or highly impracticable. In this situation, the party who has run into trouble is neither a bad person trying to take advantage of the promisor nor an imprudent person trying to escape the consequences of a bad bargain. Therefore, the courts enforce the modification in the interest of fairness, although technically no new consideration has been given. You should note, however, that strikes, increases in the costs of raw materials, and bad weather are not considered unforeseeable. A revolution in Central America that caused supplies to be cut off would be foreseeable; a revolution in France would not. A building contractor who, in excavating the foundation of a new building, strikes bedrock in an area where bedrock formations are not usually found so close to the surface could also rely on this exception to the general rule.

Modifications and the Code

The Code has made a major change in the traditional rule in the case of agreements to modify existing contracts. Agreements to modify contracts for the sale of goods *need no consideration* to be binding (2-209 [1]). People often freely agree to modify their agreements and believe that such modifications are binding. The Code chose to reward these people's expectations.

For example, assume Plastex Corporation enters a contract to supply The Picnic Place with plastic dishes and utensils for $3.50 a setting. After the contract is made, the price of oil suddenly rises, and Plastex's manufacturing costs are greatly increased. Plastex notifies Picnic Place that it can no longer afford to supply the articles at $3.50 a setting and is raising the price to $4. Picnic Place can, of course, refuse to pay $4 a setting and hold Plastex liable for breach of contract if it does not deliver the goods at the original price. However, Picnic Place may believe that paying $4 is better than taking a chance that it won't have dishes and utensils in time for the summer season. Picnic Place may therefore agree to pay the new price. If it does, Plastex can enforce the agreement to pay $4 per setting because it was voluntarily entered into, even though no new consideration was given.

Several points should be noted concerning the way this section of the Code operates. First, there is *no duty* to agree to a modification. Picnic Place could have refused to agree to Plastex's increased price and enforced the original contract. Second, the exception applies only to *existing contracts*. Third, only one term of the existing contract was altered. The other terms under the contract remained in force. Finally, modifications are subject to review under the Code's principles of good faith and fair dealing. Unfair agreements or agreements that result from coercion are unlikely to be enforced.

The Code contains two provisions to protect people from fictitious claims that an agreement has been modified. If the original agreement requires any modification to be in writing, an oral modification is unenforceable (2-209 [2]). Regardless of what the original contract says, if the price of the goods in the modified agreement is $500 or more, the modification is not enforceable unless it is in writing or other requirements of the Code's statute of frauds are met (2-201).

PROMISES TO DISCHARGE DEBTS FOR PART PAYMENT

In many cases, a debtor offers to pay a creditor a sum less than the creditor is demanding in exchange for the creditor's promise to accept the part payment as full payment of the debt. If the creditor later sues for the balance of the original debt, is the creditor's promise to take less enforceable? The answer depends on the nature of the debt and the circumstances of the debtor's payment.

Liquidated Debts

The general rule is that a promise to discharge a **liquidated debt** for part payment of the debt at or after its due date is unenforceable due to lack of consideration. A liquidated debt is one that is *due* and *certain,* which means that there is no dispute about the existence or the amount of the debt. If a debtor does nothing more than agree to pay less than an amount clearly owed, how can that be valid consideration for the creditor's promise to take less? The debtor has actually done less than he or she already had a duty to do, namely, to pay the full amount of the debt.

For example, Beth borrows $2,000 from the First City Bank, payable in six months. When the time for payment arrives, Beth sends the bank a check for $1,800 marked: "In full payment for any and all claims First City has against me." First City cashes the check (impliedly promising to accept it as full payment by cashing it) and later sues Beth for $200. First City can recover the $200, since Beth has given no consideration to support its implied promise to accept $1,800 as full payment.

On the other hand, if Beth had done something she had no duty to do in exchange for First City's promise, she could enforce First City's promise against it and avoid paying the $200. If Beth had *paid early* (before the loan contract called for payment), or *at a different place* from that called for in the loan contract, or in a *different medium of exchange* from that called for in the loan contract (e.g., a car worth $1,800) in exchange for First City's promise, she has given consideration and can enforce the promise.

Unliquidated Debts

An honest dispute about the existence or amount of a debt makes the debt an **unliquidated** one. Assume Tom and Mark are involved in an automobile accident. Tom claims that Mark is at fault and that his total losses from the accident are $9,500. Mark denies responsibility for the accident and argues that Tom's losses are far less than $9,500. There are only two ways to finally settle this dispute: (1) allow a court to determine the nature and extent of the parties' liabilities or (2) reach a private settlement agreement. If Mark offers to pay Tom $2,000 in full payment of all claims Tom has against him and Tom accepts, Tom has entered a binding **accord and satisfaction—** the legal term for settling a disputed claim. Both Mark and Tom have given up their right to have a court decide their liability in exchange for the other's promise to settle their dispute for a definite amount. Therefore, their mutual promises are supported by consideration and enforceable.

Code Section 1-207

This section states: "A party who with explicit reservation of rights performs . . . in a manner demanded or offered by the other party does not thereby prejudice the rights reserved." Some courts have interpreted this language to mean that sellers of goods can cash checks marked "payment in full" and still collect for the unpaid amount if they have attempted to reserve their rights through phrases such as "under protest" or "without prejudice." Courts that take this approach thereby avoid the operation of the accord and satisfaction rule. A majority of courts, though, hold that cashing a "payment in full" check discharges the obligation under the Code. Additionally, several states have enacted a new version of 1-207, which specifically states that 1-207 does not apply to accord and satisfaction.

Composition Agreements

Compositions are agreements between a debtor and two or more creditors who agree to accept a stated percentage of their liquidated claims against the debtor at or after the due date, in full satisfaction of their claims. They are generally treated as binding on the parties to the agreement, despite the fact that doing so appears to be contrary to the general rule on liquidated debts. Creditors usually enter compositions when they believe that failure to do so may result in the debtor's bankruptcy, in which case they might ultimately recover a smaller percentage of their claims than that agreed to in the composition.

CONCEPT SUMMARY   **Preexisting Duties**

Type	Reason	Exception
1. Promises not to commit crimes or torts	Since every member of society has this duty, the promise lacks consideration.	
2. Promises by public officials to perform official duties	Since public officials are bound to perform their official duties, these promises lack consideration.	
3. Promise to perform preexisting contractual duties a. Common law rule	Since the promisee is already under contract to perform the promise, it lacks consideration.	Unforeseeable difficulties that made performance impossible or highly impractical can make promise enforceable.
b. Uniform Commercial Code Rule (2-209)	If commercially reasonable and freely agreed to, promise to alter existing contract for sale of goods is enforceable.	No additional consideration is needed.
4. Promise to pay part of a debt a. Liquidated debt	Since the amount is due and certain, a promise to pay less lacks consideration.	Composition agreements enforced without additional consideration.
b. Unliquidated debt	Since the amount is genuinely in dispute, an agreement resulting in accord and satisfaction is enforceable.	Under UCC ß1-207, *some courts* allow collection of the remainder if checks marked "payment in full" are cashed with reservation.

PAST CONSIDERATION

The courts generally hold that past consideration is no consideration. This rule of consideration basically focuses on the "bargained for and given in exchange" part of our definition of consideration. If a promisee's performance was rendered *before* the promisor's promise was made, then it can never serve as consideration, even though it may meet the "legal value" part of the test. This is so because it was not "bargained for and given in exchange" for the promisor's promise. Return to our earlier example with Frank and his grandmother, but assume that in this case Frank's grandmother says to him, "I'm glad you quit smoking last year, so I'll give you $500 for your birthday." If she later refuses to pay, can Frank enforce her promise? No; he has not given consideration because he did not quit smoking in exchange for her promise.

IN RE LOVEKAMP
24 P. 3d 894 (Okla. Civ. App. 2001)

FACTS

Louise Serrato and Donald Lovekamp were divorced in 1975 after a 10-year marriage. Several months after the divorce, they began living together again. Serrato alleged that in 1981, after Lovekamp began feeling ill, he talked about selling his house and ranch for $120,000. He gave her a check for $60,000 for coming back and staying with him after the divorce. He told her she could cash the check after he sold the property or if something happened to him. When Lovekamp died in 1999, the check was too old to cash. Serrato then filed a claim against the estate for $60,000.

ISSUE

Is Serranto's return to live with Lovekamp sufficient consideration to enforce the promise to pay $60,000?

DECISION

No. Past consideration is no consideration. A past consideration is an act or forbearance in time past by which a person has benefited. If afterward, whether from good feeling or interested motives, the person who benefited makes a promise to pay for that act or forbearance, that promise is gratuitous and cannot be legally enforced.

Moral Obligation

Some courts and legislatures have created an exception to the past consideration rule for **moral obligations.** These cases usually contain promises made by a promisor to pay for board and lodging previously provided to a needy relative or a very close friend, or a promise to pay the debts of a relative. Some courts have found it distressing that such promises would not be enforced and have enforced them despite their lack of consideration. In addition, a few states have passed statutes making promises to pay for past benefits enforceable if the promise is contained in a writing that clearly expresses the promisor's intent to be bound.

FORBEARANCE TO SUE

Forbearance occurs when someone promises not to file a legal suit in exchange for a promise to pay a certain sum of money or some other consideration. The promise not to file suit is valid consideration because the promisor has given up a legal right, the right to sue. There are, however, some qualifications on this rule.

The courts clearly do not want to sanction extortion by allowing people to threaten to file spurious (unfounded) claims in the hope that others will agree to some payment to avoid the expense or embarrassment of suit. On the other hand, we have a strong public policy favoring private settlement of disputes and do not want to require people to second guess the courts. Therefore, it is generally said that in order for forbearance to be valid consideration, the promisee must in *good faith* believe he or she has a valid claim.

DUNCAN v. DUNCAN
553 S.E.2d 925 (N.C. Ct. App. 2001)

FACTS

Pagie P. Duncan made a will dividing her property among her five children. It provided that if her son Lawrence predeceased her, his share of the estate should go to his wife Mildred. At the same time, she entered into a separate agreement with the children that she would not revoke or alter the will in exchange for their promise not to challenge the will or make any claim against the estate. Lawrence died three months later. Several months later Pagie gave two of her children powers of attorney, and they conveyed all of her real property to the remaining four children. That same year she made a new will revoking the old one and leaving all her property to her four surviving children. She died a month later. Mildred sued for a one-fifth interest in the estate.

ISSUE

Does the agreement not to revoke the will lack consideration?

DECISION

No. In order for a contract to be enforceable, it must be supported by consideration. Consideration exists if the promisee, in return for the promise, refrains from doing anything that he has a right to do. Forbearance, or a promise to forbear the exercise of a legal right, is a sufficient consideration for a promise made on account of it. Pagie promised not to revoke or alter her will in exchange for her children's promise not to file against the estate. Each side had a legal right to do those things. The execution of a later will is a breach of the previous, legally enforceable agreement.

MUTUALITY OF OBLIGATION

Generally, a bilateral contract that lacks mutuality is unenforceable due to lack of consideration. As you learned earlier, in a bilateral contract the mutual promises of the parties form the consideration for the agreement. However, the fact that a party made a promise in exchange for the other party's promise is not enough to provide consideration. The promise made must also meet the "legal value" part of our consideration definition. The parties must have bound themselves to do something they had no duty to do, or not to do something they had a right to do.

This issue is raised in some cases because what first looks like a binding promise turns out to be an **illusory promise.** Illusory promises are worded in a way that allows the promisor to decide whether or not to perform the promise. A promise to "buy all the wheat I want" is illusory. A bilateral agreement based on an illusory promise is unenforceable due to lack of mutuality. This means that an illusory promise cannot serve as consideration.

ADDITIONAL EXCEPTIONS TO THE REQUIREMENT OF CONSIDERATION

PROMISSORY ESTOPPEL

The doctrine of promissory estoppel, which was discussed in Chapters 6 and 7, is increasingly being used to enforce promises that are not supported by consideration. Such liberal use is encouraged by the *Restatement (Second) of Contracts.* If the three elements required for estoppel are present (a *promise* likely to induce reliance, *reliance* on that promise, and *injustice* as a result of reliance), the promisor may be *estopped* from raising the defense of lack of consideration. For example, a tenant tells her landlord that she is considering remodeling her apartment and asks if he intends to allow her to renew her lease. He says yes but later refuses to honor his promise. If the tenant has actually spent a substantial sum remodeling in reliance on the landlord's promise, his promise is probably enforceable against him.

FIRM OFFER

Remember that under the Code, an offer by a merchant in a signed writing to keep an offer open is good without additional consideration. This concept was discussed in Chapter 7.

CHARITABLE SUBSCRIPTIONS

A promise to make a gift for a charitable or educational purpose is unenforceable unless and until the institution to which the promise was made incurs obligations by relying on the promise. This exception is usually justified on the basis of either estoppel or public policy.

DEBTS BARRED BY BANKRUPTCY DISCHARGE OR THE STATUTE OF LIMITATIONS

Once a bankrupt debtor is granted a discharge (bankruptcy is discussed in Chapter 39), creditors no longer have a legal right to collect the discharged debts. Similarly, a creditor who fails to file suit to collect a debt within the time limit set by the appropriate statute of limitations loses the right to collect it. However, many states enforce *new promises* by debtors to pay these kinds of debts even though technically they are not supported by consideration, since the creditors have no rights to give up in exchange for the debtors' new promises. This is a source of great potential danger to debtors and great temptation for creditors. Many states recognize this fact by requiring such promises to be in writing to be enforceable. The Bankruptcy Act requires a reaffirmation promise to be made prior to discharge; the promise can be revoked within 30 days after it becomes enforceable, and the Bankruptcy Court must approve it. In addition, the Bankruptcy Court must counsel individual debtors about the legal effects of reaffirmation.

CONCEPT SUMMARY   Consideration

There is valid consideration if there is:
1. A bargained for exchange

---

2. of a promise, act, or forbearance

---

3. that had legal value
   a. not preexisting duty
   b. not past consideration
   c. not illusory promise or

---

4. A recognized exception:
   a. Promise to perform preexisting contractual duties under §2-209, or unforeseen difficulties
   b. Accord and satisfaction of an unliquidated debt
   c. "Payment in full" check for goods cashed with reservation under §1-207
   d. Composition agreement
   e. Past consideration recognized as a moral obligation
   f. Promissory estoppel
   g. Relied on charitable subscription
   h. New promise to pay discharged debt if in writing or meets requirements of Bankruptcy Act

---

QUESTIONS AND PROBLEM CASES

1. Explain the concept of *legal value.*
2. What is the difference between the common law rule and Code rule regarding promises to perform preexisting contractual duties?
3. Explain the difference between a liquidated and an unliquidated debt and its importance for consideration purposes.
4. Explain why past consideration is not good consideration.
5. In 1977 Dairy Specialties, Inc. (DSI), hired Gross for 15 years as general manager and to develop nondairy products. His compensation included annual cost-of-living increases, a reversionary ownership of his inventions and formulas, and a 2 percent royalty on them after the 15-year term. Diehl bought DSI. A condition of the sale was that Gross's contract be renegotiated. Gross agreed even though he received nothing from the sale and was not a party to the sale. The new contract eliminated the annual increase, royalty, and ownership terms. When he was subsequently fired, Gross sued for compensation, arguing that it should be

calculated under the DSI contract terms. Is he correct?
6. Slattery, an independent, licensed polygraph operator, was employed by law enforcement authorities to question a suspect. During the testing, which was conducted over two days, the suspect confessed to killing a guard in a Wells Fargo robbery, a crime about which the suspect was not being questioned. The suspect was convicted and sentenced for the murder. Slattery claimed a $25,000 reward Wells Fargo had offered for information leading to the arrest and conviction of the person or persons participating in the shooting. Is Slattery entitled to the reward?
7. Crookham & Vessels was the general contractor on a project to build an extension of a railroad for the Little Rock Port Authority. Larry Moyer Trucking (Moyer) was subcontracted to do the excavation and dirt work for the project. Moyer dug several ditches as part of its work, but they kept collapsing due to drainage problems. After redigging the ditches several times, Moyer

refused to continue work unless he received extra pay for again redigging the ditches. Crookham & Vessels agreed to do this but later refused to pay. Was there consideration for Crookham & Vessels' promise to pay more to have the ditches redug?

8. Arrow Employment sent Arthur Seides to a job interview with Futuronics Corporation. Seides was told that the job was a "fee paid" position and that Futuronics would pay the 10 percent recruiting fee. Futuronics refused to pay the full 10 percent fee and paid only 5 percent. Seides took the job and agreed to pay the remaining 5 percent but later refused to pay. Arrow filed suit and Seides moved to dismiss, arguing lack of consideration. Is Seides's promise enforceable?

9. In 1917, a building in Des Moines was leased for 99 years, the annual rent to be $18,000 for the final 45 years payable in gold coin at the lessor's option. Monetary policy changed, and Congress in 1933 declared that gold clauses were against public policy and were therefore payable in U.S. currency. In 1977, policy changed again, and gold clauses were made enforceable if they were part of an obligation issued after October 27, 1977. The lease was assigned to American Life & Casualty Insurance Co. in 1990. The assignment stated that American Life "hereby accepts, assumes and agrees to be bound by all of the terms and conditions to be performed by the lease . . . from and after August 1, 1990." In 1993 the lessor, Trostel, demanded that American Life pay its rent in gold coin. In 1996, Congress passed an amendment that specifically prohibited gold clauses dated before 1977 unless both parties agreed to them. When American Life refused to pay in gold coin, Trostel sued. Was the assignment of the lease a novation of the old contract, and the agreement to assume the terms of the old contract a new agreement to pay in gold?

10. Gorham was a store manager for LensCrafters when he received a phone call from Benson Optical offering him a job. After an interview, he was offered the job of area manager for half of North Carolina plus stores in Kentucky and Florida for several thousand dollars more in salary. Terms were discussed over the phone, and he was told a confirming letter and packet would follow. When he received nothing, he phoned and was told they were in the mail and that he should quit his job with LensCrafters, which he did. He declined further negotiations with LensCrafters, flew to Chicago at his own expense, and reported for a nationwide sales meeting, which was his first day of employment. At this meeting Gorham was "reinterviewed" and then terminated. When he sued for breach of contract, Benson defended by arguing there was no consideration because the promise of employment was unenforceable. Gorham had been promised employment at will, which gave the employer the right to fire him at any time for any reason, including on the first day of work. Is Benson correct?

11. Dyer lost his foot in a job related accident. When he returned to work 10 months later, Dyer alleged that his employer promised to employ him for life in exchange for his forbearance to sue about his injury. Dyer was fired seven months later. When Dyer sued, his employer defended by arguing that since Dyer was covered by workers' compensation, he had no legal grounds on which to base a suit. Therefore, his forbearance to sue was not good consideration for the promise of lifetime employment. Was Dyer's good faith forbearance to sue adequate consideration?

12. Barondes made a charitable pledge of $2,000 to the Jewish Federation that he later refused to pay. Can the pledge be enforced despite the lack of consideration?

CHAPTER 10

Capacity to Contract

Webster Street Partnership leased an apartment to Matt and Pat, both minors, for one year. After paying rent for two months, Pat and Matt were unable to pay the third month's rent, and they were asked to move out. Webster Street was unable to rerent the apartment for two months. It sued the boys for this lost rent, as well as for other fees and damages. Matt and Pat refused to pay, and countersued for the return of the rent they had already paid.

- *Can Matt and Pat avoid paying damages because they were minors when they made the contract?*
- *Can Matt and Pat disaffirm the contract and recover what they had already paid while they lived in the apartment?*
- *Could Webster Street disaffirm the rental contract when it discovers Matt and Pat are minors?*

FIGURE 10–1   Capacity

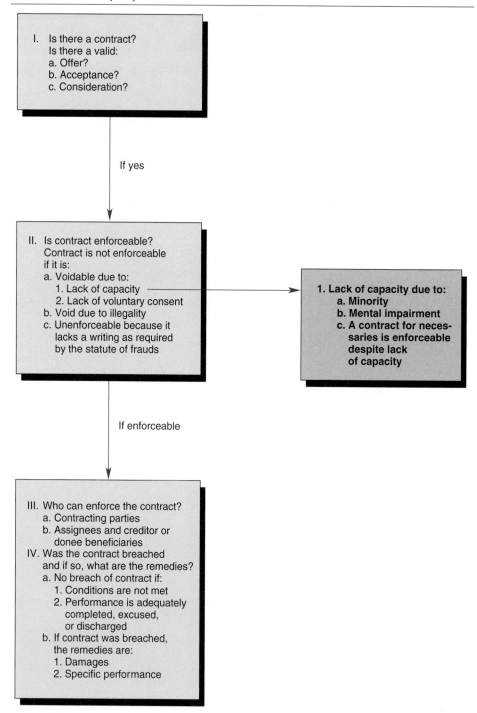

The law uses the word **capacity** to describe the ability of a person to do a legally valid act. Certain classes of persons have traditionally been treated as having a limited capacity to contract because the law sought to protect them in their contractual relations with others. Three major classes of persons are given this special protection: minors, people who are mentally impaired, and intoxicated persons.

If either party entering a contract lacks the capacity to contract, the contract is **void** or **voidable,** depending on the kind of incapacity involved. Capacity to contract, however, is *presumed,* which means that the party who claims incapacity must prove it.

········ *MINORS' CONTRACTS* ········

THE REASON FOR MINORS' INCAPACITY

The idea behind minors' incapacity is that a minor (a person who is not legally considered to be an adult) may not be able to bargain effectively with older, more experienced persons. The courts responded to this idea by making minors' contracts *voidable*—that is, the minor is given the right to **disaffirm** (cancel) his or her contracts. Since the idea is to protect the minor, *only* the minor can disaffirm; adults who contract with minors are bound to the agreement unless the minor chooses to disaffirm. Thus, Webster Street, the landlord in the opening case, would not be able to disaffirm its rental contract with Matt and Pat if they wished to continue living in the apartment and continued to pay the rent.

MITCHELL V. MIZERSKI
1995 Neb. App. LEXIS 99 (Ct. App. Neb. 1995)

FACTS

Travis Mitchell, 16, brought a 1970 Pontiac GTO into Mizerski's body shop to get an estimate on repairs. Mizerski estimated the cost at $1,550.35, and required Mitchell to pay a deposit of $1,000. Travis paid the $1,000 with a cashier's check when he left the car with Mizerski. Some weeks later Travis and his father went to the shop to check on the progress of the repairs and authorize additional repairs costing $300–$400. Two months later they returned, and the father got into a "heated" argument with Mizerski over the amount due. They subsequently compromised on $850, which was paid by a cashier's check drawn on Travis' parents' account when Travis picked up the car. Travis returned the car several times to have repairs done on Mizerski's work. Mizerski then received a letter from Travis and his father complaining about the poor workmanship and asking how Mizerski intended to resolve the problem. He did not reply, and Travis filed suit to disaffirm the contract and to have all amounts paid under the contract returned to him. Mizerski argued that the repair contract was really with the father and thus could not be disaffirmed.

ISSUE

Can Travis disaffirm the contract?

DECISION

Yes. Mizerski's contract was with Travis, not the father. Travis brought the car in for the estimate, delivered it for the repairs, picked it up when it was completed, and paid for it through money he deposited into his parents' account because he did not have a checking account. When Travis delivered the car, he accepted the contract for repairs, and Mizerski began work on that basis. He had no reason to believe he was entering into a contract with anyone other than Travis. While Travis's father did accompany him to the shop on two occasions and argued with Mizerski on one of these occasions, a worker testified that Mizerski stated that the contract was with Travis, not the father. The fact that the father holds title to the car, negotiated the compromise on the amount due, and cosigned the letter of complaint does not change this decision. An individual is not transformed into a party to a contract merely by negotiating certain terms of the

(continued)

MITCHELL V. MIZERSKI
(concluded)

contract or reaching agreement as to the balance due. The father was merely acting as an agent for Travis.

As a general rule, an infant does not have the capacity to bind himself absolutely by contract. The right to avoid the contract is conferred by law for the minor's protection against his own improvidence and the designs of others. The policy of the law is to discourage adults from contracting with minors. The result may seem hardly just to the adult, but persons dealing with minors do so at their peril. Safety lies in refusing to transact business with them. While the minor must return so much of the

consideration still in his possession upon disaffirmance, he does not have to return the equivalent of what has been disposed of during minority. The law is designed to protect the young and inexperienced, and to make them pay back an equivalent for property wasted or squandered during minority would be ineffectual for its intended purpose. Travis has nothing of value that can be returned to Mizerski; paint and body work cannot be returned, and the car is owned by the father. Mizerski's cost of dealing with a minor is returning all of Travis' payments.

ABILITY TO DISAFFIRM

The general rule is that minors may disaffirm their contracts at any time during their minority and for a reasonable time after attaining majority. In most states, a minor becomes an adult at 18 (the age of majority). What constitutes a "reasonable time" after majority depends on the facts and circumstances of each case. Generally, a minor may disaffirm by doing anything that clearly indicates to the other party an intent not to be bound by the terms of the contract. No one but the minor or the minor's personal representative (a guardian or the administrator of a deceased minor's estate) may exercise the right to disaffirm.

If the minor's contract involves title to real estate, the minor cannot disaffirm until reaching majority. This is due to the special importance the law has traditionally accorded to ownership of real property. The rule is designed to protect a minor from improvidently disaffirming a transaction involving such property.

RATIFICATION

The minor who does not disaffirm within a reasonable time after attaining majority is held to have **ratified** the contract and thereafter loses the right to disaffirm. The idea behind ratification is that adults who indicate an intent to be bound by contracts entered while still minors should be bound to those contracts and denied the right to disaffirm thereafter. As adults, they are assumed to have sufficient knowledge and experience to judge the wisdom of those contracts. By the same reasoning, minors, lacking such traits, cannot ratify contracts while still minors.

Any words or conduct on the part of a minor after reaching majority that clearly indicates an intent to be bound by the contract are enough for ratification. If the minor, after attaining majority, sells or gives away the consideration he or she received under the agreement, this is probably enough for ratification. Performing part of the contract after attaining majority, such as making payments or accepting some performance under the contract, is often treated as evidence of an intent to ratify. However, some states require a formal statement by the minor before they find ratification.

THE CONSEQUENCES OF DISAFFIRMING

Minors who successfully disaffirm a contract are entitled to the return of any consideration they have given the adult party to the contract. In return, minors are obligated

---

FLETCHER V. MARSHALL
632 N.E.2d 1105 (Ill. Ct. App. 1994)

FACTS

Kirsten Fletcher and John Marshall rented an apartment for a year. After a couple of months, the couple was not getting along and Marshall had a chance to go to college, so he moved out. Marshall signed the lease on April 29, 1991; he turned 18 by June 30, 1991. Fletcher sued him for half the rent, arguing that although he was a minor when he signed the contract, he ratified it by moving in and paying rent after attaining majority.

ISSUE

Has Marshall ratified the contract?

DECISION

Yes. A contract is not void *ab initio* but merely voidable at the election of the minor upon his attaining majority. After attaining majority, a minor is deemed to have ratified the contract if he fails to disaffirm it within a reasonable time and/or if he does any distinct and decisive act which clearly shows an intent to affirm. Once he has ratified, he cannot then disaffirm. Two weeks after turning 18, Marshall moved into the apartment and paid rent. He lived in the apartment about one and one-half months and never took any action before moving, evidencing an intention to disaffirm. This shows ratification, and he cannot disaffirm after moving out.

---

to return to the adult any consideration still in their possession that they received from the adult.

Under common law, minors are entitled to the return of their property given as consideration, even if that property is possessed by a third party at the time of disaffirmance. Suppose, for example, that Katie trades in her motorcycle on the purchase of a car from B-2 Used Cars. B-2 then sells the motorcycle to Leann. After experiencing several problems with the car, Katie decides to disaffirm the car sales contract. She must return the car but is entitled to reclaim the motorcycle from Leann. Leann, in turn, has to try to get her money back from B-2. In order to protect innocent third parties such as Leann, the Uniform Commercial Code changed the common law. Minors whose contracts involve goods can no longer reclaim those goods from innocent third parties.

A difficult problem arises when the minor is no longer in possession of the consideration the adult gave, or when the consideration has been partially consumed or damaged, or has otherwise declined in value. For example, Rebecca (age 17) buys a 1998 Toyota from B-2 Used Cars. Two months later, she totally wrecks the car. Rebecca then calls B-2 and says she is disaffirming the contract and wants her $300 down payment back, plus the two $125 monthly payments she has made. The question is: Must Rebecca place B-2 in *status quo ante* (the position B-2 would be in if the contract had never come into existence) by paying the reasonable value of the car? The traditional common law answer, and the one adopted by the *Mitchell v. Mizerski* court is that the minor who no longer has the consideration the adult gave does not have any duty to place the adult in status quo. In the context of the case at the beginning of the chapter, Matt and Pat, who have used the apartment for two months, have nothing to return to Webster Street. They can still get their rent back.

Ethical Implications   Is it ethical for minors to disaffirm otherwise fair contracts when they know they will be unable to return the adult to the status quo?

BARRIERS TO DISAFFIRMANCE

As you can see, the disaffirmance rule places severe hardship on adults in some cases. It was probably adopted as a deterrent, for what was to prevent adults from contracting with minors if the worst thing that could happen if the minor disaffirmed was that adults would get back whatever consideration they gave under the contract? Many courts today are reacting against the harshness of this rule by requiring the disaffirming minor to place the adult in status quo in some circumstances. This is especially true in cases where the minor is close to 18, the contract is fair, the adult was not at fault in contracting with the minor, and the adult would suffer an important loss if not returned to status quo.

Because of the potential unfairness to adults, a growing number of courts are also creating exceptions to the general rule that minors can disaffirm their contracts. This has happened, for example, in cases where minors have lied about their age. Similarly, state legislatures have passed statutes denying minors the right to disaffirm certain kinds of contracts. These statutes typically involve things such as contracts for medical care, life insurance, bank accounts, loans for college tuition, agreements to support children, contracts made while running a business, and employment contracts of minor professionals such as actors and athletes. Such contracts are usually required to be fair and sometimes require court approval.

SHELLER V. FRANK'S NURSERY & CRAFTS, INC.
957 F. Supp. 150 (N.D. Ill. 1997)

FACTS

When Sheller, a minor, applied for employment, she signed an application that said, "any claim that I may wish to file against the Company . . . must be submitted for binding and final arbitration . . . arbitration will be the exclusive remedy for any and all claims . . . I have reviewed, understand and agree to the above." Following her discharge by Frank's Nursery, Sheller filed a sexual harassment suit.

ISSUE

Can Sheller avoid arbitrating her claim because of her minority?

DECISION

No. The minority rule allows minors to disaffirm their contracts. As with most rules of law, however, there are exceptions. The right is to be used as a shield, not a sword. A minor's right to disaffirm should be exercised with some regard to the rights of others. Permitting Sheller to void the contract would be inconsistent with the public policy reasons underlying the infancy law doctrine. Arbitrating a statutory claim does not mean an individual forgoes substantive rights afforded by the statute; it only submits the claim to an arbitral rather than a judicial forum. Whether Sheller was a minor is irrelevant to her signing of the application agreement. Defendant required all its employees, including adults, to sign the same agreement.

EMANCIPATION

Emancipation is the term used to describe the termination of a parent's right to receive services and wages from a child and to generally control him. Emancipation can occur, for example, when a minor marries or gets a job and moves away from home and the parent does not object. No formalities are required. Emancipation does not usually give the minor the capacity to contract, as is shown by the following *Mitchell* case.

MITCHELL V. STATE FARM MUTUAL AUTOMOBILE INSURANCE CO.
963 S. W. 2d 222 (Ky. Ct. App. 1998)

FACTS

When Sherri Mitchell was 17, she was injured in a car accident. She signed a release with State Farm stating she agreed to settle her injury claim for $2,500. She later sought to repudiate the agreement, arguing lack of capacity. State Farm asserted that since Sherri was emancipated because of her marriage, she had the capacity to contract.

ISSUE

Does emancipation give a minor capacity to contract?

DECISION

No. A person under 18 lacks capacity to contract and can avoid contracts made by her during that time. Although parental emancipation may free the infant from parental control, it does not remove all of the disabilities of infancy. The capacity rule may seem antiquated in view of the arguable maturity of today's youth. It may seem ironic that a minor can drive a car yet not be bound by the contract to purchase the car. The distinction to be made is that too frequently a contract involves negotiation and thought beyond the maturity of most people under the age of 18. We cannot adopt a rule that marriage by the minor somehow classifies her as more mature and intelligent than her unmarried counterpart. Indeed, marriage by a minor too frequently may itself be indicative of a lack of wisdom and maturity.

MISREPRESENTATION OF AGE BY MINORS

Often, an adult faced with a minor's attempt to disaffirm a contract argues that the minor misrepresented his or her age. If the adult can prove this charge to the court's satisfaction, a question arises about what effect the misrepresentation should have on the minor's right to disaffirm. In theory, the right to disaffirm should not be affected, since one who lacks capacity cannot acquire it merely by claiming to have capacity.

In reality, however, the minor who misrepresents his or her age is not allowed to defraud adults by doing so. The courts have used several different methods to achieve this result. Some courts allow the minor to disaffirm but require the minor to place the adult in status quo. Others hold that the minor is *estopped* from raising the defense of minority and is therefore bound by the terms of the agreement. Many states allow the minor to disaffirm but hold the minor liable to the adult in tort for *deceit*.

NECESSARIES

Necessaries are generally defined as those things that are essential to a minor's continued existence and general welfare. Things that have traditionally been treated as necessaries include food, clothing, shelter, medical care, basic educational and/or vocational training, and the tools of a minor's trade. Items sold to a minor are not considered necessaries if the minor's parent or guardian has supplied or is willing to supply similar items. The court in the *Webster Street* case found that the apartment rental was not a necessary because the boys' parents were perfectly willing to have them live at home.

Minors are generally held liable on a *quasi contract* basis for the *reasonable value* of necessaries furnished to them. This is so because penalizing adults who supply minors with necessaries would not only produce an unfair result but also discourage other adults from supplying minors with necessaries. Since minors are liable for only the reasonable value of necessaries they actually receive, they do not have to pay the contract price of necessaries if it is greater than their reasonable value.

FIGURE 10-2   Necessaries

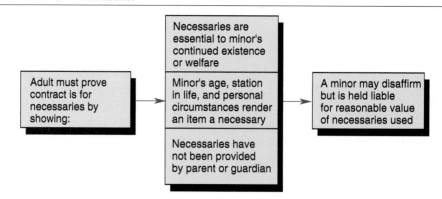

Minors also are not liable for the value of necessaries they have purchased under a contract but have not received at the time they disaffirm. For example, Mary Smith, a minor, rented an apartment in Tudor Village for $800 a month. She signed a one year lease. After living there three months, Mary decided to move to another apartment complex. Mary can disaffirm her lease because she lacked capacity to contract. She is liable for the reasonable value of three months' rent at Tudor Village, but she is not liable for the remaining nine months' rent (she has not actually received any benefits from the remainder of the lease). If she could convince the court that the reasonable value of living at Tudor Village was less than $800 a month, she would be liable only for the lesser amount.

Whether a given item is considered a necessary depends on the facts of the particular case. The minor's age, station in life, and personal circumstances are all relevant to this issue. Thus, a car may be considered a necessary for a minor who needs it to get to work but not for a high school student who merely wishes to avoid riding the school bus. As a general rule, the definition of necessary is widening to include things commonly considered important by today's standards. The adult has the burden of proving that an item is a necessary.

SCHMIDT V. PRINCE GEORGE'S HOSPITAL
784 A.2d 1112 (Md. Ct. App. 2001)

FACTS

In 1997, when Schmidt was 16, she was involved in a car accident. She was taken to the emergency room of Prince George's Hospital. Because she was unconscious, the hospital could not contact her parents, but it provided necessary emergency medical care for a brain concussion and an open scalp wound. When she was discharged the next day, Schmidt's bill totaled $1,756.24. Schmidt was insured under her father's policy, and the insurance company sent her father a check for $1,756.24. The check was cashed but the father did not pay the hospital; he used the money to buy a replacement car for

Schmidt. After unsuccessful attempts to get Schmidt to pay, the hospital sued her for the amount owed soon after she reached the age of majority.

ISSUE

Was the hospital's treatment a necessary for which Schmidt is liable?

DECISION

Yes. The prevailing rule is that a minor's contracts are voidable. Normally, people who deal with minors deal

(continued)

SCHMIDT V. PRINCE GEORGE'S HOSPITAL
(concluded)

with them at their peril. The law takes care of minors to prevent them from being imposed upon or overreached by persons of more years and experience. However, minors are liable for necessaries such as board, apparel, and medical treatment. The services rendered here were reasonable and fair, and possibly life-saving. They were a necessary. If the parent is able and willing to pay for the provision of such services, the necessaries doctrine does not apply because parents are responsible for their children's necessaries. Here it can be shown that the parent is unwilling to pay, and thus Schmidt can be held liable. While this might seem unfair to the minor, it is more important as a matter of public policy to not place hospitals and other emergency health care providers in a situation where apparently financially able individuals may avoid paying for necessary medical treatment.

FIGURE 10-3   Minors' Right to Disaffirm

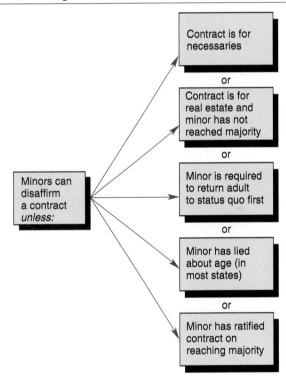

CONTRACTS OF MENTALLY IMPAIRED AND INTOXICATED PERSONS

THEORY OF INCAPACITY

Like minors, people suffering from mental impairment can lack the capacity to contract. Often referred to as "insanity" in cases and books, lack of mental capacity can be induced by a variety of causes such as mental illness, brain damage, retardation, or senility. The basic reason for holding that such persons lack the capacity to contract is that we presume they are unable to bargain effectively with those who do not share their disability. Many states treat intoxicated persons like people who lack mental capacity if, at the time they entered the agreement, they were so intoxicated from drugs or alcohol that they were unable to understand the nature of the business at hand.

THE TEST OF INCAPACITY

The test usually applied in contract law is whether a party, at the time the contract was entered into, had sufficient mental capacity to understand the nature and effect of the contract. A person could be medically insane (e.g., suffering from paranoid delusions) but still have the legal capacity to contract. A person could be periodically insane but enter a binding contract during a lucid moment. A person could be senile, of less-than-ordinary intelligence, or highly neurotic but still be able to understand the nature of the transaction.

THE EFFECT OF INCAPACITY

If a court later finds that a person lacked mental capacity at the time the contract was entered into, the contract is *voidable* at the election of that person (or his or her guardian or administrator). A distinction is made between such agreements and those made by persons who had been adjudicated insane before entering the agreement. *Adjudicated* in this context means a general hearing was held on the person's mental competency, and the court determined that the person was of unsound mind and appointed a guardian or conservator of the person's estate. In most states, the agreements of persons who have been adjudicated insane are *void.*

NECESSARIES

People lacking mental capacity are liable for the *reasonable value* of necessaries on the same basis and for the same reasons as minors.

THE RIGHT TO DISAFFIRM

Like minors, people lacking mental capacity can disaffirm their contracts, and on disaffirmance, must return any consideration they received that they still have. Must they also place the other party in status quo? The answer depends on whether the other party was on notice of the person's lack of capacity. If there was no reason to know of the other party's lack of capacity, the contract cannot be disaffirmed without placing him or her in status quo. If, on the other hand, he or she knew or should have known of the other party's incapacity, the person lacking such capacity is allowed to disaffirm without restoring the status quo. This rule punishes those who may try to take advantage of people who lack capacity but protects those who have no such intent.

RATIFICATION

People who regain their capacity can ratify their contracts just like a minor who attains majority. If the person dies or is adjudicated insane, his or her personal representative may ratify the contract. Ratification has the same effect in this context that it does in minors' contracts.

SARVER V. BELLSOUTH TELECOMMUNICATIONS, INC.
1996 U.S. Dist. LEXIS 12148 (D.E. La. 1996)

FACTS

After working for BellSouth for 22 years, Sarver resigned pursuant to a plan offered by the company. He signed a release waiving all potential claims against the company pertaining to his termination. In exchange for signing the release, he received $14,085. Eight months later he filed suit against BellSouth, alleging it violated the Americans with Disabilities Act (ADA). BellSouth argued that his suit was barred by the release and that Sarver had ratified the release by keeping the $14,085. Sarver defended his right to sue by alleging that he lacked capacity to execute the release, that he was intimidated into making his decision, and that he was financially unable to return the money.

ISSUE

Did Sarver ratify the waiver?

DECISION

Yes. Sarver was treated for alcoholism at various times while working for BellSouth. However, Sarver does not allege this as affecting his capacity; rather, he cites depression and suicidal tendencies at the time of his signing. A contract made by a person deprived of reason at the time of contracting is either null or voidable. However, the person can cure the contractual defect by confirming or ratifying the agreement. Several courts have held that failure to return the consideration received for a release after learning that it is voidable ratifies the release. Sarver has manifested an intent to be bound by the waiver and has made a new promise to abide by the terms of the release. Even if Sarver attempted to return the payment now, it would be "too little, too late." He knew of the voidability when he filed his suit. To avoid ratification, he had to return it "soon after."

CONCEPT SUMMARY   **Lack of Capacity**

A contract is voidable due to:
1. Lack of capacity because of minority.
   Exceptions (i.e., situations where contracts are not voidable):
   a. Contract is for necessaries.
   b. Contract is ratified on reaching majority.
   c. Minor lied about age (in some states).

2. Lack of capacity because of mental impairment.
   Exceptions (i.e., situations where contracts are not voidable):
   a. If adjudicated insane, contract is void.
   b. Contract is for necessaries.
   c. Contract is ratified on regaining capacity.

.... *QUESTIONS AND PROBLEM CASES* ....

1. Explain why minors are allowed to disaffirm their contracts.
2. Explain three limitations on a minor's right to disaffirm a contract.
3. Explain the test for mental incapacity in contract law.
4. Dodson, 16, bought a truck for $4,900 in cash from Shrader. After driving it for nine months, he took it to a mechanic to check out a problem and was told there was a burned valve in the engine. Dodson drove the truck for two

more months without repairs, until the engine "blew up." Later, the inoperable truck was struck while parked and damaged further. Dodson tendered the truck to Shrader and demanded his $4,900 back. Shrader refused to return the money without being paid the difference between the value of the truck as tendered, which was $500, and the $4,900. Must Dodson put Shrader in status quo?
5. When Reynaldo Garay was 2½, he walked between two parked cars and into the path

of a car driven by Overholtzer. Reynaldo was seriously injured. Five years later, his parents sought damages from Overholtzer. However, their suit was barred by the statute of limitations. They then brought suit in Reynaldo's name for medically related expenses he might incur because his claims were not barred until a reasonable time after he reached majority. Overholtzer defended by arguing that Reynaldo had no claim because his parents were liable for his medical expenses. Is Overholtzer excused under the doctrine of necessaries?

6. Michaelis, 17, consulted Dr. Schori for pregnancy-related medical care. During her first visit she signed a binding arbitration agreement. When she went into labor, Schori told her another doctor would attend her at the hospital, but he never showed up. Michaelis's pregnancy-induced hypertension was not detected, and her baby was stillborn. When Michaelis sued for malpractice, Schori asserted the matter had to be arbitrated. Can Michaelis disaffirm the arbitration agreement?

7. When actress Brooke Shields was 10, she posed nude in a bathtub for a series of photographs taken by Gary Gross for Playboy Press. Shields's mother signed a consent form that gave Gross the right to use the photos at any time for any purpose. The pictures were used several times, including use in a book by Shields about her life. When she was 17, Shields attempted to stop additional use of the photos by disaffirming the consent. Gross defended by citing a New York statute that allowed parents to give consent for minor models. Did New York's statute deny Shields her common law right to disaffirm the contract?

8. Rotondo bought a diamond ring from Kay Jewelry Company. He told Kay that he was a minor and that he was buying it as an engagement ring. He made a part payment of $94.49 on the ring and on that same day presented the ring to his fiancée. Eight months later, the engagement was ended but the ring was not returned. Rotondo asked Kay to repossess the ring shortly after the engagement was broken, but there was no evidence that it was repossessed. Rotondo sought to disaffirm the contract for the ring, and Kay argued that he could not do so without returning the ring. Can Rotondo disaffirm?

9. The Home Saving and Loan Association loaned Haith money to refinance her mortgage and remodel her home. Haith was later adjudicated incompetent and a guardian was appointed for her. The guardian sought to have the loan set aside on the basis of Haith's incompetency despite the fact that Haith could not return what she had received. Will the guardian succeed?

10. After staying home and raising four children, Adams became an employee at Lehigh University. Ten years later, after the end of a secret five-year homosexual relationship, she realized her marriage was in trouble and began psychological counseling. She later separated from her husband but continued therapy. During a session, at which her husband was present, he asked his wife, "What do you want?" She wrote on a piece of paper that she wanted the house, her car, the joint bank accounts, and a computer. The husband took the note to his attorney, who drafted a property settlement on its basis. Karen, ignoring the advice of her psychologist to hire her own attorney, signed the agreement. She later challenged the agreement on the ground of incapacity. Will she succeed?

CHAPTER 11

Voluntary Consent

Johnson bought a house from Davis for $310,000. He had noticed peeling plaster and ceiling stains in the family room but the sellers implied they were caused by a minor window problem that had been repaired. A few days later, after a heavy rain, he discovered water gushing into the house, and was told that $25,000 in repairs to the roof and walls were required.

- *Do buyers have a duty to make their own investigations before entering contracts?*
- *Do sellers have a duty to disclose latent defects?*
- *Can Johnson disaffirm the contract?*

FIGURE 11–1   Voluntary Consent

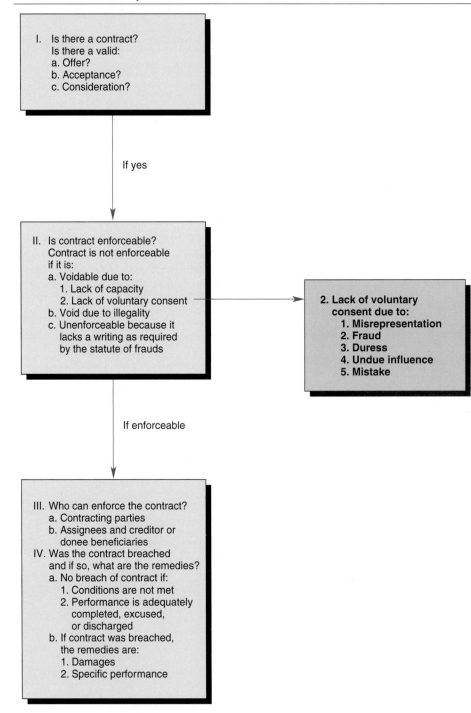

. . . . *INTRODUCTION* . . . .

THE NEED FOR REAL CONSENT

Even if the facts and circumstances surrounding a case indicate that the parties reached an agreement, that agreement must be **voluntary** to be enforceable. This is so because the idea that a contract is a voluntary agreement between the parties is the basis of contract law. The common law came to recognize several kinds of behavior that could operate to take away a person's ability to freely enter into a contract: misrepresentation, fraud, duress, and undue influence. The courts also came to recognize that a mistake of fact on the part of one or both of the parties could sometimes prevent a true agreement from being reached.

THE PARTIES' DUTY OF CARE

People who enter into contracts are required to exercise reasonable caution and judgment. The rules requiring voluntary consent are designed to protect a party to a contract from innocent errors on his or her own part and from unacceptable behavior by the other party to the agreement. A person should use reasonable care to discover everything relevant to the contract he or she is about to enter. Rarely do the courts allow a party to avoid responsibility for a carelessly made promise.

THE REMEDY

Contracts entered into as a result of misrepresentation, fraud, duress, undue influence, and certain kinds of mistakes are **voidable.** The injured party (or parties) may **rescind** (cancel) the contract. The injured person returns what he or she has received and recovers what he or she has given under the contract. If no performance has yet been rendered when the grounds for rescission are discovered, the injured party may notify the other party that he or she **disaffirms** (denies the validity of) the contract. If the other party sues for breach of contract, the injured party can use lack of voluntary consent as a defense.

RATIFICATION

Those who discover that they have been the victim of misrepresentation, fraud, duress, undue influence, or mistake must act promptly to rescind or disaffirm their contracts. The person who waits for an unreasonable time after discovery to complain may be held to have **ratified** the contract and may lose the power to rescind. The idea behind the doctrine of ratification is simple: One who waits too long to complain has indicated satisfaction with the agreement despite the initial lack of true consent.

. . . . *MISREPRESENTATION* . . . .

The basic idea of misrepresentation is that one of the parties to a contract created in the mind of the other party a mistaken impression about an important fact or facts concerning the subject of the contract. Acting in reliance on this mistaken belief, the victimized party entered into a contract he or she would not otherwise have entered if the full truth had been known. The elements of **misrepresentation** are ordinarily given as *misrepresentation* of a *material fact justifiably relied on* to the *detriment* of (causing harm to) the person relying. Note that a mere untrue assertion is not sufficient. A person seeking to avoid a contract on the ground of misrepresentation must prove all of these elements.

KNOWLEDGE OF FALSITY

Note also that none of the elements listed above requires any proof that persons guilty of the misrepresentation know that their statement is untrue. Misrepresentation can result from an honest mistake or negligence on the part of the misrepresenter. This is so because of the long-standing equitable principle that one who makes a statement bears the risk of its truth.

MATERIALITY

A *material* fact is one that would contribute to a reasonable person's decision to enter the contract. Materiality is determined by the circumstances of each particular case. For example, assume that Bob, who was living in Illinois, bought real estate by mail through Fran, a Florida real estate agent. Fran sent Bob several pictures of the house and a general description of the house and its neighborhood. Included in the description was the statement that the house was "within easy walking distance of schools, churches, and shopping centers." After moving in, Bob discovers that the closest school is four miles away. Is this misrepresentation sufficiently material to justify rescission?

The answer depends on who Bob is. If Bob is a retired, childless widower, the misrepresentation could be judged to be immaterial. On the other hand, if Bob has a child in school, the nearness of schools could well be considered material.

FACT VERSUS OPINION

In addition to being material, an actionable misrepresentation must concern a present or past *fact*. This is another way of saying that the subject of the misrepresentation must be *knowable*. Statements about future events ("This stock will double in price in the next two years") or statements of opinion ("This is the most attractive house in the neighborhood") do not serve as a basis for rescission, although people may, in fact, rely on them. One of the constant problems in this area is whether a given statement was mere *puffing* (a term used to indicate sales talk) or amounted to an actionable misstatement of material fact. For example, the seller who says, "This is a good car" is probably puffing, whereas the seller who says, "This car was owned by an elderly man

---

SPERAU V. FORD MOTOR CO.
1995 Ala. LEXIS 263 (Sup. Ct. Ala. 1995)

FACTS

Ford Motor Company had a program to recruit African-Americans to be franchise dealers. Sperau was working in the construction business in North Carolina when Ford recruited him to open a dealership in Alabama. He was initially reluctant, but Ford reduced the capital required to operate from $632,000 to $535,000 and increased the estimated return on capital from 56 percent to 64.5 percent. They also told him that a vast majority of black dealers were successful and making a profit. At that time Ford reports showed that return on investment for black dealers was substantially lower than the average for all dealers and that a higher percentage of black dealers

were in a loss position. Ford did not reveal this. Sperau opened a dealership in 1988; it went bankrupt in 1991. When Sperau sued, Ford's defenses, among others, were that the representations regarding sales and return on profit were not facts but merely opinions regarding future events which could not be relied on, and that race-based figures were not material.

ISSUE

Were the statements regarding estimated return on capital merely opinions? Was the race-based data immaterial?

(continued)

SPERAU V. FORD MOTOR CO.
(concluded)

DECISION

No. Where the facts are not equally known to both parties, a statement of opinion by one who knows the facts better often involves a statement of material fact that justifies the opinion, so that an action can be based on the statement. There was substantial evidence that Ford occupied a superior position with respect to historical information, as evidenced by its reports, which could predict future sales and profits. Additionally, Ford had established its own guidelines regarding initial capital requirements. Sperau did not have this information at his disposal and thus had to rely on the statements made by

Ford regarding the dealership. Ford manipulated the information to aggressively recruit Sperau. A Ford executive testified that if he were called upon to prepare a profit and sales forecast and/or capital requirement for a newly appointed black dealer, he would certainly take the fact the dealer was a minority into consideration. Sperau was an educated, sophisticated businessman. However, Ford had superior and historical knowledge regarding the expected performance of its new dealers and knew that minority dealers were predicted to be loss dealers. This was material information.

who drove it only twice a week" is probably guilty of misrepresentation if the car was actually used by a drag racer. Often the result will turn on whether the person making the statement had superior knowledge and bargaining power.

JUSTIFIABLE RELIANCE

There are basically two ideas behind making justifiable reliance an element of misrepresentation. The first is the idea that there should be some *causal connection* between a misrepresentation and the complaining party's entry into the contract. If the complaining party knew the truth, or for some other reason did not in fact rely on the misrepresentation, why should it be a basis for canceling the contract? The second idea behind justifiable reliance is that parties who enter a contract must take reasonable steps to discover the facts about the contracts they enter into. So, if the facts are readily discoverable by either party (e.g., by reasonable inspection or because they are a matter of public record), a party generally is not allowed to rely on the other party's statements about them.

The *Restatement (Second) of Contracts* and many courts are placing less stress on the justifiable reliance requirement. However, as a general rule, people are still required to make a reasonable effort to watch out for themselves.

GRIESI V. ATLANTIC GENERAL HOSPITAL
756 A.2d 548 (Md. Ct. App. 2000)

FACTS

Griesi, a physical therapist, applied for a job at Atlantic General (AG). Slater, AG's acting chief executive officer (CEO), interviewed Griesi, told him he wanted to train and mentor him, and took him on a tour of the hospital. Two weeks later Griesi called Slater, and Slater said he expected to make a job offer soon. Griesi then received a job offer from another company and called Slater to see whether AG was going to offer him a job. After discussing

starting dates and salary over the next several days, Slater called Griesi and offered him a job. He stated that it had been approved by the chairman of the board. Griesi accepted the job the next day and turned down other job offers. Five days later Griesi received a written contract, signed by Slater, on AG's letterhead. AG then got a new CEO, and questions were raised about Griesi's employment, but Slater assured him he still was hired.

(continued)

GRIESI v. ATLANTIC GENERAL HOSPITAL
(concluded)

AG subsequently told Griesi it was not hiring him and that Slater did not have the authority to do so.

ISSUE

Did Griesi justifiably rely on Slater's representations?

DECISION

Yes. AG, through its agent, employee, and acting CEO, Slater, misrepresented several related facts at the time the offer of employment was made including (1) that Slater was authorized to make an offer of employment and hire employees for AG, (2) that the interviewing and selection process was complete, and (3) that Griesi could rely on AG's performance after he accepted the job. Griesi justifiably relied on these misrepresentations to his detriment.

It is not unreasonable to rely on information provided by a CEO in making a career decision about which corporation could best meet a job candidate's present and future personal and professional needs and plans. Businesspeople routinely rely on statements made about the workings of a corporation by its CEO. It is clear that if the CEO voluntarily gave specific, relevant, and persuasive information to Griesi about the corporation in the course of their serious and deliberate negotiations, and Griesi relied on that information to make a decision about whether to enter into a contract with AG, and that information was false, foreseeable, and considerable harm would befall him.

DETRIMENT

The courts do not allow a person who claims to have been victimized by a misrepresentation to cancel the contract unless he or she can show some *detriment* (injury) as a result of the misrepresentation. Ordinarily, however, if one can prove the other elements of misrepresentation (particularly the "material fact" element), it is fairly easy to show injury. All that must be shown is that the complaining party would be in a better position if things were as they had been represented. See Figure 11–2.

FIGURE 11–2   Misrepresentation

Defendant:	Misrepresented a fact	→	The fact was material		
Plaintiff:	Relied on the fact	→	Reliance was justified	→	Plaintiff was harmed by reliance

FRAUD

In some cases, the complaining party may be able to prove that the party who made the misstatement knew or should have known that it was untrue. **Fraud** is intentional misrepresentation. To prove fraud, one must prove all the elements of misrepresentation plus two additional elements: that the misrepresentation was (1) *knowingly* made with the (2) *intent to deceive* (technically called *scienter*).

WHAT IS A "KNOWINGLY MADE" MISSTATEMENT?

Clearly, if it can be shown that a defendant actually knew that what he or she said was untrue, a "knowing" misstatement has been proven. It is also sufficient to show that the defendant possessed enough information so that he should have known the truth, even if he actually did not. So, if Acme Used Cars tells Mary that the Pinto is in excellent running order although Acme has not bothered to check out the statement of the previous owner that the car was making strange noises and there might be something wrong with it, Mary could probably show fraud. Acme should have known, based on the prior owner's statements, that something was probably wrong and should have checked it out. Mary could also show that Acme made the statement *recklessly.* Making statements without sufficient information to believe they are true (recklessness) is sufficient to constitute fraud.

In the *Johnson* case at the beginning of this chapter, the seller of the home must have known, or at least was recklessly ignorant of the fact that there were major problems with the roof. When Johnson inquired about the stains, and the seller implied the problem was due to a window that had been fixed, the response was sufficient for fraud and Johnson could rescind the contract.

INTENT TO DECEIVE

Scienter refers to the mental state of the defendant. The courts generally infer an intent to deceive from the fact that the defendant knowingly made a misstatement to a plaintiff who was likely to rely on it. The defendant's motivation is irrelevant; she may actually believe that she is doing the plaintiff a favor. For example, Beth is trying to sell her friend Mike a car. Beth thinks that the car is a good one and that the price is a real bargain. Beth knows, however, that the car's odometer was disconnected for a year and that the car has much higher mileage on it than the odometer indicates. She tells Mike that the car "has only 20,000 miles on it" (the figure the odometer shows). Beth is guilty of fraud.

Taking action to conceal a fact also indicates *scienter.* So if Beth turned back the odometer from 30,000 to 20,000 miles but said nothing about the mileage to Mike, she would be guilty of fraud. Likewise, concealing something in fine print in the middle of a lengthy document in the reasonable belief that the other party will not read it can be evidence of fraud.

HORD V. ENVIRONMENTAL RESEARCH INSTITUTE OF MICHIGAN
579 N.W.2d 133 (Mich. Ct. App. 1998)

FACTS

Hord was working at G.E. when he started looking for another job. At a job interview with ERIM in 1992, he was given a copy of its financial summary for the 1991 fiscal year instead of the one for 1992. The financial position of ERIM had significantly deteriorated during that time. ERIM discussed hiring Hord to develop a new program in high-performance computing, and there was a discussion of how long ERIM would be willing to support such a program before it became self-sustaining. ERIM hired Hord in January 1993. In January 1994 his employment was reduced to 80 percent, and in June he was notified of a layoff. He then resigned and sued ERIM for fraud, alleging that ERIM knowingly made false representations

regarding its disposition and ability to fund long-range projects in order to induce Hord to work for it.

ISSUE

Was Hord fraudulently induced to enter an employment contract with ERIM?

DECISION

There are six essential elements of a fraud claim: (1) that defendant make a material misrepresentation; (2) that is false; (3) that the defendant knew it was false or made it recklessly; (4) that defendant made it with the intention that plaintiff should rely on it; (5) that the plaintiff acted

(continued)

HORD V. ENVIRONMENTAL RESEARCH INSTITUTE OF MICHIGAN
(concluded)

in reliance; and (6) that the plaintiff thereby suffered injury. ERIM showed the 1991 statement as a representation that it was a reflection of its current financial strength. This was obviously a material statement. It had a more current statement that showed it was in a much weaker financial condition. This is evidence that ERIM knew its representation was false when it made it. Hord would not have accepted the job had he known of ERIM's financial status. There is evidence for all the elements of fraud.

FRAUD BY SILENCE

Does a party to a contract have a duty to disclose to the other party all the material facts he or she knows about the subject of the contract? The original common law position on this issue was *caveat emptor* (let the buyer beware). The seller could remain silent without fear of being found guilty of fraud. Only actual statements by the seller could serve as a basis for fraud. The duty, therefore, was placed on buyers to ask the right questions of the seller, forcing the seller to make statements about the subject of the sale.

Today, however, many courts recognize that *caveat emptor* often produced unfair results. Some buyers simply do not know enough to ask the right questions about the subject of the sale, so many courts are recognizing a limited duty on the part of the seller to disclose material facts. Generally, this duty is limited to material facts that the buyer could not have discovered by reasonable inspection and would be unlikely to inquire about.

Some courts consider the duty to disclose to be especially important in the consumer real estate sales area. Since the purchase of a home is the largest investment most consumers make, courts are increasingly protecting that investment by holding knowledgeable developers, sellers, and their agents liable when they fail to reveal defects or problems that seriously undermine the value of the home. In the introductory *Johnson* case, the seller may have had a duty to disclose major defects in the roof that allowed water to "cascade in" even if Johnson had not inquired about the stains.

STAMBOVSKY V. ACKLEY
572 N.Y.S.2d 672 (App. Div. N.Y. 1991)

FACTS

Stambovsky, to his horror, discovered that the house he had recently contracted to buy was commonly reputed to be possessed by poltergeists. Ackley, the seller of the house, had widely publicized their presence including stories in both *Reader's Digest* and the local press, and on a walking tour of the Village of Nyack, New York, where the house was located. Stambovsky sought to rescind the contract of sale.

ISSUE

Did the seller have a duty to disclose the fact that the house was haunted to the buyer?

DECISION

Yes. Whether the source of the spectral apparitions seen by Ackley are parapsychic or psychogenic, having reported them on a national and local level, she is estopped from denying their existence. From the perspective of Stambovsky, a very practical problem arises regarding the discovery of paranormal phenomenon: "Who you gonna call?" While in New York *caveat emptor* normally rules in real estate transactions, where fairness and common sense dictate that an exception should be created, the evolution of the law should not be stiffed by

(continued)

STAMBOVSKY V. ACKLEY
(concluded)

rigid application of a legal maxim. The impact of the reputation of the house, as created by Ackley, goes to the very essence of the bargain between the parties. As a resident of New York City, Stambovsky could not be expected to have any familiarity with the folklore of Nyack. Ackley acted reasonably in inspecting the premises and doing a title search. The most thorough search, however, would not unearth the property's ghoulish reputation. Where a condition that has been created by the seller materially impairs the value of the contract and is peculiarly within the knowledge of the seller and unlikely to be discovered by the prudent buyer, rescission is called for. The court was "moved by the spirit of equity to allow rescission."

Legislatures are also expanding the situations in which persons must make disclosures. For example, the Truth in Lending Act[1] and the federal securities laws[2] both mandate that certain information be disclosed. Additionally, several states have passed laws requiring specific disclosures in real estate transactions.

Ethical Implications	When does a party have an ethical duty to disclose information to the other party to the contract?

FRAUD IN THE EXECUTION

Fraud in the execution involves misstatements about the content or legal effect of something usually contained in a form or preprinted contract. People who relied on the misstatement rather than reading the document for themselves were seen as not having justifiably relied and thus usually could not claim fraud. While this rule is still true, if the signer was in some way prevented or discouraged from reading the contract, or if a special relationship involving trust and confidence existed between the parties and this led to the person not understanding the nature of the document she was signing, fraud in the execution resulted. This type of fraud generally prevents a contract from being created.

THE REMEDY FOR FRAUD

The buyer who can prove fraudulent misstatements or failure to disclose on the part of the seller has a choice of remedies. He or she may *rescind* the contract, like the buyer who can only prove misrepresentation. A defrauded buyer also has the option of *affirming* the contract and suing in tort for damages resulting from the fraud. This is so because the elements of fraud are the same as the elements for the tort of **deceit.** The buyer could recover actual damages resulting from the fraud (usually the difference between the true value of what the buyer bought and its represented value). So, if Bob bought a car from Frank for $500 and Frank told him it was in excellent condition, knowing its transmission was bad, Bob can choose his remedies. He can rescind the contract, return the car, and get back his $500; or he can keep the car and sue for $100 (the difference between the purchase price and the true value of the car with a

---

[1]See Chapter 42 for further discussion of this act.
[2]See Chapter 25 for further discussion of these laws.

FIGURE 11–3   Fraud

Defendant:	*Intentionally* misrepresented a fact	→	The fact was material		
Plaintiff:	Relied on the fact	→	Reliance was justified	→	Plaintiff was harmed by reliance

defective transmission). Bob might also be able to get punitive damages since fraud is intentional wrongdoing. See Figure 11–3.

DURESS AND UNDUE INFLUENCE

GENERAL NATURE

Duress and *undue influence* are terms used to describe situations in which one party to an agreement interfered with the other party's ability to resist entering into the agreement. The basic idea of **duress** is that one of the parties, by making some *threat of harm,* forced the other party to enter an agreement he or she would not otherwise have entered. **Undue influence** is closely related to duress, but it exists only when the parties had some confidential relationship at the time of the contract. The basic idea of undue influence is that the dominant person in a confidential relationship took advantage of the other party to the relationship by getting the other party to enter into an unfavorable agreement.

Contracts made under duress and undue influence are *voidable* because the injured party has been deprived of the ability to make a free choice. Their promise is not a voluntary one as required by contract law. Note that both duress and undue influence must be exerted at the time the contract is entered into; exerting such force later will not make the contract voidable.

DURESS

The common law courts originally required a threat of physical injury before they would find duress. Modern courts require only that the *threat* be a *wrongful* one.

Whether an act is wrongful depends on the facts and circumstances of the particular case. A threat to breach a contract can be wrongful if it appears that the person making the threat is attempting to extort additional payments when he has no reasonable justification for breaching the contract. Threatening economic harm or withholding someone's property without justification can also be wrongful. To be sufficient for duress, the threatened harm must be such that a disastrous loss would occur if the threat were carried out. It is not wrongful to take advantage of someone's difficult financial condition to drive a hard bargain if the bargainer did not create the difficulty.

The *Restatement* and most courts take the position that a threat of criminal prosecution is wrongful pressure even though the person making the threat has good reason to believe that the other person has committed a crime.

The courts have generally held that the threat of a well-founded civil suit is not duress. If this were not so, every party who settled a suit out of court could later argue duress. If, however, the threat is used to force the party to enter an unfair transaction that is unrelated to the rights involved in the threatened suit, this can be duress. For example, a husband in the process of divorcing his wife may threaten to sue for custody of their children (something he has a legal right to do) unless she gives him stock she

FIGURE 11–4   Duress

Defendant:	Threatened	→	Threat was wrongful
Plaintiff:	Free will was overcome	→	Entered into a contract that would not otherwise have been entered into

owns in his company. The threat of an unfounded civil suit could also constitute duress if the fear of the expense of defending the suit forced the threatened party to enter an agreement against his or her will.

If the act is wrongful, the basic question the courts ask is whether that act effectively deprived the other party of his or her ability to resist entering the agreement. Did the wrongful act leave the person with no reasonable alternative but to enter the contract? See Figure 11–4.

CROSSTALK PRODUCTIONS, INC. v. JACOBSON
65 Cal. Rptr. 2d 615 (Cal. Ct. App. 1998)

FACTS

Keith and Cross were employees of CBS. They approached their supervisor, Jacobson, about their idea of forming an outside company to provide video promotion spots. He was in charge of selecting outside vendors, and he told plaintiffs he thought they could get a contract with CBS. They met with Jacobson and his supervisor, who approved an exclusive contract to provide spots. Plaintiffs were asked to remain at CBS until replacements could be hired; they agreed but told management they were leaving to form their company, CrossTalk Productions. The next day Jacobson told plaintiffs he wanted them to "help him out" because he had done them a favor and asked for $500 per month. Plaintiffs, although shocked and distressed, reluctantly agreed because Jacobson had the ability to fire them and to kill the contract once they were out on their own; he had their economic future in his hands. They were intimidated by him and his power at CBS, and feared they would lose their jobs and the contracts if they told anyone; they felt they had no alternative. They made three payments, and then Jacobson demanded they pay $1,000 per month. When they could not pay the $1,000, Jacobson raised problems with CrossTalk's work and a cancellation of their contract seemed imminent. Plaintiffs told CBS about Jacobson's demands. CBS fired Jacobson, and a few months later, canceled CrossTalk's contract on the basis of "admitted wrongdoing." Plaintiffs sued under a theory of economic duress, among others.

ISSUE

Are plaintiffs' claims sufficient to allow them to proceed under a theory of economic duress?

DECISION

Yes. Plaintiffs believed that they had no reasonable alternative under the circumstances but to accede to defendant's demands in order to make sure the contract they had negotiated with CBS would be finalized. This was necessary due to Jacobson's extortionate threats. Whether there was a reasonable alternative must be judged against whether a reasonably prudent person would follow the same course.

UNDUE INFLUENCE

The basic idea behind undue influence is to protect the old, the timid, and the physically or mentally weak from those who gain their confidence and attempt to take advantage of them. Victims of undue influence must have the mental capacity to contract but lack the ability to adequately protect themselves against unscrupulous persons who gain their confidence. In most states, a confidential relationship raises a presumption of undue influence that the benefiting party must disprove.

Most of the cases in which undue influence is charged involve relatives, friends, or long-time advisors (such as lawyers or bankers) of an elderly or sick person, who are alleged to have gotten the victim to make gifts or sales at unfair prices. For example, Marge Johnson, age 84, spent her last five years living with her daughter Joan. Marge had been in poor health and was unable to care for herself. When Marge died, her other heirs discovered that two weeks before her death, Marge had sold her house to Joan for $90,000. The market value of the house at the time of the sale was $150,000. The other heirs may attempt to have the sale set aside, arguing that it is the product of undue influence. Joan will probably argue that Marge knew the true value of the house but sold it to her at the lower price as a reward for taking care of her for so many years. Whether this was, in fact, undue influence depends on Marge's mental state, Joan's behavior, and Marge's knowledge of the value of the property.

Ethical Implications	The undue influence rules generally are used to protect the very old or very young. Do we have special ethical duties to these classes of people? Why or why not? Are there other classes to which we owe special duties of care?

.... *MISTAKE* ....

THE NATURE OF MISTAKE

The term *mistake* is used in contract law to describe the situation in which one or both of the parties to an agreement acted under an untrue belief about the existence or nonexistence of a *material fact.* The things that were said about materiality and fact in the section on misrepresentation hold true in mistake cases. In **mistake** cases, unlike fraud and misrepresentation cases in which the victim is also acting under a mistaken belief about the facts, the mistaken belief about the facts is not the product of a misstatement by the other party. Mistake in this sense does not include errors of judgment, ignorance, or a party's mistaken belief that he or she will be able to fulfill certain obligations under a contract.

The reason behind the idea of mistake is that mistake may prevent the "meeting of the minds" required by contract law. In deciding mistake cases, courts often seem to be trying more obviously to "do justice" than in other kinds of cases. This is why decisions in mistake cases sometimes seem to depart from the announced rules of law dealing with mistake.

MUTUAL MISTAKE

Mistake cases are classed as **mutual** or **unilateral,** depending on whether both or only one of the parties was acting under a mistaken belief about a material fact. Mutual mistake is always a basis for granting rescission of the contract at the request of either party. Clearly, no meeting of the minds took place and therefore no true contract was ever formed.

Mutual mistake can arise in many different ways. The parties may unintentionally use a term in their agreement that is *ambiguous*—capable of being honestly understood in two different ways. For example, on August 13, 2002, Apex Imports, Inc., of New York City, orders a shipment of Oriental rugs from Bristol Carpets, Ltd., of Bristol, England. Apex requests that the carpets be shipped on the *China Seas,* a ship scheduled to leave Liverpool, England, on August 15, 2002, for New York. Bristol accepts Apex's order, thinking Apex means another ship with the same name scheduled to leave Liverpool on December 1, 2002. Since Apex was unaware of the second ship, its order did not specify a shipment date. Neither party to the agreement is at fault, and either may elect to rescind the agreement. The test for determining the existence of a mutual mistake is, however, an *objective* one. This means that objective factors may remove what first looks like ambiguity.

The parties may also be mistaken about the subject matter of their agreement. For example, Kathy owns a Mercedes and a Porsche. Bob has always wanted a Porsche and knows Kathy owns one. Kathy decides to sell her Mercedes and buy a BMW. A mutual friend of Bob and Kathy tells Bob, "Kathy's selling her car." Thinking Kathy is selling the Porsche (he does not know she also has a Mercedes), Bob calls Kathy and says, "I'll give you $9,500 for your car." Kathy, thinking Bob is talking about the Mercedes, says, "You've got a deal." Obviously, there is not meeting of the minds in this case.

STATE OF ALASKA V. CARPENTER
268 P. 2d 1181 (Alaska Sup. Ct. 1994)

FACTS

Carpenter made two separate contracts to buy two parcels of land from the state of Alaska. Both contracts contained the following language, "The Seller makes no warranty, express or implied, nor assumes any liability whatever, regarding the social, economic, or environmental aspects of the Parcel [including] the soil conditions, water drainage, or natural or artificial hazards." The contracts also required the buyer to develop the land as a working farm but did not warrant it was suitable for that use. Carpenter signed a statement saying he had inspected the parcel, or had voluntarily declined to do so, and was satisfied with its description. He borrowed money from the Agricultural Revolving Loan Fund (ARLF), a state agency that loaned money to farmers to help them develop their land. Carpenter's repeated efforts to develop the land and grow crops were unsuccessful due to spring flooding. He eventually abandoned the effort, and the land was reclassified as unsuitable for agriculture. At that point Carter quit making payments on the loans, and ARLF sued him. He claimed he was excused from payment due to a mistake about the suitability of the land for farming.

ISSUE

Should Carpenter be excused from repaying the loans under the doctrine of mutual mistake?

DECISION

No. Judicial relief from a contract on the basis of mutual mistake is proper where there was a mistake of both parties at the time of contracting as to a basic assumption on which the contract was made, the mistake had a material effect on the performance, and the party seeking relief did not bear the risk of the mistake. Where there is a conscious uncertainty, there is an assumption of the risk that the resolution of the uncertainty may be unfavorable. The detailed disclaimers in the contracts made Carpenter aware that there were uncertainties regarding the condition of the land. Although both parties may have intended for the land to be developed for agricultural purposes, they were uncertain that this was possible. Additionally, Carpenter contractually bore the risk of that uncertainty. He is not excused from his contractual obligations.

UNILATERAL MISTAKE

The basic rule is that if only one of the parties to the agreement is acting under a mistaken belief, this is not grounds for rescission. The reasoning behind the rule is that the law does not want to give all people who want to get out of a contract an easy exit by allowing them to argue mistake. It also wants to encourage people to exercise reasonable care to find out all the facts when entering their agreements. Therefore, it is often said that if a person's own negligence is the cause of his or her mistake, relief will not be granted.

However, when one looks at the cases involving unilateral mistake, it appears that the courts often grant rescission if they are convinced that a person was truly mistaken and that a serious injustice would result from enforcing the agreement. This is sometimes true even when the mistaken party was slightly negligent.

Other factors that the courts weigh when deciding whether to grant relief are whether relief can be granted without causing the other party to suffer a material loss and whether the nonmistaken party knew or should have known of the mistake. If the nonmistaken party will not be hurt by allowing rescission, the courts are more inclined to do so. If someone must bear a loss as a result of the agreement, the courts are inclined to impose the loss on the mistaken party by not granting rescission unless it appears that the other party should have known of the mistake. In such a case, the courts are likely to grant rescission rather than allow one party to take advantage of the other's mistake. This is so even if the nonmistaken party must bear a loss as a result of rescission, since he or she could have avoided the loss by acting in good faith (by informing the mistaken party of the error) or by exercising reasonable care (to discover the mistake when the facts should have indicated that the other party was mistaken). See Figure 11–5.

FIGURE 11–5   Unilateral Mistake

Plaintiff:	Made mistake nonnegligently or with slight negligence	→	Mistake was of a fact	→	Promptly notified defendant when mistake was discovered	→	Serious injustice would result if contract is enforced
Defendant:	Will not suffer much harm if rescission allowed		or		Knew or should have known of the mistake and instead tried to take advantage of it		

CONCEPT SUMMARY   **Voluntary Consent**

There is no voluntary consent if there is

1. Misrepresentation
   a. Misrepresentation of a material fact.
   b. Justifiably relied on to the plaintiff's harm.

2. Fraud
   a. Intentional misrepresentation of a material fact.
   b. Justifiably relied on to the plaintiff's harm.

3. Duress
   a. Wrongful threat.
   b. Plaintiff's free will was overcome.

4. Undue Influence
   a. Confidential relationship.
   b. Plaintiff was induced to make an unfavorable agreement.

5. Mistake
   a. Mutual
      1. Untrue belief by both parties about a material fact.
      2. Either party can rescind.
   b. Unilateral
      1. Mistaken party may be able to rescind if meets certain conditions, or
      2. If other party knew or should have known of the mistake and is trying to take unfair advantage of it.

.... **QUESTIONS AND PROBLEM CASES** ....

1. Explain the concept of *scienter.*
2. Why do the courts require justifiable reliance in misrepresentation and fraud?
3. Give the elements of undue influence and explain the types of people it is designed to protect.
4. Explain the differences between a unilateral and mutual mistake.
5. Reed bought a house from King. He was not told before the sale that a woman and her four children had been murdered there 10 years earlier. He learned this from a neighbor after the sale. Reed sued King and his real estate agent seeking to rescind the sale. Can he rescind the contract?
6. Sarnifil had a comprehensive general liability insurance policy and a commercial umbrella insurance policy with Peerless Insurance Co. The agent that sold him the policies told him that they covered expenses for loss prevention measures. Sarnifil did not read the three-page policy. In reliance on the agent's statement, he canceled another policy that did contain such coverage. Later, when Sarnifil sought reimbursement for loss prevention expenses, Peerless refused to pay because the policies did not cover such expenses. Sarnifil sued for misrepresentation, arguing he justifiably relied on the agent's statement. Is he correct?
7. Blubaugh was summoned to his employer's office and told he could resign or be fired. If he resigned and signed a letter releasing the employer from any claims he might have against it, he would get outplacement counseling and $4,560 in addition to his separation pay. Blubaugh resigned and signed the release. Later, he requested and received moving expenses. Blubaugh later sued for wrongful termination. The employer argued his suit was barred by the release. Blubaugh argued the release should be set aside on the ground of economic duress since he was in a state of shock and distraught about losing his job when he signed it, he had no opportunity to negotiate terms, and he was not told he could consult with a lawyer. Should the release be set aside on these grounds?
8. Wyers, a 59-year-old recently widowed woman with no income, met Gilreath, a 29-year-old who told her he loved her and offered to marry her. He also offered to help her with her finances. He took Wyers, who had a limited ability to read and write and who was taking several medications that impaired her reasoning ability, to a lawyer's office to sign some papers. She thought she was signing for a loan; she actually conveyed her home to Gilreath. He then tried to get a loan on the house from United Companies Financial Corp. United became suspicious after doing a title search and required Gilreath to bring Wyers in to sign the mortgage. After Wyers signed, a check for $13,775 was made out to her, but it was given to him. He cashed it and disappeared. Can Wyers set aside the transaction on the basis of undue influence?
9. In 1973, Exxon Corporation signed a 20-year lease for the rental of a gas station from Wooldridge. The annual rent was $28,700 plus 1.5 cents per gallon for gallons of gas sold in excess of 950,000 gallons per year. In 1979, Wooldridge sued to rescind the contract, alleging the parties were mutually mistaken as to the amount of motor fuel that could be sold on the premises and to whether Exxon could supply the amount of fuel "necessary to provide adequate consideration to the parties." Were the mistaken beliefs the kind that will support rescission?
10. When Olga Mestrovic died, the 1st Source Bank was appointed as her estate's representative. She owned many art works created by her husband, Ivan Mestrovic, an internationally known sculptor and artist. Her will stated the art was to be sold and the proceeds distributed to family members. Olga also owned real estate, which the bank arranged to sell to the Wilkins. The sale agreement included such personal property as appliances, drapes, and French doors in the attic. After the closing, the Wilkins complained that the premises were left in a cluttered condition and would require substantial cleaning. The bank said the Wilkins could clean the property and keep any items of personal property they wanted, or they could hire a rubbish removal service. Neither party knew art works remained on the premises. During the clean-up, the Wilkins found eight drawings and a plaster sculpture by Ivan Mestrovic. The bank sued them for the return of the art works. Can it recover them on the basis of mistake?

CHAPTER 12

Illegality

Mary Beth Whitehead agreed to be impregnated by William Stern's sperm, to carry the child to term, and to turn the child over to William and his wife when it was born. The Sterns agreed to pay Whitehead $10,000 for her services. After the child was born, Whitehead refused to turn the child over to the Sterns, and they sued to enforce the contract.

- *Can a contract be declared illegal if there is no law prohibiting it?*
- *Should the courts refuse to enforce this type of agreement because it violates public policy?*
- *If the agreement is declared illegal, can the Sterns recover any payments they may have made to Whitehead?*

FIGURE 12–1   Illegality

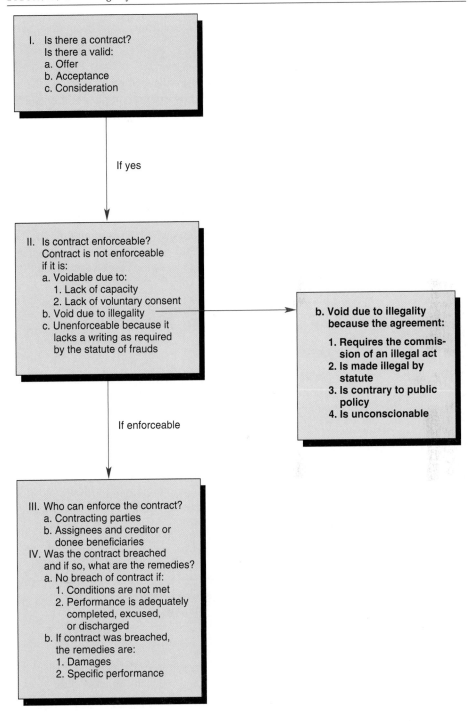

.... *INTRODUCTION* ....

ILLEGALITY

Even if the parties to an agreement have met every other requirement for a valid contract, their agreement is unenforceable if either its formation or its performance is illegal or contrary to the public interest. The public welfare is simply more important than the right of individuals to bargain freely. No sensible legal system would enforce bargains that undermine its authority or its basic objectives.

TYPES OF ILLEGALITY

An agreement is illegal if it calls for behavior that violates a statute or a rule of common law. Also, certain kinds of agreements are themselves made illegal by statutes. An agreement that is contrary to a general rule of public policy is also illegal. The *Whitehead* agreement featured at the beginning of this chapter, could be illegal under any of these. It could violate existing laws outlawing the selling of human beings. In addition, some states have passed laws making surrogate mother contracts illegal. Finally, some courts have held surrogacy agreements to be against public policy.

THE PRESUMPTION OF LEGALITY

When determining the legality of an agreement, the courts presume the parties intended a legal result and interpret their agreement accordingly. All doubts are resolved in favor of the legality of the agreement unless the parties clearly intended an illegal bargain.

THE EFFECT OF ILLEGALITY

GENERAL RULE

Hands off illegal agreements is the general position taken by the courts. A court will not enforce illegal agreements but will leave the parties where it finds them. This means that a party to an illegal agreement generally cannot recover damages for breach of the agreement, recover consideration given to the other party, or recover in quasi contract for benefits conferred on the other party. The basic reason for this rule is to further the public interest, not to punish the parties to an illegal agreement. Since the public interest is most important, courts will sometimes allow recovery if this would best serve the public interest in a particular case. Two such exceptions to the hands-off approach are discussed later in this chapter.

TROTTER V. NELSON
684 N.E.2d 1150 (Ind. Sup. Ct. 1997)

FACTS

Nelson was a clerical who worked for Trotter, an attorney. Trotter allegedly agreed to pay Nelson 5 percent of any fees generated by personal injury or workers' compensation cases she referred to him. Such an agreement is in violation of the Indiana Rules of Professional Conduct. After quitting, Nelson sued Trotter for fees due under the contract.

ISSUE

Does the doctrine of illegality prevent Nelson from getting the promised fees?

DECISION

Yes. While there is a very strong presumption of the enforceability of contracts, the freedom to contract may

(continued)

Contracts Made Illegal by Statute

Type of Statute	Actions Affected	Remedy
Wagering Statutes	Betting	None
Usury Statutes	Interest charged for the use of money	Forfeiture of excess or all interest, or interest and principal
Sunday or "Blue Laws"	Selling certain goods such as alcohol, or performing certain acts on Sunday	Weekday ratification usual
Contracts with Persons Who:		
1. Have **failed** to obtain a **license**	1. Contracts in jobs that require proof of character or skill	1. None
2. Have **failed** to pay a **licensing fee**	2. Licensing required for revenue-raising purposes	2. Contracts generally enforceable

.... *CONTRACTS CONTRARY TO* ....
PUBLIC POLICY

THE IDEA OF PUBLIC POLICY

Public policy is a broad concept that is impossible to define precisely. Perhaps the only realistic way to define it is to say that a court's view of public policy is determined by what the court believes is in the best interests of society. Public policy may change with the times; changing social and economic conditions may make behavior that was acceptable in an earlier time unacceptable today, or vice versa.

There is therefore no simple rule for determining when a particular bargain is contrary to public policy and illegal. Public policy is contradicted by immoral and unethical agreements, even though they may not call for the performance of an illegal act. The courts have broad discretion in ruling on questions of public policy, and this discretion can provide the legal system with a degree of healthy flexibility.

A.Z. v. B.Z.
725 N.E. 2d 1051 (Mass. 2000)

FACTS

After several years of fertility problems, B.Z. and A.Z. went to a clinic and had preembryos (the four-to-eight cell stage of a developing fertilized egg) created from their eggs and sperm. Excess preembryos were held in cryopreservation at the clinic. In order to participate in the clinic program, the clinic required egg and sperm donors to sign consent forms including one regarding the ultimate disposition of any frozen preembryos. This included what would happen under certain contingencies including the wife becoming infertile, one of the parties dying, and the parties separating. The couple signed that if they became separated, the embryos should be returned to the wife for implant. During subsequent implantation procedures, forms were again presented. The husband signed the blank forms, and the wife filled in the disposition stating that the embryos should be returned to her. Before the last vial of preembryos was used, the husband filed for divorce. He also sought a permanent injunction preventing the preembryos from being used for implantation. The wife sought enforcement of the contract.

(continued)

A.Z. v. B.Z.
(concluded)

ISSUE

Would enforcement of the contract be against public policy?

DECISION

Yes. Only three states have passed legislation on this issue, and there is little common law. What law there is is split. We believe that in this case the agreement should not be enforced. First, we believe the agreement applies only to the parties' intent at the time the form was signed. It does not speak to what the parties later intended if they disagreed. It also states no duration. Here the former wife is seeking to enforce the agreement four years after it was signed. We also cannot conclude that "separation" applies to divorce. Additionally, since the wife filled in the term, we cannot assume the husband meant to be bound by it. Finally, and most importantly, even if we found that it was an unambiguous agreement, as a matter of public policy we cannot enforce it. An agreement that compels one to become a parent against his will is against public policy. Prior agreements to enter into familial relationships, whether marriage or parenthood, should not be enforced against individuals who subsequently reconsider their decisions.

Courts may differ in their views of what constitutes desirable public policy—a difference that can make a contract legal in one state and illegal in another. This is true of surrogacy contracts such as that involved in the *Whitehead* case at the beginning of the chapter. The following are additional examples of contracts that courts frequently find to be contrary to public policy.

CONTRACTS INJURIOUS TO PUBLIC SERVICE

The public interest is best served when public officials fully and faithfully perform their duties. It should come as no surprise, then, that agreements that induce public servants to deviate from their duties are illegal. For example, agreements to pay public employees more or less than their lawful salary are unlawful. Agreements that create a conflict between a public employee's personal interests and public duties are also illegal. A good example of this kind of case would be an agreement between a state highway department employee and a real estate speculator who pays the public employee for advance notice of the planned routes of new highway construction. Agreements to pay public servants to influence their decision making are also illegal.

CONTRACTS TO INFLUENCE FIDUCIARIES

Any agreement that tends to induce a **fiduciary** (a person in a position of trust or confidence like a trustee, agent, or partner) to breach his or her fiduciary duties is illegal. This is so because such an agreement operates as a fraud on the principal or beneficiary who is entitled to the fiduciary's loyalty. This applies to agreements by fiduciaries that favor the interests of a third person at the expense of their principals' interests, and agreements that produce a conflict between fiduciaries' personal interests and their principals' interests. The only way a fiduciary may lawfully enter such an agreement is by fully and fairly disclosing the conflict to his or her principal or beneficiary in advance.

EXCULPATORY CLAUSES

An **exculpatory clause** is a provision in a contract that attempts to relieve one party to the contract from liability for the consequences of his or her own negligence.

Public policy generally favors holding people responsible for their own behavior. In addition, courts are concerned that a party relieved of liability for his negligence will not have the incentive to be careful to avoid injuring others. On the other hand, if no duty to the public is involved and the parties have freely and knowingly agreed, the exculpatory clause may be enforceable. Exculpatory clauses that seek to avoid liability for willful misconduct or fraud, however, are generally unenforceable.

KYRIAZIS V. UNIVERSITY OF WEST VIRGINIA
450 S.E.2d 649 (Ct. App. W.Va. 1994)

FACTS

The University of West Virginia has both intramural and club athletics. The University takes no role in the organization, regulation, or supervision of club sports, but it actively controls the intramural sports and regulates them for safety. Recognition as a club sport entitles the club to get money from the school, to join the sports club federation and get more money, and to use the school's facilities. Students participating in club sports are required to sign a release stating they recognize the hazards involved in the activity and that they waive any claims they may have against the University for injuries or death occurring as a result of their participation in the sport. Kyriazis played the club sport of rugby and was injured. When he sued, the University said the suit was barred by the exculpatory agreement.

ISSUE

Should the court refuse to enforce the agreement on the ground of public policy?

DECISION

Yes. When exculpatory agreements are freely and fairly made between two people of equal bargaining power, and there is no public interest with which the agreement interferes, it will generally be upheld. It will not be enforced on the grounds of public policy, though, when the agreement exempts a party charged with a duty of public service and the injured person is one to whom the duty is owed. There are several criteria used to determine whether the release violates the public policy exceptions.

The courts consider whether the party seeking exculpation: (1) is concerned with a business of a type generally thought suitable for public regulation; (2) is engaged in performing a public service of great importance to the public; (3) holds itself out as willing to perform such service to the public; (4) possesses more bargaining power; (5) exercises that power and gives the public a standardized adhesion contract of exculpation; and (6) the person seeking the service is placed under its control. The University argues it does not meet these criteria because rugby is not an essential service but a recreational activity and that the student freely entered the agreement. In this it is wrong.

Athletics are integral and important elements of the educational mission of the University. In providing recreational activities, it fulfills its educational mission and performs a public service. As an enterprise charged with a duty of public service, the University owes a duty of due care to its students when it encourages them to participate in any sport. The University had superior bargaining power. The University's *Code of Student Rights and Responsibilities* requires students to follow the instructions of representatives of the administration. The release was prepared by a lawyer and nothing in it reveals the student had benefit of counsel when he signed it. If the student wished to play club rugby, he had to sign it. Because the University qualifies as a public service and it possessed a decisive bargaining advantage over the student when he signed the release, the release is void as a matter of public policy.

CONTRACTS IN RESTRAINT OF TRADE

One of the basic assumptions underlying our economic system is that the public interest is, in most cases, best served by free competition. On the other hand, the courts have recognized that there are some situations where limited restrictions on competition are justifiable. The courts therefore look very closely at agreements that attempt to limit competition to see whether the restraint imposed is reasonable or should be struck down for violating public policy. In Chapter 41 you will also learn that some agreements in restraint of trade are specifically made illegal by the anti-trust laws.

Agreements whose *sole* purpose is to restrain trade are illegal. However, a restraint that is merely *ancillary to* (supplementary to) a contract may be legal if it is designed to protect interests created by the contract and it is *no broader than is reasonably necessary* to protect those interests. For example, it is common for a contract for the sale of a business to provide that the seller will not compete with the buyer for a specified period of time after the sale. If the restriction covers a reasonable geographic area and a reasonable time period, it will probably be upheld. Similarly, employment contracts often provide that employees will not compete with or work for a competitor of their employer after they have ceased their employment. If such a restriction is reasonably necessary to prevent an employee from disclosing trade secrets or taking away the employer's customers, and it has reasonable geographic and time limitations, it is also likely to be upheld.

Courts also consider the degree of hardship a covenant not to compete would have on the public and on the party who would be restrained from competing. Restrictions on competition work a greater hardship on an employee than on someone who has sold a business. Therefore employee agreements not to compete are often judged by a stricter standard than are similar agreements that accompany the sale of a business.

The courts do not agree on how to treat a restriction that is unreasonably broad. Some courts enforce the restraint for a reasonable period of time and within a reasonable geographic area. Others strike the entire restriction and refuse to grant the buyer or employer any protection. Some states bar enforcement through a statute.

ADVANCED MARINE ENTERPRISES, INC. v. PRC INC.
256 Va. 106 (Va. Sup. Ct. 1998)

FACTS

Pirrera was a senior manager in PRC's marine engineering department. He signed an agreement that for eight months after leaving PRC's employment he would not solicit customers for whom he had performed services nor render competing services within 50 miles of any office of PRC. Pirrera and others in the marine engineering department resigned and immediately started working for Advance Marine, a PRC competitor. They also took a significant amount of proprietary information with them. PRC sued Advanced Marine, Pirrera, and the other employees. When the court enjoined the employees from working for PRC until the eight-month period had run, they challenged the agreement as being unreasonable because it was unreasonably broad, unduly harsh, and oppressive.

ISSUE

Is the restrictive covenant unreasonably broad and oppressive, and therefore unenforceable?

DECISION

No. Even though PRC has 300 offices worldwide, the geographical limitation is not unreasonable because the restriction lasts for only a brief period and because it narrowly defines the activity which is prohibited. The restriction on solicitation of customers is also reasonable because it is limited to particular specialized engineering areas and persons for whom they had performed services. Finally, it does not contain a blanket prohibition against working for a competitor. The agreement is not unduly harsh and oppressive in curtailing the legitimate efforts of former PRC employees to earn a livelihood, nor is it too broad.

It also has been traditionally held that agreements restricting the free *alienation* (sale) of land are contrary to public policy, which favors a free market in land.

UNEQUAL BARGAINS

As you saw in Chapter 6, the courts were historically unwilling to consider arguments that a contract was the product of unequal bargaining power. As long as all the legal elements of a contract were present and the agreement was free from misrepresentation, fraud, duress, undue influence, or mistake, the common law courts would enforce it, despite the fact that its terms might be grossly unfair to one of the parties. This was justified by the doctrine of *freedom of contract.*

The changing nature of our society, however, has produced many contract situations in which the bargaining power of the parties may be grossly unequal. This may make it possible for one of the parties to effectively dictate the terms of the agreement and to take advantage of this power by dictating terms that are unfair to the other party. The legal system has responded to these changes in two major ways.

First, there has been an increasing "public" input through legislation into many previously private contract situations. Wage and hour laws, workers' compensation laws, usury laws, and rent control laws are just a few of the many kinds of statutes aimed at placing limits on the exercise of private bargaining power.

Second, today's courts are responding to the problem by recognizing the idea of **unconscionable contracts** and **contracts of adhesion**—contracts in which the only choice for one of the parties is between "adhering" to the terms dictated by the other party or not contracting at all. A court may refuse to enforce such an agreement as contrary to public policy. Clauses in fine print or in such technical language that an ordinary person would not understand their meaning have also been stricken on this basis. Unequal bargaining power standing alone is not enough to justify unenforceability, however. It must also appear that the party with superior power used it to take unfair advantage of the other party to the agreement. The courts are especially likely to find such inequality in cases involving consumer contracts with businesses, although there are also numerous cases in which contracts between small companies and large industrial giants have been held to be adhesion contracts. While courts are increasingly willing to prevent oppression and unfair surprise by finding agreements to be unconscionable or contracts of adhesion, they will not use such doctrines to relieve people of their bad bargains.

The *Restatement (Second) of Contracts* urges broad powers on the courts to deal with unconscionability. The Uniform Commercial Code specifically grants courts these broad powers.

Ethical Implications	A large bank required customers to sign a signature card. In extremely small type the card stated that the depositor agreed that the account was subject to the bank's present and future rules, regulations, practices, and charges. On the basis of this agreement, the bank charged depositors $6 for each check returned for insufficient funds. The actual cost to the bank for processing each check was 30 cents. Thus, there was a 2,000 percent differential between the bank's actual cost and the fee it charged. Is it ethical for a business to make this kind of return in this manner?

Common Contracts Contrary to Public Policy

Type of Contract	Action Involved	Conditions under Which Contract Sometimes Enforced
Contracts Injurious to Public Service	Bribes	
Contracts to Influence Fiduciaries	Prize, reward, or other inducement	Full disclosure to, and agreement of, beneficiary
Exculpatory Clauses	Release of liability for negligence	No duty to public involved, and free agreement by other party
Contracts in Restraint of Trade	Agreement not to compete	If ancillary to contract for sale of a business, or for employment, and is no broader than necessary and not injurious to public
Contracts Resulting from Unequal Bargaining Power	Unconscionable or adhesion contracts	

THE CODE AND UNCONSCIONABLE CONTRACTS

Section 2-302 recognizes the idea of an **unconscionable contract.** The drafters of the Code knew that many contracts today are not truly consensual, even though the classic forms of lack of voluntary consent (like fraud, duress, undue influence, and mistake) are not present, and that they are often the products of unequal bargaining power between the parties. Many consumer contracts are created on preprinted forms drawn by one party's attorney. These form contracts sometimes contain provisions that are unreasonably favorable to the party whose attorney drafted them. In addition, these contracts are sometimes so filled with legalese (technical legal wording) that consumers in reality do not understand the nature of the contract they have signed.

The Code gives the courts considerable power to deal with these problems by giving them freedom to remedy unconscionable contracts. If a court finds a contract to be unconscionable, it can refuse to enforce it entirely, enforce it without any unconscionable clause, or enforce it in a way that avoids an unconscionable result.

The Code does not define *unconscionable,* leaving it instead for the courts to define. In doing so, the courts have tended to follow the path charted by those earlier courts that refused to enforce "adhesion contracts" on the grounds that they were contrary to public policy. Unconscionable contracts are often described as those that are so unfair that they "shock the conscience of the court." This unfairness may result from the fact that one of the parties did not either notice or truly understand a clause of the contract (because it was too technically worded, in fine print, on the back of the contract, etc.). A finding of unconscionability may also result when a party with superior bargaining power imposes unfair terms on the other party.

HARRIS V. GREEN TREE FINANCIAL CORP.
183 F.3d 173 (3rd Cir. 1999)

FACTS

The Harrises claimed to be victims of a fraudulent home improvement scheme perpetrated by Green Tree Finan-cial Corp. Green Tree recruited home improvement contractors, told the contractors to obtain high-interest

(continued)

HARRIS V. GREEN TREE FINANCIAL CORP.
(concluded)

second mortgages contracts on home improvements by targeting relatively unsophisticated, low- to middle-income, senior citizens, promising that the work would be performed at an affordable cost and that no payment would be due until the customer was completely satisfied. The form contracts allowed Green Tree to charge exorbitant amounts for collateral protection insurance. They obtained these contracts by using high-pressure sales tactics such as in-home sales and telemarketing. After the Harrises signed the forms, the contractors either did not do the promised work or did it in an unsatisfactory manner. When the Harrises sued, Green Tree sought to enforce an arbitration clause in the contracts. This clause was contained in the secondary mortgage contract which appeared in small print on the back and near the bottom of the one-page form contract. In the clause Green Tree reserved the right to sue but the Harrises did not have that right.

ISSUE

Is the clause unconscionable and therefore unenforceable?

DECISION

No. The doctrine of unconscionability relieves a person from an unfair contract or an unfair term of a contract. There are generally two kinds of unconscionability—procedural, or unfair surprise, and substantive. *Procedural* pertains to the process by which an agreement is reached, and the form of an agreement including the use of fine print and convoluted or unclear language. *Substantive unconscionability* refers to terms that are unreasonably or grossly favorable to one side. The Harrises argue that the contract is procedurally unfair because the arbitration clause is in fine print on that back of the form. However, since this was a one-page contract, there was no procedural unconscionability here. The Harrises also argue that the clause is substantively unconscionable because Green Tree retains the right to sue but they can't, and Green Tree can choose the arbitrator without their consent. We find that arbitration agreements are still enforceable even though one party can still litigate issues. Finally, we read the arbitration term to mean that if the Harrises object to Green Tree's choice of an arbitrator, they can petition the court to appoint another one. The arbitration agreement is enforceable.

Unconscionability will probably not apply to any terms of an agreement that were truly bargained for, even though one of the parties made a "bad deal." Consumers who are dealing with merchants are generally more successful in arguing unconscionability than merchants who are dealing with other merchants because the courts are more likely to assume that, as compared to consumers, merchants have more bargaining power, better access to legal advice, and more knowledge about the nature of the transactions they enter. In those few cases in which merchants have successfully argued unconscionability, they were usually small businesspeople (who in reality had no more bargaining power than a consumer) dealing with large corporations.

Current Issues   Today many illegality issues facing courts involve public policy questions about family relationships. The family has long been considered to be a crucial social institution, and it is therefore protected by the courts. The nature and role of the family in our society is changing, however, and courts are being asked to recognize these changes. You already saw one example of this in the cases dealing with division of property between couples who live together without getting married.

(continued)

Another example is raised by the *Whitehead* case. What are the permissible ways for people to bring children into the family unit? Should the courts recognize contracts involving surrogacy, or *in vitro* fertilization? The *A.Z. v. B.Z.* case raises the question of who "owns" the frozen embryos created through *in vitro* fertilization if the couple whose eggs and sperm were used to create the embryo separates before transplantation. The courts and legislatures are split in their answers to these difficult questions.

Another area in transition involves *antenuptial agreements*. Antenuptial agreements are entered into by a couple before marriage and determine how property should be divided if there is later a divorce. Traditionally, courts held such agreements to be void as against public policy because they might facilitate or induce a divorce and because they usually left the woman financially needy. Many courts are now allowing such agreements, however, because they recognize that attitudes toward divorce have changed, as has the ability of women to support and protect themselves. In addition, rather than encouraging divorce, they recognize that such agreements may actually promote marital stability by making clear the expectations and responsibilities of the parties.

QUESTIONS AND PROBLEM CASES

1. Explain the different kinds of illegality.
2. Explain the difference between an illegal wagering statute and a legitimate property insurance policy.
3. Explain a contract of adhesion and give an example.
4. Explain the requirements for an enforceable employment contract that is in restraint of trade.
5. Blum contracted with the city of Niagara Falls, New York, to lease an arena for a "bloodless" bull fight. The city canceled the lease after being advised by its corporate counsel that such a performance would violate state law. Can the city be held liable for canceling the contract?
6. Todd wanted to have a child but did not want to get married. Straub agreed to have intercourse with her after she signed an agreement stating that she would hold him harmless for emotional and financial support of a child that might result from their relationship. Eleven months later, Todd gave birth to B.M.T. After three years of raising B.M.T. without any support from Straub, Todd filed suit for B.M.T. seeking a declaration of paternity and child support. Is Straub's agreement unenforceable on the basis of public policy?
7. Myers operated the Greendoor tavern under a sole-owner liquor license. Clouse, a patron of the bar, agreed to buy it. They labeled their purchase agreement an "Employment/Management Contract," and stated that Clouse would manage the business for four years and receive 60 percent of the profits as salary. Clouse paid $7,500 at the signing of the agreement and was to pay $7,500 later. Two weeks after Clouse started operating the bar, the liquor license was lost because Myers had not applied for a new partnership license as required by law. Clouse sued to get his $7,500 back, and Myers countersued to collect the remaining $7,500. Can either collect?
8. Representatives of Sho-Pro of Indiana visited Brown's home in order to sell him replacement windows. They got his name through an entry in a "sweepstakes contest" to win, with no obligation, a house full of windows or $500, plus a "turkey platter." After a four- to five-hour sales pitch, including an inquiry into his financial background, Brown signed a number of documents. Three days later a representative of Sho-Pro left a card in his door, and when he contacted the company, he was informed that he had purchased four replacement windows on credit for $4,322. Brown protested that he had not bought any windows, that he could not afford them, and that he did not own the house. The woman on the phone told him that there would be no problem and that the order would

be stopped. No windows were ever installed, but a week or two later a representative of Sho-Pro arrived to measure windows. When Brown said that he did not order any windows, he was assured that the measuring was being done only in case he changed his mind or someone else moved into the house. Brown was asked to sign a document saying the man had been to the house that the man said he needed in order to get paid for the work. Sho-Pro then sued Brown for several thousand dollars. One of the documents signed by Brown was a contract for the sale of windows for $4,322 that would have cost Sho-Pro a total of $1,080.50. The remainder was for "lead costs," management and administrative costs, sales commission, and profit. In addition, Sho-Pro was seeking to collect attorneys' fees and interest. Should the contract be enforced? Explain.

9. Wilson was a licensed architect who had failed to pay the annual $15 registration fee required by the licensing statute. He had done $33,900 of good architectural work for Kealakekua Ranch, which refused to pay. He sued for his fee, and Kealakekua raised the defense of illegality. Did Wilson's failure to pay the annual registration fee make his contract with Kealakekua illegal?

10. Griffin, who was an expert skier and certified ski instructor, entered the Ironman Decathlon at a ski resort run by Big Valley. In order to participate, he had to sign a "General Release of Claim," which said that he assumed all risk of competition and released all claims against the resort and the race sponsors. During the first event, a downhill ski race, Griffin was found unconscious, probably a result of losing control of his skis and hitting a tree. He died a few hours later. Griffin's estate filed a wrongful death suit against Big Valley. Is the suit barred by the exculpatory clause?

11. Parker, a pediatric endocrinologist, was hired by Nalle Clinic. He signed an agreement stating that he would not practice medicine in the county for 25 months after leaving the clinic's employ. After working for two years, Parker quit and opened a medical practice a few blocks from the clinic. The clinic challenged Parker's right to practice. Will it be successful?

CHAPTER 13

The Form and Meaning of Contracts

M & M Flying Service, Inc., entered into a written contract with the Andalusia-Opp Airport Authority to run management and commercial activities from January 1, 1983, to December 31, 1987. The Authority came under new management on January 1, 1988. When the new management and M & M failed to agree on the terms of a renewal of M & M's contract, the Authority sought to stop M & M from operating at the airport. M & M argued that at the same time it had signed the management contract in 1983, it had also signed a 10-year lease, and that the Authority had orally promised that M & M could continue to operate commercial activities for the life of the lease.

- *Is the oral promise that commercial activities could continue for five years enforceable without a writing?*
- *Was the fact that M & M operated commercial activities from 1983 to 1988 sufficient evidence that it was promised another five years so that no writing is required for that promise?*
- *Did the promise about allowing commercial activities for five years have to be in writing because it was to take place on the Authority's land?*

FIGURE 13-1   When a Contract Is Unenforceable

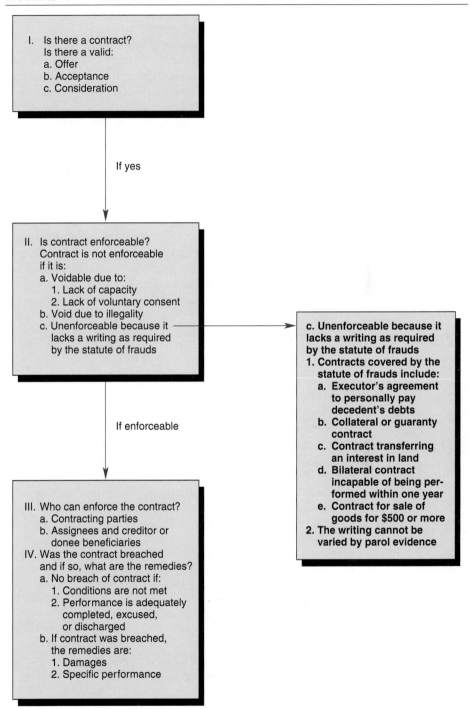

Many people mistakenly believe that oral contracts are not binding and enforceable. How many times have you heard someone say, "I agreed, but they didn't get it in writing"? The truth is that oral contracts are generally every bit as binding and enforceable as written ones.

There are, however, some exceptions to this general rule. As you will see later in this chapter, all states have *statutes of frauds* that require certain kinds of contracts to be evidenced by a writing to be enforceable.

Even if a contract is not one of those that the statute of frauds requires to be in writing, written contracts are more desirable than oral contracts for several reasons. The parties are less likely to misunderstand the terms of their agreement if they have reduced them to written form. If a dispute about the parties' obligations should arise at a later date, the writing is better evidence of the terms of their agreement than their memories, which may fail or be distorted by wishful thinking. Likewise, the existence of a written agreement may provide protection against intentional misstatements about the terms of the agreement.

Parties who put their contracts in writing should try to make the writing as complete and unambiguous (clear) as possible. This reduces the potential for later disagreement and makes it easier for a court to construe or interpret the agreement if a dispute arises. A court that is called on to interpret an ambiguous agreement relies on rules of construction (interpretation) that the law has created for this purpose. These will be discussed later in this chapter.

The parties to a written agreement should also be sure that the writing is complete and covers all the important terms of their agreement for another important reason. As you will see in a later part of this chapter, a rule of law called the *parol evidence rule* often prevents a party to a written contract from trying to prove terms that were left out of the writing.

The Statute of Frauds

The statutes of frauds adopted by the states are patterned after the original statute of frauds adopted in England in 1677. At that time, parties to a lawsuit could not testify in their own cases. Thus, in order to prove a contract, the parties had to rely on the testimony of third persons who were often paid witnesses or friends, and false testimony was common. In an effort to stop the widespread fraud and perjury, Parliament required those contracts in which the potential for fraud was great, or the consequences of fraud were especially serious, to be in writing to be enforceable. A **statute of frauds** essentially says that in some cases, the law will require more evidence (a writing) that the parties had an agreement than the oral testimony of the party claiming that a contract existed.

Among those classes of contracts traditionally required to be in writing by the statute of frauds are:

1. Contracts by the executor or administrator of a deceased person's estate to be personally liable for a debt of the deceased person.
2. Contracts by one person to answer for the debt or default of another.
3. Contracts for the transfer of an interest in land.
4. Bilateral contracts that have not been fully performed by either party and are not capable of being performed within a year of their formation.

Several additional classes of contracts have been added to the traditional categories covered by the statute. For example, the Uniform Commercial Code states that contracts for the sale of goods costing $500 or more are not enforceable without a writing or other specified evidence. This is illustrated in the *Lee* case later in the chapter. Many states also require contracts to pay debts barred by a bankruptcy discharge or the statute of limitations to be evidenced by a writing. In addition, many states require contracts to pay a commission on the sale of real estate to be evidenced by a writing.

The U.N. Convention on the International Sale of Goods, the "international UCC," has decided not to require the formality of a writing. While countries could choose to require a writing and still sign the Convention, most countries throughout the world have opted to do away with strict form requirements. Thus, oral international contracts between companies in signatory countries will be enforced without a writing. (See the *MCC–Marble* case later in the chapter for a discussion of the CISG.)

THE EFFECT OF FAILURE TO COMPLY

In most states, the statute of frauds makes oral contracts that come within its provisions **unenforceable,** not void or voidable. This means several things. If the parties to such an oral contract have both fully performed their obligations, neither is allowed to rescind the contract. Their mutual performance is ample evidence that a contract in fact existed. If one of the parties to an executory oral contract files suit to enforce the contract and the other party does not raise the statute of frauds as a defense, the court will enforce the agreement.

If an oral contract is declared to be unenforceable under the statute of frauds, and one of the parties has rendered some performance under the contract that conferred benefits on the other party, he or she can recover the reasonable value of the performance in *quasi contract.* In some instances that will be discussed later, part performance of a contract is sufficient to take the contract outside the scope of the statute or to satisfy the statute's requirement by providing the extra element of proof of a contract's existence beyond the mere oral testimony of a party.

One of the troubling things about the statute is its potential for injustice. It can as easily be used to defeat a contract that was actually made as to defeat a fictitious agreement. In recent years, some courts have begun to try to prevent such injustices by using the equitable doctrine of *promissory estoppel* to allow some parties to recover under oral contracts that the statute of frauds would ordinarily render unenforceable. If the plaintiff has *materially relied* on the oral promise and will suffer *serious losses* if the promise is not enforced, courts in these states hold that the other party is estopped from raising the statute of fraud as a defense. The idea behind these decisions is that the statute, which is designed to prevent injustice, should not be allowed to work an injustice. These cases also impliedly recognize the fact that the reliance required by promissory estoppel to some extent provides evidence of the existence of a contract between the parties, since it is unlikely that a person would materially rely on a nonexistent promise.

Ethical Implications	Is it ethical to challenge the enforceability of an oral contract on statute of frauds grounds when all of the other elements of a contract clearly are in existence?

CONTRACTS COVERED BY THE STATUTE OF FRAUDS

EXECUTORS' AGREEMENTS TO PERSONALLY PAY THEIR DECEDENTS' DEBTS

When a person dies, an executor or administrator is appointed by the probate court to settle the deceased person's (the decedent's) estate. Basically, this involves paying all outstanding claims against the estate and distributing any remainder to the decedent's heirs. The executor or administrator is often a relative or close friend of the decedent.

Creditors of the decedent who fear that the decedent's estate will not be great enough to cover their claims may try to get the executor to agree to be personally responsible for the decedent's debts. Executors who are relatives or close friends may feel morally obligated to make such promises, although they have no legal obligation to do so. In extreme cases, creditors who would otherwise suffer a great loss may be tempted to lie and claim the executor made such a promise. To prevent such fraud and to guard against ill-considered promises by executors, such promises must be in writing to be enforceable.

CONTRACTS TO ANSWER FOR THE DEBT OF ANOTHER

In addition to the executor's contracts just discussed, there are many other common situations in which one person agrees to be responsible for the debts or default of another. Such contracts are called **collateral** or **guaranty contracts.** The essence of such contracts is that a third person (the *guarantor*) agrees to perform the contractual duties another person (the *obligor*) owes under another contract, *if* the obligor does not perform. The person to whom the obligor and the guarantor are contractually liable is called the *obligee.* These situations, then, involve three parties and two promises, one of which is conditional. Only the conditional promise by the guarantor to the obligee to be responsible for the obligor's debt must be in writing.

If, for example, a clothing store (the obligee) that has opened a credit account with Mike, a college student (the obligor), gets Mike's older brother Tom (the guarantor) to agree to pay the amount owed on the account if Mike fails to do so, this is a guaranty contract. Tom's contract must be in writing to be enforceable.

FIGURE 13–2   Guaranty Contract

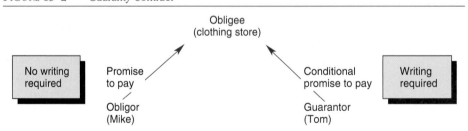

Many three-party transactions are not guaranty contracts but are instead *original contracts* of the third party. The distinction between an original contract and a guaranty contract is important because original contracts do not need to be evidenced by a writing to be enforceable. The major difference between the two is that a party to an original contract is *primarily* liable (absolutely liable under the terms of the contract) to perform his or her contractual duties, while a guarantor is only *secondarily* liable (liable only if the obligor does not perform).

For example, Bob and Joe agree to buy a television set from Frank's TV Service for $189.95, payable over 24 months. Bob and Joe are **co-obligors** on the sales agreement and are both *primarily* liable to make the payments. Frank's TV can collect the amount due under the agreement from *either* Bob or Joe without first showing a demand for payment from the other. Bob and Joe's promises are therefore *original* ones and need not be evidenced by a writing to be enforceable.

FIGURE 13–3   Original Contract

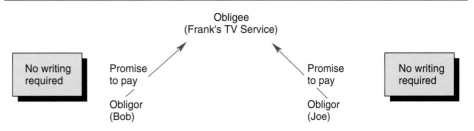

NAKAMURA V. FUJII
67 N.Y.S.2d 113 (N.Y. App. Div. 1998)

FACTS

In August 1992, the Fujiis told Nakamura they could not pay their daughter's tuition at University of Southern California (USC) and asked him to pay "certain tuition invoices" for her. He orally agreed in exchange for their express promise to repay the money on demand. He issued five checks to USC between August 1992 and December 1993, totaling $40,339.33. In 1993 they made the same request for their younger daughter, and Nakamura again orally agreed, subject to the same conditions. He issued six checks for her tuition between August 1993 and January 1996, totaling $60,964.20. When Nakamura demanded payment, the Fujiis refused to pay and he

then sued. The Fujiis raised the statute of frauds as a defense.

ISSUE

Were these oral promises to pay for debt of another that are barred by the statute of frauds?

DECISION

No. This is not a guaranty to repay the debt of another if she does not pay. Rather, the Fujiis made an independent promise to repay monies advanced by Nakamura at their express request. Their daughters owed no debt to Nakamura, and therefore the statute of frauds is inapplicable.

In some cases, what would at first glance appear to be a guaranty contract within the statute will be treated as an original contract outside the statute's scope. This is due to the **leading object** doctrine, which says that the promises of those who are primarily motivated by a desire to secure some personal benefit fall outside the statute. Thus, if people promising to pay for the debt of another are primarily motivated to make the promise because they expect some personal benefit by so doing, their conditional promise does not need to be in writing to be enforceable.

CONTRACTS TRANSFERRING AN INTEREST IN LAND

Our legal system has historically treated land as being more important than other forms of property. This special treatment stems from the time when land was the primary basis of wealth. As a result of this special status, contracts transferring ownership rights in real estate must be evidenced by a writing to be enforceable. Therefore, oral contracts to sell or mortgage real estate, to permit the mining and removal of minerals from land, and to grant easement (access) rights to land are generally unenforceable. Most states have a separate statute of frauds covering leases. Generally, these statutes require a writing only for long-term leases (e.g., for leases of a year or longer). A contract to erect a building or to insure a building does not come under the real estate provision of the statute of frauds because such contracts do not involve the transfer of ownership rights.

In some cases, **part performance** of a contract for the sale of land takes the contract out of the coverage of the statute. In order for part performance to have this effect, it must clearly indicate the existence of a contract of sale and not be consistent with any other interpretation. Ordinarily, this requires that the buyer either has made substantial improvements to the property or has taken possession of the property and paid part or all of the purchase price. There are two primary reasons for allowing part performance to substitute for the statute's writing requirement. First, the courts are preventing the injustice that would occur to the party who has acted in reliance on the oral contract. Also, the nature of the reliance required in part performance cases tends to furnish good evidence that the parties did, in fact, have a contract. The only other instance where part performance has this effect is in the case of sales contracts under the Uniform Commercial Code.

BILATERAL CONTRACTS NOT CAPABLE OF BEING PERFORMED WITHIN ONE YEAR

Long-term bilateral contracts must be in writing because contracts that call for performance over a considerable period of time increase the risk of faulty or willfully inaccurate recollection of their terms in subsequent disputes. Unfortunately, attempts at line drawing such as this can produce apparently silly results in many cases.

The first thing to note is that these statutes are generally worded to include only executory bilateral contracts "not to be performed within one year" or "not capable of being performed within one year." This means that if it is *possible* for the contract to be performed within a year, it need not be evidenced by a writing, despite the fact that performance *is not likely to be* or *is not in fact* completed within a year. The M & M Flying Service contract, discussed in the introductory case, was alleged to be for five years. By its terms, then, it could not be performed within a year, and had to be in writing to be enforceable.

POPANZ V. PEREGRINE CORP.
710 A.2d 250 (Maine 1998)

FACTS

Popanz, the associate director of Peregrine Corp., was offered the position of director. She refused the position based on the oral promise made by the director when Popanz had been hired that she could retain her current position until she reached age 65, which would happen in several years. Three years later Peregrine terminated Popanz when it eliminated her position. She sued for breach of the promise of employment until 65.

ISSUE

Is the promise unenforceable because it was not in writing?

DECISION

Yes. The statute of frauds requires that promises that cannot be performed within one year from the making thereof to be in writing to be enforceable. By its terms, this promise cannot be performed within one year. Popanz cannot avoid the statutory requirement by arguing promissory estoppel. Reliance solely on an oral promise of continued employment is not sufficient to avoid the statute of frauds.

Also note that the statutes apply only to *executory bilateral* contracts. Therefore, most courts hold that if a contract has been fully performed by one side, the promise of the other party is enforceable even if it cannot be performed within a year. Thus, if

Fran lends Craig $500 and Craig orally promises to repay the loan within 18 months, Fran can enforce the promise even though it is oral.

The one-year period is computed from the time the contract comes into existence, not from the time performance is to begin. Most states begin counting on the day after the contract comes into existence (parts of days are not counted), a few on the day it is formed.

When a contract states an indefinite time for performance, it need not be evidenced by a writing if it is possible to perform the contract within one year. So, oral contracts to perform "for life" are generally enforceable, since one of the parties concerned could die within a year and have thereby fully performed.

WHAT KIND OF WRITING IS REQUIRED?

While the statutes of frauds of all the states are not the same, most states require only a *memorandum* of the parties' agreement; they do not require that the entire contract be in writing or that the writing be in a single document. The writing can be in any form, including letters, telegrams, receipts, or any other writing indicating that the parties had a contract. It can be made any time before the suit is filed.

Although there is a general trend away from requiring complete writings to satisfy the statute of frauds, an adequate memorandum must still contain several things. The identity of the parties to the contract must be indicated in some way, and the subject matter of the contract must be identified with reasonable certainty. These things can be contained in several documents, so long as it is clear that the documents all relate to the same agreement. The requirement that the subject matter be identified with reasonable certainty causes particular problems in contracts for the sale of land, since many states require a detailed description of the property to be sold. The statutes of the states vary on whether the memorandum must state the consideration agreed to by the parties.

CONNER V. LAVACA HOSPITAL DIST.
267 F.3d 426 (5th Cir. 2001)

FACTS

Dr. Conner was a family practitioner at a rural health clinic operated by Lavaca. She worked under one-year contracts. At the expiration of her 1995 contract, she entered negotiations for a new contract. The IRS had notified Conner that she had dramatically underestimated her income. To solve this problem, she asked that in the new contract, funds earned from her time in the clinic be separated from her time in the hospital. At the end of her contract, she continued to work under three-month stopgap contracts, and after the last of those expired, continued to work without a contract while negotiations continued. She finally presented her case before the board of directors, who passed a motion to enter into an agreement to offer a three-year contract that spelled out monthly salary and vacation days. They encouraged the administrator, attorneys, and the doctor's representative to get together to work out the separate charges and to come back to the board for approval. Four days later the board met in emergency session and voted to rescind the earlier motion. The board then made offers to other doctors for less lucrative contracts while continuing to employ Dr. Conner. After working for several more months without a written contract, she sued. The hospital defended by arguing the statute of frauds.

ISSUE

Were the minutes of the board meeting a sufficient writing to satisfy the statute of frauds?

(continued)

Conner v. Lavaca Hospital Dist.
(concluded)

Decision

No. A promise that is not enforceable within a year is within the statute of frauds. Dr. Conner is attempting to enforce a three-year employment contract. Thus, it must be reflected in an adequate writing. This writing or memorandum must be complete within itself in every material detail. While minutes of a meeting could meet the statute of frauds writing requirement, they do not do so in this case. Generally, duration, compensation, and the employee's duties are essential elements of an employment contract. Terms left open for future negotiation cannot be essential or material elements because leaving such terms open renders the contract unenforceable under the statute of frauds. While the doctor argues that the separate charges issue is merely a ministerial detail, we find otherwise. She continued to negotiate because she considered this to be a necessary term in the new contract. Thus, the minutes are not complete enough to meet the statute of frauds requirement.

One point on which the states generally agree is that the memorandum needs to be signed only by the party to be bound (or his or her agent). This means that both parties' signatures do not have to appear in the writing. The idea here simply is that it is the defendant who needs protection against fraud, so it is his or her signature that is required to satisfy the statute. It is, however, in the best interests of both parties for both signatures to appear on the writing; otherwise, the contract evidenced by the writing is enforceable only against the signing party. In most instances, the signature can appear anyplace on the memorandum. Any writing, mark, initials, stamp, engraving, or other symbol placed or printed on a memorandum will suffice as a signature if it was intended to authenticate (indicate the genuineness of) the writing.

The increasing number of contracts transacted over the Internet caused Congress to pass the Electronic Signatures in Global and National Commerce Act (E-Sign) in 2000. It provides that a contract or signature may not be denied legal effect "solely because it is in electronic form." This gives a digital signature the same effect as one written in ink on paper. E-Sign defines an electronic signature as "any electronic sound, symbol, or process attached to or logically associated with a contract or other record and executed or accepted by a person with the intent to sign the records." Such signatures are already in common use. A PIN number used to access an ATM and a password used to enter a website would meet this definition. By creating a uniform national law, Congress intended to promote the use of the Internet for electronic commerce. It also intended for it to work in conjunction with the Uniform Electronic Transactions Act, which has been adopted by about half the states. The UETA is further discussed in Chapter 48.

The Code's Statute of Frauds

The Code has its own statute of frauds section (2-201), which applies to contracts for the sale of goods for $500 or more. The unique thing about the Code's approach to the statute of frauds issue is that the Code recognizes that the basic purpose of the statute of frauds (to provide more evidence that a contract existed than the mere oral testimony of one of the parties) can be satisfied by several kinds of things *other than a writing*.

If the goods are *specially manufactured for the buyer* and "not suitable for sale to others in the normal course of the seller's business," and the seller has made a substantial beginning in manufacturing them or has entered a binding agreement to acquire them for the buyer before learning that the buyer is denying the existence of a contract, the buyer loses the statute of frauds defense (2-201[3][a]).

The Code permits other exceptions to the writing requirement when it has other reliable proof of the existence of a contract. For instance, if a party being sued on a contract *admits the existence* of the contract in testimony in court or in any of the pleadings filed during the course of the lawsuit, that satisfies the statute (2-201[3][b]).

Partial performance also creates an exception. If a party accepts goods or accepts payment for goods, the statute of frauds is satisfied *to the extent of the payment made or the goods accepted* (2-201[3][c]). For example, Mary and John have an oral contract for the sale of 100 pairs of boots at $10 a pair. If Mary delivers the boots and John accepts them, or if John pays for the boots and Mary accepts payment, neither can raise the statute of frauds as a defense. If, however, only some of the boots are delivered (50 pairs) or only a partial payment is made ($500), the remainder of the agreement is unenforceable.

The basic Code writing requirement (2-201[1]) is that there be evidence of the parties' contract in the form of a written memorandum that indicates the existence of a contract between the parties, indicates the quantity of goods sold, and is signed by the party to be charged. So, a letter that said:

> I agree to sell to John Smith 200 wrenches.
> (Signed)
> Steve Jones

would be sufficient to satisfy the Code's writing requirement against Steve.

In most cases, however, John Smith would have a good statute of frauds defense against Steve because John did not sign the writing. The Code provides, however, that if John is a *merchant* and he receives this writing from Steve and does not object in writing within 10 days after receiving it, he loses his statute of frauds defense (2-201[2]). Steve still must convince the court that the parties had a contract, but he is not prevented by the statute of frauds from trying to do so. The idea behind this subsection of the Code is that the natural response of a person who did not have a contract would be to object. John's failure to object satisfies the statute's requirement of some extra proof (beyond Steve's oral testimony) that a contract existed.

LEE V. VOYLES
898 F. 2d 76 (7th Cir. 1990)

FACTS

King Leopold III of Belgium was forced to abdicate the throne in 1950, and he lived in exile in Switzerland. Time passes slowly for exiled monarchs, and Leopold turned to the simple pleasures of life, such as cars capable of speeds of 200 mph. One of these was his 1954 custom-designed 375 Pinin Farina Cabriolet, known as the "King Leopold Ferrari." When he tired of the car, he sold it, and it eventually fell into deplorable mechanical condition. In 1969 Golomb bought the car and shipped it to Illinois where he, his family, and his girlfriend, Voyles, spent more than a decade restoring it. Lee, an exotic car fancier, saw a picture of the car in 1985 and asked how much it would take to buy it. When told $275,000, Lee countered with $175,000, which was refused. Lee made several other, higher offers, all of which were rejected. He finally offered $275,000. Lee claims Golomb accepted. Golomb, however, claims he said he would have to check with his family but had Lee make out four checks, one to him,

(continued)

LEE V. VOYLES
(concluded)

one to Voyles, and two to family members, which Lee did. Voyles endorsed her check. The family decided they could not bear to part with the car, and Golomb returned the checks to Lee. Lee sued to have the court order specific performance of the alleged contract to sell the car.

ISSUE

Was Voyles's signature on the check, along with written offers, sufficient for a "signed writing"?

DECISION

No. Sometimes fascinating facts bring with them exciting legal issues. This is not such an occasion. Even if there was a contract here (which we do not find), it would not be enforceable under the UCC's statute of frauds provision. The contract was for the sale of a good worth more that $500. It had to be evidenced by a signed writing. Although Lee sent several letters to Golomb, including a letter summarizing their "agreement," Golomb never signed any of them. While Voyles did endorse her check, the contract needed Golomb's signature to be binding. In the future, those seeking a royal car for their collections had best negotiate with all the Golombs.

CONCEPT SUMMARY   Statute of Frauds

Type of Contract Required to Be in Writing	Exception (besides Promissory Estoppel)
1. Executor's agreements to personally pay decedent's debts.	
2. Collateral guaranty contracts.	Leading object rule.
3. Transfers of interest in land.	Part performance.
4. Bilateral contracts incapable of performance within one year.	(Construe as possible to perform within a year.)
5. Contract for sale of goods for $500 or more.	Specially manufactured goods.
	Admission.
	Part performance.
	Merchant's failure to object to memo within 10 days.

.... *INTERPRETING CONTRACTS* ....

THE NECESSITY OF INTERPRETATION

Many times the parties to a contract disagree about the meaning of one or more terms of their agreement. When this occurs, the courts must interpret or construe the contract to determine the rights and duties of the parties. The interpretation of uncertain or ambiguous terms is a question for the jury. The basic standard of interpretation is objective: The courts attempt to give the agreement the meaning that a reasonable person would be expected to give it in light of the surrounding facts and circumstances.

RULES OF CONSTRUCTION

The courts have created certain basic rules to guide them in interpreting contracts. Most of these are simply matters of common sense. The first thing a court does is attempt to determine the *principal objective* of the parties. Every clause of the contract is then interpreted in light of this principal objective. Ordinary words are given their usual meaning and technical words their technical meaning unless a different meaning was clearly intended.

If the parties are both members of the same trade, profession, or community in which certain words are commonly given a particular meaning (this is called *usage*), the courts presume the parties intended the words' meanings to be controlled by that trade usage. For example, if the word *dozen* in the bakery business means 13 rather than 12, a contract between two bakers for the purchase of 10 dozen loaves of bread will be presumed to mean 130 loaves rather than 120. Usage can also add provisions to the parties' agreement. If the court finds that a certain practice is a matter of common usage in the trade, profession, or community of the parties, the court assumes that the parties intended to include that practice in their agreement. Parties who are members of a common business, profession, or community and who intend not to be bound by usage should specifically say so in their agreement.

If the parties used a form contract, or the contract is partly printed and partly written, the *written terms control the printed terms* if the two conflict. If one of the parties drafted the contract, ambiguities are resolved *against the party who drafted the contract*. As the *Farm Bureau Insurance* case shows, this is especially true in insurance contracts.

CURTIS O. GRIESS & SONS, INC. V. FARM BUREAU INS. CO. OF NEBRASKA
528 N.W.2d 329 (Sup. Ct. Neb. 1995)

FACTS

Curtis O. Griess & Sons (Griess) was insured by Farm Bureau against physical loss of its livestock caused directly by a covered peril, including windstorms. While there were some exclusions, infectious diseases were not excluded. Griess's swine herd became infected by a pseudorabies virus carried during a tornado from an infected herd downwind. When he sought compensation from Farm Bureau for his $149,000 loss, it refused to pay. Farm Bureau argued that the direct cause of the swine loss was the virus, and that the windstorm was merely a prior condition contributing to the loss.

ISSUE

Should the insurance contract be interpreted to cover the swine loss?

DECISION

Yes. The insured was protected from loss of its swine due to wind damage. The wind need not pick up the swine and throw them to the earth in order to be a direct cause of the loss. If wind-borne materials cause a loss, that loss is considered a direct result of a windstorm. There is no reason to treat a wind-borne virus differently from other wind-borne objects. The windstorm was the dominant, efficient cause that set the virus in motion. Absent the windstorm, there would have been no infection of the swine.

THE PAROL EVIDENCE RULE

THE PURPOSE OF THE RULE

The basic idea behind the parol evidence rule is that when the parties to an agreement have expressed their agreement in a complete, unambiguous writing, the writing is the best evidence of their intent. This is generally true since the terms of the writing are known and irrefutable, whereas oral statements by the parties after a dispute has arisen regarding what they had agreed to may be affected by faulty memory, wishful thinking, or outright bad intent. Even prior writings made by the parties may represent only preliminary subjects of negotiation on which the parties never agreed.

FIGURE 13–4   Parol Evidence Rule

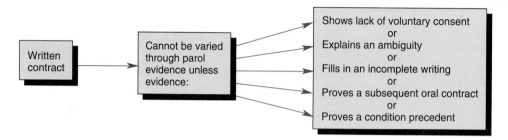

So, the **parol evidence rule** says that a party cannot vary the terms of a written contract by introducing evidence of terms allegedly agreed on *prior to, or contemporaneous with* (at the same time as), the writing. (See Figure 13–4.)

The parol evidence rule is a potential source of danger for parties who reduce their agreements to written form, since it can operate to prevent proof of terms that the parties did, in fact, agree to. For example, Bob buys a house from Susan. They orally agree that Susan will pay for any major repairs the house needs for the first year Bob owns it. The written contract of sale, however, does not include this term, and when the furnace breaks down three months after the sale, Susan refuses to pay the cost of repair. If the written contract is complete and unambiguous, Bob will probably be barred from proving the oral repair term.

The lesson to be learned from this example is that parties who put their agreements in writing should make sure that all the terms of their agreement are included in the writing.

BOGINIS v. MARRIOTT OWNERSHIP RESORTS, INC.
855 F. Supp. 862 (E.D. Va. 1994)

FACTS

Marriott Ownership Resorts, Inc. (MORI), was developing a time-share conversion of the Barbados Beach Club and hired Boginis to be the project director. Boginis signed a letter of employment that said, "This agreement supersedes all prior agreements, written or oral, and sets forth the entire agreement between you and Marriott Ownership Resorts relating to the terms of your employment and may not be orally changed, modified, renewed, or extended." Boginis also signed a clause that said, "I, Herbert Boginis, further understand that no such promise or guarantee of any type concerning the terms and/or conditions is binding upon the Company unless made in writing." Shortly after he assumed his duties in Barbados, Boginis asserted that he realized that MORI has misrepresented the project and his position. Later, after a dispute with his supervisor, he was terminated, allegedly due to downsizing. Boginis sued MORI on several theories including that it fired him in violation of its contractual

policy of not terminating employees for performance-related reasons without written warnings and counseling, and for misrepresenting the position and project. MORI asserted the parol evidence rule, citing the letter of employment.

ISSUE

Can Boginis rely on promises outside the written agreement?

DECISION

No. The integration clause prevents any recovery on oral promises. Boginis signed the contract, clearly understanding that there were no promises outside the agreement. The asserted terms were not consistent oral terms, additional to the contract, and cannot be introduced. Boginis had an individual management contract. It contains no requirement to terminate for cause or to follow

(continued)

BOGINIS V. MARRIOTT OWNERSHIP RESORTS, INC.
(concluded)

certain procedures. The merger clause makes it clear that the written agreement contains all the promises and supersedes any oral promises. The agreement allows for written modifications, and Boginis understood this. It was, in fact, amended to adjust his compensation. If a general employment manual containing disciplinary and termination measures had been intended to be part of the agreement, it could have been made a provision of the contract as were the other conditions. There is no evidence of fraudulent misrepresentation. The statements made to Boginis were statements of expectations about the project. At the time they were made, Boginis knew that discussions about the position were not part of the job offer because he knew MORI was still interviewing others for the position. This and the integration clause bar Boginis's claims.

EXCEPTIONS TO THE PAROL EVIDENCE RULE

There are many situations in which either the writing is not the best evidence of the agreement between the parties, or a party is not challenging the writing but instead is challenging the underlying contractual obligation that the writing represents. These are the bases of the following exceptions, where oral testimony regarding the meaning of the written contract is allowed.

Lack of Voluntary Consent

A party is always allowed to introduce oral proof that the contract the writing represents was entered into as the result of fraud, misrepresentation, duress, undue influence, or mistake. This sort of proof is allowed because it does not seek to contradict the terms of the writing and because of our strong public policy against enforcing such agreements. For the same reasons, oral testimony that attempts to show that the contract is illegal is also allowed.

Ambiguous Contracts

If the terms of the writing are unclear, oral testimony can be introduced to aid the court in interpreting the writing. A party can introduce testimony about the facts and circumstances surrounding the agreement without contradicting its terms.

Incomplete Writings

If the writing is clearly incomplete, a party can introduce proof of consistent oral terms that "fill the gaps" in the writing. A party is never allowed, however, to use this exception to alter, vary, or contradict the written terms of the contract.

Subsequent Oral Contracts

A party can always introduce proof of an oral agreement made after the writing was created. A writing made on the 5th of the month is plainly not the best evidence of an agreement made on the 10th of the month. You should note, however, that subsequent oral modifications of contracts may sometimes be unenforceable due to lack of consideration or failure to comply with the statute of frauds. In addition, the courts look closely at the evidence of the claimed oral modification.

Conditions Precedent

If the written agreement is silent about the date it is to take effect or about any conditions that must occur before it becomes effective, oral testimony can be introduced to prove these facts. Such proof merely elaborates on, but does not contradict, the terms of the writing.

Contracts controlled by the U.N. Convention on the International Sale of Goods also allow oral testimony about the meaning of the contract. While the CISG does not specifically mention parol evidence, courts are interpreting the convention to allow it, as the MCC–Marble case shows.

MCC–Marble Ceramic Center v. Ceramica Nuova D'Agostino, S.P.A.
144 F. 3d 1384 (11th Cir. 1998)

FACTS

MCC–Marble ordered ceramic tile from Ceramica Nuova, an Italian manufacturer, based on samples seen at an Italian trade fair. The price, quality, quantity and delivery terms were put on the front of Ceramica's order form. The back of the form allowed cancellation for default or delay in payment, and required that complaints about defects be made in writing within 10 days. Ceramica did not fulfill several orders, and MCC–Marble sued for breach of contract. Ceramica defended by arguing that MCC–Marble had defaulted on some payments. MCC–Marble then argued that it reduced its payments because some of the tiles were defective; however, it did not give written notice of this. MCC–Marble asserted that it and Ceramica intended not to be bound by the terms on the back of the order form.

ISSUE

Can a court consider parol evidence in a contract dispute governed by the U.N. Convention for the International Sale of Goods?

DECISION

Yes. The CISG differs from the UCC. The drafters of the CISG were comfortable with permitting parties to rely on oral contracts because they did not include any statute of frauds provision and expressly provided for the enforcement of oral contracts. The CISG also directs courts to give due consideration to all relevant circumstances of the case including the negotiations. Although the CISG does not have a statement on parol evidence, it does require the court to consider evidence of a party's subjective intent when signing a contract if the other party to the contract was aware of that intent at the time. The court in this case can consider the parol evidence regarding the parties' intent.

CONCEPT SUMMARY	**Form and Meaning of Contracts**

1. A contract is unenforceable if it lacks a writing as required by the statute of frauds. Contracts covered by the statute of frauds include:
   a. Executor's agreement to personally pay decedent's debts.
   b. Collateral or guaranty contract.
   c. Contract transferring an interest in land.
   d. Bilateral contract incapable of being performed within one year.

2. A contract may be enforceable if promissory estoppel or other exception applies.

3. A written contract cannot be varied by parol evidence (unless exception applies).

QUESTIONS AND PROBLEM CASES

1. Explain the rationale behind the statute of frauds.

2. What is a collateral contract, and how does it differ from a contract that is cosigned?

3. Explain the exceptions to the writing requirement under the UCC.

4. Explain the parol evidence rule.

5. In the *Nakamura v. Fujii* case described in the chapter, Nakamura issued five checks to USC between August 1992 and December 1993, totaling $40,339.33. The Fujiis requested that he also pay tuition for their younger daughter, and Nakamura issued six checks for her tuition between August 1993 and January 1996, totaling $60,964.20. When Nakamura demanded payment, the Fujiis refused to pay, and he then sued. The Fujiis raised the statute of fraud as a defense, arguing that the contract could not be performed within a year. Are they correct?

6. Valentine, an adult, was charged with criminal assault. His parents contacted the Crozier law firm about representing him, and the firm agreed. It claimed the parents orally agreed to guarantee payment for the legal fees incurred by their son. Valentine's mother paid a retainer fee of $250. The firm represented the son until the parents asked it to stop. The firm claimed it was owed $4,200, and sued the parents for that amount. The parents defended by citing the statute of frauds. Is the parents' oral promise enforceable?

7. Dr. Rangle started dating Temple in 1968 when he was 52 and she was 26. In 1971, Rangle employed her in his medical office. In 1976, Rangle and Temple became engaged but Rangle kept avoiding marriage. This avoidance caused Temple to leave him for several short periods. In 1980, they got a marriage license but it expired without being used. In 1982, when she turned 40, Temple was particularly upset about not being married and said she was leaving for good. Rangle pleaded with her to return and promised her that he would leave her his estate, including his real property, in exchange for her returning to work and continuing their relationship. She did, but when Rangle died suddenly in 1983 there was not a properly signed writing conveying the property to Temple. His estate went to his nephew, Unitas. Can Temple show part performance to enforce the promise to convey her the property?

8. Tomson, a clerk in the Kansas Attorney General's office, sued Kansas Attorney General Robert Stephan and others for sexual harassment. The case was settled and the terms of the settlement were not released. There was much speculation in the media about the settlement and whether public funds were involved. Stephan, who was considering running for governor, was concerned about the publicity and held a press conference in which he revealed details of the settlement. Tomson sued him for breach of contract, alleging that a requirement of the settlement agreement was that its terms be kept confidential. The agreement was not in writing, and Stephan defended by raising the statute of frauds. Is the agreement not enforceable since it was intended to last for more than a year?

9. Biggle and Knight, well-known science fiction writers, wanted to write an eight-volume science fiction anthology for Harper & Row. On May 16, 1975, a senior editor sent a typed, unsigned interoffice memo to another editor, Jakab, stating, in part, "I talked to Biggle and agreed to do the books. We need to do a separate contract for each book." On July 28, 1975, Jakab wrote to Biggle acknowledging receipt of contracts for three books, forwarding three additional contracts for different volumes, and noting that there were two more contracts to come. Contracts for the first four volumes were signed by both parties; contracts for three other volumes were signed by Biggle and Knight, but not by Harper & Row. Harper & Row issued an announcement of the series, identifying Biggle and Knight as the editors, describing it as "a complete science fiction textbook in eight topically oriented paperback volumes," and described the contents. In November, Jakab wrote to Biggle suggesting that the series be done in four volumes. When he refused, the senior editor wrote saying they should get another publisher if they were going to insist on eight volumes, and Biggle sued.

Both parties agreed the statute of frauds applied to the contract because it could not be performed within a year. Harper & Row argued there was no writing signed by it that committed it to eight volumes, that the four signed contracts related only to individual volumes, not to an entire anthology. Are the writings, taken together, sufficient under the statute of frauds to enforce an eight-volume contract?

10. French was the president and 25 percent owner of two companies that served the Northtown Mall in Spokane. At the request of the mall owner, French helped arrange its sale to Sabey. To ensure continuity in mall operations, Sabey offered to hire French as vice-president of its retail division. The terms they allegedly negotiated included a five-year term of employment, renewable for another five years, with termination at the option of either party on six months' written notice. French wrote some of the terms up in a letter that Sabey orally agreed to but never signed. French worked for Sabey for 11 months and then was fired without notice. Can French enforce the contract? Explain.

11. Davis, while helping a neighbor free a car stuck in the snow, was severely injured by a board that was thrown out from beneath the wheels of the car. Davis had medical coverage under a Preferred Risk Mutual insurance policy for injuries caused by an accident from being struck by a car. Preferred rejected his claim for the board-related injuries. Are Davis's injuries covered by the insurance contract?

12. MacFarlane met Rich while he was vacationing in England. A year later they agreed to be married, and Rich agreed to give up her jobs and home in England and move to New Hampshire. MacFarlane insisted that Rich sign an antenuptial agreement, she refused, and the wedding was called off. Later they again set a wedding date, but three days before the wedding MacFarlane again insisted on Rich's signing the agreement. Rich signed it on the day they wed. Fourteen months later MacFarlane and Rich were in the Cayman Islands having Christmas dinner when MacFarlane left the table "to change his clothes" and never returned. Rich did not see him again until he appeared for the divorce hearing several months later. At the hearing MacFarlane argued that the agreement was voided due to a clause stating that if MacFarlane left Rich for another woman (which he claimed he had), the agreement would be null and void. Rich sought to introduce oral evidence showing that a literal reading of the clause was not what was intended; it was intended to protect her from a philandering husband by allowing her, at her option, to void the agreement if he ran off with another woman, and to thereupon ask the court to award her more than the agreement would have given her. Should Rich be allowed to orally alter the plain meaning of the language?

CHAPTER 14

Third Parties' Contract Rights

Peterson had a three-year employment contract as a newscaster–anchorman on WTOP-TV. After one year under this contract, the station was sold, and Peterson's contract was assigned to the new owner. Peterson subsequently negotiated a contract with another station and resigned. When he was sued by the new owner for breach of contract, Peterson claimed the new owner had no rights under his contract with the former owners of the station and therefore could not sue him.

- *Can someone pursue rights under another person's contract?*
- *Did Peterson have a right not to have his contract assigned to someone with whom he had not contracted?*
- *Could Peterson hold the original owners liable if the new owners breached the contract with him?*

FIGURE 14–1   Third Parties' Contract Rights

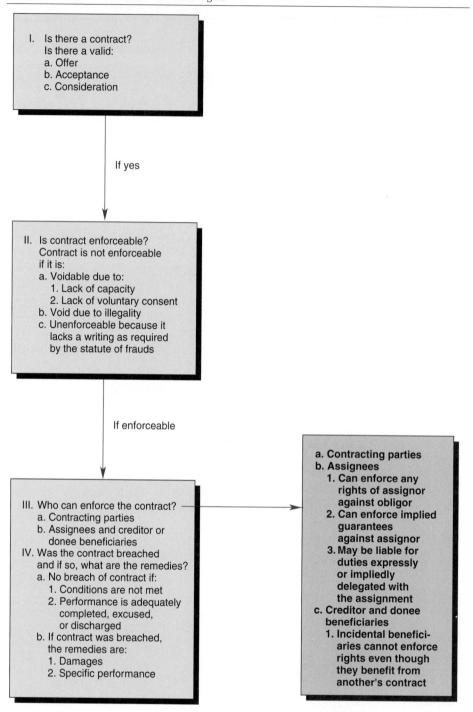

Up to this point our discussion of contracts has focused on the rights and duties of the original parties to the contract. There are, however, two kinds of situations in which persons who were not originally parties to a contract may claim some interest in it: These concern assignments of contracts and third-party beneficiaries of contracts.

.... **ASSIGNMENT OF CONTRACTS** ....

DEFINITION

A contract consists of both rights and duties. A contracting party has the duty to perform his or her own promise and the right to receive the other party's promised performance. These rights and duties can usually be transferred to third persons. When *rights* under a contract are transferred, this is called an **assignment.** The transfer of *duties* is called a **delegation.** Delegations will be discussed later in this chapter.

The person who makes an assignment is called the **assignor,** and the person who accepts the assignment is called the **assignee.** After an assignment, the assignee is entitled to whatever performance the assignor had a right to under the original contract. The other original party to the contract (called the *promisor* or *obligor*) must render all performance to the assignee. For example, Bill owes Frank $100, payable in six months. Frank, who needs money today, assigns his rights to the payment to Mary for $80. Bill (the promisor or obligor) must now pay Mary (the assignee) the $100 he previously owed a duty to pay to Frank (the assignor). (See Figure 14–2.)

No particular formalities are required to create an assignment. It can be done orally or in writing, so long as the assignor's intent to assign is clear. In addition, consideration is generally not required. Rights can be given away as well as sold.

FIGURE 14–2   Assignment Obligations

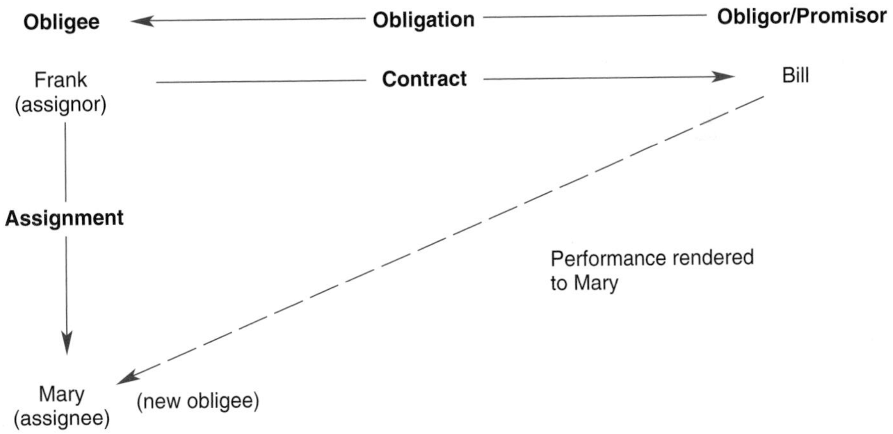

WHAT CONTRACTS ARE ASSIGNABLE?

Not all contracts are assignable over the objection of the promisor. Any assignment that would *materially alter* the duties of the promisor is unenforceable, since the promisor cannot be required to do something significantly more than, or different from, what he or she originally agreed to do. So, if Acme Sugar Company has entered a "requirements" contract to supply all the sugar requirements of Goody Candy Company, a small candy manufacturer, Goody could not assign its contract rights to

Yummy Candy Corporation, a much larger candy manufacturer. Clearly, Yummy's sugar requirements would be much greater than Goody's.

Contracts involving *personal rights* are also generally nonassignable. These are contracts in which some element of personal skill, credit, character, or judgment is an essential part of the agreement. In such a case, the substitution of the assignee for the assignor would materially change the nature of the performance required of the promisor. Employment contracts are therefore generally held nonassignable. In the *Peterson* case, however, the court found that Peterson's contract was assignable since his duties did not change and the sale merely substituted one corporate owner for another. The corporate owners did not render personal services to Peterson.

Contracts that *expressly forbid assignment* are also generally nonassignable. However, some states refuse to enforce such clauses where the rights assigned would otherwise be assignable. Other states interpret nonassignment clauses very strictly. For example, a court may say that a clause barring assignment of the contract prohibits only the delegation of duties. The *Restatement* and the Uniform Commercial Code take this latter approach. Bankruptcy filings can also cause a court to assign a contract despite nonassignment clauses.

CLAREMONT ACQUISITION CORP. v. GENERAL MOTORS CORP.
113 F.3d 1029 (9th Cir. 1997)

FACTS

The Cadillac, Pontiac/GMC Truck, Ford, Isuzu, and Hyundai dealerships at the Claremont Auto Center filed for bankruptcy under Chapter 11. The bankruptcy court approved Worthington as the purchaser of the dealership's assets, including the dealer franchises. However, the franchises could not be assigned without the consent of the manufacturer. G.M. refused to consent, and the dealership sought an order compelling the assignment.

ISSUE

Can the franchise contracts be assigned?

DECISION

Yes. Although it is technically more accurate to speak of the assignment of a party's rights under a contract and the delegation of duties, we follow the more common use of the term "assign" as encompassing both assignment of rights and delegation of duties. Notwithstanding a provision in an executory contract or in applicable law that prohibits, restricts, or conditions the assignment of the contract, a bankruptcy trustee may assign the contract so long as the assignee gives adequate assurance of future performance. Worthington, however, did not meet the requirements necessary for assignment; the contract is not assigned to them.

Assignments *contrary to public policy* are also not effective. *Assignments of future wages* are an example. In order to protect wage earners from unwisely impoverishing themselves, some states prohibit wage assignments by statute. Others allow such assignments but regulate them in various ways, such as limiting the amount that may be assigned.

Generally, all other kinds of assignments that do not involve personal relationships or increase the promisor's burden are enforceable. Promises to pay money, deliver goods, or sell land are generally assignable. Contracts not to compete with a buyer of a business or an employer are also generally assignable with the sale of the business. The purpose of such contracts is to protect the *goodwill* of the business (the value of the business as a going concern), an asset that can be sold with the business.

.... **THE CONSEQUENCES OF ASSIGNMENT** ....

THE RIGHTS AND DUTIES OF ASSIGNEES

An assignee is entitled to all the rights his or her assignor had under the assigned contract, including the right to the promisor's performance. If the promisor does not perform, the assignee can sue for nonperformance. An assignee, however, cannot acquire any greater rights than the assignor has. Therefore, if the promisor has a good defense against the assignor (e.g., fraud, lack of consideration, or lack of capacity), that defense is also good against the assignee.

Assignees should promptly notify the promisor of the assignment. This is necessary because the promisor who renders performance to the assignor without notice of the assignment has no further liability under the contract. Promisors with notice of the assignment who render performance to the assignor or to any third party remain liable to the assignee under the assigned contract. Assignors who accept performance from the promisor after the assignment hold any benefits they receive as trustee for their assignees.

Notice to the promisor may be important in one other situation. If the assignor later wrongfully assigns the contract to a second assignee who pays for it without notice of the first assignment, a question of priority results. Who is entitled to the promisor's performance, and who is stuck with a lawsuit against the assignor? The majority of states follow the *American rule,* which holds that the first assignee has priority. Some states, however, follow the *English rule,* which gives priority to the first assignee to give notice of assignment. In both types of states, a potential assignee should contact the promisor before taking the assignment.

Assignors who are *paid* for making an assignment are potentially liable to assignees for certain **implied guarantees.** These guarantees are imposed by law unless the assignment agreement clearly indicates to the contrary. They are:

1. The assigned claim is valid, which means that:
    a. The promisor has capacity to contract.
    b. The contract is not illegal.
    c. The contract is not voidable for any other reason known to the assignor (such as fraud or misrepresentation).
    d. The contract has not been discharged prior to assignment.
2. The assignor has good title to the rights assigned.
3. The assignor will not do anything to impair the value of the assignment.
4. Any written instrument representing the assigned claim is genuine.

Assignors who wrongfully assign the same claim more than once are therefore liable to an assignee who is later held to have acquired no rights against the promisor. The assignor does not impliedly warrant the solvency of the promisor.

DELEGATION OF DUTIES

When a promisor appoints another to perform his duties under a contract, this is called a *delegation.* Like assignments, not all duties are delegable. If the duty to be performed could be performed fully by many different persons, it is delegable. If performance depends on the personal skill, character, or judgment of the promisor, however, it may not be delegated. Thus, in the *Peterson* case that opened the chapter,

Peterson would not have been able to delegate his duties to another newscaster-anchorman since they involved his personal skill. Public policy can also prevent the delegation of duties.

BLOCHER V. DEBARTOLO PROPERTIES MANAGEMENT, INC.
760 N.E.2d 229 (Ind. Ct. App. 2001)

FACTS

DeBartolo, a construction management company, was hired as the general contractor to renovate the Richmond Square Mall. Its sole role was to manage the construction activities performed entirely by the contractors it hired. One of those subcontractors, Smither, was hired under an agreement whereby it agreed to comply with laws, rules, and regulations including those of the Occupational Safety and Health Administration (OSHA). It agreed to pay any fines or penalties related to its work arising from breach of such rules and regulations. In order to complete its work, Smither had to cut holes in the mall's roof to install skylights. In its contract with subcontractors, DeBartolo specifically retained jurisdiction over roof penetration for bonding purposes. While working on the roof, Blocher fell through a hole cut by another worker and died. The next day an OSHA inspector visited the site and issued several citations to Smither. Blocher's estate sued DeBartolo. DeBartolo defended by saying that Smither was the responsible party.

ISSUE

Did DeBartolo successfully delegate its safety duties as a supervisory contractor to Smither?

DECISION

No. A principal is not liable for the negligence of an independent contractor unless the principal is charged by law or contract with performing the specific duty. Blocher alleged that DeBartolo had assumed the duty for workplace safety at the mall, including the subcontractors' compliance with OSHA regulations. While one can delegate the performance of the work to a subcontractor, it can never delegate the responsibility or legal liability for the work.

Sometimes it is not clear whether a delegation was intended. Does an assignment of the assignor's rights carry with it an implied delegation of the assignor's duties under the contract? Unless the assignment agreement clearly indicates a contrary intent, courts today tend to interpret assignments as including a delegation of the assignor's duties. A promise on the part of the assignee to perform these duties is implied, and this implied promise is enforceable by *either* the promisor or the assignor. Both the Code and the *Restatement* support this interpretation. If general assignment language is used, such as an assignment of "the contract," or of "all my rights under the contract," courts following the Code or *Restatement* would interpret it as creating both an assignment and a delegation.

The promisor who delegates duties is *still liable* to the promisee if the party to whom the duties were delegated fails to satisfactorily perform them. This rule is necessary to make contracts truly binding; otherwise, a promisor could avoid virtually all liability by merely delegating duties she did not want to perform.

The only exception to this rule is when the parties enter into a novation. A **novation** is a new, separate agreement by the promisee to release the original promisor from liability in exchange for a third party's agreement to assume the promisor's duties. To have a novation requires more than the obligee's consent to having the delegate perform the duties. The language used by the parties or the circumstances surrounding the transaction must show that the obligee consented to the *substitution* of one obligor for another.

ROSENBERG V. SON, INC.
491 N.W.2d 71 (Sup. Ct. N.D. 1992)

FACTS

In 1980, Pratt contracted to buy the Rosenbergs' Dairy Queen in Grand Forks, N.D., for $62,000—$10,000 down and the remaining $52,000 in quarterly payments at 10 percent interest. In 1982 Pratt assigned her rights and delegated her duties under the contract to Son, Inc. (Son), and moved to Arizona. The Rosenbergs consented to the assignment. In the assignment contract Son promised to indemnify Pratt against all claims brought under the contract. In 1984 Son assigned the contract to Merit Corporation. Merit used the inventory and equipment of the Dairy Queen as collateral on a loan. Merit paid the Rosenbergs the quarterly payments due until 1988, when it filed for bankruptcy. At that time $17,326.24 was due. The bank repossessed the Dairy Queen equipment and inventory to satisfy the loan, and the Rosenbergs sued Pratt and Son for the $17,326.24. Pratt defended by arguing that there had been a novation, and only Son, Inc., was liable.

ISSUE

Was the consented-to assignment a novation?

DECISION

No. It is well established that a contracting party cannot escape its liability under a contract by merely assigning its duties and rights to a third party. The original debtor remains liable on the contract in spite of the delegation, and the seller can seek the amount due from either the assignor or the assignee. It is not, however, legally impossible to rid oneself of an obligation under a contract. A party can seek approval from the other original party for a release and substitute a new party in its place. This is called a novation. However, a novation must be clearly stated by the terms of the agreement. It is clear that the assignment agreement between Pratt and Son was only an assignment, not a novation. There was no mention of discharging Pratt, and the indemnity clause shows that Pratt contemplated the possibility of being held liable if Son did not pay. The Rosenbergs assented to an assignment only, not a novation. The agreement between Pratt and Son does not unilaterally affect the Rosenbergs' rights.

THIRD-PARTY BENEFICIARY CONTRACTS

Generally, those who are not parties to a contract have no rights in the contract even though they may benefit from its performance. If the parties to the contract *intended* to benefit a third party, however, the third party can enforce the contract. There are two classes of **third-party beneficiaries** that have such enforcement rights: **donee beneficiaries** and **creditor beneficiaries.** If the third party only incidentally benefits from the contract and was not an intended beneficiary, he or she is an **incidental beneficiary** and cannot enforce it.

A factor that is often considered in determining intent to benefit is whether the person making the promise to perform was to render performance directly to the third party. For example, if Mary contracts with Greetings Galore to have balloons delivered to Joe on his birthday, the fact that the balloons were to be delivered to Joe would be good evidence that the parties intended to benefit Joe. Once a donee or creditor beneficiary has accepted the contract, or relied on it, the original parties cannot cancel or modify the contract without the third party's consent, unless the original contract gives them the right to do so. Generally, life insurance contracts give the insured the right to change the beneficiary without the beneficiary's consent.

DONEE BENEFICIARIES

A third person is a *donee beneficiary* if the promisee's *primary purpose* in contracting was to make a *gift* of the contracted performance to the third party. Either the promisee or the donee beneficiary can sue the promisor for not performing the promise. The beneficiary can recover the value of the promised performance, while the promisee can recover damages resulting from nonperformance (usually only nominal damages). In the example above, Joe was a donee beneficiary of Galore and Mary's contract, and he as well as Mary could sue if Galore failed to perform. (See Figure 14–3.)

FIGURE 14–3   Donee Beneficiary

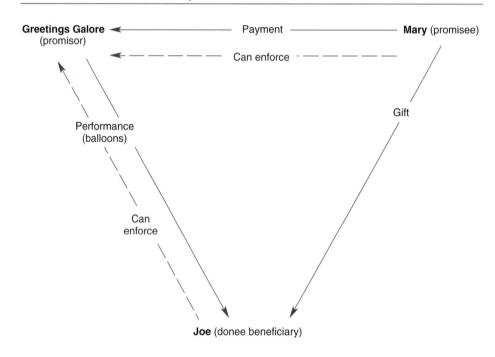

CHERRY v. CROW
845 F. Supp. 1520 (M.D. Fla. 1994)

FACTS

Cherry was booked into Polk County Jail to serve a sentence for driving under the influence. At that time, he informed PHS medical staff, the group which had been hired to provide health care services for jail inmates, that he consumed a case of beer a day. Over the next two days, he repeatedly asked for medical attention for symptoms related to alcohol withdrawal. The next day his wife informed PHS that her husband had a history of delirium tremens, a sometimes lethal form of delirium induced by

withdrawal, and that he needed immediate medical attention. A few hours later his cellmates called for medical attention for him, and he was transferred to the infirmary for observation. Due to his hallucinations, he was shackled to his bed. Later, Cherry walked or jumped off the end of the bed, and due to the shackles, landed head first on the concrete floor. He died five days later from head injuries. Cherry's estate sued PHS for breach of contract, among other claims.

(continued)

CHERRY V. CROW
(concluded)

ISSUE

Was Cherry a donee beneficiary of the contract between Polk County and PHS?

DECISION

Yes. When it is manifest from the nature or terms of a contract that the parties thereto intended its provisions to be for the benefit of a third party as well as for the benefit of the parties themselves, the third party can maintain an action on the contract. The contract between PHS and Polk County stated:

WHEREAS, the SHERIFF has the statutory and constitutional duty to provide necessary and proper medical . . . care services for persons remanded to his care, custody and control . . .

WHEREAS, the SHERIFF is desirous of contracting with PHS and PHS is desirous of contracting with the SHERIFF to provide total health care services *for the inmates/detainees* . . . housed within the county correctional system . . .

The Sheriff and PHS intended to benefit inmates through their contract, including Cherry. He can sue for its breach.

Life insurance contracts are a common form of donee beneficiary contract. The insurance company (the promisor), in return for payment of a premium, contracts with the owner of the policy (the promisee) to pay benefits to a beneficiary on the death of the insured (who may or may not be the promisee). If the insured dies and the company does not pay, the beneficiary can sue for the policy amount.

CREDITOR BENEFICIARIES

If the promisor's performance will *satisfy a legal duty* that the promisee owes a third party, the third party is a *creditor beneficiary*. The duty owed can be any kind of legal duty and need not necessarily be the payment of money. The creditor beneficiary has rights against *both* the promisee and the promisor.

For example, Bill buys a car on time from Honest Bob's Motors. Bill then sells the car to Sue, who agrees to make the remaining payments Bill owes Honest Bob's. Honest Bob's is a creditor beneficiary of Bill (the promisee) and Sue's (the promisor) contract and can recover the balance due from either Bill or Sue. (See Figure 14–4.) In the *Rosenberg* case, the Rosenbergs were the creditor beneficiaries of the contract between Pratt and Son, Inc., and they could collect from either Pratt or Son.

INCIDENTAL BENEFICIARIES

Occasionally, the performance of a contract intended solely for the benefit of the promisee will also incidentally benefit a third person. These *incidental beneficiaries* acquire no rights under the contract and so cannot sue for nonperformance.

For example, Dave's house is in bad condition. He hires Ace Construction Company to paint and reroof the house. Dave's neighbor Aimee would benefit from this contract, since Dave's house is an eyesore that may affect the value of Aimee's property. Aimee, however, is an incidental beneficiary of Dave's contract with Ace and has no right to sue Ace if it breaches the contract. Members of the general public are generally held to be incidental beneficiaries of contracts such as street repair contracts entered into by municipalities or other government units. The specific terms of the contract in the *Cherry* case altered this general rule.

Figure 14–4   Creditor Beneficiary

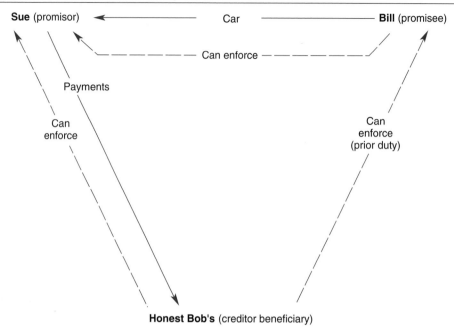

Mortise v. United States
102 F. 3d 693 (2d. Cir. 1996)

Facts

Bernard and Cheryl Mortise and another couple were riding their all terrain vehicles (ATVs) on a Saturday night in early March on land owned by Oneida County in New York. As they had before, they sported on logging roads. As before, they did not notice any fences or signs restricting use. Unknown to them, the county had given the Army National Guard permission to use the land for field training exercises; one was occurring that night. The United States agreed to pay the county for any damages caused by the exercises. The Guardsmen set up trip wires near their mortar placements so that when faux enemies approached, smoke flares would be set off, revealing the "enemy" position. After the ATVs went up a road, a guardsman rigged a trip wire across the road. When they came back down single file, Bernard, in the lead, tripped the wire, igniting a flare that spewed debris over him. Instantly, Guardsmen in camouflage came out of the woods, pointed their guns at him, and "dry fired" (i.e., no bullets). He pleaded with them not to shoot. One of the Guardsmen fired a blank round. Cheryl thought her husband had been shot and started screaming. They

were told to shut up and shut off their ATVs. The Guardsmen, convinced they were "enemy" decoys, treated them brusquely, cursing and telling them they were prisoners. Soon a lieutenant arrived, realized the mistake, explained what had happened, and allowed them to go. The Mortises sued for assault, a claim for which the U.S. has not waived sovereign immunity, and therefore the claim was barred. They then claimed to be beneficiaries of the indemnity contract between the county and the U.S.

Issue

Were the Mortises incidental beneficiaries of the indemnity agreement between the county and the U.S., and therefore barred from suit?

Decision

Yes. The Mortises argue that they are third-party beneficiaries of the agreement between the county and the U.S., and that they can therefore sue the U.S. for their damages. Generally, only an intended beneficiary of a contract may assert a claim. There is no indication that

(continued)

MORTISE V. UNITED STATES
(concluded)

the agreement between the federal government and Oneida County was intended to confer a benefit on the Mortises. Indeed, there is no evidence that the government or the county even knew of their existence. The agreement conferred no benefit on any entity other than the county.

CONCEPT SUMMARY   Enforcing the Contract

Who can enforce the contract?

1. Contracting parties.

2. Assignees.
   a. Can enforce any rights of assignor against obligor.
   b. Can enforce implied guarantees against assignor.
   c. May be liable for duties expressly or impliedly delegated with the assignment.

3. Donee and creditor beneficiaries.
   Incidental beneficiaries cannot enforce rights even though they benefit from another's contract. Members of the general public are usually incidental beneficiaries of governmental contracts for goods and services.

········ *QUESTIONS AND PROBLEM CASES* ········

1. What is an *implied guarantee?* Give two examples.
2. What is required for a novation of a contract?
3. What is a *creditor beneficiary?* Can she enforce the contract?
4. Douglas, an employee of Page–Wilson Corp. (P–W), signed agreements stating that he would not use intellectual property or customer lists to P–W's disadvantage and that he would not work or consult for a competitor for one year after leaving. Four years later P–W was sold, and several months later Douglas quit. He was subsequently sued by the new owner for soliciting customers and establishing a competing business. Douglas argued that he had no contractual relationship with the new owners and that therefore they could not enforce his agreements with P–W. Is he correct?
5. In 1981 Cooper sold the Blackwell Sand Company, including its goodwill, to Stewart. The sales agreement contained a covenant not to compete that prohibited Cooper from entering in any manner into the sand business within 100 miles of Meridian, Mississippi, for 10 years.

   In 1982 Stewart assigned all his interest in the company to Gidden, his former partner. Subsequently, Cooper reentered the sand business, and Gidden sought to enforce the covenant not to compete against Cooper. Cooper claimed the covenant was a personal covenant between himself and Stewart and thus could not be assigned. Is a covenant not to compete accompanying the sale of a business assignable?

6. Smith, owner of an apartment complex, was converting the complex to a cooperative by selling individual units. Each purchaser was required to pay Smith an extra $15 per month for utilities, taxes, and insurance. Smith sold all his rights in the complex to Roberts and assigned the purchasers' contracts to him. Roberts failed to pay the applicable property tax, and Radley, a purchasing tenant, sued him to compel payment of the tax. Roberts argued that in purchasing Smith's interests, all he bought was the right to collect the payments made by tenants and that he assumed no duties. Is Roberts liable for the property tax?

7. Theresa and Ricky LaShelle divorced in 1985. Theresa was awarded the house, where she resided with the couple's two children. She was responsible for paying the first mortgage contract on the home, and Ricky for paying the second mortgage. His assumption of the second mortgage was in lieu of his paying maintenance and child support. At the time of the divorce, Ricky was losing $40,000 per year; Theresa was earning $12,000 per year. Ricky continued to lose money in 1986 and finally sold his tractor to Ostendorf in return for Ostendorf's paying off the second mortgage contract, which he failed to do. Ricky later filed for bankruptcy and sought to be discharged from his duty to pay off the second mortgage. Was Ricky's duty to make the mortgage payments delegable?

8. In 1974 Spiklevitz loaned money to the Herons. The Herons signed a note, promising to repay $4,800 by January 15, 1975. In 1980 the Herons sold their business to the Markmill Corporation. In conjunction with the sale, Markmill signed an "Assumption of Obligation" in which it agreed to assume and pay debts of the business. The outstanding balance of $3,510 still owed to Spiklevitz was listed as one of these debts. When Markmill failed to pay, Spiklevitz sued. Can Spiklevitz collect the debt from Markmill?

9. Anderson went to Monahan Beaches Jewelry Center to look for an engagement ring for his fiancée, Warren. The salesman discussed various attributes of rings to help define what might be pleasing to Warren. Anderson later bought a "diamond" ring and gave it to Warren on Christmas. Shortly thereafter, Warren noticed a chip in the stone and returned it to Monahan, which agreed to replace it with a stone of equal or greater value. Warren then took the ring to another store for appraisal, at which time she discovered the alleged diamond was really cut glass or cubic zirconia. Can Warren sue Monahan for breach of contract under Anderson and Monahan's contract?

10. In 1983 an underground water main burst in Manhattan and flooded the building where Con Edison had an electricity supply substation. A fire resulted and disrupted electric power for four days. This occurred during the biannual "Buyers Week" when merchandisers from around the world were there to visit fashion showrooms and place orders for future seasons. Some 200 Garment Center businesses brought suit against Con Edison, among others. Some of the businesses had no direct contractual relationship with Con Edison. They argued their lease agreements with their landlords, who were the direct contracting entities with Con Edison, obligated them to pay an apportioned share of the electricity expenses to the landlords and that therefore they could sue under the contracts between the landlords and Con Edison. Are they correct?

CHAPTER 15

Performance and Remedies

Kapenis put in a bid to buy the Gildeas' house. The contract contained a clause stating that the offer was subject to Kapenis "obtaining suitable financing interest rate no greater than 12¾ percent." Kapenis rejected all loan programs offered to him as having monthly payments that were too high, as not being assumable, or as having terms that were not satisfactory. Kapenis then withdrew his offer. The Gildeas sued him for breach of contract.

- *Did the interest rate condition have to be met before there would be an enforceable contract?*
- *Did Kapenis breach the contract by rejecting all financing programs available?*
- *If the contract was breached, what are the appropriate remedies?*

FIGURE 15–1   Performance and Remedies

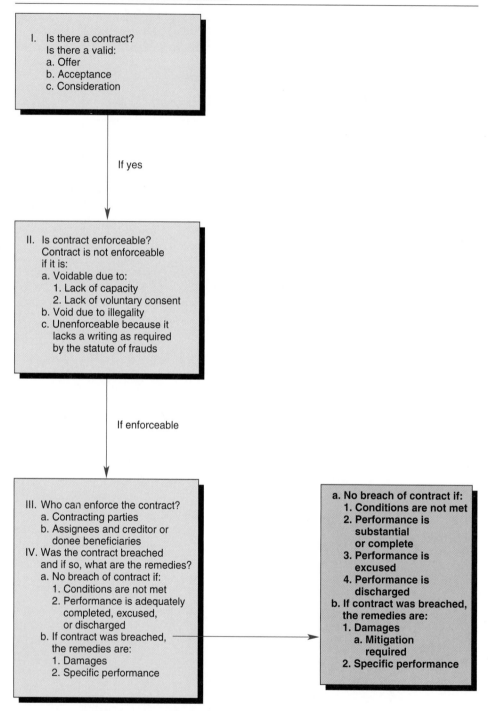

In Chapter 6, the introductory chapter to this part of the text, we defined contracts as *legally enforceable agreements*. If an agreement meets all the requirements we have discussed in previous chapters, it is a contract and therefore enforceable. In the majority of contract situations, issues of enforceability never even arise because the parties perform their duties voluntarily and fully.

If a dispute arises between the parties to a contract, however, several important questions may be raised. Many of these questions deal with the parties' duties of performance under the contract. Are there any *conditions* in the contract that affect the parties' duties? If so, have these conditions been met? Have parties who have rendered performance under the contract satisfied their contractual duties, or is their performance so defective that it amounts to a *material breach* of the contract? Does a party who has failed to perform satisfactorily have some legal *excuse* for not performing, or has his or her duty to perform been *discharged* in some way?

Even if it is clear that one of the parties has materially breached the contract, a dispute may still arise about the *remedies* to which the other party is entitled. The answers to these questions can be very important in determining the rights of the parties.

CONDITIONS

DEFINITION

Generally, a party's contractual duty to perform arises at the time the contract is formed, even though the time for performing is set for a future date. The parties may, however, provide that a party's duty to perform is qualified by the happening of some event, or **condition.**

TYPES OF CONDITIONS

If the event must occur before a party's duty to perform arises, this is called a **condition precedent.** For example, Tom promises to buy Mary's race car for $350,000 if the car wins the Indianapolis 500 race. The car's winning the race is a condition precedent to Tom's duty to buy. If the car does not win, a *failure of condition* has occurred, and Tom has no duty to buy the car. Likewise, Kapenis' condition of suitable financing, described in the introductory case, had to be met before he was obligated to buy the Gildeas' house.

If the happening of a condition discharges an existing duty to perform, this is called a **condition subsequent.** For example, Joan and Mike enter a contract requiring Joan to mow Mike's grass on July 3, the day before his big party on July 4, unless it rains. If it rains, Joan does not have to mow the grass, and Mike's duty to pay Joan is discharged.

If the contract calls for the parties to perform their duties at the same time, each party's duty to perform is conditioned on the other party's performance. These conditions are called **concurrent conditions.** Neither party can enforce the other party's promise without performing or *tendering* (offering) performance. For example, Pete agrees to buy Wendi's cookie store for $150,000. Pete does not have a duty to pay the $150,000 unless Wendi tenders the store. Wendi does not have a duty to give Pete the store unless Pete tenders the $150,000.

THE CREATION OF CONDITIONS

Conditions may be expressly or impliedly created. **Express conditions** are created by oral or written statements in the contract. No special words are necessary to create an express condition, but they are often created by words such as *provided that, on condition that, if, when, while, after,* and *as soon as.*

The nature of the parties' contract may also lead the courts to imply a **constructive (implied) condition** on the parties' duties of performance. For example, in bilateral contracts that call for an exchange of performances at the same date, or that do not state a time for performance, the law infers that each party's performance is a *constructive concurrent condition* of the other party's duty to perform. So, in a contract between Sam and Jan for the sale of a car, Sam's duty to pay for the car is conditioned on Jan's delivery of the car, and Jan's duty to deliver is conditioned on Sam's tender of the purchase price. If, however, their contract had called for Jan to deliver the car on a stated date and Sam to pay for the car two weeks later, Jan's delivery would be a *constructive condition precedent* of Mike's duty to pay.

CONCEPT SUMMARY	Conditions	
	Conditions	
Condition Precedent	Performance excused *unless* condition occurs.	
Condition Subsequent	Performance excused *if* condition occurs.	
Concurrent Conditions	*Tender* of performance precedes right to demand performance.	

STANDARDS OF PERFORMANCE

A common source of dispute between contracting parties is whether the parties have fulfilled their duties of performance under the contract. Promisors must perform their contractual duties in the manner they have promised to perform them. If they do not, they are liable for breach of contract, they are not entitled to payment under the contract, and the contract can be terminated. The courts have attempted to create practical, commonsense standards for evaluating the parties' performance They recognize three basic degrees of performance: *complete or satisfactory performance, substantial performance,* and *material breach* of contract.

COMPLETE OR SATISFACTORY PERFORMANCE

Some kinds of contractual duties can be completely and perfectly performed. The payment of money, the delivery of a deed, and the delivery of certain goods are all duties that can be performed to a high degree of perfection. Promisors who completely perform such duties are entitled to receive the full contract price in return. Promisors in complete performance contracts who do not completely perform cannot recover the contract price. They may, however, recover in quasi contract for benefits conferred on the other party. In the education context, as the *Ross* case illustrates, courts will recognize breach of contract claims only for failure of a private institution to render satisfactory performance of very specific promises.

ROSS v. CREIGHTON UNIVERSITY
957 F.2d 410 (7th Cir. 1992)

FACTS

Ross was recruited to play basketball at Creighten. He came from an academically disadvantaged background, and at the time he enrolled, Ross was at an academic level far below that of the average Creighton student. For example, he scored in the bottom fifth percentile of college-bound seniors taking the ACT, while the average freshman admitted to Creighton with him scored in the upper 27 percent. Creighton realized Ross's academic limitations when it admitted him, and, to induce him to attend and play basketball, assured him that he would receive sufficient tutoring so that he "would receive a meaningful education while at Creighton." Ross attended

(continued)

ROSS v. CREIGHTON UNIVERSITY
(concluded)

Creighton from 1978–82. He maintained a D average and earned 96 of the 128 credits needed to graduate. On the advice of the athletics department, he took many of these credits in courses such as marksmanship and the theory of basketball, which did not count toward a University degree. He also alleged that the University hired a secretary to read his assignments and prepare and type his papers. When he left Creighton, Ross had the overall language skills of a fourth-grader and the reading skills of a seventh-grader. He took remedial classes for a year at a preparatory school at Creighton's expense, attending classes with grade-school children, and then enrolled at Roosevelt University. He was forced to withdraw from there for lack of funds. In 1987 he suffered a "major depressive episode" during which he barricaded himself in a motel room and threw furniture out the window. He claimed the furniture "symbolized" Creighton. Ross sued Creighton for breach of contract, among other theories.

ISSUE

Can Ross sue Creighton for breach of contract?

DECISION

Yes. It is generally held that the basic legal relationship between a student and a private university or college is contractual in nature. The catalogs, bulletins, circulars, and regulations of the institution made available to the matriculant become a part of the contract. It is clear, however, that not all aspects of a university–student relationship are subject to remedy through a breach-of-contract claim. For example, a decision of the school regarding the academic qualifications of the student will not be reviewed by the courts because they are not qualified to judge this. Likewise, courts will not judge the general quality of education provided to the student. Thus, plaintiff must allege more than that the institution did not provide a good enough education. He must point to an identifiable contractual promise that was breached. If the school took tuition money and provided no education, promised a set number of hours of instruction and did not deliver, or promised a course of instruction that would qualify the student as a journeyman and did not present the fundamentals necessary, a breach of contract suit would be available. Ross alleges more than that the University failed to provide him with an education of a certain quality. He alleges it knew he was not academically qualified to participate in its curriculum and specifically promised him he would be able to participate in a meaningful way by providing specific services to him. The court does not have to judge whether Creighton provided deficient services but whether it failed to provide any real access to its academic curriculum at all. Ross can sue for breach of contract.

SUBSTANTIAL PERFORMANCE

Some kinds of contractual duties are very difficult to perform perfectly due to their nature and the limits of human ability. Examples of these are found in construction projects, agricultural contracts, and many contracts for personal or professional services. Such duties are, however, capable of being substantially performed in most cases. **Substantial performance** is performance that falls short of complete performance in minor respects but does not deprive the promisee of a material part of the consideration that was bargained for. Promisors may make an honest attempt to perform, but due to lack of ability or factors beyond their control, they may fall short of complete performance. If their performance is such that it cannot be returned to them, and there was no express condition for complete performance, they will be held to have substantially performed their duties. This allows the promisor to be compensated for his or her performance.

An example of substantial performance is a building that deviates slightly from the contract's specifications. What constitutes substantial performance depends on the circumstances of each case. The promisor who substantially performs is generally entitled to the contract prices less any damage the other party has suffered as a result of the defective performance. If the promisor willfully failed to completely perform, the doctrine of substantial performance will not apply.

MATERIAL BREACH

The promisor is guilty of **material breach** of contract if his or her performance fails to reach the degree of perfection the other party is justified in expecting under the circumstances. Such a promisor has no right of action under the contract and is liable to the other party for damages resulting from the breach. If the promisor's defective performance conveyed some benefits to the party that cannot be returned, the promisor may, under a quasi contract theory, be able to recover the reasonable value of benefits conferred from the other party.

M. J. OLDENSTEDT PLUMBING CO., INC. V. K-MART CORP.
629 N.E.2d 214 (Ill. Ct. App. 1994)

FACTS

Oldenstedt was a subcontractor on a new store for K-Mart. In its contract, Oldenstedt agreed to supply adequate personnel, material, and equipment at all times to meet the project schedule, and to cooperate with the contractor in scheduling and performing the work to avoid conflict, delay in, or interference with others' work. Oldenstedt started work over two weeks late. The project supervisor told it several times and wrote several letters stating that the work was going too slowly and that it was in breach of the subcontract. Oldenstedt was given another month to complete the work, but it fell significantly behind again. Finally, the supervisor hired someone else to finish the work and to correct deficient work by Oldenstedt. The supervisor then canceled the contract with Oldenstedt, and Oldenstedt sued for breach of contract.

ISSUE

Did Oldenstedt substantially perform, and is it therefore entitled to payment under the contract?

DECISION

No. Oldenstedt promised to comply with the project's time schedule, to supply adequate resources, and to cooperate with the contractor to avoid delay. It did not do these things. It did not even comply with the revised schedule, which gave it an additional month. The pace of Oldenstedt's work was so slow that it materially breached the contract. Since it did not substantially perform, Oldenstedt is not entitled to the contract price less damages for any harm done. Its claim lies in *quantum meruit*, and it can recover the reasonable value of any benefit conferred on K-Mart. This means it will get what the work was worth, not what it cost Oldenstedt.

ANTICIPATORY BREACH

A promisor may also be held to have breached the contract under the doctrine of **anticipatory repudiation** or **anticipatory breach.** If the promisor, prior to the time for performance, indicates an intent not to perform his or her duties under the contract, the other party may treat the contract as breached and sue for that breach immediately if he or she so chooses. Anticipatory repudiation may take the form of an express statement by the promisor, or it may be implied from actions by the promisor that indicate an intent not to perform. For example, John, who has contracted to sell a car to Bill, sells the car to Marla two weeks before the delivery date set by his contract with Bill. Impliedly, John has repudiated his contract with Bill.

SPECIAL PERFORMANCE PROBLEMS

There are two special problem areas relating to performance that should be discussed in detail. These are contracts where the promisor agrees to perform to the **personal satisfaction** of the promisee, and construction contracts that condition the property owner's duty to pay on the builder's obtaining an **architect's** or **engineer's certificate** certifying that the builder satisfactorily performed.

When the promisor agrees to perform to the promisee's personal satisfaction in contracts involving matters of personal taste, comfort, or judgment, the promisee who is honestly dissatisfied may reject the performance without liability, even if doing so is unreasonable. If, on the other hand, the contract involves issues of mechanical fitness, utility, or marketability, most courts require the promisee to accept performance that would satisfy a reasonable person.

Building and construction contracts commonly require the builder to give the owner a certificate issued by a specific engineer or architect before the owner has a duty to pay the builder. These certificates, which are often issued at each stage of completion, indicate that the work is done to the satisfaction of the architect or engineer. Contractors who are unable to produce a required architect's or engineer's certificate cannot recover under the contract unless their failure is excused. This may be done by showing that the named architect or engineer is dead, ill, or insane; that the architect or engineer is acting in bad faith; or that the other party has prevented the issuance of the certificate. If the architect or engineer who denies certification is acting in good faith, even if he or she is being unreasonable in doing so, the majority of courts hold that the owner has no duty to pay under the contract. A minority of courts recognize unreasonable refusal as an excuse where the contract has been substantially performed.

THE TIME FOR PERFORMANCE

Failure to perform on time is a breach of the contract. In some cases, the failure may be serious enough to constitute a material breach. If the contract does not expressly or impliedly state a time for performance, performance must be completed within a reasonable time. What constitutes a "reasonable time" depends on the circumstances of each case.

In contracts in which failure to perform on time is a material breach, it is said that **time is of the essence.** A contract may expressly provide that time is of the essence. If so, the courts enforce this provision unless doing so would impose an unjust penalty on the promisor. The courts may also imply that time is of the essence if late performance is of little or no value to the promisee. For example, Ted contracts

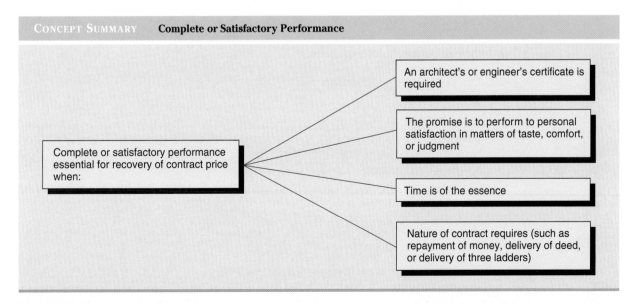

CONCEPT SUMMARY   Complete or Satisfactory Performance

Complete or satisfactory performance essential for recovery of contract price when:

- An architect's or engineer's certificate is required
- The promise is to perform to personal satisfaction in matters of taste, comfort, or judgment
- Time is of the essence
- Nature of contract requires (such as repayment of money, delivery of deed, or delivery of three ladders)

with the *Morning Tribune* to run an ad for Christmas trees from December 21 to December 24, but the paper does not start running Ted's ad until December 26. Clearly, time is of the essence in this contract and the *Morning Tribune* has materially breached.

If time is not of the essence of a contract, the promisee must accept late performance rendered within a reasonable time of when performance was due. The promisee is then entitled to deduct or set off from the contract price any losses suffered due to the delay.

.... **EXCUSES FOR NONPERFORMANCE** ....

Promisors who fail to perform satisfactorily may be able to avoid liability for breach of contract if they can show some *legal excuse* for their failure. Prevention of performance and impossibility of performance are the two traditionally accepted forms of excuse.

PREVENTION

The basic idea of prevention is that the promisee who causes the promisor's failure of performance cannot complain about the failure. Promisees owe promisors a duty of cooperation in the performance of a contract. Promisees who breach this duty by failing to cooperate or actively hindering or delaying performance are themselves guilty of a material breach of the contract. This relieves the promisor of any duty of further performance under the contract.

IMPOSSIBILITY

If it becomes impossible for a promisor to perform his or her contractual duties, the duty to perform is discharged and the promisor is not liable for material breach. **Impossibility** in the legal sense of the word, however, means "it cannot be done," not "I cannot do it." Promisors who find they have agreed to perform duties that are beyond their capabilities, or that have become unprofitable or difficult to perform, are generally not excused from their duty to perform. However, if some event arises after the formation of the contract that renders performance objectively impossible, nonperformance will be excused. The courts have traditionally recognized three kinds of impossibility: incapacitating illness or death of the promisor in a personal service contract, intervening illegality, and destruction of the subject matter essential to performance. Some courts today also recognize a fourth kind of impossibility called *commercial impracticability* or *commercial frustration*.

Illness or Death of Promisor

Personal service contracts are the only contracts that the promisor's death terminates. For example, if Dave contracts to sell his house to Terry and dies before the closing date, Terry can enforce the contract against Dave's estate. However, if Dave, a concert pianist, dies before giving a concert he has agreed to perform, his estate is not liable for breach of contract.

Illness may also excuse the promisor's failure to perform if the nature of the required performance and the seriousness and duration of the illness make it impossible for the promisor to substantially perform.

Intervening Illegality

If a statute or government regulation enacted after a contract's creation makes performance of a party's contractual duties illegal, the promisor is excused from performing.

Statutes or regulations that merely make performance more difficult or less profitable do not excuse nonperformance.

Destruction of Subject Matter

If, through no fault of the promisor, something that is essential to the promisor's performance is destroyed, the promisor is excused from performing. For example, Jill, a skating champion, is hired by the owners of the civic arena to put on a skating demonstration. If the arena is destroyed by fire prior to the date of Jill's performance, Jill's nonperformance will be excused. The destruction of items that the promisor intends to use in performing does not excuse nonperformance if substitutes are available, even though securing them makes performance more difficult or less profitable.

Commercial Impracticability

Some courts are relaxing the strict common law position on impossibility of performance by recognizing as an excuse for nonperformance circumstances that do not amount to impossibility. These courts recognize **commercial impracticability** as an excuse when unforeseeable developments make performance highly or unreasonably expensive, or of little value to the promisee. Assume, for example, that Biggs rented a boat from Maritime, Inc. The contract required Maritime to keep the boat in repair. While Biggs was loading the boat, it was rammed by another boat, causing severe damage. Estimates showed that it would cost more to fix the boat than the boat was worth prior to the collision. The court might well find it was unreasonable to require Maritime to repair the boat under these circumstances.

Commercial impracticability only acts as an excuse if the promisor did not expressly or impliedly assume the risk that the event would occur. The *Restatement* has adopted the commercial impracticability standard, as has the Uniform Commercial Code for contracts involving the sale of goods.

Commercial Frustration

Commercial frustration or *frustration of venture* is very similar to impracticability. Under this doctrine, performance is excused when events occur after the formation of the contract that would make the return performance of the other party worthless to the promisor. Like impracticability, the event must not have been foreseeable, and the promisor must not have expressly or impliedly assumed the risk that the event would occur.

·········· **DISCHARGE** ··········

THE NATURE OF DISCHARGE

Parties who have been released from their obligations under a contract are said to be **discharged.** Normally, both parties to a contract are discharged when they have completely performed their contractual duties. There are, however, several other things that can operate to discharge a party's duty of performance.

Earlier in this chapter you saw several situations in which a party's duty to perform could be discharged: the occurrence of a condition subsequent, the nonoccurrence of a condition precedent, material or anticipatory breach by the other party, and excused nonperformance. There are several other ways discharge can occur.

DISCHARGE BY AGREEMENT

Since contracts are created by mutual agreement, they may also be discharged by **mutual agreement.** An agreement to discharge must be supported by consideration to be enforceable.

DISCHARGE BY WAIVER

A party to a contract may **waive** his or her right to insist on complete performance. Waiver occurs when a party accepts incomplete performance without objection, knowing that the defects in performance will not be remedied. In order to avoid waiving their rights, parties who receive incomplete performance should give the other party prompt notice that they expect complete performance and will seek damages if defects are not corrected.

DISCHARGE BY ALTERATION

If the parties' agreement is represented by a written instrument, a material, **intentional alteration** of the instrument by one of the parties discharges the other party. If a party consents to an alteration or does not object to it after learning of it, he or she is not discharged. Alterations by third parties without the knowledge or consent of either contracting party do not affect the parties' rights.

DISCHARGE BY STATUTE OF LIMITATIONS

Courts have long refused to allow people to sue if they delay an unreasonable time in bringing their lawsuit. All states statutorily establish the reasonable time within which a lawsuit must be brought. These statutory time limits are called **statutes of limitations.**

One who has breached a contractual duty may be discharged from liability for breach if the other party does not bring suit within the statute of limitations for contracts. The time period for enforcing contracts varies from state to state, and many states distinguish between oral and written agreements. The UCC statute of limitations for contracts involving the sale of goods is four years from the time the goods are tendered. The statutory period ordinarily begins to run from the date of the breach, but it may be delayed if the party with the right to sue is incapacitated (e.g., insane).

REMEDIES

THE THEORY OF REMEDIES

If a party does not perform as promised under the contract, and performance has not been excused or discharged, then the other party is entitled to a remedy for the breach of the contractual promise. A court that awards a remedy for breach of contract tries to put the injured party in the same position he or she would have been in if the contract had been performed. Ordinarily, this may be done by awarding the injured person a judgment for money damages. If the loser in the suit does not pay the judgment, the winner is entitled to the court's help in enforcing it, as described in Chapter 2.

DAMAGES IN CONTRACT CASES

There are several kinds of damages that may be recoverable in contracts cases. The amount and kind of damages that may be recovered in a given dispute depend on the

---

TRISTAR COSMETICS, LTD. V. WESTINGHOUSE BROADCASTING
1992 U.S. Dist. LEXIS 3248 (E.D. Pa. 1992)

FACTS

Tristar bought a 30-second commercial for its new skin care product on *PM Evening Magazine* on February 27, 1991, because that program was scheduled to air a news segment on skin care. The segment talked about products containing "Nayad," an ingredient in Tristar's product. The contract provided that the ad "must run on Tuesday February 27, 1991." The ad did not run during the show, and Tristar sued for damages, including lost profits. Westinghouse sought a summary judgment, arguing that lost profits of a new company are too speculative to be recovered.

ISSUE

Are lost profits too speculative to be recovered as damages?

DECISION

No. The once generally accepted rule precluding all new businesses from recovering damages for lost profits has been replaced with a rule of evidence. Lost profits are now recoverable in contracts where there is enough evidence to establish them with reasonable certainty. While it is difficult for a new business to establish lost profits with the requisite degree of certainty, it can be done. Tristar has the expert testimony of a Wharton School marketing professor as to the profits that could be expected. While there is some skepticism about such projections, the jury should be allowed to decide its probity. The summary judgment is denied.

---

circumstances of the case. However, damages must be proved with reasonable certainty. Losses that are purely speculative are not recoverable.

Compensatory Damages

A party suing for breach of contract who has suffered actual losses as a result of the breach is entitled to recover **compensatory damages.** These damages are designed to place the plaintiff in the same position as if the contract had been performed. Compensatory damages ordinarily are measured by the loss in value of the promised performance. They are the difference between the value of performance that the plaintiff actually received and the value of the performance he or she had the right to expect. If no performance is rendered, the damages would be the value of the promised performance. The court will subtract from this amount any cost or loss the plaintiff was able to avoid by not having to perform his or her own promises. For example, Don agrees to sell his guitar worth $200 to Jane for $150, but he later refuses to go through with the deal. Jane's loss in value would be $200 less the $150 she did not pay Don, so her damages would be $50. Compensatory damages are normally limited to losses that would ordinarily occur as a result of breaching the contract.

Consequential Damages

In some cases the special circumstances of the plaintiff cause him or her to suffer losses that would not ordinarily be foreseeable as a result of the breach. Normally, such **consequential damages** are not recoverable unless the defendant had reason to foresee them at the time the contract was created. Generally, this means that the defendant must have known of the special circumstances that caused the loss. So, if Speedy Trucking Company contracts to deliver parts to Apex Manufacturing's plant without knowing that Apex is shut down waiting for the parts, Speedy is not liable for the consequential damages Apex suffers as a result of late delivery of the parts.

DELI V. UNIVERSITY OF MINNESOTA
578 N.W.2d 779 (Minn. Ct. App. 1998)

FACTS

Deli was head coach of the University of Minnesota women's gymnastics team, and her husband was an assistant coach. Deli and her husband used University equipment to tape a game in Florida. Her husband also used the equipment to videotape the couple having sexual relations during the stay in Florida. On the plane home, a player asked to see the tape to review the team's performance, and the husband gave it to her. Before Deli could recover the tape, several students and another assistant coach watched it; a parent of one of the students complained to the athletic director about the sexually explicit tape. The athletic director demanded the tape and promised she would not view it. At the direction of the University's legal counsel, the director viewed it and took notes on the tape's contents. Deli, who was fired for reasons unrelated to the tape, sued for breach of contract and promissory estoppel. Deli was awarded $675,000 for the emotional distress resulting from the breach of promise. The University appealed.

ISSUE

Are emotional distress damages recoverable in contract, or must a tort be proved?

DECISION

Deli cannot recover for emotional distress. Under contract law, extra-contractual damages, such as emotional distress, are not recoverable for breach of contract except in exceptional cases where the breach is accompanied by a tort. This is to ensure that contract law will not be swallowed by tort law. The preservation of a boundary between the two is necessary to protect the specific interests and expectations each embodies. The tort remedy is often more advantageous because it will permit greater recovery. The only possible tort Deli suffered is invasion of privacy, but Minnesota does not recognize this tort. To allow Deli to recover for emotional distress would be to allow her to accomplish in contract what she cannot in tort. We will not subvert the law of contract to allow recovery of such damages.

Nominal Damages

Nominal damages are very small damages that the court may award the plaintiff when a technical breach of contract has occurred without causing any actual loss. Typically, they are no more than $1.

Liquidated Damages

The parties to a contract may provide in advance that a specific sum shall be recoverable if the contract is breached. Such provisions are called **liquidated damage** provisions. If the amount specified is reasonable and if the nature of the contract is such that actual damages would be difficult to determine, liquidated damage provisions are enforced. When liquidated damage provisions are enforced, the amount of damages agreed on is the injured party's exclusive remedy. If the amount specified is unreasonably great in relation to the probable loss or injury, however, or if the amount of damages could be determined easily in the event of breach, the courts declare the provision to be a *penalty* and refuse to enforce it.

GUILIANO V. CLEO INC.
995 S.W.2d 88 (Tenn. 1999)

FACTS

The president and CEO of Cleo sent a letter of employment to Guiliano in 1992, promoting him to Vice President of Marketing for a three-year term. It spelled out several terms of employment including the following paragraph:

> In the event the Company terminates this Agreement and your employment without cause, you shall continue to be paid your then current salary from the date of termination through October 31, 1995.

In 1994 Cleo had several changes in upper management, and Guilano's new boss found his work to be unsatisfactory. He eventually was relieved of all duties, told to stay home, all phone calls were screened, and those that were work related were handled by the new V.P., who had moved into Guilano's old office. The company told Guilano it would contact him when there was something he could do and it would continue to pay him. After three months without contact, Guilano took a job elsewhere and sued Cleo for constructive firing without cause, seeking his salary through October 31, 1995. Guilano's new salary was $7,000 more than his salary at Cleo, and Cleo paid him until he obtained the new job. They therefore argued that the $90,125 due under the clause was a penalty since Guilano suffered no monetary damages and should not be paid.

ISSUE

Does the paragraph represent a liquidated damages clause that is punitive and therefore unenforceable?

DECISION

No. Liquidated damages are a stipulated sum agreed on by the parties at the time they enter their contract, to be paid to compensate for injuries should a breach occur. The stated amount should represent an estimate of potential damages in cases where damages are likely to be uncertain and not easily proven. The paragraph here states the amount due if Cleo breaches the contract. Cleo did wrongfully constructively fire Guilano. However, if the stipulated amount is unreasonable in relation to the potential or estimated damages, it will be treated as a penalty for breach and not be enforced. The penalty issue can be looked at from the point of view of what the parties knew at the time the contract was made, or the court can look at the amount of the liquidated damages compared to the actual damages suffered. We believe the better approach is the former. The amount is a reasonable estimate of damages at the time the contract was entered. Neither party knew at that time whether Guilano would be able to get a job at a similar salary if the contract was breached. Damages would be difficult to prove including losses due to loss of professional status, prestige, and advancement opportunities.

Punitive Damages

Ordinarily, **punitive damages** are not recoverable for breach of contract. They are recoverable only when extreme circumstances justify penalizing the defendant, such as if the breach of contract is willful, wanton, or malicious. Punitive damages also are sometimes specifically authorized by statute, as is the case with some consumer protection statutes.

While punitive damages are not ordinarily available in contract cases, they are available if the plaintiff can sue in tort for a bad faith breach, as discussed above. In these cases plaintiffs not only can collect damages for injuries such as emotional distress but also are likely to get large punitive damage awards because defendants' actions have been especially wrongful. Bad faith breach of contract actions have been most commonly allowed in suits against insurers for bad faith nonpayment of legitimate claims, and, more recently, against employers for wrongful firing of employees. Because these types of suits tend to blur the traditional line between tort and contract law, courts are moving cautiously in adopting the reasoning, and a few courts have decided to disallow punitive damages in certain bad faith cases.

THE DUTY TO MITIGATE DAMAGES

Plaintiffs who have been injured by a breach of contract have a duty to **mitigate** (avoid or minimize) the damages they suffer if they can do so without undue risk, expense, or humiliation. They are not able to recover damages for injuries they could have easily avoided. For example, an employee who has been wrongfully fired would be entitled to damages equal to his or her wages for the remainder of the employment period. Such an employee, however, has a duty to make reasonable efforts to seek a similar job elsewhere and thereby minimize damages.

CURTIS O. GRIESS & SONS, INC. v. FARM BUREAU INSURANCE
528 N.W.2d 329 (Sup. Ct. Neb. 1995)

FACTS

[This case was also discussed in Chapter 13 regarding interpretation of contracts.] Griess's swine were infected with pseudorabies virus carried downwind by a tornado from an infected herd. He sought recovery for his losses under his insurance contract with Farm Bureau, which covered damage due to windstorms. In addition to compensation for the death and damage to his swine, Griess sought recovery for $128,732.38 in veterinary expenses for testing, treating, and management of the pseudovirus in order to prevent further damage to the herd. The insurance company claimed it had no liability for the cost of preventing further damages.

ISSUE

Should Griess be reimbursed for fulfilling his duty to mitigate damages?

DECISION

Yes. Parties to contracts have a duty to mitigate their damages. In addition, the insurance contract states, under a clause entitled, "WHAT YOU MUST DO AFTER A LOSS: In the event of a loss to which this insurance may apply you shall . . . b. PROTECT THE PROPERTY FROM FURTHER DAMAGE. This includes making reasonable and necessary repairs to protect the property, and keeping accurate records of repair expenses." This implies that the insurer will pay for such expenses. Payment is also consistent with the promisee's general duty to mitigate. Without treatment the animals would have died and the insurer would have been required to cover a greater loss. Defendant is liable for the veterinary fees.

EQUITABLE REMEDIES

If the legal remedies for breach of contract (usually money damages) are not adequate to fully remedy a party's injuries, a court has the discretionary right to grant an **equitable remedy.** Whether equitable relief is granted depends on the equities of a particular case. By applying "maxims" of equity such as "He who seeks equity must do equity," and "He who comes to equity must come with clean hands," the courts grant equitable relief only when justice is served by doing so. The two most common equitable remedies are specific performance and injunction. (See Table 15–1.)

Specific Performance

If the subject matter of a contract is *unique* so that a money damage award will not adequately compensate a buyer whose seller has refused to perform, a court may order the seller to **specifically perform** the contract. Real estate traditionally has been treated as unique and is the most common subject of specific performance decrees. For example, Frank enters a contract to sell his house to Dorothy for $90,000. When he

TABLE 15-1   Remedies

Damages	
Compensatory	Loss in value of promised performance
Consequential	Foreseeable losses from special circumstances of particular contract
Nominal	Award for purely technical breach of contract (usually $1.00)
Liquidated	Damages specified in contract for breach
Punitive	Usually unavailable—sometimes awarded for bad faith breach
Equitable Remedies	
Specific Performance	Promisor ordered to perform contract where subject matter is unique
Injunction	Ordered to prevent irreparable injury

learns that the market value of the house is $95,000, Frank decides not to go through with the sale. Dorothy sues Frank for breach of contract. Her normal legal remedy would be her lost profit on the sale (the market price less the contract price—$5,000 in this example). However, since real estate is generally treated as unique, Dorothy could get the court to order Frank to specifically perform his duties under their contract by giving her a deed to the property.

Personal property is generally not considered unique, but antiques, heirlooms, and works of art may merit specific performance. Specific performance is generally not granted in personal service contracts because it would require a form of involuntary servitude and would probably be ineffective in giving the promisee what was bargained for.

I.LAN SYSTEMS, INC. v. NETSCOUT SERVICE LEVEL CORP.
2002 U.S. Dist LEXIS 209 (D. Mass. Jan. 2, 2002)

FACTS

I.Lan entered into a Value Added Reseller (VAR) agreement with NetScout to resell NetScout's software to its customers. I.Lan claimed it purchased the unlimited right to use the software, replete with perpetual upgrades and support, whereby it effectively could rent, rather than sell, the software to its customers. It points to the purchase order to support its claim. NetScout points to the VAR agreement and the clickwrap license agreement contained in the software to refute this. The clickwrap license states that "[NetScout's] liability for damages to licensee for any cause whatsoever, regardless of the form of any

claim or action, shall be limited to the license fees paid for the licensed product." However, another section states that each party has the right to bring judicial proceedings to enforce its rights under the agreement, and specifically mentions specific performance. I.Lan sought specific performance of the agreement for perpetual upgrades and unlimited support.

ISSUE

Is the subject matter of the contract sufficiently unique to warrant specific performance?

(continued)

I.Lan Systems, Inc. v. NetScout Service Level Corp.
(concluded)

DECISION

No. Specific performance is allowed when the items are unique or not replaceable as a practical matter. I.Lan argues that the software is unique because it is copyrighted and took years to develop. The same could be said of any mass-produced item, and a mass-produced product is the antitheses of the word "unique." More importantly, the software is one of several competing software packages in the market that run on ordinary computers and perform substantially the same functions. They are interchangeable as a practical matter. I.Lan could purchase comparable software on the open market and reconfigure its systems to run that software. Since the software is not unique, I.Lan cannot have specific performance.

Injunctions

Injunctions are available when a breach of contract threatens to produce an *irreparable injury.* A court can order a party to do certain acts (a **mandatory injunction**) or to refrain from doing certain acts (a **prohibitory injunction**). For example, an employee with special skills who has agreed not to work for a competitor may be *enjoined* from breaching his or her contract and working for that competitor. Like specific performance, an injunction cannot be used to compel personal service.

CONCEPT SUMMARY   **Performance and Remedies**

Was the contract breached and what are the remedies?
I. No breach of contract if
   a. Conditions are not met
      1. Condition precedent does not occur
      2. Condition subsequent occurs
   b. Performance excused due to
      1. Prevention by promisee
      2. Impossibility due to
         (a) Illness or death of promisor
         (b) Intervening illegality
         (c) Destruction of subject matter
         (d) Commercial impracticability
         (e) Commercial frustration
   c. Performance discharged due to
      1. Agreement
      2. Waiver
      3. Alteration
      4. Running of statute of limitations
   d. Contract completely or substantially performed

II. If contract was breached, remedies are
   a. Damages
      1. Compensatory
      2. Consequential
      3. Nominal
      4. Liquidated
      5. Punitive
   b. Equitable remedies
      1. Specific performance
      2. Injunction

.... **QUESTIONS AND PROBLEM CASES** ....

1. Explain the effect of a condition subsequent on the enforcement of a contract.

2. Explain the difference between substantial performance and satisfactory performance.

3. Explain the duty to mitigate damages.

4. Weiss paid Nurse Midwifery Associates (Midwifery) $750 for prenatal and postnatal care, and to attend at the birth of his son. Although the Weisses received services on at least a dozen occasions, the midwife was not present at the birth because the birth came too soon after labor started. Weiss sued for return of the $750 he had paid. Did Midwifery substantially perform the contract?

5. In 1857, the *Central America,* which was loaded with gold from California, sank off Cuba. Thompson organized the Columbus–American Discovery Group, an organization that won the race to locate the sunken ship. In 1983, Thompson, Standefer, and Doering entered a contract contemplating the salvage of the ship. It stated, "It is agreed that a corporation . . . will be formed between [us]. The object of forming [it] is to carry out the duties of the . . . Group under the joint venture with Mr. John." The agreement further provided that if the joint venture discontinued operations for any reason, the corporation or individuals therein would still receive a share of any salvage from the ship. John was to finance the search and salvage procedures. John, however, never signed the contract or the joint venture agreement, and a corporation was never chartered. After the failure of the joint venture, Standefer had virtually no active participation in the location of the ship or the salvage operation. Nonetheless, Standefer sought to assert rights under the contract and share in the treasure that was salvaged by Thompson. Thompson alleged that the creation of the joint venture was a condition precedent to the contract's effectiveness. Is he correct? Explain.

6. Miceli contracted to buy Dieberg's Island. The contract required the closing to be on May 16 at 10:00 AM at Community Title's office. It stated time was of the essence. Miceli was not there at 10:00; at 10:20 Dieberg declared the contract breached and left. Dieberg planned to use the money from Miceli to close on another property and had to arrange alternative financing. At 10:30 Miceli appeared without the money. He did not tender payment until 1:30, and Dieberg refused to accept it. Miceli sued for specific performance, arguing that closing sometime on the 16th was adequate. Is he correct?

7. Arabian Score, a limited partnership, contracted to buy a colt, Score, from Lasma Arabian Ltd. Arabian agreed to pay $1 million for Score and for Lasma's promotion of it. Lasma was required to spend $250,000 over five years promoting Score as a "2 Star Stallion" for stud purposes. The contract also provided that all risk passed to Arabian on the purchase of Score, and Arabian took out mortality insurance on the horse. Score died within the year, having sired two foals. The insurance company went broke. Arabian sued Lasma for the part of the $250,000 it had not spent promoting Score. Does impossibility or commercial frustration excuse performance of the contract?

8. The Boston Symphony Orchestra (BSO) contracted with actress Vanessa Redgrave to narrate a series of performances of Stravinsky's "Oedipus Rex" in Boston and New York. Prior to the performances, Redgrave had come out in support of the Palestine Liberation Organization. When the contract with Redgrave was announced, BSO subscribers and community leaders strongly protested. BSO canceled Redgrave's contract and she sued for damages, including wages lost on subsequent offers she did not receive due to the cancellation. Are lost opportunities the kind of consequential damages that can be compensated?

9. In November and December 1979, Stock Shop, Inc., sent Bozell & Jacobs, Inc. (Bozell), 697 stock photographs of U.S. scenes for Bozell to consider for use in an ad campaign for one of its clients. The pictures came with a statement that provided that the damages for loss of a photograph would be a minimum of no less than $1,500. Thirty-nine of the pictures were

never returned, and Stock Shop sued for $1,500 for each picture. Is the liquidated damage clause enforceable?

10. When Nancy (Gilbo) Hawkins and William Gilbo were divorced, they entered a separate agreement providing that William would be entirely responsible for all of his son's undergraduate college tuition plus reasonable incidental and daily living expenses while he was a student. The agreement stated that it was not part of the divorce decree and that William was binding himself on an independent contractual basis. The son's expenses were $39,342.68, of which William paid $8,392.50. When Nancy brought suit for the difference, William defended by arguing that only the son could seek the damages since the contract was made for his benefit and that Nancy's only remedy was specific performance. Is he correct?

P A R T   I I I

Sales

CHAPTER 16

Formation and Terms of Sales Contracts

Suppose the Red Balloon Toy Store places an order over the telephone with the Red Wagon Company for 25 large red wagons at $24.95 each. Red Wagon sends a document entitled "Order Acknowledgment" to Red Balloon in which it notes the sale to it, the quantity of wagons ordered, and the price per wagon. It also goes on to state that the price is F.O.B. Red Wagon's factory and that the sale is subject to the terms and conditions set forth on the back of the form. Three weeks later, Red Wagon ships the 25 wagons to Red Balloon. A number of the wagons are damaged en route when the truck carrying them is involved in an accident. This situation raises a number of questions:

- *Was a contract formed between Red Balloon and Red Wagon even though the offer and acceptance are not mirror images of each other?*
- *If a contract was formed, what are its terms?*
- *Was the contract required to be in writing to be enforceable?*
- *When would title to the wagons pass to Red Balloon?*
- *When would Red Balloon obtain an insurable interest in the wagons?*
- *Between Red Wagon and Red Balloon, who had the risk of loss or damage to the wagons while they were in the hands of the carrier?*

In this chapter, we will address these and other questions concerning the formation and terms of contracts.

######### *INTRODUCTION* ....

In Part II, "Contracts," we introduced the common law rules that govern the creation and performance of contracts generally. Throughout much of history, special rules, known as the *law merchant,* were developed to control mercantile transactions in goods. Because transactions in goods commonly involve buyers and sellers located in different states—and even different countries—a common body of law to control these transactions can facilitate the smooth flow of commerce. To address this need, a Uniform Sales Act was drafted in the early 1900s and adopted by about two-thirds of the states. Subsequently, the Uniform Commercial Code (UCC or Code) was prepared to simplify and modernize the rules of law governing commercial transactions.

This chapter reviews some Code rules that govern the formation of sales contracts previously discussed. It also covers some key terms in sales contracts, such as delivery terms, title, and risk of loss. Finally, it discusses the rules governing sales on trial, such as sales on approval and consignments.

SALE OF GOODS

The **sale of goods** is the transfer of ownership to tangible personal property in exchange for money, other goods, or the performance of services. The law of sales of goods is codified in Article 2 of the Uniform Commercial Code. While the law of sales is based on the fundamental principles of contract and personal property, it has been modified to accommodate current practices of merchants. In large measure, the Code discarded many technical requirements of earlier law that did not serve any useful purpose in the marketplace and replaced them with rules that assure merchants and consumers of goods that laws will be applied in keeping with commercial expectations.

Article 2 of the Code applies only to *transactions in goods.* Thus, it does not cover contracts to provide services or to sell real property. However, some courts have applied the principles set out in the Code to such transactions. When a contract appears to call for the furnishing of both goods and services, a question may arise as to whether the Code applies. For example, the operator of a hair salon may use a commercial solution intended to be used safely on humans that causes injury to a person's head. The injured person then might bring a lawsuit claiming that there was a breach of the Code's warranty of the suitability of the solution. In such cases, the courts commonly see whether the sale of goods is the *predominant* part of the transaction or merely an *incidental* part; where the sale of goods predominates, courts normally apply Article 2.

Thus, the first question you should ask when faced with a contracts problem is: Is this a contract for the sale of goods? If it is not, then the principles of common law that were discussed in Part II, "Contracts," apply. If the contract is one for the sale of goods, then the Code applies.

LEASES

A lease of goods is a transfer of the right to possess and use goods belonging to another. Although the rights of one who leases goods (a lessee) do not constitute ownership of the goods, leasing is mentioned here because it is becoming an increasingly important way of acquiring the use of many kinds of goods, from automobiles to farm equipment. In most states, Article 2 and Article 9 of the UCC were applied to such leases by analogy. However, rules contained in these articles sometimes were inadequate to resolve special problems presented by leasing. For this reason, a new article of the UCC dealing exclusively with leases of goods, Article 2A, was written in 1987. Article 2A has been adopted by 48 states and the District of Columbia as of the time of this writing. Because of space limitations, it is not covered in detail in this textbook.

HIGHER STANDARDS FOR MERCHANTS

The Code recognizes that buyers tend to place more reliance on professional sellers and that professionals are generally more knowledgeable and better able to protect themselves than nonprofessionals. Therefore, the Code distinguishes between merchants and nonmerchants by holding merchants to a higher standard in some cases (Sections 2-201[2], 2-205, 2-207[2], and 2-314).[1] The Code defines **merchant** (2-104[1]) on a case-by-case basis. If a person regularly deals in the kind of goods being sold, or purports to have some special knowledge about the goods, or employed an agent in the sale who fits either of these two descriptions, that person is a merchant for the purposes of the contract in question. So, if you buy a used car from a used-car dealer, the dealer is a merchant for the purposes of your contract. But if you buy a refrigerator from a used-car dealer, the dealer is probably not considered to be a merchant for purposes of that sale.

CODE REQUIREMENTS

The Code requires that parties to sales contracts act in *good faith* and in a *commercially reasonable manner*. Further, when a contract contains an unfair or unconscionable clause, or the contract as a whole is unconscionable, the courts have the right to refuse to enforce the unconscionable clause or contract (2-302). The Code's treatment of unconscionability is discussed in detail in Chapter 12, "Illegality."

A number of the Code provisions concerning the sale of goods were discussed in the chapters on contracts. The Concept Summary below lists some of the important provisions discussed earlier, together with the chapters in the text where the discussion can be found.

CONCEPT SUMMARY	Formation of Contracts
Offer and Acceptance (Chapters 8 and 9)	1. A contract can be formed in any manner sufficient to show agreement, including conduct by both parties that recognizes the existence of a contract.
	2. The fact that the parties did not agree on all the terms of their contract does not prevent the formation of a contract.
	3. A firm written offer by a merchant that contains assurances it will be held open is irrevocable for a period of up to three months.
	4. Acceptance of an offer may be made by any reasonable manner and is effective on dispatch.
	5. A timely expression of acceptance creates a contract even if it contains terms different from the offer or states additional terms *unless* the attempted acceptance is expressly conditioned on the offer's agreement to the terms of the acceptance.

(continued)

---

[1]The numbers in parentheses refer to sections of the Uniform Commercial Code.

CONCEPT SUMMARY	Formation of Contracts *(concluded)*
	6. An offer inviting a prompt shipment may be accepted either by a prompt promise to ship or a prompt shipment of the goods.
Consideration (Chapter 10)	1. Consideration is not required to make a firm offer in writing by a merchant irrevocable for a period of up to three months.
	2. Consideration is not required to support a modification of a contract for the sale of goods.
Statute of Frauds (Chapter 14)	1. Subject to several exceptions, all contracts for the sale of goods for $500 or more must be evidenced by a writing signed by the party against whom enforcement of the contract is sought. It is effective only as to the quantity of goods stated in the writing.
	2. A signed writing is not required if the party against whom enforcement is sought is a merchant, received a written memorandum from the other party, and did not object in writing within 10 days of his receipt of it.
	3. An exception to the statute of frauds is made for specially manufactured goods not suitable for sale to others on which the seller has made a substantial beginning in manufacturing or has entered into a binding contract to acquire.
	4. An exception to the statute of frauds is made for contracts that a party admits the existence of in court testimony or pleadings.
	5. If a party accepts goods or payment for goods, the statute of frauds is satisfied to the extent of the payment made or the goods accepted.
Unconscionability (Chapter 13)	If a court finds a contract for the sale of goods to be unconscionable, it can refuse to enforce it entirely, enforce it without any unconscionable clause, or enforce it in a way that avoids an unconscionable result.

TERMS OF SALES CONTRACTS

GAP FILLERS

The Code recognizes the fact that parties to sales contracts frequently omit terms from their agreements or state terms in an indefinite or unclear manner. The Code deals with these cases by filling in the blanks with common trade practices or by giving commonly used terms a specific meaning that is applied unless the parties' agreement clearly indicates a contrary intent.

PRICE TERMS

A fixed price is not essential to the creation of a binding sales contract. Of course, if price has been the subject of a dispute between the parties that has never been resolved, no contract is created because a "meeting of the minds" never occurred. However, if the parties omitted a price term or left the price to be determined at a future date or by some external means, the Code supplies a price term (2-305). Under the common law, such contracts would have failed due to "indefiniteness." If a price term is simply omitted, or if the parties agreed to agree on price at a later date but cannot, or if the parties agreed that price would be set by some external agency (like a particular market or trade journal) that fails to set the price, the Code says the price is a *reasonable price at the time for delivery* (2-305[1]). If the agreement gives either party the power to fix the price, that party must do so in *good faith* (2-305[2]). If the surrounding circumstances clearly indicate that the parties did not intend to be bound in the event that the price was not determined in the agreed-on manner, no contract results (2-305[4]).

QUANTITY TERMS

Output/Requirements Contracts

In some cases, the parties may state the quantity of goods covered by their sales contract in an indefinite way. Contracts that obligate a buyer to purchase a seller's *output* of a certain item or all the buyer's *requirements* of a certain item are commonly encountered. These contracts caused frequent problems under the common law because of the indefiniteness of the parties' obligations. If the seller decided to double its output, did the buyer have to accept the entire amount? If the market price of the item soared much higher than the contract price, could the buyer double or triple its demands?

The Code limits quantity in such cases to "such actual output or requirements as may occur in good faith" (2-306[1]). Even good faith amounts may not be tendered or demanded if they are "unreasonably disproportionate" to any stated estimate in the contract or to "normal" prior output or requirements if no estimate is stated (2-306[1]).

Exclusive Dealing Contracts

The Code takes a similar approach to *exclusive dealing* contracts that obligate dealers to deal only in one manufacturer's product line. Under the common law, these contracts were sources of difficulty because the parties' duties were indefinite. Did the dealer have to make any effort to sell the manufacturer's products, and did the manufacturer have any duty to supply the dealer? The Code says that unless the parties agree to the contrary, sellers have a duty to use their *best efforts* to supply their buyers, who have a duty to use their *best efforts* to sell the goods (2-306[2]).

DELIVERY TERMS

Unless the parties agree to the contrary, the Code says that the goods ordered are to be delivered in a *single-lot shipment* (2-307). If the contract is silent about the place for delivery, the goods are to be delivered at the *seller's place of business* (2-308[a]). The only exception to this rule is in the case of contracts dealing with identified goods that both parties at the time of contracting know are located someplace other than the seller's place of business. In such a case, the *site of the goods* is the place for delivery (2-308[b]).

TIME TERMS

The Code takes the same position as the common law when the parties' contract is silent about the time for performance. Performance in such cases must be tendered within a *reasonable time* (2-309[1]). If the parties' contract calls for a number of performances over an indefinite period of time (e.g., an open-ended requirements contract), the contract is valid for a *reasonable time* but may be terminated at any time by either party after giving *reasonable notice* (2-309[2] and [3]).

Finally, the Code also provides for the time and place of payment. Unless the parties agreed on some other payment terms, payment for the goods is due at the "time and place at which the buyer is to receive the goods" (2-310[a]).

.... **TITLE AND THE CODE** ....

CODE CHANGES

The Code also deals with many important questions about the **ownership (title)** of the goods in sales contracts. This is important for several reasons. If the goods are lost, stolen, damaged, or destroyed, who must bear the **risk of loss,** the seller or the buyer? Whose creditors (the seller's or the buyer's) have the legal right to seize the goods to satisfy their claims? What are the rights of those who buy goods that are subject to the **claims of third parties** (for example, their rightful owner or secured creditors)? Who has the **insurable interest** that the law requires before a party can purchase insurance protection for the goods?

Under the common law, most problems concerning risk of loss, insurable interest, and the rights of various third parties to the goods were answered by determining who had title to the goods. The Code, to clarify these questions, has specific rules that generally do not depend on who has title.

GENERAL TITLE RULES

Physical Delivery

The Code does have a general title section. It provides that title passes to the buyer when the seller has completely performed his or her duties concerning *physical delivery* of the goods (2-401[2]). So, if the contract merely requires the seller to *ship* the goods, title passes to the buyer when the seller delivers the goods to the carrier. If the contract requires *delivery* of the goods by the seller, title passes to the buyer when the goods are delivered and tendered to the buyer.

The case that follows, *Butler v. Beer Across America,* illustrates the principle that title to beer passed to the buyer when the seller transferred it to the carrier because the seller was not required to make delivery at the destination.

BUTLER V. BEER ACROSS AMERICA
40 UCC Rep.2d 1008 (U.S.D.C., N.D. Ala. 2000)

FACTS

In April 1999 while his parents were away from home on vacation, Hunter Butler, a minor, used a credit card in his name to order 12 bottles of beer through Beer Across America's Internet site on the World Wide Web. When his mother, Lynda Butler, returned home, she found several bottles from the shipment of beer remaining in the refrigerator. Lynda Butler then filed a civil lawsuit against Beer Across America seeking damages under Section 6-5-70 of the Alabama Civil Damages Act. The Civil Damages Act provides for a civil action by the parent or guardian of a minor against anyone who knowingly sells or furnishes liquor to the minor. A threshold issue in the lawsuit was whether the sale of the beer had taken place in Alabama so that a court in Alabama would have personal jurisdiction over Beer Across America.

Beer Across America was an Illinois corporation involved in the marketing and sale of alcoholic beverages and other merchandise. The beer was brought by carrier from Illinois to Alabama. The sales invoice and shipping documents provided that the sale was FOB the seller, with the carrier acting as the buyer's agent. Moreover, the invoice included a charge for sales tax but no charge for beer tax; Alabama law requires that sales tax be collected for out-of-state sale of goods that are then shipped to Alabama but requires beer tax be collected only on sales within Alabama.

(continued)

Butler v. Beer Across America
(concluded)

Issue

Did the sale of the beer take place in Alabama?

Decision

No, the sale took place in Illinois. The court noted that under the versions of the Uniform Commercial Code in effect in both Illinois and Alabama, a sale consists in the passing of title from the seller to the buyer. Title to goods passes at the time and place of shipment when the contract does not require the seller to make delivery at the destination. Accordingly, ownership to the beer passed to Hunter Butler upon tender of the beer to the carrier.

Author's Note

The court went on to transfer the case to the U.S. District Court for the Northern District of Illinois.

Delivery without Moving the Goods

If delivery is to be made without moving the goods, title passes at the *time and place of contracting,* if the goods have been identified to the contract. **Identification** occurs when the surrounding circumstances make it clear that the goods are those "to which the contract refers" (2-501). This may result from the contract description of the goods (if they are distinct from other goods in the seller's possession) or from actions of the seller, such as setting aside or marking the goods.

Negotiable Document of Title

Sometimes when the goods are being shipped by a professional carrier, the parties will use a **negotiable document of title.** For instance, a seller may ship the goods to the buyer with payment due on delivery. The document of title (a negotiable bill of lading) serves as the contract between the seller and the shipper as well as identifies who has title and control of the goods. The document of title (signifying the right to control the goods) will not be surrendered to the buyer until she pays for the goods. If the contract calls for the seller to deliver a negotiable document of title to the goods (like a warehouse receipt or a bill of lading) to the buyer, title passes when the document of title is delivered.

BUYER'S REJECTION

In some instances, the buyer will **reject** the goods, perhaps because he does not believe that they conform to the contractual specifications. Whatever the reason, if the buyer rejects tender of the goods, title will automatically be revested in the seller.

TITLE AND THIRD PARTIES

A basic rule of property law is that a person can transfer no greater rights (title) in property than he himself possesses. So, if Bob steals a stereo from Mary and sells it to Mike, Mike has no greater title to the stereo than Bob possessed. Thus, Mary could recover the stereo from Mike just as she could have recovered it from Bob. The Code, however, makes three important exceptions to this rule in order to protect the rights of innocent buyers.

TRANSFERS OF VOIDABLE TITLE

A seller who has voidable title can pass good title to a **good faith purchaser for value** (2-403[1]). Sellers may obtain voidable title by impersonating another person when acquiring the goods from their rightful owner, paying for the goods with a bad check, failing to pay for goods sold on a "cash sale" basis, or obtaining the goods in some other fraudulent manner. **Good faith** means "honesty in fact in the transaction concerned" (1-201[19]), and a buyer has given "value" if he or she has given any consideration sufficient to support a simple contract (1-201[44]).

The primary reason for this exception is to place the burden of loss on the party who had the best opportunity to avoid the harm. Good faith purchasers can do nothing to avoid injury. However, the rightful owners of goods at least have the opportunity to protect themselves by taking steps to assure themselves of the buyer's identity, accepting only cash or certified checks, refusing to part with the goods until they have cash in hand, or taking steps to discover fraud before parting with the goods. In view of their greater relative fault, the Code requires the original owners of the goods to bear the burden of collecting from their fraudulent buyers. This principle is illustrated in *Alsafi Oriental Rugs v. American Loan Co.*

ALSAFI ORIENTAL RUGS V. AMERICAN LOAN CO.
864 S.W.2d 41 (Ct. App. Tenn. 1993)

FACTS

In December 1990, Arlene Bradley entered Alsafi Oriental Rugs and advised the owner that she was an interior decorator and that she was interested in selling some of his rugs to one of her customers. Alsafi did not know Bradley and had never done business with her. However, he allowed her to take three rugs out on consignment with the understanding that she would return them if her customer was not interested. In fact, however, Bradley was not obtaining the rugs for a "customer" but was instead working for another individual, Walid Salaam, a rug dealer.

A friend of Bradley's had introduced her to Salaam earlier. Salaam had advised the two women that he was the owner of a recently closed oriental rug store that he was attempting to reopen. He offered to teach them how to become decorators and told them that when his store reopened, they could operate out of the store. Salaam advised them that until he got his store restocked, however, he wanted them to "check out" rugs on approval from other rug dealers in town. As they had no experience with oriental rugs, Salaam instructed them which rugs to look for. He then instructed them to go to rug dealers in Memphis and advise them that they were

interior decorators with customers that wanted to purchase oriental rugs.

After Bradley obtained possession of the three rugs from Alsafi, she turned them over to Salaam, who in turn took them to a pawnshop operated by the American Loan Company. There Salaam pawned the rugs, obtaining approximately $5,000 after filling out the required paperwork. Salaam failed to redeem the rugs. Following the default, the pawnshop gave the appropriate notice that it intended to dispose of them.

In April 1991 Alsafi learned that his rugs were at the pawnshop. After visiting the pawnshop and identifying the three rugs as his, he brought suit to recover possession of them.

ISSUE

Was Alsafi entitled to recover the rugs from the pawnshop?

DECISION

No. Under Section 2-403 (1), a person with voidable title has power to transfer a good title to a good faith purchaser for value. Where goods have been delivered under

(continued)

ALSAFI ORIENTAL RUGS V. AMERICAN LOAN CO.
(concluded)

a transaction of purchase, the purchaser has this power even though the delivery was procured through fraud punishable as larcenous under the criminal law. Here, Bradley obtained the goods through a voluntary transfer of possession described as a "consignment"—and not through any wrongful nonpermissive taking of the goods. As such Bradley was a purchaser of the goods—albeit with voidable title to them—and was empowered by her transaction with Alsafi to pass title to Salaam, who in turn passed title to the American Loan Company, which was found by the court to be a good faith purchaser for value, having no actual knowledge or reason to believe that Salaam was not the true owner of the rugs.

BUYERS IN THE ORDINARY COURSE OF BUSINESS

The second exception made by the Code concerns **buyers in the ordinary course of business.** A "buyer in the ordinary course of business" is one who, in good faith, buys goods from a person dealing in goods of that type without knowing that the sale violates the ownership rights of any third party (1-201[9]). Under the Code, buyers in the ordinary course take goods free of any security interest in the goods that their seller may have given a third party (9-307).

For example, Art's Jeep Sales borrows money from First Financial Services and gives First Financial a security interest in all its inventory. The security interest gives First Financial the right to seize Art's inventory if it defaults on the loan. If Bob buys a new Jeep from Art's, he takes the Jeep free and clear of First Financial's security interest if he is a "buyer in the ordinary course." The basic purpose of this exception is to protect those who innocently buy from merchants, thereby promoting confidence in such commercial transactions. Security interests and the rights of buyers in the ordinary course of business are discussed in more detail in Chapter 41, "Secured Transactions."

ENTRUSTING GOODS

The Code's third major exception to the general common law rule on title is the "entrusting rule" (2-403[2] and [3]). Anyone who entrusts goods to a merchant who regularly deals in such goods gives that merchant the power to give good title to a "buyer in the ordinary course." So, if Mary takes her watch to Precious Jewelers, Inc., for repair, Precious could give good title to a buyer in the ordinary course who buys the watch. In such a case, Mary would have to sue Precious for conversion of the watch; she could not get her watch back from the buyer. The purpose of this exception is to promote commerce by giving buyers the knowledge that they will get good title to goods they purchase in the ordinary course of their sellers' business.

CONCEPT SUMMARY	Title and Third Parties
General Rule	A seller cannot pass better title to goods than he has.
Exceptions to General Rule	1. A person who has voidable title to goods can pass good title to a bona fide purchaser for value. 2. A buyer in the ordinary course of a retailer's business takes free of any interests in the goods that the retailer has given to others. 3. A person who buys goods in the ordinary course of a dealer's business takes free of any claims of a person who entrusted those goods to the dealer.

Ethical Implications	Suppose you are the owner of a small jewelry store that sells new and antique jewelry. A customer leaves a family heirloom—an elaborate diamond ring—with you for cleaning and resetting. By mistake a clerk in your store sells it to another customer. What would you do? If you were the buyer of the ring and had given it to your fiancé as a gift and then were informed of the circumstances, what would you do?

RISK OF LOSS

OVERVIEW

The transportation of goods from sellers to buyers is a risky business. The carrier of the goods may lose, damage, or destroy them; floods, tornadoes, and other natural catastrophes may take their toll; thieves may steal all or part of the goods. If neither party is at fault for the loss, who should bear the risk? If the buyer has the risk when the goods are damaged or lost, the buyer is liable for the contract price. If the seller has the risk, he or she is liable for damages unless substitute performance can be tendered.

The common law placed the risk on the party who had technical title at the time of the loss. The Code rejects this approach and provides specific rules governing risk of loss that are designed to provide certainty and place the risk on the party best able to protect against loss and most likely to be insured against it. Risk of loss under the Code depends on the terms of the parties' agreement, the moment the loss occurs, and whether one of the parties was in breach of contract when the loss occurred.

THE TERMS OF THE AGREEMENT

The parties have the power to control who has the risk of loss by specifically saying so in their agreement (2-509[4]). This they may do directly or by using certain commonly accepted shipping terms in their contract. In addition, the Code has certain general rules on risk of loss that amplify specific shipping terms and control risk of loss in cases in which specific terms are not used (2-509).

SHIPMENT CONTRACTS

If the contract requires the seller to ship the goods by carrier but does not require that the seller guarantee their delivery to a specific destination, the risk passes to the buyer when the goods are delivered to the carrier (2-509[1][a]). The following are commonly used shipping terms that create **shipment contracts:**

FOB (Free on Board) **FOB (Free on Board)**   calls for the seller to deliver the goods free of expense and at the seller's risk to the place designated. So, if the contract term is "FOB Chicago" or some other place of *shipment,* the seller bears the risk and expense of delivering the goods *to the carrier* (2-319[1][a]). If the term is "FOB vessel, car, or other vehicle," the seller must *load* the goods on board at his or her own risk and expense (2-319[1][c]).

FAS (Free Alongside) **FAS (Free Alongside)**   is commonly used in maritime contracts and is normally accompanied by the name of a specific vessel and port. The seller must deliver the goods alongside the vessel at his or her own risk and expense (2-319[2]).

CIF (Cost, Insurance, and Freight) **CIF (Cost, Insurance, and Freight)**   means that the price of the goods includes the cost of shipping and insuring them. The seller bears this expense and the risk of loading the goods (2-320).

C&F (Cost and Freight) **C&F (Cost and Freight)**   is the same as CIF except that the seller is not obligated to *insure* the goods.

DESTINATION CONTRACTS

If the contract requires the seller to guarantee delivery of the goods to a specific destination, the seller bears the risk and expense of delivery to that destination (2-509[l][b]). The following are commonly used shipping terms that create **destination contracts:**

FOB Destination An **FOB** term coupled with the place of **destination** of the goods puts the expense and risk of delivering the goods to that destination on the seller (2-319[l][b]).

Ex-Ship **Ex-Ship** does not specify a particular ship but places the expense and risk on the seller until the goods are *unloaded* from whatever ship is used (2-322).

No Arrival, No Sale **No Arrival, No Sale** places the expense and risk during shipment on the seller. If the goods fail to arrive through no fault of the seller, the seller has no further liability to the buyer (2-324).

GOODS IN THE POSSESSION OF THIRD PARTIES

When, at the time of contracting, the goods are in the hands of a third-party bailee (like a carrier or warehouseman) and are to be delivered without being moved, the risk passes to the buyer when the buyer has *the power to take possession* of the goods (2-509[2]). If the goods are covered by a document of title (negotiable or nonnegotiable), the risk passes when the buyer *receives the document of title*. When no document of title is involved, the risk passes when the bailee *acknowledges the buyer's right to possession*. This is illustrated in the case that follows, *Harmon v. Dunn.*

HARMON V. DUNN
1997 WL 13462 (Ct. App. Tenn. 1997)

FACTS

Bess Harmon was the owner of a two-year-old stallion named Phantom's Recall that was stabled at Bud Dunn and Sons Stable in Florence, Alabama. Steve Dunn was responsible for the general care (supplies and shoeing) of the animal and its training for and transport to various horse shows. Mrs. Harmon indicated to Dunn that she desired to sell the horse and instructed him to sell it for a purchase price of $25,000. Dunn began communicating with various parties, and Toby Scarborough agreed to purchase it.

On June 30, 1994, Dunn took Scarborough's check dated June 29, 1994, in the amount of $25,000 payable to Harmon to Harmon's home. Harmon was anxious to complete the transaction that afternoon as she and her family were about to depart for vacation. A "transfer of ownership" document, dated June 30, 1994, was signed by Mrs. Harmon, along with the stallion's certificate of registration. Dunn, however, instructed Mrs. Harmon to leave the space for the buyer's name blank because Scarborough had several businesses and Dunn was not sure

(continued)

HARMON V. DUNN

(concluded)

which he preferred to designate as owner. Mrs. Harmon also paid Dunn his commission on the sale.

That evening Dunn saw Scarborough at a horse show in Lewisburg, Tennessee, and told him that he had given Scarborough's check to Mrs. Harmon. However, he did not deliver the papers to him at that time, forgetting to do so, and Scarborough did not ask for them. Dunn also saw Scarborough the next evening at another show but again did not deliver the papers. Scarborough knew that Dunn had the papers and that Phantom's Recall was stabled at Dunn's barn. At that time, Scarborough told Dunn that the horse would be transported to another stable on July 5.

A veterinarian was called to treat the horse on June 26 because it was not eating well and had a cough and a fever. When she examined the horse the next day, it was doing much better. She next saw the horse on July 3, and because of its "extremely grave condition" she had it transported to the veterinary hospital, where it died the next day. The horse had acute colitis-x and was acutely endotoxic, a condition under which a horse can go from ok to dead in a very few hours.

Scarborough stopped payment on his check the next day. Mrs. Harmon returned home on July 9 to discover the horse had died and that Scarborough's bank had not honored the check. Harmon then brought suit against Scarborough to recover the purchase price of the horse.

ISSUE

Did Scarborough have the risk of loss of the horse when it died before it had been physically delivered to him?

DECISION

Yes. Under the UCC when goods are held by a bailee to be delivered without being moved, the risk of loss passes to the buyer (a) on his receipt of a negotiable document of title covering the goods or (b) on acknowledgment by the bailee of the buyer's right to possession of the goods. Here, there was a bailor–bailee relationship between Mrs. Harmon and Dunn. Scarborough knew that the horse had been sold to him and that Dunn had the transfer papers and was holding the horse for him. By July 1, Scarborough had the ability to control the horse—and in fact gave Dunn instructions as to the transfer of the horse that was to take place on July 5. Thus the risk of loss had passed to Scarborough.

AUTHOR'S NOTE

The court rejected Scarborough's assertion that he had been misled as to the condition of the horse because the veterinarian could not say with any degree of certainty that the colitis was present in the horse on June 30 or July 1.

RISK GENERALLY

If none of the special rules that have just been discussed applies, the risk passes to the buyer on receipt of the goods if the seller is a merchant. If the seller is not a merchant, the risk passes to the buyer when the seller tenders (offers) delivery of the goods (2-509[3]). For example, Frank offers to sell Susan a car, and Susan sends an e-mail accepting Frank's offer. When he receives the e-mail, Frank calls Susan and tells her she can "pick up the car anytime." That night, the car is destroyed when a tree falls on it during a storm. If Frank is a used car salesman, he must bear the loss. If Frank is an accountant, Susan must bear the loss.

BREACH OF CONTRACT AND RISK OF LOSS

The Code follows the trend set by earlier law of placing the risk of loss on a party who is in breach of contract. There is no necessary reason why a party in breach should bear the risk, however. In fact, shifting the risk to parties in breach sometimes produces results contrary to some of the basic policies underlying the Code's general

CONCEPT SUMMARY	Risk of Loss

The point at which the risk of loss or damage to goods identified to a contract passes to the buyer is as follows:

1. If there is an agreement between the parties, the risk of loss passes to the buyer at the time they have agreed to.

2. If the contract requires the seller to ship the goods by carrier but does not require that the seller guarantee their delivery to a specific destination (shipment contract), the risk of loss passes to the buyer when the seller has delivered the goods to the carrier and made an appropriate contract for their carriage.

3. If the contract requires the seller to guarantee delivery of the goods to a specific destination (destination contract), the risk of loss passes to the buyer when the goods are delivered at the designated destination.

4. If the goods are in the hands of a third person and are to be delivered without being moved, the risk of loss passes to the buyer when the buyer has the power to take possession of the goods; for example, when he receives a document of title.

5. In any situation other than those noted above where the seller is a merchant, the risk of loss passes to the buyer on his receipt of goods.

6. In any situation other than those noted above where the seller is not a merchant, the risk of loss passes to the buyer on the tender of delivery to the buyer by the seller.

7. When a seller tenders goods that the buyer could lawfully reject because they do not conform to the contract description, the risk of loss stays on the seller until the defect is cured or the buyer accepts them.

8. When a buyer rightfully revokes acceptance of goods, the risk is on the seller to the extent it is not covered by the buyer's insurance.

9. If a buyer repudiates a contract for identified, conforming goods before risk of loss has passed to the buyer, the buyer is liable for a commercially reasonable time for any loss or damage to the goods that is not covered by the seller's insurance.

rules on risk by placing the risk on the party who does not have possession or control of the goods. When the seller tenders goods that the buyer could lawfully reject because they do not conform to the contract description, the risk of loss remains on the seller until the defect is cured or the buyer accepts the goods (2-510[1]). When a buyer rightfully revokes acceptance of the goods, the risk of loss is on the seller from the beginning to the extent that it is not covered by the buyer's insurance (2-510[2]).

Buyers who repudiate a contract for identified, conforming goods before risk of loss has passed to them are liable for a commercially reasonable time for any damage to the goods that is not covered by the seller's insurance (2-510[3]). For example, Trendy Shoe Stores contracts to buy 1,000 pairs of shoes from Acme Shoe Manufacturing Company. Acme crates the shoes and stores them in its warehouse pending delivery to Trendy. Trendy then tells Acme it will not honor its contract for the shoes, and they are destroyed by a fire in Acme's warehouse shortly thereafter. If Acme's insurance covers only part of the loss, Trendy is liable for the balance.

INSURABLE INTEREST

The Code rules that govern risk of loss are supplemented by rules that give the parties an **insurable interest** in the goods, which allows them to insure themselves against most of the risks they must bear. Buyers may protect their interest in goods before they obtain title to them, since they have an insurable interest in goods at the moment the goods are *identified to the contract* (2-501[1]). Sellers have an insurable interest in their goods as long as they have title to the goods or a security interest in them (2-501[2]).

SALES ON TRIAL

There are several common commercial situations in which a seller entrusts goods to another person. This may be done to give a potential buyer the chance to decide whether or not to buy the goods or to give the other party a chance to sell the goods to a third party. These cases present difficult questions about who has the risk of loss of the goods and whose creditors may attach the goods. The Code provides specific rules to answer these questions depending on the nature of the parties' agreement.

SALE OR RETURN

In a **sale or return** contract, the goods are delivered to the buyer *primarily for resale* with the understanding that the buyer has the right to return them (2-326[1][b]). Unless the parties agreed to the contrary, title and risk of loss rest with the buyer. Return of the goods is at the buyer's risk and expense (2-327[2][b]), and the buyer's creditors can attach the goods while they are in the buyer's possession (2-326[2]). Placing the risk on the buyer in these cases recognizes the fact that sale or return contracts are generally *commercial* transactions.

SALE ON APPROVAL

In a **sale on approval,** the goods are delivered to the buyer *primarily for the buyer's use* (2-326[1]a]). The buyer is given the opportunity to examine or try the goods so as to decide whether to accept them. Risk of loss and title to the goods do not pass to the buyer until the buyer accepts the goods (2-327[1][a]). Any use of the goods that is consistent with a trial of the goods is not an acceptance, but the buyer who fails to give reasonable notice of an intent to return the goods may be held to have accepted them (2-327[l][b]).

The buyer's creditors cannot reach goods held on approval (2-326[2]), and return of the goods is at the seller's risk and expense (2-327[1][c]). These provisions recognize the fact that sales on approval are primarily *consumer* transactions.

SALE ON CONSIGNMENT

Frequently, a seller (a consignor) places goods in the hands of a merchant (a consignee) who has agreed to act as the seller's agent in selling the goods. These are called **sales on consignment** or **sales on memorandum.** Since consigned goods still belong to the consignor, the consignor has title to and risk of loss of the goods. One potential danger in such cases is that the consignee's creditors may incorrectly assume that the consigned goods belong to the consignee and extend credit on that basis. Accordingly, the Code gives the consignee's creditors the power to attach consigned goods unless the consignor takes steps to notify them of his or her interest in the goods (2-326[3]).

Consignors may do this either by prominently posting a sign at the consignee's place of business indicating their interest in the goods or by filing a financing statement covering the goods pursuant to Article 9 of the Code. (Finance statements are discussed in Chapter 41.) Consignors who fail to take either of these steps may defeat the claims of a consignee's creditors by proving that the consignee "is generally known by his creditors to be substantially engaged in selling the goods of others" (2-326[3][b]). The risk taken by a consignor who does not take appropriate steps to protect his interest is illustrated in the following case, *In re Auclair.*

IN RE AUCLAIR MCGREGOR V. JACKSON
131 BR 185 (Bankr. M.D. Ala. 1991)

FACTS

Edd and Diane Auclair maintained a place of business in Covington County, Alabama, where they operated a gun shop and convenience store named Heath Grocery and Final Chapter Firearms. In November 1989, Luke Jackson delivered about 70 firearms to the Auclairs to sell on consignment. The consignment agreement provided as follows: "I Edd Auclair have received a number of guns, of which a list will be attached and I will sign. As I sell a gun I will pay James E. "Luke" Jackson or Betty King with them giving me a receipt for that particular gun. If something should happen to Luke Jackson the guns are to be returned to Betty King or at that time Betty King and Edd Auclair can enter into an agreement. If something should happen to Edd Auclair, Diane agrees to return all guns that have not been paid for to Luke Jackson or Betty King and pay for any that has [*sic*] been sold." The agreement was signed by Jackson, King, and the Auclairs.

On June 28, 1990, the Auclairs filed a petition in bankruptcy under Chapter 11 of the Bankruptcy Act. Shortly thereafter Jackson removed the firearms he had consigned from the Auclairs' store. The bankruptcy trustee representing the Auclairs' creditors claimed that the firearms were the property of the bankruptcy estate.

ISSUE

Were the firearms that Jackson had delivered to the Auclairs pursuant to the consignment agreement subject to the claims of the Auclairs' creditors?

DECISION

Yes. Under section 2-326(3) of the Uniform Commercial Code, goods delivered on consignment are deemed to be on sale or return. Thus, by deeming the consignee a purchaser of the goods, the consignor is precluded from asserting an ownership claim to the goods vis-à-vis the consignee's creditors. A consignor can avoid having the consigned goods being subject to the claims of the consignee's creditors only if he (1) complies with an applicable law providing for his interest to be evidenced by a sign; (2) establishes that the person conducting the business is generally known by his creditors to be selling the goods of others; or (3) complies with the filing provisions for secured transactions. In this instance, Jackson is not protected because Alabama has no sign law, only one of the Auclairs' creditors, at best, had knowledge of the consignment, and Jackson had not complied with the filing requirements for secured transactions.

.... *QUESTIONS AND PROBLEM CASES* ....

1. What are the differences between a "sale or return" and a "sale on approval"?

2. Suchy Funeral Home brought suit against Waldenmaier to recover the contracted price for a funeral, including the providing of a casket. Waldenmaier claimed that the lawsuit was commenced more than four years after the funeral and thus was barred by the Code's four-year statute of limitations (2-725). Suchy contended that the Code's statute of limitations did not apply because no "sale of goods" was involved. Should the court apply the Code provisions to this contract?

3. *Video Case.* See "Software Horror Story." Chuck Mason, a computer consultant, was hired to develop customized software for a business. His plan was to purchase off-the-shelf software and to modify it to meet the customer's need. After identifying several software packages that might

meet his need, he contacted a retailer, Bits and Bytes, by phone and explained his need to be able to modify the package at the source code level and to have the source code. He then asked Bits and Bytes to recommend a package that would meet these criteria and be easy to modify. After receiving the recommended software (D-Base Hit) from Bits and Bytes, Chuck modified the software but was unable to get it to work as envisioned. Bits and Bytes refused to take it back because Chuck's modifications prevented it from being resold or returned to the software publisher. Chuck refused to pay Bits and Bytes for the package. Chuck then purchased a different software package (Customized Amazing Base) and customized it for his customer. However, the customized software never functioned satisfactorily for the client, and she refused to pay Chuck for it. Does the UCC apply to the sale of the software by the retailer? Does it apply to the sale of the customized software by Chuck to the customer?

4. On June 3, 1991, Donald and Sonna Hummel executed a written purchase order invoice for the purchase of a 1989 Chevrolet Corsica from Raisor Pontiac in Lafayette, Indiana. The purchase order indicated that the total retail price of the Corsica would be $7,681.98, that the Hummels would make a cash down payment of $624.50, and that the Purdue Employees Federal Credit Union would be the lienholder for the $7,057.48 balance. The Hummels signed a Retail Installment Contract and Security Agreement with Raisor Pontiac, presented a check for $350.00, and took delivery of the Corsica. The next day the Hummels gave Raisor Pontiac a second check for $274.50. On June 5. 1991, Donald Hummel was driving the Corsica when it collided with a vehicle driven by Matthew Lyons. At the time of the accident, Raisor Pontiac held the certificate of title to the Corsica and the vehicle bore an interim license plate. Lyons was injured in the accident and Sean O'Donnell, a passenger in the Lyons vehicle, died in the collision.

   The day after the accident, the Hummels' $274.50 check to Raisor Pontiac was debited to their account and on June 7, the $350.00 check was debited. Also on June 7, Raisor Pontiac assigned the Installment Contract with the Hummels to the Credit Union, which remitted a check to Raisor Pontiac for $7,057.48, the amount financed. Raisor Pontiac transferred the Certificate of Title to the Hummels on June 11. At the time of the accident, Raisor Pontiac was insured by American Employers Insurance Co. under a policy that covered its ownership, maintenance, or use of covered automobiles. Sean O'Donnell's parents sued Hummel for the wrongful death of their son, alleging that he was negligent in his operation of the automobile at the time of the collision. They also sought a declaratory judgment that the American Employers' policy covered this situation on the grounds that Raisor Pontiac was the owner of the vehicle at the time of the accident. Was Raisor Pontiac the owner or title holder of the Corsica at the time of the accident?

5. Club Pro Golf Products was a distributor of golf products. It employed salesmen who called on customers to take orders for merchandise. The merchandise was sent by Club Pro directly to the purchaser and payment was made by the purchaser directly to Club Pro. A salesman for Club Pro, Carl Gude, transmitted orders for certain merchandise to Club Pro for delivery to several fictitious purchasers. Club Pro sent the merchandise to the fictitious purchasers at the fictitious addresses where it was picked up by Gude. Gude then sold the merchandise, worth approximately $19,000, directly to Simpson, a golf pro at a golf club. Gude then retained the proceeds of sale for himself. Club Pro discovered the fraud and brought suit against Simpson to recover the merchandise. Did Simpson get good title to the merchandise he purchased from Gude even though Gude had obtained it by fraud?

6. *Video Case.* See "TV Repair." Arnold took his old TV to an appliance store for repair. The appliance store developed financial problems and was unable to pay its debts to its creditors as they became due. Facing bankruptcy, the appliance store held a going-out-of-business sale and sold everything in the store, including Arnold's TV, to individual customers who had no knowledge of anyone else's interest in the goods. Does Arnold have the legal right to recover the TV from the person who bought it at the going-out-of-business sale?

7. In June, Ramos entered into a contract to buy a motorcycle from Big Wheel Sports Center. He paid the purchase price of $893 and was given the papers necessary to register the cycle and get insurance on it. Ramos registered the cycle but had not attached the license plates to it. He left on vacation and told the salesperson for Big Wheel Sports Center that he would pick up the cycle on his return. While Ramos was on vacation, there was an electric power blackout in New York City and the cycle was stolen by looters. Ramos then sued Big Wheel Sports Center to get back his $893. Did Big Wheel Sports Center have the risk of loss of the motorcycle?

8. *Video Case.* See "Sour Grapes." Jelly Manufacturer, a food processor in Chicago, placed a phone order with Grape Grower, a grower in California, for a quantity of perishable produce. The shipping term was "CIF" with payment to be made on delivery (C.O.D.). Grower delivered the goods called for in the

contract to a carrier and contracted for their shipment. However, it neglected to provide that the goods be shipped under refrigeration. The goods were loaded on a nonrefrigerated boxcar and as a result the produce was spoiled when it reached Chicago. Who had the risk of loss, Grape Grower or Jelly Manufacturer?

9. Richard Burnett agreed to purchase a mobile home with a shed from Betty Jean Putrell, Executrix of the Estate of Lena Holland. On Saturday, March 3, 1990, Burnett paid Putrell $6,500 and was given the certificate of title to the mobile home as well as a key to it but no keys to the shed. At the time the certificate of title was transferred, the following items remained in the mobile home: the washer and dryer, mattress and box springs, two chairs, items in the refrigerator, and the entire contents of the shed. These items were to be retained by Putrell and removed by her. To facilitate removal she retained one key to the mobile home and the only keys to the shed. On Sunday, March 4, the mobile was home was destroyed by fire through the fault of neither party. At the time of the fire, Putrell still had a key to the mobile home as well as the keys to the shed and she had not removed the contents of the mobile home or of the shed. The contents of the shed were not destroyed and were subsequently removed by Putrell. Burnett brought suit against Putrell to recover the $6,500 he had paid for the mobile home and shed. Did the seller, Putrell, have the risk of loss of the trailer?

10. Collier, a retail store operator, accepted a delivery of stereo tapes, cartridges, and equipment from B&B Sales. The invoice noted that the goods had been "sold to" Collier and stated: "Terms 30-60-90; this equipment will be picked up if not sold in 90 days." Shortly thereafter, Collier's store was burglarized and all the merchandise was stolen. B&B filed suit against Collier for the purchase price of the merchandise, claiming that the transaction was a sale and that Collier was liable to pay for the merchandise. Collier argued that the transaction was a consignment and that B&B had the risk of loss. Did Collier or B&B have the risk of loss of the merchandise?

CHAPTER 17

Warranties and Product Liability

When you buy a product from a merchant, you have certain expectations relating to its quality and safe use. For example, if a Ford dealer sells you a new Explorer, you might expect:

1. *After you discount certain statements as sales talk, the vehicle will perform as well as the salesperson promised.*
2. *The vehicle will perform as well as the manufacturer—Ford—said it would in its advertisements.*
3. *The vehicle will conform to any written guarantees that were made by the manufacturer or dealer.*
4. *The vehicle will be suitable for driving on the highway and for other uses to which such cars are usually put, and its quality will be similar to that of other cars.*
5. *The vehicle has been properly designed and manufactured and does not have any dangerous defects or unusual problems of which you have not been warned.*

Suppose you are driving your 16-month-old SUV on an interstate highway when a tire blows out with the tread separating from the rest of the tire. The SUV, which is susceptible to rollovers, rolls over, the vehicle is badly damaged, and you are seriously injured. Who is responsible for the accident and for the damages you have sustained? You, the manufacturer of the SUV, the manufacturer of the tire, and/or the dealer from whom you purchased the vehicle?

If it can be shown that the vehicle and/or tire were defective at the time you purchased the vehicle, liability might be placed on one or both of the manufacturers and/or the dealer based on one or more of a number of legal theories: (1) express warranty, (2) implied warranties that are imposed by law, (3) negligence, or (4) strict liability. In this chapter, we will explore the legal rules for holding manufacturers and sellers liable for product quality.

INTRODUCTION: HISTORICAL DEVELOPMENT OF THE LAW

Prior to 1900, the sale of goods was commonly made in a face-to-face negotiation between the buyer and the seller. The goods were relatively simple and could be examined on the spot. Frequently, the seller was a peddler who would leave for parts unknown as soon as he had sold his wares. The sale was often looked on as a test of wits; the seller did his best to drive a sharp bargain. Similarly, the buyer did everything possible to get a good buy. In this situation, neither the buyer nor the seller placed much faith in the statements of the other. The statements made by the seller were taken by the buyer to be sales talk. These statements were not binding on the seller unless he clearly assumed responsibility for the quality of the goods he was selling.

Business methods have changed over time. Today, sales to businesspeople are frequently made by a salesperson calling on the customer. The salesperson either describes the goods or displays samples of the goods. The selling of many kinds of consumer goods is done through advertising on television, in newspapers and magazines, or on the Internet. These changes in the way sales of goods are made have led to changes in the law providing more protection to buyers of these goods. Manufacturers and sellers are also held much more accountable for the quality and safety of the goods they sell because of changes in society's concept of who can best bear the responsibility for the quality of goods.

In the next section of this chapter, we will cover the obligations and rules concerning seller responsibility for product quality that arise under the Uniform Commercial Code's warranty provisions. Later in the chapter, we will cover obligations that arise under the federal Magnuson-Moss Act, the common law of negligence, and the doctrine of strict liability.

WARRANTIES

In general, a **warranty** is a contractual promise by the seller regarding the quality, character, or suitability of the goods he has sold. In a product liability suit based on breach of warranty, the plaintiff is claiming that the product did not live up to the seller's promise. If the seller, through words or behavior, makes promises about the goods, he has created an **express warranty.** In addition, certain responsibilities for the quality of goods sold are imposed on the seller by the Uniform Commercial Code. These warranties arise whether or not the seller has made express promises as to the quality of the goods. The warranties imposed by law are known as **implied warranties.**

EXPRESS WARRANTIES

In order to create an express warranty, it does not matter whether the seller uses the words *warranty* or *guarantee* or whether the seller *intends* to make a warranty. The critical elements for creation of an express warranty are that the seller make a *statement of fact or a promise* to the buyer *concerning the goods* that *become part of the bargain* between the buyer and seller (2-313[1][a]).[1] Sellers who merely give an opinion or recommend the goods do not create an express warranty. Thus, sellers are not considered to have made an express warranty if they confine their statements to "sales

---

[1]The numbers in parentheses refer to sections of the Uniform Commercial Code.

talk." Some examples of sales talk are: "It is a good buy"; "These goods are first class"; and "You should be happy with this."

Whether a statement made by a seller is interpreted as an opinion or as an express warranty often depends on the relative experience and knowledge of the buyer and seller. If the seller deals in the type of goods she is selling and the buyer does not deal in such goods and knows little about them, a statement by the seller about the quality or character of the goods might be interpreted as a warranty. On the other hand, if the buyer is a dealer in such goods and has had experience and knowledge similar to that of the seller, the same statement might be interpreted as an expression of an opinion.

For example, if a used car dealer who is very familiar with the mechanical operation of cars is selling a car to a person who is not knowledgeable about cars, the dealer's statements about the condition of the car and its performance are likely to be treated as statements of fact or promises creating an express warranty. However, if that same dealer is selling a car to another dealer who is equally knowledgeable about cars, the seller's statements are less likely to be treated as promises on which the dealer would rely in deciding to purchase the car.

Health problems related to the sale and use of tobacco products have spurred considerable litigation. One of the most celebrated cases was brought by a smoker, Rose Cipollone, against a number of tobacco companies seeking to recover damages arising out of her use of cigarettes.

CIPOLLONE V. LIGGETT GROUP, INC.
893 F.2d 541 (3rd Cir. 1990)

FACTS

Rose Cipollone was born in 1925 and began to smoke in 1942. From 1942 until 1955, she smoked Chesterfield brand cigarettes manufactured by Liggett. In 1955 she stopped smoking Chesterfields and began to smoke L&M filter cigarettes, also manufactured by Liggett. In 1968 she started smoking the Virginia Slims brand manufactured by Philip Morris; in the 1970s she switched to the Parliament brand, also manufactured by Philip Morris; and in 1974 she switched from Parliament to the True brand manufactured by Lorillard, Inc. From 1942 until the early 1980s, Cipollone smoked between one and two packs of cigarettes a day. In 1981 she was diagnosed as having lung cancer and in 1982 she had a lung removed. She continued to smoke until 1983 when she became terminally ill. She died on October 21, 1984, after bringing suit for damages against Liggett, Philip Morris, and Lorillard. The lawsuit was continued by her husband, Antonio, after her death. One of the claims in the lawsuit was for breach of express warranties, which she asserted had been made concerning the health effects of smoking.

Cipollone testified that she began smoking the Chesterfield brand to be glamorous like the pretty girls and movie stars depicted in the Chesterfield ads and because the ads stated that Chesterfields were "mild," which she understood to mean safe. Subsequent Chesterfield ads (in 1952) included the words, "PLAY SAFE Smoke Chesterfield. NOSE, THROAT, and Accessory Organs Not Adversely Affected by Smoking Chesterfields." She also frequently listened to the Arthur Godfrey show on the radio. The Chesterfield brand was the sponsor of the show and was marketed on it. During one show in 1952, Godfrey read a commercial that noted, "You hear stuff about cigarettes being harmful to you . . . Here's an ad . . . if you smoke, it will make you feel better," and went on to say that following a six-month "medical" study of Chesterfield smokers, a medical specialist had stated the smokers were not adversely affected by smoking Chesterfield cigarettes. Godfrey then asserted, "I never did believe they [Chesterfield cigarettes] did you any harm and now we've got the proof. So—Chesterfields are the cigarette for you."

When Cipollone switched to L&M cigarettes, she recalled seeing ads that stated the L&M filter tips were safer and that doctors recommend you smoke. During the years she smoked L&M cigarettes, some of their ads indicated that the "miracle tip filters" were "just what the

(continued)

CIPOLLONE V. LIGGETT GROUP, INC.
(concluded)

doctor ordered." The "miracle tip" was advertised as "removing the heavy particles, leaving you a Light and Mild smoke." She testified that her switch to Parliament was in part due to its recessed filter, which she thought would be healthier. The change to True, a cigarette advertised as being low in tar, was prompted by advice of her doctor.

ISSUE

Could these advertisements create an express warranty?

DECISION

Yes. The court held that the statements in the advertisements could create express warranties but that they had to be shown in part of the "basis of the bargain" on which Cipollone had purchased the cigarettes. Thus (1) Anto-

nio Cipollone had to prove that his wife had read, seen, or heard the advertisements in question and (2) Liggett had to have an opportunity to prove that any advertisements read, seen, or heard by Cipollone were not believed by her. Earlier, the court had held that the Federal Cigarette Labeling and Advertising Act of 1966, which required health warnings on labels and advertisements, had preempted all post-1965 warranty claims based on cigarette advertising.

AUTHOR'S NOTE

In 1992, in *Cippollone v. Liggett Group, Inc.*, 112 S. Ct. 2608, the U.S. Supreme Court held that the Federal Cigarette Labeling and Advertising Act did not preempt claims under state law for breach of express warranty.

Ethical Implications

The causal relationship between smoking and lung cancer is now well documented. In light of this, is it ethical for a company to manufacture and market cigarettes and other tobacco products? How justifiable are advertisements for tobacco products that are aimed at teenagers and young adults? What about targeting sales to people in other countries who may have less knowledge about the health effects of smoking?

In negotiating a sale, a seller may use descriptive terms to convey to the buyer an idea of the quality or characteristics of the goods; for example, Brand X is "a skin cream for oily skin." Similarly a seller might use pictures, drawings, blueprints, or technical specifications, or in some cases a sample or model. When a seller uses descriptive terms and the buyer takes them into consideration when making the purchase, the seller has expressly warranted that the goods she delivers will meet that description. If a sample or model is part of the basis of a bargain of a contract, the seller has expressly warranted that the goods delivered will conform to the sample or model (2-313 [1][b], [c]).

IMPLIED WARRANTIES

Nature of Implied Warranties

Under present methods of merchandising, the buyer commonly has little or no opportunity to examine goods carefully before making a decision to purchase them. In addition, because of the complexity and nature of many of the goods that are sold today, buyers are often not in a position to test the goods adequately to determine their quality prior to buying them. The merchant dealing in the goods or the manufacturer of such goods is in a much better position to make a thorough examination or test of the goods to determine their adequacy and quality. Therefore, in the interest of promoting higher standards in the marketplace, the law imposes certain responsibilities on the seller for the quality, character, and suitability of the goods sold. This is particularly true where the seller is a merchant dealing in goods of that kind.

Implied warranties imposed by law are not absolute. They arise only under certain circumstances, and the seller may include a clause in the contract that excludes them. The courts, however, favor implied warranties. If the seller wishes to be relieved of the responsibility for implied warranties, the sales contract must clearly provide that the parties did not intend the implied warranties to become part of the contract.

There are two implied warranties of quality imposed under the Code: (1) the implied warranty of merchantability and (2) the implied warranty of fitness for a particular purpose. These two warranties overlap, and under some circumstances the seller may be held liable for breach of both warranties.

Implied Warranty of Merchantability

If the seller is a merchant who deals in the kind of goods sold, there is an *implied warranty* that the goods are **merchantable,** or fit for their ordinary purpose. If the person who sells the goods does not deal in goods of that kind, the implied warranty of merchantability is not involved. For example, if your occupation is selling clothing and you sell your used 1994 Chevrolet to a neighbor, there is no implied warranty that the car is merchantable.

The common test for **merchantability** is whether the goods are *fit for the ordinary purpose* for which such goods are used (2-314[2][c]). Thus, a person of normal weight who buys a chair should be able to sit on it without it collapsing. The chair should also withstand other things people commonly do with chairs, such as occasionally standing on them or dragging them across the floor.

The other tests of merchantability for all sales contracts are:

1. The goods conform to any promises or statements of fact made on the container or label.
2. The goods are adequately packaged and labeled.
3. The goods are of the same kind, quality, and quantity within each unit (case, package, carton).
4. Fungible goods (mixed goods that are identical and cannot be separated, such as grain and coal) are of average quality for the kind of goods described in the contract.
5. The goods conform closely enough to the description in the contract to be acceptable to others in the trade or business (2-314[2]).

The case that follows, *Denny v. Ford Motor Co.,* involves a claim that a small sports utility vehicle was not fit for the ordinary purposes for which it was to be used driving on a highway.

DENNY V. FORD MOTOR CO.
662 N.E.2d 730 (Ct. App. N.Y. 1995)

FACTS

Nancy Denny was severely injured when the Ford Bronco II that she was driving rolled over. The accident occurred when Denny slammed on her brakes in an effort to avoid a deer that had walked directly into her motor vehicle's path. Denny and her husband brought an action against Ford Motor Company, the vehicle's manufacturer, asserting a claim for, among other things, breach of the implied warranty of merchantability.

(continued)

DENNY V. FORD MOTOR CO.
(concluded)

The evidence at the trial centered on the particular characteristics of utility vehicles, which are generally made for off-road use on unpaved and often rugged terrain. Such use often necessitates climbing over obstacles such as fallen logs and rocks. While utility vehicles are traditionally considerably larger than passenger cars, some manufacturers have created a category of downsized "small" utility vehicles, which are designed to be lighter, to achieve better fuel economy, and to appeal to a wider consumer market. The Bronco II in which Denny was injured falls into this category.

Denny produced evidence showing that small utility vehicles in general, and the Bronco II in particular, present a significantly higher risk of rollover accidents than do ordinary passenger automobiles. She showed that the Bronco II had a low stability index attributable to its high center of gravity and relatively narrow track width. The vehicle's shorter wheel base and suspension system were additional factors contributing to its instability. Ford had made minor design changes in an effort to achieve a higher stability index, but none of the changes produced a significant improvement in the vehicle's stability.

Ford argued at the trial that the design features of which Denny complained were necessary to the vehicle's off-road capabilities. According to Ford, the vehicle had been intended to be used as an off-road vehicle and had not been designed to be sold as a conventional passenger automobile. Ford's own engineer stated that he would not recommend the Bronco II to someone whose primary interest was to use it as a passenger car, because the features of a four-wheel drive utility vehicle were not

helpful for that purpose and the vehicle's design made it inherently less stable.

A Ford marketing manual, however, predicted that many buyers would be attracted because utility vehicles were "suitable to contemporary life styles" and were "considered fashionable" in some suburban areas. According to the manual, the sales presentation should take into account the vehicle's "suitability for commuting and for suburban and city driving." Additionally, the vehicle's ability to switch between two-wheel and four-wheel drive would "be particularly appealing to women who may be concerned about driving in snow and ice with their children." The Dennys testified that the perceived safety benefits of its four-wheel drive capacity were what attracted them to the Bronco II and that they were not at all interested in its off-road use.

ISSUE

Did Ford breach the implied warranty of merchantability when it sold the Bronco II for use as an on-road vehicle when it had a propensity to roll over in such use?

DECISION

Yes. The law implies a warranty by a manufacturer that places its product on the market that the product is reasonably fit for the ordinary purpose for which it was intended. Here the Dennys claim that the Bronco was not fit for its ordinary purpose because of its alleged propensity to roll over and the lack of warnings to the consumer of this propensity. The jury found that Ford had breached the implied warranty of merchantability.

Under the Code, the implied warranty of merchantability applies to the selling of food or drink (2-314[1]). Thus, if food or drink sold in a restaurant is not wholesome, the seller may be held liable for breach of this warranty. The courts, however, disagree on how to judge whether food is wholesome if it contains a naturally occurring but unexpected substance. Some courts, using a "foreign-natural" test, say that the warranty is breached if the substance is "foreign" to the food but not if it is natural to it. Thus, if Carl bought a chicken sandwich with a piece of metal in it that injured his mouth, he would be able to recover. If, however, his mouth were instead injured by a piece of chicken bone in the sandwich, he would not be able to recover. A growing number of courts have adopted a different test. Under this test, plaintiffs can recover if they could not reasonably expect the substance to be in the food, even if it is naturally occurring. Courts using this test would allow Carl to recover if he could show that a reasonable person would not expect to find a chicken bone in a chicken sandwich. These issues are addressed in the *Mexicali Rose* case with the court's majority and the dissenting justices reaching different conclusions.

MEXICALI ROSE V. SUPERIOR COURT
16 UCC Rep.2d 607 (Sup. Ct. Cal. 1992)

FACTS

Jack Clark was a customer at the Mexicali Rose restaurant. He ordered a chicken enchilada and sustained throat injuries when he swallowed a one-inch chicken bone. He brought an action for damages based on breach of the implied warranty of merchantability, negligence, and strict liability. He alleged that Mexicali Rose negligently left the bone in the enchilada and the food was unfit for human consumption. He also asserted that he did not expect to find a bone and that it is not common knowledge that there may be bones in a chicken enchilada.

ISSUE

Was Mexicali Rose liable for breach of the implied warranty of merchantability because of the presence of the chicken bone in the enchilada?

DECISION

No. The court applied the foreign–natural test and held that if an injury-producing substance is natural to the preparation of the food served, then it can be said that it was reasonably expected by its very nature and the food cannot be determined unfit or defective. In such a case the injured person does not have a cause of action for breach of implied warranty or for strict liability. The court went on to say that if the presence of the natural substance is the consequence of a restaurateur's failure to exercise due care in food preparation, the injured patron can sue under a negligence theory. Alternatively, if the injury-causing substance is foreign to the food served, then the injured patron may sue on the grounds of breach of warranty and strict liability and the court must determine whether the substance (1) could be reasonably expected by the average consumer and (2) rendered the food unfit or defective.

DISSENT

The dissenting justices took a different view, noting that a majority of the court had held that processed food containing a sharp, concealed bone is fit for consumption, though no reasonable consumer would anticipate finding the bone. They noted that the majority had declared, in effect, that the bone is natural to the dish and therefore the dish is fit for consumption. The rule created by the majority seems bizarre in application to mass producers and distributors of processed food, irrational in differentiating between natural and unnatural contaminants, and unfair in saddling the objectively reasonable—and truthful—consumer with costs he or she had no way of protecting against. In applying the implied warranty of merchantability, courts should consider "natural" to mean that the consumer should anticipate finding the object in the meal. The focus should be on whether the object should reasonably be anticipated in the dish as served.

Implied Warranty of Fitness for a Particular Purpose

At times, the seller may know the *particular purpose* for which the buyer needs the goods and know that the buyer is *relying* on the seller to select goods suitable for that purpose. If these two conditions are met, then the seller makes an **implied warranty** that the goods will be *fit for that particular purpose* (2-315).

In some instances, the buyer will tell the seller the particular purpose for which the goods are needed. For example, a farmer goes to a feed store and tells the clerk that he needs a pesticide that will kill corn borers. If the clerk knows the farmer is depending on her to pick a suitable pesticide, there is an implied warranty that the product selected will be fit for the farmer's needs. If, when properly used, the product selected kills the farmer's corn or is ineffective against corn borers, the implied warranty is breached.

In other instances, the particular purpose is implied from the circumstances. For example, when Carl buys a roast beef sandwich, it is implied that he is going to eat it. Therefore, the sandwich is sold with an implied warranty that it will be fit for the particular purpose of eating. If it is contaminated, the warranty of fitness for a particular purpose is breached. While the warranty of merchantability and warranty of fitness for a particular purpose can both accompany the sale of a good, as in Carl's case, they are not the same. The implied warranty of merchantability applies only to merchants, while the warranty of fitness for a particular purpose can also apply to nonmerchants. The warranty of merchantability focuses on whether the goods are fit for the ordinary purposes for which such goods are used; the warranty of fitness for a particular purpose on the buyer's individual purpose. Thus, if a 350-pound man tells the clerk he needs a chair that will not collapse under his weight and is sold one that will support a person of only average weight, the warranty of fitness for a particular purpose is breached but not the warranty of merchantability.

If the buyer gives the seller technical specifications of the goods she wishes to buy or clearly indicates the particular goods desired, there is no implied warranty of fitness for a particular purpose. Under these circumstances, there is no evidence that the buyer is relying on the seller's judgment or expertise.

In the case that follows, *Klein v. Sears Roebuck & Co.*, Sears was found to have made and breached a warranty for a particular purpose.

KLEIN V. SEARS ROEBUCK & CO.
41 UCC Rep. 1233 (4th Cir. 1985)

FACTS

Shortly after Steven Klein was married and moved into a new home, he went to a local Sears store to consult with a salesman about the purchase of a riding lawn mower. He explained to the salesman that he had no experience with lawn mowers and that the property on which the mower was to be used was a ¾-acre tract containing numerous hills. The salesman recommended a Sears Craftsman 8-horsepower, electric-start, rear-engine riding mower with a 30-inch cutting deck. The sale, however, was conditioned on an inspection of Klein's property, to be conducted at the time of delivery of the mower. A few days later, the Sears salesman delivered the mower to Klein's residence, inspected the property, and pronounced the mower suitable for mowing the property. He did warn Klein that the mower should be driven vertically up and down the hills.

Klein used the mower without incident for about a year. However, one day when he was mowing vertically up a 19-degree slope, the mower tipped over backward and his hand was severely injured when it came in con-

tact with the rotating blades. He suffered an 80 percent impairment of his right arm and hand and was unable to continue in his employment as a jeweler. He brought suit against Sears to recover for his injuries, claiming, among other things, breach of the warranty of fitness for a particular purpose. Sears argued, among other things, that the owner's manual stated that the mower should not be used on a slope in excess of 15 degrees and thus that Klein's injury was due to improper operation, not breach of warranty.

ISSUE

Was Sears liable for breach of the warranty of fitness for particular purpose?

DECISION

Yes. The court found that the warranty of fitness for a particular purpose was made in this case because Sears had knowledge of the particular purpose for which the mower was to be used and that Klein was relying on its

(continued)

KLEIN V. SEARS ROEBUCK & CO.
(concluded)

judgment to select or furnish suitable goods. The warranty was breached when Klein was injured while operating the mower in a manner consistent with the representations made by the Sears salesman—that is, vertically on a slope that was pronounced safe.

Implied Warranty of Title

The **implied warranty of title** differs from other warranties in that it protects the buyer in his ownership of the goods bought. In contrast, the other warranties discussed in this chapter relate to the quality of the goods sold. The general rule is that in any contract for the sale of goods, the seller warrants to the buyer that he has the right to sell them (2-312). If, for example, the seller stole the goods, the seller does not have good title to them, and the warranty of title is breached when he sells them to the buyer.

Under the implied warranty of title, the seller also warrants that the goods are *free of any liens or claims of other parties* unless the buyer was given notice of the liens or claims at the time the contract was made (2-312). Suppose John puts his car up for sale. John originally borrowed the money to buy the car from his bank, and the bank took a security interest or lien on it to secure John's repayment of the loan. If John still owes $600 to the bank at the time he sells the car to Ann, John must either pay off the bank before he transfers title to Ann or specifically provide in his agreement with Ann that the automobile is being sold subject to the bank's lien.

When the seller of goods is a merchant, the implied warranty of title also covers a claim by a third party that the sale or use of the goods infringes a patent held by that third party.

The implied warranty of title is not made where there is specific language in the contract or circumstances giving the buyer reason to know that the seller does not claim to have title—such as a sheriff's sale. This principle is illustrated in the case that follows, *Marino v. Perna.*

MARINO V. PERNA
629 N.Y.S.2d 669 (Civ. Ct. N.Y.C. 1995)

FACTS

On January 31, 1992, Joseph Perna purchased a 1981 Oldsmobile at a traffic auction from the city marshall, Alfred Locascio. The certificate of sale, signed by Perna, indicated that the car had been seized pursuant to execution issued on an action brought by the New York City Parking Violations Bureau against Jose Cruz. Perna bought the car for $1,800 plus tax and towing fees "subject to the terms and conditions of any and all chattel mortgages, rental agreements, liens, conditional bills of sale, and encumbrances that may be on the motor vehicle." The automobile had 58,103 miles on the odometer at the time.

On May 7, 1993, Perna sold the car to Eli Marino, a co-worker, for $1,200. The vehicle had approximately 65,000 miles on its odometer at the time of sale. During the period in which he owned the automobile, Marino made a number of repairs to the car, including replacing the

(continued)

MARINO V. PERNA
(concluded)

radiator ($270), repair of the power steering and a valve cover ($117), and replacement of a door lock ($97.45).

Marino registered and insured the vehicle, and a valid certificate of title was issued to him. In February of 1994, Marino's son was driving the Oldsmobile when he was stopped by the police and subsequently arrested for driving a stolen vehicle. His son was kept in jail overnight and released after arraignment. The charges eventually were dismissed but not without a further court appearance and $600 attorney fees paid by claimant. The Oldsmobile was never returned to Marino. At the time it was seized, the odometer reflected about 73,000 miles.

Marino brought an action for breach of warranty of title against Perna, seeking to recover the cost of the automobile, the costs of restoring it, and the legal fees arising from the arrest of his son for possession of a stolen vehicle. Perna, in turn, brought an action against Locascio, the city marshall who sold him the car.

ISSUE

Was Perna liable for breach of warranty in the resale of the automobile he had bought at a public auction conducted by a marshall?

DECISION

Yes. Under the UCC, a contract for the sale of goods contains an implied warranty of title. The statute, however, excludes contracts from warranting title when "specific

language or circumstances give the buyer reason to know that the person selling does not claim title in himself or that he is purporting to sell only such right or title as he or a third person might have." Sales by a sheriff or marshall have long been recognized as being out of the ordinary course and do not carry a warranty of title. Here, not only was the sale at a public auction by a marshall but also the certificate of sale informed Perna that he was purchasing subject to any encumbrances of Cruz, the judgment debtor. Thus the marshall has no liability for breach of warranty. However, there is a clear breach of the warranty of title by Perna in his sale to Marino, as the marshall's exception does not apply to this sale.

AUTHOR'S NOTE

The court held that Marino was entitled to recover the market value of the car at the time it was surrendered to the authorities ($1,200), but that he could not directly recover the cost of the improvements as they were reflected in the market value of the car. Marino also was not able to recover the consequential damages (the cost of the arrest and of defending the arrest) because they were not reasonably foreseeable as Perna had no reason to suspect the car had been stolen, having registered and insured it. Damages available for breach of warranty are discussed in more detail in Chapter 19, Remedies for Breach of Contract.

EXCLUSIONS AND MODIFICATIONS OF WARRANTIES

GENERAL RULES

Under the Code, the parties to a contract have, within certain limits, the right to agree to relieve the seller from all or part of the liability for express or implied warranties. Frequently, sellers try to exclude or limit their responsibility for these warranties; however, such exclusions and modifications are not looked on with favor by the courts. The seller must satisfy a number of strict requirements in order to be successful in excluding or modifying an express or implied warranty. These requirements are designed to make it likely that the buyer is aware of the clause modifying or excluding the warranty and freely consents to it. In a dispute, the court considers the reasonableness of the particular exclusion or modification and will refuse to enforce an exclusion it finds to be unreasonable or unconscionable.

LIMITATION OF EXPRESS WARRANTIES

If sellers do not want to be liable for express warranties, they should try to avoid making any. This is difficult, however, because the seller is likely to make statements about the goods or use models or samples. A seller who makes an express warranty and who also tries to disclaim all express warranties by including a disclaimer clause in the contract is not likely to succeed. The disclaimer will probably be disregarded on the ground that it is inconsistent with the express warranty (2-316[1]). In the case that follows, *Thacker v. Menard*, the court found that the seller did effectively disclaim any express warranties.

THACKER V. MENARD
31 UCC Rep.2d 734 (7th Cir. 1997)

FACTS

Darrell and Sharon Thacker were interested in building a vacation home. They obtained a large book from National Plan Service that contained a plan for a "Vacation A-Frame Home LakePoint," which included blueprints with all the specifications for building the house. They took the book to Menard's to shop for the necessary materials. They spoke to Mark Rhinehart, a salesman, and asked him how much it would cost them to purchase what they needed to build the house. Rhinehart looked at the book, found the plan number, and entered it into the store's computer. The computer generated a six-page estimate of what was needed and how much it would cost.

Each page of the estimate contained the following disclaimer:

> This is an estimate. It is given only for general price information. This is not an offer and there can be no legally binding contract between the parties based on this estimate . . . **MENARD'S IS NOT RESPONSIBLE FOR ANY LOSS INCURRED BY THE CUSTOMER WHO RELIES ON PRICES SET FORTH HEREIN OR ON THE AVAILABILITY OF ANY OF THE MATERIALS STATED HEREIN.** All information on this form, other than price, has been provided by customer and Menard's is not responsible for any errors in the information on this estimate, including but not limited to, quantity, dimension and quality. Please examine this estimate carefully. **MENARD'S MAKES NO REPRESENTATIONS ORAL, WRITTEN OR OTHERWISE THAT THE MATERIALS LISTED ARE SUITABLE FOR ANY PURPOSE BEING CONSIDERED BY THE CUSTOMER. BECAUSE OF WIDE VARIATIONS IN CODES, THERE ARE NO REPRESENTATIONS THAT THE MATERIALS LISTED HEREIN MEET YOUR CODE REQUIREMENTS.**

The Thackers did not read this language, either when the estimate was generated or at any time prior to agreeing to purchase the materials. It was relatively inconspicuous, appearing on the form in type approximately one-half the size of the type on the remainder of the form. The bottom-line price on the estimate was $13,151.87.

The estimate was significantly lower than two other estimates the Thackers had received. Rhinehart assured them, however, that the estimate contained all the materials they would need. The Thackers were suspicious of the low price but were assured that the favorable price was due to Menard's high volume business. These assurances were repeated on two other occasions by Menard employees. The Thackers then placed an order for the materials.

When the materials were delivered to the Thacker's construction site, they discovered that the list was incomplete. It omitted items like the 2-by-12 beams necessary to build the center of the house and some of the glass windows called for by the plans. The Thackers claimed that they had to spend $147,398—more than 10 times the original $13,151.87 bid—trying to build the home (excluding the construction of the foundation, floor coverings, plumbing, heating and electrical wiring, which the Thackers were handling separately).

The Thackers brought suit against Menard, claiming, among other things, breach of contract, breach of express warranty, and breach of warranty for a particular purpose.

(continued)

THACKER V. MENARD
(concluded)

ISSUE

Was there a contract between the Thackers and Menard's that contained an express or implied warranty that everything the Thackers needed to build the house was listed on the estimate?

DECISION

No. The written estimate clearly disclaimed any warranty that the materials were fit for any purpose and negated any intent that the parties intended to make the em- ployee assurances part of the basis of the bargain. Even if the agreement was considered to be an oral contract, the majority of its terms could be ascertained only by reference back to the written estimate, which would have been incorporated in it. And the written estimate contains a clear disclaimer. There was no contract between the Thackers and Menard's that contained a promise that the materials would be sufficient to build the house, nor did it contain either an express warranty or a warranty for a particular purpose.

EXCLUSION OF IMPLIED WARRANTIES

In order to exclude the implied warranty of merchantability, the seller must specifically mention *merchantability* in the exclusion. The exclusion does not have to be in writing but if it is in writing, the clause that excludes all or part of the warranty of merchantability must be *conspicuous* (2-316[2]). Thus, the exclusion clause must be printed or written into the contract in large type or letters, or in an ink of a different color, so that the person reading the contract is not likely to overlook it. If the seller is particularly concerned that the exclusion clause be enforced, the seller should have the buyer separately initial the exclusion clause.

To exclude the implied warranty of fitness for a particular purpose, the exclusion must be in *writing* and it must be *conspicuous* (2-316[2]). Thus, a general disclaimer such as, "ALL IMPLIED WARRANTIES ARE HEREBY DISCLAIMED," if sufficiently conspicuous, would disclaim the warranty of fitness for a particular purpose. It would not, however, exclude the warranty of merchantability because the word *merchantability* was not used.

Warranties can also be excluded by the circumstances of the sale. Goods sold "as is" or "with all faults" are sold without the implied warranties of merchantability and fitness for a particular purpose. These phrases, which usually accompany the sale of used or damaged goods, call the buyer's attention to the warranty exclusion and make it clear that there are no warranties (2-316[3][a]). A seller can also limit both implied warranties by making goods available for examination and demanding that the buyer examine them. If the buyer takes the goods without examining them, the buyer has no implied warranty with regard to defects that should have been discovered through inspection (2-316[3][b]).

UNCONSCIONABLE DISCLAIMERS

The Code gives the court the authority to refuse to enforce a particular clause or even an entire contract if it finds it is *unconscionable* (2-302). Disclaimers of warranty that are not conspicuous would be seen as unconscionable. Disclaimers of warranty can also be unconscionable if there is a great disparity of bargaining power between the buyer and the seller and if the court believes that the disclaimer was forced on the buyer with no chance to bargain over its form. A court is most likely to find a disclaimer unconscionable in the case of a personally injured consumer, and somewhat less likely to do so when the consumer has suffered only property damage or economic loss. It is least likely to find the disclaimer unconscionable where the plaintiff is a merchant trying to recover for property damage or economic loss.

LIMITATION OF WARRANTIES

Sellers may try to limit their liability for breach of warranty. For example, the seller might agree to be responsible for only repairing or replacing a product that is not as it is warranted to be. Such a limitation may be enforced unless a court finds that it is *unconscionable* or that the limitation causes the warranty to *fail of its essential purpose*. A court is most likely to find a failure of essential purpose where a defect in a small part causes serious injury to a consumer and the seller is claiming that his responsibility is only to replace the defective part. Likewise, most states hold that where a consumer good has caused personal injury to the consumer, a limitation or exclusion of consequential damages is unconscionable.

WHO BENEFITS FROM A WARRANTY?

PURCHASER

When a product is defective and injures someone, the question arises as to whether the injured person can benefit from the warranty and recover from the seller or manufacturer for breach of warranty. For example, suppose Molly buys an electric table saw for her husband Joe as a birthday present. She purchases the saw at Ace Hardware. The saw was made by the Blake Manufacturing Company. While Joe was using this saw, the blade flew off, severely injuring Joe's arm. This happened because the saw had been improperly designed. The saw came with a warranty that it was guaranteed against defects in material and workmanship for a period of 90 days.

Suppose Joe tries to sue Ace Hardware, claiming breach of an express warranty or breach of the implied warranty of merchantability. The hardware store might try to claim that Joe should not be able to sue it for breach of warranty because he did not purchase this saw from the hardware store. Remember that warranties arise as part of a contract, and the contract in this case was between Molly and the hardware store.

A similar problem could arise if either Joe or Molly tried to sue Blake to recover for the injuries on the grounds that the manufacturer had breached either an express warranty or the implied warranty of merchantability. The manufacturer might claim that it had sold the saw to the hardware store but that it had not dealt with either Joe or Molly. The manufacturer would say it had no contract or warranty responsibility to either of them.

PRIVITY OF CONTRACT

In the past, the courts applied the general rule of contract law that a person who was not a party to the contract has no right to enforce it. A person had to be in **privity of contract** to enforce the contract. Unless a person had purchased the defective goods, he or she had no cause of action for breach of warranty. Furthermore, even the purchaser of defective goods was able to sue only the immediate seller and not the manufacturer, with whom there had been no contract.

Today, most courts allow an injured purchaser to recover directly from the manufacturer of the goods. This is true even though the version of the Code adopted in some states does not expressly authorize such a suit. In most cases, the manufacturer had control over the condition of the product when it reached the buyer's hands and should be held liable for any defects in it. The fact that the consumer may bring suit against the manufacturer in no way relieves the retailer of its responsibility for the fitness or merchantability of the goods. In most states, the buyer is permitted to sue both the retailer and the manufacturer in the same suit. This is true both for implied warranties and for express warranties that may have been made by the manufacturer.

NONPURCHASERS

The Code also extends some of the benefits of warranties to persons who did not themselves purchase the particular defective goods. One alternative version of the Code extends warranty protection to "*any natural person who is in the household of the buyer or who is a guest in his house* if it is reasonable to expect that such person may use, consume, or be affected by the goods and who is injured in his person by breach of warranty" (2-318, Alternative A). Moreover, the seller is not permitted to exclude or limit this liability. Thus, in the example involving the table saw, the Code would allow Joe to sue for breach of warranty because he is a member of the buyer's household.

A more difficult question is raised when the injured person is an employee of the buyer of the goods or a bystander. The decisions concerning bystanders and employees are not consistent among all states; however, there is a growing tendency for the courts to allow persons who have been injured as a result of breach of warranties of goods to claim the benefit of the warranties. This problem is directly addressed in an alternative version of the Code that has now been enacted by a significant number of states (2-318, Alternative C). It provides:

> A seller's warranty whether express or implied extends to any person who may reasonably be expected to use, consume, or be affected by the goods and who is injured by breach of the warranty. A seller may not exclude or limit the operation of this section with respect to injury to the person of the individual to whom the warranty extends.

This version of the Code would allow bystanders or employees to recover for breach of warranty if they could have reasonably been expected to be affected by the goods and were in fact injured as a result of the breach. In the case that follows, involving a crash of an airliner, the court held that a passenger was not entitled to the protection of a warranty extended to the purchaser of a component of the plane.

IN RE AIR CRASH DISASTER AT SIOUX CITY, IOWA, ON JULY 19, 1989
BANKS V. UNITED AIRLINES, INC.
760 F.Supp. 1283 (N.D. Ill. 1991)

FACTS

On July 19, 1989, United Airlines Flight 232 from Denver to Chicago crashed during an attempted emergency landing at Sioux City, Iowa. The crash resulted from engine failure and a loss of hydraulic power. Of the 296 passengers on board, 111 were killed in the crash. The aircraft, owned and operated by United Airlines, was a DC-10 manufactured by McDonnell Douglas. General Electric manufactured the aircraft's engines; Parker Hannifin Corporation manufactured the hydraulic system installed in the airplane. The hydraulic system was manufactured at Parker Hannifin's Control Systems Division in Irvine, California.

Lois Banks was a fare-paying passenger on Flight 232 and was killed in the crash. Her husband and two daughters filed a lawsuit in the federal district court in Califor-

nia against United Airlines, McDonnell Douglas, General Electric, and Parker Hannifin seeking damages under theories of negligence, recklessness, strict liability, breach of warranty, and breach of contract. One of the issues in the lawsuit was whether the Bankses could maintain a claim against Parker Hannifin for breach of the implied warranty of fitness for the hydraulic system's intended use and purpose. Parker Hannifin took the position that the claim could not be maintained because there was no privity between it and Lois Banks. The Bankses sought to circumvent the privity requirement by invoking the exception in California law for employees who are injured while using equipment purchased by their employers.

(continued)

IN RE AIR CRASH DISASTER AT SIOUX CITY, IOWA, ON JULY 19, 1989
BANKS V. UNITED AIRLINES, INC.
(concluded)

ISSUE

Did the lack of privity between Lois Banks and Parker Hannifin bar the claim for breach of warranty of fitness for a particular purpose?

DECISION

Yes. Initially, the court noted that under California law, privity between plaintiff and defendant is a requirement for actions based on implied warranty of fitness. While an exception is made for employees who are injured while using equipment purchased by their employers, Lois Banks was a passenger on the flight, and not an employee, and thus the exception is not applicable here. Neither the California legislature nor the courts have extended the warranty to others not in privity, even if they are affected by its use, and the court explicitly declined to extend the rationale for protecting employees to the relationship of passenger that Lois Banks had with United Airlines.

CONCEPT SUMMARY	**Warranties under the UCC**	
Warranty	**Creation**	**Defense/Disclaimer**
Express Warranty (2-313)	An express warranty is created where: 1. Seller makes an *affirmation of fact* or *promise* concerning the goods that becomes part of the *basis of the bargain.* 2. Descriptive terms, drawings, or technical specifications are used. 3. A sample or model is used as the basis for the contract.	1. Seller may defend on grounds that statement was an *opinion* or *recommendation,* or that it did *not* become part of the basis of the bargain (e.g., it was made after the sale). 2. Any disclaimer must be consistent with the express warranty made or it may be disregarded.
Implied Warranty of Merchantability (2-314)	The implied warranty of merchantability is an implied warranty of quality imposed by law on *merchants* dealing in goods of that kind. Goods must be fit for the *ordinary purpose* for which such goods are used.	1. Disclaimer may be oral or in writing but must mention *merchantability* and, if in writing, must be *conspicuous.* 2. Disclaimer is effective if the sale is stated to be "as is" or "with all faults." 3. If buyer inspects, or is offered opportunity to inspect, then she is bound by defects that were found, or should have been found. 4. Court may refuse to enforce an unconscionable disclaimer.
Implied Warranty of Fitness for a Particular Purpose (2-315)	The implied warranty of fitness for a particular purpose is imposed by law on sellers (including nonmerchants) who: 1. Know the purpose or use for which the buyer is acquiring the goods. 2. Know that the buyer is relying on the seller to select goods suitable for that purpose.	1. Disclaimer must be in *writing* and *conspicuous.* 2. Disclaimer is effective if the sale is stated to be "as is" or "with all faults." 3. If buyer inspects, or is offered opportunity to inspect, then she is bound by defects that were found, or should have been found. 4. Court may refuse to enforce an unconscionable disclaimer.
Implied Warranty of Title (2-312)	In any sale of goods, seller impliedly warrants that she has the right to sell the goods, that buyer will get good title, and that the goods are free of liens or claims by third parties unless buyer is given notice of them.	Warranty may be limited or excluded by specific language or by circumstances (e.g., police auction).

FEDERAL TRADE COMMISSION
WARRANTY RULES

MAGNUSON-MOSS WARRANTY ACT

In the late 1960s and early 1970s, Congress conducted a number of investigations into consumer product warranties and their terms. It concluded that the warranties were frequently confusing, misleading, and frustrating to consumers, and that the law governing warranties should be changed to encourage manufacturers to market more reliable products for competitive reasons. Congress based its findings in part on the fact that consumer products are typically sold with a form contract dictated by the seller, that the consumer cannot bargain with the seller over terms, and that the remedies stated in these contracts are sometimes not useful to the consumer. For these reasons, Congress passed the Magnuson-Moss Warranty Act, which became effective in 1975.

PURPOSE OF THE ACT

The Magnuson-Moss Warranty Act is intended to (1) provide minimum warranty protection for consumers, (2) increase consumer understanding of warranties, (3) ensure warranty performance by providing useful remedies, and (4) encourage better product reliability by making it easier for consumers to choose among products on the basis of their likely reliability. The act applies to all sellers of a "consumer product" that costs more than $5 who give the consumer a written warranty. It does not require the seller to make a warranty. In fact, it may have led to fewer warranties being made.[2]

REQUIREMENTS OF THE ACT

Under the act and the warranty regulations of the Federal Trade Commission (FTC), the seller is not required to give a written warranty. If the seller does give a warranty, however, it must comply with the act and the regulations. The seller must disclose in a single document, in simple and understandable language, the following items of information:

1. The persons who can enforce or use the warranty (for example, the original purchaser or any subsequent owner of the item during the term of the warranty).
2. A clear description of the products, parts, components, characteristics, and properties covered by the warranty, and, if necessary, the items excluded from the warranty.
3. A statement of what the maker of the warranty will do and what items or services will be paid for if the product is defective, malfunctions, or does not conform to the warranty, and (if needed for clarity) a statement of what the warrantor will not pay for.
4. The time the warranty begins (if it begins on a date other than the purchase date) and its duration.
5. A step-by-step explanation of how to obtain warranty service and information about any *informal dispute settlement mechanisms* (for example, arbitration) made available by the seller.

---

[2]The act covers consumer products that cost more than $5 but the regulations adopted by the Federal Trade Commission to implement the act cover only products that cost more than $15.

6. Any limitations on the duration of implied warranties and any exclusions or limitations on relief, such as consequential or incidental damages (for example, not paying to drain the basement after the water heater breaks), and an explanation that under some state laws those exclusions or limitations may not be allowed.

7. A statement that the consumer has certain legal rights under the warranty as well as other rights that may vary from state to state.

FULL WARRANTIES

The maker of the warranty must state whether the warranty is a **full warranty** or a **limited warranty.** A full warranty means:

1. The warrantor will fix or replace any defective product, including removal and reinstallation if necessary, free of charge.

2. It is not limited in time (say, to one or two years).

3. It does not either exclude or limit payment for consequential damages unless the exclusion or limitation is printed conspicuously on the face of the written warranty.

4. If the product cannot be repaired or has not been repaired after a reasonable number of efforts to repair it, the consumer may choose between a refund and a replacement.

5. The warrantor cannot impose duties on the consumer except reasonable duties (for example, the warranty cannot require the consumer to ship a piano to the factory) or a duty not to modify the product.

6. The warrantor is not required to fulfill the warranty terms if the problem was caused by damage to the product through unreasonable use.

A full warranty does not have to cover the whole product. It may cover only part of the product, such as the picture tube of a television set. Also, anyone who owns the product during the warranty period may invoke or use the warranty.

LIMITED WARRANTIES

A limited warranty is any other warranty covered by the act that does not meet the standards for a full warranty. For example, a limited warranty may cover only parts, not labor, or may require the purchaser to return a heavy product to the seller or service representative for service. It may also require the purchaser to pay for handling or allow only a pro rata refund or credit, depending on the length of time since the product was purchased. Often, a limited warranty protects only the first purchaser.

AVAILABILITY OF WARRANTIES

The act requires the seller to make the written warranty terms available to the prospective buyer before the sale. For example, the text of the warranty might be displayed next to the product, or on the package in which the product is enclosed. Warranty terms can also be collected in notebooks in the department that sells the goods and may even be microfilmed, so long as the prospective buyer can readily use the microfilm reader. The maker of the warranty is required to make the text of the warranty available to sellers in forms that sellers can readily use, such as providing copies of the written warranty with each product, or on a tag, sticker, label, or other attachment to the product, or on a sign or poster. These warranty requirements also cover catalog and door-to-door sales.

ENFORCEMENT

The FTC enforces the disclosure provisions of the warranty act and regulations; for example, it enforces the seller's obligation to make the terms available before the sale and the format requirements imposed on all makers of warranties (manufacturers or sellers). Consumers have the right to sue the maker for failure to fulfill the terms of the warranty. Consumers can sue the manufacturer if the manufacturer offers the warranty, or the retailer if the retailer grants the warranty.

. . . . *NEGLIGENCE* . . . .

PRODUCT LIABILITY IN GENERAL

Liability of a seller based on breach of warranty is only one of the theories of liability that courts have used to impose liability on the manufacturer or seller of goods for personal injury or property damage that results from the use of the goods. Two other legal bases for product liability are negligence and strict liability.

NEGLIGENCE

In Chapter 5, you studied the general rules concerning negligence. The basic rule is that a person owes a *duty of care* to avoid *foreseeable injury to others.* As long ago as 1916, courts held that a manufacturer could be liable to a consumer of a defective product on the grounds that the manufacturer was negligent in not adequately *inspecting* the product. Subsequently, courts have held manufacturers liable for negligence not only for failing to inspect but also for:

1. *Improperly manufacturing* the goods.
2. *Misrepresenting* the character of goods or their fitness for a particular purpose.
3. Failing to *disclose known defects,* adequately *warn about known dangers,* or *instruct about proper use.*
4. Failing to use *due care in designing* the goods.

In the *Griggs v. BIC Corp.* case that follows, the court held that a company was potentially liable for failure to design and manufacture a childproof lighter.

GRIGGS v. BIC CORP.
981 F.2d 1439 (3rd Cir. 1992)

FACTS

On October 10, 1985, Zachary Griggs, then 11 months old, sustained serious injuries in a fire at his Pennsylvania home that his three-year-old stepbrother, Kenneth Hempstead, ignited with a disposable butane lighter manufactured by BIC Corporation. Kenneth removed the lighter from his stepfather's pants pocket in the early hours of the morning and set fire with it to Zachary's bedding while the rest of the household slept. Two incidents within six months preceded this fire, in which Kenneth attempted to light either matches or a lighter, of which his parents were aware and for which they disciplined Kenneth. Prior to Zachary's injuries, his mother had seen warnings

(continued)

GRIGGS V. BIC CORP.
(concluded)

that BIC placed on the packaging of its lighters to keep them away from children. She was also independently aware that lighters should be kept out of the reach of children.

Timothy and Catherine Griggs, as parents and guardians of Zachary, sued BIC alleging that its failure to manufacture a childproof lighter constituted both defective and negligent design.

ISSUE

Is BIC potentially liable to the Griggs for failure to manufacture a childproof lighter?

DECISION

Yes. Initially, it should be noted that the lighter was not considered to be defective under Pennsylvania's strict liability law. A product would be considered defective only if it left the manufacturer's control lacking an element necessary to make it safe for its intended use or possessing any feature that rendered it unsafe for the intended use. Because children were not the intended users, the failure to design it to be childproof did not render it "defective." However, under general negligence principles, if a manufacturer of cigarette lighters can reasonably foresee that they will fall into the hands of children, who, albeit unintended users, can ignite them with the probability of serious injury to themselves and others, and if childproofing lighters is economically feasible, then the manufacturer has a duty to guard against unreasonable risk of harm by designing the lighter to be childproof.

DUTIES

Middlemen such as retailers, distributors, and wholesalers have no duty to inspect new, prepackaged goods unless they know of or have reason to know of a defect.

Traditionally, there was no duty to warn of obvious dangers. Thus, a knife manufacturer did not have to put a warning on its knives cautioning users that they could cut themselves. While this is still somewhat true, an increasing number of courts hold that the **obvious danger** rule is no longer a complete defense. To these courts, the obviousness of the danger is merely one of the factors to be considered in determining liability. Courts also hold that there is a duty to warn *after* the sale, where practicable, when a manufacturer learns that the product may be dangerous. For example, the manufacturer of canned vegetables has a duty to warn the public if it discovers that some of its cans are contaminated, even if it does not discover this until several months after the cans have left its plant.

PRIVITY AND DISCLAIMERS DO NOT APPLY

Because liability based on negligence does not involve a contractual relationship, it does not matter whether or not the buyer dealt directly with the manufacturer. The manufacturer's duty of care extends to all persons who might foreseeably be injured if the manufacturer does not exercise its duty of care. It is foreseeable that the ultimate consumer of goods or a bystander might be hurt if goods are not properly designed or built. Likewise, disclaimers in contracts are usually not effective to shield a manufacturer or seller against liability for negligence to consumers. Usually such clauses are held to be against public policy.

.... *STRICT LIABILITY* ....

REASONS FOR DEVELOPMENT OF STRICT LIABILITY

Persons injured by defective products were not always able to recover for their injuries under negligence or breach of warranty. Often, contributory negligence on the part of the plaintiff completely barred recovery for injuries sustained as a result of negligence on the part of the defendant. While this is generally not true today because of the adoption of comparative negligence, it was a very important factor at the time strict liability developed. In addition, it was often difficult for the plaintiff to prove negligence because the evidence was in the defendant's control.

Similarly as you have seen, a person who is injured by a defective product may have trouble in bringing a successful lawsuit based on breach of warranty if he or she was not the buyer, in the buyer's family or household, or the buyer's guest. In addition, warranties were often excluded. As a result of these barriers to recovery, many people were unable to recover when injured by defective products.

In the mid-1960s, courts increasingly took note of the limitations inherent in both breach of warranty and negligence as a means for redressing product-caused injuries, and began to apply strict liability in tort to product liability cases. Under this theory, sellers are held liable regardless of whether or not they exercised reasonable care. If the product is inherently dangerous so that no amount of due care could make it safe, then the manufacturer is required to give the user notice of the unreasonable danger. Privity, disclaimers, and contributory negligence do not bar recovery.

Application of strict product liability has grown until today the theory is the one most commonly used to hold manufacturers liable when products they place on the market are defective and cause injuries to people. The purpose of strict product liability is to ensure that the costs of injuries from defective products are borne by the seller who put the products on the market, rather than by the injured person. The sellers can pass on these costs in the form of higher prices, and thereby socialize the risk by spreading the cost back through society.

ELEMENTS OF STRICT LIABILITY

The essential element for strict product liability is that the product be defective. Generally, to be successful under this theory, the plaintiff must show that:

1. A product has been sold in a *defective condition* that makes it *unreasonably dangerous* to the user or consumer.
2. The seller is engaged in the business of selling such a product.
3. The product is expected to and does reach the consumer without substantial change in the condition in which it is sold.
4. The consumer or other person sustains physical harm or property damage because of the defective condition.

A product can be defective in the same way that it caused harm due to the manufacturer's negligence; that is, it can be defective because it was mismanufactured, misdesigned, lacked proper warnings or instructions, or was misrepresented. The primary difference between the two theories is that negligence focuses on the manufacturer's conduct, and asks whether the manufacturer acted reasonably. Strict liability focuses on the product, and asks whether the product is unreasonably dangerous because of its defect. Often the answer to both questions is the same.

While strict liability is currently accepted by most states, its application varies among the states. Some states may apply it to situations involving the sale of services, used merchandise, or real estate; others may not. Some courts apply strict liability to retailers as well as manufacturers. Other courts will not hold the retailer liable if the manufacturer is available for suit. Several states have passed legislation that absolves a seller from liability if the manufacturer can be held liable. Most states hold that plaintiffs cannot recover for purely economic losses under strict liability. A growing number of states, however, allow such recovery if the defect caused the product to be unreasonably dangerous, even if it did not result in physical injury.

Ethical Implications	Assume you are the chief executive officer (CEO) of a company that manufactures baby pillows filled with foam pellets. After the pillows have been on the market for about three months and you have sold about 10,000 of them, you receive reports implicating your pillow in the suffocation deaths in their cribs of two infants under the age of three months. What, if anything, would you do about the products already sold? What, if anything, would you do about the products you have in inventory?

STATE OF THE ART

In determining whether a product is **inherently dangerous** or has been **defectively designed,** the courts look to the "state of the art" in existence at the time of manufacture. Under the decisions in most states, this does not mean simply what other companies in the industry are doing; rather, the focus is on whether anything else could have been done to make the product safer, given the practical and technological limitations of the time. In some instances, design changes or improvements made subsequently by a manufacturer have been used as evidence of what the manufacturer should have done earlier.

These principles are illustrated in the case that follows, *Uniroyal Goodrich Tire Co. v. Martinez.*

UNIROYAL GOODRICH TIRE CO. V. MARTINEZ
977 S.W.2d 328 (Sup. Ct. Texas 1998)

FACTS

Roberto Martinez was injured while installing a Goodrich tire on a motor vehicle. The injury occurred after the 16-inch tire exploded while Martinez was attempting to mount it on a 16.5-inch rim. He did so despite the presence of a prominent warning label on the tire. The warning specifically stated that one should never mount a 16-inch tire on a 16.5-inch rim and that doing so could cause severe injury or death because the tire would explode.

Martinez sued Goodrich under strict liability. His theory was not that the warning was inadequate, but rather

that the exploding tire was defective because Goodrich had failed to use a safer alternative bead design that would have it kept from exploding. Martinez introduced evidence that Goodrich's competitors—and eventually Goodrich itself—had adopted a safer tire bead design. Goodrich argued that the alternative design was not in fact safer because if the tire was matched to a wrong rim size, the bead would not seat on the rim and would inevitably explode during use. Martinez, however, produced counter evidence that the alternative design not only would have prevented the injury he sustained but

(continued)

Uniroyal Goodrich Tire Co. v. Martinez
(concluded)

would not have introduced other dangers of equal or greater magnitude.

Issue

Is a manufacturer strictly liable for injuries caused by a plaintiff's failure to follow a suitable warning if the manufacturer knows of a safer alternative product design?

Decision

Yes. To establish a design defect under section 402A of the *Restatement (Third) of Torts*, a claimant must establish that the defendant could have provided a safer alternative design. This design must be reasonable—that is, it must be able to be implemented without destroying the utility of the product. In determining whether a reasonable alternative design exists, the court can weigh various factors bearing on the risk and utility of the product, including whether the product contains suitable warnings and instructions. However, instructions and warnings may be ineffective because users of the product may not be adequately reached, may be likely to be inattentive, or may be insufficiently motivated to follow the instructions or heed the warnings. Thus, warnings are not a substitute for a reasonably safe design. Here the jury could reasonably find that a reasonable alternative design existed.

Defenses

Most states that have adopted strict liability do not allow the injured party to recover if the injuries resulted from the **misuse** of the product. This means that if the plaintiff used the product in a manner that was not intended or foreseeable, he may not recover. So, for example, if April decides to trim the sides of her hedge with her electric lawn mower and is injured, she would probably not be able to recover.

Plaintiffs are also denied recovery when their injuries result from the alteration of the product after it left the manufacturer. However, if the alteration and the danger it created were foreseeable, the manufacturer can be held liable for not designing the product so that it could not be altered, or for failing to warn against alteration.

Finally, knowingly assuming an obvious risk of injury is a defense to strict product liability in most states.

Industrywide Liability

Industrywide liability is an outgrowth of strict product liability. Like strict liability, it was adopted to allow a larger number of people who were injured by products to recover. It carries out the policies behind strict liability because it is designed to take the risk of product-related injuries off the consumer and place them on the manufacturer, who can spread the cost back through society. The need for the theory of industrywide liability arose because an increasing number of people were being injured by standardized products that did not cause the injury until after a number of years. Because of the time lapse and the fact that different manufacturers' products were interchangeable, plaintiffs were unable to identify which of the manufacturers making that kind of product made the product that injured them.

For example, many manufacturers have produced asbestos. Often, those working with asbestos could not tell which manufacturer processed the asbestos they were working with. Many of the asbestos-related diseases these workers suffered did not occur until 20 to 40 years after they had worked with the asbestos. Thus, they were unable to successfully identify the particular manufacturer that made the asbestos that injured them. In order to overcome such problems, several courts have decided to apportion liability among the firms in that industry that could have produced the product rather than make the plaintiff identify a particular manufacturer. While the details differ from state to state, most courts apportion the liability between the manufacturers on the basis of their market share. Not all courts faced with the issue have chosen to adopt industrywide liability. However, it is possible that more will as discoveries grow about widely used products that injure over long periods of time.

A manufacturer who is sued on the basis of industrywide liability may try to defend on the grounds that: (1) it did not manufacture the product that caused the injury to the plaintiff, (2) that its market share was less than alleged by the plaintiff, or (3) that the risks from its product were lower than those from other manufacturers.

POSSIBLE LIMITATIONS ON STRICT LIABILITY

The broad expansion of seller's liability for defective products has generated claims that the law has gone too far. Some manufacturers and insurance companies contend that product liability law now so favors the consumer that it is stifling the development of new products and putting unreasonable cost burdens on manufacturers—and, in turn, on consumers. As a result, many state legislatures have passed laws limiting the seller's liability. Frequently, these laws have focused on (1) defining what is state of the art, (2) protecting a manufacturer if its products meet government safety standards, (3) protecting subsequent sellers from suit if the manufacturer is available, and (4) using comparative fault to reduce a damage award if the plaintiff contributed to his or her own injury.

STATUTES OF REPOSE

The most commonly adopted reform, however, was a statute of repose. A **statute of repose** bars the bringing of a tort-based product liability suit after a certain number of years—usually 10—from the date the product is first sold to a user. This is a significant change in the law for people who are injured by products such as asbestos or DES that do not cause injury until many years later. In most states, the tort statute of limitations gives people one or two years *from the time they discover* their injury in which to bring their suit. People covered by statutes of repose now cannot bring suit if their injury is not discovered within the statutory period. A few state courts have declared their state's statute of repose unconstitutional because it denies people the right to seek redress for their injuries when they had no chance to discover their injuries within the statutory period.

CONCEPT SUMMARY   Bases for Product Liability

	Express Warranty	Implied Warranties of Merchantability or Fitness for a Particular Purpose	Negligence	Strict Liability
Basis	Included by parties in the contract of sale.	Imposed by law in the contract of sale.	Duty to use due care to avoid foreseeable injury. Includes duty concerning design, inspection, manufacture, representation, disclosure of defects, and instruction as to safe use.	Liability without fault imposed on manufacturers and sellers of unreasonably dangerous products.
Who Benefits/ Who Can Use	Buyer, members of his family, and, in some states, any person who may reasonably be expected to use, consume, or be affected by the goods and who is injured by the breach.	Buyer, members of his family, and, in some states, any person who may reasonably be expected to use, consume, or be affected by the goods and who is injured by the breach.	Person to whom duty of care is owed and who is injured by breach. Privity of contract is not required.	Person injured by using or consuming product where the defect is the proximate cause of the injury or damage. Privity of contract is not required.
Defenses	Warranty was not made or was effectively disclaimed or limited.	The warranty was effectively disclaimed or limited.	1. Seller exercised reasonable care. 2. Buyer assumed the risk. 3. Buyer was contributorily negligent.	1. Product has been substantially changed since it left the manufacturer or seller. 2. Buyer was adequately warned about the unreasonable danger. 3. Product was state of the art when designed or manufactured. 4. Buyer used product in an unintended or unforeseen manner. 5. Buyer assumed all obvious risk of injury.
Disclaimers	Possible to the degree it is not inconsistent with the express warranty made.	Possible so long as it is not unconscionable.	Generally not effective to shield against liability for negligence to consumers.	Generally not effective.

QUESTIONS AND PROBLEM CASES

1. John Klages, the night auditor at a motel, was working one evening when the motel was held up. When he was unable to open the safe, one of the robbers pointed a gun at Klages's head and pulled the trigger. However, the gun was a starter pistol and he was not seriously injured.

Klages decided he needed something to protect himself against future robberies. He went to the Market Supply Company to see about using mace and was shown a leaflet distributed by General Ordnance Equipment Corporation concerning its mace weapons. The leaflet contained this description:

> Rapidly vaporizes on face of assailant effecting *instantaneous incapacitation* . . . It will *instantly stop and subdue* entire groups . . . *instantly stops assailants in their tracks* . . . an attacker is *subdued instantly,* for a period of 15 to 20 minutes. . . . *Time* magazine stated that chemical mace is "for police the first, if not the final, answer to a nationwide need—a weapon that *disables as effectively* as a gun and yet does no permanent injury." The effectiveness is the result of a unique, *incapacitating formulation* (patent pending), projected in a shotgunlike pattern of heavy liquid droplets that, upon contact with the face, cause extreme tearing, and a *stunned,* winded condition, often accompanied by dizziness and apathy.

Based on this description, Klages purchased the weapon. Several months later, some people posing as potential guests held up the motel at gunpoint and ordered Klages to open the safe. Using the cash register as a shield, Klages squirted the mace at one of the robbers, hitting him beside the nose. Klages then ducked but the robber followed him down and shot him in the head, causing Klages to lose the sight in his right eye. He then sued Market Supply Company and General Ordnance, claiming, among other things, breach of express warranty. Were the statements in the leaflet promises or affirmations of fact constituting an express warranty?

2. Custom Concepts designed a product known as the Magic Crystal Ball as a premium for use by McDonald's restaurants in some of its children's selections on its menu. As designed, the Magic Crystal Ball was to be a hollow plastic ball enclosing a paper cube. The child-player was to "ask a question" of the ball, shake it, and turn it upside down to read an answer printed on one of the faces of the paper cube. Plastic Products agreed to manufacture the Magic Crystal Balls for Custom. Working from drawings supplied by Custom, Plastic produced a prototype that was approved by Custom and McDonald's and passed a safety test by U.S. Testing, a laboratory that evaluates consumer products for quality and safety. Plastic then accepted a purchase order to make 1,785,500 of the crystal balls and began production. However, the production-run crystal balls failed the safety test because Plastic had thinned the edges of the walls so that its injection molds would fill uniformly. Custom had Plastic hold production, and then McDonald's canceled its order because of time constraints in the promotional campaign of which the Magic Crystal Ball was to be a part. Custom notified Plastic that the project was off and brought suit against Plastic alleging breach of warranty. Did Plastic breach an express warranty when the production crystal balls did not conform to the prototype?

3. Irma Virgil bought a pint-sized thermos bottle from "Kash N' Karry." After a couple of months of use, she poured coffee into it one morning and was adding some milk when it imploded, throwing hot coffee and glass into her face and injuring her eye. Irma testified that she had not dropped the thermos and had not abused it. She sued "Kash N' Karry," claiming, among other things, breach of warranty of merchantability. Was the warranty of merchantability breached?

4. Phillips, a high school senior, bit into a turkey bone in a bite-sized cube of white turkey meat ladled, along with gravy and peas, onto a mound of mashed potatoes in a high school cafeteria in West Springfield, Massachusetts. He felt something in his throat, and after some effort expelled "a small, 1½ inch hooked bone." He sustained injury to his esophagus and was hospitalized for four days. Phillips brought suit against the town, claiming breach of warranty of merchantability in the food served to him in the cafeteria. What test should be applied to determine whether there was a breach of warranty of merchantability because of the presence of a bone in the meal served to Phillips?

5. Beck, a high school baseball coach, ordered six pairs of flip-type baseball sunglasses from Rayex Corporation. Rayex had advertised the sunglasses as baseball sunglasses that would give "instant eye protection." While one of his baseball players, Michael Filler, was using a pair

of the glasses, the glasses were hit by a fly ball. The glasses shattered, and as a result, Filler lost his right eye. Filler then brought a lawsuit against Rayex, claiming, among other things, a breach of the implied warranty of fitness for a particular purpose. Was the manufacturer liable for breach of the implied warranty of fitness for a particular purpose?

6. Paul Brokke purchased a Pentax Super Program camera for $89.95 from Albert Williams, the operator of a pawnshop in Bozeman, Montana. Shortly after the purchase, Brokke was notified by the Bozeman police department that the camera was stolen property; he was directed to surrender it to the police department, which he did. He then returned to the pawnshop and requested a refund for his purchase of the stolen merchandise. Williams denied the request, and Brokke brought suit to recover the purchase price. Williams argued that he had no knowledge that the camera was stolen property and asserted that he disclaimed any warranty of title of goods sold in his business by way of a large sign posted in his store stating that all merchandise is sold "as is." Brokke denied having seen any such sign. Is Williams liable to Brokke for breach of the warranty of good title in the sale of the stolen camera?

7. *Video Case.* See "Car Deals." Jake, a car salesman, is discussing a particular car with Jones, a customer at Jake's dealership. Jake tells Jones, "You won't find a car like this at any price. This car is a crown jewel." Later Jake says that he bought the car at an auction in Kentucky. Influenced by these statements, Jones buys the car. The bill of sale conspicuously says that the car is being sold "AS IS" and that no warranties or representations concerning the car have been made or given, except as stated in the bill of sale. Later, Jones discovers that the car's brakes are so defective that the car is unsafe to drive.

Which, if any of Jake's statements are express warranties? Which, if any, have been breached here? Does the language in the bill of sale disclaim any express warranties that might exist? Does the language in the bill of sale disclaim the implied warranty of merchantability? Assuming that the implied

warranty of merchantability has not been disclaimed, is it breached here?

8. Mark Hemphill was a football player for Southern Illinois University. He sustained injuries to his spine when he was hit while wearing a helmet manufactured by Riddell Sporting Goods, Inc. He brought suit against the university's athletic director (Gale Sayers), the football coach, the trainer, the manufacturer of the helmet, and the merchant from whom the helmet was purchased by the university. He sought to recover based on claims of negligence, strict liability, and breach of implied warranties. Riddell sought to have the claim of breach of implied warranties against it dismissed on the grounds there was no privity of contract between it and Hemphill. Should Hemphill's breach of warranty claims against Riddell be dismissed on the grounds there was no privity of contract between it and Hemphill?

9. Connie Daniell locked herself in the trunk of a 1973 Ford LTD in an attempt to commit suicide. At some point she changed her mind but she was unable to get out. She was released nine days later. She subsequently sued Ford Motor Company for the psychological and physical injuries she sustained because the trunk did not have an internal release or opening mechanism that would have allowed her to escape. She alleged, among other theories, that the company was negligent in its design of the car because it lacked such a mechanism, and negligent because it failed to warn users that the trunk did not have such a mechanism. Was Ford negligent for failing to warn, or failing to include a release in its design of the car?

10. From 1987 to 1992 Wilma Carlin took Halcion, a drug manufactured and distributed by Upjohn Company for the treatment of insomnia. The drug was prescribed for her by her physician. Carlin claimed that she suffered serious permanent physical, mental, and emotional injuries because of her use of Halcion. She brought suit against Upjohn based, among other things, on strict liability. She claimed that Halcion was unavoidably unsafe (i.e., that it could cause emotional, physical, and psychic instability, distress, and injuries), that its dangerous propensities were known to Upjohn,

or were reasonably knowable scientifically at the time that she received the Halcion, and that Upjohn failed properly to warn users of the dangerous propensities.

Upjohn contended that under California law no cause of action for strict liability could be stated against a prescription drug company based on failure to warn. The trial court accepted Upjohn's position and Carlin asked the court of appeals to order the trial court to allow the cause of action. Can a claim for strict liability against a prescription drug company be based on failure to warn a consumer about dangerous propensities that are known to the manufacturer?

11. Douglas Bratz and Bradley Baughn were injured while riding a Honda mini–trail bike. At the time, they were eight years old. Douglas was driving and Bradley was the passenger when the bike hit a truck. Douglas had run three stop signs and was looking behind him at a girl riding another mini–trail bike at the time of the accident. Bradley was not wearing a helmet, and while Douglas was wearing one, it flew off when the bike hit the truck because it was not fastened. The minibike contained a warning label prominently posted in front of the operator. It read: READ OWNER'S MANUAL CAREFULLY. THIS VEHICLE WAS MANUFACTURED FOR OFF-THE-ROAD USE ONLY. DO NOT OPERATE ON PUBLIC STREETS, ROADS OR HIGHWAYS. The operator's manual contained a similar admonition as well as a statement urging the user to wear a helmet. The fathers of both boys owned motorcycles and had purchased minibikes for their children. The parents of the injured boys filed suit against Honda, claiming, among other things, that the mini–trail bike was unreasonably dangerous. Honda maintained that it had provided sufficient warning as to the danger of improper operation. Should Honda be held strictly liable for the injuries?

CHAPTER 18

Performance of Sales Contracts

Suppose that Frank Farmer agrees to sell 1,000 bushels of U.S. Grade #1 Delicious apples to George Grocer for $10 per bushel, with delivery to be made in three installments on September 1, October 1, and November 1. A variety of questions may arise as to the obligations of the two parties in performing this contract. For example:

- *If George Grocer sells his business and assigns his contract with Farmer to Supermarket on August 15, does Supermarket have the right to delivery of the apples by Farmer and does it have the obligation to honor the contract and pay for them?*
- *If nothing was said about delivery, is Farmer obligated to deliver the apples or is Supermarket obligated to pick them up at Farmer's place of business?*
- *If some of the apples in the September 1 delivery are Jonathan, rather than Delicious, apples, what options are open to Supermarket?*
- *If Supermarket rejects some of the apples in the September delivery, what obligations does it have with respect to the rejected apples?*
- *If Supermarket accepts the October 1 shipment and later discovers that the apples are not Grade #1, what options are open to it?*
- *If a severe early frost damages Farmer's apple crop, to what extent will he be excused from performing the contract?*

These questions and others will be addressed in this chapter.

.... *INTRODUCTION* ....

In the two previous chapters, we have discussed the formation and terms of sales contracts, including those terms concerning express and implied warranties. In this chapter, the focus is on the legal rules that govern the performance of contracts. Among the topics covered are the basic obligations of the buyer and seller with respect to delivery and payment, the rights of the parties when the goods delivered do not conform to the contract, and the circumstances under which the performance of a party's contractual obligations are excused.

.... *GENERAL RULES* ....

The parties to a contract for the sale of goods are obligated to perform the contract according to its terms. The Code gives the parties great flexibility in deciding between themselves how a contract will be performed. The practices in the trade or business as well as any past dealings between the parties are used to supplement or explain the contract. The Code provides both buyer and seller with certain rights. It also sets out what is expected of the buyer and seller on points the parties did not deal with in their contract. Keep in mind that the Code changes basic contract law in a number of respects.

GOOD FAITH

The buyer and seller must act in *good faith* in the performance of a sales contract (1-203).[1] **Good faith** is defined to mean "honesty in fact" in performing the duties assumed in the contract or in carrying out the transaction (1-201[9]). Thus, if the seller is required by the contract to select an assortment of goods for the buyer, the selection must be made in good faith; the seller should pick out a reasonable assortment (2-311). It would not be good faith to include, for example, only unusual sizes or colors.

COURSE OF DEALING

The terms in the contract between the parties are the primary means for determining the obligations of the buyer and seller. The meaning of those terms may be explained by looking at any performance that has already taken place. For example, a contract may call for periodic deliveries of goods. If a number of deliveries have been made by the buyer without objection by the seller, the way the deliveries were made shows how the parties intended them to be made. Similarly, if there were any past contracts between the parties, the way they interpreted those contracts is relevant to the interpretation of the present one. If there is a conflict between the express terms of the contract and the past **course of dealing** between the parties, the express terms of the contract prevail (2-208[2]).

---

[1]The numbers in parentheses refer to the sections of the Uniform Commercial Code.

USAGE OF TRADE

In many kinds of businesses, there are **customs and practices of the trade** that are known by people in the business. These customs and practices are usually assumed by parties to a contract for goods of that type. Under the Code, these trade customs and practices can be used in interpreting a contract (1-205). If there is a conflict between the express terms of the contract and trade usage, the express terms prevail (2-208[2]).

The case that follows, *Weisz Graphics v. Peck Industries,* illustrates how both course of dealing and usage of trade can affect the interpretation of a contract.

WEISZ GRAPHICS DIVISION OF THE FRED B. JOHNSON CO., INC. V. PECK INDUSTRIES, INC.
403 S.E.2d 146 (Ct. App. S.C. 1991)

FACTS

Weisz Graphics is a custom manufacturer and seller of decals, markings, and other graphic materials and competes in a national market. Weisz manufactures its products to customer specifications based on blueprints, samples, art, or mechanical drawings. It manufactures only to order and does not maintain a general inventory. However, it regularly engages in what are known as "release programs" with its customer; such programs are common in the industry. Under a release program, Weisz manufactures a large quantity of goods to customer order, and then warehouses it for the customer. As the customer needs the goods, Weisz releases them in specified lots that are billed when shipped. Release programs in the industry are generally limited to one year, due in part to the shelf life of the goods.

Peck Industries, a manufacturer of commercial signs for national and Memphis, Tennessee, accounts, uses pressure-sensitive vinyl letter, numbers, and other products purchased from Weisz. Beginning in 1985, Peck began purchasing some of its requirements from Weisz; some contracts were for immediate manufacture and delivery while others were for extended delivery under a release program. A November 1985 order provided: "BREAK UP INTO MULTIPLE SHIPMENTS." Weisz's acknowledgment contained the following shipment terms: "On Releases Bill & Ship on release for 12 months." In April 1986, Peck sent a purchase order for a quantity of goods that provided "TO BE BILLED AND SHIPPED AS RELEASED." Weisz sent back its standard acknowledgment form on which a clerk had typed "On Releases over 12 months." Another order was placed by Peck that stated on its face: "ORDER AS NEEDED FOR A PERIOD OF 1 YEAR." In each case Weisz immediately manufactured the items ordered and over a period of a year released and billed shipments at Peck's request. At the end of the 12 months, Weisz refused to make further shipments until Peck paid in full the remaining balance on the shipments. Peck refused to pay, choosing instead to obtain its requirements from other manufacturers at higher prices. Weisz then brought suit for the balance due on the goods sold to Peck.

ISSUE

Was the 12-month period for releases incorporated into the contract through usage of trade and course of dealing?

DECISION

Yes. The court found that even though Peck's purchase order did not contain a release deadline, a time limitation of 12 months on such release arrangements was standard in the industry. It also found that Weisz's prior course of dealing with Peck has been to ship on a 12-month release and that none of its prior release contracts with Peck has exceeded 12 months. Finally, the court concluded that the 12-month term had become part of the November 1985 and April 1986 contracts when Peck did not object to the term contained in the acknowledgments.

<table>
<tr><td>***Ethical Implications***</td><td>When supplies of goods that are the subject of a contract are in significantly shorter supply than when the agreement was made and the price has risen, the seller may be tempted to look for an excuse to cancel the contract so that he can sell to someone else at a higher profit. Similarly, if the goods are in significantly more plentiful supply than when a contract was made, the buyer might be tempted to create an excuse to cancel so that he can buy elsewhere at a lower price. When, if ever, is a seller or buyer ethically justified in trying to find a way out of a contractual obligation because the supply or market conditions have so changed that he can make a better deal elsewhere? Concomitantly, are there circumstances under which the other party, acting in an ethically responsible manner, should voluntarily release the disadvantaged party from his or her contractual commitment?</td></tr>
</table>

WAIVER

In a contract in which there are a number of instances of partial performance (such as deliveries or payments) by one party, the other party must be careful to object to any later deliveries or payments. If the other party does not object, it may be waiving its right to cancel the contract if other deliveries or payments are late (2-208[3] and 2-209[4]).

For example, a contract calls for a fish market to deliver fish to a restaurant every Thursday and for the restaurant to pay on delivery. If the fish market regularly delivers the fish on Friday and the restaurant does not object, the restaurant will be unable later to cancel the contract for that reason. Similarly, if the restaurant does not pay cash but rather sends a check the following week, then the fish market must object if it may want to rely on the late payment as grounds for later canceling the contract.

A party who has waived rights to a portion of the contract not yet performed may *retract the waiver* by giving reasonable notice to the other party that strict performance will be required. The retraction of the waiver is effective unless it would be unjust because of a *material change* of position by the other party in *reliance* on the waiver (2-209[5]).

ASSIGNMENT

Under the Code, the duties of either the buyer or the seller generally may be delegated to someone else. If there is a strong reason for having the original party perform the acts, such as that the quality of the performance might be different if another party performed them, then duties cannot be delegated. Also, if the parties agree in the contract that there is to be no assignment, then duties cannot be delegated. However, the right to receive performance—such as to receive goods or payment—can be assigned (2-210).

DELIVERY

BASIC OBLIGATIONS

The basic duty of the seller is to *deliver* the goods called for by the contract. The basic duty of the buyer is to *accept and pay for the goods* if they conform to the contract (2-301). The buyer and seller may agree that the goods are to be delivered in several lots or installments. If there is no agreement for delivery in installments, then all the goods must be delivered to the buyer in a single delivery.

PLACE OF DELIVERY

The buyer and seller may agree on the place where the goods will be delivered. If no such agreement is made, then the goods are to be delivered at the seller's place of business. If the seller does not have a place of business, then delivery is to be made at her home. These rules do not apply if the goods are located somewhere other than the seller's place of business or home. In those cases, the place of delivery is the place where the goods are located (2-308).

SELLER'S DUTY OF DELIVERY

The seller's basic obligation is to tender delivery of goods that conform to the contract with the buyer. **Tender of delivery** means that the seller must make the goods available to the buyer. This must be done during reasonable hours and for a reasonable period of time so that the buyer can take possession of the goods (2–503).

The contract of sale may require the seller merely to ship the goods to the buyer but not to deliver the goods to the buyer's place of business. If it does, the seller must put the goods into the possession of a carrier such as a trucking company or a railroad. The seller must also make a **reasonable contract** with the carrier to take the goods to the buyer. Then the seller is required to **notify** the buyer that the goods have been shipped.

If the seller does not make a reasonable contract for delivery or notify the buyer and a material delay or loss results, the buyer has the right to reject the shipment. For example, suppose the goods are perishable, such as fresh produce, and the seller does not have them shipped in a refrigerated truck or railroad car. If the produce deteriorates in transit, the buyer can reject the produce on the grounds that the seller did not make a reasonable contract for shipment of it (2-504).

In some situations, the goods sold may be in the possession of a bailee such as a warehouse. If the goods are covered by a negotiable warehouse receipt, the seller must indorse the receipt and give it to the buyer (2-503[4][a]). This enables the buyer to obtain the goods from the warehouse. This type of situation exists when grain being sold is stored at a grain elevator. If the goods are with a bailee but no negotiable warehouse receipt was issued, the seller must notify the bailee of the sale. The seller must then obtain the bailee's agreement to hold the goods for the buyer, or the seller must have the goods released to the buyer (2-503[4][b]).

.... INSPECTION AND PAYMENT

BUYER'S RIGHT OF INSPECTION

Normally, the buyer has the right to inspect the goods before she accepts or pays for them. The buyer and seller may agree on the time, place, and manner in which inspection will be made. If no agreement is made, then the buyer may inspect the goods at any reasonable time and place and in any reasonable manner (2-513[1]).

If the shipping terms are **cash on delivery (COD),** then the buyer must pay for the goods before inspecting them unless they are marked "Inspection Allowed." However, if it is obvious even without inspection that the goods do not conform to the contract, the buyer may reject them without paying for them first (2-512[1][a]). For example, if a farmer contracted to buy a bull and the seller delivered a cow, the farmer would not have to pay for it. The fact that a buyer may have to pay for goods before inspecting them does not deprive the buyer of remedies against the seller if the goods do not conform to the contract (2-512[2]).

PAYMENT

The buyer and seller may agree in their contract that the price of the goods is to be paid in money or in other goods, services, or real property. If all or part of the price of goods is payable in real property, then only the transfer of goods is covered by the law of sales of goods. The transfer of the real property is covered by the law of real property (2-304). The contract may provide that the goods are sold on credit to the buyer and that the buyer has a period of time to pay for them. If there is no agreement for extending credit to the buyer, the buyer must pay for them on delivery. The buyer can usually inspect the goods before payment except when they are shipped COD, in which case the buyer must pay for them before inspecting them.

Unless the seller demands cash, the buyer may make payment by personal check or by any other method used in the ordinary course of business. If the seller demands cash, the seller must give the buyer a reasonable amount of time to obtain it. If payment is made by check, the payment is conditional on the check's being honored by the bank when it is presented for payment (2-511[3]). If the bank refuses to pay the check, the buyer has not satisfied the duty to pay for them. In that case, the buyer does not have the right to retain the goods and must give them back to the seller.

.... *ACCEPTANCE, REVOCATION, AND REJECTION*

ACCEPTANCE

Acceptance of goods occurs when a buyer, after having reasonable opportunity to inspect the goods, either indicates that he will take them or fails to reject them. To **reject** goods, the buyer must **notify** the seller of the rejection and **specify** the defect or nonconformity. If a buyer treats the goods as if he owns them, the buyer is considered to have accepted them (2-606).

For example, Ace Appliance delivers a new television set to Beth. Beth has accepted the set if, after trying it and finding it to be in working order, she says nothing to Ace or tells Ace that she will keep it. Even if the set is defective, Beth is considered to have accepted it if she does not give Ace timely notice that she does not want to keep it because it is not in working order. If she takes the set to her vacation home even though she knows it does not work properly, this also is an acceptance. In the latter case, the use of the television set would be inconsistent with its rejection and the return of ownership to the seller.

If a buyer accepts any part of a *commercial unit* of goods, he is considered to have accepted the whole unit (2-606[2]). A **commercial unit** is any unit of goods that is treated by commercial usage as a single whole. It can be a single article (such as a machine), a set of articles (such as a dozen, bale, gross, or carload), or any other unit treated as a single whole (2-105[6]). Thus, if a bushel of apples is a commercial unit, then a buyer purchasing 10 bushels of apples who accepts 8½ bushels is considered to have accepted 9 bushels.

In the case that follows, *Weil v. Murray,* the buyer was considered to have accepted a painting that he had returned after inspection and had handled inconsistently with ownership of the seller.

WEIL V. MURRAY
2001 WL 345222 (U.S.D.C. S.D.N.Y. 2001)

FACTS

On October 19, 1997, Mark Murray, a New York art dealer and gallery owner, traveled to Montgomery, Alabama, to view various paintings in the art collection owned by Robert Weil. Murray examined one of the paintings under ultraviolet light—a painting by Edgar Degas entitled "Aux Courses." Murray discussed the Degas with Ian Peck, another art dealer, who indicated an interest in buying it and asked Murray to arrange to have it brought to New York.

Murray and Weil executed an agreement which provided for consignment of the Degas to Murray's gallery "for a private inspection in New York for a period of a week from November 3" to be extended only with the express permission of the consignor. The director of Murray's Gallery picked up the painting, which was subsequently shown by Murray to Peck. Peck agreed to purchase the painting for $1,225,000 with Murray acting as a broker. On November 8, Murray advised Weil that he had a buyer for the Degas and they orally agreed to the sale. Subsequently, they entered into a written agreement for the sale of the painting for $1 million that indicated, among other things, that if Weil did not receive full payment by December 8, Murray would disclose the name of the undisclosed principal on whose behalf he was acting.

Neither Murray nor anyone else ever paid Weil the $1 million. Nonetheless, Murray maintained possession of the Degas from November 3, 1997, through March 25, 1998, when Weil requested its return. At some point in mid-November, Weil and Peck took the Degas to an art conservator. A condition report prepared by the conservator and dated December 3, 1997, showed that the conservator had cleaned the painting and sought to correct some deterioration. Weil brought an action to recover the price of the painting from Murray.

ISSUE

Did Murray "accept" the painting and thus become liable for the purchase price?

DECISION

Yes. Goods that a buyer has in its possession necessarily are accepted or rejected by the time a reasonable time for inspecting them passes. Murray first inspected the painting in Montgomery, and then had it in his possession in his gallery and was present when it was examined by an expert. Thus, he not only had a reasonable time to inspect the Degas, he actually did inspect it and is deemed to have accepted it because he did not reject it. Moreover, when Murray permitted the painting to be cleaned and altered, he had committed an act inconsistent with the seller's ownership of the painting. Murray accepted the painting and was liable for the agreed-upon purchase price.

EFFECT OF ACCEPTANCE

Once a buyer has accepted goods, he cannot later reject them unless at the time they were accepted, the buyer had reason to believe that the nonconformity would be cured. By accepting goods, the buyer does not forfeit or waive remedies against the seller for any nonconformities in the goods. However, if the buyer wishes to hold the seller responsible, he must give the seller **timely notice** that the goods are nonconforming.

The buyer is obligated to pay for goods that are accepted. If the buyer accepts all the goods sold, he is, of course, responsible for the full purchase price. If only part of the goods are accepted, the buyer must pay for that part at the contract rate (2-607[1]).

REVOCATION OF ACCEPTANCE

Under certain circumstances, a buyer is permitted to **revoke** or undo the acceptance. A buyer may revoke acceptance of nonconforming goods where (1) the nonconformity *substantially impairs the value* of the goods and (2) the buyer accepted them *without knowledge* of the nonconformity due to the difficulty of discovering the nonconformity or the buyer accepted the goods because of *assurances* by the seller (2-608[1]).

The right to revoke acceptance must be exercised within a reasonable time after the buyer discovers or should have discovered the nonconformity. Revocation is not effective until the buyer notifies the seller of the intention to revoke acceptance. After a buyer revokes acceptance, he has the same rights as if the goods had been rejected when delivery was offered (2-608). The *North River Homes, Inc. v. Bosarge case*, which appears below, illustrates some of the considerations involved in determining whether a buyer acted reasonably to revoke acceptance.

The right to revoke acceptance could arise, for example, where Arnold buys a new car. While driving it home, he discovers that the car has a seriously defective transmission. When Arnold returns the car to the dealer, the dealer promises to repair it, so Arnold decides to keep the car. If the dealer does not fix the transmission after repeated efforts to do so, Arnold could revoke his acceptance on the grounds that the nonconformity substantially impairs the value of the car, that he took delivery of the car without knowledge of the nonconformity, and that his acceptance was based on the dealer's assurances that he would fix the car. Similarly, revocation of acceptance might be involved where a serious problem with the car that was not discoverable by inspection shows up during the first month's use.

Revocation must be invoked prior to any *substantial change in the goods*, however, such as serious damage in an accident or wear and tear from use over a period of time. What constitutes a "substantial impairment in value" and when there has been a "substantial change in the goods" are questions that courts frequently have to decide when an attempted revocation of acceptance results in a lawsuit.

North River Homes, Inc. v. Bosarge
17 UCC Rep.2d 121 (Sup. Ct. Miss. 1992)

Facts

On August 20, 1983, Elmer and Martha Bosarge purchased from J & J Mobile Home Sales a furnished mobile home manufactured by North River Homes. The mobile home, described by a J & J salesman as the "Cadillac" of mobile homes, cost $23,900. Upon moving into their new home, the Bosarges immediately discovered defect after defect. The defects included: a bad water leak that caused water to run all over the trailer and into the insulation, causing the trailer's underside to balloon downward; loose moldings; warped dishwasher door; warped bathroom door; holes in the walls; defective heating and cooling system; cabinets with chips and holes in them; furniture that fell apart; rooms that remained moldy and mildewed; a closet that leaked rainwater; and spaces between the doors and windows and

their frames that allowed the elements to come in. The Bosarges had not been able to spot the defects before taking delivery because they had viewed the mobile home at night on J & J's lot and there was no light on in the mobile home.

The Bosarges immediately and repeatedly notified North River Homes of the defects, but it failed to satisfactorily repair the home. In November of 1983 the Bosarges informed North River of their decision to revoke their acceptance of the defective home. On some occasions, repairmen came but did not attempt to make repairs, saying they would come back. Other times, the repairs were inadequate. For example, while looking for the water leak, a repairman cut open the bottom of the mobile home and then taped it back together with masking tape

(continued)

North River Homes, Inc. v. Bosarge

(concluded)

which failed to hold and resulted in the floor bowing out. Another inadvertently punctured a septic line and did not properly repair the puncture, resulting in a permanent stench. Other repairmen simply left things off at the home, like a new dishwasher door and a countertop, saying they did not have time to make the repairs.

In June 1984 the Bosarges provided North River with an extensive list of problems that had not been corrected. When they did not receive a satisfactory response, they sent a letter on October 4, 1984, saying they would make no further payments. North River made no further efforts to correct the problems. In March 1986 the Bosarges' attorney wrote to North River, formally revoking acceptance of the mobile home because of its substantially impaired value, tendering the mobile home back to it, and advising North River that it could pick the home up at its earliest convenience. They then brought a lawsuit requesting return of the purchase price and seeking damages for breach of various warranties.

ISSUES

Did the Bosarges effectively revoke their acceptance of the mobile home and were they barred from revoking acceptance because of their continued use?

DECISION

The court held that the Bosarges had effectively revoked their acceptance of the mobile home. The defects here constituted a substantial impairment of the goods. Once notified of the revocation of acceptance, the seller has a right to attempt to cure the defect. However, the seller cannot postpone revocation in perpetuity by trying to fix everything that goes wrong. There is a time when enough is enough and the buyer is not required to give the seller additional time to bring the goods into conformance with the contract. The continued use of the home after revocation did not constitute a waiver of the right to revoke as the Bosarges were not in a financial position to own two homes. At most the continued use gave the seller a right to a set-off.

Buyer's Rights on Improper Delivery

If the goods delivered by the seller do not conform to the contract, the buyer has several options. The buyer can (1) reject all of the goods, (2) accept all of them, or (3) accept any commercial units and reject the rest (2-601). The buyer, however, cannot accept only part of a commercial unit and reject the rest. The buyer must pay for the units accepted at the price per unit provided in the contract.

Where the contract calls for delivery of the goods in separate installments, the buyer's options are more limited. The buyer may reject an installment delivery only if the nonconformity *substantially affects the value of that delivery* and *cannot be corrected* by the seller. If the defect or nonconformity is relatively minor, the buyer must accept the installment. The seller may offer to replace the defective goods or give the buyer an allowance in the price to make up for the nonconformity (2-612).

Rejection

If a buyer has a basis for rejecting a delivery of goods, the buyer must act within a reasonable time after delivery. The buyer must also give the seller notice of the rejection, preferably in writing (2-602). The buyer should be careful to state all of the defects on which he is basing the rejection, including all that a reasonable inspection would disclose. This is particularly important if the defect is one that the seller might cure (remedy) and the time for delivery has not expired. In that case, the seller may notify the buyer that she intends to redeliver conforming goods.

If the buyer fails to state in connection with his rejection a particular defect that is ascertainable by reasonable inspection, he will not be permitted to use the defect to justify his rejection if the seller could have cured the defect had she been given reasonable notice of it. In a transaction taking place between merchants, the seller has, after rejection, a right to a written statement of all the defects in the goods on which the buyer bases his right to reject, and the buyer may not later assert defects not listed in justification of his rejection (2-605).

RIGHT TO CURE

If the seller had some reason to believe the buyer would accept nonconforming goods, then the seller can take a reasonable time to reship conforming goods. The seller has this opportunity even if the original time for delivery has expired. For example, Ace Manufacturing contracts to sell 200 plain red baseball hats to Sam's Sporting Goods, with delivery to be made by April 1. On March 1, Sam's receives a package from Ace containing 200 red baseball hats with blue trim and refuses to accept them. Ace can notify Sam's that it intends to cure the improper delivery by supplying 200 plain red hats, and it has until April 1 to deliver the plain red hats to Sam's. If Ace thought Sam's would accept the red hats with blue trim because on past shipments it did not object to the substitution, then Ace has a reasonable time even after April 1 to deliver the plain red hats.

WRONGFUL REJECTION

If the buyer wrongfully rejects goods, he is liable to the seller for breach of the sales contract (2-602[3]).

BUYER'S DUTIES AFTER REJECTION

If the buyer is a merchant, then the buyer owes certain duties concerning the goods that he rejects. First, the buyer must follow any reasonable instructions the seller gives concerning disposition of the goods. The seller, for example, might request that the rejected goods be shipped back to the seller. If the goods are perishable or may deteriorate rapidly, then the buyer must make a reasonable effort to sell the goods. The seller must reimburse the buyer for any expenses the buyer incurs in carrying out the seller's instructions or in trying to resell perishable goods. In reselling goods, the buyer must act reasonably and in good faith (2-603). Problem case 9 at the end of this chapter illustrates the decisions that a buyer who receives nonconforming, perishable goods must make.

If the rejected goods are not perishable or the seller does not give the buyer instructions, then the buyer has several options. First, the buyer can store the goods for the seller. Second, the buyer can reship them to the seller. Third, the buyer can resell them for the seller's benefit. If the buyer resells the goods, the buyer may keep expenses and a reasonable commission on the sale. Where the buyer stores the goods, the buyer should exercise care in handling them. The buyer must also give the seller a reasonable time to remove the goods (2-604).

If the buyer is not a merchant, then his obligation after rejection is to hold the goods with reasonable care to give seller an opportunity to remove them. The buyer is not obligated to ship them back to the seller (2-602).

CONCEPT SUMMARY	Acceptance, Revocation, and Rejection
Acceptance	1. Occurs when buyer, having had a reasonable opportunity to inspect goods, either (1) indicates he will take them or (2) fails to reject them. 2. If buyer accepts any part of a commercial unit, he is considered to have accepted the whole unit. 3. If buyer accepts goods, he cannot later reject them *unless* at the time they were accepted the buyer had reason to believe that the nonconformity would be cured. 4. Buyer is obligated to pay for goods that are accepted.
Revocation	1. Buyer may revoke acceptance of nonconforming goods where (1) the nonconformity *substantially impairs the value* of the goods and (2) buyer accepted the goods without knowledge of the nonconformity because of the difficulty of discovering the nonconformity or buyer accepted because of assurances by the seller. 2. Right to revoke must be exercised within a *reasonable* time after buyer discovers or should have discovered the nonconformity. 3. Revocation must be invoked before there is any *substantial change* in the goods. 4. Revocation is not effective until buyer notifies seller of his intent to revoke acceptance.
Rejection	1. Where the goods delivered do not conform to the contract, buyer may (1) reject all of the goods, (2) accept all of the goods, or (3) accept any commercial unit and reject the reset. Buyer must pay for goods accepted. 2. Where the goods are to be delivered in installments, an installment delivery may be rejected *only* if the nonconformity substantially affects the value of that delivery and cannot be corrected by the seller. 3. Buyer must act within a reasonable time after delivery. 4. Buyer must give the seller *notice* of the basis for the rejection.

.... ASSURANCE, REPUDIATION, AND EXCUSE ....

ASSURANCE

The buyer or seller may become concerned that the other party may not be able to perform required contract obligations. If there is a reasonable basis for that concern, the buyer or seller can demand **assurance** from the other party that the contract will be performed. If such assurances are not given within 30 days, then the party is considered to have repudiated the contract (2-609).

For example, a farmer contracts to sell 1,000 bushels of apples to a canner, with delivery to be made in September. In March, the canner learns that a severe frost has damaged many of the apple blossoms in the farmer's area and that 50 percent of the crop has been lost. The canner has the right, in writing, to demand assurances from the farmer that she will be able to fulfill her obligation in light of the frost. The farmer must provide those assurances within 30 days. For example, she might advise the canner that her crop sustained only relatively light damage or that she had made commitments to sell only a small percentage of her total crop and expects to be able to fill her obligations. If the farmer does not provide such assurances in a timely manner, then she is considered to have repudiated the contract. The canner then has certain remedies against the farmer for breach of contract. These remedies are discussed in the next chapter.

The *LNS Investment Company, Inc. v. Phillips 66 Company* case, which follows, illustrates a situation where a buyer became concerned about the seller's ability to perform and demanded assurances from the seller.

LNS INVESTMENT CO., INC. V. PHILLIPS 66 CO.
731 F. Supp. 1484 (D. Kan. 1990)

FACTS

LNS Investment Company is the successor to the CompuBlend Corporation (CBC) which blended, labeled, and packaged quart plastic bottles of motor oil for, among others, the Phillips 66 Company. On July 29, Peter Buhlinger, Phillip's manager of lubricants, wrote a letter to CBC that read as follows:

> This will confirm our verbal agreement whereby Phillips will purchase additional quantities of plastic bottles from CBC during 1986.
>
> CBC, in an effort to increase their packaging capacity, has committed to purchase several additional molds to blow the Phillips one-quart container. In order to amortize the cost of the additional equipment, Phillips has agreed to take delivery of a maximum of 4,000,000 bottles to be made available by December 31, 1986. This agreement includes the production available now and to be supplemented by the additional equipment. Should CBC not be able to produce the full 4,000,000 quarts by December 31, 1986, this agreement shall be considered satisfied.
>
> Phillips' desire is to receive as many bottles packaged with Phillips motor oil in 1986 from CBC as possible. It is our intention to change to a different type of plastic one-quart container beginning in 1987 and therefore this agreement cannot extend past the December 31, 1986 deadline. All production would have to be of high resaleable [*sic*] plastic quarts filled with the appropriate Phillips products and labeled accordingly. The production would be required to be available on an even weekly basis in order to facilitate movement of the product to the warehouse and customers.

Although the agreement called for CBC to increase its production capacity, CBC experienced numerous problems in maintaining even its precontract capacity. Moreover, the quality of goods CBC was able to deliver was frequently unacceptable to Phillips. On September 18, a Phillips representative wrote to CBC complaining about the quality of goods Phillips was receiving, specifically mentioning neck finish and label application problems. The letter also noted that if Phillips had known how CBC would perform, it would not have committed to purchase CBC's hoped-for increase in production. CBC's

chairman responded on September 29, acknowledging certain deficiencies, offering a number of reasons for the inability to perform, and stating that he was sure CBC would be showing "marked improvement in deliveries in the coming week and even more in another two or three weeks."

On October 15, the Phillips representative reiterated its continued dissatisfaction with CBC's products, indicating "we definitely do not want bottles on the shelf of the quality submitted." And, on December 16, he advised CBC that Phillips would not renew any commitments to purchase goods from CBC after March 31, 1987, because of CBC's poor performance under the July 29 agreement. In May 1987, CBC brought suit against Phillips, alleging that Phillips breached the July 29 agreement by failing to purchase CBC's full output of plastic bottles through December 31, 1986. Phillips contended that it was entitled to suspend its performance of the contract because it did not receive reasonable assurances from CBC that it would perform its obligations under the contract.

ISSUE

Was Phillips entitled to suspend its performance of the contract because it did not receive reasonable assurances from CBC that it would perform its obligations under the contract?

DECISION

Yes. Phillips had reasonable grounds for insecurity regarding CBC's performance and was justified in demanding assurances from CBC concerning its future performance. CBC failed to provide Phillips with adequate assurance. CBC's continual excuses for failing to perform, unaccompanied by corresponding remedial action, cannot be considered adequate. Accordingly, Phillips was entitled to suspend its own performance of the contract by refusing to place further orders and/or canceling previously placed orders. Phillips did not breach the contract by suspending its performance.

ANTICIPATORY REPUDIATION

Sometimes one of the parties to a contract repudiates the contract by advising the other party that he does not intend to perform his obligations. When one party repudiates the contract, the other party may suspend his performance. In addition, he may either await performance for a reasonable time or use the remedies for breach of contract that are discussed in the next chapter (2-610).

Suppose the party who repudiated the contract changes his mind. Repudiation can be withdrawn by clearly indicating that the person intends to perform his obligations. The repudiating party must do this before the other party has canceled the contract or materially changed position by, for example, buying the goods elsewhere (2-611).

EXCUSE

Unforeseen events may make it difficult or impossible for a person to perform his contractual obligations. The Code rules for determining when a person is excused from performing are similar to the general contract rules. General contract law uses the test of **impossibility.** However, in most situations, the Code uses the test of **commercial impracticability.**

The Code attempts to differentiate events that are unforeseeable or uncontrollable from events that were part of the risk borne by a party. If the goods required for the performance of a contract are destroyed without fault of either party prior to the time the risk of loss passed to the buyer, then the contract is voided (2-613).

Suppose Jones agrees to sell and deliver an antique table to Brown. The table is damaged when Jones's antique store is struck by lightning and catches fire. The specific table covered by the contract was damaged without fault of either party prior to the time the risk of loss was to pass to Brown. Under the Code, Brown has the option of either canceling the contract or accepting the table with an allowance in the purchase price to compensate for the damaged condition (2-613).

COMMERCIAL IMPRACTICABILITY

If unforeseen conditions cause a delay or inability to make delivery of the goods (make performance *impracticable*), the seller is excused from making delivery. However, if a seller's capacity to deliver is only partially affected, then the seller may allocate production among his customers. If the seller chooses to allocate production, notice must be given to the buyers. When a buyer receives this notice, the buyer may either terminate the contract or agree to accept the allocation (2-615).

For example, United Nuclear contracts to sell certain quantities of fuel rods for nuclear power plants to a number of electric utilities. If the federal government limits the amount of uranium United has access to, so that United is unable to fill all its contracts, United is excused from full performance on the grounds of commercial impracticability. However, United may allocate its production of fuel rods among its customers and give them notice of the allocation. Then, each utility can decide whether to cancel the contract or accept the partial allocation of fuel rods.

In the absence of compelling circumstances, courts do not readily excuse parties from their contractual obligations, particularly where it is clear that the parties anticipated a problem and sought to provide for it in the contract.

.... *QUESTIONS AND PROBLEM CASES* ....

1. What is the difference between a buyer's rejection of goods and revocation of acceptance?

2. Baker was a buyer and distributor of popcorn. Ratzlaff was a farmer who grew popcorn. Baker and Ratzlaff entered into a written contract pursuant to which Ratzlaff agreed that in the current year he would raise 380 acres of popcorn and sell the popcorn to Baker. Baker agreed to furnish the seed popcorn and to pay $4.75 per hundred pounds of popcorn. The popcorn was to be delivered to Baker as he ordered it, and Baker was to pay for the popcorn as it was delivered. At Baker's request, the first delivery was made on February 2 of the following year and the second on February 4. On neither occasion did Raztlaff ask Baker to pay or Baker offer to pay. During that week, Ratzlaff and Baker had several phone conversations about further deliveries, but there was no discussion about payments. On February 11, Ratzlaff sent written notice to Baker that he was terminating the contract because Baker had not paid for the two loads of popcorn that had been delivered. In the meantime, Ratzlaff sold his remaining 1.6 million pounds of popcorn to another buyer at $8 per 100 pounds. Baker then sued Ratzlaff for breach of contract. Did Ratzlaff act in good faith in terminating the contract?

3. Harold Ledford agreed to purchase three used Mustang automobiles (a 1966 Mustang coupe, a 1965 fastback, and a 1966 convertible) from J. L. Cowan for $3,000. Ledford gave Cowan a cashier's check for $1,500 when he took possession of the coupe, with the understanding he would pay the remaining $1,500 on the delivery of the fastback and the convertible. Cowan arranged for Charles Canterberry to deliver the remaining vehicles to Ledford. Canterberry dropped the convertible off at a lot owned by Ledford and proceeded to Ledford's residence to deliver the fastback. He refused to unload it until Ledford paid him $1,500. Ledford refused to make the payment until he had an opportunity to inspect the convertible, which he suspected was not in the same condition that it had been in when he purchased it. Canterberry refused this request and returned both the fastback and the convertible to Cowan. Cowan then brought suit against Ledford to recover the balance of the purchase price. Was Ledford entitled to inspect the car before he paid the balance due on it?

4. Spada, an Oregon corporation, agreed to sell Belson, who operated a business in Chicago, Illinois, two carloads of potatoes at "$4.40 per sack, FOB Oregon shipping point." Spada had the potatoes put aboard the railroad cars; however, he did not have floor racks used in the cars under the potatoes as is customary during winter months. As a result, there was no warm air circulating and the potatoes were frozen while in transit. Spada claims that his obligations ended with the delivery to the carrier and that the risk of loss was on Belson. What argument would you make for Belson?

5. In the spring of 1991 Vince Ford, a retailer, contracted with a wholesaler, Starr Fireworks, for the purchase of various types of fireworks at an agreed price of $6,748.86. In May 1991, Starr delivered the 138 cases of fireworks in one lot to Ford's warehouse in Lusk, Wyoming. Ford did not immediately inspect the fireworks; instead, he distributed them to his retail outlets throughout Wyoming for resale to the public.

   Approximately 10 days after the fireworks were distributed to the retail outlets, Ford discovered that some fireworks were unsalable because of water damage and packaging problems. However, Ford did not inspect the remainder of the fireworks from the shipment. Ford telephoned Starr's representative to report the problems. Although Ford claimed that he instructed his employees not to sell any products received from Starr, a month later one of his stores sold several cases of the fireworks that had been purchased from Starr to another fireworks retailer. The buyer reported no problem with those fireworks, and they were subsequently resold to customers without reported problems.

   After several unsuccessful attempts by Starr representatives to pick up the fireworks, they did pick up 10 cases of fireworks, worth $1,476.87, on August 3, 1991; at that time Ford signed an acknowledgment that he still owed $5,251.99 to Starr. Ford claimed to have returned the remaining fireworks to Starr's Denver office on August 13, 1991. He said that no one was available in the office so he left the fireworks outside a side door; Starr never received those fireworks.

Starr brought suit to recover the balance due on the fireworks that Ford had acknowledged retaining. Ford claimed that he had rejected the entire shipment on the grounds they were unmerchantable and counterclaimed for damages he asserted he had sustained. Ford contended that his inspection of some of the fireworks disclosed packages with torn wrappings, mold or mildew on some fireworks, and paper wrapping which fell apart exposing the fireworks. Ford argued that from this sampling it was reasonable to assume all the goods delivered by Starr were unmerchantable. Did Ford make an effective rejection of the entire shipment?

6. Maxwell Shoe Co., a wholesale shoe distributor, ordered a quantity of shoes from Martini Industries. When Maxwell Shoe received the shipment, it discovered that all of the shoes were cracked and peeling. Maxwell Shoe contacted Martini Industries and stated that it was rejecting the shipment because the shoes were defective. Maxwell Shoe wanted to ship the shoes back to Martini Industries but received no communication from Martini Industries regarding what was to be done with the shipment. Maxwell Shoe did not pay the remainder owed for the shipment and stopped payment on the check that had been initially issued for the order. Subsequently, Maxwell Shoe had the shoes refinished by another company and distributed and sold the shoes. Martini Industries sued for the value of the shipment. Did Maxwell Shoe accept the shipment of shoes and owe Martini Industries for the goods?

7. On May 23, Deborah McCullough, a secretary, purchased a Chrysler LeBaron from Bill Swad Chrysler-Plymouth. The automobile was covered by both a limited warranty and a vehicle service contract (extended warranty). Following delivery, McCullough advised the salesman that she had noted problems with the brakes, transmission, air conditioning, paint job, and seat panels, as well as the absence of rustproofing. The next day, the brakes failed and the car was returned to the dealer for the necessary repairs. When the car was returned, McCullough discovered that the brakes had not been properly repaired and that none of the cosmetic work had been done. The car was returned several times to the dealer to correct these problems and others that developed subsequently. On June 26, the car was again returned to the dealer, who kept it for three weeks. Many of the defects were not corrected, however, and new problems with the horn and brakes arose. While McCullough was on a shopping trip, the engine abruptly shut off and the car had to be towed to the dealer. Then, while she was on her honeymoon, the brakes again failed. The car was taken back to the dealer with a list of 32 defects that needed correction. After repeated efforts to repair the car were unsuccessful, McCullough sent a letter to the dealer calling for rescission of the purchase, requesting return of the purchase price, and offering to return the car on receipt of shipping instructions. She received no answer and continued to drive it. McCullough then filed suit. In May of the next year, the dealer refused to do any further work on the car, claiming that it was in satisfactory condition. By the time of the trial two years later, it had been driven 35,000 miles, approximately 23,000 of which had been logged after McCullough mailed her notice of revocation. By continuing to operate the vehicle after notifying the seller of her intent to rescind the sale, did McCullough waive her right to revoke her original acceptance?

8. Haralambos Fekkos purchased from Lykins Sales & Service a Yammar Model 165D, 16-horsepower diesel tractor and various implements. On Saturday, April 27, Fekkos gave Lykins a check for the agreed-on purchase price, less trade-in, of $6,596, and the items were delivered to his residence. The next day, while attempting to use the tractor for the first time, Fekkos discovered it was defective. The defects included a dead battery requiring jump starts, overheating while pulling either the mower or tiller, missing safety shields over the muffler and the power takeoff, and a missing water pump. On Monday, Fekkos

contacted Lykins's sales representative who believed his claims to be true and agreed to have the tractor picked up from Fekkos's residence; Fekkos also stopped payment on his check. Fekkos placed the tractor with the tiller attached in his front yard as near as possible to the front door without driving it onto the landscaped area closest to the house. Fekkos left the tractor on the lawn because his driveway was broken up for renovation and his garage was inaccessible, and because the tractor would have to be jump-started by Lykins's employees when they picked it up. On Tuesday, Fekkos went back to Lykins's store to purchase an Allis-Chalmers tractor and reminded Lykins's employees that the Yammar tractor had not been picked up and remained on his lawn. On Wednesday, May 1, at 6:00 A.M., Fekkos discovered that the tractor was missing, although the tiller had been unhitched and remained in the yard. Later that day, Lykins picked up the remaining implements. The theft was reported to the police. On several occasions, Fekkos was assured that Lykins's insurance would cover the stolen tractor, that it was Lykins's fault for not picking it up, and that Fekkos had nothing to worry about. However, Lykins subsequently brought suit against Fekkos to recover the purchase price of the Yammar tractor. Was Fekkos liable for the purchase price of the tractor that had been rejected and was stolen while awaiting pickup by the seller?

9. Walters, a grower of Christmas trees, contracted to supply Traynor with "top-quality trees." When the shipment arrived and was inspected, Traynor discovered that some of the trees were not top quality. Within 24 hours, Traynor notified Walters that he was rejecting the trees that were not top quality. Walters did not have a place of business or an agent in the town where Traynor was. Christmas was only a short time away. The trees were perishable and would decline in value to zero by Christmas Eve. Walters did not give Traynor any instructions, so Traynor sold the trees for Walters' account. Traynor then tried to recover from Walters the expenses he incurred in caring for and selling the trees. Did the buyer act properly in rejecting the trees and reselling them for the seller?

10. Whelan ordered fuel oil from Griffith to be delivered to his farm home, which was located on a country road. The oil was to be delivered on a COD basis. Griffith made two attempts to deliver the oil, but each time no one was found at home. The morning after a heavy snow, the heaviest in 20 years, Griffith equipped the truck with chains and made a third attempt to deliver the oil but found on arrival that the driveway to the house was impassable due to snowdrifts approximately 6 feet high. When the driver drove past the house and attempted to turn around, the truck became stuck in the snow and had to be towed back to the main highway. Whelan ran out of oil and, as a result of having no fuel, his heating plant froze, causing substantial damage to it. Whelan sued Griffith to recover for the damage to the heating plant, claiming the breach of the contract to deliver the oil was the cause of the damage. Should Griffith be held liable?

11. *Video Case.* See "Sour Grapes." Jelly Manufacturer, a food processor in Chicago, placed a phone order with Grape Grower, a grower in California, for a quantity of perishable produce. The shipping term was "CIF" with payment to be made on delivery (C.O.D.). Grower delivered the goods called for in the contract to a carrier and contracted for their shipment. However, it neglected to provide that the goods be shipped under refrigeration. The goods were loaded on a nonrefrigerated boxcar and as a result the produce was spoiled when it reached Chicago. Jelly Manufacturer, as required by the C.O.D. term, paid for the produce by check before discovering the spoilage. By paying for the produce, has Jelly Manufacturer "accepted" the goods so that it cannot subsequently "reject" them as nonconforming?

When Jelly Manufacturer called Grower to complain, Grower offered to rush a replacement shipment. Jelly Manufacturer declined the offer, stating that it would not arrive in time for the produce to be processed and delivered to Grocery Chain in time to meet Jelly Manufacturer's contract with Grocery Chain. Was Jelly Manufacturer required to accept Grower's promise to make a replacement shipment?

CHAPTER 19

Remedies for Breach of Sales Contracts

Suppose that Kathy is engaged to be married. She contracts with the Bridal Shop for a custom-designed bridal gown in size 6 with delivery to be made by the weekend before the wedding. Kathy makes a $500 deposit against the contract price of $1,500. If the dress is completed in conformance with the specifications and on time, then Kathy is obligated to pay the balance of the agreed-on price. But what happens if either Kathy or the Bridal Shop breaches the contract? Consider these examples:

- *If Kathy breaks her engagement and tells the Bridal Shop that she is no longer interested in having the dress before the shop has completed making it, what options are open to the Bridal Shop? Can it complete the dress or should it stop work on it?*
- *If the Bridal Shop completes the dress but Kathy does not like it and refuses to accept it, what can the Bridal Shop do? Can it collect the balance of the contract price from Kathy, or must it try to sell the dress to someone else?*
- *If the Bridal Shop advises Kathy that it will be unable to complete the dress in time for the wedding, what options are open to Kathy? If she has another dress made by someone else, or purchases a ready-made one, what, if any, damages can she collect from the Bridal Shop?*
- *If the Bridal Shop completes the dress but advises Kathy it plans to sell it to someone else who is willing to pay more money for it, does Kathy have any recourse?*

These questions, and others, will be addressed in this chapter.

.... ***INTRODUCTION*** ....

REMEDIES IN GENERAL

Usually, both parties to a contract for the sale of goods perform the obligations they agreed to in the contract. Occasionally, however, one of the parties to a contract fails to perform his obligations. When this happens, the injured party has a variety of remedies for breach of contract. The objective of these remedies is to put the injured person in the *same position as if the contract has been performed.* The remedies that are made available to the injured party by the Uniform Commercial Code are discussed in this chapter.

AGREEMENTS AS TO REMEDIES

The buyer and seller may provide their own remedies, to be applied in the event that one of the parties fails to perform. They can also limit either the remedies that the law makes available or the damages that can be recovered (2-719[1]).[1] If the parties agree on the amount of damages that will be paid to the injured party, this amount is known as **liquidated damages.** An agreement for liquidated damages is enforced if the amount is reasonable and if actual damages would be difficult to prove in the event of breach of the contract. The amount is considered reasonable if it is not so large as to be a penalty or so small as to be unconscionable (2-718[1]).

For example, Carl Carpenter contracts to sell a display booth for $3,000 to Hank Hawker for Hawker to use at the county fair. Delivery is to be made to Hawker by September 1. If the booth is not delivered on time, Hawker will not be able to sell his wares at the fair. Carpenter and Hawker might agree that if delivery is not made by September 1, Carpenter will pay Hawker $1,750 as liquidated damages. The actual sales Hawker might lose without a booth would be very hard to prove, so Hawker and Carpenter can provide some certainty through the liquidated damages agreement. Carpenter then knows what he will be liable for if he does not perform his obligation. Similarly, Hawker knows what he can recover if the booth is not delivered on time. The amount ($1,750) is probably reasonable. If it were $500,000, it likely would be void as a penalty because it would be way out of line with the damages that Hawker would reasonably be expected to sustain. And if the amount were too small, say $1, it might be considered unconscionable and therefore not enforceable.

If a liquidated damages clause is not enforceable because it is a penalty or unconscionable, then the injured party can recover the actual damages that were suffered.

Liability for **consequential damages** resulting from a breach of contract (such as lost profits or damage to property) may also be limited or excluded by agreement. The limitation or exclusion is not enforced if it would be unconscionable. Any attempt to limit consequential damages for injury caused to a person by consumer goods is considered prima facie unconscionable (2-719[3]). Suppose an automobile manufacturer makes a warranty as to the quality of the automobile. Then it tries to disclaim responsibility for any person injured if the car does not conform to the warranty and to limit its liability to replacing any defective parts. The disclaimer of consequential injuries in this case would be unconscionable and therefore would not be enforced. Exclusion of or limitation on consequential damages is permitted where the loss is commercial, as long as the exclusion or limitation is not unconscionable.

---

[1]The numbers in parentheses refer to sections of the Uniform Commercial Code.

In the *Moore v. Coachmen Industries, Inc.* case that follows, the court found that consequential damages had been excluded by agreement between the parties.

MOORE V. COACHMEN INDUSTRIES, INC.
34 UCC Rep.2d 758 (Ct. App. N.C. 1998)

FACTS

In September 1989, Luther and Sudie Moore purchased a new 1989 Sportscoach Cross Country recreational vehicle manufactured by Coachmen Industries and Sportscoach Corporation of America from Carolina Country RV, Inc., an authorized distributor of Coachmen and Sportscoach. The vehicle was covered by a New Recreational Vehicle Limited Warranty that provided, in pertinent part:

> Sportscoach Corporation of America will, for one year from the retail purchase date, or for the first 15,000 miles of use, whichever comes first, make repairs which are necessary because of defects in material or workmanship. We will repair or replace any defective part at no cost to you . . .
>
> * * * *
>
> WE SHALL NOT BE LIABLE FOR INCIDENTAL OR CONSEQUENTIAL DAMAGES, such as your expenses for transportation, lodging, loss or damage to your personal property, inconvenience, or loss of income. Some states do not allow exclusion or limitation of incidental or consequential damages, so the above limitation may not apply to you.
>
> IMPLIED WARRANTIES, INCLUDING ANY WARRANTY OF MERCHANTABILITY OR FITNESS FOR A PARTICULAR PURPOSE ARE LIMITED IN DURATION TO THE TERM OF THIS WRITTEN WARRANTY. Some states do not allow limitations on how long an implied warranty lasts, so the above limitation may not apply.

The vehicle was equipped with two electrical systems, a 120-volt alternating current system (AC), and a 12-volt direct current (DC) system, and an AC to DC converter system. The power converter unit had been manufactured by Magne Tek, Inc.

In November 1993, the Moores loaned their recreational vehicle to Linda and Harvey Reep for a weekend. During the Reeps' travels, they turned on the vehicle's generator and the fan in the vehicle's air conditioner unit. Approximately five minutes later, the Reeps noticed heavy smoke and flames in the rear of the vehicle, in front of the bedroom area. The Reeps pulled the vehicle to the shoulder of the interstate and narrowly escaped, before the vehicle and all of its contents were destroyed by fire. The contents included a satellite dish and receiver box purchased in September 1990 at a cost of $4,100 as well as personal property. At the time of the fire, the vehicle had approximately 10,000 miles on its odometer. Several experts in the cause and origin of fires concluded that the fire began at the vehicle's converter box and was due to a fault in the wiring or an electrical fault in the converter box.

The Moores brought suit against Coachmen, Sportscoach, and Magne Tek, claiming among other things, breach of express and implied warranties and negligence. One of the issues in the lawsuit was the effect of the limited warranty.

ISSUE

Was the limited warranty effective in limiting the manufacturer's liability to repair and replacement for a year or 15,000 miles and in excluding consequential and incidental damages?

DECISION

Yes. The limited warranty expressly limited claims for breach of express or implied warranties to one year or 15,000 miles, whichever came first, and the Moore's claims in this instance were untimely. Moreover, because this case did not involve personal injury, there was no presumption that the limitation of damages was unconscionable, and the Moores were not able to make a showing that the limitation was unconscionable.

STATUTE OF LIMITATIONS

The Code provides that a lawsuit for breach of a sales contract must be filed within four years after the breach occurs. The parties to a contract may shorten this period to one year, but they may not extend it to longer than four years (2-725). A breach of warranty normally is considered to have occurred when the goods are delivered to the buyer. However, if the warranty covers future performance of goods (for example, a warranty on a tire for four years or 40,000 miles), then the breach occurs at the time the buyer should have discovered the defect in the product. If, for example, the buyer of the tire discovers the defect after driving 25,000 miles on the tire over a three-year period, he would have four years from that time to bring any lawsuit to remedy the defect.

In the case that follows, *Painter v. General Motors Corp.,* the court rejected a claim that a warranty excluded to "future performance" and applied the four-year statute of limitations.

PAINTER V. GENERAL MOTORS CORP.
974 P. 2d 924 (Sup. Ct. Wyoming 1999)

FACTS

Rebecca Painter purchased a GMC "Jimmy" from Rolly Creech. Creech had originally acquired it from a dealer on September 28, 1990. The vehicle was covered by a three-year, 50,000 mile "bumper to bumper" warranty.

On December 22, 1991, the "Jimmy" was being driven by Painter's mother-in-law, who heard a loud explosion, pulled the vehicle into the emergency lane, and stopped. The vehicle burst into flames immediately and was destroyed in the fire. The odometer reading at that time was approximately 14,500 miles.

Painter filed suit against General Motors, alleging, among other things, breach of warranty. The action was filed on December 20, 1995, more than four years after delivery of the vehicle, but two days short of four years after the explosion and fire. General Motors moved for summary judgment in its favor on the grounds that the

warranty claim was barred by the four-year statute of limitations. Painter contended that the "bumper to bumper" warranty was a warranty for future performance and thus was timely filed.

ISSUE

Was Painter's suit barred by the statute of limitations?

DECISION

Yes. Under section 2-725(2), a breach of warranty occurs—and the four-year statute of limitations begins to run—on delivery of the goods unless the warranty extends to future performance. The warranty in this case did not extend to future performance. The "repair or replace" warranty merely recognized that there might be future problems and was not a warranty that there would be no problems for three years after delivery.

SELLER'S REMEDIES

REMEDIES AVAILABLE TO AN INJURED SELLER

A buyer may breach a contract in a number of ways; the most common are (1) by wrongfully refusing to accept goods, (2) by wrongfully returning goods, (3) by failing to pay for the goods when payment is due, and (4) by indicating an unwillingness to go ahead with the contract.

When a buyer breaches a contract, the seller has a number of remedies under the Code, including the right to:

1. Cancel the contract.
2. Withhold delivery of any undelivered goods.
3. Resell the goods covered by contract and recover damages from the buyer.
4. Recover from the buyer the profit the seller would have made on the sale or the damages the seller sustained.
5. Recover the purchase price of goods delivered to or accepted by the buyer.
6. Reclaim goods in the possession of an insolvent seller.

CANCELLATION AND WITHHOLDING OF DELIVERY

When a buyer breaches a contract, the seller has the right to cancel the contract and to hold up his own performance of the contract. The seller may then set aside any goods that were intended to fill the seller's obligations under the contract (2-704).

If the seller is in the process of manufacturing the goods, the seller has two choices. The seller may complete manufacture of the goods or stop manufacturing and sell the uncompleted goods for their scrap or salvage value. In choosing between these two alternatives, the seller should choose the one that will minimize the loss (2-704[2]). Thus, the seller would be justified in completing the manufacture of goods that could be resold readily at the contract price. However, a seller would not be justified in completing specially manufactured goods that could not be sold to anyone other than the buyer who ordered them. The purpose of this rule is to permit the seller to follow a reasonable course of action to **mitigate** (minimize) the damages. These principles are illustrated in *Madsen v. Murrey & Sons Company.*

MADSEN V. MURREY & SONS CO., INC.
743 P. 2d 1212 (Sup. Ct. Utah 1987)

FACTS

Murrey & Sons Company, Inc. (Murrey), was engaged in the business of manufacturing and selling pool tables. Erik Madsen was working on an idea to develop a pool table that, through the use of electronic devices installed in the rails of the table, would produce lighting and sound effects in a fashion similar to a pinball machine. Murrey and Madsen entered into a written contract whereby Murrey agreed to manufacture 100 of its M1 4-foot by 8-foot six-pocket coin-operated pool tables with customized rails capable of incorporating the electronic lighting and sound effects desired by Madsen. Under the agreement, Madsen would design the rails and provide the drawings to Murrey, who would manufacture them to Madsen's specifications. Madsen was to design, manufacture, and install the electronic components for the tables. Madsen agreed to pay $550 per table or a total of $55,000 for the 100 tables and made a $42,500 deposit on the contract.

Murrey began the manufacture of the tables while Madsen continued to work on the design of the rails and electronics. Madsen encountered significant difficulties and notified Murrey that he would be unable to take delivery of the 100 tables. Madsen then brought suit to recover the $42,500 he had paid Murrey.

Following Madsen's repudiation of the contract, Murrey dismantled the pool tables and used salvageable materials to manufacture other pool tables. A good portion of the material was simply used as firewood. Murrey made no attempt to market the 100 pool tables at a discount or at any other price in order to mitigate its damages. It claimed the salvage value of the materials it reused was $7,448. There was evidence that if Murrey had completed the tables, they would have had a value of at least $21,250 and could have been sold for at least that much, and that the changes made in the frame to accommodate the electrical wiring would not have adversely affected the quality or marketability of the pool tables. Murrey said it had not completed manufacture because its reputation for quality might be hurt if it dealt in "seconds" and that the changes in the frame might weaken it and subject it to potential liability.

ISSUE

Was Murrey justified in not completing manufacture of the pool tables?

DECISION

No. The court held that Murrey's action in dismantling the tables and using the materials for salvage and firewood was not commercially reasonable. It had a duty to mitigate its damages, which it could have done by marketing the tables at full or discounted prices.

RESALE OF GOODS

It the seller sets aside the goods intended for the contract or completes the manufacture of such goods, the seller is not obligated to try to resell the goods to someone else. However, the seller may resell them and recover damages. The seller must make any resale in *good faith* and in a *reasonable commercial manner.* If the seller does so, the seller is entitled to recover from the buyer as damages the *difference* between the *resale price* and the *price the buyer agreed to pay* in the contract (2-706).

If the seller resells, he may also recover incidental damages but must give the buyer credit for any expenses the seller saved because of the buyer's breach of contract. **Incidental damages** include storage charges and sales commissions paid when the goods were resold. Expenses saved might be the cost of packaging and/or shipping the goods to the buyer (2-710).

If the seller intends to resell the goods in a private sale to another buyer, the seller must give the first buyer reasonable notice of the proposed resale. If the resale will be at a public sale such as an auction, the seller generally must give the buyer notice of the time and place of the auction. The seller may make a profit at the resale if the goods bring more than the contract price. If the seller makes a profit, the seller may keep it and does not have to give the profit to the buyer (2-706).

RECOVERY OF THE PURCHASE PRICE

In the normal performance of a contract, the seller delivers conforming goods (goods that meet the contract specifications) to the buyer. The buyer accepts the goods and pays for them. The seller is entitled to the purchase price of all goods *accepted* by the buyer. The seller is also entitled to the purchase price of all goods that *conformed* to the contract and were *lost or damaged after the buyer assumed the risk for their loss* (2-709). For example, a contract calls for Dell to ship 35 computers to Maxwell's Office Supply with shipment "FOB Dell's manufacturing facility." If the computers are lost or damaged while on their way to Maxwell's, Maxwell's is responsible for paying Dell for them.

The seller may also recover the purchase or contract price from the buyer in one other situation. This is where the seller has made an honest effort to resell the goods and was unsuccessful or where it is apparent that any such effort to resell would be unsuccessful. This might happen where the seller manufactured goods especially for the buyer and the goods are not usable by anyone else. Assume Sally's Supermarket sponsors a bowling team. It orders six green-and-red bowling shirts to be embroidered with "Sally's Supermarket" on the back and the names of the team members on the pocket. After the shirts are completed, Sally's wrongfully refuses to accept them. The seller will be able to recover the agreed-on purchase price if it cannot sell the shirts to someone else.

If the seller sues the buyer for the contract price of the goods, the seller must hold the goods for the buyer. Then the seller must turn the goods over to the buyer if the buyer pays for them. However, if resale becomes possible prior to the time the buyer pays for the goods, the seller may resell them. Then the seller must give the buyer credit for the proceeds of the resale (2-709[2]).

DAMAGES FOR REJECTION OR REPUDIATION

When the buyer refuses to accept goods that conform to the contract or repudiates the contract, the seller does not have to resell the goods. The seller has two other ways of determining the damages that the buyer is liable for because of the buyer's breach of contract: (1) the difference between the contract price and the market price at which the goods are currently selling, and (2) the "profit" the seller lost when the buyer did not go through with the contract (2-708).

The seller may recover as damages the *difference* between the *contract price* and the *market price* at the time and place the goods were to be delivered to the buyer. The seller may also recover any incidental damages but must give the buyer credit for any expenses the seller has saved (2-708[1]). This measure of damages is most commonly sought by a seller when the market price of the goods dropped substantially between the time the contact was made and the time the buyer repudiated the contract.

For example, on January 1, Toy Maker, Inc. contracts with the Red Balloon Toy Shop to sell the shop 100,000 Beanie Babies at $3.50 each, with delivery to be made in Boston on June 1. By June 1, the Beanie Baby fad has passed and Beanie Babies are selling for $1 each in Boston. If the shop repudiates the contract on June 1 and refuses to accept delivery of the 100,000 Beanie Babies, Toy Maker is entitled to the difference between the contract price of $350,000 and the June 1 market price in Boston of $100,000. Thus, Toy Maker could recover $250,000 in damages plus any incidental expenses but less any expenses saved by it in not having to ship the Beanie Babies to the Red Balloon Toy Shop.

If getting the difference between the contract price and the market price would not put the seller in as good a financial position as if the contract had been performed, the seller may choose an alternative measure of damages based on the lost profit and overhead the seller would have made if the sale had gone through. The seller can recover this *lost profit and overhead* plus any incidental expenses. However, the seller must give the buyer credit for any expenses saved as a result of the buyer's breach of contract (2-708[2]).

Using the Beanie Baby example, assume that the direct labor and material cost to Toy Maker of making the Beanie Babies was 55 cents each. Toy Maker could recover as damages from Red Balloon the profit Toy Maker lost when Red Balloon defaulted on the contract. Toy Maker would be entitled to the difference between the contract price of $350,000 and its direct cost of $55,000. Thus Toy Maker could recover $295,000 plus any incidental expenses and less any expenses saved.

LIQUIDATED DAMAGES

If the seller has justifiably withheld delivery of the goods because of the buyer's breach, the buyer is entitled to recover any money or goods he has delivered to the seller over and above the agreed amount of liquidated damages. If there is no such agreement, the seller will not be permitted to retain an amount in excess of $500 or 20 percent of the value of the total performance for which the buyer is obligated under the contract, whichever is smaller. This right of restitution is subject to the seller's right to recover damages under other provisions of the Code and to recover the amount of value of benefits received by the buyer directly or indirectly by reason of the contract (2-718).

SELLER'S REMEDIES WHERE BUYER IS INSOLVENT

Unless the seller has agreed to extend credit to the buyer, the buyer must pay for the goods at the time they are delivered. When the seller is ready to make delivery of the goods, the seller may withhold delivery until the payment is made (2-511[1]).

Suppose a seller has agreed to extend credit to a buyer and then before making delivery the seller discovers the buyer is insolvent. A buyer is insolvent if he cannot

CONCEPT SUMMARY	Seller's Remedies (on Breach by Buyer)

Problem	Remedy
Buyer refuses to go ahead with contract and seller has goods	1. Seller may cancel contract, suspend his performance, and set aside goods intended to fill the contract. 　a. If seller is in the process of manufacturing, he may complete manufacture or stop and sell for scrap, picking the alternative that in his judgment at the time will minimize the seller's loss. 　b. Seller can resell goods covered by contract and recover difference between contract price and proceeds of resale. 　c. Seller may recover purchase price where resale is not possible. 　d. Seller may recover damages for breach based on difference between contract price and market price, or in some cases based on his lost profits.
Goods are in buyer's possession	1. Seller may recover purchase price. 2. Seller may reclaim goods in possession of insolvent buyer.
Goods are in transit	1. Seller may stop any size shipment if buyer is insolvent. 2. Seller may stop carload, truckload, planeload, or other large shipment for reasons other than buyer's insolvency.

pay his bills when they become due. The seller then has the right to withhold delivery until the buyer pays cash for the goods and for any goods previously delivered for which payment has not been made. The seller also has the right to require the buyer to return any goods the insolvent buyer obtained from the seller within the previous 10 days. If the buyer told the seller she was solvent at any time in the previous three months—and in fact she was not solvent—the seller can reclaim goods received by the buyer even earlier than the last 10 days (2-702).

If a seller discovers a buyer is insolvent, the seller has the right to stop delivery of any goods that are being shipped to the buyer. This would involve notifying the carrier, for example, the trucker, or the airline, in time to prevent delivery to the buyer (2-705).

BUYER'S REMEDIES

BUYER'S REMEDIES IN GENERAL

A seller may breach a contract in a number of different ways. The most common are (1) failing to make an agreed delivery, (2) delivering goods that do not conform to the contract, and (3) indicating an intention not to fulfill the obligations under the contract.

A buyer whose seller breaks the contract is given a number of remedies. These include:

1. Canceling the contract and recovering damages where the buyer rightfully rejected goods or justifiably revoked acceptance.
2. Buying other goods ("covering") and recovering damages from the seller based on any additional expense the buyer incurs in obtaining the goods.
3. Recovering damages based on the difference between the contract price and the current market price of the goods.
4. Recovering damages for any nonconforming goods accepted by the buyer based on the difference in value between what the buyer got and what the buyer should have gotten.
5. Obtaining specific performance of the contract where the goods are unique and cannot be obtained elsewhere.

In addition, the buyer can in some cases recover consequential damages (such as lost profits) and incidental damages (such as expenses incurred in buying substitute goods).

BUYER'S RIGHT TO DAMAGES

Where a buyer has rightfully rejected goods or has justifiably revoked acceptance of goods, the buyer may cancel the contract, recover as much of the purchase price as has been paid, and recover damages. Thus, while the Code does not explicitly use the common law contract term *rescission* (discussed in Chapter 15), it does incorporate the concept. In the *Baker v. Burlington Coat Factory Warehouse* case that follows, the buyer was entitled to recover the purchase price paid for a coat that was defective.

BAKER v. BURLINGTON COAT FACTORY WAREHOUSE
34 UCC Rep.2d 1052 (N.Y. City Ct. 1998)

FACTS

Catherine Baker purchased a fake fur coat from the Burlington Coat Factory Warehouse store in Scarsdale, New York, paying $127.99 in cash. The coat began shedding profusely, rendering the coat unwearable. The shedding was so severe that Baker's allergies were exacerbated, necessitating a visit to her doctor and to the drugstore for a prescription.

She returned the coat to the store after two days and demanded that Burlington refund her $127.99 cash payment. Burlington refused, indicating that it would give her a store credit or a new coat of equal value, but no cash refund. Baker searched the store for a fake fur of equal value and found none. She refused the store credit, repeated her demand for a cash refund, and brought a lawsuit against Burlington when it again refused to make a cash refund.

In its store, Burlington displayed several large signs which state, in part,

WAREHOUSE POLICY
Merchandise in New Condition, May be Exchanged Within 7 Days of Purchase for Store Credit and Must Be Accompanied by a Ticket and Receipt. No Cash Refunds or Charge Credits.

On the front of Baker's sales receipt was the following language:

Holiday Purchases May Be Exchanged Through January 11th, 1998, In House Store Credit Only No Cash Refunds or Charge Card Credits.

On the back of the sales receipt was the following language:

We Will Be Happy To Exchange Merchandise In New Condition Within 7 Days When Accompanied By Ticket and

Receipt. However, Because of Our Unusually Low Prices: No Cash Refunds or Charge Card Credits Will Be Issued. In House Store Credit Only.

At the trial, Baker claimed that she had not read the language on the receipt and was unaware of Burlington's no-cash-refunds policy. The court found that Burlington had breached the implied warranty of merchantability when it sold the defective coat to Baker.

ISSUE

Where the seller breaches the implied warranty of merchantability and the buyer returns the defective goods, is the buyer entitled to a refund of the purchase price paid for the goods?

DECISION

Yes. While under New York law, a retail merchant is permitted to establish a no-cash and no-credit-card refund policy and enforce it when it has been prominently displayed, the policy cannot be applied in the case of defective goods. Here, Burlington breached the implied warranty of merchantability by selling Baker a defective product and under section 2-714 of the Uniform Commercial Code, Baker is entitled to the return of the purchase price in cash.

AUTHOR'S NOTE

The court went on to hold that Burlington's failure to inform buyers of their right to a cash or credit charge refund when the goods are defective, and hence breach the implied warranty of merchantability, is misleading and deceptive under the state's general business law.

BUYER'S RIGHT TO COVER

If the seller fails or refuses to deliver the goods called for in the contract, the buyer can purchase substitute goods; this is known as **cover.** If the buyer does purchase substitute goods, the buyer can recover as damages from the seller the *difference* between the *contract price* and the *cost of the substitute goods* (2-712). For example, Frank Farmer agrees to sell Ann's Cider Mill 1,000 bushels of apples at $8.00 a bushel. Farmer then refuses to deliver the apples. Cider Mill can purchase 1,000 bushels of similar apples, and if it has to pay $8.50 a bushel, it can recover the difference (50 cents a bushel) between what it paid ($8.50) and the contract price ($8.00). Thus, Cider Mill could recover $500.00 from Frank.

The buyer can also recover any incidental damages sustained but must give the seller credit for any expenses saved. In addition, the buyer may be able to obtain consequential damages. The buyer is not required to cover, however. If the buyer does not cover, the other remedies under the Code are still available (2-712[3]).

The case that follows, *KGM Harvesting Co. v. Fresh Network,* illustrates a situation in which the aggrieved buyer chose to seek damages based on its cost of cover from the defaulting seller.

KGM HARVESTING CO. V. FRESH NETWORK
26 UCC Rep.2d 1028 (Ct. App. Cal. 1995)

FACTS

KGM Harvesting Company, a California lettuce grower and distributor, and Fresh Network, an Ohio lettuce broker, began dealing with each other in 1989, and over the years the terms of the agreement were modified. As of May 1991, their agreement called for KGM to deliver 14 "loads" of lettuce a week at a price of 9 cents a pound. A load of lettuce consists of 40 bins, each of which weighs 1,000 to 1,200 pounds. At an average of 1,100 pounds, one load would equal 44,000 pounds, and the 14 loads called for in the contract would weigh 616,000 pounds. At 9 cents per pound, the cost would be approximately $55,440 per week.

Fresh Network, in turn, resold all of the lettuce to another broker (Castellani Company), who sold it to Club Chef, a company that chopped and shredded it for the fast-food industry (specifically, Burger King, Taco Bell, and Pizza Hut). The transactions between Fresh Network and Castellani, and in turn between Castellani and Club Chef, were on a cost plus basis. This meant each paid its buyer its actual cost plus a small commission.

In May and June 1991, when the price of lettuce went up dramatically, KGM refused to supply Fresh Network with lettuce at the contract price of 9 cents per pound. Instead, it sold the lettuce to others at a profit between $800,000 and $1,100,000. Fresh Network then went out

on the open market and purchased lettuce to satisfy its obligations to Castellani Company. Castellani covered all of Fresh Network's extra expense except for $70,000. Fresh Network then sought to recover from KGM as damages the difference between what it was forced to spend to buy replacement lettuce and the contract price of 9 cents a pound (approximately $700,000). KGM objected on the grounds that Fresh Network had been able to pass some of the increased cost along to Castellani.

ISSUE

Was Fresh Network, as the aggrieved buyer, entitled to recover as damages from the defaulting seller, KGM, the difference between its cost of cover and the contract price?

DECISION

Yes. The court held that the objective of the remedies in the UCC was to give the aggrieved party the nearest possible equivalent to the benefits of performance. In this case, only by receiving reimbursement for the additional costs incurred could the buyer truly receive the benefits of the bargain. In determining the measure of damages under Section 2-712, it is not necessary to consider all subsequent events impacting the buyer's ultimate profit

(continued)

KGM Harvesting Co. v. Fresh Network
(concluded)

or loss. The courts have not held that the damages recoverable under a "cover" approach are limited to an amount that would place the buyer in the same position which it would have been in had the seller fully performed the agreement.

Incidental Damages

Incidental damages include expenses the buyer incurs in receiving, inspecting, transporting, and storing goods shipped by the seller that do not conform with those called for in the contract. Incidental damages also include any reasonable expenses or charges the buyer has to pay in obtaining substitute goods (2-715[1]).

Consequential Damages

In certain situations, an injured buyer is able to recover **consequential damages,** such as the buyer's lost profits caused by the seller's breach of contract. The buyer must be able to show that the seller knew or should have known at the time the contract was made that the buyer would suffer special damages if the seller did not perform his obligations. The buyer must also show that he could not have prevented the damage by obtaining substitute goods (2-715[2]).

Suppose Knitting Mill promises to deliver 20,000 yards of a special fabric to Dora by September 1. Knitting Mill knows that Dora wants to acquire the material to make garments suitable for the Christmas season. Knitting Mill also knows that in reliance on the contract with it, Dora will enter into contracts with department stores to deliver the finished garments by October 1. If Knitting Mill delivers the fabric after September 1 or fails completely to deliver it, it may be liable to Dora for any consequential damages she sustains if she is unable to acquire the same material elsewhere in time to fulfill her October 1 contracts.

Consequential damages can also include an injury to a person or property caused by a breach of warranty. For example, an electric saw is defectively made. Hank purchases the saw, and while he is using it, the blade comes off and severely cuts his arm. The injury to Hank is consequential damage resulting from a nonconforming or defective product.

Damages for Nondelivery

If the seller fails or refuses to deliver the goods called for by the contract, the buyer has the option of recovering damages for the nondelivery. Thus, instead of covering, the buyer can get the *difference* between the *contract price* of the goods and their *market price* at the time the buyer learns of the seller's breach. In addition, the buyer may recover any incidental damages and consequential damages but must give the seller credit for any expenses saved (2-713).

Suppose Bill agreed on June 1 to sell and deliver 5,000 bushels of wheat to a grain elevator on September 1 for $7 per bushel and then refused to deliver on September 1 because the market price was then $8 per bushel. The grain elevator could recover $5,000 damages from Bill, plus incidental damages that could not have been prevented by cover.

DAMAGES FOR DEFECTIVE GOODS

If a buyer accepts defective goods and wants to hold the seller liable, the buyer must give the seller *notice* of the defect within a *reasonable time* after the buyer discovers the defect (2-607[3]). Where goods are defective or not as warranted and the buyer gives the required notice, the buyer can recover damages. The buyer is entitled to recover the *difference* between the *value of the goods received* and the *value the goods would have had if they had been as warranted*. The buyer may also be entitled to incidental and consequential damages (2-714).

For example, Al's Auto Store sells Anne an automobile tire, warranting it to be four-ply construction. The tire goes flat when it is punctured by a nail, and Anne discovers that the tire is really only two-ply. If Anne gives the store prompt notice of the breach, she can keep the tire and recover from Al's the difference in value between a two-ply and a four-ply tire. The *Jetpac* case, which follows, illustrates a situation where the aggrieved buyer was entitled to recover damages based on the reduced value of the goods received plus consequential and incidental damages.

JETPAC GROUP, LTD. V. BOSTEK, INC.
942 F. Supp 716 (D. Mass 1996)

FACTS

Jetpac Group, Ltd., is an export/import company based in Shreveport, Louisiana. Formed in 1988, Jetpac's business generally involved selling food products, such as frozen chicken, in various countries around the world, including Russia. In 1992, it partnered with Natashquan Korotia Systems (NKS), a Canadian company headed by a former citizen of what had been the Soviet Republic of Georgia. NKS held a contract to sell 3,000 computers—in a configuration known as "Russian 286s"—to a buyer in Russia at a price of $1,050 per unit.

Jetpac contacted Bostek, Inc., a Hanover, Massachusetts, supplier of computer hardware and software that, among other things, built integrated systems to customer's specifications, buying the components from various sources and then assembling them. On June 11, 1992, Jetpac and Bostek agreed that Bostek would build a "test shipment" of 100 units that would be shipped to the Russian customer on June 15. Bostek's price was to be $630 per unit for this smaller production run; it's quote for the larger number eventually desired was $605 per unit. The parties agreed on the components to be included in the computers, including a 286/16 motherboard, a 220-volt power supply, a VGA monitor, a mouse, and a Cyrillic/English keyboard. Bostek was to ship the units directly to the customer in Russia with Jetpac paying the freight costs for shipping from Boston of

$8,184. NKS and Jetpac were to split the profit on the Russian sale.

When the computers arrived in Russia, the customer notified NKS that there were significant problems. Not all the specified components were included; for example, no "mice" were shipped, although the specifications called for them. Some of the wiring in the central processing unit was either missing or disconnected. Further, the monitors did not switch automatically from 100 to 220 volts, and as a result, several of them "blew up" when initially switched on. When Jetpac's president went to Russia to meet with the very dissatisfied customer, he observed the wiring problems, and when he tried to turn on five separate systems that had been in the shipment, only one booted up. In short, the "test shipment" that had been designed to impress the Russian customer and open the way to more sales was a disaster. In an effort—unsuccessful it turned out—to regain the customer's confidence, NKS and Jetpac bought and supplied the customer with another 200 units from another supplier.

The Russian customer refused to pay fully for the first shipment and refused to buy the balance of the 3,000 computers. Thus reasonably probable sales of 2,700 computers at $1,050 were lost. NKS charged back to Jetpac its share of the shortfall on the first shipment ($23,517). Jetpac brought suit against Bostek, claiming

(continued)

Jetpac Group, Ltd. v. Bostek, Inc.
(concluded)

damages for breach of warranty, consequential damages in the form of lost profits and incidental expense, including the cost of its president's travel to Moscow to try to mollify the unhappy customer, and additional shipping expenses it incurred to get components to the customer that had been omitted from the initial shipment.

ISSUE

Is Jetpac, as the aggrieved buyer, entitled to recover damages for breach of warranty, consequential damages for lost profits, and incidental expenses incurred as a result of Bostek's breach of contract?

DECISION

Yes. Bostek breached the contract by failing to furnish goods that conformed to the contract description and, because the goods were defective, there was a breach of the warranty of merchantability. For breach of warranty, Jetpac is entitled to damages in the amount of the difference "between the value of the goods accepted and the value they would have had if they had been as warranted." (2-714). Here, this measure of damages can be determined by Jetpac's share of the loss ($23,517) when the customer in Russia refused to pay the full price for the computers. In addition, Jetpac is entitled to recover incidental and consequential damages (2-715). Recoverable consequential damages include "any loss resulting from general or particular requirements and needs of which the seller at the time of contracting had reason to know and which could not reasonably be prevented by cover or otherwise." Such damages include "prospective profits lost as the natural and probable consequence of the breach." In this case, Bostek had reason to know that a defective initial shipment could jeopardize the business opportunity and profit on the full sale of 3,000 units. Finally, Jetpac is also entitled to recover the incidental expenses it incurred as a result of Bostek's breach, including the cost of the trip to Moscow and the additional shipping expenses.

Ethical Implications	In problem case 7, how would you assess the ethicality of the representations made by the salesperson to the purchaser in response to his question? In a case like this, should it be incumbent on a purchaser to ask the "right" questions in order to protect himself, or should there be an ethical obligation on the seller to disclose voluntarily material facts that may be relevant to the purchaser's making an informed decision?

CONCEPT SUMMARY	Buyer's Remedies (on Breach by Seller)

Problem	Buyer's Remedy
Seller fails to deliver goods or delivers nonconforming goods that buyer rightfully rejects or justifiably revokes acceptance of	1. Buyer may cancel the contract and recover damages. 2. Buyer may "cover" by obtaining substitute goods and recover difference between contract price and cost of cover. 3. Buyer may recover damages for breach based on difference between contract price and market price.
Seller delivers nonconforming goods that are accepted by buyer	Buyer may recover damages based on difference between value of goods received and value they would have had as warranted.
Seller has goods but refuses to deliver them and buyer wants them	Buyer may seek specific performance if goods are unique and cannot be obtained elsewhere.

BUYER'S RIGHT TO SPECIFIC PERFORMANCE

Sometimes the goods covered by a contract are **unique** and it is not possible for a buyer to obtain substitute goods. When this is the case, the buyer is entitled to specific performance of the contract. **Specific performance** means that the buyer can require the seller to give the buyer the goods covered by the contract (2-716). Thus, the buyer of an antique automobile such as a 1910 Ford might ask a court to order the seller to deliver the specified automobile to the buyer because it was one of a kind. On the other hand, the buyer of grain in a particular storage bin could not get specific performance if he could buy the same kind of grain elsewhere.

BUYER AND SELLER AGREEMENTS AS TO BUYER'S REMEDIES

As mentioned earlier in this chapter, the parties to a contract may provide for additional remedies or substitute remedies for those expressly provided in the Code (2-719). For example, the buyer's remedies may be limited by the contract to the return of the goods and the repayment of the price or to the replacement of nonconforming goods or parts. However, a court looks to see whether such a limitation was freely agreed to or whether it is unconscionable. In those cases, the court does not enforce the limitation and the buyer has all the rights given to an injured buyer by the Code.

.... *QUESTIONS AND PROBLEM CASES* ....

1. What is the objective of the remedies that the Code makes available to a party to a contract who has been injured when the other party breached its obligations?

2. International Record Syndicate (IRS) hired Jeff Baker to take photographs of the musical group Timbuk-3. Baker mailed 37 "chromes" (negatives) to IRS via the business agent of Timbuk-3. When the chromes were returned to Baker, holes had been punched in 34 of them. Baker brought an action for breach of contract to recover for the damage done to the chromes.

   A provision printed on Baker's invoice to IRS stated: "[r]eimbursement for loss or damage shall be determined by a photograph's reasonable value which shall be no less than $1,500 per transparency." Baker testified that he had been paid as much as $14,000 for a photo session, which resulted in 24 photographs, and that several of them had already been resold. He also had received as little as $125 for a single photograph. He once sold a photograph taken in 1986 for $500 and sold several reproductions of it later for a total income of $1,500. Was the liquidated damages provision enforceable by Baker?

3. Lobianco contracted with Property Protection, Inc., for the installation of a burglar alarm system. The contract provided in part:

   > Alarm system equipment installed by Property Protection, Inc., is guaranteed against improper function due to manufacturing defects of workmanship for a period of 12 months. The installation of the above equipment carries a 90-day warranty. The liability of Property Protection, Inc., is limited to repair or replacement of security alarm equipment and does not include loss or damage to possessions, persons, or property.

   As installed, the alarm system included a standby battery source of power in the event that the regular source of power failed. During the 90-day warranty period, burglars broke into Lobianco's house and stole $35,815 worth of jewelry. First, they destroyed the electric meter so that there was no electric source to operate the system, and then they entered the house. The batteries in the standby system were dead, and thus the standby system failed to operate. Accordingly, no outside siren was activated and a telephone call that was supposed to be triggered was not made. Lobianco brought suit, claiming damage in the amount of her stolen jewelry because of the failure of the alarm system to work properly. Did the disclaimer effectively eliminate any liability on the alarm company's part for consequential damages?

4. Parzek purchased from New England Log Homes a log home kit consisting of hand-peeled logs, window frames and door frames. The brochure that Parzek had seen before buying the log home kit contained a statement that the logs were treated with a preservative "to protect the treated wood against decay, stain, termites, and other insects." Other statements indicated the maintenance-free nature of the logs, and there was a guarantee against any materials and engineering defects. The logs were delivered in May 1974 to the construction site, where they were stored in stacks covered by heavy tarpaulins. By fall of 1976, the walls were erected and the roof was on. In 1979, Parzek discovered 15 medium-sized blue metallic beetles on the interior walls of the home. He was assured by the dealer for New England Log Homes that the problem was not serious. The following April, however, Parzek observed hundreds of beetles and discovered larvae and "excavation channels" in the logs. When he contacted New England Log Homes, he was told that it did not guarantee that its logs were insect free. Parzek had the home treated by an exterminator and then brought suit against New England Log Homes. Relying on Section 2-725 of the Code, New England Log Homes contended that the lawsuit was barred by the statute of limitations because it was filed more than four years after the date of delivery. Was the lawsuit barred by the statute of limitations because it was filed more than four years after the date of delivery?

5. Bechtel ordered an alabaster-colored mink coat from Pollack Furs. The coat had been specially made because she required an unusually large size and requested a particular styling. The coat cost $5,500, of which Bechtel paid $250. Several months later, she decided that she did not want the coat and canceled the order, even though Pollack Furs had completed the coat. Pollack Furs then filed suit for the balance of the purchase price. What can Bechtel argue in defense?

6. Cohn advertised a 30-foot sailboat for sale in the *New York Times*. Fisher saw the ad, inspected the sailboat, and offered Cohn $4,650 for the boat. Cohn accepted the offer. Fisher gave Cohn a check for $2,535 as a deposit on the boat. He wrote on the check, "Deposit on aux sloop, D'arc Wind, full amount $4,650." Fisher later refused to go through with the purchase and stopped payment on the deposit check. Cohn readvertised the boat and sold it for the highest offer he received, which was $3,000. Cohn then sued Fisher for breach of contract. He asked for damages of $1,679.50. This represented the $1,650 difference between the contract price and the sale price plus $29.50 in incidental expenses in reselling the boat. Was Cohn entitled to recover the difference between the contract price and the resale price plus his incidental expenses?

7. Barr purchased from Crow's Nest Yacht Sales a 31-foot Tiara pleasure yacht manufactured by S-2 Yachts. He had gone to Crow's Nest knowing the style and type yacht he wanted. He was told that the retail price was $102,000 but that he could purchase the model they had for $80,000. When he asked about the reduction in price, he was told that Crow's Nest had to move it because there was a change in the model and they had new ones coming in. He was assured that the yacht was new, that there was nothing wrong with it, and that it had only 20 hours on the engines. Barr installed a considerable amount of electronic equipment on the boat. When he began to use it, he experienced tremendous difficulties with equipment malfunctions. On examination by a marine expert, it was determined that the yacht had earlier been sunk in salt water, resulting in significant rusting and deterioration in the engine, equipment, and fixtures. Other experts concluded that significant replacement and repair were required, that the engines would have only 25 percent of their normal expected life, and that following its sinking, the yacht would have only half of its original value. Barr then brought suit against Crow's Nest and S-2 Yachts for breach of warranty. To what measure of damages is Barr entitled to recover for breach of warranty?

8. De La Hoya bought a used handgun for $140 from Slim's Gun Shop, a licensed firearms dealer. At the time, neither De La Hoya nor Slim's knew that the gun had been stolen prior to the time Slim's bought it. While De La Hoya was using the gun for target shooting, he was questioned by a police officer. The officer traced the serial number of the gun, determined that it had been stolen, and arrested De La Hoya. De La Hoya had to hire an attorney to defend himself against the criminal charges. De La Hoya then brought a lawsuit against Slim's Gun Shop for breach of warranty of title. He sought to recover the purchase price of the gun plus $8,000, the amount of his attorney's fees, as "consequential damages." Can a buyer who does not get good title to the goods he purchased recover from the seller consequential damages caused by the breach of warranty of title?

9. Schweber contracted to purchase a certain new black Rolls Royce Corniche automobile from Rallye Motors. He made a $3,500 deposit on the car. Rallye later returned his deposit to him and told him the car was not available. However, Schweber learned that the automobile was available to the dealer and was being sold to another customer. The dealer then offered to sell Schweber a similar car but with a different interior design. Schweber brought a lawsuit against the dealer to prevent it from selling the Rolls Corniche to anyone else and to require that the car be sold to him. Rallye Motors claimed that he could get only damages, not specific performance. Approximately 100 Rolls Royce Corniches were being sold each year in the United States, but none of the others would have the specific features and detail of this one. Was the remedy of specific performance available to Schweber?

10. *Video Case.* See "Sour Grapes." Jelly Manufacturer, a food processor in Chicago, placed a phone order with Grape Grower, a grower in California for a quantity of perishable produce. The shipping term was "CIF" with payment to be made on delivery (C.O.D.). Grape Grower delivered the goods called for in the contract to a carrier and contracted for their shipment. However, it neglected to provide that the goods be shipped under refrigeration. The goods were loaded on a nonrefrigerated boxcar and as a result the produce was spoiled when it reached Chicago. Jelly Manufacturer, as required by the C.O.D. term, paid for the produce by check before discovering the spoilage. When Jelly Manufacturer called Grape Grower to complain, Grower offered to rush a replacement shipment. Jelly Manufacturer declined the offer, stating that it would not arrive in time for the produce to be processed and delivered to Grocery Chain in time to meet the processor's contract with Grocery Chain. Jelly Manufacturer arranged for a rush replacement shipment from a nearby source, but had to pay 150 percent of the prevailing market price for the produce. Even so, Jelly Manufacturer was unable to deliver the finished products to Grocery Chain and was required to pay a penalty for late delivery as provided in its contract with Grocery Chain. Can Jelly Manufacturer recover damages from Grape Grower for breach of contract? If so, what elements can be recovered? Can Grocery Chain recover the penalty from Jelly Manufacturer?

PART IV

Agency and Employment

CHAPTER 20

The Agency Relationship— Creation, Duties, and Termination

Mary Fletcher entered into an exclusive listing agreement with Robert Hicks, a licensed real estate broker, to sell some land and buildings. They agreed on a sale price of $1.6 million. During the period of the listing agreement, Hicks was in contact with a number of prospective purchasers, including Walter Steere. When the property was still unsold when the listing agreement expired, Fletcher and Hicks agreed that Hicks would continue to market the property. In April, Hicks told Fletcher that he had an offer from Walter Steere for $1.1 million. Fletcher agreed to accept that amount. She later discovered that Hicks and Steere had purchased the property together as partners.[1]

- *Was Hicks acting as Fletcher's agent? How are such relationships created?*
- *What duties did Hicks owe Fletcher? Were any of these duties violated?*
- *How does one properly terminate an agency relationship? What duties do agents owe principals after the agency has been terminated?*

---

[1]Petition of Contoocook Valley Paper Company, 529 A.2d 1388 (Sup. Ct. NH 1987).

INTRODUCTION

An agency relationship arises when one person (the **agent**) acts for the benefit of and under the direction of another (the **principal**). You have no doubt been involved in agencies numerous times. You may have assisted a friend by making some purchase on her behalf. While doing so, you were acting as her agent. If you have ever employed an attorney to represent you in court or to negotiate some claim against someone else, the attorney acted as your agent. Agency law especially focuses on the relations between principals and agents and the third persons with whom agents deal in making contracts on behalf of principals. Because it has developed primarily from the decisions of courts, most agency rules spring from the common law.

Agency law addresses three basic questions:

1. What duties do a principal and agent owe each other?
2. What is the liability of the principal and the agent on contracts made by the agent?
3. When is the principal liable for the torts of the agent?

Answers to the last two questions will be deferred until Chapter 21. This chapter will focus on the first question—determining the duties that principals and agents owe each other. This discussion will be preceded by an examination of how agency relationships are created. The chapter will end with a discussion of the proper ways of terminating an agency.

CREATION OF AN AGENCY

NATURE OF AGENCY

Agency relationships usually are formed by contract, although they may be found in the absence of a contractual agreement. An agency may be either written or oral[2] and either compensated or uncompensated. In fact, a court may find that there is an agency relationship even though the parties have expressly agreed that they do not intend to create one. For example, a manufacturer may control the selling activities of a franchised retailer so closely that the retailer is treated as the agent of the manufacturer. Even a statement in the franchise agreement declaring that the retailer is not an agent of the manufacturer is not binding on the court.

An agency results from any indication of consent by the principal that the agent may act on the principal's behalf and under her control. This can be proven not only by direct evidence between the parties but also by the surrounding circumstances such as the words and conduct of the parties. Consider the following case and the factors the court used in denying the existence of an agency relationship.

Compare the following case with the case that opened the chapter. There, Hicks certainly appeared to be an agent of Fletcher. Real estate brokers generally are agents of the seller of land rather than of the buyer. Thus, for the duration of the exclusive listing agreement, Hicks seemed to be acting on behalf of and under the control of Fletcher. This agency appears to have continued even after the expiration of the listing agreement, since Hicks's words and actions indicated that he would continue to represent Fletcher in the sale of the property.

---

[2]Some states, however, have an "equal dignity rule" that holds that if the contract the agent forms must be in writing, the agency agreement also must be in writing. Thus, in the case that opened this chapter, the agreement between Hicks and Fletcher may need to be in writing since the statute of frauds generally requires a written agreement to sell land. See Chapter 13 for a discussion of the statute of frauds.

BASILE V. H&R BLOCK
761 A.2d 1115 (Pa. Sup.Ct. 2000)

FACTS

H&R Block provides tax preparation services nationwide through a network of retail offices operated through subsidiaries. As a part of its service, Block offers a program, known as "Rapid Refund," which involves electronic filing of tax returns with the IRS, resulting in quicker refunds than a taxpayer filing a paper return would receive. Block also arranged for Mellon Bank to provide a refund anticipation loan (RAL) program to Block's qualified Rapid Refund customers. Specifically, Block customers who filed their returns electronically and met the lender's eligibility requirements were informed of the availability of loans in the amount of their anticipated refunds from Mellon Bank. If the customer was interested in the loan, Block would simultaneously transmit the taxpayer's income tax return information to the IRS and Mellon Bank. Within a few days of the transmittal, the taxpayer, if approved, would receive a check in the amount of the loan minus a bank transaction fee. The taxpayer could also elect to have Block's tax preparation and electronic filing fees withheld by the lender from the RAL check so that the taxpayer would not have to advance any money. When the taxpayer's actual tax refund was ready, usually within a matter of weeks, the IRS would deposit the refund check into an account at Mellon Bank to repay the loan. In exchange for the RAL, the taxpayer paid to Mellon a flat rate finance charge of $29 or $35, which Block employees presented to the taxpayer as a flat dollar amount rather than as a percentage interest rate on the short term loan. Block did not disclose to its RAL customers that it received a payment from Mellon Bank for each loan, shared in the profits of the RALs in other ways, or that the taxpayer's endorsement on the back of the loan proceeds check constituted a signature on a loan agreement on the reverse side of the check. Sandra Basile, one of Block's RAL customers, filed an action against Block, claiming that Block breached its fiduciary duty to her by failing to disclose that the refund anticipation payment was a loan and that Block had a financial interest in arranging the program. Basically, the gist of Basile's claim was that a principal-agent relationship existed between Block and its RAL customers and that, as an agent, Block had a fiduciary duty to fully disclose to its customers the nature of the RAL program and Block's participation in the profits generated from it.

ISSUE

Did an agency relationship exist between H&R Block and its customers?

DECISION

No. The three basic elements of agency are (1) the manifestation by the principal that the agent shall act for him, (2) the agent's acceptance of the undertaking, and (3) the understanding of the parties that the principal is to be in control of the undertaking. In all matters affecting the subject of the agency, the agent must act with the utmost good faith in furthering and advancing the principal's interests, including a duty to disclose to the principal all relevant information. However, there is no agency in this case. There is no showing that the customers intended Block to act on their behalf in securing the RALs. To the contrary, Block offered its customers the opportunity to file their tax returns electronically with several options, only one of which involved RALs. Customers were not required to apply for an RAL in order to have their returns prepared by Block or filed electronically through Block. It was the customer alone who decided to take advantage of the RAL option. Block was neither authorized to, nor did in fact, act on its customers' behalf in this regard. If a customer elected to apply for an RAL, Block simply facilitated the loan process by presenting customers to Mellon Bank as viable loan candidates. Block neither applied for the loan on behalf of customers nor determined that customers should apply; customers undertook that procedure themselves. The RAL program was merely another distinct and separate service offered by Block to its customers. Simply introducing customers to a lender willing to provide a loan is not sufficient to create an agency relationship. The special relationship arising from an agency agreement, with its concomitant heightened duty, cannot arise from any and all actions, no matter how trivial, arguably undertaken on another's behalf. Rather, the action must be a matter of consequence or trust, such as the ability to actually bind the principal or alter the principal's legal relations. Such power decidedly did not exist here with regard to facilitating the RALs. Therefore, no agency existed between Block and its customers.

CAPACITY TO BE A PRINCIPAL

Generally, a person can do anything through an agent that he or she could legally do personally. The legal effect of the agent's action on behalf of the principal is usually the same as if the principal had done the act. For example, minors and insane persons are bound on contracts made by their agents only to the extent that they would have been bound if they had taken the action in person. This is true even though the agent has full capacity to contract.

Business organizations and groups of people can also act through an agent. Each partner is an agent of the other partner(s) in carrying on partnership business. A corporation is a legal entity that can act only through agents. An unincorporated association such as a club or neighborhood association is not viewed as a legal entity. Although its members may appoint an agent and will be bound by the agent's acts, the association itself does not become a party to a contract made by an agent.[3]

CONCEPT SUMMARY	Creation of an agency
Test	Is one party (agent) acting: 1. For the benefit of *and* 2. Under the control of another (principal)?
Evidence	Look at the parties' words, actions, and the surrounding circumstances.
Formalities	Generally, none are required: 1. No contract is necessary. 2. Agreement may be oral. 3. Agent need not be compensated.
Capacity	No legal capacity necessary to serve as an agent (some regulatory exceptions). (Incapacitated agent may avoid agency agreement.) Any "person" with legal capacity may be a principal.
Power	Agent may do anything that the principal could do (with some exceptions).

CAPACITY TO BE AN AGENT

A person can have the capacity to act as an agent although he or she does not have the legal capacity to contract. For example, Helen, a minor, may serve as an agent to make a contract that is binding on William, the adult principal. Note, however, that while Helen has the capacity to bind William on a contract with a third person, she may be able to release herself from the agency agreement at her option. Partnerships, as well as corporations, may act as agents. Marriage does not automatically establish an agency relationship; however, a person may be appointed as an agent by his or her spouse.

DUTIES OF AGENTS TO PRINCIPALS

The duties of an agent to the principal normally derive from either the contract, if any, between them or from the common law of agency. While most agency relationships arise out of contract, the agency contract, especially if it is oral, may state little more than the general purpose of the agency. For example, Patrick may merely tell Angie to

---

[3]Many states have enacted statutes making unincorporated associations' assets subject to suit.

sell his car after he goes into the Army. In such cases, the duties the agent owes to the principal must be found in the common law.

The following duties exist at the common law even when the agency agreement is silent:

1. Duty of loyalty.
2. Duty to obey instructions.
3. Duty to exercise care and skill.
4. Duty to communicate information.
5. Duty to account for funds and property.

DUTY OF LOYALTY

Of all of the common law duties an agent owes the principal, the most important is the fiduciary duty of loyalty. A **fiduciary** is one who is trusted to act in the best interests of another rather than pursuing his or her own interests. While all of the other common law duties can be reduced by agreement, the duty of loyalty cannot be eliminated. In fact, courts are hesitant to enforce an agreement that diminishes this duty in even the slightest way.

Conflicts of Interest

The agent's **duty of loyalty** requires complete honesty from the agent in all dealings with the principal. Further, the duty requires either avoidance of conflicts between the interests of the agent and those of the principal or full disclosure of any such conflict to the principal. If, after such advance disclosure, the principal is willing to continue the agency relationship, the agent is shielded from liability for breach of the duty of loyalty.

Such disclosure should include notification of all compensation that the agent expects to receive in the course of fulfilling the agency functions, because the agent is not permitted to make a secret profit from the agency. Anything of value that comes to the agent because of the agency relationship belongs to the principal. Thus, if Alfred is a purchasing agent for General Electric Company and receives kickbacks or secret gifts from suppliers from whom he purchases goods for GE, the company is entitled to those gifts.

Agents breach their duty of loyalty by buying for the principal from themselves even if they charge a fair price. The duty of loyalty demands that the agent avoid even the **appearance of impropriety.** Such purchases are permissible only when the agent has informed the principal, in advance, of the potential conflict of interest and fully discloses other pertinent facts. The same is true of sales to the agent. Suppose Karen agrees that Andrew, her real estate agent, may himself purchase the acreage she listed with him. If he did not tell her that a new highway was planned that would run beside it, she could recover the acreage. This would be true even though no other offer for the property had been received.

Further, in the course of carrying out her agency duties, an agent is not permitted to seize any opportunities available to her principal. For example, suppose Bill authorizes Alice, who is going to an antique car rally, to buy a car for him if she finds a bargain. She learns of a very good deal but takes it for herself instead of buying it for Bill. Bill would be able to get the car from Alice at her cost. If Alice had already sold the car to someone else, Bill could recover damages for the loss of the bargain. Likewise, an agent is not permitted to enter into any business in competition with the principal.

Consider the following case and its discussion of the agent's duty of loyalty. In particular, notice the court's recognition that the actual scope of the duty of loyalty may depend on the nature of the particular agency relationship. Don't be frustrated if this seems ambiguous. Pay particular attention to the court's advice on how agents can avoid the possibility of violating the duty of loyalty.

CAMECO V. GEDICKE
724 A.2d 783 (N.J. Sup.Ct. 1999)

FACTS

Cameco, a producer of food products, employed Gedicke as a salaried traffic manager at a salary of approximately $38,000 per year. Gedicke's primary duty was arranging transportation of Cameco's food products to retail stores by common carrier. His duties included coordinating Cameco's shipping schedules, negotiating the lowest possible shipping rates, and supervising the warehouse employees who loaded the trucks. Cameco's shipping costs comprised 15 to 20 percent of its operating expenses. Gedicke's duties also included inspecting Cameco's off-site warehouses for cleanliness and temperature maintenance. Because of his position, Gedicke became familiar with the identity of Cameco's suppliers, customers, and common carriers, as well as its delivery routes and rates, all of which Cameco considers to be confidential information. Without telling Cameco, Gedicke and his wife formed Newton Transport Service, which Gedicke operated primarily out of his home. Acting on behalf of distributors or truckers, Gedicke arranged for the transportation of food products to retailers. After several years, Newton Transport's profits exceeded $62,000 a year. Two of the distributors for which Newton Transport arranged transportation sold the same products as Cameco. On over 600 occasions, Gedicke arranged for a trucker transporting Cameco's goods also to transport goods for Newton Transport's customers. However, the addition of Newton Transport freight actually enabled Gedicke to negotiate lower rates for Cameco. Gedicke admitted that he engaged in telephone conversations relating to Newton Transport's business during his scheduled hours with Cameco. However, he took no more than 15 minutes per day for such matters and used his personal credit card in making such calls. After learning of Gedicke activities, Cameco asked the court to declare, as a matter of law, that Gedicke had breached his duty of loyalty to Cameco.

ISSUE

Should the court find, as a matter of law, that Gedicke has breached his duty of loyalty?

DECISION

No. This case is not one in which an employee, while employed by one employer, advanced his interest by seeking other employment. Nor is it one in which the employee surreptitiously tried to capture the employer's business, disparage its products, or divert its business to another. Rather, the case is one in which a salaried employee, while working for his employer, supplemented his income by establishing a business that, although it did not compete directly with his employer, may have assisted certain of the employer's competitors. Hence, the question focuses on the level of assistance to a competitor that would justify a finding that an employee breached the duty of loyalty owed to his or her employer. The scope of the duty of loyalty that an employee owes to an employer may vary with the nature of their relationship. Employees occupying positions of trust and confidence, for example, owe a higher duty than those performing low-level tasks. Assisting an employer's competitor can constitute a breach of the employee's duty of loyalty. Similarly, an employee's self-dealing may breach that duty. To avoid the possibility of charges of disloyalty, employees generally should inform employers of their plans before establishing an independent business that might conflict with that of the employer. To an employee, the possibility of conflict with the employer's interests may seem remote; to the employer, the possibility may seem more immediate. The greater the possibility that another occupation will conflict with the employee's duties to the employer, the greater the need for the employee to alert the employer to that possibility. In sum, various considerations affect determination of an

(continued)

CAMECO V. GEDICKE
(concluded)

employees breach of loyalty. One consideration is the possible existence of contractual provisions. A provision might permit an employee to seek a second source of income, whether through a second job or an independent business. Conversely, a noncompetition covenant might limit an employee's economic activities both during and after employment. A second consideration is whether the employer knew of or agreed to its employee's secondary profit-seeking activities. An employee's disclosure of an intention to pursue a second source of income alerts the employer to potential problems and protects the employee from a charge of disloyalty. The third consideration concerns the status of the employee and his or her relationship to the employer. An officer, director, or key executive, for example, has a higher duty than an employee working on a production line. Fourth, the nature of the employee's second source of income and its effect on the employer are relevant. An employee's duty of loyalty to an employer generally precludes acts of direct competition. Employees should not engage in conduct that causes their employers to lose customers, sales, or potential sales. Nor should they take advantage of their employers by engaging in secret self-serving activities, such as accepting kickbacks from suppliers or usurping their employer's corporate opportunities. Employees who defraud their employers or engage in direct competition with them run the risk of discharge, forfeiture of the right to compensation, and other legal and equitable remedies. Among the facts supporting a recovery for Cameco are that Gedicke never informed the company he had established an independent business as a truck broker; that Gedicke spent some time during his normal work hours engaged in Newton Transport's business; and that his dealings put Gedicke in a position where he could assist, perhaps unintentionally, the truckers and Cameco's competitors. Facts suggesting that Gedicke did not breach his duty of loyalty are that he was a low- or mid-level salaried employee; that during his employment, Gedicke was not subject to any contractual limitations preventing him from establishing an outside business; that he did not cause Cameco to lose any customers, sales, potential sales, or profits; and that he did not compete directly with Cameco or render substantial assistance to any of its competitors. This case must now be remanded to the trial court so it can determine if Gedicke has breached his duty of loyalty.

Ethical Implications   Suppose that a client contracted for the principal's services specifically because of its desire to draw from the agent's special expertise. Is the agent breaching an ethical duty to the client by allowing it to contract with the principal, knowing that he will soon terminate his relationship with the principal's company?

Dual Agency

Usually one cannot serve as agent for both parties to a transaction; however, the principals may consent to such a dual role if the parties are both fully informed. Suppose Pamela employs Allen as a real estate broker to find a buyer for her residence. Patti wants to buy some houses as rental property and has agreed to pay Allen a commission on those she buys through him. Allen arranges a sale of Pamela's house to Patti. If he has not informed both of them of his dual role, he is not entitled to a commission from either. If only Patti is aware of and approves the arrangement, Allen may collect a commission from her but not from Pamela. A principal who was not informed of the agent's dual role also retains the right to rescind any contract made by the agent in his dual role.

Courts make an exception when the dual agent is employed merely as a **middleman.** If an agent is employed to find a buyer for one party and a seller for the other and the parties intend to and do negotiate their own transaction, the agent is only a middleman. If neither party relies on the agent for advice or negotiation, there is no breach of loyalty. Real estate brokers normally just bring the parties together rather than actually negotiating a contract of sale. However, the party first employing the broker usually expects to and does in fact rely on the broker for advice. Therefore, it is a breach of duty if the agent also purports to advise the other party.

Consider the case opening the chapter in this context. Hicks purported to be representing Fletcher in the sale of her land and buildings. It was therefore a breach of his duty of loyalty if he simultaneously represented Steere's or his own interests without her consent. If he was indeed secretly acting as Steere's partner in the purchase of Fletcher's property, he was serving as an undisclosed dual agent in violation of his fiduciary duty to Fletcher.

Confidential Information

Another aspect of the duty of loyalty is the duty of agents to avoid disclosing or using the principal's secrets. Agents breach this duty if they either disclose confidential information to others or use it to benefit themselves. Trade secrets such as formulas, processes, and mechanisms are included within this duty; so are customer lists, special selling techniques, and sales manuals. However, agents may use the general knowledge and skills they have acquired while employed by their principal. This is true even when a former agent is competing with her former principal after termination of the agency relationship. A principal claiming a trade secret must be able to show that the information was protected and treated as a secret within the agency. This usually means that only a few people were allowed access to it and that it was never disclosed to anyone else except on a confidential basis.

CONCEPT SUMMARY	**The Agent's Duty of Loyalty**	
Nature	Fiduciary duty: • Action in best interests of principal. • Complete honesty. • Cannot be eliminated by agreement.	

Proscriptions	Agent should avoid:
	• Conflicts of interest:
	  self-dealing.
	  secret profits.
	  usurping principal's opportunities.
	• Dual agencies.
	• Misuse of confidential information.	

Exception	Agent may engage in otherwise prohibited activity: • With principal's consent. • After full and open disclosure.	

DUTY TO OBEY INSTRUCTIONS

An agent is not entitled to substitute her personal judgment for that of the principal. The agent may not ignore instructions just because they seem unwise or not truly in the best interests of the principal. If no instruction is given, the agent should exercise her best judgment to further the interests of the principal.

The agent has a duty to obey the principal and will be liable for any loss to the principal caused by failure to follow such instructions. Suppose Joe instructs Alma, a clerk in his store, to sell goods only for cash except to those customers who have previously established accounts with him. While Joe is gone, Alma sells goods on credit to a very well-dressed customer. Later, Joe is unable to collect. Alma is liable to Joe for the price of the goods. The fact that Alma thought Joe would benefit from her action is not a defense since she acted contrary to his instructions.

There are a few situations in which the agent may act contrary to the principal's instructions without incurring liability. Suppose Joe had told Alma not to obligate him for any goods or services during his absence. While he was gone and out of contact with Alma, a tornado damaged the roof of his store. Alma would have implied authority to obligate Joe for any reasonable roof repairs that she might arrange. It is reasonable for Alma to believe that, in the emergency and despite the instructions, Joe would have wanted her to have the roof repaired. (Implied authority will be discussed more fully in Chapter 21.)

Ethical Implications	Suppose that you are a sales representative for a major manufacturer with responsibility over the company's independent (franchised) retail dealers. The manufacturer instructs you to pressure the retailers to adhere to its suggested retail prices. Specifically, you are told to "threaten and cajole" them if that is what it takes to get their compliance. Retail price-fixing agreements between manufacturers and retailers violate the antitrust laws, while voluntary compliance with suggested prices does not. What should you do?

DUTY TO EXERCISE CARE AND SKILL

Unless changed by agreement, the agent has a duty to act with ordinary care and with the skill common for the kind of work he is hired to do. An agent who is authorized to receive goods or to make collections has a duty to use customary practices to protect the principal's property. While the agent who makes loans is not an insurer of their collectibility, the agent must use care to investigate the credit standing of any borrowers. If it is usual to require security, the agent must investigate the adequacy of the security.

If the agent is acting without pay—a **gratuitous agent**—that fact is taken into account by the courts. The standard of care and skill required generally is less for a gratuitous agent than it is when the agent is to be compensated.

DUTY TO COMMUNICATE INFORMATION

The agent has a duty to inform the principal of knowledge the agent gains in the course of her responsibilities. This duty will be violated if the agent does not promptly notify the principal of anything of relevance to the agency that she knows or should know are of concern to the principal.

CTC COMMUNICATIONS v. BELL ATLANTIC CORPORATION
14 F. Supp. 2d 133 (D.C. Me. 1998)

FACTS

Bell Atlantic is a telecommunications carrier that sells telecommunications services in New York and the New England states. CTC Communications is in the business of selling telecommunication services to customers in the same territory. Beginning in 1984, CTC sold intra-LATA services through an agency agreement with Bell

(continued)

CTC COMMUNICATIONS V. BELL ATLANTIC CORPORATION
(concluded)

Atlantic. Approximately 90 percent of CTC's income was generated by its agency relationship with Bell Atlantic. Under the agency, CTC sold Bell Atlantic's products to end users and was paid a commission on each such sale. Bell Atlantic also paid fees to CTC to manage the relationship between Bell Atlantic and its customers by providing information and service to each customer at no additional charge to the customer. (CTC acted as Bell Atlantic's face to the designated customers.) The agency agreement was negotiated during the months leading up to the enactment of the Telecommunications Act of 1996—a period of great uncertainty in the telecommunications industry. That Act imposes certain obligations on local exchange carriers to foster the growth of competition for telecommunication services involving calls that originate and terminate within a local access and transport area (LATA). One of the results of the Act was the emergence of resale of telecommunications services in intra-LATA markets. The original agency agreement contained a noncompetition clause. However, in light of the pending telecommunications legislation, CTC had that clause renegotiated to state that if, within 12 months after termination of the agency agreement, CTC became a reseller, it was permissible for CTC to resell Bell Atlantic services to otherwise forbidden customers. The agency relationship between CTC and Bell Atlantic was terminated in December of 1997. Twelve months later CTC began soliciting Bell Atlantic's customers for its own reselling operations. Bell Atlantic then brought suit against CTC, claiming that it had breached its fiduciary duty to Bell Atlantic by failing to disclose all material information (i.e., its intentions regarding the possibility of resale with respect to the customers it serviced for Bell Atlantic) during the renegotiation of the noncompetition clause.

ISSUE

Did CTC breach its fiduciary duty during the renegotiation by failing to disclose its intent to become a reseller if the opportunity to do so arose?

DECISION

No. Bell Atlantic argues that the fiduciary relationship between Bell Atlantic and CTC at the time of the renegotiations obligated CTC to disclose all information which

CTC had reason to believe would be material to Bell Atlantic, but was not already known to Bell Atlantic during the negotiations. CTC was aware of the possibility that federal law might create both opportunities for reselling and incentives on Bell Atlantic's behalf to terminate the agency agreement. Given this atmosphere, CTC used the renegotiation to try and ensure its continuing livelihood by preserving an option to resell Bell Atlantic services to those customers constituting 90 percent of CTC's revenues. The critical question for the court is whether Bell Atlantic knew of CTC's intentions through information provided by CTC during the course of the negotiations. Bell Atlantic correctly asserts that an agent is subject to the duty to use reasonable efforts to give his principal information which is relevant to affairs entrusted to him and which, as the agent has notice, the principal would desire to have and which can be communicated without violating a superior duty to a third person. A fiduciary owes a duty of undivided and undiluted loyalty to those whose interests the fiduciary is to protect. This is a sensitive and inflexible rule of fidelity, barring not only blatant self-dealing, but also requiring avoidance of situations in which a fiduciary's personal interest possibly conflicts with the interest of those owed a fiduciary duty. Although an agent has no duty after termination of the agency not to compete with the principal, during the continuance of the agency he has a duty not to do disloyal acts looking to future competition. Thus, it is apparent that an agent owes a duty to its principal to disclose information which is material to the interests of the principal, including situations in which silence on the part of the agent places the principal at a disadvantage in dealings with its own agent. However, this fiduciary duty was not breached in this particular case. The obligation to disclose any intentions regarding the possibility of becoming a reseller upon termination of the agency agreement was satisfied by CTC's negotiation of the change in the post termination noncompetition language. The act of negotiating a favorable term in the eventuality that CTC's agency relationship with Bell Atlantic was terminated, especially in light of the uncertain state of federal communications law at the time of the renegotiation, gave sufficient notice to Bell Atlantic.

TABLE 20–1   Tips for Complying with Duty to Account

---

1. Keep complete and accurate records of all relevant transactions.

2. Have principal inspect all records at regular intervals and certify, in writing, as to their accuracy.

3. Have a mutually agreed-upon CPA inspect all records.

Warning: None of these steps will help the agent if the principal is able to prove embezzlement or falsification.

DUTY TO ACCOUNT FOR FUNDS AND PROPERTY

Property

An agent frequently is given money or property (tools, an automobile, or samples) by the principal. If so, the agent has a duty to return them or to account for his inability to do so on request by the principal. Included among the property for which the agent must account are any secret profits he received in violation of the duty of loyalty as well as any bribes or kickbacks that he might have received from third persons in the scope of the agency.

An Accounting

If the job of the agent includes receiving payments or operating a farm or business for the principal, the agent must periodically give the principal an accurate record of receipts and expenditures. The contract that establishes the agency normally states when such records are due. It may be as often as each day, or it may be only once a year. However, an **accounting** is more than just giving the principal a record of receipts and expenditures. It also involves an agreement, express or implied, between the agent and the principal that the record is correct. The principal may ask a court for a formal accounting if she is dissatisfied with the agent's records. (See Table 20–1.)

Commingling

An agent has a duty to keep the principal's property separate from her own. If the agent fails to do this, she is liable for any loss to the principal. If the agent **commingles** goods that are fungible—that is, if she mixes goods that are identical and cannot be separated—the agent bears the risk of any loss. For example, suppose Amy is carrying in her purse $1,000 in expense money that belongs to RCA Corporation, her employer. Mixed with it is $500 of her own money. She is robbed. Later, the thief is caught and the police recover $900. RCA will be entitled to the $900 if Amy cannot identify which of the bills belonged to RCA and which belonged to her.

An agent has the duty to deposit funds of the principal in a separate bank account. This should be either an account in the principal's name or a special account in the form: "Ames, in trust for Parker." Professional agents who serve a number of clients often maintain an account in the form: "Ames's Clients' Trust Fund."

Embezzlement

Agents are often given property of the principal for use in the principal's business. If the agent takes the property with the intent to deprive the principal of it, the agent is guilty of the crime of **embezzlement.** Whether or not the property of the principal is wrongfully used, the agent must return it or be liable for its value in an action for **conversion.**

If an agent uses the money of the principal for the agent's purposes, the principal may choose either to sue for the money or to obtain whatever was purchased with it. Suppose Andrew, as agent, is paid $5,000 owed by a debtor of Perkins, Andrew's principal. Instead of giving it immediately to Perkins, Andrew invests it in the stock of Golden Mining Company. Luckily, the market price of the stock rises to $10,000 before Perkins learns of the wrongdoing. Perkins is entitled to all of the stock. If instead the value of the stock had decreased, Perkins could recover the $5,000.

.... *DUTIES OF PRINCIPALS TO AGENTS* ....

A well-drafted agency contract would be expected to set out the duties the principal owes to the agent. However, if the contract is poorly drafted or if there is no contract at all, the courts look to the common law of agency for guidance. The following duties generally are imposed on the principal by the common law:

1. The duty to compensate.
2. The duty to reimburse and indemnify.
3. The duty to keep accounts.

DUTY TO COMPENSATE

Normally, a duty to pay the agent is implied unless special circumstances or the relationship of the parties suggest that a gratuitous agency was intended. The agency agreement should specify the amount of compensation due the agent and when it has been earned. Many disputes arise because no clear agreement has been reached. In the absence of agreement, the agent is entitled to the customary or reasonable value of the services performed. Custom is sometimes quite clear. For example, in most communities, real estate brokers all charge the same commission rate. If there is no clear custom and the amount is in dispute, expert witnesses may testify as to what a reasonable amount would be.

Contingent Compensation

Compensation is often made contingent on results. Sales agents are frequently paid an agreed-on percentage of the value of the sales they make. Stockbrokers are also usually paid on a commission basis. Lawyers in the United States, especially when serving plaintiffs in tort actions such as automobile claims, often agree to contingent fees. If they win the case for the plaintiff, they get some share (often one-third) of the recovery. The plaintiff has only expenses and court costs to pay if there is no recovery. An agent is entitled to be paid if the agreed-on result is obtained even though the principal does not benefit. For example, Albert is employed by Pierce Manufacturing Company as a salesperson. As a result of material shortages, Pierce is unable to produce and ship several large orders taken by Albert and accepted by Pierce. Albert is entitled to his commission on those orders. However, if Pierce had informed Albert of the shortage and had stopped approving orders he sent in, Pierce would have no liability to Albert.

It is common to give agents who are compensated on a commission basis a monthly or weekly "draw" against commissions to be earned. This gives the agent money for living expenses. At some longer interval, such as quarterly or once a year, the agent is paid the amount by which the commissions exceed the draw. If it is not clear from the employment contract whether the agent must reimburse the principal if the draw exceeds the commissions, courts generally hold that overpayments cannot be recovered.

Procuring Cause

Generally, agents do not receive commissions on transactions that occur after termination of the agency relationship. However, when an agent was the primary factor in a purchase or sale, the **procuring cause** rule may entitle the procuring agent to her commission regardless of who eventually completes the sale. This rule is designed to permit agents to collect commissions on sales completed after termination of the agency relationship if the sale primarily resulted from the agent's efforts. Without the rule, the principal easily could escape paying the agent's commissions while enjoying the fruits of her labors.

CHRISTENSEN SALES AGENCY V. GENERAL TIME CORPORATION
1998 U.S. Dist. LEXIS 11796 (W.D. Mich. 1998)

FACTS

Spartus Corporation, a former manufacturer of clocks, entered into a sales representative agreement with Christensen Sales Agency. Under the terms of the agency agreement, Christensen was to earn sales commissions on clocks sold within its sales region. Either party could terminate the agreement without cause by giving seven days notice. In the event of termination by Spartus, the agreement further stated that Spartus would pay to Christensen sales commissions on clocks "solicited by . . . [Christensen] prior to the effective date of termination and accepted by Spartus prior to the effective date of the termination, provided that they are delivered by Spartus within thirty (30) days after the effective date of termination." On April 17, 1996, General Time Corporation bought the assets of Spartus. It immediately sent a letter to Christensen, reassuring the agent that there would be no changes to its status as a sales representative as to the Spartus merchandise. During ensuing discussions, there was no mention of post-termination commissions. However, General Time stated that Christensen would continue to receive commissions at the rate paid by Spartus. With these assurances in mind, Christensen launched a large annual sales effort of Spartus wall clocks to Meijer stores. This work included time calling General Time's representatives about pricing, samples, and displays of the merchandise. On May 31, 1996, General Time informed Christensen by letter that the company had decided to make changes in its sales territories and that Christensen was terminated as a sales representative.

After the termination, General Time continued to sell Spartus wall clocks to Meijer. Christensen claimed that its sales effort was the procuring cause of the post-termination sales of the Spartus merchandise to Meijer and demanded that it receive commission for all of the sales. General Time agreed that Christensen was the procuring cause but insisted that it was only responsible for commissions for products shipped within 30 days of May 31, 1996.

ISSUE

Is Christensen entitled to commission beyond the 30-day period after termination of the agency relationship?

DECISION

Yes. Agency law has long recognized the rights of agents to receive commissions for sales after their agency terminates where their promotion was the procuring cause of a later sale. This creates an implied-in-law contract that agents receive post-termination sales commissions in those instances where the agency contract is silent or undecided as to whether post-termination commissions will be paid. The question becomes, therefore, whether the parties to this oral agency contract demonstrated an intent that post-termination commissions not be paid. Christensen says that the oral contract is silent on this term because the parties' agreement to continue compensation under the Spartus agreement only referred to the commission rate and not post-termination

(continued)

CHRISTENSEN SALES AGENCY V. GENERAL TIME CORPORATION
(concluded)

commissions. General Time argues that the parties are bound by all the terms of the Spartus agreement. Whether the parties' oral agreement contains all terms of the Spartus agreement is a question of fact which depends in part on the parties' post-contract actions. In this instance, General Time has not acted as if bound by all terms of the Spartus agreement. The termination letter sent by General Time did not give seven days notice as required by the Spartus agreement. Also, assuming that

General Time meant to treat Christensen fairly, the fact that it encouraged and facilitated Christensen's Meijer promotion at a time when it was contemplating discontinuing the agency relationship argues against construing the parties' oral contract as containing a term limiting post-termination commissions. Thus, a jury could reasonably believe the parties did not intend to include the posttermination commission limitation in their oral agreement.

Duration of Employment

Sometimes an agent is expected to incur substantial expenses that are to be recouped through a commission on completion of the agency. When no duration is agreed on and the agent has made the expenditures, a court may hold that the principal cannot terminate the agency until after the agent has had a reasonable time to try to earn the expected commission. Suppose a developer gives Ralph, a real estate broker, an exclusive right to sell residential lots. It is customary for brokers to use extensive advertising and to establish an office in the subdivision. Ralph does this even though the agreement with the developer does not specify its duration. The developer cannot cancel the contract until Ralph has had a reasonable opportunity to recover his costs.

Real Estate Commissions

A real estate broker who represents a seller normally earns the commission when he finds a buyer "ready, willing, and able" to make the purchase on the offered terms. "Able," of course, means that the buyer has or can borrow the asking price for the property. If the seller has not given the broker specific terms of price, closing date, or other important items, then the commission is not earned until the contract of purchase has been made.

Insurance Commissions

In the life insurance business, it is customary for the company to pay the agent a commission on all premiums paid on the insurance contracts sold. This encourages the agent to provide continued service to policyholders and to recognize the fact that the value of the sale is greater than the first payment. In other lines of business, including casualty insurance, the agent is paid a commission on renewals by, or repeated transactions with, a customer first sold by the agent. Such agreements should clearly state whether the agent or the agent's representative is entitled to such payments after the agent's death or termination of employment.

DUTY TO REIMBURSE AND INDEMNIFY

Sometimes agents make advances from their own funds in conducting the principal's business. If the agent is acting within the scope of her authority, the principal has a duty to reimburse the agent for expenses incurred for the principal. Also, if the agent suffers losses while acting for the principal within the scope of the agent's authority, the principal has a duty to indemnify the agent.

For example, suppose Abby is a salesperson for Pruitt Company. She is in Cleveland when she is asked by Pruitt to go to a foreign trade show. She uses her own funds to pay workers to set up the company's booth at the show. In order to ship the exhibit back to Pruitt, she is required to pay a $500 export fee, again out of her own funds. Pruitt has a duty to reimburse her for her expenses and to indemnify her for the export fee.

However, if some fault of the agent causes a loss, the principal will not be required to indemnify the agent for the amount of the loss. And, of course, the principal is not liable for unauthorized expenses incurred by the agent.

DUTY TO KEEP ACCOUNTS

The principal has a duty to keep records from which the compensation due the agent can be determined. This duty is reinforced by tax laws that require such recordkeeping. For example, an employer must keep and make available to a salesperson a record of the sales on which commissions have been earned.

ENFORCEMENT OF LIABILITIES BETWEEN PRINCIPALS AND AGENTS

BREACH OF DUTY BY AGENT

When an agent's breach of duty causes harm to the principal, the principal may deduct the loss from the amount due the agent. If no compensation is due the agent, the principal can bring an action in court. If the breach of duty is serious enough, the principal may have no duty to compensate the agent even though the principal can show no actual damages. The agent may even be discharged without liability in spite of an unexpired contract.

BREACH OF DUTY BY PRINCIPAL

In most situations, an agent who is in lawful possession of property that belongs to the principal has a lien on it for the compensation due him for his performance of the agency responsibilities. For example, if a stockbroker has purchased a security for a client, he may hold the certificate until he is paid. Likewise, an attorney has a lien on the documents of the client while they are in the attorney's possession. Of course, the agent may also bring a lawsuit against the principal for any injuries suffered as a result of a breach of duty by the principal. (See Figure 20–1.)

TERMINATION OF AGENT'S POWERS

TERMINATION BY WILL OF PARTIES

A well-drafted agency agreement usually will discuss when or how the agency is to end. The relationship then will terminate at the time or on the happening of an event stated in the contract. For example, the agency may be for one year, or the principal and agent may agree that the agency is to last until the principal's new plant is complete and ready to operate. If no time or event is specified, then the agency automatically ends when the result for which the agency was created has been accomplished.

FIGURE 20-1   Agency Duties

Of course, both parties may mutually agree to modify their agency contract and accelerate or extend the termination date.

AGENCY AT WILL

Notwithstanding the agency agreement, either party generally may terminate the agency at any time, since the relationship is based on mutual consent. This gives each party the **power to terminate** even if there is no contractual right to do so. For example, suppose the agency agreement provides that the agency will continue for five years. Despite this language, either the agent or the principal can end it before then— say, in two years. This doctrine—known as **agency at will**—stems from the judicial reluctance to force people to continue personal relationships against their will. Of course, whenever one party exercises the *power to terminate* in violation of the *right to terminate,* the other party may recover monetary damages in a breach of contract suit.

There are several exceptions to the rule that one possesses the power to terminate the agency at any time. Two such instances will be discussed below: (1) agency coupled with an interest and (2) certain legislative restrictions.

Agency Coupled with an Interest

An **agency coupled with an interest** is one exception to the general rule that either party has the power to terminate an agency. It arises when the power is given as a security. Such an agency is irrevocable without the consent of the agent. A common example of this type of agency is where a creditor is authorized to sell property pledged as security for a loan. Suppose Paula borrows $1,000 from Adam. She gives Adam authority as her agent to sell her diamond ring to satisfy his claim if she does not pay the loan back as promised. Paula cannot revoke Adam's power to sell the ring. Even her death does not terminate the agency so long as the debt remains unpaid. (See Table 20–2.)

TABLE 20–2   Power versus Right to Terminate

Power	Right	Consequence
Yes	Yes	May terminate without penalty
Yes	No right if violation of contract	May terminate but liable for contract damages
No power if agency coupled with interest or violation of law	No right if there is no power	May *not* terminate

Legislative Restrictions

Termination of an agency based on race, color, sex, religion, national origin, and age generally are prohibited by state and federal legislation. Statutes also may prevent termination of an agent for engaging in labor union activities or reporting unsafe working conditions. These and other public policy exceptions will be developed more fully in Chapter 22.

INDUSTRIAL REPRESENTATIVES V. CP CLARE CORPORATION
74 F. 3d 128 (7th Cir. 1996)

FACTS

CP Clare, a manufacturer of electrical components, engaged Industrial Representatives, Inc. (IRI) in April 1991 to solicit orders for its products. By Fall 1994, CP Clare's sales in IRI's territory exceeded $6 million annually, a tenfold increase since IRI's engagement. CP Clare decided to take promotion in-house and sent IRI a letter terminating the agency at the end of October 1994. CP Clare gave IRI 42 days' notice (their agency agreement required only 30). The contract contained a further obligation: CP Clare had to pay IRI a commission for all products ordered before the termination date that were delivered in the next 90 days. CP Clare kept this promise. However, IRI believed it had not been paid enough for the work it did in boosting CP Clare's sales. IRI argued that the termination violated public policy because CP Clare was trying to take "opportunistic advantage" of the goodwill IRI's services created for CP Clare's products. In short, IRI felt that it had made a substantial investment in the product sales and that the anticipated future sales were now like an annuity that CP Clare wrongfully decided to capture.

ISSUE

Has CP Clare unlawfully terminated the agency relationship?

DECISION

No. No one, least of all IRI, could have thought that a contract permitting termination on 30 days' notice, with payment of commissions for deliveries within 90 days thereafter, entitled the agent to the entire future value of the goodwill built up by its work. The terms on which the parties would part ways were handled expressly in this contract, and IRI got what it bargained for. Contracts allocate risks and opportunities. If things turn out well, the party to whom the contract allocates the upper trail of outcomes is entitled to reap the benefits. This agreement provides explicitly for what has come to pass: termination with substantial outstanding business. IRI knew or should have recognized that the 90-day period created a risk, and it could have responded by demanding a higher commission rate to compensate.

CONCEPT SUMMARY	Events That Properly Terminate the Agency	
Operation of Law	Death or insanity of either party. Bankruptcy affecting the agency. Illegality or impossibility of agency objective. Destruction of subject matter of the agency. Material change in business conditions.	
Will of the Parties	Terms of the contract. Agency objective is accomplished. Mutual agreement of the parties.	

TERMINATION BY OPERATION OF LAW

The law terminates an agency if certain events occur. Among these are the death or insanity of either party and the bankruptcy of either party if it affects the agency. Where an agent's credit does not affect the agency (for example, a salesperson in a retail store), the agency is not terminated by bankruptcy. Further, banks generally continue to have the authority to act as a depositor's agent for check-cashing purposes for a limited period of time after the depositor/agent's death. (This exception will be discussed in greater detail in Chapter 39.)

Termination also occurs if the objective of the agency becomes impossible or illegal or if the subject matter of the agency is lost or destroyed. For example, a real estate broker may be hired as a rental agent for a house. If the house burns down, the agency ends.

A substantial change in market values or business conditions that affects the subject of the agency ends it if a reasonable agent would believe that termination is desired by the principal. For example, assume that a broker is authorized to sell a large block of stock in an aircraft manufacturer at a fixed price. If war breaks out and the president announces a large increase in aircraft purchases that would greatly benefit the manufacturer, the agency authority to sell at the original price would terminate.

NOTICE TO THIRD PERSONS

An agent still may be able to bind the principal on contracts with third persons after termination of the agency if the third person is unaware that the agency has ended. This is because an agency continues in existence as to a third person until that person has notice or knowledge of its termination.[4] To avoid being bound by acts of the agent after termination, the principal must give **actual notice** to those who have dealt with the former agent. A written notification generally is most desirable because it is easy to prove its existence. **Constructive notice** is sufficient for persons who may have been aware of the agency but have never formally dealt with it. A notice in a newspaper of general circulation in the area is normally sufficient for such persons. Suppose a husband has permitted his wife to charge things to his account at several stores. He then publishes an advertisement in the local newspaper: "After November 1, I shall no longer accept responsibility for the debts incurred by my wife." This would be effective against stores that had not yet charged him for goods bought by his wife, but he should send letters to stores where he has already paid such bills in order to avoid further liability. (See Table 20–3.)

---

[4]This notion—called *apparent authority*—will be developed more fully in Chapter 21.

TABLE 20-3   Notice of Agency Termination*

Third Person	Type of Notice	Example
Those who dealt with agent before termination	Actual	Direct personal communication (e.g., letter)
Those who knew of agency but had never dealt with it before termination	Constructive	Newspaper announcement
Those who never knew of existence of the agency	None	

Notification is not necessary when termination is due to principal's death, loss of capacity, or impossibility of performing agency objective.

JOHNSON V. NATIONWIDE INSURANCE COMPANY
1998 U.S. App. LEXIS 22392 (2d Cir. 1998)

FACTS

Shelly A. Johnson claimed that her brother-in-law, Michael P. Donnelly, a former employee of Nationwide, induced her to invest $70,000 in a Nationwide tax-free mutual fund. At the time she made the investment, Shelly was unaware that Michael was no longer an actual or implied agent of Nationwide. After she discovered that Michael had misappropriated the funds, Shelly sued Nationwide. She contended that Michael still had apparent authority to represent Nationwide because the company had failed to properly notify her of his termination.

ISSUE

Is Nationwide liable to Shelly for her investment?

DECISION

Yes. Apparent authority arises from conduct of the principal which, reasonably interpreted, causes a third person to believe that the principal consents to having the purported agent act on the principal's behalf. In order to defeat apparent authority, the principal must provide notice that it wishes to terminate the agent's authority. Where the third person has not previously dealt with the principal through the agent, but knows of the authority by reputation, the principal must give "publicity" through some method reasonably adapted to give the information to such third person. This could be by advertising the fact in a newspaper of general circulation in the place where the agency is regularly carried on. In the present action, Nationwide widely advertised Michael's agency and provided him with various indicia of authority which cloaked him with an aura of authority on which Shelly reasonably relied. Because Nationwide did not publicize its termination of Michael to his previous customers, much less to those members of the public who, like Shelly, would be justified in believing the agency still existed, it is liable to Shelly.

Several exceptions to the notice rules do exist. Notice is not necessary when the agency is terminated due to death of the principal, loss of legal capacity by the principal, or impossibility of performance.

.... **INTERNATIONAL AGENCY AGREEMENTS** ....

INTERNATIONAL
business

This chapter has examined the common law rules of agency that supplement any special rights or obligations that the principal and agent may include in an agency contract. In the United States, there are few restrictions on what terms may be included in such an agreement. That is not the case, however, in many countries throughout the world. Those nations reserve special protections for local agents irrespective of any contract entered into with the foreign principal.

Most of the world does not share the United States' notion of agency at will. Accordingly, it may be extremely difficult to terminate an overseas agent without good cause. And, even when such terminations are permitted, the principal may be required to give reasonable notice and offer some amount of severance pay.

.... *QUESTIONS AND PROBLEM CASES* ....

1. Distinguish between the right to terminate an agency and the power to do so. When does the principal not have the power to terminate the agency?

2. What are the limitations placed on an agent who is contemplating terminating the agency relationship in order to go into direct competition with the principal?

3. For approximately eight years, Van Matre was employed as an insurance agent for Prudential Insurance Company. During his employment, Van Matre sold several types of life insurance policies to various customers throughout the central Illinois area. He also serviced those policyholders as well as others assigned to him by Prudential. In the course of his employment, Van Matre was given access to information on each of the policyholders with whom he dealt. After terminating his employment with Prudential, Van Matre became an agent for Transamerica Insurance Company. He then succeeded in inducing several of his former customers to terminate their Prudential policies and to purchase instead policies issued by Transamerica. Prudential argued that Van Matre's postemployment use of information about policyholders obtained while he was employed by Prudential was a breach of his fiduciary duty to avoid using confidential information in competition with a former principal. Accordingly, it sued to enjoin his future interference with his former customers and for $100,000 in damages for the terminations he had already caused. Did Van Matre breach his fiduciary duty of loyalty?

4. *Video Case.* See "Martin Manufacturing." Mr. Martin, the president of Martin Manufacturing, fires a purchasing agent named Mitch. The reason is that Mitch has also been taking kickbacks from suppliers. Martin also withholds Mitch's last paycheck until Martin

can determine how much Mitch's misbehavior has cost him. Has Mitch breached any fiduciary duties to Martin? If so, identify which ones. Will Mitch be required to give Martin the amount of any kickbacks he has received? Can Martin fire Mitch under these circumstances without incurring liability? Finally, is Martin legally justified in withholding Mitch's paycheck?

5. Consumers Insurance Service was Lang's insurance agent on a 1986 Toyota that was insured with Interstate Bankers Mutual Casualty Company. Lang later purchased a 1988 Toyota from Nugent Toyota Dealership but, before he was allowed to remove it from the dealership, the dealer's credit manager called Consumers to verify that the new car would be insured. A Consumers' employee indicated that the 1988 Toyota was insured by Interstate. Based on these assurances, Lang took delivery of the new car, started driving it, and paid the insurance premiums when they became due. Several months later Lang wrecked the 1988 Toyota and filed an insurance claim. Interstate denied coverage on the grounds that it had never agreed to insure the car. Lang sued Interstate, alleging that the agency relationship between Interstate and Consumers bound the insurer to the assurances made by its agent. Interstate denied that an agency relationship existed. Should Lang's suit be dismissed because no agency relationship existed between Interstate and Consumers?

6. Willis was employed to find buyers for Haveg Industries' wire products. His agency contract permitted either party to terminate the agreement on 30 days' written notice. In the event of such a termination, the agreement entitled Willis to commissions only on orders accepted by Haveg up to and including the termination date. During his employment, Willis convinced Boeing Company to choose Haveg's

product as its general-purpose wire. However, before Boeing made any orders, Haveg terminated Willis's contract. Boeing's first major order did not occur until more than a year and a half after his termination and the company continued to make major purchases during the next five years. Willis argued that Haveg terminated him in bad faith in order to avoid paying his commissions on the Boeing orders. He sued Haveg to recover his commissions on all purchases made by Boeing during the five years following his termination. Is Willis entitled to the commissions as the procuring cause of the orders?

7. Ronald Chernow is in the business of auditing telephone bills for customers. He determines whether the customer's phone equipment is in place, properly billed, and in working order. He also checks for overcharges and receives half of any overcharge refund the customer receives from the telephone company. Chernow hired Angelo Reyes as an auditor. During his employment, Reyes, without Chernow's knowledge, took various steps to establish a business that competed with Chernow's. He obtained three auditing contracts and performed work under those agreements while still employed by Chernow. He also solicited a fourth account but did no work for that firm until after terminating his employment with Chernow. None of the businesses with whom Reyes contracted was one of Chernow's existing customers. Further, Reyes' personal soliciting and auditing activities did not take place during his regular working hours. He devoted that time exclusively to Chernow's business. Did Reyes breach the duty of loyalty he owed Chernow?

8. For two years, Bobby and Modell Warren took their cotton crops to certain cotton gins that ginned and baled the cotton. After being so instructed by the Warrens, the gins obtained bids for the cotton from prospective buyers and the Warrens told the gins which bids to accept. Then the gins sold the cotton to the designated buyers, collecting the proceeds. At the Warrens' instruction, the gins deferred payment of the proceeds to the Warrens until the year after the one is which each sale was made. The Warrens did not report the proceeds as taxable income for the year when the gins received the proceeds, instead including the proceeds in their return for the following year. After an IRS audit, the Warrens were compelled to treat the proceeds as taxable income for the year when the proceeds were received by the gins. This was because the IRS considered the gins to be the agents of the Warrens and, therefore, considered the money to be received by the Warrens when it was received by the gins. Is the IRS correct in treating the agreement between the Warrens and the gins to be an agency relationship?

9. In May, Ingersoll submitted his resignation from RTV, a media monitoring business. Although Ingersoll indicated that he wished to leave by the end of May, RTV persuaded him to stay until the end of August. Sometime during July, Ingersoll decided to launch his own business, called TransMedia, which would compete with RTV. One of RTV's major clients, the Department of Defense, put out a new bid solicitation in late July. During early August, while he was still with RTV, Ingersoll submitted a bid for the Department of Defense contract on behalf of TransMedia. After TransMedia won the contract, RTV learned that the company was operated by Ingersoll. RTV sued Ingersoll for breach of his fiduciary duties. Ingersoll defended on the grounds that if RTV had not persuaded him to stay beyond his announced resignation date, this conflict never would have arisen. Did Ingersoll breach his duty of loyalty to RTV?

10. *Video Case.* See "Martin Manufacturing." Immediately after being fired by Martin Manufacturing (see problem case 4 above), Mitch decided to squeeze one last bit of profit from his relationship with Martin. Thus, he calls a customer with whom he has dealt on many occasions, and orders several cases of fasteners on Martin's behalf. Later, he resells the fasteners himself, pocketing the money. Is Martin liable to the supplier for the fasteners? Later, he resells the fasteners himself, pocketing the money. Is Martin liable to the suppliers for the fasteners? In any event, what should Martin do to protect itself against cases like this?

CHAPTER 21

Liability of Principals and Agents to Third Parties

After suffering pain in his chest and left arm while lifting weights, Jack Gilbert visited the emergency room of Sycamore Municipal Hospital. Dr. Frank, the emergency room doctor, ran several tests and informed Gilbert there was no evidence of heart disease. Gilbert was prescribed pain medication and discharged that day. He died later that evening. An autopsy revealed signs of heart disease. The hospital contended it was not liable for the doctor's alleged malpractice because he was not the hospital's agent or employee. It argued that the emergency room staff were independent contractors, although emergency room patients were not advised of this fact. The court held that the hospital could be held vicariously liable for the doctor's alleged malpractice under a doctrine of apparent agency.[1]

- *What is meant by vicarious liability? When does it arise?*
- *What is an apparent agency and how does it arise?*
- *What is an independent contractor? How does it differ from an agent or employee?*

[1]Gilbert v. Sycamore Municipal Hospital, 622 N.E.2d 788 (Sup. Ct. Ill. 1993).

.... *INTRODUCTION* ....

This chapter will examine the various types of liability that principals and agents may owe to third persons who deal with the agency. It will begin with a discussion of the contract law issues that generally arise in agency situations. This will include an exploration of the authority that an agent must possess before she may bind her principal to a contract with a third person. Closely related to these authority issues are the principal's contractual liability for an agent's misrepresentations, the agent's knowledge, and the actions of subagents appointed by the agent, which will be discussed briefly. The focus then will shift to a discussion of the contractual liability that the agent may incur in carrying out his agency functions. The chapter will close with an examination of the tort and criminal liability that may be imposed on principals and agents for the actions of agents in carrying out their agency responsibilities.

THE AGENT'S AUTHORITY TO BIND THE PRINCIPAL ON CONTRACTS

A principal is bound on a contract entered into on his behalf by an agent if the agent had authority to act for the principal. Such authority may be either actual or apparent. Actual authority may be expressed or implied. Even if no actual authority has been given, the principal may be held liable because he either appeared to give authority to the agent (apparent authority) or ratified the act of the agent (or one posing as an agent).

Thus, a clear understanding of the contractual liability of a principal to a third person for a contract created by an agent requires an examination of the following concepts:

1. Actual authority
   a. Express authority
   b. Implied authority
2. Apparent authority
3. Ratification

However, before considering these specific agency concepts, read the following case. It may prove useful for several reasons. First, it provides a special application of the concept of authorization within the Internet context. Second, it touches on the issue of an agent's duty of loyalty that was discussed in the previous chapter. Finally, it offers a general guidance on the outer parameters of the notion of authorization.

SHURGARD STORAGE CENTERS V. SAFEGUARD SELF-STORAGE
119F.Supp.2d 1121 (W.D. Wash. 2000)

FACTS

Shurgard Storage Centers is the industry leader in full and self-service storage facilities in both the United States and Europe. Its growth in the last 25 years is primarily due to the development and construction of top-quality storage centers in "high barrier to entry" markets. Pursuant to this strategy, Shurgard has developed a sophisticated system of creating market plans, identifying appropriate development sites, and evaluating whether a site will provide a high return on an investment. It invests significant resources in creating a marketing team to carry out these tasks for each potential market. These teams become familiar with the market,

(continued)

SHURGARD STORAGE CENTERS V. SAFEGUARD SELF-STORAGE
(concluded)

identify potential acquisition sites, and develop relationships with brokers and sellers in the market so that Shurgard has the best opportunity to acquire a preferred site. Safeguard Self-Storage is a direct competitor of Shurgard. In late 1999, Safeguard approached Eric Leland, Shurgard's regional development manager and offered him employment. Because of his position with Shurgard, Leland had full access to Shurgard's confidential business plans, expansion plans, and other trade secrets. While still employed by Shurgard but acting as an agent for Safeguard, Leland sent e-mails to Safeguard containing various trade secrets belonging to Shurgard. Leland did this without Shurgard's knowledge or approval. After learning of Leland's activities, Shurgard sued Safeguard for civil damages under the Computer Fraud and Abuse Act (CFAA). That statute specifically permits the recovery of compensatory damages from anyone who "intentionally accesses a computer without authorization or exceeds authorized access and thereby obtains . . . information from any protected computer." The CFAA defines the term "exceeds authorized access" to include accessing "a computer with or without authorization and to use such access to obtain or alter information in the computer that the accesser is not entitled to obtain or alter."

Safeguard argued that the statute was not violated because Leland's behavior was neither with nor without authorization and nor in excess of his authorized access.

ISSUE

Were Leland's activities without authorizations or in excess of his authorized access?

DECISION

Yes. Safeguard's challenge to Shurgard's claim under the CFAA is based on the belief that Leland had authorized access to the information in question. Specifically, Safeguard claimed that Leland had full access to all the information transferred to Safeguard. However, this argument ignores general agency law, which holds that "unless otherwise agreed, the authority of an agent terminates if, without knowledge of the principal, he acquires adverse interests or if he is otherwise guilty of a serious breach of loyalty to the principal." Under this rule, the authority Shurgard had granted Leland ended the instant he secretly became an agent for Safeguard. Therefore, for the purposes of this lawsuit under the CFAA, Leland lost his authorization and was "without authorization" when he obtained and sent trade secrets to Safeguard via e-mail.

ACTUAL AUTHORITY

Actual authority is the true authority granted to the agent by the principal. It is proper authority in the sense that an agent acting within her actual authority is not in violation of her agency duty to the principal. Actual authority may be either express or implied.

Express Authority

Authority is **express** when the principal specifically describes the extent of the agent's powers. Generally, this may be done orally, although some states have statutes that require the authority of an agent who is to buy or sell land to be in writing. An **attorney-in-fact** is the technical label given to an agent whose authority is in writing. Suppose that Paul plans to be in Europe for the summer and wishes to sell his car. He may appoint Anne as his attorney-in-fact to sign the necessary papers on his behalf. Anne is said to possess his **power of attorney.** The test of an agent's express authority is *the specific language the principal used in granting the authority*.

Implied Authority

Often express authority is incomplete and does not cover every contingency because the principal can seldom foresee every circumstance in which the agent may need to act. Therefore, an agent also possesses the **implied authority** to do whatever else is reasonably necessary to accomplish the objectives of the agency. This may include what is customary for agents to do in the particular business of the principal or in similar transactions in the community. However, implied authority is limited by any specific prohibitions or other indications of the principal's wishes.

The test used by a court in determining the extent of the agent's implied authority is the *justifiable belief of the agent*. Suppose that Herb is left in charge of Joe's store while Joe is out of town on business. Joe's instructions to Herb said nothing about the arrival of merchandise. Herb would have implied authority to sign a delivery receipt for any arriving goods if he could reasonably believe that they had in fact been ordered.

Agents also have implied power to act in emergencies (sometimes called *inherent agency power*). If a tornado breaks the windows and tears off part of the roof of the store, Herb has implied authority to make necessary repairs if he cannot reach Joe for further instructions. This is true even if Joe told Herb not to make purchases of any kind. Each of these exercises of implied authority would be binding on Joe as if he had personally performed the acts himself.

The terms *general agent* and *special agent* frequently arise in discussions of implied authority. A general agent is a person who acts for the principal in a number of transactions over a period of time. A special agent, on the other hand, is authorized by the principal to do a specific act or to handle one or a few of certain types of business transactions. Her authority to act is limited to that single transaction. Thus, one might expect general agents to have a broader range of implied authority than special agents.

APPARENT AUTHORITY

Apparent authority is created by the conduct of the principal that causes a third person reasonably to believe that another has the authority to act for the principal. It may exist if a principal has intentionally or by want of ordinary care induced and permitted third persons to believe a person is her agent even though no actual authority has been conferred on the agent. The source of apparent authority is the principal, just as it is for express and implied authority. Words or acts of an agent alone cannot create apparent authority.

The test used for determining the extent of an agent's apparent authority is the *justifiable belief of a third party* dealing with the agent. Remember, if the agent justifiably believed she had authority, her authority would be *implied, not apparent*. This distinction can be very important because an agent's exercise of apparent authority, in the absence of actual authority, is in violation of the agent's duty to the principal. Thus, a principal who is bound to a contract with a third person based on an agent's apparent authority may sue the agent for damages.

Apparent authority may arise from customs in the trade. Thus, when a principal wishes to impose limitations on an agent's authority that are not customary, it is important that such restrictions be communicated to third persons in order to avoid apparent authority. Former agents also may possess apparent authority if the principal does not notify third persons of the termination of the agency relationship. (Termination and notice were discussed in Chapter 20.)

Apparent Agent

A person may have apparent authority although he never has been appointed an agent by the principal. The apparent authority arises from the principal's failure to inform third persons that the relationship is not what it appears to be. Consider the medical malpractice case that opened this chapter. The hospital considered its emergency room doctors to be independent contractors rather than agents or employees. However, it failed to advise emergency room patients of this arrangement. Although the doctrine of apparent authority normally is applied in contract cases, the court found in this tort suit that the patient's reasonable belief made the doctor an **apparent agent** of the hospital. Specifically, the court held that the hospital and its doctors behaved in a manner that would lead a reasonable person to believe an agency existed.

Duty of Third Persons to Determine Agent's Authority

Generally, people who deal with an agent or a purported agent have a duty to determine the extent, if any, of the agent's authority. The fact that an agent may have some implied or apparent authority does not end the inquiry. The specific question is whether the agent or purported agent had implied or had apparent authority to make the particular agreement.

STANDARD FUNDING CORP. V. LEWITT
678 N.E.2d 874 (N.Y. Ct. App. 1997)

FACTS

Standard Funding Corporation, an insurance premium financing company, entered into a series of financing agreements with Jeffrey Lewitt to finance the premiums on insurance policies of Public Service Mutual Company. Standard Funding had provided Lewitt with its financing agreement forms which Lewitt and the prospective insureds were to complete and sign. Before entering into the first financing agreement with Lewitt, Standard Funding contacted Public Service Mutual whose personnel confirmed that Lewitt was an agent in good standing with the company, licensed to sell all lines of business. Pursuant to the financing agreements, Standard Funding would finance the bulk of an insured's initial insurance policy premium in exchange for a security interest in all unearned premiums. The insured would agree to repay Standard Funding on an installment schedule; if the insured defaulted, the financing agreement gave Standard Funding the authority to cancel the insurance policy and assert a right to all unearned premiums due under the policy. After Lewitt tendered two executed financing agreements to Standard Funding indicating that Public Service Mutual had issued policies to the insureds, Standard Funding issued two checks to Lewitt totaling $23,325. Standard Funding then sent Public Service Mutual notice of financing forms containing copies of the checks issued to Lewitt. Later, Lewitt completed two additional financing agreements for the financing of Public Service Mutual premiums and received two checks from Standard Funding in the total amount of $204,000. Again Standard Funding sent notice of financing forms with copies of the checks to Public Service Mutual. The insurer did not respond to any of the notices. After Standard Funding failed to receive payments from the alleged insureds, it contacted Public Service Mutual who investigated the matter and discovered that the four financing agreements covered fictitious policies and false insureds. No policies were ever issued in connection with those agreements and Public Service Mutual received no premiums for them. Public Service Mutual thereafter terminated Lewitt's agency contract. Standard Funding sued Public Service Mutual on the theory that the insurer was liable for the fraudulent acts of Lewitt acting as its agent. Public Service Mutual argued that Lewitt did not have the authority to enter into the premium financing agreements on its behalf.

ISSUE

Did Lewitt have authority to bind Public Service Mutual to the premium financing agreements with Standard Funding?

(continued)

STANDARD FUNDING CORP. V. LEWITT
(concluded)

DECISION

No. There is no basis to conclude that the agency contract between Lewitt and Public Service Mutual endowed Lewitt with actual authority to procure on behalf of Public Service Mutual the financing of premiums for proposed insureds. The agency agreement granted Lewitt authority to "solicit and accept proposals for insurance covering such risks as the Company may authorize to be insured in the agent's territory." He also was endowed with "full power and authority to receive, collect and receipt for premiums on insurance tendered by the agent to and accepted by the company." Thus, Lewitt was expressly authorized only to issue policies and to receive and collect premiums. Nothing in the agency agreement authorized him to negotiate or enter into premium financing agreements on behalf of Public Service Mutual. Lewitt had no implied authority because we reject Standard Funding's contention that premium financing is an activity incidental to or reasonably necessary for the performance of Lewitt's express powers. Nor do we find any support for a determination that Lewitt had apparent authority to enter into or procure financing agreements on behalf of the insurer.

Essential to the creation of apparent authority are *words or conduct of the principal*, communicated to a third party, that give rise to the appearance and belief that the *agent* possesses authority to enter into a transaction. Public Service Mutual made no representations regarding Lewitt's authority to procure on its behalf premium financing for its proposed insureds. Rather, the insurer's representations were limited to Lewitt's power to write insurance policies and accept premiums for them. Moreover, all representations in the premium financing agreements were purely those of the *agent*. Correspondingly, the checks issued by Standard Funding pursuant to the financing agreements were payable solely to Lewitt. Finally, Standard Funding's reliance on the fact that Public Service Mutual received notices of financing as a basis for imposing liability on the insurer also is without merit. The notices of financing stated that payment from Standard Funding was "subject to your acceptance of the terms and conditions of the premium financing agreement." Public Service Mutual never signified any acceptance of the terms and conditions of the financing agreements, as the notices required.

RATIFICATION

Nature of Ratification

One may become liable through **ratification** for an unauthorized act that was done by an agent. Ratification may be either an act of an agent who has exceeded the authority given or an act by someone who has not been appointed an agent at all. For example, suppose Alex is a buyer for Polly's furniture store, Scandinavian Imports. While in Norway, Alex finds a classic MG sports car for sale. Although his authority is limited to buying furniture, he contracts to buy it as agent for Polly, who is a collector of antique cars. She, not Alex, is liable on the contract if she ratifies it by instructing the seller to ship the car.

Any act that the principal could have authorized at the time the act was done may be ratified. Generally, the effect of ratification is the same as if the act had been authorized in the first place.

Ratification is basically a question of the **intent** of the principal. However, the principal need not express that intent; it may be implied by his acts or failure to act. Often

CONCEPT SUMMARY Agency Authority			

Category		Definition	Test	Contractual Liability*
Actual	**Express**	Special authority (oral or written)	The explicit agency agreement between the principal and the agent	Principal is liable to the third party.
	Implied	Supplemental authority reasonably necessary to accomplish the agency objectives	The justifiable belief of the agent	Principal is liable to the third party.
Apparent		Appearance of authority in the agent created by the principal	The justifiable belief of the third party dealing with the agent	Principal is liable to the third party; but the agent is liable to the principal.

*Liability is based on a fully disclosed agency. Fully disclosed, partially disclosed, and undisclosed agencies are discussed later in this chapter.

ratification is inferred by a court from the fact that the principal accepted the benefits of an unauthorized contract. It may also be inferred from the principal's failure to repudiate an unauthorized contract after becoming aware of it.

Requirements for Ratification

For ratification to be effective, the agent or purported agent must have *acted on behalf of the principal.* (This requires that the principal has been disclosed to the third person.) The principal must have had **capacity** to do the act both at the time it was done in the principal's name by the agent and when ratification occurs. Thus, there can be no ratification of an act done in the name of a corporation that was not in existence when the act was done. Only the **entire act** of the agent can be ratified; the principal may not ratify what is beneficial and deny what is burdensome. Ratification of a contract must be done before cancellation by the third person. Before ratification, the third person may usually withdraw from an unauthorized transaction. A requirement that frequently causes disputes is that the principal must have had *knowledge of all material facts* at the time of ratification. It is not necessary, however, that the principal fully understand the legal significance of those facts.

Effect of Ratification

Ratification releases the agent from liability to both the principal and the third person for having exceeded his or her authority. It also gives the agent the same right to compensation that he or she would have had if there had been prior authorization. Simultaneously the principal is entitled to the full benefit of the contract. Likewise, the principal is bound in the same manner and to the same extent as if the agent had been fully authorized from the beginning. (See Table 21–1.)

TABLE 21-1   Ratification

When Necessary	Requirements	When Occurs	Effect

1. Agent exceeds authority
 	
2. Nonagent acts as an agent
	1. Agent or nonagent acts on behalf of principal
	2. Principal had capacity to do act:
	  a. At time it was done, *and*
	  b. At time of ratification
	3. Must ratify the entire act
	4. Must ratify before third party cancels
	5. Principal must have knowledge of all material facts
		Principal demonstrates intent to ratify:
		1. Express
		2. Implied:
		  a. Acceptance of benefits of act
		  b. Failure to repudiate after discovering act
			Same as if the act was originally authorized:
			1. Agent or nonagent released from liability
			2. Principal is bound to the contract with the third party:
			  a. Gains full benefits
			  b. Assumes all liabilities

HUPPMAN V. TIGHE
642 A.2d 309 (Md. Ct. App. 1994)

FACTS

Harry Tighe opened an investment account with an investment firm, Legg Mason Wood Walker, Inc. Tighe's authorization was required for all investments on his account. One month after opening the account, Tighe discovered that L. Reed Huppman, his Legg Mason broker, had made an unauthorized purchase of units in a limited partnership for more than $220,000. When Huppman came to Tighe's home to explain the situation, he convinced Tighe that he should hold onto the limited partnership units because they were not readily marketable. In reality, they probably were marketable. Despite this unauthorized purchase, Tighe did not close out his Legg Mason account and continued to buy securities through Huppman for over two years. During this time, he received over $52,000 in distributions from the limited partnership units, which were deposited in his Legg Mason account. Tighe finally complained to a Legg Mason compliance officer about the deal and, ultimately, he sued the investment firm for damages. Legg Mason argued that it was not liable because, by his subsequent behavior, Tighe ratified the unauthorized purchase.

ISSUE

Did Tighe ratify the unauthorized purchase by his agent?

DECISION

No. A principal will be bound by the unauthorized acts of his agent if the transaction is ratified. Such ratification occurs if a principal, with knowledge of the material facts surrounding the agent's unauthorized act, receives and retains the benefits of the act. In this case, there is sufficient evidence that Tighe was not made aware of the material facts of the unauthorized transaction. Huppman intentionally misled Tighe into believing he could not get his money returned immediately because there was no market into which to sell the limited partnership units. Thus, Tighe believed he had no choice but to hold onto the investment until Legg Mason and Huppman could sell it. Thus, Tighe did not have all of the material facts undergirding the unauthorized transaction and thus could not have ratified the purchase.

RELATED CONTRACTUAL LIABILITY ISSUES

PRINCIPAL'S LIABILITY FOR THE AGENT'S REPRESENTATIONS

The principal is bound by representations that the agent is expressly authorized to make. Likewise, the principal also is liable for representations that are reasonably necessary for the agent to make in order to accomplish the purpose of the agency since they would be impliedly authorized. Finally, the principal is bound on representations that are customary in the kind of business being transacted by the agent. The agent has apparent authority to make such statements. If the representation is a usual one, the principal is bound even though she has told the agent not to make such a statement. This is not true, of course, if the third person knows that the agent has exceeded his actual authority. So if the principal wishes to avoid such potential liability, she must be certain to inform third persons of any restrictions on the agent's actual authority. (Remember, of course, that the agent will be required to indemnify the principal for any losses the principal suffers as a result of the agent exceeding her actual authority.)

A person who is induced to enter a contract by the misrepresentation of an agent has the same remedies as if he had contracted with any person who made a misrepresentation. As was discussed in Chapter 11, the remedy of rescission is available when a misrepresentation occurs. If the misrepresentation is considered to be a warranty or guaranty, the principal is liable for damages when the product or service is not as represented. Misrepresentations by an agent made with the intent to deceive will also make the agent liable to the third person. (Of course, the third person is entitled to only a single recovery.)

Exculpatory Clauses

To give notice of lack of authority in the agent, sellers often use an **exculpatory clause** in the printed offer forms they furnish their salespeople. The form has a provision that says, in effect, "It is understood and agreed that salespersons have no authority to make any representation other than those printed herein and that none has been made in connection with this sale." However, many courts permit a third person to rescind a contract when the person has relied on a misrepresentation by the agent even though the contract contains an exculpatory clause.

The use of printed offer forms is itself a device sellers use to control the contracts their sales agents make. This is done by arranging the transaction so that the salesperson merely solicits an order that is, by its terms, "subject to approval of the home office." There is no contract then until the seller has received the written offer and decided to accept it. The printed form makes it clear that the salesperson is only taking an order (offer). It also usually contains an exculpatory clause limiting the salesperson's authority.

PRINCIPAL'S LIABILITY FOR NOTICE AND PAYMENTS TO THE AGENT

Effect of Notice

Generally, notice to the agent is notice to the principal if it relates to the business of the agency. This is because the agent has a duty to inform the principal of knowledge the agent gains in the course of his or her responsibilities. However, if the information does not relate to the scope of the agent's responsibilities and authority, the principal is bound only by the information that is actually passed on by the agent. For example, Gomez has a standing order to purchase fresh fish for his restaurant from Lee, a fish supplier. Gomez tells a janitor at Lee's office that he is revoking the order. This notice is not binding on Lee if the janitor fails to pass the message on.

Payments to the Agent

Payment to the agent of a debt owed to the principal discharges the debt if the agent has authority to receive such payments. This is true even if the agent steals the money. An agent who makes over-the-counter sales is viewed as having apparent authority to collect for the goods. The same is true of a selling agent who is given possession of the goods for delivery. However, these agents do not usually have apparent authority to collect on account for goods sold at an earlier time. Other salespersons generally have no authority to collect unless it is expressly or impliedly given to them. An agent who has negotiated a loan or sold property and has been permitted by the principal to keep the negotiable instrument payable to the principal has apparent authority to receive payment on that instrument.

Effect of Conflicts of Interest

Sometimes an agent does not tell the principal things learned while acting within the scope of the agency because it is to the agent's advantage not to do so. Likewise, the agent may withhold payments received on behalf of the agency. When this is the case, the principal will not be bound if the agent colludes with the third person to withhold knowledge or money from the principal or if the third person should otherwise be aware that the agent is likely to withhold such information or money.

FEDERAL KEMPER INSURANCE COMPANY v. BROWN
674 N.E.2d 1030 (Ind. Ct. App. 1997)

FACTS

Carl Brown spoke to an insurance agent about obtaining automobile liability insurance for a Chevrolet Cavalier for which his stepson, who lived with Brown, would be the primary driver. Brown needed to obtain a new insurance policy for the car because the insurance company that had insured the stepson planned to cancel the stepson's insurance due to his poor driving record. (His license had been suspended on more than one occasion.) Brown informed the insurance agent that the stepson had accumulated more than one speeding ticket in the previous five years. The agent told Brown that the insurance on the stepson alone would cost more than $1,000 per year. However, in order to save Brown money, the agent filled out an application for insurance which misrepresented that Brown's wife was the only other person in Brown's household over the age of 12 and that no operator of the Cavalier had any moving violations or

had had his or her license suspended within the previous five years. The policy contained a provision in which the applicant certified that all statements in the application were true and correct. Brown signed the application without reading it. Kemper Insurance issued Brown an automobile liability policy for the Cavalier based on the false application. It is not disputed that the insurer would not have issued the policy had it known that the stepson was the primary driver of the car. Later, the stepson was involved in an automobile accident that resulted in a fatality. Kemper denied coverage under Brown's automobile liability policy based upon the fraudulent application and sought to rescind the policy. Brown insists that, because he had disclosed all material information to the insurance agent, he cannot be charged with the agent's fraud in obtaining insurance from Kemper and the policy cannot be rescinded.

(continued)

FEDERAL KEMPER INSURANCE COMPANY V. BROWN
(concluded)

ISSUE

Should the knowledge of the agent be imputed to Kemper?

DECISION

No. Generally, the law imputes an agent's knowledge, acquired while the agent was acting within the scope of his agency, to the principal, even if the principal does not actually know what the agent knows. When an agent authorized to solicit and take applications for insurance fraudulently inserts false answers without the knowledge of the applicant, the insurance company must suffer the loss, not the insured, who is without fault. Knowledge will not be imputed to the principal in cases where the agent colludes with the person who claims the benefit of the principal's knowledge in a fraudulent scheme to defraud the principal. Brown knew that obtaining automobile insurance for his stepson would be difficult and/or expensive. Nevertheless, the agent obtained insurance for Brown from Kemper at a lower premium by misrepresenting on the application. Most importantly, Brown signed the application that omitted his stepson as the primary driver, knowing that his stepson was, in fact, the primary driver. As Brown is chargeable with the misrepresentation of facts material to the risk, Kemper may rescind the policy and avoid liability with respect to Brown and his stepson.

PRINCIPAL'S LIABILITY FOR ACTS OF SUBAGENTS

AGENT'S AUTHORITY TO APPOINT SUBAGENTS

A **subagent** is an agent of the agent. When a corporation is made an agent, of necessity the principal is served by subagents. Such authority is implied. (This is because a corporation can act only through agents.) Other agents may be given express authority to hire subagents to do some or all of the work of the agent. Such authority may also be either implied or apparent. If the agent is found to have such authority, both the principal and the agent are bound to a third party by acts of the subagent. Between the agent and the principal, however, it is the agent who is ultimately liable for the acts of the subagent. (It is possible for the agent to limit this liability to the principal through the use of an exculpatory clause.)

Some agents are given authority to employ agents for the principal rather than subagents. For example, a sales manager for a corporation would probably have authority to hire sales agents for the corporation. Such agents are not subagents; they are agents of the corporation. The sales manager would not be bound by their acts unless their failings were due, in part, to his negligence in their selection or supervision.

AGENTS MAY HAVE EMPLOYEES

Agents may delegate to employees acts for the principal that involve no judgment or discretion. These are called **ministerial acts**. The principal is normally not bound by acts of employees of agents unless these employees are also subagents whose appointment by the agent has been authorized. This is a fairly confusing area of the law. But basically the principal will be liable for the acts of an agent's employees only if he would have been liable if the agent had performed the act herself.

.... *CONTRACT LIABILITY OF THE AGENT* ....

INTRODUCTION

Generally, the agent is representing the principal when making contracts and all three parties (the agent, the principal, and the third party) intend that the agreement bind only the principal and the third party. As a result, the agent usually will not be liable on the agreement. There are, however, some special situations in which the agent may become personally liable on the contract with the third person. These basic circumstances arise when there are:

1. Unauthorized actions by the agent.
2. Nonexistent or incompetent principals.
3. Agreements by the agent to assume liability.
4. An undisclosed principal.
5. A partially disclosed principal.

UNAUTHORIZED ACTIONS

A person who represents that he or she is making a contract on behalf of a principal but who has no authority to do so does not bind the principal. Therefore, the agent is liable to the third person for damages suffered if the principal refuses to perform the contract. The same is true whenever agents exceed their authority—express, implied, or apparent.

Liability is imposed on an agent who has exceeded his authority on the basis of an **implied warranty of authority.** The agent is treated as if he had guaranteed to the third party that he had authority to make the contract. Suppose that you are employed as a sales agent for Acme Machine Tool Company and guarantee that a machine that you sell to a customer will eliminate the need for three employees. If you have no express authority from Acme to make such a guaranty (and such a guaranty is not common in the machine tool industry), then you, not Acme, will be liable to the customer if the machine fails to replace the employees.

The intent, knowledge, and good faith of the agent are immaterial in deciding whether the implied warranty of authority applies. If the agent exceeds his or her authority, liability results—unless the principal ratifies the act. Knowledge on the part of the third person that the agent is not authorized to make the guaranty also relieves the agent of liability. (See Figure 21–1.)

NONEXISTENT OR INCOMPETENT PRINCIPAL

A person who acts as an agent for a principal that is not in existence at the time of the act is personally liable on the contract. Therefore, if an agent acts for a corporation that is not yet formed or for an entity that has no legal existence, such as an unincorporated association, the agent is liable.

Assume that a community jogging club makes arrangements to hold a marathon run. One of its members makes contracts for renting certain equipment for the group. If the club is not incorporated, he is an agent for a nonexistent principal. If the contracts are not performed by the club, he will be personally liable on them.

The same is true if the principal has been judged insane or is a minor. The law imposes an implied warranty by the agent that the principal has the capacity to be bound. However, if the third person is aware of the lack of capacity of the principal, the agent is protected.

FIGURE 21-1   Implied Warranty of Authority

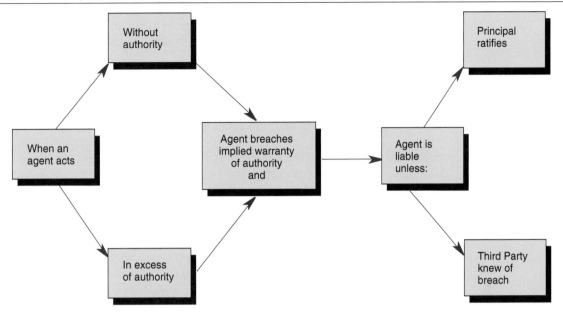

AGREEMENTS BY THE AGENT TO ASSUME LIABILITY

Of course, an agent may make a contract in her own name while being employed as an agent. An agent may also become a party to a contract along with the principal, thus assuming joint liability. Or an agent may guarantee a contract made for the principal, in which case the agent becomes liable as a surety—that is, liable if the principal defaults.

To avoid liability because of confusion as to whether or not an agent is acting for herself or for the principal, the agent should sign all documents carefully. If she intends to act for a principal, the agent should:

1.   Fully disclose the identity of the principal.
2.   Clearly indicate her capacity as an agent.

DISCLOSED PRINCIPAL

Usually, a person who is dealing with an agent is aware of the fact and knows for whom the agent is acting. If a salesperson comes to your door and announces that "Avon is calling," you know that the person is an agent for a principal—Avon Products. In such a case, Avon Products is a **disclosed principal.**

Rights and Liabilities of Agent

When the principal is disclosed, all parties intend the contract to be between the principal and the third party. In ordering from the Avon agent, both you and the agent intend that you contract with Avon, not the agent. Therefore, the agent is not a party to the contract. If the agent has acted within his or her authority, the agent has no liability on the contract.

Generally, agents for disclosed principals cannot bring suit on contracts they make for principals. There are a few exceptions, however. For example, only the agent can bring an action on a negotiable instrument payable to her unless it is endorsed to the principal. Also, by custom an auctioneer is permitted to sue a buyer for breach of contract.

Rights and Liabilities of Principal

Since the principal rather than the agent is the intended party to the contract, the principal may enforce it. Likewise, the principal rather than the agent is liable on the contract. Suppose that goods you have ordered from the Avon agent are shipped and you fail to pay. Avon, not the agent, will be able to recover from you. If Avon fails to deliver, you may recover from Avon, not the agent.

UNDISCLOSED PRINCIPAL

Sometimes principals do not want their identities known to those who deal with their agents. A common example is when a large and well-known corporation wants to acquire a plot of ground, perhaps for a new plant. If it were known that General Motors Corporation wanted to buy 160 acres on the edge of a city, owners of suitable land would probably expect a higher price than if some local individual or small company were interested. If plots owned by several different people are desired, GM would be even more likely to have to pay more than its normal value for the last plot. The owner would think GM would be willing to pay a high price to complete the purchases. To avoid the extra cost, GM is likely to purchase through several agents, each purporting to be buying personally. In such cases, GM is an **undisclosed principal.**

Rights and Liabilities of Agent

When the principal is undisclosed, the third party who deals with the agent believes the agent is acting personally and accordingly expects the agent to be a party to the contract. Therefore, the agent is held liable on contracts entered into on behalf of an undisclosed principal. The agent is also permitted to sue on such a contract as a party to it. Of course, whenever an agent is found liable on a debt that he or she rightfully incurred on behalf of an undisclosed principal, the agent may in turn recover from the principal. This right of indemnification protects the agent in all instances except when the principal is unable to reimburse the agent due to insolvency.

Rights and Liabilities of Principal

Since the contract was made for his benefit, an undisclosed principal is permitted to enforce it. Further, if the third person learns of the principal's identity, she may elect to sue the principal instead of the agent. The third person cannot, of course, recover damages from both the principal and the agent. (If the third person elects to recover from the agent, the principal is then required to indemnify the agent.)

Ethical Implications

One reason a principal remains undisclosed is because the third party might demand a larger payment for the goods or services if she knew she was dealing with the principal. Yet contract law principles suggest that a party has a duty to disclose all material facts to his contracting partner. Is it ethical to contract through an undisclosed agency when it is clear that the third party would behave differently if she knew of this fact?

PARTIALLY DISCLOSED PRINCIPAL

A principal is **partially disclosed** when the third person knows he is dealing with an agent but does not know the identity of the principal. This is likely to occur when an agent signs a contract or negotiable instrument, indicating her status as an agent, but forgetting to identify her principal.

The rights and duties of the parties when the principal is partially disclosed basically are the same as when the principal is undisclosed. If the principal is unknown, the third person must rely on the credit and trustworthiness of the agent. Therefore, the agent is held liable on the contract. (See Figure 21–2.)

FIGURE 21–2   Disclosed, Undisclosed, and Partially Disclosed Agency*

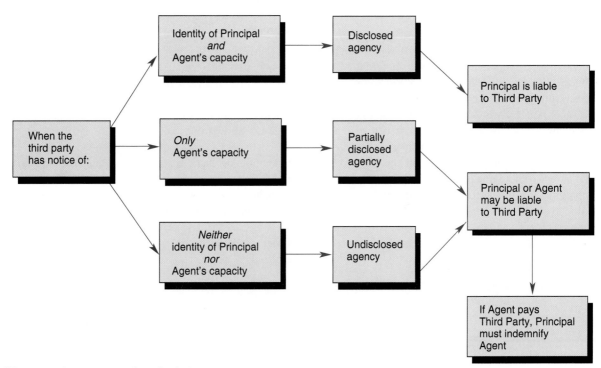

This assumes the agent possessed actual authority.

CONCEPT SUMMARY	Contractual Liability of Principals and Agents	
Circumstance	**Principal's Liability**	**Agent's Liability**
Nonexistent or incompetent principal	Cannot be liable since lacks capacity or does not exist	Liable to third party
Unauthorized action	Not liable to third party unless act is ratified	Liable to third party unless act is ratified
Actual authority	Liable to third party	Not liable to third party unless undisclosed or partially disclosed agency (principal would then have to indemnify agent)
Apparent authority	Liable to third party	Not liable to third party but liable to principal for exceeding actual authority
Undisclosed or partially disclosed (actual authority)	May be liable if third party discovers identity (otherwise must indemnify agent)	May be liable if third party does not pursue principal (may then recover from principal)
Agent agrees to shared liability	Jointly liable with agent to third party (must indemnify agent in surety situations)	Jointly liable with principal to third party (may be indemnified by principal in surety situations)

AFRICAN BIO-BOTONICA V. LEINER
624 A.2d 1003 (N.J. Sup. Ct. 1993)

FACTS

Sally Leiner was the sole shareholder, director, and president of a corporation, Ecco Bella, Inc. When Leiner bought merchandise from African Bio-Botonica, she paid with checks which bore the name Ecco Bella. Likewise, in her contacts with African, she used Ecco Bella stationery. However, she never indicated that the firm was a corporation. Initially, African's records listed Leiner as its customer, although this was later changed to Ecco Bella, but without any indication that Ecco Bella was a corporation. When Ecco Bella did not pay for shipment, African sued Leiner personally. Leiner's defense was that she was merely an agent and, therefore, only her principal, Ecco Bella, was liable on the account.

ISSUE

Is Leiner personally liable for the shipment from African?

DECISION

Yes. Unless the parties agree otherwise, an agent who enters into a contract for an undisclosed or a partially disclosed principal is personally liable on the contract. An authorized agent who contracts on behalf of a disclosed principal generally is not personally liable on the contract. African was not informed and did not know that Ecco Bella was a corporation. The agent who seeks protection from his status as an agent has the means and the motive to communicate that status to the person with whom he is dealing. If the person with whom the agent is dealing does not know of the agency and has no reasonable way to know except by asking, the agent has the burden of disclosing his agency and the identity of his principal in order to avoid liability on contracts he makes. Because Leiner was acting as an agent for an undisclosed or partially disclosed principal, she was therefore personally liable on the purchase contracts with African.

.... ***LIABILITY FOR TORTS*** ....

INTRODUCTION

Principals frequently will be liable for the torts committed by their agents. Unfortunately, where and when such liability arises is not always clear. However, there are some legal concepts that guide us in determining if tort liability should be imposed on the principal. Three important distinctions that generally prove vital in this determination are:

1. Direct liability versus respondeat superior.
2. Employee versus independent contractor.
3. Negligence versus intentional torts.

DIRECT LIABILITY VERSUS RESPONDEAT SUPERIOR

The principal may be liable to third persons for the torts of an agent under either direct liability or respondeat superior.

Direct Liability

Under **direct liability** the principal is basically liable because of her own tort. This may be because the principal personally directed the agent's tortious conduct or otherwise intended that it occur. Direct liability can also arise when the principal is negligent in controlling the agent. Generally, the principal is directly liable when she is *negligent in the hiring or supervision of the agent.*

Respondeat Superior

Principals may be liable to third persons injured by the torts of their agents under the doctrine of **respondeat superior**, which means "let the master answer." This theory of imputed liability generally applies to principals who are employers, making them liable for the torts of their employees. Unlike direct liability, it imposes such liability on employers without regard to whether or not they are at fault. Even proof that the employee violated specific instructions of the employer in committing the tort generally will not relieve the principal from liability. A principal's liability under respondeat superior often is called **vicarious liability.**

WHITE v. REVCO DISCOUNT DRUG CENTERS
33 S. W. 3d 713 (Tenn. Sup.Ct. 2000)

FACTS

On May 4, James E. Woodfin entered a Revco Discount Drug Store. While inside Revco, he caused a considerable disruption and was issued a misdemeanor citation for disorderly conduct by Danny Boone, Revco's security guard. After issuing the citation, Boone, who was also an off-duty police officer with the Knoxville Police Department (KPD), warned Woodfin never to return to Revco. One month later, the manager of Revco approached Boone, who was working that day as Revco's security guard, and informed him that Woodfin had entered the store a few days earlier, contrary to Boone's earlier warning. Boone, under the direction of the Revco manager, called the KPD and inquired about the status of the May 4 citation. From this call, Boone learned that Woodfin had failed to report to the jail for "booking" as ordered by the citation and that a bench warrant had been issued

for Woodfin's arrest. Revco's manager then allegedly directed Boone to go to Woodfin's apartment to serve the bench warrant, to prevent Woodfin from ever returning to Revco, and to punish Woodfin for disregarding Revco's no trespass order. Before proceeding, however, Boone arranged for several uniformed KPD officers to accompany him from Revco to Woodfin's apartment. Upon arriving at the apartment, Boone and the uniformed officers discovered that Woodfin had locked himself in and would not allow anyone to enter. After obtaining a key, Boone and the other officers entered the apartment. Woodfin, who was locked in the bathroom, warned them that he had a shotgun and would shoot anyone who entered. One of the uniformed officers then kicked in the bathroom door and fired his weapon, mortally wounding Woodfin. The officers then for the first

(continued)

WHITE V. REVCO DISCOUNT DRUG CENTERS
(concluded)

time called a police supervisor to tell him what had happened. Woodfin's family filed a wrongful death suit against Revco based on the theory of respondeat superior because Boone was allegedly acting as an agent for Revco during the events giving rise to Woodfin's death. Revco asked the court to dismiss the complaint because Boone, as a matter of law, was acting solely within the scope of his duty as a police officer. Thus, according to Revco, Boone could not be considered Revco's agent while the officers were at Woodfin's apartment.

ISSUE

Should the court dismiss the respondeat superior claim?

DECISION

No. In the typical case involving the doctrine of respondeat superior, an employer may be held liable for the torts committed by his or her employees while performing duties within the scope of employment. Of course, the issues stemming from the private employment of off-duty policemen do not fit precisely within the typical framework of respondeat superior. Still, agency principles can be used to resolve such disputes. Important in the concept of agency is that a principal is generally bound by its agent's acts done in its behalf and within the actual or apparent scope of the agency. The focus of this inquiry is placed upon the actions and consent of the principal, rather than upon the agent's actions or the willingness of the agent to perform those actions.

Indeed, a principal may be held liable for an agent's tortious act, even if that act occurs outside of the scope of the agency if the act was commanded or directed by the principal. It is also well settled that an agent may serve two masters simultaneously, so long as the objectives of one master are not contrary to the objectives of the other. In so doing, the person serving two masters may cause both employers to be responsible for an act if the act is within the scope of employment for both. To summarize these agency principles in terms of the application to the issue in this case, we conclude that private employers may be held vicariously liable for the acts of an off-duty police officer employed as a private security guard under any of the following circumstances: (1) the actions taken by the off-duty officer occurred within the scope of private employment; (2) the action taken by the off-duty officer occurred outside of the regular scope of employment, if the action giving rise to the tort was taken in obedience to orders or directions of the employer and the harm proximately resulted from the order or direction; or (3) the action was taken by the officer with the consent or ratification of the private employer and with an intent to benefit the private employer. This complaint has made sufficient allegations to assert a cause of action against Revco for vicarious liability under each of these three circumstances. Accordingly, the case is remanded to the circuit court so a jury can determine whether the facts support recovery under any of these theories.

EMPLOYEES VERSUS INDEPENDENT CONTRACTORS

Employers may be liable for the negligence of their employees under the theory of respondeat superior. However, principals are less likely to be liable for the torts of an independent contractor unless they were negligent in selecting or supervising the independent contractor or where the work of the independent contractor involved extrahazardous activities such as blasting or crop dusting. Such liability is derived from the principal's direct liability, rather than from respondeat superior. Thus, the distinction between whether the agent was an employee or an independent contractor often is crucial in determining the liability of the principal.

Independent Contractor

Independent contractors are persons or firms that contract to do work according to their own methods. They are under the control of the principal as to the **result** to be obtained but not as to the means used to accomplish that result.

FIGURE 21–3   Employees versus Independent Contractors

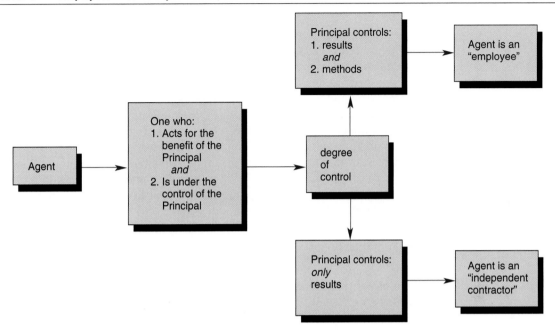

Consider the medical malpractice case that opened this chapter. In reality the emergency room doctors were independent contractors rather than employees. The hospital did not pay them any salary or control their diagnosis or treatment. The doctors set their own fees, billed separately, kept their profits and losses, and bore the losses from their practice. They determined their own work schedules, salaries, vacations, and maximum absences. It was only because the patients were not aware of these facts that the court used apparent agency to treat the doctors as agents or employees.

Employee

Employees are under the control of the employer as to both the **objective** of their work and the **means** used to achieve it. Employers may give detailed directions to employees about their physical activities on the job. In effect, the employer is buying the time of the employee. This is, of course, much less true of high-level managers and those with professional training such as accountants and attorneys than it is for blue-collar workers. (See Figure 21–3.)

Scope of Employment

The employer is liable under respondeat superior only if the tort of the employee was committed *within the scope of employment.* This is often difficult to ascertain. Several factors are looked at in making the decision.

1. Whether the tort was committed within the time and space limits of the employment. If the act is done during off-hours or at a distance from the workplace, it is not within the scope of employment except in unusual cases.
2. Whether the employee intended to serve the employer in doing the act. If the act is directed at some personal objective, such as settling a personal dispute, the employer is not liable.

3.   Whether the act is of the same general nature as (or incidental to) some
      authorized conduct.

Courts distinguish between a **mere deviation** and a situation in which an employee temporarily abandons the employment. For example, if Ellen, a truck driver
for United Parcel Service, takes a one-block detour while making deliveries in order
to mail a personal letter, it is a mere deviation. If Ellen negligently injures a pedestrian
just before reaching the mailbox, UPS would be liable. However, if Ellen and a friend
decide to take a break to visit the zoo and the pedestrian is struck on the way there,
Ellen alone, not UPS, would be liable.

Courts disagree as to when an employee has returned to the employment after a
temporary abandonment. In the zoo example, some courts would impose liability on
the employer for the negligence of Ellen as soon as she started toward her next delivery. Others would make the employer liable only if Ellen were at or near a point on
the original route when the accident occurred.

Degree of Control

The factor that distinguishes an employee from an independent contractor is the
degree of control of the principal. Compare these two examples: James, a delivery
truck driver for a retail shop, may be told when to start work, in what order to make
deliveries, what routes to use, and how long to take for lunch. James is an employee,
and his employer will be responsible for the injuries he inflicts on third persons while
carrying out his job. Bill, on the other hand, operates his own delivery service. A retailer hiring his services will probably tell him where and about when the deliveries
for the retailer are to be made. However, the starting time, the routes to be used, and
the order of delivery are left to Bill's discretion. Bill is an independent contractor and
his principal, the retailer, generally will not be liable for Bill's torts unless the retailer
also is negligent in some way.

Since the right to control is not always clearly expressed in the agency agreement,
disputes about liability for torts committed on the job are frequent. Even if there is an
agreement that there is no right to control, the principal will be liable if she is actually
directing the work at the time the tort is committed.

When the right to control and even the degree of actual control are unclear, courts
look to other factors to determine whether the person committing the tort is an
employee or an independent contractor. Some of these factors are whether the one
employed is engaged in a distinct occupation or business, the degree of skill required, who furnishes the equipment used, and whether the work in the locality is
usually done by employees or independent contractors. Not infrequently, some factors point toward finding that the tortfeasor was an employee while others indicate
that he or she was an independent contractor, thus making the determination extremely difficult.

Loaned Employee

It is not uncommon for an employee to be directed to do work for another employer,
with the original employer being paid for the services of the employee. The question
then arises as to which employer is liable for a tort committed by the **loaned employee.** Generally, the original employer is liable. However, if the primary right of
control has shifted to the special employer, he is liable under the **borrowed employee** doctrine.

NEGLIGENCE VERSUS INTENTIONAL TORTS

Courts frequently find principals liable for the negligence of their agents. Consider the medical malpractice case that opened this chapter. Once the court used apparent agency to create a principal–agent relationship between the hospital and the emergency room doctor, it had no difficulty holding the hospital vicariously liable for the doctor's malpractice.

While liability for the negligence of agents is common, courts are less likely to assess liability against principals for their agents' intentional torts. Unless an intentional tort was encouraged by the principal, courts tend to find that it was committed outside the scope of the agency. However, many courts now are finding an employer liable if she should have foreseen the intentional tort. For example, a tavern that employs a bouncer is likely to be held responsible for any assault or battery that the bouncer commits on a customer. (See Figure 21–4.)

A careful examination of the cases finding such liability under respondeat superior reveals a strong resemblance to direct liability analysis. Under direct liability, a

FIGURE 21–4   Principal's Liability for the Torts of the Agent*

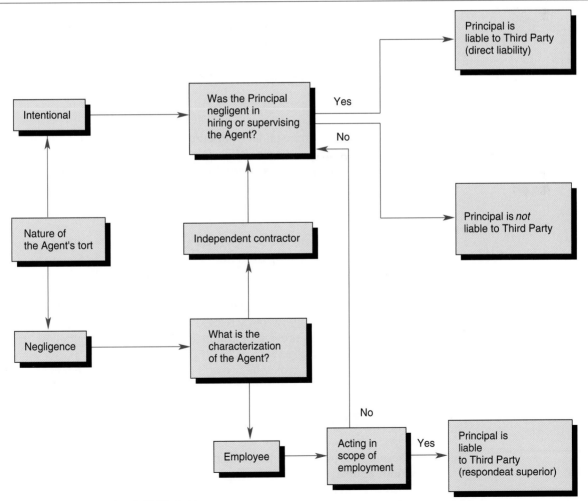

In all cases, the agent is not relieved of liability for his torts.

principal clearly is liable for intentional torts when the principal's negligence in hiring or supervising the agent increases the likelihood of the tort occurring.

Ethical Implications	United Airlines has a policy of regularly returning alcoholic pilots to the job after treatment. The company's medical director stated: "You either have practicing alcoholics in the cockpits, or you have recovering ones." What are the legal problems with returning alcoholics to safety-sensitive positions? What ethical concerns are raised by this policy?[2]

LIABILITY OF THE AGENT

The fact that an agent was acting within his authority normally does not relieve him of personal liability for a tort he committed. This is true even if he acted at the direction of the principal or employer. An agent has no duty to comply with orders if they are wrongful and he has a duty to society not to commit torts. In a suit against the agent, the fact that the principal will ultimately be liable is no defense. But if an agent is found liable for negligence committed in the scope of the agency, he may be indemnified by the principal.

Of course, a third party who is injured through the tortious conduct of an agent can get only one recovery. Thus, the injured person is more likely to sue the principal since there is a greater likelihood that the principal will have liability insurance.

LIABILITY FOR CRIMES

LIABILITY OF AGENT

A person who commits a crime under instructions from her principal is guilty of that crime. It is no defense that the agent is following the principal's instructions. This is because the agent's duty to society overrides the duty to follow the direction of the principal.

LIABILITY OF PRINCIPAL

It was once difficult to convict the employer for a crime committed by an employee. The view was that the commission of a crime was generally outside the scope of employment unless directed by or participated in by the employer. Employers were often held liable for nonphysical crimes defined by statute, such as price fixing or securities violations. However, they generally were not found guilty for physical crimes such as trespass or battery. Newly revised criminal codes are more likely to impose liability on the employer even for criminal physical acts committed by an employee with decision-making power that occur during the employee's work. Here, as in the tort cases, courts have broadened what is considered to be within the scope of employment.

FOREIGN REPRESENTATIVES

U.S. businesses often will retain overseas agents to facilitate their international transactions. Those agents over whom the principal has a great deal of control are known as **dependent agents,** while agents who retain a great deal of discretion are called

---

[2]"Firms Debate Hard Line on Alcoholics," *The Wall Street Journal*, April 13, 1989, p. B1, col. 3.

independent agents. Most foreign nations impose stringent responsibilities under their criminal, tax, and labor laws on U.S. companies that have dependent agents doing business within their borders.

.... *QUESTIONS AND PROBLEM CASES* ....

1. Distinguish between the tests for implied and apparent authority. How does the liability of the agent exercising implied authority differ from the liability of the agent exercising apparent authority?

2. After the Bartons and Snellson were involved in an automobile accident, the Bartons retained Griffiths as an attorney to negotiate an out-of-court settlement. After lengthy discussion with Snellson's insurance company, Griffiths settled the case for $3,000. The Bartons, however, personally rejected the $3,000 offer. Snellson filed suit to enforce the settlement, claiming that Griffiths was authorized to accept the settlement on behalf of the Bartons. Was Griffiths authorized to bind the Bartons to the settlement offer?

3. Ralph and Annie Hazelton engaged Alphonse Geronda, a realtor, to sell their variety store. Geronda represented to Michael Arbour that "this was a typical general store," selling gas, oil, hardware, beer, and groceries. He reported that the store had an annual gross income of over $100,000. Geronda failed to inform Arbour that one-third of the store's profit was attributable to an accompanying lawn and garden equipment distributorship that the Hazeltons were not including in the sale. When Arbour visited the business, Geronda directed him away from the garage area where the lawn and garden equipment was stored. Throughout all of these negotiations, the Hazeltons were unaware of Geronda's misrepresentations. After purchasing the store, Arbour learned of the importance of the equipment sales from the Hazeltons. He sued, asking for rescission of the contract. Is Arbour entitled to a rescission because of Geronda's misrepresentation?

4. *Video Case*. See "In the Cards." Jack runs a card shop. Linda, who knows little or nothing about baseball or baseball cards, agreed to run the shop for Jack while he went out for dinner. Jack told Linda she could sell any card for the price marked on the card. Then, he pointed to a case containing the more expensive cards, and said that he might negotiate the price on those cards if customers would wait until he returned. Shortly, after Jack left, Linda sold a small boy an Ernie Banks rookie card for $12. The card bore a price sticker that stated: "1200." The boy apparently was unaware of the card's true value and did not try to negotiate its price. Did Linda have authority to sell the card for $12? Does Jack have any basis for suing her for his losses if the boy is able to keep the card?

5. Lisa M. visited the hospital for an ultrasound examination. After conducting the ordered examination, the technician left the ultrasound room for about 10 minutes to develop the photographic results. On his return, he asked Lisa if she wanted to know the sex of the baby, and she said she did. He told her, falsely, that he would need to scan "much further down," and that it would be uncomfortable. With her cooperation, the technician inserted the ultrasound-generating wand in her vagina. After a while he put down the wand and fondled her with his fingers. While fondling her, the technician explained that he needed to excite her to get a good view of the baby. After discussing the examination with her regular obstetrician, Lisa discovered that the technician's actions were improper. She sued the technician and the hospital. Is the hospital vicariously liable under the theory of respondeat superior?

6. Arthur Jensen, Inc., was a corporation engaged in the housing construction business. Arthur Jensen owned over half of the corporation's stock and served as its president. Alaska Valuation Service (AVS) conducted housing appraisals for Jensen on numerous occasions over the years. When AVS took the orders for appraisals, it was not aware that it was dealing with a corporation. It believed that it was dealing directly with Jensen. Jensen never specifically informed AVS of his status as an agent for Arthur Jensen, Inc. AVS attempted to

hold Jensen personally liable for the appraisal services. Is Jensen personally liable as an agent for an undisclosed principal?

7. *Video Case.* See "Martin Manufacturing." Mr. Martin, the president of Martin Manufacturing, was talking with Arnold, a new traveling salesman, about Arnold's first week on the road. Arnold told Martin he hit one of Martin's customers in the customer's store, causing the customer some physical harm. The blow came after Arnold and the customer got into an argument, during which the customer ordered Arnold out of his store. In striking the customer, Arnold was motivated, at least in part, by a feeling that no Martin employee should have to endure such disrespect. Shortly after this, Martin also learned from Arnold that Arnold had gotten into an accident while driving the company van. The accident came after Arnold negligently ran a stop sign while thinking about the fight. The driver of the other car was seriously injured in the accident. Assuming that Arnold is an employee, is Martin liable to the customer for any battery Arnold committed? Is Martin liable to the victim in the accident?

8. Equilease retained Douglas Quinn, an attorney, to repossess several utility trailers, with authority to take whatever steps were necessary to recover the trailers. Quinn hired James McCann, a specialist in repossessing cars, to locate the equipment. After orally reporting to Quinn that he had found the trailers in Iowa, Quinn instructed McCann to have them towed to Nebraska. McCann hired Neff Towing to carry out this request. Neff Towing stored the trailers on its lot in Omaha, Nebraska, and McCann notified Quinn of this fact. When it was not paid, Neff Towing sued Equilease for its towing and storage services, arguing that McCann was a subagent capable of binding Equilease to the towing and storage contracts. Was McCann a subagent with authority to bind Equilease to the towing and storage contract?

9. James Gravois purchased The Captain's Raft restaurant and then sold it to Computer Tax Service, Inc., a corporation owned by him and his wife. Gravois never informed the managers, employees, or suppliers of The Captain's Raft that the restaurant was owned by the corporation. You'll See Seafood supplied fresh seafood to the restaurant. You'll See's president, William Hayward, likewise thought that Gravois owned the restaurant as he was never informed otherwise and checks for seafood were signed by Gravois with no indication of a corporate capacity. The checks themselves as well as the menus were printed with the name "The Captain's Raft" with no indication it was a corporate entity. You'll See sued Gravois to collect $24,161 owed for seafood delivered to the restaurant. Gravois denied liability, claiming that he was merely an agent and that Computer Tax Service, which by this time was bankrupt, was liable for the debt. You'll See argued that Gravois was personally liable as an agent for an undisclosed principal. Was Gravois liable as an agent for an undisclosed principal?

10. Victory Tabernacle Baptist Church hired Ladison, gave him keys that enabled him to lock and unlock all of the Church's doors, and entrusted him with duties that encouraged him to have frequent unsupervised contact with children. On numerous occasions during his employment, Ladison raped the plaintiff's 10-year-old daughter both at the Church and at other locations. The mother sued the Church for negligent hiring. She claimed that when the Church hired Ladison it knew or should have known that he had recently been convicted of aggravated sexual assault on a young girl, that he was on probation for that offense, and that a condition of his probation was that he not be involved with children. The Church argued that it could not be liable because the rapes did not occur within the scope of Ladison's employment. Will the Church escape liability because the rapes did not occur within the scope of Ladison's employment?

CHAPTER 22

Employment Laws

Luedtke worked on oil drilling rigs on Alaska's North Slope. His employer required employees to take a drug test during their next week of "R&R" after their names appeared on a list. Luedtke refused to take the test, and he was fired.

- *Can employees be forced to take drug tests to keep their jobs?*
- *Would Luedtke's job protection rights be different if he worked for the government?*
- *If Luedtke was wrongfully fired, what recourse does he have against his employer?*

.... *INTRODUCTION* ....

If you operate a business that employs even one person outside your own family, you must comply with a myriad of statutes. These statutes impose duties on employers that supplement and greatly increase the duties imposed by the common law of agency. Many of the statutes require you to keep records and often to make reports to both state and federal agencies. In addition, recent changes in the common law doctrine of employment at will may impose new duties on you as an employer. This chapter will briefly discuss some of the most important of these statutes, as well as recent developments in the common law relating to employment.

.... *HISTORICAL BACKGROUND* ....

There have long been statutes to govern the employment relationship. The objective of the early statutes in both England and the United States was to *control and restrict workers*. For example, the earliest statutes on wages set maximums rather than minimums. A statute of Edward VI in 1549 prohibited joint actions such as strikes or the formation of unions by workers.

The Industrial Revolution changed the nature and conditions of work. As more power machinery was used and the size of mining, manufacturing, and processing activities grew, accidents and industrial disease killed and disabled many workers. Women and children as well as men were drawn off the farms to work in factories. Hours were long—often 14 hours a day, six days a week.

Despite the fact that the workplace had become much more dangerous, both tort and contract law were interpreted in a manner that made it virtually impossible for workers to recover for workplace injuries, or to keep their jobs if they complained. Several states passed statutes whose aim was to protect workers. Many also passed laws setting 10 hours as the maximum workday for women and prohibiting the employment of young children in mining and manufacturing. However, these laws were often declared unconstitutional because they were interpreted as interfering with freedom of contract as guaranteed by the Due Process Clause of the Fourteenth Amendment of the U.S. Constitution.

The 20th century has seen a change in these conditions brought about by state and federal laws. Today, as discussed in Chapter 43, the Constitution is interpreted to put few limits on the power of both state and federal governments to regulate business. The regulation of the employment relationship itself is an important part of such power. These laws recognize the importance of the employment relationship to most individuals, the power that the employer has over the worker, and the abuses of that power that often occurred.

.... *HEALTH AND SAFETY LEGISLATION* ....

WORKERS' COMPENSATION

In the 19th century, it was very hard for an employee who was injured on the job to recover damages from the employer. This was true although the common law and some state statutes imposed a duty on the employer to furnish a reasonably safe workplace. It was difficult to prove that the employer had been negligent. Even if negligence could be proved, the common law defenses of *contributory negligence and assumption of risk* (discussed in Chapter 5) by the employee usually barred recovery. In addition, the employer could claim the *fellow-servant rule* as a defense. This rule declared that if the injury was the result of negligence by another worker, the employer had no liability.

In the period between 1917 and 1925, most states enacted workers' compensation laws. These put *liability* for injuries occurring within the scope of employment on the employer *without regard to fault*. The laws represent a compromise between the employer's and employee's interests. The employee gives up the right to sue the employer in exchange for the high probability of recovering without the cost of a lawsuit. The employer gives up the right to use the traditional negligence defenses in exchange for limited payments to the employee. Punitive damages and emotional damages such as pain and suffering cannot be recovered.

The statutes require the employer to furnish the employee with medical treatment and a fixed level of income during disability. Scheduled amounts are awarded for death or loss of limb. Generally, they also include some rehabilitation services. Disability income payments tend to be low. Although many statutes specify a rate of two-thirds of wages, they also establish a maximum that, because of inflation, has become quite low. The payments are funded through employer contributions to a state compensation fund, through insurance purchased by employers, or through self-insurance by large employers. Workers' compensation is administered by a state agency.

Not everyone is covered by workers' compensation. Employers with three or fewer employees are frequently exempted. Employees in certain types of employment, such as farming, charitable organizations, and household service, are also often excluded. Anyone not covered can sue the employer in tort. In addition, many states cover only certain occupational diseases. There is no federal law requiring injury compensation that applies to employers generally. Railroads and mining are covered by such federal legislation, however. Because of rather substantial differences in coverage and benefits under various state workers' compensation statutes, mandatory federal standards have often been proposed to Congress.

Employees can recover only for *work-related injuries*. This means that they must **arise out of employment** or be related to the type of employment involved. Thus, a secretary whose husband comes to her office and shoots her during work would not be able to recover under workers' compensation because her injury was not related to her work. The injuries must also happen **in the course of employment.** Generally, injuries occurring on the way to and from the job are not within the course of employment. Disputes as to the employer's liability are initially heard by an administrative board.

OSHA

Worker compensation laws were designed to compensate for workplace injuries, not primarily to make the workplace safer. Most employers insure their risks under these statutes, and premiums vary according to the safety of the industry and the individual employer. Despite this fact and the efforts to promote safety in the workplace by insurance companies and some employers, many employers tolerated unsafe practices by workers, and workplaces were often hazardous.

The first federal safety statute that applied to all types of businesses was the Occupational Safety and Health Act of 1970. It applies to all businesses that affect interstate commerce, even those with only one employee. It seeks to protect the safety and health of employees through duties imposed on the employer and through enforcement by the Occupational Safety and Health Administration (OSHA).

The act imposes a *general duty* on covered employers to *prevent workplace hazards* that may cause death or serious physical harm. In addition, employers are required to report on-the-job fatalities and injuries that require hospitalization to the Secretary of Labor within 48 hours. Employers with more than 10 employees are required to keep a log of all work-related deaths, injuries, and illnesses.

The act also delegates to the Secretary of Labor authority to establish detailed *health and safety standards* that must be complied with by employers. Under this authority, the Secretary has set maximum levels of exposure for certain hazardous substances such as asbestos and lead. Another regulation requires that manufacturing workers be informed of hazardous chemicals in the workplace. Regulations also protect workers from retaliation if they refuse to do work that they reasonably believe might cause their death or serious injury and if they reasonably believe no less drastic alternative is available.

The Occupational Safety and Health Administration, a division of the Department of Labor, enforces the act. Its inspectors may enter the workplace at any reasonable time and without advance notice. However, if an employer objects to the inspection, a search warrant must be obtained. Inspectors usually check workplaces after fatalities have occurred, often in response to complaints of workers, and occasionally on just a random basis. Violations of the act may result in citations, fines, and even criminal penalties for willful violations that result in death.

The statute permits states to develop and enforce their own health and safety programs. Such programs must provide protection to employees at least as great as that established by OSHA. Many states have approved programs.

FAMILY AND MEDICAL LEAVE ACT

The Family and Medical Leave Act, passed in 1993, is designed to provide job security to employees with serious health conditions as well as to provide reasonable leave periods for family-related health issues. Another important goal is to make the workplace more accommodating to women and families.

Employers with 50 or more employees are required to give covered employees up to 12 *unpaid* workweeks of leave per year to deal with the care of themselves, a child, a spouse, or a parent with a serious health condition. Leave is also granted for the birth or adoption of a child. In most instances, the employee's job is protected during the leave, and benefits are continued. In order to be eligible for the leave, an employee must have worked at least 1,250 hours during the previous 12 months. Table 22–1 on page 364 contains additional details.

CALDWELL V. HOLLAND
208 F.3d 671 (8th Cir. 2000)

FACTS

Caldwell worked for Holland's Kentucky Fried Chicken restaurant, where she had an excellent record. On Saturday, her three-year-old son awoke with a high fever, pain in his ears, and congestion. Caldwell notified her manager that she would be absent because she had to take her son to the doctor. At the emergency clinic, the son was diagnosed with an acute ear infection and put on a 10-day course of antibiotics and a two-day

(continued)

CALDWELL V. HOLLAND
(concluded)

decongestant. Caldwell was also informed that he would need surgery to prevent permanent hearing loss. That night Caldwell, a single mother, worked the night shift at another KFC owned by Holland while her elderly mother cared for her son. When Caldwell reported to work on Monday, she was summarily fired. On a follow-up visit the son had to have another course of antibiotics, and two weeks later had surgery.

ISSUE

Did the son have a "serious health condition," therefore causing Caldwell's leave to be covered by the FMLA?

DECISION

Yes. The FMLA's purpose is to allow working men and women to balance the conflicting demands of work and personal life. It thus allows intermittent leave, and the cumulative effects of illness to be considered. The FMLA allows eligible employees to take up to 12 workweeks of leave per year for serious health conditions that afflict their immediate family members. A serious health condition occurs when a family member suffers a condition that requires inpatient care or continuing treatment by a health care provider. The family member must be incapacitated for three consecutive days and then receive subsequent treatment. In making this determination for a three-year-old child, we must assess whether the illness demonstrably affected his normal activity. Here, the son's infection was severe enough to warrant emergency treatment, he was kept inside and in bed as much as possible for more than three days, and on continuing medication. It was also a persistent condition that could be treated only by surgery. His illness can be found to qualify.

HEALTH INSURANCE

The President and Congress have recently turned their attention to extending the availability of health insurance to all Americans. A limited step in this direction is Public Law 99-272, shown in Table 22–1, which continues the availability of health care insurance at the employer's group rate to certain terminated employees and their families for up to 36 months.

WAGES AND PENSIONS

FAIR LABOR STANDARDS ACT

In 1938, Congress passed the Fair Labor Standards Act (FLSA), which requires covered employers to pay their employees a minimum hourly wage and to pay time and a half for hours worked in excess of 40 in one week. Generally, employers are covered if they are engaged in interstate commerce or if their annual gross sales exceed $500,000 and their business affects interstate commerce.

Certain employees who are usually higher paid are exempt from the act. They include executive, administrative, and professional employees and outside salespeople. To be exempt as an executive, one's primary duty must be to manage a business or a recognized subdivision. Such an employee must be involved in hiring and firing decisions. An administrative employee must have special expertise. Examples would be a credit or personnel manager. For exemption as a professional employee, one must be in a recognized profession or an occupation requiring special intellectual instruction. Examples would be lawyers, engineers, and actuaries (in an insurance company).

Time worked includes the time an employee is "suffered or permitted" to work. Therefore, employers may be liable for pay even when an employee works voluntarily,

TABLE 22–1   Health and Safety Regulation and Compensation

Workers' Compensation (state legislation)

Compensates employee for work-related injury if injury arises: 1. Out of employment 2. In the course of employment	Compensable injuries include: 1. Accidental injuries 2. Occupational diseases (most) 3. Emotional illness (much) 4. Stress-related injury or illness (much)	Benefits include: 1. Medical expenses 2. Percentage of income 3. Death benefits 4. Rehabilitation 5. Scheduled payment for loss of bodily part	Special issue—in some states employee is allowed to sue for additional compensation if: 1. The employer recklessly or intentionally caused injury, or 2. The employer was acting in another capacity (such as manufacturer of employee-injuring product)

Occupational Safety and Health Act (federal legislation)
(Many states have an equivalent act.)

Employer duties: 1 Provide workplace free from hazards likely to cause serious injury or death 2. Comply with agency rules and regulations 3. Keep records and make them available to employees and agency 4. Notify and instruct employees regarding hazardous chemicals in the workplace	Employee rights: 1. Can refuse to work if reasonably fears for safety 2. Can initiate safety complaints with agency	Agency duties: 1. Set health and safety standards 2. Investigate complaints and inspect for compliance 3. Bring enforcement actions and levy fines and penalties	Special issue—cutbacks and lack of enforcement in 1980s led to increases in injuries and criminal prosecutions

Family and Medical Leave Act (federal legislation)

Protects job and benefits while employee is on unpaid leave for up to 12 weeks	Protections include:
	
	1. Employee's same or similar job upon return
	2. Group life insurance
	3. Health insurance
	4. Disability insurance
	5. Vacation
	6. Educational benefits
	7. Pensions
		Protected reasons for leave include:
		
		1. Serious health condition of employee
		2. Serious health condition of child, spouse, or parent
		3. Birth or adoption of a child
			1. *Serious health condition* is any physical or mental illness, injury or condition that involves
			  a. Inpatient care (e.g., hospital, hospice)
			  b. Continuing treatment of a health care provider
			2. Employee can be required to use accumulated vacation, personal, or family leave time as part of 12-week period

Public Law 99-272 (federal legislation)

Continues health insurance coverage under group rates for terminated employee and/or family	People covered include: 1. Terminated or reduced hours employee (unless terminated for gross misconduct) 2. Divorced or separated spouse of employee 3. Spouse of deceased, terminated, or medicare-eligible employee 4. Dependent child of deceased, terminated, divorced, separated, or medicare-eligible employee	Coverage is: 1. Same coverage as that provided employees under group plan 2. At 102 percent of cost 3. Up to 18 months for terminated or reduced-hours employee (and spouse/family); up to 36 months for other causes	Coverage ceases when: 1. No group plan available for employees 2. Coverage is obtained under another plan 3. Person becomes eligible for medicare 4. Person fails to pay premium

perhaps to increase his or her knowledge. Under the act, employees must be paid for time "on call." They must also be paid for short rest periods when they cannot use the time effectively for their own purposes. Employers are required to keep records that include the time worked by covered employees. Either the Department of Labor, which administers the act under its Wage and Hour Division, or an aggrieved employee can bring suit for violations. The employer must pay twice any amount wrongfully withheld from the employee.

The FLSA also prohibits *oppressive child labor*. Generally, this means employment of children under the age of 14 and the employment of older children in hazardous jobs.

STATE WAGE STATUTES

States also have minimum wage and overtime statutes. These statutes have become less important as coverage under the FLSA has increased. Some statutes specify how soon wages must be paid to the employee after they are earned. For example, a California statute requires the employer to pay off a discharged employee immediately. It also provides that in most types of employment, employees must be paid every two weeks and within seven days following the last day of the pay period.

Most states also have statutes dealing with the garnishment of wages. **Garnishment** is a court order that makes money or property held by a debtor (the *garnishee*) subject to the claim of a creditor. The statutes usually limit the amount of wages subject to garnishment. For example, Illinois limits attachment to 15 percent of gross wages. It also prohibits the firing of employees because their wages have become subject to garnishment.

EMPLOYMENT RETIREMENT INCOME SECURITY ACT

Almost half the civilian work force is covered by pension plans. Before the passage of the Employment Retirement Income Security Act (ERISA) in 1974, abuses and injustices under these plans were common. The act is designed to prevent problems such as underfunding, dishonest or careless management of funds, and the loss of benefits by long-service employees who change employers, who are fired, or whose employers go out of business. The act does not require employers to establish pension plans or to meet specific benefit levels. It primarily regulates the management and vesting of established plans. Pension funds **vest** when the employee's legal right to them cannot be taken away.

The act covers both employer- and union-sponsored pension plans. Under the act, existing and new plans must comply with certain standards, which are listed in Table 22–2 on page 366. The act also established the Pension Benefit Guaranty Corporation to provide insurance for plans whose total assets are insufficient to pay promised benefits. This might occur because of termination of the employer's business or certain other causes. The corporation is funded by a small premium for each covered employee, paid by the pension plan. Recently, the premiums were raised because of the bankruptcies of several large employers whose plans were not fully funded.

The language describing the coverage of ERISA is broad. There has been much litigation regarding ERISA's impact on nonpension benefits such as health insurance. Generally, the act has been interpreted to limit employer discretion and state regulation regarding such benefits.

The Department of Labor and the Internal Revenue Service share in enforcing the act. Violations are subject to criminal and civil penalties. In addition, plan participants and beneficiaries may enforce their rights under the act.

TABLE 22-2   WAGE AND RETIREMENT INCOME REGULATION

Fair Labor Standards Act (FLSA) (federal legislation)
(Every state has its own wage and hour law; most regulate garnishment.)

Regulates wages and hours:	Some covered times:	Employees not covered:	Some employers not covered:
1. Establishes minimum wage for covered employees 2. Minimum overtime rate of 1.5 percent of regular wages 3. Regulates employment of minors	1. When on call 2. Brief rest periods 3. Required briefings 4. Staying to fill out reports 5. Incidental, integral preparatory activity	1. Executives, administrators, and professionals 2. Outside salespeople 3. Many agricultural workers 4. Self-employed and unpaid family workers 5. Members of armed forces	1. Employers with less than $500,000 annual sales affecting interstate commerce 2. Railroads and carriers 3. Some fishery and forestry businesses

Employment Retirement Income Security Act (ERISA) (federal legislation)

Regulates pension plans voluntarily provided by employer	Participation and vesting rules:	Employer must:	The Pension Benefit Guaranty Corporation, created by the act and funded by employer contributions, insures pension fund participants against loss of pension funds.
	1. Participation in the plan must begin within one year of employment (unless immediate full vesting) 2. Voting rights must follow one of three plans implemented by the 1986 ERISA amendments	1. Manage the fund as a fiduciary and the managers must fulfill fiduciary duties 2. Provide required information about the plan to employees and the secretary of labor 3. Keep records 4. Provide sufficient funding for employees' credited service	

Unemployment Compensation (state legislation under federal supervision)

Provides replacement income through experience-based tax on employers	Eligible recipients— unemployed due to lack of suitable employment who:	Covered termination examples:
	1. Are making reasonable effort to find suitable employment 2. Were not discharged for misconduct or did not voluntarily quit without good cause	1. Termination due to incompetence generally covered 2. Quit to follow transferred spouse 3. Quit due to harassment

Social Security (FICA) (mainly financed by the Federal Insurance Contributions Act)

Provides old-age, survivors, and disability benefits, and medicare	A flat percentage tax is imposed on all income below a certain base figure; the employer is required to pay a matching amount.

COLLECTIVE BARGAINING AND UNION ACTIVITIES

The first recorded organized action by workers in America was a strike for a $6-per-week wage by printers in Philadelphia in 1786. Workers in certain trades, including shoemakers, weavers, and tailors, organized unions in the early years of the 19th century to seek higher wages and shorter hours. Employers were able to get some of these workers prosecuted for conspiracy; the courts held that such activities were criminal because they restrained trade.

Although later they were unable to get criminal actions brought against union activity, most employers remained strongly opposed to unions. One device they developed was the "yellow-dog contract," which required a worker taking a job to promise not to join a union. Courts were often quick to enjoin a strike if the employer could show that there might be violence or that other persons' interests would be hurt. In addition, the employment at will doctrine allowed employers to fire pro-union employees, and blacklisting of such employees was common. Finally, periodic economic depressions sapped the growth and power of unions.

In 1932, when union membership and influence had been hurt severely by the Great Depression, Congress passed the Norris-LaGuardia Act to help unions offset some of the advantage held by employers. The act prohibited the federal courts from issuing injunctions against lawful strikes, picketing, and certain other activities, and prohibited the enforcement of yellow-dog contracts. It did not give workers the right to organize and bargain collectively, though.

THE NATIONAL LABOR RELATIONS ACT

The right of workers to organize and bargain collectively was expressly recognized in the National Labor Relations Act (Wagner Act) in 1935. The act also prohibited certain actions by employers that were thought to deter union organizing and bargaining. These were declared to be unfair labor practices. It established the National Labor Relations Board (NLRB) to administer the act. The NLRB's major functions are to conduct elections for employees to decide whether to be represented by a union, and to hear charges of unfair labor practices.

An election is held after a petition is filed with the NLRB by a group of employees, a labor union, or an employer. Sometimes more than one union is on the ballot. The board determines what group of employees will be allowed to vote. This becomes the **bargaining unit.** A board of representatives supervises the election. If a union receives a majority of the votes of the employees who vote, the board certifies it as the exclusive bargaining representative for the unit. It then represents all employees in the unit whether or not they voted for or belong to the union.

THE LABOR–MANAGEMENT RELATIONS ACT

Union membership and power grew rapidly as World War II approached. After the war (1947), Congress amended the Wagner Act by the Taft-Hartley Act, presently known as the Labor–Management Relations Act (LMRA). It was passed to limit what was seen to be the excessive power of unions. The coverage of the act is very broad. For NLRB jurisdiction, out-of-state purchases or sales of goods and services need equal only $50,000. However, federal, state, and local government employees, as well as agricultural laborers and household employees, are excluded.

Under the act, certain union and employer practices are declared to be unfair labor practices. Examples of unfair labor practices are listed in Table 22–3 on page 368. The act also prohibits an employer and union from agreeing that the employer will refrain from dealing in the products of another employer who is considered to be unfair to the union. Such contracts are called *hot-cargo agreements*. Recently, there has been much litigation regarding whether it is an unfair labor practice for an employer

TABLE 22–3   Examples of Unfair Labor Practices under the LMRA

Employer	Union
1. Interfering with the right of employees to form or join a labor union or to engage in concerted activities for their mutual aid or protection. 2. Establishing or dominating a labor union. 3. Discriminating against employees in hiring or any other terms of employment because of their union membership. 4. Discriminating against employees who have filed charges with the NLRB. 5. Refusing to bargain collectively with a union that represents the employees.	1. Coercing an employer to join a union and coercing an employer in the selection of representatives for collective bargaining. 2. Coercing an employer to discriminate against an employee who is not a union member, except for failure to pay union dues under a union shop agreement. 3. Refusing to bargain collectively with the employer. 4. Picketing or conducting a secondary boycott or strike (that is, against someone other than the employer with whom the union has a dispute) for an illegal purpose. 5. Setting excessive initiation fees under a union shop agreement. 6. Forcing an employer to pay for work not performed (featherbedding). 7. Picketing to require an employer to recognize or bargain with a union that has not been certified as the bargaining agent.

to avoid its union contract by closing a plant, moving work to a nonunion site, or declaring bankruptcy. Generally, such actions have been allowed as long as they are not motivated by antiunion animus, and the employer has bargained with (although it does not have to come to agreement with) the union.

The NLRB processes unfair practice charges brought against unions and employers. If the board finds that the employer or union has committed an unfair labor practice, it orders the offending party to "cease and desist," or it may order affirmative action to remedy the harm caused by the violation. Suppose Jacob was discharged because he was trying to get co-workers to join a union. The employer would be ordered to reinstate him with back pay. An employer who has committed an unfair practice by making threats or promises before an election might be required to mail an NLRB notice to the employees, and a new election might be directed.

LOCAL 14 UNITED PAPERWORKERS INT'L UNION, AFL-CIO v. NLRB
1993 U.S. App. Lexis 22017 (1st Cir. Aug. 19, 1993)

FACTS

During a strike against it, International Paper Company (IP) continued operations by employing nonstriking union members and nonunion replacement workers. There were periodic outbreaks of violence, threats, and other strike-related misconduct. After the strike, IP discharged some employees for strike-related misconduct. The union claimed that IP discriminated against the striking employees by firing strikers for strike-related misconduct while failing to dismiss nonstriker Barclay, who had engaged in equally serious or more serious misconduct but had only received a warning. During the strike, Barclay and his son, carrying baseball bats, confronted a group of strikers who were attending a party near Bar-

clay's home. He complained to them about being harassed and constantly called a "scab," and said he was there to clean them out. When a scuffle ensued after he refused to leave, one of the guests received a cut. This behavior was compared to that of the fired strikers. Striker Chicoine accosted a nonstriker and told her he would kill her for crossing the picket line, and used a megaphone to threaten replacement workers by telling them he had a .44 and would blow their heads off. Striker Flagg threatened to kill a replacement worker. Striker Hamlin attempted to run replacement workers off the road with his truck. Striker Storer threw a rock at a replacement worker's car, kicked the car, and jumped on

(continued)

Local 14 United Paperworkers Int'l Union, AFL-CIO v. NLRB
(concluded)

the bumper. The NLRB upheld the firings, and the union appealed that decision to the circuit court.

Issue

Did the employer unfairly discriminate against the striking employees?

Decision

No. Under Article 7 of the NLRA, employees have the right to peacefully strike, picket, and engage in other activities for the purpose of collective bargaining. They also have the right to refrain from such activities. At the end of a strike, the employer must reinstate striking employees so they are not penalized for exercising their rights.

However, behavior that reasonably tends to coerce or intimidate nonstriking employees in the exercise of their right to refrain from strike activities is serious strike-related misconduct that can justify discharge. Employers may not tolerate misconduct by nonstrikers that is as serious or more serious than that of the strikers who were fired. Here, Barclay's behavior was provoked. Barclay had been harassed at his home. Strikers had blown air horns in front of his house, shouted obscenities, threatened him, and fired a projectile through his window, showering his son with glass. Only then did Barclay confront the strikers at the party. The actions of the dismissed strikers were not in response to provocations. The firings were not discriminatory.

The LMRA further provides for an 80-day "cooling-off" period in strikes that the president finds likely to harm national safety or health. During this period, employees must return to work or continue working. A Federal Mediation and Conciliation Service provides skilled people to help unions and employers in their bargaining so as to prevent strikes or lockouts. A *lockout* occurs when the employer discontinues operations during a labor dispute.

The Labor–Management Reporting and Disclosure Act

The Labor–Management Reporting and Disclosure Act (Landrum-Griffin Act) was passed in 1959 as a further check on the unions. Congressional hearings during the 1950s uncovered much corruption and undemocratic procedures within the unions. The act was designed to promote honesty and democracy in running the union's internal affairs. It requires a union to have a constitution and bylaws, and it sets forth a "bill of rights" for union members. It also requires certain reports to the Secretary of Labor. These reports must disclose a great deal about the financial situation of the union and its internal procedures.

Union membership, and therefore union power, have dramatically decreased in the past decade. Membership has fallen from a high of 39 percent of the private workforce in 1955 to less than 12 percent today. This decline is due to a variety of reasons including loss of traditionally unionized jobs in the manufacturing sector, court recognition of worker rights such as job security outside the union setting, the passage of worker protection legislation by Congress and the states, and union abuse of power and participation in criminal activities.

.... *DISCRIMINATION IN EMPLOYMENT* ....

The Equal Pay Act of 1963

The Equal Pay Act, passed as an amendment to the FLSA, prohibits sex discrimination in pay. It requires covered employers to pay employees of both sexes equally for jobs that require equal skill, effort, and responsibility, and that are performed under similar working conditions. The result is to raise the lower pay rate. Different rates of pay are permitted under seniority and merit systems as well as under piecework or other incentive systems. In addition, different rates are allowed for "any factor other than sex." Included within this catchall category would be differences based on factors such as shift differentials or bonuses paid because the job is part of a training program. The act is administered by the Equal Employment Opportunity Commission (EEOC). The employers covered are the same as those covered by the Wage and Hour Act.

BARTGES V. UNIVERSITY OF NORTH CAROLINA AT CHARLOTTE
908 F. Supp. 1312 (W.D.N.C. 1995)

FACTS

Bartges volunteered to be an assistant coach for the women's basketball team. She did well and was later paid for that part-time work. Subsequently, Bartges was offered the part-time position of head coach of the women's softball team. In that job she replaced Wiseman, a male, and was paid as much or more as he. Later, after a dispute with UNCC's athletic director, a woman, Bartges filed suit claiming she was being paid less than male coaches at UNCC because she was a woman. Bartges sued under the Equal Pay Act, among other theories.

ISSUE

Does Bartges have a claim under the Equal Pay Act?

DECISION

No. In an EPA suit, the comparitor must be a particular employee working for the same employer, not some hypothetical composite employee. While the jobs don't have to be identical, they should have a common core of tasks in common. When Wiseman was head softball coach, he was paid $7,950 for coaching, and $7,950 for teaching two courses. When Bartges took over, she received $12,000 for coaching softball and $8,000 for coaching basketball. She was paid more even though she was much less qualified than Wiseman. Bartges, however, does not want to compare herself to him but to other male coaches. These are not appropriate comparitors, however, because their jobs do not require substantially equal skill, effort, and responsibility, or they do not have substantially equal working conditions. For example, the men's baseball coach has a 32-member team as opposed to the 15-member softball team; he must recruit, monitor, and coach more than twice as many student athletes as Bartges. In addition, he supervises another full-time coach. Because the position requires more work, it is full time. Although Bartges did have another part-time job, she made no showing that her combined positions were the same as those of any of the full-time coaches with whom she seeks comparison. Additionally, men's basketball is the most marketable and largest revenue-producing sport at UNCC. This makes the assistant coaching positions, which are full-time, considerably more important to the university, and the positions entail greater public relations, recruiting, and other coaching responsibilities with much more pressure to produce winning teams. These differences in responsibilities and expectations render the work performed different in kind and create different working conditions. Even if Bartges had proved the jobs of the male coaches were equal, she would still lose, for the university is able to show factors other than sex are responsible for the differences. Bartges had less experience, the sport she coached was of relatively less importance to the university, and the prevailing wage for coaches in her sport all justify the difference.

TITLE VII, THE CIVIL RIGHTS ACT OF 1964

The major piece of legislation outlawing discrimination in employment is Title VII of the Civil Rights Act of 1964 (as amended in 1972). It prohibits discrimination on the basis of race, color, religion, sex, or national origin. Covered employers cannot use any of these human differences to make distinctions for purposes of hiring, firing, promoting, or fixing pay rates or other terms and conditions of employment including "fringe benefits" such as pensions and medical insurance. The act applies to employers engaged in an industry affecting interstate commerce that have at least 15 employees, to unions, and to employment agencies. It also applies to state and local government positions.

Discrimination is not defined in the act. It has gained meaning through interpretation by the EEOC, the agency that administers the act, and the courts. They have interpreted the act to include not only **intentional discrimination** (e.g., refusing to hire women) but also acts that have **discriminatory impact.** An example would be a neutral rule requiring police officers to be at least 5 feet 7 inches tall and weigh 140 pounds. Even though this rule is applied equally to all, it keeps a larger number of women and certain ethnic minorities from qualifying for the job than it does white males. If it can be shown that these requirements were not necessary to perform the job, the employer is in violation of Title VII when it uses them. Most such height and weight requirements have been struck down under this interpretation, as have many other employment screening devices and tests.

The act has more recently been interpreted to encompass **sexual harassment** as a form of prohibited discrimination. The first kind of sexual harassment to be prohibited, *quid pro quo* harassment, involves some express or implied connection between the employee's submission to sexually oriented behavior and job benefits. For example, the refusal by Sondra's supervisor to promote her unless she has sexual relations with him would be quid pro quo harassment. The *Faragher* case illustrates the other kind of sexual harassment, a *sexually harassing environment. Faragher* also points out that if a company institutes and effectively enforces a sexual harassment policy, it may not be liable in a harassing environment case.

FARAGHER V. BOCA RATON
118 S. Ct. 2275 (U.S. Supreme Ct. 1998)

FACTS

Beth Ann Faragher worked as an ocean lifeguard in Boca Raton, Florida. Faragher alleged that two of her immediate supervisors subjected her and other female lifeguards to uninvited and offensive touching, lewd remarks, and offensive comments about women. The lifeguards and supervisors were stationed at the city beach and worked out of a small one-story building. There was a clear chain of command, and the lifeguards had no significant contact with higher city officials. The city had a sexual harassment policy, but it failed to disseminate the policy among employees of the lifeguard section, and many of the supervisors and lifeguards were unaware of it. Faragher did not complain to higher management about the two supervisors. Although she spoke of their behavior to a third supervisor, Gordon, she did not regard these discussions as formal complaints to a supervisor but as conversations with a person she held in high

esteem. Because he did not feel it was his place to do so, Gordon did not report these complaints to his own supervisor or to any city official. Two months before Faragher resigned, a former female lifeguard complained to the city's personnel director about the supervisors' conduct; following an investigation, they were reprimanded. Faragher sued for sexual harassment after she resigned.

ISSUE

Is the city liable for the sexually hostile work environment created by the supervisors?

DECISION

Yes. An employer is liable for a hostile environment created by a supervisor with authority over the employee. An employer can defend itself by showing (a) that the

(continued)

FARAGHER V. BOCA RATON
(concluded)

employer exercised reasonable care to prevent and correct promptly any sexually harassing behavior, and (b) that the plaintiff employee unreasonably failed to take advantage of any preventive or corrective opportunities provided by the employer or to otherwise avoid harm. No affirmative defense is available, however, when the supervisor's harassment results in a tangible employment action such as discharge, demotion, or undesirable reassignment. It is undisputed that these supervisors were granted virtually unchecked authority over their subordinates, directly controlling and supervising Faragher's day-to-day activities. It is also clear that Faragher and her colleagues were completely isolated from the city's higher management. The city has no affirmative defense. It entirely failed to disseminate its policy against sexual harassment among the beach employees and its officials made no attempt to keep track of the conduct of the supervisors. The city's policy also did not include any assurance that the harassing supervisors could be bypassed in registering complaints. Under such circumstances, the city could not be found to have exercised reasonable care to prevent the supervisors' harassing conduct. Unlike the employer of a small workforce, who might expect that sufficient care to prevent tortious behavior could be exercised informally, those responsible for the city operations could not reasonably have thought that precautions against hostile environments in any one of many departments in far-flung locations could be effective without communicating some formal policy against harassment and having a sensible complaint procedure.

Sexual harassment has recently been recognized in countries outside the United States. A successful sexual harassment case was litigated in Japan in 1992. Several other countries, including Canada, Australia, the United Kingdom, and France, have sexual harassment laws. As more women enter the workforce worldwide, more litigation in this area can be expected.

Discrimination based on religion, sex, or national origin is permitted where one of these characteristics is a bona fide occupational qualification (BFOQ). A Christian church would not have to consider a Muslim as an applicant for choir director. A health club could limit its employment of attendants in its men's locker room to men. The courts have given a very narrow interpretation to this exception, however. Discrimination based on stereotypes (e.g., that women are less aggressive) or the preferences of co-workers or customers is not permitted. No BFOQ exception is permitted with respect to discrimination based on race or color.

Affirmative action has also been upheld by the courts. The term refers to plans for increasing the proportion of minorities or women in an employer's workforce or in higher-level positions. The aim is to encourage an employer to apply greater effort in finding and promoting qualified minority and female candidates. A typical plan might involve hiring of one minority member for each white worker until a certain percentage of the workforce is composed of minorities. Generally, such plans must be temporary (until the goal is reached), must not unduly restrict the job opportunities of those not included in the plan, and must not involve the hiring or promotion of unqualified workers.

Such plans have resulted in gains in many fields and industries. However, these gains can be eroded when layoffs and reductions in the workforce occur. Since the first to be let go are traditionally those with least seniority, and since women and minorities are a large percentage of those most recently hired under such plans, their number in the workforce is drastically reduced. Bona fide seniority systems are specifically protected under Title VII, however; thus, applying affirmative action to seniority plans is particularly troublesome. In general, the Supreme Court has been more reluctant to allow protective actions in layoffs than it has in hiring.

Ethical Implications	Affirmative action, unless court ordered, is entirely voluntary. Does an employer have an ethical duty to help overcome the effects of societal discrimination by voluntarily implementing a program? What are the ethical implications of giving preference to a person simply because of that person's membership in a racial, ethnic, or gender group?

The EEOC can initiate action in response to complaints of discrimination by applicants or employees, or it can act on its own. It first attempts conciliation of discrimination charges. If attempts at settlement fail, the EEOC or the individual alleging discrimination may bring an action in the federal courts to require steps to correct discrimination that is found to exist. This may involve payment of lost wages and benefits to those discriminated against, "affirmative action" hiring or promotion plans, or other remedial measures such as reinstatement in the job.

A trend among employers is to have employees sign mandatory arbitration agreements as a condition of getting or keeping a job. These agreements keep employees from suing about any workplace dispute, including discrimination claims. The EEOC, which strongly supports ADR (alternative dispute resolution), objects to mandatory binding arbitration as a condition of employment because it denies employees the right to bring independent discrimination claims. The Supreme Court, however, has strongly supported such agreements. The case that follows upholds the EEOC's independence to pursue discrimination claims. This is even more important in light of individual employees' arbitration agreements.

EEOC v. WAFFLE HOUSE INC.
122 S. Ct. 754 (2002)

FACTS

All Waffle House employees are required to sign an agreement that they will settle any dispute or claim concerning employment through binding arbitration. Baker signed such an agreement, and 16 days after beginning work as a grill operator suffered a seizure. He was soon fired. He then filed a claim with the EEOC. After conciliation efforts failed, the EEOC brought suit against Waffle House, alleging that it fired Baker in intentional or reckless violation of the Americans with Disabilities Act (ADA). Waffle House asserted that since Baker had signed a mandatory arbitration agreement, the issue could not be litigated by the EEOC for his benefit.

ISSUE

Can the EEOC file a claim for damages for an employee against a company when the company's employees have signed mandatory arbitration agreements?

DECISION

Yes. Congress gave the EEOC the same enforcement powers under the ADA that it gave it under Title VII. In 1972, Congress amended Title VII to give the EEOC power to bring its own enforcement actions. Indeed, it was intended to carry the main burden of Title VII litigation. When Congress again amended the Act through passage of the Civil Rights Act in 1991 and broadened the available remedies, it authorized the EEOC to seek those remedies. The existence of a private arbitration agreement between the employee and employer does not change the EEOC's status.

Most states also have fair employment laws and enforcement schemes. In those states, employees must first file charges with the state agency. If no settlement results at this level, then the employee can file with the EEOC.

THE CIVIL RIGHTS ACT OF 1991

In the late 1980s the Supreme Court decided several cases in a manner that reduced the ability of employees to successfully bring discrimination claims. Congress reacted to the Court's decisions by passing the Civil Rights Act of 1991. The act, in effect, overturned the Court's decisions and restored the law to the way it had been. In addition, the act extended Title VII coverage to U.S. citizens working for U.S. companies overseas, and established that an employment decision based partly on discriminatory motives and partially on legitimate reasons is still illegal discrimination. Remedies for people harmed by discrimination were also expanded. The act allows claimants to sue for damages, including punitive damages, in cases of intentional discrimination, and provides for jury trials in such cases. The total amount of damages is limited by the size of the employer.

AGE DISCRIMINATION IN EMPLOYMENT ACT

The Age Discrimination in Employment Act (ADEA) prohibits employers of 20 or more people from refusing to hire, paying less to, discharging, or otherwise discriminating against employees because of their age. Employment agencies are also covered by the act, as are labor unions, which are prohibited from excluding from their membership or otherwise discriminating against persons because of age. The protection given is to persons 40 years old and older. A BFOQ exemption is provided. For example, a drama company would be able to limit its casting for a teenager's part to young people. Like the Equal Pay Act and Title VII, the statute is enforced by the EEOC.

Retirement of employees less than 70 years old under a mandatory pension plan was made illegal by the 1978 amendments. There is an exception for executives and others receiving very high pension benefits. Earlier retirement for inability to do the work is permitted.

MAHONEY V. RFE/RL INC.
47 F.3d 447 (D.D.C. 1995)

FACTS

RFE/RL, a nonprofit corporation that operates Radio Free Europe and Radio Liberty, employed 300 U.S. citizens at its facility in Munich, Germany. Employees were terminated when they reached age 65 in accordance with the terms of the union contract. While RFE/RL admitted that the mandatory retirement age would otherwise be in violation of the ADEA, it argued it was allowed in this case under an exception in the act that states:

It shall not be unlawful for an employer . . . to take any action otherwise prohibited . . . where such practices involve an employee in a workplace in a foreign country, and compliance . . . would cause such employer . . . to violate the laws of the country in which such workplace is located.

RFE/RL claimed a mandatory retirement age was a deeply embedded concept in German labor practices equivalent to a law.

(continued)

MAHONEY V. RFE/RL INC.
(concluded)

ISSUE

Can the mandatory retirement age be justified under the exception in the ADEA?

DECISION

Yes. When RFE/RL entered the contract with the union in 1982, the ADEA had no extra territorial reach, and the retirement provision, which was modeled after a nationwide agreement in the German broadcast industry, was entirely lawful. Congress amended the ADEA in 1984 to cover American citizens working for American companies overseas. After the amendment, RFE/RL applied to the "Works Council" (the Betriebstre) for a limited exception to the contract to allow U.S. workers to continue working past age 65. A *Betriebstre*, which exists in every German firm with 20 or more workers, is a body elected by employees. One of its duties is to ensure that management adheres to all provisions of the union contract. Departures from the contract are illegal without the Council's approval. The Betriebstre determined that

allowing U.S. citizens to work longer would both violate the contract's provision and discriminate on the basis of nationality. RFE/RL appealed the decision to the Munich Labor Court and lost. After negotiations with the union to change the contract failed, Mahoney was forced to retire. The retirement was legal under the Act's exception. Although a labor contract is not a law, a contract depends on laws to enforce it and make it effective. When a company fails to comply with a labor contract, it breaks the law. If RFE/RL had retained Mahoney, it would have violated the German laws standing behind such contracts, as well as the decisions of the Munich Labor Court. Congressional legislation cannot set aside the laws of foreign countries. The ADEA solves the dilemma faced by an overseas employer whose obligations under foreign law conflict with the ADEA by exempting it from compliance in such circumstances. The exception saves RFE/RL from the impossible position of having to conform to two inconsistent legal regimes.

AMERICANS WITH DISABILITIES ACT

The enactment of the Americans with Disabilities Act of 1990 (ADA) extended comprehensive federal coverage against discrimination on the basis of disability. The previous federal law, the Rehabilitation Act of 1973, applied only to employers with federal contracts. Most of the provisions of the ADA are very similar to those of the Rehabilitation Act.

The ADA protects a *qualified individual with a disability* from discrimination on the basis of that disability. A disability is defined as (1) a physical or mental impairment that substantially limits one or more of a person's major life activities, (2) a record of such an impairment, or (3) being regarded as having such an impairment. People with AIDS or AIDS-related conditions are specifically covered; people addicted to drugs or alcohol are not. Mental disease is covered, but certain sex-related traits such as bisexuality and transvestism are not. As the *Toyota* case shows, the Supreme Court has interpreted the ADA to limit its application to fewer employees.

A qualified individual is one who can perform the essential functions of a job with or without *reasonable accommodation* for his or her disability. Reasonable accommodation involves a determination of what the employer can do to enable the disabled person to perform the job without undue hardship to the employer. In determining undue hardship the courts consider several factors such as the cost of the accommodation in relation to the size of the employer, the employer's income, how many people would be helped, and whether it would be a one-time expense. Accommodation would include making the facility readily accessible, restructuring jobs, and providing adaptive equipment such as amplification devices and electronic readers.

TOYOTA MOTOR MANUFACTURING, KENTUCKY, INC. V. WILLIAMS
122 S. Ct. 681 (2001)

FACTS

Williams, an assembly line worker at Toyota, developed carpal tunnel syndrome. As a result, she was put on restrictions regarding how much she could lift, what kinds of tools she could use, and movements she could make. She was given modified duty jobs for two years, but she continued to have problems. After bringing a suit against Toyota, which was settled, she was put on an inspection team and did the job satisfactorily for two years. Then the duties of the team were expanded, and some of the new duties put a strain on her neck and shoulders, which led to further injury. Williams requested that Toyota accommodate her by allowing her to return to the prior duties that she could do successfully. This did not happen, and Williams began to regularly miss work. She was then fired. Williams filed a discrimination claim with the EEOC for Toyota's failure to reasonably accommodate her impairments as required by the ADA. Williams claimed that she was "disabled" under the ADA because her physical impairments substantially limited her in manual tasks, housework, gardening, playing with her children, lifting, and working. She claimed these were major life activities under the ADA.

ISSUE

Was Williams substantially impaired, and therefore covered by the ADA?

DECISION

No. The ADA defines a disability as, "a physical or mental impairment that substantially limits one or more of the major life activities" of an individual. Merely having an impairment does not make one disabled under the ADA. The impairment must also limit a major life activity. The term "substantially" precludes impairments that interfere in only a minor way with the performance of manual tasks from qualifying as a disability. "Major" refers to those activities that are of central importance to daily life. These terms must be strictly interpreted in order to make the Act fit with the legislative findings of Congress when it passed the law. This interpretation is also consistent with our decision in *Sutton v. United Air Lines* where we held that Congress did not intend to include people with corrected physical limitations among those covered by the Act. Thus, to be substantially limited in performing manual tasks, an individual must have an impairment that prevents or severely restricts the individual from doing activities that are of central importance to most people's daily lives. The impairment's impact must also be permanent or long term. An individualized assessment of the effect of an impairment is necessary, especially when, as with carpal tunnel syndrome, symptoms vary widely from person to person. The assessment must ask whether the person is excluded from a wide range of jobs, not just a specific job. Additionally, the manual tasks unique to any particular job are not necessarily important parts of most people's lives. Williams was not excluded from major life activities such as household chores, brushing one's teeth, and bathing. She was not disabled for purposes of the Act.

The ADA is administered by the EEOC. The Civil Rights Act of 1991 allows the disabled who suffer intentional discrimination to sue for damages, including punitive damages. Most states also have statutes protecting disabled persons from discrimination in employment.

········· *EMPLOYMENT AT WILL* ·········

The **employment-at-will** doctrine has been in existence for over 100 years. This doctrine allows employers to fire an employee who was not hired for a specific term (at-will employees) for any reason—good or bad. It is based on the laissez-faire values of the 19th century, for it leaves both the employer and employee with maximum freedom. The employee is free to quit at any time, and the employer can adjust its workforce as it sees fit. It also puts the risks of an uncertain economy on the employee and has led to many abuses. While the employment-at-will doctrine had been eroded in the past 50 years by statues such as Title VII, the NLRA, and the ADEA, the majority of employees were still unprotected against arbitrary and unfair firing.

Over the past several years, courts have been creating exceptions to the employment-at-will doctrine in an attempt to curb some of these abuses. They have used three different theories to do so: (1) the firing is against public policy, (2) the firing is in violation of implied terms of the employment contract, and (3) the firing violates an implied covenant of good faith and fair dealing. Over 40 states recognize at least one of these exceptions. However, application is far from uniform.

Under the public policy exception, firing someone for exercising a statutorily recognized duty, right, or privilege such as filing a worker compensation claim, serving jury duty, or refusing to commit perjury for the employer would be a wrongful discharge. Additionally, as illustrated by the *Paralegal case*, employees who report employer wrong-doing to appropriate agencies and personnel are protected under this theory. This activity, called *whistleblowing*, is also protected by statute in a majority of states.

PARALEGAL V. LAWYER
783 F. Supp. 230 (E.D. Pa. 1992)

FACTS

The plaintiff, a paralegal, worked for the defendant, a lawyer. The lawyer was under investigation for alleged misdeeds by the Disciplinary Board of the Supreme Court of Pennsylvania. Plaintiff revealed that the lawyer had written and back-dated a letter in order to deceive the Board into thinking he had communicated with his client earlier, thereby hoping to avoid the disciplinary complaint. The paralegal was fired after the lawyer learned of her revelation.

ISSUE

Was the firing a wrongful firing in violation of public policy?

DECISION

Yes. Plaintiff was, in today's parlance, a whistleblower. An at-will employee can sue in tort for wrongful firing if the firing contravenes a clear mandate of public policy. The public policy protecting whistleblowers is expressed in both statutes and court decisions. This case is similar to the case of a barmaid who was fired for refusing to serve an obviously intoxicated patron. Her refusal was in compliance with public policy as expressed in Pennsylvania's Dram Shop Act. Here, a lawyer has a duty not to falsify material facts or evidence, or to forge documents. The public policy underlying these rules is so obvious as to need no discussion. Plaintiff refused to countenance these acts by blowing the whistle and was fired. She can sue for that wrongful firing.

In implied contract cases, the courts find promises of job security and fair dealing made to employees in personnel manuals, handbooks, job interviews, and so on. Such actions as having a disciplinary procedure, a probationary period, or calling a job a career position have been sufficient for the court to imply the contract promises. In the third kind of case, which has been recognized by few courts, the employee argues that the firing is unlawful because it was done in bad faith. Generally, these cases involve terminations made on bases that have nothing to do with job performance but involve improper ulterior motives.

Employee Privacy

In addition to the erosion of employment at will, employee rights are being expanded by a growing recognition of an employee's right to privacy. Congress has recently given protection to this right through passage of the Employee Polygraph Protection Act, and the courts through drug-testing decisions.

Lie Detector Tests

Increasing liability of employers for employee actions and rising employee theft were two of the reasons that polygraph examination of employees and applicants had risen to over 2 million per year. Because of invasive questions asked before and during such tests, and because the polygraph records answers whether or not the individual responded verbally, the tests can be very invasive of privacy. In addition, most workers had no meaningful way to refuse to take them or control over use of the results. In response to these problems, Congress passed the Employee Polygraph Protection Act in 1988.

The act prohibits private employers from using mechanical lie detector tests to screen applicants. It also prohibits employers from using these tests on employees unless the employer is engaged in an investigation of economic losses due to theft, embezzlement, industrial espionage, or similar causes. Even in this instance, the employer cannot use the test unless it can show that the employee had access to the material under investigation and some reasonable ground to believe the employee was involved. The act allows manufacturers and distributors of controlled substances and security service firms wider use of these tests.

Many states also have laws prohibiting or regulating the use of lie detector tests. Most establish minimum qualifications for those who administer the tests. If the state law is stricter than the federal law, it is not preempted.

Drug Testing

Privacy is at the center of challenges to the employer's right to test for drug use. By their nature such tests invade privacy: The tests can reveal such private facts as whether a person is pregnant, and they can reveal off-duty usage that had no impact on job performance. Most court cases so far have involved public employees or applicants who are protected by a constitutional right to privacy under the Fourth Amendment's search and seizure provisions. Use of drug tests in this context has generally been held to be violative of the right to privacy unless the employer can show a reasonable basis for suspecting that the individual employee was using drugs or that drug use in a particular job could threaten public safety or interest.

Bennett v. Massachusetts Bay Transportation Authority
1998 Mass. Super LEXIS 164 (Mass. Superior Ct. 1998)

Facts

Bennett was a motorperson for the MBTA. In 1990, the MBTA gave Bennett a copy of its new Drug and Alcohol Policy which called for random drug testing of employees in safety-sensitive positions. A motorperson is a safety-sensitive position. The policy also urged employees to self-refer to an employee counseling service for drug use. Those who complied with treatment and made progress would not be fired. Thirty months later, Bennett

(continued)

BENNETT V. MASSACHUSETTS BAY TRANSPORTATION AUTHORITY
(concluded)

was required to take a random drug test. Her test came back positive for cocaine, and she was fired.

ISSUE

Did the drug test violate Bennett's Fourth Amendment protection against unreasonable search and seizure?

DECISION

No. The MBTA has a ridership of 700,000 people a day. Its riders depend on operators to perform in a safe and responsible manner; safety is a paramount MBTA concern. In the late 1980s, the federal Urban Mass Transportation Authority proposed regulations requiring all public transportation systems, as a condition of receiving federal funding, to implement pre-employment, probable cause,

return to work, random, and post-accident drug testing. As a result, the MBTA adopted its drug testing policy. The collection and testing of urine are searches under the Fourth Amendment. However, the search of Bennett was not unreasonable because the MBTA has a compelling interest in deterring drug use by safety-sensitive employees. As the Supreme Court pointed out, these employees "discharge duties fraught with such risk of injury to others that even a momentary lapse of attention can have disastrous consequences." Bennett's urine test was conducted in a manner as consistent with protecting her privacy interests as feasible. Random drug testing is an effective deterrent to drug abuse by safety-sensitive employees.

Private employees can challenge drug testing under tort theories such as invasion of privacy or infliction of emotional distress (discussed in Chapter 4), or as a wrongful firing under one of the theories eroding employment at will. So far, however, such challenges have met with limited success. For example, in the *Luedtke* case that opened this chapter, the court found that the employer's firing of Luedtke for refusing to take the drug test was not a breach of the implied covenant of good faith and fair dealing in his employment contract. The court recognized a right to privacy, but in highly dangerous jobs such as Luedtke held, his privacy interests were secondary to the employer's concern that Luedtke not be impaired by off-the-job drug use.

Some states have responded to the lack of protection for private employees by passing laws that extend to these employees protections similar to those constitutionally granted to public employees. They also regulate how a statutorily permitted test must be administered. A few states have taken the opposite approach and have passed laws making it easier for private employers to conduct drug tests. In addition, federal law requires drug testing of certain employees, such as those occupying safety-sensitive or security-related jobs in the transportation industry.

OTHER PRIVACY CONCERNS

Modern technology has given employers a variety of means to monitor employees' reliability and work performance. Congress and state legislatures are considering and enacting legislation regulating an employer's use of phone, computer, or video and other electronic monitoring because of its invasive and overreaching potential. There is also increasing litigation regarding employer searches of areas such as desks, lockers, offices, briefcases, and other things that an employee might reasonably believe are private. In such cases the courts weigh the employer's need to do the search against the intrusiveness on the employee's reasonable expectation of privacy.

Personnel and medical records are another area of privacy concern to employees. Congress recently enacted the Health Insurance Portability and Accountability Act (HIPPA) to help maintain the privacy and security of health information. Employers who obtain identifiable information from health plans they administer are regulated regarding what information they share and with whom it can be shared. The Department of Health and Human Services is proposing final regulations, and compliance with those regulations will be required by 2003. Many states allow both public and private employees access to their personnel files, and some limit third-party access to those files.

Employee privacy is an area of growing concern to both employees and employers. It is likely to continue to be the subject of litigation, legislation, and expansion.

.... *QUESTIONS AND PROBLEM CASES* ....

1. Explain what is necessary to show that an injury is work related under workers' compensation.
2. How does ERISA protect an employee's retirement benefits?
3. Explain what a BFOQ is and give an example.
4. Explain when an employer can use a lie detector test.
5. Define "reasonable accommodation" and explain what courts consider in determining it.
6. Gayler, a semitractor-trailer driver for North American Van Lines, was injured during her work and received workers' compensation benefits. Ten months later she was still undergoing treatments when her doctor prescribed a medical device to aid her recovery. North American authorized the purchase of the device. Gayler was driving her car to pick up the device at a medical supplier when she was seriously injured in a head-on collision. Gayler claimed that the accident arose out of her employment because she was obtaining an employer-authorized treatment at the time it occurred. Is she correct?
7. Johnson and Jump were members of General Teamsters Local 162. The union was on strike against Western-Pacific Construction Materials Company (Materials). During the strike, Johnson harassed a security guard, spit at vehicles, carried weapons, cursed and threatened employees as they crossed the picket line, and threw a baseball-sized rock at a car, denting it. Jump ran a car driven by a strike replacement employee off the road, and assaulted and threatened him. Materials fired Johnson and Jump for this conduct. The union filed unfair labor practice charges contesting the firings. Were the firings by the company unfair labor practices?

8. Perry Jordan voluntarily resigned her employment with the North Carolina National Bank after she became a member of the Seventh-Day Adventists. A belief of this sect is that its members should not work from sunset Friday to sunset Saturday. Later, she sought reemployment by the bank. She stated in her application that she must be guaranteed never to be called on to work on Saturday. Is refusal to employ because of this condition a violation of Title VII by North Carolina National Bank?

9. During Harris's two-and-one-half years of work at Forklift Systems, the president, Hardy, made frequent gender-based insults and sexual innuendoes to Harris. For example, Hardy would say things like, "You're a woman, what do you know?" and "We need a man as the rental manager." He suggested that he and Harris negotiate her raise at the local Holiday Inn, and he asked her and other female employees to retrieve coins from his front pants pocket. He would drop objects and ask the female employees to bend over and pick them up. When Harris complained, Hardy promised to stop, but soon thereafter, in front of a customer, he asked her if she had promised the customer sex in order to get the contract. Harris quit and sued for sexual harassment. Harris's claim was unsuccessful because the lower court found that Hardy's actions were not sufficiently severe to seriously affect Harris's psychological well-being. Harris appealed. Will she be successful?

10. Between 1986 and 1993, Smith was employed by Midland Brake in light assembly. During this time, he had problems with chronic dermatitis on his hands and some muscular injuries. As a result, his physicians placed restrictions on his work activities and on several occasions

ordered him to stop working for limited periods. Midland Brake attempted to accommodate Smith's limitations by assigning him to duties within the light assembly department that involved less lifting and less exposure to irritants. After Smith had been on a leave of absence for almost 10 months, Midland Brake terminated his employment, citing an inability to accommodate his skin sensitivity. Smith contended that there were numerous job openings in other areas of Midland Brake that should have been made available to him. He sued for discrimination under the ADA. Was Smith's discharge in violation of the ADA?

11. Blocker became a CPA in 1979. After working as a staff auditor and accountant for other companies, she was hired as a junior auditor by AT&T in 1983. When she was hired, there were four male auditors in her area who had been with the company for several years and were classified as senior auditors. In 1984, Blocker complained that she was not receiving the same salary as a new male senior auditor, Bradshaw, even though she was doing the same work. When Bradshaw was brought in, AT&T was in the process of divestiture of the Bell System, and its policy was to fill positions with lateral transfers from other areas because of a promotion and hiring freeze. In 1985, Blocker filed a complaint with the EEOC claiming that she was not being paid equally for equal work. Did AT&T violate the Equal Pay Act by paying Blocker less than the male accountants?

12. Von Raab, the Commissioner of Customs, instituted a drug-screening program for certain positions within the Customs Service because drug interdiction had become the service's primary enforcement mission. Employees directly involved with drug interdiction or enforcement and employees who carried firearms were to be tested. The initial test was a monitored urine test. If it proved positive, a gas chromatography/mass spectrometry test was done. If that test also proved positive, and the employee could offer no satisfactory explanation, he or she would be fired. The National Treasury Employees Union, which represented Customs employees, challenged the program as violative of the Fourth Amendment. Is it correct?

PART V

Business Organizations

CHAPTER 23

Which Form of Business Organization?

George, Kim, and Martha have decided to open a Polynesian restaurant that specializes in oriental food and tropical drinks. George has no personal savings; however, he has a bartender's license as well as seven years of experience as an assistant manager at a large restaurant. Kim recently inherited a large sum of money and is interested in investing some of it in a business opportunity. However, as a full-time medical student, Kim has neither the time nor the desire to operate the business. Martha has personal savings of almost $20,000 and is willing to invest some of it in the restaurant. However, she also wants to set some money aside for her son's future college expenses. She plans on working full-time with George as co-manager of the restaurant. George, Kim, and Martha are now trying to decide which form of business organization they should select for the restaurant.

- *Which form of business will be easiest for them to organize?*
- *Which will provide the greatest protection for Kim's and Martha's uncommitted savings?*
- *Which form will provide the greatest relief from tax liability?*
- *Which form will be best suited for raising necessary operating capital if Kim's and Martha's contributions should prove inadequate?*
- *What are the potential risks and advantages of becoming a franchisee in a national restaurant chain?*

Consider these issues as you read through this chapter.

The legal form of a business can have great bearing on the successful operation and resulting profitability of the business venture. Accordingly, it is important to have a general understanding of the fundamental features of each of the basic types of business organization. This chapter will offer a general examination of:

1. Sole proprietorships
2. Partnerships (both general and limited)
3. Corporations (publicly held and close)
4. Limited liability companies
5. Limited liability partnerships
6. Franchising

SOLE PROPRIETORSHIP

A **sole proprietorship** is a business operated by a person as his own personal property. The enterprise is merely an extension of the individual owner. Agents and employees may be hired, but the owner has all the responsibility; all the profits and losses are the owner's. For example, one might conduct a computer service business as an individual proprietorship. It would be very much like buying a house as an investment and renting it out. The person operating the business need not use his or her own name as the name of the business; it may be operated under an assumed or trade name, such as the Data Experts Company. Such a trade name would have to be registered with the proper state or local official, however. Employees of the business are the personal employees of the owner. The salaries and wages paid to employees of the business and other business expenses are deductible in determining taxable income.

PARTNERSHIPS

General Partnership

A **partnership** is a voluntary association designed to carry on a business for profit. However, no express agreement to create a general partnership is necessary. All that is required is that the parties intend to have the relationship that the law defines as a partnership. In a **general partnership,** each of the partners is an owner and has a right to share in the profits of the business. Unless otherwise agreed, a partner is not considered an employee and not is entitled to wages for the services he or she renders to the partnership. As with a sole proprietorship, each partner is personally liable for any losses suffered by the partnership business, even if the losses exceed the individual partner's contributions to the enterprise.

Limited Partnership

The **limited partnership,** a variation of the ordinary or general partnership, was designed to combine the informalities of the partnership with the capital-raising advantages of the corporation. It permits investors (the limited partners) who do not engage in management to share in the profits of the business without becoming personally liable for its debts.

CORPORATIONS

A **corporation** is treated as an entity separate and distinct from its owners. By incorporating, it is easier to hold property over long periods of time since corporate existence is not generally threatened by the death, bankruptcy, or retirement of an individual owner. A corporation can acquire, hold, and convey property in its own name. It can also sue and be sued in its own name. The principal reason to incorporate a business today, however, is the limited liability of its shareholders. Ordinarily, the owners (shareholders) of a corporation are not personally liable for its debts; their loss is limited to their investment.

Corporations often are divided into publicly held and close corporations. The stock of the **close corporation** is held by a family or small group of people who know one another. A **publicly held** corporation sells shares to people who may have little interest in it except as investors.

One's status as a shareholder gives one certain ownership rights in the corporate business, although this does not include an automatic right to be an employee. However, in numerous instances, the employees of a publicly held corporation will become shareholders, and the shareholders in a close corporation will serve as employees.

See Figure 23–1 for a summary of the basic forms of business organization.

FIGURE 23–1   The Basic Forms of Business Organization

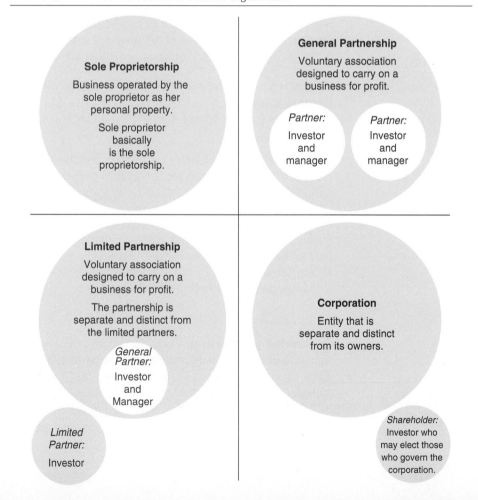

FACTORS TO CONSIDER IN CHOOSING FORMS OF BUSINESS ORGANIZATION

Each type of business structure possesses certain advantages and disadvantages that must be considered in deciding which form of business organization to select. Some of these important attributes are:

1. Limited liability
2. Taxation
3. Formalities
4. Financing
5. Management
6. Life of the business
7. Liquidity of investment

LIMITED LIABILITY

Safety is a prime consideration for most investors, particularly when they are not major participants in the enterprise. Limited partners who do not participate in management and shareholders in a corporation may lose their investment if the business fails. However, they have no further liability to creditors of the business or to victims of torts that are attributable to the business. In contrast, partners in a general partnership may lose not only their investment but also may be required to pay partnership debts from personal assets. Sole proprietors have the same risk of unlimited personal liability.

In many instances, shareholders in a small corporation may be induced to voluntarily waive their unlimited liability. Credit to such corporations, especially new ones without strong earnings records, may be granted only if the debt is guaranteed by one or more of the shareholders. Lending banks often require shareholders to cosign corporate notes. Suppliers may require shareholders to guarantee accounts. These acts are seldom demanded of limited partners because the general partners are liable. This exception to limited liability seldom occurs outside of the contractual context. For example, a victim of the negligence of an employee in driving the corporation's delivery truck cannot get the wealthiest shareholder to agree to assume liability after an accident. Therefore, from a risk standpoint, a shareholder or limited partner is better off than a general partner. (See Figure 23–2 on page 389.)

Sometimes courts strip corporate shareholders of their limited liability to prevent unfair results. This concept, known as "piercing the corporate veil," is more thoroughly discussed in Chapter 25. Consider the following case, where the court refuses to pierce the veil.

NLRB. v. GREATER KANSAS CITY ROOFING
2 F. 3d 1047 (10th Cir. 1993)

FACTS

Greater Kansas City Roofing (GKC) had been operated as a sole proprietorship owned by Judy Clarke and managed by her husband, Charlie Clarke. In 1983, because of numerous violations of the labor laws, the National Labor Relations Board (NLRB) ordered the business to pay a total of $133,742.47. Tina Clarke, Charlie's sister, began loaning money to GKC in 1984 to help it out of its financial difficulties. Finally, when the business was unable to pay Tina the more than $38,000 it owed her, she decided to set up a new corporation and run the business herself. Tina Clarke became the sole shareholder, officer, and director of The New Greater Kansas City Roofing Corporation (New GKC). She was unaware at the time this corporation was formed that GKC had committed labor law violations and that the NLRB had an outstanding judgment against the business. New GKC basically took over the assets of its predecessor and retained many of its former customers. New GKC's staff was composed

(continued)

NLRB. v. GREATER KANSAS CITY ROOFING
(concluded)

almost exclusively of the former employees of GKC, including Charlie Clarke, who was employed to manage the corporate business. Tina failed to adhere to corporate formalities in her dealings with New GKC. She used a trade name associated with the corporation, as well as its address and telephone number, to establish a credit card collection account and to open a checking account for her escort service, Affaire d'Amour. There is no evidence New GKC had bylaws, accounts, stock, corporate records, or held meetings. In 1988 the NLRB attempted to collect its outstanding judgment against GKC. It alleged that New GKC was the alter ego of GKC and that its corporate veil should be pierced so that Tina Clarke could be held personally liable on the claim.

ISSUE

Should the court pierce the veil and find Tina Clarke liable on the corporate debt?

DECISION

No. The corporate structure is an artificial construct of the law, a substantial purpose of which is to create an incentive for investment by limiting exposure to personal liability. Only in extreme circumstances will the corporate form be disregarded so the personal assets of a controlling shareholder may be attached to pay the debts of the corporation. However, the corporate veil should be pierced only in situations where it is essential to avoid impropriety or injustice. This is an alter ego case. That is, the NLRB seeks to pierce the corporate veil because Tina Clarke disregarded New GKC as a separate entity and operated the company as if it were her own personal activity. Under the alter ego theory a shareholder will have personal liability for corporate debts only if a two-prong test is met. First, the shareholder must disregard the corporation's separate identity. Second, adherence to the corporate fiction would sanction a fraud or promote an injustice. While Tina Clarke's sloppy manner of conducting business under New GKC might have disregarded the corporation's separate identity, there is no evidence that she committed fraud, either in the formation of the corporation or in the misuse of the corporate form. There is nothing to indicate New GKC was created to avoid the judgment since she was unaware of it when she formed the corporation. Further, there is no showing that Tina Clarke used the corporate form to work an injustice. She already had loaned GKC over $38,000 and, after incorporation, continued to loan her own money to the business.

Refer to the case that opened this chapter. There, Kim and Martha both were concerned about minimizing the risk of losing more than their investments in the restaurant business. Kim, not desiring to become actively involved in the operation of the restaurant, may prefer to organize the business as a limited partnership. Martha, on the other hand, wishes to actively manage while simultaneously safeguarding her personal savings. She may favor the corporate form of organization.

TAXATION

The wealth-increasing potential of an investment in a business is greatly affected by the income tax laws. These laws change from time to time; however, the basic principles tend to remain constant. Changes in rates of taxation may shift the tax advantage between the partnership and corporate forms in certain circumstances. Since earnings projections for a business are also uncertain, the possibility of tax rate changes seldom affects the final choice of the form of organization.

The basic difference is between taxation as a partnership and taxation as a corporation. A corporation is a taxable entity. It pays income taxes on its own income, and its shareholders generally must pay income taxes on dividends from the corporation although they are paid out of income already taxed to the corporation. On the other hand, a partnership is not treated as a taxable entity. Income (or loss) is passed

FIGURE 23-2   Liability Features of the Basic Forms of Business Organization

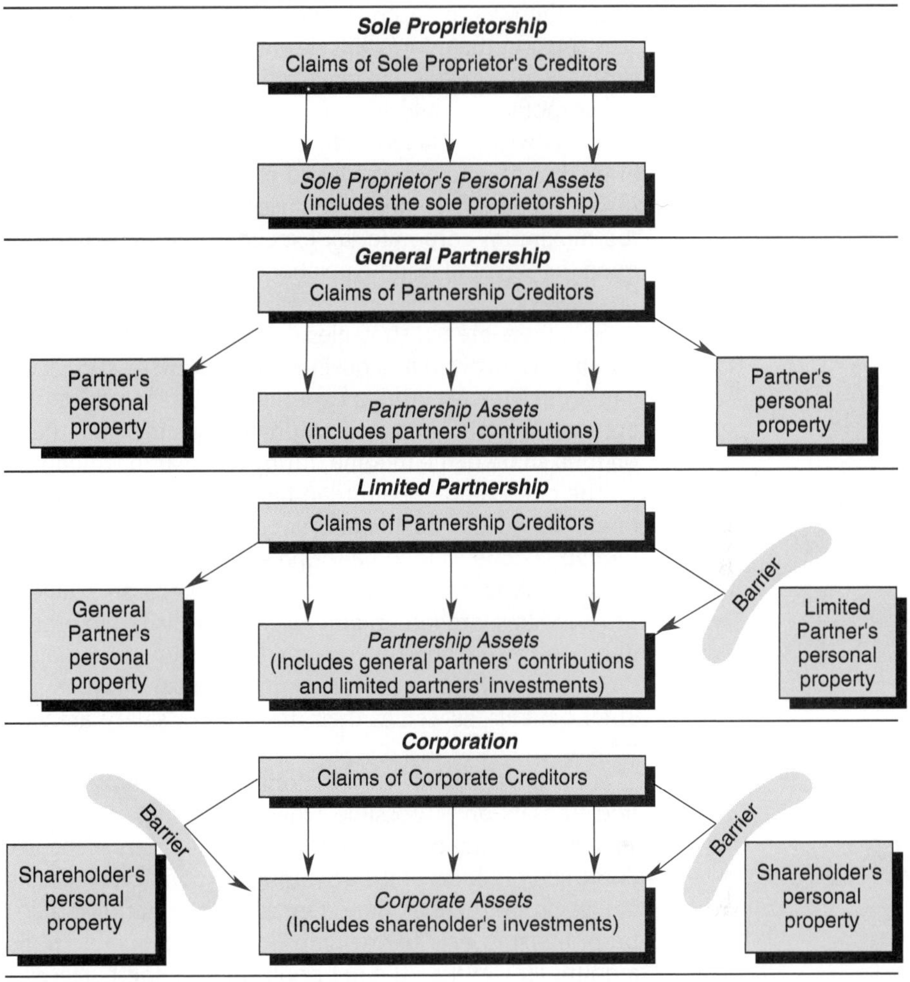

through pro rata to the partners and taxed to them. Likewise, a sole proprietorship is not a taxable entity.

S Corporations

S Corporations, or Subchapter S corporations, represent an important variation that should be considered by certain closely held corporations. They are taxed very much like a partnership in that no corporate tax is paid. Instead, shareholders directly report their share of the corporation's losses or earnings on their individual tax returns. This can provide an important advantage over ordinary corporations. Several requirements (only a few of which will be mentioned here) must be maintained or the Subchapter S corporation loses its tax status:

1. There can be no more than 75 shareholders.
2. The shareholders must all be individuals or estates.
3. Shareholders must consent in writing to having the corporation taxed as a partnership.

Advantages of Corporate Taxation

When the maximum corporate tax rate was less than the maximum individual tax rate, the corporate form was desirable despite the threat of a double tax. If corporate profits were reinvested in expansion of the business rather than paid out in dividends, the corporation could serve as a tax shelter. The shareholder's interest in the retained earnings was not taxed until the stock was sold or the corporation was dissolved. Then the shareholder was taxed at a capital gains rate, which was lower than the ordinary income rate applied to dividends. However, in 1988, for the first time in history, the maximum corporate tax exceeded the maximum individual rate. This strengthened the threat of double taxation and discouraged the use of the corporate form of business.

Still, there are tax strategies that can minimize such disadvantages. When the corporation is involved in a business that has wide swings in income from year to year, it can reduce the tax burden experienced by shareholders by keeping the dividend rate constant. Partners and sole proprietors, on the other hand, will be individually taxed on their share of the income during the year in which it was earned.

The corporation tax burden can be lessened if the shareholders are active in the operation of the business. Shareholder–employees may be paid salaries that, although taxable as income to the shareholders, are deductible expenses for the corporation. Also, fringe benefits, such as pension plans or health insurance, can be provided to shareholder–employees if furnished to other employees. The cost can be deducted by the corporation, and there is no immediate taxation to the employees of the value to them of the plans. In contrast, partners are not treated as employees. Their benefits, as well as their drawings or salary, are viewed as distributions of partnership profits.

A tax advantage of corporations may be realized when the business is sold. A tax-free transaction is possible when the shares of a corporation are exchanged for shares of another corporation. The shareholders of the acquired corporation then become shareholders of the acquiring corporation without being required to pay a capital gains tax at that time. On the other hand, a sale of the business of a sole proprietorship or a partnership is usually a taxable transaction. If the sale is for an amount greater than the net book value of the business, an immediate capital gains tax will be due. (See Figure 23–3.)

Advantages of Sole Proprietorship and Partnership Taxation

If losses are anticipated in the early years of a business and the owners have other income, the sole proprietorship and partnership forms will save taxes during that period. The owners can reduce their tax liability on their other income by the amount of the partnership losses.

Partnerships and individual proprietorships are not required to pay corporate franchise taxes. Usually, taxes on their operations (other than income taxes) are set at a lower level than those on corporations. Also, they do not need to pay privilege taxes to do intrastate business in another state.

FORMALITIES

An individual proprietorship or a general partnership can be formed without the formalities required of a corporation or a limited partnership; no filing with a government official is necessary. The same is true at termination. Cancellation of the certificate is necessary for limited partnerships and corporations.

FIGURE 23-3   Lessening the Burden of Corporate Taxation

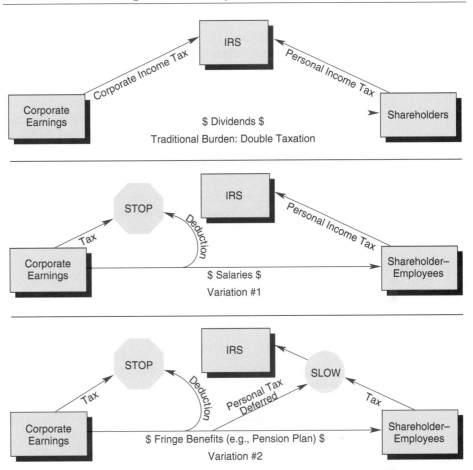

Less is also required when proprietorships and partnerships operate in other states. A corporation must be qualified if it wants to do interstate business in any state except the state in which it is incorporated. For example, if a corporation wanted to operate a retail shop in another state, it would have to file its articles of incorporation in the new state, appoint a local representative to accept legal papers for the corporation, and pay annual privilege or franchise taxes as well as pay for the privilege of qualification. None of this is required of an individual proprietorship or a general partnership.

FINANCING

For larger businesses, the corporate form makes financing easier. The wide variety of equity and debt securities available allows flexibility. Limited liability and the tendency of investors to relate corporate securities to familiar "blue chip" companies make them appear safer. For small corporations, the continuity factor may make it easier for the business to borrow money from a bank. If the principal shareholders put up their stock as collateral, the loan may be more acceptable. This would give the lender a chance to take control of the management or to sell the corporation as a going business rather than be forced to liquidate if the loan becomes uncollectible.

MANAGEMENT

The corporation can be very flexible in management arrangements. Day-to-day operating management can be given to one or more officers, while the board of directors retains general policy control. Shareholders who are not directors have a very limited voice in corporate decision making; however, they seldom risk liability by participating in management.

Limited partners, on the other hand, generally cannot participate in management at all without the danger of losing limited liability. General partners usually are free to take an active role in management, although they can delegate routine management decisions to one or more partners. Nevertheless, all general partners are likely to have apparent authority to bind the partnership. Because partners seldom give up their right to participate in management, business decisions may be delayed by time-consuming consultation, and deadlocks may occur.

The close corporation is no freer of serious problems than a partnership when owners cannot agree on management. Since it is more traditional in the corporate form to assign everyday management to a chief executive officer, conflicts and disputes may arise less often under that form.

Of course, the sole proprietorship provides the greatest ease of management. There, the proprietor is free, within the limits of the law, to unilaterally determine the destiny of the organization.

Freeze-Outs in Close Corporations

A minority shareholder in a close corporation has little power and, thus, may be "frozen out" (left out of important opportunities) by the majority regarding such issues as a reduction or elimination of dividends as well as a loss of employment. Traditionally, minority shareholders have had an uphill battle fighting such a freeze-out in court. Even if no attempt at freeze-out is made, without power to terminate the corporation (as is readily available in a partnership), the minority shareholder is at best "locked in" to the investment.

BROOKS V. HILL
717 So.2d 759 (Ala. Sup. Ct. 1998)

FACTS

Raymond Brooks owned a 19 percent interest in H & B, a closely held corporation. Leroy Hill, Raymond's brother-in-law, owned the remaining interest. In 1993, Leroy persuaded Raymond to sell his shares in the corporation for $1.2 million ($62,987.00 per share). One year later, Raymond died and his widow, Dorothy, was appointed executrix of his estate. She filed a lawsuit against Leroy (her brother), asserting that he had breached his fiduciary duties as an officer and majority shareholder of H & B by using the assets of the corporation to benefit his own personal interests. This included having corporate employees perform personal services for himself and borrowing the corporate airplane for purposes unrelated to the business. Dorothy alleged that Leroy did these things as part of a scheme to devalue the corporation's stock so he could purchase it from Raymond at a deflated price. She claimed that Leroy knew that the value of the stock was far in excess of $62,987 per share and that he misrepresented its actual value to Raymond when he made the offer to buy Raymond's holdings. Specifically, Dorothy filed a complaint against Leroy for minority shareholder "oppression."

(continued)

BROOKS V. HILL
(concluded)

ISSUE

Is Leroy liable for minority shareholder oppression?

DECISION

No. Our courts have recognized that majority shareholders of a closely held corporation owe a duty to at least act fairly to the minority interests. This is because where several owners carry on a business together (as they usually do in a close corporation), their relationship should be considered a fiduciary one similar to the relationship among partners. The fact that the enterprise is incorporated should not substantially change the picture. However, the minority oppression or "freeze-out" cause of action is not a panacea for any and all conduct undertaken by majority shareholders of a close corporation that could be deemed unfair to the minority. Rather, the underpinnings of the freeze-out cause of action demonstrate that it is meant to be a remedy for a more specific type of unfairness that may arise from the hybrid nature of close corporations. Dorothy alleges that Leroy devalued Raymond's stock in H & B by wasting corporate assets and that in making an offer to purchase his shares Leroy misrepresented their actual value. However, a minority shareholder cannot recover on his own behalf for a director's waste of corporate assets, even in the close corporation context. Thus, Leroy's alleged waste of H & B's assets cannot be the basis of a freeze-out claim in Dorothy's favor. We similarly conclude that Leroy's alleged misrepresentation as to the value of H & B does not rise to a freeze-out claim. One could certainly deem it "unfair" for a majority shareholder of a close corporation to misrepresent a material fact to a minority shareholder in connection with a purchase of his shares. But while such wrongdoing suggests that minority shareholder might have been defrauded, it does not suggest that the minority shareholder has also been "frozen out" of the corporation. Dorothy has not asserted that Raymond was deprived of his fair share of corporate gains, such as salaried employment, dividends, or other corporate privileges he reasonably might have expected to receive by virtue of his position as a stockholder. Nor has she alleged that Leroy used his right of control in an attempt to coerce or "squeeze" Raymond into accepting an unreasonably low price for his shares, either by threatening to deprive him of income flowing from the corporation or even by "stonewalling" in purchase negotiations in an attempt to take advantage of the practical difficulty Raymond might have had in selling his interest to a third party. Rather, the complaint asserts that Leroy simply made a misrepresentation of material fact, upon which Raymond relied to his detriment. Clearly, however, the duty to refrain from making false representations does not spring from the vulnerability of a minority shareholder in the context of a close corporation. Thus, the complaint does not state a cause of action for a claim of minority shareholder freeze-out.

Ethical Implications   Suppose that you are the majority shareholder in a close corporation. Rather than generously distributing dividends to all of the shareholders, the corporation, under your direction, hires you as a well-paid management consultant. Is this ethical?

LIFE OF THE BUSINESS

Legally, a corporation is not affected by the death or insolvency of a shareholder. Of course, if the knowledge or skill of the deceased was the principal reason for the corporation's success, the corporation may not remain profitable very long. A great advantage of the corporation in providing continuity is the ease of transferring ownership of the shares. Ownership of a family or other close corporation can be shifted gradually by gift or sale of shares to those who will succeed the present managers. This may minimize the tax consequences at death that would otherwise result from selling the business. Those who will not participate as employees can be given a claim to income through dividends. Two or more classes of stock can be established to separate the major share of ownership from control.

Generally, it is easier to preserve goodwill in a corporation as owners change than it is in a partnership or sole proprietorship. This results from the continuity of the corporation, which may be very important in a business that serves the public.

The business of a partnership may be continued when a partner dies, becomes insolvent, or wishes to retire. Nevertheless, the law treats the partnership as dissolved. Special agreements to keep the business operating must be made in advance of these events, or it may be difficult to attain agreement to form a new partnership. A partner can terminate an ordinary partnership at will. However, termination in violation of the partnership agreement may subject the terminating partner to liability for damages.

The success of an individual proprietorship usually depends on its owner. Therefore, successful continuation of the business by a widow, widower, son, or daughter is less likely than in a partnership.

LIQUIDITY OF INVESTMENT

The ease of selling one's investment in a publicly held corporation is one of the major advantages of the corporate form. Theoretically, the minority shareholders in a close corporation can also sell their shares. However, unless at least a seat on the board of directors can be obtained through cumulative voting, there may be little that is attractive to a potential buyer. Shareholders of the corporation have little incentive to buy out the minority interest because of the freeze-out potential discussed earlier. Shareholders in close corporations are often restricted in the sale of their stock. This may also make the investment less marketable and therefore less liquid.

General partners can sell their partnership interests but the purchaser does not become a partner unless he or she is accepted unanimously by the other general partners into what is essentially a new partnership. The partner who wants to sell out before the end of the agreed-on term of the partnership is in a weak bargaining position. Unless the partnership agreement changes the generally prevailing rules, such a partner is not entitled to force the partnership business to be liquidated. Nor is the departing partner entitled to share in the goodwill value of the business if the other partners exercise their right to continue it.

Limited partnership interests can be sold without such adverse effects; however, there seldom is a public market, such as a stock exchange, where they can be sold. Publicly offered partnership interests generally are designed to serve as tax shelters for the original purchasers during the early years of ownership and are generally unattractive to investors during their later years.

MAKING THE CHOICE

Rarely do all of these factors point toward the choice of one form of business organization. For instance, in the case that opened this chapter, Kim may have favored either the corporate or the limited partnership form in order to shelter her private savings from business debts. However, under the corporate form, she faces the problem of double taxation when dividends are declared. George and Martha could lessen this problem for themselves by steering corporate earnings toward salaries and fringe benefits rather than toward dividend payments. George and Martha also could draw salaries and benefits under the limited partnership form. Kim, on the other hand, could not. And, as a passive investor, she could be taxed immediately on her share of any undistributed partnership earnings. Accordingly, each factor needs to be analyzed separately and then all the advantages and disadvantages need to be weighed together.

It is possible that a single factor such as limited liability will be so important as to outweigh other factors. However, if the business involves little risk or the owners have few other assets, this factor should be given little weight. In our restaurant case, Kim and Martha will want to give great weight to the limited liability factor. A restaurant, particularly one selling alcoholic beverages, would continually be faced with the risk of large personal injury suits.

Likewise, in starting a small business, financing a corporation will be no easier than financing a partnership or an individual proprietorship. If several years of substantial losses are expected and the owners have other income that can be offset by the losses, being taxed as a partnership may be the primary factor. The partnership can be changed to a corporation later, when profits are assured. At that time, pension plans and other employee fringe benefits and reinvestment of profits in the business will probably result in minimizing taxes through the corporate form.

It is wise to consult a public accountant and a lawyer who have had experience with businesses faced with these choices and who are familiar with the latest IRS rules. Certainly this should be done before forming a corporation if the business is beyond minimal size or capitalization. There are likely to be adverse tax consequences from liquidating a corporation or selling its assets to another form of business.

LIMITED LIABILITY COMPANIES

Forty-seven states have statutes that permit businesses to operate **limited liability companies** (LLCs). These statutes grant LLCs the taxation benefits of partnerships and the limited liability advantages of corporations. Unlike limited partnerships, all of the investors are able to share in management and, unlike S corporations, there are no restrictions on the number of members an LLC can have.

CREATION

LLCs are similar to corporations and limited partnerships in that they require the filing of articles of organization with the secretary of state. The name of an LLC must include the words "limited liability company" or some other clear indication of its limited liability feature so the public is made aware of this fact. Some states require LLCs to file annual reports with the Secretary of State.

LEGAL STATUS

Like a corporation, an LLC is a separate entity with a legal existence apart from its individual owners. It may sue or be sued in its own name and it can buy, hold, or sell property. Similarly, it may enter into contracts and incur liabilities in its own name.

Because of the LLC's separate legal identity, it generally is liable for its own obligations. In short, the members have limited liability. This means they risk no more than their investment in the LLC. However, as with corporations, courts will pierce the veil between the LLC and its members if an LLC is created with the intent to defraud its creditors. In those instances, the members will be personally liable on LLC debts.

OPERATION

Like corporations, LLCs are separate and distinct from their members. Thus, one member has no personal liability for the wrongful acts of others. This is an appealing feature for partners in professional firms (doctors, lawyers, accountants, and so on) where malpractice suits are skyrocketing. However, at least four states (California, Delaware, Oregon, and Rhode Island) prohibit professionals from organizing their businesses as LLCs.

Individuals, partnerships, corporations and even other LLCs can become LLC members. All that is required is that the member make the agreed-upon capital contributions. Members then share in the management of the entity in proportion to their capital contributions. Often they will appoint managers to carry out the actual operation of the business.

Because the members of an LLC often share management power, they frequently have considerable implied and apparent authority to bind the LLC on transactions in the ordinary course of business. They also are fiduciaries of the LLC. As such, they must manage the business in the best interest of the LLC.

TRANSFERABILITY

State statutes generally permit LLCs to restrict their members' ability to transfer their interests in the LLC. Transferees usually have no right to become a member and share in the management of the LLC unless the other members consent. A transferee who does not become a member is entitled only to the transferring member's share of the profits.

When a member withdraws from the LLC, she is entitled to receive either the value of her interest or a return of her capital investment. However, a distribution of assets to a departing member will occur only if the LLC's assets would exceed its liabilities after the distribution.

DISSOLUTION

States frequently require limited liability companies to have a stated duration (generally no more than 30 years). Further, the LLC must be set up so that it can be easily dissolved. Otherwise it will not qualify for the single tax treatment available to partnerships under the federal tax laws. Thus, dissolution generally is caused by the death, retirement, bankruptcy, or dissolution of any member. However, the mere act of dissolution does not necessarily terminate the LLC's business. The remaining members may avoid liquidation by unanimously agreeing to continue the business operations.

BARBIERI V. SWING-N-SLIDE CORP.
1997 Del. Ch. LEXIS 9 (Del. Ch. Ct. 1997)

FACTS

Richard Mueller, the president, chief executive officer, and director of Swing-N-Slide Corporation (SNS), joined with several officers of the corporation to form Greengrass Management, a limited liability company. Mueller and those officers were the sole members of the LLC. They formed the entity solely for the purpose of serving as one of two general partners in Greengrass Holdings (Holdings), a partnership that was created to make a

(continued)

BARBIERI V. SWING-N-SLIDE CORP.
(concluded)

public tender offer to buy 60 percent of SNS's common shares from the SNS shareholders. Robert Barbieri, a shareholder in SNS, sued Mueller, the other members of the LLC, and the LLC, claiming that they had breached their fiduciary duty to the SNS shareholders because they had a conflict of interest during the tender offer negotiations. The LLC moved to dismiss the claim against it on the grounds that it owed no fiduciary duty to the SNS shareholders.

ISSUE

Does the LLC owe a fiduciary duty to the SNS shareholders?

DECISION

Yes. The underlying theory in support of this lawsuit is that because Mueller and the other SNS officers are owners of the LLC, which in turn is one of the general partners of Holdings, the LLC owes fiduciary duties to the SNS shareholders. We start with the basic proposition that directors and officers of a corporation owe fiduciary duties to the corporation and its shareholders. Thus, Mueller and the other LLC members (officers of SNS) owed fiduciary duties to SNS. However, the LLC argued

that since it is an independent legal entity and did not own or control SNS at the time of the tender offer, it did not have fiduciary obligations to SNS or its shareholders. But this argument answers only the question of when an otherwise unaffiliated entity becomes a fiduciary. Barbieri asserted that the LLC had existing fiduciary obligations to SNS from the instant Mueller formed it. Accordingly, the LLC's argument fails to address the very different question of whether a legal entity must take on the preexisting fiduciary duties of those who form and control it. We conclude that the fiduciary duties of Mueller and the other SNS officers must be imputed to the LLC they formed. Neither Mueller nor the others would escape their fiduciary obligations to SNS had they not formed the LLC. To allow them to use this state's laws allowing the formation of the limited liability company as a vehicle to avoid those very duties would be unconscionable. Therefore, where, as here, the allegations of a complaint support the conclusion that an entity was formed and controlled by fiduciaries for purposes solely related to the entity to which those persons owed fiduciary duties, the entity may be considered to take on the same fiduciary obligations.

LIMITED LIABILITY PARTNERSHIPS

Facing growing numbers of costly lawsuits, the major accounting firms sought a new kind of business structure to shield partners' personal assets from malpractice claims. The states responded by permitting the formation of **limited liability partnerships** (LLPs). In recent years, many law firms have begun joining the accounting profession in making the switch from general partnerships and professional corporations to limited liability partnerships.

CREATING AN LLP

LLPs are relatively easy to organize around an existing partnership. The partners need merely file an LLP form with the state and then maintain an adequate amount of professional liability insurance. After this is done, the personal assets of partners not involved in wrongdoing by other members of the firm will be sheltered from malpractice claims against the firm. Partners who are directly involved in the litigation (those who actually committed the malpractice) still have unlimited personal liability.

MANAGING THE LLP

As with general partnerships, all of the partners in an LLP have equal say in its management. Of course, this can be altered by agreement. New partners cannot join the LLP without the unanimous consent of the current partners. Thus, anyone who buys the interest of an LLP partner is not a partner unless the other partners unanimously agree.

LLP TAXATION

LLPs are taxed as general partnerships. The LLP pays no income taxes. Instead, each partner reports her share of the LLP's profits and losses on her personal tax return.

FRANCHISING

THE NATURE OF FRANCHISING

Franchising has become one of the most common ways of conducting business in the United States. Automobiles, gasoline, and certain home appliances like refrigerators and washing machines have long been sold through franchise arrangements. The great growth of franchising, however, has come in the last quarter century. It has become the most common arrangement in providing certain services. This is particularly true in the fast-food industry (for example, McDonald's Corporation) and motels (Holiday Inns, Inc.), but franchises are also used in many other fields. A few examples include Century 21 real estate brokerage firms, Culligan water softeners, H & R Block, Inc., tax-preparing services, and Muzak sound systems.

The franchising relationship is contractual. The franchisor has developed a product or service or a particular pattern of marketing it, and the franchisee becomes an outlet in what appears to be a regional or national (or even international) chain. The franchisor may conduct its business as a sole proprietorship, partnership, or corporation and so may the franchisee. Typically, the franchisor is a corporation, and often the franchisee forms a corporation to own and operate the franchised business.

ADVANTAGES OF FRANCHISING

Franchising may combine the advantages of a small business managed by its owner with the resources, especially marketing impact, available only to large firms. The franchisee may be interested mainly in securing the privilege of selling a highly advertised product. Usually, one of the most important advantages of a franchise to the franchisee is the right to use a trademark owned by the franchisor that is well known and/or highly advertised. In addition, many franchisors have developed a standardized and tested method of conducting the business, whether it is producing hamburgers, operating an employment service, or replacing automobile mufflers.

From the franchisee's standpoint, especially if he or she has had little or no experience in the business being franchised, the most important services of the franchisor are likely to be advertising, training in the business, and advice after the business is underway. Some franchisors also assist with financing. They may build and equip the place of business and lease it to the franchisee—a so-called **turnkey operation.**

One of the major advantages of franchising for the franchisor is the possibility of rapid expansion by using the financial resources of the franchisees. Through franchising, the franchisor can gain considerable control over the distribution of its products

CONCEPT SUMMARY   Factors to Consider in Selecting the Form of Business Organization

	Sole Proprietorship	General Partnership	LLP	Limited Partnership	S Corporation	Corporation	LLC
Liability	Unlimited	Unlimited	Unlimited for general obligations. Limited for other partners' malpractice	Unlimited for general partners; limited for limited partners	Limited	Limited	Limited
Taxation	Single tax	Single tax	Single tax	Single tax	Single tax	Double tax	Single tax
Formalities	None	None	Comply with statute	Comply with statute; requires at least one limited and one general partner	Create corporation with no more than 75 shareholders; make an election with the IRS	Comply with statute	Comply with statute
Financing	Poor	Poor	Poor to average	Average to strong	Poor to average	Strong	Average to strong
Management	Right to manage	Right to manage	Right to manage	General partners may manage; limited partners may *not* manage	Shareholders may not manage unless elected to board	Shareholders may not manage unless elected to board	Right to manage
Life of Business	Ends on death or termination by sole proprietor	Dissolves on death or retirement of partner. (business *may* continue)	Dissolves on death or retirement of partner (business *may* continue)	Dissolves on death or retirement of general partner (business may continue)	Perpetual	Perpetual	Fixed term. Dissolves on death or retirement of member (business may continue)
Liquidity of Investment	Poor to average	Poor	Poor	Poor to average	Average (transfer may be restricted)	High	Poor to average

or services without owning the retail outlets. By carefully controlling the number and location of outlets, the franchisor can reduce competition among them and perhaps encourage them not to carry competitive products. This may make the franchise organization's competition against similar products (or services) more effective by encouraging bigger investments and more aggressive marketing by franchisees. Efforts may also be made to influence prices charged by the franchisee. Where the franchisee prepares a product such as food, or offers a service, the franchisor usually maintains a high degree of control over operations to standardize quality.

FRANCHISEE COMPLAINTS

Although many franchisees have been very successful, some have quickly lost their life savings. Of course, there are risks in any business; not all of McDonald's franchises have been profitable. However, some franchisors have grossly misrepresented the opportunities for success of their franchisees and the assistance that the franchisor will actually provide. Most franchise contracts are typical "contracts of adhesion" (see Chapter 11). Some contain terms that may bring hardship to franchisees that are acting in good faith and performing reasonably well under the contract. Termination clauses frequently give broad discretion to the franchisor. The term of the contract may be short—only a year for the typical service station contract—with no assurance of the right to renew or to transfer a going business to another person. Some contracts even prohibit franchisees from joining franchisee associations.

Ethical Implications	Suppose that a franchisor now can make more money by owning its own retail outlets than by marketing its product through independent franchisees. However, language in its franchise agreements prohibits it from unilaterally terminating the franchisees. Could it ethically open franchisor-owned outlets in the territories presently served by the independently owned franchisees and sell to the public at prices lower than the wholesale prices available to the franchisees?

FRANCHISOR PROBLEMS

In an attempt to control distribution to maximize its profits and perhaps those of its franchisees, the franchisor runs the risk of violating federal and state antitrust laws. Attempts to require franchisees to buy products, equipment, and supplies exclusively from the franchisor may violate the prohibition in the Clayton Act against tie-in sales. Attempts to require adherence to prices set by the franchisor and prohibitions against sales to customers outside an assigned sales territory may violate the Sherman Act. (These risks can be better understood after studying Chapter 44.)

Franchise contracts usually declare that the franchisee is an independent contractor and is not an agent or employee of the franchisor. However, in an effort to maintain the quality of the product or service offered by the franchisee, and thus the value of its trademark, the franchisor often exerts considerable control over many aspects of the franchisee's operations. This control has been sufficient in many cases to cause courts to hold that the franchisee is not an independent contractor. Thus, the franchisor becomes liable for torts committed by the franchisee's employees, as discussed in Chapter 21. Although insurance can cover this risk in most cases, lawsuits against the franchisor can be damaging to reputation as well as time consuming for the franchisor's executives.

GOVERNMENT REGULATION

Many inexperienced people have been ruined financially by believing extravagant claims of the wealth-building potential of franchises. Others have suffered unfair terminations, causing them large losses. As a result, both the federal and state governments now generally regulate the franchise relationship.

Federal Legislation

At the federal level, legislation has been passed specifically to protect automobile and service station franchisees. These laws aim to protect dealers from coercive practices, including abrupt terminations and unfair competition by their franchisors. The Federal Trade Commission has issued rules designed to give prospective franchisees more information. These rules require franchisors to explain the termination, cancellation, and renewal provisions of the franchise contract. Franchisors must disclose the number of franchisees terminated in the past year and the reasons for termination. All restrictions on franchisees must be included in the agreement. Finally, all representations made to prospective franchisees must have a "reasonable basis." Violations are subject to a $10,000-per-day civil penalty, and the FTC can sue on behalf of injured franchisees.

State Legislation

Numerous states have enacted comprehensive laws governing the franchisee–franchisor business relationship. Several others have implemented legislation with general application to these business arrangements. These vary widely in their provisions. Often, they prohibit certain contract provisions and franchisor practices thought to be unfair to franchisees. Usually, they seek to prevent deceptive advertising of franchise opportunities and to limit the franchisor's power to terminate franchises. Others govern how close to an existing franchisee a new outlet can be.

ZEIDLER V. A&W RESTAURANTS
2001 U.S. Dist. LEXIS 653 (N.D. Ill. 2001)

FACTS

In 1991, Russell Zeidler and A&W Restaurants entered into a written License Agreement under which A&W granted Zeidler a license to operate an A&W restaurant in the Stratford Square Mall in Bloomingdale, Illinois. The License Agreement was to last until December 31, 2011, unless otherwise terminated in accordance with the terms of the agreement. A&W was entitled to terminate the License Agreement if, among other things, Zeidler defaulted "in the performance or observance of any of [his] obligations . . . and such default continued for a period of thirty (30) days after written notice to the Licensee." To assist Zeidler in obtaining financing for the franchise, A&W provided him with a pro forma financial statement reflecting anticipated annual sales. However, as the years passed, the restaurant consistently lost money. Early in 1997, Zeidler complained to A&W about the restaurant's failure to attain the financial goals set forth in the pro forma financial statement. Later that year, A&W's franchise area manger, David Martin, visited the restaurant. In a memorandum sent to Zeidler, Martin listed several areas of concern regarding the cleanliness and management of the restaurant. He advised Zeidler that his concerns were serious and directed him to remedy the defects within 30 days, at which time Martin would return to perform a Quality Assurance Report (QAR) on the restaurant. When the QAR was completed one month later, Martin gave the restaurant a score of 59 percent, far below the passing grade of 80 percent.

(continued)

ZEIDLER V. A&W RESTAURANTS
(concluded)

Additionally, the mall manager informed Martin that Zeidler had been unable to provide proof of insurance. Martin sent Zeidler a detailed memorandum informing him of A&W's concerns regarding the condition of the restaurant. He also informed Zeidler that his failure to carry insurance violated the License Agreement. Six days after sending the memorandum, Martin returned to the restaurant and found no improvement. A&W then sent Zeidler a Notice of Intent to Terminate the franchise, citing the operational deficiencies noted in the QAR and the failure to carry insurance. The letter gave Zeidler until February 16, 1998 (40 days), to get back into the compliance with the License Agreement to avoid termination. Despite receiving another letter from A&W requesting that Zeidler advise A&W of his plan to correct the problems, Zeidler did not respond. On March 11, 1998, Martin again visited the restaurant. Although there were some improvements, he still found some operational defaults. On March 25, A&W terminated the franchise relationship. Zeidler sued A&W for wrongful termination under the Illinois Franchise Disclosure Act, claiming that neither the failure to obtain insurance nor the QAR were valid reasons for termination. In its defense, A&W argued that is had good cause to terminate Zeidler's franchise.

ISSUE

Did A&W have good cause to terminate the franchise?

DECISION

Yes. The termination of the License Agreement was justified on the basis of the insurance default alone. Zeidler's failure to obtain insurance for the restaurant constituted a clear violation of the License Agreement and was a valid reason for termination since that document permitted termination for violation of "any" of the provisions of the agreement. Zeidler had argued that the termination for the insurance default was unlawful because A&W had not terminated any other franchises on that basis. However, this argument is not persuasive. A&W's treatment of its other franchises is irrelevant to its treatment of Zeidler. He also argued that the insurance default was merely a pretext for termination and that A&W had an ulterior motive, namely, that is wished to retaliate against Zeidler for complaining about the allegedly inaccurate pro forma financial statement. This argument fails as well because A&W's motives are immaterial since the insurance default was a sufficient and legitimate ground for termination. Even if the insurance default did not provide sufficient lawful grounds for the termination, the termination was justified because Zeidler failed to meet A&W's quality assurance standards. If the QAR were the only evidence of operational deficiencies in Zeidler's restaurant, and if A&W had terminated the franchise based on the QAR without making any attempt to work with Zeidler, the court might agree that the termination was unlawful. However, Zeidler's failure to respond to A&W's notice lead to the conclusion that A&W had sufficient lawful grounds for the termination. The Illinois Franchise Disclosure Act provides that a franchisor may not effect a termination without "good cause." Under that statute, "good cause" includes the franchisee's failure to comply with a lawful contract provision. The requirement that its franchisees supply insurance is a lawful contract provision.

.... *FRANCHISING IN FOREIGN COUNTRIES* ....

During the past 20 years, more than 400 U.S. franchisors have opened over 31,000 outlets around the world. While most of this expansion has occurred across the border into Canada, many opportunities also are being found in Western Europe and East Asia. During the next several years, we should expect to see a flurry of American franchising efforts in Mexico.

Differences in language, culture, business practices, and laws from one country to the next will raise new problems for franchisors in establishing and operating these overseas networks. More than ever franchisors will need to carefully investigate the target market, looking for signs of political and economic instability. They must be familiar with each legal system since many countries impose stringent limitations on franchise agreements in order to protect local franchisees.

QUESTIONS AND PROBLEM CASES

1. What are the principal factors that should be considered in determining which form of business organization to use?

2. What is *limited liability*? Which forms of business organization have a limited liability feature?

3. Scott entered into a five-year employment contract with Baca Grande Corporation, a resort that was owned by AZL Resources, Inc. During Scott's employment Baca Grande owned some assets; however, it maintained separate corporate and financial records at AZL's corporate offices. Because Baca Grande often operated with a "zero bank account," it frequently required loans from AZL. When Scott was fired from his position he sued AZL (Baca Grande's sole shareholder) for breach of contract. Is AZL liable for Baca Grande's financial obligations to Scott?

4. *Video Case.* See "The Reunion." When friends reunite at a wedding, they reveal their plans for business ventures. Al and Amy, an unmarried couple, propose opening a Thai restaurant. Al is a dentist and Amy is director of public relations for a publishing company. Amy will quit her job eventually to manage the restaurant. They will hire a chef whose restaurant is about to close. Carl is a successful real estate agent who wants to open his own real estate firm. Bob has tried several business ventures, but all have failed, including a venture to manufacture ski racks for motorcycles. Dave and Donna, the newly married couple, plan to quit their jobs, move to Wyoming, and open a software development business. They want the business to have few investors. They have lined up potential clients who will finance their initial efforts in return for software customization. What business forms should each of these individuals use for their business ventures? What additional questions do you want to ask to help you determine the best business forms for their ventures?

5. James Coduti was a minority shareholder in the Hudson Tool & Die Corporation (Hudson). Werner Hellwig, the majority shareholder in Hudson, had been feuding with Coduti for some time. Coduti brought suit against Hellwig for refusing to authorize bonuses or dividends while Hudson was amassing large cash reserves. At the time of the suit, Hudson had

certificates of deposit of approximately $775,000. Coduti argued that reserves of between $350,000 and $400,000 were sufficient for a business of this type. Hellwig claimed the accumulations were necessary to protect against dislocations if a major account was lost, to cover replacement costs for equipment, and to permit plant expansion. Should the court compel Hudson to declare a dividend?

6. Margo Neff is disabled and requires a wheelchair to gain mobility. She filed suit against American Dairy Queen Corporation, alleging that the Dairy Queen retail outlets in San Antonio had numerous barriers that made those stores inaccessible to the disabled. The Americans with Disabilities Act requires an individual who "operates a place of public accommodation" to provide full and equal enjoyment of its facilities. American Dairy Queen argued that it was not responsible for removing the barriers because it did not own, lease, or operate the stores. As evidence it offered copies of its franchise agreements with the local franchisees who ran the retail outlets. Neff contended the terms of the franchise agreements supported her claim that American Dairy Queen retained sufficient control over the operation of San Antonio stores to make it an operator of the stores for purposes of the statute. Specifically, the franchise agreement gave American Dairy Queen the power to veto modifications to the stores' facilities. Does American Dairy Queen's veto power make it an "operator" of the restaurant who is responsible for compliance with the equal access requirements of the federal statute?

7. George Mims was executive director of the Greater Fort Worth and Tarrant County Community Action Agency (CAA). The board of directors called a special meeting at which time Mims was terminated as executive director of the corporation. He refused to vacate the premises and, as a result, CAA filed suit to enjoin him from interfering with the day-to-day activity at the corporation. Mims argued his dismissal was not binding since the board was illegally constituted. The bylaws of CAA required that 42 directors be in attendance to dismiss the executive director. However, at the

time of Mims's dismissal there were only 32 members on the board and only 18 of them attended the meeting. Did the board have authority to dismiss Mims?

8. Herb Jones started making tooled leather belts as a hobby. Later, he learned how to cast bronze belt buckles. He had little trouble selling them to friends. He was taking some art classes while seeking a degree in business at the local college. His belts, which he sold on weekends at craft shows, paid his tuition and provided spending money. Now he has been able to get a few men's clothing stores to stock his belts on a consignment basis. Demand has increased beyond his ability to fill it. As he completes his program at the college, he decides he would like to get into the business of making and selling belts and other leather goods. He learns of the availability of a small shop location in a popular shopping mall. A friend, Bill Williams, who has another year to go at the college, is willing to help him in his spare time. Suburban Bank and Trust Company is willing to lend Herb $8,000, the amount he thinks he needs to pay rent for one year, to buy a stock of leather and brass from which to make the belts, and to pay Bill to work weekends for three months. The loan is conditional on Herb's father cosigning the note. Herb's Uncle Joe, who works for a large corporation, suggests that Herb should incorporate the business. Do you agree?

9. Assume that Herb's business in the preceding problem case has been operating for a year and has made a profit. Herb has expanded by purchasing other leather products to sell. All of the profit has been reinvested in the business. Herb has, however, paid off $2,000 of the loan to the bank. The bank is willing to renew the loan and even to increase it to $10,000 if Herb's father cosigns again. Bill Williams would like to join the firm full time but has no money or credit to contribute. Herb and Bill think that if they had a salesman to visit men's clothing shops and perhaps other retailers, they could increase their sales substantially. A mutual friend, George Robbins, has had sales experience and would be willing to join the business. He could invest $10,000. The workshop in the back of the shop is already too small. Herb would like to rent a loft or other low-rent space for belt production where there would be no interruptions and enough space for several workers. Herb would also like to have Bill supervise this operation. Herb estimates that minimum capital of $40,000 is necessary. What he owns in equipment, supplies, and inventory is worth $10,000 at cost, and he believes that the value of his going business is at least $10,000 in addition. His father is willing to invest $5,000 but wants no further liability. Uncle Joe is also willing to invest $5,000 on the same basis. What form of business organization is appropriate? How should it be capitalized?

10. Morley-Murphy served as a distributor of Zenith's consumer electronic products under a series of annual distributorship agreements. During its 58-year association with Zenith, Morley-Murphy was apparently a very successful dealer, and in 1994, Zenith products accounted for 54 percent of Morley-Murphy's total business. Around that time, however, business was not rosy for Zenith. It had reported a net operating loss in 9 of the last 10 years prior to the events here. This dismal trend inspired efforts at corporate reorganization. One aspect of Zenith's business that came under the microscope was its distribution system. It formerly had relied principally on a network of independent distributors, like Morley-Murphy, who sold Zenith products to small specialized retailers and a few large department stores. However, since the mid-1980s, large discount consumer electronic retailers began to account for more and more sales. Many of these companies operated their own distribution centers and insisted on dealing directly with manufacturers. By 1994, Zenith's 15 remaining independent distributors sold only 20 percent of its product, and Zenith had to subsidize these sales through extra discounts that cost it millions of dollars a year. In 1994, a Zenith task force reported that the company could probably reap substantial savings if it converted to "one-step distribution," in which its products would be shipped directly from its factories to the retailers' warehouses. Zenith adopted this recommendation and informed Morley-Murphy that is would be formally terminated as a distributor. This

notification did not suggest any way in which Morley-Murphy could "cure" the problem that lay behind the decision to terminate, and it did not identify any deficiency in Morley-Murphy's performance as a dealer. Further, Zenith never bothered to determine whether Morley-Murphy, standing alone, was a profitable dealer. Morley-Murphy sued Zenith, claiming the termination of its dealership violated the *Wisconsin Fair Dealership Law*. That statue prohibits the termination of the dealership agreement without *good cause*. It further defines *good cause*, in part, as "*failure by a dealer to comply substantially with essential and reasonable requirements which requirements are not discriminatory.*" Zenith argued that it did not violate the statute because it terminated Morley-Murphy as part of systemwide, nondiscriminatory change from two-step to one-step distribution intended to stem overall losses and improve financial performance. Morley-Murphy claimed that the statute did not tolerate market withdrawal as a term that could be imposed for good cause. Does the Wisconsin statute permit a franchisor to terminate a dealership agreement for the kind of reason Zenith offered?

CHAPTER 24

Partnerships

Digges persuaded Levin and Wharton to join him in forming a law partnership. They enthusiastically agreed because Digges came from a long line of prominent Maryland attorneys dating back to the 17th century. Levin and Wharton devoted most of their time to trial work and left all of the money matters to Digges. According to Wharton, "[I]f you don't trust your partner, you ought not to be partners." Digges later pled guilty to stealing over $1 million from a client, Dresser Industries, by padding and falsifying invoices during a 3½-year period. He then stole the proceeds from the law firm and used the money to restore his mansion. Neither Levin nor Wharton was accused of any wrongdoing. However, since Digges was found to be acting within the scope of the partnership, both Levin and Wharton, as partners, were held individually liable for the money that Digges stole from Dresser.[1]

- *What is the fundamental nature of the partnership form of business organization and how does it arise?*
- *What are the rights and responsibilities of partners?*
- *How do courts determine the contractual authority of partners?*
- *When is one partner individually liable for the torts and crimes committed by another partner?*

---

[1]"A Well-Born Lawyer Falls from Eminence," *The Wall Street Journal*, December 27, 1989, p. B4; "Prominent Maryland Lawyer," *The Wall Street Journal*, January 15, 1990, p. B5.

.... ***INTRODUCTION*** ....

This chapter examines the partnership form of business organization. It demonstrates the ease with which partnerships may be created and explores the basic structure of this type of business. This includes a discussion of the authority generally vested in partners as well as a distinction between the rights of partnership creditors and those belonging to creditors of the individual partners. After a survey of the rights and duties of partners, there is a discussion of the procedures involved in terminating a partnership. The chapter closes with a brief examination of the legal aspects of limited partnership.

.... ***CREATION OF A PARTNERSHIP*** ....

Most people are surprised to discover that there are amazingly few legal formalities involved in creating a partnership. In fact, a court may find two persons to be partners even though neither had the specific intent to create a partnership. This is so because no express agreement is necessary to create a partnership. All that is required is that the parties intended to have the relationship that the law defines as a partnership. The Uniform Partnership Act (UPA) simply describes a partnership as "an association of two or more persons to carry on as co-owners of a business for profit."

AN ASSOCIATION OF TWO OR MORE PERSONS

A partnership is a voluntary and consensual association involving two or more persons. Nobody can be forced to become a partner, although one can engage unwittingly in behavior that gives rise to the creation of a partnership. The UPA is extremely liberal in that it permits individuals, partnerships, and corporations to qualify as persons that can form a partnership.

CARRYING ON A BUSINESS FOR PROFIT

The UPA definition of a partnership applies only to instances in which two or more persons carry on a business for profit. However, any trade, occupation, or profession is treated as a business in determining the existence of a partnership. The key element in this definition is the fact that the objective must be to make a **profit.** People who are involved in a nonprofit association are not partners.

CONCEPT SUMMARY	Establishing the Existence of a Partnership
Definition	**Key Elements**
1. **Association of two or more persons**	• May be natural or artificial (corporate) persons. • Must be at least two partners.
2. **Carrying on a business**	• Objective must be to make a profit.
3. **As co-owners**	• Must have a community of interest. This is evidenced by: a. Sharing losses. b. Sharing profits. c. Sharing management.

CO-OWNERSHIP

For there to be a partnership there must be **co-ownership,** which means ownership of the business as such. It does not require that the property used in the business be owned by the partnership or in equal shares by the partners. In fact, the property and capital used in the business of a partnership can be supplied entirely by a single partner or the property may be leased from others and the working capital borrowed.

DISPUTES ON THE EXISTENCE OF A PARTNERSHIP

There are often disputes as to whether or not there is or has been a partnership. A court that is forced to determine whether a business is a partnership must look at all the facts. If, overall, there appears to be a community of interest, a partnership is found. Usually a sharing in both the profits and the important management decisions results in a partnership.

PARTNERSHIP BY ESTOPPEL

You can be liable as a partner without being a partner. If you go with a friend to a bank to borrow money and tell the banker that you and the friend are partners in a business, the banker can hold you liable as a partner. The same result would occur if the friend stated that you were his partner and you failed to correct the statement. However, if the friend went alone to the bank and told the banker you were his partner, you would not be liable.

The legal concept that is applicable is *estoppel*. The person who seeks to hold another liable as a partner must prove that she relied on the holding out or consent. The reliance must be justifiable and must result in loss to the person who sold goods or otherwise relied on the credit of the person held out as a partner. If reliance is justifiable, the defendant is estopped from claiming that there was, in fact, no partnership.

ARTICLES OF PARTNERSHIP

Although generally not required, it is highly desirable to have written articles of partnership. (Partnership agreements may need a writing when they create an interest in real property or have a term in excess of one year.) A written contract tends to minimize misunderstanding and disagreement. The process of preparing such an agreement is likely to cause the parties to provide for contingencies they might not otherwise consider. This is especially true if a lawyer is called on who is experienced in drafting partnership agreements.

It should be noted that lawsuits raising the question of whether or not there is a partnership usually arise where arrangements among the partners have been casual. Disputes are more likely when there are no written articles of partnership.

Articles of partnership usually state how profits and losses are to be shared. They should provide a means for continuing the business on the death or disability of a partner. Other matters usually included in articles of partnership are the name of the firm, the business to be carried on, the term for which the partnership is to exist, salary and drawing accounts, the authority of the partners to bind the firm, and provisions for withdrawal of partners.

JOINT VENTURES

Many courts distinguish a **joint venture** from a partnership. The elements of a joint venture are (1) an express or implied agreement to carry on an enterprise; (2) a manifestation of intent by the parties to be associated as joint venturers; (3) a joint interest as reflected in the contribution of property, finances, effort, skill, or knowledge by each party to the joint venture; (4) a measure of proprietorship of joint control of the enterprise; and (5) a provision for the sharing of profits or losses.

The major distinction between a joint venture and partnership is that a joint venture relates to a single enterprise or transaction and a partnership relates to a continuing business. Both require a meeting of the minds and contract formation. However, some courts hold that the requirement for joint ventures is less formal and may be implied entirely by conduct. Further, they state that, with joint ventures, any agreement that does exist need not cover as many terms as are necessary for a partnership. For instance, an agreement to jointly buy, develop, and resell one particular plot of land may be considered a joint venture. On the other hand, an agreement to jointly buy, develop, and resell land on a long-term basis may well be construed as a partnership.

For the purposes of this chapter, the distinction between a partnership and a joint venture is not very important. This is so because courts generally apply partnership law to joint ventures. Perhaps the only significant difference is that joint venturers sometimes are held to have less implied and apparent authority than partners. This is because of the more limited scope of the joint venture enterprise.

CHEN V. WANG
1998 U.S. Dist. LEXIS 600 (N.D. Ill. 1998)

FACTS

From 1977 through 1989, Thomas Wang was the manager and part owner of a hotel in Aurora, Illinois. His sister-in-law, Irene, was aware that Thomas was interested in acquiring another hotel and expressed interest in investing in such a purchase. Irene subsequently wired $1,000,000 to Thomas to use for that purpose. Thomas was told that $750,000 of this amount was provided by Irene's sister, Kuei-Ying Chen. Thomas had decided the North Aurora Inn would be a good property to purchase. Its sale price was approximately $1,750,000. Thomas and his wife, Susanna, discussed the purchase with Kuei. In this conversation, Susanna informed Kuei that she would contribute $1,000,000 of her own money so they could then afford to buy the property and have an additional $250,000 for renovations and working capital. Ownership of the Hotel and profits therefrom were to be shared proportionately to the promised contributions, 50 percent for Susanna, 37.5 percent for Kuei, and 12.5 percent for Irene. Thomas was to manage the Hotel without compensation until the business became profitable. It also was agreed that title to the property would be in all three sisters' names. The Hotel was purchased on May 1, 1990, for the $1,750,000 price. However, Susanna did not contribute any cash. It was purchased with $900,000 of Kuei's and Irene's money, with the other $850,000 being financed by a mortgage provided by the seller. The title to the Hotel was only in the name of Susanna and

Thomas. They formed North Aurora Inn, Inc., a corporation owned by Susanna and Thomas only to manage the Hotel. All subsequent losses generated by the business were reported only on Thomas's and Susanna's tax returns. All lease payments that North Aurora Inn, Inc., paid to the Hotel were kept by Thomas and Susanna. When Kuei questioned Thomas about the deed, he told her that it had not yet been recorded, even though it actually had been recorded one month earlier. The following August, a document drafted in Chinese was signed by the three sisters listing each of their contributions. During the next two years, Thomas borrowed $940,000 from Kuei. She thought the money was for personal loans to Thomas when in reality he was using the money for Hotel renovations and to make mortgage payments. He later began repaying these loans with funds from the business. When Kuei finally discovered what was occurring, she sued Susanna for breach of her fiduciary duties as a partner.

ISSUE

Has Susanna violated her partnership duties to Kuei?

DECISION

No. There was no partnership. When there is no written agreement sufficiently establishing a partnership, the intent of the parties is considered as well as the facts and

(continued)

CHEN V. WANG
(concluded)

circumstances surrounding the alleged formation of the entity. There must be a meeting of the minds to create a partnership. The sharing of profits is prima facie evidence of the existence of a partnership, but not sufficient evidence of such a relationship. Other factors to consider include the manner in which the parties have dealt with each other; the mode in which each has, with the knowledge of the other, dealt with third parties in a partnership capacity; whether the entity has been held out as a partnership or advertised using the partnership name; whether profits have actually been shared; whether a partnership certificate has been filed with the county clerk; and whether partnership tax returns have been filed. Additionally, an agreement to form a partnership does not itself create a partnership; the partnership does not arise until the parties actually join together to carry out a common venture, each contributing property or services and each having a community of interest in the profits. Here, the written agreement certainly does not establish that the parties intended to create a partnership. It states only that amount of capital contributed by each sister and does not use the Chinese word for partner or partnership. Moreover, once the money was invested, Thomas's and Susanna's conduct was inconsistent with the creation of a partnership. The Hotel was never held out as being owned by a partnership; the deed for the property was recorded in Thomas's and Susanna's names only; Thomas and Susanna used all lease payments as their own; no partnership certificate was filed; and Thomas and Susanna reported all losses on their own tax returns. Even if the testimony to be held is sufficient to show that the sisters intended to enter a partnership, the evidence is insufficient to show

that a partnership was actually created. Since there is insufficient proof of a partnership, Kuei's claims cannot be considered on behalf of a partnership. However, it is not always necessary to define or categorize the form of the joint entity created. Some cases indicated that a joint venture is essentially a partnership, but one that concerns a single enterprise or transaction. However, a joint venture does differ from a partnership in that, although a meeting of the minds and contract formation is required, (a) the requirement is less formal and may be implied entirely by conduct and (b) any agreement that exists need not cover as many terms as is necessary for a partnership to exist. The elements of a joint venture are (1) an express or implied agreement to carry on an enterprise; (2) a manifestation of intent by the parties to be associated as joint venturers; (3) a joint interest as reflected in the contribution of property, finances, effort, skill, or knowledge by each party to the joint venture; (4) a measure of proprietorship or joint control of the enterprise; and (5) a provision for the sharing of profits or losses. Here, there is certainly evidence of an agreement to carry on the Hotel enterprise. It is undisputed that there was an agreement as to the sharing of profits. Although the deed was recorded in Thomas's and Susanna's names, they do not dispute Kuei and Irene also have a proprietary interest in the property. Finally, there was an agreement as to responsibilities; Thomas was to manage the Hotel. There is sufficient evidence of a meeting of the minds as to an intent to join together in a common venture. Ultimately, there is adequate evidence of a joint venture and, as a matter or law, the relationship between joint venturers is a fiduciary relationship.

.... *MANAGEMENT AND AUTHORITY* ....
OF PARTNERS

VOICE IN MANAGEMENT

Each partner normally has an equal voice in managing the business. A vote of the majority prevails if there are more than two partners. This may be changed by agreement, however. One or a group of partners may, by agreement of the partners, be granted authority to make the day-to-day operating decisions of the business. These might include making usual contracts for goods and services, and hiring and firing employees.

Unanimous agreement is required to act contrary to the partnership agreement or to fundamentally change the nature of the partnership business. Assume you are a member of a retail partnership. You decide that it would be a good investment to buy a nearby residence for rental purposes. Approval of all the partners is necessary. Likewise, unanimity would be required for an agreement to guarantee the debt of another, such as that of a partner, if contracts of surety or indemnity fall outside the scope of the partnership's usual business. Such approval would also be required to authorize a sale of the store's entire inventory or the building in which the business is conducted.

When a certain action is proposed and there is an even split among the partners, the action cannot be taken. If it is an important matter and the deadlock continues, it may be impossible to continue the business. In such a case, any partner may petition a court for dissolution of the partnership.

AUTHORITY

Authority to act for a partnership may be of three types: express, implied, and apparent. These concepts have the same meaning as under agency law, and the tests for implied and apparent authority are the same. Both implied and apparent authority are influenced by customs and usages of the particular partnership and those of similar businesses in the area.

Express Authority

A partner has express authority to do whatever he or she is authorized to do by the articles of partnership. In addition, express authority stems from any other agreement of the partners.

Implied Authority

The UPA states: "Every partner is an agent of the partnership for the purpose of its business." He or she can bind the partnership on contracts that are usually appropriate to that business. For example, if your partnership runs a women's ready-to-wear clothing store, any partner has the authority to buy dresses for resale. However, this implied authority may be abolished or limited by agreement of the partners.

UNITED STATES LEATHER V. H&W PARTNERSHIP
60 F.3d 222 (5th Cir. 1995)

FACTS

Dean Wilkerson and Walter Helms created a corporation, DWA, that operated a furniture factory. They then formed the H&W Partnership for the purpose of buying DWA's facility and leasing it back to the corporation. After purchasing several leather shipments from United States Leather, DWA fell behind in its payments. Wilkerson then met with U.S. Leather officials and gave them a promissory note for the $438,000 balance on DWA's account. He signed the note on behalf of DWA. However, a few days before the first payment was due, Wilkerson requested an extension of time. U.S. Leather agreed to the extension on the condition that H&W was included as a maker of the note. Wilkerson consented and signed the note on behalf of DWA and H&W. When DWA went out of business without ever making a payment, U.S. Leather sued H&W on the note. The partnership argued that it was not liable on the note because Wilkerson did not have authority to bind it.

(continued)

UNITED STATES LEATHER V. H&W PARTNERSHIP
(concluded)

ISSUE

Did Wilkerson have authority to bind H&W on the note?

DECISION

Yes. The Uniform Partnership Act holds that "every partner is an agent of the partnership for the purpose of its business, and the act of every partner . . . for apparently carrying on in the usual way the business of the partnership . . . binds the partnership." Under the statute, the determinative issue is whether Wilkerson acted within the scope of the partnership business. The appropriate test for determining if a partner's acts were within the scope of the partnership business, and therefore binding on the partnership, is if the acts were done to further or benefit the partnership. It is not disputed here that there is direct relationship between DWA and H&W. The partnership's own viability depended on the continuation of DWA because H&W relied on the rental income from the

corporation to pay its mortgages. DWA needed raw materials, including leather, and it was the business of the partnership to ensure that the corporation had access to financing so it could acquire these materials. The acts of Wilkerson in executing the promissory note in favor of U.S. Leather indirectly, but with certainty, benefited the partnership. Finally, the evidence revealed that H&W had executed similar agreements with suppliers in the past in order to facilitate financing for DWA. What is reasonably apparent from these transactions is that H&W Partnership had a continued and necessary interest in obtaining financing for DWA that would subsequently benefit the partnership. Those transactions further substantiate that this practice was an ordinary and consistent manner in which the partnership carried out its business. Wilkerson's actions were within the scope of the partnership business when he executed the note in favor of U.S. Leather.

Apparent Authority

When the agency authority of a partner is abolished or limited by agreement, the partner may still have apparent authority. Suppose, in the clothing store example, that you and your partners, Roger and Jane, have agreed that all merchandise buying will be done by Jane. Suppose further, as is likely, that it is customary for all partners in this type of business to give merchandise orders. A manufacturer takes and fills an order given by Roger. If the manufacturer is unaware of the restriction, the partnership and, ultimately, you are bound.

RATIFICATION

Generally, the partnership will not be liable for contracts created by a partner acting outside the scope of her authority. An exception to this rule arises when the other partners ratify the unauthorized action. (Ratification was discussed previously in Chapter 21.) It occurs when the partners, either expressly or implicitly, demonstrate the intent to accept the action of the partner who was lacking actual or apparent authority. Any act that the partnership could have authorized at the time it was done may be ratified. Ratification releases the partner from liability for having exceeded her authority and binds the partnership to the contract as if it had been authorized all along.

PROPERTY OF PARTNERSHIPS

WHAT IS PARTNERSHIP PROPERTY?

Disputes often arise among both partners and creditors over what property actually belongs to the partnership and what property belongs to individual partners. Partnership property includes all property that originally was contributed to the partnership as well as anything purchased then or later for the partnership. In addition, any property acquired with partnership funds is partnership property unless a contrary intent is clearly shown. The fact that property is used in the business does not make it partnership property; however, assets that appear on the account books of the partnership are presumed to be partnership property. Payment by the partnership of taxes or insurance on property is presumptive but not conclusive evidence that the property is owned by the partnership. The same is true if improvements are made on the property by the partnership.

OWNERSHIP AND POSSESSION

Partnership property is held by the partners as tenants in partnership. Partners have no separate interest in partnership property. They have no right to sell, mortgage, or devise to an heir any individual item of the firm's property.

A partner has a right to take possession of the firm's property for partnership purposes but not for personal use. For example, if you are a partner, you have no right to use the firm's automobile for your vacation. Permission of a majority of the partners would be required. You may, however, without special permission, drive the car to the bank to deposit the firm's receipts. (See Figure 24–1.)

CREDITORS OF PARTNERS

A creditor of a partner may not attach any of the property owned by the partnership; however, a partner may assign her partnership interest to a creditor or to anyone else. This entitles the assignee to receive that partner's share of the profits. It does not give the assignee a right to any information about partnership affairs or a right to look at its books.

FIGURE 24–1   Partnership Property

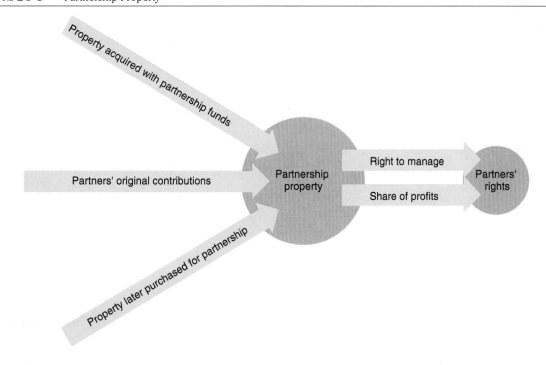

A creditor who gets a judgment against a partner may obtain from the court a **charging order** against the partner's interest in the firm. The court may appoint a receiver to look after the creditor's interests. If profits are insufficient to pay off the creditor, the court may order that the partner's interest be sold. The purchaser may dissolve the partnership if it is to exist for an indefinite time. If it is for a term of years that has not expired, the partnership will continue as originally agreed. The purchaser will not be a partner, nor can she exercise any of the partner's rights except to receive that share of the profits. The partnership or any partner may purchase the debtor's partnership interest by paying the debt. (See Figure 24–2.)

PARTNERS' RIGHTS AND DUTIES

RIGHT TO COMPENSATION

A partner is not ordinarily entitled to salary or wages. The compensation is presumed to be the partner's share of profits. This is true even if one partner spends much more time than another on partnership business. The same principle applies to rent to a partner for use of the partner's property and to interest on a capital contribution. An exception is made by the UPA when a partner dies. Then any surviving partner is entitled to reasonable compensation for winding up partnership affairs.

Of course, the partners may agree that one or more of them is to be paid salary, rent, interest, or wages in addition to sharing in profits. Often, drawing accounts for

FIGURE 24–2   Rights of Creditors

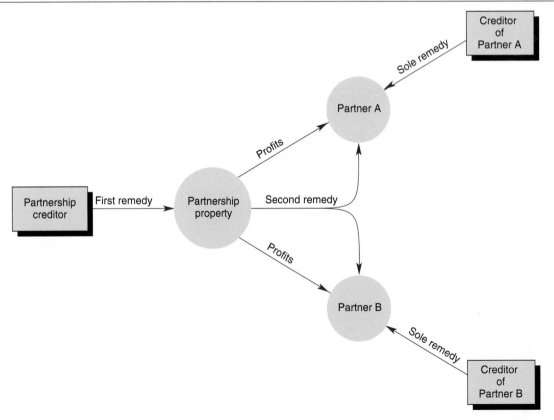

all partners are agreed on, or perhaps regular monthly payments are made. These are then deducted from the partner's share of profits when year-end settlements are made. In the absence of a contrary agreement, profits are shared equally even if capital contributions are unequal. The sharing of losses is the same as the sharing of profits unless there is a different agreement.

Ethical Implications

The relative ease with which a partnership may be formed often results in creation of this form of business organization without any real planning by the partners. Consequently, a partner who contributes considerably more time and money to the business than the other partners often is shocked to discover that, in the absence of agreement, she is not entitled to a salary or a greater share of the profits. Is it ethical for the other partners to oppose compensation for such a partner merely because of the failure to draft a more comprehensive agreement?

DUTY OF LOYALTY AND GOOD FAITH

Partners not only must be honest but also must not permit self-interest to come before duty to the partnership. Partners may buy from or sell to the partnership. However, if they do, they must make full disclosure of any facts relevant to the deal that are not known to the other partners. Partners may not make secret profits from their position as members of a partnership.

In the absence of a contrary understanding, each partner owes a duty to devote full time and his or her best efforts to the affairs of the partnership. A partner must not engage in activities that are in competition with or otherwise likely to injure the partnership. For example, suppose you join with a friend in forming a real estate brokerage partnership. If your partner accepts commissions for arranging sales of property not listed with the firm, the partnership is entitled to those commissions. A partner is also liable to the partnership for the value of partnership property that he or she uses for individual purposes.

SILVERBERG V. COLANTUNO
1998 Colo. App. LEXIS 199 (Colo. Ct. App. 1998)

FACTS

First Denver Corporation (FDC) was organized in 1981 by Silverberg, Colantuno, and Isham. The corporation borrowed $2.8 million to purchase the stock of a bank (stock loan). The loan was secured, in part, personally by Silverberg, Colantuno, and Isham. E&A Associates (E&A), a partnership, was formed by those same three individuals and others. The partnership owned the building and leased it to the bank. Silverberg ultimately became the president of FDC, the managing partner of E&A, and a director of the bank. In 1987, because of the bank's poor financial condition, the Office of Comptrol-

ler of the Currency (OCC) issued a cease and desist order against the bank, preventing it from paying dividends. Such dividends had been the sole source of funds for FDC's interest payments on the stock loan and, without such proceeds, Silverberg had to commence assessments against the E&A partners. In 1989, the original stock loan was assigned to another bank and was assigned to the Tennebaum company, which was owned by a relative of Silverberg. Because it was considered to be a "problem" loan, the assignment was for a substantially discounted amount. In October 1990, the OCC

(continued)

SILVERBERG V. COLANTUNO
(concluded)

reduced the bank's equity capital considerably because it believed the bank was at a substantial risk of immediate failure. From that time through spring 1991, Silverberg unsuccessfully explored various options to secure additional capital. Present E&A partners were unwilling to raise the necessary funds, and the E&A partnership had a negative net worth. To avoid a takeover of the bank by the Federal Deposit Insurance Corporation (FDIC), Silverberg proposed that a group of investors (made up, in part, of current E&A partners) contribute $1 million to capitalize the bank. In return they would acquire the building, the bank business, and the shares of FDC. He labeled this the Go Forward plan. Existing E&A partners were invited to participate in the Go Forward plan. As a condition, each would be first required to pay their pro rata share of the Tennebaum obligation. Ten of the existing partners, including Silverberg, elected to join. Colantuno and Isham did not. The partnership was also requested to approve the Go Forward plan and 82 percent, including Isham, but not Colantuno, consented. After the plan was finalized, Colantuno charged that Silverberg's accomplishment of the Go Forward plan breached his fiduciary duties to the E&A partners who declined to participate.

ISSUE

Is Silverberg liable for breaching his fiduciary duties?

DECISION

No. Partners in a business enterprise owe fiduciary duties to one another that encompass the highest duty of loyalty. They stand in a relationship of trust and confidence to each other and are bound by standards of good conduct and square dealing. Each partner has the right to demand and expect from the other a full, fair, open, and honest disclosure of everything affecting the relationship. This includes a duty to exercise sound business judgment. A partner must make full disclosure of all material facts within his or her knowledge in any way relating to partnership affairs. This duty requires that partners not misrepresent or intentionally conceal material facts, as well as make timely affirmative disclosures without prompting. Here there was no breach of a fiduciary duty by Silverberg. In light of economic conditions, the impaired financial position of the bank, and the regulatory pressure, the Go Forward plan constituted a reasonable business decision by Silverberg in a good-faith effort to protect partnership assets. Silverberg fully disclosed information concerning the bank's precarious financial condition and the actions needed to rectify the situation, thereby meeting his fiduciary disclosure obligation as the Go Forward plan. At the time of the plan, the bank had no value. An FDIC takeover of the bank would have been more damaging to E&A and its partners than was the Go Forward plan.

DUTY OF CARE IN PARTNERSHIP BUSINESS

Partners have a duty to exercise reasonable care and skill in transacting business for the partnership. A further duty is not to exceed the authority granted to them by the partnership. Partners are liable for their negligence while acting for the partnership but not for honest errors of judgment.

DUTY TO INFORM

Partners owe a duty to pass on to the other partners all information coming to them that may be important to the operation of the partnership. This is because a notice by a third person to any partner is treated as having been given to the partnership. This rule stems from the agency relationship arising among partners. It is presumed that an agent will disclose to the principals all matters that it is his or her duty to disclose to them. Outsiders dealing with the agent are entitled to rely on this presumption whether or not the agent in fact communicates the knowledge to the principals. Of course, this is not true if the third person has been told that all notices must be given to a certain partner.

DUTY TO ACCOUNT

Partners have a duty to account for any expenditure of partnership funds they make. They must also account for the sale or other disposal of partnership property. The same is true for any benefit or profit coming to them as partners. They also have a right to be reimbursed by the partnership for expenses on its behalf.

The duty of keeping the account books is usually assigned to one partner. He then has a duty to keep them accurately. If the records do not properly show the application of the funds coming to the firm, the partner will be liable.

ENFORCEMENT OF PARTNERSHIP RIGHTS AND LIABILITIES

LIABILITY ON CONTRACTS

Partnerships were not considered legal entities at common law. They could not sue or be sued in the firm name; rather, all partners had to be joined as plaintiffs or defendants. This requirement of joinder (naming and serving all parties as defendants or naming all as plaintiffs) made it hard for creditors to sue on partnership contracts. Today, under the UPA, "the firm is primarily liable if a contract is made by a partner" or other agent who has express, implied, or apparent authority. If the partnership does not pay off the liability, then the partners become **jointly liable.** When liability is joint, all of those liable must be sued in the same suit at common law. However, at common law any partner is liable for the entire debt if the other partners are dead, beyond the jurisdiction of the court, or judgment proof (without property that can be seized for debt).

Most states today have a **common name** statute that permits suits against a partnership in the name under which it commonly does business. These statutes eliminate the common law requirement to get personal service on (to deliver the summons to) each partner. Common name statutes permit a plaintiff who is suing on a partnership contract to get a judgment if one or more of the partners are served.

LIABILITY FOR TORTS

The doctrine of respondeat superior imposes liability on the partnership for torts committed by any partner or employee of the firm while engaged in partnership business. The principles of agency law (see Chapter 21) apply in determining whether a tort is committed within the scope and during the course of the partnership business. The liability of the partners for partnership torts is *joint and several*. This permits the injured person to sue any partner individually or all of them together.

In the case that opened this chapter, Dresser Industries could sue the law firm or any of the attorneys individually for Digges's overbilling since it occurred within the scope of the partnership. Thus, Wharton and Levin could be liable even though they were accused of no wrongdoing. After being found liable, however, Wharton or Levin could seek indemnification from the partnership.

A partner who commits a tort against another partner is, of course, liable for the resulting injury. Therefore, Wharton and Levin will have an action for an accounting against Digges in order to recover the money that he stole from the partnership.

LIABILITY FOR CRIMES

A partnership may commit a crime by the manner in which it carries on its business. Examples of such crimes would include violating antitrust laws, failing to obtain a necessary business license, or discharging a prohibited pollutant. The firm is liable for the resulting fines. The individual partners are liable if the firm has inadequate assets.

The other partners are not subject to imprisonment for a crime committed by a partner. This is true even if the crime was committed by the wrongdoing partner while acting for the partnership. Some direct participation or encouragement would be necessary for imprisonment.

DISSOLUTION OF THE PARTNERSHIP

Dissolution occurs when any partner ceases to be associated in the carrying on of the business. However, a partner's demand for a dissolution does not automatically terminate the partnership business. Instead, it may be carried on by the remaining partners through a **continuation.** There are four basic ways in which a dissolution occurs: nonwrongful; wrongful; automatically by law; or by court decree.

NONWRONGFUL DISSOLUTION

A partnership established for a certain period of time dissolves at the end of that period. A partnership that is formed for a certain objective, such as to subdivide a certain plot of ground and then to develop and sell residential lots, dissolves when that objective is reached. Of course, the partners can at any time unanimously agree to dissolve a partnership. They can do this although they earlier agreed on some specific time or the attainment of some objective not yet reached. Where no period of time or specific undertaking is agreed on, the partnership is a **partnership at will.** Such a partnership may be dissolved at any time by any partner. All that is necessary is for a partner to notify the other partners.

In the partnership agreement, the partners also may provide for expelling a partner. If so, and if the agreed-on procedure is followed, a partner may be forced out without violation of the agreement. Such a provision eliminates the right the expelled partner would otherwise have to insist on liquidation.

Each nonwrongful partner (including the partner demanding the dissolution) may demand that the business of the partnership be wound up and liquidated. Thus, the partnership business cannot be continued in the absence of the unanimous approval of all of the nonwrongful partners. Furthermore, nonwrongful partners have the right to participate fully in the winding up process.

WRONGFUL DISSOLUTION

A partner has the *power* to dissolve a partnership even though she does not have the *right*. However, if a partner exercises the power to dissolve when she does not possess the right, she has caused a wrongful dissolution. Refusal by partners to carry out their obligations under a partnership agreement also may constitute a wrongful dissolution. So, if a partner fails to pay his partnership contribution or refuses to furnish the services agreed on, he may be treated as a wrongfully dissolving partner.

A partner who wrongfully dissolves loses the right to demand a winding up and liquidation. In addition, the wrongful partner forfeits the right to participate in the winding up process should any nonwrongful partner decide on one. The innocent partners are given the right by the UPA to continue the business by themselves or with a new partner or partners. If this is done, the partner who breaches the agreement must still be paid the value of his interest less damages for the breach. As an alternative, which is often necessary when the partnership or remaining partners do not have enough cash, the partnership must secure a bond to ensure that the departing partner will be paid off and indemnified against partnership liabilities. The wrongdoing partner is not entitled to anything for goodwill in computing the value of his partnership share.

AUTOMATIC DISSOLUTION

The death or bankruptcy of any partner automatically dissolves the partnership. The same is true if the conduct of the partnership business becomes illegal, as it would, for example, if in time of war one of the partners were an enemy alien. It also occurs if a member of the partnership loses her license to practice the profession or carry on the business of the partnership.

DISSOLUTION BY COURT ORDER

A court may also dissolve a partnership by judicial decree. This usually occurs on petition by one or more partners. Several grounds for such action are given by the UPA: *insanity* of a partner, *permanent disability* of a partner, and *willful or continuing breach* of the partnership agreement. Mere personal friction or antagonism is usually not considered a basis for dissolution when the business continues to be profitable. However, the prospect of long-continuing losses may be a sufficient ground for court dissolution even if there is no wrongdoing or inability to work together. A partner who seeks dissolution by a court is viewed as voluntarily dissolving the partnership.

.... *WINDING UP* ....

Normally, the partners themselves wind up—that is, liquidate the assets of the business—after dissolution. If the partnership is dissolved by the death or bankruptcy of a partner, the remaining partners have the right to wind up. If a partnership has been dissolved in violation of the partnership agreement, the innocent partners have the right to liquidate the partnership assets. These rights to wind up, which are granted by the UPA, may be modified by the partnership agreement.

Where dissolution is by court order, the court usually appoints a representative as *receiver* to wind up the business. When disputes arise during the winding up, a partner may ask a court to appoint a receiver.

POWERS DURING WINDING UP

The purpose of the winding up is to liquidate the assets at their highest value and bring the affairs of the partnership promptly to an end. This may involve completing partnership contracts. For example, in a partnership involved in the construction business, it may be desirable to finish contracts for constructing large buildings that may take two or three years to complete. In order to finish these jobs, the winding-up partners would have authority to enter into new contracts with subcontractors, with material suppliers, and with workers. As a result, it may be necessary that the winding-up partners borrow money on behalf of the partnership in order to complete these contracts.

It is possible, however, that the partners may desire to assign such long-term contracts to other contractors. In most cases, they would be authorized to make such assignments. Of course, the winding-up partners have no authority to enter contracts for new business. They would be liable to the partnership for any loss suffered on such contracts.

DUTIES OF PARTNERS DURING WINDING UP

Partners continue to have fiduciary duties to their copartners during winding up. A partner who is entitled to participate in the winding up cannot be excluded, nor can a partner claim specific partnership property without the agreement of the others.

COMPENSATION FOR WINDING UP

Under the UPA, the partners who wind up a partnership business are not entitled to be paid for that work. They are limited to their share of the profits unless there is an agreement to compensate. However, surviving partners are entitled to reasonable compensation when the winding up follows the death of a partner.

Ethical Implications	In the absence of an agreement permitting compensation, partners generally are not entitled to be paid for their work during the winding-up process. Still, as a fiduciary they have a duty to act in the best interests of all of the partners, including those who are not taking an active part in the winding up. Is it ethical for a partner to let the other partners do the work during the winding up without compensating them for their efforts?

CONTINUATION

The general rule is that there is no right to continue a partnership beyond the originally agreed-on term. If a partnership is established for a term of 10 years, none of the partners has a right to continue the business beyond that time except with the unanimous agreement of all. Further, in a partnership at will, the remaining partners have no right to continue the business when one of the partners chooses to have it liquidated. Accordingly, in order to preserve the value of the goodwill developed by the business, the partnership agreement often will include language modifying the right to insist on liquidation.

CONTINUATION WITHOUT WINDING UP

Some courts take the view that there is an automatic dissolution of the partnership on the withdrawal or death of a partner. However, many partnership agreements declare that there will be no dissolution at such an event even if a new partner or partners enter into the partnership. This usually is beneficial to all concerned because it preserves the value of the going business. Whether or not there has been a technical dissolution, courts enforce partnership agreements that provide for a continuation of the business. There is then no winding up or termination.

Partners may agree at any time that the interest of one partner shall be purchased by the partnership or by one or more of the other partners. They also may agree to take in an additional partner. Or they may agree to permit a partner to sell his or her interest to another and to accept that person as a substitute partner. These agreements are called **buyout agreements.** Normally, they include provisions seeking to protect the financial interests of the partners who are leaving (and those who are entering) the partnership. Usually, life insurance is bought to fund the purchase of the interests of partners who die.

LIABILITY FOR PRIOR OBLIGATIONS

The continuing partnership becomes liable for the debts incurred by the original partnership. A withdrawing partner or the representative of a deceased partner remains liable for those debts if the continuing partnership does not or cannot pay them.

Usually, the continuing partners agree to relieve the withdrawing partners of liability on the debts of the old partnership. However, such agreements are not binding on creditors unless they have joined in a *novation*. This involves an agreement by the creditor with both the withdrawing partners (or representatives of deceased partners) and the continuing partners. The continuing partners agree to assume the obligation, and the creditor agrees to hold only them liable and to release the withdrawing partners or their representatives.

A novation is sometimes inferred by courts from the conduct of the creditor of the original partnership. Acceptance of a check or other negotiable instrument from a continuing partner has been held to be a novation if it is in full settlement of the claim and the creditor had knowledge of the change of membership. This would not apply to a partial payment.

A person who joins an existing partnership becomes liable for all previous obligations of the partnership as if he or she had been a partner. However, liability is limited to the partnership assets.

CITIZENS BANK V. PARHAM–WOODMAN MEDICAL ASSOCIATES
874 F. Supp. 705 (E.D. Va. 1995)

FACTS

Citizens Bank and Parham–Woodman Medical Associates, a general partnership, entered a construction loan agreement on April 30, 1985. The loan, in the principal amount of $2 million, was to fund construction of a medical office building for the partnership. Nilda Ante and Larry King were the general partners when the loan was extended. As contemplated by the agreement, the bank made advances from time to time during the construction of the building. Between April 1985 and June 1986, the advances totaled $1,457,123.15. On June 25, 1986, Nada Tas and her husband, Joseph Tas, also became general partners. From that date until November 17, 1986, Citizens Bank made additional advances in the amount of $542,876.85. After the medical office building was built, the partnership defaulted on the loan. Ante and King went into bankruptcy and their personal liability was eliminated. The bank then sued Nada and Joseph Tas, claiming they were personally liable for the $542,876.85 in advances made after their admission to the partnership.

ISSUE

Are Nada and Joseph Tas personally liable for the advances made after their admission to the partnership?

DECISION

No. Nada and Joseph Tas have personal liability for the advances only if the advances represent partnership debt that arose after they became general partners. On April 30, 1985, the bank became obligated to lend the partnership the total sum of $2 million to be advanced from time to time upon satisfaction of contractually specified conditions. At the same time, the partnership agreed to borrow the $2 million from the bank. The loan agreement required the advances to be applied to the limited purpose of building construction and the partnership was obligated contractually to complete the construction. The bank was not free after April 1985 to impose additional conditions on its making future advances. Notwithstanding the somewhat contingent arrangement respecting disbursement of the loan, the

(continued)

CITIZENS BANK V. PARHAM–WOODMAN MEDICAL ASSOCIATES
(concluded)

debt arose on April 30, 1985. Partnership law makes an incoming partner liable for all obligations arising before his admission, but provides that this liability shall be satisfied only out of partnership property. Thus, existing and subsequent creditors have equal rights against partnership property and the separate property of all the previously existing partners, while only the subsequent creditors have rights against the separate estate of newly admitted partners. This rule enables potential creditors of the partnership to know that what they see of a partnership is what they can reach and it permits potential incoming partners to avoid surprise liabilities.

LIABILITY FOR NEW OBLIGATIONS

Former partners may be held liable for the new obligations of a continuing partnership when the new or continuing partners have apparent authority to bind the former partner. Such authority is likely to arise when creditors of the old partnership have not been notified of the departure of the former partner and rely on his continued presence in the partnership when extending new credit. Accordingly, withdrawing partners should protect themselves by notifying the world of their departure through actual and constructive notice. (These concepts were discussed earlier in Chapter 21.)

RIGHTS OF NONCONTINUING PARTNER

The noncontinuing partner (or his estate) becomes a creditor of a continuing partnership. The obligations to the noncontinuing partner are subordinate to those of other creditors. So, if a person withdraws from a partnership business that continues, he would get what the business owes him only if the partnership can pay all other debts first. The value of the partnership interest of the noncontinuing partner is determined as of the time he leaves the partnership.

CONCEPT SUMMARY	Liability to Creditors	
	Prior Obligations	**New Obligations**
Continuing Partners	Liable	Liable
Withdrawing Partners	Liable (unless released by a novation)	Not liable (if they have given notice of withdrawal)
New Partners	Liable only to extent of contribution unless they agree to greater liability	Liable

In the absence of a provision in the partnership agreement, the UPA gives a retiring partner or the representative of a deceased partner an option. The noncontinuing partner can take either her partnership interest at the time of dissolution plus interest or her partnership interest plus her share of profits gained from the use of her property. The choice need not be made until after an accounting. At that time it can be determined which choice is more favorable.

FIGURE 24–3   Dissolution of the Partnership

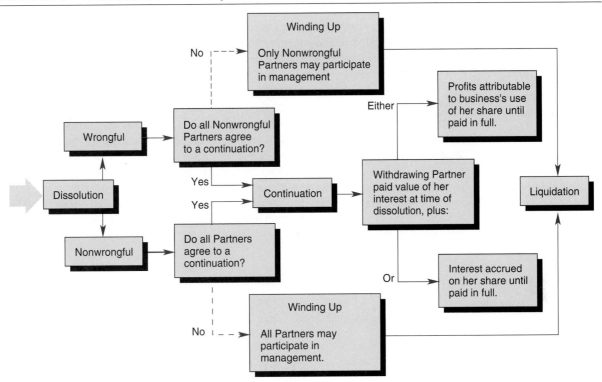

The UPA gives the other partners a right to continue the business (with or without additional partners) when a partner decides to withdraw before its agreed term or objective has been reached. The withdrawal, of course, would be a breach of the partnership agreement. In this case, the remaining partners have two options: they must either pay the breaching partner his interest promptly or continue the business only for the agreed-on term and then settle with all partners during winding up. (See Figure 24–3.)

DISTRIBUTION OF ASSETS

ORDER OF DISTRIBUTION

The final act of winding up a partnership is the distribution of assets. There is no problem if the partnership business has been profitable; creditors and partners will be paid in full. Where there have been losses, however, it is crucial to determine the order in which the various claimants are entitled to be paid their claims from the remaining assets. The UPA has established the following priorities:

1. Outside creditors (other than partners) of the firm.
2. Debts owed to a partner either for loans or advances made to the firm or for liabilities of the firm paid by the partner.
3. The return of each partner's capital contribution.
4. The remaining assets are divided as profits according to the partnership agreement.

A distinction is made between money or property that a partner lends to the firm and that which the partner contributes as capital. In winding up, the loans from partners are paid after debts due other creditors. It is only after all debts are paid that the partners are entitled to the return of their capital investment. Therefore, if a partner makes a loan, it is important that the firm's account books clearly show this.

Unless the agreement specifies that a certain value has been placed on a partner's labor, a partner who has contributed no cash or other property would normally receive nothing under step 3. However, a value may by agreement be put on a nonproperty contribution of a partner and set up as capital on the firm's books. For example, a partner may have spent a great deal of time developing the basic ideas on which the business operates. Or he or she may have the friendships or other contacts on which the business depends. Special knowledge or skill in operating the partnership business might also be recognized in this way.

The order of distribution among partners, stated in the rules above, can be varied by agreement among the partners. However, creditors of the firm who are not partners must always be paid first.

VARGO V. CLARK
1998 Ohio App. LEXIS 2957 (Ohio Ct. App. 1998)

FACTS

Nancy Clark and Ruth Vargo are sisters. Those two, along with Nancy's husband, Wayne, decided to open a grocery store in Arabia, Ohio. The Clarks owned real estate, and Nancy had worked in the grocery business, but they lacked the financial resources to build and run a grocery. Ruth provided funds for the business, incurring $35,081 in credit card debt. The Clarks deposited the money in an account for C&C Grocery. Ruth then quit her job and moved from Michigan to Ohio to live with the Clarks. They never entered into a written contract. On April 1, 1996, C&C Grocery opened for business. Ruth and each of the Clarks spent about the same amount of time in the store. However, due to personal and/or financial difficulties between Ruth and the Clarks, Ruth returned to Michigan in July 1996 and the partnership was dissolved. The Clarks borrowed $22,000 from a finance company and $35,000 from Wayne's father to contribute to the business. Wayne testified that he never entered into a written contract with Ruth because he did not want anyone to have an interest in his land. The Clarks' home and their daughter's home also sit on the six-acre tract that they used for the grocery. The store and the land it occupies is worth $75,000, the inventory $11,000, and the equipment $20,000 (totaling $106,000). In distributing the partnership assets, the court gave Ruth $53,000 (50 percent of $106,000 in assets) plus another $17,540.50 (50 percent of her financial contribution to the business). The Clarks appealed the judgment of the trial court, claiming that Ruth had no right to any of the assets and that the court failed to compensate them for their financial contributions to the business.

ISSUE

Did the court distribute the assets correctly?

DECISION

No. The court was correct in awarding Ruth 50 percent of the real estate and other assets. The Clarks wanted to use the land to build the grocery but lacked the necessary capital for construction. Ruth contributed the funds that eventually paid for substantial portions of the grocery and its inventory. This provides competent, credible evidence to support the trial court's finding that the Clarks intended to contribute their land to the partnership in return for Ruth's contribution of capital. However, the trial court did err in failing to account for the debt incurred by the Clarks when it figured the debts of the joint venture. Nancy and Wayne incurred debts of $22,000 and $35,000 in furtherance of the partnership. These amounts must be taken into account when dividing the debts and assets of the partnership.

LIQUIDATING AN INSOLVENT PARTNERSHIP

The order of distribution takes on even more importance when the partnership has suffered losses and is unable to fully repay its outside creditors. Then the burden of paying off the partnership creditors may fall on the individual partners, creating competition between the partnership creditors and the creditors of the individual partners for the assets of the partners. The general rule for resolving such disputes (known as **marshalling of assets**) is that partnership creditors have first claim on partnership assets and creditors of individual partners have first claim on the assets of individual partners.

TERMINATION

The winding up process is complete when the partnership assets are entirely distributed and the claims of the partnership creditors are satisfied. Only after completion of this liquidation process is the partnership terminated.

LIMITED PARTNERSHIPS

The purpose of the limited partnership form of business organization is to permit some partnership investors to have limited liability. The limited partner gives up the right to participate in the management of the partnership business in return for limited liability. Like a corporate shareholder, the limited partner may lose his investment but no more.

CHARACTERISTICS

Limited partnerships have one or more general partners and one or more limited partners. Normally, limited partners have no obligation for the debts of the partnership. Management of the business of the partnership is in the hands of the general partner or partners. Because limited liability is a privilege given by the state, limited partnerships can be created only under a state statute. All states have such statutes.

FORMALITIES

The statutory formalities must be complied with to form a limited partnership. A certificate must be filed with the Secretary of State or the county recorder. The certificate must describe the nature of the business, its location, and the term of its existence. It must also give the names and addresses of all partners and their capital contributions, listing separately the limited and general partners. A description and a statement of the agreed value of contributions in property other than cash must be included. Certain other information must be provided, such as whether the partnership may admit additional partners and whether limited partners may assign their interests to others. The certificate should also include a statement of the events permitting a partner to withdraw from the limited partnership. Note that the withdrawal of a limited partner does not automatically dissolve the limited partnership. (See Figure 24–4 on page 426.)

RIGHTS AND LIABILITIES

Partnership law applies to limited partnerships except to the extent changed by the applicable limited partnership statutes. One fundamental difference from general

FIGURE 24–4   Certificate of a Limited Partnership

Limited Partnership Certificate

I. The name of the Limited Partnership is Sunset Acres Estates, Limited Partnership.

II. The business of the Limited Partnership shall be the development and operation of a mobile home park in Monroe County, Indiana.

III. The location of the principal place of business of the Limited Partnership shall be 400 North Walnut Street, Bloomington, IN 47401, or wherever the General Partner may from time to time designate.

IV. The name and address of each Partner are as follows:

    A. The name of the General Partner is Bloomington Realty, Inc., 400 North Walnut Street, Bloomington, IN 47401.

    B. The names and residences of the Limited Partners are:
       George E. Ash, 4210 Saratoga Avenue, Bloomington, IN 47401
       Helen V. Brown, 4203 E. 3d Street, Bloomington, IN 47401
       Alice A. Jones, 468 Elm Street, Bloomington, IN 47401
       Roger S. Smith, 1807 E. 2d Street, Bloomington, IN 47401

V. The Limited Partnership shall continue until dissolved by any one of the following events:

    A. The mutual consent of all Partners,

    B. The sale of the Partnership business,

    C. The adjudication that the General Partner is bankrupt or the filing of a voluntary petition of bankruptcy or an admission by the General Partner that it is unable to pay its debts.

    D. Or in any event, at midnight, December 31, 2004.

VI. The initial capital contribution of the General Partner is $20,000, the agreed value of its services in acquiring the tract to be developed by the Partnership. The initial contribution of each of the Limited Partners is $50,000 in cash.

VII. Each Limited Partner agrees to contribute an additional $30,000 on or before May 1, 1999, and an additional $20,000 on or before May 1, 2000. In addition, each Limited Partner agrees to make an additional capital contribution not to exceed $20,000 on or before May 1, 2001, if in the sole discretion of the General Partner additional capital is needed for the proper development, maintenance, or sale of the property.

VIII. The capital contribution of the Partners shall be repaid upon dissolution and winding up of the Partnership.

IX. The net profits and net losses of the Partnership for any calendar year shall be allocated among the Partners in the same proportion as their capital contributions. However, the profit, it any, from the sale of the property shall be divided equally among the General Partner and the Limited Partners. If any Limited Partner has failed to make any of the capital contributions called for in Articles VI or VII, his share shall be proportionately reduced and reallocated to the other Partners.

X. A Limited Partner or his legal representative may assign his partnership interest at any time and substitute the assignee as a Limited Partner upon notification to the General Partner and all Limited Partners, with a copy of the assignment furnished to the General Partner.

XI. Additional Limited Partners may be added upon the approval of the General Partner and a majority of the then existing Limited Partners.

XII. No Limited Partner shall have priority over any other Limited Partner as to the return of his capital contributions.

IN WITNESS WHEREOF, the Partners have executed this Certificate this 5th day of January, 1999.

LIMITED PARTNERS:

George E. Ash
George E. Ash

Helen V. Brown
Helen V. Brown

Alice A. Jones
Alice A. Jones

Roger S. Smith
Roger S. Smith

GENERAL PARTNER:

Bloomington Realty, Inc.

by *William Glass*
   President

partnership principles, however, is that limited partners are not fiduciaries. The rights and liabilities of general partners are essentially the same as those of partners in an ordinary partnership. However, without the approval of all the limited partners, the general partners cannot admit other general partners, and they may not add other limited partners unless this right is given in the certificate.

Liabilities When Formalities Are Absent

Formerly, if the limited partnership failed to file the proper certificate, it would be treated as a general partnership. This resulted in all of the partners, limited and general alike, being personally liable on all partnership debts, Now, however, those who erroneously believe they are limited partners may escape liability under certain conditions. In some states those intended to be limited partners must renounce any interest in the profits of the firm on discovering the error. In others, they must cause a proper certificate to be filed or withdraw from participation in future distributions of profits. However, the limited partners are liable as general partners to any person who extended credit to the partnership before the proper filing of the certificate and who was under the good faith belief that the limited partners were general partners.

Gregg v. S. R. Investors, Ltd.
1998 U.S. Dist. LEXIS 6191 (N.D. Ill. 1998)

Facts

Jerry Gregg engaged in business as a railroad consultant. S. R. Investors, Ltd. (SRI) was formed in 1983 purportedly as a limited partnership to own and operate the Sierra Railroad. Gregg entered into a consulting agreement with SRI, pursuant to which he was to provide services to Sierra. After SRI terminated the relationship, Gregg claimed that he had not been paid for his services. He sued Russell J. Barron and Richard Cohn, claiming they were personally liable on the debt. While Barron and Cohn both invested in SRI as limited partners, Gregg argued that Illinois law does not allow limited partnerships to operate a railroad. Specifically, the state law provides: "a limited partnership may carry on any business that a partnership without limited partners may carry on except . . . the operation of railroads." According to Gregg, because SRI could not be formed properly as a limited partnership, all the "limited partners," including Barron and Cohn, must be construed to be general partners. As general partners, Gregg alleges they are liable for all debts of the partnership. Barron and Cohn assert that they cannot be held liable as general partners because once they learned of Gregg's argument that SRI could not be formed as a limited partnership, they timely withdrew from the partnership pursuant to state law.

Issue

Did Barron and Cohn lose their limited liability?

Decision

No. Illinois law provides that "a person who makes a contribution to a business enterprise and erroneously but in good faith believes that he or she has become a limited partner in the enterprise is not a general partner in the enterprise and is not bound by its obligations . . . if within a reasonable time after ascertaining the mistake, he or she . . . withdraws from the future equity participation in the enterprise." Barron and Cohn were both passive investors in SRI and exercised no control over the enterprise and did not participate in management or decision making. Gregg did not know either of them and, accordingly, did not base any of his decisions on the fact that either was a general partner. The information that Barron and Cohn received repeatedly indicated that SRI would be formed as a limited partnership and neither realized that the business could not be legally formed as a limited partnership. Finally, both Barron and Cohn filed for and received certificates of withdrawal from the Office of the Secretary of State soon after discovering Gregg's argument. Gregg further argued that the withdrawal provision

(continued)

GREGG v. S. R. INVESTORS, LTD.
(concluded)

in Illinois law does apply to this case because it is applicable only when a partnership could legally be created as a limited partnership in the first place. This argument is rejected because the withdrawal provision should be construed broadly. Finally, Gregg asserts that the defendants did not assert that they in good faith believed they were investing as limited partners. He suggests that ignorance of the law is no excuse and, accordingly, the court should presume that every investor is aware of the statutory limits on forming limited partnerships. Such a holding is untenable. Only someone well versed in railroad and/or partnership law would likely be aware of such a statutory prohibition. Certainly the ordinary investor would have no occasion to suspect that such a prohibition exists.

CONTROL BY LIMITED PARTNERS

A limited partner who takes part in the control of the business becomes liable to partnership creditors like a general partner. There have been few cases, but it appears that *control* means participation in day-to-day management decisions. If a limited partner is acting substantially like a general partner, she has the liability of a general partner to all creditors of the limited partnership. If she takes part in control of the business but does not act substantially like a general partner, she is liable only to those persons who deal with the limited partnership with actual knowledge of her participation in control.

DISSOLUTION OF A LIMITED PARTNERSHIP

As with an ordinary partnership, a limited partnership may be dissolved and its business wound up. However, not all events that would have dissolved a general partnership will have the same effect on a limited partnership. This is so because the limited partners are not involved in the actual management of the partnership business. Accordingly, the personality of the limited partners will not always be vital to the existence of the limited partnership.

The death or bankruptcy of a limited partner does not result in dissolution; neither does the addition or substitution of a limited partner. However, the limited partnership certificate must be canceled when all limited partners have died or withdrawn. The retirement, death, or insanity of a general partner usually dissolves a limited partnership. But dissolution can be avoided if the right to continue is granted in the certificate or if all other general and limited partners agree.

QUESTIONS AND PROBLEM CASES

1. Union Switch manufactures and sells switching and signaling systems to railroads and other transportation industries. In 1985 it decided to select outside vendors to provide certain parts and focus its own efforts on assembling the final product. Accordingly, Union met with Gulf South Marine regarding the selection of Gulf as an outside vendor. Union indicated that it preferred to do business with a limited number of vendors rather than to bid work out on a project-by-project basis. Eventually, Union chose Gulf as a preferred vendor and began placing orders during 1986. The exact terms of the association between the two companies were

never formalized into a written contract. However, on several occasions, Union officials referred to the firm's relationship with Gulf as a "partnership" and called Gulf one of its "partner–vendors." Union also indicated by letter that it intended Gulf to be its sole source for machined detail parts and subassemblies. Gulf alleges that it relied on Union's assurances regarding the "partner" nature of the relationship and that Gulf would be the exclusive source of certain parts to make initial investments to enable it to satisfy Union's orders. During 1987, the two parties unsuccessfully attempted to agree to a formal contract to define their relationship. However, they did sign a pricing agreement in which Union promised Gulf prices to ensure Gulf "equitable profitability (based on industry norms)." When Gulf later expressed dissatisfaction with the pricing agreement, Union agreed to make retroactive payment to Gulf for services during 1987, including a $200,000 incentive payment to be made at the end of 1988 if Gulf performed in a satisfactory manner. In March 1989, Union informed Gulf that it had not earned the incentive bonus because of late deliveries, high rejection rates for Gulf parts, and slow response to price quotations. In the same letter, Union terminated Gulf as a "partner-vendor" and began to greatly reduce its purchases from Gulf. When Union ultimately terminated its business relationship with Gulf in 1993, Gulf sued. According to Gulf, the events of 1986 and 1987 gave rise to an oral partnership agreement, which was violated when Union withdrew from the relationship in bad faith. Union argued that a legal partnership did not exist. Was the relationship between Union and Gulf a partnership?

2. Linda and William Bass began dating in 1974 and started living together the following year. At that time she was working and he was unemployed. Later William acquired a restaurant where Linda worked 17 hours a day while he was employed at a beer store. When he quit that job, Linda and William each worked 12-hour shifts in the restaurant in order to keep it open 24 hours a day. She was never compensated for her efforts. At this same time, William started several other businesses that

became quite successful. In 1980 Linda and William were married. Even though they were divorced that same year, they immediately began living and working together again. While Linda was not listed as a partner or co-owner of any of the businesses, she wrote and signed most of the checks for the operations. She was never paid wages or a salary for her efforts. All of the businesses and property were listed exclusively in William's name. When William died in 1986, Linda claimed a right to one-half of his assets as his business partner. His son disputed her claim. Were Linda and William business partners?

3. Levy and Disharoon formed a partnership for the purpose of purchasing a jet and operating a charter airline service. Disharoon located a jet and informed Levy that it could be purchased for $963,000. After securing Levy's approval, Disharoon arranged to have the partnership borrow $975,000 to make the purchase. In reality and unknown to Levy, Disharoon had contracted to buy the jet for only $860,000. When the sale was completed, Disharoon had arranged to have $860,000 paid to the seller and $103,000 deposited in his personal bank account. Upon discovering Disharoon's misrepresentation, Levy sued for both actual and punitive damages on a theory of breach of loyalty and good faith. Is Disharoon liable for breaching a duty of loyalty?

4. *Video Case.* See "The Partnership." Art, Ben, and Diedre are partners of Alphabet Builders, a partnership in the construction business. They meet at a restaurant with a prospective new partner, Don, who says he will decide whether to enter the partnership after discussing the matter with his wife. During the meeting, they are approached by John, with whom the partnership has been attempting to do business. Art introduces Don to John, stating, "We're celebrating Don's joining Alphabet Builders." Don and John shake hands, and John says, "Congratulations! Alphabet Builders has a very good reputation. In fact, I'm about to become one of your new clients. I signed the contract this morning." Don says nothing in response to John's statement. Subsequently, Don decides not to join Alphabet Builders. Nonetheless, when Alphabet Builders breaches

its contract with John, John sues Don on the contract. Is Don liable to John?

5. *Video Case.* See "The Partnership." Art is a partner of Alphabet Builders, a partnership in the construction business. The three partners of Alphabet Builders have agreed that the partnership may not borrow money unless all the partners approve the borrowing. In the name of the partnership, but without the consent of his partners, Art borrows money from a bank. Art tells the bank that the partnership will use the money for general purposes. Art endorses the loan check in the name of the partnership but deposits the money in his personal account. Art uses the money to purchase commodities futures. Art loses the money on the futures and is unable to repay the loan. The bank sues Alphabet Builders and its partners. Are Alphabet Builders and its partners liable to the bank on the loan? Does Art have any liability to the other two partners?

6. *Video Case.* See "The Partnership." Art retires from Alphabet Builders, a partnership with Ben and Diedre. Zack agrees to replace Art in the partnership. Zack signs an agreement with Art in which Zack assumes Art's liability for all partnership obligations. After Art leaves the partnership, Alphabet Builders falls behind in payments to its creditors, including the following: (a) The bank from which Art obtained a loan in the name of the partnership prior to his leaving the partnership. Art pocketed the money and used it for personal investments. Art did not disclose the loan to his partners or to Zack; (b) The creditor who leases office equipment to Alphabet Builders. The lease agreement predates the time Art left the partnership; (c) Subcontractors owed money on contracts entered into after Art left and Zack entered the partnership. What is Art's liability on these obligations? What liability does Zack have? What other facts might you need to help answer these questions?

7. Schymanski and Conventz entered into an oral partnership agreement for the purpose of building and operating a fishing lodge. The partnership was on a 50–50 basis, with each to contribute equal shares of cash and equal shares of personal services according to their respective expertise. Conventz was to supervise the construction of the lodge and to handle the advertising in Alaska. Schymanski was to conduct a promotional campaign in Germany. After numerous delays and disagreements, Conventz expressed his desire to terminate the partnership. He claimed that he was entitled to compensation for his architectural efforts. Schymanski denied that there was ever an agreement for such compensation. In the absence of an agreement, is Conventz entitled to compensation for the architectural efforts?

8. Clarkson, Beck, and Clegg entered into an agreement to form a partnership, known as C.B.C. Investments, for the purpose of building and developing a warehouse. The partnership intended to lease the warehouse to Spring City Knitting Co. Several months later Clarkson withdrew from C.B.C. and informed Beck that she would be developing the warehouse project on her own. Soon after this, Clarkson entered into a lease agreement with Spring City. Beck sued Clarkson for wrongful dissolution. Clarkson claimed that, since the partnership agreement did not fix a definite time for termination, it was a partnership at will which could be properly dissolved at any time. Could the court find that Clarkson wrongfully dissolved the partnership?

9. Gershunoff, Silk, and Oliker became equal partners in a business designed for the syndication and management of apartment houses. They never executed a written agreement setting forth the term of the partnership. Later, when Oliker voluntarily withdrew from the partnership, Gershunoff and Silk continued to operate the business, acquiring new assets and incurring new obligations. For the next two and one-half years, the parties met on numerous occasions to discuss the financial details of Oliker's withdrawal. Finally, Oliker demanded that the business be liquidated and that he be paid a one-third interest in the partnership assets at the time of termination. Silk and Gershunoff argued that Oliker's interest should be based on the value of the partnership at the time of dissolution and should not include the increase in partnership property that occurred during the two and one-half years after his withdrawal.

May Oliker now compel a liquidation and receive one-third of the assets at the time of termination?

10. After Henefeld withdrew from the partnership H&K Garage Doors, the firm made several purchases from Taylor Building Products on credit. Taylor extended the credit without knowing that Henefeld had withdrawn from the partnership. Taylor had extended credit to H&K on several occasions prior to Henefeld's withdrawal. When H&K was unable to pay Taylor's claims, Taylor sought to recover from Henefeld. Is Henefeld liable for the obligations incurred by H&K after his withdrawal?

CHAPTER 25

Formation and Termination of Corporations

Jane Vosseller decided to operate a retail establishment. She intended to organize the business as a corporation that would be named Pottery Warehouse, Inc. On February 28, she executed a lease with Company Stores Corporation for rental of store premises for a five-year term. She signed the lease, "THE POTTERY WAREHOUSE, INC., a corporation to be formed under the laws of the State of Tennessee. By Jane M. Vosseller, Its President." Pottery Warehouse was not incorporated until March 29. Later, when the corporation breached the terms of the lease, Company Stores attempted to hold Vosseller personally liable on the lease.[1]

- *What is a corporate promoter? When is she liable for preincorporation contracts? How can this potential liability be reduced?*
- *What is a defectively formed corporation? When are people personally liable for the debts of defectively formed corporations?*
- *How much capitalization and what level of formalities must be met before a corporation will be treated as an entity separate and apart from its owners? When will a court "pierce the veil" and make shareholders personally liable on corporate obligations?*

---

[1]Company Stores Development Corporation v. The Pottery Warehouse, Inc., 733 S.W.2d 886 (Ct. App. Tenn. 1987).

.... **INTRODUCTION** ....

Corporations are extremely important in today's society. The growth of the modern corporation has been largely responsible for the dynamic economic development attained by this country over the last century. Through corporations, people are able to invest money in a business enterprise without worrying about unlimited liability or management responsibilities. Thus, corporation law gives business the capability to raise the capital necessary to achieve the economics of scale vital to economic efficiency.

If you plan to form a new business, you may very well decide that it should be a corporation. After all, not all corporations are huge economic entities; most of them are small businesses. Further, today it is very easy to form a corporation.

This chapter will look at the basic issues that arise in the incorporation process. Specifically, it will examine:

1. The nature of a corporation.
2. The preincorporation process.
3. The actual incorporation.
4. Liability for defective incorporation.
5. When courts will pierce the corporate veil.
6. Close corporations.
7. The termination process.

.... **NATURE OF A CORPORATION** ....

THE PRINCIPAL CHARACTERISTICS OF THE CORPORATION

The concept of a corporation developed in early law. One advantage of the corporate form of business is that it makes it easier to hold property for long periods of time. This is because the corporation is treated as an intangible being with a life separate from the lives of its owners.

Other powers also came to be associated with the corporate form of organization early on. Because of its separate identity, the corporation can hold and convey property in its own name. Further, it can sue and be sued in its own name. Finally, a corporation possesses the right to make bylaws to govern the relations among its members.

TYPES OF CORPORATIONS

Today, three principal types of corporations are commonly recognized.

Governmental Corporations

The **governmental corporation** is often called a **municipal corporation.** Examples are a city, a school corporation, and a sewage district. Such governmental corporations usually, although not always, have the power to tax. They frequently operate much like business corporations except that they do not seek to make a profit. Examples are the Tennessee Valley Authority and the Federal Home Loan Bank.

Nonprofit Corporations

Nonprofit corporations are similar to nontaxing governmental corporations. They differ, however, in that they are formed and operated by private persons. Examples include hospitals, clubs, and some very large businesses such as Blue Cross-Blue Shield Association. Their founders and members are not permitted to make a profit from the operation of the corporation, although the officers and employees are paid salaries. Each of the states has a special statute under which nonprofit corporations are to be formed and operated.

For-Profit Corporations

For-profit corporations are by far the most common of the various types. The aim of such corporations is usually to make a profit that may be distributed to the shareholders as dividends. Sometimes, however, most or all of the profits are reinvested in the corporation in order to make the business grow. Then, at a later time, shareholders may sell their stock or the entire business may be sold. In this way, the shareholders receive their profits while paying only the lower capital gains tax rather than an income tax on the retained profits.

For-profit corporations are often divided into publicly held and close corporations. The stock of a **close corporation** is generally held by a small group of people who know one another. Usually some or all of them intend to be active in management. An example is a family-owned and -operated retail shop. The close corporation can be contrasted with the **publicly held corporation,** which sells shares to people who often have little interest in it except as investors. General Motors Corporation is a good example. Of course, most publicly held corporations are much smaller than GM. However, most of the largest corporations are publicly held. In a large corporation with stock owned by many scattered shareholders, ownership of less than 10 percent of the shares may be enough to control the enterprise.

From here on we shall discuss only the for-profit corporation. However, many of the legal principles and rules are the same for all types of corporations. Therefore, some of the cases may involve nonprofit corporations. (See Table 25–1.)

REGULATION OF CORPORATIONS

The Model Business Corporation Act (MBCA), prepared by the Corporation, Banking, and Business Law Section of the American Bar Association, was drafted as a model statute for adoption by the legislatures of the various states. The MBCA has been amended many times and was completely revised in 1984. While the old MBCA is still

TABLE 25–1   Types of Corporations

Government Corporation	• Examples: city, school corporation • Generally don't seek profit • Often have power to tax
Nonprofit Corporation	• Examples: hospital, club • Not permitted to make profit • Members may draw salaries • Incorporated under special statute
For-Profit Corporation **Publicly Held**	• Public investors • Profits generally distributed as dividends • Formed under general incorporation statutes
Close	• Small group of investors • Earnings often reinvested • Greater management flexibility is permitted

the basis for the statutes of the majority of the states, most of the provisions of the revised MBCA do represent the rule of the majority of the courts in the United States. Accordingly, this book will concentrate on the revised MBCA, although the old MBCA provisions will be noted when they deviate greatly from the revised model statute.

THE PREINCORPORATION PROCESS

PROMOTERS

Promoters are people who bring a corporation into being. Thus, promotion is a vital activity in a free enterprise system. The promoter is the person who has the idea for a business. She finds people who are willing to finance it—to buy shares of stock and/or to lend money and credit. Contracts must be made for building or leasing space, buying or renting equipment, hiring employees, buying supplies and advertising, and whatever else is required for the early operation of the business. Most state incorporation statutes permit reserving a name for a proposed corporation. This is also done by the promoter. She must arrange for the filing of the legal papers to incorporate the business, and she will usually guide the corporation through the early months or years before the new company is a "going concern."

While the promoter may start with an idea and build a corporate business around it, this is not always the case. In many instances, the promoter will take a sole proprietorship or partnership and convert it into the corporate form. And, of course, rather than always having a single promoter, frequently the corporation will be created through the vision and efforts of a group of promoters.

LEGAL LIABILITY OF PROMOTERS

Liability to the Corporation

The relation of promoters to the corporation, to its shareholders, and to those with whom they contract is unique. Promoters are not agents of the corporation prior to its incorporation because the corporation (the principal) is not yet in existence. Promoters are not agents of the persons who are interested in the venture because the promoters were not appointed by them and are not under their control.

Nevertheless, promoters owe a fiduciary duty to the corporation and to the persons interested in it. This includes the duties of full disclosure, good faith, and absolute honesty to the corporation and to the original shareholders. Thus, it would be a breach of duty to use money received on stock subscriptions to pay the expenses of forming the corporation unless this intent were disclosed.

A promoter often takes an option on property or makes an outright purchase on behalf of the corporation. If he or she misrepresents the price paid or to be paid, the corporation may recover the secret profit made by the promoter. However, if the promoter makes a full disclosure of the expected profit to an independent board of directors, the corporation cannot recover. Of course, if the board of directors is under the control of the promoter, the corporation could rescind the contract or recover damages for breach of the fiduciary duty.

Liability to Third Parties

Promoters are generally held liable on contracts they make on behalf of corporations that are not yet formed. If the corporation is never formed, or if it fails to adopt the promoter's preincorporation agreement, the promoter is liable. This is based on agency law: An agent who makes a contract for a nonexistent principal is personally liable on it. If there is more than one promoter, they are all liable under a joint enterprise theory. Promoters sometimes attempt to escape this potential liability by having the third party agree, when the preincorporation contract is made, that the promoter is not to be liable. The disadvantage of this strategy, however, is that neither the promoter nor the corporation can force the third party to perform such a contract. This results from the rule for bilateral contracts that if one party is not bound, neither is the other because such contracts lack *mutuality*.

After the corporation comes into existence, it may agree to assume liability for the promoter's preincorporation contracts. Such an agreement between the promoter and the corporation, in and of itself, is not sufficient to relieve the promoter from all liability on the contracts. This is so because the third party contracted directly with the promoter. The promoter is released from liability on the preincorporation contracts only if the corporation, the promoter, and the third party all agree that the corporation will be substituted for the promoter. This agreement is called a *novation*.

In the case that opened this chapter, Vosseller acted as a promoter in negotiating the preincorporation contract for The Pottery Warehouse. However, the court held that she was not personally liable on the contract. This is so because many courts find against personal liability when a contract is made in the name and solely on the credit of the proposed corporation and the other contracting party knows that the corporation does not yet exist.

LIABILITY OF THE CORPORATION

Liability to the Promoter

As a general rule, corporations are not required to compensate promoters for the services they render during the preincorporation period. However, there is nothing illegal or wrong if promoters are paid for their services. Profit to the promoters is illegal only if it is not disclosed. After formation of the corporation, it may agree to pay the promoters not only for their expenses but also for their services. Frequently, promoters are issued shares of the stock of the new corporation for their services. In the past, many states had not permitted promotional services to be used as consideration for shares in the new corporation. However, the current trend in law, as evidenced by the revised MBCA, is to permit the corporation to issue shares in return for the promoters' preincorporation services.

Liability to Third Parties

When the corporation comes into existence, it is not automatically liable on the contracts made by the promoter. As indicated above, the corporation cannot be liable as principal since it was not in existence. The same fact prevents the corporation from ratifying the promoter's contracts; ratification requires capacity to contract at the time the contract was made.

Nevertheless, all American courts except those of Massachusetts have held corporations liable if, after incorporation, the *board acts to adopt the contract* (adoption is similar to ratification in its effect). Mere acceptance of the benefits of the contract is generally sufficient to bind the corporation. Massachusetts, however, requires that the parties expressly create a novation before the corporation can be held liable for the preincorporation contracts.

CRYE-LEIKE REALTORS V. WDM, INC.
1998 Tenn. App. LEXIS 641 (Tenn. Ct.App. 1998)

FACTS

On November 10, 1993, George C. Richert appointed Colman Borowsky, a real estate broker with Crye-Leike Realtors, as his sole and exclusive real estate broker to aid him in the leasing and/or acquisition of industrial property. In executing the agreement, Richert agreed to inform Borowsky of any property of which he became aware in order for Borowsky to contact the owner or the owner's broker. Richert also agreed that, if he entered into any lease or purchase agreement within 24 months after the period of the agreement, Richert would recognize and provide for Borowsky as the broker in the transaction. The agreement provided that after an initial term of 12 months, either party could terminate the arrangement by giving 30 days written notice. At the time they executed the agreement, the parties understood that Richert would be forming a new corporation that would actually acquire the property. Richert represented that he would be the chief executive officer of the new corporation and that he would have authority to execute agreements on its behalf. Because the corporation was not yet in existence, however, Richert signed the agreement in his individual capacity. Borowsky signed the agreement on behalf of Crye-Leike. On December 7, 1993, Richert formed WDM, Inc. Richert became WDM's president and chief executive officer. A short time later, Borowsky showed Richert a potential space at an industrial park. In January 1994, Borowsky prepared a written offer to lease the space and submitted it to the Belz Enterprises, the property owner. Although Borowsky thought the lease was a "done deal," as the negotiations began to drag on, he suspected that Richert and WDM were "bailing out" on him. On February 22, 1994, Richert, on behalf of WDM, executed a lease agreement for a different piece of property with Memphis Zane May Associates. Contrary to the original agreement between Crye-Leike and Richert, neither Borowsky nor Crye-Leike received a commission. By letter dated February 23, 1994, Richert terminated his agreement with Crye-Leike and Borowsky. He wrote the letter on WDM stationery, and he signed it on behalf of WDM as its president and chief executive officer. Some time after receiving the termination letter, Borowsky learned of the lease transaction. As a result, Crye-Leike filed an action against WDM for breach of contract. WDM argued that it was not liable on the contract because it neither adopted nor ratified the contract between Richert and Crye-Leike.

ISSUE

Is WDM liable on the preincorporation contract?

DECISION

Yes. A corporation may become liable on a preincorporation contract executed by its promoter if the corporation subsequently ratifies or adopts the contract. Ratification is the express or implied adoption and confirmation by the corporation of a contract entered into on the corporation's behalf by a promoter who purported to have authority to act as the corporation's agent. For ratification to occur, the corporation, having full knowledge of the facts, must accept the benefits of the promoter's contract. Moreover, the corporation, either by circumstances or by its affirmative election, must indicate an intention to adopt the contract as its own. The record contains evidence that, after it was incorporated, WDM began to receive the benefits of Richert's contract with Crye-Leike. It is undisputed that Borowsky continued to search for suitable property for WDM to conduct its business. These efforts included contacting various landlords and other brokers, showing different properties to WDM and, on at least one occasion, preparing an offer to lease space on behalf of WDM. The corporation also had full knowledge of the facts in this case because Richert, WDM's president and chief executive officer, had full knowledge of the contract he executed with Crye-Leike and of Borowsky's subsequent efforts to find suitable space for WDM. Finally, the record contains evidence that the corporation intended to adopt the contract. Pursuant to contract, in January 1994 Borowsky submitted an offer to Belz Enterprises on behalf of WDM for the lease of industrial space. Richert signed the offer on behalf of WDM, as the corporation's president. Even when Richert sent the letter to Borowsky notifying him that the agreement was being terminated, Richert used WDM stationery and signed the letter as WDM's president and chief executive officer. This evidence supports Crye-Leike's claim that WDM ratified or adopted the contract after its incorporation and that, in actuality, Borowsky was representing WDM, not Richert. Although, as a general rule, the knowledge of a single promoter cannot be imputed to the corporation, exceptions to this rule have been found whether the promoters become directors and stockholders in corporation.

Ethical Implications	When might a corporation refuse to adopt a preincorporation contract? Is it right for a corporation to refuse to adopt a contract entered on its behalf by a corporate promoter?

.... INCORPORATION ....

THE RIGHT TO INCORPORATE

All business corporations derive their existence from the state in which they are incorporated. The earliest business corporations in the American colonies obtained charters from the King of England, since the colonies were governed by the English monarch. The Constitutional Convention of 1797 considered giving this power to the federal government; however, no such power was included in the Constitution. Therefore, this power was left to the states. To form a corporation, the promoters had to find a legislator who was willing to introduce a bill. The legislature then decided whether to grant a charter.

Early legislators feared the growth of corporate power. Charters, therefore, tended to be for short periods of time. For example, a charter might have to be renewed after 10 years. The powers granted and the amount of capital involved were generally rather limited. Most of the earliest corporations were formed to supply public facilities such as bridges, tool roads, and waterworks. A few, however, were mining and manufacturing businesses.

As commercial and industrial development progressed in the United States, legislators were impressed by the resultant benefits brought to the people and, accordingly, they wanted to encourage corporations. At this time, there was also an expanding belief in greater freedom and equality for all people. These factors resulted in the passage of **general incorporation laws,** which made incorporation a right instead of a legislative privilege. Under these statutes, all that is necessary to form a corporation is to prepare **articles of incorporation** that comply with the state's incorporation statute. If they do, a state official—usually the Secretary of State—has a duty to issue a certificate of incorporation.

DECIDING WHERE TO INCORPORATE

Frequently, the corporation will be incorporated in the state where most of its business will be conducted. However, if the enterprise is conducting its affairs in interstate commerce, the promoters may decide to incorporate in a state other than the state in which the principal offices are located. Many large corporations "shop around" for the state that will offer the most benefits to the enterprise.

Two fundamental considerations frequently arise when the promoters are trying to decide where to incorporate. First, the business may be incorporated in a state where the incorporation fees, taxes, annual fees, and other charges tend to be lower. Second, the promoters may decide to incorporate in a state where the corporation statute and judicial decisions grant management considerable freedom from shareholder interference in the operation of corporate affairs. Traditionally, Delaware and, more recently, Ohio, have been attractive states for incorporation. (See Table 25–2.)

STEPS IN INCORPORATION

The following steps governing the incorporation process are included in the MBCA:

TABLE 25-2   Deciding Where to Incorporate

Expenses	Restrictions on Internal Governance
Incorporation fees	Incorporation statute
Annual fees	Judicial decisions
Taxes	General regulations

1. Preparation of the articles of incorporation.
2. Signing and authenticating the articles by one or more of the incorporators.
3. Filing the articles with the Secretary of State and paying all required fees.
4. Issuance of the certificate of incorporation by the Secretary of State.
5. Holding an initial organizational meeting.

Different states may vary slightly in exactly what they require in order to incorporate; however, the above requirements are included in the corporation laws of most states. Further, many states require that a minimum of $1,000 be contributed to the business before it can receive a certificate of incorporation. Some states have an additional requirement directing that a copy of the articles of incorporation be filed in the county where the corporation has its principal place of business.

CONCEPT SUMMARY   **Liability on Preincorporation Contracts**

	Before Incorporation	After Incorporation, before Adoption	After Incorporation, after Adoption
Promoter Contracts with Third Party	Promoter: liable to third party.	Promoter: liable to third party.	Promoter: liable until novation.
Third Party Unaware That Contract Is for Corporation	Corporation: no liability.	Corporation: no liability.	Corporation: liable to third party.
	Third party: liable to promoter.	Third party: liable to promoter.	Third party: liable to corporation after novation.
Promoter Contracts with Third Party	Promoter: no liability.	Promoter: no liability.	Promoter: no liability.
	Corporation: no liability.	Corporation: no liability.	Corporation: liable to third party.
Third Party Agrees to Hold Only the Corporation Liable	Third party: no liability.	Third party: no liability.	Third party: liable to corporation.
Promoter Contracts with Third Party for Benefit of Corporation without Disclaiming Liability	Promoter: liable to third party.	Promoter: liable to third party.	Promoter: no liability.
	Corporation: no liability.	Corporation: no liability.	Corporation: liable to third party.
	Third party: liable to promoter.	Third party: liable to promoter.	Third party: liable to corporation.

FIGURE 25-1   Articles of Incorporation of Universal Enterprises, Inc.

Article I. The name of the corporation is Universal Enterprises, Inc.

Article II. The purpose of the Corporation is to engage in any lawful activity for which corporations may be organized under the Domestic Corporations for Profit Act of Indiana.

Article III. The term of existence of the Corporation shall be perpetual.

Article IV. The post office address of the principal office of the Corporation is 205 North College Avenue, Bloomington, IN 47401. The name of its Resident Agent is Charles Smith, 205 North College Avenue, Bloomington, IN 47401.

Article V. The total number of authorized shares shall be 1,000 common shares, each with a par value of $100.

Article VI. The shares may be issued in one (1) or more classes. Each class shall have such relative rights, preferences, and limitations, and shall bear such designations, as shall be determined by resolution of the Board of Directors prior to the issuance of any shares of such classes.

Article VII.

(*a*) Each share shall be entitled to one (1) vote on all matters.

(*b*) Cumulative voting shall not be permitted on any matter.

Article VIII. The Corporation will not commence business until at least $1,000 has been received for the issuance of shares.

Article IX. (*a*) The initial Board of Directors of the Corporation shall be composed of three members. The number of Directors may from time to time be fixed by the Bylaws of the Corporation at any number not less than three (3). In the absence of a Bylaw, the number shall be three (3).

(*b*) Directors need not be shareholders of the Corporation.

Article X. The initial Board of Directors of the Corporation and their post office addresses are as follows:

Alvin B. Cortwright, 1234 Saratoga Drive, Bloomington, IN 47401

Douglas E. Fenske, 567 East 9th Street, Bloomington, IN 47401

Gordon H. Inskeep, 8910 East 10th Street, Bloomington, IN 47401

Article XI. The name and post office address of the Incorporator is: P.D. Quick, 1112 North Walnut Street, Bloomington, IN 47401.

Article XII. Provisions for the conduct of the affairs of the Corporation shall be contained in the Bylaws. The Bylaws may be amended from time to time by the affirmative vote of the majority of the Board of Directors.

   IN WITNESS WHEREOF, the undersigned, being the Incorporator designated in Article XI, has executed these Articles of Incorporation and certifies to the truth of the facts above stated, this 12th day of November, 1999.

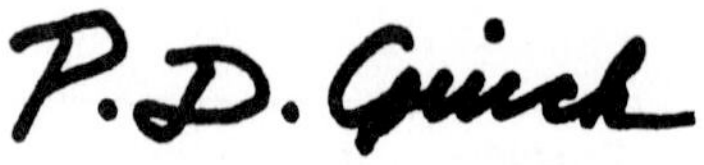

P.D. Quick

P. D. QUICK

CONTENTS OF THE ARTICLES OF INCORPORATION

The articles of incorporation serve the same function as a charter. They are rather like a constitution in that they are the basic document of the corporation and a major source of its powers. The articles will generally be prepared for the corporation by a lawyer because most states have statutes that prescribe the general form of the document; however, these requirements may vary from state to state. (See Figure 25–1.)

Mandatory Contents

The MBCA lists the following matters that *must* be included in the articles of incorporation:

1. The name of the corporation, which must not be deceptively similar to that of any other corporation registered earlier. (It must contain the word *corporation, incorporated, company,* or *limited,* or an abbreviation.)

2. The number of shares of capital stock that the corporation shall have authority to issue.

3.   The address of the initial registered office of the corporation and the name of its registered agent.
4.   The name and address of each incorporator.

Optional Contents

Under the MBCA, the following matters *may* be included in the articles:

1.   The duration of the corporation, which may be, and usually is, perpetual.
2.   The purpose of the corporation. Frequently, this is stated very broadly, such as to "engage in any lawful activity."
3.   The par value of the shares of the corporation.
4.   The number and names of the initial board of directors.
5.   Any additional provisions that are not inconsistent with the state's corporation law. These may include dividend rights and quorum requirements, as well as procedures for the election and removal of directors.

WHO MAY BE INCORPORATORS?

Some states require that at least three natural persons who are adults serve as the incorporator. The MBCA relaxes this rule by permitting a single person, a partnership, an unincorporated association, or even another corporation to act as an incorporator. The incorporator does not incur any special liabilities as a result of her status. She really has no function beyond lending her name and signature to the incorporation process.

THE CERTIFICATE OF INCORPORATION

The Secretary of State reviews the articles of incorporation in order to ensure that they comply with the requirements of the state's incorporation statute. If they do, the Secretary of State issues a certificate of incorporation, which certifies that the corporation is in existence.

ORGANIZATION MEETING

After approval of the articles of incorporation, the MBCA requires that an organization meeting be conducted by the board of directors. In some states, this first meeting is to be held by the incorporators rather than by the directors. The MBCA specifies that bylaws shall be adopted and officers elected at the organization meeting. Usually a corporate seal is adopted, the form of stock certificates is approved, stock subscriptions are accepted, and issuance of stock is authorized. Other business may include adoption of the promoter's contracts, authorization of payment of or reimbursement for expenses of incorporation, and determination of the salaries of officers.

CORPORATE SEAL

Generally, a corporation will adopt a seal. In many states, the corporation must authenticate all real estate documents (deeds and mortgages) by affixing the seal to them. The seal is usually kept by the corporate secretary.

BYLAWS

The function of bylaws is to establish rules for the conduct of the internal affairs of the corporation. The bylaws usually supplement the articles of incorporation by more precisely defining rights and responsibilities of the parties. (If the articles of incorporation are analogous to a constitution, the bylaws are analogous to statutes.)

The bylaws usually set out the duties and authority of the officers and the conduct of meetings. This would include the time and place of the annual shareholders' meeting and how special meetings of shareholders are to be called. They may establish the quorum necessary for the meetings and how elections to the board of directors shall be conducted. They also provide for the organization of directors into committees, if desired, and for the frequency and conduct of board meetings. The bylaws usually set up the procedures for the transfer of shares, for the keeping of stock records, and for declaring and paying dividends.

Occasionally, particularly in close corporations, some of these matters are included in the articles. However, some managerial freedom is lost if too many detailed issues are included in the articles rather than in the bylaws. This is because amendment of the articles of incorporation can be expensive and requires a filing with the Secretary of State. Amendments to bylaws, however, usually can be made by the directors at any time without special formalities.

To be valid, bylaws must be consistent with state law and the articles of incorporation. Directors, officers, and shareholders of the corporation are bound by bylaws that are properly adopted. Others, including corporate employees, are not bound by them unless they have notice or knowledge of them.

The MBCA gives the directors the power to adopt the initial bylaws. Some statutes give this power to the incorporators or the initial shareholders. The MBCA and most statutes give the power of amendment and repeal to the directors; however, shareholders have an inherent right to make bylaws. Thus, if they choose to do so, the shareholders may amend or repeal the bylaws adopted by the directors.

THE *ULTRA VIRES* DOCTRINE

A corporation obtains its legal powers from the state in which it is incorporated. These powers come from the corporation statute, the court decisions of that state, and the articles of incorporation. Simultaneously, there are limitations imposed on the powers of the corporation and its management. Such constraints generally arise in statutes, the articles of incorporation, and the bylaws.

For many years, courts took the view that acts done by corporations that were beyond the authority given them by either the state of incorporation or their articles were void and of no effect. A transaction that was beyond the corporation's powers was said to be **ultra vires.** The state (through the Attorney General), a shareholder, or the corporation itself, could prevent the enforcement of an *ultra vires* contract. This view was often used by the corporation to avoid a contract that later looked unattractive because of a change of conditions; unfairness to the other party to the contract was often the result.

Courts have not all agreed in handling these cases. Most of them have refused to enforce wholly executory contracts but have let stand contracts that had been performed by both parties. Contracts that had been partially executed were the most difficult for the courts. The majority of courts have held that such a contract is enforceable if one of the parties has received a benefit.

The MBCA has eliminated the use of *ultra vires* as a defense to the enforcement of a contract. However, it permits a shareholder to seek a court injunction to stop a corporation from carrying out a proposed action beyond its powers. It also permits the corporation itself, a shareholder, or a receiver in a bankruptcy to bring a suit for damages to the corporation against the officers and/or directors who entered into an *ultra vires* contract. The state's attorney general is also permitted to enjoin the corporation from entering into unauthorized transactions.

DEFECTIVE INCORPORATION

Many times, corporate promoters and others will claim to be acting for a corporation before all of the incorporation requirements have been met. When such misrepresentations arise, it is important to determine the liability of parties involved in the defectively formed corporation. There are several approaches currently being used to resolve these situations.

MODERN APPROACHES

Liability under the Old MBCA

A majority of the states follow the "old MBCA." It holds that the *issuance of the certificate of incorporation* is conclusive proof of incorporation in all challenges to the corporate status except a *quo warranto* action brought by the Secretary of State. (A *quo warranto* action is a suit brought by the state attempting to force the business to stop acting as a corporation.)

Under the old MBCA approach, all persons who assume to act as a corporation when the certificate of incorporation has not been issued are jointly and severally liable for the business debts. It is not altogether clear whether this personal liability would attach to all shareholders or only to those people involved in managing the business.

Liability under the Revised MBCA

The *filing* of the articles of incorporation, evidenced by the return of the copy stamped by the Secretary of State, is conclusive proof of incorporation under the revised MBCA. As with the old MBCA, however, this presumption may be overcome in a quo warranto proceeding brought by the state.

The revised MBCA somewhat clarifies exactly who will be jointly and severally liable for the business debts after the defective incorporation. Such liability would be imposed only on promoters, managers, and shareholders who both (1) participated in management and policy decisions and (2) knew of the defective incorporation. All others would be released from any liability in excess of their initial investment.

Shareholders and others who take no active part in a defectively formed corporation frequently are able to avoid personal liability. Similarly, those who mistakenly believe that the corporation is in existence have no personal liability. Consider the following case.

SIVERS V. R&F CAPITAL CORPORATION
858 P. 2d 895 (Ore. Ct. App. 1995)

FACTS

Roy Rose signed a contract to lease a warehouse from Dennis Sivers. In signing the lease, Rose was acting on behalf of R&F Capital Corporation in his position of chairman. However, the corporation was not in existence at the time the lease was signed. In fact, it did not come into existence until one month later. When R&F breached the

(continued)

SIVERS V. R&F CAPITAL CORPORATION
(concluded)

lease, Sivers sued Rose, claiming that those who prematurely act on behalf of a corporation are personally responsible for liabilities incurred before incorporation. Rose testified that he was a businessman who created financing packages to buy companies. His highest net worth at one point was $56 million. He had been involved in setting up many corporations. However, he had no specific experience with incorporating because his attorneys handled those aspects of the business. He argued that he was not liable because he honestly believed the corporation was in existence at the time he signed the lease.

ISSUE

Is Rose personally liable on the lease?

DECISION

No. Oregon law holds that "all persons purporting to act as or on behalf of a corporation, knowing there was no corporation, are jointly and severally liable for liabilities created while so acting." This is a codification of the judicial exceptions to the general rule that those who prematurely act as, or on behalf of, a corporation are personally liable on all transactions entered into or liabilities incurred before incorporation. The statute protects participants who act honestly but subject to the mistaken belief that the articles of incorporation have been filed. The wording clearly indicates that the test for imposition of personal liability is one of actual knowledge. With respect to R&F, Rose had no participation in its daily operations, other than attending board meetings and signing documents as chairman. He entrusted Flaherty, another director, with those daily duties. Rose did not even read the articles of incorporation until after he was sued. Flaherty was assigned the responsibility of incorporating R&F prior to the lease signing, but he failed to do so. Rose stated that he believed that R&F was incorporated and that he would not have signed any document on behalf of the corporation if he had known that incorporation had not occurred. In light of Rose's honest belief, he is not personally liable on the corporate debt.

HISTORICAL APPROACHES

The MBCA approaches to defective incorporation brought greater clarity than existed under the traditional approaches to the problem. Historically, a defective incorporation might lead to personal liability on the part of promoters, managers, and shareholders, as well as rescission of contracts made on behalf of the defectively formed business. In deciding what consequences should arise, the courts often made their determination based on the intent of the parties and their amount of compliance with the incorporation statute. The consequences that attended the failure to properly incorporate depended on whether the business was described as a *de jure* corporation, a *de facto* corporation, or a corporation by estoppel.

CONCEPT SUMMARY	Liability for Defective Incorporation				
	Old MBCA	**Revised MBCA**	**De Jure**	**De Facto**	**Corporation by Estoppel**
Time When Incorporation Occurs	Issuance of certificate of incorporation	Return of "stamped" articles of incorporation	Substantial compliance with all mandatory provisions	Honest attempt to comply with mandatory provisions	Reliance on representation of incorporation
Liability for Defective Attempt to Incorporate	All who assume to act as a corporation	All who: 1. Participate in management *and* 2. Knew of defect	Generally, nobody (a few states permit a quo warranto action)	May be quo warranto action	Active managers (tort liability on everyone)

De Jure *Corporation*

In a *de jure* corporation, the promoters substantially complied with all *mandatory* provisions. (Mandatory provisions are those that the corporation statute says "must" be done in order to protect the public interest. Other provisions are merely directory and their omission will not destroy the enterprise's corporate identity.) In these instances, the business was treated as a corporation in all instances except a quo warranto proceeding.

De Facto *Corporation*

A *de facto* corporation existed when there was an honest attempt to comply with the mandatory provisions of the corporate statute, yet the attempt still failed in some material respect (e.g., the business failed to hold an organizational meeting). The *de facto* corporation could not be challenged by a third party, and the corporation itself was not permitted to deny its corporate existence.

Corporation by Estoppel

Sometimes people hold themselves out as representing a corporation when no real attempt to incorporate has been made. In these instances, the courts would not let either of the parties to the contracts avoid them due to the misrepresentation of the corporation status. This is so because the promoter pretending to represent a corporation should not be able to benefit from his misrepresentation and the other party suffers no undue harm since he intended to contract with a business possessing only limited liability.

. . . . *PIERCING THE CORPORATE VEIL* . . . .

EFFECT

Normally, shareholders in corporations are not personally liable for the debts of the corporation. This limited liability probably is the principal reason that people incorporate a business today. Through incorporation, the owners' loss is limited to the extent of their investment in the corporation. However, in some instances, a creditor may be able to persuade a court to disregard this separateness between shareholder and corporation. If so, it is said that the court has pierced the corporate veil. This is done by the court in order to give the creditor a judgment against one or more of the shareholders. The shareholders held personally liable on the debt usually are only those who are active in the management of the business.

COMMON SITUATIONS

There are several situations in which a court may pierce the veil. One is when the corporation is given so few assets by its promoters that it could not be expected to pay its debts. Starting a corporation "on a shoestring" (called **undercapitalization**) is not in itself unlawful. However, it may amount to fraud if the objective seems to be to operate a risky business while avoiding the foreseeable claims of creditors.

A number of cases have held shareholders personally liable where they mixed their personal dealings and corporate transactions as if all were personal. The corporation is then viewed as the **alter ego** of the shareholder–manager. The likelihood of the court piercing the veil is greater if there is undercapitalization coupled with the absence of strict adherence to corporate formalities such as holding shareholders' and directors' meetings.

Similar principles are followed by courts in dealing with suits against corporations that operate a part of their business through a subsidiary corporation. (A subsidiary corporation is one in which a majority of stock is owned by a parent corporation.) If the subsidiary is given a few assets and most decisions are made by the parent, the parent corporation may be held liable for the subsidiary's debts.

REQUIREMENTS

The traditional judicial rule is that the court will pierce the veil when two requirements are met.

1. There must be *domination* of the corporation by one or more of its shareholders.
2. The domination must result in an *improper* purpose.

The improper purpose most frequently arises when the corporation defrauds its creditors by not having sufficient assets available to meet expected claims. (See Figure 25–2.)

CRANE V. GREEN & FREEDMAN BAKING COMPANY
134 F3d 17 (1st Cir. 1998)

FACTS

The terms of a collective bargaining agreement required Green & Freedman Baking Company, a corporation, to make periodic payments on behalf of its unionized drivers to an insurance fund. However, after experiencing financial difficulties, Green & Freedman ceased to make the agreed-upon contributions. Sandra Crane, the insurance fund manager, sued the corporation's two controlling shareholders, Richard Elman and Stanley Elman, to recover the payments owed by Green & Freedman. The Elmans claimed that, as shareholders, they were not personally liable for corporate debts. Crane argued that they were personally liable as the "alter egos" of Green & Freedman.

ISSUE

Should the court pierce the corporate veil and hold the Elmans personally liable on the corporate debt?:

DECISION

Yes. Because a rigid test cannot account for all the factual variety, this circuit's standard for measuring a veil-piercing claim is somewhat open ended. Courts should consider the respect paid by the shareholders themselves to the separate corporate identity, the fraudulent intent of the individual defendants, and the degree of injustice that would be visited on the litigants by recogniz-

ing the corporate identity. Using this test, we find ample evidence that there exists a legally sufficient basis to reach beyond Green & Freedman's corporate identity and hold the Elmans liable for the corporation's unpaid contributions. There was evidence that the Elmans, through their domination of Green & Freedman, caused the corporation to make payments to themselves and their relatives at a time when the corporation was known to be failing and could be expected to default, or was already in default, on its obligations to the insurance fund. These payments lacked any business justification. Courts have routinely viewed the wrongful diversion of corporate assets to or for controlling individuals at a time when the corporation is in financial distress as a fraud that can justify piercing the corporate veil. The fraudulent self-dealing was probative not only of fraudulent intent but also of another element, disregard of the corporate identity. For example, the Elmans mixed their own finances with those of Green & Freedman's. Their undocumented and interest-free loans could be found to show a disregard for the corporate form. Further, there was evidence of inadequate and, indeed, fraudulent record keeping. They falsified corporate minutes to state that their wives, who served as nominal directors, attended meetings and authorized corporate borrowing,

(continued)

CRANE V. GREEN & FREEDMAN BAKING COMPANY
(concluded)

when in fact their wives did neither. We accept the Elmans' contention that a closely held corporation need not hew to every corporate formality in order to maintain its shareholders' immunity from the corporation's debts. A veil-piercing plaintiff will not prevail if the evidence shows only that the closely held defendant corporation was run without the strict formalities of its publicly held counterpart. But in this case, there were practices that went beyond mere informalities. Important transactions between the corporation and its controlling shareholders went undefined, and the Elmans appear to have created false minutes. Thus, we conclude that sheltering the Elmans from Green & Freedman's liability to the insurance fund would be manifestly unjust.

Ethical Implications   Suppose that Smith incorporates his restaurant and is the sole shareholder of the corporation. While he has purchased the normal insurance coverage for a restaurant of this size and type, the policy is not large enough to satisfy the claims of his many injured customers after the ceiling collapses causing substantial personal injury when the restaurant was particularly crowded. Is it ethical for Smith to oppose the efforts of the injured patrons to reach his personal assets when the corporate assets prove insufficient?

FIGURE 25-2   Piercing the Corporate Veil

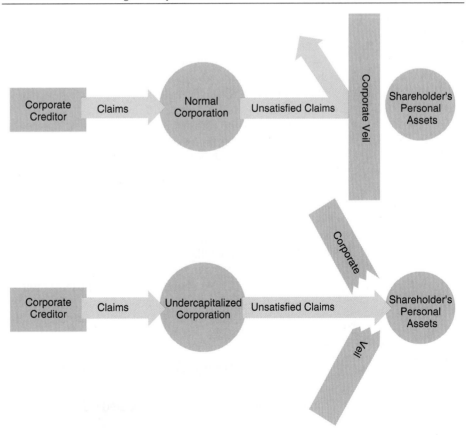

········ *CLOSE CORPORATIONS* ········

Most incorporated businesses are close corporations. In fact, most of the firms listed among the Fortune 500 began as close corporations. Generally, businesses do not start out as publicly traded corporations. Instead, they originally are organized as close corporations and go public only after several years.

While there is no uniform definition for a close corporation, most such entities do share certain characteristics. Four traits are common:

1. The shareholders are few in number.
2. Shareholders usually live in the same geographic area and know one another and their skills.
3. All or most of the shareholders are active in the business.
4. There is no established market for the stock.

UNSUITABILITY OF TRADITIONAL CORPORATION LAW

Those establishing businesses usually form corporations rather than partnerships. They seek limited liability, certain tax consequences, and perhaps other perceived or actual advantages for shareholders. However, because relationships among shareholders are frequently close and informal, they often believe that they should be able to work their problems out in any manner they wish, as can usually be done in a partnership. One of the basic principles of corporation law is that majority rule applies to both shareholder and director action. Another is that the directors, not the shareholders, are given the authority to manage the business. Also, the general rule is that shareholders are free to dispose of their shares by sale or gift. This is, of course, consistent with the common law principles that the owner of property is free to transfer it at will.

The application of these rules is often inconsistent with the objectives of the shareholders of close corporations. Usually, one of their main objectives is employment for themselves in a managerial position in the business. They fear leaving their tenure in that position to the discretion of the board of directors. If their goal is income, they are faced with the rules of corporate law that the directors have almost complete discretion in determining whether and when to pay a dividend. Both of these goals indicate that control of the corporation is important to shareholders in close corporations. Yet, since corporation law calls for majority rule, a minority shareholder is particularly vulnerable to oppression. This may involve discharge from employment with a resulting loss of salary, or the minority shareholder may even be frozen out of ownership through a merger or reorganization of the corporation.

Loss of position and salary would be serious enough if minority shareholders could sell the shares like shareholders in a publicly held corporation. However, due to the vulnerability of minority shareholders in close corporations, it is usually very difficult for dissatisfied shareholders to dispose of their investment at a price consistent with its economic value. Often the only persons interested in buying the shares are the majority shareholders—the very ones causing the owners of the minority interests to want to sell.

MODERN REGULATION OF CLOSE CORPORATIONS

Today, most states have enacted corporation laws that recognize the close corporation and the special problems associated with it. These statutes may be classified into three types:

1. A special section or chapter in the general incorporation statute that deals exclusively with close corporations.
2. Scattered provisions throughout the general corporation act that permit close corporations to voluntarily adopt less rigid organizational and operational arrangements.
3. Statutes that do not specifically mention close corporations but permit corporations to adopt in their articles or bylaws provisions that are particularly attractive to close corporations.

In general, all three types of statutes give legal recognition to some or all of the devices developed by lawyers to ensure private ownership and to protect minority shareholders.

TRANSFERABILITY OF SHARES

Close corporation shares are seldom intended to be sold to the public at large. Usually, the shareholders in such corporations desire not only to choose their original business associates but future owners as well. Likewise, few people are interested in buying into a small business dominated by strangers. These similarities between the close corporation and a partnership create compelling reasons for the shareholders of close corporations to demand special rules governing the transferability of shares.

There are several basic types of transfer restrictions. Under the **right of first refusal,** either the corporation or its shareholders are given the right to buy shares offered for sale to an outsider willing to purchase them. This device generally is employed to maintain the balance of power in a close corporation. However, it also is useful in preventing unwanted persons from buying into the corporation. One way of dealing with the problem of guaranteeing that a shareholder receives the value of her investment upon death or retirement is through a **buy-and-sell agreement.** The shareholder or her estate is required to sell and the corporation is obligated to purchase the shares at an agreed-upon price. A way of keeping unwanted persons out of the corporation is through a **consent restraint.** With this arrangement, a would-be seller must gain the permission of the corporation's board of directors or shareholders for any sale of shares other than to the corporation or pro rata to present shareholders. Consider the following case examining the enforceability of a right of first refusal restriction.

STUFFT V. STUFFT
916 P. 2d 104 (Mont. Sup. Ct. 1996)

FACTS

Stufft Farms, Inc., was a corporation that owned and operated a family farm. Esther Stufft owned 17,077 of the corporation's shares, and Carmen Stufft owned 17,018 shares, while Carol Stufft Larsen, Dorene Stufft Badgett, and David Stufft each owned 20 shares. To ensure that the corporation remained in the hands of the family, the corporate bylaws included a right of first refusal restriction. This provision stated that "no shareholder shall

have the right or power to pledge, sell or otherwise dispose of, except by will, any share or shares of this company without first offering the said share or shares to the company and shareholders at the then book value." On February 24, Neil Johnson offered to buy all of Stufft Farms's shares. However, the offer was contingent upon all the shareholders selling their shares to Johnson. All the shareholders, except David Stufft, agreed to accept

(continued)

STUFFT V. STUFFT
(concluded)

Johnson's offer. On March 9, David attempted to invoke the right of first refusal to buy the other shareholders' shares at book value. They refused his demand to sell their shares to him at book value, but instead, on March 10 offered to sell them to him at the same price Johnson offered. David rejected that offer. Finally, on March 27, the board of directors voted to dissolve the corporation and sell all of its assets to Johnson. David sued to void the sale on the grounds that this sale violated his rights under the right of first refusal.

ISSUE

Has there been a violation of David's right of first refusal?

DECISION

No. To trigger a right of first refusal there must be more than a willingness to sell on the part of the shareholders;

there must also be an actual agreement to sell. In this case, there was no such agreement to sell the stock. Johnson's offer to purchase the shares was an offer to buy *all* of the stock in the corporation. That offer was not accepted by David. Therefore, no agreement was reached. Similarly, the other shareholders' March 10 offer to sell the stock to David on the same terms as those offered by Johnson was not accepted. David's right of first refusal to purchase the corporate stock was not triggered because the other shareholders did not "pledge, sell or otherwise dispose of" their shares of stocks. They still own their stock in the corporation. The sale of the corporate assets to Johnson did not trigger the right of first refusal. The language in the bylaws suggests that the transfer restriction does not apply to an intended sale of the entire corporation or its assets.

.... *GOVERNANCE ISSUES* ....

Minority shareholders in close corporations are particularly vulnerable. The very nature of the close corporation greatly reduces the marketability of their shares, eliminating the option of selling out if things get too unbearable. For this reason, minority shareholders frequently fear leaving corporate decisions to a majority vote. They could be outvoted on a matter they believe to be crucial to their interests. This may apply to basic decisions that must be made by shareholders, such as amendment of the articles of incorporation. It may also be true of matters that are decided by the directors, such as employment and salary decisions as well as dividend policy.

JUDICIAL PROTECTION OF MINORITY SHAREHOLDERS

Courts have begun to recognize a fiduciary duty in corporate officers and majority shareholders to treat minority shareholders fairly. This has resulted in a greater willingness on the part of the judiciary to intervene to protect minority shareholders in intracorporate conflicts. Such intervention has occurred even in the absence of statutory authority for it.

Circumstances in which many courts will act without specific statutory authority include the following:

1. The officers or majority shareholders have been guilty of fraud, have oppressed minority shareholders, or have grossly mismanaged the business.
2. A deadlock among shareholders has resulted in a failure to hold corporate meetings, or one or more shareholders have taken control to the exclusion of other shareholders.
3. The business cannot be carried on profitably because of deadlock or dissension.

Courts have even turned to partnership law to determine the rights and duties of shareholders to one another in a close corporation. This has occurred when the parties themselves have acted as if they viewed their relationship as one between partners rather than investors in a corporation.

SENNERIKUPPAM V DATEL ENGINEERING
1998 U.S. App. LEXIS (6th Cir. 1998)

FACTS

Datel Engineering Company was incorporated in 1989. Naren Patel contributed all of Datel's initial capital. Sennerikuppam was an officer and member of the board of directors of Datel and was involved in its formation. He also had primary responsibility for Datel's day-to-day business operations. Datel distributed shares of stock to 10 of its employees and directors in accordance with a stock purchase agreement. The 113 shares that were distributed were the only outstanding shares in Datel. Sennerikuppam received nine shares and paid $2,500 per share. Sixty shares were distributed to a trust established by and for the benefit of Naren Patel, making him the majority shareholder. A provision in the stock purchase agreement which governs the redemption of shares by the corporation provides, if the corporation buys back shares, "The price per share shall be . . . $2,500.00 per share, which may be adjusted annually by agreement in writing of the shareholders holding 60 percent of the shares." After the redemption of 27 shares by the corporation in 1990, Naren Patel controlled more than 60 percent of the outstanding shares and could have unilaterally adjusted the share price. However, no adjustment was made. In 1994, Sennerikuppam announced his resignation. He then sold his nine shares back to Datel and was paid $2,500 per share. However, he also requested that he be paid his pro rata share of the corporation's retained earnings, which he estimated to be $2,325,751 or $27,362 per outstanding share. At the time Sennerikuppam sold his shares, payments had been made to five other shareholders who had previously sold their shares. They each received $2,500 per share pursuant to the stock purchase agreement. However, those payments were made in 1990, at a time when the corporation was not yet financially successful. Sennerikuppam filed a suit against Naren Patel for breach of fiduciary duty. This claim is based on the fiduciary duty owed by majority shareholders to minority shareholders in a corporation. It hinges on the fact that Naren Patel controlled more than 60 percent of the outstanding shares in Datel, such that he could have unilaterally adjusted the share price. Sennerikuppam alleges that Naren Patel's failure to do so, despite the undisputed increase in the actual value of the shares, constituted a breach of his fiduciary duty as majority shareholder.

ISSUE

Has Naren Patel breached his fiduciary duty as a majority shareholder?

DECISION

No. For his claim to succeed, Sennerikuppam must demonstrate that Naren Patel used his majority control of the corporation to his own advantage without providing minority shareholders with an equal opportunity to benefit. This is so because when courts have dealt with breach of fiduciary duty in a close corporation, they have focused on the denial of equal opportunities to minority shareholders. Yet Sennerikuppam has not alleged that Naren Patel sold his shares at a price which was unavailable to him. In fact, Naren Patel did not sell his own shares at all. Similarly, Naren Patel did not receive any distribution of Datel's earnings beyond what any shareholder received. There is no meaningful support in case law for concluding, as Sennerikuppam would have us do, that Naren Patel can be found to have breached his fiduciary duty merely by failing to compensate Sennerikuppam for the true value of his shares. First, it is clear that Naren Patel did not violate the stock purchase agreement when the corporation paid Sennerikuppam $2,500 per share for his stock. The agreement makes absolutely no reference to the fair value of shares nor to the distribution of retained earnings upon sale of shares. Second, Naren Patel did nothing to mislead Sennerikuppam about the price he would receive if he sold his shares or to make him believe that he would get a percentage of Datel's retained earnings when he sold the shares. Third,

(continued)

SENNERIKUPPAM V DATEL ENGINEERING
(concluded)

Sennerikuppam has not alleged that he was coerced in any way into selling his shares or even into resigning from Datel. Moreover, he does not and cannot contend that he sold his shares out of desperation after requests for an increase in share price or the distribution of retained earnings were refused, because he did not request either action before selling his shares. We also note that Sennerikuppam was under no obligation to sell his shares when he resigned from Datel.

CORPORATIONS IN A GLOBAL ENVIRONMENT

Businesses engaging in international commerce frequently will choose the corporate form for carrying out their global operations. A corporation domiciled in another country but doing business in the United States is called an **alien corporation.** Most of the rules governing foreign corporations apply equally to alien corporations. U.S. corporations doing business in other countries frequently will be protected against discriminatory treatment by *bilateral investment treaties* that are in force between the United States and many of its trading partners.

In many circumstances, a U.S. investor will choose to incorporate its business in the country where it is conducting its overseas operations. It may establish such a subsidiary in order to avoid exposing its domestic assets to foreign tax laws and potential product liability suits. Further, many nations will require that foreign investors maintain no more than a minority interest in certain sensitive sectors of their economy (i.e., telecommunications, natural resources, or transportation). In those instances, the U.S. investor may become a minority shareholder in an incorporated joint venture in which a foreign company holds the controlling interest.

TERMINATION OF THE CORPORATION

DISSOLUTION BY AGREEMENT

Since the corporation is an entity created by the state, it must have the state's consent to dissolve. If the articles of incorporation provide for a limited rather than an indefinite life, the corporation automatically terminates at the end of the designated time. This is so rare that the MBCA does not even make clear whether any statement must be filed with the Secretary of State after such automatic dissolution.

Incorporation statutes establish procedures for other situations in which termination is voluntary. The MBCA provides for dissolution by a majority of the incorporators if the corporation has not begun business or issued any shares. The corporation may also be dissolved by written consent of all shareholders. The MBCA authorizes the board of directors to propose dissolution and hold a shareholders' meeting. Dissolution results if a majority of the shareholders entitled to vote do so in favor of the proposal. Corporations with more than one class of shareholders sometimes provide for voting on dissolution and other matters by class. In such a case, the majority of each class must vote in favor of dissolution.

A corporation that merges into another is dissolved. If two corporations consolidated into a new corporation, both of the old ones are dissolved.

INVOLUNTARY DISSOLUTION

A corporation may be dissolved by a judgment of a court. Under the MBCA, the Attorney General of the state may file an action for dissolution. Grounds for dissolution include failure to pay the annual franchise tax and failure to file the corporation's annual report with the Secretary of State. Failure to appoint or maintain a registered agent in the state is also grounds for dissolution.

A shareholder may ask a court to dissolve a corporation. The MBCA allows this where the directors are in conflict, their deadlock cannot be broken by the shareholders, and the corporation faces ruin as a result. If directors are acting illegally or are being very unfair to shareholders, a court may dissolve the corporation. Misapplication or waste of corporate assets is also a basis for dissolution. Finally, a creditor may be able to convince a court to dissolve a corporation if it is insolvent and cannot pay its debts.

Of course, when dealing with deadlocked corporations, courts often have the discretion to order remedies other than dissolution. Consider the following case where the court orders one shareholder to sell his 50 percent interest to the owner of the other one-half of the stock.

BALSAMIDES V. PERLE
712 A.2d 673 (N.J. Super. Ct. 1998)

FACTS

Leonard N. Perle was the owner of one-half of the stock in Protameen Chemicals, Inc. Emanuel Balsamides owned the other one-half interest. These two men built up a successful chemical business by utilizing Perle's technical talents and administrative skills and Balsamides' sales acumen and knowledge of the market. This was a classic case of an inside man and outside man, each doing his job superbly, but each also viewing his job as the more important in the company. Each had two sons who eventually came into the business. Balsamides' sons worked in the field and earned substantial salaries and commissions. Perle's sons started learning the administrative areas, intending eventually to be salesmen, with Perle attempting to see that their remuneration matched that of the Balsamides sons. It was alleged that during their final years together, Perle engaged in numerous instances of wrongful conduct which ultimately deadlocked the corporation. Specifically, there were allegations of Perle's purposeful refusal or delay in providing technical information requested for Balsamides' customers; his refusal to provide product samples when requested by Balsamides' customers; a refusal to stock materials in the company warehouse that he knew Balsamides' customers would be ordering; and his denial of Balsamides' access to the company's computer system.

All of these actions were allegedly done in an effort to embarrass Balsamides with his customers. The trial court directed Perle to sell his stock in the deadlocked corporation to Balsamides for $1,960,500.

ISSUE

Should Perle be required to sell his stock to Balsamides?

DECISION

Yes. We are well aware that the record is not one sided. We have seen significant provocations and even alleged ethnic disparagement on the part of Balsamides, which obviously heightened the estrangement of these erstwhile friends and close business associates. The court, however, after first attempting to preserve the integrity of the corporation by appointing a provisional director, determined that the corporation would have to be sold or have one partner buy out the other. The trial court determined that the buyout presented the greatest possibilities of resolving this matter in the near future, of maximizing the benefit to both parties, and in preserving Protameen and its business to the greatest extent possible. It believed that Balsamides was crucial to the company's growth over the years. He brought the major accounts and customers into the fold as a result of his

(continued)

BALSAMIDES V. PERLE
(concluded)

contacts in the cosmetic business and his ability as a salesman. This is not meant to demean the contribution of Perle to Protameen's success. However, the primary reason for the corporation's amazing growth lies in the skill with which Balsamides handles the sales side of Protameen. Further, Balsamides is the outward presence of Protameen in the cosmetics industry. When people in the cosmetics field think of Protameen, they think of Balsamides. Finally, the decision to permit Balsamides to buy the interest of Perle is supported by the conduct of

Perle. While Balsamides is not blameless in this entire controversy, his behavior was not injurious to the business of the corporation. On the other hand, Perle conducted himself in his vendetta against Balsamides in a way that was harmful to the business of Protameen, and he displayed little or no regard for the welfare of his own company and the interests of his partner. There is no question that the trial court's order is consistent with its discretion under New Jersey law.

CONCEPT SUMMARY   **Involuntary Dissolution**

Petition Filed By	Justification for Involuntary Dissolution
Attorney General	1. Failure to pay franchise tax. 2. Failure to pay corporation's annual fee. 3. Failure to appoint or maintain a registered agent in the state.
Shareholder	1. Directors are in conflict *and* deadlock cannot be broken by shareholders *and* corporation faces ruin. 2. Directors are acting illegally or unfairly. 3. Misapplication or waste of corporate assets.
Creditor	Corporation is insolvent *and* not paying its debts.

.... *QUESTIONS AND PROBLEM CASES* ....

1. What are the principal characteristics of a close corporation?

2. Paul Swanson owned 25 shares and Robert Shockley owned 75 shares in North Central Adjustment Co., Inc. Shockley, the majority shareholder, sold his shares to John Davis, who was not and never had been a shareholder in the corporation. Davis agreed to pay $90,000 for the stock in installments payable over a 10-year period. Swanson brought suit, alleging that the sale was in violation of a bylaw restricting sales of the shares. The bylaw permitted sale of the stock only after the corporation and the other shareholders had been given the right of first refusal to purchase the shares at a formula price. The formula price for Shockley's 75 shares at the time of the sale to Davis was $7,500. Shockley defended his sale to Davis on

the grounds that eight months prior to the sale, the bylaw containing the right of first refusal was repealed. In that vote, Shockley voted his shares in favor of the repeal while Swanson, the minority shareholder, abstained. Is Swanson entitled to buy Shockley's shares at the formula price under the right of first refusal?

3. Koch and Czeschin decided to go into the business of commercially processing aloe vera plant leaves. They intended to form a corporation, Quality Aloe Vera Labs, Inc., under which they would carry out this plan. On April 25, Czeschin entered into an agreement to purchase aloe vera leaves at a set price from a grower, Aloe Limited. Czeschin signed the contract on behalf of Quality Aloe Vera Labs, Inc., although the company actually was not incorporated until the following June 3. From

the date of the contract until the following August, Quality placed and paid for 10 orders of aloe vera leaves. Then, from August until December, it made 10 more orders but failed to pay for any of them. Quality filed a petition in bankruptcy while owing Limited over $30,000 on its account. Limited sued Czeschin on the account under a theory of promoter liability. Is Czeschin liable as a promoter on a preincorporation contract?

4. Cook Construction, a general contractor, entered into a subcontract providing that Bryant Construction was to perform certain portions of work on a highway project for Cook. The two corporations signed the contract on October 19, 1984. Later, after Bryant had completed its work, Cook refused to pay the prices that Cook had quoted. Bryant filed suit. In preparing to defend the suit, Cook discovered that on January 27, 1984, the chairman of the Mississippi State Tax Commission had suspended Bryant's corporate charter for failure to file annual reports and pay franchise taxes. Cook argues that the actual effect of the suspension was that Bryant was deprived of its power and capacity to act and, therefore, the contract was unenforceable because it was *ultra vires*. Was the subcontract unenforceable because it was an *ultra vires* act?

5. Monogram, Inc., wished to buy a company that produced and sold smoke detectors. Accordingly, Monogram formed Monotronics, Inc., for the sole purpose of buying and operating the business. Monogram contributed $1.8 million cash to Monotronics and held 100 percent of its stock. After several profitable months, Monotronics's sales began to fall until its total assets dwindled to $10,000. Monotronics finally ceased doing business altogether, although it owed its largest creditor, Edwards Company, $352,000. Edwards Company attempted to hold Monogram liable for Monotronic's debts. Should the court pierce the corporate veil and hold Monogram liable on Monotronics' contractual obligations?

6. Joseph Bitter and two brothers, Joseph Smith and Steve Smith, became good friends. As a result of their friendship, they decided to go into the tavern business together. The parties bought an existing tavern and took title in the name of their corporation, Gomer's, Inc. Soon, the brothers began feuding with Bitter and, because of their combined two-thirds interest, assumed virtual control of the business. In response, Bitter claimed that he and the brothers (the promoters), not the corporation, held title to the real estate. He claimed that Gomer's, Inc., could not own the building because the corporation was not yet in existence when the contract was made. Do the promoters, rather than the corporation own the building?

7. Jacobson, as promoter for A.L.W., Inc., contracted with Stern, an architect, to draw plans for a new hotel and casino to be built on the north shore of Lake Tahoe. It was to be known as King's Castle. About 19 months after King's Castle opened, A.L.W., Inc., filed for bankruptcy. At that time, only $120,000 of the $250,000 fee for Stern's services had been paid by A.L.W., Inc. Stern brought suit against Jacobson, as promoter, for the balance due. Was Jacobson liable to Stern for the amount unpaid for his services?

8. Cusack was an officer and director of Quality Steel, Inc., a closely held corporation. Basically, Cusack had complete control over the corporation, making every important decision, controlling its day-to-day operations, and exercising unlimited access to its funds. Later, the corporation and Cusack were indicted for violating two occupational health and safety standards at a construction project. Cusack was specifically charged with violating a federal statute that provided that "[a]ny employer who willfully violates any standards . . . shall . . . be punished by a fine of not more than $10,000." Cusack defended on the basis that he was not an employer. He claimed that the corporation was the employer. Was Cusack the employer?

9. Davidson Industries sold materials to Capital Components. Capital ceased operations and Kwik Set Components made an agreement with Capital to finish certain of its contracts. Some of the materials purchased by Capital from Davidson were used for this purpose. After Capital's demise, materials continued to be purchased in the name of Capital but were used entirely by Kwik Set. Ira Salter was the president of both Capital and Kwik Set. Both corporations

had the same board of directors and used the same address. Davidson sued Kwik Set for payment. Kwik Set claimed that it was not liable because it and Capital were separate corporations. Should the court pierce the corporate veil and hold Kwik Set liable for the materials purchased in the name of Capital?

10. Following the death of L. E. Ward in 1969, his widow, three children, and a grandson formed a corporation for the purpose of holding the family farmlands. Leroy Ward controlled 50 percent of the corporation, Ward Farms, Inc. Throughout the life of the corporation, numerous conflicts existed between Leroy and the other shareholders. The corporation had never declared a dividend. Several lawsuits were instituted among the shareholders concerning the corporation. Leroy had been enjoined from entering the property despite his control of 50 percent of the corporate stock. Leroy petitioned the court to dissolve the corporation on the grounds that it was deadlocked and its assets were being wasted. Should the corporation be dissolved by the court?

CHAPTER 26

Management of the Corporate Business

John R. Park was the chief executive officer of Acme Markets, Inc., a national retail chain with over 36,000 employees, 874 retail outlets, and 16 warehouses. The Food and Drug Administration (FDA) notified Park of certain unsanitary conditions at Acme's Baltimore warehouse. After receiving the complaint, Park conferred with Acme's vice president for legal affairs, who assured him that the Baltimore division vice president was investigating and would be taking corrective action. Two months later, a subsequent FDA inspection of the warehouse found improved sanitary conditions; however, there was still evidence of rodent infestation. The FDA filed criminal charges against both Acme and Park, citing evidence of an earlier letter informing Park of similar problems in the company's Philadelphia warehouse. Acme pleaded guilty to the charges but Park refused to do so. The United States Supreme Court upheld Park's criminal conviction and the resulting fine of $250.[1]

- *What are the responsibilities that directors and officers owe to their corporations?*
- *When are officers and directors liable for the torts and crimes committed by the corporation?*
- *What protections are available to officers and directors when they are charged with torts or crimes?*

---

[1]United States v. Park, 421 U.S. 658 (U.S. Sup. Ct. 1975).

The shareholders are the owners of the corporation. They can affect the way the business is run through their power to elect directors and to amend the articles of incorporation. They do not, however, have the power to make management decisions. All statutes of incorporation give that power to the directors. The directors, in turn, usually delegate the making of at least the day-to-day operating decisions to the officers.

If the shareholders are dissatisfied with those decisions, they can replace the directors, who in turn will probably replace the officers. The shareholders generally have no right to instruct the directors or the officers on the operating decisions they should make. Shareholders must approve certain extraordinary corporate transactions such as a merger, a sale or lease of substantially all the assets of the corporation, or the dissolution of the corporation. However, the Model Business Corporation Act (MBCA) requires that the proposal for these actions come from the board of directors.

As this discussion should make clear, the board of directors and officers of a publicly held corporation have broad management authority. However, their managerial discretion is not unlimited. There are limits placed on this power beyond the voting rights of the shareholders. Basically, the directors and officers must act in a manner consistent with the powers and objectives of the corporation and with the state and federal laws that govern corporate activities.

.... *THE BOARD OF DIRECTORS* ....

POWERS AND DUTIES

Most state incorporation statutes declare that "the business of the corporation shall be managed by a board of directors." Of course, in a large corporation, especially where a number of the directors have full-time jobs elsewhere, this is impossible. The directors tend to ratify management decisions made by the top executives rather than to take the initiative in making the decisions. Recognizing this, the MBCA now says: "All corporate powers shall be exercised by or under the authority of, and the business and affairs of a corporation shall be managed under the direction of, a board of directors."

General Powers of the Board

Certain corporate actions can be taken by the board of directors acting alone. Statutes of the states vary on this. The MBCA permits the board to take the following actions by itself: declaring a dividend; establishing the price for the sale of shares of stock; electing and removing officers; filling vacancies on the board of directors; and selling, leasing, and mortgaging assets of the corporation outside the normal course of its business.

Actions Requiring Board Initiative

Some corporate actions can be taken only through **board initiative.** The initiative process requires that the board of directors propose the matter to the shareholders, who then must approve the action. Board initiative is generally required for any fundamental changes in the corporation; for example, amendment of the articles of incorporation, merger of the corporation, sale of all or substantially all of the corporation's assets, and voluntary dissolution of the corporation.

ONLINE COMMUNICATIONS

During the year 2000, the Delaware General Corporation Law was amended to enable Delaware corporations to make use of the Internet. The amendments eliminated language from the corporation statutes that blocked the use of modern communications technology. Thus, directors can now legally communicate official business by e-mail since electronic communications are permitted for corporate business. Specifically, the term "electronic communications" includes forms of communication that do not involve the physical transmission of paper if the communication creates a record that can be retained, retrieved, or reviewed by the recipient and can be reproduced in paper form.

While the statute does not allow board meetings to take place electronically, it does permit director resignations to be transmitted electronically. Further, director actions taken by unanimous consent may be taken by electronic transmission.

POWERS AND RIGHTS OF A DIRECTOR AS AN INDIVIDUAL

Directors are not agents for the corporation by virtue of that office. They have power to act for the corporation only as a part of the board, not as individuals. Of course, a director can become an agent if she is also serving as an employee of the corporation.

A director has the right to inspect the corporate books and records. This right is necessary to carrying out the director's duty of overseeing the management. However, the right to inspect can be denied where it can be shown that the director has an interest that conflicts with that of the corporation. If such an adverse interest arises, it would probably be a sound reason for removal of the director.

ELECTION OF DIRECTORS

Number of Directors

Some states require corporations to have a minimum of three directors. The MBCA requires only one, recognizing that it would be superfluous to have more than one director when a single individual or another corporation owns all the stock. The MBCA allows the number of directors to be fixed in either the articles or the bylaws. If it is fixed in the bylaws, the directors can easily vary the number as conditions change. It is not necessary to go to the trouble and expense of amending the articles when a director dies or resigns and the directors are not ready to nominate a successor.

Qualifications

A few state statutes require directors to be shareholders. Some require that a certain percentage of the directors be citizens of the state of incorporation or of the United States. Qualifications for directors can be set out in the articles, if desired.

Nomination

Directors are elected by the shareholders at their annual meeting. Usually, they are nominated by the current directors, although nominations can be made from the floor during the shareholders' meeting. However, candidates nominated from the floor seldom are elected in large corporations that solicit proxies, as will be discussed in Chapter 27.

Term of Office

Directors normally hold office only until the next annual meeting, or until a successor has been elected and qualified. The MBCA permits corporations to provide for staggered terms in their articles. A corporation that has a board of nine or more members may establish either two or three nearly equal classes of directors. Then only one class of directors is elected at each annual meeting unless there are vacancies. Staggered terms are said to ensure that experienced directors remain on the board; however, they are usually adopted to make a corporate takeover more difficult.

Vacancies

Vacancies on the board can be filled only by a vote of the shareholders unless the state statute, the articles, or the bylaws give this power to the board itself. The MBCA permits a majority of the remaining directors, even though less than a quorum, to elect directors to serve out unexpired terms. It also permits the board to increase the size of the board and then to elect a director to the vacancy created. Such a director may serve only until the next shareholders' meeting.

REMOVAL OF DIRECTORS

A director may not be removed without cause unless this is permitted by statute or by articles or bylaws adopted prior to the director's election. The MBCA permits shareholders to remove directors with or without cause. A director who has failed to or is unable to attend and participate in directors' meetings or who has acted contrary to the interests of the corporation can be removed for cause. Shareholders can remove a director for cause at any time even though the power of removal has been given by the articles or bylaws to the directors. Before being removed for cause, a director must be given notice and a hearing. (See Figure 26–1.)

DIRECTORS' MEETINGS

Frequency

Boards of directors usually schedule regular meetings. Today, boards of large corporations typically meet monthly; however, some corporations have regular meetings

FIGURE 26–1   Removal of Directors

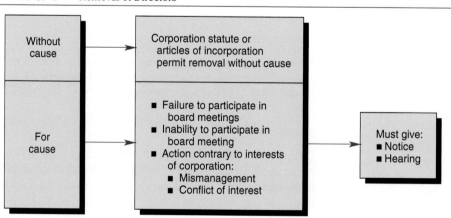

only quarterly. Small corporations, in which most of the directors are active in the business, may have only one formal meeting each year. The directors' other meetings are informal, with no minutes kept.

Notice

Reasonable notice must be given for special meetings. If all of the directors attend a meeting, this cures any defect in or failure to give notice. However, a director who has not received a proper notice may attend solely to complain of the notice. In this case, he or she would not be held to have been in attendance. Directors may also cure a defect in the notice by waiving notice. The corporate secretary usually prepares and gets such waivers signed if notice is late or otherwise defective. Under common law, a waiver of notice has to be signed by all of the directors either before or during the meeting. The MBCA permits the waiver to be signed after the meeting.

Formality

Under common law, directors could act only when properly convened as a board and could not vote by proxy. This rule was based on belief in the value of mutual counsel and collective judgment. Today, the MBCA permits directors to act without a meeting if all of the directors consent in writing to the action taken. It also permits a director to attend a meeting through the use of a telephone hookup. The only requirement is that the directors be able to hear one another simultaneously.

Quorum

Each director has only one vote, regardless of his or her shareholdings. Actions taken by a board are ineffective unless a quorum is present. Normally, a quorum is a majority of the number of directors fixed by the articles or bylaws. The articles or bylaws may set the quorum at a higher figure. If there is a quorum present, the vote of a majority of the directors is the act of the board.

COMPENSATION OF DIRECTORS

Under the common law, directors had no power to fix their own salaries and were not entitled to compensation for their ordinary duties as directors. The MBCA permits directors to fix their compensation unless this is prohibited by the articles of incorporation. Outside directors (those who are not employees of the corporation) are paid rather modest fees even in the largest corporations. However, directors' fees have been rising rapidly in recent years as the duties and liabilities of directors have become greater.

GRIMES v. DONALD
673 A.2d 1207 (Del. Sup. Ct. 1996)

FACTS

James Donald was the chief executive officer of DSC Communications. The corporation's board of directors entered into an employment contract with Donald that ran until his 75th birthday. Under the terms of the agreement, Donald was responsible for the general management of the corporation and for reporting to the board of directors. The agreement further provided that his employment could be terminated by death, disability, for

(continued)

GRIMES V. DONALD
(concluded)

cause, and without cause. However, Donald could declare a "constructive termination without cause" if he believed in good faith that the board or a substantial shareholder in the corporation engaged in "unreasonable interference" with his carrying out his duties and responsibilities. If a termination without cause were to occur, Donald was entitled to his base salary ($650,000) for the remainder of the contract and his annual incentive award ($300,000). The total amount of payments and benefits for the remainder of the agreement totaled approximately $20 million. A DSC shareholder, C. L. Grimes, demanded that the court invalidate the employment agreement with Donald. Grimes argued that the potentially severe penalties which DSC would incur if the board interfered with Donald's management would inhibit the board from exercising its duties. He believed this to be an illegal delegation of the duties and responsibilities of the board of directors.

ISSUE

Has the board of directors unlawfully delegated its duties and responsibilities?

DECISION

No. Grimes has pleaded, at most, that Donald would be entitled to $20 million in the event of a constructive termination. In light of the financial size of DSC, this would amount to no more that a *de facto* abdication. Directors may not delegate duties which lie at the heart of the management of the corporation. They may not delegate their duty to use their own best judgment on management matters. However, the employment agreement with Donald does not formally preclude the board from exercising its statutory powers and fulfilling its fiduciary duty. Generally, an informed decision to delegate a task is as much an exercise of business judgment as any other. Further, business decisions are not an abdication of directional authority merely because they limit a board's freedom of future action. If the market for senior management, in the business judgment of the board, demands significant severance packages, boards will inevitably limit their future range of action by entering into employment agreements like the one here. Large severance packages will deter boards, to some extent, from dismissing senior officers. Here, we have only a rather unusual contract, but not a case of abdication.

OFFICERS OF THE CORPORATION

POWERS

The MBCA provides that a corporation shall have a president, one or more vice presidents (as stated in the bylaws), a secretary, and a treasurer. Any two or more offices may be held by the same person except the offices of president and secretary. This permits dual signatures on corporate documents. Many corporations have established the office of chairman of the board; the chairman of the board may be the chief executive of the corporation. Occasionally, this is only a part-time position.

PRESIDENT OR CHAIRMAN

The power of the officers to bind the corporation on contracts they make on its behalf is the same as that of any agent. In addition to their express authority, they have implied and apparent authority. Certain officers may also have ***ex officio*** authority—that is, authority by virtue of their offices. This, however, is more restricted than is generally believed. The president or chairman of the board has no power to bind the corporation solely because of his position. However, if he is also the chief executive, then broad authority is implied to make contracts and do other acts appropriate to the ordinary business of the firm. A corporate officer is liable to the corporation for resulting losses if he acts beyond his authority.

VICE PRESIDENT

A vice president has no authority by virtue of that office. However, if the title indicates that the person is the principal officer of some area of the business, she has considerable implied authority. For example, the vice president of marketing has implied authority to do those acts normally done by a manager of sales.

CORPORATE SECRETARY

The corporate secretary (called *clerk* in some states) keeps the minutes of meetings of the shareholders and directors and other general corporate records such as stockholder records. The office gives the secretary no authority to bind the corporation on contracts. However, there is a presumption that a document to which the secretary has affixed the corporate seal has been properly authorized.

TREASURER

The treasurer has charge of the funds of the corporation. He or she has power to pay out corporate funds for proper purposes and is the person who receives payments to the corporation. The treasurer binds the corporation on receipts, checks, and endorsements. However, the treasurer does not have authority by virtue of the office alone to borrow money or issue negotiable instruments.

········ DUTIES OF DIRECTORS AND OFFICERS ········

Unlike directors, the corporate officers are agents of the corporation. However, the directors share with the officers the same fiduciary duties that an agent owes the principal. The recent trend has been to raise the standard of conduct required of directors and officers. This has been done through the SEC and the federal securities laws it administers. It has also been done by courts in interpreting the common law.

The fiduciary duties that officers and directors owe the corporation include:

1. The duty to act within one's authority and within the powers of the corporation.
2. The duty to act diligently and with due care in conducting the affairs of the corporation.
3. The duty to act with loyalty and good faith for the benefit of the corporation.

DUTY TO ACT WITHIN AUTHORITY

Directors and officers must act within the authority given to them and to the corporation by statute, the articles, and the bylaws. Directors or officers may be liable to the corporation if it is damaged by an act exceeding their authority or if they act outside of the scope of the corporation's authority. However, if they enter an *ultra vires* transaction, justifiably believing it to be within the scope of the corporation's business, they are not held liable. (*Ultra vires* transactions were discussed in Chapter 25.)

Ratification

Like any principal, a corporation may ratify an unauthorized act by its officers or other agents. This may be done through a resolution of the board of directors or of the shareholders. It may also be implied from acceptance of benefits from the unauthorized act. Ratification, when it occurs, releases the officer or director from liability to the corporation and binds the corporation as if the act originally had been authorized.

DUTY OF DUE CARE AND DILIGENCE

Prudent Person Standard

Directors and officers may be liable to the corporation for failure to act with due care and diligence. The MBCA requires that a director or officer discharge his duties with "such care as an ordinarily prudent person in a like position would use under similar circumstances." Thus, officers and directors are not liable to the corporation if they act with the *common sense, practical wisdom,* and *informed judgment* that could be expected of an ordinarily prudent person. Of course, the greater the actual qualifications of the individual, the greater the level of the duty that would be expected.

There are three dimensions to this prudent person standard. An officer or director will be found to have discharged her duty of care if she acts:

1. In good faith.
2. As would an ordinarily prudent person under like circumstances.
3. Under the reasonable belief that she is acting in the best interests of the corporation.

The duty of care requires that directors and officers make a reasonable investigation before making any corporate decisions. These standards, however, take into consideration the complexities of many corporate decisions and understand that it would be impossible for any manager to personally investigate every facet of every business decision. As a result, the MBCA standard permits directors and officers to rely on the opinions, reports, and statements of persons who reasonably appear to be competent and reliable.

Business Judgment Rule

Directors are not liable for mere errors of judgment when they act with care and good faith. This is the **business judgment rule.** The rule precludes the courts from substituting their business judgment for that of the corporation's managers. In short, it protects officers and directors from personal liability for honest mistakes in judgment.

In order to obtain the protection of the business judgment rule, the directors must meet three requirements in arriving at their decision:

1. An informed decision
2. No conflict of interest
3. Rational basis

First, they must make an informed decision. As stated above, they may rely on information collected and presented by other persons. Second, the decision makers must be free from conflicts of interest. Any self-dealing on the part of the directors in the course of making the decision would deprive them of the shelter provided by the business judgment rule. Third, the board of directors must have a rational basis for believing that the decision is in the best interests of the corporation. Generally, this means that the decision must not be "manifestly unreasonable." (Many courts hold that the directors' decision is not rational if their actions amount to "gross negligence.")

If the business decision violates any of these requirements, the officers or directors are stripped of the protection provided by the business judgment rule. Courts would then feel freer to substitute their judgment for that of the corporate decision makers. Further, if the court found the decision to be unwise, the officers or directors would be liable unless they could prove that the transaction at issue was intrinsically fair to the corporation.

McMullin v. Beran
765 A.2d 910 (Del. Sup.Ct. 2000)

FACTS

Mary McMullin was a shareholder of ARCO Chemical Company (Chemical) until its purchase by Lyondell Acquisition Corporation. Prior to this purchase, more than 80 percent of Chemical's common stock had been owned by Atlantic Richfield Company (ARCO). On February 17, 1998, ARCO received a call from Lyondell in which Lyondell expressed an interest in acquiring Chemical. From February until June of that year, ARCO and its chief financial officer contacted a number of entities to gauge their interest in participating in a bidding process. In mid-March, ARCO informed Chemical's directors about Lyondell's interest, and the directors authorized ARCO to explore the sale of the entire company. Throughout May and June, Lyondell made several offers to purchase all of Chemical's outstanding shares, each of which was rejected by ARCO as being too low. Finally, on June 13, 1998, Lyondell offered $57.75 per share for all outstanding shares. The following day, Chemical's board of directors met to consider the latest proposal. Representatives of ARCO made presentations regarding the terms of the proposal and the sale process. After Chemical's financial advisor made a presentation and expressed the opinion that the price was fair to all of Chemical's shareholders, the board of directors unanimously approved the transaction. After the sale was completed, McMullin filed suit against the board, claiming that the members breached their fiduciary duties by failing to maximize shareholder value. McMullin did not dispute ARCO's right to sell its own 80 percent interest for whatever consideration it might desire. Instead, she argued that the board breached its duty of care and its duty of loyalty by failing to act in an informed and deliberate manner before submitting a proposal to the stockholders. She alleged that ARCO initiated and timed the transaction to benefit itself because it needed quick cash infusion. Further, she argued that the board

wrongfully delegated its managerial responsibilities by authorizing ARCO unilaterally to negotiate without any procedural safeguards to protect the interests of minority shareholders. According to her complaint, ARCO not only conducted the negotiations but also placed its own cash restrictions on potential bidders. McMullin complained that Chemical's directors met only once to consider the merits of the transaction and, at that time, made its decision solely on the basis of the presentation by ARCO's financial advisor. The trial court dismissed her claim on the basis that the directors were justified in delegating control of the sale process to ARCO because, due to ARCO's large stock holdings, no transaction could proceed without its approval. McMullin appealed.

ISSUE

Should McMullin's claims against the director's be dismissed?

DECISION

No. One of the fundamental principles of corporation law is that the business affairs of a corporation are managed by or under the direction of its board of directors. The business judgment rule is a corollary common law precept to this statutory provision. It is a presumption that in making a business decision, the directors of a corporation acted on an informed basis, in good faith, and in the honest belief that the action taken was in the best interests of the corporation. The business judgment rule operates as both a procedural guide for litigants and a substantive rule of law. Procedurally, the initial burden is on the shareholder plaintiff to rebut the presumption of the business judgment rule. To meet that burden, the shareholder plaintiff must effectively provide evidence that the defendant board of directors, in reaching its challenged decision, breached any *one* of its triad of

(continued)

McMullin v. Beran
(concluded)

fiduciary duties—loyalty, good faith, or due care. Substantively, if the shareholder plaintiff fails to meet that evidentiary burden, the business judgment rule attaches and operates to protect the individual director-defendants from personal liability for making the board decision at issue. Burden shifting does not create *per se* liability on the part of directors. It is a procedure by which the judiciary determines the standard of review that is applicable to measure the board of directors' conduct. If the shareholder plaintiff succeeds in rebutting the presumption of the business judgment rule, the burden shifts to the defendant directors to prove the entire fairness of the transaction. Chemical's directors were obliged to make an informed, deliberate judgment, in good faith, that the transaction terms, including the price, were fair. They were also obliged to disclose with entire candor all material facts concerning the transaction, so that the minority shareholders would be able to make an informed decision whether to accept the tender offer price or to seek judicial remedies such as appraisal or an injunction. The directors' duties of care, loyalty, and good faith are owed to all Chemical shareholders in recommending the sale of the entire corporation. When the entire sale is proposed, negotiated, and timed by a majority shareholder, the board cannot realistically seek any alternative because the majority shareholder has the right to vote its shares in favor of the transaction. Nevertheless, in such situations, the directors still are obliged to make an informed and deliberate

judgment, in good faith, about whether the sale to the third party will result in maximization of value for the minority shareholders. This duty required that the directors act on an informed basis to independently ascertain how the transaction being offered compared to Chemical's value as a going concern. The board cannot abdicate that duty by leaving it to the shareholders alone to approve or disprove the transaction because the majority shareholder's voting power makes the outcome a preordained conclusion. When a majority of a corporation's voting shares are owned by a single entity, there is a significant diminution in the voting power of the minority shareholders. Consequently, minority shareholders must rely for protection on the fiduciary duties owned to them by the board of directors. This responsibility required the Chemical board to first, conduct a critical assessment of the Lyondell proposal; and, second, make an independent determination whether that transaction maximized value for all shareholders. The substantive protections of the business judgment rule can be claimed only by disinterested directors whose conduct otherwise meets the tests of the rule's procedural requirements. Finally, McMullin's complaint alleged that 6 of the 12 Chemical directors were employed by ARCO and 2 others held positions with ARCO subsidiaries. Yet none of those 8 abstained from the discussions or the vote concerning the proposed transaction. Accordingly, the case should be remanded so the trial court can examine McMullin's claim.

The Business Judgment Rule in the Takeover Context

The newspapers often report the legal and economic controversies surrounding attempts by outsiders to acquire control of publicly held corporations. Generally, the outsiders make a tender offer (offer to purchase shares at prices above market price) for the controlling shares of the target corporation. (Tender offers will be discussed in Chapter 27.) The corporation's current management often will oppose such offers and may employ various defenses to defeat the tender offer. Successful defenses frequently trigger complaints from shareholders that the directors fought the tender offer solely to preserve their corporate positions.

Generally, directors are protected from liability for such opposition under the business judgment rule. However, recent judicial decisions have taken note of the greater risk of a conflict of interest in the tender offer context. Accordingly, there seems to be a preliminary burden that the directors must meet before they are accorded the business judgment rule defense when they oppose takeover attempts. First, the directors must demonstrate that they had reasonable grounds for believing that a danger to the corporation existed. And second, they must establish that their defensive measures were reasonable in relation to the threat to the corporate interest.

Ethical Implications	The inside directors' financial interests may be directly assaulted by a takeover attempt from outsiders. Outside directors do not have such an apparent conflict of interest in evaluating the merits of a tender offer. Should the board ever fight a takeover when less than a majority of the outside directors is opposed to the offer?

Legislative Responses to Increased Director Liability

At one time, the business judgment rule appeared to automatically shelter directors from liability for their decisions as long as they avoided self-dealing. And yet, even then, corporations were having difficulty attracting and retaining outside directors. In the wake of cases such as *Stepak v. Addison*, insurance premiums for directors' policies have skyrocketed, precipitating what many states have perceived to be a real director liability crisis.

State legislatures across the country have responded by enacting legislation designed to limit directors' liability for breach of the duty of care. From this flurry of legislative activity, three fundamental types of statutory limitations have appeared. The most popular (pioneered by Delaware and adopted by over 30 states) are **charter option statutes.** This amendment to the state corporation law authorizes any corporation to adopt a specific amendment to its articles of incorporation that removes breach of duty as a cause of action for monetary damages against directors. Under this approach, both the board of directors and the shareholders would have to approve the limitation on director liability. Even then, officers and directors still would be liable for intentional misconduct, failure to act in good faith, self-interest, knowing violations, and breach of the duty of loyalty.

A second type of amendment to the state corporation law provides that directors will have no liability for breach of the duty of care in the absence of willful misconduct or recklessness. The state of Ohio has such a statute with an added provision—it presumes that a director acted in good faith unless it can be demonstrated by clear and convincing evidence that he did not. These types of statutes (in force in at least five states) are called **self-executing statutes** because they are automatically effective. No board or shareholder action is necessary to trigger their applicability.

A final type of limitation was adopted by the state of Virginia. It is a **cap on monetary damages statute.** Specifically, the law holds that the maximum liability that may be imposed on directors is the greater of $100,000 or the amount of cash compensation that the director received from the corporation during the previous 12 months. This approach shares certain aspects of the previous two types. It is self-executing in that the cap automatically applies in the absence of board and shareholder action. However, it has a charter option quality in that the board and shareholders of a corporation may amend the corporate charter to reduce the cap (they may not increase it). (See Figure 26–2 on page 468.)

DUTY OF LOYALTY AND GOOD FAITH

Directors and officers must act in the best interests of the corporation. They breach their duty if they try to profit personally at the expense of the corporation.

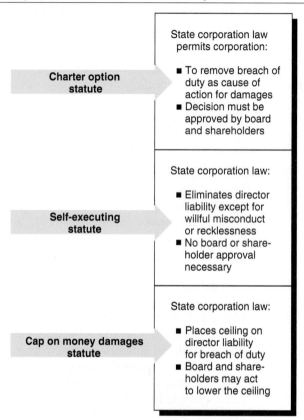

FIGURE 26–2   Legislative Limitations on Director Liability

Self-Dealing

Directors and officers are not prohibited from entering into transactions with the corporation. At one time, courts held that such deals were voidable by the corporation but today the majority of courts hold them voidable only if unfair to the corporation. However, before a director (or another business organization in which she has a major interest) enters a contract with the corporation, the director should make a *full disclosure* of his or her interest. This requires that the director or officer disclose all material facts of the transaction, including her interest in it.

After full disclosure, the disinterested members of the board or the shareholders themselves must approve the transaction. However, such approval does not automatically relieve the self-dealing director or officer from liability to the corporation. Under the MBCA, the initial burden of proving the fairness of the transaction lies with the self-dealing director or officer. After proper approval by the board of directors or shareholders, the burden of establishing unfairness merely shifts to the corporation.

Usurping Corporate Opportunities

Directors and officers may not usurp a corporate opportunity. Such usurpation occurs when a business opportunity comes to them in their official capacities and the opportunity is within the corporation's normal scope of business. For example, directors may not buy the right to sell a product that would fit into the corporation's line of goods. If the corporation is financially unable to pursue the opportunity, a director or officer may take it.

Three elements must be met before directors or officers may be found to have usurped a corporate opportunity:

1. The opportunity must have come to them in their corporate capacity.
2. The opportunity must be related to the corporate business.
3. The corporation must have been able to take advantage of the opportunity.

Even when these three requirements are met, the director may still avoid liability if she can show that the corporation waived its rights to the opportunity. Thus, if the director offered the opportunity to the corporation with full disclosure of all material terms and a disinterested majority of the board rejected the transaction, the director may take it. In some instances, a court may find an implied waiver if the corporation knew of the opportunity and failed to act on it in a timely manner.

A. Teixeira & Co. v. Teixeira
699 A.2d 1383 (R.I. Sup. Ct. 1997)

FACTS

Teixeira & Co., Inc., is a corporation formed by six shareholders for the purpose of acquiring and operating Pop's Liquors, a retail liquor store. In terms of corporate organization and management structure, the corporation was not a model of clarity. For instance, its articles of incorporation failed to indicate that it was a close corporation pursuant to state law, it had no board of directors, and Honorato Custodio, one of the six shareholders, served as the president, vice president, secretary, and treasurer. In December of 1982, Custodio learned that Mendon Liquors was going to be offered for sale. He called a meeting of the shareholders, and they agreed he should pursue the idea of purchasing Mendon Liquors. However, the purchase never materialized. In fact, the negotiations from December 1982 to March 1983 never reached a formal or serious stage, and Custodio concluded that the owners of Mendon Liquors were uninterested in his inquiries. According to Custodio, the owners would not return his telephone calls with sales terms or a price for the purchase. Custodio then learned that Mendon Liquors had been purchased in June 1983 by Act, Inc., a corporation composed of three individuals. One of those three, Armenio Teixeira, was one of the six shareholders in Teixeira & Co. Believing the sale of Mendon Liquors was initiated by Armenio, Custodio sued. He alleged that the purchase of Mendon Liquors was a corporate opportunity that rightfully belonged to Teixeira & Co., but it had been diverted by Armenio.

ISSUE

Has Armenio violated the corporate opportunity doctrine?

DECISION

No. Custodio's claim is premised on what has come to be known as the doctrine of corporate opportunity. Stated succinctly, this legal doctrine prohibits a corporate fiduciary from diverting a business opportunity away from the corporation and taking it for himself. To successfully state a claim then, a plaintiff must demonstrate that the defendant was a corporate fiduciary and that he diverted a corporate opportunity. Corporate officers and directors of any corporate enterprise, public or close, have long been recognized as corporate fiduciaries who owe a duty of loyalty to the corporation and its shareholders and are thereby prohibited from diverting corporate opportunities to themselves. In this case, however, Armenio was neither an officer nor a director. Pursuant to its articles of incorporation, the corporation had no board of directors and Custodio held the positions of president, vice president, secretary, and treasurer. It might be argued that Armenio was not a fiduciary. We do not believe, however, that the question of who is a corporate fiduciary is subject to such facile analysis. We conclude on the basis of the small number of shareholders in the corporation, the active participation by those shareholders in management decisions, and their close and intimate working relations, that all six shareholders, by acting as if they were partners, thus assumed a fiduciary duty toward one another and their corporation. Having concluded that Armenio, like a director or officer, was a fiduciary, we next examine the question of whether he diverted a corporate opportunity in violation of his fiduciary duty of loyalty. We conclude that Armenio

(continued)

A. Teixeira & Co. v. Teixeira
(concluded)

did not breach that fiduciary duty because Teixeira & Co. was financially unable to avail itself of the opportunity of purchasing Mendon Liquors. Armenio then, as anyone, was able to participate in the acquisition by Act, without accountability to Teixeira & Co. Where the corporation is unable to avail itself of the business opportunity, there can be no usurpation of a corporate opportunity.

Freeze-Outs, Oppression, and Bad Faith

There have been many lawsuits in which minority shareholders complain that they have been unfairly treated by the directors. Usually, these involve close corporations. The suits may claim a freeze-out. This occurs when the corporation is merged with a newly formed corporation under terms by which the minority shareholders receive cash or other securities for their shares, rather than receiving stock in the new corporation. Sometimes they claim oppression of minority shareholders. This frequently occurs when the majority shareholders refuse to pay dividends even though the corporation is able to do so. Others allege that the corporation will not hire minority shareholders while unreasonably high salaries have been paid to controlling shareholders and their friends. Still others involve purchases by or sales of assets to controlling shareholders where the price is said to be unfair. Usually, minority shareholders win such suits only where the acts of directors have clearly been in bad faith or have clearly abused the discretion given the directors under the business judgment rule.

Trading on Inside Information

When directors and officers buy or sell the corporation's stock, they may be in violation of their fiduciary duties. Any disclosure of the confidential information they have acquired through their position with the corporation might have a profound effect on the value of the corporation's securities. Yet current judicial trends point toward a greater and greater duty to disclose all material information to the buyers and sellers of stock. As a result, the federal securities laws prohibit **insiders,** those with confidential material information concerning the corporation, from buying or selling its stock. Insider trading, as well as the other duties imposed on directors and officers by the securities laws, will be discussed in greater detail in Chapter 28.

DIRECTORS' RIGHT TO DISSENT

A director who assents to the actions of the board of directors may be held liable if the board has failed to abide by its duties to the corporation. Any director who attends a board meeting is held to have assented to the board's actions unless he specifically dissents. Under the MBCA, a director will not have dissented unless he refuses to vote for the proposed course of action and makes this dissent clear to the other board members by having it appear in the minutes or by giving a written notice of dissent to the chairman or secretary immediately following the meeting.

Ethical Implications	A dissenting director will be held liable for the actions of the board unless she formally registers her dissent. What are the practical problems that a director faces in complying with this process?

.... *LIABILITY FOR TORTS AND CRIMES* ....

CORPORATE LIABILITY

Tort Liability

A corporation is liable for all torts committed by its employees while acting in the course of and within the scope of their employment. This may be true even when the corporation has instructed the employee to avoid the act. This rule is a simple application of the agency concept of respondeat superior (discussed in Chapter 21).

Crimes

Many criminal statutes clearly are intended to apply to corporations. Examples include the securities acts, the antitrust laws, and the numerous laws regulating the employment relationship. The traditional view was that a corporation could not be guilty of a crime involving intent. However, today, courts are especially likely to find criminal liability when a crime is committed, requested, or authorized by the board of directors, an officer, or a high-level manager.

STATE V. SMOKEY'S STEAKHOUSE, INC.
478 N.W.2d 361 (Sup. Ct. N.D. 1991)

FACTS

During an inspection of Smokey's Steakhouse, a restaurant and bar, police officers arrested two 20-year-old women for being in the bar while underage. Neither woman had been asked for proof of age by any Smokey's employee and both had been served alcoholic beverages. Smokey's Steakhouse was charged with commission of a criminal act for allowing a person under the age of 21 to remain on premises where alcoholic beverages were being sold. Smokey's contended that, as a corporate defendant, it could not be liable for the crime because its bartender was acting outside of the scope of her employment in serving the women. Specifically, it asserted that one of the women was the bartender's underage sister and that the bartender intentionally violated Smokey's company policy against serving underage patrons.

ISSUE

Is the corporation criminally liable in spite of its employee's violation of company policy?

DECISION

Yes. A corporation can be convicted of a crime when the offense is committed by an employee acting within the scope of her employment. An employee is acting within the scope of her employment for criminal law purposes when (1) she has authority to do the particular corporate business that was conducted illegally and (2) she was acting, at least in part, in furtherance of the corporation's business interests. However, a corporation is not insulated from criminal liability merely because it published instructions and policies that are violated by its employee. The corporation must place the acts outside the scope of an employee's employment by adequately enforcing its rules. There is no evidence that Smokey's ever attempted to enforce its policy that employees not serve underage patrons. Accordingly, the bartender was acting within the scope of employment when she served the two underage women and allowed them to remain on the premises.

LIABILITY OF OFFICERS AND DIRECTORS

Torts

Modern courts are much more willing to find negligence on the part of corporate directors and officers. Accordingly, where corporate activities cause injury or economic damage to others, the officer in charge, or even the directors, may be held liable. An officer or director may be held liable for the torts of employees of the corporation if she authorizes or participates in the commission of the tort.

Crimes

The criminal liability of officers has leaped to the attention of business leaders as state courts have upheld state criminal prosecutions against corporate officials for workplace injuries. Similarly, officers and directors both have been held personally liable under federal statutes imposing liability for hazardous waste cleanup costs. Directors and officers traditionally could be found guilty of crimes if they requested, authorized, or assisted in the commission of a crime by an employee. Now, they may be held criminally liable for failing in their supervisory duties.

Specifically, an officer can be found criminally liable for the illegal behavior of a subordinate when the officer (1) knew of or should have known of the illegal conduct and (2) failed to take reasonable measures to prevent it. (See Figure 26–3.) Thus, in the case that opened this chapter, Park, the chief executive officer of Acme, was found guilty for failing to see that the rodent infestation was removed. The Supreme Court held that he was not justified in relying on the employees to whom he had delegated the task since they had previously failed to adequately resolve the matter.

INDEMNIFICATION

The cost of defending and/or settling a suit or criminal charge brought against a director, officer, or employee may be very high. To encourage people to become officers and directors, corporations often indemnify them for such expenses. Today, however, all of the states place some limitations on the ability of corporations to indemnify officers and directors in order to strengthen the deterrence element of tort and criminal law.

In all instances, indemnification is *mandatory* if the officer or director prevails on the merits of the suit against him. When that occurs, the corporation must reimburse him for all of his costs and expenses. In cases in which the officer or director is found guilty, he still may be indemnified under **voluntary indemnification** if he acted in a manner that he believed not to be opposed to the corporation's best interests and had no reasonable cause to believe his conduct was unlawful. Such optional indemnification will occur if a majority of disinterested directors, an independent legal counsel, or the shareholders decide it to be appropriate. Many times, directors and corporations will have agreed in advance that indemnification should be mandatory

FIGURE 26–3   Liability for Torts and Crimes

If:	Employee commits a crime or tort	While:	Acting in scope of employment	Then:	Corporation is liable
When:	Corporate officer:		Knew of employee's crime or tort and could have prevented it	Then:	Officer may be liable

under such circumstances. Such agreements are permissible and provide greater certainty and security for officers and directors. In the case that opened this chapter, it is extremely likely that Park would be indemnified by Acme corporation.

An officer or director who has acted in bad faith or who is found liable to the corporation may not be indemnified under any circumstances. Further, the SEC will oppose on public policy grounds indemnification of damages sustained as a result of violations of the federal securities laws. (See Figure 26–4.)

CONCEPT SUMMARY	Duties of Officers and Directors
Act within Authority	Unauthorized actions may be ratified by disinterested board.
Due Care and Diligence	Due care met by prudent person standard. Informed, disinterested, and rational decisions sheltered by business judgment rule.
Loyalty and Good Faith	Avoid self-dealing or usurping corporate opportunities unless they are fair to corporation.

FIGURE 26–4   Indemnification of Officers and Directors

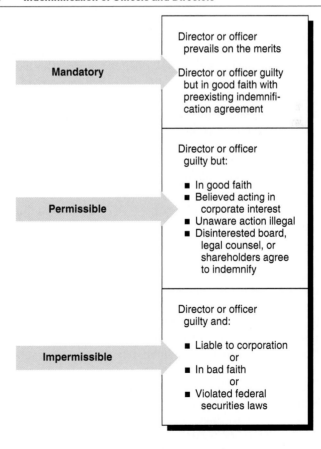

QUESTIONS AND PROBLEM CASES

1. Explain the difference between the authority of the board of directors and the authority of individual directors.

2. Barnet Stepak was a shareholder in Southern Company, a corporation whose subsidiaries provide electricity to consumers in the southern United States. Stepak demanded that Southern's board of directors bring suit to recover damages from two groups of current and former directors and officers for various illegal activities they committed in connection with their duties at the corporation. The board of directors investigated Stepak's charges. However, it entrusted the investigation to the law firm of Troutman Sanders, which had previously represented the suspected officers and directors in criminal investigations carried out by the Justice Department, the IRS, and the SEC. After various presentations dominated by Troutman Sander's attorneys, the outside directors of the board voted unanimously to reject Stepak's demand. When Stepak claimed that the board had wrongfully refused his demand, the board argued that its decision was protected by the business judgment rule. Was the board's decision protected by the business judgment rule? Explain.

3. On February 10, the board of directors of HBO designated that the annual meeting of the corporation would be held on April 30. Proxy materials were distributed with management recommending reelection of the present board. On March 28, a committee was formed to oppose the reelection of the six directors. The committee proposed an alternate slate of directors and further proposed a program that would allegedly maximize the value of the corporation. On April 25, the incumbent board decided to embrace the committee's program and began attempts to convince the shareholders that it would be better able to carry out the plan than would the committee. On April 29 (the day before the scheduled date of the meeting and election), the directors received information that the committee might win the election. On that afternoon, the board announced that the annual meeting would be postponed until September 22 so that shareholders would have time to evaluate the board's proposal to embrace the committee's program. The committee requested an injunction preventing the board from further delaying the annual meeting. Should the board be enjoined from further delaying the annual meeting and board elections?

4. Evertson and others formed a Wyoming corporation to engage in oil well servicing. Evertson served as the corporation's vice president. The funds obtained for the corporation's initial capitalization were insufficient to purchase all the equipment that it needed to function fully. Therefore, Evertson formed and was the only shareholder of another corporation (Rental) that would purchase the equipment that the Wyoming corporation lacked. Evertson enjoyed substantial profits from leasing equipment to the Wyoming corporation. The Wyoming corporation alleged that in forming Rental, Evertson wrongfully appropriated for himself an opportunity that properly belonged to it. Should Evertson be liable for having usurped a corporate opportunity?

5. Donald Trapp was president, a director, and the largest shareholder in Leson Chevrolet, Inc., a family-owned corporation. There were three shareholders, and the articles of incorporation provided that directors must be shareholders and established a minimum of three directors. Trapp was removed from his position as president by the board of directors, with his being the only dissenting vote. (The provision requiring three directors who are also shareholders prevented the others from removing him from the board.) The board appointed Griffin general manager, authorizing him to take over direction of the business from Trapp. However, Trapp continued to act as if he were the manager, giving directions to Griffin and the sales manager. Griffin told the board that he could not function under these conditions and would leave the company if Trapp were not removed from the premises. The corporation then sought to enjoin Trapp from interfering with the operation of the business or coming on the premises. Trapp argued that such an order would be illegal because it would prevent him from carrying on

his duties as a director of the corporation. Can Trapp, a director, be enjoined from coming on the corporate premises or interfering with the operation of the business?

6. Following one year of negotiations, James McDougal signed an agreement to purchase the Bank of Kingston. The sellers were the majority shareholders in First National Bank of Huntsville, the only other bank in the county. The sales agreement included a provision prohibiting the buyer from moving the bank to Huntsville for a period of 10 years. McDougal signed the agreement to purchase the bank stock as "James B. McDougal, Agent." About three months after the purchase, the board of directors of the Bank of Kingston changed the name of the bank to Madison Bank and Trust. Shortly thereafter, they began efforts to move the bank's main office from Kingston to Huntsville. The sellers sought an injunction to force the bank to comply with the provision in the sales agreement that prohibited such a move. The bank defended on the grounds that McDougal, its president, acted outside of his authority in signing the agreement. Is the covenant not to move to Huntsville enforceable against the bank? Explain.

7. After numerous private discussions, Jerome Van Gorkom, Trans Union's chairman and chief executive officer, convinced Jay Pritzker to make a merger offer for the purchase of Trans Union. Van Gorkom scheduled a meeting of the Trans Union board of directors for the following day to discuss the proposal. Van Gorkom began the special meeting of the board with a 20-minute oral presentation of his understanding of the offer, although he had not yet seen it. Copies of the proposed merger agreement were delivered too late for study before or during the meeting. Van Gorkom did not disclose how the purchase price was arrived at or that he had first proposed the price in his negotiations with Pritzker. Trans Union's chief financial officer presented a brief oral statement of his preliminary study of the buyout, although he did not purport to make a valuation of Trans Union's worth. After two hours, the directors approved the proposed merger agreement. Shareholders of Trans Union brought suit seeking recission of the merger

and damages from the members of the board of directors. The directors claimed that their decision was protected by the business judgment rule. Does the business judgment rule apply to the board's decision?

8. Loft, Inc., manufactured and sold candies, syrups, and beverages. It also operated 115 retail candy and soda fountain stores. Loft sold Coca-Cola at all of its stores, purchasing its 30,000-gallon annual requirement of the syrup and mixing it with carbonated water at its various soda fountains. In May 1931, Charles Guth, the president and general manager of Loft, became dissatisfied with the price of Coca-Cola syrup and suggested to Loft's vice president that Loft buy its syrup from National Pepsi-Cola Company. Soon thereafter, Guth bought Pepsi's secret formula and trademark for only $10,000. He organized a new corporation, Pepsi-Cola Company, of which he and his family owned a majority interest. From 1931 to 1935, without the knowledge or approval of Loft's board of directors, Guth used Loft's working capital, its credit, its plant and equipment, and its key personnel to produce Pepsi-Cola syrup. In addition, by dominating Loft's board of directors, Guth made Loft the chief customer of Pepsi-Cola. By 1935, the value of Pepsi-Cola's business was several million dollars. Loft brought suit, charging Guth with usurping a corporate opportunity and demanded that Guth give his Pepsi-Cola shares to Loft. Did Guth usurp a corporate opportunity?

9. Richmond Plasma Corporation (RPC), a wholly owned subsidiary of Automated Medical Laboratories (AML), has twice been closed by the Food and Drug Administration (FDA) for overbleeding of blood donors. Following the first closing, Partucci, a regional manager, was made chief compliance officer for RPC. While RPC was closed and awaiting an FDA inspection, Partucci and his compliance team discovered serious problems. The compliance team instructed RPC employees to falsify various records and, in some instances, falsified documents themselves. The Department of Justice prosecuted AML for making and using false documents. Can the corporation be found guilty for the crimes of its employees?

10. McLean, a former vice president of International Harvester's international division, was charged with violation of the Foreign Corrupt Practices Act (FCPA). Harvester pleaded guilty and admitted that the government had adequate evidence that two of its employees had aided and abetted violations of the FCPA. McLean believed that Harvester's plea negotiations and guilty plea implicated him in the bribery scheme, making him a scapegoat. At the trial, all of the substantive counts against him were dismissed because of a rule providing that an employee could not be convicted of violating the FCPA unless his employer was also convicted. (This rule was later repealed by the 1988 amendments to the FCPA.) McLean was then tried and acquitted of conspiring to violate the FCPA. He requested indemnification of $158,000 in legal fees and expenses incurred in defending himself. Harvester claimed that McLean waived any right to indemnification because he refused the services of the attorney that Harvester offered him. Must Harvester indemnify McLean for his legal fees?

CHAPTER 27

Financing the Corporation and the Role of the Shareholders

Holmes A. Court had a reputation for taking over a corporation, extracting quick profits, and leaving the company and its remaining shareholders staggering. Accordingly, Asarco's board of directors was alarmed to discover that Court was buying up the company's common stock. In preparation for a full-fledged assault, the board fashioned a formidable takeover defense. It unanimously approved the issuance of a new preferred stock series to be distributed as a dividend. The voting rights of this new stock were such that if Court acquired 20 percent of the common and 20 percent of the Series C Preferred, he would have only 4.1 percent of the total vote although he owned one-fifth of the stock.[1]

- *Will a court uphold the board's defensive tactics?*
- *What is common stock? How does it differ from preferred stock?*
- *What are the rights and obligations of the holders of various types of stock?*

---

[1]Asarco, Inc. v. Court, 611 F. Supp. 468 (D. N.J. 1985).

Financing the Corporation

Sources of Corporate Financing

One of the major reasons that promoters select the corporate form of business is the variety of funding sources available to businesses that incorporate. The initial funds and property may come directly from the promoters or it may come from many diverse types of investors. An important source of financing is the sale of corporate securities in the form of shares, debentures, bonds, and long-term notes.

Other sources of funding are also prevalent. Short-term bank loans may provide at least part of the operating capital of the corporation. (Frequently, the promoters and major shareholders will be required to cosign these notes.) Often, this short-term funding will come in the form of accounts receivable financing and inventory financing. Of course, once the corporation is operating profitably, retained earnings may generate an important source of funds.

The remainder of the discussion of corporate funding in this chapter will be confined to the two types of corporate securities. The first type, **equity securities,** arises through the sale of ownership interests in the business in the form of shares of corporate stock. The second, **debt securities,** is typified by bonds and other obligations of the enterprise.

Equity Securities

A corporation must issue some common stock. It may also, if authorized by its articles, issue preferred stock. Both kinds of stock are equity securities. Certificates are issued to represent the shares of stock but they are not the stock; they are merely evidence of ownership.

Common Stock

If a corporation has only one class of stock, it is **common stock.** If there is more than one class, the common shareholders usually bear the major risks of the business and will benefit most from success. They receive what is left over after the preferences of other classes have been satisfied. This is usually true for both income available for dividends and for net assets on liquidation. Common stock usually carries voting rights. There may be more than one class of common stock, however, such as Class A and Class B. One class may have no right to vote.

Preferred Stock

Any stock that has a preference over another class of stock is call **preferred stock.** Usually, preferred shareholders have a preference as to dividends and the distribution of assets when the corporation is dissolved. (The dividend rights of various types of preferred stock will be discussed more fully later in this chapter.)

The rights of preferred shareholders may vary from corporation to corporation. In some instances, preferred stock may be made convertible into common stock. And sometimes preferred stockholders will be given voting rights. However, usually the right to vote is granted only in the event that dividends due are not paid. In the case that opened this chapter, the defensive tactics of the Asarco board of directors were not permitted by the court. They were prohibited because the corporation had no power to issue preferred stock that would result in differing voting rights within the same class.

Preferred stock can be **redeemed**—that is, paid off and canceled by the corporation—if the articles permit. Under the Model Business Corporation Act (MBCA), the redemption price must be stated in the articles. Redemption permits the corporation to buy back the shares even if the holders do not wish to sell. It is very common for a corporation to issue preferred shares subject to redemption at the option of the corporation. Although it is not as common, a corporation may also have a redeemable class of common shares. Redemption will not be permitted, however, if the cost would make the corporation insolvent.

CONSIDERATION FOR SHARES

Shares of stock are generally issued in exchange for money, property, or services already performed for the corporation. The board of directors is entrusted with the authority to decide what is the proper amount and form of consideration for the shares. Corporation statutes, however, will frequently place some limitations on the discretion of the board of directors in order to protect the rights of creditors and other shareholders.

Presently, most states follow the old MBCA approach, which requires that shares be issued only for money, tangible or intangible property, and services already performed for the corporation. Most of these states do not permit the promoter's preincorporation services to be proper consideration for shares because the services were not technically rendered to the corporation. (The corporation was not in existence at the time of these services.) Likewise, these states do not consider promissory notes or pledges of future services to be acceptable forms of consideration for shares in the corporation. This is so because such promises may overstate the value of the corporation since they may never be performed.

The revised MBCA permits promises of future services and promissory notes to be exchanged for shares since they do have value to a corporation. (Of course, because of the risk of nonperformance, the value may not be as great as the value of services that have already been rendered to the corporation.) Further, the new MBCA allows the corporation to issue shares to the promoters in exchange for their preincorporation efforts because the corporation has benefited from such services. (Without these services, the corporation would probably not exist.)

VALUE OF SHARES

Sometimes, a value is assigned to the shares in the articles of incorporation. This arbitrary amount is referred to as **par value.** If the stock has no par value, the board of directors may assign a **stated value** when the shares are issued.

Stated Capital

Par value and stated value reflect the minimum amount of consideration for which the shares can be issued. This is so because the stated capital of the corporation is determined by multiplying the number of outstanding shares times the par or stated value of each share. If the shares were issued for less than the par or stated value, the stated capital of the corporation would exaggerate the actual value of the corporation. As a result, the board of directors as well as the purchasers of shares are liable to the corporation when shares have been issued for less than the par or the stated value.

FIGURE 27–1   Stated Capital and Capital Surplus

$$\text{Stated capital} = (\text{Par value}) \times \left(\begin{matrix} \text{Number of shares} \\ \text{outstanding} \end{matrix}\right)$$

$$\text{Capital surplus} = \left(\begin{matrix} \text{Amount received} \\ \text{per share} \end{matrix} - \text{Par value}\right) \times \left(\begin{matrix} \text{Number of shares} \\ \text{outstanding} \end{matrix}\right)$$

Capital Surplus

Many times, the shares are actually worth more than the par or the stated value. In these instances, the directors have a duty to the corporation to receive the *fair value* of the stock. In order to avoid liability to the corporation, the directors must exercise good faith and the care of ordinary prudent directors in determining the amount of consideration that is to be collected for the shares. When the shares sell for more than their par or stated value, the excess amount is referred to as *capital surplus*. While the MBCA has abandoned the use of the terms *stated value* and *capital surplus*, most states still use the concepts. (See Figure 27–1.)

OPTIONS, WARRANTS, AND RIGHTS

The MBCA expressly permits directors to issue options to purchase shares of the corporation. These may be given in connection with the sale of other securities, or they may be issued to employees as an incentive to increase profitability in order to maximize the market value of the corporation's stock. Shareholder approval is required under the MBCA for employee and director stock option plans.

Options represented by certificates are known as *warrants*. They are sometimes part of a package of securities sold as a unit; for example, they may be given along with notes, bonds, or even shares. The term *rights* is usually applied to short-term and often nonnegotiable options. Rights are used to give present security holders a right to subscribe to some proportional quantity of the same or a different security of the corporation. Often they are given in connection with a preemptive right requirement.

TREASURY STOCK

A corporation may purchase its securities from any willing seller. It does not need specific authority to do so in its articles. However, the MBCA permits such purchases only out of unrestricted earned surplus. Earned surplus arises when a corporation retains all or part of its operating profit rather than paying it out in dividends. Capital surplus may be used only on a two-thirds vote of shareholders. Capital surplus can come from several sources. One is sales of shares above par value. Repurchased shares become treasury shares. They cannot be voted in elections, and they can be resold without regard to par value or original issue price.

The MBCA recommends abolishing the concept of treasury shares. Under this approach, repurchased shares are restored to unissued status. They may then be reissued unless the articles of incorporation require cancellation.

DEBT SECURITIES

Corporations have the power to borrow money necessary for their operations by issuing debt securities. This power is inherent; it need not appear in the articles of incorporation. Unlike equity securities, debt securities do not transfer an ownership interest in the corporation. They create a debtor–creditor relationship. Accordingly, the corporation/debtor is obligated to pay a periodic interest charge as well as the

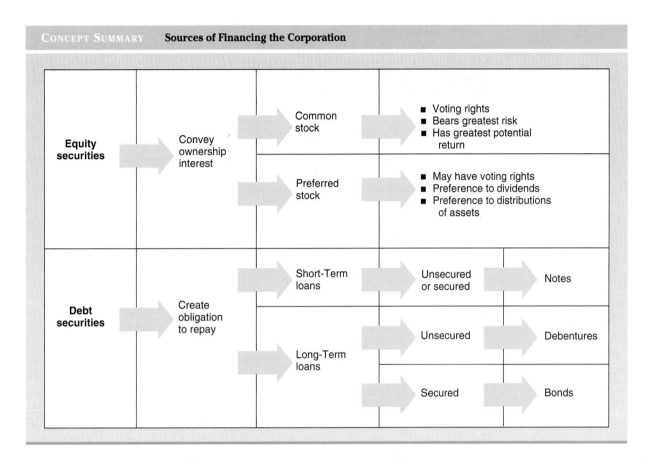

| CONCEPT SUMMARY | Sources of Financing the Corporation |

balance of the debt on the maturity date. Debt securities arise in the form of notes, debentures, or bonds.

Notes

Short-term debt instruments are called **notes.** They seldom have terms in excess of five years. Notes may be either secured or unsecured. When they are secured, the creditor may force the sale of the collateral if the debt is not paid according to the terms of the agreement.

Debentures

Long-term unsecured debt instruments are called **debentures.** They may have a term of 30 years or more. Frequently, debentures will have an indenture. An **indenture** is a contract protecting the rights of the debenture holders. It will define what acts constitute default by the corporation as well as stipulate the rights of the holder on default. In many instances, it will place restrictions on the corporation's right to issue other debt securities in order to prevent the corporation from overextending itself.

Bonds

Long-term, secured debt securities are called **bonds.** They generally have indentures and, therefore, differ from debentures only because they are secured. The security may be real property such as a building or personal property such as machinery, raw materials, or even accounts due from customers. Bondholders, as well as holders of secured notes, have priority as to the assets securing the debt. Therefore, they are more likely than unsecured noteholders and debenture holders to receive greater portions of their claims should the corporation be forced to liquidate.

BECOMING A SHAREHOLDER

If you are not already the owner of shares of stock in a corporation, you may wish to become one. No large investment is necessary. Many shares sell for less than $10 per share, although those of companies with good financial prospects usually sell for more. Although you will find in this chapter that shareholders have a number of rights, most shareholders are interested in only one—the right to share in the profits of the corporation.

FUNCTIONS OF SHAREHOLDERS

Although owners of the corporation, shareholders have few functions, and in most publicly held corporations they exercise little influence. Normally, their principal function is the election of the directors. In large corporations, the proxy system of voting and the tendency of most shareholders to follow the recommendations of management usually result in the election of persons nominated by management.

Shareholders are also required to approve unusual or extraordinary corporate transactions such as a merger, sale of substantially all corporate assets, or a voluntary dissolution. In addition, their favorable vote is necessary to amend the corporate articles. Some states require shareholder approval for other matters as well. For example, the MBCA requires shareholder approval of stock option plans for corporate officers and other managers. It also requires approval of loans to officers by the corporation. These functions are performed at shareholders' meetings. The meetings may be either the regular annual meeting or special meetings.

MEANS OF ACQUIRING STOCK

One can become a shareholder by several means. One is by subscribing to shares in a new corporation being formed. Another is by subscribing to shares that are being issued by an existing corporation. A more common method is to buy newly issued shares that have been underwritten by an investment banker and sold through a stockbroker. (An underwriter of a stock issue agrees to market it to investors and usually guarantees to sell the entire issue at an agreed-on price.) The most common way of becoming a shareholder is by buying previously issued shares from a former owner, either directly or through a broker.

Subscriptions to buy stock in a corporation that is not yet in existence are usually treated as offers until incorporation is completed. The MBCA makes such subscriptions irrevocable for six months. Generally, corporate acceptance of preincorporation subscriptions occurs by action of the board of directors after incorporation. It is at this time (the time of acceptance) that the subscriber becomes a shareholder. (Some state statutes provide that the acceptance automatically occurs at the time of the issuance of the certificate of incorporation.)

A subscription for unissued shares in an existing corporation is usually treated as an offer. A contract is formed, and the subscriber becomes a shareholder when the corporation accepts the offer. The making of the subscription contract is called **issuing stock.** The stock certificate cannot, under the MBCA, be issued until the shares are fully paid for.

.... **SHAREHOLDERS' MEETINGS** ....

ANNUAL MEETING

All of the state laws except Delaware's require corporations formed in the state to have an annual meeting. A Delaware corporation can use a mail ballot instead of holding a meeting. The main purpose of the annual meeting is the election of directors. Many larger corporations ask the shareholders to approve the selection of public auditors. There may be other proposals by management for shareholder approval, such as an executive stock option or profit-sharing plan or an amendment to the articles of incorporation. There may also be resolutions proposed by shareholders to be voted on. It is customary for the chief executive and perhaps other officers to give brief reports on the corporation's operations during the past year and its prospects for the current year. Shareholders may ask questions of the top officers, usually during a question period scheduled to follow the officer reports.

SPECIAL MEETINGS

Special meetings of shareholders are quite rare in most corporations. One is called when shareholder approval of a corporate action is necessary between annual meetings. The most common purpose is probably to get approval of a proposal by the directors to merge with another corporation.

The MBCA provides that a special meeting may be called by the president, the board of directors, or the holders of one-tenth or more of the shares entitled to vote at the meeting. Under the MBCA, the bylaws may provide that other officers or persons (such as the chairman of the board) may call a special meeting of shareholders.

NOTICE OF MEETINGS

The MBCA requires **notice** of all shareholders' meetings to be given not less than 10 or more than 50 days before the meeting. The notice must give the place, day, and hour of the meeting. For special meetings, the purpose of the meeting must be given. If an extraordinary corporate transaction such as a merger is to be voted on, notice of the proposal must be given to *all* shareholders, even if there are shareholders who own a class of stock not usually entitled to vote. The shareholders entitled to notice are those "of record." They are the people whose names appear on the stock-transfer book of the corporation.

If the required notice is not given, actions taken at a meeting are of no effect. However, shareholders who did not get proper notice may **waive** notice. As in the case of directors' meetings (discussed in the previous chapter), attendance at the meeting is an automatic waiver. However, there is no waiver if the shareholder attends only to object to the holding of the meeting. Waiver is effective only if all shareholders who did not get proper notice either attend or waive in writing.

REMOTE PARTICIPATION

Amendments to Delaware's corporation laws now permit directors to allow shareholders who are not physically present at a meeting to participate by remote communication. In fact, the directors may dispense with a physical location entirely and conduct the entire meeting by modern communications technology. Four requirements must be met if a shareholder meeting is to be conducted remotely: (1) the corporation must have implemented some reasonable means for ensuring that those persons participating are indeed shareholders, (2) those participating shareholders and proxy holders must be afforded a reasonable opportunity to both participate and vote, (3) some means must be provided so that participants have the opportunity to read or hear the ongoing proceedings, and (4) the corporation must keep a record of any remote votes or other actions taken at the meeting.

The rules governing remote participation by shareholders do not have to meet the same retention, retrieval, review, and reproduction requirements imposed on directors' actions. Thus, while a directors' action by remote transmission would not be valid unless it could be reproduced in paper form (see Chapter 26), shareholder meetings may now be conducted by conference call.

For many years, corporations were required to maintain and make available a list of all shareholders during the 10 days prior to a shareholder meeting. The new amendments to Delaware law now permit the corporation to maintain the list either at its principal place of business or to post it on an electronic network. For meetings that are conducted entirely by remote communications, the list is to be made available throughout the meeting on an accessible electronic network.

SHAREHOLDERS ENTITLED TO VOTE

Sources of the Right to Vote

If you are a shareholder, your right to vote at a shareholders' meeting depends on the incorporation statute and the articles and bylaws of the corporation. If you own common stock and have it listed in your name, you probably have a right to vote.

Determining Who May Vote

The person who has legal title to the stock is the one usually entitled to vote. Directors of publicly held corporations usually establish a record date prior to each shareholders' meeting. Those who are shareholders of record on that date are allowed to vote. Those who are owners of shares held in the name of another, such as a stock broker, may obtain a proxy from the record holder. SEC rules require brokers to mail proxy material to customers for whom they hold shares.

Nonvoting Stock

Owners of a nonvoting class of stock have a right to vote only under certain circumstances. The MBCA gives holders of such stock the right to vote on extraordinary corporate transactions, which are discussed later in this chapter. Neither a corporation nor its subsidiary may vote treasury shares. Unissued stock, of course, carries no vote.

ELLIOTT ASSOCIATES L.P. v. AVATEX CORPORATION
715 A.2d 843 (Del. Sup. Ct. 1998)

FACTS

Avatex is a corporation that has both common and preferred stock outstanding. It created and incorporated Xetava Corporation as its wholly owned subsidiary and the following day announced its intention to merge with and into Xetava. Under the terms of the proposed merger, Xetava is to be the surviving corporation. Once the transaction is consummated, Xetava will immediately change its name to Avatex Corporation. The proposed merger will cause a conversion of the preferred stock of Avatex into common stock of Xetava. The merger

(continued)

ELLIOTT ASSOCIATES L.P. V. AVATEX CORPORATION
(concluded)

will effectively eliminate Avatex's certificate of incorporation, which includes the certificate of designations creating the Avatex preferred stock and setting forth its rights and preferences. The terms of the merger do not call for a class vote of these preferred stockholders. The preferred stockholders filed suit to enjoin the proposed merger, arguing that the transaction required the consent of two-thirds of the holders of the preferred stock. Under the terms of the Avatex certificate of incorporation, preferred stockholders have no right to vote except on "any amendment, alteration or repeal of the certificate of incorporation whether by merger, consolidation or otherwise, that . . . materially and adversely affects the rights of the . . . [preferred] stockholders." The text of the terms governing the voting rights of the preferred stockholders required that such an alteration or repeal of the certificate required "the consent of the holders of at least two-thirds of the shares" of the preferred stock.

ISSUE

Did this corporate action require the consent of two-thirds of the preferred stockholders?

DECISION

Yes. The narrow legal question in this case is whether the "amendment, alteration or repeal" of the certificate of incorporation is caused "by merger, consolidation or otherwise" thereby requiring a two-thirds class vote of the preferred stockholders. Here the preferred stock of Avatex is converted to common stock of the surviving corporation, Xetava, a newly formed corporation that is admittedly a wholly owned subsidiary of Avatex created for the sole purpose of effecting this merger and eliminating the Avatex preferred stock. The operative events here are that the proposed downstream merger of Avatex into Xetava results in the conversion of Avatex stock to Xetava stock and the elimination "by merger" of the certificate protections granted to the preferred stockholders. Thus, it is *both* the stock conversion *and* the repeal of the Avatex certificate that causes the adverse effect to the preferred stock. Avatex argues that the voting rights of the preferred stockholders would be triggered only in the circumstances where Avatex survives the merger and its certificate is amended thereby. The difficulty with this reading is that it fails to account for the word *consolidation*, which appears in the certificate of incorporation. A consolidation cannot entail an amendment because in a consolidation there is no surviving corporation whose preexisting certificate is subject to amendment. The resulting corporation in a consolidation is a completely new entity with a new certificate of incorporation. All the certificates of the constituent corporations simply would become legal nullities in a consolidation. In short, Avatex's proposed reading of the relevant provisions would render the word *consolidation* mere surplusage, and it is problematic for that reason. Here, Avatex disappears, just as it would in a consolidation. In our view, this constitutes repeal, if not an amendment or alteration. Thus, the proposed merger is within the class of events that trigger preferred stockholders' voting rights because the merger materially and adversely affects the preferred stockholders by rendering the Avatex certificate that protects them a legal nullity.

PROXY VOTING

As a shareholder, you may appoint another person, known as a *proxy*, to vote for you. The MBCA requires a written document appointing the proxy as an agent to vote for you. This document is also, rather confusingly, called a **proxy.** Some states permit an oral proxy. A proxy may generally be revoked at any time; it is automatically revoked if you later give another proxy on the same shares of stock.

Modern corporation statutes permit creation of irrevocable proxies. These statutes usually specifically define when a proxy may be irrevocable. The MBCA allows a proxy to be irrevocable if it so states and if it is "coupled with an interest." A proxy will be coupled with an interest when, among other things, the proxy holder is a party to a shareholder voting agreement or has agreed to purchase the shares under a "buy-and-sell agreement."

Solicitation of Proxies

As indicated above, usually in publicly held corporations only a small proportion of the shares are owned by persons who attend shareholders' meetings. Management then solicits proxies. It asks the shareholders who do not expect to attend to appoint, as their proxy, one or more of the directors or some other person friendly to management. Most shareholders sign and return their proxies.

Regulation of Proxies

The SEC has power under the 1934 act to make rules about proxy statements. The proxy statement must give certain information. For example, if directors are to be elected, information must be given about any employment contract and pension or stock option benefits and any material transaction between a nominee and the corporation. An annual statement must be mailed with or before the proxy statement for an annual meeting.

The proxy document, under SEC rules, must permit shareholders a choice of voting for or withholding their vote from all of the management slate of directors. They may also exempt one or more directors from their favorable vote. They must also be permitted to abstain or vote for or against any resolutions that have been proposed.

Finally, SEC rules require corporations subject to them to furnish a shareholder list to any shareholder who desires to solicit proxies. As an alternative, the corporation may mail the proxy material for the soliciting shareholder. (The regulation of proxies will be discussed in greater detail in Chapter 28.)

Expenses

The corporation pays for the preparation and mailing of a proxy statement on behalf of management. If someone else or a group wants to nominate directors, that group must bear the expense of soliciting proxies. A proxy battle tends to be very expensive, and relatively few challengers win. If they do, they are entitled to be reimbursed by the corporation for their expenses because it is assumed from their shareholder support that the corporation has benefited.

Effect

Shareholders usually follow the recommendation of management in their voting or merely sign the proxy without voting. The proxy also usually gives management authority to vote the shares on any other matter coming before the meeting. The effect, of course, is to determine the outcome of the meeting before it is held. Argument made for or against a resolution at the meeting can affect only the votes of those present. A resolution made from the floor has no chance of passing unless the management votes its proxies in favor of it. Through the proxy system, management is able to control the corporation without owning many shares itself.

LOUDON V. ARCHER-DANIELS-MIDLAND COMPANY
700 A.2d 135 (Del. Sup. Ct. 1997)

FACTS

Archer-Daniels-Midland Company (ADM), a publicly held corporation, was the subject of a federal criminal investigation into possible antitrust violations. In July of 1995, it was disclosed that ADM director Mark E. Whitacre had been acting at the behest of the FBI, covertly videotaping and sound recording various ADM meetings and conferences. The FBI investigation, with the assistance of Whitacre's espionage, allegedly revealed an extensive pattern of market manipulation and price-fixing engaged in by ADM's chief executive officer, Dwayne Andreas, and other corporate insiders. On July 19, 1995, ADM issued a press release disclosing the board's election of Gaylord O. Coan to the ADM board. The release made no mention, however, of the resignation of Howard M. Buffet, whom Coan had replaced on the board and on the management slate presented to the stockholders for election. Prior to his resignation, Mr. Buffet had been an employee of the company as well as a director, having served as a corporate vice president, assistant to ADM chairman Andreas, and ADM's corporate spokesperson. On August 7, 1995, ADM removed Mr. Whitacre from the board and publicly announced that he had misappropriated some $2.5 million while acting as an FBI operative. Mr. Whitacre has repeatedly professed his innocence and continues to claim that the $2.5 million was a portion of the purported $6 million in improper bonuses paid by ADM to its officers and directors. On September 13, 1995, ADM issued its proxy statement in connection with the company's upcoming annual stockholder meeting. The proxy statement contained disclosures concerning the FBI investigation. However, it made no mention of the circumstances surrounding the resignation of former ADM director Howard M. Buffet. At the annual meeting, ADM's proposed slate of directors ran unopposed and was overwhelmingly re-elected. Dwayne Andreas allegedly presided over the meeting in an extremely autocratic and domineering manner. He refused to allow stockholders to ask questions and abruptly dismissed any efforts by stockholders to comment or question the current affairs of ADM. A stockholder filed a lawsuit contending that the ADM board breached its fiduciary duty by failing to disclose the facts surrounding Howard Buffet's resignation. The complaint averred that Buffet resigned because he refused to participate in Dwayne Andreas's plan to stonewall ADM stockholders, the media, and Wall Street and did not believe the information he was receiving from ADM officials about the government's probe and related litigation.

ISSUE

Did the ADM Board have a legal duty to disclose the circumstances surrounding Buffet's resignation in the proxy statement?

DECISION

No. It is well established that directors of Delaware corporations are under a fiduciary duty to disclose fully and fairly all material information within the board's control when it seeks shareholder action. An omitted fact is material if there is a substantial likelihood that a reasonable stockholder would consider it important in deciding how to vote. There must be a substantial likelihood that the disclosure of the omitted fact would have been viewed by the reasonable stockholder as having significantly altered the total mix of information made available. However, the directors' duty of disclosure does not oblige them to characterize their conduct in such a way as to admit wrongdoing. Thus, even where material facts must be disclosed, negative inferences or characterizations of misconduct or breach of fiduciary duty need not be articulated. The complaint contends that it is material that Buffet allegedly tendered his resignation in response to the wrongdoing of other board members and that this is a fact that a reasonable ADM stockholder would want to know in deciding how to vote. This argument presents a novel disclosure theory. To be sure, it might be better practice for directors of a public corporation to be more candid and forthcoming in their communications to stockholders when presenting a slate for election to the board. However, it is a leap of logic for this court to fashion a bright line of disclosure for directorial elections. The complaint before us does not state a well-pleaded claim that the nondisclosure of the background of Buffet's omission from the management slate was material or actionable.

FIGURE 27–2   Shareholder Rights

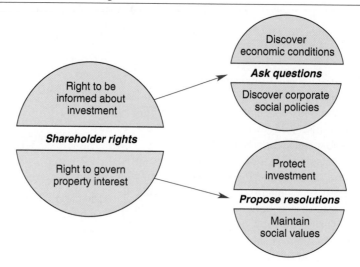

SHAREHOLDER PROPOSALS AND RIGHT TO SPEAK

Sources of Shareholder Rights

Shareholders have the right both to ask questions and to propose resolutions at shareholders' meetings. The first right is that of an owner to be informed about his or her investment. The second is the right of an owner to participate in establishing the framework within which the directors exercise their powers of management. It is related to the shareholders' rights to make bylaws. (See Figure 27–2).

Shareholder Resolutions

In recent years, shareholder activists have submitted resolutions at the annual meetings of quite a number of the largest corporations. They generally fall into two types. One type aims to protect or enhance the interests of small shareholders. Proposals to amend the corporate articles to permit cumulative voting for directors (discussed in the next section), to put ceilings on the salaries of top executives, and to limit corporate gifts to charitable and educational organizations are of this type. The other type had its beginnings about 1970. Proposals of this type are usually offered by groups that have goals of social or political change or that oppose certain corporate activities. A few shares may be purchased solely to permit making the proposal. Other such groups, particularly church groups, may have owned quite a few shares as an investment for some time.

Some resolutions seeking a change in corporate policy asked the directors of corporations to withdraw from South Africa until apartheid ended. Some have merely asked the corporation to publicize certain information withheld as confidential, such as statistics on minority employment.

Ethical Implications	Do shareholders have a moral responsibility to monitor the activities of the corporations in which they hold stock? Do they have a responsibility to urge those corporations to behave in a socially responsible manner?

CUMULATIVE VOTING

Most corporations elect directors on the basis that each share is entitled to one vote for each director. Many corporations, however, permit shareholders to cumulate their votes. By using all their votes to support one director, a group of minority shareholders may be able to elect a director of their choice. If they spread their votes among all nominees, on the other hand, they would not be able to elect any.

A number of states require businesses incorporated in them to permit shareholders to cumulate their votes for directors. Few large publicly held corporations are incorporated in these states. The purpose of **cumulative voting** is to give minority shareholders an opportunity to be represented on the board. Opponents say that this is likely to be divisive and to cause friction among board members that will damage the firm.

The formula for determining the number of shares, *X*, required to elect one director under cumulative voting is:

$$X = \frac{S}{D + 1} + 1$$

where *S* is the number of shares voting and *D* is the total number of directors to be elected. Clearly, the fewer directors to be elected, the greater is the percentage of shares required to elect one director. Dividing directors into three classes, one class to be elected each year, makes it more difficult for minority shareholders to attain representation on the board.

RIGHTS OF INSPECTION AND PREEMPTIVE RIGHT

THE SHAREHOLDER'S RIGHT TO INSPECT

The MBCA requires a corporation to send its latest financial statements to any shareholder on request. It also requires the corporation to permit a shareholder, on written request, to examine in person, or through an agent such as a lawyer or an accountant, its "relevant books and records of account, minutes, and record of shareholders." The shareholder or agent may make extracts from these records.

Proper Purpose

The shareholder must have a proper purpose for examining the records. To learn business secrets or to gain a competitive advantage is not a proper purpose. To determine the value of one's shares or to identify fellow shareholders in order to communicate with them concerning corporate affairs is a proper purpose. It is a proper purpose to make a copy of the shareholder list in order to wage a proxy contest to unseat present management.

SHAW V. AGRI-MARK, INC.
663 A.2d 464 (Del. Sup.Ct. 1995)

FACTS

Agri-Mark is a cooperative stock corporation in the business of processing, handling, and marketing the milk and other dairy products of its "producer members," farmers in the New England states and New York. Each

(continued)

SHAW V. AGRI-MARK, INC.
(continued)

dairy farmer who wishes to become a member is required to sign a Member Marketing Agreement with Agri-Mark. This agreement is a contract by which the member agrees to sell all of his or her milk products to Agri-Mark, and, in exchange, Agri-Mark agrees to market the dairy products to the public. Agri-Mark's equity base is comprised entirely of member contributions to the corporation and retained earnings from the proceeds of its milk marketing operations. The cooperative is divided into geographical regions containing between 100 and 275 members. At regional meetings, each member is entitled to one vote. The board of directors for Agri-Mark is selected at these regional meetings with members from each region electing one director. All of the stock of the Agri-Mark is held by those elected to its board of directors. Each director is issued one share of Agri-Mark stock in exchange for one dollar. The directors constitute the only Agri-Mark shareholders of record. At the expiration of each director's term, he or she must sell his or her share back to Agri-Mark for one dollar. Only directors are permitted to vote at annual or special meetings of the shareholders. Thus, although the individual members of Agri-Mark supply the corporation with its equity and directly elect its directors, they are not shareholders of record, since the corporate by-laws limit that status to directors. Karen Shaw, an Agri-Mark member, brought an action in court to compel Agri-Mark to allow her to inspect its books and records. Specifically, she sought to inspect the corporation's membership list, as well as salary information concerning the five highest paid executives of Agri-Mark. The corporation argued that, since Shaw was not a shareholder of record, she had no right to inspect the corporation's books and records.

ISSUE

Does Shaw have a right to inspect the corporation's books and records?

DECISION

No. It is well established that, as a matter of common law, a shareholder possessed a qualified right to inspect or examine the stock ledger, as well as the books and records of the corporation. This common law right of inspection was not absolute. In order to enforce inspection, the shareholder demanding inspection had to show that the inspection was for proper purposes. A proper purpose was viewed under the common law as a purpose relating to the interest the shareholder sought to protect by seeking inspection. Thus, a proper purpose in seeking inspection was considered as a purpose germane to shareholder's interest or status as a shareholder. In short, a shareholder's right to inspection is status related. In this regard, inspection rights have been viewed as an incident to the shareholder's ownership of corporate property. As an equitable owner of the corporation's assets, a shareholder possessed a right to reasonable information concerning the conduct of corporate management, as well as the condition of the corporation's business and affairs. As a matter of self-protection, the shareholder was entitled to know how his or her agents were conducting the affairs of the corporation of which he or she was a part owner. In addition to the common law right of inspection, the right has been codified in corporation statutes. These statues limit the right to inspect shareholder lists or other corporate books and records to shareholders of record. In fact, establishing oneself as a shareholder of record is a mandatory condition precedent to the right to make a demand for inspection. In this regard, the corporation may look to its stock ledger as the sole evidence in identifying those shareholders of record who are entitled to inspection. Shaw now argues that members of a corporation should be treated synonymously with shareholders of record for purposes of the common law right of inspection. However, this argument that, as a matter of equity, the members should be recognized as shareholders of Agri-Mark since they are the "real" owners of the cooperative is unconvincing. Corporate law has traditionally limited the rights of shareholders to shareholders of record. Only if a corporation fails in its affirmative duty to maintain a stock ledger may a court look to extrinsic evidence in deciding whether a party possesses record shareholder status. Although Shaw is a member, she is not a shareholder of Agri-Mark, let alone a shareholder of record. Agri-Mark has issued one share of stock to each member of its board of directors. As the only shareholders of Agri-Mark, the directors exclusively enjoy the rights incident to share ownership. The court is not unmindful of the situation in which Shaw finds herself as an equity owner

(continued)

SHAW V. AGRI-MARK, INC.
(concluded)

who is denied the right to inspection, while those who have the status of shareholders have only a nominal ownership interest in the corporation. But her plight is of her own making. She voluntarily chose to become a member of Agri-Mark while others were designed as shareholders, and, presumably, she was or should have been aware that her rights would be governed by the Marketing Agreement she executed.

Ethical Implications	Is it ethical for a businessperson to purchase shares of stock in a competing company in order to gain access to its books and records?

Denials

The MBCA gives shareholders an absolute right to inspect the shareholder list. In order to discourage the denial of proper demands to inspect, the MBCA makes a corporate official who denies a proper demand liable for a penalty of 10 percent of the value of the shares of the demanding shareholder. Many state statutes have no such penalty provision and, as a result, denials are common.

PREEMPTIVE RIGHTS

A number of states require corporations domiciled there to give their current shareholders an option to purchase their proportionate share of any new issue of stock. This enables the shareholder to maintain the same relative interest in the corporation as before. Granting such a preemptive right creates difficult problems in large corporations that have several classes of stock. Generally, courts do not apply preemptive rights to treasury shares, shares issued in connection with a merger or consolidation, or shares issued in exchange for property or past services. Further, most of the states provide that there is no preemptive right unless the articles of incorporation create such a right.

DIVIDENDS

DIRECTORS' DISCRETION TO PAY DIVIDENDS

Shareholders have a right to share in the net income of the corporation; however, the declaration of dividends is subject to the business judgment of the board of directors. They may not pile up unneeded cash in the treasury or pay it out in unreasonably high salaries to management. However, the burden of proof is on the shareholder to show that the directors have abused their discretion.

TYPES OF DIVIDENDS

Cash and Property Dividends

Dividends are usually paid in cash. However, in some instances the corporation may distribute corporate assets other than cash. These property dividends may take the form of shares of stock that the corporation owns in another corporation or any other noncash asset of the corporation.

Stock Dividends

Distributions of shares in the corporation itself are called **stock dividends.** They are usually paid when management wants to retain all or an unusually high proportion of earnings for reinvestment. A large stock dividend may have as its main purpose a reduction in the market price per share to encourage greater investor interest in the stock. Stock dividends payable in the same class of shares do not change a shareholders' stake in the corporation. The proportion of shares owned remains the same; the shareholder just has a higher number of shares.

LEGAL LIMITS ON DIVIDENDS

Incorporation statutes all put limits on the dividends a corporation may pay. The MBCA permits paying dividends only out of retained earnings. It also prohibits the payment of a dividend that would make the corporation insolvent. A business is *insolvent* when it cannot pay its debts as they become due.

STOCK SPLITS

A **stock split** is not a dividend; it merely changes the par value or stated value of the shares and the number outstanding, not the retained earnings account. A stock split increases the number of shares outstanding; a reverse stock split reduces the number of shares outstanding. The reason for either action is to adjust the price of the stock to one that the management of the corporation believes is more appropriate. Brokers' commissions tend to be lower on 100-share lots. If the stock price is high, this may discourage investors from buying it. If it is too low, it may appear to be less than a sound investment.

If the articles of incorporation have not previously authorized a share split, it cannot be made until they are amended to permit it. Therefore, there must be a favorable vote of shareholders. Only the vote of the directors is necessary for a stock dividend unless additional shares must be authorized. An amendment of the articles of incorporation is required to increase the number of authorized shares.

LOHNES V. LEVEL 3 COMMUNICATIONS
2001 U.S. App. LEXIS 25447 (1st Cir. 2001)

FACTS

In February 1998, Paul Lohnes, as part of the consideration for a lease he extended, was issued a stock warrant to purchase 8,541 share of Level 3 Communications's common stock. Both the exercise price and the expiration date were formalized in the warrant document. The warrant also contained a two-paragraph antidilution provision, which, upon the occurrence of certain described events, automatically adjusted the number of shares to which Lohnes would be entitled upon exercise of the warrant. In all, share adjustments were engendered by five separate contingencies: capital reorganization, reclassification of common stock, merger, consolidation, and sale of all (or substantially all) capital stock or assets. However, the warrant did not explicitly provide for an adjustment of shares in the event of a stock split. On July 14, 1998, Level 3's board of directors authorized a

(continued)

LOHNES V. LEVEL 3 COMMUNICATIONS
(concluded)

two-for-one stock split to be effectuated in the form of a stock dividend granting common shareholders one new share of stock for each share held. The board set the record date as July 30, 1998. On July 20, Level 3 issued a press release announcing the stock split, but it did not provide Lohnes with any personalized notice. The split then occurred as scheduled. Despite the sharp reduction in the share price that accompanied the stock split, Lohnes paid no heed until approximately three months after the record date. When he then discovered what had transpired, Lohnes attempted to purchase 17,082 shares (twice the number of shares specified in the warrant). Lohnes argued that he was entitled to the additional shares based on the warrant's antidilution provision because he believed the stock split could be equated with a capital reorganization and/or a reclassification. However, Level 3 refused to sell that number, arguing that the warrant did not provide for any share adjustment based upon the occurrence of a stock split effected as a stock dividend. Dissatisfied with this response, Lohnes then exercised the warrant and received 8,541 shares of Level 3's common stock and sued Level 3, alleging breach of both the warrant and the implied duty of good faith.

ISSUE

Should Lohnes be permitted to purchase the additional shares of Level 3's common stock?

DECISION

No. A stock warrant is an instrument that grants the warrantholder an option to purchase shares of stock at a fixed price. In this case, Lohnes has forwarded the premise that either "capital reorganization" or "reclassification of stock" encompasses a stock split. Thus, in his mind, Level 3's stock split activated the share adjustment mechanism set forth in the stock warrant. However, the meaning of the term "capital reorganization" belies Lohne's ambitious definition. A "reorganization" is a general term describing corporate amalgamations or readjustments occurring, for example, when one corporation acquires another in a merger or acquisition, a single corporation divides into two or more entities, or a corporation makes a substantial change in its capital structure. The first two prongs of this definition clearly do not apply here. That leaves only the question of whether a stock

split entails a "substantial change in a corporation's capital structure." It does not. First and foremost, the accounting mechanics that accompany a stock split are mere window dressing. To be sure, a stock split effected through the distribution of shares in the form of a stock dividend results in an increase in the common stock at par account and an offsetting decrease in additional paid-in capital, but this subtle set of entries has no effect on total shareholder equity or on any other substantive aspect of the balance sheet. Because a stock split does not entail a substantial change in a corporation's capital structure, the unelaborated term "capital reorganization" cannot plausibly include a stock split effected as a stock dividend. Further, a stock split is not a "reclassification of stock." The essence of a "reclassification of stock" is the modification of existing shares into something fundamentally different. Stock splits, effected as stock dividends, do not entail any such fundamental alteration of the character of an existing security. For example, Level 3's stock split in no way altered its shareholders' proportionate ownership interest, varied the class of securities held, or revised any of the attributes associated with the stock. What is more, the stock split did not have a meaningful impact on either the corporation's balance sheet or capital structure. For those reasons, there is no principled basis on which to stretch the definition of "reclassification of stock" to encompass a stock split. The court also rejects Lohnes's claim that Level 3 breached an implied duty of good faith by failing to provide him with personalized, advance warning of the stock split and by failing to advise him specifically about the adverse impact the stock split would have on the warrant if he did not exercise it before the record date. The most prominent flaw in this argument is that Lohnes misperceives the fruits of the bargain that he struck. After all, a warrantholder does not become a shareholder unless and until he exercises his purchase option. Consequently, a warrantholder's right to insist that the corporation maintain the integrity of the shares described in the warrant, if it exists at all, must be found in the text of the warrant itself. An examination of the warrant reveals quite clearly that Level 3 was not contractually bound to provide Lohnes with individualized notice of the stock split.

TABLE 27–1   Dividends on Preferred Stock

Noncumulative	Has preference to dividends actually paid in year earned
Cumulative	Receives omitted dividends from previous years before others are paid
Cumulative to the extent earned	Has right to all dividends, not declared but previously earned, before others are paid
Participating	Receives usual preference plus right to share income left after common shares paid normal dividend

DIVIDENDS ON PREFERRED STOCK

The contract with preferred shareholders usually gives them a preference in dividends over common shareholders. This preference means that common shareholders cannot receive any dividends until preferred shareholders have been fully paid. Dividends on **cumulative preferred** stock, if not paid in any year, will be payable later when funds are available. Dividends on **noncumulative preferred** stock need not be paid later if they are not earned and paid in the year due. Sometimes, **participating preferred** stock is issued. Holders of such stock get their usual dividend. Then, after the common shareholders receive a prescribed "normal" dividend, the preferred shareholders participate with the common shareholders in income available for dividends. Of course, if there are no funds available for dividends, none will be paid to either class. If the preference is **cumulative to the extent earned,** the preferred shareholder has a right, before common shareholders receive any dividends, to be paid all dividends that were not declared when earned in prior fiscal years. (See Table 27–1.)

EFFECT OF DIVIDEND DECLARATION

Once the directors have voted to pay a lawful dividend, it becomes a debt of the corporation. It may treat as the shareholder the persons registered as such on its records; therefore, directors usually set a record date. If a sale of the stock is made on a stock exchange, the purchaser is entitled to the dividend unless the sale occurs on or after the *ex dividend date,* which is two business days before the record date for the dividend.

SHAREHOLDER RIGHTS IN EXTRAORDINARY CORPORATE TRANSACTIONS

AMENDMENT OF ARTICLES

Any amendment to the articles of incorporation must be approved by the shareholders. The MBCA requires approval by a majority of the shares entitled to vote but permits the articles of incorporation to impose a higher requirement. If the amendment would affect the rights of a class of shares, then shareholders of that class have a right to vote as a class even though those shareholders normally have no vote. For example, if the proposal is to eliminate a provision for cumulative dividends on a class of preferred stock, a majority of the shares of that class must approve.

OTHER EXTRAORDINARY TRANSACTIONS

Under the MBCA, approval of all classes of shares is required for a merger or consolidation. A *merger* occurs when one corporation is absorbed into another existing corporation. A *consolidation* occurs when two or more corporations become part of a new corporation. A sale of most of the corporation's assets or a voluntary dissolution of the corporation also requires the favorable vote of the shareholders.

APPRAISAL RIGHTS

The statutes in many states give appraisal rights to shareholders who vote against certain transactions. Suppose you vote against a proposal to merge your corporation with another but the majority supports the merger. If you have an appraisal right, you may demand that the corporation pay you the fair value of your shares.

Actions Covered

Under the MBCA, the **right of appraisal** applies in cases of mergers or a sale of most of the corporate assets. It would also apply to amendments to the articles of incorporation that would materially affect liquidation, dividend, redemption, preemptive, or voting rights. Some state statutes permit an appraisal right when there is a consolidation.

Procedures

The MBCA as well as most state statutes limit the right of appraisal to shareholders who have a right to vote. Further, shareholders can exercise the right only if they did not vote in favor of the transaction triggering the right of appraisal. (Some state laws require that they have actually voted against the action.) Next, most statutes insist that the dissenting shareholders notify the corporation of their intent to exercise the right before the actual vote has taken place. If these steps are met, the corporation will instruct them where they may demand payment. Finally, they must actually demand payment. If the shareholders and the corporation cannot agree on the value of the shares, they may ask a court to determine ("appraise") their value.

Exclusions

Most state statutes deny the right of appraisal to shares that are traded on a recognized securities exchange. This exclusion is grounded on the belief that the securities market is the best determinant of the value of the shares. No such exclusions are recommended by the MBCA.

CEDE & COMPANY V. CINERAMA
684 A.2d 289 (Del. Sup. Ct. 1996)

FACTS

Technicolor, Inc., engaged in a number of businesses including videocassette duplicating, photographic film processing for professionals, and motion picture licensing. In 1981, the corporation's board of directors approved a plan to develop a nationwide network of one-hour consumer film processing stores. However, this new

(continued)

CEDE & COMPANY v. CINERAMA
(concluded)

venture fell behind schedule and Technicolor reported an 80 percent decline in net income. In the summer of 1982, MacAndrews & Forbes Group (MAF) and Technicolor agreed that MAF would acquire Technicolor in a two-step acquisition. The first step was an all-cash tender offer of $23 per share for all of Technicolor's outstanding shares. If not all of Technicolor's shareholders tendered their shares to MAF, the second step was a merger of MAF and Technicolor, by which all remaining Technicolor shareholders would receive $23 per share and Technicolor would merge with MAF. By December 3, 1982, MAF had acquired 82 percent of Technicolor's shares under the first step of the acquisition. Immediately, as controlling shareholder, MAF began looking for buyers for Technicolor's less profitable divisions, including the one-hour consumer film processing business. On January 24, 1983, Technicolor's shareholders approved the second step. Cinerama, a Technicolor shareholder, dissented from the merger and sought to have the court appraise its shares under its statutory dissenters' rights. Cinerama argued that the court should value Technicolor with regard to the strategies that had been conceived and implemented by MAF as of the merger date. Technicolor argued that the court should consider the value of the shares only as Technicolor existed prior to the discussion of the two-step acquisition (with the unprofitable consumer film processing division).

ISSUE

Should the appraisal of the Technicolor shares include the value added by the merger plan?

DECISION

Yes. The underlying assumption in an appraisal valuation is that the dissenting shareholders would be willing to maintain their investment position had the merger not occurred. Accordingly, the court's task in an appraisal proceeding is to value what had been taken from the shareholder—the proportionate interest in the going concern. To that end, the corporation must be valued as an operating entity. In a two-step merger, to the extent that value has been added following a change in majority control before cash-out, it is still value attributable to the going concern on the date of the merger. Consequently, value added to the going concern by the majority acquirer during the transient period of a two-step merger accrues to the benefit of all shareholders and must be included in the appraisal process on the date of the merger. By failing to accord Cinerama full proportionate value of its shares in the going concern on the date of the merger, the court would be imposing a penalty on Cinerama for lack of control. Consequently, MAF would reap a windfall profit from the appraisal process by cashing out a dissenting shareholder for less than the fair value of its interest in Technicolor as a going concern on the date of the merger.

LAWSUITS BY SHAREHOLDERS

INDIVIDUAL ACTIONS

Shareholders may sue the corporation for a breach of their shareholder contract, the basis for the relationship between the corporation and the shareholder. The contract is a product of the corporate articles and bylaws and any board of directors resolution applicable to the particular stock issue, as well as the corporation statute. It is not a document signed by the shareholder and the corporation. Suppose you are a shareholder and other shareholders of the same class are paid a dividend but you are not. You as an individual could sue the corporation to get the same dividend on your shares because you have not received a benefit to which you are entitled as a shareholder.

CLASS ACTIONS

When a number of people have a right or claim against the same defendant growing out of essentially the same set of facts, a class action may be brought by any one of them. For example, if the corporation did not pay a preferred dividend that was due, you could bring a suit demanding that the dividend be paid. If you win, the corporation would have to pay the dividend to all of the preferred shareholders of the class. You would then be able to recover from the corporation your expenses in bringing suit. If you lose, there would be no reimbursement.

DERIVATIVE ACTIONS

Shareholders are not usually able to sue to enforce a right of the corporation. Suppose an officer of the corporation has breached his duty by setting up a business to compete with the corporation and has made $1 million at the expense of the corporation. A shareholder could not sue him to recover the proportionate share of that loss. This is so because the corporation is a legal entity separate from the shareholders.

However, under certain conditions, a shareholder is permitted to sue as a representative of the corporation. There are two basic requirements: first, the shareholder must have owned shares at the time of the wrong; second, the shareholder must urge the directors and, if appropriate, the other shareholders to direct that such a suit be brought by the corporation. A shareholder is permitted to bring suit only if the directors refuse or have a conflict of interest that is likely to keep them from suing. If the shareholder wins, the damages normally go to the corporation, not to the shareholder directly. However, as in the case of a successful class action, the shareholder will be reimbursed for her expenses in bringing the suit.

In 1997, the Pennsylvania supreme court made it more difficult for shareholders to bring derivative suits in that state. The decision, which appears below, follows a series of recommendations issued by the American Law Institute on how corporations should handle derivative suits. Note, however, that the Pennsylvania decision is at variance with the rules in most other states where shareholders may more liberally bring derivative suits on behalf of their corporations. Consider the reasoning of the Pennsylvania court.

CUKER V. MIKALAUSKAS
692 A.2d 1042 (Penn. Sup. Ct. 1997)

FACTS

PECO Energy Company is a publicly regulated utility incorporated in Pennsylvania which sells gas to residential, commercial, and industrial customers. It is required to conform to public utility commission regulations which govern the provision of service to residential customers, including opening, billing, and terminating accounts. A 1991 audit prepared for the public utility commission recommended changes in 22 areas, including criticisms and recommendations regarding PECO's credit and col-

lection function. Minority shareholders thereafter alleged wrongdoing by some PECO directors and officers, asserting that they had damaged the corporation by mismanaging the credit and collection function, particularly as to the collection of overdue accounts. The shareholders demanded that PECO authorize litigation against the wrongdoers to recover monetary damages sustained by the corporation. The board of directors responded by creating a special litigation committee to

(continued)

CUKER V. MIKALAUSKAS
(concluded)

investigate the allegations. Only the 12 nondefendant members of the PECO board acted to create the special committee. The committee was aided in its investigation by a law firm and the corporation's regular outside auditor. The report of the special committee concluded there was no evidence of bad faith, self-dealing, concealment, or other breaches of the duty of loyalty by any of the defendant officers. It also concluded that the defendant officers exercised sound business judgment in managing the affairs of the corporation. The report concluded that proceeding with a derivative suit would not be in the best interests of PECO. When it received the report of the special litigation committee, the board debated the recommendations at two meetings. The 12 nondefendant directors then voted unanimously to reject the demand that the corporation bring litigation against the defendant directors and officers. The minority shareholders then filed a derivative lawsuit on behalf of the corporation. The corporation argued that the business judgment rule permits the board of directors to terminate the derivative lawsuit brought by the minority shareholders.

ISSUE

Does the business judgment rule permit the board of directors to terminate the derivative lawsuit?

DECISION

Yes. The business judgment rule insulates an officer or director of a corporation from liability for a business decision made in good faith if he is not interested in the subject of the business judgment, is informed with respect to the subject of the business judgment to the extent he reasonably believes it to be appropriate under the circumstances, and rationally believes that the business judgment is in the best interests of the corporation.

The business judgment rule encourages competent individuals to become directors by insulating them from liability for errors in judgment. It also recognizes that business decisions frequently entail some degree of risk and consequently provides directors broad discretion in setting policies without judicial or shareholder second-guessing. Finally, the doctrine prevents courts from becoming enmeshed in complex corporate decision making, a task they are ill-equipped to perform. Decisions regarding litigation by or on behalf of a corporation, including shareholder derivative actions, are business decisions as much as any other financial decisions. As such, they are within the province of the board of directors. Such business decisions of a board of directors are, unless taken in violation of a common law or statutory duty, within the scope of the business judgment rule. Assuming that an independent board of directors may terminate shareholder derivative actions, what is needed is a procedural mechanism for implementation and judicial review of the board's decision. Without considering the merits of the action, a court should determine the validity of the board's decision to terminate the litigation; if that decision was made in accordance with appropriate standards, then the court should dismiss the derivative action prior to litigation on the merits. Factors bearing on the board's decision will include whether the board or its special litigation committee was disinterested, whether it prepared a written report, whether it was independent, whether it conducted an adequate investigation, and whether it rationally believed its decision was in the best interests of the corporation. If all of these criteria are satisfied, the business judgment rule applies and the court should dismiss the derivative suit.

SHAREHOLDER LIABILITY

LIABILITY ON SHARES

If a person buys stock that was fully paid for when issued, he normally has no further liability to the corporation or its creditors. The same is true of subsequent buyers of the stock regardless of the price paid. However, a shareholder who did not pay the full subscription price for newly issued shares is liable for the balance due. This would include "watered stock" situations where property exchanged for shares is overvalued.

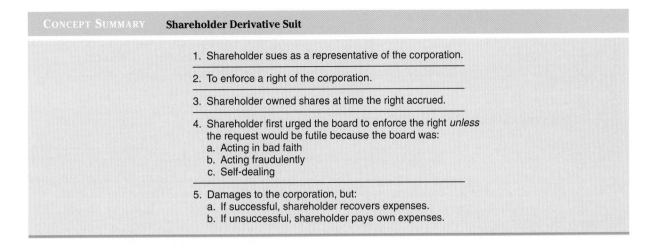

The shareholder is also liable if the consideration given for the shares is not lawful payment under the incorporation statute. Remember, most states follow the rule that permits property or services actually performed to be exchanged for stock but does not permit the exchange of a promissory note or the promise of future services. Those states adopting the revised MBCA do permit promissory notes and promises of future services as consideration for shares.

LIABILITY FOR ILLEGAL DIVIDENDS

A dividend that was paid illegally may be recovered from a shareholder who received it knowing it was illegal. If the corporation was insolvent at the time, the shareholder is liable even if he was unaware of the illegality.

TRANSFER AND REDEMPTION OF SHARES

RESTRICTIONS

A shareholder has a right to sell or give away her shares unless there is a valid restriction. Under SEC rules, selling may be restricted because the shares were part of a private offering. In close corporations, the original shareholders may not want to have to deal with strangers. An agreement by all of them to require any shareholder who desires to sell to give the corporation or the other shareholders a first right to purchase the shares would be upheld by courts. Notice of a restriction on the right of sale must be conspicuously placed on the stock certificate to be effective against a purchaser who is unaware of it.

TRANSFER PROCEDURE

To transfer the stock, the owner endorses the assignment form usually printed on the back of the stock certificate. An assignment may also be made by a separate document called a *stock power*. Banks usually use such assignment forms when stock is put up as collateral. If no transferee is named, the certificate and the shares it represents are transferable by mere delivery. Sending such a certificate through the mails would be risky.

DUTY TO RECORD

The corporation has a duty to record the transfer of its stock and its other registered securities. It is liable to the transferee if it fails to do so. Of course, this duty depends on the certificate being properly endorsed and without any valid restrictions.

.... *QUESTIONS AND PROBLEM CASES* ....

1. In order to prevent Edward Carey from taking over Pennsylvania Enterprises, the corporation's board of directors announced a proposal to widen the distribution of its shares. Because the proposal required shareholder approval, the board scheduled a special shareholder meeting for October 12 and announced that only shareholders of record on September 2 would be permitted to vote. At the special meeting the board's proposal passed by a margin of almost 24,000 votes. However, 79,000 of the shares voted in support of the proposal were recorded in the names of Loriot and Cede, but were voted by other persons. The disputed shares belonged to corporate shareholders who were permitted to reinvest their cash dividends with Pennsylvania Enterprises for new shares. Instead of registering the new shares in the name of the individual shareholders, the corporation registered them to Loriot or Cede. However, under the reinvestment plan, the individual shareholders, not Loriot or Cede, were able to vote the shares. Carey sued to invalidate the election, claiming that only shareholders of record may vote at shareholder meetings. The corporation argued that, as beneficial owners, the individual shareholders should be permitted to vote the shares. Should the election be invalidated?

2. Morely Brothers Corporation ran into financial difficulties and, rather than declare bankruptcy, it negotiated a takeover by S & T Industries, Inc. The agreement, which was approved by a majority of the shareholders, provided for the purchase by S & T of newly authorized and issued shares. The effect of this was to diminish the ownership of all other holders of Morely Brothers stock from 100 percent to 19.9 percent. Thomas Clark and other minority shareholders who owned 9.1 percent of the stock before the transaction occurred voted against the agreement and demanded a right of appraisal. They claimed that because Morely Brothers stock was not publicly traded, there was no ready market for their shares. Assuming that the shareholders followed the proper procedures, should the right of appraisal be granted?

3. Kamen was a shareholder of Cash Equivalent Fund, Inc. (Fund), a mutual fund whose investment adviser was Kemper Financial Services. Kamen brought a shareholders' derivative action on behalf of Fund against Kemper, claiming that Kemper had obtained shareholder approval of the investment-adviser contract by causing Fund to issue a materially misleading proxy statement. Kamen stated that she had made no presuit demand on Fund's board of directors because doing so would have been futile. In support of this allegation, Kamen stated that all of the directors were under the control of Kemper and that the board had voted unanimously to approve the misleading proxy statement. The lower court dismissed Kamen's suit by adopting a federal common law "universal demand" rule that prevents derivative suits unless the shareholder first makes a presuit demand on the corporate board of directors. Kamen appealed to the U.S. Supreme Court, arguing that a futility exception should excuse presuit demands if permitted by state law. May states offer futility exceptions for shareholders who fail to make presuit demands on the board of directors before bringing derivative suits?

4. *Video Case.* See "The Stock Option." An employee of FAMCO purchases common shares of FAMCO through its fringe benefit plan. Transfer of the shares purchased under the plan is restricted in two ways. First, when employment terminates for any reason, FAMCO has an option to purchase the shares at book value. Second, if an employee attempts to sell the shares while employed, FAMCO has a right of first refusal to purchase the shares at the sale

CHAPTER 28

Securities Regulation

Robert Willis was a psychiatrist. During a therapy session, one of his patients explained that she was upset because her husband, the chief executive officer of Shearson Leob Rhodes, was seeking to become BankAmerica's chief executive officer. Based on this information, Willis bought BankAmerica stock and made a profit of $27,475. As a result, Dr. Willis was charged with securities fraud for trading on inside information.[1]

- *What is a security?*
- *What liabilities do the federal securities acts impose on those who deal in securities?*
- *What is insider trading? What limits are placed on those who obtain inside information?*

---

[1]"Insider Trading Rule Extends to Therapy," *The Wall Street Journal*, May 17, 1990, p. B10.

.... *INTRODUCTION* ....

The federal securities laws have two purposes. First, they provide investors with more information to help them make buying and selling decisions. Second, they prohibit some of the unfair, deceptive, and manipulative practices that caused substantial losses to the less informed and less powerful investors during the stock market debacle at the end of the 1920s.

OVERVIEW OF THE FEDERAL LEGISLATION

THE SECURITIES ACT OF 1933

The Securities Act of 1933 (1933 Act) is concerned primarily with **public distributions** of securities. It regulates the sale of securities while they are passing from the hands of the issuer into the hands of the public investors. Issuers selling securities publicly must make necessary disclosures at the time the issuer sells the securities to the public. The 1933 Act is chiefly a **one-time disclosure** statute, although some of its liability provisions purport to cover all fraudulent sales of securities.

Securities Exchange Act of 1934

By contrast, the mandatory disclosure provision of the Securities Exchange Act of 1934 (1934 Act) require **periodic disclosures** from issuers of securities. An *issuer with publicly traded equity securities* must report annually and quarterly to its shareholders. Any other material information about the issuer must be disclosed as it is obtained by the issuer, unless the issuer has a valid business purpose for withholding disclosure.

Securities and Exchange Commission

The Securities and Exchange Commission (SEC) was created by the 1934 Act. Its responsibility is to administer the 1933 and 1934 Acts and five other securities statutes. Like other federal administrative agencies, the SEC has legislative, executive, and judicial functions. Its legislative branch promulgates rules and regulations, its executive branch brings enforcement actions against alleged violators of the statutes and their rules and regulations, and its judicial branch decides whether a person has violated the securities statutes.

What Is a Security?

If a transaction involves no security, the securities regulations do not apply. Thus, it is important to understand the precise definition of a **security.** The 1933 Act broadly defines the term *security* as:

> any note, stock, . . . bond, debenture, evidence of indebtedness, certificate of interest of participation in any profit-sharing agreement, . . . preorganization certificate or subscription, . . . investment contract, voting trust certificate, . . . fractional undivided interest in oil, gas, or mineral rights, . . . or, in general, any interest or instrument commonly known as a "security."

The 1934 Act definition is similar except that it excludes notes and drafts that mature not more than nine months from the date of issuance. Many state statutes are equally broad in their interpretation of what constitutes a security.

Disclosure: 1933 Act versus 1934 Act

1933 Act	1934 Act
One-time disclosure	Periodic disclosure
Occurs when new securities are issued	Occurs throughout the life of the securities
• File registration statement with SEC • Make prospectus available to buyers	• File 10-K annually • File 10-Q quarterly • File 8-K monthly* *(when special events occur)

Investment Contracts

Sales of limited partnerships, Scotch whisky receipts, live animals with contracts to care for them, restaurant properties and citrus groves with management contracts, and franchises have all been held to be securities. They are all examples of an **investment contract,** a device that is specifically included in the definition of a security. The term *investment contract* is broadly defined by the courts as an *investment of money* in a *common enterprise* with an *expectation of profits from the efforts of others*. The fact that there is no certificate or that what is being offered for sale is labeled tangible property is immaterial.

SEC v. SG LTD.
265 F.3d 42 (1st Cir. 2001)

FACTS

SG Ltd. And its affiliate SG Trading Ltd. operated a "StockGeneration" website offering online users the opportunity to purchase shares of 11 different "virtual companies" listed on the website's "virtual stock exchange." SG arbitrarily set the purchase and sale prices of each of these imaginary companies in biweekly "rounds" and guaranteed that investors could buy or sell any amount of shares at posted prices. SG placed no upper limit on the amount of funds that an investor could squirrel away in its virtual offerings. SG advised potential purchasers to pay particular attention to shares in a "privileged company" and boasted that investing in those shares was a "game without any risk." To this end, its website announced that the privileged company's shares would unfailingly appreciate, boldly proclaiming that the share price of the privileged company is supported by the owners of SG and, for that reason, its value constantly rises on average at a rate of 10 percent monthly. To add

plausibility to this representation and to allay anxiety about future pricing, SG published prices of the privileged company's shares on month in advance. While SG conceded that a decline in the share price was theoretically possible, it assured prospective participants that under the rules governing the fall in prices, the share price for the privileged company could not fall by more than 5 percent in a round. To bolster this claim, it vouchsafed that shares in the privileged company were supported by several distinct revenue streams. According to SG's representations, capital inflow from new participants provided liquidity for existing participants who might choose to sell their virtual shareholdings. As a backstop, SG pledged to allocate an indeterminate portion of the profits derived from its website operations to a special reserve fund designed to maintain the price of the privileged company's shares. At least 800 U.S participants, paying real cash, purchased virtual shares in the

(continued)

SEC V. SG Ltd.
(continued)

virtual companies listed on SG's virtual stock exchange. In the fall of 1999, more than $4.7 million in participants' funds was deposited in an SG Trading Ltd. Bank account. The following spring, more than $2.7 million was deposited in accounts held by SG Trading and SG Ltd. In late 1999, participants began to experience difficulties in redeeming their virtual shares. These difficulties crested on March 20, 2000, when SG unilaterally suspended all pending requests to withdraw funds. Two weeks later, SG announced a reverse stock split, which caused the share prices of all companies listed on the virtual stock exchange, including the privileged company, to plummet to 1/10,000 of their previous values. At the same time, SG stopped responding to participant requests for a return of funds yet continued to solicit new participants through its website. Ultimately, the SEC undertook an investigation of SG's activities, which culminated in filing a civil action alleging that SG's operations constituted a fraudulent scheme in violation of the registration and antifraud provision of the federal securities laws. SG argued that the securities rules did not apply to its operations because its virtual shares were not securities because they were a clearly marked and defined game lacking a business context. Accordingly, SG moved to have the claim dismissed.

Issue

Should the claim against SG be dismissed because the virtual shares were games, not securities.

Decision

No. Congress intended the definition of a security under the federal securities statutes to encompass a wide array of financial instruments, ranging from well-established investment vehicles (e.g., stocks and bonds) to much more arcane arrangements. Included in this array is the elusive concept of an investment contract. Judicial efforts to delineate what is—and what is not—an investment contract are grounded in the seminal case of *SEC v. W.J. Howey Co*. The Howey court established a tripartite test to determine whether a particular financial instrument constitutes an investment contract (and, hence, a security). This test has proven durable. Under it, an investment contract comprises (1) the investment of money (2) in a common enterprise (3) with the expectation of profits to be derived solely from the efforts of the

promoter or a third party. The Supreme Court has long espoused a broad construction of what constitutes an investment contract. Characterizing purchases of the privileged company's shares as a "clearly marked and defined game" does not resolve the issue. As long as the three-pronged *Howey* test is satisfied, the instrument must be classified as an investment contract. The first component of the *Howey* test focuses on the investment of money. The determining factor is whether an investor chose to give up a specific consideration in return for a separable financial interest with the characteristics of a security. The SEC has sufficiently alleged the existence of this factor since it is quite reasonable to assume that participants who invested money for virtual shares did so in anticipation of investment gains. The second component of the Howey test involves the existence of a common enterprise. Courts are in some disarray as to the legal rules associated with the ascertainment of a common enterprise. Many courts require a showing of horizontal commonality—a type of commonality that involves the pooling of assets from multiple investors so that all share in the profits and risks of the enterprise. Other courts have modeled the concept of common enterprise around fact patterns in which an investor's fortunes are tied to the promoter's success rather than to the fortunes of his or her fellow investors. This doctrine, known as *vertical commonality*, has two variants. Broad vertical commonality requires that the well-being of all investors be dependent upon the promoter's expertise. In contrast, narrow vertical commonality requires that the investor's fortunes be interwoven with and dependent upon the efforts and success of those seeking the investment of third parties. Thus far, neither the Supreme Court nor this court has authoritatively determined what type of commonality must be present to satisfy the common enterprise element. However, this case requires us to now take a position. We hold that a showing of horizontal commonality—the pooling of assets from multiple investors in such a manner that all share in the profits and risks of the enterprise—satisfies the common enterprise component of the *Howey* test. Adopting this rule aligns us with the majority view. Here, the pooling element of horizontal commonality jumps off the screen. SG unambiguously represented to its clientele that participants' funds

(continued)

SEC V. SG LTD.
(concluded)

were pooled in a single account used to settle participants' online transactions. Of course, horizontal commonality requires more than pooling alone; it also requires that investors share in the profits and risks of the enterprise. We conclude, without serious question, that SG's arrangement can fairly be characterized as a pyramid scheme that provides the requisite profit-and-risk sharing to support a finding of horizontal commonality. The final component of the *Howey* test—the expectation of profits solely from the efforts of others—is itself divisible. The Supreme Court has recognized an expectation of profits in two situations: (1) capital appreciation from the original investment and (2) participation in earnings resulting from the use of investors' funds. These situations are to be contrasted with transactions in which an individual purchases a commodity for personal use or consumption. SG's profit-related guarantees constitute a not-very-subtle form of economic inducement that played upon greed and fueled expectations of profit sufficient to meet the *Howey* test. However, the third step of

Howey is not met unless the expected profits can be said to result solely from the efforts of others. The courts of appeals have been unanimous in declining to give literal meaning to the word "solely" in this context, instead holding that the requirement is satisfied as long as the efforts made by those other than the investor are undeniably significant ones (those essential managerial efforts which affect the failure or success of the enterprise). SG was responsible for all the important efforts that undergirded the 10 percent guaranteed monthly return. As the sole proprietor of the StockGeneration website, SG enjoyed direct operational control over all aspects of the virtual stock exchange. This court need go no further. Giving due weight to the economic realities of the situation, the SEC has alleged a set of facts, which, if proven, support the three-part *Howey* test and support its assertion that the opportunity to invest in the privileged company constituted an invitation to enter into an investment contract within the reach of the federal securities laws.

THE SECURITIES ACT OF 1933

The 1933 Act has two principal regulatory components: (1) registration provisions and (2) antifraud provisions. The registration requirements of the 1933 Act are designed to give investors the information they need to make intelligent decisions about whether to purchase securities. The issuer of the securities is required to file a registration statement with the Securities and Exchange Commission and to make a prospectus available to prospective purchasers. The various antifraud provisions in the 1933 Act impose liability on sellers of securities for mistaking or omitting facts of material significance to investors.

REGISTRATION REQUIREMENTS OF THE 1933 ACT

The 1933 Act requires the issuer of securities to register the securities with the SEC prior to their offer or sale to the public. Historical and current data about the issuer and its business (including certified financial statements), full details about the securities to be offered, and the use of the proceeds of the issuance, among other information, must be included in a **registration statement** prepared by the issuer of the securities. The issuer must file the registration statement with the SEC.

The registration statement becomes effective after it has been reviewed by the SEC. The SEC review involves only the completeness of the registration statement and whether it contains **per se fraudulent** statements. Examples of **per se fraudulent** statements are those that tout the securities ("these are the best securities you can buy") and forecasts that are not reasonably based (a new company promising a 35 percent annual return on investment on its common stock).

FIGURE 28-1   Periods in the Life of a New Security

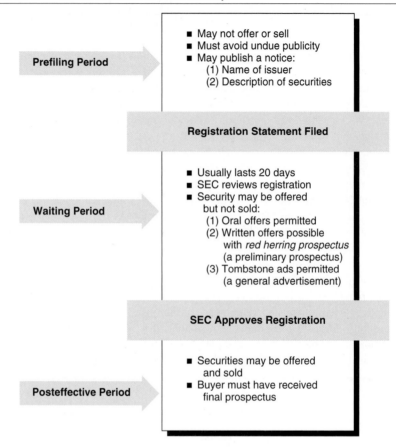

Prefiling Period
- May not offer or sell
- Must avoid undue publicity
- May publish a notice:
  (1) Name of issuer
  (2) Description of securities

Registration Statement Filed

Waiting Period
- Usually lasts 20 days
- SEC reviews registration
- Security may be offered but not sold:
  (1) Oral offers permitted
  (2) Written offers possible with *red herring prospectus* (a preliminary prospectus)
  (3) Tombstone ads permitted (a general advertisement)

SEC Approves Registration

Posteffective Period
- Securities may be offered and sold
- Buyer must have received final prospectus

Most of the information in the registration statement must be included in the **prospectus,** which is the basic selling document of a 1933 Act registered offering. It must be furnished to every purchaser of the registered security prior to or concurrently with the delivery of the security to the purchaser. The function of the prospectus is to allow an investor to make his investment decision based on all relevant data concerning the issuer, not merely the favorable information that the issuer would be inclined to disclose voluntarily.

The 1933 Act restricts the issuer's ability to communicate with prospective purchasers of the securities. It includes basic rules regarding the timing, manner, and content of offers and sales. (See Figure 28–1.)

Electronic Filing

During 1992, the SEC's new computerized system for corporate filings became operational. Known as **EDGAR,** the Electronic Data Gathering, Analysis, and Retrieval system permits corporations to download their SEC-required reports on their quarterly and annual finances and other matters directly into a government computer. While EDGAR does not save the SEC or corporate filers much money, it provides tremendous savings for the public because reports going into the SEC electronically now are retrievable electronically. This provides access within hours or minutes rather than days. The SEC's Internet homepage (www.sec.gov) provides access to the EDGAR database.

Exemptions from the Registration Requirements

Complying with the registration requirements of the 1933 Act is a burdensome and time-consuming process. It is also expensive. An issuer's first public offering may consume six months and cost in excess of $1 million. It is understandable why some issuers prefer to avoid registration when they sell securities. Fortunately for them, there are several exemptions from registration available for issuers. However, every student must learn the most important rule of the 1933 Act: *Every transaction in securities must be registered with the SEC or be exempt from registration.*

There are two types of exemptions from the registration requirements of the 1933 Act: securities exemptions and transaction exemptions. **Exempt securities** never need to be registered, regardless of who sells the securities, how they are sold, or to whom they are sold. Securities sold in **exempt transactions** are exempt from the registration requirements for those particular transactions only. Each transaction stands by itself. A security sale may be exempt today because it is sold pursuant to a transaction exemption, yet tomorrow it may have to be registered when the security is offered or sold again in a transaction for which there is no exemption.

Exempt Securities

Some securities are exempted from the registration provisions of the 1933 Act either because (1) the character of the issuer makes registration unnecessary, (2) the issuance of such securities is subject to regulation under another statutory scheme, or (3) the purchasers of the securities can adequately protect themselves. The following are the most important securities exemptions.

1. Government-issued or -guaranteed securities.
2. Short-term notes and drafts.
3. Securities of nonprofit issuers.
4. Financial institution securities.
5. ICC-regulated issuers.
6. Insurance policies and annuity contracts.

Although these securities are exempt from the registration provisions of the 1933 Act, they are *not* exempt from the antifraud provisions of the act. Therefore, any fraud committed in the course of selling these securities can be attacked by the SEC and by those persons who were defrauded.

Transaction Exemptions

The most important 1933 Act exemptions are the *transaction exemptions*. A security may be sold pursuant to a transaction exemption but only that sale, not subsequent sales, will be covered by the exemption. Future sales must be made pursuant to a registration or another exemption. As with the securities exemptions, the transaction exemptions are exemptions from the registration provisions only. The antifraud provisions of the 1933 Act apply equally to exempted and nonexempted transactions.

The most important transaction exemptions are those available for **issuers.** They are the private offering, the intrastate offering, and the small offerings. There also are several exemptions that allow **nonissuers**—average investors, usually—to offer and sell the securities they own, yet avoid the need to have the issuer register the securities. One provision exempts "transactions by any person other than an issuer, underwriter, or dealer." This exemption is used by most investors when they sell securities.

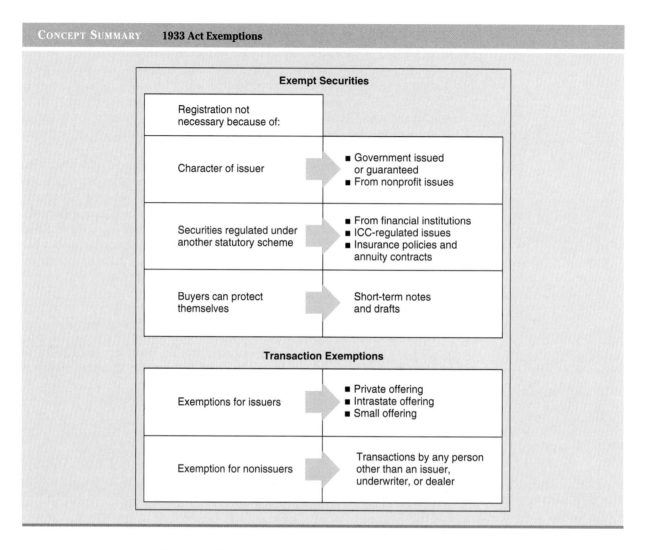

For example, if you buy General Motors Corporation common shares on the New York Stock Exchange, you may freely resell them without a registration. You are not an issuer (GM is); you are not an underwriter (because you are not helping GM distribute the shares to the public); and you are not a dealer (because you are not in the business of selling securities).

ANTIFRAUD PROVISIONS OF THE 1933 ACT

To accomplish its objective of preventing fraud and unfair, deceptive, or manipulative practices and providing remedies to the victims of such practices, Congress included a number of liability provisions in the Securities Act of 1933. Violations of the act may subject the defendant to both civil and criminal actions.

Liability for Improper Offers and Sales

Section 12(1) of the 1933 Act imposes liability on any person who has violated the timing, manner, and content restrictions on offers and sales of new issues. The purchaser's remedy is rescission or damages. These violations occur when a person offers or sells unregistered and nonexempt securities in violation of the 1933 Act.

FIGURE 28–2   Section 11 of the 1933 Act

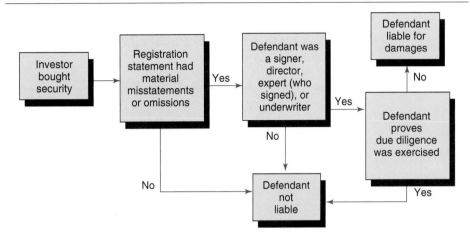

Liability for Defective Registration Statements

Section 11 of the 1933 Act provides civil liabilities for damages resulting to an investor who finds, after purchasing the security, that the registration statement for the security contained an untrue statement or omitted a material fact. Potentially liable for such misleading or false information in the registration statement are all of its signers, all directors (whether or not they signed), all "experts"who gave consent to be named in the registration statement as having prepared or certified part of it (such as auditors, lawyers, geologists, or engineers), and the underwriters of the distribution of the security. The purchasers remedy under Section 11 is for damages caused by the misstatement or omission.

Section 11 was a radical liability section when it was enacted and remains so today. It is radical for three reasons. First, reliance is not usually required. The purchaser need not show that she relied on the misstatement or omission in the registration statement. In fact, the purchaser need not have even read the registration statement or seen it. Second, privity is not required. A purchaser need not prove that she purchased the securities from the defendant. All she need prove is that the defendant is in one of three classes of persons liable under Section 11. Third, the purchaser need not prove that the defendant negligently or intentionally misstated or omitted a material fact. Instead, the defendant has the burden of proving that he exercised **due diligence.** (The only other defense available to a defendant is to prove that the purchaser knew of the misstatement or omission when she purchased the security.) (See Figure 28–2.)

Other Liability Provisions

Section 12(2) prohibits misstatements or omissions of material fact made in a prospectus or in an oral communication related to the prospectus or an initial offering (except government-issued or -guaranteed securities). Its reach is significant because mere *negligence*, rather than *scienter*, is enough to trigger liability under Section 12(2). (Scienter is the intent to deceive, manipulate, or defraud the purchaser.)

Section 12(2) has a *privity* requirement; this means that the purchaser may sue only those persons from whom she purchased the security. Further, she must show that she *relied* on the misstatement or omission and that she did not know of the untruth or omission. The defendant may escape liability by proving that he did not know and could not reasonably have known of the untruth or omission. The purchaser's remedy is rescission or damages, as it is under Section 12(1). Recoveries are available to purchasers of initial distributions, not to those trading in the secondary market.

GUSTAFSON V. ALLOYD COMPANY
115 S.Ct. 1061 (U.S. Sup. Ct. 1995)

FACTS

Gustafson, McLean, and Butler (collectively Gustafson) were in 1989 the sole shareholders of Alloyd, Inc., a manufacturer of plastic packaging and automatic heat-sealing equipment. Alloyd was formed, and its stock issued, in 1961. In 1989, Gustafson decided to sell Alloyd and engaged KPMG Peat Marwick to find a buyer. In response to information distributed by KPMG, Wind Point agreed to buy substantially all of the issued and outstanding stock of the corporation. In preparation for negotiating the contract with Gustafson, Wild Point undertook an extensive analysis of the company, relying in part on a formal business review prepared by KPMG. After the sale, the year-end audit of Alloyd revealed that Alloyd's actual earnings for 1989 were lower than the estimates relied upon by the parties. Wind Point claimed that the contract of sale was a prospectus, so that any misstatements contained in the agreement gave rise to liability under Section 12(2) of the 1933 Act. Wind Point sued under Section 12(2), seeking rescission of the contract.

ISSUE

Is the contract of sale a prospectus that creates Section 12(2) liability?

DECISION

No. As this case reaches us, we must assume the stock purchase agreement contained material misstatements of fact made by the sellers. On this assumption, the buyer would have the right to obtain a rescission if those misstatements were made "by means of a prospectus or oral communication (related to a prospectus)." The 1933 Act created federal duties—for the most part, registration and disclosure obligations—in connection with public offerings of securities. It does not extend to a private sales contract, such as this. When the 1933 Act was drawn and adopted, the term "prospectus" was well understood to refer to a document soliciting the public to acquire securities from the issuer. It is understandable that Congress would provide buyers with a right to rescind, without proof of fraud or reliance, as to misstatements contained in a document prepared with care, following well-established procedures relating to investigations with due diligence and in the context of a public offering by an issuer or its controlling shareholders. It is not plausible to infer that Congress created this extensive liability for every casual communication between buyer and seller in the secondary market. In sum, the word "prospectus" is a term of art referring to a document that describes a public offering of securities by an issuer or controlling shareholder. This contract of sale, and its recitations, were not held out to the public and were not a prospectus as the term is used in the 1993 Act.

Section 17(a) broadly prohibits the use of any device or artifice to defraud and the use of any untrue or misleading statement in connection with the offer or sale of any security. Two of the subsections of Section 17(a) require that the defendant merely act negligently, while the third subsection requires proof of scienter. The Supreme Court has not decided whether a buyer has a private right of action for damages under Section 17(a), and the courts of appeals are split on the issue.

.... **SECURITIES EXCHANGE ACT OF 1934** ....

The Securities Exchange Act of 1934 is chiefly concerned with disclosing material information to investors. Unlike the 1933 Act, which is primarily a one-time disclosure statute, the 1934 Act requires *periodic disclosure* by issuers with publicly held equity securities. In addition, the 1934 Act regulates insiders' transactions in securities, proxy solicitations, tender offers, brokers and dealers, and securities exchanges. Finally, the 1934 Act has several sections prohibiting fraud and manipulation in securities transactions.

REGISTRATION OF SECURITIES UNDER THE 1934 ACT

Two types of securities must be registered under the 1934 Act. First, an issuer must register a class of equity securities with at least 500 shareholders if the issuers' total assets exceed $3 million. The securities must be traded in interstate commerce. Second, an issuer must register any security traded on a national security exchange, such as common shares traded on the American Stock Exchange. The information required in the 1934 Act registration statement is similar to that required under the 1933 Act.

PERIODIC REPORTS

To maintain a steady flow of material information to investors, the 1934 Act requires that those issuers required to register under the 1934 Act, as well as any issuer who has made a registered offering under the 1933 Act, file periodic reports with the SEC. These issuers must regularly file several types of reports; however, the most important are the annual and quarterly reports.

The 10-K annual report must include audited financial statements for the fiscal year plus current information about the conduct of the business, its management, and the status of its securities. In effect, the 10-K report is intended to update the information required in the 1934 registration statement.

The quarterly report, the 10-Q, requires only a summarized, unaudited operating statement and unaudited figures on capitalization and shareholders' equity. An 8-K monthly report is required within 15 days of the end of any month in which any specified event occurs, such as a change in the amount of securities, a default under the terms of an issue of securities, acquisition or disposition of assets, a change in control of the corporation, or any materially important event.

GALLAGHER V. ABBOTT LABORATORIES
269 F. 3d 806 (7th Cir. 2001)

FACTS

For many years the FDA inspected the Diagnostic Division of Abbott Laboratories and found deficiencies in manufacturing quality control. Despite numerous warnings, Abbott never made sufficient changes to satisfy the FDA's concerns. On March 17, 1999, the FDA sent Abbott another letter demanding compliance with all regulatory requirements and threatening severe consequences. Despite publication of this warning in the financial periodicals, Abbott's stock prices remained firm. By September 1999, the FDA began insisting on substantial penalties plus changes in Abbott's methods of doing business. On September 29, 1999, after the markets had closed, Abbott issued a press release describing the FDA's

position, asserting that Abbott was in substantial compliance with federal regulations and revealing that the parties were engaged in settlement talks. Abbott's stock fell more than 6 percent the next business day. On November 2, 1999, Abbott and the FDA resolved their differences, and a court entered a consent decree requiring Abbott to remove 125 diagnostic products from the market until it improves its quality control and to pay a $100 million civil fine. The next business day Abbott's stock slumped, which together with the earlier drop implied that shareholders saw the episode as costing Abbott (in cash plus future compliance costs and lost sales) more than $5 billion. Lena Gallagher, representing a class of

(continued)

GALLAGHER V. ABBOTT LABORATORIES
(concluded)

Abbott shareholders, contended that Abbott committed fraud by deferring public revelation of the problems with the FDA.

ISSUE

Did Abbott have a duty to disclose all information relating to the FDA investigation as soon as it was available to the corporation?

DECISION

No. Gallagher's argument supposes that firms have an absolute duty to disclose all information material to stock prices as news comes into their possession. Yet that is not the way the securities laws work. We do not have a system of continuous disclosure. Instead firms are entitled to keep silent (about good news as well as bad) unless positive law creates a duty to disclose. The 1933 Act requires firms to reveal information only when they issue securities. The 1934 Act adds that the SEC may require issuers to file annual and other periodic reports—with the emphasis on *periodic* rather than continuous. Regulations do require comprehensive annual filing, the Form 10-K, and less extensive quarterly supplements on Form 10-Q. The supplements need not bring up to date everything contained in the annual 10-K report and nothing in Regulation S-K (the SEC's list of required disclosure) requires disclosure in a supplemental report of information about a corporation's regulatory problems. Updating documents has its place in securities law. A registration statement and a prospectus for a new issue of securities must be accurate when they are used to sell stock, not just when they are filed. Material changes in a company's position thus must be reflected in a registration statement promptly. But this does not imply changes in a 10-K annual report, even when that report is used as the principal disclosure document.

SHORT-SWING TRADING BY INSIDERS

The 1934 Act requires that insiders individually file a statement disclosing their holdings of any class of equity securities of the issuer. An **insider** is an officer of a corporation with equity securities registered under the act; a director of such a corporation; or an owner of 10 percent or more of a class of equity securities registered under the 1934 Act. In addition, these insiders must report any transaction in such securities within 10 days following the end of the month in which the transaction occurs. Purchases and sales made six months before and six months after one becomes an officer, director, or 10 percent holder must also be reported.

Under the 1934 Act, any profit made by an insider is recoverable by the issuer if the profit resulted from the purchase and sale (or the sale and purchase) within less than a six-month period of any class of the issuer's equity securities. This regulation of **short-swing profits** is designed to stop speculative insider trading on the basis of information that "may have been obtained by such owner, director, or officer by reason of his relationship to the issuer." The application of the provision is without regard to intent or actual use of insider information.

REGULATION OF PROXY SOLICITATIONS

As was discussed in Chapter 27, shareholders of public corporations rarely attend shareholder meetings. As a result, the only way many shareholders can vote at these meetings is by proxy, through which the shareholders direct other persons to vote their shares. Just as investors need information to be able to make intelligent investment decisions, so too do shareholders need information to determine whether to give a proxy to another person and how to direct that person to vote. Accordingly,

SEC rules require that any person soliciting proxies from holders of securities registered under the 1934 Act furnish each shareholder with a proxy statement containing certain information. Usually the only party soliciting proxies is the corporation's management, which is seeking proxies in order to reelect itself to the board of directors.

If the management of the corporation does not solicit proxies, it must nevertheless inform the shareholders of material information affecting matters to be put to a vote of shareholders. This information statement, which contains about the same information as a proxy statement, must be sent to all shareholders entitled to vote at the meeting.

.... LIABILITY PROVISIONS OF THE 1934 ACT ....

Congress included several liability provisions in the 1934 Act. These provisions provide remedies to victims of fraudulent, deceptive, or manipulative practices.

MANIPULATION OF A SECURITY'S PRICE

Section 9 specifically prohibits a number of deceptive practices that may be used to cause security prices to rise or fall by fraudulently stimulating market activity. This violation may occur when a person simultaneously buys and sells the same stock in order to stimulate substantial trading activity and thereby affect the price of the security. This type of illegal practice is called a **wash sale.**

LIABILITY FOR FALSE STATEMENTS IN FILED DOCUMENTS

Section 18 is the 1934 Act counterpart to Section 11 of the 1933 Act. Section 18 imposes liability on any person responsible for a false or misleading statement of material fact in any document filed with the SEC. (Filed documents include the 10-K, 10-Q, and proxy statements.) Any person who relies on a false or misleading statement may sue for damages. As with Section 11, the purchaser need not prove that the defendant was negligent or acted with scienter (bad motive). However, the defendant has a defense that he acted in good faith and had no knowledge that the statement was false or misleading. This defense is easier to meet than the Section 11 due diligence defense, requiring only that the defendant prove that he did not act with scienter. Partly for this reason, Section 18 is rarely used.

SECTION 10(b) AND RULE 10b-5

The most important liability section in the 1934 Act is Section 10(b). Section 10(b) is an extremely broad provision prohibiting the use of any manipulative or deceptive device in contravention of any rules the SEC may prescribe as "necessary or appropriate in the public interest or for the protection of investors." Rule 10b-5 was adopted by the SEC under Section 10(b). Securities need not be registered under the 1933 Act or the 1934 Act for Rule 10b-5 to apply. The rule applies to transactions executed on a securities exchange as well as face-to-face transactions.

The most important elements of a Rule 10b-5 violation are a misstatement or omission of material fact, scienter, and reliance. In addition, private persons suing under the rule must be purchasers or sellers. Finally, the wrongful action must be accomplished by the mails, an instrumentality of interstate commerce (use of a telephone within one state has been held to meet this requirement), or a national securities exchange.

Misstatement or Omission

The essence of fraud, deception, and manipulation is falsity or nondisclosure when there is a duty to speak. Rule 10b-5 imposes liability on persons who **misstate material facts.** For example, if a manager of an unprofitable business induces shareholders to sell their stock to him by representing that the business will fail, although he knows that the business has become potentially profitable, he violates Rule 10b-5.

In addition, a person is liable if he **omits material facts** when he has a duty to disclose. For a person to be liable for an omission, there must be duty of trust or confidence breached either by a nondisclosure or by the selective disclosure of confidential information. For example, a securities broker is liable to his customer for not disclosing that he owns the shares he recommends to the customer. As an agent of the customer, he owes a fiduciary duty to his customer to disclose his conflict of interest. In addition, a person is liable for omitting to tell all the material facts after he has chosen to disclose some of the facts. His selective disclosure created the duty to disclose all the material facts.

SAN LEANDRO EMERGENCY MEDICAL GROUP v. PHILIP MORRIS
Fs F.3d 801 (2nd Cir. 1996)

FACTS

In recent years, cigarette sales have been declining because of health concerns and changing demographics. The entry of discount brands into the marketplace has led to a further decline in the sales of premium brands such as Philip Morris's Marlboro line. Historically, in order to sustain or increase its profit levels, Philip Morris has responded to decreasing demand for Marlboro by raising Marlboro's price and at the same time narrowing the price gap between its discount and premium brands in order to make the discount brands less attractive. Philip Morris engaged in this strategy through the first quarter of 1993 and implemented price increases on discount cigarettes during that period. However, retailers foiled the company's strategy by deciding to absorb the price increases rather than pass them on to consumers, thus maintaining the large retail price gap between discount and premium brand cigarettes. At the end of the first quarter of 1993, in the face of declining sales volume and decreasing market share for Marlboro, Philip Morris adopted a new marketing strategy. Philip Morris announced that it would cut the price of Marlboro by $0.40 per pack, a move estimated to reduce its earnings by $2 billion in 1993. Following this announcement, Philip Morris stock dropped almost 25 percent. This prompted the filing of numerous lawsuits under Rule 10b-5, alleging that Philip Morris misrepresented or failed to disclose to the market that Marlboro sales were declining at such a rate that raising prices would not compensate for the loss of sales and that the company was actively considering a new and alternative strategy of cutting Marlboro prices at the expense of short-term profits.

ISSUE

Did Philip Morris violate Rule 10b-5 through the omission of a material fact?

DECISION

No. To state a cause of action under Section 10(b) and Rule 10b-5, the plaintiffs must plead that Philip Morris made a false statement or omitted a material fact, with scienter, and that plaintiffs' reliance on that action caused injury. Plaintiffs contend that prior to April 2, 1993, Philip Morris misstated and failed to disclose that it was planning a radical change in pricing strategy for Marlboro that would reduce the company's 1993 profits by $2 billion. Specifically, the plaintiffs argued that Philip Morris had made numerous statements that it would continue its historic strategy of raising the price of Marlboro in order to sustain profits. Further, the revised marketing plan in this case marked a sharp break from the company's historic practices and was important enough that a reasonable investor probably would want to know about it. However, we are concerned about interpreting the securities laws to force companies to give their competitors advance

(continued)

SAN LEANDRO EMERGENCY MEDICAL GROUP V. PHILIP MORRIS
(concluded)

notice of sensitive pricing information. Thus, absent a showing that Philip Morris's earlier public statements were materially misleading, the company had no duty to disclose its new marketing plan. During the first quarter of 1993, the company pursued its historic marketing strategy and there was no reason to believe its optimistic assessments of that course of action were unreasonable given the past success of that strategy.

Materiality

The misstated or omitted fact must be **material.** In essence, material information is any information that is likely to have an impact on the price of a security in the market. Such matters as proposed mergers, tender offers for the corporation's stock, plans to introduce an important new product, or indications of an abrupt change in the expectations of the company are examples of what would be considered material facts.

Scienter

For fraud, deception, or manipulation to exist, the defendant must have acted with **scienter.** Mere negligence is not enough under Rule 10b-5. **Scienter** is an intent to deceive, manipulate, or defraud. Recklessness ("the pretense of knowledge where knowledge there is none") may constitute scienter.

Purchaser or Seller

In order to seek damages under Rule 10b-5, the private plaintiff must be an actual *purchaser or seller* of securities. Thus, a person who was deterred from purchasing a security because of false statements cannot recover his lost profits because he was not an actual purchaser.

Reliance

Private plaintiffs using Rule 10b-5 must prove that they relied on the misstatement of material fact. However, **reliance** is not usually required in *omission* cases; the investor need merely prove that the omitted fact was material. The reliance element also might be met where material misrepresentations were available to the public. Under this *fraud-on-the-market* theory the investor's reliance on the integrity of the market was found to justify a presumption of reliance on the misrepresentation.

Statute of Limitations

For many years, fraud claims under Section 10(b) and Rule 10b-5 were governed by statutes of limitations established under the various state laws. (A statute of limitation establishes the period of time within which a lawsuit will be permitted to be brought.) The policy of borrowing from state law was quite controversial because of the multistate nature of most securities violations and the lack of uniformity from state to state. Accordingly, the U.S. Supreme Court established a uniform federal statute of limitations that requires that litigation be commenced within one year after discovery of the facts constituting the violation and no more than three years after the violation has occurred.

Conduct Covered by Rule 10b-5

Numerous activities are prohibited by Rule 10b-5. However, while one can easily see that actual fraud and price manipulation are covered by the rule, two other areas are less obvious: the corporation's continuous disclosure obligation and insider trading.

Continuous Disclosure of Material Information

The purpose of the securities acts is to ensure that investors have the information to make intelligent investment decisions at all times. The periodic reporting requirements of the 1934 Act are designed to accomplish this result. If important developments arise between the disclosure dates of reports, however, investors will not have all the information they need to make intelligent decisions unless the corporation discloses immediately the material information. Rule 10b-5 may be read to require a corporation to immediately and accurately disclose material information unless it has a valid business purpose for withholding disclosure.

Trading on Inside Information

Many interesting Rule 10b-5 cases involve the failure to disclose nonpublic, corporate information known to an insider. Some of these cases involve face-to-face transactions between an insider and another shareholder. For example, a corporation's president acquires at a low price all of the corporation's outstanding shares. His failure to tell the sellers about contracts that would increase the value of the shares violates Rule 10b-5. In other cases, the buyer and seller have not met face-to-face. Instead, the transaction has been executed on a stock exchange. The trading on an exchange by a person in possession of confidential corporate information has been held to violate Rule 10b-5, even though the buyer and seller never met.

The essential rule is that a person with inside information must either disclose the information before trading or refrain from trading. Thus, it is a violation of Rule 10b-5 to buy or sell either on an exchange or in a direct transaction when one is privy to material information that is not generally available to the investing public. This applies to almost anyone, not just to those who are usually viewed as insiders, such as directors, officers, and owners of a major interest in the company. It includes secretaries, such employees as researchers or geologists, and their supervisors. It also includes outside consultants, lawyers, engineers, financial and public relations advisors, and others who are given "inside" information for special purposes, such as news reporters and personnel of government agencies. Furthermore, **tippees** (those who are given or acquire the information without the need to know), such as stockbrokers or financial analysts and even relatives or friends of those with access to the inside information, are forbidden to trade on the information.

In the case that opened this chapter, Dr. Willis received the information that his patient's husband was seeking to become BankAmerica's chief executive officer in a confidential setting. Thus, according to the court, Willis should have known that the information was to remain secret. As a result, he was found guilty of trading on inside information. For violation of the insider trading rules, the SEC may seek a civil penalty of three times the profit gained or loss avoided. This treble penalty is paid to the Treasury of the United States. Since Dr. Willis made a $27,475 profit, under the treble damages provisions, he must pay the Treasury Department $82,425. He could also be punished by criminal fines of up to $1 million and a 10-year prison term. Unlike the rest of Section 10(b) and Rule 10b-5, the statute of limitations for insider trading permits lawsuits to be instituted up to five years after the violations occurred.

UNITED STATES V. O'HAGAN
117 S.Ct. 2199 (U.S. Sup. Ct. 1997)

FACTS

James Herman O'Hagan was a partner in the law firm of Dorsey & Whitney. In July 1988, Grand Metropolitan retained Dorsey & Whitney as legal counsel for a potential tender offer for the common stock of the Pillsbury Company. Both Grand Metropolitan and Dorsey & Whitney took precautions to protect the confidentiality of Grand Metropolitan's tender offer plans. While Dorsey & Whitney was still representing Grand Metropolitan, O'Hagan began purchasing call options for Pillsbury stock. Each option gave him the right to purchase 100 shares of Pillsbury stock by a specified date in 1988 at a price just under $39 per share. When Grand Metropolitan announced its tender offer, the price of Pillsbury stock rose to nearly $60 per share. O'Hagan then sold his Pillsbury call options and common stock, making a profit of more than $4.3 million. After the SEC investigated O'Hagan's transactions, it claimed that he defrauded his law firm and its client, Grand Metropolitan, by using for his own trading purposes material nonpublic information regarding Grand Metropolitan's planned tender offer. O'Hagan was charged with securities fraud in violation of Section 10(b) and Rule 10b-5. He claimed that criminal liability under Section 10(b) and Rule 10b-5 could not be predicated on the misappropriation theory.

ISSUE

Could O'Hagan's criminal liability be based on the misappropriation theory?

DECISION

Yes. Section 10(b) proscribes (1) using any deceptive device (2) in connection with the purchase or sale of securities, in contravention of rules prescribed by the SEC. The provision, as written, does not confine its coverage to deception of a purchaser or seller of securities; rather, the statute reaches any deceptive device used "in connection with the purchase or sale of any security." Liability under Rule 10b-5 does not extend beyond conduct encompassed by Section 10(b)'s prohibition. Under the "traditional" or "classical theory" of insider trading liability, Section 10(b) and Rule 10b-5 are violated when a corporate insider trades in the securities of his corporation on the basis of material, nonpublic information. Trading on such information qualifies as a "deceptive device" under Section 10(b) because a relationship of trust and confidence exists between the shareholders of a corporation and those insiders who have obtained confidential information by reason of their position with that corporation. That relationship gives rise to a duty to disclose (or to abstain from trading) because of the necessity of preventing a corporate insider from taking unfair advantage of uninformed stockholders. The classical theory applies not only to officers, directors, and other permanent insiders of a corporation, but also to attorneys, accountants, consultants, and others who temporarily become fiduciaries of a corporation. The "misappropriation theory" holds that a person commits fraud in connection with a securities transaction and thereby violates Section 10(b) and Rule 10b-5 when he misappropriates confidential information for securities trading purposes, in breach of a duty owed to the source of the information. Under this theory, a fiduciary's undisclosed, self-serving use of a principal's information to purchase or sell securities, in breach of a duty of loyalty and confidentiality, defrauds the principal of the exclusive use of that information. The two theories are complementary, each addressing efforts to capitalize on nonpublic information through the purchase or sale of securities. The classical theory targets a corporate insider's breach of duty to shareholders with whom the insider transacts; the misappropriation theory outlaws trading on the basis of nonpublic information by a corporate outsider in breach of a duty not to a trading party but to the source of the information. The misappropriation theory is thus designed to protect the integrity of the securities markets against abuses by outsiders to a corporation who have access to confidential information that will affect the corporation's security price when revealed, but who owe no fiduciary or other duty to that corporation's shareholders. We hold that O'Hagan's misappropriation satisfies Section 10(b)'s requirement that chargeable conduct involve a "deceptive device or

(continued)

UNITED STATES V. O'HAGAN
(concluded)

contrivance" used "in connection with" the purchase or sale of securities. Misappropriators deal in deception. A fiduciary who pretends loyalty to the principal while secretly converting the principal's information for personal gain dupes or defrauds the principal. The misappropriation theory is also well-tuned to an animating purpose of the SEC Act: to insure honest securities markets and thereby promote investor confidence. Although information disparity is inevitable in the securities markets, investors likely would hesitate to venture their capital in a market where trading based on misappropriated nonpublic information is unchecked by law.

Ethical Implications

Suppose that you overhear a lunchtime conversation between the presidents of two corporations in which they are discussing an upcoming yet still unannounced takeover. Is it ethical for you to purchase shares of the target company's stock based on this information without disclosing the reason for your decision to your sellers?

SAFE HARBOR LEGISLATION

At the end of 1995, Congress passed new legislation designed to curb lawsuits against companies whose stock performance fails to live up to expectations. Specifically, the law discourages the filing of lawsuits by requiring that plaintiffs plead specific facts that corporate insiders knew they were committing fraud when they made statements projecting a company's future performance.

Perhaps most importantly, the new law also erects a **safe harbor** for companies that make optimistic forecasts about future earnings or new products. As long as companies warn the public about factors that might undermine their forecasts, they will be immune from liability if the predictions prove false. Unfortunately, the legislation is vague about how specific the warning must be and fails to define exactly what types of factors must be identified in the cautionary statements. It remains to be seen how the courts will resolve these ambiguities.

CONCEPT SUMMARY	Provisions of the 1934 Act	
Disclosure	Registration of securities Periodic reports by issuers Holdings and transactions reports by insiders	
Proxies	Regulation of proxy statements and proxy contests	
Antifraud	Fraudulently stimulating market activity False statements in filed documents Manipulative or deceptive devices Continuous disclosure Insider trading	
Tender offers	Reporting and procedural requirements	

INTERNATIONAL COOPERATION

Several factors have brought about a tremendous surge in the internationalization of securities markets. Technological advances in communications and computers are partially responsible for this increase. Similarly, the world has witnessed a growing liberalization and deregulation movement that has removed restrictions on foreign participation in most developed securities markets. Finally, many investors subscribe to the view that international diversification of investments will reduce risks and enhance stable returns.

In spite of these trends toward international investment, regulation of securities markets is largely subject to national law. Because the national systems vary tremendously in their enforcement activities, the SEC has pursued two strategies to protect U.S. investors throughout the world. First, it has asserted broad extraterritorial jurisdiction over global transactions that affect U.S. commerce. Partially because many nations have strongly resisted these intrusions into their domestic affairs, the SEC has pursued a second approach. This has involved the formation of mutual legal assistance treaties and memoranda of understanding between the United States and its trading partners. Basically, these efforts seek cooperation between the SEC and securities regulators from other countries in securities law investigations and enforcement.

TENDER OFFER REGULATION

HISTORY

Until the early 1960s, the predominant procedure by which one corporation acquired another was the merger, a transaction requiring the cooperation of the acquired corporation's management. Since the 1960s, the tender offer has become an often-used acquisition device. A **tender offer** is a public offer by a bidder to purchase a target company's equity securities directly from its shareholders at a specified price for a fixed period of time. The offering price is usually well above the market price of the shares. Such offers often are made even though there is opposition from the target company's management. These are called **hostile tender offers.**

THE WILLIAMS ACT

In 1968, the Williams Act amendments to the 1934 Act were passed to provide investors with more information to make tender offer decisions. The aim of the amendments is to give the bidder (usually a corporation) and the target company equal opportunities to present their cases to the shareholders. Strict reporting and procedural requirements are established for both parties. The Williams Act applies only when the target company's equity securities are registered under the 1934 Act.

A bidder making a tender offer must file a tender offer statement with the SEC before the offer is made. The information in this statement includes the terms of the offer (for example, the price), the background of the bidder, and the purpose of the tender offer (including whether the bidder intends to control the subject company). An SEC rule requires the bidder to keep the tender offer open for at least 20 business days and prohibits any purchase of shares during that time. The purpose of this rule is to give shareholders adequate time to make informed decisions to tender their shares. If the bidder increases the offering price during the term of the tender offer, all shareholders must be paid the higher price even if they tendered their shares at a lower price. If more shares are tendered than the bidder offered to buy, the bidder must prorate purchases among all the shares tendered. This proration rule is designed to foster careful shareholder decisions about whether to sell shares.

STATE REGULATION OF TENDER OFFERS

Most of the states have enacted statutes regulating tender offers. Generally, such legislation has been enacted to protect local corporations from hostile takeovers, requiring long periods of advance notice to the target company and long minimum offering periods. Despite early questions concerning the constitutionality of such legislation, the Supreme Court has made clear that a properly worded statute will be permitted.

STATE SECURITIES LEGISLATION

PURPOSE AND HISTORY

State securities laws are frequently referred to as **blue-sky laws,** since the early statutes were designed to protect investors from promoters and security salespersons who offered stock in companies organized to pursue visionary schemes. All of the states have such legislation, and all provide penalties for fraudulent sales and permit the issuance of injunctions to protect investors from additional or anticipated fraudulent acts. Most statutes grant broad power to investigate fraud to some state official—usually the Attorney General or his appointee as securities administrator. All statutes provide criminal penalties for selling fraudulent securities and conducting fraudulent transactions.

BROKER–DEALER REGISTRATION

Most of the state securities statutes regulate professional sellers of securities, notably securities brokers and dealers. These statutes register securities brokers and require proof of the financial responsibility of dealers. Dealers must disclose pertinent facts about the securities they are selling and avoid sales of fraudulent securities.

UNIFORM SECURITIES ACT

In August 1985, the National Conference of Commissioners on Uniform State Laws adopted a new Uniform Securities Act. The new act replaced the Uniform Securities Act of 1956. Both acts contain antifraud provisions, require the registration of securities, and demand broker–dealer registration.

Both Uniform Securities Acts permit an issuer to register its securities by coordination. Instead of filing a registration statement under the 1933 Act and a different one as required by state law, registration by coordination allows the issuer to file the 1933 Act registration statement with the state securities administrator. Registration by coordination decreases the issuer's expense of complying with state law when making an interstate offering of its securities.

QUESTIONS AND PROBLEM CASES

1. What is the major difference between the registration requirements of the 1933 Act and those of the 1934 Act?

2. Scienter is an essential element in a Rule 10b-5 violation. What is meant by *scienter?*

3. Life Partners, Inc., facilitates the sale of life insurance policies from AIDS victims to investors at discount. The investors then recover the face value of the policy after the policy holder's death. Meanwhile, the terminally ill

sellers secure much needed income in the final years of life when employment is unlikely and medical bills are often staggering. This process is known as "viatical settlements." For acceptance into the standard Life Partners program, an insured must meet the following criteria: (1) be diagnosed with "Full Blown AIDS"; (2) have a life expectancy of 24 months or less as determined by Life Partners' "independent reviewing physician"; and (3) be certified as mentally competent. Life Partners also represents that a policy qualifies for purchase only if it is issued by an insurance company rated "A-" or higher by a national rating service. In addition, the policy must be in good standing. The policies are assigned to Life Partners, not to investors. After the insured's death, the benefits are also paid directly to Life Partners, which then pays the investors. Investors have no direct contractual rights against the insurance companies that issue the policies. Whether they receive a return on their investment or even recover their principal depends upon Life Partners' ability to honor its contractual obligations to them. The SEC claims that Life Partners sold unregistered securities and made untrue and misleading statements in violation of the federal securities laws. Life Partners argues that the viatical settlements are not securities within the scope of the securities laws. Are the viatical settlements investment contracts that qualify as securities?

4. A&P was prepared to make a tender offer to Waldbaum, Inc., a supermarket chain, for $50 per share. Ira Waldbaum, president and founder of the target company, called his sister and told her to gather her stock certificates for delivery. Being elderly and in frail health, the sister called her daughter to drive her to the bank. The daughter asked her sister, Susan, to pick up her children from school so she could take their mother to the bank. That sister told her husband, Keith Loeb, about the plans. Loeb then discussed what he had heard about the planned offer with Robert Chestman, his broker. Chestman bought 11,000 shares of Waldbaum shares for himself, Mr. Loeb, and other clients. For this, Chestman was charged with illegally using inside information, sentenced to two years in prison, and ordered to pay approximately $250,000 in restitution. Chestman appealed this Rule 10b-5 conviction. Did

Chestman violate Rule 10b-5 by illegally trading on inside information?

5. The Co-Op, an agricultural cooperative, raised money to support its general business operations by selling promissory notes payable on demand by the holder. The Co-Op marketed the scheme as an *investment program* and paid a variable rate of interest that was adjusted monthly to keep it higher than the rate paid by local financial institutions. The notes were offered to both members and nonmembers and regularly were advertised as safe investments. After the Co-Op filed for bankruptcy, holders of the notes sued the cooperative's auditor, claiming that it had violated the antifraud provisions of the 1934 Act by failing to follow generally accepted accounting principles in its audit. The auditor argued that the 1934 Act did not apply because the notes were not securities. Were the notes securities?

6. Robert D. Johnson operated a fraudulent scheme under the name of Ridge Associates. He borrowed money from investors for the purported reason of importing industrial wines. In fact, the business was a hoax, and Johnson merely used the money from some investors to pay off others. Johnson did not register the securities as required by the 1933 Act. Frank Mower asked Thomas Gilliam to introduce him to Johnson so that he could invest in Ridge Associates. Gilliam told him that he could not do that but offered to represent him in investing money with Johnson. Under this arrangement, Mower invested several hundred thousand dollars with Johnson through Gilliam. Mower was forced into bankruptcy and Joseph Lawler, his bankruptcy trustee, sued Gilliam under Section 12(1) of the Securities Act of 1933. Is Gilliam liable under Section 12(1)?

7. Escott and other investors brought suit to recover the loss of their investment in debentures issued by BarChris Construction Corporation. BarChris became bankrupt when the owners of bowling alleys built by the corporation failed to make their payments. The defendants were those who had signed the registration statement filed with the SEC. In its prospectus for the debentures, BarChris overstated sales and earnings and its current assets. It also understated its liabilities on some sales contracts and failed to disclose that a large part of the proceeds from the sale of the

debentures would be used to pay off the old debts. It also failed to disclose that it was in the business of operating bowling alleys. (It had begun operating some of the alleys when the owners defaulted on their payments to the corporation.) Some of the defendants were unaware of the misleading statements and omissions. Auslander was an outside director who had just joined the board before the debentures were registered and had not read the registration statement. Trilling, a junior officer who was controller, also claimed that he had been unaware of the false and misleading statements. Another defendant was Peat, Marwick, Mitchell & Co., the public accounting firm that had prepared an audit for the corporation. Were those who had signed the registration statement liable because of the misleading statements and omissions even if they were unaware of them?

8. R. Foster Winans was coauthor of a *Wall Street Journal* investment advice column ("Heard on the Street") that, because of its perceived quality and integrity, had an impact on the market prices of the stocks it discussed. Winans was familiar with the *Journal's* rule that the column's contents were the *Journal's* confidential information prior to publication. In spite of this, he gave advance information to Felis, a stockbroker, as to the timing and contents of the column. Felis bought and sold stocks based on the column's probable impact on the market and shared the profits with Winans. The court did not find that the content of any of the columns was altered to further the profits of this stock-trading scheme. Both were convicted of violating Section 10(b) and Rule 10b-5. (They also were found guilty of violating the federal mail and wire fraud statutes.) Should the insider trading convictions be upheld?

9. Dynamics Corporation owned 9.6 percent of the common stock of CTS Corporation. Dynamics announced a tender offer for another million shares of CTS, which would have increased its ownership interest in CTS to 27.5 percent. The board of directors of CTS elected to be governed by the provisions of a law that had just been enacted in Indiana. This statute provided that if a person made an offer that would give him a certain percentage of control shares, those shares would not have voting rights unless the other shareholders voted to give such rights to the shares. The practical effect of this requirement is to condition acquisition of control of a corporation on approval of the preexisting disinterested shareholders. Dynamics challenged the Indiana statute on the grounds that it was unconstitutional because it conflicted with the Williams Act. Should the Indiana statute be upheld?

10. In December 1978, Combustion Engineering, Inc., and Basic, Inc., agreed to merge. During the preceding two years, representatives of the two companies had held various meetings and conversations regarding the possibility of a merger. During that time, Basic made three public statements denying that any merger negotiations were taking place or that it knew of any corporate developments that would account for heavy trading activity in its stock. At the time of the initial discussions between the two corporations, Basic's common stock was trading at $27 per share. Combustion ultimately agreed to purchase Basic's outstanding stock at $46 per share. Former Basic shareholders who had sold their stock between the times of the first public denial of merger activity and the merger announcement brought suit, alleging that Basic's statements had been false or misleading in violation of Section 10(b) and Rule 10b-5. The district court granted summary judgment for Basic on the theory that Basic's statements were immaterial because it was not clear that the merger was going to be consummated. The court of appeals reversed, finding that the statements issued by Basic were so incomplete as to mislead. Further, it adopted a fraud-on-the-market theory to create a rebuttable presumption that the former shareholders relied on the misstatements and omissions by trading on a market that was artificially depressed by Basic's denials of any merger discussions. Did the court of appeals correctly apply the materiality and reliance elements?

CHAPTER 29

Legal Liability of Accountants

Steve Noles relied on his trusted accountant, James Checksfield, to keep him out of trouble with the IRS. That was a serious mistake. Checksfield ended up being a controlled informant for the government. Based on evidence revealed by Checksfield that Noles skimmed untaxed income from his restaurant, Noles was indicted on six counts of income tax evasion and faced up to 24 years in prison and $900,000 in fines. During the time Checksfield was gathering evidence for the IRS, he received more than $20,000 in accounting fees from Noles. According to Mr. Noles, "Jim Checksfield often sat in my living room with my wife and two children. We treated him like family. I trusted him. Why, I even gave him power of attorney to represent me before the Internal Revenue Service!"[1]

- *Did Checksfield breach a duty owed to Noles for which he could be liable in contract or tort?*
- *What are the ethical implications of accountants voluntarily disclosing the improprieties of their clients to the government?*
- *To what extent does an accountant–client privilege protect people like Noles?*

---

[1]"Accountant's Sideline as an IRS Informant Brings Grief to Client," *The Wall Street Journal*, February 22, 1990, p. A1.

.... *INTRODUCTION* ....

BASES FOR LIABILITY

There are numerous legal theories under which an accountant might be found liable. Many of the previous chapters in this book have offered fairly detailed discussions of these causes of action. However, the main basis of liability for accountants is the *duty to exercise ordinary skill and care.* Breach of this duty may lead to an action grounded in the tort of negligence (see Chapter 5). Closely related are the suits stemming from the agency relationship (see Chapters 20 and 21) between the accountant and the client. Because this relationship is contractual in nature, breach of the duty might also trigger an action in breach of contract (see Chapter 15). Sometimes, the violation by the accountant is fraudulent (see Chapter 11) and perhaps even criminal (see Chapter 3). Further, many suits brought against accountants in recent years have been based on violations of the provisions of the federal securities laws (see Chapter 28). Finally, many times the accountant involved in the action will be a partner in a public accounting firm. If so, the law of partnership (see Chapter 24) will be involved, probably resulting in liability for all of the partners in the firm. (If the accountant is an employee and not a partner, the firm may still be liable under the doctrine of respondeat superior (see Chapter 21).)

The liability of the accountant can be both civil and criminal. (In Chapter 28 we examined how violations of the federal securities laws could subject the defendant to both civil and criminal remedies.) Further, when an accountant violates a duty, he may be called before a judicial body, an administrative body, or both. In addition, the accountant's liability may be to a client, a third person, or both. These and other issues will be discussed in this chapter.

GAAP AND GAAS

Organizations representing the public accounting profession have developed and issued guidelines for conducting accounting work. Generally accepted accounting principles (GAAP) apply to the way business transactions should be recorded. Generally accepted auditing standards (GAAS) give directions to accountants in auditing the books of an enterprise. Accountants are rarely held liable if they have followed these standards, but failure to comply may constitute negligence. However, compliance with the standards is not always a sufficient defense. In a few cases, courts have refused to recognize this defense where they believed the accountants' work was misleading. This is particularly true in securities cases. There courts insist that financial statements, taken as a whole, fairly present the financial condition of the company and the results of its operations.

.... *COMMON LAW LIABILITY* ....
               TO CLIENTS

A business may have several reasons for employing an outside accountant to review its books. Often a formal audit is demanded by a creditor or prospective creditor. However, assurance that the internal bookkeeping of the business is accurate and that periodic financial statements are reliable are almost certain to be among the major reasons for the employment.

CONTRACTUAL LIABILITY

Like anyone, accountants have a duty to perform their contractual obligations. If an accountant agrees to complete an engagement by a certain time and fails to do so, there will be liability for whatever damages result. For example, suppose an accounting firm agrees to complete an audit by February 15 because it has been informed of a deadline set by a prospective lender to the client. If the audit report is not finished until March and the lender has no more funds available at that time, the accountant would be liable for the client's resulting loss. The fact that the accounting firm had other deadlines would not be a defense. Of course, the firm would not be liable if it could be shown that the delay was due to the client's having obstructed performance of the audit. This might occur if the client refused to give the firm access to needed records.

Ordinarily, an accountant may not delegate her responsibilities without the consent of the client. This is because the contract is a personal one, based on the skill, training, and personality of the accountant. The **no delegation rule** frequently becomes an issue at tax return time when demand for the accountant's services becomes overwhelming and there is a temptation to take on more work than can possibly be accomplished in a timely manner. (Again, as in the late audit report example, an accountant who files a late return cannot defend on the ground that she had too much work to perform.)

TORT LIABILITY

Negligence

Even when there is no express agreement, the law imposes a duty of care on public accountants engaged to provide services to a client. The law implies that the public accountants have promised to exercise the skill, knowledge, and care generally used by accountants. Failure to comply with these standards might lead to an action against the accountant grounded in *negligence* if, as a result, the client suffers damages. For certified public accountants, a court would look to the higher standards that certification implies. These standards would include following GAAP and GAAS. Further, an accountant's failure to follow the instructions of her firm in performing the job is also likely to be treated by a court as negligence. (These standards would be applicable whether the suit is brought in contract or tort.)

The failure of an accountant to discover fraud by the client's employees or others is not in itself proof of negligence by the accountant. The investigative techniques used by accountants will not always uncover the fraud of a skillful and careful crook. However, accountants cannot overlook questionable entries or omissions in the accounts and supporting records of the client. For example, if the application of GAAS should raise the suspicions of a careful person trained as an accountant, an auditor who fails to follow through with appropriate inquiries and tests is negligent. (If the purpose of an audit is to look for suspected irregularities, more would be expected of an accountant.)

The individual circumstances will determine what action the accountant is required to take when he discovers irregularities. Certainly, it is necessary to notify an appropriate person in management if an accountant has a basis for suspicion of fraud. Notifying a person thought to be a participant in the suspected fraud would never be appropriate.

The traditional defenses of *contributory negligence* and *comparative negligence* may apply in a negligence action against an accountant. (See Chapter 5 for discussion of these defenses.) However, many courts hesitate to allow the client's contributory negligence to excuse the accountant's negligence because of the accountant's superior skills. The defense is more likely to succeed in an instance in which the client failed to follow the accountant's advice or in which the client already was aware of the irregularities before the accountant failed to discover them.

Fraud

The intentional misrepresentation of material facts or the intentional failure to disclose such information to a client may result in the accountant being found liable for fraud. In Chapter 28, we described such behavior as acting with *scienter—the knowledge of an untruth or the reckless disregard for the truth*. Suppose that an accountant represents that he completed an audit of the client when in reality he merely accepted the accuracy of the client's books without investigation. A careful audit would have discovered that an employee of the client was regularly embezzling funds from the client. The accountant may be liable in fraud for any losses suffered by the client from the time when the audit should have discovered the embezzlement.

Generally, in a negligence or contract action, the client is limited to recovering compensatory damages. That is, the damage award is limited to the amount that will replace the actual loss caused by the accountant's wrong. If the accountant is found liable in fraud, however, the client may be able to recover punitive damages as well. (Under a punitive damage award, the client will receive an amount in excess of his actual loss. This award is designed to punish the accountant for her fraudulent conduct.)

COMMON LAW LIABILITY TO THIRD PERSONS

Creditors, shareholders, and other investors often rely on financial statements that have been prepared or certified by public accountants. Sometimes firms engage an accountant to do an audit solely because this has been requested by a prospective or present creditor. Historically, third-party suits against accountants were generally barred by the **privity doctrine.** (This doctrine limited recovery to those with a direct contractual relationship to the accountant.)

CONTRACT

At common law, recovery by a creditor was possible on the theory that the creditor was a third-party beneficiary of the contract employing the accountant. (See Chapter 14 for a discussion of such contracts.) This required showing that the accountant was aware that the audit was ordered to satisfy the demand of a creditor or prospective creditor. Then, the exception extended only to that person or firm. In the absence of these special circumstances, contract law has not been widely used by third persons (nonclients) suffering damages as a result of an accountant's breach.

NEGLIGENCE

Many courts carried the privity doctrine over to negligence suits against an accountant by third persons who may have relied on her work. Thus, these nonclients—creditors, shareholders, and other investors of the accountant's client—were prevented from recovering damages caused by her negligence. In effect, this meant that accountants did not owe a duty of care and skill to nonclients.

CURRENT APPROACHES TO THIRD-PARTY NEGLIGENCE ACTIONS

Many courts today have refused to apply the privity doctrine to third-party negligence suits against accountants. Currently, there are five major judicial approaches for handling such suits. They are:

1. The *Ultramares* approach.
2. The Near Privity approach.
3. The *Restatement* approach.
4. The Reasonably Foreseeable Users approach.
5. The Balancing approach.

The Ultramares *Approach*

The rationale for the application of the privity doctrine in suits against accountants stems from the landmark case of *Ultramares v. Touche.*[2] In *Ultramares*, the auditor had not been told that Ultramares Corporation was to receive 1 of the 32 signed copies of the certified balance sheet. Yet the auditors were clearly negligent in making their audit. They had accepted without question as accounts receivable $700,000 in fictitious sales, although these and other entries should have aroused their suspicions. Judge Cardozo refused to hold the accounting firm liable, and his rationale has been much quoted. He said: "If liability for negligence exists, a thoughtless slip or blunder, the failure to detect a theft or forgery beneath the cover of deceptive entries, may expose accountants to a liability in an indeterminate amount for an indeterminate time to an indeterminate class."

The Near Privity Approach

In contrast to the strict privity rule of *Ultramares*, several courts have adopted a near privity approach. It grew out of a case in which a seller employed a weigher to certify the weight of beans and to provide a copy of the certification to the buyer. Judge Cardozo, the author of *Ultramares*, held for the buyer in a suit against the weigher for inaccurately certifying the weight of the beans. Drawing from this opinion, several recent courts have held that accountants may be liable in negligence to third parties when three prerequisites are satisfied: (1) The accountants must have been aware that the financial reports were to be used for a particular purpose. (2) The accountant must have known the identity of the third parties and that they would rely on the reports. (3) There must have been some conduct on the part of the accountant linking her to the third party that evidences the accountant's understanding of the third party's reliance.

The Restatement *Approach*

A third theory of liability is set forth in the *Restatement (Second) of Torts*. Under this theory, the accountant is liable only to those third parties who are "specifically foreseeable." This standard imposes greater liability on accountants than does the *Ultramares* rule. However, the *Restatement* requires that the accountant be aware of the third parties and also know of the possibility that the third parties will rely on the

---

[2]174 N.E. 441 (N.Y. Ct. App.; 1931).

financial statements. Thus, this approach does not protect the typical investor who was unknown to the accountant and her client when the financial statements were prepared. Of the state courts that have abandoned the *Ultramares* approach, the majority has chosen to replace it with the *Restatement* approach.

The Reasonably Foreseeable Users Approach

This theory exposes a negligent accountant to greater liability than do the *Ultramares* and *Restatement* approaches. Under this approach, the accountant could be liable to unknown but reasonably foreseeable users if three conditions are met. First, the user must have received the financial statements from the accountant's client for a proper business purpose. Second, the third person must have reasonably relied on the accuracy of those financial statements. And third, the damages suffered by the third party must be a foreseeable result of the accountant's negligence.

NYCAL CORPORATION V. KPMG PEAT MARWICK
688 N.E.2d 1368 (Mass. Sup. Jud. Ct. 1998)

FACTS

Gulf Resources & Chemical Corporation retained Peat Marwick to audit its 1990 financial statements. The completed auditor's report was included in Gulf's annual report, which became publicly available on February 22, 1991. One year before that date (February 1990), D.S. Kennedy & Company had reported to the SEC that it had acquired over two million shares of Gulf common stock and that it intended to acquire a controlling interest in Gulf. Peat Marwick was aware of this SEC filing. In fact, Gulf's management discussed with Peat Marwick the potential for purchasing Kennedy's shares. Thus, Peat Marwick was aware of Kennedy's interest in acquiring a controlling interest in Gulf and that Gulf intended to treat Kennedy as a hostile takeover threat. In March 1991, Kennedy entered into discussions with Gulf concerning the possible purchase of a large block of Gulf shares, and during the course of those discussions, Gulf provided Kennedy with a copy of its 1990 annual report. Thereafter, Kennedy purchased almost four million shares of Gulf and gained operating control of the corporation. Peat Marwick first learned of this transaction a few days prior to the July 12, 1991, closing. Gulf filed for bankruptcy protection in October 1993, rendering Kennedy's investment worthless. Kennedy then filed a civil complaint against Peat Marwick as a result of its alleged reliance on the auditors' report. Kennedy claimed the report materially misrepresented the financial condition of Gulf.

ISSUE

Did Peat Marwick owe a legal duty to Kennedy?

DECISION

No. Kennedy urges our adoption of the broad standard of liability encompassed in the foreseeability test. Pursuant to this test an accountant may be held liable to any person whom the accountant could reasonably have foreseen would obtain and rely on the accountant's opinion, including known and unknown investors. We refuse to hold accountants susceptible to such expansive liability, and conclude that this state's law does not protect every reasonably foreseeable user of an inaccurate audit report. We also reject the near-privity test, which limits an accountant's liability exposure to those with whom the accountant is in privity or in a relationship sufficiently approaching privity. Under the near-privity test, an accountant may be held liable to noncontractual third parties who rely to their detriment on an inaccurate financial report if the accountant was aware that the report was to be used for a particular purpose, in the furtherance of which a known party (or parties) was intended to rely, and if there was some conduct on the part of the accountant creating a link to that party, which evinces the accountant's understanding of the party's reliance. Rather than the foreseeability or near-privity tests, we adhere instead to the test taken from Section 552 of the Restatement (Second) of Torts. It limits the accountant's

(continued)

NYCAL CORPORATION V. KPMG PEAT MARWICK
(concluded)

negligence liability to losses suffered (a) by the person or one of a limited group of persons for whose benefit and guidance he intends to supply the information or knows that the recipient intends to supply it; and (b) through reliance upon it in a transaction that the accountant intends the information to influence or knows that the recipient so intends, or in a substantially similar transaction. We believe that the *Restatement* test properly balances the indeterminate liability of the foreseeability test and the restrictiveness of the near-privity rule. The better-reasoned decisions interpret the *Restatement* test as limiting the potential liability of an accountant to noncontractual third parties who can demonstrate "actual knowledge on the part of accountants of the limited—though unnamed—group of potential third parties that will rely upon the report, as well as actual knowledge of the particular financial transaction that such information is designed to influence." The accountant's knowledge is to be measured at the moment the audit report is published, not by the foreseeable path of harm envisioned by litigants years following an unfortunate business decision. In this case, Peat Marwick did not prepare the audit report for Kennedy's benefit and Kennedy was not a member of any limited group of persons for whose benefit the report was prepared. At the time the audit was being prepared, Kennedy was an unknown, unidentified potential future investor in Gulf. Peat Marwick was not aware of the existence of the transaction between Gulf and Kennedy until after the stock purchase agreement had been signed and only a few days before the sale was completed. Further, Peat Marwick neither intended to influence the transaction entered into by Kennedy and Gulf nor knew that Gulf intended to influence the transaction by use of the audit report. While Peat Marwick was aware of the circumstances surrounding Kennedy's earlier purchases, which had occurred prior to the completion of the audit report, Kennedy's purchase of the controlling shares of Gulf stock did not resemble those earlier transactions. Moreover, the audit report was prepared for inclusion in Gulf's annual report and not for the purpose of assisting Gulf's controlling shareholders in any particular transaction. The rule we adopt here today will preclude accountants from having to insure the commercial decisions of nonclients where, as here, the accountants did not know that their work product would be relied upon by the plaintiff in making an investment decision.

The Balancing Approach

Some courts have identified the need for a more flexible and equitable standard for resolving third-party negligence suits against accountants. They believe that the determination of whether a defendant will be held liable to a third person not in privity is a matter of policy and involves the balancing of various factors. Accordingly, they have devised a six-factor balancing test that examines (1) the extent to which the transaction was intended to affect the plaintiff; (2) the foreseeability of harm to the plaintiff, (3) the degree of certainty that the plaintiff suffered injury; (4) the closeness of the connection between the defendant's conduct and the injury suffered; (5) the moral blame attached to the defendant's conduct; and (6) the policy of preventing future harm. (See Figure 29–1 on page 532.)

FRAUD

Because of its reprehensible nature, most courts have extended an accountant's liability for fraudulent conduct to all foreseeable users of her work product who suffered damages that were proximately caused by the accountant's fraud. Thus, third persons have a much greater likelihood of success in suits against an accountant if they can prove that in making the mistatement or omission in a report, the accountant committed fraud. To prove fraud it must be shown that the accountant acted with

Figure 29–1   Third-Party Negligence Suits

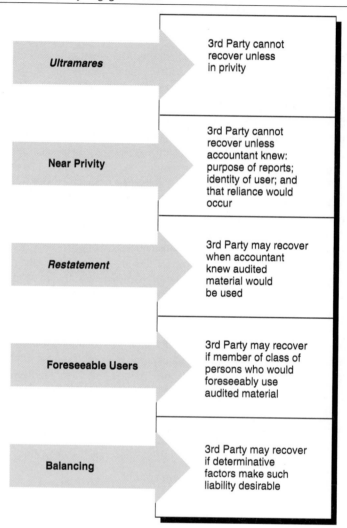

a special type of intent, called **scienter.** An accountant acts with scienter when he knows of the falsity of a statement or when making the statement, he recklessly disregards the truth.

Thus, the scienter standard of fraud would be met if an accountant, rather than examining the current figures in a client's books (perhaps because he was overwhelmed with other clients' work as well), relies on the previous year's figures. It would also include recognizing obvious evidence of embezzlement yet failing to notify a client of its existence.

Courts throughout the country are not entirely consistent on the precise test that a third party must meet in order to recover for an accountant's fraud. Yet all seem to be in agreement that the third party's path to recovery is easier once fraud has been proven than it would be for mere negligence. Consider the following case, where the Texas Supreme Court argues that, because of the intent requirement that is part of a fraud case, a third party must prove something more than mere foreseeability to recover from an accountant.

ERNST & YOUNG, L.L.P. v. PACIFIC MUTUAL LIFE INSURANCE CO.
51 S.W.3d 573 (Tex. Sup.Ct. 2001)

FACTS

In 1982, InterFirst issued a series of notes scheduled to mature in 1989. By 1986, InterFirst was in financial difficulty, and it began to negotiate a merger with Republic-Bank, which appeared at the time to be a stronger, more profitable bank. Ernst & Young audited RepublicBank's financial statements for the year ending December 31, 1986, and gave an unqualified opinion that those statements fairly presented the bank's financial position. RepublicBank incorporated Ernst & Young's audit report and the audited financial statement in the 1986 annual report it made to its shareholders and Form 10-K it filed with the SEC. The banks merged in June 1987. Republic-Bank offered several securities as part of the merger, including notes and two classes of stock in the merged entity. Together with InterFirst, RepublicBank issued a Joint Proxy and Prospectus soliciting their respective shareholders' proxies to approve the merger. The Joint Proxy and Prospectus also discussed the common stock and one series of preferred stock to be issue in connection with the merger. To promote another series of preferred stock and capital notes, RepublicBank issued two other prospectuses. These two prospectuses incorporated by reference the Joint Proxy and Prospectus. All three prospectuses incorporated RepublicBank's 1986 Form 10-K, which incorporated by reference in a section of the prospectuses entitled, "Experts," which stated that the RepublicBank's financials were incorporated in reliance upon the audit report and upon the authority of Ernst & Young as experts in auditing and accounting. Finally, RepublicBank included the three prospectuses in the registration statements filed with the SEC to register the securities described in the prospectuses. Ernst & Young consented to including its audit opinion and the financial information that had been the subject of its report in the prospectuses and to having its name mentioned in the "Experts" section. The underwriters who were seeking buyers for merger-related securities contacted Pacific Mutual Life Insurance Company. At the time, Pacific was considering whether to purchase the 1982 InterFirst notes. It was initially reluctant to do so because of its experience with other InterFirst notes, which it had placed on its problem asset list due to InterFirst's poor financial condition. But after reviewing the public information relating to the merger, including the merger

prospectuses and newspaper articles, Pacific decided that the InterFirst notes were a good investment because they would be backed by the merged bank. Pacific bought $400,000 worth of the 1982 InterFirst notes one month after the merger and then bought nearly $8 million worth a few months later. However, Pacific did not buy any of the securities offered in the three prospectuses. Shortly after Pacific completed buying the InterFirst notes, the merged entity, First RepublicBank Corporation, disclosed serious financial problems with its real estate portfolio and filed for bankruptcy. Alleging that it had been misled by fraudulent representations in the three prospectuses, Pacific sued Ernst & Young. It claimed that Ernst & Young's audit opinion contained misrepresentations, including statements that the audit complied with generally accepted accounting standards (GAAS). Specifically, Pacific argued that the financial statements did not accurately reflect RepublicBank's financial condition as of December 31, 1986, because they understated RepublicBank's real estate liabilities. Pacific further alleged that Ernst & Young violated the independence standards imposed by GAAS by failing to disclose that, at the time it issued its opinion, several of its partners had significant outstanding RepublicBank loans. Ernst & Young moved for summary judgment because the accounting firm had no reason to expect that a third party, such as Pacific, would rely on its audit report in making its decision to buy the notes that were issued by InterFirst before the banks merged.

ISSUE

Should the court dismiss Pacific's fraud claim against the accounting firm?

DECISION

Yes. To prevail on its fraud claim, Pacific must prove that (1) Ernst & Young made a material representation that was false; (2) it knew the representation was false or made it recklessly as a positive assertion without any knowledge of its truth; (3) it intended to induce Pacific to act upon the representation; and (4) Pacific actually and justifiably relied upon the representation and thereby suffered injury. Ernst & Young claims that in order to prevail, a nonclient, such as Pacific, must show

(continued)

ERNST & YOUNG, L.L.P. v. PACIFIC MUTUAL LIFE INSURANCE CO.
(concluded)

that the accounting firm, in auditing RepublicBank's 1986 financial statements, specifically intended to induce Pacific to buy the InterFirst notes. Ernst & Young likens the direct-intent requirement to the doctrine of "privity," which requires a direct relationship between the fraudulent accounting firm and a specific known person. Ernst & Young is wrong. Our fraud jurisprudence focuses not on whether an intentional misrepresentation is directly transmitted to a known person alleged to be in privity with the accountant but on whether the intentional misrepresentation was intended to reach a third person and induce reliance. Where a party makes a false representation to another with the intent or knowledge that it should be exhibited or repeated to a third party for the purpose of deceiving him, the third party, if so deceived to his injury, can maintain an action in tort against the party making the false statement for the damages resulting from the fraud. Thus, a misrepresentation made through an intermediary is actionable if it is intended to influence a third person's conduct. Our jurisprudence focuses on the accountant's knowledge and intent to induce reliance by a third party or class of persons. This requirement of an actual purpose or desire to induce reliance requires a degree of certainty that does beyond mere foreseeability. Even an obvious risk that a

misrepresentation might be repeated to a third party is not enough to satisfy the reason-to-expect standard; rather the fraudulent accountant must have information that would lead a reasonable man to conclude that there is an especial likelihood that it will reach those persons and will influence their conduct. It is not enough that a defendant intends or has reason to expect that its representation will reach and be relied upon by one who receives it. The plaintiff must have incurred pecuniary loss in the type of transaction in which the accountant intends or has reason to expect his conduct to be influenced. Although the transaction sued upon need not be identical to that the defendant contemplates, it must have the same essential character. In sum, the reason-to-expect standard requires more than mere foreseeability; the claimant's reliance must be especially likely and justifiable, and the transaction sued upon must be the type the defendant contemplated. Ernst & Young is entitled to summary judgment because it has negated the intent requirement of the claim as a matter of law. The accounting firm did not have reason to expect that Pacific would rely on an audit report relating to the sale of securities offered as a part of a merger when it bought the InterFirst notes that were issued some four years earlier.

DUTY TO DISCLOSE NEW INFORMATION

It has been held that the duty of care of accountants extends beyond their actions during the audit itself. In one case, an accounting firm learned through further work for a client that figures in financial statements that it had certified a short time earlier were false and misleading. The court held that the accountants had a duty to disclose the unreliability of the earlier report to anyone who they knew was relying on it. Liability for failure to comply with this duty may be based on either negligence or fraud.

Ethical Implications	How far should an accountant's liability to disclose the unreliability of earlier reports extend? Should the accountant contact all persons who might possibly be using the inaccurate statements although they were not foreseen users at the time the audit was performed?

STATUTORY LIABILITY OF ACCOUNTANTS

FEDERAL SECURITIES ACTS

In Chapter 28, we discussed the federal and state securities laws and the various causes of action that arise when they are violated. Generally, violations of the statutes give the injured person a right to sue in negligence or fraud. Because of the privity rules, third persons (nonclients) frequently sue under these laws. And, as we will discuss, both the 1933 Act and the 1934 Act contain criminal penalties.

Civil Actions under the 1933 Act

Section 11(a) of the Securities Act of 1933 explicitly imposes liability on accountants for *misstatements or omissions of material facts* in the information they furnish for *registration statements* required by the 1933 Act. It also applies to lawyers and other "experts" such as engineers and consulting geologists. If this information is misleading, these experts are liable unless they can prove that they exercised due diligence. In other words, an accountant is liable for a defective registration statement unless she can prove that she made a reasonable investigation and reasonably believed that the certified financial statements were accurate. This lack of negligence can usually be proved by demonstrating that the accountant was in compliance with GAAS and GAAP.

The accountant is liable to any purchaser of securities issued pursuant to a defective registration statement. Reliance is not essential. Thus, the purchaser can recover even if he had not read the registration statement containing the material misstatements or omissions. As a general rule, the accountant is liable for the purchaser's entire loss. Of course, if the accountant can demonstrate that the purchaser was aware of the misstatements or omissions in the registration statement before buying the securities, the purchaser could not recover. Further, recovery would be denied if the losses were the result of a general downturn in the price of the securities that was totally unrelated to the accountant's negligence.

The accountant's duty is to have a reasonable belief in the accuracy of the figures at the time the registration statement becomes effective. Frequently, the effective date is several months after the audit has been completed. Therefore, the accountant has a continuing duty to review the audited statements until the effective date. If there is any material change in conditions following the audit, the figures must be reexamined and corrected before the registration becomes effective.

Section 11 has a statute of limitations that limits the period of time for which an accountant might be held liable for a defective registration statement. The purchaser

CONCEPT SUMMARY	Accountant's Liability to Third Persons
Legal Theory	**Summary of Accountant's Liability**
Common Law Liability	
Contract	Liable for breach of contract to third-party beneficiary only if accountant was aware that the audit was ordered for the third party's benefit.
Negligence	Liability is generally barred by the privity doctrine unless the accountant should have foreseen that the third party would rely on the audit.
Fraud	Liable to anyone injured by an intentional misstatement or an intentional omission.
Statutory Liability	
1933 Act Section 11(a)	Liable to any purchaser of a security when there is a misstatement or omission of a material fact in the registration statement. Purchaser need not prove reliance. Burden is on accountant to prove he exercised due diligence.
1934 Act Rule 10b-5	Liable for misstatement or omission of a material fact in connection with the purchase or sale of a security. Plaintiff must prove accountant acted with scienter.
1934 Act Section 18(a)	Liable for damages resulting from any false or misleading information in any report filed with the SEC. Plaintiff must prove reliance.

must sue the accountant within one year after the time the misstatement or omission was or should have been discovered. However, a suit may not be brought more than three years after the securities were offered to the public.

Other provisions of the 1933 Act and the Securities and Exchange Act have also been used against accountants. These sections are designed to protect investors. Therefore, there are no privity requirements, that bar common law suits in many states. (See Chapter 28 for a detailed discussion of these provisions.)

Endo V. Arthur Andersen & Company
163 F.3d 463 (7th Cir. 1999)

FACTS

Fruit the Loom hired Arthur Andersen to audit its financial statements for 1985. Andersen did this and reported to Fruit of the Loom's management that the financial statements were complete and accurate so far as Andersen could determine through the use of sound auditing methodology. The statements contain a footnote, reviewed and approved by Andersen as part of the audit, to the effect that Fruit of the Loom is contesting in the Tax Court $105 million in deficiencies assessed by the IRS for a period in the 1970s. The note includes a warning that the cash payment to the IRS, including interest, may exceed the amount of alleged deficiencies. This warning does not appear in the note on tax liabilities in Fruit of the Loom's 1986 financial statements, although other ominous warnings not included in the previous statement relating to tax liabilities for the 1980s do appear. The 1986 statements were audited by Ernst & Young, which had replaced Andersen as Fruit of the Loom's auditor. In the public documents accompanying the 1987 IP, Fruit of the Loom was required to disclose its financial reports for 1985 as well as 1986. It asked Andersen to consent to the republication of the report of the 1985 audit. Sound accounting practice required Andersen to read the offering documents and check with its successor auditor, Ernst & Young, to make sure that Ernst & Young had not discovered anything to falsify the 1985 financial statements that Andersen had certified. Andersen duly obtained from Ernst & Young letters certifying that Ernst & Young discovered nothing that warranted changing the 1985 financial statements. It then consented to the republication of its audit report in the offering documents without the original footnote. In March 1987, Fruit of the Loom made an initial public offering of common stock and other securities. Endo and other purchasers of these securities lost money on their investment when the IRS fined Fruit of the Loom for more than the $105 million in actual tax deficiencies. Endo argued that, because Andersen consented to republication of the 1985 statements without the footnote, investors who purchased the securities were mislead into thinking that Andersen had changed its mind about the danger of the IRS fining Fruit of the Loom for more than the actual deficiencies. Endo sued Andersen under Section 11(a) of the 1933 Act..

ISSUE

Is Andersen liable to the investors for a misleading omission under Section 11(a) because it consented to republication of the 1985 statements without the warning footnote?

DECISION

No. So far as Andersen's compliance with applicable auditing standards is concerned, there is no issue. It did exactly what those standards require of a former auditor asked to consent to the republication of its audit report had not been accurate. If investors were misled, it was not because they mistakenly relied on Andersen to exercise reasonable care to discover such information; Andersen used all the requisite care and discovered no such information—there was none to discover. The question, rather, is whether by permitting Fruit of the Loom to omit from the IPO documents the warning sentence from the footnote to the 1985 financial statements, Andersen mislead investors into thinking that the tax liability picture had brightened—that Fruit of the Loom's maximum tax liability for the years during the 1970 would be confined to the $105 million figure. The key to answering this question lies in the difference between historical and predictive information in a former auditor's audit report.

(continued)

ENDO V. ARTHUR ANDERSEN & COMPANY
(concluded)

The text, as distinct from the footnotes, of the 1985 financial statements that Andersen approved shows the revenues and costs that the company actually experienced that year. This was "history" so far as the successor auditor was concerned. Because Fruit of the Loom was required in its IPO documentation to report its 1985 financial results and because information obtained since Andersen had audited those results might show that they were inaccurate, it was important to Fruit of the Loom and to investors that Andersen, which, unlike Ernst & Young, had investigated the 1985 results, check to make sure they were still accurate. That is what Andersen did by checking with Ernst & Young, which had audited the next year's statements and so would know whether anything had happened during that year to require revision of the previous year's statements. The footnote at issue, however, talks about the future—specifically, about what might happen as a result of the unresolved litigation in the Tax Court. As to that, Andersen had no continuing responsibility arising from its role as a former auditor. The current auditor would know much more about the future. The investor is not interested in the former auditor's continued confidence in the figures, which the auditor has approved, but in the current auditor's opinion regarding contingencies that, no yet having materialized, are not reflected in the historical data. The investor who reads the documentation accompanying Fruit of the Loom's IPO sees a column for the company's 1985 financial results, a column for its 1986 results, a set of footnotes dealing with contingent liabilities not reflected in the columns, and notations that Andersen audited the 1985 results and continues to stand by them and that Ernst & Young audited the 1986 results. The investor will assume that Andersen is standing by the numbers in the column for 1985, not standing by prophesies in the footnotes, which are about today speaking of tomorrow rather than about today speaking of yesterday. The footnotes are, it is true, a part of the financial statements. But remember that an accountant's liability for misleading representations in a registration statement is limited to the portion of any financial statements that purports to have been prepared or certified by him. Andersen did not purport to certify the footnotes to Fruit of the Loom's 1986 financial statements, though it did purport to certify that, on the basis of information received from Ernst & Young, it had no reason to revise the 1985 financial results shown in the 1986 statements. The investor does not expect the same financial data and estimates to be audited by two separate audit companies. He expects the current data, including the current estimates of contingent liabilities, to be audited by the current auditor, and data for periods prior to the hiring of this auditor to be audited by a former auditor. Ernst & Young did not audit 1985 financials; Andersen did. Andersen did not audit the 1986 predictions; Ernst & Young did.

Civil Liability under the 1934 Act

Section 10(b) and Rule 10b-5, discussed in Chapter 28, have been the basis of most of the suits by investors against accountants. Rule 10b-5 prohibits any person from making a *misstatement or omission of a material fact* in connection with the purchase or sale of any security. One element of this action is that the purchaser or seller must *rely* on the misstatement or omission. However, in recent years, the courts have greatly eroded this notion of reliance and allowed plaintiffs to recover even though they had not read the report containing the omissions.

The popularity of Rule 10b-5 among plaintiffs is somewhat diminished by the requirement that something more than negligence must be shown to make a defendant liable for damages. That something more was scienter. This means that there must have been an intentional or at least knowing misrepresentation before the accountant can be found liable under Rule 10b-5. And, as we noted above, a reckless disregard of facts known to the accountant that would cast doubt on the information she provides would probably also be sufficient for liability. Requiring scienter has greatly reduced the number of successful suits against accountants.

The 1934 Act has several other provisions under which an accountant might be held liable. Section 18(a) (discussed in Chapter 28) imposes liability on accountants who furnish false or misleading information in any report or document filed with the SEC. While privity is not a defense in a Section 18 action, it is still not widely used because it contains a stringent *reliance* requirement. The purchaser or seller must have actually read the false information. This is a major hurdle since investors seldom read many of the documents filed with the SEC.

Finally, accountants may be liable for assisting others in violating the securities laws. It is illegal to encourage or participate in the publication of misleading information. Even if the information were prepared by others, the accountant may be found liable for *aiding and abetting*. In 1994 the Supreme Court stripped the SEC of authority to pursue accountants who aided or abetted corporate fraud. However, at the end of 1995, Congress enacted legislation restoring this power to the SEC and federal prosecutors. Thus, the SEC may file disciplinary cases against accountants or lawyers who aid and abet others who commit fraud. The new legislation specifically requires accounting firms to report any illegal activities uncovered during an audit.

At the same time, the new legislation shields accountants from the joint-and-several-liability system that plagued them for many years. Under joint and several liability, an accounting firm could be held liable for the full amount of a judgment if the defendant corporation became insolvent. The new regulatory scheme limits the accounting firm's liability to the proportion of the fraud for which the accountants were responsible, plus a 50 percent premium when the main defendant is insolvent.

Criminal Liability

Both the 1933 and 1934 Securities Acts have criminal provisions. Although the criminal provisions do not specifically mention accountants, they may be and have been used against them. A willful (intentional) misrepresentation, including an omission, in a registration statement is made a criminal act under the 1933 Act. The 1934 Act makes it a crime to willfully make a false or misleading statement in reports that are required to be filed under the act. A willful violation of Rule 10b-5 is also a crime.

STATE SECURITIES ACTS

Each of the 50 states has a securities statute that contains liability provisions. In addition, some of the states have provisions that specifically impose criminal penalties on accountants for willful falsification of financial statements and other reports. In the past, few actions have been brought against accountants under these statutes. However, this may well change as plaintiffs begin to recognize the difficulty in proving the scienter requirement of Rule 10b-5 and some of the other federal provisions.

LIABILITY FOR TAX WORK

Accountants may be held liable for negligence in preparing tax returns and giving tax advice. For example, an accountant may be required to reimburse a client for a penalty imposed for late filing if the delay is caused by the accountant. An accountant who erroneously tells a client that a transaction is nontaxable may be liable for the extra costs incurred because of the bad advice. This is also true of losses suffered by a client who has participated in a tax shelter scheme on the erroneous advice of an accountant.

ADMINISTRATIVE PROCEEDINGS

An accountant who violates the federal securities acts may be subjected to an administrative hearing conducted by the SEC. Under this procedure, an administrative law judge will first hear the case and make a determination. The SEC commissioners will then issue a final order. Through this procedure, the SEC possesses the authority to temporarily or permanently bar an accountant from practicing before it. The final order of the SEC may be appealed to a federal court of appeals.

PROFESSIONAL CONDUCT

Most states also have licensing boards that regulate the ethical conduct of the accounting profession. These state agencies may suspend or revoke the accountant's license to practice in that state if she commits illegal or unethical acts. Historically, the state licensing boards regulated accountants' right to advertise their services to the public. However, as the following case suggests, strict regulation of advertising in the accounting profession may be a thing of the past.

FANE V. EDENFIELD
507 U.S. 761 (U.S. Sup. Ct. 1993)

FACTS

Fane, a certified public accountant, moved to Florida to set up an accounting practice. In order to establish a client base, he intended to solicit business via in-person contacts with businesses he felt would be interested in his services. Fane was unable to carry out this plan, however, because in-person solicitation by CPAs was forbidden in Florida. Other financial professionals, such as noncertified accountants, bookkeepers, and tax preparers, were not prohibited from utilizing personal contacts to solicit new clients. Fane sued in an effort to have the prohibition of in-person solicitation by CPAs declared unconstitutional.

ISSUE

Should prohibition against in-person solicitation be upheld?

DECISION

No. In soliciting potential clients, Fane seeks to communicate no more than truthful, nondeceptive information proposing a lawful commercial transaction. It is clear that this type of personal solicitation is commercial expression to which the protections of the First Amendment apply. In denying CPAs and their clients the advantages of commercial solicitation, Florida's law threatens societal interests in broad access to complete and accurate commercial information that First Amendment coverage of commercial speech is designed to safeguard. This is not to say that the state does not have substantial reasons for regulating personal solicitations by CPAs. Florida certainly has a legitimate interest in protecting consumers from fraud and overreaching and in maintaining both the fact and appearance of CPA independence in auditing a business and attesting to its financial statements. However, the state has not demonstrated that its ban on CPA solicitation advances those interests in any direct and material way. It presents no studies that suggest personal solicitation of prospective business clients by CPAs creates the dangers of fraud, overreaching, or compromised independence. Thus, the ends sought by the state are not advanced by the speech restriction, and legitimate commercial speech is suppressed. For this reason, the no solicitation rule infringes on the First Amendment rights of CPAs.

QUALIFIED OPINIONS AND DISCLAIMERS

Normally, after performing an independent audit, the accountant **certifies** the financial statements by issuing an **opinion letter.** This letter states whether the audit was performed in conformity with GAAS and if the financial statements accurately reflect the client's financial condition in compliance with GAAP. The accountant issues an **unqualified opinion,** meaning that in her opinion there has been compliance with GAAS and GAAP.

QUALIFIED OPINION

In some instances, the accountant will issue a **qualified,** or **clean, opinion.** For example, there may be litigation pending against the client. The uncertainty over how the litigation will be decided may cast a cloud of doubt over the financial picture of the client. The accountant will be relieved from any responsibility for major changes in the client's financial position due to an unfavorable verdict if he clearly stated his qualification in an opinion letter.

DISCLAIMER

An accountant may have conducted such a limited audit that she does not feel able to offer an opinion as to the accuracy of the client's financial statements. In this situation, she may **disclaim** any opinion. However, she would still be liable for any irregularities that her limited audit should have revealed. She may avoid liability for these irregularities by discovering them and issuing an **adverse opinion.** Merely issuing an **unaudited** statement does not create a disclaimer as to the financial statement's accuracy. The fact that they were unaudited only lowers the level of inquiry for which the accountant will be responsible.

PROTECTION OF ACCOUNTANTS' PAPERS

WORKING PAPERS

The working papers that an accountant prepares in making an audit belong to the accountant, not the client. This is so because the accountant may need to justify his work before the IRS or a court. Working papers include many different kinds of notes. Among the items included might be plans for the audit, results of testing to determine the reliability of accounts, notes as to the handling of unusual matters, and comments about the client's internal controls and accounting policies. Although these papers do not belong to the client, the accountant must get the client's permission before they can be transferred to another accountant. Also, the client has a right of access to the working papers for any reasonable purpose. This would include use of the papers by an attorney defending the client in a tax case.

ACCOUNTANT–CLIENT PRIVILEGE

Communications between lawyers and their clients are treated by the courts as privileged. That is, under most circumstances they are protected from discovery procedures in a lawsuit. Generally, lawyers cannot be required to tell what their clients have said to them, nor can they be required to produce their working papers as exhibits in court or during discovery proceedings before trial. However, no such privilege has been generally recognized in the case of accountants.

Many states have statutes that grant protection to accountants' working papers and also to conversations, letters, and memorandums between accountants and their clients. However, federal courts do not always recognize such state statutes. For example, a privilege of confidentiality has not, in the past, been recognized in federal tax cases. An accountant may be forced by a subpoena to make available to the IRS working papers involving a client who is being investigated. The accountant may also be forced to testify about the client's records and about conversations that the accountant had with the client. The same is true in SEC investigations.

In 1998, a federal statue extended the attorney–client privilege to "a federally authorized tax practitioner." That term encompasses a nonlawyer who is nevertheless authorized to practice before the Internal Revenue Service. The new privilege protects communications between a taxpayer and this federally authorized tax practitioner to the extent the communication would be considered a privileged communication if it were between a taxpayer and an attorney. It does not protect work product. Further, nothing in the statute suggests that these nonlawyers are entitled to privilege when they are doing other than lawyers' work. Consider the following case.

UNITED STATES V. FREDERICK
182 F.3d 496 (7th Cir. 1999)

FACTS

Richard Frederick is both a lawyer and an accountant. He both provides legal representation to and prepares the tax returns of Randolph and Karin Lenz and their company, KCS Industries. The IRS is investigating the Lenzes and their company. As a part of this investigation, it has issued summonses directing Frederick to hand over hundreds of documents that may be germane to the investigation. Frederick has balked at handing over all of the documents, claiming that some were protected by either the attorney–client privilege or the lawyer's work-product privilege (or both). Most of the documents in issue were created in connection with Frederick's preparation of the Lenzes' tax returns. They are drafts of the returns (including schedules), worksheets containing the financial data and computations required to fill in the returns, and correspondence relating to the returns. The IRS argues that these documents are not privileged because they are the kinds of documents that accountants and other preparers generate as an incident to preparing their clients' returns or that the taxpayers themselves generate if they prepare their own returns. Frederick claims that, because he is simultaneously acting as the Lenzes' attorney, all of the requested documents are protected from discovery.

ISSUE

Does the fact that Frederick is the Lenzes' attorney automatically render the documents privileged?

DECISION

No. There is no common law accountant's or tax preparer's privilege, and a taxpayer must not be allowed, by hiring a lawyer to do the work that an accountant, or other tax preparer, or the taxpayer himself, normally would do to obtain greater protection from government investigators that a taxpayer who did not use a lawyer s his tax prepare. To rule otherwise would be to impede tax investigations, reward lawyers for doing nonlawyers' work, and create a privileged position for lawyers in competition with other tax preparers—and to do all this without promoting the legitimate aims of the attorney–client and work-product privileges. The attorney–client privilege is intended to encourage people who find themselves involved in actual or potential legal disputes to be candid with any lawyer they retain to advise them. The hope is that this will assist the lawyer in giving the client good advice and will also avoid the disruption of the lawyer–client relationship that is brought about when a lawyer is made a witness against his client. The

(continued)

UNITED STATES V. FREDERICK
(concluded)

work-product privilege is intended to prevent the a litigant from taking a free ride on the research and thinking of his opponent's lawyer and thus avoid deterring a lawyer's committing his thoughts to paper. Communications from a client that neither reflect the lawyer's thinking nor are made for the purpose of eliciting the lawyer's professional advice or other legal assistance are not privileged. The information that a person furnishes the prepare of his tax return is furnished for the purpose of enabling the preparation of the return, not the preparation of a legal brief or an opinion letter, and therefore is not privileged. A complicating factor is that when Frederick was doing the worksheets and filling out the Lenzes' tax returns, he knew that the IRS was investigating the Lenzes and their company, albeit in connection with different tax years, and he was representing them in that investigation. But people who are under investigation and represented by an attorney have the same duty as anyone else to file tax returns. They should not be permitted by using a lawyer in lieu of another type of tax preparer to obtain greater confidentiality than other taxpayers. By using Frederick as their tax preparer, the Lenzes ran the risk that his legal thoughts born out of his legal representation of them would creep into his worksheets and so become discoverable by the government. The Lenzes

undoubtedly benefited from having their lawyer do their returns, but they must take the bad with the good; if his legal thinking infects his worksheets, that does not cast the cloak of privilege over the worksheets; they are still accountants' worksheets, unprotected no matter who prepares them. The most difficult question presented by this appeal, and one on which we cannot find any precedent, relates to documents prepared in connection with audits of the taxpayers' returns. An audit is both a stage in the determination of tax liability, often leading to the submission of revised tax returns, and a possible predecessor to litigation. Normally, however, taxpayers in audit proceedings are represented by accountants, or not represented at all, rather than by lawyers; and so the principal effect of equating audits to litigation and thus throwing a cloak of privilege over the audit-related work of the taxpayer's representative would be to create an accountant's privilege usable only by lawyers. The federal statute extending the attorney–client privilege to federally authorized tax practitioners does not help Frederick. First, it extends the privilege to nonlawyers, not lawyers. Second, nothing in the statute indicates that it would extend to nonlawyer practitioners when they are doing other than lawyers' work. As we have noted, preparing for an audit is not traditionally lawyers' work.

Ethical Implications

An accountant may be forced by subpoena to reveal the contents of working papers to the IRS. Is it ethical for the accountant to voluntarily reveal this information in the absence of a subpoena when he discovers that his client has engaged in tax fraud? Should the accountant voluntarily reveal such findings to other persons who might be injured by the client's fraudulent content?

········ *QUESTIONS AND PROBLEM CASES* ········

1. Osborne Computer Corporation planned the initial public offering of its stock in 1983. Accordingly, it retained Arthur Young to perform audits on its 1981 and 1982 financial statements. The auditor issued unqualified (clean) opinions on those financial statements, showing a modest net operating profit for 1982. Later, the company experienced manufacturing problems with its new model product and sales plummeted. When the corporation filed for bankruptcy, Bily and other investors sued Arthur Young for professional negligence, asserting that the accounting firm did not perform the audit in accordance with generally accepted auditing standards. Bily claimed that he paid more than $1.5 million for shares of Osborne stock in reliance on the audit opinions. Is a court adhering to the *Ultramares* approach

likely to find Arthur Young liable to the third-party investors for its negligence in performing the audit? Explain.

2. Under California law, accounting activities that fall within the statutory definition of the "practice of public accountancy" are reserved to licensed accountants. A person is deemed to be practicing public accountancy if she holds herself out to the public in any manner as one skilled in the knowledge, science, and practice of accounting and as qualified and ready to render professional service as a public accountant; offers to perform professional services that require an audit, examination, verification, investigation, certification, presentation, or review of financial transactions and accounting records; or, in general, renders professional services to clients in any or all matters relating to accounting procedure and to the recording, presentation, or certification of financial information or data. Unlicensed persons can offer to the public only a limited category of basic accounting services when performed as part of bookkeeping operations. Furthermore, they cannot use any title likely to be confused with the two official titles reserved or licensed for accountants: *certified public accountant* and *public accountant.* A new regulation prohibits unlicensed persons from using either the title "accountant" or the description of services offered as "accounting." Is this new regulation permissible? Explain.

3. Max Mitchell, a certified public accountant, went to First Florida Bank for the purpose of negotiating a loan on behalf of his client, C.M. Systems. After informing the bank vice president that he was a CPA, Mitchell gave the vice president audited financial statements of C.M. Systems for the two previous years, assuring the bank that he was thoroughly familiar with his client's financial condition. In reliance on these statements the bank granted the loan. When C.M. Systems failed to repay the loan, the bank discovered that Mitchell had overstated his client's assets, understated his client's liabilities, and overstated his client's net income. Is Mitchell liable to the bank in negligence under the *Restatement* approach?

4. *Video Case.* See "Cafeteria Conversation." Steve has authority to write checks on the account of his employer, a public company under the Securities Exchange Act of 1934. Because Steve is a compulsive gambler and substance abuser, he needs a constant supply of cash to finance his habits. Steve regularly issues checks payable to actual suppliers who are not currently owed money. He then steals the checks, signs the names of the payees, and cashes the checks. Because Steve also is in charge of reconciling his employer's bank statements, his embezzlement scheme is not discovered by the employer's independent auditor during a routine audit. Is the independent auditor liable to the employer for its losses resulting from Steve's embezzlement?

5. Greenstein Logan had performed Burgess Marketing's annual audit since the company's inception. Further, based on Greenstein Logan's representations of competence, Burgess hired Dunham, one of Greenstein Logan's certified public accountants, as its comptroller. During his tenure with Burgess, Dunham underaccrued and underpaid Burgess's federal excise tax. When Dunham's irregularities were uncovered by his successor, Burgess terminated its relationship with Greenstein Logan. An investigation revealed that audited financial statements prepared by Greenstein Logan had grossly understated Burgess's excise tax liability and expenses and overstated its net profit and net worth. Instead of a net profit and a positive net worth (as shown by Greenstein Logan's audited statements), Burgess had been operating at a substantial monthly deficit, was bankrupt, and had a negative net worth of $1.7 million. After the IRS levied a $2.7 million tax lien against Burgess, the company sued Greenstein Logan for its negligent audit and its negligent representation of Dunham's competence as a comptroller. Should Greenstein Logan be liable in negligence to Burgess?

6. Silvia Ibanez was a member of the Florida bar and licensed CPA in the state of Florida. In addition, she was authorized by the Certified Financial Planner Board of Standards, a private organization, to use the trademarked designation "Certified Financial Planner" (CFP). Ibanez referred to these credentials in her advertising and other communication with the

public. She placed CPA and CFP next to her name. Notwithstanding the truthful nature of her communication, the state of Florida reprimanded her for engaging in "false, deceptive, and misleading advertising." Specifically, the state concluded that the word "certified" used in the CFP designation misleads the public into believing state approval and recognition exists. However, it gathered no evidence to verify this conclusion. Should the decision to discipline Ibanez be upheld?

7. Giant Stores Corporation hired Touche Ross & Co. to audit its financial statements. It was later discovered that Giant had manipulated its books by falsely recording assets that it did not own and omitting substantial amounts of accounts payable so that the financial information that Touche had certified was incorrect. The Rosenblums, allegedly relying on the correctness of the audits, acquired Giant stock in conjunction with the sale of their business to Giant. That stock subsequently proved to be worthless after the financial statements were found to be false. The Rosenblums claimed that Touche negligently conducted the audits and that Touche's negligence proximately caused their loss. If the court uses the reasonably foreseeable users approach, could Touche be liable to the Rosenblums in spite of the lack of privity?

8. In March 1971, Lawrence and Theodore Oleck sold their shares in Blue Circle Telephone Answering Service, Inc., to Sherwood Diversified Services, Inc., in exchange for cash and promissory notes of Sherwood. In negotiating and concluding the transaction, the Olecks were given and relied on Sherwood's 1970 financial statements that had been audited and certified by Arthur Andersen & Co. Before the notes were paid in full, Sherwood became insolvent. The Olecks alleged that Andersen failed to disclose adequately (1) the high probability that Sherwood would not be able to collect on $2.5 million of notes issued by U.S. New Media International Corporation and (2) that Sherwood would have to pay an additional $2 million as guarantor on New Media's bank loan. Sherwood's risk in these transactions depended on New Media's ability to collect its accounts receivable. Andersen had studied the collectibility of the accounts receivable and concluded that they were more than adequate security to cover the bank debt and the Sherwood notes. Will the Olecks be able to prove that Andersen acted with scienter and therefore be able to recover under Rule 10b-5?

9. Jerome Riker, manager for 1136 Tenants' Corporation, hired Max Rothenberg & Co. to prepare financial reports for the corporation. Audit services were also to be performed. A Rothenberg employee discovered that several invoices were missing from the financial records of the corporation. He noted the missing invoices on his worksheet. The invoices were needed to prove that payments of $44,000 were made to creditors and not embezzled by someone in the corporation. The Rothenberg employee failed to notify anyone in the corporation that there were missing invoices. In reality, there were no invoices. Riker had embezzled the money. He embezzled even more money after the audit was completed. Is Rothenberg liable to the corporation in negligence for not informing it of the embezzlement?

10. Amerada Hess Corporation hired Arthur Young Co. (AY) to review its financial statements in connection with required disclosures under federal securities laws. AY also signed but did not prepare the company's tax returns. The IRS issued a summons requiring AY to make all of its Amerada Hess files (approximately 1 million pages of documents) available to it. For securities act purposes, AY had to determine whether Amerada Hess had contingent tax liabilities. Therefore, AY's working papers included notes as to which of the positions on income tax matters taken by the company might be questionable. The working papers also indicated the accountant's impression of the firm's willingness to fight in court and its settlement positions on matters that might be contested. May the audit working papers be withheld from the IRS as a part of an accountant–client privilege of confidentiality?

PART VI

Property

CHAPTER 30

Personal Property

Claudio is a skilled craftsman employed by Goldcasters Jewelry to make handcrafted jewelry. Working after his normal working hours and using materials he paid for himself, Claudio crafts a fine ring by skillfully weaving together strands of gold wire. He presents the ring to his fiancèe, Cheryl, as an engagement ring in anticipation of their forthcoming marriage. While visiting the restroom in a steak and ribs restaurant, Cheryl removes the ring so she can wash some barbeque sauce from her hands. In her haste to get back to her table, she leaves the ring on the washstand when she exits the restroom. Sandra, a part-time janitor for the restaurant, finds the ring and slips it into her purse. When Cheryl realizes she is missing the ring and returns to the restroom to look for it, neither the ring nor Sandra is still there. Later that evening Sandra sells the ring to her cousin, Gloria, who gives her $200 for it. Several days later, Cheryl breaks her engagement to Claudio, telling him that she no longer loves him. Claudio asks Cheryl to return the ring, indicating that he intended for her to have it only if their engagement led to marriage.

This situation raises a number of questions concerning rights and interest in personal property that will be discussed in this chapter. They include:

- *Who was the owner of the ring at the time Claudio created it, Goldcasters or Claudio?*
- *Did Claudio make an effective gift of the ring to Cheryl? Or was it a conditional gift that he could revoke when Cheryl decided to call off the marriage?*
- *What was Sandra's responsibility when she found the ring? Between Sandra and the restaurant, who had the better right to the ring?*
- *Did Cheryl have the right to recover the ring from Sandra?*
- *Did Gloria become the owner of the ring when she paid the $200 to Sandra?*
- *Does Cheryl have the right to recover the ring from Gloria if she finds that Gloria has it?*

········ *NATURE AND CLASSIFICATION* ········

PROPERTY

The concept of property has special importance to the organization of society. The essential nature of a particular society is often reflected in the way it views property, including the degree to which property ownership is concentrated in the state, the extent to which the state permits individual ownership of property, and the rules that govern such ownership. History is replete with wars and revolutions that arose out of conflicting claims to, or views concerning, property. And significant documents in our own Anglo-American legal tradition, such as the Magna Carta and the Constitution, deal explicitly with property rights.

The word **property** has a variety of meanings. It may refer to an object such as a building, or it may refer to legal rights connected with an object such as are found in the lease of a building, giving the tenant the right to occupy and use the building. However, the word *property* can also refer to legal rights that have economic value but are not connected with an object. A patent is an example of this kind of property.

When we talk about **ownership** of property, we are talking about a *bundle of legal rights* recognized and enforced by society. For example, ownership of a building includes the exclusive right to use, enjoy, sell, mortgage, or rent the building. If someone else tries to use the property without your consent, you can use the courts and legal procedures to eject the person. Ownership of a patent includes the rights to sell it, to license others to use it, or to produce the patented article personally.

In the United States, private ownership of property is of considerable importance and is protected by the Fifth Amendment to the Constitution, which provides that no person shall be deprived by the state of "life, liberty, or property, without due process of law." We recognize and encourage the rights of individuals to acquire, enjoy, and use property. These rights, however, are not unlimited. For example, a person cannot use the property in an unreasonable manner to the injury of others. Also, the state has the "police power" to impose reasonable regulations on the use of property, to tax it, and to take it for public use by paying compensation for it to the owner.

REAL AND PERSONAL PROPERTY

Property can be divided into different classes based on its characteristics. The same piece of property may fall into more than one class. The most important classification is that of real property and personal property. **Real property** is the earth's crust and all things firmly attached to it. **Personal property** includes all other objects and rights that can be owned.

Real property can be turned into personal property if it is detached from the earth. Similarly, personal property can be attached to the earth and become real property. For example, marble in the ground is real property. When the marble is quarried, it becomes personal property, but if it is used in constructing a building, it becomes real property again. Perennial vegetation, such as trees, shrubs, and grass, that does not have to be seeded every year is usually treated as part of the real property. When trees and shrubs are severed from the land, they become personal property. Crops that must be planted each year, such as corn, oats, and potatoes, are usually treated as personal property. However, if the real property on which they are growing is sold, the new owner of the real property also becomes the owner of the crops.

When personal property is attached to, or used in connection with, real property in such a way as to be treated as part of the real property, it is known as a **fixture.** The law concerning fixtures is discussed in Chapter 32.

Tangible and Intangible Property

Tangible property has a physical existence; land, buildings, and furniture are examples. Property that has no physical existence is called **intangible property;** patent rights, easements, and bonds are examples of intangible property.

The distinction between tangible and intangible property is important primarily for tax and estate-planning purposes. Generally, tangible property is subject to tax in the state in which it is located, whereas intangible property is usually taxable in the state where its owner lives.

Public and Private Property

Property is also classified as public or private based on the ownership of the property. If the property is owned by the government or a government unit, it is classified as **public property;** but if the property is owned by an individual, group of individuals, a corporation, or some other business organization, it is **private property.**

Acquiring Ownership of Personal Property

Production or Purchase

The most common ways of obtaining ownership of property are by producing it or by purchasing it. A person owns the property he makes unless the person has agreed to do the work for someone else. In that case, the employer is the owner of the product of the work. For example, a person who creates a painting, knits a sweater, or develops a computer program is the owner unless she was hired by someone to do the painting, knit the sweater, or develop the program.

Another major way of acquiring property is by purchase. The law of sale of goods was discussed in Chapters 16–19.

Possession of Unowned Property

In very early times, the most common way of obtaining ownership of personal property was simply by taking possession of unowned property. For example, the first person to take possession of a wild animal became its owner. Today, one can still acquire ownership of personal property by possessing it if the property is unowned. The two major examples of unowned property that can be acquired by possession are wildlife and abandoned property. Thus, a person with a fishing license fishing in a public lake who catches a fish, a hunter with a hunting license who shoots a deer in a state forest, or a person with a shellfish permit who recovers clams or mussels would become the owner of the fish, deer, clams or mussels, provided they were taken in accord with the provisions of the license. The ownership of the property on which the wild animal is taken is a factor in the ownership of a captured wild animal. For example, a trespasser on private property normally would not have a better right to a fish caught in a private lake than the owner of the lake who would be considered its owner.

Rights of Finders of Lost, Mislaid, and abandoned Property

The old saying "finders keepers, losers weepers" is not a reliable way of predicting the legal rights of those who find personal property that originally belonged or still belongs to another.

The rights of the finder will be determined by whether the property he finds is classified as abandoned, lost, or mislaid.

1. **Abandoned property.** Property is considered to be abandoned if the owner intentionally placed the property out of his possession with the intent to relinquish ownership of it. For example, Kristin takes her television set to the city dump and leaves it there. The finder of abandoned property who takes possession of it with the intention of claiming ownership becomes the owner of the property. This means he acquires better rights to the property than anyone else in the world including the original owner. For example, if Todd finds the TV set, puts it in his car, and takes it home, Todd becomes the owner of the TV set.

Additional issues are presented when abandoned property is found on property owned by another person. First, when abandoned property is embedded in the soil, it belongs to the owner of the soil. Second, when the owner of the land where the property is found (whether on or embedded in the soil) has constructive possession of the property such that the property is not "lost" or abandoned, it belongs to the owner of the land.

2. **Lost property.** Property is considered to be lost if the owner did not intend to part with possession of the property. For example, if Barbara's camera fell out of her handbag while she was walking down the street, it would be considered lost property. The person who finds lost property does not acquire ownership of it, but he acquires better rights to the lost property than anyone other than the true owner. For example, suppose Laura finds Barbara's camera in the grass where it fell. Leslie then steals the camera from Laura's house. Barbara is still the owner of the camera. She has the right to have it returned to her if she discovers where it is or if Laura knows that it belongs to Barbara. As the finder of lost property, Laura has a better right to the camera than anyone else except its true owner (Barbara). This means that she would have the right to require Leslie to return it to her if she finds out that Leslie has it.

If the finder of lost property knows who the owner of it is and refuses to return it, the finder is guilty of conversion and must pay the owner the fair value of the property.

A finder who sells the property that he has found can pass to the purchaser only those rights that he has; he cannot pass any better title to the property than he himself has. Thus, the true owner could recover the property from the purchaser.

3. **Mislaid property.** Property is considered mislaid if the owner placed the property somewhere and accidentally left it there, not intending to relinquish ownership of the property. For example. Sam places his backpack on a coatrack at Campus Bookstore while shopping for textbooks. Forgetting the backpack, Sam leaves the store and goes home. The backpack would be considered to be mislaid rather than lost because Sam intentionally and voluntarily placed it on the coatrack. The consequences of property's being classified as mislaid are that the finder acquires no rights to the property. Rather, the person in possession of the real property on which the personal property was mislaid has the right to hold the property for the true owner. For example, if Sarah found Sam's backpack in Campus Bookstore, Campus Bookstore would have the right to hold the mislaid property for Sam. Sarah would acquire neither possession nor ownership of the backpack.

The rationale for this rule is that it increases the chances that the property will be returned to its real owner. A person who knowingly put it down but forgot to pick it up might well remember later where the property had been left and return for it.

Some states have a statute, known as an **estray statute,** that allows finders of property to clear their title to the property after taking steps to see whether the true owner can be located. The statutes generally provide that the person must give public notice of the fact that the property has been found, perhaps by putting an ad in a local newspaper. All states have **statutes of limitations** that require the true owner of property to claim it or bring a legal action to recover possession of it within a certain number of years. A person who keeps possession of lost or unclaimed property for longer than that period of time will become its owner.

In the case that follows, *Corliss v. Wenner and Anderson*, the court awarded found property to the owner of the land on which it was found.

CORLISS V. WENNER AND ANDERSON
2001 Ida. App. Lexis 79 (Ct. App. Idaho 2001)

FACTS

In the fall of 1996, Jann Wenner hired Anderson Asphalt Paving to construct a driveway on his ranch. Larry Anderson, the owner of Anderson Asphalt Paving, and his employee, Gregory Corliss, were excavating soil for the driveway when they unearthed a glass jar containing paper-wrapped rolls of gold coins. Anderson and Corliss collected, cleaned, and inventoried the gold pieces dating from 1857 to 1914. The 96 coins weighed about 4 pounds. Initially, Anderson and Corliss agreed to split the coins between themselves, with Anderson retaining possession of all the coins. Subsequently, Anderson and Corliss argued over ownership of the coins, and Anderson fired Corliss. Anderson later gave possession of the coins to Wenner in exchange for indemnification on any claim Corliss might have against him regarding the coins.

Corliss sued Anderson and Wenner for possession of some or all of the coins. Corliss contended that the coins should be considered "treasure trove" and awarded to him pursuant to the "finders keepers" rules of treasure trove. Wenner, defending both himself and Anderson, contended that he had the better right to possession of the gold coins. The trial court held Idaho did not recognize "treasure trove" and that the coins, having been carefully concealed for safekeeping, fit within the legal classification of mislaid property, to which the right of possession goes to the land owner. Alternatively, the court ruled that the coins, like the topsoil being excavated, were a part of the property owned by Wenner and that Anderson and Corliss were merely Wenner's employees. Corliss appealed.

ISSUE

Does the finder of the buried gold coins have a better right to the coins than the owner of the property on which they were found?

DECISION

No. The court of appeals affirmed the district court's decision. The court noted that at common law, all found property is generally categorized in one of five ways: (1) abandoned property—that the owner had discarded or voluntarily forsaken with the intention of terminating his ownership but without vesting ownership in any other person; (2) lost property—that property the owner has involuntarily and unintentionally parted with through neglect, carelessness, or inadvertence, and does not know the whereabouts; (3) mislaid property—that the owner has intentionally set down in a place where he can resort to it and then forgets where he put it: (4) treasure trove—a category reserved exclusively for gold or silver in coin, plate, bullion, and sometimes its paper money equivalents, found concealed in the earth or in a house or other private place, normally under circumstances indicating the treasure has been concealed for so long as to indicate that the owner is probably dead or unknown; and (5) embedded property—that personal property which has become a part of the natural earth such as pottery, the sunken wreck of a steamship, or a rotted away sack of gold-bearing quartz rock buried or partially buried in the ground.

Here, the coins had been wrapped in paper and buried in a glass jar, evidencing a desire to keep them safe and clearly not lost or abandoned. The court then declined to adopt the rule of treasure trove, finding it out of harmony with modern notions of fair play. It noted the rule invited trespassers to roam over the property of others with metal detecting devices and to claim whatever was found to be theirs; it found this notion to be repugnant to the normal common laws treatment of trespassers. Accordingly, the court held that the owner of land has constructive possession of all personal property

CORLISS V. WENNER AND ANDERSON
(concluded)

secreted in, on, or under his land and that the landowner is entitled to possession to the exclusion of all but the true owner absent a contract between the landowner and finder.

CONCEPT SUMMARY   **Rights of Finders of Personal Property**

Character of Property	Description	Rights of Finder	Rights of Original Owner
Lost	Owner unintentionally parted with possession.	Rights superior to everyone except the owner.	Retains ownership; has the right to the return of the property.
Mislaid	Owner intentionally put property in a place but unintentionally left it there.	None; person in possession of real property on which mislaid property was found holds it for the owner, and has rights superior to everyone except owner.	Retains ownership; has the right to the return of the property.
Abandoned	Owner intentionally placed property out of his possession with intent to relinquish ownership of it.	Finder who takes possession with intent to claim ownership acquires ownership of property.	None.

GIFTS

Title to personal property can be obtained by **gift.** A gift is a voluntary transfer of property to the **donee** (the person who receives a gift), for which the **donor,** (the person who gives the gift), gets no consideration in return. To have a valid gift, all three of the following elements are necessary:

1. The donor must *intend* to make a gift.
2. The donor must make *delivery* of the gift.
3. The donee must *accept* the gift.

The most critical requirement is delivery. The person who makes the gift must actually give up possession and control of the property to either the *donee* or a third person to hold it for the donee. Delivery is important because it makes clear to the donor that she is voluntarily giving up ownership without getting something in exchange. A promise to make a gift is usually not enforceable; the person must actually part with the property. In some cases, the delivery may be symbolic. For example, handing over the key to a strongbox can be symbolic delivery of the property in the strongbox.

There are two kinds of gifts: gifts *inter vivos* and gifts *causa mortis*. A gift *inter vivos* is a gift between two living persons; a gift *causa mortis* is a gift made in contemplation of death. For example, Uncle Ernie is about to undergo a serious heart operation. Ernie gives his watch to his nephew Ted and tells Ted he wants him to have it if he does not survive the operation. A gift *causa mortis* is a conditional gift. It is not effective if (1) the donor recovers from the peril or sickness under fear of which the gift was made; (2) the donor revokes or withdraws the gift before he dies; or (3) the donee dies before the donor. If one of these events takes place, ownership of the property goes back to the donor. The case that follows, *Worrell v. Lathan*, illustrates a situation in which a claimed gift was not upheld either as an *inter vivos* gift or as a gift effective on death of the donor.

WORRELL v. LATHAN
478 S.E.2d 287 (Ct. App. S.C. 1996)

FACTS

Barbara Worrell and Elizabeth Brisendine enjoyed a long-term friendship. Brisendine often spent time at the beach with Worrell's family; they saw each other at social events and occasionally traveled together. After Brisendine became terminally ill, Worrell drove her to and from the hospital and to doctors' appointments. On a number of occasions Brisendine attempted to give Worrell money, but she never accepted it.

While Worrell was visiting Brisendine at her home in September 1993, Brisendine wrote a check, made an entry in her checkbook, and attempted to give the check to Worrell. Worrell refused the check, telling Brisendine that she looked after her out of friendship and did not desire payment for helping a friend. Brisendine returned the check and checkbook to her pocketbook. Worrell did not see the actual check and did not know the amount for which it was written. She was later told that the check "would be in the mail to her."

Henry Meyer, who took care of Brisendine's finances, saw an entry for $10,000 to Barbara Worrell in Brisendine's checkbook and was told by Brisendine that she was going to mail the check to Worrell. Brisendine died on October 21, 1993. Worrell did not hear anything else about the check until January 1994, when Meyer, who was then serving as one of the personal representatives of the estate, contacted her. Meyer told Worrell that a third party had endorsed her signature on the check and was trying to cash the check at NationsBank. Worrell then took an interest in the check, learned of the amount, and tried to ascertain what Brisendine had intended with the check. Worrell then filed a claim against the estate for $10,000, alleging the check was intended as a gift. The claim was denied by the personal representatives (Ray Lathan and Henry Meyer), and Worrell brought suit.

ISSUE

Did Brisendine make a gift of the $10,000 to Worrell?

DECISION

No. The established rule is that gifts *inter vivos* and *causa mortis* must be fully and completely executed; that is, there must be donative intent to transfer title to the property, a delivery by the donor, and an acceptance by the donee. Here there was evidence that Brisendine intended to make a gift to Worrell. She indicated such to both Worrell and Meyer and she entered the information in her own hand in her checkbook. However, there was no evidence showing any form of delivery of the check to Worrell. To be effective, there must be a complete and unconditional delivery; the transfer of possession and title must be absolute and go into immediate effect so far as the donor can make it. Moreover, acceptance by the donor of the gift is also required. Here the absence of evidence of delivery and acceptance means the gift was not completed and, in any event, Brisendine's death effectively revoked the uncompleted gift.

CONDITIONAL GIFTS

Sometimes a gift is made on condition that the donee comply with certain restrictions or perform certain actions. A conditional gift is not a completed gift, and it may be revoked by the donor before the donee complies with the conditions. However, if the donee has partially complied with the conditions, the donor cannot withdraw the gift without giving the donee an opportunity to comply fully.

Gifts in contemplation of marriage, such as engagement rings, have given rise to much litigation. Generally, gifts of this kind were considered to have been made on an implied condition that they are to be returned if the donee breaks the engagement without legal justification or if it is broken by mutual consent. If the engagement was unjustifiably broken by the donor, the traditional rule generally bars the donor from recovering gifts made in contemplation of marriage. As illustrated in the *Lindh v. Surman* case, an increasing number of courts have rejected the traditional approach and its focus on fault. Some states have enacted legislation prescribing the rules applicable to the return of engagement presents.

LINDH V. SURMAN
742 A.2d 643 (Sup. Ct. Pa. 1999)

FACTS

In August 1993, Roger Lindh proposed marriage to Janis Surman. Roger presented her with a diamond engagement ring that he had purchased for $17,400. Janis accepted the marriage proposal and the ring. Two months later Roger broke the engagement and asked Janis to return the ring. She did so. Roger and Janis reconciled, with Roger again proposing marriage and again presenting Janis with the engagement ring. Again, Janis accepted the proposal and the ring. In March 1994, Roger again broke the engagement and asked Janis to return the ring. This time, however, she refused. Roger sued her, seeking recovery of the ring or a judgment for its value. Roger contended that the ring was a conditional gift that he had the right to have returned to him when the marriage did not take place. Janis took the position that a donor who prevents the occurrence of the condition when the donee was ready and willing to perform should have to right of recovery of the gift.

ISSUE

When the donor of a engagement ring breaks the engagement, must the donee return the ring or its equivalent value?

DECISION

Yes. The majority rejected the fault-based approach suggested by Janis and adopted a no-fault rule. Under this approach, there is no investigation into the motives or reasons for the cessation of the engagement and the donee must return the engagement ring simply upon the nonoccurrence of the marriage. The court indicated that a fault-based approach would require an inquiry into complex circumstances and have to consider not only who ended the engagement but also that person's reasons, which in some cases might entirely justify the action. This kind of inquiry would invite bitter and unpleasant accusation against those they nearly made their spouse. A ring-return rule based on fault principles would inevitably invite acrimony and encourage parties to present their exfiances in the worst possible light. Trial courts likely would not be presented with situation where fault was clear and easily ascertained. The no-fault approach is the modern trend and is consistent with the movement away from the notion of fault in divorce statutes.

DISSENT

The adoption of the no-fault approach by the majority in order to relieve trial courts from having the onerous task of sifting through the debris of broken engagements to ascertain who is truly at fault is not well founded. Broken engagements are no more disturbing than cases where judges and juries are asked to discern possible abuses in nursing homes and day care centers or criminal cases involving horrific, irrational injuries to innocent victims. The subject matter that trial courts address on a daily basis is certainly of equal sordidness as any fact pattern they may need to address in a simple case of who broke the engagement and why. One can envision a scenario where a prospective bride and her family have expended thousands of dollars in preparation for the culminating event of matrimony and she is, through no fault of her own, left standing at the altar holding the catering bill. The majority would add insult to injury by stripping her of her engagement ring. There is no need to modernize the relatively simple fault-based rule determining possession of the engagement ring under the conditional gift law.

Uniform Gifts to Minors Act

The Uniform Gifts to Minors Act, which has been adopted in one form or another in every state, provides a fairly simple and flexible method for making gifts of money and securities to minors. Under it, an adult can make a gift of money to a minor by depositing the money with a broker or a bank in an account in the donor's name, or with another adult or a bank with trust powers, as custodian for the minor under the Uniform Gifts to Minors Act. Similarly, a gift of registered securities can be made by registering the securities in the name of another adult, a bank trustee, or a broker as custodian for the minor. A gift of unregistered securities can be made by delivering the securities to another adult or a bank trustee along with a statement that the adult, trustee, or broker is to hold the securities as custodian and then obtaining a written acknowledgment from the custodian. The custodian is given fairly broad discretion to use the gift for the minor's benefit but may not use it for the custodian's benefit. If the donor fully complies with the Uniform Act, the gift is considered to be irrevocable.

Will or Inheritance

Ownership of personal property can also be transferred on the death of the former owner. The property may pass under the terms of a will if the will was validly executed. If there is no valid will, the property is transferred to the heirs of the owner according to state laws. Transfer of property at the death of the owner will be discussed in Chapter 34, "Estates and Trusts."

Confusion

Title to personal property can be obtained by **confusion.** Confusion is the intermixing of goods belonging to different owners in such a way that the goods cannot later be separated. For example, suppose wheat belonging to several different people is mixed in a grain elevator. If the mixing was by agreement or if it resulted from an accident without negligence on anyone's part, then each person owns his proportionate share of the entire quantity of wheat.

However, a different result would be reached if the wheat was wrongfully or negligently mixed together. Suppose a thief steals a truckload of Grade 1 wheat worth $8.50 a bushel that belongs to a farmer. The thief dumps the wheat into a storage bin that contains a lower-grade wheat worth $4.50 a bushel. Once mixed, the wheat cannot be separated into the two grades, so it is worth only $4.50 a bushel. The farmer has first claim against the entire mixture to recover the value of his wheat that was mixed in. The thief, or any other person whose intentional or negligent act results in confusion of goods, must bear any loss caused by the confusion.

Accession

Title to personal property can also be obtained by **accession.** Accession means increasing the value of property by adding materials and/or labor. As a general rule, the owner of the original property becomes the owner of the improvements. For example, Harry takes his automobile to a shop that replaces the engine with a larger engine and puts in a new four-speed transmission. Harry is still the owner of the automobile as well as the owner of the parts added by the auto shop.

Problems can arise if materials are added or work is done on personal property without the consent of the owner. If property is stolen from one person and improved by the thief, the original owner can get it back and does not have to reimburse the thief for the work or materials in improving it. For example, a thief steals Ralph's used car, puts a new engine in it, replaces the tires, and repairs the muffler. Ralph is entitled to get his car back from the thief and does not have to pay him for the engine, tires, or muffler.

The result is more difficult to predict, however, if property is mistakenly improved in good faith by someone who believes that he is its owner. Then two innocent parties—the original owner and the person who improved the property—are involved. Usually the person who improved the property in good faith is entitled to recover the cost of the improvement made to it. Alternatively, the improver can keep the property and pay the original owner the value of the property as of the time that he obtained it. Whether the original owner has the right to recover the property after paying for the improvements depends on several factors. First, what is the relative increase in value? Second, has the form or identity of the property been changed? Third, can the improvements be separated from the original property? This is illustrated in the case that follows, *Ballard v. Wetzel*.

BALLARD V. WETZEL
1997 WL 650878 (Ct. App. Tenn. 1997)

FACTS

Faith Ballard's Corvette was substantially damaged in an accident and was being stored in her garage. Her son, Tyrone Ballard, told her that he would take the vehicle and have it restored. Instead he sold it to Lambert Auto Parts. Johnny Wetzel purchased the Corvette "hull" for $900 from Lambert, whose regular business is selling parts. Wetzel obtained a receipt documenting the purchase of the parts. He also checked the VIN numbers through the county clerk's office to make sure the parts were not stolen. Wetzel spent approximately $5,000 and 100 hours of labor restoring the vehicle. When completed, the restoration had a market value of $7,950.

George Martin, an employee of Lambert, testified that he purchased only a "hull" of a car—rather than a whole vehicle—from Tyrone Ballard. Martin also testified that he usually received a title when he bought a "whole" vehicle but had not received one in this case where he had purchased only part of one. Under Tennessee law, a certificate of title is not required to pass ownership of a motor vehicle, but any owner dismantling a registered vehicle is to send the certificate of title back to the state.

Faith Ballard brought suit against Wetzel to recover possession of the Corvette. Wetzel contended that he was a good faith purchaser for value and had become the owner of the restored auto hull by accession.

ISSUE

Did Wetzel become the owner of the Corvette by accession?

DECISION

Yes. The sale of the vehicle by Tyrone constituted theft and normally a buyer from a thief gets only the title which the thief has, which is a void title. However, the courts have held that title may pass to an innocent purchaser where there is a great disparity in the value between the original article and the new product resulting from the purchaser's labor and/or materials. Here, Wetzel acquired title to the Corvette by accession because his labor significantly increased the value of the vehicle.

.... **QUESTIONS AND PROBLEM CASES** ....

1. What are the differences between a gift *inter vivos* and a gift *causa mortis*?

2. In 1945, Lieber was serving in the U.S. Army. He was one of the first soldiers to occupy Munich,

Germany. He and some other soldiers entered Adolf Hilter's apartment and removed various items of Hitler's personal belongings. Lieber brought his share to this home in Louisiana. It included Hitler's uniform jacket and cap and some of his decorations and personal jewelry. Leiber's possession of these items was well known. There were several feature articles about them, and they were occasionally displayed to the public. Many years later, Lieber's chauffeur stole the collection and sold it to a dealer of historical material in New York. The dealer sold it to Mohawk Arms, which had no knowledge that it had been stolen. Lieber learned that Mohawk Arms had the collection and demanded that the company return it. Mohawk Arms claimed that it did not have to return the collection to Lieber because the collection properly belonged to the occupational military authority or to the Bavarian government, not to Lieber. Was Lieber entitled to the return of the collection that had been stolen from him?

3. Heath Benjamin, an employee of Lindner Aviation, found $18,000 in currency inside the wing of an airplane owned by State Central Bank. The bank acquired the airplane in April 1992 when it repossessed it from its prior owner who had defaulted on a loan. In August, the bank took the plane to Lindner Aviation for a routine annual inspection.

As part of the inspection Benjamin removed panels from the undersides of the wings. Although the panels were to be removed annually as part of an inspection, it appeared that the panel had not been removed for several years and several screws were so rusty they had to be drilled out. Inside the left wing Benjamin discovered two packages approximately four inches high wrapped in tin foil. Inside the packages was paper currency, tied in string. The currency was primarily twenty-dollar bills with mint dates before the 1960s, primarily from the 1950s, smelling musty.

Benjamin reported what he had found to his supervisor and offered to divided the money with him. However, the supervisor reported the discovery to the owner of Lindner Aviation, who insisted that they contact the authorities. The money was turned over to the local police

department. Two days later, Benjamin filed an affidavit with the county auditor claiming that he was the finder of the currency under the provisions of the Iowa Code (Chapter 644). Lindner Aviation and State Central Bank also filed similar claims. The notices required under the Iowa Code were published and posted. No one came forward within 12 months claiming to be the true owner of the money.

Benjamin then filed a declaratory judgment action against Lindner Aviation and the bank to establish his right to the money under the Iowa Code provision that vested ownership of property in the finder if the true owner did not claim it within 12 months. The district court held that the statue applied only to "lost" property and the money here was mislaid. Accordingly, it awarded the money to the bank, holding that it was entitled to possession of the money to the exclusion of all but the true owner. However, it also found that Benjamin was a "finder" within the meaning of the statute and awarded Benjamin a 10 percent finder's fee as authorized by the statute. Benjamin appealed. Was Benjamin the finder of the lost property and thus entitled to ownership of the money?

4. Leonard Charrier was an amateur archeologist. After researching colonial maps and records, he concluded that the Trudeau Plantation near Angola, Louisiana, was the possible site of an ancient village of the Tunica Indians. Charrier obtained the permission of the caretaker of the Trudeau Plantation to survey the property with a metal detector for possible burial locations. At the time, he mistakenly believed that the caretaker was the Plantation's owner. He located and, over the next three years, excavated approximately 150 burial sites containing beads, European ceramics, stoneware and glass bottles; iron kettles, vessels, and skillets; knives, muskets, gunflints, balls, and shots; crucifixes, rings, and bracelets; and native pottery. He began discussions with Harvard University to sell the collection to its Peabody Museum. While the University inventoried, cataloged, and displayed the items pursuant to a lease agreement, it was unwilling to go through with a sale unless Charrier could establish title to the artifacts. He then brought

suit against the owners of the Trudeau Plantation seeking a declaratory judgment that he was the owner of the artifacts. The state of Louisiana intervened in the litigation to assert the rights of the lawful heirs of the artifacts. Charrier argued that the Indians abandoned the artifacts when they moved from the Trudeau Plantation in 1764. He contended that they were unowned property until he found them and reduced them to his possession. He compared them to wild game and fish, which are unowned until someone takes possession of them. Were the artifacts abandoned property of which Charrier could become the owner by taking possession?

5. First National Bank of Chicago sold a number of used file cabinets on an "as is" basis to Zibton, a dealer in new and used office furniture. In the summer of 1983, Zibton sold some of the cabinets to Charles Straye. Straye gave one of the cabinets, a locked one with no keys, to his friend Richard Michael. About six weeks later, Michael was moving the file cabinet in his garage when it fell over and several of the locked drawers opened. Inside were more than 1,600 certificates of deposit (CDs), including 7 that had not been canceled or stamped paid and that were worth a total of $6,687,948.85, with maturity dates ranging from October 1982 to January 1983. Six of the CDs were payable to "Bearer." First Chicago had placed the CDs in the cabinet between March and May of 1983 when the responsibility for storing paid CDs was changed to a different unit of the bank. The CDs were moved from a vault to file cabinets at that time. Each drawer had been labeled with a card stating "Paid Negotiable CDs" and indicating the numbers of the CDs contained in the drawer. The new unit responsible for storing CDs determined that they could not use the file cabinets, so the CDs were transferred to tote boxes. First Chicago employees randomly checked to determine if the contents were gone and then transferred the file cabinets to the warehouse for sale. Michael called the FBI, which took possession of all of the CDs. He then filed an action for a declaratory judgment that he should be awarded ownership of the CDs. In his lawsuit, Michael argued that he was entitled to possession of the CDs because they were the subject of a sale from First Chicago. Alternatively, he claimed that the CDs were abandoned property, as opposed to lost or mislaid property, which he as finder was entitled to keep. Is Michael entitled to ownership of the CDs that he found in the file cabinets that were given to him?

6. Bernice Paset, a customer of the Old Orchard Bank, found $6,325 in currency on the seat of a chair in an examination booth in the bank's safe-deposit vault. The chair was partially under a table. Paset notified officers of the bank and turned the money over to them. She was told by the bank officials that the bank would try to locate the owner and that she could have the money if the owner was not located within one year. The bank wrote to everyone who had been in the safe-deposit vault area either on the day of, or on the day preceding, the discovery, stating that some property had been found and inviting the customers to describe any property they might have lost. No one reported the loss of any currency and the money remained unclaimed a year after it had been found. The bank refused to deliver the money to Paset, contending it was mislaid, not lost, property and that it had a better right to it. Was the money found on the chair in the safe-deposit vault mislaid property?

7. Hunter Taylor lived with Hattie Smith. Taylor rented a safe-deposit box at the Crown Center Bank in the name of Hattie Smith and gave her both keys to the box. Smith signed a card that authorized and directed the bank to allow Hunter Taylor to enter "my box" at any time. On several occasions, Taylor borrowed the keys to the box without explanation and then returned them to Smith. Smith claimed that Taylor told her he had put money in the box for her. Smith did not see Taylor put any money in the box, and none was put in the day the box was rented. Taylor was murdered, and at the time of the murder he had both of the keys to the box in his possession. Smith had the box opened by the bank, and $8,000 was found in it. The administer of Taylor's estate claimed the money was for the estate. Smith claimed that the money was a gift to her. Had Taylor made a valid gift of the money to Smith?

8. Jack Patterson hired Dondee Blanton to perform cleaning services in connection with his fire restoration business. The business relationship evolved into a romantic one which lasted through November 1991. Both were married at the time and each knew of the other's marital status. Sometime between April and July 1991, Patterson proposed to Blanton and she accepted. Each agreed to divorce his or her spouse to make the contemplated marriage possible. Over the next few months, Patterson gave Blanton several gifts of jewelry, including bracelets, watches, and a pair of engagement rings, with a value of $46,500. In October, Patterson's wife filed for divorce, but Blanton remained married to her spouse. In November, Patterson and Blanton took a Caribbean cruise together, during which Patterson purchased further jewelry for Blanton. Shortly after they returned from the cruise, the two quarreled and ended their affair. Patterson requested that Blanton return the jewelry, but she refused. Patterson then brought suit, alleging that the jewelry was a conditional gift given in contemplation of marriage, that Blanton had converted the jewelry to her own use, and that the jewelry or its value should be returned to him. Was Patterson entitled to the return of the jewelry on the grounds that it was a conditional gift given in contemplation of marriage that had to be returned when the engagement was broken.

9. Ochoa's Studebaker automobile was stolen. Eleven months later the automobile somehow found its way into the hands of the U.S. government, which sold it at a "junk" auction for $85 to Rogers. At the time it was purchased by Rogers, no part of the car was intact. It had no top except a part of the frame; it had no steering wheel, tires, rims, cushions, or battery; the motor, radiator, and gears were out of the car; one wheel was gone, as was one axle; the fenders were partly gone; and the frame was broken. It was no longer an automobile but a pile of broken and dismantled parts of what was once Ochoa's car. Having purchased these parts, Rogers used them in the construction of a delivery truck at an expense of approximately $800. When the truck was completed, he put it to use in his furniture business. Several months later, Ochoa was passing Rogers's place of business and recognized the machine from a mark on the hood and another on the radiator. He discovered that the serial and engine numbers matched those on the car he had owned. Ochoa demanded the car from Rogers, who refused to surrender it. Ochoa brought suit to recover possession of the property. In the alternative, he asked for the value at the time of the suit, which he alleged to be $1,000 and for the value of the use of the car at the rate of $5 per day from the time that Rogers had purchased it from the government. Was Ochoa entitled to recover possession of his property, which Rogers had substantially improved?

CHAPTER 31

Bailments

You take your car to a parking garage where the attendant gives you a claim check and then drives the car down the ramp to park it. While eating at a restaurant, you leave your coat with an attendant in a coatroom. Frank rents a van to move his household goods to a new apartment. Charlie borrows his neighbor's lawn mower to cut his grass. Ann asks Kathy, who lives in the next apartment, to take care of her cat while she goes on vacation. These are everyday situations that involve bailments. This chapter will focus on the legal aspects of bailments. Among the questions we will cover are:

- *What are your rights if your car is damaged or if property is stolen from the trunk while the car is parked in the parking garage?*
- *How effective are the signs you may see near checkrooms that say, "Not responsible for loss or damages to property"?*
- *What are your responsibilities if you borrow or rent items such as a van or a lawn mower from someone else?*
- *What obligations does the person from whom you rent or borrow an item have to insure the safety of that item or to warn you about any known defects?*
- *What are your responsibilities if you agree to take care of someone else's personal property?*

.... **NATURE OF BAILMENTS** ....

ELEMENTS OF A BAILMENT

A **bailment** is the delivery of personal property by one person (the **bailor**) to another person (the **bailee**) who accepts it and is under an express or implied agreement to return it to the bailor or to someone designated by the bailor. The essential elements are:

1. The bailor must own or have the right to possess the item of property.
2. The bailor must deliver exclusive possession and control of the property, but not title, to the bailee.
3. The bailee must knowingly accept the property with the understanding that he owes a duty to return the property as directed by the bailor.

CREATION OF A BAILMENT

A bailment is created by an express or implied contract. Whether the elements of a bailment have been fulfilled is determined by examining all the facts and circumstances of a particular situation. A critical requirement in the creation of a bailment is whether the person to whom the property was delivered *intended to assume possession and control over the property.* Suppose you go into a restaurant and hang your hat and coat on an unattended rack. It is unlikely that this created a bailment because the restaurant owner never assumed control over the hat and coat. However, if there is a checkroom and you check your hat and coat with the attendant, a bailment will arise.

If you park your car in a parking lot, keep the keys, and can drive the car out yourself whenever you wish, a bailment has not been created. The courts treat this situation as a lease of space. Suppose you take your car to a parking garage where an attendant gives you a claim check and then parks the car. In this case, there is a bailment of your car since the parking garage has accepted delivery and possession of your car. However, a distinction is made between the car and some packages locked in the trunk. If the parking garage was not aware of the packages, it would probably not be a bailee of them as it did not knowingly accept possession of them.

The case that follows, *Detroit Institute Arts v. Rose and Smith*, illustrates a situation in which no bailment was found to exist.

DETROIT INSTITUTE OF ARTS v. ROSE AND SMITH
127 F.Supp.2d 117 (U.S.D.C. D.Conn. 2001)

FACTS

The Howdy Doody Show was a television program beloved by millions of children in what is now known as the "baby boom generation." It was produced and broadcast by the National Broadcasting Company, Inc. (NBC), from 1947 to 1960. Hosted by Robert "Buffalo Bob" Smith, the show's main character was Howdy Doody, a puppet in the image of a freckled-faced boy in cowboy clothing.

Beginning in 1952, Rufus Rose served as the puppet master, puppeteer, and caretaker for many of the puppets that appeared on the show. While the show was on the air, he created, stored, and made repairs to the puppets in his workshop in Waterford, Connecticut—and was compensated accordingly. When the show ended in 1960, Rose, pursuant to an informal agreement, kept

(continued)

DETROIT INSTITUTE OF ARTS V. ROSE AND SMITH
(concluded)

possession of the puppets at his workshop until final arrangements were made for them. Rose acknowledged that the puppets belonged to NBC.

In 1965, Rose began a series of correspondence with NBC about payment for his maintenance and storage of the puppets, including Howdy Doody, since the end of the show in 1960. In a letter to NBC, Rose proposed that (1) NBC pay him for storage and upkeep of all the puppets since the end of the show (2) he be allowed to keep the minor puppets but with the understanding he would not use them as Howdy Doody Show characters and (3) the main puppets from the show, including Howdy Doody, would be turned over to a museum, the Detroit Institute of Arts (DIA), that was the recognized museum of puppetry in America. Subsequently, he signed a release acknowledging payment for past fees and indicating his agreement to send Howdy Doody to the DIA.

In 1970, Rose, in response to a request from his friend Buffalo Bob, who was making personal appearances throughout the country, sent Howdy Doody to Buffalo Bob. In an accompanying letter, Rose explained to Buffalo Bob that he had agreed with NBC that the puppet would "eventually" be placed in the DIA and that it would never be used in a commercial manner—and that the original Howdy Doody was being sent to Buffalo Bob "with this mutual understanding and responsibility." For the next fifteen years, Buffalo Bob kept Howdy Doody and used the puppet in his personal appearances.

In 1992, Buffalo Bob's attorney contacted Rose's widow, NBC, and DIA, requesting that they waive the requirement that Howdy Doody be placed in the DIA. He indicated that Buffalo Bob had fallen on difficult financial times and now wished to sell the puppet and keep the proceeds. Rose's son Christopher replied on behalf of his mother, stating that it was his father's intention that Buffalo Bob honor the "condition" that Howdy Doody be given to the DIA. NBC refused to release Howdy Doody to him, and the DIA declined to let him sell the puppet. Buffalo Bob then informed the DIA that he would transfer Howdy Doody to the museum "when he no longer wished to keep the puppet."

In 1998, Buffalo Bob and Christopher Rose executed an agreement to sell the puppet and split the proceeds 50–50. They "certified" that Christopher had received the puppet from Buffalo Bob and Christopher entered into a consignment agreement with an auction house to sell the "original Howdy Doody." A few days later Buffalo Bob died, and the DIA brought a lawsuit to prevent the Rose family from selling the puppet and to gain possession of it. One of the questions in the lawsuit was whether the 1970 letter created a bailment to Buffalo Bob that obligated him to turn the puppet over to the DIA.

ISSUE

Did the 1970 letter agreement between Rose and Buffalo Bob create a gratuitous bailment pursuant to which Buffalo Bob was required to turn Howdy Doody over to the DIA?

DECISION

Yes. The court noted that a bailment arises when the owner or bailor delivers personal property to another for some particular purpose with an express or implied contract to redeliver the goods when the purpose has been fulfilled, or to otherwise deal with the goods according to the bailor's directions. The bailor has a property interest in the goods while the bailee merely possesses them. Here the bailment was for the sole benefit of the bailee, a type of bailment known as a *gratuitous bailment* and one that typically involves no consideration. However, the bailor suffers a detriment by giving up possession. Bailments involve certain implied obligations that are implied in the absence of an express condition. One general obligation is to return the bailed property to the owner—or as directed by him. A bailee can also become liable to a third party when the bailment contract includes provisions that were incorporated for the third party's special benefit and interest.

Here the evidence establishes that Rufus Rose's 1970 letter to Buffalo Bob created an enforceable bailment whereby Buffalo Bob assumed a duty to turn over Howdy Doody to the DIA. Buffalo Bob's use of the puppet was specifically conditioned on the same two requirements that NBC imposed on Rufus Rose, including the requirement that Howdy Doody eventually be placed in the care of the Detroit Institute of Arts. Rose gave up possession of the puppet in reliance on Buffalo Bob's promise to redeliver the puppet. The DIA has the right to enforce that promise.

CUSTODY

A distinction is made between delivering **possession** of goods and merely giving **custody** of goods. If a shopkeeper entrusts goods to a clerk in the store, the shopkeeper is considered to have given the clerk custody of the goods but to have retained possession of them. Because the shopkeeper has retained legal possession, there has not been a bailment of goods to the clerk.

TYPES OF BAILMENTS

Bailments are commonly divided into three different categories:

1. Bailments for the sole benefit of the bailor.
2. Bailments for the sole benefit of the bailee.
3. Bailments for mutual benefit.

The type of bailment can be important in determining the liability of the bailee for loss of or damages to the property. However, some courts no longer rely on these distinctions for this purpose.

Bailments for Benefit of Bailor

A bailment for the sole benefit of the bailor is one in which the bailee renders some service but does not receive a benefit in return. For example, you allow your neighbor to park her car in your garage while she is on vacation and she does not pay you anything for the privilege. Your neighbor (bailor) has received a benefit from you (bailee), but you have not received a benefit in return.

Bailments for Benefit of Bailee

A bailment for the sole benefit of the bailee is one in which the owner of the goods allows someone else to use them free of charge. For example, you loan your lawn mower to your neighbor so he can cut his grass.

Mutual Benefit Bailments

If both the bailee and the bailor receive benefits from the bailment, it is a mutual benefit bailment. For example, you rent a U-Haul trailer from a store. You, the bailee, benefit by being able to use the trailer while the store benefits from your payment of the rental charge. Similarly, if you store some furniture at a commercial warehouse, it is a mutual benefit bailment. You get the benefit of having your goods cared for while the storage company benefits from the storage charge you pay. On some occasions, the benefit to the bailee is less tangible. Suppose you check your coat at an attended coatroom at a restaurant. Even if no charge is made for the service, it is likely to be treated as a mutual bailment because the restaurant is benefiting from your patronage.

RIGHTS AND DUTIES

DUTIES OF THE BAILEE

The bailee has two basic duties: (1) to take reasonable care of the property that has been entrusted to him and (2) to return the property at the termination of the bailment.

BAILEE'S DUTY OF CARE

The bailee is responsible for using **reasonable care** to protect the property during the time he has possession of it. If the bailee does not exercise reasonable care and the property is lost or damaged, the bailee is liable for negligence. Thus, the bailee would have to reimburse the bailor for the amount of loss or damage. If the property is lost or damaged without the fault or negligence of the bailee, the bailee is not liable to the bailor.

Whether the bailee in a particular case exercised reasonable care depends in part on who is benefiting from the bailment. If it is a mutual benefit bailment, then the bailee must use ordinary care, which is the same kind of care a reasonable person would use to protect his own property in that situation. If the bailee is a professional that holds itself out as a professional bailee—such as a warehouse—it must use the degree of care a person in that profession would use. This is likely to be more care than the ordinary person would use. In addition, there is usually a duty on a professional bailee to explain any loss or damage to property, that is, to show it was not negligent. If it cannot do so, it will be liable to the bailor.

If the bailment is solely for the benefit of the bailor, then the bailee may be held to a somewhat lower degree of care. If the bailee is doing you a favor, it is not reasonable to expect him to be as careful as when you are paying a bailee for keeping your goods. Usually, the bailee in this situation is liable only for gross negligence. On the other hand, if the bailment is for the sole benefit of the bailee, it is reasonable to expect that the bailee will use a higher degree of care. If you loan your sailboat to your neighbor, you probably expect her to be even more careful with it than you would be. In this situation, a bailee is liable for even slight negligence.

Who benefits from a bailment is one consideration in determining what is reasonable care. Other factors include the nature and value of the property, how easily it can be damaged or stolen, whether the bailment was paid for or free, and the experience of the bailee. Using reasonable care includes using the property only as was agreed between the parties. For example, you loan your lawn mower to your neighbor to cut his lawn. However, if he uses it to cut the weeds on a trash-filled vacant lot and the mower is damaged, he would be liable because he was exceeding the agreed purpose for the bailment—that is, to cut his lawn.

BAILEE'S DUTY TO RETURN THE PROPERTY

One of the essential elements for a bailment is the duty of the bailee to return the property at the termination of the bailment. The bailee must return the goods in an undamaged condition to the bailor or to someone designated by the bailor. If the goods have been damaged or lost, there is a rebuttable presumption of negligence on the part of the bailee. To overcome the presumption, the bailee has the burden of showing that the accident, damage, or loss resulted from some cause consistent with the exercise of the relevant level of due care on his part. This principle is illustrated in the case of Institute of *London Underwriters v. Eagle Boats, Ltd.*, that appears below.

In most instances, the bailee must return the identical property that was bailed. If you loan your 1999 Jeep to your friend, you expect to have that particular car returned to you. In some cases, the bailor does not expect the identical goods back. For example, if a farmer stores 1,500 bushels of wheat at a local grain elevator, that farmer expects to get back 1,500 bushels of similar wheat when the bailment is terminated, but not the identical wheat that he deposited.

The bailee is also liable to the bailor if she misdelivers the bailed property at the termination of the bailment. The property must be returned to the bailor or to someone specified by the bailor.

INSTITUTE OF LONDON UNDERWRITERS V. EAGLE BOATS, LTD.
918 F. Supp. 297 (E.D. Mo. 1996)

FACTS

In early 1991, William Seebold, the president of Eagle Boats, Ltd., was approached by a boating magazine, Trailer Boats, about doing a feature on a motorboat manufactured by Eagle Boats. The magazine feature would include a written article and photographs of the boat on Grand Lake near Ketchum, Oklahoma. Seebold expressed interest in the idea to the magazine's representative.

At the time, a motorboat owned by Hoppies Village Marina was at Eagle Boat's facility in Fenton, Missouri, undergoing minor paint repairs. The motorboat was a 1991 Seebold Eagle 265 Limited Edition; a 26-foot, 4,000 to 4,500 pound, 600-horsepower supercharged motorboat capable of attaining a speed of 80 mph. It was considered to be the "Cadillac" of motorboats in its class. Seebold called Hoppies about using its motorboat for the magazine article, which would include information not only about the motorboat and Eagle Boats, but also about Hoppies Village Marina. Hoppies agreed. The arrangement was for Seebold to transport the boat to Ketchum and then return it to Hoppies' custody.

After the touch-up work on the motorboat was finished, the boat was loaded onto a custom-built trailer owned by Hoppies. The trailer did not have a locking device on it—a device capable of locking the trailer to the truck. The trailer was then hooked up to an Eagle Boats truck, and Seebold drove it to Ketchum. He arrived at the Grand Lodge Inn about 9:30 PM. The demonstration for the magazine was scheduled for 6:00 AM the next morning.

Seebold parked the truck, boat, and trailer on the motel's parking lot, parallel to a fence at the end of the lot, facing away from the highway. There was one dusk-to-dawn light shining in front of the motel, and the boat was parked across the lot from this light. The parking lot was small and narrow, making it difficult for the boat

and trailer to be turned around. There were other boats parked on the lot, but this was the closest to the road and also the most expensive. Behind the motel were storage units. Seebold was awakened about 4:30 the next morning with the news that the boat and trailer were missing.

At the time of the theft, the motorboat and trailer had a combined fair market value of more than $60,000. Hoppies' insurance carrier, Institute of London Underwriters, paid Hoppies' insurance claim. Then as the subrogee of Hoppies' claim against Eagle Boats, it brought suit against Eagle and Seebold for their failure to use reasonable care of the bailed motorboat and trailer to prevent their theft.

ISSUE

Were Eagle Boats and Seebold, as bailees, liable to Hoppies Village Marina for their failure to use reasonable care to prevent the theft of the motorboat and trailer?

DECISION

Yes. There is no dispute that Seebold and Hoppies entered into a bailment arrangement. The duty of the bailee is to exercise ordinary care in the handling and safekeeping of the bailed property, including ordinary care to prevent theft of the bailed property. In a mutual benefit bailment, the bailee is not an insurer but does have a duty of ordinary care. Here, the only precaution taken by Seebold was to park the boat/trailer where it would be inaccessible and difficult to move. However, he chose the parking space closest to the roadway. He did not put a chain around the boat and trailer to lock it to the truck. He did not hire anyone to guard the boat overnight. And he did not inquire about the use of the storage units behind the motel. Accordingly, Seebold failed to demonstrate that he exercised due care of the boat/trailer while it was in his custody and is liable for his negligence.

LIMITATIONS ON LIABILITY

Bailees may try to limit or relieve themselves of liability for the bailed property. Common examples include the signs near checkrooms, "Not responsible for loss or damage to checked property" and **disclaimers** on claim checks, "Goods left at owner's risk." Any attempt by the bailee to be relieved of liability for intentional wrongful acts is against public policy and will not be enforced.

A bailee's ability to be relieved of liability for negligence is also limited. The courts look to see whether the disclaimer or limitation of liability was *communicated* to the bailor. Did the attendant point out the sign near the checkroom to the person when the coat was checked? Did the parking lot attendant call the person's attention to the disclaimer on the back of the claim check? If not, the court may hold that the disclaimer was not communicated to the bailee and did not become part of the bailment contract. Even if the bailee was aware of the disclaimer, it still may not be enforced on the ground that it is contrary to public policy.

Courts do not look with favor on efforts by a person to be relieved of liability for negligence. We expect people to use reasonable care and to be liable if they do not and someone or something is injured as a result. If the disclaimer was offered on a take-it-or-leave-it basis and was not the subject of arm's-length bargaining, it is not likely to be enforced. A bailee may be able to limit liability to a certain amount. Ideally, the bailee will give the bailor a chance to declare a higher value and to pay an additional charge to be protected up to the declared value of the goods. Common carriers such as railroads and trucking companies often take this approach.

In the case that follows, *Collins v. Click Camera & Video, Inc.*, the court enforced a clause that limited a bailee's liability to the replacement cost of the bailed property.

COLLINS V. CLICK CAMERA & VIDEO, INC.
621 N.E.2d 1294 (Ct. App. Ohio 1993)

FACTS

Leo Collins deposited 28 reels of Super 8 movie film with Click Camera & Video, Inc., to have the images contained on the film transferred onto video tape. At least 50 percent of the film depicted images of Collins's daughter during her early childhood.

At the time he deposited his movie film, Collins signed a video transfer "order form" which detailed the type of service desired, cost of the service ($234.28), deposit required, and expected completion date. The "order form" also included a box in the lower left hand corner entitled "Customer's receipt" which included a customer signature and stated in extremely small print, among other things,

> [the customer] acknowledge[s] and agree[s] that the video transfer center or its agents [*sic*] liability for any loss, damage or delay to material during the requested service will be limited to the replacement cost of a non-exposed roll of film

or replacement. The video center or its agents shall not be liable for any other loss or damage, direct, consequential, or incidental arising out of its customers use of the video transfer center facilities.

Collins was asked to sign the line under this provision and he did so. He was not asked to read the limitations clause, nor were its provisions explained to him. Collins did not read the limitations clause and was not aware of its provisions. However, at his deposition he indicated that he would have signed it even had he been cognizant of its content.

When Collins attempted to collect his film, Click Camera was unable to account for its whereabouts. Collins filed suit against Click Camera alleging breach of a bailment contract and/or negligence for Click Camera's failure to redeliver the bailed property. He sought damages of more than $25,000. Click Camera filed a motion for

(continued)

COLLINS V. CLICK CAMERA & VIDEO, INC.
(concluded)

summary judgment in its favor, asserting that the limitation clause limited Collins's recovery to replacement cost of the film deposited.

ISSUE

Was Click Camera's liability to Collins for its failure to redeliver the bailed film limited to its replacement value by the limitations clause?

DECISION

Yes. Where a bailee fails to return bailed property, he can escape liability only by showing that he exercised ordinary care in safeguarding the bailed property or that the bailor accepted responsibility for its loss. Here, assent to the limitations clause was specifically and separately required. The use of the clause in video transfer contracts is commercially reasonable because the charge for the service is minimal compared to the potential liability for negligence. In addition, given the nature of film processing, the extent of potential liability is unpredictable because the processor is generally unaware of the content of the film when it is delivered and unable to replace that content should the film be lost or destroyed. Here, this particular clause has some attributes that could lead to a finding of unconscionability; the title of the clause "Customer Receipt" is misleading, and the print is very small and not distinguished by type size or spacing. However, Collins saw the limitations clause but failed to read it. He also indicated that he would have signed it even if he had known its contents. This is not a case where Collins was required as a practical matter to enter into this bailment contract. The clause is not unconscionable as applied to him.

RIGHT TO COMPENSATION

Whether a bailee is paid for keeping property or must pay for the right to use it depends on the bailment contract or the understanding of the parties. If the bailment is a favor, then the bailee is not entitled to compensation even though the bailment is for the benefit of the bailor. If the bailment is the rental of property, then the bailee must pay the agreed-on rental rate. If the bailment is for the storage or repair of property, then the bailee is entitled to the contract price for the storage or repair services. If no price is agreed on, the bailee gets the reasonable value of the services provided.

In many instances, the bailee will have a **lien** on the bailed property for the reasonable value of the services. Suppose you take a chair to an upholsterer to have it recovered. This is a mutual benefit bailment. When the chair has been recovered, the upholsterer has the right to keep it until you pay the agreed price or—if no price was set—the reasonable value of the work. (Artisan's liens are discussed in Chapter 40.)

BAILOR'S LIABILITY FOR DEFECTS IN THE BAILED PROPERTY

When personal property is rented or loaned, the bailor makes an **implied warranty** that there are no hidden defects in the property that make it unsafe for use. If the bailment is for the sole benefit of the bailee, then the bailor is liable for injuries that result from defects in the bailed property only if the bailor knew about the defects and did not tell the bailee. For example, Paul loans his car, which has bad brakes, to Sally. If Paul does not tell Sally about the bad brakes and if Sally is injured in an accident because the brakes fail, Paul is liable for Sally's injuries.

If the bailment is a mutual benefit bailment, then the bailor has a larger obligation. The bailor must use reasonable care in inspecting the property and seeing that it is safe for the purpose for which it is rented. The bailor is liable for injuries suffered by the bailee because of defects that the bailor either knew about or should have discovered by reasonable inspection. For example, Frank's Rent-All rents trailers. Suppose Frank's does not inspect the trailers after they come back from being rented. A wheel has come loose on a trailer that Frank's rents to Harold. If the wheel comes off while Harold is using the trailer and the goods Harold is carrying in the trailer are damaged, Frank's is liable to Harold.

In addition, product liability doctrines that apply a higher standard of legal responsibility have been applied to bailors who are commercial lessors of personal property. This includes express and implied warranties of quality under either Article 2 or Article 2A of the UCC. Thus, if goods are rented to someone (mutual benefit bailment) for her personal use, there may be an *implied warranty* that the goods are fit for the purpose for which they are rented. Liability does not depend on whether the bailor knew about or should have discovered the defect. The only question is whether the property was fit for the purpose for which it was rented.

Some courts have also imposed **strict liability** on lessors/bailors of goods that turn out to be more dangerous than the lessee/bailee would have expected. This liability is imposed regardless of whether the lessor was negligent or at fault. Implied warranties and strict liability were discussed in detail in Chapter 17. In the case below, *Samuel Friedland Family Enterprises v. Amoroso*, a bailor in a bailment for mutual benefit was held strictly liable for injuries sustained by the bailee.

SAMUEL FRIEDLAND FAMILY ENTERPRISES V. AMOROSO
630 So.2d 1067 (Sup. Ct. Fla. 1994)

FACTS

The Diplomat Hotel is a waterfront property in Hollywood, Florida. Sunrise Water Sports, Inc., leased part of the Diplomat's property and operated a sailboat rental stand there, renting sailboats which it owned. Paula Amoroso and her family were guests at the Diplomat and rented sailboats on three occasions. The third time, she was injured when a sailboat's crossbar broke.

As a result of her injuries Amoroso sued the Diplomat, Sunrise, and a welder who had repaired the crossbar a few days before the accident. She asserted claims for negligence and breach of warranties of fitness and strict liability against the Diplomat and Sunrise and for negligence against the welder. She also asserted a claim in strict liability against the Diplomat and Sunrise. The trial court directed a verdict in favor of the defendants on the strict liability claim. On appeal, this was reversed by the court of appeals, and the Diplomat and Sunrise appealed the decision to the Florida Supreme Court.

ISSUE

Can the lessor of a defective sailboat that injures a person as well as the hotel that provides space to the lessor be held strictly liable to the person injured?

DECISION

Yes. The court held that the doctrine of strict liability that applies to manufacturers and distributors of defective products also applies to commercial lessors of such products. In both instances the consumer uses the product without having an opportunity to discover the defect, and the same rationale supports holding the lessor of a defective product strictly liable. It found that Sunrise was in the business of leasing sailboats which it owned and should be held strictly liable for leasing a defective sailboat to the Amorosos. The court also found that the Diplomat leased property to Sunrise specifically for the purpose of leasing sailboats and that it was actively involved in marketing the sailboats to its guests. In turn, it concluded that the hotel's involvement was sufficient to sustain a strict liability cause of action against it as a lessor engaged in the business of leasing the sailboats.

CONCEPT SUMMARY	Duties of Bailees and Bailors	
Type of Bailment	**Duties of Bailee**	**Duties of Bailor**
Sole Benefit of Bailee	1. Must use great care; liable for even slight negligence. 2. Must use goods consistent with bailment agreement. 3. Must return goods to bailor or dispose of them at his direction. 4. May have duty to compensate.	1. Must notify the bailee of any known defects.
Mutual Benefit	1. Must use reasonable care; liable for ordinary negligence. 2. Must use goods consistent with bailment agreement. 3. Must return goods to bailor or dispose of them at his direction. 4. May have duty to pay reasonable compensation.	1. Must notify bailee of all known defects and any hidden defects that are known or could be discovered on reasonable inspection. 2. Commercial lessors may be subject to warranties of quality and/or strict liability in tort. 3. May have duty to compensate bailee.
Sole Benefit of Bailee	1. Must use at least slight care; liable for gross negligence. 2. Must use goods consistent with bailment agreement. 3. Must return goods to bailor or dispose of them at his direction.	1. Must notify bailee of all known defects and any hidden defects that are known or could be discovered on reasonable inspection. 2. May have duty to compensate bailee.

SPECIAL BAILMENT SITUATIONS

COMMON CARRIERS

Bailees who are **common carriers** are held to a higher level of responsibility than bailees who are private carriers. Common carriers are persons who are licensed by government agencies to carry the property of anyone who requests the service. Airlines licensed by the Department of Transportation (DOT) and trucks and buses that formerly were licensed by the Interstate Commerce Commission (ICC) are examples of common carriers. The rates and terms under which a common carrier will carry property are normally subject to the approval of these government agencies. **Private contract** carriers are persons who carry goods only for persons selected by the carrier.

Both common carriers and private contract carriers are bailees. However, the law makes the common carrier the **absolute insurer** of the goods it carries. The common carrier is responsible for any loss or damage to goods entrusted to it. The common carrier can avoid responsibility only if it can show that the loss or damage was caused by (1) an act of God, (2) an act of a public enemy, (3) an act or order of the government, (4) an act of the person who shipped the goods, or (5) the nature of the goods themselves.

The common carrier is liable if goods entrusted to it are stolen by some unknown person but not if the goods are destroyed when a tornado hits its warehouse. If the shipper improperly packages or crates the goods and this results in their being damaged, then the carrier is not liable. Similarly, if perishable goods are not in suitable condition to be shipped and deteriorate in the course of shipment, the carrier is not liable so long as it used reasonable care in handling them. Common carriers are usually permitted to limit their liability to a stated value unless the bailor declares a higher value for the property and pays an additional fee.

HOTELKEEPERS

Hotelkeepers are engaged in the business of offering lodging and/or food to transient persons. They hold themselves out to serve the public and are obligated to do so. Like the common carrier, the hotelkeeper is held to a higher standard of care than the ordinary bailee.

The hotelkeeper is not a bailee in the strict sense of the word. The guest does not usually surrender the exclusive possession of her property to the hotelkeeper. However, the hotelkeeper is treated as the virtual insurer of the guest's property. The hotelkeeper is not liable for loss of or damage to property if he can show that it was caused by (1) an act of God, (2) an act of a public enemy, (3) an act of government authority, (4) the fault of a member of the guest's party, or (5) the nature of the goods.

Most states have passed laws that limit the hotelkeeper's liability. Commonly, they require the hotel owner to post a notice advising guests that any valuables should be checked into the hotel vault. The hotelkeeper's liability is then limited for valuables that are not so checked. The following case, *Gooden v. Days Inn*, illustrates a situation in which a hotel complied sufficiently with the law to be able to gain the benefit of the limitation of liability.

SAFE-DEPOSIT BOXES

If you rent a safe-deposit box at a local bank and place some property in the box, the box and the property are in manual possession of the bank. However, it takes both your key and the key held by the bank to open the box, and in most cases the bank does not know the nature, amount, or value of the goods in your box. Although a few courts have held the rental of a safe-deposit box to be a lease, not a bailment, most courts have found that the renter of the box is a bailor and the bank a bailee. As such, the bank is not an insurer of the contents of the box. However, it is obligated to use due care and to come forward and explain loss or damage to the property entrusted to it.

GOODEN V. DAYS INN
385 S.E.2d 876 (Ct. App. Ga. 1990)

FACTS

Marvin Gooden checked into a Days Inn in Atlanta, Georgia, on March 3, 1988, paying in advance for two days' lodging. The next day he temporarily left his room, leaving a paper bag filled with approximately $9,000. Shortly thereafter, Mary Carter, a housekeeper, went into Gooden's room to clean it and found the bag of money. Seeing no other personal effects, she assumed that Gooden had checked out. Accordingly, she turned the bag over to her immediate supervisor, Vivian Clark, who in turn gave the bag of money to Dempsey Wilson, who was responsible for general supervision and the maintenance of the grounds. Wilson had been employed by Days Inn for approximately three years, and during that time he was occasionally given items of value to turn

into the office. He always did so until this occasion when he decided to abscond with the bag of money.

A safe was located on the premises of the Days Inn for the use of the guests. Days Inn posted a notice concerning the availability of the safe on the door of the room which Gooden occupied. Pursuant to this notice, Days Inn disclaimed liability for guests' valuables unless they were placed in the safe. At no point did Gooden seek the use of the safe.

Georgia law provides in pertinent part that: "The innkeeper may provide a safe or other place of deposit for valuable articles and, by posting a notice thereof, may require the guests of the innkeeper to place such valuable

(continued)

GOODEN V. DAYS INN
(concluded)

articles therein or the innkeeper shall be relieved from responsibility for such articles."

Gooden brought a tort action against, among others, Days Inn seeking damages in the amount of $9,000. Days Inn contended that it could not be held responsible for the loss of Gooden's money since it had posted notice concerning the availability of the safe and Gooden had failed to take advantage of it. Gooden, in turn, argued that the Georgia statue could not insulate an innkeeper from liability where the loss of a guest's valuables is occasioned by the negligent or tortious conduct of the innkeeper's employees.

ISSUE

Was the innkeeper shielded from liability by the statute?

DECISION

Yes. The court noted that the statute carves out no exception for losses occasioned by the negligence of the innkeeper. Thus, if the innkeeper posts notice of a safe pursuant to the statute, it is not liable for articles stolen from a guest's room even if its negligence contributed to the loss. The court went on to note that any bailment in this case was for the mutual benefit of the parties and that the degree of diligence required of Days Inn and its employees was ordinary diligence. It stated that Days Inn, Carter, and Clark demonstrated they acted with ordinary care and diligence with respect to the bag of money—and Wilson, whom they had no reason to distrust, was nowhere to be found.

INVOLUNTARY BAILMENTS

Suppose you own a cottage near a lake. After a violent storm, you find a sailboat washed up on your beach. You may be considered the **involuntary bailee** or **constructive bailee** of the sailboat. This relationship may arise when you find yourself in possession of property that belongs to someone else without having agreed to accept possession.

The duties of the involuntary bailee are not well defined. The bailee does not have the right to destroy the property or to use it. If the true owner shows up, the property must be returned to the owner. Under some circumstances, the involuntary bailee may be under an obligation to assume control of the property and/or to take some minimal steps to ascertain who the owner is.

.... *QUESTIONS AND PROBLEM CASES* ....

1. What are the critical elements that determine the degree of care that a bailee is required to exercise?

2. Hallman and his family were taking an automobile trip to Florida. They stopped at the New Colonial Hotel to spend the night. Hallman asked the registration clerk if the hotel had parking facilities. He was told that the bellboy would take care of the car. The bellboy took the luggage needed by the Hallmans from the car and put it in their room. Then he took the car to a nearby parking lot that was not owned by the hotel. The bellboy left the car with the attendant, who locked it and kept the keys. When the car was taken to the lot, it still contained some luggage on the rear seat and several garments hung on racks. When the bellboy returned to the hotel, he gave Hallman a claim check bearing the name of the parking lot and the stamped name "New Colonial." The next morning Hallman went to pick up his car and discovered that the side window was broken. Personal property worth $557 had been stolen from the car. Hallman then sued the hotel to recover for the personal property and for repair of the damage to his car. Was the hotel the bailee of the car and its contents?

3. Weinberg was the holder of a "Parkard" issued by Wayco, for which he paid $100.00 per month and which entitled him to park his automobile

at Wayco's garage, located in St. Louis. The garage had five stories, and entrance was gained by inserting the Parkard into a slot, causing the entrance gate to open. It was a so-called self-park garage, and there were no attendants on duty at the time Weinberg parked his automobile at about 11:30 PM on September 25. After securing admission to the garage with the Parkard, Weinberg parked his car, locked it, and took the keys with him. When he returned to his automobile on the evening of September 27, he found that it had been broken into and that certain personal property had been stolen from it. The automobile had not been moved. The Parkard stated: "This card licenses the holder to park one automobile in this area at holder's risk. Lock your car. Licensor hereby declares himself not responsible for fire, theft, or damage to or loss of such automobile or any article left therein. Only a license is granted hereby, and no bailment is created." Weinberg had read the language on the card and knew what it said. Is Wayco liable for the stolen property?

4. Thompson discovered that the automatic transmission in his car was leaking even though it otherwise was operating properly. He took the car to Mr. Transmission, a transmission repair business, told the people there he wanted the transmission seals replaced because the automatic transmission was leaking, signed a work order, and left the car with them expecting to pay their advertised fee of $69.95. When he returned to the shop several hours later, he found that the transmission, which did not have to be taken apart to replace the seals, had been removed from his car and was disassembled. An employee told him the fluid was burnt out and had metal particles in it. He also broke one of the transmission parts in Thompson's presence. Thompson was told that the transmission would have to be rebuilt or replaced and that installing a rebuilt transmission at a cost of $377 would be the quickest. In order to get his car back, Thompson had Mr. Transmission install a replacement rebuilt transmission and paid for it under protest as he had not authorized his transmission to be disassembled. The replacement transmission began to leak, and Thompson brought an action for unauthorized

disassembly and destruction of his operating transmission resulting in his forced purchase of another transmission. He also sought punitive damages. Was Mr. Transmission liable to Thompson for the acts it took with respect to his transmission that had been entrusted to it?

5. George Pringle, the head of the drapery department at Wardrobe Cleaners, went to the home of Dr. Arthur Axelrod to inspect some dining room draperies for dry-cleaning purposes. He spent about 30 minutes looking at the drapes and inspected both the drapes and the lining. He pointed out some roach spots on the lining that could not be removed by cleaning, but this was not of concern to the Axelrods. He did not indicate to them that the fabric had deteriorated from sunburn, age, dust, or air conditioning so as to make it unsuitable for dry cleaning. He took the drapes and had them dry cleaned. When the drapes were returned they were unfit for use. The fabric had been a gold floral design on an eggshell-white background. When returned, it was a blotchy gold. Wardrobe Cleaners stated that it was difficult to predict how imported fabrics would respond to the dry-cleaning process and that the company was not equipped to pretest the fabric to see whether it was colorfast. The Axelrods sued Wardrobe Cleaners for $1,000, the replacement value of the drapes. Should the cleaner be liable for the damage caused to the drapes during the dry-cleaning process?

6. Georgie Simon entrusted 14 gold and silver coins to her ex-husband, Hardie Maloney, to take to a coin show in Atlanta, Georgia. He was to try to sell the coins, for which he would receive a 7 percent commission. Maloney traveled to the coin show along with his girlfriend, Ann Williams, and a male friend, Herbert Pellegrini, with whom he had previously traveled to 40 or 50 coin shows. Just before they got ready to leave the Waverly Hotel, where the show had been held, Maloney and Williams went up to Pellegrini's room. Pellegrini would not permit Williams to use the bathroom because he wanted to check out before the deadline and avoid being charged for another day. Williams and Maloney helped Pellegrini carry his three pieces of luggage to the lobby. While Pellegrini checked out, Williams went to the ladies' room in the lobby

of the hotel. While Williams was in the bathroom, Maloney went to get his car, on the suggestion and insistence of Pellegrini. He resisted the suggestion because he was carrying a briefcase containing Georgie Simon's coins, as well as the coins he had brought to, and purchased at, the show. Maloney wanted to wait until they could all walk over to the car together for protection. However, after being assured by Pellegrini that he would watch the briefcase, Maloney went to get the car, setting the briefcase down beside Pellegrini's three bags in front of the hotel. When Maloney returned with the car, Pellegrini walked up to the vehicle carrying all three pieces of his own luggage but had left Maloney's briefcase in front of the hotel. When Maloney asked about the whereabouts of the briefcase, Pellegrini replied that he did not know where it was. It was never found. Georgie Simon brought suit against Maloney for $19,000, the value of the coins she had entrusted to him, and Maloney, in turn, filed a claim against Pellegrini for the loss of those coins as well as for the $12,300 in coins that he had entrusted to Pellegrini. Was Pellegrini liable for the loss of the coins entrusted to him?

7. In April, Mrs. Carter brought her fur coat to Reichlin Furriers for cleaning, glazing, and storage until the next winter season. She was given a printed form of receipt, on the front of which an employee of the furrier had written $100 as the valuation of the coat. There was no discussion of the value of the coat, and Carter did not realize that such a value had been written on the receipt, which she did not read at the time. A space for the customer's signature on the front of the receipt was left blank. Below this space in prominent type appeared a notice to "see reverse side for terms and conditions." The other side of the receipt stated that it was a storage contract and that by its acceptance the customer would be deemed to have agreed to its terms unless notice to the contrary was given within 10 days. Fifteen conditions were listed. One of the conditions was as follows: "Storage charges are based on valuation herein declared by the depositor, and amount recoverable for loss or damage to the article shall not exceed its actual value or the cost of

repair replacement with materials of like kind and quality or the depositor's valuation appearing in this receipt, whichever is less." In the fall of the year, after Carter had paid the bill for storage and other services on the coat, Reichlin Furriers informed her that the coat was lost. The fair market value of the coat at the times was $450. Carter sued Furrier for loss of the coat and sought $450 damages. Furrier claimed that its liability was limited to $100. Was the limitation of liability on the claim check effective to limit Furrier's liability?

8. Stanley Hartmann, a mechanical engineer, was employed as a draftsman and designer of hydraulic equipment by J & S Hydraulics, Inc. (J & S), a company that designed, manufactured, and repaired hydraulic equipment. J & S maintained on its premises numerous machines used in the course of its business, including a radial arm saw manufactured by Black & Decker. One evening, Hartmann was operating the radial arm saw for a personal project, the construction of a workbench. Such after-hours personal use of machinery was permitted by J & S, was frequently exercised by its employees, and was regarded as a fringe benefit of employment. Earlier that day, Hartmann had obtained specific permission, as was required, to use a company vehicle to drive to a nearby lumberyard and purchase lumber for the construction of the workbench. At the end of the workday, Hartmann and several of his co-workers carried the lumber from the truck into the shop and onto a mezzanine level on which the saw was located. Management was aware of his planned use of the saw, but he did not obtain explicit permission to use it. While Hartmann was operating the saw, it kicked back and pulled his left hand into the saw, severing his fingers and thumb. The saw, as manufactured, was equipped with a removable antikickback device, which was not in place at the time Hartmann was operating the saw. Following the accident, an antikickback device was placed on the saw by J & S. Hartmann brought suit against J & S and Black & Decker. He claimed that J & S owed him a duty of reasonable care as to the condition of the saw and to warn him of any defects. In particular, he

Rottermich v. Union Planters National Bank
40 UCC Rep.2d 1110 (Ct. App. Missouri 2000)

FACTS

Kenneth Rottermich and Herman Toebben owned St. Charles Bowling Lanes, Inc., a bowling alley in St. Charles, Missouri. Rottermich and Toebben operated St. Charles Bowl from the early 1960s when the building housing the lanes was constructed through 1987 when the business was sold. In January 1972, St. Charles Bowl entered into a lease agreement with AMF, Inc., for the installation of pinspotters in the building. The pinspotters were manufactured in three pieces and then assembled inside the bowling alley. They were placed in the step-down portion of the alley lane that was designed for them and screwed, bolted, and riveted to the concrete floor.

The lease agreement provided in pertinent part:

Upon termination of this agreement, AMF shall immediately have the right to possession of the machines and AMF may enter upon the premises where the machines are located, take possession without previous demand or notice and without legal process, and remove them to the manufacturer's factory or other place of storage. . . . The machines shall at all times remain the sole and exclusive property of AMF . . . and operator shall have no right, title or interest to the machines but only the right to use them under this agreement. The machines shall remain personal property and shall not be deemed otherwise by reason of becoming attached to the premises.

In 1987, St. Charles Bowl, Inc., was sold to a corporation, Weber's St. Charles Lanes, whose owners included Toebben's son. The purchase agreement was expressly contingent upon an assignment to Weber's Bowl of the lease agreement between St. Charles Bowl and AMF. The price paid to Rothermich and Herman Toebben did not include consideration for the pinspotters because they were considered by all parties to be the property of AMF pursuant to the terms of the lease agreement. The purchase price was financed in part through promissory notes payable to Rothermich, Toebben, and Boatmen's Bank secured by a deed of trust covering "all buildings, fixtures and appurtenances now or hereafter to the same belonging. . . ."

In 1989, Weber's purchased the pinspotters from AMF, financing the purchase through a loan from Union Planters National Bank and granting Union Planters a security interest in the pin spotters. Subsequently, Weber's defaulted on its loans to Rothemrich, Toebben, Boatmen's, and Union Planters. By agreement among the parties, the pinspotters were sold at a foreclosure sale and removed from the bowling alley premises with no physical or structural damage to the property. The AMF pinspotters were resold to another bowling alley operator outside the United States. The purchaser of the bowling alley real estate at the foreclosure sale installed replacement pinspotters.

Rothermich and Toebben claimed that they were entitled to the proceeds from the sale of the pinspotters because the pinspotters had been fixtures subject to their deed of trust. Union Planter's argued that it was entitled to the proceeds because the pinspotters were personal property subject to its security interest.

ISSUE

Were the pinspotters fixtures?

DECISION

No. The court focused on the intent of the parties. The original lease agreement and its extension stated that the pinspotters were to remain personal property. When the bowling alley was sold, the purchase did not include consideration for the pinspotters, and the sale was made contingent on the lease agreement for the pinspotters being assigned. The new owner affirmed the intent by granting a security interest in them in connection with their purchase. Although the pinspotters were screwed, bolted, and riveted to the floor, they were shown to be readily removable and were resold for reuse at another location. The purchaser at the foreclosure sale of the bowling alley real estate was able to install replacement pinspotters without difficulty, showing that there was no particular adaptation of the pinspotters to the premises.

Security Interests in Fixtures

Special rules apply to personal property subject to a lien or security interest at the time it is attached to real property. Assume, for example, that a person buys a dishwasher on a time-payment plan from an appliance store and has it installed in his kitchen. To protect itself, the appliance store takes a security interest in the dishwasher and perfects that interest by filing a financing statement in the appropriate real estate records office within the period of time specified by the Uniform Commercial Code. The appliance store then is able to remove the dishwasher if the buyer defaults in his payments. The store could be liable, however, to third parties such as prior real estate mortgagees for any damage removal of the dishwasher caused to the real estate. The rules governing security interest in personal property that will become fixtures are explained more fully in Chapter 41.

CONCEPT SUMMARY	**Fixtures**
Concept	A *fixture* is an item of personal property attached to or used in conjunction with real property in such a way that it is treated as being part of the real property.
Significance	A conveyance of the real property will also convey the fixtures on that property.
Factors Considered in Determining Whether Property Is a Fixture	1. Attachment: Is the item physically attached or closely connected to the real property? 2. Adaptation: How necessary or beneficial is the item to the use of the real property? 3. Intent: Did the person who installed the item manifest intent for the property to become part of the real property?
Express Agreement	Express agreements clearly stating intent about whether property is a fixture are generally enforceable.
Trade Fixtures (Tenants' Fixtures)	Definition of *trade fixtures:* personal property attached to leased real property by a tenant for the purpose of carrying on his trade or business. Trade fixtures can be removed and retained by the tenant at the termination of the lease except when one or more of the following apply: 1. Removal would cause substantial damage to the landlord's real property. 2. Tenant fails to remove the fixtures by the end of the lease (or within a reasonable time, if the lease is for an indefinite period of time). 3. An express agreement between the landlord and tenant provides otherwise.

RIGHTS AND INTERESTS IN REAL PROPERTY

When we think of ownership of real property, we normally think of somebody owning all the rights in a particular piece of land. However, a variety of different interests can be created in a particular piece of land, and it is possible to divide those interests among a number of people. The interests include leases, licenses, easements, life estates, and mineral or timber rights.

FEE SIMPLE

The **fee simple** is the basic land ownership interest in the United States. A person who owns real property in fee simple has the right to the entire property for an unlimited period of time and the unconditional power to dispose of it either during his lifetime or on his death. If the person does not make a will, the land will automatically pass to the person's heirs on his death. A person who owns land in fee simple may grant many rights to others without giving up the ownership of his fee simple interest.

For example, Arnold, who has a fee simple interest in land, may give Bob a mortgage on the land, grant Cindy an easement or right-of-way across the land, and lease the land to a farmer for a period of time. Arnold has granted rights to Bob, Cindy, and the farmer, but Bob still owns the land in fee simple. When the rights of Bob, Cindy, and the farmer terminate, they pass back to Arnold and again become part of his bundle of ownership rights.

LIFE ESTATE

A **life estate** is a property interest that gives a person the right to use property only for his own lifetime or for a time that is measured by the lifetime of somebody else. A person who has a life estate in a piece of real property has the right to use the property but does not have the right to commit acts that will result in permanent injury to the property.

LEASEHOLD

A **lease** gives the tenant the right to occupy and use a particular piece of property. This right may be for a fixed period of time such as a month or year. If no time period is specified, then it is known as a **tenancy at will.** Under a tenancy at will, either the landlord or the tenant can terminate the leasehold after giving notice to the other person of her intention to do so. The law of landlord and tenant will be discussed in Chapter 33.

EASEMENT

A person may have the right to use or enjoy the land of another person but not to actually occupy it on a long-term basis; this is known as an **easement.** An easement can be either an affirmative or a negative easement. An **affirmative easement** is the right to make certain uses of the land of another. The right to drive across another person's property to reach your property, to run a sewer line across it, or to drill for oil and gas on the land of another person is an affirmative easement.

A **negative easement** is the right to have someone who owns an adjoining piece of property refrain from making certain uses of his or her land. The right to have your neighbor refrain from erecting a building on his property that would cut off light and air from your building is a negative easement.

Easements may be acquired in a number of ways. They may be bought or sold, or they may be held back when the owner of a piece of property sells other rights to the property. Sometimes an easement is implied even though the parties did not specifically grant or purchase it. For example, Arthur owns 80 acres of land fronting on a dirt road and bounded on the other three sides by a limited-access highway. If Arthur sells the back 40 acres to Byron, Byron will get an easement by **necessity** across Arthur's remaining property because that would be the only way he could get to his property.

An easement can also be created by **adverse possession** (prescription). Obtaining a property interest by adverse possession is discussed later in this chapter. As an example, if someone without your permission openly uses a shortcut across a corner of your property for the statutory period of time, that person will obtain an easement. She will have a continuing right to engage in that activity. The true owner of the property must assert his rights during that period and stop the other person or end up losing an interest in his property.

Because an easement is a type of interest in land, it is within the coverage of the statute of frauds. An express agreement granting or reserving an easement must be in writing to be enforceable. Under the statutes of most states, the grant of an easement must be executed with the same formalities as are observed in executing the grant of a fee simple interest in real property. However, easements not granted expressly, such as easements by prior use, necessity, or prescription or adverse possession are enforceable even though they are not in writing.

The *Lee v. Lozier* case, which follows, illustrates the creation of an easement by prescription or adverse possession.

LEE V. LOZIER
945 P. 2d 214 (Ct. App. Wash. 1997)

FACTS

Fogelman's Lake Washington Tracts is an 11-lot subdivision on the banks of Lake Washington. Lots 7 through 11 of the development border the lake; Lots 1 through 6 are inland lots. Lot 9 is a community beach lot, of which each lot owner owns an undivided one-tenth interest.

In 1981, the owners of Lots 1–6 ("the neighbors") equally divided the cost of building a community dock extending into the lake from the shore of Lot 9 with William Fogelman, who owned and lived on Lot 10, which borders Lot 9 to the south. As constructed, the dock generally followed the border dividing Lots 9 and 10 and widened at its end into an 80-foot long "T" shaped water ski pier. Approximately one foot of the width of the dock stem, and half the width of the water ski pier lie within Lot 10; the remainder of the dock lies entirely within Lot 9. The dock has five moorage slips: three community slips that lie within Lot 9 and two that lie within Lot 10 to be used exclusively by the owner of Lot 10.

At the time the dock was built, Fogelman agreed to allow the neighbors to use the portions of the dock that extend onto Lot 10, apart from the two moorage slips. The minutes of the homeowners meeting between the neighbors and Fogelman stated that "Bill Fogelman agreed to give [the neighbors] a letter that he [would] never deny lot owners access to the water ski pier that crosses his property line." He also stated that as soon as the dock was completed the letter would appear on Lot 10's title. However, Fogelman never recorded an easement against the title to Lot 10.

In the years following the completion of the dock, the neighbors used it for various activities including, fishing, sailing, waterskiing, strolling, picnicking, temporarily tying up boats to unload goods and passengers, and mooring boats. In the summer, the neighbors also used the dock for sunbathing and swimming.

In 1989 Lozier purchased Lot 10 from Fogelman and began making extensive renovations to the house on the lot. Prior to purchasing the lot, Lozier was aware of the covenants and bylaws of the association concerning the community dock but did not review the homeowners' association minutes or speak with any of the neighbors about the dock before purchasing the property. Lozier took up residence in 1992. On several occasions he noticed people, including the neighbors, using the Lot 10 portion of the dock and requested that they move to the Lot 9 portion of the dock. Eventually, Lozier drew a chalk line on the dock separating Lot 10 from Lot 9 and put up a "private property" sign advising others to stay off the Lot 10 portion of the dock.

The neighbors confronted Lozier and insisted they were entitled to use the entire dock, including the portion lying within Lot 10. When they were unable to come to a resolution with Lozier, the neighbors filed suit requesting an order establishing their entitlement to a prescriptive easement to use the entire dock, including the portions extending onto Lot 10. Lozier filed a counterclaim requesting a permanent injunction preventing the neighbors from entering the Lot 10 portions of the dock.

ISSUE

Did the neighbors obtain an easement by prescription to use the portion of the dock on Lot 10?

DECISION

Yes. The neighbors openly used the Lot 10 portions of the dock for at least 10 years [the statutory period]; their use began under a claim of right adverse to Fogelman; Fogelman was aware of the adverse use by the neighbors at a time when he could have asserted his rights but did not do so; and the neighbors' seasonal use was "continuous" given that the use of a dock inevitably has a seasonal character. This satisfies the elements necessary for a prescriptive easement to use portions of the dock stem and water ski pier lying on Lot 10.

LICENSE

A **license** is usually a temporary right to use another person's land for a limited and specific purpose. A license is similar in some ways to an easement; however, it is not considered to be an interest in land and usually does not have to be in writing to be enforceable. It may be created orally. A common example of a license is obtaining permission to hunt or fish on another person's land.

PRIVATE RESTRICTIONS

Within certain limits, a person who sells real estate may obtain the agreement of the buyer to certain restrictions on the subsequent use of the land. Similarly, the owner of real estate may, by agreement or by a declaration in trust, impose restrictions on the use that will be made of that property.

For example, Frank owns two adjacent lots. He sells one to Rose but gets Rose to promise not to operate any business involving the sale of liquor on the property. This commitment is included in the deed Frank gives to Rose along with a statement that the property is to revert to Frank if the commitment is broken. Similarly, suppose that a developer sells lots in a subdivision and puts a restriction in each deed concerning the minimum size and cost of houses that can be built on the property. He might also restrict the types of design. Alternatively, the restrictions may be put in the plat for the subdivision that is filed in the local land records office.

The validity and enforceability of such private restrictions on the use of real property depend on the *purpose, nature, and scope* of the restriction. If a restraint is so great that it effectively prevents the sale or transfer of the property to anyone else, it is not enforceable. If a restriction is reasonable and its purpose is not against public policy, it is enforceable. For example, a restriction that prohibits future sale of the property to a non-Caucasian is not enforceable. However, restrictions that relate to the minimum size of lots, maintenance of the area as a residential community, or the cost, size, and design of buildings are frequently enforceable.

These restrictions are usually enforceable by the parties to the agreement or by persons who are intended to benefit by them. If the restriction is contained in a subdivision plat in the form of a general building scheme, other property owners in the subdivision may be able to enforce it. Restrictions can be waived; the right to enforce them can be lost by abandonment; or they can end by their own terms. If a restriction is invalid, waived, abandoned, or lost due to dramatically changed circumstances, the basic deed remains valid but the deed is treated as if the restriction had been stricken from it. The case that follows, *Mains Farm Homeowners Association v. Worthington,* illustrates the enforcement of a restriction.

MAINS FARM HOMEOWNERS ASSOCIATION V. WORTHINGTON

854 P. 2d 1072 (Sup. Ct. Wash. 1993)

FACTS

Mains Farm is a platted subdivision. A declaration of restrictive covenants for the subdivision was recorded in 1962. Worthington purchased a residential lot in Mains Farms in 1987. At that time a house already existed on the property. Before purchasing, Worthington obtained and read a copy of the restrictive covenants, which stated, in pertinent part, that all lots in Mains Farm "shall be designated as 'Residential Lots' and shall be used for single family residential purposes only."

(continued)

MAINS FARM HOMEOWNERS ASSOCIATION V. WORTHINGTON
(concluded)

Worthington later began occupying the residence along with four adults who paid her for 24-hour protective supervision and care. The four adults, who were not related to Worthington, were unable to do their own housekeeping, prepare their own meals, or attend to their personal hygiene. In providing this supervision and care on a for-profit basis, Worthington complied with the licensing and inspection requirements established by Washington law governing such enterprises.

When her intended use of property became known, other property owners objected. Despite that knowledge, she applied for a building permit to add a fifth bedroom to the house. She was advised that her intended facility did not comply with applicable zoning. Worthington later obtained the permit by stating that only her family would be living with her. In her words: "I told them what they wanted to hear."

The Mains Farm Homeowners Association (Association), which consisted of owners of property in the subdivision, filed suit against Worthington and asked the court to enjoin her from using her property as an adult home business. The Association asserted that Worthington's use violated the restrictive covenants.

The trial court issued an injunction against Worthington's use and the decision was affirmed by the court of appeals. Worthington appealed to the Washington Supreme Court, and several organizations representing the interests of disabled adults submitted *amicus curiae* (friend of the court) briefs urging reversal.

ISSUE
Should Worthington's use of her property as an adult home business be enjoined as a violation of the restrictive covenant?

DECISION
Yes. The court noted that Worthington had read the restrictive covenants before she bought the property and that she was aware of her neighbor's objections to her proposed use of the property. Conducting a state-licensed business involving 24-hour supervision and care of four individuals, unrelated to Worthington by birth or marriage and brought together by referral from a state agency, does not come within the definition of a single-family residence. The use exceeded the reasonable expectations of the other lot owners who had purchased their family houses in reliance on the recorded covenants. Accordingly, equitable considerations warrant the issuance of an injunction against Worthington's continued use of her property as a group home business.

CONCEPT SUMMARY	Interests in Real Property
Possessory Interests	**Description**
Fee Simple	The basic and highest form of land ownership. Owner has the absolute power to possess and use the property (subject to government regulation and private restrictions), the right to dispose of it during his lifetime or on his death, and ability to grant many subsidiary interests to others without giving up his basic ownership.
Life Estate	The right to possess and use property for a time measured by the person's lifetime or that of another person.
Leasehold (see Chapter 33)	The right to possession for a time specified by contract or by law as in tenancies for years, periodic tenancies, and tenancies at will.
Nonpossessory Interests	**Description**
Easement	The right to make certain uses of another person's property or the right to prevent another person from making certain uses of his own property.
Private Restrictions	A restraint imposed by contract on the subsequent use of land, which may be enforceable against subsequent owners depending on the purpose, nature, and scope of the restriction.
License	*Not* an interest in land but a temporary right to use another's land for a limited and specific purpose.

CO-OWNERSHIP OF REAL PROPERTY

Co-ownership of real property exists when two or more persons share the same ownership interest in certain property. The co-owners do not have separate rights to any portion of the real property; each has a share in the whole property. Seven types of co-ownership are recognized in the United States.

TENANCY IN COMMON

Persons who own property under a **tenancy in common** have undivided interests in the property and equal rights to possess it. When property is transferred to two or more persons without specification of their co-ownership form, it is presumed that they acquire the property as tenants in common. The respective ownership interests of tenants in common may be, but need not be, equal. One tenant, for example, could have a two-thirds ownership interest in the property with the other tenant having a one-third interest.

Each tenant in common has the right to possess and use the property. Individual tenants, however, cannot exclude the other tenants in common from also possessing and using the property. If the property is rented or otherwise produces income, each tenant is entitled to share in the income in proportion to her ownership share. Similarly, each tenant must pay her proportionate share of property taxes and necessary repair costs. If a tenant in sole possession of the property receives no rents or profits from the property, she is not required to pay rent to her cotenant unless her possession is adverse to or inconsistent with her cotenant's property interests.

A tenant in common may dispose of his interest in the property during life and at death. Similarly, his interest is subject to his creditors' claims. When a tenant dies, his interest passes to his heirs or, if he has made a will, to the person or persons specified in the will. Suppose Peterson and Sievers own Blackacre as tenants in common. Sievers dies, having executed a valid will in which he leaves his Blackacre interest to Johanns. In this situation, Peterson and Johanns become tenants in common.

Tenants in common may sever the cotenancy by agreeing to divide the property or, if they are unable to agree, by petitioning a court for *partition*. The court will physically divide the property if that is feasible, so that each tenant receives her proportionate share. If physical division is not feasible, the court will order that the property be sold and that the proceeds be appropriately divided.

JOINT TENANCY

A **joint tenancy** is created when equal interests in real property are conveyed to two or more persons by means of a document clearly specifying that they are to own the property as joint tenants. The rights of use, possession, contribution, and partition are the same for a joint tenancy as for a tenancy in common. The joint tenancy's distinguishing feature is that it gives the owners the **right of survivorship,** which means that upon the death of a joint tenant, the deceased tenant's interest automatically passes to the surviving joint tenant(s). The right of survivorship makes it easy for a person to transfer property at death without the need for a will. For example, Devaney and Osborne purchase Redacre and take title as joint tenants. At Devaney's death, his Redacre interest will pass to Osborne even if Devaney did not have a will setting forth such an intent. Moreover, even if Devaney had a will that purported to leave his Redacre interest to someone other than Osborne, the will's Redacre provision would be ineffective.

A joint tenant may mortgage, sell, or give away his interest in the property during his lifetime. If one of the joint tenants does sell or convey his interest to someone else, the joint tenancy is broken as to the share sold. The new person comes into the joint ownership as a tenant in common rather than as part of a joint tenancy. The rights of use, possession, contribution, and partition of joint tenants are the same as those of tenants in common. This is illustrated in *Frank v. Frank.*

FRANK V. FRANK
1992 Conn. Super. Lexis 1064 (Super. Ct. Conn. 1992)

FACTS

Rudolph A. Frank, Sr., was born in 1927. He had four children, Rudolph Jr., Denise, Diane, and Dorian, by his first wife, LaVerne. On December 3, 1975, Rudolph married Greta, a woman with whom he had been living. In July 1976, they purchased a single-family residence for $35,000. The warranty deed by which they took title conveyed the property to "RUDOLPH FRANK and GRETA FRANK, and unto the survivor of them, and unto such survivors (*sic*) heirs and assigns forever."

The Frank family at this time was not a particularly happy one. Greta and Rudolph Sr.'s children never got along. Rudolph and Greta occasionally fought so violently that the police had to be called. In the summer of 1977, Greta left the home. About that time, Rudolph Sr. decided to convey his share in the house to his children, doing so by way of a quitclaim deed conveying all his right, title, and interest in the property to his four children. The deed was filed with the town clerk on August 29, 1977. He also told his children that no matter how much he asked for it, they were never to give the house back to him.

In the fall of 1977, Greta returned to Rudolph Sr. and asked him to get the property back. An attorney retained by Rudolph Sr. wrote the children asking that they reconvey the property to him. However, they heeded his earlier command and refused to do so.

Greta and Rudolph Sr. lived together until May 1987 when he had to be placed in a convalescent home; he died in August 1987. Greta continued to live in the house,

paying the mortgage and maintaining the house without support from Rudolph Sr.'s children.

In 1989, the four children filed a petition seeking to partition the property and to have it sold so that they could realize their share. Greta contended that the children had no interest in the property because Rudolph Sr., as a joint tenant with right of survivorship who happened not to survive, could convey only a life interest in the property to his children and that interest expired when he died.

ISSUE

Do the children have an interest in the property and are they entitled to have the property partitioned and sold?

DECISION

Yes. Rudolph Sr. and Greta acquired the property as joint tenants, with the right of survivorship. A joint tenancy can exist only as long as there is a unity of (1) interest, (2) title, (3) time, and (4) possession. When any of these unities is broken, the joint tenancy is destroyed. A unilateral act of conveyance breaks the unity of title. Rudolph Sr.'s conveyance of his interest to his children severed the joint tenancy, and his children hold the interest he conveyed as tenants in common with the remaining joint tenant—Greta. As to tenants in common, on petition the court may order the partition or sale of any property, real or personal, owned by two or more persons. Here partition is not practicable, so the court ordered the property sold and the proceeds distributed to the tenants in common.

TENANCY BY THE ENTIRETY

Approximately half of the states permit married couples to own real property under a **tenancy by the entirety.** This tenancy is essentially a joint tenancy with the added requirement that the owners be married. As does the joint tenancy, the tenancy by the entirety features the right of survivorship. Neither spouse can transfer the property by will if the other is still living. Upon the death of the husband or wife, the property passes automatically to the surviving spouse.

A tenancy by the entirety cannot be severed by the act of only one of the parties. Neither spouse can transfer the property unless the other also signs the deed. Thus, a creditor of one tenant cannot claim an interest in that person's share of property held in tenancy by the entirety. Divorce, however, severs a tenancy by the entirety and transforms it into a tenancy in common. The Concept Summary that follows compares the features of tenancy in common, joint tenancy, and tenancy by the entirety.

CONCEPT SUMMARY	Tenancy in Common, Joint Tenancy, and Tenancy by the Entirety		
	Tenancy in Common	**Joint Tenancy**	**Tenancy by the Entirety**
Equal Possession and Use?	Yes	Yes	Yes
Share Income?	Yes	Yes	Presumably
Contribution Requirement?	Generally	Generally	Generally
Free Conveyance of Interest?	Yes; transferee becomes tenant in common	Yes, but joint tenancy is severed on conveyance and reverts to tenancy in common	Both must agree; divorce severs tenancy
Effect of Death?	Interest transferable at death by will or inheritance	Right of survivorship; surviving joint tenant takes decedent's share	Rights of survivorship; surviving spouse takes decedent's share

COMMUNITY PROPERTY

A number of western and southern states recognize the **community property** system of co-ownership of property by married couples. This type of co-ownership assumes that marriage is a partnership in which each spouse contributes to the family's property base. Property acquired during the marriage through a spouse's industry or efforts is classified as *community* property. Each spouse has an equal interest in such property regardless of who produced or earned the property. Because each spouse has an equal share in community property, neither can convey community property without the other's joining in the transaction. Various community property states permit the parties to dispose of their interests in community property at death. The details of each state's community property system vary, depending on the specific provisions of that state's statutes.

Not all property owned by a married person is community property, however. Property a spouse owned before marriage or acquired during marriage by gift or inheritance is *separate* property. Neither spouse owns a legal interest in the other's separate property. Property exchanged for separate property also remains separately owned.

TENANCY IN PARTNERSHIP

When a partnership takes title to property in the partnership's name, the co-ownership form is called **tenancy in partnership.** Co-ownership of property in the partnership form of organization is discussed in Chapter 24.

CONDOMINIMUM OWNERSHIP

Condominiums have become very common in the United States in recent years, even in locations outside urban and resort areas. Under condominium ownership, a purchaser takes title to her individual unit and becomes a tenant in common with other unit owners in shared facilities such as hallways, elevators, swimming pools, and parking areas. The condominium owner pays property taxes on her individual unit and makes a monthly payment for the maintenance of the common areas. She may generally mortgage or sell her unit without the other unit owners' approval. For federal income tax purposes, the condominium owner is treated as if she owned a single-family home and is thus allowed to deduct her property taxes and mortgage interest expenses.

COOPERATIVE OWNERSHIP

In a cooperative, a building is owned by a corporation or group of persons. One who wants to buy an apartment in the building purchases stock in the corporation and holds his apartment under a long-term, renewable lease called a *proprietary lease*. Frequently, the cooperative owner must obtain the other owners' approval to sell or sublease his unit.

ACQUISITION OF REAL PROPERTY

Among the different methods of obtaining title to real property are:

1. Purchase
2. Gift
3. Will or inheritance
4. Tax sale
5. Adverse possession

Original title to land in the United States was acquired either from the federal government or from a country that held the land prior to its acquisition by the United States. The land in the 13 original colonies had been granted by the king of England either to the colonies or to certain individuals. The land in the Northwest Territory was ceded by the states to the federal government, which in turn issued grants or patents of land. Original ownership of much of the land in Florida and in the Southwest came by grants from the rulers of Spain.

ACQUISITION BY PURCHASE

The right to sell one's property is a basic ownership right. In fact, any restriction on the right of an owner to sell his property is usually considered to be against public policy and is not enforced. Most people who own real property acquired title by buying it from someone else. Each state sets the requirements for transferring a piece of real property located in that state. The various elements of selling and buying real property, including broker agreements, contracts to buy real estate, and deeds, will be covered in the next section of this chapter.

ACQUISITION BY GIFT

Ownership of real property may be acquired by *gift*. For such a gift to be valid, the donor must *deliver* a properly executed deed to the property to the donee or to some third person to hold it for the donee. It is not necessary that the donee or the third person take possession of the property. The essential element of the gift is the delivery of the deed. Suppose a man makes out a deed to the family farm and leaves it in a safe-deposit box for delivery to his son when he dies. The attempted gift will not be valid because there was no delivery of the gift during the donor's lifetime.

ACQUISITION BY WILL OR INHERITANCE

The owner of real property generally has the right to dispose of that property by **will.** The requirements for making a valid will are discussed in Chapter 34. If the owner of real property dies without making a valid will, the property will go to his heirs as determined under the laws of the state in which the real property is located.

ACQUISITION BY TAX SALE

If the taxes assessed on real property are not paid, they become a lien on the property. This lien has priority over all other claims of other persons to the land. If the taxes remain unpaid for a period of time, the government sells the land at a tax sale, and the purchaser at the tax sale acquires title to the property. However, in some states the original owner has the option for a limited time (perhaps a year) to buy it from the purchaser at the tax sale for her cost plus interest.

ACQUISITION BY ADVERSE POSSESSION

East state has a statute of limitations that provides an owner of land only a fixed number of years to bring a lawsuit to regain possession of his land from someone who is trespassing on it. This time period generally varies between 5 and 20 years, depending on the state. Thus, if someone moves onto your land and acts as if he is the owner, you must take steps to have that person ejected from your land. If you do not do so during the statutory period, you will lose your right to do so. The person who stayed in possession of your property for the statutory period will be treated as the owner. He will have acquired title to it by *adverse possession* or *prescription*.

    To acquire title by adverse possession, a person must possess land in a manner that puts the true owner on notice that he has a cause of action against that person. There must be actual occupancy that is hostile to the real owner's title, with an open claim to title (i.e., not with the owner's permission) continuously for the statutory period. In some states, the person in possession of land who is claiming the right to be there must also pay the taxes. It is not necessary that the same person occupy the land for the statutory period; however, the possession must be continuous for the necessary time.

    Adverse possession can take place in some fairly common situations. For example, Buzz Miller and Claire Alton own adjoining lots on which they have built houses. In 1978 Alton builds a fence to separate the two lots; however, she erects it about four feet onto Miller's land. She also builds a driveway that extends into the four-foot strip even though Miller did not give her permission to do so. He does not take steps to have the fence moved to its rightful position on the line between their lots. For 10 years Alton acts as if she owns the four-foot strip. Then she sells her lot to Edgar Gray, who also uses it and acts as if he is the owner. If the statute of limitations in that state is 20 years, in 1998 Gray will be the owner of the four-foot strip by adverse possession. The case that follows, *Appalachian Regional Healthcare, Inc. v. Royal Crown Bottling Company*, involves the acquisition of ownership of a small parcel of land by a company that believed it already was the owner of the land and was surprised to learn that someone else had a claim to it.

APPALACHIAN REGIONAL HEALTHCARE, INC. v. ROYAL CROWN BOTTLING COMPANY
824 S.W.2d 878 (Sup. Ct. Ky. 1992)

FACTS

In 1957 Royal Crown Bottling Company (RC) leased a small plot of land from Stumbo Supply Company, Inc. RC erected a billboard advertising Royal Crown Cola which was approximately 8 by 24 feet in size and was located approximately 20 feet from the edge of the highway. The plot of land was very small but was wide enough for the sign. On October 30, 1967, RC purchased the plot of land from Arnie Stumbo and recorded the deed in the local courthouse. Over the years, RC maintained the sign on the property, cutting weeds and brush from around the sign and going on the property to restore it. In 1986 Appalachian Regional Healthcare, Inc. (ARH), requested permission from RC to place a sign on the property, a request which RC granted. Shortly afterward, ARH asserted legal title to the property and demanded that RC remove its sign. ARH based its claim on a deed dated September 30, 1963. RC agreed that ARH had the superior record title but continued to claim ownership of the property by adverse possession. In Kentucky, the statutory period for recovering possession of real property from an adverse claimant is 15 years.

ISSUE

Did RC obtain title by adverse possession to the property on which the sign is located?

DECISION

Yes. The court stated that one may obtain title to real property by adverse possession for the statutory period of 15 years even when there is no intention by the adverse possessor to claim land not belonging to him. There are, however, five elements, all of which must be satisfied before adverse possession will bar record title: (1) possession must be hostile and under a claim of right; (2) it must be actual; (3) it must be exclusive: (4) it must be continuous; and (5) it must be open and notorious. The court found that RC had met these conditions. Among other things it had made a conspicuous use of the property continuously over the statutory period sufficient to put ARH on notice of the adverse use being made of its property. RC's defective or invalid deed was sufficient to afford it color of title. Accordingly, at the end of the 15 years, it had become the title holder to the real property described in the deed on which its sign was located.

TRANSFER BY SALE

STEPS IN A SALE

The major steps normally involved in the sale and purchase of real property are:

1. Contracting with a real estate broker to sell the property or to locate suitable property for sale.
2. Negotiating and signing a contract to sell the property.
3. Arranging for the financing of the purchase and the satisfaction of other contingencies such as a survey or an acquisition of title insurance.
4. Closing the sale, at which time the purchase price is usually paid and the deed is signed and delivered.
5. Recording of the deed.

REAL ESTATE BROKERS

Although engaging a real estate broker is not a legal requirement for the sale of real property, it is common for one who wishes to sell his property to "list" the property with a broker. A listing contract empowers the broker to act as the seller's agent in procuring a ready, willing, and able buyer and in managing details of the property transfer. A number of states' statutes of frauds require listing contracts to be evidenced by a writing and signed by the party to be charged.

Real estate brokers are regulated by state and federal law. They owe *fiduciary duties* (duties of trust and confidence) to their clients. Chapter 20 contains additional information regarding the duties imposed on such agents.

Types of Listing Contracts

Listing contracts specify such matters as the listing period's duration, the terms on which the seller will sell, and the amount and terms of the broker's commission. There are different types of listing contracts.

1. *Open listing.* Under an open listing contract, the broker receives a *nonexclusive* right to sell the property. This means that the seller and third parties (for example, other brokers) also are entitled to find a buyer for the property. The broker operating under an open listing is entitled to a commission only if he was the first to find a ready, willing, and able buyer.

2. *Exclusive agency listing.* Under an exclusive agency listing, the broker earns a commission if he *or any other agent* finds a ready, willing, and able buyer during the period of time specified in the contract. Thus, the broker operating under such a listing would have the right to a commission even if another broker actually procured the buyer. Under the exclusive agency listing, however, the seller has the right to sell the property himself without being obligated to pay the broker a commission.

3. *Exclusive right to sell.* An exclusive right to sell contract provides the broker the exclusive right to sell the property for a specified period of time and entitles her to a commission no matter who procured the buyer. Under this type of listing, a seller must pay the broker her commission even if it was the seller or some third party who found the buyer during the duration of the listing contract.

CONTRACT FOR SALE

The principles regarding contract formation, performance, assignment, and remedies that you learned in earlier chapters are applicable to contracts for the sale of real estate. The agreement between the seller and the buyer to purchase real property should be in writing to be enforceable under the statute of frauds. The agreement commonly spells out such things as the purchase price, the type of deed the purchaser will get, and what items of personal property such as appliances and carpets are included. It may also make the "closing" of the sale contingent on the buyer's ability to obtain financing at a specified rate of interest and the seller's procurement of a survey, title insurance, and termite insurance. Because they are within the statute of frauds, real estate sales contracts must be evidenced by a suitable writing signed by the party to be charged in order to be enforceable.

FINANCING THE PURCHASE

Various arrangements for financing the purchase of real property, such as mortgages, land contracts, and deeds of trust, are discussed in Chapter 40.

FEDERAL DISCLOSURE LAWS

Congress has enacted several statutes designed to protect purchasers of real estate. The federal Real Estate Settlement Procedures Act (RESPA) requires that a buyer receive advance disclosure of the settlement costs that will be incurred in settlement. RESPA also requires that a record be kept of the actual settlement charges in all real estate transactions involving federally related loans such as Veterans Administration and Federal Housing Administration loans. The required settlement/disclosure statement itemizes each settlement cost charged to the buyer and each charged to the seller. These settlement charges commonly include (1) real estate broker's commissions, (2) loan origination fees, (3) loan discount points, (4) appraisal fees, (5) credit report fees, (6) lender's inspection fees, (7) insurance premiums, (8) settlement closing/escrow fees, (9) prepaid interest and taxes, (10) title search fees, (11) notary's and/or attorney's fees, (12) survey fees, (13) title insurance premiums, and (14) transfer and recording fees.

Among the purposes of the settlement statement are to give the buyer notice of the cash needed at settlement and an opportunity to engage in "comparison shopping" of settlement terms so that the buyer can arrange the most favorable terms.

RESPA prohibits a number of practices, including kickbacks or payments for referral of business to title companies. It also prohibits any requirement by the seller that title insurance be purchased from any particular company.

In response to fraud and misrepresentations made by some sellers of land, particularly retirement and vacation properties, Congress enacted the Interstate Land Sales Full Disclosure Act. The act generally applies to developers who subdivide property into 50 or more lots and who use interstate means such as the mails and the telephone to sell the property. The act requires that a "property report" be prepared disclosing certain kinds of information about the property and the developer's plans regarding it. The report is filed with the U.S. Department of Housing and Urban Development and must be made available to prospective buyers. Developers who violate the law are subject to civil and criminal penalties.

FAIR HOUSING ACT

The Fair Housing Act, enacted by Congress in 1968 and substantially revised in 1988, is designed to prevent discrimination in the housing market. Its provisions apply to real estate brokers, sellers (other than those selling their own single-family dwellings without the use of a broker), lenders, lessors, and appraisers.

Originally, the act prohibited discrimination on the basis of race, color, religion, sex, and national origin. The 1988 amendments added handicap and "familial status" to the list. The familial status category was intended to prevent discrimination in the housing market against pregnant women and families with children. "Adult" or "senior citizen" communities restricting residents' age do not violate the Fair Housing Act even though they do exclude families with children so long as the housing meets the requirements of the act's "housing for older persons" exemption.

The act prohibits discrimination on the above-listed bases in a wide range of matters relating to the sale or rental of housing. These matters include refusals to sell or rent, representations that housing is not available for sale or rental when in fact it is, and discriminatory actions regarding the provision of services and facilities involved in sale or rental. The act also prohibits discrimination in connection with brokerage services, appraisals, and financing of dwellings.

A violation of the Fair Housing Act can result in a civil action brought either by the government or the aggrieved individual. If the aggrieved individual brings suit and prevails, the court may issue injunctions, award actual and punitive damages, assess attorney's fees and costs, and grant other appropriate relief.

TRANSFER BY DEED

Each state has enacted statutes that set out the formalities for transferring land located within its borders. As a general rule, the transfer of land is accomplished by the execution and delivery of a **deed.** A deed is an instrument in writing whereby the owner of an interest in real property (the **grantor**) conveys to another (the **grantee**) some right, title, or interest in that property. Two types of deeds, the quitclaim deed and the warranty deed, are in general use in the United States.

Quitclaim Deeds

When the grantor conveys by a **quitclaim deed,** she conveys to the grantee whatever title she has at the time she executes the deed. However, in a quitclaim deed the grantor does not claim to have good title or, in fact, any title. If the title proves to be defective or if the grantor has no title, the grantee has no right to sue the grantor under the quitclaim deed. Quitclaim deeds are frequently used to cure a technical defect in the chain of title to property. In such a case, the grantor may not be claiming any right, title or interest in the property. See Figure 32–1 on page 592 for an example of a quitclaim deed.

Warranty Deeds

A **warranty deed** contains covenants of warranty; that is, the grantor, in addition to conveying title to the property, guarantees to make good any defects in the title he has conveyed (see Figure 32–2 on page 593). A warranty deed may be a deed of general warranty or of special warranty. In a **general warranty deed** the grantor warrants against all defects in the title and all encumbrances (such as liens and easements). In a **special warranty deed,** the grantor warrants against only those defects in the title or those encumbrances that arose after he acquired the property. If the property conveyed is mortgaged or subject to some other encumbrance such as an easement or a long-term lease, it is a common practice to give a special warranty deed that contains a provision excepting those specific encumbrances from the warranty.

Form and Execution of Deed

Some states have enacted statutes setting out the form of deed that may be used in these states. However, a deed may be valid even though it does not follow the statutory form. The statutory requirements of the different states for the execution of deeds are not uniform, but they do follow a similar pattern. As a general rule, a deed states the name of the grantee, contains a recitation of consideration and a description of the property conveyed, and is signed by the grantor. In most states the deed, to be eligible for recording, must be acknowledged by the grantor before a notary public or other officer authorized to take an **acknowledgment.**

No technical words or conveyance is necessary. Any language is sufficient that indicates with reasonable certainty an intent to transfer the ownership of the property. The phrases "give, grant, bargain, and sell" and "convey and warrant" are in common use. A consideration is recited in a deed for historical reasons. The consideration recited is not necessarily the purchase price of the real property. It is sometimes stated to be "one dollar and other valuable consideration."

The property conveyed must be described in such a manner that it can be identified. In urban areas, descriptions are as a general rule given by lot, block and plat. In

FIGURE 32–1   A Quitclaim Deed

Quitclaim Deed

THIS DEED, made the 15th day of August, 2002, BETWEEN Frances B. Pearce, a married woman, of No. 150 Oaklawn Street, City of Baltimore, State of Maryland, party of the first part, and Kathleen M. Sparks, a single woman of No. 300 Maryland Avenue, City of Annapolis, State of Maryland, party of the second part.

WITNESSETH, that the party of the first part, in consideration of One Hundred Dollars ($100.00) lawful money of the United States, paid by the party of the second part, does hereby release and quitclaim unto the party of the second part, the heirs, successors and assigns of the party of the second part forever.

ALL the certain plot, piece or parcel of land, with the buildings and improvements thereon erected, situate and lying in the City of Annapolis, Anne Arundel County, State of Maryland, described as follows:

BEGINNING for the same at the Northeast corner of the building numbered 197 Main Street on the Southwest side of Main Street (formerly Church Street) and running thence with the partition wall between the building hereby conveyed and that of Mary J. Moss et al., Liber S. H. 15, folio 97; (1) South 15° 09′ 11″ West 30.67 feet to the junction of the partition walls; thence with the division line between the lot hereby conveyed and that of before-mentioned Mary J. Moss; (2) South 18° 13′ 02″ West 66.70 feet to a fence corner; thence with the fence line; (3) North 68° 01′ 58″ West 18.75 feet to an iron pipe found; thence (4) North 27° 42′ 20″ East 10.79 feet to a fence corner; thence with a fence line (5) North 71° 34′ 50″ West, 7.75 feet to an iron pipe found; thence with a fence line (6) North 12° 42′ 30″ East 23.67 feet to the Southeast corner of the building numbered 199 Main Street; thence with the partition wall between the building hereby conveyed; and No. 199 Main Street (7) North 14° 57′ 30″ East 60.33 feet to the Northwest corner of the building hereby conveyed and the Southwest side of Main Street; thence with the Southwest side of Main Street (8) South 75° 02′ 30″ East 28.79 feet to the place of beginning. Containing 2,537 square feet of land, more or less, as surveyed by C. D. Meekins and Associates, Annapolis, Maryland.

TOGETHER with all right, title and interest, if any, of the party of the first part in and to any streets and roads abutting the above described premises to the center lines thereof; together with the appurtenances and all the estate and rights of the party of the first part in and to said premises.

TO HAVE AND TO HOLD the premises herein granted unto the party of the second part, the heirs or successors and assigns of the party of the second part forever.

IN WITNESS WHEREOF, the party of the first part has duly executed this deed the day and year first above written.

In presence of:

Charles S. Reinhart   *Frances B. Pearce*

Witness   Grantor

ACKNOWLEDGEMENT OF DEED

State of Maryland   )

County of Anne Arundel) ss

I, an officer authorized to take acknowledgements according to the laws of the State of Maryland, duly qualified and acting, HEREBY CERTIFY that Frances B. Pearce to me personally known, this day personally appeared and acknowledged before me that she executed the foregoing Deed, and I further certify that I know the said person making said acknowledgement to be the individual described in and who executed the said Deed.

Edward A. Smith

Edward A. Smith
Notary Public

FIGURE 32–2   A Warranty Deed

Warranty Deed

THIS DEED, made in the City of Washington, District of Columbia on the 8th day of September, two thousand and two,

BETWEEN William S. Clark, an unmarried man, party of the first part, and Samuel D. Butler, party of the second part.

WITNESSETH, that the party of the first part, in consideration of Eighty-seven Thousand Five Hundred Dollars ($87,500.00) lawful money of the United States, paid by the party of the second part, does hereby grant and release unto the party of the second part, his heirs and assigns forever.

ALL that certain plot, piece or parcel of land located in the District of Columbia and known and described as Lot numbered Thirty-nine (39) in William D. Green's subdivision of part of Lot numbered Twenty-two (22) in Square numbered Twelve Hundred Nineteen (1219), as per plat recorded in the Office of the Surveyor for the District of Columbia in Liber 30 at folio 32, together with the buildings and improvements thereon and all the estate and rights of the party of the first part in and to said property.

TO HAVE AND TO HOLD THE premises herein granted unto the party of the second part, his heirs and assigns forever.

And the party of the first part covenants as follows:

FIRST—That the party of the first part is seized of the said premises in fee simple, and has good right to convey the same.

SECOND—That the party of the second part shall quietly enjoy the said premises.

THIRD—That the premises are free of encumbrances.

FOURTH—That the party of the first part will execute or procure and further necessary assurances of the title to said premises.

FIFTH—That the party of the first part will forever warrant the title to said premises.

IN WITNESS WHEREOF, the party of the first part has set his hand and seal the day and year above written.

In presence of:

Millicent A. Fenton   *William S. Clark*   (SEAL)

Millicent A. Fenton   William S. Clark

ACKNOWLEDGEMENT OF DEED

District of Columbia, ss:

I, an officer authorized to take acknowledgements according to the laws of the District of Columbia, duly qualified and acting, HEREBY CERTIFY that William S. Clark to me personally known, this day personally appeared and acknowledged before me that he executed the foregoing Deed, and I further certify that I know the said person making said acknowledgement to be the individual described in and who executed the said Deed.

Kathryn R. Cole

Kathryn R. Cole
Notary Public

---

rural areas, the land, if it has been surveyed by the government, is usually described by reference to the government survey; otherwise, it is described by metes and bounds, which is a surveyor's description using distances and angles measured in the survey (see Figure 32–1).

A deed must be delivered to be valid. Suppose a woman executes a deed to her home and puts it in her safe-deposit box together with a note directing that the deed be delivered to her son after her death. The deed is not effective to pass title after the woman's death. A deed, to be valid, must be delivered in the lifetime of the grantor.

RECORDING DEEDS

The delivery of a valid deed conveys title from a grantor to a grantee. Nevertheless, in order to prevent his interest from being defeated by third parties who may claim an interest in the same property, the grantee should immediately **record** the deed. When a deed is recorded, it is deposited and indexed in a systematic way in a public office, where it operates to give notice of the grantee's interest to the rest of the world.

Each state has a recording statute that establishes a system for the recording of all transactions that affect the ownership of real property. The statutes are not uniform in their provisions. In general, they provide for the recording of all deeds, mortgages, and other such documents and declare that an unrecorded transfer is void as against an innocent purchaser or mortgagee for value.

METHODS OF ASSURING TITLE

One of the things that a person must be concerned about in buying real property is whether the seller of the property has *good title* to it. In buying property, a buyer is really buying the seller's ownership interests. Because the buyer does not want to pay a large sum of money for something that turns out to be worthless, it is important for him to obtain some assurance that the seller has good title to the property. This is commonly done in one of three ways.

In some states, it is customary for the seller to give the buyer an **abstract of title** certified to the date of closing. The abstract is a history of the passage of title of the real property according to the records but is not a guarantee of title. The buyer, for his or her own protection, should have the abstract examined by a competent attorney who will give an opinion as to the title held by the grantor. The opinion will state whether or not the grantor has a **merchantable title** to the property. A merchantable title is one that is readily salable and not subject to objection because of defects in it. If the title is defective, the nature of the defects will be stated in the title opinion.

In many states, the buyer obtains protection against defects in the title by acquiring **title insurance.** This insurance is designed to reimburse the buyer for loss if the title turns out to be defective. When the purchase of the property is being financed by a third party, the lender often requires that a policy of title insurance be obtained for the lender's protection.

Several states have adopted the **Torrens system.** Under this system, the person who owns the land in fee simple obtains a certificate of title. When the real property is sold, the grantor delivers a deed and certificate of title to the grantee. The grantee then delivers the deed and certificate of title to the designated government official and receives a new certificate of title. All liens and encumbrances against the property are noted on the certificate of title, and the purchaser is assured that the title is good except as to the liens and encumbrances noted on it. However, it should be noted that some claims or encumbrances, such as adverse possession or easements by prescription, do not appear on the records. They must be discovered by making an *inspection* of the property. In some states, certain encumbrances, such as liens for taxes, short-term leases, and highway rights, are good against the purchaser even though they do not appear on the certificate.

WARRANTIES IN THE SALE OF A HOUSE

Traditionally, unless there was an express warranty of the habitability or condition of a house, or unless there was some fraud or misrepresentation involved, the purchaser of a house was subject to the doctrine of **caveat emptor** (that the buyer must beware at his own risk). This was based on the fact that the buyer and seller dealt at arm's length and the buyer had the opportunity to become acquainted with the condition and quality of the property being acquired. Thus, the buyer had a choice: Either obtain an express warranty from the seller as to the quality of the property or take the property at his own risk.

Courts in the majority of states have abandoned the *caveat emptor* doctrine in the sale of new homes by builder–sellers. Where latent or undiscoverable defects are involved, they have adopted the doctrine of **caveat venditor** (that the responsibility is on the seller). This tends to put the buyer of a new home in roughly the same position as the buyer of goods. The buyer gets an *implied warranty of habitability* (or merchantable fitness) of the house.

The implied warranty of habitability is basically a guarantee that the house is free of *latent* (that is, hidden) defects that would render it unsafe or unsuitable for human habitation. A breach of the warranty will subject the defendant to liability for damages, measured by either the cost of repairs or the loss in value of the house. If the breach is so serious that it constitutes a material breach, it can even lead to rescission of the sale. The application of the warranty has been limited to builders, builder–vendors, and developers. That is, an ordinary seller of a house who is not the builder or developer does not make a warranty of habitability.

One further issue that has caused a great deal of litigation is whether the warranty extends to subsequent purchasers of the house. For example, XYZ Development Company builds a house and sells it to Smith. If Smith later sells the house to Jones, can Jones sue XYZ for breach of warranty if a serious defect renders the house uninhabitable? The earlier cases limited the warranty to *new* houses and held that the subsequent purchasers had no cause of action for breach of warranty against the original builder. A considerable number of more recent cases, however, have extended the implied warranty to subsequent purchasers for a reasonable time. The decisions in these cases recognize that the purchase of a house is one of the largest investments a buyer will ever make and that buyers have justifiable expectations about the durability of a house. Naturally, the extension of the warranty to subsequent purchasers greatly increases the legal vulnerability of builders and developers. This is illustrated in the *Hershey v. Rich Rosen Construction Company* case that follows.

HERSHEY V. RICH ROSEN CONSTRUCTION COMPANY
817 P. 2d 55 (Ct. App. Ariz. 1991)

FACTS

Rich Rosen Construction company completed construction of a single-family home with a stucco exterior and sold it to the initial purchaser on April 1, 1976. In 1985 the initial owner sold the house to the second owner, who later added a room onto a corner of the house. In November 1985 James and Marjatta Hershey rented the house and lived there for six months prior to purchasing it in May 1986. During that period the Hersheys did not experience any problems with the stucco. Prior to the purchase, James Hershey performed a "walk-around in-

spection," during which he did not see any cracks or defects in the stucco on the exterior of the house.

In April or May 1987 Hershey first noticed some bulging of the stucco on the southwest side of the house but did not do anything about it at the time because it did not appear to be a major problem. After a heavy rainstorm in August 1987, he heard what he thought to be water running behind a bedroom wall; the next day he discovered more stucco bulging from the wall and a small hole where a piece had dropped out. He filed a

(continued)

HERSHEY V. RICH ROSEN CONSTRUCTION COMPANY
(concluded)

claim with his insurance company for rain damage. The insurer denied the claim based on the opinion of an architect that the various cracks and loose stucco resulted from the exterior stucco application being improperly done at the time of construction. The materials used were not weather approved, and neither the materials nor the construction methodology met the local building code. An expert retained by the Hersheys concluded that the stucco exterior on their home was "one of the worst examples of material selection and application I have encountered in the past 10–12 years" and categorized the workmanship as "below average to almost criminal." Hershey discovered the name of the builder, Rich Rosen Construction Company, from a neighbor who was an original owner of a Rosen-built home and who had a similar problem with his stucco in 1979.

The Hersheys contacted Rich Rosen Construction Company and requested that it repair the damage, but it declined. The Hersheys then filed a complaint for breach of implied warranty, seeking repair costs.

ISSUE

Was there an implied warrant of habitation in the construction of the new house that ran to a subsequent purchaser when a breach of the warranty was discovered 12 years later?

DECISION

Yes. First, the court observed that Arizona recognizes implied warranties of workmanship and habitability for original owners of residential structures and that the warranties were extended to subsequent purchasers by the Arizona Supreme Court in 1984. However, the warranties are limited to latent defects that would not have been discoverable had a "reasonable inspection" been made prior to the purchase. The testimony in this case indicated that the defects could have been discovered by a trained person engaged in the business of home inspection, but that a lay person would not be likely to key in on any of the problems until they began to manifest themselves. The court concluded that the Hersheys had met the requirement for making a reasonable inspection and that they were not required to have retained an expert at the time they purchased the home. The court also concluded that because a stucco exterior has a normal life expectancy in the Arizona desert of 30 to 50 years, it was reasonable to conclude that it should have been expected to last more than 12 years on the Hershey's house. Accordingly, the court found that based on the expected life of the defective component of the house, 12 years was not an unreasonable period for an implied warranty of habitability and workmanship to exist.

Another issue that has arisen regarding the implied warranty of habitability is whether the warranty can be *disclaimed* or *limited* in the contract of sale. Subject to the doctrine of unconscionability, concerns about public policy, and legal rules of interpretation and constructions, it appears that the warranty can be validly disclaimed or at least limited by appropriate provisions in a contract. However, such clauses are strictly construed against the builder–vendor.

Other courts have imposed a duty on sellers of property to disclose any known defects in the premises that are not discoverable by reasonable inspection by the buyer. If the seller does not make such disclosure, such silence may be held to constitute **misrepresentation.** In a few states, the courts have gone even further and protected buyers where the seller of a used house was not aware of a defect. For example, the buyers of a used house in Louisiana discovered extensive termite infestation after they bought the house. The termite problem was not readily apparent to the naked eye, and the sellers were not aware of it. The court said that the buyers could recover the cost of repairing the hidden defect where the defect was so serious that the purchasers would not have bought the house had it been known.

.... **PUBLIC CONTROLS ON** ....
THE USE OF LAND

SOCIETAL RESTRAINTS

Although the owner of an interest in real property may generally make such use of her property as she desires, the owner does not have an unlimited right to do so. Society places a number of restraints on the owner of real property: (1) the owner cannot use the property in such a way as to unduly injure others; (2) through the use of the "police power," government units have the right to impose reasonable regulations on the use of property; and (3) the government has the right to take the property through the power of **eminent domain.**

NUISANCE LAW

One's enjoyment of her own land depends to a great extent on the uses her neighbors make of their land. When the uses of neighboring landowners conflict, the aggrieved party sometimes institutes litigation to resolve the conflict. A property use that unreasonably interferes with another person's ability to use or enjoy her own property may lead to an action for **nuisance** against the landowner or possessor engaged in the objectionable use.

The term *nuisance* has no set legal definition. It is often regarded, however, as encompassing any property-related use or activity that unreasonably interferes with the rights of others. Property uses potentially constituting nuisances include uses that are inappropriate to the neighborhood (such as using a vacant lot in a residential neighborhood as a garbage dump), bothersome to neighbors (such as keeping a pack of barking dogs in one's backyard), dangerous to others (such as storing large quantities of gasoline in 50-gallon drums in one's garage), or of questionable morality (such as operating a house of prostitution or a drug den).

To amount to a nuisance, a use need not be illegal. The fact that relevant zoning laws allow a given use does not mean that the use cannot be a nuisance. The fact that a use was in existence before complaining neighbors acquired their property does not mean that the use may not be considered a nuisance, although it does lessen the likelihood that the use would be held to be a nuisance.

The test for determining the presence or absence of a nuisance is highly dependent on the facts in the individual case. Nuisance actions involve a balancing of the various interests and rights involved. For example, the courts may weigh the social utility of the objectionable conduct and the burden of stopping it against the degree to which the conduct is infringing on the rights of other property owners.

Nuisances may be private or public. To bring a *private nuisance* action, the plaintiff must be a landowner or occupier whose enjoyment of his own land is substantially lessened by the alleged nuisance. The remedies for private nuisance include damages and injunctive relief designed to stop the offending use.

A *public nuisance* occurs when a nuisance harms members of the public, who need not be injured in their use of property. For example, if a power plant creates noise and emissions posing a health hazard to pedestrians and workers in nearby buildings, a public nuisance may exist even though the nature of the harm involves no loss of enjoyment of property. Public nuisances involve a broader class of affected parties than do private nuisances. The action to abate a public nuisance must usually be brought by the government. Remedies generally include injunctive relief and civil penalties that resemble fines. This is illustrated in the case that follows, *United States v. Wade*. Private parties may sue for abatement of public nuisances or for damages caused by public nuisances only when they suffer unique harm different from that experienced by the general public.

UNITED STATES V. WADE
992 F.Supp. 6 (D.C.D.C. 1997)

FACTS

Beginning in early 1994, the Washington D.C. Metropolitan Police Department received reports that individuals were selling drugs in front of a brick row house at 647 G Street, S.E. From April 1995 through January 1997, the police received 42 complaints about the alleged drug-trafficking activity. The local citizen's association took their complaints about the recurring drug transactions to their D.C. councilman and to the United States Attorney for the District of Columbia.

In October 1994, the police began an undercover investigation of the alleged narcotic trafficking inside and in front of 647 G Street. According to police reports written in conjunction with the investigation, the distribution of the drugs usually took place in front of the house, with the distributor coming out of the house with a small quantity of drugs to sell either to pedestrians or to individuals who were driving by the house. Upon making the sale, the distributor would take the money into the house and would retrieve additional drugs for sale. Over the course of the two-year investigation, the police made purchases from seven different individuals on ten different occasions; they also confiscated drugs from the house on three occasions.

On December 19, 1996, a grand jury indicted seven individuals, including Charles, Eugene, James, and Love Wade, for narcotics and other violations. Charles and Eugene pled guilty to a number of the charges, including keeping a disorderly house. The court entered an order requiring abatement of the nuisance of keeping a disorderly house. The order directed the United States Marshal to (1) effectively close the house and to keep it closed for a period of a year, (2) to remove all fixtures, furniture, and movable property used in conducting the nuisance; (3) to give the residents the opportunity to take all personal items and property that are not contraband, paraphernalia, or plainly used in conducting the nuisance of unlawfully selling crack cocaine base; and (4) to provide public notice that anyone who breaks and enters the house shall be punished for contempt of court, including by fine or imprisonment.

The Wades—and a number of other residents/owners of the house—objected to the abatement order and sought to have it vacated. This group included Dorothy, Shelton, Angel, and Jean Wade, all related by blood or marriage to Rosie B. Wade, the last titled owner of the house at 647 G Street, who died intestate (see Chapter 34—Estates and Trusts) in 1994. They contended that abatement of the nuisance of a "disorderly house" was inappropriate in this case: (1) it should be limited to situations where the property was being used for lewdness or prostitution; (2) the nuisance had been effectively abated because all of the alleged offenders were either sentenced, awaiting trial, or no longer at, or near, 647 G Street; and (3) the nondefendant owners were without guilty knowledge that any drug-trafficking activity was taking place on the premises. At the hearing, Charles and Eugene expressed great concern about where their mother, father, and sister, who was retarded, would relocate.

ISSUE

Should the house be closed as a public nuisance?

DECISION

Yes. The concept of a public nuisance in the form of a "disorderly house" includes a variety of different kinds of establishments, including bawdy houses, gambling houses, unlicensed taverns, and places where stolen goods are received. The common element is that the premises are used to commit illegal acts and either disturb the public peace or corrupt the morals of the community. Here, the multiplicity of public complaints along with statements from nearby residents that they were fearful of venturing outside because of the drug traffic amply demonstrates that the activity at the house constitutes a public nuisance. The owners had sufficient grounds to be aware of the illegal activity taking place on the premises. And the argument that the nuisance had been abated was dismissed by the court because some of those indicted in connection with activity near the house were not currently in the custody of the law.

OTHER PROPERTY CONDITION–RELATED OBLIGATIONS OF REAL PROPERTY OWNERS AND POSSESSORS

In recent years, the law has increasingly required real property owners and possessors to take steps to further the safety of persons on the property and to make the property more accessible to disabled individuals. This section discusses two legal developments along these lines: the trend toward expansion of *premises liability* and the inclusion of property-related provisions in the Americans with Disabilities Act.

Expansion of Premises Liability

Premises liability is the name sometimes used for negligence cases in which property owners or possessors (such as business operators leasing commercial real estate) are held liable to persons injured while on the property. As explained in Chapter 5, property owners and possessors face liability when their *failures to exercise reasonable care* to keep their property reasonably safe result in injuries to persons lawfully on the property. The traditional premises liability case was one in which a property owner's or possessor's negligence led to the existence of a potentially hazardous condition on the property (e.g., a dangerously slick floor or similar physical condition at a business premises), and a person justifiably on the premises (e.g., a business customer) sustained personal injury upon encountering that unexpected condition (e.g., by slipping and falling).

Security Precautions against Foreseeable Criminal Acts   Recent years have witnessed a judicial inclination to expand premises liability to cover other situations in addition to the traditional scenario. A key component of this expansion has been many courts' willingness to reconsider the once-customary holding that a property owner or possessor had no legal obligation to implement security measures to protect persons on the property from the wrongful acts of third parties lacking any connection with the owner or possessor. Today, courts frequently hold that a property owner's or possessor's duty to exercise reasonable care includes the obligation to take reasonable security precautions designed to protect persons lawfully on the premises from foreseeable wrongful (including criminal) acts by third parties.

This expansion has caused hotel, apartment building, and convenience store owners and operators to be among the defendants held liable—sometimes in very large damage amounts—to guests, tenants, and customers on whom violent third-party attackers inflicted severe physical injuries. In such cases, the property owners' or possessors' negligent failures to take security precautions restricting such wrongdoers' access to the premises served as at least a *substantial factor* leading to the plaintiffs' injuries. The security lapses amounting to a lack of reasonable care in a particular case may have been, for instance, failures to install deadbolt locks, provide adequate locking devices on sliding glass doors, maintain sufficient lighting, or employ security guards.

Determining Foreseeability   The security precautions component of the reasonable care duty is triggered only when criminal activity on the premises is foreseeable. It therefore becomes important to determine whether the foreseeability standard has been met. In making this determination, courts look at such factors as whether previous crimes had occurred on or near the subject property (and if so, the nature and frequency of those crimes), whether the property owner or possessor knew or should have known of those prior occurrences, and whether the property was located in a high-crime area. The fact-specific nature of the foreseeability and reasonable care determinations makes the outcome of a given premises liability case difficult to predict in advance. Nevertheless, there is no doubt that the current premises liability climate gives property owners and possessors more reason than ever before to be concerned about security measures.

Americans with Disabilities Act   In 1990, Congress enacted the broad-ranging Americans with Disabilities Act (ADA). This statute was designed to eliminate long-standing patterns of discrimination against disabled persons in matters such as employment, access to public services, and access to business establishments and similar facilities open to the public. The ADA's Title III focuses on places of *public accommodation*. It imposes on certain property owners and possessors the obligation to take reasonable steps to make their property accessible to disabled persons (individuals with a physical or mental impairment that substantially limits one or more major life activities).

Places of Public Accommodation   Title III of the ADA classifies numerous businesses and nonbusiness enterprises as places of **public accommodation.** These include hotels, restaurants, bars, theaters, concert halls, auditoriums, stadiums, shopping centers, stores at which goods are sold or rented, service-oriented businesses (running the gamut from gas stations to law firm offices), museums, parks, schools, social services establishments (day care centers, senior citizen centers, homeless shelters, and the like), places of recreation, and various other enterprises, facilities, and establishments. Private clubs and religious organizations, however, are not treated as places of public accommodation for purposes of the statute.

Modifications of Property   Under the ADA, the owner or operator of a place of public accommodation cannot exclude disabled persons from the premises or otherwise discriminate against them in terms of their ability to enjoy the public accommodation. Avoiding such exclusion or other discrimination may require alteration of the business or nonbusiness enterprise's practices, policies, and procedures.

Prohibited discrimination may also include the "failure to remove architectural barriers and communication barriers that are structural in nature," if removal is "readily achievable." When the removal of such a barrier is not readily achievable, the property owner or possessor nonetheless engages in prohibited discrimination if he, she, or it does not adopt "alternative methods" to ensure access to the premises and what it has to offer.

New Construction   Newly constructed buildings on property used as a place of public accommodation must contain physical features making the buildings *readily accessible* to disabled persons. The same is true of additions built on to previous structures.

Remedies   A person subjected to disability-based discrimination in any of the respects discussed above may bring a civil suit for injunctive relief. An injunction issued by a court must include "an order to alter facilities" to make the facilities "readily accessible to and usable to individuals with disabilities to the extent required" by the ADA. The court has discretion to award attorney's fees to the prevailing party. The U.S. Attorney General also has the legal authority to institute a civil action alleging a violation of Title III of the ADA. In such a case, the court may choose to grant injunctive and other appropriate equitable relief, award compensatory damages to aggrieved persons (when the Attorney General so requests), and assess civil penalties (up to $50,000 for a first violation and up to $100,000 for any subsequent violation) "to vindicate the public interest." When determining the amount of any such penalty, the court is to give consideration to any good faith effort by the property owner or possessor to comply with the law. The court must also consider whether the owner or possessor could reasonably have anticipated the need to accommodate disabled persons.

ZONING ORDINANCES

State legislatures commonly delegate to counties, cities, towns, and other local governments the **police power** to impose reasonable regulations designed to promote the public health, safety, morals, and general welfare of the community. **Zoning ordinances** are an exercise of such a power to regulate. Generally, zoning ordinances divide a city or town into a number of districts, specify or limit the use to which property in those districts can be put, and restrict improvements on and use of the land.

Such restrictions and controls may be of four basic types:

1. *Control of use.* The activity on the land may be regulated or limited, for example, to single- or multifamily dwellings, commercial establishments, light industry, or heavy industry.
2. *Control of height and bulk.* The regulation may control the height of buildings; the setback from front, side, and rear lot lines; and the portion of a lot that can be covered by a building.
3. *Control of population density.* The regulation may provide how much living space must be provided for each person and may specify the maximum number of persons who can be housed in a given area.
4. *Control of aesthetics.* These regulations are commonly used to control billboards but may also be used to enforce similarity and dissimilarity of buildings as well as to preserve historic areas.

When a zoning ordinance is passed, it has only a prospective effect, so existing uses and buildings are permitted to continue. However, the ordinance may provide for the gradual phasing out of such uses and buildings that do not conform to the general zoning plan. If a property owner later wants to use the property in a way other than that permitted by the zoning ordinance, the owner must try to have the ordinance amended. To do this, the owner must show that the proposed changes are in accordance with the overall plan or must try to obtain a **variance** on the ground that the ordinance creates an undue hardship by depriving him of the opportunity to make a reasonable use of the land. Such attempts to obtain amendments or variances often conflict with the interests of nearby property owners who have a vested interest in the zoning status quo. These conflicts sometimes produce heated battles before the zoning authorities.

A disgruntled property owner might also attack the constitutionality of a zoning ordinance. Zoning ordinances have produced a great deal of litigation in recent years as cities and towns have used their zoning power as a means of social control. For example, a city might create a special zone for adult bookstores or other uses that are considered moral threats to the community. This has given rise to challenges that such ordinances unconstitutionally restrict freedom of speech.

Another type of litigation has involved ordinances designed to restrict single-family residential zones to living units of traditional families related by blood or marriage or to no more than two unrelated adults. Many cities and towns have attempted to "zone out" such other living groups as groups of unrelated students, communes, religious cults, and group homes by specifically defining the word *family* in a way that excludes these groups. In the case of *Belle Terre v. Boraas,*[1] the Supreme Court upheld such an ordinance as applied to a group of unrelated students. It subsequently held, however, that an ordinance that defined "family" in such a way as to prohibit a grandmother from living with her grandsons was an unconstitutional intrusion on personal freedom regarding marriage and family life. In some cases, restrictive definitions of the term *family* have been held unconstitutional under state constitutions. In others, such definitions have been narrowly construed by the courts.

Subdivision Ordinances

Many local governments also have ordinances that deal with proposed subdivisions. The ordinances often require that the developer meet certain requirements as to lot size, street and sidewalk layout, and sewers and water. The ordinances commonly require city approval of the proposed development before it can be started. In some cases the developer may be required to dedicate land to the city for streets, parks, and schools. The purpose of such ordinances is to protect the would-be purchasers in the subdivision as well as the city population as a whole by ensuring that minimum standards are met by the developer.

Some urban planners believe that it is undesirable to segregate totally the living, working, shopping, and entertainment areas, as is commonly done with a zoning scheme. They argue that a more livable environment is one that combines these uses so as to ensure the vitality of an area for the vast part of each day. In response to this philosophy, cities and counties are allowing "planned unit developments" and "new towns" that mix such uses so long as the plans are submitted to the authorities and approved pursuant to general guidelines established for such developments.

People are also becoming more aware of the shortcomings of making land-use decisions on a piecemeal basis at the local level. Airports, major shopping centers, highways, and new towns require a regional rather than a local planning focus. Moreover, sensitive ecological areas such as marshes can be destroyed readily if encroached on in a piecemeal manner. Accordingly, a number of states and the federal government have passed, or are considering, legislation to put some land-use planning on a regional or a statewide basis.

EMINENT DOMAIN

The Constitution provides that private property shall not be taken for public use without just compensation. Implicit in this statement is the power of the state to take property for public use by paying just compensation to the owner of the property. This power, which is called the power of **eminent domain,** makes possible our highways, water control projects, municipal and civic centers, public housing, and urban renewal.

Although the eminent domain power is probably necessary for efficient government, there are several major problems inherent in its use. One of them is the question of what is meant by "just compensation." The property owner now receives the "fair market value" of the property. Some people believe that this falls short of reimbursing the owner for what is lost because it does not cover the lost goodwill of a business or the emotional attachment a person may have to his or her home.

---

[1]416 U.S. 1 (U.S. Sup. Ct. 1974).

A second problem is deciding when a "taking" has occurred—easy when the owner is completely dispossessed by government, but much more difficult if (1) the zoning power has been utilized to restrict the permissible use of a given piece of property to a narrow publicly beneficial use such as a parking lot or (2) the government uses nearby land in such a way as to almost completely destroy the usefulness of adjoining privately owned land, as sometimes occurs in the case of municipal airports. When the government effectively takes land without having paid for it, the owner of the land can bring an action for **inverse condemnation** to obtain compensation for the taking. This problem is illustrated in the case that follows, *Dolan v. City of Tigard.*

A third problem is determining when the eminent domain power is properly exercised. Clearly, when the government unit itself uses the property, as in the case of a municipal building or a public highway, the use of the power is proper. However, in other cases, such as urban renewal, where condemned property may be resold to a private developer or the condemned property is not substandard, the use of the power is not so clearly justified.

DOLAN v. CITY OF TIGARD
114 S.Ct. 2309 (U.S. Sup. Ct. 1994)

FACTS

The State of Oregon enacted a comprehensive land use management program in 1973 that required all Oregon cities to adopt new comprehensive land use plans that were consistent with statewide planning goals. The city of Tigard, a community of some 30,000 residences on the southwest edge of Portland, developed a comprehensive plan and codified it as its Community Development Code (CDC). The CDC required property owners in the area zoned as the Central Business District to comply with a 15 percent open space requirement, limiting total site coverage including all structures and paved parking to 85 percent of the parcel. It also required that any new development facilitate a plan for a pedestrian/bicycle pathway by dedicating land for that purpose wherever required in the plan. The city also adopted a Master Drainage Plan that suggested a series of improvements to the Fanno Creek Basin.

Florence Dolan owned a plumbing and electric supply store located on Main Street in the Central Business District of Tigard. The 1.67-acre property was adjacent to Fanno Creek and a portion of it was in the 100-year floodplain and unusable for commercial development. Dolan applied to the city for a permit to redevelop the site, proposing to nearly double the size of her store and pave a 39-space parking lot.

The City Planning Commission granted the permit application, subject to conditions imposed by the city's

CDC. The Commission required Dolan to dedicate the portion of her property lying within the 100-year floodplain for improvement of a storm drainage system along Fanno Creek and to dedicate an additional strip of land adjacent to the floodplain as a pedestrian/bicycle pathway. The dedication required by the condition encompassed approximately 7,000 square feet, or roughly 10 percent, of the property. Dolan requested variances from the CDC standards, as permitted in case of undue or unnecessary hardship, but the request was denied. The Commission found that customers and employees of the store could utilize the pathway, that it would offset some of the traffic demand the store created on nearby streets, and that the increased storm water runoff from the parking lot would add to the public need to manage the stream channel and floodplain for drainage purposes.

Dolan appealed to the Land Use Board of Appeals on the ground that the city's dedication requirements were not related to the proposed development, and therefore, those requirements constituted an uncompensated taking of her property under the Fifth Amendment. The Board denied the appeal, finding a "reasonable relationship" between alleviating the impacts of the proposed development and the required dedications. The Oregon

(continued)

DOLAN V. CITY OF TIGARD
(concluded)

Court of Appeals and its Supreme Court affirmed, and Dolan appealed to the United States Supreme Court.

ISSUE

Did the condition placed by the city of Tigard constitute an unconstitutional taking of Dolan's property for public purposes without payment of just compensation?

DECISION

Yes. Initially, the Supreme Court found that the city's requirement that Dolan dedicate a portion of her property lying within the flood plain for improvement of a storm drainage system and property adjacent to the flood plain as a bicycle/pedestrian pathway as a condition for a building permit had a nexus with a legitimate public purpose. However, the city did not show the reasonable relationship between the effects of the proposed development and the required dedication. While the city found that the paved parking lot would increase storm water flow from the property, it never explained why a public greenway, as opposed to a private one, was required in the interest of flood control. Similarly, the city failed to show that the additional number of vehicle and bicycle trips generated by the proposed development were reasonably related to the requirement of a dedication of a pedestrian/bicycle pathway easement as a condition for granting the permit; there was no finding that the pathway was likely to offset traffic demand.

.... *QUESTIONS AND PROBLEM CASES* ....

1. If you hire a real estate broker to sell your house, what must the broker normally do to earn a commission?

2. On September 30, 1985, J. E. Carson leased a building to Melvin and Jeffrey Craven. They in turn allowed the Living Word Outreach Ministries, Inc. (the Church), to occupy the building with the rent payments being made by the Church. After the Church moved in, a number of improvements were made, including remodeling of the interior and the installation of heating and air conditioning units, chandeliers, a water cooler, outside floodlights, and carpet. The air conditioning system was put in the building around May of 1986, and the Church paid for it by borrowing funds from a bank. The air conditioning units were connected to the building by electrical wire, pipes, and duct systems.

   In September of 1989, the Church moved out of the building taking all of the air conditioning units and the duct work, the chandeliers, and the water cooler. Carson contended that in removing these items, the Church damaged the ceiling by cutting the overhead joists and completely destroyed the duct work and the casing around a stairway. Carson and the Cravens brought suit against the Church, claiming that the air conditioning system was a fixture that had become part of the building and seeking damages for its removal. The Church claimed that the air conditioning system was not an improvement that had become an integral part of the building and that it had not damaged the building by removing it. Was the air conditioning system a fixture that had become part of the building so that the Church was not entitled to remove it?

3. William D. Robinson left a will in which he gave his real estate as follows: "I give all of my real estate to my wife, Lela S. Robinson, and at her death it goes to Frank M. Robinson, and at his death to his two boys, David Robinson and Richard Robinson." Does Lela have a *fee simple* interest in the property or a *life estate*?

4. Sewell and Reilly owned adjoining lots. They entered into a written agreement whereby each agreed to allow the other to use the south 10 feet of his lot for alley purposes "for so long as the alley" over the other party's lot remained open. Did this agreement create an easement or a license?

5. Flynn and Korsalk own adjoining lots, and a strip of land 11 to 12 feet wide separates the houses on the lots. The distance from Flynn's house to the front boundary of the property is 71 feet. Flynn's predecessor in title, Mrs. Brewer, and her husband owned automobiles from 1947 to 1969 and drove them on the strip, including the portion owned by their neighbors, because it could not be avoided and because it was impossible to tell where the lot line was. Flynn purchased the property from the Brewers in 1969 and continued to drive across the strip. Korsalk had purchased his lot in 1968. In 1972, Korsalk began to protest Flynn's driving on this land, and in 1974 erected a chain link fence on the lot line that effectively prevented Flynn from driving his car across the strip to get to his garage. Flynn sought an injunction ordering Korsalk to remove the fence and other obstructions in the driveway and enjoining him from placing obstructions in the future. Should the injunction be granted?

6. On February 7, C. L. Hollaway, a real estate broker, obtained an open listing to sell Forshee's residence. The property was listed for sale at $55,000, and Hollaway was to receive a 6 percent commission if he sold it. On May 17, Elaine Sparks, a real estate agent who worked for Hollaway, showed the Forshee property to Mr. and Mrs. Corris Bell. She told the Bells where Forshee lived. She also offered to help the Bells find financing but was told that they were obtaining financing themselves. On May 23, Sparks learned that the Forshee property had been sold to the Bells. Hollaway then brought a lawsuit against Forshee to recover a commission. Was Hollaway entitled to a commission on the grounds that his sales agent had been the effective procuring cause of the sale?

7. William and Alice Carter purchased two lots in a subdivision called Payson Ranchos in Payson, Arizona. Each lot in the subdivision had a restriction in the deed that prohibited the use of house trailers on the lots except for a period of up to 90 days during the time that a house was being constructed on the lot. The Carters moved a trailer onto one of their lots. They removed the tongue and wheels and set the trailer up on concrete blocks. They also connected it to a septic tank and attached power and water lines. A number of Carters' neighbors brought a lawsuit to require them to remove the trailer because it was in violation of the deed restriction. The Carters claimed that the restriction did not apply because their home was no longer a trailer. They also claimed that other neighbors were violating other deed restrictions concerning the erection of fences, so they should not be able to enforce the trailer restriction against the Carters. Could the restriction against trailers be used to force the Carters to remove their trailer?

8. The Schlemeyers purchased a frame apartment house and discovered shortly after the purchase that there was substantial termite infestation. They undertook some of the steps suggested by a specialist in pest control but did not take all the measures he indicated would be necessary to ensure success. Six years later, the Schlemeyers sold the apartment house to Fred Obde but did not advise him of the termite condition. When Obde later discovered the termite infestation, he brought a lawsuit for damages against the Schlemeyers, contending that they had fraudulently concealed the infestation from him when they had been under a duty to disclose it. Can Obde recover?

9. Hartford Penn-Cann Service, Inc., operated a gas station, restaurant, and truck wash directly across the highway from a gas station and truck stop operated under the name "Hartford 65." It brought suit against the operators of Hartford 65, contending that dust from their property was blowing onto the Penn-Cann Service property to the detriment of its business and to the health of its employees. Dust from Hartford 65 frequently blew onto Penn-Cann Service's property and prevented some of its employees from wearing contact lenses and one had to wear a dust mask; its machinery, including its gas pumps, had to be replaced more frequently; the windows in its restaurant could not be opened; dust collected on packages of food in the restaurant and the packages had to be wiped off before they could be opened; and business at its truck wash fell off. Should the owners of Hartford 65 be enjoined from operating a gas station or truck stop on the ground such use constitutes a nuisance?

10. James and Marilyn Nollan own a beachfront lot in Ventura County, California. A quarter mile north of their property is Faria County Park, an oceanside public park with a public beach. Another public beach area, known as "the Cove" lies 1,800 feet south of their lot. A concrete seawall separates the beach portion of the Nollans' property from the rest of the lot. The historic mean high-tide line determines the lot's oceanside boundary. The Nollans wanted to tear down a small bungalow that was on the property and build a three-bedroom house on the lot. California law required that they obtain a coastal development permit from the California Coastal Commission to do this. They submitted the permit application and were later informed that they could have the permit on condition that they allow the public an easement to pass across a portion of their property bounded by the mean high tide line on one side and their seawall on the other. This would make it easier for the public to get to Faria County Park and the Cove. The Nollans challenged the access condition but the Commission affirmed it. On appeal, the California Court of Appeals upheld the action of the Coastal Commission. The Nollans appealed to the United States Supreme Court. Did the imposition of the public access condition constitute a taking of the Nollans' property for public use without just compensation?

CHAPTER 33

Landlord and Tenant

Chances are that during your lifetime you will be involved in the rental of property. Perhaps as a student you might rent an apartment; after graduation you might rent a house; and, during a vacation period, you might rent a condominium at a beach or a ski resort. It is also possible that you might rent some property in order to conduct a business, or you might own and rent out some residential or commercial property.

Suppose, for example, that you, along with several friends, are looking to rent a house for the next school year. You see an ad for a rental house near the campus, and orally agree with the landlord on a one-year lease to begin the following September with a monthly rent of $650. You leave him a security deposit of $1,000. When you arrive in September, the current tenants are still in possession. They move out several days later, leaving the house a mess. The landlord tells you to move in and that he'll clean it up later; however, he does not do so, despite your repeated requests to him. You complain to the city housing department, which conducts an inspection and finds numerous violations of the city's housing code. The city gives the landlord 15 days to make the necessary repairs. Before any of the repairs are made, a friend who is coming to visit you is injured when she falls through some rotten boards on the front porch. At the end of September, you and your friends move out but the landlord refuses to return your security deposit. What rights, duties, and obligations do you have in this situation?

In this chapter, you will cover the legal rules that control the landlord–tenant relationship, rules that build on contract, tort, and property law.

.... *LEASES AND TENANCIES* ....

LANDLORD–TENANT RELATIONSHIP

Landlord–tenant law has undergone dramatic change during the past four decades, owing in large part to the changing nature of the relationship between landlords and tenants. In England and in early America, farms were the most common subject of leases. The tenant sought to lease land on which to grow crops or graze cattle. Accordingly, traditional landlord–tenant law viewed the lease as primarily a conveyance of land and paid relatively little attention to its contractual aspects.

In today's society, however, the landlord–tenant relationship is typified by the lease of property for residential or commercial purposes. The tenant occupies only a small portion of the total property. He bargains primarily for the use of structures on the land rather than for the land itself. He is likely to have signed a landlord-provided form lease, the terms of which he may have had little or no opportunity to negotiate. In areas with a shortage of affordable housing, a residential tenant's ability to bargain for favorable lease provisions is further hampered. Because the typical landlord–tenant relationship can no longer be characterized fairly as one in which the parties have equal knowledge and bargaining power, it is not always realistic to presume that tenants are capable of negotiating to protect their own interests.

Although it was initially slow to recognize the changing nature of the landlord–tenant relationship, the law now tends to place greater emphasis than it once did on the contract components of the relationship. As a result, modern contract doctrines such as unconscionability, constructive conditions, the duty to mitigate damages, and implied warranties are sometimes applied to leases. Such doctrines may operate to compensate for tenants' lack of bargaining power. In addition, state legislatures and city councils have enacted statutes and ordinances that increasingly regulate leased property and the landlord–tenant relationship.

This chapter's discussion of landlord–tenant law focuses on the nature of leasehold interests, the traditional rights and duties of landlords and tenants, and recent statutory and judicial developments affecting those rights and duties.

NATURE OF LEASES

A **lease** is a contract by which an owner of property, the **landlord** (also called the *lessor*), conveys to the **tenant** (also called the *lessee*) the exclusive right to possess property for a period of time. The property interest conveyed to the tenant is called a **leasehold estate.**

TYPES OF TENANCIES

The duration of the tenant's possessory right depends upon the type of **tenancy** established by or resulting from the lease. There are four main types of tenancies.

1. *Tenancy for a term.* In a **tenancy for a term** (also called a *tenancy for years*), the landlord and tenant have agreed on a specific duration of the lease and have fixed the date on which the tenancy will terminate. For example, if Amber, a college student, leases an apartment for the academic year ending May 25, 2003, a tenancy for a term will have been created. The tenant's right to possess the property ends on the date agreed upon without any further notice unless the lease contains a provision permitting extension.

2. *Periodic tenancy.* A **periodic tenancy** is created when the parties agree that rent will be paid in regular successive intervals until notice to terminate is given but do not agree on a specific lease duration. If the tenant pays rent monthly, the tenancy is from month to month; if the tenant pays yearly, as is sometimes done under agricultural leases, the tenancy is from year to year. (Periodic tenancies therefore are sometimes called *tenancies from month to month* or *tenancies from year to year.*) To terminate a periodic tenancy, either party must give advance notice to the other. The precise amount of notice required is often defined by state statutes. For example, to terminate a tenancy from month to month, most states require that the notice be given at least one month in advance.

3. *Tenancy at will.* A **tenancy at will** occurs when property is leased for an indefinite period of time and either party may choose to conclude the tenancy at any time. Generally, tenancies at will involve situations in which the tenant either does not pay rent or does not pay it at regular intervals. For example, Kim allows her friend Eric to live in the apartment over her garage. Although this tenancy's name indicates that it is terminable "at [the] will" of either party, most states require that the landlord give reasonable advance notice to the tenant before exercising the right to terminate the tenancy.

SCHULTZ v. WURDLOW
1995 Ohio App. Lexis 333 (Ct. App. Ohio 1995)

FACTS

Emily Schultz and Kerri Minnich submitted a "Rental Application and Agreement" to rent an apartment owned and managed by Earl Wurdlow. Both Schultz and Minnich were students at Ohio State University and wished to rent the apartment only during the school year (September through June). Schultz had rented the same apartment during the preceding school year.

Wurdlow informed both women that it would be necessary to have their parents complete and sign a "Parent Agreement," which was basically identical to the lease documents. Although it was his policy not to permit residents to move in before providing him with a signed copy of the parental agreement, he permitted Schultz to move in because her mother promised to sign and return the form to him. Minnich provided him a copy of the form; however, it included her signature rather than those of her parents. Both women moved into the apartment.

After realizing that neither of the women's respective parents were willing to complete the agreement, Wurdlow gave them 30 days' notice to move out of the apartment. Both did so but requested that Wurdlow return the $410 security deposit they had paid on signing the rental agreement. Wurdlow refused to return it. He did not as-

sert that there was any rent past due or damage to the apartment; however, he did claim that they were responsible for rerental expenses and loss of rent revenue. Schultz and Minnich then filed an action in small claims court to recover the security deposit.

ISSUE

Was a tenancy at will created where there was no valid written lease but the party took possession of the premises?

DECISION

Yes. Under the statute of frauds in Ohio, a lease, whether for a short term or for a long term, must be in writing. Where, as here, there is an agreement purporting to be a lease that has a defect and the tenant enters into possession and pays rent, a tenancy at will is created. The tenancy is subject to all other terms of the purported lease except duration. Duration is determined by the period covered by the expected rent payment. Because rent was paid here on a monthly basis, a month-to-month tenancy resulted. Therefore, either party had the right to terminate the lease with one month's notice. Wurdlow gave such notice. When the women moved out of the

(continued)

SCHULTZ V. WURDLOW
(concluded)

apartment, Wurdlow would be permitted to deduct any past due rent or any damages that he sustained as a result of the tenants' noncompliance with the housing code or the rental agreement. Wurdlow here was not claiming any past due rent or damages. His only claim

was for rerental expenses and loss of rent revenue; however, these are not recoverable under a properly terminated month-to-month tenancy, and the tenants were entitled to the return of their full security deposit.

4. *Tenancy at sufferance.* A **tenancy at sufferance** occurs when a tenant remains in possession of the property (holds over) after a lease has expired. In this situation, the landlord has two options: (1) treating the holdover tenant as a trespasser and bringing an action to eject him and (2) continuing to treat him as a tenant and collecting rent from him. Until the landlord makes her election, the tenant is a tenant at sufferance. Suppose that Frank has leased an apartment for one year from Jim. At the end of the year, Frank holds over and does not move out. Frank is a tenant at sufferance. Jim may have him ejected or may continue treating him as a tenant. If Jim elects the latter alternative, a new tenancy is created. The new tenancy with be either a tenancy for a term or a periodic tenancy, depending on the facts of the case and any presumptions established by state law. Thus, a tenant who holds over for even a few days runs the risk of creating a new tenancy he might not want.

CONCEPT SUMMARY   **Types of Tenancies**

Type of Lease	Characteristics	Termination
Tenancy for a Term	Landlord and tenant agree on a specific duration of the lease and fix the date on which the tenancy will end.	Ends automatically on the date agreed upon; no additional notice necessary.
Periodic Tenancy	Landlord and tenant agree that tenant will pay rent at regular, successive intervals (e.g., month to month).	Either party may terminate by giving the amount of advance notice required by state law.
Tenancy at Will	Landlord and tenant agree that tenant may possess property for an indefinite amount of time, with no agreement to pay rent at regular, successive intervals.	May be terminated "at will" by either party, but state law requires advance notice.
Tenancy at Sufferance	Tenant remains in possession after the termination of one of the leaseholds described above until landlord has brought ejectment action against tenant or collected rent from him.	Landlord has a choice of: 1. Treating tenant as a trespasser and bringing ejectment action against him, or 2. Accepting rent from tenant, thus creating a new leasehold.

EXECUTION OF A LEASE

As transfers of interests in land, leases may be covered by the statute of frauds. In most states, a lease for a term of more than one year from the date it is made is unenforceable unless it is evidenced by a suitable writing signed by the party to be charged. A few states, however, require leases to be evidenced by a writing only when they are for a term of more than three years.

Good business practice demands that leases be carefully drafted to make clear the parties' respective rights and obligations. Care in drafting leases is especially important in cases of long-term and commercial leases. Lease provisions normally cover such essential matters as the term of the lease, the rent to be paid, the uses the tenant may make of the property, the circumstances under which the landlord may enter the property, the parties' respective obligations regarding the condition of the property, and the responsibility (as between landlord and tenant) for making repairs. In addition, leases often contain provisions allowing a possible extension of the term of the lease and purporting to limit the parties' rights to assign the lease or sublet the property. State or local law often regulates lease terms. For example, the Uniform Residential Landlord and Tenant Act (URLTA) has been enacted in a substantial minority of states. The URLTA prohibits the inclusion of certain lease provisions, such as a clause by which the tenant supposedly agrees to pay the landlord's attorney's fees in an action to enforce the lease. In states that have not enacted the URLTA, lease terms are likely to be regulated at least to a moderate degree by some combination of state statutes, common law principles, and local housing codes.

RIGHTS, DUTIES, AND LIABILITIES OF THE LANDLORD

LANDLORD'S RIGHTS

The landlord is entitled to the *agreed rent* for the term of the lease. Upon expiration of the lease, the landlord has the right to the *return of the premises in as good a condition as when leased* except for normal wear and tear and any destruction by an act of God.

Security Deposits

Landlords commonly require tenants to make security deposits or advance payments of rent. Such deposits operate to protect the landlord's right to receive rent as well as her right to reversion of the property in good condition. In recent years, many cities and states have enacted statutes or ordinances designed to prevent landlord abuse of security deposits. These laws typically limit the amount a landlord may demand and require that the security deposit be refundable, except for portions withheld by the landlord because of the tenant's nonpayment of rent or tenant-caused property damage beyond ordinary wear and tear. Some statutes or ordinances also require the landlord to place the funds in interest-bearing accounts when the lease is for more than a minimal period of time. As a general rule, these laws require landlords to provide tenants a written accounting regarding their security deposits and any portions being withheld. Such an accounting normally must be provided within a specified period of time (30 days, for example) after the termination of the lease. The landlord's failure to comply with statutes and ordinances regarding security deposits may cause the landlord to experience adverse consequences that vary state by state.

LANDLORD'S DUTIES

Fair Housing Act

As explained in Chapter 33, the Fair Housing Act prohibits housing discrimination on the basis of race, color, sex, religion, national origin, handicap, and familial status. The Fair Housing Act prohibits discriminatory practices in various transactions affecting housing, including the rental of dwellings. The act does provide an exemption for certain persons who own and rent single-family houses. To qualify for this exemption, owners must not use a real estate broker or an illegal advertisement and cannot own more than three such houses at one time. It also exempts owners who rent rooms or units in dwellings in which they themselves reside if those dwellings house no more than four families.

Included within the act's prohibited instances of discrimination against a protected person are refusals to rent property to such a person; discrimination against him or her in the terms, conditions, or privileges of rental; publication of any advertisement or statement indicating any preference, limitation, or discrimination operating to the disadvantage of a protected person; and representations that a dwelling is not available for rental to such a person when, in fact, it is available.

The act also makes it a discriminatory practice for a landlord to refuse to permit a tenant with a handicap to make—at his own expense—reasonable modifications to leased property. The landlord may, however, make this permission conditional on the tenant's agreement to restore the property to its previous condition upon termination of the lease, reasonable wear and tear excepted. In addition, landlords are prohibited from refusing to make reasonable accommodations in rules, policies, practices, or services if such accommodations are necessary to afford a handicapped tenant equal opportunity to use and enjoy the leased premises. When constructing certain types of multifamily housing for first occupancy, property owners and developers risk violating the act if they fail to make the housing accessible to persons with handicaps.

Because of a perceived increase in the frequency with which landlords refused to rent to families with children, the act prohibits landlords from excluding families with children. If, however, the dwelling falls within the act's "housing for older persons" exception, this prohibition does not apply.

Implied Warranty of Possession

Landlords have certain obligations that are imposed by law whenever property is leased. One of these obligations stems from the landlord's **implied warranty of possession.** This warranty guarantees the tenant's right to possess the property for the term of the lease. Suppose that Pat rents an apartment from Julia for a term to begin on September 1, 2002, and to end on August 31, 2003. When Pat attempts to move in on September 1, 2002, she finds that Sam, the previous tenant, is still in possession of the property. In this case, Julia has breached the implied warranty of possession.

Implied Warranty of Quiet Enjoyment

By leasing property, the landlord also makes an **implied warranty of quiet enjoyment** (or *covenant of quiet enjoyment*). This covenant guarantees that the tenant's possession will not be interfered with as a result of the landlord's act or omission. In the absence of a contrary provision in the lease or an emergency that threatens the property, the landlord may not enter the leased property during the term of the lease. If he does, he will be liable for trespass. In some cases., courts have held that the covenant of quiet enjoyment was violated when the landlord failed to stop third parties, such as trespassers or other tenants who make excessive noise, from interfering with the tenant's enjoyment of the leased premises.

LANDLORD'S RESPONSIBILITY FOR CONDITION OF LEASED PROPERTY

The common law historically held that landlords made no implied warranties regarding the *condition* or quality of leased premises. As an adjunct to the landlord's right to receive the leased property in good condition at the termination of the lease, the common law imposed on the *tenant* the duty to make repairs. Even when the lease contained a landlord's express warranty or express promise to make repairs, a tenant was not entitled to withhold rent if the landlord failed to carry out his obligations. This was because a fundamental contract performance principle—that a party is not obligated to perform if the other party fails to perform—was considered inapplicable to leases. In recent years, however, changing views of the landlord–tenant relationship have resulted in dramatically increased legal responsibility on the part of landlords for the condition of leased residential property.

Implied Warranty of Habitability

The legal principle that landlords made no implied warranty regarding the condition of leased property arose during an era when tenants used land primarily for agricultural purposes. Buildings existing on the property were frequently of secondary importance. They also tended to be simple structures lacking modern conveniences such as plumbing and wiring. These buildings were fairly easily inspected and repaired by the tenant, who was generally more self-sufficient than today's typical tenant. In view of the relative simplicity of the structures, landlord and tenant were considered to have equal knowledge of the property's condition upon commencement of the lease. Thus, a rule requiring the tenant to make repairs seemed reasonable.

The position of modern residential tenants differs greatly from that of an earlier era's agricultural tenants. The modern residential tenant bargains not for the use of the ground itself but for the use of a building (or portion thereof) as a dwelling. The structures on land today are complex, frequently involving systems (such as plumbing and electrical systems) to which the tenant does not have physical access. Besides decreasing the likelihood of perceiving defects during inspection, this complexity compounds the difficulty of making repairs—something at which today's tenant already tends to be less adept than his grandparents were. Moreover, placing a duty of tenants to negotiate for express warranties and duties to repair is no longer feasible. Residential leases are now routinely executed on standard forms provided by landlords.

For these reasons, statutes or judicial decisions in most states now impose an **implied warranty of habitability** on many landlords who lease residential property. According to the vast majority of cases, this warranty is applicable to *residential* property, not to property leased for commercial uses. The implied warranty of habitability's content in lease settings is basically the same as in the sale of real estate: The property must be safe and suitable for human habitation. In lease settings, however, the landlord not only must deliver a habitable dwelling at the beginning of the lease but must also *maintain* the property in a habitable condition during the term of the lease. Various statues and judicial decisions provide that the warrant includes an obligation that the leased property comply with any applicable housing codes.

Remedies for Breach of Implied Warranty of Habitability

From a tenant's point of view, the implied warrant of habitability is superior to constructive eviction because a tenant does not have to vacate the leased premises in order to seek a remedy for breach of the warranty. The particular remedies for breach of the implied warranty of habitability differ from state to state. Some of the remedies a tenant may pursue include these.

1. *Action for damages.* The breach of the implied warranty of habitability violates the lease and renders the landlord liable for damages. The damages generally are measured by the diminished value of the leasehold. The landlord's breach of the implied warranty of habitability may also be asserted by the tenant as a counterclaim and defense in the landlord's action for eviction and/or nonpayment of rent.

2. *Termination of lease.* In extreme cases, the landlord's breach of the implied warranty of habitability may justify the tenant's termination of the lease. For this remedy to be appropriate, the landlord's breach must have been substantial enough to constitute a material breach.

3. *Rent abatement.* Some states permit rent abatement, a remedy under which the tenant withholds part of the rent for the period during which the landlord was in breach of the implied warranty of habitability. Where authorized by law, this approach allows the tenant to pay a reduced rent that reflects the *actual* value of the leasehold in its defective condition. There are different ways of computing this value. State law determines the amount by which the rent will be reduced.

4. *Repair-and-deduct.* A growing number of states have statutes permitting the tenant to have defects repaired and to deduct the repair costs from her rent. The repairs authorized in these statutes are usually limited to essential services such as electricity and plumbing. They also require that the tenant give the landlord notice of the defect and an adequate opportunity to make the repairs himself.

SOLOW V. WELLNER
569 N.Y.S.2d 882 (Civ. Ct. City of N.Y. 1991)

FACTS

Sheldon Solow, doing business as Solovieff Gallery Company, was the owner of a 300-unit luxury apartment building on the upper east side of Manhattan that had received awards for architectural design. Rents, which were subject to a city rent-stabilization law, ranged from $1,064.89 per month for a 4th-floor studio apartment to $5,379.92 per month for a two-bedroom on the 44th floor. A brochure shown to prospective tenants before they signed a lease touted the high-quality features in the building and apartments including the roof-top pool club, 24-hour attended lobby, video-monitored service and garage entrances, four high-speed elevators with direct access to the attended underground garage, 46th-floor laundry with spectacular city view, and a four-pipe heating and air conditioning system in the public areas as well as individual apartments.

(continued)

SOLOW V. WELLNER
(concluded)

In 1987 approximately 80 tenants joined in a rent strike to protest against what they viewed as deteriorating conditions and services. Among their complaints were (1) malfunctioning elevators that consistently skipped floors, opened on the wrong floors, and were often out of service, causing interminable delays, lateness, and missed appointments; (2) stench of garbage stored between the package room and the garage as well as rodent and roach infestation; (3) frequently inoperative lobby air conditioning; (4) fire alarms that did not function; (5) a dirty laundry room with overflowing sinks, a collapsed ceiling, and missing floor tiles; (6) soiled carpets in the lobby and other public areas; (7) unlocked door separating the garage and the building; (8) exposed wiring in public areas; (9) several floods that made ingress and egress to the building difficult, caused floors to buckle, and seeped into mailboxes and the package room; (10) missing caulking that allowed water to seep into apartments; (11) standing water in the boiler room; and (12) graffiti on some walls. Solow brought suit against the tenants to recover rent, and the tenants sought an abatement of rent for breach of warranty of habitability.

The Real Property Law of New York creates an implied warranty of habitability in residential housing and provides, in pertinent part, that "In every written or oral lease or rental agreement for residential premises the landlord or lessor shall be deemed to covenant and warrant that the premises so leased or rented and all areas used in connection therewith, in common with other tenants or residents, are fit for human habitation and for the uses reasonably intended by the parties and that the

occupants of such premises shall not be subjected to any conditions which would be dangerous, hazardous, or detrimental to their life, health or safety."

ISSUE

Did the conditions present in the apartment building constitute a breach of the implied warranty of habitability?

DECISION

Yes. The court found that the conditions present here constituted a breach of the implied warranty of habitability. It noted that the warranty of habitability in residential tenancies parallels the warranty of fitness in commercial transactions, meaning that premises are to be maintained in accordance with the reasonable expectations of tenants. Certain amenities, while not life threatening, that are consistent with the nature of the bargain—such as air conditioning—fall under the protection of the warranty of habitability. Similarly, predictability and reliability of services are factors to consider in determining whether there has been a breach of the warranty. Here, the location of the premises, amenities that were touted to go with the apartment, and representations made by the landlord consistent with the lease are factors that enter into the tenants' reasonable expectations. In addition, higher rents paid by these tenants in a luxury apartment building justify their increased expectations of a well-run, impeccably clean building of consistent and reliable service. Accordingly, the court found that the conditions in the public areas breached the warranty of habitability.

Constructive Eviction

The doctrine of **constructive eviction** may aid a tenant when property becomes unsuitable for the purposes for which it was leased because of the landlord's act or omission, such as the breach of a duty to repair or the convenant of quiet enjoyment. Under this doctrine, which applies both to residential and commercial property, the tenant may terminate the lease because she has effectively been evicted as a result of the poor condition or the objectionable circumstances there. Constructive eviction gives a tenant the right to vacate the property without further rent obligation if she does so *promptly* after giving the landlord reasonable notice and an opportunity to correct the problem. Because constructive eviction requires the tenant to vacate the leased premises, it is an unattractive option for tenants who cannot afford to move or do not have a suitable alternative place to live.

The principle of constructive eviction is illustrated in *Weingarden v. Eagle Ridge Condominiums.*

WEINGARDEN V. EAGLE RIDGE CONDOMINIUMS
653 N.E.2d 759 (Toledo Mun. Ct., Ohio 1995)

FACTS

On February 14, 1994, Don Weingarden entered into a written rental agreement with Eagle Ridge Condominiums for an apartment in Maumee, Ohio. Weingarden paid $150 as a security deposit with a monthly rental rate of $750 payable on the first of each month; the month of March was rent free. The parties also agreed that the landlord would replace the bedroom door, repair the electrical outlet in the bedroom, and replace the boards in the basement.

Weingarden took possession on March 1, 1994. On March 23, he notified the apartment manager in writing that the basement of the apartment would leak when snow melted and also after a rain. The leak would saturate the carpeting in the basement and render the basement useless. When wet, the carpet would become mildewed and odorous. Weingarden also indicated that the stairway in the unit was not in compliance with the Ohio Basic Building Code and that he had fallen as a result and, further, that the door in the bedroom had not been repaired and/or replaced and that the frame on the master bedroom door was cracked. Weingarden indicated that as a result he would vacate the premises on or before July 1, 1994.

The landlord attempted to remedy the basement leak by applying cement to the interior basement walls; however, the basement continued to leak and soak the carpet. On April 1, 1994, the landlord replied to Weingarden that it would not release him from his obligations under the lease agreement. On June 16, Weingarden surrendered his keys to the apartment and indicated in writing that his deposit should be forwarded to the address in Michigan that was on the application he had submitted for the lease.

The landlord did not return any security deposit to Weingarden and did not send any itemization of disbursements to him. The landlord spent the security deposit on a water bill of $27.11 and for the cost of carpet cleaning, with the balance being applied to unpaid rent pursuant to the terms of the lease.

Weingarden brought suit against the landlord to recover the balance of his security deposit and damages of $250 per month for the diminution in value of the rental unit because of the inability to utilize the basement which constituted one-third of the apartment. The landlord counterclaimed for the unpaid rent due for the balance of the lease term. One of the issues in the case was whether the conditions in the basement amounted to a constructive eviction of Weingarden.

ISSUE

Did the wet conditions in the basement substantially affect the habitability of the apartment and amount to a constructive eviction of the tenant?

DECISION

Yes. The lease agreement contains an implied warranty of habitability, and the landlord also has a statutory duty to maintain the premises in habitable condition. The warranty of habitability is not a warranty against all discomfort and inconvenience, and a breach of the warranty must be so substantial as to amount to constructive eviction if it is to excuse the tenant from the lease. Most of the defects cited by Weingarden do not meet the test of substantiality. However, the leaking basement which resulted in thoroughly soaked carpet and its odor significantly affected the habitability of the apartment and resulted in constructive eviction. Thus, Weingarden is entitled to the return of his security deposit (less the $27.11 water bill), was excused from any further obligation for rent, and is entitled to recover damages for the diminished value of the apartment during his tenancy.

Housing Codes

Many cities and states have enacted housing codes that impose duties on a property owner with respect to the condition of leased property. Typical of these provisions is Section 2304 of the District of Columbia Housing Code, which provides: "No person shall rent or offer to rent any habitation or the furnishing thereof unless such habitation and its furnishings are in a clean, safe, and sanitary condition, in repair and free from rodents or vermin." Such codes also commonly call for the provision and maintenance of necessary services such as heat, water, and electricity, as well as suitable bathroom and kitchen facilities. Housing codes also tend to require that specified minimum space–per–tenant standards be met, that windows, doors, floors, and screens be kept in repair, that the property be painted and free of lead paint, that keys and locks meet certain specifications, and that the landlord issue written receipts for rent payments. A landlord's failure to comply with an applicable housing code may result in a fine or in liability for injuries resulting from the property's disrepair. The noncompliance may also result in the landlord's losing part or all of his claim to the agreed-upon rent. Some housing codes establish that tenants have the right to withhold rent until necessary repairs have been made and the right to move out in cases of particularly egregious violations of housing code requirements.

Americans with Disabilities Act

Landlords leasing property constituting a *place of public accommodation* (primarily commercial property as opposed to private residential property) must pay heed to Title III of the American's with Disabilities Act. Under Title III, owners and possessors of real property that is a place of public accommodation may be expected to make reasonable accommodations, including physical modifications of the property, in order to allow disabled persons to have access to the property. Chapter 32 contains a detailed discussion of Title III's provisions.

LANDLORD'S TORT LIABILITY

Traditional No-Liability Rule

There are two major effects of the traditional rule that a landlord had no legal responsibility for the condition of the leased property. The first effect—that the uninhabitability of the premises traditionally did not give a tenant the right to withhold rent, assert a defense to nonpayment, or terminate a lease—has already been discussed. The second effect was that landlords normally could not be held liable in tort for injuries suffered by tenants on leased property. This state of affairs stemmed from the notion that the tenant had the ability and responsibility to inspect the property for defects before leasing it. By leasing the property, the tenant was presumed to take it as it was, with any existing defects. As to any defects that might arise during the term of the lease, the landlord's tort immunity was seen as justified by his lack of control over the leased property once he had surrendered it to the tenant.

Traditional Exceptions to No-Liability Rule

Even before the current era's protenant legal developments, however, courts created exceptions to the no-liability rule. In the following situations, landlords have traditionally owed the tenant (or an appropriate third party) a duty, the breach of which could constitute a tort:

1. *Duty to maintain common areas.* Landlords have a duty to use reasonable care to *maintain the common areas* (such as stairways, parking lots, and elevators) over which they retain control. If a tenant or a tenant's guest sustains injury as a result of the landlord's negligent maintenance of a common area, the landlord is liable.

2. *Duty to disclose hidden defects.* Landlords have a duty to disclose hidden defects about which they know if the defects are not reasonably discoverable by the tenant. The landlord is liable if a tenant or appropriate third party suffers injury because of a hidden danger that was known to the landlord but went undisclosed.

3. *Duty to use reasonable care in performing repairs.* If a landlord repairs leased property, he must *exercise reasonable care in making the repairs.* The landlord may be liable for the consequences stemming from negligently performed repairs, even if he was not obligated to perform them.

4. *Duty to maintain property leased for admission to the public.* The landlord has a duty to suitably maintain property that is leased for *admission to the public.* A theater would be an example.

5. *Duty to maintain furnished dwellings.* The landlord who rents a *fully furnished dwelling* for a short time impliedly warrants that the premises are safe and habitable.

Except for the above circumstances, the landlord traditionally was not liable for injuries suffered by the tenant on leased property. Note that none of these exceptions would apply to one of the most common injury scenarios—when the tenant was injured by a defect in her own apartment and the defect resulted from the landlord's failure to repair rather than from negligently performed repairs.

Current Trends in Landlord's Tort Liability

Today, there is a strong trend toward abolition of the traditional rule of landlord tort immunity. The proliferation of housing codes and the development of the implied warranty of habitability have persuaded a sizable number of courts to impose on landlords the duty to use *reasonable care* in their maintenance of the leased property. As discussed earlier, a landlord's duty to keep the property in repair may be based on an express clause in the lease, the implied warranty of habitability, or provisions of a housing code or statute. The landlord now may be liable if injury results from her negligent failure to carry out her duty to make repairs. As a general rule, a landlord will not be liable unless she had *notice* of the defect and a reasonable opportunity to make repairs.

The duty of care landlords owe tenants has been held to include the duty to take reasonable steps to protect tenants from substantial risks of harm created by other tenants. Courts have held landlords liable for tenants' injuries resulting from dangerous conditions (such as vicious animals) maintained by other tenants when the landlord knew or had reason to know of the danger.

It is not unusual for landlords to attempt to insulate themselves from negligence liability to tenants by including an *exculpatory clause* in the standard form of leases they expect tenants to sign. An exculpatory clause purports to relieve the landlord from legal responsibility that the landlord could otherwise face (on negligence or other grounds) in certain instances of premises-related injuries suffered by tenants. In recent years, a number of state legislatures and courts have frowned upon exculpatory clauses when they are included in leases of residential property. There has been an increasing judicial tendency to limit the effect of exculpatory clauses or declare them unenforceable on public policy grounds when they appear in residential leases.

In the case that follows, *Howard v. Horn,* the court found that a landlord had not breached his duty to a tenant and was therefore not liable for his injuries.

HOWARD V. HORN
810 P.2d 1387 (Ct. App. Wash. 1991)

FACTS

In 1984 William Horn purchased a duplex that had been constructed in 1974. In September 1987 Horn rented one unit to Larry and Patricia Howard. On October 15, approximately two weeks after the Howards moved onto the premises, Mr. Howard stumbled on the uneven cement walkway between the porch and the driveway. He fell across three steps leading to the front door. The accident occurred just after dusk while the Howards were unloading groceries and carrying children from their car. The porch light was on, and Mr. Howard acknowledged that the uneven edge of the cement was visible "if you were looking for it." The Howards brought suit against Horn for alleged negligence. They contended that the uneven sidewalk and the failure to install a handrail along the front steps and safety glass in the window panel were evidence of a breach of duty of care on the part of Horn.

The rental agreement required the Howards to accept the premises in their present condition and to inform the landlord of any necessary repairs. The agreement further provided that the Howards would maintain the grounds, including the sidewalks, which were to be kept "in a safe condition."

Washington state law requires that a landlord has a duty to keep leased residential premises fit for human habitation. Specifically, the landlord must "(1) maintain the premises to substantially comply with any applicable code, statute, ordinance, or regulation governing their maintenance or operation, which the legislative body enacting the applicable code, statute, ordinance or regulation could enforce as to the premises rented if such condition substantially endangers or impairs the health or safety of the tenant; . . . and (5) except where the condition is attributable to normal wear and tear, make repairs and arrangements necessary to put and keep the premises in as good condition as by law or rental agreement it should have been at the commencement of the tenancy." Failure to carry out the duties gives rise to certain remedies, provided the landlord has notice of the defect. The remedies are limited to (1) the tenant's right to repair and deduct the cost from the rent, (2) a decrease in the rent based upon the diminished value of the premises, (3) payment of rent into a trust account, or (4) termination of the tenancy.

ISSUE

Is the landlord liable for the injuries sustained by the tenant?

DECISION

No. First, the terms of the rental agreement included acceptance of the premises in their present condition, the duty to inform the landlord of any needed repairs, and the duty to maintain the grounds. Thus, it found that no duty was imposed on the landlord by the rental agreement. Second, the court said that common law negligence encompasses four basic elements: duty, breach, proximate cause, and injury. A commercial or residential landlord may be liable for personal injury to a tenant if the injury is caused by a latent defect known to the landlord. Here, the uneven cement and lack of a handrail were clearly observable patent defects. The failure to use safety glass was a latent defect that Mr. Horn was unaware of until it was broken and he learned that it had to be replaced with an acrylic glass. Finally, while the state law does incorporate into all residential leases a covenant to repair, it predicates the landlord's duty upon notice and a reasonable time to repair. Moreover, the defects alleged here do not impact the livability of the dwelling so as to render it unfit for habitation.

Landlord's Liability for Injuries Resulting from Others' Criminal Conduct

Another aspect of the trend toward increasing landlords' legal accountability is that many courts have imposed on landlords the duty to take reasonable steps to protect tenants and others on their property from foreseeable criminal conduct. Although landlords are not insurers of the safety of persons on their property, an increasing number of courts have found them liable for injuries sustained by individuals who have been criminally attacked on the landlord's property if the attack was facilitated by the landlord's failure to comply with housing codes or maintain reasonable security. This liability has been imposed on residential and commercial landlords (such as shopping mall owners). Some courts have held that the implied warranty of habitability includes the obligation to provide reasonable security. In most states that have imposed this type of liability, however, principles of negligence or negligence per se furnish the controlling rationale. The law of negligence is covered in detail in Chapter 5.

In the case that follows, *Morgan v. 253 East Delaware Condominium Association,* the court found that the landlord had not been negligent and was, therefore, not liable for a criminal attack on a tenant.

MORGAN V. 253 EAST DELAWARE CONDOMINIUM ASSOCIATION
595 N.E.2d 36 (Ct. App. Ill. 1992)

FACTS

Donna Marie Morgan resided in an apartment building owned by the 253 East Delaware Condominium Association and managed by Joseph Moss Realty. One evening at about 8:30 PM Morgan walked from her class at Loyola University's downtown campus to the building, where she entered the lobby, checked her mail, and entered the elevator in the lobby. As she had first entered the building, she had observed a man talking to the doorman. The man followed her into the elevator. When it arrived at the 10th floor, he poked a gun into her back, forced her off the elevator, and robbed her and beat her with the gun, causing severe injuries. Morgan brought a lawsuit against the Association and Moss alleging that they were negligent for failing to protect her from the criminal acts of the unknown third party because they under-

took to provide security and performed it in a negligent fashion. Morgan testified that when she first rented the apartment she was told the neighborhood was safe and the building had security, including a 24-hour doorman. The doorman testified that the man had responded to an inquiry as to whether he could help him by replying, "Unit 13G." The doorman had then called the tenant in Unit 13G, told him his guest was here, and was told by the tenant to "let him up." The tenant had earlier told the doorman he was expecting guests.

ISSUE

In these circumstances did the Association and Moss have a legal duty to protect Morgan from the criminal act of the third party?

(continued)

MORGAN V. 253 EAST DELAWARE CONDOMINIUM ASSOCIATION
(concluded)

DECISION

No. The court noted that the general rule is that a landlord does not owe a tenant or guest a duty to protect them from criminal acts. This is based on the principle that the landlord is not an insurer and cannot be held liable to the tenant for every criminal act. However, liability can be imposed on a landlord who voluntarily undertakes to provide security, but performs it negligently, if the negligence is the proximate cause of the harm. Here, the landlord appeared to have acted in a reasonable manner by providing a doorman who followed the normal procedure of asking guests their business and then using the in-house phone to inform the tenant that his guest had arrived. The harm in this case did not result from any breach of duty.

CONCEPT SUMMARY   **Rights, Duties, and Liabilities of Landlords**

Rights	1. To receive the agreed-on rent for the term of the lease.
	2. To return the property at the expiration of the lease in as good a condition as it was when leased, except for normal wear and tear and any destruction by the weather or an act of God.
Duties	1. To assure the tenant the right to possess the property for the term of the lease (implied warranty of possession).
	2. To guarantee that the tenant's possession will not be interfered with as a result of any act or omission on the landlord's part.
	3. To provide and maintain, in the case of residential property, a habitable dwelling (implied warranty of habitability).
	4. To conform to any relevant housing codes or regulations that apply to the leasing of property, including provisions that concern the condition of property, duty to repair, handling of security deposits, control of rents, and eviction of tenants.
	5. To maintain common areas, to disclose hidden defects that they know about if the defects are not reasonably discoverable by tenants, and to use reasonable care in making repairs.
	6. To use reasonable care to protect tenants and others on their property from foreseeable criminal conduct.
	7. To comply with the terms of the lease agreement.
Liabilities	1. To persons, including the tenant, who suffer personal injury or property damage as a result of the landlord's failure to perform a duty that proximately results in a foreseeable injury.
	2. To the tenant for failure to perform duties required by law or by the lease agreement.
	3. To government agencies for failure to comply with applicable codes, regulations, or law.

RIGHTS, DUTIES, AND LIABILITIES
OF THE TENANT

RIGHTS OF THE TENANT

The tenant has the right to *exclusive possession* and *quiet enjoyment* of the property during the term of the lease. The landlord is not entitled to enter the leased property without the tenant's consent unless an emergency threatens the property or the landlord is acting under an express lease provision giving her the right to enter. The tenant may use the leased premises for any lawful purpose that is reasonable and appropriate unless the purpose for which it may be used is expressly limited in the lease. Furthermore, the tenant has both the right to receive leased residential property in a habitable condition at the beginning of the lease and the right to have the property maintained in a habitable condition for the duration of the lease.

DUTY TO PAY RENT

The tenant, of course, has the duty to pay rent in the agreed amount and at the agreed times. If two or more persons are cotenants, their liability under the lease is *joint and several*. This means that each cotenant has complete responsibility—not just partial responsibility—for performing the tenants' duties under the lease. For example, Allan and Bob rent an apartment from Cyndi, with both Allan and Bob signing a one-year lease. If Allan moves out after three months, Cyndi may hold Bob responsible for the entire rent, not just half of it. Naturally, Bob remains liable on the lease—as well as to Allan under any rent-sharing agreement the two of them had—but Cyndi is free to proceed against Bob solely if she so chooses.

DUTY NOT TO COMMIT WASTE

The tenant also has the duty not to commit **waste** on the property. This means that the tenant is responsible for the routine care and upkeep of the property and that he has the duty not to commit any act that would harm the property. In the past, fulfillment of this duty required that the tenant perform necessary repairs. Today, the duty to make repairs has generally been shifted to the landlord by court ruling, statute, or lease provision. The tenant now has no duty to make major repairs unless the relevant damage was caused by his own negligence. When damage exists through no fault of the tenant and the tenant therefore is not obligated to make the actual repairs, the tenant nonetheless has the duty to take reasonable interim steps to prevent further damage from the elements. This duty would include, but not necessarily be limited to, informing the landlord of the problem. The duty would be triggered, for instance, when a window breaks or the roof leaks.

ASSIGNMENT AND SUBLEASING

As with rights and duties under most other types of contracts, the rights and duties under a lease may generally be assigned and delegated to third parties. **Assignment** occurs when the landlord or the tenant transfers all of her remaining rights under the lease to another person. For example, a landlord may sell an apartment building and assign the relevant leases to the buyer, who will then become the new landlord. A tenant may assign the remainder of his lease to someone else, who then acquires whatever rights the original tenant had under the lease (including, of course, the right to exclusive possession of the leased premises).

    Subleasing occurs when the tenant transfers to another person some, but not all, of his remaining right to possess the property. The relationship of tenant to sublessee then becomes one of landlord and tenant. For example, Donald a college student whose 18-month lease on an apartment is to terminate on December 31, 2003, sublets his apartment to Wendy for the summer months of 2003. This is a sublease rather than an assignment, because Donald has not transferred all of his remaining rights under the lease.

    The significance of the assignment–sublease distinction is that an assignee acquires rights and duties under the lease between the landlord and the original tenant, but a sublessee does not. An assignee steps into the shoes of the original tenant and acquires any rights she had under the lease. For example, if the lease contained an option to renew, the assignee would have the right to exercise this option. The assignee, or course, becomes personally liable to the landlord for the payment of rent.

    Under both an assignment and a sublease, the original tenant remains liable to the landlord for the commitments made in the lease. If the assignee or sublessee fails to

TABLE 33–1   Comparison of Assignment and Sublease

	Assignment	Sublease
Does the tenant transfer to the third party *all* his remaining rights under the lease?	Yes	No
Does the tenant remain liable on the lease?	Yes	Yes
Does the third party (assignee or sublessee) acquire rights and duties under the tenant's lease with the landlord?	Yes	No

pay rent, for example, the tenant has the legal obligation to pay it. Table 33–1 compares the characteristics of assignments and subleases.

Lease Provisions Limiting Assignment

Leases commonly contain limitations on assignment and subleasing. This is especially true of commercial leases. Such provisions typically require the landlord's consent to any assignment or sublease, or purport to prohibit such a transfer of the tenant's interests. Provisions requiring the landlord's consent are upheld by the courts, although some courts hold that the landlord cannot withhold consent unreasonably. Total prohibitions against assignment may be enforced as well, but they are disfavored in the law. Courts usually construe them narrowly, resolving ambiguities against the landlord.

TENANT'S LIABILITY FOR INJURIES TO THIRD PERSONS

The tenant is normally liable to persons who suffer harm while on the portion of the property over which the tenant has control *if the injuries resulted from the tenant's negligence.*

CONCEPT SUMMARY   Rights, Duties, and Liabilities of Tenants

Rights	1. To the exclusive possession of the property for the term of the lease. 2. To the quiet enjoyment of the property so that his possession is not interfered with as a result of any act or omission on the landlord's part. 3. To be able to assign his interest in the leased property, consistent with any reasonable limitations in the lease agreement.
Duties	1. To pay the rent in the amount and at the times agreed on. 2. To use the property consistent with the agreed-on purpose of the lease and in conformance with any applicable housing and zoning codes or regulations. 3. To return the property at the termination of the lease in the same condition as it was when leased, except for normal wear and tear and any destruction caused by the weather or an act of God. 4. Not to commit waste on the property and to take reasonable steps to protect it from further damage from the elements when there is an accident or act of God. 5. To use reasonable care in his maintenance and use of the property so as to avoid foreseeable injuries to other persons or property. 6. To comply with the terms of the lease agreement.
Liabilities	1. To persons who suffer foreseeable physical injury or property damage as a proximate result of the tenant's failure to exercise due care on the property over which the tenant has control. 2. To the landlord for failure to comply with the duties imposed by the lease or by law. 3. To government agencies for failure to comply with applicable codes, regulations, and law.

TERMINATION OF THE .... *LEASEHOLD*

A leasehold typically terminates because the lease term has expired. Sometimes, however, the lease is terminated early because of a party's material breach of the lease or because of mutual agreement.

EVICTION

If a tenant breaches the lease (most commonly, by nonpayment of rent), the landlord may take action to **evict** the tenant. State statutes usually establish a relatively speedy **eviction** procedure. The landlord who desires to evict a tenant must be careful to comply with any applicable state or city regulations governing evictions. These regulations usually forbid self-help measures on the landlord's part, such as forcible entry to change locks. They may also prohibit the landlord from evicting a tenant under circumstances in which the eviction is deemed to be in retaliation for a tenant's complaints to a government agency about the condition of the premises.

At common law, a landlord had a lien on the tenant's personal property. The landlord therefore could remove and hold such property as security for the rent obligation. This lien has been abolished in many states. Where the lien still exists, it is subject to constitutional limitations requiring that the tenant be given notice of the lien, as well as an opportunity to defend and protect his belongings before they can be sold to satisfy the rent obligation.

AGREEMENT TO SURRENDER

A lease may terminate prematurely by mutual agreement between landlord and tenant to **surrender** the lease (i.e., return the property to the landlord prior to the end of the lease). A valid surrender discharges the tenant from further liability under the lease.

ABANDONMENT

Abandonment occurs when the tenant unjustifiably and permanently vacates the leased premises before the end of the lease term and defaults in the payment of rent. If a tenant abandons the leased property, he is making an offer to surrender the leasehold. As shown in Figure 33–1 on page 626, the landlord must make a decision at this point. If the landlord's conduct shows acceptance of the tenant's offer of surrender, the tenant is relieved of the obligation to pay rent for the remaining period of the lease. If the landlord does not accept the surrender, she may sue the tenant for the rent due until such time as she rents the property to someone else, or, if she cannot find a new tenant, for the rent due for the remainder of the term.

At common law, the landlord had no obligation to mitigate (decrease) the damages caused by the abandonment by attempting to rent the leased property to a new tenant. In fact, taking possession of the property for the purpose of trying to rent it to someone else was a risky move for the landlord—her retaking of possession might be construed as acceptance of the surrender. As the *Stonehedge* case illustrates, some states still adhere to the rule that the nonbreaching landlord has no duty to mitigate damages. Many states, however, now place the duty on the landlord to attempt to mitigate damages by making a reasonable effort to rerent the property. These states also hold that the landlord's retaking of possession for the purpose of rerenting does not constitute a waiver of his right to pursue an action to collect unpaid rent.

STONEHEDGE SQUARE LIMITED PARTNERSHIP V. MOVIE MERCHANTS, INC.
715 A.2d 1082 (Sup. Ct. Penn. 1998)

FACTS

Stonehedge Square Limited Partnership owns and operates a shopping center in Carlisle, Pennsylvania. Stonehedge originally entered into a five-year lease with General Video Corporation for a lease beginning on July 6, 1990, and ending on July 5, 1995. The lease contained a clause allowing the lease interest to be assigned or sublet only with the approval of the landlord, which was not to be unreasonably withheld. On July 31, 1992, General Video assigned its rights, duties, and liabilities under the lease to Movie Merchants, Inc., which operated a video rental store on the premises from July of 1992 through October 27, 1994.

In late August 1994, Movie Merchants discussed with Stonehedge the possibility of terminating its lease prior to the expiration of the remaining term of the lease. Stonehedge listed the premises for rent but was unable to find a tenant. Movie Merchants expressed a desire to buy out the lease, but no agreement could be reached as to a buyout amount. Stonehedge indicated to Movie Merchants that until a new tenant could be secured, Movie Merchants was liable on the lease. On October 27, 1994, Movie Merchants vacated the premises and failed to pay any rent thereafter. Stonehedge then sued for rent due based on an acceleration clause in the lease, seeking unpaid rent from November 1, 1994, to July 5, 1995.

ISSUE

Was Stonehedge, as a nonbreaching landlord, obligated to mitigate damages when the tenant abandoned the property in violation of the lease?

DECISION

No. A tenant cannot relieve himself of the liability to pay rent by vacating the demised premises during the term and sending the key to the landlord. This rule has the virtue of simplicity and avoids the potential for litigation over whether the landlord was diligent in seeking tenants, including issues of whether he should have made repairs, hired more or different agents, or have accepted certain potential tenants. Moreover, there would be a fundamental unfairness in depriving the landlord of the benefit of his bargain, forcing him to expend time, energy, and money to respond to the tenant's breach, and putting the landlord at risk of further expense of lawsuits and counterclaims in a matter which he justifiably thought was closed. Here, the tenant could have provided the landlord with a sublessee, and the landlord had a duty not to unreasonably withhold consent. The duty to mitigate damages should rest on the breaching party.

FIGURE 33–1   Termination of a Leasehold by Abandonment

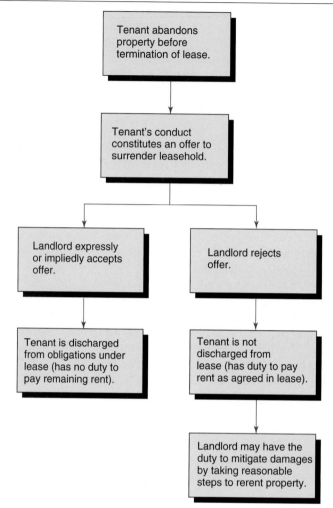

QUESTIONS AND PROBLEM CASES . . . .

1. Under what circumstances can a tenant invoke the doctrine of constructive eviction?

2. In October 1981, Mary Elizabeth Cook entered into an oral lease to Rivard Melson of a residence owned by Cook. Melson agreed to pay $400 per month in advance as rent. On November 11, 1987, Cook sent Melson a letter advising that the rent would be increased to $525 per month, effective January 1, 1988, and asking Melson if he was going to pay. On December 10, 1987, Melson stated he would not pay the increased rent. On January 2, 1988, Melson sent Cook a check for $400 as rent for January. Cook returned the check and stated

that the rent was now $525. Melson did not vacate the premises until February 1, 1988. Cook brought a suit against Melson for $525 for the unpaid rent. Was the tenant liable for the increased rent?

3. Pines was a student at the University of Wisconsin. In May, he and some other students asked Perssion if he had a house they could rent for the next school year. Perssion showed them a house that was in filthy condition, saying he would clean and fix it up, provide the necessary furniture, and have it in good condition by September. Pines agreed to rent the house. When Pines and the other tenants

arrived in the fall, the house was still filthy and there were no student furnishings. They began to clean up the house themselves and to paint it using some paint supplied by Perssion. However, they became discouraged with their progress. They contacted an attorney who advised them to request the city building inspector to check the building. The inspector found numerous violations of the building code, including inadequate electric wiring and the kitchen sink and toilet in need of repair. The inspector gave Perssion two weeks to make the repairs. Pines and the other tenants moved out of the house. They then sued Perssion to get their deposit returned to them along with payment for the work they had done in cleaning the house. Was there an implied warranty of habitability that was breached in the lease of the house?

4. A tenant rented an apartment from the landlord pursuant to a lease that required her to surrender the premises in "as good a state and condition as reasonable use and wear and tear will permit" and to make a refundable security deposit. After the lease was executed, the landlord notified the tenants in the building that no tenant was to shampoo the wall-to-wall carpet on surrender of the lease because the landlord had retained a professional carpet cleaner to do it. The cost of the carpet cleaner's services was to be automatically deducted from the security deposit. When the tenant left the building, a portion of her security deposit was withheld to cover carpet cleaning and she sued for a refund of the full deposit. Is the tenant entitled to a refund?

5. Garcia rented an apartment from Freeland Realty under an oral lease. There was no agreement as to who would make repairs to the property. Garcia had two small children, and he discovered that the children were eating paint and plaster that was flaking off the walls in two rooms in the apartment. Garcia complained about the situation to the landlord. When the landlord did not make the necessary repairs, Garcia purchased some paint and plaster. He repaired the walls and then sued the landlord to recover for the work. He claimed $29.35 for materials and $1.60 an hour (the minimum wage at the time) for each of the 10 hours he

spent doing the work. Under the "Multiple Dwelling Law" in New York City, a landlord is obligated to keep his property repaired and painted. However, the law gives only the city—not the tenant—the right to force the landlord to obey this law. Could the tenant recover the cost of making these repairs from the landlord where the lease did not require the landlord to make repairs?

6. Linda Schiernbeck rented a house from Clark and Rosa Davis for the sum of $150 per month. Approximately one month after she moved in, Schiernbeck noticed a discolored circular area on one of the walls. There was a screw in the middle of this area. Schiernbeck determined that a smoke detector had been attached to the wall. No smoke detector was present, however, during the time Schiernbeck lived in the house. Schiernbeck later contended that she notified the Davises about the missing smoke detector, but the Davises denied this. Approximately one year and three months after Schiernbeck's tenancy began, a fire broke out in the house. Schiernbeck and her daughter were severely injured. Contending that the Davises should have installed a smoke detector, Schiernbeck sued them on negligence and breach of contract grounds. Did the Davises owe Schiernbeck a duty to install a smoke detector?

7. Mary Ajayi and Wemi Alakija were tenants in an apartment complex managed for the landlord by Lloyd Management, Inc. Neighboring tenants complained on various occasions to Lloyd about repeated disturbances that continued late into the night and included yelling and loud noises coming from the apartment shared by Ajayi and Alakija. The sounds of running could also be heard during these disturbances. Neighbors whose apartment walls adjoined those of the Ajayi-Alakija apartment also complained that items were knocked off their walls as a result of banging and jarring coming from the Ajayi-Alakija apartment. Do Lloyd and the landlord have any obligation to take responsive action? If so, Why? What course(s) of action might they pursue?

8. In order to rent an apartment in a building owned by Tobe McKenzie and McKenzie Development Corporation (MDC), Linda Crawford was required to sign a standard form

lease provided by McKenzie and MDC. This lease contained an exculpatory clause stating that McKenzie and MDC "shall not be liable" to Crawford "for any injury to [Crawford's] person or loss of or damage to property for any cause." Two months after Crawford rented the apartment, which was located on the building's second floor, a fire broke out in the first-floor apartment of Debra and Larry Buckner. The fire spread to Crawford's apartment and blocked Crawford from escaping through the front—and only—door of her apartment. To escape the fire, Crawford jumped from a second-story window. When she landed, she sustained numerous injuries, partly due to debris that had accumulated on the ground behind the building. Crawford filed a negligence action against the Buckners, McKenzie, and MDC. McKenzie and MDC argued that the exculpatory clause in the lease barred her negligence claim against them. Should the exculpatory clause be given effect?

9. Florence Trentacost, who was 61 years old, was mugged in the hallway of the apartment house where she was a tenant. The incident happened about 4 o'clock in the afternoon about 25 feet into the building at the foot of some stairs. She suffered a number of injuries, including a dislocated shoulder, a broken leg, a broken ankle, and several other fractures and cuts. She sued the landlord to recover for her personal injuries. She claimed that the landlord had been negligent by failing to maintain the safety of the common areas of the building and by failing to have a lock on the front door entrance to the building. The apartment building was located in an area where there had been civil disturbances in 1969–71, and the neighborhood was considered by the police to be a high-crime area. Unauthorized persons had previously been seen in the building and reported to the landlord. Was the landlord liable to the tenant for the injuries she sustained when she was mugged in the apartment house?

10. On March 1, Sharon Fitzgerald entered into an oral lease of a house owned by Parkin. The lease was on a month-to-month basis, and the rent was set at $290 per month. Parkin also agreed to make certain repairs to the house. On July 1, Fitzgerald notified Parkin by mail of the repairs that needed to be made. These included repairs of leaky pipes, the kitchen ceiling, and the back porch. Fitzgerald also said she would withhold the rent if the repairs were not made within 30 days. On July 13, Fitzgerald had the premises inspected by a city housing inspector who found eight violations of the city code. Parkin was given notice of these violations. On July 29, Parkin served Fitzgerald with a formally correct notice to vacate the premises within 30 days. In September, he brought a lawsuit to have Fitzgerald evicted. A Minnesota statute gives a tenant a defense to an eviction action if the eviction is in retaliation for the reporting of a housing violation in good faith to city officials. Could the landlord evict the tenant from the house under these circumstances?

11. Kridel entered into a lease with Sommer, owner of the Pierre Apartments, to lease apartment 6-L for two years. Kridel, who was to be married in June, planned to move into the apartment in May. His parents and future parents-in-law had agreed to assume responsibility for the rent because Kridel was a full-time student who had no funds of his own. Shortly before Kridel was to have moved in, his engagement was broken. He wrote Sommer a letter explaining his situation and stating that he could not take the apartment. Sommer did not answer the letter. When another party inquired about rental apartment 6-L, the person in charge told her that the apartment was already rented to Kridel. Sommer did not enter the apartment or show it to anyone until he rented apartment 6-L to someone else when there were approximately eight months left on Kridel's lease. He sued Kridel for the full rent for the period of approximately 16 months before the new tenant's lease took effect. Kridel argued that Sommer should not be able to collect rent for the first 16 months of the lease because he did not take reasonable steps to rerent the apartment. Was Sommer entitled to collect the rent he sought?

CHAPTER 34

Estates and Trusts

During your lifetime you may accumulate a sizable amount of property. This commonly includes real property such as a home and a variety of personal property such as a car, furniture, clothes, cash, and stocks and bonds. You may also develop a number of obligations—either legal or self-created—to others such as husband or wife, children, parents, and other family members or close friends, and even to institutions such as churches, colleges, and charities. During your lifetime, you may dispose of some of your property to meet these obligations. On your death, it is desirable that your property go, to the extent possible, to the individuals and institutions of your choosing. Among the questions we will deal with in this chapter are:

- *What will happen to your property on your death, if you have not left a valid will?*
- *What are the requirements for executing a valid will?*
- *What are the most common grounds used to challenge wills?*
- *Under what circumstances can oral wills or documents that do not formally comply with the normal requirements be recognized?*
- *What are the major steps in the administration of an estate of a deceased person?*
- *What is required to establish a trust?*
- *What are the duties of a trustee?*

.... *INTRODUCTION* ....

One of the basic features of the ownership of property is the right to dispose of the property during life and at death. You have already learned about the ways in which property is transferred during the owner's life. The owner's death is another major event occasioning the transfer of property. Most people want to be able to choose who will get their property when they die. There are numerous ways in which a person may control the ultimate disposition of his property. He may take title to the property in the form of joint ownership that gives his co-owner a right of survivorship. He may create a trust and transfer property to it to be used for the benefit of a spouse, child, elderly parent, or other beneficiary. He may execute a will in which he directs that his real and personal property be distributed to persons named in the will. If, however, a person makes no provision for the disposition of his property at his death, his property will be distributed to his heirs as defined by state laws. This chapter focuses on the transfer of property at death and on the use of trusts for the transfer and management of property, both during life and at death.

This area of the law is commonly known as **estate planning** or estates and trusts. State and federal tax laws are an important factor in this area but will not be discussed in detail. There are also many state statutes that affect estate planning. While this chapter will outline some of the considerations involved, it is important that you develop your estate plan with a competent attorney who is familiar with federal tax laws and the laws of the state where you reside or your property is located.

.... *WILLS* ....

RIGHT OF DISPOSITION BY WILL

The right to control the disposition of property at death has not always existed. In the English feudal system, the king owned all land. The lords and knights had only the right to use land for their lifetime. A landholder's rights in land terminated on his death, and no rights descended to his heirs. In 1215, the king granted the nobility the right to pass their interest in the land they held to their heirs. Later that right was extended to all property owners. In the United States, each state has enacted statutes that establish the requirements for a valid will, including the formalities that must be met to pass property by will.

NATURE OF A WILL

A **will** is a document that is executed with specific legal formalities by a person and contains her instructions about the way her property will be disposed of at her death. A man who makes a will is known as a **testator** and a woman who makes one is a **testatrix.** A will can dispose only of property belonging to the testator at the time of his death. Furthermore, wills do not control property that goes to others through other planning devices (such as life insurance policies) or by operation of law (such as by right of survivorship). For example, property held in joint tenancy or tenancy by the entirety is not controlled by a will because the property passes automatically to the surviving cotenant by right of survivorship. In addition, life insurance proceeds are usually controlled by the insured's designation of beneficiaries, not by any provision of a will.

COMMON WILL TERMINOLOGY

Some legal terms commonly used in wills include the following:

1. *Bequest.* A **bequest** (also called **legacy**) is a gift of personal property or money. For example, a will might provide for a bequest of a family heirloom to the testator's daughter. Since a will can direct only property that is owned by the testator at the time of his death, a specific bequest of property that the testator has disposed of before his death is ineffective. This is called **ademption.** For example, Samuel's will states that Warren is to receive Samuel's collection of antique guns. If the guns are destroyed before Warren's death, however, the bequest is ineffective because of ademption.

2. *Devise.* A **devise** is a gift of real property. For example, the testator might devise her family farm to her grandchild.

3. *Residuary.* A **residuary** is the balance of the estate that is left after specific devises and bequests are made by the will. After providing for the disposition of specific personal and real property, a testator might provide that the residuary of his estate is to go to his spouse or be divided among his descendants.

4. *Issue.* A person's **issue** are her lineal descendants (children, grandchildren, great-grandchildren, and so forth). This category of persons includes adopted children.

5. *Per capita.* This term and the next one, *per stirpes,* are used to describe the way in which a group of persons are to share a gift. **Per capita** means that each of that group of persons will share equally. For example, Grandfather dies, leaving a will that provides that the residuary of his estate is to go to his issue or descendants *per capita.* Grandfather had two children, Mary and Bill. Mary has two children, John and James. Bill has one child, Margaret. Mary and Bill die before Grandfather (in legal terms, *predecease* him), but all three of Grandfather's grandchildren are living at the time of his death. In this case, John, James, and Margaret would each take one-third of the residuary of Grandfather's estate.

6. *Per stirpes.* When a gift is given to the testator's issue or descendants **per stirpes** (also called **by right of representation**), each surviving descendant divides the share that her parent would have taken if the parent had survived. In the preceding example, if Grandfather's will had stated that the residuary of his estate was to go to his issue or descendants *per stirpes,* Margaret would take one-half and John and James would take one-quarter each (that is, they would divide the share that would have gone to their mother).

TESTAMENTARY CAPACITY

The capacity to make a valid will is called **testamentary capacity.** To have testamentary capacity, a person must be *of sound mind* and *of legal age,* which is 18 in most states. A person does not have to be in perfect mental health to have testamentary capacity. Because people often delay executing wills until they are weak and in ill health, the standard for mental capacity to make a will is fairly low. To be of "sound mind," a person need only be sufficiently rational to be capable of understanding the nature and character of her property, of realizing that she is making a will, and of knowing the persons who would normally be the beneficiaries of her affection. A person could move in and out of periods of lucidity and still have testamentary capacity if she executed her will during a lucid period.

Lack of testamentary capacity is a common ground upon which wills are challenged by persons who were excluded from a will. *Fraud* and *undue influence* are also common grounds for challenging the validity of a will. In assessing a claim of undue influence, the court looks to see whether a bequest appears to be made on the basis of natural affection or of some improper influence. The actions of fiduciaries such as attorneys are scrutinized carefully, particularly for improper influence. This is especially true if the fiduciaries are not related to the deceased person, were made beneficiaries, and had a critical role in preparing the will.

EXECUTION OF A WILL

Unless a will is executed with the formalities required by state law, it is *void.* The courts are strict in interpreting statutes concerning the execution of wills. If a will is declared void, the property of the deceased person will be distributed according to the provisions of state laws that will be discussed later.

The formalities required for a valid will differ from state to state. For that reason, an individual should consult the laws of his state before making a will. If he should move to another state after having executed a will, he should consult a lawyer in his new state to determine whether a new will needs to be executed. All states require that a will be *in writing.* State law also requires that a formal will be *witnessed,* generally by two or three *disinterested* witnesses (persons who do not stand to inherit any property under the will), and that it be *signed* by the testator or by someone else at the testator's direction. Most states also require that the testator *publish* the will—that is, declare or indicate at the time of signing that the instrument is his will. Another formality required by most states is that the testator sign the will in the presence and the sight of the witnesses and that the witnesses sign in the presence and the sight of each other. As a general rule, an **attestation clause,** which states the formalities that have been followed in the execution of the will, is written following the testator's signature. These detailed formalities are designed to prevent fraud. Commonly, a will must be in writing, signed by the testator (or in the testator's name by some other individual in the testator's conscious presence and by the testator's direction), and signed by at least two individuals, each of whom signed within a reasonable time after she witnessed either the signing of the will or the testator's acknowledgment of that signature or will. Also, any individual who is generally competent to be a witness usually may witness a will. See Figure 34–1 for an example of a will.

In some situations, a lawyer might arrange to have the execution of a will *videotaped* to provide evidence relating to the testator's capacity and the use of proper formalities. (Note that the will is executed in the normal way; the videotape merely records the execution of the will.) Some state probate codes specifically provide that videotapes of the executions of wills are admissible into evidence.

JOINT AND MUTUAL WILLS

In some circumstances, two or more people—a married couple, for example—decide together on a plan for the disposition of their property at death. To carry out this plan, they may execute a **joint will** (a single instrument that constitutes the will of both or all of the testators and is executed by both or all) or they may execute **mutual wills** (joint or separate, individual wills that reflect the common plan of distribution).

Underlying a joint or mutual will is an agreement on a common plan. This common plan often includes an express or implied contract (a contract to make a will or not to revoke the will). One issue that sometimes arises is whether a testator who has made a joint or mutual will can later change the will. Whether joint and mutual wills

FIGURE 34-1   Example of a Will

LAST WILL AND TESTAMENT
OF
WILLIAM R. FOLGER

I, WILLIAM R. FOLGER, of McLean, County of Fairfax, Commonwealth of Virginia, being of sound and disposing mind and memory, do make this to be my Last Will and Testament, hereby revoking all former wills and codicils made by me.

FIRST. I direct that the expenses of my funeral and burial, including a grave site, gravestone, and perpetual care, be paid out of my estate in such amount as my Executrix may deem proper and without regard to any limitation in the applicable law as to the amount of such expenses and without necessity of prior Court approval.

SECOND. I direct that all estate, inheritance, succession, and other death taxes and duties occasioned by my death, whether incurred with respect to property passing by this Will or otherwise, shall be paid by my Executrix out of the principal of my residuary estate with no right of reimbursement from any recipient of any such property.

THIRD. I further direct my Executrix to pay all of my legal obligations and debts (exclusive of any debt or debts secured by a deed of trust or mortgage on real estate, not due at the time of my death or becoming due during the period of administration of my estate). In determining what are my obligations and debts, I direct my Executrix to avail herself of every defense that would have been available to me.

FOURTH. I hereby confirm my intention that the beneficial interest in all property, real or personal, tangible or intangible (including joint checking or savings accounts in any bank or savings and loan association), which is registered or held, at the time of my death, jointly in the names of myself and any other person (including tenancy by the entireties, but excluding any tenancy in common), shall pass by right of survivorship or operation of law and outside of the terms of this Will to such other person, if he or she survives me. To the extent that my intention may be defeated by any rule of law, I give, devise, and bequeath all such jointly held property to such other person or persons who shall survive me.

FIFTH. I give my tangible personal property, including furniture, clothing, automobiles and their equipment, and articles of personal or household use or ornament, but not including money, securities, or the like, to my wife Kristin A. Folger, if she survives by thirty (30) days, and if she does not so survive me, I give the same absolutely to my issue who so survive me, such issue to take *per stirpes*.

I express the hope that my wife or my issue will dispose of my tangible personal property according to my wishes, however my wishes may be known to her or to them, but I expressly declare that I do not intend to create any trust in law or in equity with respect to my tangible personal property.

SIXTH. I give the sum of $10,500 to St. Christopher's Church, McLean, Virginia, for its unrestricted use.

SEVENTH. I give, bequeath, and devise all the rest and residue of my estate, of whatsoever nature and wheresoever situated, to my wife Kristin A. Folger, if she survives me by more than thirty (30) days. If she does not so survive me, I give the same absolutely to my issue who so survive me, such issue to take *per stirpes*.

EIGHTH. I nominate, constitute, and appoint my wife Kristin A. Folger, to be the Executrix of this my Last Will and Testament. My Executrix shall have full power in her discretion to do any and all things necessary for the complete administration of my estate, including the power to sell at public or private sale, and without order of court, any real or personal property belonging to my estate, and to compound, compromise, or otherwise to settle or adjust any and all claims, charges, debts, and demands whatsoever against or in favor of my estate, as fully as I could do if living.

(continued)

FIGURE 34–1   *(concluded)*

NINTH. I direct that no bond or other security be required of my Personal Representative appointed hereunder in any jurisdiction, any provision of law to the contrary notwithstanding.

IN WITNESS WHEREOF, I have set my hand and seal to this Last Will and Testament, typewritten upon two (2) pages, each one of which has been signed by me this 15th day of August, 2002, at McLean, Virginia.

William R. Folger

William R. Folger

The foregoing instrument consisting of two (2) typewritten pages was signed, published, and declared by the testator to be his Last Will and Testament in the presence of us, who, at his request, in his presence, and in the presence of each other, have subscribed our names as witnesses this 15th day of August, 2002.

Carole H. Carson of *McLean, Virginia*
Robert A. Carson of *McLean, Virginia*
Sandra H. Somers of *Falls Church, Virginia*

are revocable depends on the language of the will, on state law, and on the timing of the revocation. For example, a testator who made a joint will with his spouse may be able to revoke his will during the life of his spouse because the spouse still has a chance to change her own will, but he may be unable to revoke or change the will after the death of his spouse. The Uniform Probate Code (UPC), which has been adopted by a number of states, provides that the mere fact that a joint or mutual will has been executed does *not* create the presumption of a contract not to revoke the will or wills.

INFORMAL WILLS

Some states recognize certain types of wills that are not executed with these formalities. These are:

1. *Nuncupative wills.* A **nuncupative** will is an oral will. Such wills are recognized as valid in some states but only under limited circumstances and to a limited extent. In a number of states, for example, nuncupative wills are valid only when made by soldiers in military service and sailors at sea, and even then they will be effective only to dispose of personal property that was in the actual possession of the person at the time the oral will was made. Other states place low dollar limits on the amount of property that can be passed by a nuncupative will.

2. *Holographic wills.* **Holographic wills** are wills that are written and signed in the testator's handwriting. The fact that holographic wills are not properly witnessed makes them suspect. They are recognized in about half of the states and by section 2–502(b) of the UPC, even though they are not executed with the formalities usually required of valid wills. For a holographic will to be valid in the states that recognize them, it must evidence testamentary intent and must actually be *handwritten* by the

testator. A typed holographic will would be invalid. Some states require that the holographic will be *entirely* handwritten, other states require only that the signature and material portions of the will be handwritten by the testator, and some also require that the will be dated.

In the case that follows, *Estate of Rowell v. Hollingsworth*, the court required strict compliance with the state statute governing wills and refused to recognize a holographic will that was not signed at the end of the document.

ESTATE OF ROWELL V. HOLLINGSWORTH
585 So.2d 731 (Sup. Ct. Miss. 1991)

FACTS

Mildred Rowell died on August 6, 1989. She was 65 years old, a widow, and possessed a 10th-grade education. She was survived by seven children. On December 21, 1989, one of the children, Evelyn Hollingsworth, filed a Petition for Letters of Administration, alleging that her mother had left no will and asking that she be named administratrix of her mother's estate, which she subsequently was.

On February 6, 1990, another daughter, Kathey Amyotte, filed a Petition for Probate of Will. She alleged that her mother had left a holographic will, handwritten on two sides of one sheet of paper. The will began "I Mildred Rowell of Route 2 Box 210 Vossburg Miss 39366 of Clark County Mississippi, being of sound and disposing mind and memory, do hereby make, ordain, publish and declare this instrument to be my last will and testament. . . ." The purported will left most of the property either to her two sons or to Kathey's son (Mildred's grandson). It was not signed at the end of the document.

At a hearing, Paul Rowell testified that his mother had given him a blue plastic folder approximately two years before her death and asked him to keep it for her. A few days after she died, Paul examined the folder and found the holographic will, which appeared to be fairly accurate as to Mildred Rowell's possessions. Mildred's sons and Kathey testified that they were familiar with their mother's handwriting and that the will had been written by her. The other sisters sought to dismiss the Petition on the grounds that the will had not been subscribed as required by statute.

The Mississippi Code sets forth the following requirements for execution of wills: "Who may execute. Every person eighteen (18) years of age or older, being of sound and disposing mind, shall have power, by last will and testament, or codicil in writing, to devise the estate . . . and personal estate of any description whatever, provided such last will and testament, or codicil, be signed by the testator or testatrix, or by some other person in his or her presence and by his or her express direction. Moreover, if not wholly written and subscribed by himself or herself, it shall be attested by two or more credible witnesses in the presence of the testator or testatrix."

ISSUE

Was the document handwritten by Mildred Rowell a valid holographic will?

DECISION

No. While the court found that the document in question was in the handwriting of Mildred Rowell, it found that it had not been subscribed (signed at the end or beneath the will) as required by law. Although her name appeared in the first line of the document, it did not appear again. Thus, the court concluded that the statutory requirement had not been met. It noted that some other jurisdictions sometimes allow more flexibility in the case of holographic wills, but that Mississippi had adopted a *bright-line rule* concerning signing that made for easy and sure application—even though it might in some cases lead to an unfair or unjust result.

LIMITATIONS ON DISPOSITION BY WILL

A person who takes property by will takes it subject to all outstanding claims against the property. For example, if real property is subject to a mortgage or other lien, the beneficiary who takes the real property gets it subject to the mortgage or lien. In addition, the rights of the testator's creditors are superior to the rights of a beneficiaries under her will. Thus, if the testator was insolvent (her debts exceeded her assets), persons named as beneficiaries do not receive any property by virtue of the will.

Under the laws of most states, the surviving spouse of the testator has statutory rights in property owned solely by the testator that cannot be defeated by a contrary will provision. This means that a husband cannot effectively disinherit his wife and vice versa. Even if the will provides for the surviving spouse, he can elect to take the share of the decedent's estate that would be provided by state law rather than the amount specified in the will. In some states, personal property, such as furniture, passes automatically to the surviving spouse.

At common law, a widow had the right to a life estate in one-third of the lands owned by her husband during their marriage. This was known as a widow's **dower** right. A similar right for a widower was known as **curtesy.** A number of states have changed the right by statute to give a surviving spouse a one-third interest in fee simple in the real and personal property owned by the deceased spouse at the time of her death. (Naturally, a testator can leave her spouse more than this if she desires.) Under UPC 2–201, the surviving spouse's elective share varies depending on the length of the surviving spouse's marriage to the testator—the elective share increases with the length of marriage.

As a general rule, a surviving spouse is given the right to use the family home for a stated period as well as a portion of the deceased spouse's estate. In community property states, each spouse has a one-half interest in community property that cannot be defeated by a contrary will provision. (Note that the surviving spouse will obtain *full* ownership of any property owned by the testator and the surviving spouse as joint tenants or tenants by the entirety.)

Children of the testator who were born or adopted after the will was executed are called **pretermitted** children. There is a presumption that the testator intended to provide for such a child unless there is evidence to the contrary. State law gives pretermitted children the right to a share of the testator's estate. For example, under section 2–302 of the Uniform Probate Code, a pretermitted child has the right to receive the share he would have received under the state intestacy statute unless it appears that the omission of this child was intentional, the testator gave substantially all of her estate to the child's other parent, or the testator provided for the child outside of the will.

IN RE PETITION OF SHIFLETT
490 S.E.2d 902 (Sup. Ct. W.V. 1997)

FACTS

Kenzie Shiflett married Mary Herron on July 24, 1981. A year and a half later, she abandoned the marriage and the couple lived separate and apart until Kenzie Shiflett died on December 30, 1992. By will executed November 15, 1984, Shiflett left his entire estate to his son from a prior marriage, Kenneth Shiflett, except for a clock and a trailer which he bequeathed to Mary.

At the time the will was executed, the dower rights of a husband under state law were barred if the husband or wife voluntarily left or abandoned their spouse without such cause as would entitle them to a divorce. However, about nine months prior to Kenzie's death, the West Virginia legislature passed a sweeping revision to the descent and distribution provisions in the West Virginia Code, including repeal of the abandonment provision. At the same time the legislature provided that a "surviving spouse" could elect against a will and take an "elective-share percentage of the estate." The percentage a surviving spouse

(continued)

IN RE PETITION OF SHIFLETT
(concluded)

was entitled to take was "determined by the time the spouse and decedent were married to each other."

Mary claimed an elective share of Kenzie's estate—in lieu of her rights under the will—and the Circuit Court of Randolph County awarded her a 34 percent share of the estate. Kenneth filed a petition with the court asking that Mary be barred from taking an elective-share percentage of the estate on the ground she had abandoned Kenzie approximately 10 years before his death. He argued that the statutory revisions unjustly reward Mary for her conduct and undermine his father's intent as expressed in his will. He noted that his father was legally blind and in poor health at the time the statutory revisions took effect and died approximately six months thereafter. Accordingly, he asserted that there was neither a reasonable opportunity nor a reasonable amount of time for his father

to obtain a divorce to prevent Mary from taking any part of the estate except what he intended to give her under the will.

ISSUE

Was Mary entitled to a statutory share of the estate as a surviving spouse even though she had abandoned the marriage 10 years earlier?

DECISION

Yes. The operative effect of a will and the rights of the parties under it are governed by the law in force at the time of a testator's death. The determination of whether abandonment, or some other kind of misconduct, should result in a surviving spouse's right to an estate is a determination best left to the legislature.

REVOCATION OF WILLS

One important feature of a will is that it is *revocable* until the moment of the testator's death. For this reason, a will confers *no present interest* in the testator's property. A person is free to revoke a prior will and, if she wishes, to make a new will. Wills can be revoked in a variety of ways. Physical destruction and mutilation done with intent to revoke a will constitute revocation, as do other acts such as crossing out the will or creating a writing that expressly cancels the will.

In addition, a will is revoked if the testator later executes a valid will that expressly revokes the earlier will. A later will that does not *expressly* revoke an earlier will operates to revoke only those portions of the earlier will that are inconsistent with the later will. Under the UPC, a later will that does not expressly revoke a prior will operates to revoke it by inconsistency if the testator intended the subsequent will to *replace* rather than *supplement* the prior will [2–507(b)]. Furthermore, the UPC presumes that the testator intended the subsequent will to replace rather than supplement the prior will if the subsequent one makes a complete disposition of his estate, but it presumes that the testator intended merely to supplement and not replace the prior will if the subsequent will disposes of only part of his estate [2–507(c), 2–507(d)]. In some states, a will is presumed to have been revoked if it cannot be located after the testator's death, although this presumption can be rebutted with contrary evidence.

Wills can also be revoked by operation of law without any act on the part of the testator signifying revocation. State statutes provide that certain changes in relationships operate as revocations of a will. In some states, marriage will operate to revoke a will that was made when the testator was single. Similarly, a divorce may revoke provisions in a will made during marriage that leave property to the divorced spouse. Under the laws of some states, the birth of a child after the execution of a will may operate as a partial revocation of the will.

CODICILS

A **codicil** is an amendment of a will. If a person wants to change a provision of a will without making an entirely new will, she may amend the will by executing a codicil. One may *not* amend a will by merely striking out objectionable provisions and inserting new provisions. The same formalities are required for the creation of a valid codicil as for the creation of a valid will.

CONCEPT SUMMARY	Wills

Type of Will	Requirements
Formal Will	1. Must be in writing. 2. Must be witnessed by two or three "disinterested" witnesses. 3. Must be signed by the testator or at his direction. 4. May have to be published or declared by the testator to be his will. 5. Must be signed by testator in the presence and sight of witnesses. 6. Witnesses must sign in the presence and sight of the testator and each other.
Holographic Will	1. Must be entirely written and signed in the testator's handwriting. 2. Must evidence testamentary intent. 3. Not permitted in all states.
Nuncupative Will	1. Oral will made before witnesses and valid only to transfer personal property and not real property. 2. Not permitted in all states; some limit it to soldiers or sailors or place low dollar limits on property it can govern.

ADVANCE DIRECTIVES: PLANNING FOR DISABILITY

Advances in medical technology now permit a person to be kept alive by artificial means even in many cases in which there is no hope of the person being able to function without life support. Many people are opposed to their lives being prolonged with no chance of recovery. In response to these concerns, almost all states have enacted statutes permitting individuals to state their choices about the medical procedures that should be administered or withheld if they should become incapacitated in the future and cannot recover. Collectively, these devices are called **advance directives.** An advance direction is a written document (such as a *living will* or *durable power of attorney*) that directs others how future health care decisions should be made in the event that the individual becomes incapacitated.

LIVING WILLS

Living wills are documents in which a person states in advance her intention to forgo or obtain certain life-prolonging medical procedures. Almost all states have enacted statutes recognizing living wills. These statutes also establish the elements and formalities required to create a valid living will and describe the legal effect of living wills. Currently, the law concerning living wills is primarily a matter of state law and differs from state to state. Living wills are typically included with a patient's medical records. Many states require physicians and other health care providers to follow the provisions of a valid living will. Because living wills are created by statute, it is important that all terms and conditions of one's state statute be followed. Figure 34–2 shows an example of a living will form. The case below, *Cruzan v. Director, Missouri Department of Health,* shows the consequences of not having a living will in a state in which such wills are authorized.

FIGURE 34–2   Living Will

LIVING WILL DECLARATION

Declaration made this _____ day of _____. I, _____, being at least eighteen (18) years of age and of sound mind, willfully and voluntarily make known my desires that my dying shall not be artificially prolonged under the circumstances set forth below, and I declare:

If at any time I have an incurable injury, disease, or illness certified in writing to be a terminal condition by my attending physician, and my attending physician has determined that my death will occur within a short time, and the use of life prolonging procedures would serve only to artificially prolong the dying process, I direct that such procedures be withheld or withdrawn and that I be permitted to die naturally with only the provision of appropriate nutrition and hydration and the administration of medication and the performance of any medical procedure necessary to provide me with comfort, care, or to alleviate pain.

In the absence of my ability to give directions regarding the use of life prolonging procedures, it is my intention that this declaration be honored by my family and physicians as the final expression of my legal right to refuse medical or surgical treatment and accept the consequences of the refusal.

I understand the full import of this declaration.

Signed: _____
City, County, and State of Residence

The declarant has been personally known to me, and I believe (him/her) to be of sound mind. I did not sign the declarant's signature above for or at the direction of the declarant. I am not a parent, spouse, or child of the declarant. I am not entitled to any part of the declarant's estate or directly financially responsible for the declarant's medical care. I am competent and at least eighteen (18) years of age.

Witness _____ Date _____
Witness _____ Date _____

CRUZAN V. DIRECTOR, MISSOURI DEPARTMENT OF HEALTH
110 S.Ct. 2841 (U.S. Sup. Ct. 1990)

FACTS

On the night of January 11, 1983, 25-year-old Nancy Cruzan lost control of her car while driving down Elm Road in Jasper County, Missouri. The vehicle overturned, and Cruzan was discovered lying face down in a ditch with no detectable respiratory or cardiac function. Paramedics were able to restore her breathing and heartbeat at the accident site, and she was transported to a hospital. There she was diagnosed as having sustained probable cerebral contusions, compounded by significant anoxia (lack of oxygen). She remained in a coma for three weeks and then progressed to an unconscious state in which she was orally able to ingest some nutrition. To ease feeding and further her recovery, surgeons

implanted a gastrostomy feeding and hydration tube. She then lay in a Missouri state hospital in what is commonly referred to as a *persistent vegetative state.*

After it became apparent that Cruzan had virtually no chance of regaining her mental faculties, her parents (also her legal guardians) asked hospital employees to terminate the artificial nutrition and hydration procedures, which would cause her death. The employees refused to do so without court approval. The parents then sought authorization from the state trial court for termination. Cruzan had not executed a living will, but a former roommate of Cruzan's testified that Cruzan had told her that if she were sick or injured she would not want to

(continued)

Cruzan v. Director, Missouri Department of Health
(concluded)

continue her life unless she could live at least halfway normally.

The trial court granted authorization to terminate nutrition and hydration, holding that a person in Cruzan's position had a fundamental constitutional right to refuse or direct the withdrawal of "death prolonging procedures." It also found that Cruzan's conversation with her roommate indicated that she would not want to continue with life support. The Supreme Court of Missouri reversed on the ground that no one can assume the choice regarding termination of medical treatment for an incompetent person in the absence of the formalities required under the Missouri Living Will Statute or clear and convincing evidence, which it found lacking in this case. The U.S. Supreme Court then agreed to hear the case.

Issue

Does the U.S. Constitution require the hospital to withdraw life-sustaining treatment from Cruzan under these circumstances?

Decision

No. The Court held that it was appropriate for the state to recognize that under certain circumstances a surrogate may act for a patient to have hydration and nutrition withdrawn in such a way as to cause death, but, at the same time, to establish a procedural safeguard to ensure that the action of the surrogate conforms as best it may to the wishes expressed by the patient while competent.

Durable Power of Attorney

Another technique of planning for the eventuality that one may be unable to make decisions for oneself is to execute a document that gives another person the legal authority to act on one's behalf in the case of mental or physical incapacity. This document is called a **durable power of attorney.**

A *power of attorney* is an express statement in which one person (the **principal**) gives another person (the **attorney in fact**) the authority to do an act or series of acts on his behalf. For example, Andrew enters into a contract to sell his house to Willis, but he must be out of state on the date of the real estate closing. He gives Paulsen a power of attorney to attend the closing and execute the deed on his behalf. Ordinary powers of attorney terminate upon the principal's incapacity. By contract, the *durable power of attorney* is not affected if the principal becomes incompetent.

A durable power of attorney permits a person to give someone else extremely broad powers to make decisions and enter transactions such as those involving real and personal property, bank accounts, and health care, and to specify that those powers will not terminate upon incapacity. The durable power of attorney is an extremely important planning device. For example, a durable power of attorney executed by an elderly parent to an adult child at a time in which the parent is competent would permit the child to take care of matters such as investments, property, bank accounts, and hospital admission. Without the durable power of attorney, the child would be forced to apply to a court for a guardianship, which is a more expensive and often less efficient manner in which to handle personal and business affairs.

Durable Power of Attorney for Health Care

The majority of states have enacted statutes specifically providing for **durable powers of attorney for health care** (sometimes called **health care representatives**). This is a type of durable power of attorney in which the principal specifically gives the attorney in fact the authority to make certain health care decisions for her if the principal should become incompetent. Depending on state law and the instructions given by the principal to the attorney in fact, this could include decisions such as consenting or withholding consent to surgery, admitting the principal to a nursing home, and possibly withdrawing or prolonging life support. Note that the durable power of attorney becomes relevant only in the event that the principal becomes incompetent. So long as the principal is competent, she retains the ability to make her own health care decisions. This power of attorney is also revocable at the will of the principal. The precise requirements for creation of the durable power of attorney differ from state to state, but all states require a written and signed document executed with specified formalities, such as witnessing by disinterested witnesses.

FEDERAL LAW AND ADVANCE DIRECTIVES

A federal statute, The Patient Self-Determination Act, requires health care providers to take active steps to educate people about the opportunity to make advance decisions about medical care and the prolonging of life and to record the choices that they make. This statute, which became effective in 1992, requires health care providers such as hospitals, nursing homes, hospices, and home health agencies, to provide written information to adults receiving medical care about their rights concerning the ability to accept or refuse medical or surgical treatment, the health care provider's policies concerning those rights, and their right to formulate advance directives. The act also requires the provider to document in the patient's medical record whether the patient has executed an advance directive, and it forbids discrimination against the patient based on the individual's choice regarding an advance directive. In addition, the provider is required to ensure compliance with the requirements of state law concerning advance directives and to educate its staff and the community on issues concerning advance directives.

INTESTACY

If a person dies without having made a will, or if he makes a will that is declared invalid, he is said to have died **intestate.** When that occurs, his property will be distributed to the persons designated as the intestate's heirs under the appropriate state's **intestacy** or **intestate succession** statute. The intestate's real property will be distributed according to the intestacy statute of the state in which the property is located. His personal property will be distributed according to the intestacy statute of the state in which he was domiciled at the time of his death. A **domicile** is a person's permanent home. A person can have only one domicile at a time. Determinations of a person's domicile turn on facts that tend to show that person's intent to make a specific state his permanent home.

CHARACTERISTICS OF INTESTACY STATUTES

The provisions of intestacy statutes are not uniform. Their purpose, however, is to distribute property in a way that reflects the *presumed intent* of the deceased—that is, to distribute it to the persons most closely related to her. In general, such statutes first provide for the distribution of most or all of a person's estate to her surviving spouse, children, or grandchildren. If no such survivors exist, the statutes typically provide for the distribution of the estate to parents, siblings, or nieces and nephews. If no relatives at this level are living, the property may be distributed to surviving grandparents, uncles, aunts, or cousins. Generally, persons with the same degree of relationship to the deceased person take equal shares. If the deceased had no surviving relatives, the property **escheats** (goes) to the state.

Figure 34–3 shows an example of a distribution scheme under an intestacy statute.

FIGURE 34–3   Example of a Distribution Scheme under an Intestacy Statute

Person Dying Intestate Is Survived By	Result
1. Spouse* and child or issue of a deceased child	Spouse 1/2, Child 1/2
2. Spouse and parent(s) but no issue	Spouse 3/4, Parent 1/4
3. Spouse but no parent or issue	All of the estate to spouse
4. Issue but no spouse	Estate is divided among issue
5. Parent(s), brothers, sisters, and/or issue of deceased brothers and sisters but no spouse or issue	Estate is divided among parent(s), brothers, sisters, and issue of deceased brothers and sisters
6. Issue of brothers and sisters but no spouse, issue, parents, brothers, and sisters	Estate is divided among issue of deceased brothers and sisters
7. Grandparents, but no spouse, issue, parents, brothers, sisters, or issue of deceased brothers and sisters	All of the estate goes to grandparents
8. None of the above	Estate goes to the state

Note, however, second and subsequent spouses who had no children by the decedent may be assigned a smaller share.

SPECIAL RULES

Under the intestacy statutes, a person must have a relationship to the deceased person through blood or marriage in order to inherit any part of his property. State law includes adopted children within the definition of "children" and treats adopted children in the same way as it treats biological children. (An adopted child would inherit from her adoptive parents, not from her biological parents.) Half-brothers and half sisters are usually treated in the same way as brothers and sisters related by whole blood. An illegitimate child may inherit from his mother, but as a general rule, illegitimate children. do not inherit from their fathers unless their paternity has been either acknowledged or established in a legal proceeding.

A person must be alive at the time the decedent dies to claim a share of the decedent's estate. An exception may be made for pretermitted children or other descendants who are born *after* the decedent's death. If a person who is entitled to a share of the decedent's estate survives the decedent but dies before receiving her share, her share in the decedent's estate becomes part of her own estate.

SIMULTANEOUS DEATH

A statute known as the *Uniform Simultaneous Death Act* provides that where two persons who would inherit from each other (such as husband and wife) die under circumstances that make it difficult or impossible to determine who died first, each person's property is to be distributed as though he or she survived. This means, for example, that the husband's property will go to his relatives and the wife's property to her relatives.

.... *ADMINISTRATION OF ESTATES* ....

When a person dies, an orderly procedure is needed to collect his **estate**—his property—settle his debts, and distribute any remaining property to those who will inherit it under his will or by intestate succession. This process occurs under the supervision of a probate court and is known as the **administration process** or the **probate** process. Summary (simple) procedures are sometimes available where the estate is relatively small—for example, where it has assets of less than $7,500.

THE PROBATE ESTATE

The probate process operates only on the decedent's property that is considered to be part of her **probate estate.** The probate estate is that property belonging to the decedent at the time of her death other than property held in joint ownership with right of survivorship, proceeds of insurance policies payable to a trust or a third party, property held in a revocable trust during the decedent's lifetime in which a third party is the beneficiary, or retirement benefits, such as pensions, payable to a third party. Assets that pass by operation of law and assets that are transferred by other devices such as trusts or life insurance policies do not pass through probate.

Note that the decedent's probate estate and his *taxable estate* for purposes of federal estate tax are two different concepts. The taxable estate includes all property owned or controlled by the decedent at the time of his death. For example, if a person purchased a $1 million life insurance policy made payable to his spouse or children, the policy would be included in his taxable estate but not in his probate estate.

DETERMINING THE EXISTENCE OF A WILL

The first step in the probate process is to determine whether the deceased left a will. This may require a search of the deceased person's personal papers and safe-deposit box. If a will is found, it must be *proved* to be admitted to probate. This involves the testimony of the persons who witnessed the will if they are still alive. If the witnesses are no longer alive, the signatures of the witnesses and the testator will have to be established in some other way. In some states, a will may be proved by an affidavit (declaration under oath) sworn to and signed by the testator and the witnesses at the time the will was executed. This is called a **self-proving affidavit.** If a will is located and proved, it will be admitted to probate and govern many of the decisions that must be made in the administration of the estate.

SELECTING A PERSONAL REPRESENTATIVE

Another early step in the administration of an estate is the selection of a personal representative to administer the estate. If the deceased left a will, it is likely that she designated her personal representative in the will. The personal representative under a will is also known as the **executor.** Almost anyone could serve as an executor. The testator may have chosen, for example, her spouse, a grown child, a close friend, an attorney, or the trust department of a bank.

If the decedent died intestate, or if the personal representative named in a will is unable to serve, the probate court will name a personal representative to administer the estate. In the case of an intestate estate, the personal representative is called an **administrator.** A preference is usually accorded to a surviving spouse, child, or other close relative. If no relative is available and qualified to serve, a creditor, bank, or other person may be appointed by the court.

Most states require that the personal representative *post a bond* in an amount in excess of the estimated value of the estate to ensure that his duties will be properly and faithfully performed. A person making a will often directs that her executor may serve without posting a bond, and this exemption may be accepted by the court.

RESPONSIBILITIES OF THE PERSONAL REPRESENTATIVE

The personal representative has a number of important tasks in the administration of the estate. She must see that an inventory is taken of the estate's assets and that the assets are appraised. Notice must then be given to creditors or potential claimants against the estate so that they can file and prove their claims within a specified time, normally five months. As a general rule, the surviving spouse of the deceased person is entitled to be paid an allowance during the time the estate is being settled. This allowance has priority over other debts of the estate. The personal representative must see that any properly payable funeral or burial expenses are paid and that the creditors' claims are satisfied. The case below, *Probate Proceedings, Will of Doris Duke, Deceased*, illustrates the consequences of a failure by the personal representatives to meet their responsibilities.

PROBATE PROCEEDINGS, WILL OF DORIS DUKE, DECEASED
632 N.Y.S.2d 532 (Sup. Ct., App. Div., N.Y. 1995)

FACTS

Doris Duke died leaving a will in which she designated her butler, Bernard Lafferty, as executor. He was authorized to appoint a corporate co-executor, and he appointed the United States Trust Company of New York as co-executor. As a personal assistant to Duke, Lafferty had a mother–son relationship with her and assisted her with her personal affairs, the operation of her various properties, and the supervision of over 100 employees. The property and department managers reported to Lafferty, who had a salary of $100,000 a year. Under the terms of the will, Lafferty was to receive a trust income of $500,000 a year for life and a commission of $5 million for his services as executor. The bulk of Duke's $1.2 billion estate was bequeathed primarily to charity.

Lafferty continued to live in the Duke properties, living as if they were his own, and paid himself a generous salary and lavish benefits. This was authorized only by Lafferty and the United States Trust Company as co-executor. Lafferty routinely commingled his personal assets with the estate assets. He also was hospitalized on a number of occasions after he went on drunken binges. The United States Trust Company granted Lafferty unsecured loans totaling $825,000 to pay for his "personal needs"—more luxuries.

The Surrogate's Court, New York County, summarily removed Lafferty and the United States Trust Company as co-executors and appointed temporary administrators for the estate. Lafferty and his co-executor appealed their removal.

ISSUE

Should the co-executors designated in the will be removed for failing to properly carry out their fiduciary responsibilities?

DECISION

Yes. Lafferty wasted estate assets by collecting a salary and living in the estate as if it were his own. There is no justification for these emoluments because he was also entitled to lucrative commissions as executor. The commingling of assets is a serious breach of fiduciary duty and the fact they could be repaid is no defense. Moreover, the surrogate was not obligated to expose the estate to the risk that Lafferty's drunkenness might affect his performance. Finally, the corporate co-executor created a conflict of interest when it granted Lafferty unsecured loans. This gave it a financial stake in Lafferty's continued service as executor so that he could repay the

(continued)

PROBATE PROCEEDINGS, WILL OF DORIS DUKE, DECEASED
(concluded)

loans out of his commissions. It was also improper for United States Trust Company to acquiesce in Lafferty's misconduct.

DISSENT

The testator has the right to determine who is most suitable among those legally qualified to manage his affairs and execute his will and his solemn selection should not be lightly disregarded. The residual charitable beneficiaries are not objecting to Lafferty's continued service and, at this point, it is not clear that injury to the estate has been occasioned or threatened by the alleged excesses of Lafferty or the conduct of the corporate fiduciary.

Both the federal and state governments impose estate or inheritance taxes on estates of a certain size. The personal representative is responsible for filing estate tax returns. The federal tax is a tax on the deceased's estate, with provisions for deducting items such as debts, expenses of administration, and charitable gifts. In addition, an amount equal to the amount left to the surviving spouse may be deducted from the gross estate before the tax is computed. State inheritance taxes are imposed on the person who receives a gift or statutory share from an estate. It is common, however, for wills to provide that the estate will pay all taxes, including inheritance taxes, so that the beneficiaries will not have to do so. The personal representative must also make provisions for filing an income tax return and for paying any income tax due for the partial year prior to the decedent's death.

When the debts, expenses, and taxes have been taken care of, the remaining assets of the estate are distributed to the decedent's heirs (if there was no will) or to the beneficiaries of the decedent's will. Special rules apply when the estate is too small to satisfy all of the bequests made in a will or when some or all of the designated beneficiaries are no longer living.

When the personal representative has completed all of these duties, the probate court will close the estate and discharge the personal representative.

.... *TRUSTS* ....

INTRODUCTION

A **trust** is a legal relationship in which a person who has legal rights to property has the duty to hold it for the use or benefit of another person. The person benefited by a trust is considered to have "equitable title" to the property because it is being maintained for his benefit. This means that he is regarded as the real owner even though the trustee has the legal title in his or her name. A trust may be created in a number of different ways:

1. The owner of the property may declare that he is holding certain property in trust. For example, a mother might state that she is holding 100 shares of General Motors Corporation stock in trust for her daughter.
2. The owner of property may transfer property to another person with the expressed intent that that person is not to have the use of it but rather is to hold it for the benefit of either the original owner–donor or a third person. For

example, Arthur transfers certain stock to First Trust Bank, with instructions to pay the income to Arthur's daughter during her lifetime, and after her death to distribute the stock to her children.

3. A trust may be created by operation of law. For example, where a lawyer who represents a client injured in an automobile accident receives a settlement payment from an insurance company, the lawyer holds the settlement as trustee for her client.

Most commonly, however, trusts are created through *express instruments* whereby an owner of property transfers title to the property to a trustee who is to hold, manage, and invest the property for the benefit of either the original owner or a third person. For example, Long transfers certain stock to First Trust Bank with instructions to pay the income to his daughter during her lifetime and to distribute the stock to her children after her death.

TRUST TERMINOLOGY

A person who creates a trust is known as **settlor** or **trustor.** The person who holds the property for the benefit of another person is called the **trustee.** The person for whose benefit the property is held in trust is the **beneficiary.** A single person may occupy more than one of these positions; however, if there is only one beneficiary, he cannot be the sole trustee. The property held in trust is called the **corpus** or **res.** A distinction is made between the property in trust, which is the principal, and the income that is produced by the principal.

A trust that is established and effective during the settlor's lifetime is known as an **inter vivos trust.** A trust can also be established in a person's will. Such trusts take effect only at the death of the settlor. They are called **testamentary trusts.**

WHY PEOPLE CREATE TRUSTS

Barbara owns a portfolio of valuable stock. Her husband has predeceased her. She has two children and an elderly father for whom she would like to provide. Why might it be advantageous to Barbara to transfer the stock to a trust for the benefit of the members of her family?

First, there may be income tax or estate tax advantages in doing so, depending on the type of trust she establishes and the provisions of that trust. For example, she can establish an irrevocable trust for her children and remove the property transferred to her trust from her estate so that it is not taxable at her death. In addition, the trust property can be used for the benefit of others and may even pass to others after the settlor's death without the necessity of having a will. Many people prefer to pass their property by trust rather than by will because trusts afford more privacy: unlike a probated will, they do not become an item of public record. Trusts also afford greater opportunity for postgift management than do outright gifts and bequests. If Barbara wants her children to enjoy the income of the trust property during their young adulthood without distributing unfettered ownership of the property to them before she considers them able to manage it properly, she can accomplish this through a trust provision. A trust can prevent the property from being squandered or spent too quickly. Trusts can be set up so that a beneficiary's interest cannot be reached by his creditors in many situations. Such trusts, called **spendthrift trusts,** will be discussed later.

Placing property in trust can operate to increase the amount of property held for the beneficiaries if the trustee makes good investment decisions. Another important consideration is that a trust can be used to provide for the needs of disabled beneficiaries who are not capable of managing funds.

CREATION OF EXPRESS TRUSTS

There are five basic requirements for the creation of a valid express trust, although special and somewhat less restrictive rules govern the establishment of charitable trusts. The requirements for forming an express trust follow.

1. *Capacity.* The settlor must have had the **legal capacity** to convey the property to the trust. This means that the settlor must have had the capacity needed to make a valid contract if the trust is an *inter vivos* trust or the capacity to make a will if the trust is a testamentary trust. For example, a trust would fail under this requirement if at the time the trust was created, the settlor had not attained the age required by state law for the creation of valid wills and contracts (age 18 in most states).

2. *Intent and formalities.* The settlor must *intend* to create a trust at the present time. To impose enforceable duties on the trustee, the settlor must meet certain formalities. Under the laws of most states, for example, the trustee must accept the trust by signing the trust instrument. In the case of a trust of land, the trust must be in writing so as to meet the statute of frauds. If the trust is a testamentary trust, it must satisfy the formal requirements for wills.

3. *Conveyance of specific property.* The settlor must convey *specific property* to the trust. The property conveyed must be property that the settlor has the *right to convey.*

4. *Proper purpose.* The trust must be created for a *proper purpose.* It cannot be created for a reason that is contrary to public policy, such as the commission of a crime.

5. *Identity of the beneficiaries.* The *beneficiaries* of the trust must be described clearly enough so that their identities can be ascertained. Sometimes, beneficiaries may be members of a specific class, such as "my children."

CHARITABLE TRUSTS

A distinction is made between private trusts and trusts created for charitable purposes. In a private trust, property is devoted to the benefit of specific persons, whereas in a charitable trust, property is devoted to a charitable organization or to some other purposes beneficial to society. While some of the rules governing private and charitable trusts are the same, a number of these rules are different. For example, when a private trust is created, the beneficiary must be known at the time or ascertainable within a certain time (established by a legal rule known as the **rule against perpetuities**). However, a charitable trust is valid even though no definitely ascertainable beneficiary is named and even though it is to continue for an indefinite or unlimited period.

Doctrine of Cy Pres

A doctrine known as **cy pres** is applicable to charitable trusts when property is given in trust to be applied to a particular charitable purpose that becomes impossible, impracticable, or illegal to carry out. Under the doctrine of *cy pres,* the trust will not fail if the settlor indicated a general intention to devote the property to charitable purposes. If the settlor has not specifically provided for a substitute beneficiary, the court will direct the application of the property to some charitable purpose that falls within the settlor's general charitable intention.

TOTTEN TRUSTS

A **Totten trust** is a deposit of money in a bank or other financial institution in the name of the depositor *as trustee* for a named beneficiary. For example, Bliss deposits money in First Bank in trust for his daughter, Bessie. The Totten trust creates a revocable living trust. At Bliss's death, if he has not revoked this trust, the money in the account will belong to Bessie.

POWERS AND DUTIES OF THE TRUSTEE

In most express trusts, the settlor names a specific person to act as trustee. If the settlor does not name a trustee, the court will appoint one. Similarly, a court will replace a trustee who resigns, is incompetent, or refuses to act.

The trust codes of most states contain provisions giving trustees broad management powers over trust property. These provisions can be limited or expanded by express provisions in the trust instrument. The trustee must use a *reasonable degree of skill, judgment, and care* in the exercise of her duties unless she holds herself out as having a greater degree of skill, in which case she will be held to a higher standard. Section 7–302 of the UPC provides that the trustee is held to the standard of a prudent person dealing with the property of another, and if she has special skills or is named trustee based on a representation of special skills, she is required to use those special skills. She *may not commingle* the property she holds in trust with her own property or with that of another trust.

A trustee owes a *duty of loyalty* (fiduciary duty) to the beneficiaries. This means that he must administer the trust for the benefit of the beneficiaries and avoid any conflict of interest between his personal interests and the interest of the trust. For example, a trustee cannot do business with the trust that he administers without express permission in the trust agreement. He must not prefer one beneficiary's interests to another's and he must account to the beneficiaries for all transactions. Unless the trust agreement provides otherwise, the trustee must make the trust productive. He may not delegate the performance of discretionary duties (such as the duty to select investments) to another, but he may delegate the performance of ministerial duties (such as the preparation of statements of account).

A trust may give the trustee discretion as to the amount of principal or income paid to a beneficiary. In such a case, the beneficiary cannot require the trustee to exercise her discretion in the manner desired by the beneficiary.

Allocating between Principal and Income

One of the duties of the trustee is to distribute the principal and income of the trust in accordance with the terms of the trust instrument. Suppose Wheeler's will created a testamentary trust providing that his wife was to receive the income from the trust for life, and at her death, the trust property was to be distributed to his children. During the duration of the trust, the trust earns profits, such as interest or rents, and has expenses, such as taxes or repairs. How should the trustee allocate these items as between Wheeler's surviving spouse, who is an **income beneficiary,** and his children, who are **remaindermen?**

The terms of the trust and state law bind the trustee in making this determination. As a general rule, ordinary profits received from the investment of trust property are allocated to income. For example, interest on trust property or rents earned from leasing real property held in trust would be allocated to income. Ordinary expenses such as insurance premiums, the cost of ordinary maintenance and repairs of trust property, and property taxes would be chargeable to income. The principal of the trust includes the trust property itself and any extraordinary receipts, such as proceeds or gains derived from the sale of trust property. Extraordinary expenses—for example, the cost of long-term permanent improvements to real property or expenses relating to the sale of property—would ordinarily be charged against principal.

LIABILITY OF TRUSTEE

A trustee who breaches any of the duties of a trustee or whose conduct falls below the standard of care applicable to trustees may incur personal liability. For example, if the trustee invests unwisely and imprudently, the trustee may be personally liable to reimburse the trust estate for the shortfall. The language of the trust affects the trustee's liability and the level of care owed by the trustee. A settlor might, for example, include language lowering the trustee's duty of care or relieving the trustee of some liability that she might otherwise incur.

The trustee can also have liability to third persons who are injured by the operation of the trust. Because a trust is not in itself a legal entity that can be sued, a third party who has a claim (such as a tort claim or a claim for breach of contract) must file his claim against the trustee of the trust. The trustee's actual personal liability to a third party depends on the language of the trust and of any contracts she might enter on behalf of the trust as well as the extent to which the injury complained of by the third party was a result of the personal fault or omission of the trustee.

SPENDTHRIFT TRUSTS

Generally, the beneficiary of a trust may voluntarily assign his rights to the principal or income of the trust to another person. In addition, any distributions to the beneficiary are subject to the claims of his creditors. Sometimes, however, trusts contain provisions known as **spendthrift clauses,** which restrict the voluntary or involuntary transfer of a beneficiary's interest. Such clauses are generally enforced, and they preclude assignees or creditors from compelling a trustee to recognize their claims to the trust. The enforceability of such clauses is subject to four exceptions, however:

1. A person cannot put his own property beyond the claims of his own creditors. Thus, a spendthrift clause is not effective in a trust when the settlor makes himself a beneficiary.
2. Divorced spouses and minor children of the beneficiary can compel payment for alimony and child support.
3. Creditors of the beneficiary who have furnished necessaries can compel payment.
4. Once the trustee distributes property to a beneficiary, it can be subject to valid claims of others.

TERMINATION AND MODIFICATION OF A TRUST

Normally, a settlor cannot revoke or modify a trust unless she reserves the power to do so at the time she establishes the trust. However, a trust may be modified or terminated with the consent of the settlor and all of the beneficiaries. When the settlor is dead or otherwise unable to consent, a trust can be modified or terminated by consent of all the persons with a beneficial interest but only when this would not frustrate a material purpose of the trust. Because trusts are under the supervisory jurisdiction of a court, the court can permit a deviation from the terms of a trust when unanticipated changes in circumstances threaten accomplishment of the settlor's purpose.

Implied and Constructive Trusts

Under exceptional circumstances in which the creation of a trust is necessary to effectuate a settlor's intent or avoid unjust enrichment, the law *implies* or imposes a trust even though no express trust exists or an express trust exists but has failed. One trust of this type is a **resulting trust,** which arises when there has been an incomplete disposition of trust property. For example, if Hess transferred property to Wickes as trustee to provide for the needs of Hess's grandfather and the grandfather died before the trust funds were exhausted, Wickes will be deemed to hold the property in a resulting trust for Hess or Hess's heirs. Similarly, if Hess had transferred the property to Wickes as trustee and the trust had failed because Hess did not meet one of the requirements of a valid trust, Wickes would not be permitted to keep the trust property as his own. A resulting trust would be implied.

A **constructive trust** is a trust created by operation of law to avoid fraud, injustice, or unjust enrichment. This type of trust imposes on the constructive trustee a duty to convey property she holds to another person on the ground that the constructive trustee would be unjustly enriched if she were allowed to retain it. For example, when a person procures the transfer of property by means of fraud or duress, she becomes a constructive trustee and is under an obligation to return the property to its original owner. The case that follows, *Pagliai v. del Re,* illustrates a situation in which a constructive trust was imposed.

PAGLIAI v. DEL RE
2001 U.S. Dist. LEXIS 2195 (S.D.N.Y. 2001)

FACTS

In 1952, Dr. Bruno Pagliai acquired a 15th century painting by Master Cima Da Conegliano ("Cima"). On his death in 1983, the painting passed to his son. At his request, his sister, Francesca, took the painting to Sotheby's in New York to have it appraised. Subsequently, the painting was stored at Marisa del Re Gallery, apparently pursuant to a consignment agreement with the brother. The brother later died, and ownership of the painting passed to Francesca, his sole heir, by intestate succession.

In April 1996 del Re gave the painting to James Goodman of Goodman Galleries, who was arbitrating a dispute between Marisa del Re Gallery (MDRG) and International Art Investors (IAI) concerning money MDRG owed for art work. The arbitration agreement signed by MDRG stated that it would post collateral with Goodman to secure the amount which Goodman determined due to IAI, which collateral was to be "free of all liens, encumbrances and claims of third parties." Del Re gave Goodman her verbal assurance that the painting

was free and clear of encumbrances, but Goodman did not ask for and del Re did not provide to him any record or proof of ownership of the painting.

On April 19, 1996, Goodman issued an arbitration award in which he found that MDRG owed IAI $413,650. Del Re failed to pay the award within the time stipulated and confirmed by letter that she would allow James Goodman Gallery to sell the collateral she put up against the award. She valued the Cima painting at $80,000. In November 1966, Goodman consigned the painting to Christie's for auction. The consignment agreement included a warrant by Goodman that he had the right and title to consign the painting for sale and that it was free and clear of liens, claims, and encumbrances of others. Christie's subsequently checked the Art Loss Register to see if the painting had been registered as lost or stolen— and it had not. On January 31, 1997, Christie's sold the painting at auction painting, which it had valued in its catalogue as worth between $50,000 and $80,000, at

(continued)

PAGLIAI V. DEL RE
(concluded)

auction to a purchaser from Tokyo for $65,000. The proceeds of the sale, less Christie's commission, were applied to the award owed by MDRG to IAI.

In January 1997, Pagliai spoke with del Re to ask for the return of the painting. She had forgotten about it after her brother's death and remembered its existence only at this time. Del Re indicated that she would get back to Pagliai, but she never did. In 1999 Pagliai filed suit against del Re seeking, among other things, a declaration of a constructive trust.

ISSUE

Should the court declare del Re to be the trustee of a constructive trust in favor of Pagliai for the value of the painting?

DECISION

Yes. The court noted that a constructive trust is an equitable remedy designed to prevent unjust enrichment. Commonly there are four elements of a constructive trust: (1) a confidential or fiduciary relationship, (2) a promise, (3) a transfer in reliance, and (4) unjust enrichment. However, the elements are only guideposts for

what is an equitable remedy, and the lack of a fiduciary relationship does not defeat the imposition of a constructive trust. Here, Pagliai has established the existence of a constructive trust. The painting was left in del Re's custody on her implicit representation that it would be safe to do so. Using the painting to satisfy her debt against IAI allowed del Re to reap the benefits of property which did not belong to her. Accordingly, the court imposed a constructive trust on the amount of debt which del Re satisfied by using the painting.

AUTHOR'S NOTE

Pagliai's claims in her lawsuit included a claim of conversion. However, to the extent her claim was based on the fact Pagliai had used the painting as collateral in connection with the IAI dispute, it was barred by New York's three-year statute of limitations for conversion. To the extent the claim was based on a bailment of "indefinite" duration, the court held that while Pagliai had a "reasonable time" to make a demand for return of the bailed property, the delay of 14 years in making the demand was unreasonable. This left "constructive trust" as her most viable basis for recovery against del Re.

.... *QUESTIONS AND PROBLEM CASES* ....

1. If a person dies without leaving a will, who will be entitled to his or her property?

2. For 36 years, Ward Duchett lived in Washington, D.C., with his sister Mary in her home. On numerous occasions, Mary had promised Ward she would leave him her real estate if he remained single and continued to live with her. At age 60, Mary became seriously ill and was put in a hospital. Three weeks later, her sister Maude, who was a nurse in Philadelphia, came to Washington and took Mary home even though her doctors advised against it and she did not ask to be taken home. Maude took complete charge of Mary, repeatedly prevented other relatives, including Ward, from seeing Mary, and told them she was doing it on doctor's orders. That statement was false. Mary was in a very weak physical condition, sometimes could recognize people only by their voices, and could not sit up or carry on

a conversation. Maude secretly arranged for a lawyer to come and prepare a will, which was quickly executed. It left everything to Maude in "consideration for her kindness, untiring devotion, and personal service to me during my illness when no other relative offered or came to do for me, and without hope of reward." The will was witnessed by the lawyer and by a cousin who was very close to Maude. Mary died the next day. There was no evidence that Mary had previously felt any ill will toward any of her relatives. Ward moved to set the will aside. Should the will be set aside?

3. Roy and Icie Johnson established two revocable *inter vivos* trusts in 1966. The trusts provided that upon Roy's and Icie's deaths, income from the trusts was to be paid in equal shares to their two sons, James and Robert, for life. Upon the death of the survivor of the sons, the trust was to be "*divided equally between all*

of my grandchildren, per stirpes." James had two daughters, Barbara and Elizabeth. Robert had four children, David, Rosalyn, Catherine, and Elizabeth. James and Robert disclaimed their interest in the trust in 1979, and a dispute arose about how the trust should be distributed to the grandchildren. The trustee filed an action seeking instructions on how the trusts should be distributed. What should the court hold?

4. In 1937, a testator died leaving a will in which the bulk of his estate was in trust. The will provided that the trust was to continue during the lifetime of his two sons, Orin Byers and Clifford W. Byers. On the death of either son, if he was survived "by children lawfully begotten of their bodies," the children were to share equally their father's share. If a son died without "leaving surviving children begotten of his body," the trust was to be kept intact until the death of the other son and then divided "among children of said sons who survive him." Orin died in 1941. Clifford died in 1961 leaving a legitimate daughter, Guinevere, and an illegitimate son, Raymond. Both were living when the testator died. Raymond brought an action claiming he was entitled to a half interest in the trust. Should his claim be granted?

5. On March 23, 1994, Evelyn Foster died, leaving a house and nearly 400 acres of land in Mercer County along with personal property. She had executed a holographic will, which was offered for probate. The will stated in part:

> I—Evelyn Foster—being of sound Mind and Body—do hereby declare—In the event of my death—I herby [*sic*] will the farm-house + contents to go to Judy Foster Monk—any Monies shall be divided equally—after the funeral Expenses—between Greg Foster + Judy Foster Monk—also I do herby [*sic*] request that the Farm *not be sold!* Any personal items shall be equally divided—
> Sincerely—
> Evelyn Foster

Foster's son claims that Foster willed only a "farmhouse + contents" to his sister (Judy), *not* the farm land. Is he correct?

6. Crawshaw bequeathed the bulk of his estate to two residuary beneficiaries, the Salvation Army and Marymount College. Crawshaw's will provided for 15 percent of the residue to go to the Salvation Army outright and 85 percent to Marymount College in trust. The stated purpose of this trust was to provide loans to nursing and other students at Marymount. Marymount ceased operation on June 30, 1989. It sought to have the trust funds directed to Marymount Memorial Educational Trust Fund. The Salvation Army challenged this, arguing that Crawshaw did not intend to benefit students attending colleges other than Marymount. It asked that the court distribute the trust funds to the Salvation Army as the remaining beneficiary of Crawshaw's residuary estate. What should the court do?

7. After Boyd Ruff died, his wife found in his wallet a blank check on the back of which was written, "I Boyd Ruff request that all I own in the way of personal or real estate property go to my wife Modene, Boyd Ruff." Ruff had a serious coronary condition that he knew could be fatal at any time and executed the document shortly before his death and just after a serious heart attack. Ruff was survived by his wife, three brothers, and a sister but left no children. Modene Ruff filed a petition in probate to admit the document as a will. Ruff's sister, Lois, filed a petition to set the will aside on the grounds that (1) on its face it was not a valid holographic will and (2) it did not show a valid intent to make a will. Under Arkansas state law, a holographic will entirely in the handwriting of a testator along with his signature is valid despite the lack of witnesses to it if the handwriting and signature are later established to be the testator's by three credible disinterested witnesses. Should the petition to admit the will be granted?

8. Kenneth Hotarek and Suzanne Benson were married in July 1968. Their son, Paul Hotarek, was born on October 25, 1970. Hotarek and Benson were divorced two years later, on October 26, 1972. In July 1986, at the age of 15, Paul was killed in an automobile accident. Subsequent to Paul's death, his estate settled a claim against the other driver for $20,000 and was awarded uninsured motorist's benefits in the amount of $525,000. These proceeds made up Paul's estate. Following Paul's death and during the initial stages of the probate proceedings, Suzanne Benson could not be

located. For about 13 years preceding Paul's death, she had not had any contact with Paul, did not provide any financial support to him, and did not display any interest in, nor any love and affection toward her son. Once she was located, the probate court ordered half of Paul's estate distributed to her in accordance with Connecticut law. It provides that if a person dies intestate leaving no spouse or children, the residue of the estate shall be distributed equally to the decedent's parent or parents. Kenneth Hotarek objected to the distribution to Benson on the grounds she had abandoned her minor son during his life and should not be entitled to share in his estate after his death. Is Benson entitled to share in her intestate son's estate?

9. When Peter Kaufman died, his son William reluctantly qualified to become the administrator of his father's estate. William was a farmer with relatively little schooling or experience in financial matters. He agreed to serve as administrator only on the understanding that he could hire an attorney who would do most of the work. William Kaufman retained W. L. Doolan as the attorney and put the management of the estate entirely in his hands. Doolan was a highly respected lawyer with a good reputation. Over a period of five years, Doolan systematically embezzled money from the estate. When the embezzlement was discovered, Doolan was insolvent and unable to repay the money. While Kaufman checked with Doolan about once a week, he never demanded an accounting from him. A new administrator was appointed for the estate, and he sued William Kaufman to hold him liable for the amount of the embezzlement. Was the administrator of an estate liable where an agent he appointed embezzled money entrusted to him that belonged to the estate?

10. Maggie Gaines, an elderly and infirm woman, maintained certain savings deposits and certificates in the Jefferson Federal Savings and Loan Association. During her lifetime, she had the name of her son, Billy Gaines, placed on the accounts along with her own. Her purpose in doing this was not to make a gift to Billy but to enable him to handle the funds for her support and benefit in the event she became incapacitated. Because of her deteriorating physical condition, she had to leave her residence and be cared for in Billy's home. She stayed there about two years before being moved to a nursing home for about four months immediately preceding her death.

During the time Maggie was living with Billy, he took control of and disposed of all of the funds which were formerly on deposit at Jefferson Federal together with Maggie's Social Security checks. Billy invested some of the funds in his own personal newspaper business and used some of the funds for Maggie's support and maintenance.

On Maggie's death, her estate claimed that a constructive trust arose between Billy and Maggie whereby he was obligated to reasonably use the funds for Maggie's benefit and to account for the balance. Did the placing of the son's name on the mother's account under these circumstances create a constructive trust?

CHAPTER 35

Insurance

Benjamin Born purchased an insurance policy from Medico Life Insurance
Company. As a part of the application process, Benjamin gave a complete health
history and was asked specific questions about preexisting medical conditions.
Adeline Born, his wife, answered all of the questions, stating that Benjamin had no
preexisting medical problems and was in good health. After the policy was issued,
Medico discovered that Benjamin had a history of heart disease, degenerative
arthritis, and urinary system disorders. When Medico rescinded the policy and
refunded the premiums, Born refused to cash the premium refund and claimed he
was still insured.[1]

- *What are the contractual rules governing the creation of the insurance
  relationship?*
- *How do courts determine the liability of insurers?*
- *When and how may insurers cancel insurance policies?*

---

[1]Born v. Medico Life Insurance Co., 428 N.W.2d 585 (Ct. App. Minn. 1988).

Generally, property owners must bear the risk of loss to their own property. However, throughout this book, you have seen situations in which a person might be held liable for the risk of damage or loss to the property of another. Chapters 4 and 5 are filled with examples of persons who negligently or intentionally damaged another's property and were held liable for the resulting losses. And Chapter 16 discusses instances when buyers of goods could be liable for losses involving property they do not technically own. The purpose of insurance contracts, as this chapter will discuss, is to allow people to shift to another a risk of loss that they would ordinarily have to bear.

TERMINOLOGY

In essence, the insurance relationship is a contract that may involve more than two persons. The **insurer** (usually a corporation), in exchange for the payment of consideration (called a **premium**), agrees to pay for losses caused by specific events (perils). The **beneficiary** is the person to whom the insurance proceeds are payable. The **insured** is the person whose life is covered by a life insurance policy or the person who acquires insurance on property in which she possesses an insurable interest. (Insurable interests will be discussed later in this chapter.) In most instances, the insured is also the **owner** of the policy (the person who can exercise the contractual rights set out in the insurance contract); however, this is not always the case.

A distinction is made between valid insurance contracts and wagering contracts. A *wagering contract* creates a new risk that did not previously exist and is illegal as contrary to public policy. *Insurance contracts,* on the other hand, transfer existing risks. This chapter will discuss four major types of insurance contracts: life insurance, fire insurance, liability insurance, and health insurance.

.... *LIFE INSURANCE CONTRACTS* ....

In life insurance contracts, the insurer is bound to pay a certain sum when a certain event (the death of the insured) occurs. Only the time that the event occurs is uncertain. The insurance contract is a **valued policy;** that is, the insurer is required to pay a fixed amount (referred to as the **face value** of the policy). The rate of the premiums to be paid depends on the face value of the policy. (The higher the face value, the higher will be the premiums that must be paid.) There are two basic kinds of insurance; whole life and term life.

WHOLE LIFE INSURANCE

A policy for **whole life** insurance, also called *ordinary* or *straight life* insurance, normally binds the insurer to pay the face value of the policy on the death of the insured. The insured must pay the specified premium for the duration of his or her life. In addition to its risk-shifting character, a whole life insurance policy has an important savings feature. As premiums are paid on the policy, it develops a *cash surrender value* that the insured can recover if the policy is terminated. In the same way, a whole life policy develops a loan value. This increases with the age of the policy and enables the insured to borrow money from the insurer at relatively low interest rates.

TERM LIFE INSURANCE

A **term life** insurance contract obligates the insurer to pay only the face amount of the policy if the insured dies within a specified period of time—the term of the policy. The insured is obligated to pay premiums for the term of the policy. Term contracts, unlike whole life contracts, do not build up any cash surrender value or loan value. Many term contracts have a *guaranteed renewability* feature that allows the insured to renew the policy for additional terms up to a stated age without proving insurability (good health). However, the premium rate for additional terms is likely to be higher than that for the original term. Many term contracts also contain a *guaranteed convertibility* feature that allows the insured to convert the policy to a whole life policy.

PROPERTY INSURANCE CONTRACTS

Property insurance contracts are **indemnity** contracts. The insurer is obligated to reimburse the insured for any actual losses that the insured suffered due to damage to the insured property. The loss must occur during the period of time that the policy is in force. The amount that the insured may recover is generally limited to the extent of the loss sustained as long as it does not exceed the amount of coverage that the insured purchased.

TYPES OF LOSSES COVERED

Insurers generally do not provide coverage for losses to property resulting from any and all types of causes. Instead, they usually specify certain *covered perils* or list various *excluded perils*.

Covered Perils

Property insurance contracts generally provide coverage for a broad range of perils. Losses resulting from fire, lightning, hail, wind, vandalism, aircraft or automobile crashes, and overflows from burst pipes often are included in the lists of covered perils.

Fire insurance contracts are an extremely common type of property insurance contract. These policies generally cover losses only from *hostile* fires—those that burn where no fire is intended to be (fires caused by lightning, outside sources, or electrical shorts, or fires that escape from places where they are intended to be, like a *friendly* fire in a fireplace that spreads). Fire insurance policies generally cover more than direct damage caused by the fire. They also cover indirect damage caused by smoke and heat, and the damage caused by the efforts of firefighters to put out the fire.

Excluded Perils

Flood-related damage to property is a common excluded peril. Earthquake damage and harm caused by acts of war or nuclear contamination also are typical exclusions. Losses resulting from the deliberate acts of an insured that were intended to damage the property also are likely to be excluded.

NATIONWIDE INSURANCE V. BOARD OF TRUSTEES
116 F.3d 1154 (7th Cir. 1997)

FACTS

In the early morning hours, Aleck Zavalis, Glenn Schicker, and Conor Gorman, all students at the University of Illinois, stole into the University's Memorial Stadium. They spelled out the letters "F-O-O" with lighter fluid on the playing field. ("Foo" was a word they derived from "Foofur," a lazy hound dog that appeared in a Saturday morning cartoon show during the late 1980s.) Their intent was to light the letters and leave a residue of soot on the Astroturf which would be visible on television or from the bleachers. However, the flames quickly spread, and a sizable portion of the playing surface was destroyed. The University, which incurred damages in excess of $600,000, sued the three students. At the time of the mishap, Zavalis's parents maintained a homeowner's insurance policy with Nationwide Insurance. That policy provided public liability coverage for all residents of the Zavalis household including Aleck. However, the policy expressly excluded property damage "which is expected or intended by the insured." Both Zavalis and the University argued that the students' behavior did not fall within the exclusion. Specifically, Zavalis argued that he did not "expect or intend" the damages because he did not intend to burn any part of the Astroturf. Rather, he and his friends thought that the lighter fluid alone would burn, leaving only a residue of soot on the portions of the Astroturf to which it had been applied.

ISSUE

Does the insurance company have a duty to defend and indemnify Zavalis?

DECISION

No. Sometimes common sense prevails, even in the law. This is one of those occasions. An insured "expects or intends" the injury in question when he acts with an intent or a conscious awareness that damage will result. The mere fact that the actual damage is more severe than the insured anticipated does not, by itself, necessarily establish that he did not "expect or intend" it. The inescapable fact is that Zavalis did intend to damage the Astroturf. Whether he meant to actually scorch it or merely leave a layer of soot on the turf that could be cleaned away later, common sense tells us that his purpose was to damage the field nonetheless. Damage need not be permanent to constitute damage, and defacement certainly qualifies as damage. Here, Zavalis literally played with fire, and although the resulting harm was far beyond what he expected, this was a harm that fell clearly in the policy's exclusion. Therefore, Nationwide is not obligated to defend or indemnify Zavalis.

Additional Coverages

Property owners may be able to purchase a specialized policy (such as flood insurance) to make up for gaps in a standard insurance contract. Further, many standard policies permit an insured to obtain broader coverage by paying additional premiums. This is common for people who wish to secure coverage for earthquake damages.

PERSONAL PROPERTY INSURANCE

Up to this point, the discussion of property insurance has focused on policies providing protection for *real* property. However, *personal* property also may be insured. **Homeowners' policies** often insure both the insured's dwelling and the personal property located on or inside the real property. In fact, many homeowners' policies cover personal property that was temporarily removed from the dwelling at the time it was damaged.

Automobile insurance policies are in part personal property insurance contracts because they provide coverage under their *comprehensive and collision* sections for car damages resulting from fire, wind, hail, vandalism, and collisions with animals or trees. (*Note:* Automobile insurance also is a type of liability insurance contract.) There are other types of property insurance as well. For instance, farmers may buy crop insurance to protect against the risk that crops will be damaged by wind or flooding.

TYPES OF POLICIES

Valued Policies

Some property insurance contracts are called **valued policies.** If property covered by a valued policy is totally destroyed, the insured can recover the face amount of the policy regardless of the fair market value of the building. For example, Smith bought a home with a fair market value of $100,000 in 1994 and purchased a valued policy with a face value of $100,000 to insure the house against the risk of fire. In the next few years, because of deterioration in the surrounding neighborhood, the home's fair market value decreased. In 1999, when the home had a fair market value of only $84,000, it was totally destroyed by fire. Despite the reduced fair market value, Smith is entitled to $100,000 (the face value of the policy).

Open Policies

Most property insurance policies are **open policies.** These allow the insured to recover the fair market value of the property at the time it was destroyed, up to the limits stated in the policy. Thus, in the example presented in the previous paragraph, Smith would be entitled to only $84,000 when the home was destroyed in 1999.

Suppose, instead, that Smith's home had increased in value so that at the time of the fire, its fair market value was $130,000. In this case, it does not matter what type of policy Smith had. Under both the valued and open policies, his recovery would be limited to the face value of the policy—$100,000. (See Table 35–1.)

SPECIAL TERMS

The insurance contract may contain special terms relating to the insured's rights on destruction of the property. It is common for some policies to give the insurer the option of replacing or restoring the damaged property instead of paying its fair market value.

TABLE 35–1   Insurance Recovery for a Total Loss

Face Value of Policy	Fair Market Value at Time of Loss	Valued Policy Recovery	Open Policy Recovery
$100,000	$84,000	$100,000	$84,000
$100,000	$130,000	$100,000	$100,000

Coinsurance Clause

Some fire insurance policies contain a coinsurance clause that can operate to limit the insured's right to recovery. The coinsurance provision requires the insured to insure the property to a specified percentage of its fair market value in order to fully recover the value of partial losses. Generally, most policies require that the insured purchase insurance equal to at least 80 percent of the fair market value.

For example, ABC Manufacturing Company has a fire insurance policy on its warehouse with Friendly Mutual Insurance Group. The policy has an 80 percent coinsurance clause. The warehouse had a fair market value of $100,000. (Therefore, ABC was supposed to carry at least $80,000 of insurance on the building.) However, ABC purchased a policy with a face value of only $60,000. A fire partially destroyed the building, causing $40,000 worth of damage to the structure. Because of the coinsurance clause, ABC will recover only $30,000 from Friendly. This figure was arrived at by taking the amount of insurance carried ($60,000) divided by the amount of insurance required ($80,000) times the loss ($40,000).

The coinsurance formula for recovery for partial losses is stated as follows:

$$\frac{\text{Amount of insurance carried}}{\text{Coinsurance percent} \times \text{Fair market value}} \times \text{Loss} = \text{Recovery}$$

Remember that the coinsurance formula applies only to "partial" losses of property. If the warehouse had been totally destroyed by the fire, ABC could have recovered $60,000 (the face value of the policy). The formula would not have been applicable. If it had been used, it would have indicated that Friendly owed ABC $75,000. Yet this would have been more than the face amount of the policy. This is not possible; whether the loss is total or partial, the insured can never recover more than the face value of the policy. (See Table 35–2.)

Pro Rata Clause

With the limited exception of the valued policy discussed above, the insured can never recover more than the amount of the actual loss. To allow otherwise would encourage unscrupulous people to intentionally destroy their property. Accordingly, when the insured has purchased insurance policies from more than one insurer, the loss will be apportioned among the insurance companies. The amount for which any particular insurer is liable is calculated by determining the total amount of the insurer's policy in proportion to the total amount of insurance covering the property.

For example, Andrew purchased two insurance policies to cover his home against the risk of fire. His policy from Farmers' Mutual had a face value of $50,000 while the coverage by States Insurance was for $100,000. The home was partially destroyed by

TABLE 35–2   Coinsurance Clause

Fair Market Value at Time of Loss	Face Value of Policy	Amount of Insurance Required	Actual Loss	Recovery
$100,000	$60,000	$80,000	$40,000	$30,000
$100,000	$60,000	$80,000	$100,000	$60,000

fire, with the losses amounting to $30,000. Farmers' Mutual is responsible for $10,000, while States Insurance is liable for the remaining $20,000.

The formula for determining each insurer's liability is stated as follows:

$$\frac{\text{Amount of insurer's policy}}{\text{Total coverage by all insurers}} \times \text{Loss} = \text{Liability of insurer}$$

Thus, Farmers' liability was calculated as follows:

$$\frac{\$50,000 \text{ (Farmers' policy)}}{\$150,000 \text{ (Total of both policies)}} \times \$30,000 \text{ (Loss)} = \$10,000$$

The liability of States Insurance could be similarly calculated by substituting $100,000 (States' policy) for the $50,000 (Farmers' policy) in the numerator of the equation. This formula may be used for both partial and total losses. However, note again that each company's liability is limited by the face value of the policy. Thus, Farmers' could never be liable for more than $50,000 and States' liability is limited to a maximum of $100,000. (See Table 35–3.)

Pro rata clauses do not apply to life insurance contracts. In a life insurance case, the beneficiary would recover the face value of all of the policies.

.... *LIABILITY INSURANCE CONTRACTS* ....

Under liability insurance policies the insurer agrees to pay the sums for which the insured becomes legally obligated to pay to another person. There are various types of liabilities that insurers are willing to assume. They range from personal liability policies to business liability contracts to workers' compensation policies. Some insurance contracts, such as automobile policies, combine the liability features with property insurance coverage. Typical homeowners' policies also combine these features.

LIABILITY COVERAGE

While the terms of the various liability insurance contracts may vary, they frequently share certain coverage terms. For instance, most liability policies provide coverage against the insured's liability for negligence but not for liability resulting from the insured's deliberately wrongful acts (intentional torts and crimes). Like property insurance agreements, the liability insurance policies tend to define their particular coverages by listing either covered or excluded liabilities.

Personal Liability Policies

Personal liability insurance contracts, including the liability provisions in homeowners' policies, often restrict their coverage to bodily injury and property damages suffered by third persons as a result of an *occurrence* for which the insured is legally

TABLE 35–3   Pro Rata Insurance

Policy A	Policy B	Total Insurance (Policy A plus Policy B)	Actual Loss	Liability of Insurer A	Liability of Insurer B
$50,000	$100,000	$150,000	$30,000	$10,000	$20,000

liable. They generally define "occurrence" as some type of accident that causes bodily injury or property damage.

Business Liability Policies

Business liability insurance contracts often provide broader coverage than personal liability policies. While their coverage is limited to injuries resulting from the "conduct of business," they frequently cover claims arising from the insured's intentional tort liability springing from defamation or invasion of privacy lawsuits. They may also include liability for a third person's economic losses as well as their claims for bodily injury or property damage. **Malpractice insurance** is similar to business liability coverage in that it provides protection for professionals whose negligent professional conduct causes injuries to third persons.

ZIMMERMAN V. SAFECO INSURANCE COMPANY
605 N.W.2d 727 (Minn. Sup.Ct. 2000)

FACTS

Robert Zimmerman was the president and sole shareholder of Airport & Airline Taxi-Cab Corporation. In 1991, Zimmerman and a female employee of Airport Taxi became involved in a sexual relationship; however, by late 1994 the affair had begun to tarnish. The employee began avoiding Zimmerman and no longer wanted a relationship with him because he had been making embarrassing and distressing comments to her in front of her co-workers. Although the relationship had ended, Zimmerman attempted to rekindle it. Unsuccessful, he found it difficult to see the employee on a daily basis because of his romantic feelings. He asked her to explore other job options, despite the fact that he admitted that he was satisfied with her work. The employee begged Zimmerman for her job, prompting an outburst from Zimmerman that included sexual innuendoes. In July 1995, she finally resigned her employment and sued Zimmerman, claiming sexual harassment in the workplace. The district court held that Zimmerman's conduct had constituted sexual harassment which caused the female employee emotional distress and permanent emotional damage. When Zimmerman was sued, he tendered his defense to Safeco Insurance Company under his homeowner's insurance policy. Safeco declined to accept the tender, asserting that liability for sexual harassment was not covered under the policy because it was a loss that fell within the business pursuits exclusion to coverage. The policy listed as an exclusion to liability coverage any damages "arising out of business pursuits of any insured." However, the policy also

had an exception to the exclusion for "activities which are ordinarily incident to non-business pursuits." Zimmerman then sued Safeco for breaching the insurer's duty to defend and indemnify him for the sexual harassment lawsuit. Specifically, Zimmerman claimed that the exclusion did not apply because sexual pursuits in the workplace are not conduct peculiar to or in furtherance of the interests of his business. He further contended that, even if the business pursuits exclusion does apply, the exception to the exclusion is applicable because, regardless of the label attached to sexual harassment, the sexual pursuit of another person is an activity ordinarily incident to nonbusiness pursuits.

ISSUE

Is Zimmerman's sexual harassment liability covered by his homeowner's insurance policy?

DECISION

No. Whether conduct constitutes a business pursuit depends on the relationship between the conduct in question and the business of the insured. Here, the liability-creating conduct is Zimmerman's sexual harassment of an employee. Clearly, sexual harassment of an employee falls with the general business pursuits exclusion of the policy because by definition it occurs within the workplace. In reaching this decision, we are not condoning or legitimizing sexual harassment in the workplace. Our holding, in simplest terms, is that because the sexual harassment for which Zimmerman was found

(continued)

ZIMMERMAN V. SAFECO INSURANCE COMPANY
(concluded)

liable can happen only in the workplace, by definition it falls within the "business pursuits" exclusion. The more difficult question, however, is whether the exception to the exclusion applies because the conduct is ordinarily nonbusiness-related activity. We conclude that the exception cannot apply where, by definition, the liability-creating conduct is based upon the employment relationship in the business setting. Thus, we hold that the employee's sexual harassment claims against Zimmerman are within Safeco's homeowner's policy business exclusion provision and do not fall within the exception to the exclusion as ordinarily incident to non-business pursuits.

INSURER'S OBLIGATIONS

The actual insurance contract defines the duties that each insurer assumes. However, there are several general duties common to liability insurance policies. These include a duty to defend and the duty to pay the sums owed by the insured.

Duty to Defend

Each liability insurance provider has a **duty to defend** the insured when a third party files a legal claim against the insured that falls within the coverage terms of the policy. Of course, this duty generally does not arise unless the insured notifies the insurance company of the claims against her. Such notification triggers the insurer's duty to furnish an attorney to represent the insured in any resulting litigation.

Duty to Pay

When the third party's legal claims fall within the liability coverage provisions of the insurance policy, the insurance company has a **duty to pay** the sums owed by the insured. This includes any compensatory damages as well as any court costs assessed against the insured. Of course, this liability is subject to any policy limits contained in the insurance contract. Thus, if the liability policy was for $500,000, the insurer would not be required to pay claims against the insured in excess of that amount. Those additional amounts would be the responsibility of the insured.

Insurance companies need not wait until litigation has been concluded to satisfy their duty to pay. Most policies permit the insurer to seek voluntary settlements of liability claims against the insured. These settlements involve payment of a negotiated amount of money to the third person in exchange for the third person's giving up his legal claim against the insured.

HEALTH INSURANCE CONTRACTS

Rising costs of hospitalization, medical treatment, and medication have directed widespread attention to the need for insurance protection against financially crippling costs of illness or injury. This section examines the basic features of health insurance contracts.

Coverage

Health insurance contracts provide coverage for medical expenses resulting from a wide range of illnesses and injuries suffered by the insured or members of her immediate family. As with the previously discussed insurance contracts, health insurance policies generally specify a list of covered illnesses and injuries and also include a range of excluded illnesses or injuries. Preexisting health conditions (those that befell the insured or her family before the effective date of the policy) normally will be excluded from coverage.

Group Policies

Most people receive their insurance coverage from *group policies* that are provided by employers or other organizations. Participation in group policies tends to enable people to significantly reduce the cost of the premiums they must pay for health insurance. However, these policies frequently result in an insurance crisis for the insured when his employment or other type of group membership ends. He may then be required to pay significantly higher costs for a new insurance policy or, in many cases, may find that a new insurer will not cover extended illnesses that arose while he was covered by the group policy.

Many states have enacted legislation creating *portable health insurance*. Such statutes generally try to guarantee some level of health insurance coverage to people who change or lose their jobs. They do this by limiting the waiting periods before new coverage takes effect or by requiring insurance companies to provide coverage to people who have left a job.

Further, under federal law, businesses that provide group health insurance plans must offer self-paid, continued group coverage to qualified employees for at least 18 months after termination of employment. The Consolidated Omnibus Budget Reconciliation Act (COBRA) was enacted as a legislative response to the growing number of Americans without health insurance and the reluctance of hospitals to treat the uninsured. By offering the opportunity to obtain continuation of coverage, COBRA provides an alternative to prohibitively expensive individual health care insurance policies for those people who, because of certain events such as divorce or the loss of a job, are at risk of losing their employment-related group health insurance.

Phillips v. Saratoga Harness Racing, Inc.
240 F.3d 174 (2nd Cir. 2001)

Facts

Melody Phillips married Frank Studenroth in 1985. By 1993 Frank worked for Saratoga Harness Racing and enrolled Melody and their two children in Saratoga's group health insurance plan. This health insurance covered the cost of Melody's expensive treatments for Graves' disease, a serious disorder of the thyroid gland. In July 1993, Frank abandoned his family and moved out of the marital home. In short order, Frank and Melody were communicating only through attorneys, who were unsuccessful in

negotiating a separation agreement. By summer 1994, impatient with the pace of the protracted negotiations, Frank flew to the Dominican Republic where he commenced an ex parte divorce action. Meanwhile, Melody, unaware of the proceeding in the Dominican Republic, filed for a separation in New York. Two days later, Frank obtained a default judgment of divorce in a Dominican court. Two days after that, he married his secretary. After a short honeymoon, he returned to work and informed

(continued)

PHILLIPS V. SARATOGA HARNESS RACING, INC.
(concluded)

Saratoga's health plan administrator that he had divorced and remarried. He asked the administrator to drop Melody from his medical coverage and extend coverage to his new wife. When a beneficiary's coverage under an employer's health plan is terminated in a case such as this, federal law (COBRA) requires the employer to tell the beneficiary and advise her of her right to continue coverage at the employer's group rate but at her own expense. Inexplicably, Saratoga gave the notice and other necessary forms to Frank. He never gave them to Melody, and the company concedes that it never mailed her any of the necessary paperwork, which is the standard method for delivery of such notices. One month later, Melody (still unaware of the divorce or subsequent wedding) underwent treatment for her Graves' disease under the assumption that her health coverage through Saratoga was still valid. Only then did she learn that Frank had terminated her coverage. Meanwhile, in her separation action in New York, the judge held that Frank's Dominican divorce was invalid in New York because Melody had not been given adequate notice and an opportunity to be heard. Melody then sued Saratoga for her out-of-pocket medical costs and other damages allegedly caused by the company's failure to comply with the notice requirements of COBRA. Saratoga defended on the basis that, because the Dominican divorce was declared invalid in New York, the divorce could not suffice as a "qualifying event" that would trigger its notice obligations under COBRA.

ISSUE

Did the employer violate its duty to advise Melody of her right to continue her health coverage?

DECISION

Yes. COBRA provides that each qualified beneficiary who would lose coverage under an employer's group health plan as a result of a qualifying event is entitled to elect within the election period to continue coverage under the plan. The term "qualifying event" includes divorce or legal separation of the covered employee from the employee's spouse. When coverage is being terminated as a result of a qualifying event, COBRA requires the covered employee to notify the health plan's administrator. That notice to the employer then obligates the employer to notify the beneficiary. We conclude that whether or not an invalid divorce decree is actually a qualifying event under COBRA is not the question. It is the act of the employee telling his employer that the qualifying event has occurred—not the actual occurrence of the qualifying event itself—that triggers the employer's obligations under COBRA. This interpretation makes practical sense. Whether or not a qualifying event has occurred often requires a legal determination. Employers are rarely competent to make these legal determinations. Public policy is best served by relieving health plan administrators of the responsibility for making legal judgments. Finally, even if mere notice of a qualifying event is insufficient and the qualifying event must actually have occurred to trigger COBRA obligations, there are strong arguments that a divorce did, in fact, occur. Presumably, Frank and Melody remain divorced in the eyes of the Dominican Republic. COBRA does not specify that the divorce must be valid and recognized in all jurisdictions. For these reasons, we conclude that when an employee notifies his employer that a qualifying event has occurred, the employer's obligations under the notice provisions of COBRA are triggered.

PAYMENT OBLIGATIONS

Health insurance policies generally require the insured to pay up to a certain amount each year before the insurer's payment obligation begins. This specific amount, which varies from policy to policy, is known as the **deductible.** After the insured has paid the deductible amount, the insurer must pay all of the remaining medical expenses incurred during that year.

Some policies establish a payment obligation that is a percentage of the medical expenses. While this amount may vary, health insurance contracts often require the insurer to pay 80 percent of the expenses. For long-term hospitalization or extended illnesses, the policies also may obligate the insurer to pay a designated percentage of expenses up to a certain amount. The insurer then pays all expenses that exceed that amount.

More and more insurers place a cap on the amount they will pay for certain medical treatments or procedures. These companies will not pay amounts in excess of that amount. Many insurers will not pay for experimental medical treatments.

Health insurers may make their payments in either of two ways. They may pay the insured if she already has paid the health care provider. In other instances, the health care provider bills the insurer directly and seeks payment from the insured for amounts not covered by the insurer.

INSURANCE POLICIES AS CONTRACTS

The insurance relationship is basically contractual in nature. As a result, insurance policies must satisfy all of the elements required for a binding contract.

OFFER AND ACCEPTANCE

The standard practice in insurance is to have the potential insured make an offer to enter an insurance contract by completing an application provided by the insurer's agent and submitting it and the premium to the insurer. The insurer may then either accept or reject this offer. What constitutes acceptance depends on the kind of insurance requested and the language of the application. It is very important to know the precise time when an acceptance occurs. Any losses suffered prior to this point must be borne by the insured, not the insurer.

Applications for life insurance often provide that acceptance does not occur until the insurer delivers the policy to the insured. Most courts hold that delivery occurs when the insurer has executed and mailed the policy. A few courts, to avoid hardship, have held that delivery occurred when the policy was executed, even though it was still in the insurer's hands. If the application calls for the policy to be delivered to an agent of the insured, delivery to the agent constitutes acceptance, unless the agent has discretionary power not to deliver the policy. Some recent decisions have abandoned the purely contractual approach to insurance contracts in an attempt to seek "fair" results.

In property insurance contracts, the application may be worded so that insurance coverage begins when the insured signs the application. This can provide temporary coverage until the insurer either accepts or rejects the policy. The same result may also be achieved by the use of a **binder,** an agreement for temporary insurance pending the insurer's decision to accept or reject the risk. Acceptance in property insurance contracts generally occurs when the insurer (or agent, if authorized to do so) indicates to the insured an intent to accept the application.

A common problem that occurs in insurance law is the effect of the insurer's delay in acting on the application. If the applicant suffers a loss after applying but before the insured formally accepts, who must bear the loss? As a general rule, the insurer's delay does not constitute acceptance. Some states, however, have held that an insurer's retention of the premium for an unreasonable time constitutes an acceptance. Others have allowed tort suits against insurers for negligent delay in acting on an

FIGURE 35-1   Creation of an Insurance Contract

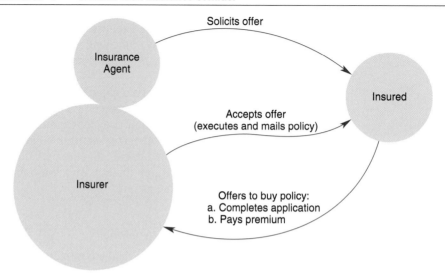

application. The theory of these cases is that insurance companies have a public duty to insure qualified applicants and that an unreasonable delay prevents applicants from obtaining insurance protection from some other source. A few states have also enacted statutes holding that insurers are bound to the insurance contract unless they have rejected the application within a specified period of time. (See Figure 35–1.)

INDEPENDENT FIRE INSURANCE COMPANY V. LEA
782 F. Supp. 1144 (E.D. La. 1992)

FACTS

Robert Lea, the owner of four apartment buildings, instructed Dick Guffey, an insurance agent, to secure fire insurance coverage for the properties. Using the standard insurance industry form, Guffey prepared an application and submitted it to Independent Fire Insurance Company. Yvonne Palmer, Independent's underwriter, mailed Guffey a written quote for a standard fire insurance policy on January 9, 1990. Her quotation letter clearly stated: "If you would like to have this policy issued, please forward written confirmation." After Guffey orally advised her that the premiums were too high, Palmer telephoned Guffey and provided a revised quotation. Guffey stated that he would discuss the amount of the premiums with Lea. There was no further contact between Palmer and Guffey until March 13, 1990, when

Guffey submitted a claim on behalf of Lea for fire damage to one of the apartments. When Independent claimed that no insurance policy existed, Lea brought suit against the insurer.

ISSUE

Was the property insured by Independent?

DECISION

No. Guffey's submission of the application constituted an offer that was not accepted by Independent. Rather, Palmer's written quotation constituted a new offer (counteroffer), which was rejected when Guffey orally requested a requote. When Palmer telephoned the new and lower quotation, she was issuing a new offer, which was never accepted by Lea. Because Guffey stated that he would have to confer with Lea, it was reasonable for

INDEPENDENT FIRE INSURANCE COMPANY V. LEA
(concluded)

Palmer to expect some sort of oral or written response unequivocally indicating acceptance. The facts are clear that Guffey never issued a binder and that Independent never billed Guffey or Lea. Guffey was acting as a broker for Lea, not as an agent for Independent. He had no authority to bind the insurance company.

Ethical Implications

Suppose that an insurance company places a 60-day waiting period in its policies in order to permit its underwriting department to determine whether the applicant is insurable. Would it be ethical for the company to delay coverage for the full 60 days in order to make sure that nothing happened to the applicant during that time even though the medical investigation is completed in much less time?

MISREPRESENTATION

Applicants for insurance have a duty to reveal fully to insurers all the material facts about the nature of the risk so that the insurer can make an intelligent decision about whether to accept the risk. Misrepresentation of material facts or failure to disclose such facts generally has the same effect in insurance cases that it does in other contracts cases; it makes the contract voidable at the election of the insurer. Thus, in the case that opened this chapter, Medico Life Insurance had the right to cancel Born's policy because of his fraudulent statements about his medical history. There are, however, two common provisions in life insurance policies that help to offset the potentially harsh effects that could otherwise result from strictly applying the general rule.

Misstatement of Age Clause

It is common for life insurance policies to contain a **misstatement of age clause.** Such clauses allow the insurer, in cases in which the insured has misstated his or her age, to adjust the benefits payable on the insured's death to reflect the amount of protection that the insured's premiums would have purchased for a person of the insured's true age. For example, Bob buys a $50,000 life insurance policy from Friendly Mutual Insurance and states his age as 35. When Bob dies, Friendly Mutual finds out that Bob was in fact 40 when he took out the policy. Since premium rates increase with the insured's age at the time the policy is taken out, Bob's premiums would have bought only $40,000 in coverage at the correct rate. Bob's estate is therefore entitled to only $40,000.

Incontestability Clause

Another common clause in life insurance policies is an **incontestability clause.** This clause bars the insurer from contesting its liability on the policy on the basis of the insured's misrepresentations if the policy has been in force for a specified period of time (often two years). Accordingly, in the chapter opener, the insurance company may have forfeited its right to cancel Born's policy if it had not discovered his misrepresentations within two years. Incontestability clauses, however, do not bar the insurer from objecting on the basis of absence of insurable interest or the purchase of the policy with the intent to murder the insured.

AMEX LIFE ASSURANCE COMPANY V. SUPERIOR COURT
930 P. 2d 1264 (Cal. Sup.Ct. 1997)

FACTS

Jose Morales applied for a life insurance policy from Amex in January 1991. Although he apparently knew he was HIV positive, Morales lied on the application form and denied having the AIDS virus. As a part of the application process, Amex required him to have a medical examination. In March 1991, a paramedic working for Amex met a man claiming to be Morales and took blood and urine samples. It is not disputed in this proceeding that this man was an imposter. On his application, Morales listed his height as five feet six inches and his weight as 142 pounds. The examiner stated that the man claiming to be Morales was five feet ten inches tall and weighed 172 pounds. The examiner also noted that the man produced no identification and appeared to be "unhealthy or older than stated age." The blood sample test was HIV negative. Amex issued Morales a life insurance policy containing a two-year incontestability clause effective May 1, 1991. All premiums were paid. Morales died of AIDS-related causes on June 11, 1993. Amex claims that after Morales died, an "informant" advised the insurer that an impostor, not Morales, appeared for the medical examination. The company conducted an investigation and then denied the claim for the policy proceeds. The letter denying the claim noted the discrepancies between the stated height and weight of the applicant and the person who appeared for the medical examination. It stated that a handwriting expert determined that the person who signed the insurance application was not the person who signed the medical test form and medical questionnaire. Amex denied payment on the basis that "when Mr. Morales applied for life insurance on his own life, but substituted another individual for himself in the examination so that the policy would be issued on the other person's medical condition, he caused Amex to issue a policy on the life of someone other than himself." The beneficiary of the policy argued that any fraud perpetrated by Morales was not excused by the policy's incontestability clause. In response, Amex urged the court to recognize an impostor defense to the incontestability clause.

ISSUE

Does the incontestability clause make the insurer liable on the policy?

DECISION

Yes. Incontestability clauses have been used by the insurance industry for more than 100 years to encourage persons to purchase life insurance. Insurance companies initially offered the incontestability clause as a policy provision because of public distrust of insurers and their promises to pay benefits in the future. Today, these clauses are required by statute in most states because without them, insurers were apt to deny benefits on the grounds of a pre-existing condition years after a policy had been issued. This left beneficiaries, particularly those in life insurance settings, in the untenable position of having to do battle with powerful insurance carriers. The clauses are designed to require the insurer to investigate and act with reasonable promptness if it wishes to deny liability on the ground of false representation or warranty by the insured. It prevents an insurer from lulling the insured, by inaction, into fancied security during the time when the facts could best be ascertained and proved, only to litigate them belatedly, possibly after the death of the insured. A few decisions have allowed an insurer to contest a claim despite the incontestability clause when an impostor claimed to be the named insured. However, those cases involved a person impersonating the named insured both in the application and the examination. The basic rationale of those cases is that when a person applies for the insurance and takes the medical examination but uses the name of someone else who then dies, no contract ever existed insuring the life of the person who has died and whose name is stated in the insurance policy.

In this case, however, there was a meeting of the minds on the identity of the person with whom Amex was dealing. Morales, the named insured, personally applied for the insurance. Amex insured his life, not someone else's. Amex did not know that an impostor appeared for the medical examination and, we may assume, would not have insured Morales's life had it known the true facts. But the fraud is similar to other frauds that the incontestability clause clearly covers. If, for example, an applicant falsely claims on the application to be healthy and then appears for the medical examination but somehow substitutes a healthy blood

(continued)

AMEX LIFE ASSURANCE COMPANY V. SUPERIOR COURT
(concluded)

sample for the tainted one, the fraud would be similar in effect to that here, but there could be no question whose life was being insured. Once Morales actually applied, his use of an impostor for the blood and urine tests did not alter the fact that he and Amex both intended to deal with each other. Instead, his misconduct was grounds for an affirmative defense based on fraud but did not preclude the existence of mutual assent, which was necessary to invoke the impostor defense. Rejecting the impostor defense under these facts furthers the policy behind incontestability clauses. When the named insured applies for the policy and the premiums are faithfully paid for over two years, the beneficiaries should be assured they will receive the expected benefits, not a lawsuit, upon the insured's death. The incontestability clause requires the insurer to investigate fraud before it issues the policy or within two years afterwards. The insurer may not accept the premiums for two years and investigate a possible defense only after the beneficiaries file a claim. Here, with minimal effort, Amex could have

discovered the fraud at the outset, as it did finally from information available before it issued the policy. To accept Amex's arguments might lead to no end of mischief as insurance companies who have taken no steps to verify the identity of their applicants or medical examinees then comb their files after the incontestability period expires, looking for some basis to contend that someone other than the named insured took part in the application or examination process.

Both the courts and the legislature have recognized the occasional inequity which the incontestability clause may allow. The inequity here is no different. While Morales's fraud was abhorrent, he did nothing more than adopt another means of supplying false information to further his own application. Amex was deceived by this but always intended to contract with Morales. We conclude that, after the incontestability period has expired, an insurer may not assert the defense that an impostor took the medical examination if, as here, the named insured personally applied for insurance.

WARRANTIES

It is important to distinguish between warranties and representations that the insured makes to induce an insurer to enter an insurance contract. Warranties are express terms in an insurance policy that are intended to operate as conditions on which insurer liability is based. Breach of such a condition by the insured terminates the insurer's duty to perform under the policy. Traditionally, this has been true whether or not the breach was material to the insurer's risk. Thus, a fire insurance policy requiring that the property owner maintain a working sprinkler system might be voided if such a system was never installed. In view of the potential harshness of this rule, some states have passed statutes providing that all statements made by applicants for life insurance are to be treated as representations, not as warranties. Also, some courts have refused to allow insurers to escape liability on the ground of breach of warranty unless such breach was material.

CAPACITY

Generally speaking, both parties to a contract must have the capacity to contract for the agreement to be enforceable. Therefore, an insurance policy taken out by a minor would be voidable at the election of the minor. Many states, however, have made the insurance contracts of minors enforceable against them by statute. Note that an insurance contract taken out on the life of a minor (the insured) by an adult (the owner) is not voidable. It is only when the minor is the owner of the policy that this rule of capacity comes into effect.

FORM AND CONTENT

Most states require that life insurance contracts be in writing. Property insurance contracts may not be required to be in writing but wisdom dictates that the parties reduce their agreement to written form.

The insurance business is highly regulated. This is due partly to the importance of the interests protected by insurance and partly to the states' recognition of the difference in bargaining power that often exists between insurers and their insureds. Many states, in an attempt to remedy this imbalance, require the inclusion of certain standard clauses in insurance policies. Some states also regulate things such as the size and style of the print used in insurance policies.

INTERPRETING INSURANCE CONTRACTS

Modern courts realize that many people who buy insurance do not have the training to fully understand the technical language contained in many policies. As a result, such courts interpret provisions in insurance contracts as they would be understood by an average person. Any ambiguities in insurance contracts are generally interpreted against the insurer that drafted the contract.

THIRD PARTIES AND INSURANCE CONTRACTS

As a general rule, contracts are assignable only when the assignment will not materially alter the promisor's burden of performance. Applying this rule to life insurance policies leads to the conclusion that a life insurance contract should be assignable because assignment will not increase the risk of the insurer since the identity of the insured will remain unchanged. If, however, the named beneficiary of the policy has been irrevocably designated because no right to change beneficiaries has been reserved in the policy, the policy may not be assigned without the beneficiary's consent. It is also common for the policy's terms to limit assignability. Many policies require notice to the insurer of any assignment. Failure to comply with such requirements renders an attempted assignment void.

An important element of the risk in property insurance policies is the character of the insured. Therefore, such policies are generally nonassignable. Those who purchase property from the insured get no interest in any policy the insured owned covering the purchased property. After a loss has occurred, however, the insured can assign the right to receive benefits under the policy, since no change in the insurer's risk is involved.

. . . . *INSURABLE INTEREST* . . . .

In order for an insurance contract not to be considered an illegal wagering contract, the person who purchases the policy (the owner) must have an **insurable interest** in the life or property being insured. A person who will suffer a financial loss from the destruction of the insured property or the death of the insured person has the required insurable interest. If no insurable interest is present, the policy is void.

INSURABLE INTEREST IN LIFE INSURANCE

In life insurance contracts, the required insurable interest must exist *at the time* the policy was issued. It need not exist at the time of the insured's death. Those who have a legitimate interest in the continuation of the insured's life have the required insurable interest.

In addition to the insured, the insured's spouse, parents, children, and any other persons who are dependents of the insured have an insurable interest in the insured's life. The insured's business associates, such as partners, employer, and fellow shareholders in a closely held corporation, may also have the required insurable interest. Likewise, the insured's creditors have an insurable interest to the extent of the debt owed them by the insured.

INSURABLE INTEREST IN PROPERTY INSURANCE

Those who have an insurable interest in property must have that interest *at the time the loss occurs.* This means that, in addition to the legal owner of the insured property, any other person who has an interest in the insured property when the loss occurs has the required insurable interest. So life tenants, lessees, secured creditors (mortgagees or lienholders), and those holding future interests in the insured property all have the required insurable interest.

The extent of a person's insurable interest in property is limited to the value of his or her interest in the property. For example, Fidelity Savings & Loan extended Marcia a $65,000 loan on her home and retained a mortgage interest in the house as security. In order to protect this investment, it obtained a $65,000 insurance policy on the property. Several years later, the house was completely destroyed by fire. At the time of the fire, the balance due on the loan was $43,000. Accordingly, $43,000 is all that Fidelity can recover under the insurance policy. That amount is the full extent of its insurable interest.

ALBERICI V. SAFEGUARD MUTUAL INSURANCE COMPANY
664 A.2d 110 (Sup. Ct. Penn. 1995)

FACTS

Joseph Alberici entered into an agreement to purchase a theatre property for a price of $210,000. The named purchaser on the purchase agreement was "Joseph Alberici or his nominee." A down payment of $21,000 was made by withdrawing funds from a savings account owned jointly by Joseph and his wife, Theresa. After signing the agreement to purchase the theatre, Alberici purchased property insurance on the property in the name of himself and Theresa. Prior to the closing of the sale, the theatre was seriously damaged by fire. Because Joseph was suspected of arson in connection with the fire and ultimately was convicted of submitting false fire loss claims, his insurance claims were denied. Theresa's insurance claims also were denied because the insurer argued she did not have an insurable interest in the property.

ISSUE

Did Theresa have an insurable interest in the property?

DECISION

Yes. Before Theresa could recover on the policy in which she had been named as an insured, it must be shown that she possessed an insurable interest in the property. A policy that insures against loss by fire is a contract of indemnity which protects the insured's interest in the property, not the property itself. One who derives monetary benefit or advantage from the preservation or continued existence of property, or who will suffer monetary loss from its destruction, has an insurable interest in the property. Upon execution of an agreement of sale, a purchaser of real estate has an equitable title to the property and may insure her interest therein. A purchaser's insurable interest is in the entire property, not merely the extent to which she has made payments toward the purchase price. Although the purchase agreement for the theatre property did not specifically identify Theresa as a purchaser, it designated the buyer as "Joseph Alberici

(continued)

ALBERICI V. SAFEGUARD MUTUAL INSURANCE COMPANY
(concluded)

or his nominee." Joseph and Theresa had always purchased property together in the past. Further, she accompanied Joseph to inspect the property prior to purchase and the monies to pay for the property had been taken from marital assets. Because Theresa was a purchaser of the property, she had an insurable interest therein. Her interest was in the value of the entire property, not merely her contribution toward the down payment.

NOTICE AND PROOF OF LOSS

A person who seeks to recover benefits under an insurance policy must notify the insurer that a loss covered by the policy has occurred and must furnish proof of loss. In life insurance contracts, the beneficiary is usually required to complete and return a proof-of-death form and may be required to furnish a certified copy of the insured's death certificate. Property insurance policies ordinarily require the insured to furnish a sworn statement of loss.

TIME LIMITS

It is common for insurance policies to specify that notice and proof of loss must be given within a specified time. The policy may state that compliance with these requirements is a condition of the insured's recovery and that failure to comply terminates the insurer's obligation. Some policies, however, merely provide that failure to comply suspends the insurer's duty to pay until proper compliance is made. Some courts require the insurer to prove it has been injured by the insured's failure to give notice before they allow the insurer to avoid liability on the ground of tardy notice.

CONCEPT SUMMARY	Insurable Interest

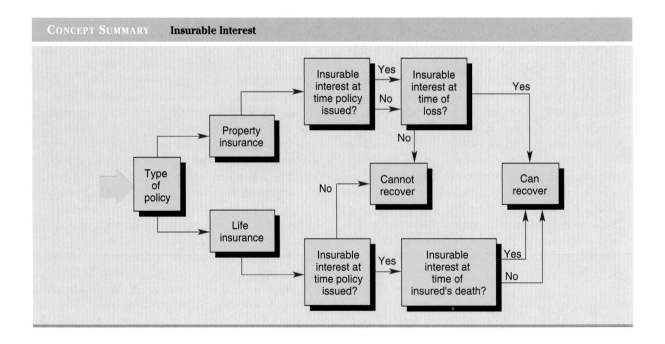

RIGHT OF SUBROGATION

The insurer may be able to exercise a right of **subrogation** if it is required to pay for the loss of property under an insurance contract. Under the right of subrogation, the insurer obtains all of the insured's rights to pursue legal remedies against anyone who may have negligently or intentionally damaged the property. For example, Ellen purchased a fire insurance policy on her home from Countywide Insurance Company. The house was completely destroyed in a fire that was caused when David threw a firecracker in the garage while Ellen was away at work. After Countywide pays Ellen the face amount of her policy, it may sue David for that amount under its right of subrogation.

A general release of the third party from liability by the insured will release the insurer from liability to the insured. Thus, in the previous example, suppose that David persuaded Ellen to sign an agreement releasing him from any liability for the fire. Because this interferes with Countywide's right of subrogation, Countywide may not have to pay Ellen for the loss. A partial release between David and Ellen will relieve Countywide of liability to Ellen to the extent of her release. (The right of subrogation is not available in life insurance contracts.)

CANCELLATION AND LAPSE

Cancellation of an insurance policy occurs when a party that has the power to terminate the policy (extinguish all rights under the policy) has exercised that power. *Lapse* occurs when the policy is permitted to expire by failure to renew it after its term has run or by some default on the part of the insured.

CANCELLATION

Ordinarily, the insurer cannot cancel a life insurance contract. Allowing insurers to do so would be unfair to insureds since insurers would be tempted to terminate old or seriously ill insureds to avoid paying benefits. The insured can cancel a life insurance policy by surrendering the policy to the insurer. The insured who surrenders a whole life policy is generally allowed under the policy provisions to recover the accumulated cash surrender value of the policy or to purchase a paid-up or extended insurance policy. A paid-up policy provides the insured with a fully paid policy in the amount that his or her cash surrender value will purchase at his or her age. An extended policy is a term policy with the same face value as the insured's original policy; the length of the term is determined by the cash surrender value of the original policy. Generally, either party may cancel a property insurance contract after giving notice to the other party. The amount and form of the notice required may be specified in the policy or regulated by state statute. Insurers that cancel must return the unearned portion of any premiums paid by the insured. Insureds who terminate are entitled to a return of the premium on a short-rate basis, which means that the insurer may compute the premiums owed for the time the policy was in effect at a slightly higher rate than the rate that would apply to the full term of the policy.

Property insurance policies frequently contain clauses that terminate the insurer's liability if the insured does anything that materially increases the insurer's risk. They may also specifically list certain kinds of behavior that will cause termination. Common examples of such behavior are keeping flammable or explosive material and allowing the premises to remain vacant for a stated period of time.

LAPSE

Insurance policies that are written for a stated period of time lapse at the expiration of the policy term. The insured's failure to pay premiums also causes a policy to lapse. The insured who allows a whole life insurance policy to lapse generally has the same rights to cash surrender value, paid-up, or extended term insurance as the insured who surrenders a policy.

Many states have passed statutes that give the insured who fails to pay a life insurance premium a grace period, usually 30 or 31 days after the date the premium was due, to pay the overdue premium and prevent policy lapse. In addition, some life insurance contracts contain a reinstatement clause that allows an insured to reinstate a lapsed policy that has not been surrendered for its cash surrender value by requesting reinstatement within a specified period after default. To secure reinstatement, the insured must pay all past-due premiums and a stated amount of interest and furnish proof of insurability (good health).

.... *QUESTIONS AND PROBLEM CASES* ....

1. Tracy Stevens hired Betty White to babysit her two daughters at Betty's home. In early 1989, Michael White, Betty's husband, sexually molested one of the children while she was in Betty's care. He was subsequently convicted of child molesting. On October 18, 1989, Tracy filed suit against Michael for unlawful touching and battery. Three months later, she amended her complaint to add Betty as a defendant, alleging that Betty was negligent in caring for her daughter. Frankenmuth Mutual Insurance Company had sold a homeowners' liability insurance policy to Michael and Betty, which was in effect at the time the molestation occurred. The first notice Frankenmuth received that Michael and Betty had been sued came in October 1990 when the company received a subpoena requiring it to produce documents for the trial. The subpoena did not specify the nature of the lawsuit. One month later, Frankenmuth sent a letter to the White's attorney stating that Michael's intentional acts were outside the scope of the policy. On April 29, 1991, Betty and Tracy settled the claim against Betty for $75,000. Tracy then attempted to collect the $75,000 from Frankenmuth. The insurance company claimed it had no duty to defend or to pay because it did not receive adequate notice of the lawsuit. Did Frankenmuth receive adequate notice of the lawsuit?

2. A severe storm struck Cheyenne, Wyoming, causing considerable damage as a result of hail and heavy rain. The hail broke sections of the basement windows at Paulson's house. The rain also caused excessive flooding in a drainage area within several blocks of the house, and the overflow from this area entered Paulson's basement through the broken windows. The high water line was several inches above the basement and most of the water damage could be attributed to water that entered through the broken windows. State Farm refused to pay for the damage to Paulson's basement, citing an exclusion in the policy that expressly stated that losses attributable to water damages ("flood, surface water, waves, tidal water, and overflow of a body of water") are not insured. Paulson contended that his loss was caused by "rain"—which was not listed under the contract definition of "water damages"—and therefore coverage existed. Are Paulson's damages covered by his insurance policy?

3. Anthony Howell was diagnosed as suffering from chronic granulocytic leukemia and told that, barring a successful bone marrow transplant, he had only a short time to live. Several months later, Howell and his ex-wife, Katherine Nyonteh, applied to Peoples Security Life Insurance for an insurance policy on Howell's life. In answering the health insurance questions on the application, both of them fraudulently concealed Howell's terminal leukemic condition. As a result, the policy was issued in Howell's name. (Ownership was later transferred to Nyonteh.) The policy contained

an incontestability clause which became effective after two years. After the policy had been in effect for more than two years, Nyonteh was late in paying her insurance premiums and the policy lapsed. She later applied for reinstatement. In the reinstatement application, both Nyonteh and Howell again concealed Howell's medical condition. The reinstatement contract also contained a two-year incontestability period. Before this incontestability period had run, Howell died. Is Nyonteh entitled to life insurance benefits?

4. League Life Insurance Company issued a life insurance policy on Barney. Premiums were paid through automatic withdrawal from Barney's credit union account on a quarterly basis. On two previous occasions, Barney did not have sufficient funds on deposit to cover the premium. When that occurred, League sent a notice to Barney and he deposited the sufficient funds. On neither of these occasions was the policy cancelled; instead, a double payment was made on the next quarterly date. In fact, the insurance company's notice indicates to its insureds that they must have sufficient funds on the next quarterly date so that a double payment can be made. Barney died on May 18, 1981, and his wife filed a life insurance claim. League denied the claim, asserting that the policy was canceled on March 1, 1981. According to League, Barney's December 1, 1980, premium was not paid, and it terminated the policy pursuant to its policy, which states that the insurance coverage terminates 92 days after the due date of any premium if payment was not remitted by the credit union. Mrs. Barney, arguing that she never received a notice that the December payment was due and unpaid, sued the insurance company. Should the claim be denied because the insurance company had no duty to inform the insured of the delinquent payment?

5. Louise Locke's husband applied for a life insurance policy with Prudence Mutual and sent a check for the first year's premium. Five days after applying for the policy, Mr. Locke became ill and was admitted to the hospital. He died two months later. Seventeen days after his death, Prudence Mutual refunded the premium. The application contained a clause that read:

"No obligation is incurred by the Company unless said application is approved by the Company at its Home Office and a contract is issued and delivered during the lifetime and good health of the applicant." Mrs. Locke, as administrator of her husband's estate, filed suit against Prudence Mutual for negligent delay in failing to act on her husband's application. Was Prudence Mutual negligent is failing to act on Mr. Locke's application?

6. Property Owners Insurance (POI) was the insurer and Thomas Cope was the insured under a business liability insurance contract for Cope's roofing business. The policy excluded coverage except in instances of liability "with respect to the conduct of the business" owned by Cope. While the policy was in force, Cope traveled to Montana with Urbanski, a person with whom Cope did significant business. While on this trip, Cope snowmobiled with a group of persons that included Gregory Johnson, who died in a snowmobiling accident. When Johnson's estate brought a wrongful death suit against Cope, POI argued that it had no obligations under the business liability insurance contract because the accident did not occur with respect to Cope's business. Should the court give POI a summary judgment because, as a matter of law, the insurance company has no liability for this claim?

7. On November 29, 1980, Billy Wayne Gillilan went to the office of Wanda Thrift, an agent of Federated Guaranty Life Insurance Company, and applied for a $40,000 policy of ordinary life insurance. The application specifically made coverage conditional on a determination by the insurer's underwriting department after an investigation that the applicant was insurable. It further stated that if the application was not accepted and approved within 60 days, no contract would be issued. On December 31, 1980, Gillilan died, and on January 9, 1981, Federated refunded his premium to his estate, rejecting his application for insurance. Gillilan's wife sued Federated, claiming that the insurer's delay in rejecting the application was unreasonable and should therefore be treated as an acceptance. Is Federated liable on the insurance policy?

8. Wheeler's church was damaged by smoke and soot when two gas heating units in the church

overheated, causing flames to leap out of the top of the units. The church's insurer refused to pay for the damage, claiming that the fire that caused it was a "friendly" one not covered by the church's fire insurance policy. Is the church entitled to payment?

9. In 1972, Betty DeWitt and her husband, Joseph, bought a house, taking title in Betty's name. On March 5, 1979, the DeWitts were divorced. As a part of the divorce settlement, Joseph was given possession of the house and Betty was ordered to sign the deed over to him. On January 29, 1980, Joseph DeWitt died. Soon thereafter, Betty moved into the house and purchased a fire insurance policy from American Family Mutual Insurance Company with a face value of $38,500. In August of 1980, the house was completely destroyed by fire. At this time, American Family learned of her divorce and the decree ordering her to convey title to Joseph. It refused to pay on the policy, arguing that she did not have an insurable interest. Betty argued that she has an insurable interest because (1) she never actually conveyed the title to Joseph and (2) she was still liable as a signer on the mortgage loan used to finance the original purchase of the house. Did Betty have an insurable interest in the house?

10. Pursuant to their partnership agreement, the law partners of the Poletti Freidin firm purchased two life insurance policies on the life of Herbert Prashker, naming the partners as beneficiaries. The policies were secured because Prashker was the most significant member of the firm in terms of his capital account and generation of business. When Prashker was struck by cancer and could no longer effectively work, the partners agreed to terminate the partnership business. Five months after the firm ceased doing business, Prashker died. His daughter claimed the $1,350,000 in life insurance proceeds, contending that the insurable interest of the former partners ended when the partnership was terminated. May the former partners recover the insurance proceeds?

PART VII

Commercial Paper

CHAPTER 36

Negotiable Instruments

Chances are that you are using a variety of negotiable instruments in your everyday life, perhaps without realizing the special qualities that have led to their widespread use in commerce and the rules that govern them. If you have a job, your employer probably pays you by check, and you likely have a checking account that you use to make purchases and pay your bills. If you have accumulated some savings, you may have invested them in a certificate of deposit at a bank. And, if you have borrowed money, you very likely were asked to sign a promissory note acknowledging the debt and committing to repay it on specified terms.

In this chapter, you will learn about:

- *The special qualities and benefits of negotiable instruments.*
- *The basic types of commercial paper.*
- *The formal requirements that must be met for instruments, such as checks, notes, and certificates of deposit, to qualify as negotiable instruments.*
- *What happens when you receive a check in which there is a conflict between the amount set forth in figures and the one written out in words.*

.... *INTRODUCTION* ....

As commerce and trade developed, people moved beyond exclusive reliance on barter to the use of money and then to the use of substitutes for money. The term **commercial paper** encompasses such substitutes in common use today as checks, promissory notes, and certificates of deposit.

History discloses that every civilization that engaged to an appreciable extent in commerce used some form of commercial paper. Probably the oldest commercial paper used in the carrying on of trade is the promissory note. Archaeologists found a promissory note made payable to bearer that dated from about 2100 BC. The merchants of Europe used commercial paper, which under the law merchant was negotiable in the 13th and 14th centuries. Commercial paper does not appear to have been used in England until about 1600 AD.

This chapter and the three following chapters outline and discuss the body of law that governs commercial paper. Of particular interest are those kinds of commercial paper having the attribute of *negotiability*—that is, they generally can be transferred from party to party and accepted as a substitute for money. This chapter discusses the nature and benefits of negotiable instruments and then outlines the requirements an instrument must meet to qualify as a negotiable instrument. Subsequent chapters discuss transfer and negotiation of instruments, the rights and liabilities of parties to negotiable instruments, and the special rules applicable to checks.

.... *NATURE OF NEGOTIABLE INSTRUMENTS* ....

When a person buys a television set and gives the merchant a check drawn on his checking account, that person uses a form of negotiable commercial paper. Similarly, a person who goes to a bank or a credit union to borrow money might sign a promissory note agreeing to pay the money back in 90 days. Again, the bank and borrower use a form of negotiable commercial paper.

Commercial paper is basically a *contract for the payment of money.* It may serve as a substitute for money payable immediately, such as a check, or it can be used as a means of extending credit. When a television set is bought by giving the merchant a check, the check is a substitute for money. If a credit union loans a borrower money now in exchange for the borrower's promise to repay it later, the promissory note signed by the borrower is a means of extending credit.

UNIFORM COMMERCIAL CODE

The law of commercial paper is covered in Article 3 (Negotiable Instruments) and Article 4 (Bank Deposits and Collections) of the Uniform Commercial Code. Other negotiable documents, such as investment securities and documents of title, are treated in other articles of the Code. The original Code Articles 3 and 4, adopted initially in the 1960s, generally followed the basic, centuries-old rules governing the use of commercial paper, but at the same time they adopted modern terminology and coordinated, clarified, and simplified the law. However, business practices continued to evolve, and new technological developments have changed the way that banks process checks. Accordingly, in 1990, a joint effort by the American Law Institute and the National Conference of Commissioners on Uniform State Laws produced a Revised Article 3 and related amendments to Articles 1 and 4. The purpose was to clarify Articles 3 and 4, to bring them into better harmony with current business practice, and to acknowledge recent technological developments.

Because virtually all of the states have adopted the 1990 revision to Article 3 and the related amendments to Article 4, we use them as the basis for this edition of the textbook. The reader should ascertain whether the state in which she lives has adopted the revised article/amendments and should keep in mind that instruments may be interpreted under the version of the Code that was in effect when the instruments were issued. Moreover, for the period between the first adoption of the revised article/amendments by a state (Arkansas) and the adoption by the last state or the District of Columbia, the "uniform law" concerning negotiable instruments will be anything but uniform.

For the student of negotiable instruments law this is an interesting—but also a particularly difficult—time to study this area of the law. Revised Article 3 and the related amendments introduce new concepts, change definitions and the wording of key elements, and delete numerous provisions from the original version of Article 3. As a result, in drafting this chapter and the three chapters that follow, the authors have relied heavily on tracking the language of the revised article and on statements by the drafters as to their intent. Further complicating the picture is the fact that in a number of respects the revision is more complex than the original version. Moreover, while more than 30 years of case law had helped flesh out the meaning of the original Article 3, the revision has diminished some of the value of that case law. Virtually all of the cases to date arose under the original version of Article 3 and are of mixed—and sometimes very limited—value in trying to assess how courts will decide issues under the revision.

Just as these factors posed a challenge to the authors of this edition of the textbook, they will pose a challenge to you and your instructor as you work your way through the material on negotiable instruments. More questions are likely to be left up in the air than is true in other, more settled areas of the law. It will take a number of years, considerable experience, and new case law to flesh out the updated law of negotiable instruments.

NEGOTIABLE INSTRUMENTS

The two basic types of negotiable instruments are *promises to pay money* and *orders to pay money.* Promissory notes and certificates of deposit issued by banks are promises to pay someone money. Checks and drafts are orders to another person to pay money to a third person. A check, which is a type of draft, is an order directed to a certain kind of person, namely a bank, to pay money from a person's account to a third person.

NEGOTIABILITY

Negotiable instruments are a special kind of commercial paper that can pass readily through our financial system and is accepted in place of money. This gives negotiable instruments many advantages.

For example, Searle, the owner of a clothing store in New York, contracts with Amado, a swimsuit manufacturer in Los Angeles, for $10,000 worth of swimsuits. If negotiable instruments did not exist, Searle would have to send or carry $10,000 across the country, which would be both inconvenient and risky. If someone stole the money along the way, Searle would lose the $10,000 unless he could locate the thief. By using a check in which Searle orders his bank to pay $10,000 from his account to Amado, or to someone designated by Amado, Searle makes the payment in a far more convenient manner. He sends only a single piece of paper to Amado. If the check is properly prepared and sent, sending the check is less risky than sending money. Even if someone steals the check along the way, Searle's bank may not pay it to anyone but Amado or someone authorized by Amado. And because the check gives Amado the right either to collect the $10,000 or to transfer the right to collect it to someone else, the check is a practical substitute for cash to Amado as well as Searle.

In this chapter and in the three following chapters, we discuss the requirements necessary for a contract for the payment of money to qualify as a negotiable instrument. We also explain the features that distinguish a negotiable instrument from a simple contract and that led to the widespread use of negotiable instruments as a substitute for money.

KINDS OF NEGOTIABLE INSTRUMENTS

PROMISSORY NOTES

The promissory note is the simplest form of commercial paper; it is simply a promise to pay money. A **promissory note** is a two-party instrument in which one person (known as the **maker**) makes an unconditional promise in writing to pay another person (the **payee**), a person specified by that person, or the bearer of the instrument a fixed amount of money, with or without interest, either on demand or at a specified, future time (3–104).[1]

The promissory note, shown in Figures 36–1 and 36–2, is a credit instrument; it is used in a wide variety of transactions in which credit is extended. For example, if a person purchases an automobile using money borrowed from a bank, the bank has the person sign a promissory note for the unpaid balance of the purchase price. Similarly, if a person borrows money to purchase a house, the lender who makes the loan and takes a mortgage on the house has the person sign a promissory note for the amount due on the loan. The note probably states that it is secured by a mortgage. The terms of payment on the note should correspond with the terms of the sales contract for the purchase of the house.

FIGURE 36–1   A Promissory Note

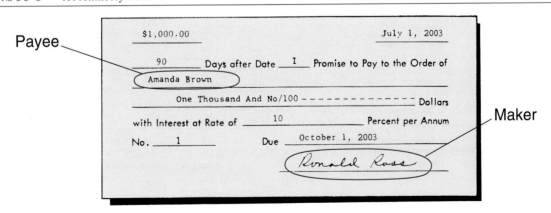

---

[1]The numbers in parentheses refer to the sections of the 1990 Revised Article 3 (and the conforming amendments to Articles 1 and 4) of the Uniform Commercial Code.

FIGURE 36–2   A Promissory Note (Consumer Loan Note)

The National
BANK OF
WASHINGTON

CONSUMER LOAN NOTE

Date_November 21,_____, 20_03_____

The words I and me mean all borrowers who signed this note. The word bank means The National Bank of Washington.

Promise to Pay

30_____ ~~months from today, I promise~~ to pay to ~~the order of~~ The National Bank of Washington
Seventy-Eight Hundred Seventy Five and no/100 ------------------ dollars ($ 7,875.00).

Payee → (pointing to "The National Bank of Washington")

Responsibility

Although this note may be signed below by more than one person. I understand that we are each as individuals responsible for paying back the full amount.

Breakdown of Loan

This is what I will pay:

Amount of loan	1.$	6,800.00
Credit Life Insurance (optional)	2.$	100.00
Other (describe)		
	3.$	-0-
Amount Financed (Add 1 and 2 and 3)	4.$	6,900
FINANCE CHARGE	5.$	975.00
Total of Payments (Add 4 and 5)	$	7,875.00
ANNUAL PERCENTAGE RATE	10.5	%

Repayment

This is how I will repay:
I will repay the amount of this note in __30__ equal uninterrupted monthly installments of $ 262.50 each on the _1st_ day of each month starting on the _1st_ day of _December_, 20_03_ and ending on ___May 1,_____, 20_07_.

Prepayment

I have the right to prepay the whole outstanding amount of this note at any time. If I do, or if this loan is refinanced—that is, replaced by a new note—you will refund the unearned finance charge, figured by the rule of 78—a commonly used formula for figuring rebates on installment loans.

Late Charge

Any installment not paid within ten days of its due date shall be subject to a late charge of 5% of the payment, not to exceed $5.00 for any such late installment.

Security

To protect The National Bank of Washington, I give what is known as a security interest in my auto and/or other: (Describe) _Ford Thunderbird_

_____ # Serial #115117-12-11974 .

See the security agreement.

Credit Life Insurance

Credit life insurance is not required to obtain this loan. The bank need not provide it and I do not need to buy it unless I sign immediately below. The cost of credit life insurance is $ 100.00 for the term of the loan.

Signed: _A. J. Smith_

Date: _November 21, 2003_

Default

If for any reason I fail to make any payment on time. I shall be in default. The bank can then demand immediate payment of the entire remaining unpaid balance of this loan, without giving anyone further notice. If I have not paid the full amount of the loan when the final payment is due, the bank will charge me interest on the unpaid balance at six percent (6%) per year.

Right of Offset

If this loan becomes past due, the bank will have the right to pay this loan from any deposit or security I have at this bank without telling me ahead of time. Even if the bank gives me an extension of time to pay this loan, I still must repay the entire loan.

Collection Fees

If this note is placed with an attorney for collection, then I agree to pay an attorney's fee of fifteen percent (15%) of the unpaid balance. This fee will be added to the unpaid balance of the loan.

Co-borrowers

If I am signing this note as a co-borrower. I agree to be equally responsible with the borrower for this loan. The bank does not have to notify me that this note has not been paid. The bank can change the terms of payment and release any security without notifying or releasing me from responsibility for this loan.

Copy Received

I received a completely filled in copy of this note. If I have signed for Credit Life Insurance. I received a copy of the Credit Life Insurance certificate.

Borrower: _A. J. Smith_ ← **Maker**
A. J. Smith
3412 Brookdale, S. W. Washington D.C.
Address

Co-borrower: _Andrea H. Smith_ ← **Co-Maker**
Andrea H. Smith
3412 Brookdale, S. W., Washington D. C.
Address

Co-borrower:_____
Address

CONSUMER CREDIT HOTLINE: If you have any questions, please call us immediately at (202) 624-3450.

1-Bank's copy   2-File copy   3-Customer's copy

CERTIFICATES OF DEPOSIT

The certificate of deposit given by a bank or a savings and loan association when a deposit of money is made is a type of note, namely a note of a bank. A **certificate of**

FIGURE 36–3   A Certificate of Deposit

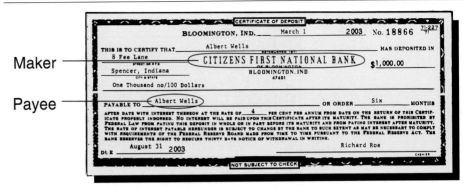

Maker

Payee

deposit is an instrument containing (1) an acknowledgment by a bank that it has received a deposit of money, and (2) a promise by the bank to repay the sum of money (3–104[j]). Figure 36–3 is an example of a certificate of deposit.

Many banks no longer issue certificates of deposit (CDs) in paper form. Rather, the bank maintains an electronic deposit and provides the customer with a statement indicating the amount of principal held on a CD basis and the terms of the CD, such as the maturity and interest rate. In these instances, the certificate of deposit is not in negotiable instrument form.

DRAFTS

A **draft** is a form of commercial paper that involves an *order* to pay money rather than a promise to pay money (3–104[e]). The most common example of a draft is a check. A draft has three parties to it: one person (known as the **drawer**) orders a second person (the **drawee**) to pay a certain sum of money to a third person (the **payee**), to a person specified by that person, or to bearer.

Drafts other than checks are used in a variety of commercial transactions. If Brown owes Ames money, Ames may draw a draft for the amount of the debt, naming Brown as drawee and herself or her bank as payee, and send the draft to Brown's bank for payment. Alternatively, Ames might send a draft providing for payment on a certain day in the future to Brown for "acceptance." Brown could "accept" the draft by signing his name to it, thereby obligating himself to pay the amount specified in the draft on that day in the future to Ames or to someone specified by Ames.

In freight shipments in which the terms are "cash on delivery," the seller commonly ships the goods to the buyer on an "order bill of lading" consigned to himself at the place of delivery. The seller then indorses the bill of lading and attaches a draft naming the buyer as drawee. He then sends the bill of lading and the draft through banking channels to the buyer's bank. A bank in the buyer's locale presents the draft to the buyer's bank for payment, and when the former bank receives payment, delivers the bill of lading to the buyer. Through this commercial transaction, the buyer gets the goods and the seller gets his money.

When credit is extended, the same procedure is followed, but the seller uses a time draft—a draft payable at some future time. (See Figure 36–4.) In such a transaction, the buyer "accepts" the draft (instead of paying it) and obligates herself to pay the amount of the draft when due. In these cases, the *drawee* (now called the **acceptor**) should date her signature so that the date at which payment is due is clear to all (3–409[c]).

FIGURE 36-4   A Draft

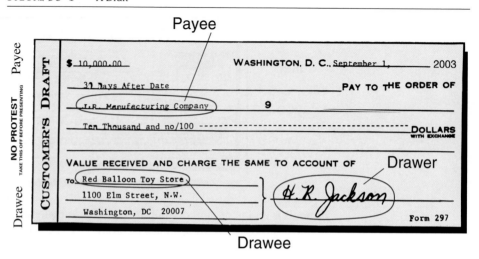

CHECKS

A **check** is a *draft payable on demand* and drawn on a bank (i.e., a bank is the drawee or person to whom the order to pay is addressed). Checks are the most widely used form of commercial paper. The issuer of a check orders the bank at which she maintains an account to pay a specified person, or someone designated by that person, a fixed amount of money from the account. For example, Elizabeth Brown has a checking account at the National Bank of Washington. She goes to Sears Roebuck & Co. and agrees to buy a washing machine priced at $459.95. If she writes a check to pay for it, she is the drawer of the check, the National Bank of Washington is the drawee, and Sears is the payee. By writing the check, Elizabeth is ordering her bank to pay $459.95 from her account to Sears or to Sear's order, that is, to whomever Sears asks the bank to pay the money. (See Figure 36–5.)

An instrument may qualify as a check and be governed by Article 3 even though it is described on its face by another term such as "money order." The Code definition of a check includes a "cashier's check" and a "teller's check." A **cashier's check** is a draft on which the drawer or drawee are the same bank (or branches of the same bank); a **teller's check** is a draft drawn by a bank (as drawer) on another bank or payable at or through a bank (3–104 [g] and [h]). For example, a check drawn by a credit union on its account at a federally insured bank would be a teller's check.

FIGURE 36-5   A Check

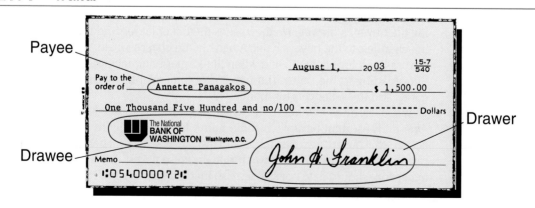

RIGHTS OF AN ASSIGNEE OF A CONTRACT

As we noted in Chapter 14, "Third Parties' Contract Rights," the assignee of a contract can obtain no greater rights than the assignor had at the time of the assignment. For example, Frank Farmer and Neam's Market enter into a contract providing that Farmer will sell Neam's a dozen crates of fresh eggs a week for a year and that Neam's will pay Farmer $14,000 at the end of the year. If at the end of the year Farmer assigns to Bill Sanders his rights under the contract—including the right to collect the money from Neam's—then Sanders has whatever rights Farmer had at that time. If Farmer has delivered all the eggs to Neam's as he promised, then Farmer would be entitled to $14,000, and Sanders would obtain that right from him. However, if Farmer has not delivered all the eggs that he had promised to deliver, or if the eggs he delivered were not fresh, Neam's might have a valid defense or reason to refuse to pay the full $14,000. In that case, Sanders would have only what rights Farmer had and also would be subject to the defense Neam's has against full payment.

Taking an assignment of a contract involves assuming certain risks. The assignee (Sanders) may not be aware of the nature and extent of any defenses that the party liable on the contract (Neam's) might have against the assignor (Farmer). An assignee who does not know what rights he is getting, or which risks he is assuming, may be reluctant to take an assignment of the contract.

RIGHTS OF A HOLDER OF A NEGOTIABLE INSTRUMENT

The object of a negotiable instrument is to have it accepted readily as a substitute for money. In order to accept it readily, a person must be able to take it free of many of the risks assumed by the assignee of a regular contract. Under the law of negotiable instruments, this is possible if two conditions are met: (1) the contract for the payment of money must meet the formal requirements to qualify as a negotiable instrument and (2) the person who acquires the instrument must qualify as a holder in due course. Basically, a *holder in due course* is a person who has good title to the instrument, paid value for it, acquired it in good faith, and had no notice of certain claims or defenses against payment. In addition, the instrument cannot bear facial irregularities (evidence of forgery or alteration or questions concerning its authenticity).

The next section of this chapter discusses the formal requirements for a negotiable instrument. Chapter 37, "Negotiation and Holder in Due Course," which follows, outlines the requirements that a person must meet to qualify as a holder in due course.

A holder in due course of a negotiable instrument takes the instrument free of all defenses and claims to the instrument except those that concern its validity. For example, a holder in due course of a note given in payment for goods may enforce the obligation in spite of the buyer's claim that the seller breached a warranty. However, if the maker of a note wrote it under duress, such as a threat of force, or was a minor, then even a holder in due course is subject to the defenses of duress or infancy to the extent other law (1) would nullify the obligation for duress or (2) would permit infancy as a defense to a simple contract. The person who holds the note could not obtain the payment from the maker but would have to recover from the person from whom he got the note.

The Federal Trade Commission (FTC) has adopted a regulation that alters the rights of a holder in due course in consumer purchase transactions. This regulation allows a consumer who gives a negotiable instrument to use additional defenses (breach of warranty or fraudulent inducement) against payment of the instrument against even a holder in due course. Similarly, some states have enacted the Uniform Consumer Credit Code (UCCC), which produces a similar result. Chapter 37 discusses the rights of a holder in due course, as well as the FTC rule.

FORMAL REQUIREMENTS FOR NEGOTIABILITY

BASIC REQUIREMENTS

An instrument such as a check or a note must meet certain formal requirements to be a negotiable instrument. If the instrument does not meet these requirements, it is non-negotiable; that is, it is treated as a simple contract, not as a negotiable instrument. A primary purpose for these formal requirements is to ensure the willingness of prospective purchasers of the instrument, particularly financial institutions such as banks, to accept it as a substitute for money.

For an instrument to be negotiable, it must:

1. Be in writing.
2. Be signed by the issuer (the "maker" in the case of a person undertaking to pay or the "drawer" in the case of a person giving an order or instruction to pay).
3. Contain an unconditional promise or order to pay a fixed amount of money, with or without interest or other charges described in the promise or order.
4. Be payable to order or to bearer at the time it is issued or first comes into possession of a holder.
5. Be payable on demand or at a definite time.
6. Not state any other undertaking or instruction by the person promising or ordering to do any act in addition to the payment of money; but it may contain (*a*) an undertaking or promise relative to collateral to secure payment, (*b*) an authorization for confession of judgment, or (*c*) a waiver of benefit of any law intended for the advantage or protection of an obligor (3–103; 3–104).

In addition, an instrument that otherwise qualifies as a check can be negotiable even if it is not explicitly payable to order or to bearer (3–104[c]). As explained later, this means that a check that reads "pay John Doe" could be negotiable even though the normal form for a check is "pay to the order of ____."

A promise or order other than a check is not a negotiable instrument if at the time it is issued or first comes into the possession of a holder it contains a conspicuous statement that the promise or order is not negotiable or is not an instrument governed by Article 3 (3–104[d]). For example, if a promissory note contained the legend "NONNEGOTIABLE," it would not qualify as a negotiable instrument even if it otherwise met the formal requirements for one.

IMPORTANCE OF FORM

Whether or not an instrument satisfies these formal requirements is important only for the purpose of determining whether an instrument is negotiable or non-negotiable. Negotiability should not be confused with validity or collectibility. If an instrument is negotiable, the law of negotiable instruments in the Code controls in determining the rights and liabilities of the parties to the instrument. If an instrument is nonnegotiable, the general rules of contract law control. The purpose of determining negotiability is to ascertain whether a possessor of the instrument can become a holder in due course.

An instrument that meets all of the formal requirements is a negotiable instrument even though it is void, voidable, unenforceable, or uncollectible for other reasons. Negotiability is a matter of form and nothing else. Suppose a person gives an instrument in payment of a gambling debt in a state that has a statute declaring that any instrument or promise given in payment of a gambling debt is void. The instrument is a negotiable instrument if it is negotiable in form even though it is absolutely void. Also, an instrument that is negotiable in form is a negotiable instrument even though it is issued by a minor. The instrument is voidable at the option of the minor if state law makes infancy a defense to a simple contract, but it is negotiable.

IN WRITING

To be negotiable, an instrument must be in writing. An instrument that is handwritten, typed, or printed is considered to be in writing (1–201[46]). The writing does not have to be on any particular material; all that is required is that the instrument be in writing. A person could create a negotiable instrument in pencil on a piece of wrapping paper. It would be poor business practice to do so, but the instrument would meet the statutory requirement that it be in writing.

SIGNED

To qualify as a negotiable instrument, an instrument in the form of a note must be signed by the person undertaking to pay (the maker) and an instrument in the form of a draft must be signed by the person giving the instruction to pay (the drawer) (3–103). An instrument has been signed if the maker or drawer has put a name or other symbol on it with the intention of validating it (3–401[b]). Normally, the maker or drawer signs an instrument by writing his name on it; however, this is not required. A person or company may authorize an agent to sign instruments for it. A typed or rubber-stamped signature is sufficient if it was put on the instrument to validate it. A person who cannot write her name might make an *X* and have it witnessed by someone else.

UNCONDITIONAL PROMISE OR ORDER

REQUIREMENT OF A PROMISE OR ORDER

If an instrument is promissory in nature, such as a note or a certificate of deposit, it must contain an unconditional promise to pay or it cannot be negotiable. Merely acknowledging a debt is not sufficient (3–103[9]). For example, the statement, "I owe you $100," does not constitute a promise to pay. An IOU in this form is not a negotiable instrument.

If an instrument is an order to pay, such as a check or a draft, it must contain an unconditional order. A simple request to pay as a favor is not sufficient; however, a politely phrased demand, such as "please pay," can meet the requirement. Checks commonly use the language, "Pay to the order of." This satisfies the requirement that the check contain an order to pay. The order is the word "pay," not the word "order." The word "order" has another function—that of making the instrument payable "to order or to bearer."

PROMISE OR ORDER MUST BE UNCONDITIONAL

An instrument is not negotiable unless the promise or order is unconditional. For example, a note that provides, "I promise to pay to the order of Karl Adams $1,000 if he replaces the roof on my garage," is not negotiable because it is payable on a condition.

In the case that follows, *Ford Motor Credit Co. v. All Ways, Inc.,* documents entitled "certified money orders" were held not to be negotiable because they did not contain an unconditional promise or order to pay.

FORD MOTOR CREDIT CO. v. ALL WAYS, INC.
546 N.W. 2d 807 (Neb. Sup. Ct. 1996)

FACTS

All Ways, Inc., and its president, Gary L. Ross, signed two retail installment contracts for the purchase of a Lincoln passenger car and a Ford truck from Seward County Ford Lincoln Mercury, Inc. The two contracts were secured by liens on the vehicles. Seward County Ford Lincoln Mercury assigned its interests in the contracts to Ford Motor Credit.

On October 27, 1993, All Ways and Ross tendered to Ford two "certified money orders" as payment in full for the two vehicles. The two documents were made out to Ford for $20,500 and $25,200. The documents stated that the sums were to be paid:

> On Demand, Money of account of the Unites States, as required by law at Section 20 of Coinage Act of 1792 from the time of official determination of said money; OR, in UCC 1201(24) Credit Money.

The documents stated they were:

> REDEEMABLE AT FULL FACE VALUE WHEN PRESENTED[;] To: O.M.B. [;] W.D. McCALL [;] P.O. BOX 500–284 [;] VICTORIA, TEXAS POSTAL ZONE 77901.

Upon receiving the documents, Ford applied the purported payments to the defendants' accounts and deposited the documents in a bank. The documents were returned by the bank as nonnegotiable because there were no bank routing numbers on the documents, and no bank was identified through which to charge. Without routing numbers, a bank would have no obligation to accept or make payment on the documents.

Ford informed All Ways and Ross that the documents were not acceptable and that they would need to pay Ford in U.S. legal tender. However, no payments were forthcoming and the account was in default. Ford brought suit to compel All Ways and Ross either to return the vehicles to Ford or to pay $35,810. One of the issues in the lawsuit was whether the documents qualified as negotiable instruments under the UCC.

ISSUE

Were the documents tendered by All Ways and Ross negotiable instruments?

DECISION

No. To be negotiable, an instrument must contain an unconditional promise or order to pay a fixed amount of money. The tendered documents do not come within the UCC's definition of a negotiable instrument. They purport to provide the creditor an unspecified "Credit Money" when presented to a post office box. This cannot be construed as an unconditional promise or order to pay a fixed sum of money.

To be negotiable, an instrument must be written so that a person can tell from reading the instrument alone what the obligations of the parties are. If a note contains the statement, "Payment is subject to the terms of a mortgage dated November 20, 1999," it is not negotiable. To determine the rights of the parties on the note, one would have to examine another document—the mortgage.

However, a reference to another document for a statement of rights with respect to collateral, prepayment, or acceleration does not destroy the negotiability of a note

(3–106[b]). For example, a note could contain the statement, "This note is secured by a mortgage dated August 30, 2002," without affecting its negotiability. In this case, the mortgage does not affect rights and duties of the parties to the note. It would not be necessary to examine the mortgage document to determine the rights of the parties to the note; the parties need only examine the note.

The negotiability of an instrument is not affected by a statement of the consideration for which the instrument was given or by a statement of the transaction that gave rise to the instrument. For example, a negotiable instrument may state that it was given in payment of last month's rent or that it was given in payment of the purchase price of goods. The statement does not affect the negotiability of the instrument.

A check may reference the account to be debited without making the check nonnegotiable. For example, a check could contain the notation, "payroll account" or "petty cash." Similarly, the account number that appears on personal checks does not make the instrument payable only out of a specific fund. Under original Article 3, a check (other than a governmental check) that stated that it was payable only out of a specific fund or account was treated as a conditional order and thus was not negotiable. Revised Article 3 changed this rule so that limiting payment to a particular fund or source does not make the promise or order conditional (3–106[b]).

Revised Article 3 also addresses the negotiability of traveler's checks that commonly require, as a condition to payment, a countersignature of a person whose specimen signature appears on the draft. Under the revision, the condition does not prevent the instrument from meeting the "unconditional promise or order" requirement (3–106[c]). However, if the person whose specimen signature appears on the instrument fails to countersign it, the failure to sign becomes a defense to the obligation of the issuer to pay. This concept will be discussed in the following chapter.

A conditional indorsement does not destroy the negotiability of an otherwise negotiable instrument. The Code determines negotiability at issuance so that later indorsements do not affect the underlying negotiability of the instrument. We discuss conditional indorsements in the next chapter.

FIXED AMOUNT OF MONEY

FIXED AMOUNT

The promise or order in an instrument must be to pay a fixed amount of money, with or without interest or other charges described in the promise or order. The requirement of a "fixed amount" applies only to principal, and the amount of any interest payable is that described in the instrument. If a variable rate of interest is prescribed, the amount of interest is calculated by reference to the formula or index referenced in the instrument. If the description of interest in the instrument does not allow the amount of interest to be ascertained, then interest is payable at the judgment rate in effect at the place of payment at the time interest first accrues (3–112). The judgment rate is the rate of interest courts impose on losing parties until they pay the winning parties.

Under the original version of Article 3, a promise or order had to be to pay a "sum certain." Generally, to meet this requirement, a person had to be able to compute from the information in the instrument the amount required to discharge—or pay off—the instrument at any given time. Among other things, this caused problems when applied to variable rate instruments that came into common commercial usage in the United States after the original Article 3 was drafted. Some state courts held that instruments providing for variable interest rates ascertainable through reference to indexes outside the instrument were not negotiable; other courts sought to interpret the Code to accommodate this new commercial practice.

PAYABLE IN MONEY

The amount specified in the instrument must be payable in money, which is a medium of exchange authorized or adopted by a domestic or foreign government and includes a monetary unit of account established by an intergovernmental organization or by agreement between two or more nations (1–201[24]). Unless the instrument otherwise provides, an instrument that states the amount payable in foreign money may be paid in the foreign money or in an equivalent dollar amount (3–107). If the person obligated to pay off an instrument can do something other than pay money, the instrument is not negotiable. For example, if a note reads, "I promise to pay to the order of Sarah Smith, at my option, $40 or five bushels of apples, John Jones," the note is not negotiable.

PAYABLE ON DEMAND OR AT A DEFINITE TIME

To be negotiable, the promise or order must be payable either on demand or at a specified time in the future. This is so that the time when the instrument is payable can be determined with some certainty. An instrument that is payable on the happening of some uncertain event is not negotiable. Thus, a note payable "when my son graduates from college" is not negotiable, even though the son does graduate subsequently.

PAYABLE ON DEMAND

A promise or order is "payable on demand" if (1) it states that it is payable on "demand" or "sight" (or otherwise at the will of the holder of the instrument) or (2) does not state any time for payment (3–108[a]). For example, if the maker forgets to state when a note is payable, it is payable immediately at the request of the holder of the note.

An instrument may be antedated or postdated, and normally an instrument payable on demand is not payable before the date of the instrument (3–113[a]). Revised Article 3 makes an important exception for checks; a payor bank (a bank that is the drawee of a draft) may pay a postdated check before the stated date *unless* the drawer has notified the bank of postdating pursuant to a procedure set out in the Code (3–113[a]; 4–401[c]).

PAYABLE AT A DEFINITE TIME

A promise or order is "payable at a definite time" if it is payable at a fixed date or dates or at a time or times readily ascertainable at the time the promise or order is issued (3–108[b]). Thus, a note dated March 25, 2003, might be made payable at a fixed time after a stated date, such as "30 days after date."

Under the Code, an instrument that names a fixed date or time for payment—without losing its negotiable character—also may contain a clause permitting the time for payment to be accelerated at the option of the maker. Similarly, an instrument may allow an extension of time at the option of the holder or allow a maker or acceptor to extend payment to a further definite time. Or the due date of a note might be triggered by the happening of an event, such as the filing of a petition in bankruptcy against the maker. The Code permits these clauses so long as one can determine the time for payment with certainty (3–108).

A promise or order also is "payable at a definite time" if it is payable on elapse of a definite period of time after "sight" or "acceptance." A draft payable at a specified time—such as "15 days after sight"—is in effect payable at a fixed time after the draft is presented to the drawee for acceptance.

If an instrument is undated, its "date" is the date it is issued by the maker or drawer (3–113[b]).

.... ## PAYABLE TO ORDER OR BEARER ....

Except for checks, to be negotiable an instrument must be "payable to order or to bearer." A note that provides, "I promise to pay to the order of Sarah Smith" or "I promise to pay to Sarah Smith or bearer" is negotiable. However, one that provides "I promise to pay to Sarah Smith" is not. The words "to the order of" or "to bearer" show that the drawer of a draft, or the maker of a note, intends to issue a negotiable instrument. The drawer or maker is not restricting payment of the instrument to just Sarah Smith but is willing to pay someone else designated by Sarah Smith. This is the essence of negotiability.

In the original version of Article 3, an order in the form of a check also had to be "payable to order or bearer" to qualify as a negotiable instrument. However, the drafters of Revised Article 3 created an exception for instruments that otherwise meet the requirements for a negotiable instrument as well as the definition of a check (3–104[c]). Under the revised article, a check that reads "Pay John Doe" could qualify as a negotiable instrument. As a result the Code treats checks, which are payment instruments, as negotiable instruments whether or not they contain the words "to the order of." The drafters explained that most checks are preprinted with these words but that occasionally the drawer may strike out the words before issuing the check and that a few check forms have been in use that do not contain these words. In these instances, the drafters preferred not to limit the rights of holders of such checks who may pay money or give credit for a check without being aware that it is not in the conventional form for a negotiable instrument.

The most common forms of a promise or order being payable to bearer use the words "payable to bearer," "payable to the order of bearer," "payable to cash," or "payable to the order of cash" (3–109[a]). A promise or order is considered to be payable "to order" if it is payable (1) to the order of an identified person or (2) to an identified person or that person's order (3–109[b]). Examples would include: "Pay to the order of Sandy Smith" and "Pay to Sandy Smith or order." A check sent with the payee line blank is payable to bearer. However, it also is considered an incomplete instrument, the rules concerning which will be discussed in the following two chapters.

In the case that follows, *Chung v. New York Racing Association*, the court found that vouchers issued by the New York Racing Association were "bearer paper" under the Uniform Commercial Code.

CHUNG v. NEW YORK RACING ASSOCIATION
714 NYS2d 429 (N.Y. Dist Ct, N.Y.C.2000)

FACTS

Doseung Chung was a Belmont Park Racetrack horse player. Belmont Park Raceway is owned and operated by the New York State Racing Authority, a nonprofit racing organization authorized by the state to stage thoroughbred horse races and to conduct pari-mutual wagering on them. While attending the track, Chung purchased from the Racing Authority a voucher for use in SAMS machines, automated machines that permit a bettor to enter his bet by inserting money, vouchers, or credit cards into the machines, thereby enabling him to select the number or combination of bets he wishes to make. A ticket is issued showing those numbers.

When a voucher is utilized for purposes of placing a bet at a SAMS machine, the SAMS machine, after deducting the amount placed by the horse player during the particular transaction, provides the horse player with, in addition to his betting ticket(s), a new voucher showing the remaining balance left on the voucher.

In this case, Chung departed the SAMS machine with his betting tickets but without his new voucher—showing thousands of dollars in remaining value—which he inadvertently left sitting in the SAMS machine. Within several minutes he realized his mistake and hurried back to the machine, only to find the voucher gone. He immediately notified the Racing Association, which, after confirming that Chung was the purchaser of the lost voucher, placed a computerized "stop" on the voucher. However, whoever had found the voucher in the machine and taken it had acted even more quickly: The voucher had been brought to a nearby track window and "cashed out" within a minute or so of Chung's having mistakenly left it in the machine.

Chung then sued the New York Racing Association, contending that it should be liable for having failed to provide any minimal protection to its customers in checking the identity and ownership of vouchers prior to permitting their "cash out." The Racing Association contended that the vouchers were "bearer paper," negotiable by anyone having possession and that it was under no obligation to purchasers of vouchers to provide any such identity or ownership checks.

Each New York State Racing Association voucher is labeled "Cash Voucher." Each voucher contains the legend "Bet against the Value or Exchange for Cash." The vouchers also are encoded with certain computer symbols, which are readable by SAMS machines.

ISSUE

Are the vouchers "bearer paper" within the meaning of the Uniform Commercial Code?

DECISION

Yes. The court stated that as opposed to instruments such as ordinary checks, which typically are made payable to the order of a specific person and are known as "order paper," bearer paper is payable to the "bearer" (i.e. to whoever walks in carrying [or "bearing"] the instrument). Under Section 3–111, an "instrument is payable to bearer when by its terms it is payable to . . . cash or the order of 'cash,' or any other indication which does not purport to designate a specific payee." Here, the vouchers by their terms—"Cash Voucher" and "Bet against Value or Exchange for Cash"—constituted "bearer paper." The court went on to note that "negotiation" of a bearer instrument occurs with change of possession, even to a finder or thief of the instrument. The subsequent possessor is then in a position to legally enforce the instrument. [These concepts are discussed in Chapter 37.]

The original payee of a check or a note can transfer the right to receive payment to someone else. By making the instrument payable "to the order of" or "to bearer," the drawer or maker is giving the payee the chance to negotiate the instrument to another person and to cut off certain defenses that the drawer or maker may have against payment of the instrument.

A check that is payable to the order of a specific person is known as "order paper." Order paper can be negotiated or transferred only by indorsement. A check payable "to bearer" or "to cash" is known as "bearer paper"; it can be negotiated or transferred without indorsement (3–201[b]). The rules governing negotiation of instruments will be detailed in the next chapter.

An instrument can be made payable to two or more payees. For example, a check could be drawn payable "to the order of John Jones and Henry Smith." Then, both Jones and Smith have to be involved in negotiating it or enforcing its payment. An instrument can also be made payable to alternative persons, for example, "to the order of Susan Clark or Betsy Brown." In this case, either Clark or Brown could negotiate it or enforce its payment (3–110[d]).

CONCEPT SUMMARY	Requirements for Negotiability
Requirement	**Basic Rules**
Must Be in Writing	1. The instrument may be handwritten, typed, or printed.
Must Be Signed by the Maker or Drawer	1. Person issuing the instrument must sign with intent of validating his or her obligation. 2. Person issuing may affix the signature in a variety of ways—for example, by word, mark, or rubber stamp. 3. Agent or authorized representative may supply the "signature."
Must Contain a Promise or Order to Pay	1. Promise must be more than acknowledgment of a debt. 2. Order requirement is met if the drawer issues an instruction to "pay."
Promise or Order Must Be Unconditional	1. Entire obligation must be found in the instrument itself and not in another document or documents. 2. Payment cannot be conditioned on the occurrence of an event.
Must Call for Payment of a Fixed Amount of Money	1. Must be able to ascertain the principal from the face of the instrument. 2. May contain a clause providing for payment of interest or other charges such as collection or attorney's fees.
Must Be Payable in Money	1. Obligation must be payable in a medium of exchange authorized or adopted by a government or by an international organization or agreement between two or more nations. 2. Maker or drawer cannot have the option to pay in something other than money.
Must be Payable on Demand or at a Definite Time	1. Requirement is met if instrument says it is payable on demand or if no time for payment is stated (then it is payable on demand). 2. Requirement is met if it is payable on a stated date, at a fixed time after a stated date, or a fixed time "after sight." 3. Instrument may contain an acceleration clause or a clause allowing maker or holder to extend the payment date.
Generally Must Be Payable to Bearer or to Order	1. Bearer requirement is met if instrument is payable "to bearer" or "to cash." 2. Order requirement is met if instrument is payable "to the order of" a specified person or persons. 3. Exception from requirement is made for instruments meeting both the definition of a check and all the other requirements for a negotiable instrument.
May Not State Any Other Undertaking or Instruction by the Person Promising or Ordering Payment to Do Any Act in Addition to the Payment of Money	1. However, it may contain (*a*) an undertaking or power to give, maintain, or protect collateral to secure payment, (*b*) an authorization or power to the holder to confess judgment or realize on or dispose of collateral, or (*c*) a waiver of the benefit of any law intended for the advantage or protection of an obligor on the instrument.

.... **SPECIAL TERMS** ....

ADDITIONAL TERMS

Generally, if an instrument is to qualify as a negotiable instrument, the person promising or ordering payment may not state undertakings or instructions in addition to the payment of money (3–104[a][3]). However, the instrument may include clauses concerning (1) giving, maintaining, or protecting collateral to secure payment,

(2) an authorization to confess judgment or to realize on or dispose of collateral, and (3) waiving the benefit of any law intended for the protection or benefit of any person obligated on the instrument.

Thus, a term authorizing the confession of judgment on an instrument when it is due does not affect the negotiability of the instrument. A confession of judgment clause authorizes the creditor to go into court if the debtor defaults and, with the debtor's acquiescence, to have a judgment entered against the debtor. However, some states prohibit confessions of judgment.

Banks and other businesses often use forms of commercial paper that meet their particular needs. These forms may include certain other terms that do not affect the negotiability of an instrument. For example, a note may designate a place of payment without affecting the instrument's negotiability. Where the instrument does not specify a place of payment, the Code sets out rules for ascertaining where payment is to be made (3–111).

Ambiguous Terms

Occasionally, a person may write or receive a check on which the amount written in figures differs from the amount written in words. Or a note may have conflicting terms or an ambiguous term. Where a conflict or an ambiguous term exists, there are general rules of interpretation that are applied to resolve the conflict or ambiguity: Typewritten terms prevail over printed terms, handwritten terms prevail over printed and typewritten terms, and where words and numbers conflict, the words control the numbers (3–114).

The following case, *Galatia Community State Bank v. Kindy,* involves a check on which there was a difference between the number on a check placed there by a checkwriting machine and those written by hand.

Galatia Community State Bank v. Kindy
307 Ark. 467 (Sup. Ct. Ark. 1991)

FACTS

Galatia Community State Bank honored a check it took for collection for $5,550, which was the amount imprinted by a checkwriting machine in the center underlined section of the check commonly used for stating the amount in words. The imprint looked like this:

```
RegistereD
No. 497345**   **5550 DOL'S 00 CTS
```

The impression made by the checkwriting machine could be felt on the front and back of the check, and "**5550 DOL'S 00 CTS" was imprinted in red ink. In the box on the right-hand side of the check commonly used for numbers, "6,550.00" appeared in handwriting. The check was in partial payment of the purchase price of

two engines that Eugene Kindy was buying from the payee on the check, Tony Hicks. Kindy postdated the check by a month and deliberately placed two different amounts on the check because he thought the bank would check with him before paying it. Kindy wanted to be sure that the engines had been delivered to Canada before he paid the $6,550 balance of the purchase price.

After the check was deposited in the Galatia Bank and Hicks was given $5,550, an employee of the bank altered the "6" by hand to read "5." Because Kindy had stopped payment on the check, the drawee bank refused to pay it to Galatia Bank. Galatia Bank then brought suit against Kindy as the drawer of the check. One of the issues in the lawsuit was how the check should be constructed. The trial court found that the rules on

(continued)

GALATIA COMMUNITY STATE BANK v. KINDY
(concluded)

construction provided in the Code were not helpful because they were contradictory.

ISSUE

Does the amount in figures imprinted by the checkwriting machine ($5,500) control over the amount written by hand in figures ($6,500)?

DECISION

Yes. Initially, the court noted that it understood the frustration of the trial court in trying to apply the Code's rules of construction to a situation in which the amount imprinted by the checkwriting machine upon the line

customarily used for words was expressed in figures, not in words. However, the court concluded that because a check-imprinting machine's purpose is to protect against alterations, the amount shown on the imprint should control whether the number is in words or in figures. The court also considered the portion written by the check-writing machine to be the equivalent of handwriting.

AUTHOR'S NOTE

Although this case was decided under the original version of Article 3, the dilemma posed, and the conclusion reached by the court on the construction of the check, would be likely to be the same under Revised Article 3.

.... *QUESTIONS AND **PROBLEM CASES*** ....

1. Is the following instrument a note, a check, or a draft? Why? If it is not a check, how would you have to change it to make it a check?

   > To: Arthur Adams January 1, 2003
   >
   > TEN DAYS AFTER DATE PAY TO THE ORDER OF: Bernie Brown
   >
   > THE SUM OF: One thousand and no/100 DOLLARS
   >
   >   SIGNED: Carl Clark

2. Frank agrees to build a garage for Sarah for $15,000. Sarah offers to sign either a contract showing her obligation to pay Frank $15,000 or a negotiable promissory note for $15,000 payable to the order of Frank. Would you advise Frank to ask for the contract or the promissory note? Explain.

3. Wiley, Tate & Irby, buyers and sellers of used cars, sold several autos to Houston Auto Sales. Houston wrote out the order for payment on the outside of several envelopes. He signed them and they were drawn on his bank, Peoples Bank & Trust Co., to be paid on the demand of Wiley, Tate & Irby. Can the envelopes qualify as negotiable instruments?

4. Is the following a negotiable instrument?

   > IOU, A. Gay, the sum of seventeen and 5/100 dollars for value received.
   >
   >   John R. Rooke

5. Is the following a negotiable instrument?

   > Subject to Approval of Title
   > Pay to the Order of Vernon Butterfield
   > $1,997.90.
   >
   >   The Culver Company
   >   By A. M. Culver

6. Holly Hill Acres, Ltd., executed a promissory note and mortgage and delivered them to Rogers. The note contained the following stipulation:

   > this note with interest is secured by a mortgage on real estate of even date herewith, made by the maker hereof in favor of the said payee, and shall be construed and enforced according to the laws of the State of Florida. The terms of said mortgage are by this reference made a part hereof.

   Is the note a negotiable instrument?

7. Olde Town Investment Corporation borrowed $18,000 from VMC Mortgage Company and signed a promissory note secured by a deed of

trust on land it owned. The note provided for interest at "three percent (3.00%) over Chase Manhattan Prime to be adjusted monthly." Is a note providing for a variable amount of interest, not ascertainable from the face of the note, a negotiable instrument?

8. Darryl Young presented five photocopied checks to the Lynnwood Check-X-Change on five different days between June 13 and June 21. Lynwood cashed the first four checks presented. The fifth check, which was presented on a Saturday, was drawn on a different account from the first four checks and was payable on the following Monday. Lynnwood's practice was to cash checks on Saturday that are dated the following Monday. Young was convicted of five counts of forgery. On appeal, Young argued that the postdated check was not a legal instrument for purposes of the forgery statute. The crime of forgery requires an instrument that, if genuine, may have legal effect or be the foundation of legal liability. Young argued that the postdated check did not meet this requirement "because the time for payment had not arrived and thus the check could not have created any legal liability on the part of any person at that time." If a check is postdated, can it qualify as a negotiable instrument and create legal liability?

9. Nation-Wide Check Corporation sold money orders to drugstores. The money orders contained the words, "Payable to," followed by a blank. Can the money order qualify as a negotiable instrument?

10. Emmett McDonald, acting as the personal representative of the estate of Marion Cahill, wrote a check payable to himself, individually, on the estate checking account in the Commercial Bank & Trust Company. The instrument contained an obvious variance between the numbers and the written words that indicated the amount of the check. It said "Pay to the order of Emmett E. McDonald $10075.00 Ten hundred seventy five . . . Dollars." The bank paid the $10,075 sum stated by the numerals to McDonald, who absconded with the funds. Yates, the successor representative, sued the bank on behalf of the estate to recover the $9,000 difference between that amount and the $1,075 that was written out. Did the bank pay the correct amount on the check?

CHAPTER 37

Negotiation and Holder
in Due Course

Suppose that Carl Cassidy agrees to sell his six-year-old Ford automobile to Sarah Smith for $6,000. When he delivers the car, she gives him a check for $6,000 drawn on the First National Bank and made payable "to the order of Carl Cassidy."

- *What does Carl have to do in order to negotiate the check to someone else?*
- *If Carl indorsed his name on the back of the check but lost it on his way to the bank where he intended to cash it, would the finder of the check be able to cash it?*
- *If Carl wants to make sure the check gets credited to his savings account at the First Federal Savings & Loan, how should he indorse it?*
- *If Carl's brother, Bob, tells him he'll give him $5,800 cash for the check, what requirements must Bob meet in order to be accorded the rights of a holder in due course of the check?*
- *If Sarah was unhappy about the automobile, believing that Carl had misrepresented its condition when he sold it to her, and stopped payment on the check so that First National refused to pay it, could Sarah assert the defense of misrepresentation if Carl sued her to collect the amount of the check? Would the answer be different if Carl had negotiated the check to Bob and he qualified as a holder in due course?*

These and other questions will be addressed in this chapter.

.... *INTRODUCTION* ....

The preceding chapter discussed the nature and benefits of negotiable instruments. It also outlined the requirements an instrument must meet to qualify as a negotiable instrument and thus possess the qualities that allow it to be accepted as a substitute for money.

This chapter focuses on negotiation—the process by which rights to a negotiable instrument pass from one person to another. Commonly, this involves an indorsement and transfer of the instrument. This chapter also develops the requirements that a transferee of a negotiable instrument must meet to qualify as a holder in due course and thus attain special rights under negotiable instruments law. These rights, which put a holder in due course in an enhanced position compared to an assignee of a contract, are discussed in some detail.

.... *NEGOTIATION* ....

NATURE OF NEGOTIATION

Under Revised Article 3, **negotiation** is the transfer of possession (whether voluntary or involuntary) of a negotiable instrument by a person (other than the issuer) to another person who becomes its *holder* (3–201). A person is a **holder** if she is in possession of an instrument (1) that is payable to bearer or (2) that is made payable to an identified person and she is that identified person (1–201[20]).[1]

For example, when an employer gives an employee, Susan Adams, a paycheck payable "to the order of Susan Adams," she is the holder of the check because she is in possession of an instrument payable to an identified person (Susan Adams) and she is that person. When she indorses (writes her name on) the back of the check and exchanges it for cash and merchandise at Ace Grocery, she has negotiated the check to the grocery store and the store is now the holder because it is in possession by transfer of a check that now is payable to bearer. Similarly, if Susan Adams indorsed the check "Pay to the Order of Ace Grocery, Susan Adams" and transferred it to the grocery store, it would be a holder through the negotiation of the check to it. The grocery store would be in possession of an instrument payable to an identified person (Ace Grocery) and would be the person identified on the check.

In certain circumstances, Revised Article 3 allows a person to become a holder by negotiation even though the transfer of possession is involuntary. For example, if a negotiable instrument is payable to bearer and is stolen by Tom Thief or found by Fred Finder, Thief or Finder becomes the holder when he obtains possession. The involuntary transfer of possession of a bearer instrument results in a negotiation to Thief or Finder.

FORMAL REQUIREMENTS FOR NEGOTIATION

The formal requirements for negotiation are very simple. If an instrument is payable to the order of a specific payee, it is called **order paper** and it can be negotiated by transfer of possession of the instrument after indorsement by the person specified (3–201[b]).

---

[1]The numbers in parentheses refer to sections of the Uniform Commercial Code (UCC).

For example, if Rachel's father gives her a check payable "to the order of Rachel Stern," then Rachel can negotiate the check by indorsing her name on the back of the check and giving it to the person to whom she wants to transfer it. Note that the check is order paper, not because the word *order* appears on the check but rather because it named a specific payee, Rachel Stern.

If an instrument is payable to bearer or to cash, it is called **bearer paper** and negotiating it is even simpler. An instrument payable to bearer may be negotiated by transfer of possession alone (3–201[b]). Thus, if someone gives you a check that is made payable "to the order of cash," you can negotiate it simply by giving it to the person to whom you wish to transfer it. No indorsement is necessary to negotiate an instrument payable to bearer. However, the person who takes the instrument may ask for an indorsement for her protection. By indorsing the check, you agree to be liable for its payment to that person if it is not paid by the drawee bank when it is presented for payment. This liability will be discussed in Chapter 38, "Liability of Parties."

NATURE OF INDORSEMENT

An indorsement is made by adding the signature of the holder of the instrument to the instrument, usually on the back of it, either alone or with other words. **Indorsement** is defined to mean "a signature (other than that of a maker, drawer, or acceptor) that alone or accompanied by other words is made on an instrument for purpose of (i) negotiating the instrument, (ii) restricting payment of the instrument, or (iii) incurring indorser's liability on the instrument" (3–204[a]). The negotiation and restriction-of-payment aspects of indorsements will be discussed below; indorser's liability will be covered in the next chapter.

The signature constituting an indorsement can be put there either by the holder or by someone who is authorized to sign on behalf of the holder. For example, a check payable to "H&H Meat Market" might be indorsed "H&H Meat Market by Jane Frank, President," if Jane is authorized to do this on behalf of the market.

WRONG OR MISSPELLED NAME

When indorsing an instrument, the holder should spell his name in the same way as it appears on the instrument. If the holder's name is misspelled or wrong, then legally the indorsement can be made either in his name or in the name that is on the instrument. However, any person who pays the instrument or otherwise gives value for it may require the indorser to sign both names (3–204[d]).

Suppose Joan Ash is issued a check payable to the order of "Joanne Ashe." She may indorse the check as "Joan Ash" or "Joanne Ashe." However, if she takes the check to a bank to cash, the bank may require her to sign both "Joanne Ashe" and "Joan Ash."

CHECKS DEPOSITED WITHOUT INDORSEMENT

Occasionally when a customer deposits a check to her account with a bank she may forget to indorse the check; also, it is common practice for depositary banks to receive unindorsed checks under what are known as "lock-box" arrangements with customers who receive a high volume of checks. Normally, a check payable to the order of an identified person would require the indorsement of that person in order for a negotiation to the depositary bank to take place and for it to become a holder. Under the original Article 3, the depositary bank (a bank that takes an item for collection), in most cases had the right to supply the customer's indorsement. Instead of actually signing the customer's name to the check as the indorsement, the bank might just stamp on it that it was deposited by the customer or credited to her account. Banks did not have the right to put the customer's indorsement on a check that the customer had deposited if the check specifically required the payee's signature. Insurance and government checks commonly require the payee's signature.

The revision to Article 3 and the conforming amendments to Articles 1 and 4 address the situation in which a check is deposited in a depositary bank without indorsement differently. The depositary bank becomes a holder of an item delivered to it for collection, whether or not it is indorsed by the customer, if the customer at the time of delivery qualified as a holder (4–205). Concomitantly, the depositary bank warrants to other collecting banks, the payor bank (drawee), and the drawer that it paid the amount of the item to the customer or deposited the amount to the customer's account.

TRANSFER OF ORDER INSTRUMENT

Except for the special provisions concerning depositary banks, if an order instrument is transferred without indorsement, the instrument has not been negotiated and the transferee cannot qualify as a holder. For example, Sue Brown gives a check payable "to the order of Susan Brown" to a drugstore in payment for some cosmetics. Until Sue indorses the check, she has not negotiated it and the druggist could not qualify as a holder of the check.

Transfer of an instrument, whether or not the transfer is a negotiation, vests in the transferee any right of the transferor to enforce the instrument. However, the transferee cannot obtain the rights of a holder in due course (discussed later in this chapter) if he is engaged in any fraud or illegality affecting the instrument. Unless otherwise agreed, if an instrument is transferred for value but without a required indorsement, the transferee has the right to the unqualified indorsement of the transferor; however, the "negotiation" takes place only when the transferor applies her indorsement (3–230[c]).

INDORSEMENTS

EFFECTS OF AN INDORSEMENT

There are three functions of an indorsement. First, an indorsement is necessary in order for the negotiation of an instrument that is payable to the order of a specified person. Thus, if a check is payable "to the order of James Lee," James must indorse the check before it can be negotiated. Second, the form of the indorsement that the indorser uses also affects future attempts to negotiate the instrument. For example, if James indorses it "Pay to the order of Sarah Hill," Sarah must indorse it before it can be negotiated further.

Third, an indorsement generally makes a person liable on the instrument. By indorsing an instrument, a person incurs an obligation to pay the instrument if the person primarily liable on it (for example, the maker of a note) does not pay it. We discuss the contractual liability of indorsers in Chapter 38. In this chapter, we discuss the effect of an indorsement on further negotiation of an instrument.

KINDS OF INDORSEMENTS

There are three basic kinds of indorsements: (1) special, (2) blank, and (3) restrictive. In addition, an indorsement may be "qualified."

Special Indorsement

A **special indorsement** contains the signature of the indorser along with the words indicating to whom, or to whose order, the instrument is payable. For example, if a check is drawn "Pay to the Order of Marcia Morse" and Marcia indorses it "Pay to the Order of Sam Smith, Marcia Morse" or "Pay to Sam Smith, Marcia Morse," it has been indorsed with a special indorsement. An instrument that is indorsed with a special indorsement remains "order paper." It can be negotiated only with the indorsement of the person specified (3–205[a]). In this example, Sam Smith must indorse the check before he can negotiate it to someone else.

Blank Indorsement

If an indorser merely signs his name and does not specify to whom the instrument is payable, he has indorsed the instrument in **blank.** For example, if a check drawn "Pay to the Order of Natalie Owens" is indorsed "Natalie Owens" by Natalie, Natalie has indorsed it in blank. An instrument indorsed in blank is payable to the bearer (person in possession of it) and from that act is "bearer paper." As such, the bearer negotiates it by transfer alone and no further indorsement is necessary for negotiation (3–205[b]).

If Natalie indorsed the check in blank and gave it to Kevin Foley, Kevin would have the right to convert the blank indorsement into a special indorsement (3–205[c]). He could do this by writing the words "Pay to the Order of Kevin Foley" above Natalie's indorsement. Then the check would have to be indorsed by Kevin before it could be negotiated further.

If Kevin took the check indorsed in blank to a bank and presented it for payment or for collection, the bank normally would ask him to indorse the check. It does this not because it needs his indorsement for the check to be negotiated to it; the check indorsed in blank can be negotiated merely by delivering it to the bank cashier. Rather, the bank asks for his indorsement because it wants to make him liable on the check if it is not paid when the bank sends it to the drawee bank for payment. Chapter 38, "Liabilities of Parties," discusses the liability of indorsers.

Restrictive Indorsement

A **restrictive indorsement** is one that specifies the purpose of the indorsement or specifies the use to be made of the instrument. Among the more common restrictive indorsements are:

1. Indorsements for deposit. For example, "For Deposit Only" or "For Deposit to My Account at First National Bank."
2. Indorsements for collection, which are commonly put on by banks involved in the collection process. For example, "Pay any bank, banker, or trust company" or "For collection only."
3. Indorsements indicating that the indorsement is for the benefit of someone other than the person to whom it is payable. For example, "Pay to Arthur Attorney in trust for Mark Minor."

Generally, the person who takes an instrument with a restrictive indorsement must pay or apply any money or other value he gives for the instrument consistently with the indorsement. In the case of a check indorsed "for deposit" or "for collection," any person other than a bank who purchases the check is considered to have **converted** the check unless (1) the indorser received the amount paid for it or (2) the bank applied the amount of the check consistently with the indorsement (e.g., deposited it to the indorser's account). Similarly, a depositary bank or payor bank (the drawee bank) that takes an instrument for deposit or for immediate payment over the counter that has been indorsed "for deposit" or "for collection" will be liable for conversion unless the indorser received the amount paid for the instrument or the proceeds or the bank applied the amount consistently with the indorsement (3–206[c]).[2]

By way of illustration, assume that Robert Franks has indorsed his paycheck "For Deposit to My Account No. 4068933 at Bank One." While on his way to the bank he loses the check, and Fred Finder finds it. If Finder tries to cash the check at a check-cashing service, the service must ensure that any value it gives for the check either is deposited to Franks' account at Bank One or is received by Franks. If it gives the money to Finder, it will be liable to Franks for converting his check. This principle is illustrated in the following case, *Lehigh Presbytery v. Merchants Bancorp, Inc.*, which involves a bank that failed to apply value given for checks consistently with restrictive indorsements on the checks.

LEHIGH PRESBYTERY v. MERCHANTS BANCORP, INC.
17 UCC Rep.2d 163 (Super. Ct. Pa. 1991)

FACTS

Mary Ann Hunsberger was hired by the Lehigh Presbytery as a secretary/bookkeeper. In this capacity, she was responsible for opening the Presbytery's mail, affixing rubber-stamp indorsements to checks received by the Presbytery, and depositing the checks into the Presbytery's account at Merchants Bancorp, Inc. Over a period of more than five years, Ms. Hunsberger deposited into her own account 153 of these checks. Each check was indorsed: "For Deposit Only to The Credit of Presbytery of Lehigh, Ernest Hutcheson, Treas." The bank credited the checks to Ms. Hunsberger's account, despite the rubber-stamp restrictive indorsement, because it relied solely on the account number handwritten on the deposit slips submitted by Ms. Hunsberger with the checks at the time of deposit. Ms. Hunsberger obtained the deposit slips in the lobby of the bank, wrote the proper account title, "Lehigh Presbytery," but inserted her

own account number rather than the account number of her employer. When the diversionary scheme was discovered, Lehigh Presbytery filed suit against the bank to recover the funds credited to Ms. Hunsberger's account.

ISSUE

Was the bank legally bound to follow the restrictive indorsements on the 153 checks deposited instead to the personal account of Ms. Hunsberger?

DECISION

Yes. First, the court noted that the indorsement stamped on each check was a restrictive indorsement within the meaning of the UCC because it included the words "for deposit" signifying a purpose of deposit or collection and it stated the instrument was to be deposited for the benefit or use of the indorser. Next, the court observed that

(continued)

---

[2]Otherwise a payor bank as well as an intermediary bank may disregard the indorsement and is not liable if the proceeds of the instrument are not received by the indorser or applied consistently with the indorsement (3–206[c][4]).

LEHIGH PRESBYTERY V. MERCHANTS BANCORP, INC.
(concluded)

under the UCC, a transferee of an instrument containing a restrictive indorsement must pay or apply any value given by it consistently with the indorsement. Accordingly, the UCC requires application of the value of the checks consistent with the indorsement—that is, for deposit to Lehigh Presbytery's account. Thus, the bank is liable to its customer for crediting checks bearing the restrictive indorsement to the personal account of Ms. Hunsberger.

AUTHOR'S NOTE

Although this case was decided under the original version of Article 3, the same result would be expected under Revised Article 3.

Some indorsements indicate payment to the indorsee as an agent, trustee, or fiduciary. A person who takes an instrument containing such an indorsement from the indorsee may pay the proceeds to the indorsee without regard to whether the indorsee violates a fiduciary duty to the indorser *unless* he is on *notice* of any breach of fiduciary duty that the indorser may be committing (3–206[d]). A person would have such notice if he took the instrument in any transaction that benefited the indorsee personally (3–307). Suppose a person takes a check indorsed to "Arthur Attorney in trust for Mark Minor." The money given for the check should be put in Mark Minor's trust account. A person would not be justified in taking the check in exchange for a television set that he knew Attorney was acquiring for his own—rather than Minor's—use.

There are two other kinds of indorsements that the original Article 3 treated as restrictive indorsements, but that the Revised Article 3 no longer considers restrictive indorsements. They are:

1. Indorsements purporting to prohibit further negotiation. For example, "Pay to Carl Clark Only."
2. Conditional indorsements, which indicate that they are effective only if the payee satisfies a certain condition. For example, "Pay to Bernard Builder Only if He Completes Construction on My House by November 1, 2003."

Under Revised Article 3, any indorsement that purports to limit payment to a particular person or to prohibit further transfer or negotiation of the instrument is not effective to prevent further transfer or negotiation (3–206[a]). Thus, if a note is indorsed "Pay to Carl Clark Only" and given to Clark, he may negotiate the note to subsequent holders who may ignore the restriction on the indorsement.

Indorsements that state a condition to the right of the indorsee to receive payment do not affect the right of the indorsee to enforce the instrument. Any person who pays the instrument or takes it for value or for collection may disregard the condition. Moreover, the rights and liabilities of the person are not affected by whether the condition has been fulfilled (3–206[b]).

Qualified Indorsement

A **qualified indorsement** is one by which the indorser disclaims her liability to make the instrument good if the maker or drawer defaults on it. Words such as "Without Recourse" are used to qualify an indorsement. They can be used with either a blank indorsement or a special indorsement and thus make it a qualified blank indorsement or a qualified special indorsement. The use of a qualified indorsement does not change the negotiable nature of the instrument. Its effect is to eliminate the contractual liability of the indorser. The next chapter, "Liability of Parties," will discuss this liability in detail.

RESCISSION OF INDORSEMENT

Negotiation is effective to transfer an instrument even if the negotiation is (1) made by a minor, a corporation exceeding its powers, or any other person without contractual capacity; (2) obtained by fraud, duress, or mistake of any kind; (3) made in breach of duty; or (4) part of an illegal transaction. A negotiation made under the preceding circumstances is subject to *rescission* before the instrument has been negotiated to a transferee who can qualify as a holder in due course (3–202). The situation in such instances is analogous to a sale of goods where the sale has been induced by fraud or misrepresentation. In such a case, the seller may rescind the sale and recover the goods, provided that the seller acts before the goods are resold to a bona fide purchaser for value.

CONCEPT SUMMARY   **Indorsements**

(Assume a check is payable "To The Order of Mark Smith.")

Type	Example	Consequences
Blank	Mark Smith	1. Satisfies the indorsement requirement for the negotiation of order paper. 2. The instrument becomes bearer paper and can be negotiated by delivery alone. 3. The indorser becomes obligated on the instrument. (See Chapter 38, "Liability of Parties.")
Special	Pay to the Order of Joan Brown, Mark Smith	1. Satisfies the indorsement requirement for the negotiation of order paper. 2. The instrument remains order paper and Joan Brown's indorsement is required for further negotiation. 3. The indorser becomes obligated on the instrument. (See Chapter 38.)
Restrictive	For deposit only to my account in First American Bank Mark Smith	1. Satisfies the indorsement requirement for the negotiation of order paper. 2. The person who pays value for the instrument is obligated to pay it consistent with the indorsement (i.e., to pay it into Mark Smith's account at First American Bank). 3. The indorser becomes obligated on the instrument. (See Chapter 38.)
Qualified	Mark Smith (without recourse)	1. Satisfies the indorsement requirement for negotiation of order paper. 2. Eliminates the indorser's obligation. (See Chapter 38.)

HOLDER IN DUE COURSE

A person who qualifies as a holder in due course of a negotiable instrument gets special rights. Normally, the transferee of an instrument—like the assignee of a contract—receives only those rights in the instrument that are held by the person from whom he received the instrument. But a holder in due course can obtain better rights. A holder in due course takes a negotiable instrument free of all **personal defenses, claims to the instrument,** and **claims in recoupment** either of the obligor or of a third party. A holder in due course does not take the instrument free of the **real defenses,** which go to the validity of the instrument or of claims that develop after he becomes a holder. We develop the differences between personal and real defenses in more detail later in this chapter and explain claims to the instrument and claims in recoupment. The following example illustrates the advantage that a holder in due course of a negotiable instrument may have.

Assume that Carl Carpenter contracts with Helen Homeowner to build her a garage for $15,500, payable on October 1 when he expects to complete the garage. Assume further that Carpenter assigns his rights to the $15,500 to First National Bank in order to obtain money for materials. If the bank tries to collect the money from Homeowner on October 1 but Carpenter has not finished building the garage, then Homeowner may assert the fact that the garage is not complete as a defense to paying the bank. As assignee of a simple contract, the bank has only those rights that its assignor, Carpenter, has and is subject to all claims and defenses that Homeowner has against Carpenter.

Now assume that instead of simply signing a contract with Homeowner, Carpenter had Homeowner give him a negotiable promissory note in the amount of $15,500 payable to the order of Carpenter on October 1 and that Carpenter then negotiated the note to the bank. If the bank is able to qualify as a holder in due course, it may collect the $15,500 from Homeowner on October 1 even though she might have a personal defense against payment of the note because Carpenter has not completed the work on the garage. Homeowner cannot assert that personal defense against a holder in due course. She would have to pay the note to the bank and then independently seek to recover from Carpenter for breach of their agreement. The bank's improved position is due to its status as a holder in due course of a negotiable instrument. If the instrument in question was not negotiable, or if the bank could not qualify as a holder in due course, then it would be in the same position as the assignee of a simple contract and would be subject to Homeowner's personal defense.

We turn now to a discussion of the requirements that must be met for the possessor of a negotiable instrument to qualify as a holder in due course.

GENERAL REQUIREMENTS

In order to become a **holder in due course,** a person who takes a negotiable instrument must be a *holder,* and take the instrument for *value,* in *good faith, without notice* that it is *overdue* or has been *dishonored* or that there is any uncured default with respect to payment of another instrument issued as part of the same series, *without notice that the instrument contains an unauthorized signature or has been altered, without notice of any claim of a property or possessory interest in it,* and *without notice* that any party has any *defense against it* or *claim in recoupment to it* (3–302[a][2]).

In addition, the revision to Article 3 requires "that the instrument when issued or negotiated to the holder does not bear such *apparent evidence of forgery or alteration* or is not otherwise so *irregular* or *incomplete* as to call into question its authenticity" (3–302[a][1]).

If a person who takes a negotiable instrument does not meet these requirements, he is not a holder in due course. Then the person is in the same position as an assignee of a contract.

HOLDER

To be a **holder** of a negotiable instrument, a person must have possession of an instrument that is either payable to "bearer" or that is payable to him. For example, if Teresa Gonzales is given a check by her grandmother that is made payable "to the order of Teresa Gonzales," Teresa is a holder of the check because it is made out to her. If Teresa indorses the check "Pay to the order of Ames Hardware, Teresa Gonzales" and gives it to Ames Hardware in payment for some merchandise, then Ames Hardware is the holder of the check. Ames Hardware is a holder because it is in possession of a check that is indorsed to its order. If Ames Hardware indorses the check "Ames Hardware" and deposits it in its account at First National Bank, the bank becomes the holder. The bank is in possession of an instrument that is indorsed in blank and thus is payable to bearer.

It is important that all indorsements on the instrument at the time it is payable to the order of someone are *authorized indorsements*. With limited exceptions (discussed later), a forged indorsement is not an effective indorsement and prevents a person from becoming a holder.

To be a holder, a person must have a complete chain of authorized indorsements. Suppose the Internal Revenue Service mails to Robert Washington an income tax refund check payable to him. Tom Turner steals the check from Washington's mailbox, signs (indorses) "Robert Washington" on the back of the check, and cashes it at a shoe store. The shoe store is not a holder of the check because its transferor, Turner, was not a holder and because it needs Washington's signature to have a good chain of authorized indorsements. Robert Washington has to indorse the check in order for there to be a valid chain of indorsements. Turner's signature is not effective for this purpose because Washington did not authorize him to sign Washington's name to the check (1–201[20]; 3–403[a]; 3–416[a][2]).

The case that follows, *Golden Years Nursing Home, Inc. v. Gabbard,* illustrates that a party in possession of a check indorsed in blank is a holder of the instrument.

GOLDEN YEARS NURSING HOME, INC. v. GABBARD
682 N.E.2d 682 731 (Ct. App. Ohio 1996)

FACTS

From 1972 until 1991, Nancy Gabbard, the office manager for the Golden Years Nursing Home, received at the nursing home Social Security checks drawn on the United States Treasury and made payable either to individual patients or to "Golden Years Nursing Home for [an individual patient]." From 1986 until 1991, Gabbard engaged in an embezzling scheme whereby she would have certain patients indorse their own checks in blank—each patient would sign his own name on the back of the check placing no restrictions on the manner in which the check could subsequently be negotiated. Gabbard would then cash the checks and either keep the cash or deposit the funds into her personal bank account.

In 1992, after Gabbard's scheme was discovered, Golden Years brought suit against Gabbard and against the Star Bank Corporation where the checks had been cashed. The patients had in other documents assigned their interests in the checks to Golden Years, and the claim against the bank alleged that it had converted Golden Years' property by cashing checks with forged indorsements. One of the issues in the lawsuit was whether the checks had been properly negotiated to Star Bank.

ISSUE

Did Star Bank become a holder of the checks that had been indorsed in blank by the payees?

(continued)

GOLDEN YEARS NURSING HOME, INC. v. GABBARD
(concluded)

DECISION

Yes. Negotiability is determined by what is on the face of the instrument, and any separate agreement with the patients does not affect the negotiability of these checks. Negotiation is the transfer of an instrument in such form that the transferee becomes a holder. If an instrument is payable to order, it is negotiated by delivery with any necessary indorsement. However, once a payee indorses a check in blank, it becomes bearer paper and can be negotiated by delivery alone. Thus, in this case, Gabbard became a holder of the checks when the checks, in-dorsed in blank by the patient–payees, were delivered to her. When Star Bank accepted the checks that were in-dorsed with the genuine signatures of the payees, the checks bore no indication that they had been assigned to Golden Years. Star Bank cashed the checks in good faith without notice of any defenses and thus became a holder in due course. This analysis does not change even if Gabbard presented the checks to the payees for their indorsement with the intent to embezzle the funds eventually.

VALUE

To qualify as a holder in due course of a negotiable instrument, a person must give **value** for it. Value is not identical to simple consideration. Under the provisions of the Revised Article 3, a holder takes for value if (1) the agreed-upon promise of perfor-mance has been performed,—for example, if the instrument was given in exchange for a promise to deliver a refrigerator and the refrigerator has been delivered; (2) he acquires a security interest in, or a lien on, the instrument; (3) he takes the instru-ment in payment of, or as security for, an antecedent claim; (4) he gives a negotiable instrument for it; or (5) he makes an irrevocable commitment to a third person (3–303). Thus, a person who receives a check as a gift or merely makes an executory promise in return for a check has not given value for it and cannot qualify as a holder in due course.

A bank or any person who discounts an instrument in the *regular course of trade* has given value for it. In this context the discount essentially is a means for increasing the return or the rate of interest on the instrument. Likewise, if a loan is made and an instrument is pledged as security for the repayment of the loan, the secured party has given value for the instrument to the amount of the loan. If Axe, who owes Bell a past-due debt, indorses and delivers to Bell, in payment of the debt or as security for its re-payment, an instrument issued to Axe, Bell has given value for the instrument. If a bank allows a customer to draw against a check deposited for collection, it has given value to the extent of the credit drawn against it.

If the promise of performance that is the consideration for an instrument has been partially performed, the holder may assert rights as a holder in due course of the instrument only to the fraction of the amount payable under the instrument equal to the partial performance divided by the value of the promised performance (3–302[d]). For example, Arthur Wells agrees to purchase a note payable to the order of Helda Parks. The note is for the sum of $5,000. Wells pays Parks $1,000 on the nego-tiation of the note to him and agrees to pay the balance of $4,000 in 10 days. Initially, Wells is a holder in due course for one-fifth of the amount of the note. If he later pays the $4,000 due, he may become a holder in due course for the full amount.

In the case that follows, *Carter & Grimsley v. Omni Trading, Inc.,* the holder of a check failed to qualify as a holder in due course because it had not taken the check for value.

CARTER & GRIMSLEY V. OMNI TRADING, INC.
716 NE2d 320 (App. Ct. Illinois 1999)

FACTS

On February 2, 1996, Omni Trading, Inc., issued Country Grain Elevators, Inc., two checks totaling $75,000 for grain it had purchased. Country Grain then endorsed the checks over to the law firm of Carter & Grimsley as a retainer for future legal services. Carter & Grimsley deposited the checks to its account on February 5, Country Grain failed the next day, and the Illinois State Department of Agriculture claimed a statutory lien on the grain in the elevator on behalf of grain producers who had sold grain to the elevator. On February 8, Carter & Grimsley was notified that Omni had stopped payment on the check. Carter & Grimsley, claiming to be a holder in due course, brought suit against Omni as the drawer of the checks that had been dishonored when presented for payment.

ISSUE

Was Carter & Grimsley a holder in due course of the checks?

DECISION

No. To qualify as a holder in due course, the holder must have taken the check, among other things, "for value." UCC section 3–303(a) states that "an instrument is issued or transferred for value if: (1) the instrument is issued or transferred for a promise of performance to the extent that the promise has been performed. . . ." This retainer was a contract for future legal services. It was a "promise of performance" not yet performed. No value was received, and Carter & Grimsley is not a holder in due course.

GOOD FAITH

To qualify as a holder in due course of a negotiable instrument, a person must take it in **good faith,** which means that the person obtained it honestly and in the observance of reasonable commercial standards of fair dealing (3–103[a][4]). If a person obtains a check by trickery or with knowledge that it has been stolen, the person has not obtained the check in good faith and cannot be a holder in due course. A person who pays too little for an instrument, perhaps because she suspects that something may be wrong with the way it was obtained, may have trouble meeting the good faith test. Suppose a finance company works closely with a door-to-door sales company that engages in shoddy practices. If the finance company buys the consumers' notes from the sales company, it will not be able to meet the good faith test and qualify as a holder in due course of the notes.

Ethical Implications

If you are in the business of buying commercial paper—such as consumer notes—from businesses such as home improvement companies, how much of an ethical obligation, if any, do you have to look into the sales practices and performance records of the companies to whom the consumers have made the notes payable?

OVERDUE OR DISHONORED

In order to qualify as a holder in due course, a person must take a negotiable instrument before he has notice that it either is **overdue** or has been **dishonored.** The reason for this is that one should perform obligations when they are due. If a negotiable instrument is not paid when it is due, the Code considers the person taking it to be on notice that there may be defenses to the payment of it.

Overdue Instruments

If a negotiable instrument is payable on demand, it is overdue (1) the day after demand for payment has been made in a proper manner and form, (2) 90 days after its date if it is a check, and (3) if it is an instrument other than a check, when it has been outstanding for an unreasonably long period of time in light of the nature of the instrument and trade practice (3–304[a]). Thus, a check becomes stale after 90 days and, for other kinds of instruments, one must consider trade practices and the facts of the particular case. In a farming community, the normal period for loans to farmers may be six months. A demand note might be outstanding for six or seven months before it is considered overdue. On the other hand, a demand note issued in an industrial city where the normal period of such loans is 30 to 60 days would be considered overdue in a much shorter period of time.

If a negotiable instrument due on a certain date is not paid by that date, normally then it is overdue at the beginning of the next day after the due date. For example, if a promissory note dated January 1 is payable "30 days after date," it is due on January 31. If it is not paid by January 31, it is overdue beginning on February 1.

As to instruments payable at a definite time, Revised Article 3 sets out four rules: (1) if the principal is not payable in installments and the due date has not been accelerated, the instrument is overdue on the day after the due date; (2) if the principal is due in installments and a due date has not been accelerated, the instrument is overdue upon default for nonpayment of an installment and remains overdue until the default is cured; (3) if a due date for principal has been accelerated, the instrument is overdue on the day after the accelerated due date; and (4) unless the due date of principal has been accelerated, an instrument does not become overdue if there is a default in payment of interest but no default in payment of principal (3–304[b]).

Dishonored Instruments

To be a holder in due course, a person must take not only a negotiable instrument before he has notice that it is overdue but also before it has been dishonored. A negotiable instrument has been *dishonored* when the holder has presented it for payment (or acceptance) and payment (or acceptance) has been refused.

For example, Susan writes a check on her account at First National Bank that is payable "to the order of Sven Sorensen." Sven takes the check to First National Bank to cash it but the bank refuses to pay it because Susan has insufficient funds in her account to cover it. The check has been dishonored. If Sven then takes Susan's check to Harry's Hardware and uses it to pay for some paint, Harry's cannot be a holder in due course of the check if it is on notice that the check has been dishonored. Harry's would have such notice if First National had stamped the check "Payment Refused NSF" (not sufficient funds).

Similarly, suppose Carol Carson signs a 30-day note payable to Ace Appliance for $500 and gives it to Ace as payment for a stereo set. When Ace asks Carol for payment, she refuses to pay because the stereo does not work properly. If Ace negotiates the note to First National Bank, First National cannot be a holder in due course if it knows about Carol's refusal to pay.

NOTICE OF UNAUTHORIZED SIGNATURE OR ALTERATION

A holder who has notice that an instrument contains an unauthorized signature or has been altered cannot qualify as a holder in due course of the instrument. For example, Frank makes out a check in the amount of $5.00 payable to George Grocer and gives it to his daughter, Jane, to take to the grocery store to purchase some groceries. The groceries Jane purchases cost $20.00 and Jane changes the check to read $25.00, giving it to Grocer in exchange for the groceries and $5.00 in cash. Grocer cannot qualify as a holder in due course if he sees Jane make the alteration to the check or otherwise is on notice of it.

NOTICE OF CLAIMS

If a person taking a negotiable instrument is *on notice of an adverse claim* to the instrument by someone else (for example, that she is the rightful owner of the instrument) or that someone is seeking to rescind a prior negotiation of the instrument, the current holder cannot qualify as a holder in due course. For example, a U.S. Treasury check is payable to Susan Samuels. Samuels loses the check and it is found by Robert Burns. Burns takes the check to a hardware store, signs "Susan Samuels" on the back of the check in the view of a clerk, and seeks to use it in payment of merchandise. The hardware store cannot be a holder in due course because it is on notice of a potential claim to the instrument by Susan Samuels.

Notice of Breach of Fiduciary Duty

One situation in which the Code considers a person to be on notice of a claim is if she is taking a negotiable instrument from a fiduciary, such as a trustee. If a negotiable instrument is payable to a person as a trustee or an attorney for someone, then any attempt by that person to negotiate it for his own behalf or for his use (or benefit) or to deposit it in an account other than that of the fiduciary puts the person on notice that the beneficiary of the trust may have a claim (3–307).

For example, a check is drawn "Pay to the order of Arthur Adams, Trustee for Mary Minor." Adams takes the check to Credit Union, indorses his name to it, and uses it to pay off the balance on a loan Adams had from Credit Union. Credit Union cannot be a holder in due course because it should know that the negotiation of the check is in violation of the fiduciary duty Adams owes to Mary Minor. Credit Union should know this because Adams is negotiating the check for his own benefit, not Mary's.

NOTICE OF DEFENSES AND CLAIMS IN RECOUPMENT

To qualify as a holder in due course, a person also must acquire a negotiable instrument without notice that any party to it has any **defenses** or **claims in recoupment.** Potential defenses include infancy, duress, fraud, and failure of consideration. Thus, if a person knows that a signature on the instrument was obtained by fraud, misrepresentation, or duress, the person cannot be a holder in due course.

A *claim in recoupment* is a claim of the obligor against the original payee of the instrument. The claim must arise from the transaction that gave rise to the instrument. An example of a claim in recoupment would be as follows: Buyer purchases a used automobile from Dealer for $8,000, giving Dealer a note for $8,000 payable in one year. Because the automobile is not as warranted, Buyer has a breach of warranty claim that could be asserted against Dealer as a counterclaim or "claim in recoupment" to offset the amount owing on the note.

IRREGULAR AND INCOMPLETE INSTRUMENTS

A person cannot be a holder in due course of a negotiable instrument if, when she takes it, it is irregular or some important or **material term** is blank. If the negotiable instrument contains a facial irregularity, such as an obvious alteration in the amount, then it is considered to be **irregular paper.** If you take an irregular instrument, you are considered to be on notice of any possible defenses to it. For example, Kevin writes a check for "one dollar" payable to Karen. Karen inserts the word "hundred" in the amount, changes the figure "$1" to "$100," and gives the check to a druggist in exchange for a purchase of goods. If the alterations in the amount should be obvious to the druggist, perhaps because there are erasures, different handwritings, or different inks, then the druggist cannot be a holder in due course. She would have taken irregular paper and would be on notice that there might be defenses to it. These defenses include Kevin's defense that he is liable for only $1 because that is the amount for which he made the check.

Similarly, if someone receives a check that has been signed but the space where the amount of the check is to be written is blank, then the person cannot be a holder in due course of that check. The fact that a material term is blank means that the instrument is **incomplete** and should put the person on notice that the drawer may have a defense to payment of it. To be material, the omitted term must be one that affects the legal obligation of the parties to the negotiable instrument. Material terms include the amount of the instrument and the name of the payee. If a negotiable instrument is completed after the obligor signed it, but before a person acquires it, the person can qualify as a holder in due course if she had no knowledge about the completion.

PAYEE AS HOLDER IN DUE COURSE

The original Article 3 provided explicitly that a *payee* could be a holder in due course if she complied with all the requirements for a holder in due course. Revised Article 3 drops the explicit statement. The drafters stated they intended no change in the law but that they were concerned that the explicit provision suggested that use of holder-in-due-course status by payees was the normal situation. It is not the normal situation because a payee usually will have notice or knowledge of any defenses to the instrument and will know whether it is overdue or has been dishonored; consequently, the payee is unlikely to qualify as a holder in due course.

For example, Drew draws a check on First Bank as drawee, payable to the order of Parks but leaves the amount blank. Drew delivers the check to Axe, his agent, and instructs Axe to fill in $300 as the amount. Axe, however, fills in $500 as the amount, and Parks gives Axe $500 for the check. Axe then gives Drew $300 and absconds with the extra $200. In such a case, Parks, as payee, is a holder in due course of the check because he has taken it for value, in good faith, and without notice of defenses.

Similarly, assume that Jarvis owes Fields $200. Jarvis agrees to sell Kirk a used television set for $200; Jarvis assures Kirk that it is in working condition. In fact, the set is broken. Jarvis asks Kirk to make her check for $200 payable to Fields and then delivers the check to Fields in payment of the debt. Fields, as the payee, can be a holder in due course of the check if he is not aware of the misrepresentation that Jarvis made to Kirk in order to obtain the check.

CONCEPT SUMMARY	Requirements for a Holder in Due Course

Requirement	Rule
1. Must be a *holder*.	A holder is a person in possession of an instrument payable to bearer or payable to him.
2. Must take for *value*.	A holder has given value: a. To the extent the agreed-on consideration has been paid or performed. b. To the extent a security interest or lien has been obtained. c. By payment of—or granting security for—an antecedent claim. d. By giving a negotiable instrument for it. e. By making an irrevocable commitment to a third person.
3. Must take in *good faith*.	Good faith means honesty in fact and the observance of reasonable commercial standards of fair dealing.
4. Must take *without notice* that the instrument is *overdue*.	An instrument payable on demand is overdue the day after demand for payment has been duly made. A check is overdue 90 days after its date. If it is an instrument other than a check and payable on demand, when it has been outstanding for an unreasonably long period of time in light of the nature of the instrument and trade practice, it is overdue. If it is an instrument due on a certain date, then it is overdue at the beginning of the next day after the due date.
5. Must take *without knowledge that the instrument has been dishonored.*	An instrument has been dishonored when the holder has presented it for payment (or acceptance) and payment (or acceptance) has been refused.
6. Must take *without notice* of any *uncured default* with respect to payment of another instrument issued as part of the same series.	If there is a series of notes, holder must take without notice that there is an uncured default as to any other notes in the series.
7. Must take *without notice* that the instrument contains an *unauthorized signature* or has been *altered*.	Notice of unauthorized signature or alteration—change in a material term—prevents holder from obtaining HDC status.
8. Must take *without notice* of any *claim of a property or possessory interest* in it.	Claims of property or possessory interest include: a. Claim by someone that she is the rightful owner of the instrument. b. Person seeking to rescind a prior negotiation of the instrument. c. Claim by a beneficiary that a fiduciary negotiated the instrument for his own benefit.
9. Must take *without notice* that any party has a *defense* against it.	Defenses include real defenses that go to the validity of the instrument and personal defenses that commonly are defenses to a simple contract.
10. Must take *without notice* of a *claim in recoupment* to it.	A claim in recoupment is a claim of the obligor on the instrument against the original payee that arises from the transaction that gave rise to the instrument.
11. The instrument must not bear *apparent evidence of forgery or alteration* or be *irregular or incomplete*.	The instrument must not contain obvious reasons to question its authenticity.

SHELTER RULE

The transferee of an instrument—whether or not the transfer is a negotiation—obtains those rights that the transferor had, including (1) the transferor's right to enforce the instrument and (2) any right as a holder in due course (3–230[b]). This means that any person who can trace his title to an instrument back to a holder in due course receives rights similar to a holder in due course even if he cannot meet the requirements himself. This is known as the **shelter rule** in Article 3.

For example, Archer makes a note payable to Bryant. Bryant negotiates the note to Carlyle, who qualifies as a holder in due course. Carlyle then negotiates the note to Darby, who cannot qualify as a holder in due course because she knows the note is overdue. Because Darby can trace her title back to a holder in due course (Carlyle), Darby has rights as a holder in due course when she seeks payment of the note from Archer.

There is, however, a limitation on the shelter rule. A transferee who has himself been a party to any fraud or illegality affecting the instrument cannot improve his position by taking, directly or indirectly, from a later holder in due course (3–230[b]). For example, Archer, through fraudulent representations, induced Bryant to execute a negotiable note payable to Archer and then negotiated the instrument to Carlyle, who took it as a holder in due course. If Archer thereafter took the note for value from Carlyle, Archer could not acquire Carlyle's rights as a holder in due course. Archer was a party to the fraud that induced the note, and, accordingly, cannot improve his position by negotiating the instrument and then reacquiring it.

.... *RIGHTS OF A HOLDER IN DUE COURSE* ....

CLAIMS AND DEFENSES GENERALLY

Revised Article 3 establishes four categories of claims and defenses. They are:

1. Real defenses—which go to the validity of the instrument.
2. Personal defenses—which generally arise out of the transaction that gave rise to the instrument.
3. Claims to an instrument—which generally concern property or possessory rights in an instrument or its proceeds.
4. Claims in recoupment—which also arise out of the transaction that gave rise to the instrument.

These defenses and claims are discussed in some detail on page 712.

IMPORTANCE OF BEING A HOLDER IN DUE COURSE

In the preceding chapter, we pointed out that one advantage of negotiable instruments over other kinds of contract is that they are accepted as substitutes for money. People are willing to accept them as substitutes for money because, generally, they can take them free of claims or defenses to payment between the original parties to the instrument. On the other hand, a person who takes an assignment of a simple contract gets only the same rights as the person had who assigned the contract.

There are two qualifications to the ability of a person who acquired a negotiable instrument to be free of claims or defenses between the original parties. First, the person in possession of a negotiable instrument must be a *person entitled to enforce the instrument* as well as a *holder in due course* (or must be a holder who has the rights of a holder in due course through the shelter rule). If the person is neither, then she is subject to all claims or defenses to payment that any party to it has. Second, the only claims or defenses that the holder in due course has to worry about are so-called real defenses—those that affect the validity of the instrument—or claims that arose after she became a holder. For example, if the maker or drawer did not have legal capacity because she was a minor, the maker or drawer has a real defense. The holder in due course does not have to worry about other defenses and claims that do not go to the validity of the instrument—the so-called personal defenses.

In the case that follows, the holder in due course of a money order that had been stolen was entitled to enforce it against the issuer.

REAL DEFENSES

There are some claims and defenses to payment of an instrument that go to the validity of the instrument. These claims and defenses are known as **real defenses.** They

---

TRIFFIN V. DILLABOUGH
670 A.2d 684 (Super. Ct. Penn. 1996)

FACTS

On December 11, 1990, two American Express money orders in the amounts of $550 and $650, respectively, which were payable to Stacey Anne Dillabough, were presented to Chuckie Enterprise, Inc. (Chuckie's), a check-cashing operation in Philadelphia. The money orders were duly indorsed, and photo identifications were provided by the payee, whereupon Chuckie's paid the face amounts minus a 2 percent fee. Dillabough was a previous customer of Chuckie's and was recognized as such by the president of Chuckie's, Charles Giunta, who handled the transaction.

The two money orders had been stolen from the premises of an American Express agent. When stolen, the money orders were signed with the preprinted signature of the chairman of American Express but were blank as to payee, date, sender, and amount. When presented to Chuckie's, however, they had been completed by persons unknown. Dillabough's role is not clear from the case. She could have been an accomplice of the thief, the thief, or even someone who bought it from the thief, but the court does not say, and it is not critical to the issue here.

The money orders were passed through the usual banking channels and were presented for payment at United Bank of Grand Junction, Colorado. American Express, having noted on its "fraud log" that the money orders were stolen, returned the money orders marked "Reported Lost or Stolen Do Not Redeposit." American Express refused to pay the amounts of the money orders.

Triffin, a commercial discounter, purchased the dishonored money orders for cash from Chuckie's and took an assignment of all of Chuckie's rights, claims, and interests in the money orders. Triffin brought suit against Dillabough and American Express; demanding payment of the stolen money orders. Judgment was entered against Dillabough by default.

The back of the money orders contained the following legend:

IMPORTANT
DO NOT CASH FOR STRANGERS
THIS MONEY ORDER WILL NOT BE PAID IF IT HAS BEEN ALTERED OR STOLEN OR IF AN INDORSEMENT IS MISSING OR FORGED. BE SURE YOU HAVE EFFECTIVE RECOURSE AGAINST YOUR CUSTOMER.
PAYEE'S INDORSEMENT

ISSUE

Where blank money orders were stolen and completed without authorization prior to their negotiation, can the transferee enforce the instruments as completed if he qualifies as a holder in due course?

DECISION

Yes. A holder in due course may enforce the instrument according to its original tenor and, when an incomplete instrument has been completed, he may enforce it as completed. Here, Chuckie's took the instrument for value by paying the face amount of the order, minus its regular fee. It took the instrument in good faith, following the customary procedure of seeking photo identification from the payee. Finally, Chuckie's had no reason to be suspicious about the instrument or whether it would be paid by American Express. Accordingly, it qualifies as a holder in due course entitled to enforce the instrument as completed. Triffin, by assignment, holds the same rights in the instrument as Chuckie's previously held.

(continued)

TRIFFIN V. DILLABOUGH
(concluded)

AUTHOR'S NOTE

Although Pennsylvania has adopted Revised Article 3, all of the transactions at issue in this case were completed prior to the effective date of the amendments and the court applied and cited the original version of Article 3. However, the same result could be expected if the court was applying Revised Article 3. The requirement under Revised Article 3 is that in order to be accorded the rights of a holder in due course, the person claiming that status must have taken the instrument in good faith. The expanded definition of good faith includes observance of reasonable commercial standards of fair dealing. See Revised Sections 3–302 and 3–103(a)(4).

can be used as reasons against payment of a negotiable instrument to any holder, including a holder in due course (or a person who has the rights of a holder in due course). Real defenses include:

1. Minority or infancy that under state law makes the instrument void or voidable; for example, if Mark Miller, age 17, signs a promissory note as maker, he can use his lack of capacity to contract as a defense against paying it even to a holder in due course.
2. Incapacity that under state law makes the instrument void; for example, if a person has been declared mentally incompetent by a court, then the person has a real defense if state law declares all contracts entered into by the person after the adjudication of incompetency to be void.
3. Duress that voids or nullifies the obligation of a party liable to pay the instrument; for example, if Harold points a gun at his grandmother and forces her to execute a promissory note, the grandmother can use duress as a defense against paying it even to a holder in due course.
4. Illegality that under state law renders the obligation void; for example, in some states, checks and notes given in payment of gambling debts are void.
5. Fraud in the essence (or fraud in the *factum*). This occurs when a person signs a negotiable instrument without knowing or having a reasonable opportunity to know that it is a negotiable instrument or without knowing its essential terms. For example, Amy Jones is an illiterate person who lives alone. She signs a document that is actually a promissory note, but she is told that it is a grant of permission for a television set to be left in her house on a trial basis. Amy has a real defense against payment of the note even to a holder in due course. Fraud in the essence is distinguished from fraud in the inducement, discussed below, which is only a personal defense.
6. Discharge in bankruptcy; for example, if the maker of a promissory note has had the debt discharged in a bankruptcy proceeding, she no longer is liable on it and has a real defense against payment (3–305[a][1]).

Real defenses can be asserted even against a holder in due course of a negotiable instrument because it is more desirable to protect people who have signed negotiable instruments in these situations than it is to protect persons who have taken negotiable instruments in the ordinary course of business.

The case that follows, *CBA Credit Services of North Dakota v. Azar,* involves an instrument issued to pay a gambling debt, which state law declared to be a void obligation.

CBA CREDIT SERVICES OF NORTH DAKOTA v. AZAR
551 N.W.2d 787 (Sup. Ct. N.D. 1996)

FACTS

James Azar, a resident of Bismarck, North Dakota, traveled to the Shooting Star Casino in Mahnomen, Minnesota. The casino is located on the reservation land of the White Earth Band of Chippewa Indians, which owns and operates the casino.

While Azar was at the casino he gambled and lost approximately $14,000 playing blackjack. Casino personnel twice approached Azar after he incurred the losses and offered him, on credit, $2,000 in blackjack chips. After Azar gambled and lost each $2,000 advance, Azar was asked to issue checks to the casino for payment of the chips. Both the checks were returned to the casino by Azar's bank marked "insufficient funds." The casino then assigned its interest in the checks to CBA Credit Services, which in turn brought suit against Azar for the amount of the checks.

Under Minnesota law, gambling debts are, in general, void and as of no effect between the parties to the debt. However, there are exceptions for legalized gambling, one of which is "gaming pursuant to the Indian Gaming Regulatory Act (IGRA)." Under the IGRA, blackjack is lawful on Indian lands only if it is conducted in conformance with a tribal–state compact entered into between the Indian tribe and the State of Minnesota. The compact between the state and the Chippewa Tribe provides in pertinent part:

All gaming shall be conducted on a cash basis. Except as herein provided, no person shall be extended credit for gaming by any gaming facility operated within the White Earth Band, and no operator shall permit any person or organization to offer such credit for a fee. This section shall not restrict the right of the Band or any other person to offer check cashing or to install or accept bank card or credit card transactions in the same manner as would normally be permitted at any retail business within the State.

ISSUE

Can CBA enforce payment of the checks issued to satisfy gambling debts incurred on credit?

DECISION

No. The gaming activity in which Azar incurred his gambling debt, the play of blackjack on credit, was not conducted lawfully under the compact and, therefore, was not conducted lawfully under IGRA. Thus, the lawful gaming exception is not applicable and the casino cannot enforce Azar's gambling debt. Moreover, as assignee, CBA has only those rights which its assignor, the casino, has. In accepting assignment of the casino's interest in the two insufficient funds checks, CBA knew the checks had been dishonored by Azar's bank and cannot qualify as a holder in due course.

In addition to the real defenses discussed above, there are several other reasons that a person otherwise liable to pay an instrument would have a defense against payment that would be effective, even against a holder in due course. They include:

1. *Forgery.* For example, if a maker's signature has been put on the instrument without his authorization and without his negligence, the maker has a defense against payment of the note.
2. *Alteration of the completed instrument.* This is a partial defense against a holder in due course (or a person having the rights of a holder in due course), and a complete defense against a non–holder in due course. A holder in due course can enforce an altered instrument against the maker or drawer according to its original tenor.
3. *Discharge.* If a person takes an instrument with knowledge that the obligation of any party obligated on the instrument has been discharged, the person takes subject to the discharge even if the person is a holder in due course.

Ethical Implications	Suppose you have given a check in payment of a gambling debt in a state that makes such obligations void. Are there any ethical considerations involved as to whether you should assert the real defense of illegality against payment of the check to a holder in due course?

PERSONAL DEFENSES

Personal defenses are legal reasons for avoiding or reducing liability of a person who is liable on a negotiable instrument. Generally, personal defenses arise out of the transaction in which the negotiable instrument was issued and are based on negotiable instruments law or contract law. A holder in due course of a negotiable instrument (or one who can claim the rights of one) is not subject to any personal defenses or claims that may exist between the original parties to the instrument. Personal defenses include:

1. *Lack or failure of consideration.* For example, a promissory note for $100 was given to someone without intent to make a gift and without receiving anything in return (3–303[b]).
2. *Breach of contract, including breach of warranty.* For example, a check was given in payment for repairs to an automobile but the repair work was defective.
3. *Fraud in the inducement of any underlying contract.* For example, an art dealer sells a lithograph to Cheryl, telling her that it is a Picasso and takes Cheryl's check for $500 in payment. The art dealer knows that the lithograph is not a genuine Picasso but a forgery. Cheryl has been induced to make the purchase and to give her check by the art dealer's fraudulent representation. Because of this fraud, Cheryl has a personal defense against having to honor her check to the art dealer.
4. *Incapacity to the extent that state law makes the obligation voidable, as opposed to void.* For example, where state law makes the contract of a person of limited mental capacity but who has not been adjudicated incompetent voidable, the person has a personal defense to payment.
5. *Illegality that makes a contract voidable, as opposed to void.* For example, when the payee of a check given for certain professional services was required to have a license from the state but did not have one.
6. *Duress, to the extent it is not so severe as to make the obligation void but rather only voidable.* For example, if the instrument was signed under a threat to prosecute the maker's son if it was not signed, the maker might have a personal defense.
7. *Unauthorized completion or material alteration of the instrument.* For example, the instrument was completed in an unauthorized manner, or a material alteration was made to it after it left the maker's or drawer's possession.
8. *Nonissuance of the instrument, conditional issuance, and issuance for a special purpose.* For example, that the person in possession of the instrument obtained it by theft or by finding it rather than through an intentional delivery of the instrument to him (3–105[b]).
9. *Failure to countersign a traveler's check* (3–106[c]).
10. *Modification of the obligation by a separate agreement* (3–117).

11.   *Payment that violates a restrictive indorsement* (3–206[f]).
12.   *Breach of warranty when a draft is accepted* (discussed in following chapter)
       (3–417[b]).

The following example illustrates the limited extent to which a maker or drawer can use personal defenses as a reason for not paying a negotiable instrument he signed. Suppose Trent Tucker bought a used truck from Honest Harry's and gave Harry a 60-day promissory note for $2,750 in payment for the truck. Honest Harry's "guaranteed" the truck to be in "good working condition," but in fact the truck had a cracked engine block. If Harry tries to collect the $2,750 from Trent, Trent could claim breach of warranty as a reason for not paying Harry the full $2,750 because Harry is not a holder in due course. However, if Harry negotiated the note to First National Bank and the bank was a holder in due course, the situation would be changed. If the bank tried to collect the $2,750 from Trent, Trent would have to pay the bank. Trent's defense or claim of breach of warranty cannot be used as a reason for not paying a holder in due course. It is a personal defense. Trent must pay the bank the $2,750 and then pursue his breach of warranty claim against Harry.

The rule that a holder in due course takes a negotiable instrument free of any personal defenses or claims to it has been modified to some extent, particularly in relation to instruments given by consumers. These modifications will be discussed in the next section of this chapter.

CLAIMS TO THE INSTRUMENT

For purposes of Revised Article 3, the term **claims** to an instrument can include:

1.   A claim to ownership of the instrument by one who asserts that he is the owner and was wrongfully deprived of possession.
2.   A claim of a lien on the instrument.
3.   A claim for rescission of an indorsement.

A holder in due course takes free of claims that arose before she became a holder but is subject to those arising when or after she becomes a holder in due course. For example, if a holder impairs the collateral given for an obligation, she may be creating a defense for an obligor.

CLAIMS IN RECOUPMENT

A *claim in recoupment* is not actually a defense to an instrument but an *offset* to *liability.* For example, Ann Adams purchases a new automobile from Dealership, giving it a note for the balance of the purchase price beyond her down payment. After accepting delivery, she discovers a breach of warranty that the dealer fails to remedy. If Dealer has sold the note to a bank that subsequently seeks payment on the note from Adams, she has a claim in recoupment for breach of warranty. If the bank is a holder in due course, the claim in recoupment cannot be asserted against it. However, if the bank is not a holder in due course, then Adams can assert the claim in recoupment to reduce the amount owing on the instrument at the time the action is brought against her on the note. Her claim could serve only to reduce the amount owing, not as a basis for a net recovery from the bank. However, if Dealer was the person bringing an action to collect the note, Adams could assert the breach of warranty claim as a counterclaim and potentially might recover from Dealer any difference between the claim and the damages due for breach of warranty.

The obligor may assert a claim up to the amount of the instrument if the holder is the original payee but cannot assert claims in recoupment against a holder in due course. In addition, the obligor may assert a claim against a transferee who does not qualify as a holder in due course but only up to the amount owing on the instrument at the time it brought the claim in recoupment.

CONCEPT SUMMARY	Claims and Defenses against Payment of Negotiable Instruments
Claim or Defense	**Examples**
Real Defense Valid against all holders, including holders in due course and holders who have the rights of holders in due course.	1. Minority that under state law makes the contract void or voidable. 2. Other lack of capacity that makes the contract void. 3. Duress that makes the contract void. 4. Illegality that makes the contract void. 5. Fraud in the essence (fraud in the *factum*). 6. Discharge in bankruptcy.
Personal Defense Valid against plain holders of instruments—but not against holders in due course or holders who have the rights on in-due-course holders through the shelter rule.	1. Lack or failure of consideration. 2. Breach of contract (including breach of warranty). 3. Fraud in the inducement. 4. Lack of capacity that makes the contract voidable (except minority). 5. Illegality that makes the contract voidable. 6. Duress that makes the contract voidable. 7. Unauthorized completion of an incomplete instrument, or material alteration of the instrument. 8. Nonissuance of the instrument. 9. Failure to countersign a traveler's check. 10. Modification of the obligation by a separate agreement. 11. Payment that violates a restrictive indorsement. 12. Breach of warranty when a draft is accepted.
Claim to an Instrument	1. Claim of ownership by someone who claims to be the owner and that he was wrongfully deprived of possession. 2. Claim of a lien on the instrument. 3. Claim for rescission of an indorsement.
Claims in Recoupment	1. Breach of warranty in the sale of goods for which the instrument was issued.

CHANGES IN THE HOLDER IN DUE COURSE RULE

CONSUMER DISADVANTAGES

The rule that a holder in due course of a negotiable instrument is not subject to personal defenses between the original parties to it makes negotiable instruments a readily accepted substitute for money. This rule can also result in serious disadvantages to consumers. Consumers sometimes buy goods or services on credit and give the seller a negotiable instrument such as a promissory note. They often do this without knowing the consequences of their signing a negotiable instrument. If the goods or services are defective or not delivered, the consumer would like to withhold payment of the note until the seller corrects the problem or makes the delivery. Where the note is still held by the seller, the consumer can do this because any defenses of breach of warranty or nonperformance are good against the seller.

However, the seller may have negotiated the note at a discount to a third party such as a bank. If the bank qualifies as a holder in due course, the consumer must pay the note in full to the bank. The consumer's personal defenses are not valid against a holder in due course. The consumer must pay the holder in due course and then try to get her money back from the seller. This may be difficult if the seller cannot be found or will not accept responsibility. The consumer would be in a much stronger position if she could just withhold payment, even against the bank, until the goods or services are delivered or the performance is corrected.

STATE LEGISLATION

Some state legislatures and courts have limited the holder in due course doctrine, particularly as it affects consumers. State legislatures limiting the doctrine typically amended state laws dealing with consumer transactions. For example, some state laws prohibit a seller from taking a negotiable instrument other than a check from a consumer in payment for consumer goods and services. Other state laws require promissory notes given by consumers in payment for goods and services to carry the words *consumer paper;* these state laws treat instruments with the legend "consumer paper" as nonnegotiable. Thus, the rights of a consumer who has signed a negotiable instrument vary from state to state.

FEDERAL TRADE COMMISSION RULES

The Federal Trade Commission (FTC) has promulgated a regulation designed to protect consumers against operation of the holder in due course rule. The FTC rule applies to persons who sell to consumers on credit and have the consumer sign a note or an installment sale contract or arrange third party financing of the purchase. The seller must ensure that the note or the contract contains the following clause:

> **NOTICE: ANY HOLDER OF THIS CONSUMER CREDIT CONTRACT IS SUBJECT TO ALL CLAIMS AND DEFENSES WHICH THE DEBTOR COULD ASSERT AGAINST THE SELLER OF THE GOODS OR SERVICES OBTAINED PURSUANT HERETO OR WITH THE PROCEEDS HEREOF. RECOVERY HEREUNDER BY THE DEBTOR SHALL NOT EXCEED AMOUNTS PAID BY THE DEBTOR HEREUNDER.[3]**

The effect of the notice is to make a potential holder of the note or contract subject to all claims and defenses of the consumer. This is illustrated in the case of *Music Acceptance Corp. v. Lofing,* which follows. If the note or contract does not contain the clause required by the FTC Rule, the consumer does not gain any rights that he would not otherwise have under state law, and the subsequent holder may qualify as a holder in due course. However, the FTC does have the right to seek a fine of as much as $10,000 against the seller who failed to include the notice.

MUSIC ACCEPTANCE CORP. v. LOFING
39 Cal. Rptr. 159 (Ct. App. Cal. 1995)

FACTS

Dan Lofing purchased a Steinway grand piano from Sherman Clay & Co., Steinway & Sons' Sacramento dealer, and received financing through Sherman Clay's finance company, Music Acceptance Corporation (MAC). The consumer note for $19,650.94 prepared by MAC and signed by Lofing included the following in bold faced type:

(continued)

---

[3]Revised Section 3–106(d) covers this clause.

MUSIC ACCEPTANCE CORP. v. LOFING

(concluded)

NOTICE

ANY HOLDER OF THIS CONSUMER CREDIT CONTRACT IS SUBJECT TO ALL CLAIMS AND DEFENSES WHICH THE DEBTOR COULD ASSERT AGAINST THE SELLER OF THE GOODS OR SERVICES OBTAINED PURSUANT HERETO OR WITH THE PROCEEDS HEREOF. RECOVERY HEREUNDER SHALL NOT EXCEED AMOUNTS PAID BY THE DEBTOR HEREUNDER.

Lofing received a warranty from Steinway which provided the company "will promptly repair or replace without charge any part of this piano which is found to have a defect in material or workmanship within five years" from the date of sale.

Lofing became disenchanted with the piano after experiencing a variety of problems with it. There was a significant deterioration in the action and tonal quality of the piano which the Sherman Clay piano technician was unable to remedy despite lengthy and repeated efforts. A Steinway representative who was called in to inspect the piano concluded that it was in "terrible condition" and expressed surprise that it had ever left the factory. He concluded that the piano would have to be completely rebuilt at the factory.

Because the piano was impossible to play and was ruining his technique, Lofing stopped making payments on the piano. To mitigate his damages, Lofing sold the piano for $7,000 and purchased a Kawai piano from another dealer. He brought suit against Sherman Clay, Steinway, and MAC for, among other things, breach of warranty. One of the issues in the litigation was whether the notice in the note allowed him to assert the breach of warranty as a grounds for not continuing to pay off the note to MAC.

ISSUE

When a promissory note contains the notice required by the FTC, can the maker assert proposed breach of warranty in the underlying transaction against the holder of the note?

DECISION

Yes. The FTC rule was adopted because the FTC believed that it was an unfair practice for a seller to employ procedures in the course of arranging the financing of a consumer sale which separated the buyer's duty to pay for goods or services from the seller's reciprocal duty to perform as promised. Here, the clear breach of warranty on the part of Sherman Clay and Steinway relieves Lofing of his duty to continue to pay the consumer note to MAC.

.... *QUESTIONS AND PROBLEM CASES* ....

1. What is the difference between a real defense and a personal defense to a negotiable instrument?

2. A bank cashed the checks of its customer, Dental Supply, Inc., presented to the bank by an employee of Dental Supply named Wilson. The checks were indorsed in blank with a rubber stamp of Dental Supply, Inc. Wilson had been stealing the checks by taking cash rather than depositing them to Dental Supply, Inc.'s account. What could Dental Supply have done to avoid this situation?

3. Raye Walker was a bookkeeper for O.K. Moving & Storage Company. She opened a checking account in her name at Elgin National Bank. She then took checks that were made payable to O.K. Moving & Storage, indorsed them "For Deposit Only, O.K. Moving & Storage Co., 80 Carson Drive, N.E., Fort Walton, Florida," and deposited them in her individual account at Elgin National Bank. In a period of one year, she deposited, and Elgin Bank accepted for deposit to her account, checks totaling $19,356.01. When O.K. Moving & Storage discovered this, it sued Elgin Bank for $19,356.01 for conversion of its checks. Should Elgin Bank have permitted the checks restrictively indorsed "For Deposit Only" to a corporation's account to be deposited to an individual account?

4. Reliable Janitorial Service, Inc., maintained a bank account with AmSouth Bank. Rosa Pennington was employed by Reliable as a bookkeeper/office manager. She deposited checks made payable to Reliable but did not have authority to write checks on Reliable's account. Beginning in January 1985, Pennington obtained counter deposit slips from

AmSouth. She wrote on the deposit slips that the depositor was "Reliable Janitorial Services, Inc.," but in the space for the account number, Pennington wrote the account number for her own personal account with AmSouth. She stamped the checks that were made payable to "Reliable Janitorial Services, Inc.," with the indorsement "For Deposit Only, Reliable Carpet Cleaning, Inc." Over an 11-month period, Pennington was able to deposit 169 checks so indorsed. AmSouth credited the deposits to Pennington, not Reliable. Pennington spent all the funds that she diverted to her account. When Reliable discovered the fraud, it brought suit against AmSouth for conversion and sought to have its account credited with the improperly paid checks. Was AmSouth Bank liable to Reliable for the value of the restrictively indorsed checks that it paid inconsistently with the indorsement?

5. Reggie Bluiett worked at the Silver Slipper Gambling Hall and Saloon. She received her weekly paycheck made out to her from the Silver Slipper. She indorsed the check in blank and left it on her dresser at home. Fred Watkins broke into Bluiett's house and stole the check. Watkins took the check to the local auto store, where he bought two tires at a cost of $171.21. He obtained the balance of the check in cash. Could the auto store qualify as a holder in due course?

6. Horton wrote a check for $20,000 to Axe, who in turn indorsed it to Halbert. In return, Halbert advanced $8,000 in cash to Axe and promised to cancel a $12,000 debt owed him by Axe. The check, when presented by Halbert to the bank, was not paid due to insufficient funds. Halbert thus never regarded the debt as canceled. To what extent can Halbert be a holder in due course of the check?

7. Charles Alcombrack was appointed guardian for his son, Chad Alcombrack, who was seven years old and the beneficiary of his grandfather's life insurance policy. The insurance company issued a check for $30,588.39 made payable to "Charles Alcombrack, Guardian of the Estate of Chad Stephen Alcombrack, a Minor." The attorney for the son's estate directed the father to take the check, along with the letters of guardianship

issued to the father, to the bank and open up a guardianship savings and checking account. Instead, the father took the check, without the letters of guardianship, to the Olympic Bank and opened a personal checking and a personal savings account. Despite the fact that the check was payable to the father in his guardianship capacity, the bank allowed the father to place the entire amount in his newly opened personal accounts. The father used all but $320.60 of the trust money for his personal benefit. A new guardian, J. David Smith, was appointed for Chad. Smith brought suit against the Olympic Bank, on Chad's behalf, to recover the amount of the check. Was the bank a holder in due course of the check?

8. Two smooth-talking salesmen for Rich Plan of New Orleans called on Leona and George Henne at their home. They sold the Hennes a home food plan. One of the salesmen suggested that the Hennes sign a blank promissory note. The Hennes refused. The salesman then wrote in ink "$100" as the amount and "4" as the number of installments in which the note was to be paid, and the Hennes signed the note. Several days later, the Hennes received a payment book from Nationwide Acceptance. The payment book showed that a total of $843.37 was due, payable in 36 monthly installments. Rich Plan had erased the "$100" and "4" on the note and typed in the figures "$843.37" and "36." The erasures were cleverly done but were visible to the naked eye. Rich Plan then negotiated the Hennes' note to Nationwide Acceptance. The Hennes refused to pay the note. Nationwide claimed that it was a holder in due course and was entitled to receive payment. Was Nationwide Acceptance a holder in due course?

9. Panlick, the owner of an apartment building, entered into a written contract with Bucci, a paving contractor whereby Bucci was to install asphalt paving on the parking lot of the building. When Bucci finished the job, Panlick gave Bucci a check for $6,500 and a promissory note for $7,593 with interest at 10 percent due six months from its date. When the note came due, Panlick refused to pay it. Bucci brought suit to collect the note, and Panlick claimed

that there had been a failure of consideration because the asphalt was defectively installed. Can Panlick assert this defense against Bucci?

10. Pedro and Paula de la Fuente were visited by a representative of Aluminum Industries, Inc., who was seeking to sell them aluminum siding for their home. They agreed to purchase the siding and signed a number of documents, including a retail installment contract and a promissory note for $9,137.24. The contract granted Aluminum Industries, Inc., a first lien on the de la Fuentes' residence; this was in violation of the Texas Civil Code, which prohibited such provisions. The promissory note contained a notice in bold type as required by the Federal Trade Commission. It read in part:

> **NOTICE: ANY HOLDER OF THIS CONSUMER CREDIT CONTRACT IS SUBJECT TO ALL CLAIMS AND DEFENSES WHICH THE DEBTOR COULD ASSERT AGAINST THE SELLER OF GOODS OR SERVICES OBTAINED PURSUANT HERETO WITH THE PROCEEDS THEREOF.**

Aluminum Industries assigned the promissory note and first lien to Home Savings Association. Aluminum Industries subsequently went out of business. Home Savings brought suit against the de la Fuentes to collect the balance due on the note. Home Savings contended that it was a holder in due course and that the de la Fuentes could not assert any defenses against it that they had against Aluminum Industries. Can an assignee of a consumer promissory note that includes the notice required by the FTC qualify as a holder in due course?

11. *Video Case.* See "TV Repair." Arnold takes his old TV set to an appliance store for repair and purchases a new TV from the store. He signs a promissory note that provides for installment payments for the balance due on the new set. The note contains the notice that the FTC requires be included in consumer credit instruments. Arnold discovers that the TV is defective after making the first payment on the note to the appliance store. The appliance store assigns the promissory note to Acme Finance Company, which notifies Arnold of its interest in the note and that he should make his payments on the note to it. Arnold advises Acme Finance that he will not make any further payments on the promissory note until the TV is repaired. If Arnold has a valid claim for breach of warranty of merchantability of the TV set, can he assert this as a defense against paying the note to the appliance store and/or to Acme Finance?

CHAPTER 38

Liability of Parties

When you sign a promissory note, you expect that you will be liable for paying the note on the day it is due. Similarly, when you sign a check and mail it off to pay a bill, you expect that it will be paid by the drawee bank out of your checking account and that if there are not sufficient funds in your account to cover it, you will have to make it good out of other funds you have. The liability of the maker of a note and of the drawer of a check is commonly understood.

However, there are other ways a person can become liable on a negotiable instrument. Moreover, some of the usual liability rules are modified when a party is negligent in issuing or paying a negotiable instrument—or otherwise contributes to a potential loss. This chapter will discuss the liabilities of the various parties to a negotiable instrument and will also cover what happens when the instrument is not paid when it is supposed to be paid. Among the issues that will be addressed are:

- *What liability do you assume when you indorse a check that is payable to your order and "cash" it at a check-cashing service?*
- *What warranties do you make when you present a check to the drawee bank for payment?*
- *What liability does a drawee bank have to its customer if it pays a check containing a forged payee's indorsement?*
- *Between you and the drawee bank, who bears the loss if you are careless in making out a check and someone is able to increase the amount stated on it?*
- *How is liability on an instrument discharged?*

Thus far in Part VI, "Commercial Paper," the focus has been on the nature of, and requirements for, negotiable instruments as well as the rights that an owner of an instrument can obtain and how to obtain them. Another important aspect to negotiable instruments concerns how a person becomes liable on a negotiable instrument and the nature of the liability incurred.

When a person signs a promissory note, he expects to be liable for paying the note on the day it is due. Similarly, when a person signs a check and mails it off to pay a bill, she expects that the drawee bank will pay it from funds in her checking account and that if her account contains insufficient funds to cover it, she will have to make it good out of other funds she has. These liabilities concerning instruments are commonly understood.

However, there are a number of other ways in which a person can become liable on a negotiable instrument. For example, a person who indorses a paycheck assumes liability on it and a bank that cashes a check with a forged indorsement on it is liable for conversion of the check. This chapter and the following chapter discuss the liabilities of the various parties to a negotiable instrument. These two chapters also cover what happens when an instrument is not paid when it is supposed to be paid. For example, a check usually should not be paid if the drawer's account contains insufficient funds or if the check has been forged. In addition, this chapter discusses the ways in which liability on an instrument can be discharged.

LIABILITY IN GENERAL

Liability on negotiable instruments flows from signatures on the instruments as well as actions taken concerning them. It can arise from the fact that a person has signed a negotiable instrument or has authorized someone else to sign it. The liability depends on the capacity in which the person signs the instrument. Liability also arises from (1) transfer or presentment of an instrument, (2) negligence relating to the issuance, alteration, or indorsement of the instrument, (3) improper payment, or (4) conversion.

.... *CONTRACTUAL LIABILITY* ....

When a person signs a negotiable instrument, whether as maker, drawer, or indorser, or in some other capacity, she generally becomes contractually liable on the instrument. As mentioned above, this contractual liability depends on the capacity in which the person signed the instrument. The terms of the contract of the parties to a negotiable instrument are not set out in the text of the instrument. Rather, Article 3 of the Uniform Commercial Code supplies the terms, which are as much a part of the instrument as if they were part of its text.

PRIMARY AND SECONDARY LIABILITY

A party to a negotiable instrument may be either primarily liable or secondarily liable for payment of it. A person who is *primarily liable* has agreed to pay the negotiable instrument. For example, the maker of a promissory note is the person who is primarily liable on the note. A person who is *secondarily liable* is like a guarantor on a contract; Article 3 requires a secondary party to pay the negotiable instrument only if a person who is primarily liable defaults on that obligation. Chapter 40, "Introduction to Security," discusses guarantors.

.... *OBLIGATION OF A MAKER* ....

The **maker** of a promissory note is primarily liable for payment of it. The maker promises unconditionally to pay a fixed amount of money and is responsible for making good on that promise. The obligation of the maker is to pay the negotiable instrument according to its terms at the time he issues it or, if it is not issued, then according to its terms at the time it first came into possession of a holder (3–412).[1] If the material terms of the note are not complete when the maker signs it, then the maker's obligation is to pay the note as it is completed, provided that the terms filled in are as authorized. If the instrument is incomplete when the maker signs it and it is completed in an unauthorized manner, then the maker's liability will depend on whether the person seeking to enforce the instrument can qualify as a holder in due course.

The case that follows, *American Federal Bank, FSB v. Parker,* illustrates a situation in which the maker of a note was negligent in signing a blank note and was required to pay the amount fraudulently filled-in by a wrongdoer.

AMERICAN FEDERAL BANK, FSB V. PARKER
392 S.E.2d 798 (Ct. App. S.C. 1990)

FACTS

Thomas Kirkman was involved in the horse business and was a friend of John Roundtree, a loan officer for American Federal Bank. Kirkman and Roundtree conceived a business arrangement in which Kirkman would locate buyers for horses and the buyers could seek financing from American Federal. Roundtree gave Kirkman blank promissory notes and security agreements from American Federal. Kirkman was to locate the potential purchaser, take care of the paperwork, and bring the documents to the bank for approval of the purchaser's loan.

Kirkman entered into a purchase agreement with Gene Parker, a horse dealer, to copurchase for $35,000 a horse named Wills Hightime, which Kirkman represented he owned. Parker signed the American Federal promissory note in blank and executed in blank a security agreement that authorized the bank to disburse the funds to the seller of the collateral. Kirkman told Parker he would cosign the note and fill in the details of the transaction with the bank. While Kirkman did not cosign the note, he did complete it for $85,000 as opposed to $35,000. Kirkman took the note with Parker's signature to Roundtree at American Federal and received two checks from the bank payable to him in the amounts of $35,000 and $50,000. Kirkman took the $35,000 and gave it to the real owner of the horse. Parker then received the horse.

Parker began making payments to the bank and called upon Kirkman to assist in making the payments pursuant to their agreement. However, Kirkman skipped town, taking the additional $50,000 with him. Parker repaid the $35,000 but refused to pay any more. He argued that he agreed to borrow only $35,000 and the other $50,000 was unauthorized by him.

ISSUE

Was Parker's liability on the note limited to the $35,000 he had authorized Kirkman to fill in?

DECISION

No. Parker was liable to American Federal for the full $85,000. Parker executed a promissory note in blank. Under the UCC the maker of a note agrees to pay the instrument according to its tenor at the time of engagement or according to the rules governing incomplete instruments. If the completion of an instrument is unauthorized, then it is considered to be an alteration. However, a subsequent holder in due course may enforce an incomplete instrument as completed. The Official Comments to the Code indicate that where

(continued)

---

[1]The numbers in parentheses refer to sections of the Uniform Commercial Code (UCC).

due course without notice of the representative nature of the signature, the representative is liable *unless* she can prove that the original parties did not intend her to be liable on the instrument (3–402[b][2]).

Thus, if an agent or a representative signs a negotiable instrument on behalf of someone else, the agent should indicate clearly that he is signing as the representative of someone else. For example, Kim Darby, the president of Swimwear, Inc., is authorized to sign negotiable instruments for the company. If Swimwear borrows money from the bank and the bank asks her to sign a 90-day promissory note, Darby should sign it either "Swimwear, Inc., by Kim Darby, President" or "Kim Darby, President, for Swimwear, Inc." If Kim Darby signed the promissory note merely "Kim Darby," she could be personally liable on the note. Similarly, if Clara Carson authorizes Arthur Anderson, an attorney, to sign checks for her, Anderson should make sure either that the checks identify Clara Carson as the account involved or should sign them "Clara Carson by Arthur Anderson, Agent." Otherwise, he risks being personally liable on them.

UNAUTHORIZED SIGNATURE

If someone signs a person's name to a negotiable instrument without that person's authorization or approval, the signature does not bind the person whose name appears. However, the signature is effective as the signature of the unauthorized signer in favor of any person who in good faith pays the instrument or takes it for value (3–403[a]). For example, if Tom Thorne steals Ben Brown's checkbook and signs Brown's name to a check, Brown is not liable on the check because Brown had not authorized Thorne to sign Brown's name. However, Thorne can be liable on the check, because he did sign it, even though he did not sign it in his own name. Thorne's forgery of Brown's signature operates as Thorne's signature. Thus, if Thorne cashed the check at the bank, Thorne would be liable to it or if he negotiated it to a store for value, he would be liable to the store to make it good.

Even though a signature is not "authorized" when it is put on an instrument initially, it can be ratified later by the person represented (3–403[a]). It also should be noted that if more than one person must sign to constitute the authorized signature of an organization, the signature of the organization is unauthorized if one of the required signatures is lacking (3–403[b]). Corporate and other accounts sometimes require multiple signatures as a matter of maintaining sound financial control.

CONTRACTUAL LIABILITY IN OPERATION

To bring the contractual liability of the various parties to a negotiable instrument into play, it generally is necessary that the instrument be *presented for payment*. In addition, to hold the parties that are secondarily liable on the instrument to their contractual liability, it generally is necessary that the instrument be *presented for payment* and *dishonored*.

PRESENTMENT OF A NOTE

The maker of a note is primarily liable to pay it when it is due. Normally, the holder takes the note to the maker at the time it is due and asks the maker to pay it. Sometimes the note may provide for payment to be made at a bank, or the maker sends the payment to the holder at the due date. The party to whom the holder presents the instrument, without dishonoring the instrument, may (1) require the exhibition of the instrument, (2) ask for reasonable identification of the person making presentment,

(3) ask for evidence of his authority to make it if he is making it for another person, (4) return the instrument for lack of any necessary indorsement, (5) ask that a receipt be signed for any payment made, and (6) require surrender of the instrument if full payment is made (3–501).

Dishonor of a note occurs if the maker does not pay the amount due when (1) it is presented in the case of (*a*) a demand note or (*b*) a note payable at or through a bank on a definite date that is presented on or after that date or (2) if it is not paid on the date payable in the case of a note payable on a definite date but not payable at or through a bank (3–502). If the maker or payer dishonors the note, the holder can seek payment from any persons who indorsed the note before the holder took it. The basis for going after the indorsers is that they are secondarily liable. To hold the indorsers to their contractual obligation, the holder must give them notice of the dishonor. The notice can be either written or oral (3–503).

For example, Susan Strong borrows $1,000 from Jack Jones and gives him a promissory note for $1,000 at 9 percent annual interest payable in 90 days. Jones indorses the note "Pay to the order of Ralph Smith" and negotiates the note to Ralph Smith. At the end of 90 days, Smith takes the note to Strong and presents it for payment. If Strong pays Smith the $1,000 and accrued interest, she can have Smith mark it "paid" and give it back to her. If Strong does not pay the note to Smith when he presents it for payment, then she has dishonored the note. Smith should give notice of the dishonor to Jones and advise him that he intends to hold Jones secondarily liable on his indorsement. Smith may collect payment of the note from Jones. Jones, after making the note good to Smith, can try to collect the note from Strong on the ground that she defaulted on the contract she made as maker of the note. Of course, Smith also could sue Strong on the basis of her maker's obligation.

PRESENTMENT OF A CHECK OR A DRAFT

The holder should present a check or draft to the drawee. The presentment can be either for payment or for acceptance (certification) of the check or draft. Under Revised Article 3, the presentment may be made by any commercially reasonable means, including a written, oral, or electronic communication (3–501). No one is primarily obligated on a check or draft, and the drawee is not obligated on a check or draft unless it accepts (certifies) it (3–408). An acceptance of a draft is the drawee's signed commitment to honor the draft as presented. The acceptance must be written on the draft, and it may consist of the drawee's signature alone (3–409).

A drawer who writes a check issues an order to the drawee to pay a certain amount out of the drawer's account to the payee (or to someone authorized by the payee). This order is not an assignment of the funds in the drawer's account (3–408). The drawee bank does not have an obligation to the payee to pay the check unless it certifies the check. However, the drawee bank usually does have a separate contractual obligation (apart from Article 3) to the drawer to pay any properly payable checks for which funds are available in the drawer's account.

For example, Janet Payne has $1,000 in a checking account at First National Bank and writes a check for $500 drawn on First National and payable to Ralph Smith. The writing of the check is the issuance of an order by Payne to First National to pay $500 from her account to Smith or to whomever Smith requests it to be paid. First National owes no obligation to Smith to pay the $500 unless it has certified the check. However, if Smith presents the check for payment and First National refuses to pay it even though there are sufficient funds in Payne's account, then First National is liable to

Payne for breaching its contractual obligation to her to pay items properly payable from existing funds in her account. Chapter 39, "Checks and Electronic Fund Transfers," discusses the liability of a bank for wrongful dishonor of checks in more detail.

If the drawee bank does not pay or certify a check when it is properly presented for payment or acceptance (certification), the drawee bank has dishonored the check (3–502). Similarly, if a draft is not paid on the date it is due (or accepted by the drawee on the due date for acceptance), it has been dishonored. The holder of the draft or check then can proceed against either the drawer or any indorsers on their secondary liability. To do so, the holder must give them notice of the dishonor (3–503). Notice of dishonor, like presentment, can be by any commercially reasonable means, including oral, written, or electronic communication. Under certain circumstances set out in Section 3–504, presentment or notice of dishonor may be excused.

Suppose Matthews draws a check for $1,000 on her account at a bank payable to the order of Williams. Williams indorses the check "Pay to the order of Clark, Williams" and negotiates it to Clark. When Clark takes the check to the bank, it refuses to pay the check because there are insufficient funds in Matthews's account to cover the check. The check has been presented and dishonored. Clark has two options: He can proceed against Williams on Williams's secondary liability as an indorser (because by putting an unqualified indorsement on the check, Williams is obligated to make the check good if it was not honored by the drawee). Or he can proceed against Matthews on Matthews's obligation as drawer because in drawing the check, Matthews must pay any person entitled to enforce the check if it is dishonored and he is given notice. Because Clark dealt with Williams, Clark is probably more likely to return the check to Williams for payment. Williams then has to go against Matthews on Matthews's liability as drawer.

TIME OF PRESENTMENT

If an instrument is payable at a definite time, the holder should present it for payment on the due date. In the case of a demand instrument, the nature of the instrument, trade or bank usage, and the facts of the particular case determine a reasonable time for presentment for acceptance or payment. In a farming community, for example, a reasonable time to present a promissory note that is payable on demand may be six months or within a short time after the crops are ready for sale because the holder commonly expects payment from the proceeds of the crops.

········· ***WARRANTY LIABILITY*** ·········

Whether or not a person signs a negotiable instrument, a person who transfers such an instrument or presents it for payment or acceptance may incur liability on the basis of certain implied warranties. These warranties are (1) **transfer warranties,** which persons who transfer negotiable instruments make to their transferees, and (2) **presentment warranties,** which persons who present negotiable instruments for payment or acceptance (certification) make to payers and drawees.

TRANSFER WARRANTIES

A person who transfers a negotiable instrument to someone else and for consideration makes five warranties to his immediate transferee. If the transfer is by indorsement, the transferor makes these warranties to all subsequent transferees. The five *transfer warranties* are:

1. The warrantor is a person entitled to enforce the instrument. (In essence, the transferor warrants that there are no unauthorized or missing indorsements that prevent the transferor from making the transferee a person entitled to enforce the instrument.)
2. All signatures on the instrument are authentic or authorized.
3. The instrument has not been altered.
4. The instrument is not subject to a defense or a claim in recoupment that any party can assert against the warrantor.
5. The warrantor has no knowledge of any insolvency proceedings commenced with respect to the maker or acceptor or, in the case of an unaccepted draft, the drawer (3–416[a]). (Note that this is not a warranty against difficulty in collection or insolvency—the warranty stops with the warrantor's knowledge.)

Revised Article 3 provides that in the event of a breach of a transfer warranty, a beneficiary of the transfer warranties who took the instrument in good faith may recover from the warrantor an amount equal to the loss suffered as a result of the breach. However, the damages recoverable may not be more than the amount of the instrument plus expenses and loss of interest incurred as a result of the breach (3–416[b]).

Transferors of instruments other than checks may disclaim the transfer warranties. Unless the warrantor receives notice of a claim for breach of warranty within 30 days after the claimant has reason to know of the breach and the identity of the warrantor, the delay in giving notice of the claim may discharge the warrantor's liability to the extent of any loss the warrantor suffers from the delay, such as the opportunity to proceed against the transferor (3–416[c]).

Although contractual liability often furnishes a sufficient basis for suing a transferor when the party primarily obligated does not pay, warranties are still important. First, they apply even when the transferor did not indorse. Second, unlike contractual liability, they do not depend on presentment, dishonor, and notice but may be utilized before presentment has been made or after the time for giving notice has expired. Third, a holder may find it easier to return the instrument to a transferor on the ground of breach of warranty than to prove her status as a holder in due course against a maker or drawer.

CONCEPT SUMMARY   **Transfer Warranties**

The five transfer warranties made by a person who transfers a negotiable instrument to someone else for consideration are:

1. The warrantor is entitled to enforce the instrument.
2. All signatures on the instrument are authentic or authorized.
3. The instrument has not been altered.
4. The instrument is not subject to a defense or a claim in recoupment that any party can assert against the warrantor.
5. The warrantor has no knowledge of any insolvency proceedings commenced with respect to the maker or acceptor or, in the case of an unaccepted draft, the drawer.

Who	What Warranties	To Whom
Nonindorsing Transferor	Makes all five transfer warranties	To his immediate transferor only
Indorsing Transferor	Makes all five transfer warranties	To all subsequent transferors

Presentment Warranties

Persons who present negotiable instruments for payment or drafts for acceptance also make warranties, but their warranties differ from those transferors make. If an unaccepted draft (such as a check) is presented to the drawee for payment or acceptance and the drawee pays or accepts the draft, then the person obtaining payment or acceptance warrants to the drawee making payment or accepting the draft in good faith that:

1. The warrantor is, or was, at the time the warrantor transferred the draft, a person entitled to enforce the draft or authorized to obtain payment or acceptance of the draft on behalf of a person entitled to enforce the draft.
2. The draft has not been altered.
3. The warrantor has no knowledge that the signature of the drawer of the draft has not been authorized (3–417[a]).

These warranties also are made by any prior transferor of the instrument at the time the person transfers the instrument; the warranties run to the drawee who makes payment or accepts the draft in good faith. Such a drawee would include a drawee bank paying a check presented to it for payment directly or through the bank collection process.

The effect of the third presentment warranty is to leave with the drawee the risk that the drawer's signature is unauthorized, unless the person presenting the draft for payment, or a prior transferor, had knowledge of any lack of authorization.

A drawee who makes payment may recover as damages for any breach of a presentment warranty an amount equal to the amount paid by the drawee less the amount the drawee received or is entitled to receive from the drawer because of the payment. In addition, the drawee is entitled to compensation for expenses and loss of interest resulting from the breach (3–417[b]). The drawee's right to recover damages for breach of warranty is not affected by any failure on the part of the drawee to exercise ordinary care in making payment.

If a drawee asserts a claim for breach of a presentment warranty based on an unauthorized indorsement of the draft or an alteration of the draft, the warrantor may defend by showing that the indorsement is effective under the *impostor* or *fictitious payee* rules (discussed later in this chapter) or that the drawer's negligence precludes him from asserting against the drawee the unauthorized indorsement or alteration (also discussed below) (3–417[d]).

If (1) a *dishonored draft* is presented for payment to the drawer or an indorser or (2) any other instrument (such as a note) is presented for payment to a party obligated to pay the instrument and the presenter receives payment, the presenter makes the following presentment warranty (3–417[d]):

> The person obtaining payment is a person entitled to enforce the instrument or authorized to obtain payment on behalf of a person entitled to enforce the instrument.

On breach of this warranty the person making the payment may recover from the warrantor an amount equal to the amount paid plus expenses and loss of interest resulting from the breach.

With respect to checks, the party presenting the check for payment cannot disclaim the presentment warranties (3–417[e]).

Unless the payor or drawee provides notice of a claim for breach of a presentment warranty to the warrantor within 30 days after the claimant has reason to know of the breach and the identity of the warrantor, the warrantor is discharged to the extent of any loss caused by the delay in giving notice of the claim of breach.

PAYMENT OR ACCEPTANCE BY MISTAKE

A long-standing general rule of negotiable instruments law is that payment or acceptance is final in favor of a holder in due course or payee who changes his position in reliance on the payment or acceptance. Revised Article 3 retains this concept by making payment final in favor of a person who took the instrument in good faith and for value. However, payment is not final—and may be recovered from—a person who does not meet these criteria where the drawee acted on the mistaken belief that (1) payment of a draft or check has not been stopped, (2) the signature of the purported drawer of the draft was authorized, and (3) the balance in the drawer's account with the drawee represented available funds (3–418[a]).

As a result, this means that if the drawee bank mistakenly paid a check over a stop-payment order, paid a check with a forged or unauthorized drawer's signature on it, or paid despite the lack of sufficient funds in the drawer's account to cover the check, the bank cannot recover if it paid the check to a presenter who had taken the instrument in good faith and for value. In that case, the drawee bank would have to pursue someone else, such as the forger or unauthorized signer, or the drawer in the case of insufficient funds. On the other hand, if the presenter had not taken in good faith or for value, the bank could, in these enumerated instances, recover from the presenter the payment it made by mistake.

The case of *Garmac Grain Co., Inc., v. Boatmen's Bank & Trust Co. of Kansas City,* which follows, illustrates the operation of presentment and transfer warranties.

GARMAC GRAIN CO., INC. v. BOATMEN'S BOAT & TRUST CO. OF KANSAS CITY
694 F. Supp. 1389 (W.D. Mo. 1988)

FACTS

Katherine Millison was employed by the Garmac Grain Company as a bookkeeper. She developed a scheme to embezzle money from Garmac whereby she would take home fully executed and valid checks payable to freight vendors and type "or L. R. Millison" (her husband's name) under the named payee with her manual typewriter. She would then indorse the check "L. R. Millison" on the back and deposit the check in a joint account she and her husband maintained at the State Bank of Oskaloosa. The altered checks were then forwarded through the Federal Reserve System, presented for payment at the drawee bank, Boatmen's Bank & Trust Company of Kansas City, and paid. Millison would then intercept the monthly bank statements from Boatmen's Bank & Trust, remove the altered checks, and obliterate

the "or L. R. Millison" on the face of the checks and the indorsement on the back.

The scheme was discovered and Millison was convicted of embezzlement. Garmac brought suit against Boatmen's Bank & Trust alleging that the altered checks were wrongfully paid. It settled with Garmac and then brought suit against the State Bank of Oskaloosa, contending that it had breached the UCC transfer warranties when it forwarded the altered checks for payment.

ISSUE

Does a depositary bank breach the transfer warranties of good title and of no material alteration when it sends a check with the payee's name altered to the drawee bank for payment?

(continued)

Garmac Grain Co., Inc. v. Boatmen's Boat & Trust Co. of Kansas City
(concluded)

Decision

Yes. A depository bank that transfers an item and receives a settlement for it warrants that (1) it has good title to the item, (2) all signatures are genuine and authorized, and (3) the item has not been materially altered. Here the warranty was breached. The State Bank of Oskaloosa did not have good title to the checks because it did not have the indorsement of the original intended payees, thus breaching the warranty of good title. The addition of an alternative payee to a check is a material alteration and thus, the warranty against material alteration was also breached. Because Millison was authorized to sign her husband's name, there was not breach of the warranty of genuineness of signatures.

Author's Note

The court found that there were issues of material fact as to whether Garmac had exercised reasonable care and promptness in examining its bank statement to discover unauthorized signatures and alterations and whether Boatmen's had exercised ordinary care in paying the checks in question. It also should be noted that this case was decided under the original version of Articles 3 and 4. Revised Article 3 and the conforming amendments to Articles 1 and 4 change the wording of the transfer and presentment warranties and the warranties appear under different section numbers. However, the result reached in this case would be the same under the revisions to the Code.

Concept Summary   Presentment Warranties

If an unaccepted draft (such as a check) is presented for payment or acceptance and the drawee pays or accepts the draft, then the person obtaining payment or acceptance warrants to the drawee:

1. The warrantor is a person entitled to enforce payment or authorized to obtain payment or acceptance on behalf of a person entitled to enforce the draft.
2. The draft has not been altered.
3. The warrantor has no knowledge that the signature of the drawer of the draft has not been authorized.

If (*a*) a dishonored draft is presented for payment to the drawer or indorser or (*b*) any other instrument (such as a note) is presented for payment to a party obligated to pay the instrument and the presenter receives payment, the presenter (as well as a prior transferor of the instrument) makes the following warranty to the person making payment in good faith: The person obtaining payment is a person entitled to enforce the instrument or authorized to obtain payment on behalf of a person entitled to enforce the instrument.

Operation of Warranties

Following are three scenarios that show how the transfer and presentment warranties shift the liability back to a wrongdoer or to the person who dealt immediately with a wrongdoer and thus was in the best position to avert the wrongdoing.

Scenario 1

Arthur makes a promissory note for $200 payable to the order of Betts. Carlson steals the note from Betts, indorses Betts's name on the back, and gives it to Davidson in exchange for a television set. Davidson negotiates the note for value to Earle, who presents the note to Arthur for payment. Assume that Arthur refuses to pay the note because Betts has advised him that it has been stolen and that he is the person entitled to enforce the instrument. Earle then can proceed to recover the face amount of the note from Davidson on the grounds that as a transferor, Davidson has warranted that he is a person entitled to enforce the note and that all signatures were authentic. Davidson, in turn, can proceed against Carlson on the same basis—if he can find Carlson. If he cannot, then Davidson must bear the loss caused by Carlson's wrongdoing. Davidson was in the best position to ascertain whether Carlson was the owner of the note and whether the indorsement of Betts was genuine. Of course, even though Arthur does not have to pay the note to Earle, Arthur remains liable for his underlying obligation to Betts.

Scenario 2

Anderson draws a check for $10 on her checking account at First Bank payable to the order of Brown. Brown cleverly raises the check amount to $110, indorses it, and negotiates it to Carroll. Carroll then presents the check for payment to First Bank, which pays her $110 and charges Anderson's account for $110. Anderson then asks the bank to recredit her account for the altered check, and it does so. The bank can proceed against Carroll for breach of the presentment warranty that the instrument had not been altered, which she made to the bank when she presented the check for payment. Carroll in turn can proceed against Brown for breach of her transfer warranty that the check had not been altered—if she can find her. Unless she was negligent in drawing the check, Article 3 limits Anderson's liability to $10 because her obligation is to pay the amount in the instrument at the time she issued it.

Scenario 3

Bates steals Albers' checkbook and forges Albers' signature to a check for $100 payable to "cash," which he uses to buy $100 worth of groceries from a grocer. The grocer presents the check to Albers' bank. The bank pays the amount of the check to the grocer and charges Albers' account. Albers then demands that the bank recredit his account. The bank can recover against the grocer only if the grocer knew that Albers' signature had been forged. Otherwise, the bank must look for Bates. The bank had the responsibility to recognize the true signature of its drawer, Albers, and not to pay the check that contained an unauthorized signature. The bank may be able to resist recrediting Albers' account if it can show he was negligent. The next section of this chapter discusses negligence.

OTHER LIABILITY RULES

Normally, a bank may not charge against (debit from) the drawer's account a check that has a forged payee's indorsement. Similarly, a maker does not have to pay a note to the person who currently possesses the note if the payee's signature has been forged. If a check or note has been altered—for example, by raising the amount—the drawer or maker usually is liable for the instrument only in the amount for which he originally issued it. However, there are a number of exceptions to these usual rules. These exceptions, as well as liability based on conversion of an instrument, are discussed below.

NEGLIGENCE

A person can be so negligent in writing or signing a negotiable instrument that he in effect invites an alteration or an unauthorized signature on it. If a person has been negligent, Article 3 precludes her from using the alteration or lack of authorization as a reason for not paying a person who in good faith pays the instrument or takes it for value (3–406). For example, Mary Maker makes out a note for $10 in such a way that someone could alter it to read $10,000. Someone alters the note and negotiates it to Katherine Smith, who can qualify as a holder in due course. Smith can collect $10,000 from Maker. Maker's negligence precludes her from claiming alteration as a defense to paying it. Maker then has to find the person who "raised" her note and try to collect the $9,990 from him.

Where the person asserting the preclusion failed to exercise ordinary care in taking or paying the instrument and that failure substantially contributed to the loss, Article 3 allocates the loss between the two parties based on their comparative negligence (3–406[b]). Thus, if a drawer was so negligent in drafting a check that he made it possible for the check to be altered and the bank that paid the check, in the exercise of ordinary care, should have noticed the alteration, then any loss occasioned by the fact that the person who made the alteration could not be found would be split between the drawer and the bank based on their comparative fault.

The case that follows, *Gulf States Section, PGA, Inc. v. Whitney National Bank of New Orleans*, illustrates a situation where a drawer's negligence in managing its checks substantially contributed to forgeries and precluded it from recovering from the drawee bank.

GULF STATES SECTION, PGA, INC. v. WHITNEY NATIONAL BANK OF NEW ORLEANS
689 So.2d 638 (Ct. App. La. 1997)

FACTS

From May through August 1992, Adrenetti Collins, an employee of the Professional Golfers Association (PGA), forged and negotiated 18 PGA checks totaling $22,699.81. The PGA brought an action against Whitney National Bank of New Orleans, which paid the checks, to recover the monies paid out of the PGA account. The bank contended that PGA should be precluded from recovering because its negligence substantially contributed to the forgeries.

Collins was hired as a temporary employee sometime in February or March 1992 by Robert Brown, the executive director of the Gulf States Section of the PGA, and then was hired as a full-time employee in May. Brown had known Collins when he hired her but was not aware that in 1982 she had been convicted of the theft of $5,445.07 from a previous employer, which she obtained by forging and negotiating 20 company checks. She also had a 1985 conviction for issuing worthless checks.

Brown had the primary responsibility in the office for signing checks, paying bills, and handling the bank accounts. The checks came in lots of 2,000, were made to be tractor-fed through a printer, and were prenumbered. They were kept in a box under the printer in Brown's office. Collins had access to the office. Brown wrote approximately 150 to 200 checks a month using a computer program, Quicken, to write and record the checks. Occasionally, there were alignment problems with the printer and checks were not printed correctly and had to be destroyed. Brown did not account for checks that he destroyed during the alignment process, but simply overrode the computer program and printed whatever check number was next in line.

Collins apparently took the first group of checks numbered 6365–6370 from Brown's office in late April, and Brown did not take note of them when he wrote check number 6371 on May 1. The computer had no record of them—and Brown overrode the computer and went on to print the next check in line. The first of the forged checks was cashed on May 4. Collins intercepted both the May and June 1992 bank statements sent by Whitney to Brown. She prepared forged statements leaving out the numbers of those checks she had stolen. The forged statements were crude replicas of the usual Whitney statements. However, when Brown received them, he simply reconciled them; they contained canceled checks, but not the ones Collins had forged and negotiated. Brown

(continued)

GULF STATES SECTION, PGA, INC. v. WHITNEY NATIONAL BANK OF NEW ORLEANS
(concluded)

did not receive any statements for July and August. On August 31, 1992, Collins asked for a leave of absence. On September 18, 1992, Brown received an overdraft notice from Whitney; this was the first inkling he had that something was wrong. He asked for copies of the July and August statements, discovered the unauthorized use, and notified Whitney.

The forgeries would have been very difficult for the bank to detect. Brown's signature on the account signature card consisted of a semilegible letter or two and a long loop. The signature on the forged checks contained a very similar semilegible letter or two followed by a long loop. Whitney's practice was to verify checks in the amount of $5,000 and over; one check fell into this category. The evidence established that Whitney had followed reasonable commercial standards in the banking industry in paying the checks.

ISSUE

Was the PGA precluded from recovering the amount of the forged checks from Whitney National Bank because its negligence substantially contributed to the forgery?

DECISION

Yes. Once a customer establishes that a bank has paid on a forged check, UCC section 3–406 shifts the burden to the bank to prove three things to preclude the customer from recovering on the check: (1) the customer negligently managed his account, (2) the negligence substantially contributed to the forgery, and (3) the bank paid the check in accord with reasonable commercial banking standards. Here the PGA was clearly negligent. The checks should have been secured, not just kept under the printer stand in a box.

Brown should have kept track of the checks more closely, and if he had, he would have known something was wrong on May 1 when he made out a check using the computer program and check number 6371 was the next check to be printed. At that point none of the forged checks had been negotiated. Brown also should have been alerted that something was wrong when he received the forged May and June statements. Brown was clearly negligent in handling the PGA account, and this substantially contributed to Collins being able to forge the checks.

IMPOSTOR RULE

Article 3 establishes special rules for negotiable instruments made payable to impostors and fictitious persons. An impostor is a person who poses as someone else and convinces a drawer to make a check payable to the person being impersonated—or to an organization the person purports to be authorized to represent. When this happens, the Code makes any indorsement "substantially similar" to that of the named payee effective (3–404[a]). Where the impostor has impersonated a person authorized to act for a payee, such as claiming to be Jack Jones, the president of Jones Enterprises, the impostor has the power to negotiate a check to Jones Enterprises.

An example of a situation involving the impostor rule would be the following: Arthur steals Paulsen's automobile and finds the certificate of title in the automobile. Then, representing himself as Paulsen, he sells the automobile to Berger Used Car Company. The car dealership draws its check payable to Paulsen for the agreed purchase price of the automobile and delivers the check to Arthur. Any person can negotiate the check by indorsing it in the name of Paulsen.

The rationale for the impostor rule is to put the responsibility for determining the true identity of the payee on the drawer or maker of a negotiable instrument. The drawer is in a better position to do this than is some later holder of the check who may be entirely innocent. The impostor rule allows that later holder to have good title to the check by making the payee's signature valid although it is not the signature of the person with whom the drawer or maker thought he was dealing. It forces the drawer or maker to find the wrongdoer who tricked him into signing the negotiable instrument or to bear the loss himself.

FICTITIOUS PAYEE RULE

A fictitious payee commonly arises in the following situation: A dishonest employee draws a check payable to someone who does not exist—or to a real person who does business with the employer but to whom the dishonest employee does not intend to send the check. If the employee has the authority to do so, he may sign the check himself. If he does not have such authority, he gives the check to his employer for signature and represents that the employer owes money to the person named as the payee of the check. The dishonest employee then takes the check, indorses it in the name of the payee, presents it for payment, and pockets the money. The employee may be in a position to cover up the wrongdoing by intercepting the canceled checks or juggling the company's books.

The Code allows any indorsement in the name of the fictitious payee to be effective as the payee's indorsement in favor of any person that pays the instrument in good faith or takes it for value or for collection (3–404[b] and [c]). For example, Anderson, an accountant in charge of accounts payable at Moore Corporation, prepares a false invoice naming Parks, Inc., a supplier of Moore Corporation, as having supplied Moore Corporation with goods, and draws a check payable to Parks, Inc., for the amount of the invoice. Anderson then presents the check to Temple, treasurer of Moore Corporation, together with other checks with invoices attached. Temple signs all of these checks and returns them to Anderson for mailing. Anderson then withdraws the check payable to Parks, Inc. Anyone, including Anderson, can negotiate the check by indorsing it in the name of Parks, Inc.

The rationale for the fictitious payee rule is similar to that for the impostor rule. If someone has a dishonest employee or agent who is responsible for the forgery of some checks, the employer of the wrongdoer should bear the immediate loss of those checks rather than some other innocent party. In turn, the employer must locate the unfaithful employee or agent and try to recover from him.

The case of *C & N Contractors, Inc. v. Community Bancshares, Inc.,* which follows, illustrates the operation of the fictitious payee rule. As you read the case, determine what the contractor should have done to prevent the loss it suffered.

C & N CONTRACTORS, INC. v. COMMUNITY BANCSHARES, INC.
646 So.2d 1357 (Sup. Ct. Ala. 1994)

FACTS

C & M Contractors is a construction and general contracting company in Gardendale, Alabama, that performs work at job sites throughout the southeastern United States. Mary Bivens was employed by C & N and performed general administrative duties for it.

Each Wednesday morning, the foreman at each job site telephoned Bivens and gave her the names of the employees working on the job site and the number of hours they had worked. Bivens then conveyed this information

to Automatic Data Processing (ADP), whose offices are in Atlanta, Georgia. ADP prepared payroll checks based on the information given by Bivens and sent the checks to the offices of C & N in Gardendale for authorized signatures. Bivens was not an authorized signatory. After the checks were signed, Bivens sent the checks to the job site foreman for delivery to the employees.

In 1991, Bivens began conveying false information to ADP about employees and hours worked. On the basis of

(continued)

C & N CONTRACTORS, INC. V. COMMUNITY BANCSHARES, INC.
(concluded)

this false information, ADP prepared payroll checks payable to persons who were actual employees but had not worked the hours Bivens had indicated. After obtaining authorized signatures from C & N, Bivens intercepted the checks, forged the indorsement of the payees, and either cashed the checks at Community Bancshares or deposited them into her account at Community Bancshares, often presenting numerous checks at one time. Bivens continued this practice for almost a year, forging over 100 checks, until Jimmy Nation, vice president of C & N, discovered the embezzlement after noticing payroll checks payable to employees who had not recently performed services for the corporation. Bivens subsequently admitted to forging the indorsements.

C & N brought suit against Community Bancshares for conversion when it cashed or accepted for deposit the numerous payroll checks containing forged payee indorsements.

ISSUE

Was Community Bancshares, as the depositary bank, liable to the drawer, C & N, for conversion because it accepted the checks containing forged payee indorsements?

DECISION

No. Generally, a depositary bank that accepts a forged check would be liable to the drawer for the loss incurred on the theory that it was in the best position to prevent the fraud by checking the authenticity of the indorsements. However, Section 3–405, commonly known as the "fictitious payee" or "padded payroll" rule, creates a narrow exception to the general rule. Where, as here, the drawer's dishonest employee conveys false information to her employer, causing him to issue checks and then after an authorized signature is placed on them, intercepts them and cashes them for her own benefit, the bank is not liable for conversion. The principle embodied in Section 3–405(1) is that the loss in this situation should fall upon the employer as a risk of its business enterprise, rather than upon the bank, because the employer is in a better position to prevent or ensure against such payroll forgeries.

AUTHOR'S NOTE

This case was decided under the original version of Article 3. Although Revised Article 3 changes the wording of the "fictitious payee rule" and sets it out in Section 3–404 of Revised Article 3, the result would be the same under the revision.

COMPARATIVE NEGLIGENCE RULE RE IMPOSTORS AND FICTITIOUS PAYEES

Revised Article 3 also establishes a comparative negligence rule if (1) the person, in a situation covered by the impostor or fictitious payee rule, pays the instrument or takes it for value or collection without exercising ordinary care in paying or taking the instrument and (2) that failure substantially contributes to the loss resulting from payment of the instrument. In these instances, the person bearing the loss may recover an allocable share of the loss from the person who did not exercise ordinary care (3–404[d]).

FRAUDULENT INDORSEMENTS BY EMPLOYEES

Revised Article 3 specifically addresses employer responsibility for fraudulent indorsements by employees and adopts the principle that the risk of loss for such indorsements by employees who are entrusted with responsibilities for instruments (primarily checks) should fall on the employer rather than on the bank that takes the check or pays it (3–405). As to any person who in good faith pays an instrument or takes it for value, a fraudulent indorsement by a responsible employee is effective as the indorsement of the payee if it is made in the name of the payee or in a substantially similar name (3–405[b]). If the person taking or paying the instrument failed to exercise ordinary care and that failure substantially contributed to loss resulting from the fraud, the comparative negligence doctrine guides the allocation of the loss.

A fraudulent indorsement includes a forged indorsement purporting to be that of the employer on an instrument payable to the employer; it also includes a forged indorsement purporting to be that of the payee of an instrument on which the employer is drawer or maker (3–405[a][2]). "Responsibility" with respect to instruments means the authority (1) to sign or indorse instruments on behalf of the employer, (2) to process instruments received by the employer, (3) to prepare or process instruments for issue in the name of the employer, (4) to control the disposition of instruments to be issued in the name of the employer, or (5) to otherwise act with respect to instruments in a responsible capacity. "Responsibility" does not cover those who simply have access to instruments as they are stored, transported, or that are in incoming or outgoing mail (3–405[a][3]).

CONVERSION

Conversion of an instrument is an unauthorized assumption and exercise of ownership over it. A negotiable instrument can be converted in a number of ways. For example, it might be presented for payment or acceptance, and the person to whom it is presented might refuse to pay or accept and refuse to return it. An instrument also is converted if a person pays an instrument to a person not entitled to payment, for example, if it contains a forged indorsement.

Revised Article 3 modifies and expands the previous treatment of conversion and provides that the law applicable to conversion of personal property applies to instruments. It also specifically provides that conversion occurs if (1) an instrument lacks an indorsement necessary for negotiation and (2) it is (*a*) purchased, (*b*) taken for collection, or (*c*) paid by a drawee to a person not entitled to payment. An action for conversion may be brought by (1) the maker, drawer, or acceptor of the instrument or (2) a payee or an indorsee who did not receive delivery of the instrument either directly or through delivery to an agent or copayee (3–420).

Thus, if a bank pays a check that contains a forged indorsement, the bank has converted the check by wrongfully paying it. The bank then becomes liable for the face amount of the check to the person whose indorsement was forged (3–420). For example, Arthur Able draws a check for $50 on his account at First Bank, payable to the order of Bernard Barker. Carol Collins steals the check, forges Barker's indorsement on it, and cashes it at First Bank. First Bank has converted Barker's property because it had no right to pay the check without Barker's valid indorsement. First Bank must pay Barker $50, and then it can try to locate Collins to get the $50 back from her. This principle is illustrated in the case that follows, *Lawyers Fund for Client Protection of the State of New York v. Bank Leumi Trust Co. of New York.*

LAWYERS FUND FOR CLIENT PROTECTION OF THE STATE OF NEW YORK
v. BANK LEUMI TRUST CO. OF NEW YORK
682 NYS2d 470 (Sup. Ct., App. Div. New York 1998)

FACTS

Following his father's death in an automobile accident, Marcial Valentin Jr. retained the law firm of Schwartz,

Gutstein & Associates (SGA) to prosecute a wrongful death action. SGA successfully negotiated a settlement

(continued)

LAWYERS FUND FOR CLIENT PROTECTION OF THE STATE OF NEW YORK v. BANK LEUMI TRUST CO. OF NEW YORK

(concluded)

with Progressive Insurance Company, which forwarded to SGA a draft payable through First National Bank of Ashland of the National City Bank. The draft was in the amount of $47,500 and was payable to Valentin and SGA.

SGA forged Valentin's indorsement on the draft and deposited it in the firm's trust account that it maintained at Bank Leumi Trust Company of New York. Even though Valentin's name was misspelled on the indorsement, Bank Leumi and Progressive accepted and honored the draft. SGA, however, never provided Valentin with his share of the proceeds, abandoned the practice of law, and filed for bankruptcy.

Valentin in turn filed a claim with the Lawyers Fund for Client Protection of the State of New York, which paid him $31,750, the net amount of the settlement proceeds after the disposition of SGA's counsel fee. In exchange, Valentin assigned his rights to the draft to the Lawyers Fund. Using its subrogation rights, Lawyers Fund brought an action for conversion against Bank Leumi and Progressive for paying the draft on a forged indorsement.

ISSUE

Was the draft converted when it was paid on a forged indorsement?

DECISION

Yes. A payee has a claim for conversion when an instrument is paid to someone else without his indorsement.

As is true under the original version of Article 3, if a check contains a restrictive indorsement (such as "for deposit" or "for collection") that shows a purpose of having the check collected for the benefit of a particular account, then any person who purchases the check or any depositary bank or payor bank that takes it for immediate payment converts the check unless the indorser receives the proceeds or the bank applies them consistent with the indorsement (3–206).

.... DISCHARGE OF NEGOTIABLE INSTRUMENTS ....

DISCHARGE OF LIABILITY

The obligation of a party to pay an instrument is discharged (1) if he meets the requirements set out in Revised Article 3 or (2) by any act or agreement that would discharge an obligation to pay money on a simple contract. Discharge of an obligation is not effective against a person who has the rights of a holder in due course of the instrument and took the instrument without notice of the discharge (3–601).

The most common ways that an obligor on an instrument is discharged from her liability are:

1. Payment of the instrument.
2. Cancellation of the instrument.
3. Alteration of the instrument.
4. Modification of the principal's obligation that causes loss to a surety or impairs the collateral.
5. Unexcused delay in presentment or notice of dishonor with respect to a check (discussed earlier in this chapter).
6. Acceptance of a draft but varying the terms from the draft as presented (this entitled the holder to treat the draft as dishonored and the drawee, in turn, to cancel the acceptance) (3–410).

In addition, as noted earlier in the chapter, a drawer is discharged of liability of a draft that is accepted by a bank (e.g., if a check is certified by a bank) because at that point the holder is looking to the bank to make the instrument good.

DISCHARGE BY PAYMENT

Generally, payment in full discharges liability on an instrument to the extent payable by or on behalf of a party obligated to pay the instrument to a person entitled to enforce the instrument. To the extent of payment, the obligation of a party to pay the instrument is discharged even though payment is made with knowledge of a claim to the instrument by some other person. However, the obligation is not discharged if (1) there is a claim enforceable against the person making payment and payment is made with knowledge of the fact that payment is prohibited by an injunction or similar legal process or (2) in the case of an instrument other than a cashier's, certified, or teller's check, the person making the payment had accepted from the person making the claim indemnity against loss for refusing to make payment to the person entitled to enforce payment. It also is not discharged if he knows that the instrument is a stolen instrument and pays someone who he knows is in wrongful possession of the instrument (3–602).

Also, if the holder has indorsed a negotiable instrument restrictively indorsed, the person who pays must comply with the restrictive indorsement to be discharged (3–603[1][b]). For example, Arthur makes a note of $1000 payable to the order of Bryan. Bryan indorses the note "Pay to the order of my account no. 16154 at First Bank, Bryan." Bryan then gives the note to his employee, Clark, to take to the bank. Clark takes the note to Arthur, who pays Clark the $1000. Clark then runs off with the money. Arthur is not discharged of his primary liability on the note because he did not make his payment consistent with the restrictive indorsement. To be discharged, Arthur has to pay the $1000 into Bryan's account at First Bank.

DISCHARGE BY CANCELLATION

A person entitled to enforce a negotiable instrument may discharge the liability of the parties to the instrument by canceling or renouncing it. If the holder mutilates or destroys a negotiable instrument with the intent that it no longer evidences an obligation to pay money, the holder has canceled the obligation (3–604). For example, a grandfather lends $5,000 to his grandson for college expenses. The grandson gives his grandfather a promissory note for $5,000. If the grandfather later tears up the note with the intent that the grandson no longer owes him $5,000, the grandfather has canceled the note.

An accidental destruction or mutilation of a negotiable instrument is not a cancellation and does not discharge the parties to it. If an instrument is lost, mutilated accidentally, or destroyed, the person entitled to enforce it still can enforce the instrument. In such a case, the person must prove that the instrument existed and that she was its holder when it was lost, mutilated, or destroyed.

Ethical Implications	See problem case 10 at the end of the chapter, in which a creditor made a mistake and returned a note marked "canceled" to the maker without collecting all of the interest due on it. Suppose, instead that the maker/borrower realized that Crown Financial Corporation had made an error in not including in the subsequent note the interest due on the original note. Should the maker/borrower feel compelled by ethical considerations to pay the interest, even if not legally required to do so?

ALTERED INSTRUMENTS; DISCHARGE BY ALTERATION

A person paying a fraudulently altered instrument or taking it for value, in good faith and without notice of the alteration, may enforce the instrument (1) according to its original terms or (2) in the case of an incomplete instrument later completed in an unauthorized manner, according to its terms as completed (3–407[c]). An alteration occurs if there is (1) an unauthorized change that modifies the obligation of a party to the instrument or (2) an unauthorized addition of words or numbers or other change to an incomplete instrument that changes the obligation of any party (3–407[a]). A change that does not affect the obligation of one of the parties, such as dotting an *i* or correcting the grammar, is not considered to be an alteration.

Two examples illustrate the situations in which Revised Article 3 allows fraudulently altered instruments to be enforced. First, assume the amount due on a note is fraudulently raised from $10 to $10,000; the contract of the maker has been changed. The maker promised to pay $10, but after the change has been made, he would be promising to pay much more. If the note is negotiated to a person who can qualify as a holder in due course who was without notice of the alteration, that person can enforce the note against the maker.

Second, assume Swanson draws a check payable to Frank's Nursery, leaving the amount blank. He gives it to his gardener with instructions to purchase some fertilizer at Frank's and to fill in the purchase price of the fertilizer when it is known. The gardener fills in the check for $100 and gives it to Frank's in exchange for the fertilizer ($7.25) and the difference in cash ($92.75). The gardener then leaves town with the cash. If Frank's had no knowledge of the unauthorized completion, it could enforce the check for $100 against Swanson.

In any other case, a fraudulent alteration **discharges** any party whose obligation is affected by the alteration *unless* the party (1) assents or (2) is precluded from asserting the alteration (e.g., because of the party's contributory negligence). Assume that Anderson signs a promissory note for $100 payable to Bond. Bond indorses the note "Pay to the order of Connolly, Bond" and negotiates it to Connolly. Connolly changes the $100 to read $100,000. Connolly's unauthorized change is fraudulent. As a result, Anderson is discharged from her primary liability as maker of the note and Bond is discharged from her secondary liability as indorser. Neither of them has to pay Connolly. The obligations of both Anderson and Bond were changed because the amount for which they are liable was altered.

No other alteration—that is, one that is not fraudulent—discharges any party, and a holder may enforce the instrument according to its *original* terms (3–407[b]). Thus, there would be no discharge if a blank is filled in in the honest belief that it is authorized or if a change is made, without any fraudulent intent, to give the maker on a note the benefit of a lower interest rate.

DISCHARGE OF INDORSERS AND ACCOMMODATION PARTIES

If a person entitled to enforce an instrument agrees, with or without consideration, to a material modification of the obligation of a party to the instrument, including an extension of the due date, then any accommodation party or indorser who has a right of recourse against the person whose obligation is modified is discharged *to the extent the modification causes a loss to the indorser or accommodation party.* Similarly, if collateral secures the obligation of a party to an instrument and a person entitled to enforce the instrument impairs the value of the collateral, the obligation of the indorser or accommodation party having the right of recourse against the obligor is discharged to the extent of the impairment. These discharges are not effective unless the person agreeing to the modification or causing the impairment knows of the accommodation or has notice of it. Also, no discharge occurs if the obligor assented to the event or conduct, or if the obligor has waived the discharge (3–605).

For example, Frank goes to Credit Union to borrow $4,000 to purchase a used automobile. The credit union has Frank sign a promissory note and takes a security interest in the automobile (i.e., takes it as collateral for the loan). It also asks Frank's brother Bob to sign the note as an accommodation maker. Subsequently, Frank tells the credit union he wants to sell the automobile and it releases its security interest. Because release of the collateral adversely affects Bob's obligation as accommodation maker, he is discharged from his obligation as accommodation maker in the amount of the value of the automobile.

QUESTIONS AND PROBLEM CASES

1. How does the contractual obligation of the maker of a promissory note differ from the contractual obligation of an indorser on a promissory note?

2. Terance Fitzgerald drew a check for $4,000 payable to New Look Auto Trim and Upholstery and delivered it to Yuvonne Goss and Benii Arrazza, the owners of New Look. Goss and Arrazza each indorsed the check in blank and deposited it in Goss's personal account at the Cincinnati Central Credit Union. When the Credit Union presented the check to Fitzgerald's bank, the check was dishonored for insufficient funds. The Credit Union then demanded that Goss and Arrazza honor the check. Are Goss and Arrazza obligated to make the check good to Credit Union?

3. Janota's signature appeared on a note under the name of a corporation acknowledging a $1,000 debt. No other wording appeared other than Janota's name and the corporate name. The holder of the note sues Janota on the note. What will Janota argue and what will be the result?

4. If checks are drawn by "McCann Industries, Inc., Payroll Account, (signed) J.Y. McCann" and the checks are not paid, who is liable— the individual or the corporation?

5. Clay Haynes was the bookkeeper for Johnstown Manufacturing, Inc. He had express check-signing authority, and his signature was on the signature card for the account that Johnstown maintained at BancOhio National Bank. Haynes was also the bookkeeper of another corporation, Lynn Polymers, Inc., which was operated by the same individuals that operated Johnstown. Over a period of a year, Haynes engaged in a check-cashing scheme from which he pocketed approximately $70,000. Haynes wrote 35 corporate checks to the order of BancOhio National Bank, and the bank, in return, gave the cash to Haynes. Johnstown brought suit against BancOhio to recover $300 for the one check written on the Johnstown account the bank paid to Haynes. Johnstown claimed that the check was written without the express authority of the corporation, and thus it contained an "unauthorized" signature. Was Haynes's signature on the check "unauthorized" as that term is used in the Uniform Commercial Code?

6. A check was drawn on First National Bank and made payable to Howard. It came into the possession of Carson, who forged Howard's indorsement and cashed it at Merchant's Bank. Merchant's Bank then indorsed it and collected payment from First National. Assuming that Carson is nowhere to be found, who bears the loss caused by Carson's forgery?

7. Mrs. Gordon Neely hired Louise Bradshaw as the bookkeeper for a Midas Muffler shop they owned and operated as a corporation, J. Gordon Neely Enterprises, Inc. (Neely). Bradshaw's duties included preparing company checks for Mrs. Neely's signature and reconciling the checking account when the company received a bank statement and canceled checks each month. Bradshaw prepared several checks payable to herself and containing a large space to the left of the

amount written on the designated line. When Mrs. Neely signed the checks, she was aware of the large gaps. Subsequently, Bradshaw altered the checks by adding a digit or two to the left of the original amount and then cashed them at American National Bank, the drawee bank. Several months later, the Neelys hired a new accountant, who discovered the altered checks. Neely brought suit against American National Bank to have its account recredited for the altered checks, claiming that American was liable for paying out on altered instruments. The bank contended that Neely's negligence substantially contributed to alterations of the instruments and thus Neely was precluded from asserting the alteration against the bank. Between Neely and American National Bank, who should bear the loss caused by Bradshaw's fraud?

8. Clarice Rich was employed by the New York City Board of Education as a clerk. It was her duty to prepare requisitions for checks to be issued by the board, to prepare the checks, to have them signed by authorized personnel, and to send the checks to the recipients. In some instances, however, she retained them. Also, on a number of occasions she prepared duplicate requisitions and checks, which, when signed, she likewise retained. She then forged the indorsement of the named payees on the checks she had retained and cashed the checks at Chemical Bank, where the Board of Education maintained its account. After the board discovered the forgeries, it demanded that Chemical Bank credit its account for the amount of the forged checks. Is Chemical Bank required to credit the board's account as requested?

9. Stockton's housekeeper stole some of his checks, forged his name as drawer, and cashed them at Gristedes Supermarket where Stockton maintained check-cashing privileges. The checks were presented to Stockton's bank and honored by it. Over the course of 18 months, the scheme netted the housekeeper in excess of $147,000 on approximately 285 forged checks. Stockton brought suit against Gristedes Supermarket for conversion, seeking to recover the value of the checks it had accepted and for which it had obtained payment from the drawee bank. Was Gristedes Supermarket liable to Stockton for conversion for accepting and obtaining payment of the stolen and forged checks?

10. Charles Peterson, a farmer and rancher, was indebted to Crown Financial Corporation on a $4,450,000 promissory note that was due on December 29, 1972. Shortly before the note was due, Crown sent Peterson a statement of interest due on the note ($499,658.85). Peterson paid the interest and executed a new note in the amount of $4,450,000 that was to mature in December 1975. The old note was then marked "canceled" and returned to Peterson. In 1975, Crown billed Peterson for $363,800 in interest that had been due on the first note but apparently not included in its statement. Peterson claimed that the interest had been forgiven and that he was not obligated to pay it. Was Peterson still obligated to pay interest on the note that had been returned to him marked "canceled"?

11. *Video Case.* See "Cafeteria Conversion." Steve, an individual with a gambling problem and a substance abuse problem, works in the accounts payable department of a company. He issues checks drawn on his employer's account that are made payable to suppliers who do business with his employer but who are not currently owed money. Then he forges the signature of the named payees, obtains payment of the checks from the drawee bank, and uses the funds to support his habits. Because Steve's responsibilities include reconciling the bank statements, his forgery scheme is not discovered for a considerable period of time. When it is discovered, is the drawee bank required to recredit the employer's account for the forged checks that were paid from it?

CHAPTER 39

Checks and Electronic Fund Transfers

If you are like most people in the United States, a checking account provides the majority of your contacts with negotiable instruments. Generally, a checking account works quite simply and smoothly. You deposit a sum of money with the bank, sign a signature card that indicates to the bank who the authorized signators on the account are, and the bank provides you with a supply of blank checks; you write checks drawing on the account, and each month the bank sends you a statement reflecting the activity in your account for the preceding month, perhaps with your canceled checks. But sometimes problems or questions arise. For example:

- *What happens if your bank refused to pay a check even though you have sufficient funds in your account?*
- *Does your bank have the right to create an overdraft in your account by paying an otherwise properly payable check?*
- *What are your rights and the bank's obligation if you stop payment on a check?*
- *When can you get your account recredited if you discover that forged or altered checks, or checks with forged or missing indorsements, have been charged to your account?*
- *What are your rights if you discover an unauthorized use has been made of your ATM card?*

This chapter focuses on the relationship between the drawer with a checking account and the drawee bank and addresses these and other questions.

········ ### THE DRAWER–DRAWEE RELATIONSHIP ········

There are two sources that govern the relationship between the depositor and the drawee bank: the deposit agreement and Articles 3 and 4 of the Code. Article 4, which governs Bank Deposits and Collections, allows the depositor and drawee bank (which Article 4 calls the "payor bank") to vary Article 4's provisions with a few important exceptions. The deposit agreement cannot disclaim the bank's responsibility for its own lack of good faith or failure to exercise ordinary care or limit the measure of damages for the lack of failure; however, the parties may determine by agreement the standards by which to measure the bank's responsibility so long as the standards are not manifestly unreasonable (4–103).[1]

The deposit agreement establishes many important relationships between the depositor and drawee/payor bank. The first of these is their relationship as creditor and debtor, respectively, so that when a person deposits money in an account at the bank, the bank no longer considers him the owner of the money. Instead, he is a creditor of the bank to the extent of his deposits and the bank becomes his debtor. Also, when the depositor deposits a check to a checking account, the bank becomes his agent for collection of the check. The bank as the person's agent owes a duty to him to follow his reasonable instructions concerning payment of checks and other items from his account and a duty of ordinary care in collecting checks and other items deposited to the account.

BANK'S DUTY TO PAY

When a bank receives a properly drawn and payable check on a person's account and there are sufficient funds to cover the check, the bank is under a duty to pay it. If the person has sufficient funds in the account and the bank refuses to pay, or dishonors, the check, the bank is liable for the actual damages proximately caused by its wrongful dishonor as well as consequential damages (4–402). Actual damages may include charges imposed by retailers for returned checks as well as damages for arrest or prosecution to the customer. Consequential damages include injury to the depositor's credit rating that results from the dishonor.

For example, Donald Dodson writes a check for $3,500 to Ames Auto Sales in payment for a used car. At the time that Ames Auto presents the check for payment at Dodson's bank, First National Bank, Dodson has $3,800 in his account. However, a teller mistakenly refuses to pay the check and stamps it NSF (not sufficient funds). Ames Auto then goes to the local prosecutor and signs a complaint against Dodson for writing a bad check. As a result, Dodson is arrested. Dodson can recover from First National the damages that he sustained because the bank wrongfully dishonored his check, including the damages involved in his arrest, such as his attorney's fees.

BANK'S RIGHT TO CHARGE TO CUSTOMER'S ACCOUNT

The drawee bank has the right to charge any properly payable check to the account of the customer or drawer. The bank has this right even though payment of the check creates an overdraft in the account (4–401). If an account is overdrawn, the customer owed the bank the amount of the overdraft and the bank may take that amount out of the next deposit that the customer makes or from another account that the depositor

---

[1]The numbers in parentheses refer to sections of the Uniform Commercial Code.

maintains with the bank. Alternatively, the bank might seek to collect the amount directly from the customer. If there is more than one customer who can draw from an account, only that customer—or those customers—who sign the item or who benefit from the proceeds of an overdraft are liable for the overdraft.

Stale Checks

The bank does not owe a duty to its customer to pay any checks out of the account that are more than six months old. Such checks are called *stale checks*. However, the bank acting in good faith may pay a check that is more than six months old and charge it to the drawer–depositor's account (4–404). This principle is illustrated in *RPM Pizza, Inc. v. Bank One–Cambridge*.

RPM PIZZA, INC. v. BANK ONE–CAMBRIDGE
869 F. Supp. 517 (E.D. Mich. 1994)

FACTS

RPM Pizza, Inc., a Domino's Pizza franchisee, maintained a checking account at Bank One–Cambridge. On May 29, 1992, RPM erroneously issued a $96,000 check drawn on its account at the bank and payable to a computer broker, Systems Marketing. After mailing the check, RPM realized its error, and on June 2, 1992, RPM placed a stop-payment order on the check. As stated in its account agreement with Bank One (and in the UCC as adopted in Ohio), written stop-payment orders (discussed later in this chapter) are effective for six months. The stop-payment order expired on December 6, 1992, and RPM failed to renew it.

On December 22, 1992, Systems Marketing deposited the check in its account at the Bank of Tampa, Florida. When the Bank of Tampa received the check, it was more than six months old and was therefore "stale" according to standard banking procedures. The Bank of Tampa credited the check to Systems Marketing's account and sent it forward to Bank One–Cambridge which charged it against RPM's checking account.

RPM brought suit against Bank One, claiming that the bank had not exercised ordinary care or acted in good faith in paying the stale check. The bank established that it routinely paid stale checks and that its internal operating procedures simply required it to perform a signature authorization on checks of more than $50,000, which it did in this case.

ISSUE

Did the bank violate the duty it owed to its customer, RPM, when it paid a check that was more than six months old?

DECISION

No. There was no showing that the bank in this case had not acted in accordance with sound banking practice when it simply checked the authenticity of the signature before paying it. The court declined to adopt a rule that payment of a stale check was a per se violation of a bank's duty to exercise ordinary care. The court noted that the reason that Systems Marketing was able to present the check was that RPM negligently mailed the check to it.

Altered and Incomplete Items

If the bank in good faith pays a check drawn by the drawer–depositor that was subsequently altered, it may charge the customer's account with the amount of the check as originally drawn. Also, if an incomplete check of a customer gets into circulation, is completed, and is presented to the drawee bank for payment, and the bank pays the check, the bank can charge the amount as completed to the customer's account even though it knows that the check has been completed, unless it has notice that the completion was improper (4–401[d]). The respective rights, obligations, and liabilities of drawee banks and their drawer–customers concerning forged and altered checks are discussed in more detail later in this chapter.

Limitations on Bank's Right or Duty

Article 4 recognizes that the bank's right or duty to pay a check or to charge the depositor's account for the check (including exercising its right to set off an amount due to it by the depositor) may be terminated, suspended, or modified by the depositor's order to stop payment (which is discussed in the next section of this chapter). In addition, it may be stopped by events external to the relationship between the depositor and the bank. These external events include the filing of a bankruptcy petition by the depositor or by the depositor's creditors and the garnishment of the account by a creditor of the depositor. The bank must receive the stop-payment order from its depositor or the notice of the bankruptcy filing or garnishment before the bank has certified the check, paid it in cash, settled with another bank for the amount of the item without a right to revoke the settlement, completed the process necessary to its decision to pay the check, or otherwise become accountable for the amount of the check under Article 4 (4–403). These restrictions on the bank's right or duty to pay are discussed in later sections of this chapter.

Postdated Checks

Under original Articles 3 and 4, a postdated check was not properly payable by the drawee bank until the date on the check. The recent amendments to Article 4 change this. Under the revision, an otherwise properly payable postdated check that is presented for payment before the date on the check may be paid and charged to the customer's account *unless* the customer has given notice of it to the bank. The customer must give notice of the postdating in a way that described the check with reasonable certainty. It is effective for the same time periods as Article 4 provides for stop-payment orders (discussed below). The customer must give notice to the bank at such time and in such manner as to give the bank an opportunity to act upon it before the bank takes any action with respect to paying the check. If the bank charges the customer's account for a postdated check before the date stated in the notice given to the bank, the bank is liable for damages for any loss that results. Such damages might include those associated with the dishonor of subsequent items (3–113[a]; 4–401[c]).

There is a variety of reasons that a person might want to postdate a check. For example, a person might have a mortgage payment due on the first of the month at a bank located in another state. To make sure that the check arrives on time, the customer may send the payment by mail several days before the due date. However, if the person is depending on a deposit of her next monthly paycheck on the first of the month to cover the mortgage payment, she might postdate the check to the first of the following month. Under the original version of Articles 3 and 4, the bank could not properly pay the check until the first of the month. However, under the revisions it could be properly paid by the bank before that date if presented earlier. To avoid the risk that the bank would dishonor the check for insufficient funds if presented before the first, the customer should notify the drawee bank in a manner similar to that required for stop payment of checks.

STOP-PAYMENT ORDER

A stop-payment order is a request made by a customer of a drawee bank instructing it not to pay or certify a specified check. As the drawer's agent in the payment of checks, the drawee bank must follow the reasonable orders of the customer/drawer about payments made on the drawer's behalf. Any person authorized to draw a check may stop payment of it. Thus, any person authorized to sign a check on the account may stop payment even if she did not sign the check in question (4–403[a]).

To be effective, a payor bank must receive a stop-payment order in time to give the bank a reasonable opportunity to act on the order. This means that the bank must receive the stop-payment order before it has paid or certified the check. In addition, the stop-payment order must come soon enough to give the bank time to instruct its tellers and other employees that they should not pay or certify the check (4–403[a]). The stop-payment order also must describe the check with "reasonable certainty" so as to provide the bank's employees the ability to recognize it as the check corresponding to the stop-payment order.

The customer may give an oral stop-payment order to the bank, but it is valid for only 14 days unless the customer confirms it in writing during that time. A written stop-payment order is valid for six months, and the customer can extend it for an additional six months by giving the bank instructions in writing to continue the order (4–403[b]). (See Figure 39–1.)

Sometimes the information given the bank by the customer concerning the check on which payment is to be stopped is incorrect. For example, there may be an error in the payee's name, the amount of the check, or the number of the check. The question then arises whether the customer has accorded the bank a reasonable opportunity to act on his request. A common issue is whether the stop-payment order must have the dollar amount correct to the penny. Banks usually take the position that the stop-payment order must be correct to the penny because they program and rely on computers to focus on the customer's account number and the amount of the check in question to avoid paying an item subject to a stop-payment order.

The amendments to Article 4 do not resolve this question. In the Official Comments, the drafters indicate that "in describing an item, the customer, in the absence

FIGURE 39–1   Stop-Payment Order

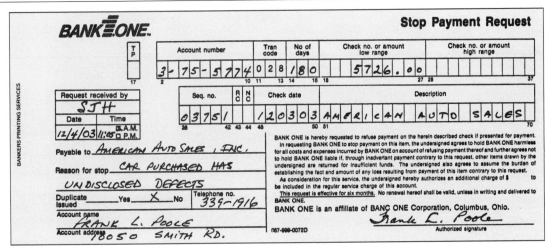

of a contrary agreement, must meet the standard of what information allows the bank under the technology then existing to identify the check with reasonable certainty."

BANK'S LIABILITY FOR PAYMENT AFTER STOP-PAYMENT ORDER

While a stop-payment order is in effect, the drawee bank is liable to the drawer of the check that it pays for any loss that the drawer suffers by reason of such payment. However, the drawer customer has the burden of establishing the fact and amount of the loss. To show a loss, the drawer must establish that the drawee bank paid a person against whom the drawer had a valid defense to payment. To the extent that the drawer has such a defense, he has suffered a loss due to the drawee's failure to honor the stop-payment order.

For example, Brown buys what is represented to be a new car from Foster Ford and gives Foster Ford his check for $15,280 drawn on First Bank. Brown then discovers that the car is in fact a used demonstrator model and calls First Bank, ordering it to stop payment on the check. If Foster Ford presents the check for payment the following day and First Bank pays the check despite the stop-payment order, Brown can require the bank to recredit his account. (The depositor–drawer bases his claim to recredit on the fact that the bank did not follow his final instruction—the instruction not to pay the check.) Brown had a valid defense of misrepresentation that he could have asserted against Foster Ford if it had sued him on the check. Foster Ford would have been required to sue on the check or on Brown's contractual obligation to pay for the car.

Assume, instead, that Foster Ford negotiated the check to Smith and that Smith qualified as a holder in due course. Then, if the bank paid the check to Smith over the stop-payment order, Brown would not be able to have his account recredited because Brown would not be able to show that he sustained any loss. If the bank had refused to pay the check, so that Smith came against Brown on his drawer's liability, Brown could not use his personal defense of misrepresentation of the prior use of the car as a reason for not paying Smith. Brown's only recourse would be to pursue Foster Ford on his misrepresentation claim.

The following case, *Seigel v. Merrill, Lynch, Pierce, Fenner & Smith, Inc.* involves a situation in which the drawer was not entitled to have his account recredited for checks paid over his stop-payment order because the drawer was unable to demonstrate he suffered any loss because of the bank's failure to honor the stop-payment order.

SEIGEL V. MERRILL, LYNCH, PIERCE, FENNER & SMITH, INC.
400 UCC Rep.2d 819 (Ct. App. D.C. 2000)

FACTS

Walter Seigel, a Maryland resident, traveled to Atlantic City, New Jersey, to gamble. While there, Seigel wrote a number of checks to various casinos, and, in exchange, received gambling chips with which to wager. The checks were drawn on Seigel's cash management account at Merrill, Lynch, Pierce, Fenner & Smith, which was established through its District of Columbia offices.

There were sufficient funds in the account to cover all checks.

Seigel eventually gambled away all the chips he had received for the checks. Upon returning to Maryland, Seigel discussed the outstanding checks with Merrill Lynch, informing his broker of the gambling nature of the transactions and his desire to avoid realizing the

(continued)

SEIGEL V. MERRILL, LYNCH, PIERCE, FENNER & SMITH, INC.
(concluded)

apparent losses. Merrill Lynch informed Seigel that it was possible to escape paying the checks by placing a stop-payment order and liquidating his cash management account. He took the advice and instructed Merrill Lynch to close his account, liquidate the assets, and not to honor any checks drawn on the account. Merrill Lynch agreed and confirmed Seigel's instructions.

Many of the checks were subsequently dishonored. However, Merrill Lynch accidentally paid several of the checks totaling $143,000 despite the stop-payment order and account closure. Merrill Lynch then debited Seigel's margin account to cover the payments.

Seigel brought suit in the District of Columbia against Merrill Lynch for paying the checks over his stop-payment order. He argued that the District of Columbia Code precluded enforcement of the checks as void gambling debts or, in the alternative, that New Jersey law prohibited the enforcement of the check. Therefore, he contended, Merrill Lynch had no rights by way of subrogation as a defense to payment over the stop-payment order. Merrill Lynch denied the applicability of the D.C. statute or any New Jersey law and contended that it stood in the shoes of the casinos to whom valid and enforceable checks had been given.

ISSUE

Was Seigel entitled to have his account recredited for the checks paid by Merrill Lynch over his stop-payment order?

DECISION

No. While the depositor has the basic right to stop payment on any item drawn on his account, the depositor also has the burden of showing the fact and amount of any loss resulting from payment of an item contrary to a stop-payment order. In this instance, Seigel is unable to establish he suffered any loss. As the payee of dishonored checks, the casino would have a prima facie right to recover its amount from Seigel as drawer, and the burden would be on Seigel to establish any defense he might have on the instrument. Seigel's argument that the casinos would have no right to enforce the check under New Jersey law because he is a compulsive gambler is without merit. Nothing in New Jersey law prohibits the cashing and redemption of checks made by "compulsive gamblers." While D.C. law might preclude the enforcement of the checks as issued out of a gambling transaction and void, Seigel gains nothing by it because the checks could be enforced in New Jersey where the transaction occurred. Moreover, the court noted that the checks could also be enforced in Maryland where Seigel lives because Maryland courts will enforce gambling debts if legally incurred in a foreign jurisdiction. Accordingly, Seigel was unable to show he ultimately suffered any loss as a result of the payment of the checks by Merrill Lynch.

The bank may ask the customer to sign a form in which the bank tries to disclaim or limit its liability for the stop-payment order. As explained at the beginning of this chapter, the bank cannot disclaim its responsibility for its failure to act in good faith or to exercise ordinary care in paying a check over a stop-payment order (4–103).

If a bank pays a check after it has received a stop-payment order and has to reimburse its customer for the improperly paid check, it acquires all the rights of its customer against the person to whom it originally made payment, including rights arising from the transaction on which the check was based (4–407). In our example involving Brown and Foster Ford, assume that Brown was able to have his account recredited because First Bank had paid the check to Foster Ford over his stop-payment order. Then the bank would have any rights that Brown had against Foster Ford for the misrepresentation.

If a person stops payment on a check and the bank honors the stop-payment order, the person still may be liable to the holder of the check. Suppose Peters writes a check for $450 to Ace Auto Repair in payment for repairs to her automobile. While driving the car home, she concludes that the car was not repaired properly. She calls her bank and stops payment on the check. Ace Auto negotiated the check to Sam's Auto Parts, which took the check as a holder in due course. When Sam's takes the check to Peters' bank, the bank refuses to pay because of the stop-payment order. Sam's then comes after Peters on her drawer's liability. All Peters has is a personal defense against payment, which is not good against a holder in due course. So Peters must pay Sam's the $450 and pursue her claim separately against Ace. If Ace were still the holder of the check, however, the situation would be different. Peters could use her personal defense concerning the faulty work against Ace to reduce or possibly to cancel her obligation to pay the check.

CERTIFIED CHECK

Normally a drawee bank is not obligated to certify a check. When a drawee bank does certify a check, it substitutes its undertaking (promise) to pay the check for the drawer's undertaking and becomes obligated to pay the check. At the time the bank certifies a check, the bank usually debits the customer's account for the amount of the certified check and shifts the money to a special account at the bank. It also adds its signature to the check to show that it has accepted primary liability for paying it. The bank's signature is an essential part of the certification: The bank's signature must appear on the check (3–409). If the holder of a check chooses to have it certified, rather than seeking to have it paid at that time, the holder has made a conscious decision to look to the certifying bank for payment and no longer may rely on the drawer or the indorsers to pay it. See Figure 39–2 for an example of a certified check.

If the drawee bank certifies a check, then the drawer and any persons who previously indorsed the check are discharged of their liability on the check (3–414[c]; 3–415[d]).

CASHIER'S CHECK

A cashier's check differs from a certified check. A check on which a bank is both the drawer and the drawee is a *cashier's check*. The bank is primarily liable on a cashier's

FIGURE 39–2   Certified Check

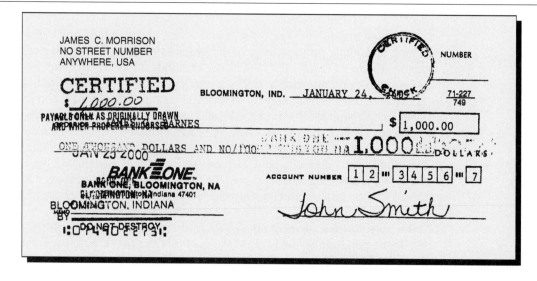

check. See Figure 39–3 for an example of a cashier's check. A teller's check is similar to a cashier's check in that it is a check on which one bank is the drawer and another bank is the drawee. An example of a teller's check is a check drawn by a credit union on its account at a bank.

DEATH OR INCOMPETENCE OF CUSTOMER

Under the general principles of agency law, the death or incompetence of the principal terminates the agent's authority to act for the principal. However, slightly different rules apply to the authority of a bank to pay checks out of the account of a deceased or incompetent person. The bank has the right to pay the checks of an incompetent person until it has notice that a court has determined that the person is incompetent. Once the bank learns of this fact, it loses its authority to pay that person's checks—because the depositor is not competent to issue instructions to pay.

Similarly, a bank has the right to pay the checks of a deceased customer until it has notice of the customer's death. Even if a bank knows of a customer's death, for a period of 10 days after the customer's death, it can pay checks written by the customer prior to his death. However, the deceased person's heirs or other persons claiming an interest in the account can order the bank to stop payment (4–405).

FORGED AND ALTERED CHECKS

BANK'S RIGHT TO CHARGE ACCOUNT

A check that bears a forged signature of the drawer or payee generally is not properly payable from the customer's account because the bank is not following the instructions of the depositor precisely as he gave them. The bank is expected to be familiar with the authorized signature of its depositor. If it pays such a check, Article 4 will treat the transaction as one in which the bank paid out its own funds rather than the depositor's funds.

Similarly, a check that was altered after the drawer made it out—for example, by increasing the amount of the check—generally is not properly payable from the

FIGURE 39–3 Cashier's Check

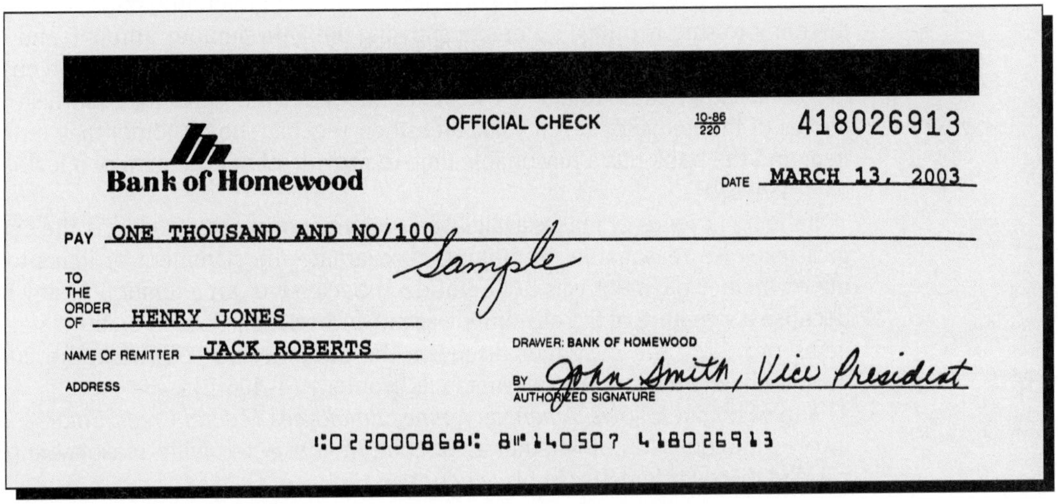
OFFICIAL CHECK 10-86/220 418026913

Bank of Homewood

DATE MARCH 13, 2003

PAY ONE THOUSAND AND NO/100

Sample

TO THE ORDER OF HENRY JONES

NAME OF REMITTER JACK ROBERTS

ADDRESS

DRAWER: BANK OF HOMEWOOD

BY John Smith, Vice President

AUTHORIZED SIGNATURE

⑆0220008681⑆ 81⑈140507 418026913

customer's account. However, as noted earlier, if the drawer is negligent and contributes to the forgery or alteration, he may be barred from claiming it as the reason that a particular check should not be charged to his account.

For example, Barton makes a check for $1 in a way that makes it possible for someone to easily alter it to read $101, and it is so altered. If the drawee bank pays the check to a holder in good faith, it can charge the $101 to Barton's account if Barton's negligence contributed to the alteration. Similarly if a company uses a mechanical checkwriter to write checks, it must use reasonable care to see that unauthorized persons do not have access to blank checks and to the checkwriter.

If the alteration is obvious, the bank should note that fact and refuse to pay the check when it is presented for payment. Occasionally, the alteration is so skillful that the bank cannot detect it. In that case, the bank is allowed to charge to the account the amount for which the check originally was written.

The bank has a duty to exercise "ordinary care" in the processing of negotiable instruments; it must observe the reasonable commercial standards prevailing among other banks in the area in which it does business. In the case of banks that take checks for collection or payment using automated means, it is important to note that reasonable commercial standards do not require the bank to examine every item if the failure to examine does not violate the bank's prescribed procedures and those procedures do not vary unreasonably from general banking practice or are not disapproved by the Code (3–103[a][7]; 4–103[c]). For example, the bank's practice may be to examine those checks for more than $1,000 and a sample of smaller checks. Thus, if it did not examine a particular check in the amount of $250 for evidence of alteration or forgery, its action would be commercially reasonable so long as (1) it followed its own protocol, (2) the protocol was not a great variance from general banking usage, and (3) the procedure followed was not specifically disallowed in the Code.

In a case in which both a bank and its customer fail to use ordinary care, a comparative negligence standard is used (4–406[e]).

CUSTOMER'S DUTY TO REPORT FORGERIES AND ALTERATIONS

A bank must send a monthly (or quarterly) statement listing the transactions in an account and commonly returns the canceled checks to the customer. Revised Article 3 recognizes the modern bank practice of truncating (or retaining) checks and permits the bank to supply only a statement showing the item number, amount, and date of payment (4–406[a]). When the bank does not return the paid items to the customer, the bank either must retain the items or maintain the capacity to furnish legible copies of the items for seven years after their receipt. The customer may request an item and the bank has a reasonable time to provide either the item or a legible copy of it (4–406[b]).

If the bank sends or makes available a statement of account or items, the customer must exercise reasonable promptness to examine the statement or items to determine whether payment was not authorized because of an alteration of any item or because a signature of the customer was not authorized. If, based on the statement or items provided, the customer discovers the unauthorized payment, the customer must notify the bank of the relevant facts promptly (4–406[c]).

The case that follows, *American Airlines Employees Federal Credit Union v. Martin,* involves the question of whether an account holder acted with "reasonable promptness" to discover forgeries in his account.

AMERICAN AIRLINES EMPLOYEES FEDERAL CREDIT UNION V. MARTIN
42 UCC Rep.2d 359 (Sup. Ct. Texas 2000)

FACTS

The American Airlines Employees Federal Credit Union is a federal credit union whose members are primarily employees of American Airlines and related entities and their spouses and families. In 1990, Tim Martin, an American Airlines employee, opened a savings account (called a "share account") at the Credit Union. He completed and signed a Credit Union membership application, which provided that the account would be "subject to any and all rules, regulations, by laws and policies of the Credit Union now in effect and as changed, amended or adopted hereafter." Martin received quarterly account statements.

In May 1994, the Credit Union adopted a Deposit Account Agreement and Disclosures, which contained the following paragraph:

> 1. *Account Statement.* You are responsible for promptly examining each account statement. Any objection that you may have respecting any item shown on the statement will be waived unless made in writing to us, and received on or before the sixtieth (60th) day following the date the statement is mailed, subject to applicable law. You agree that we will not be liable for any forged or altered items drawn on or deposited to your account if you fail to notify us within that sixty-day period.

While Martin did not receive a copy of the Deposit Agreement, he was notified about it through a newsletter and his account statements. In addition, the Credit Union specifically noted on the account statements that errors on the statement were to be reported to the Credit Union within 60 days.

On June 10, 1995, the Credit Union received a membership Account Change Card in the mail, purportedly signed by Martin, adding Molly Blair to Martin's account as a joint owner. Blair was Martin's girlfriend and a member of the Credit Union. She had recently added Martin's name to her own account. The Credit Union changed the ownership status of the account after verifying the personal and account information on the card and comparing Martin's purported signature on the change card to his original signature card. Martin's signature on the change card turned out to be a forgery.

Between June 12 and November 16, 1995, Blair transferred a total of $49,800 from Martin's account to her own. She made 14 transfers altogether—12 by telephone and 2 in person. To execute a telephone transfer, Blair would call the Credit Union and speak to a teller, who would verify Blair's identity by confirming certain personal and account information. The teller would complete the transaction by preparing and signing a "journal voucher" that identified the date of the transaction, the amount of the transfer, and the amounts involved. These journal vouchers were then mailed to Martin's address. The Credit Union also prepared journal vouchers for those transfers that Blair requested in person; these vouchers were given to Blair directly.

In addition to the 12 vouchers, the Credit Union also mailed two quarterly statements to Martin during the period that Blair made her withdrawals. The first was mailed between July 8 and July 20, 1995, and the second was mailed between October 6 and October 18, 1995. These statements documented 10 of Blair's transfers (the other 4 having been after the period covered by the second statement). The first quarterly statement listed Blair as a joint owner of the account and disclosed that she had made two withdrawals totaling $8,000. The second quarterly statement listed Blair as a joint owner and revealed that she had made eight more withdrawals totaling $36,500. Martin later denied receiving either the journal vouchers or the two statements, although there was no dispute that they were mailed to the correct address. In any event, Martin did not contact the Credit Union to request either quarterly statement.

On December 20, 1995, Martin went to the Credit Union to make a deposit and discovered that the balance in his account was not what he expected it to be. He immediately notified the Credit Union of the discrepancy. Subsequently, Martin sued the Credit Union to recover the $49,800 transferred from his account. Among other things, he claimed breach of the Credit Union's duties to him under Articles 3 and 4 of the Uniform Commercial Code. The Credit Union defended primarily on the basis of Section 4–406, which requires a bank customer to discover and report his unauthorized signature on an item within a year after the item and the account statement documenting the transaction are made available to the customer. The Credit Union maintained that the Deposit Agreement had reduced the one-year period

(continued)

AMERICAN AIRLINES EMPLOYEES FEDERAL CREDIT UNION v. MARTIN
(concluded)

set out in the statute to 60 days and that Martin was now precluded from asserting the unauthorized withdrawals because he had not given timely notice to the Credit Union.

ISSUE

Was Martin precluded from recovering the unauthorized withdrawals made to his account, which were not reported to the Credit Union within 60 days after the statement documenting them were made available to him?

DECISION

Yes, the court held that Section 4–406, which requires a bank customer to discover and report an unauthorized

signature on an item to the bank can be—and was in this case—modified to 60 days as long as the new time period is reasonable and not unconscionable. The court found no evidence suggesting the time period was unconscionable. Accordingly, the parties here had an enforceable agreement containing the 60-day provision; because Martin failed to give the Credit Union the required notice for 10 of the 14 items, he was not entitled to have them recredited to his account.

Multiple Forgeries or Alterations

Revised Article 3 provides a special rule to govern the situation in which the same wrongdoer makes a series of unauthorized drawer's signatures or alterations. The customer generally cannot hold the bank responsible for paying, in good faith, any such checks after the statement of account or item that contained the first unauthorized customer's signature or an alteration was available to the customer for a reasonable period, not exceeding 30 calendar days. The rule holds (1) if the customer did not notify the bank of the unauthorized signature or alteration and (2) the bank proves it suffered a loss because of the customer's failure to examine his statement and notify the bank (4–406[d]). Unless the customer has notified the bank about the forgeries or alterations that he should have discovered by reviewing the statement or item, the customer generally bears responsibility for any subsequent forgeries or alterations by the same wrongdoer.

Suppose that Allen employs Farnum as an accountant and that over a period of three months, Farnum forges Allen's signature to 10 checks and cashes them. One of the forged checks is included in the checks returned to Allen at the end of the first month. Within 30 calendar days after the return of these checks, Farnum forges two more checks and cashes them. Allen does not examine the returned checks until three months after the checks that included the first forged check were returned to her. The bank would be responsible for the first forged check and for the two checks forged and cashed within the 30-day period after it sent the first statement and the canceled checks (unless the bank proves that it suffered a loss because of the customer's failure to examine the checks and notify it more promptly). It would not be liable for the seven forged checks cashed after the expiration of the 30-day period.

Regardless of which party may have been negligent, a customer must discover and report to the bank any unauthorized customer's signature or any alteration within one year from the time after the statement or items are made available to him. If the customer does not do so, he cannot require the bank to recredit his account for such items. Similarly, a customer has three years from the time his statement or item is made available to discover and report any unauthorized indorsements on the item. The customer's failure to discover and report these irregularities within the one- or three-year periods specified ends his right to have his account recredited for the amount of the checks (4–406[f]).

CONCEPT SUMMARY   **Liability for Multiple Forgeries or Alterations by the Same Person**

Date First Statement Disclosing an Altered or Forged Check Is Available to Customer	Date 30 Days Later	Date Customer Gives Notice of Alteration or Forgery
Customer is not liable for forged/altered checks paid during this period unless bank suffers a loss from customer's unreasonable delay in notifying bank of forgery or alteration.	Customer is liable for forged or altered checks paid during this period unless customer gives bank notice of forgery or alteration within a reasonable time after date the first statement containing a forged or altered check was available to customer.	Customer is not liable for forged or altered checks paid during this period.

KNIGHT COMMUNICATIONS, INC. V. BOATMEN'S NATIONAL BANK OF ST. LOUIS
805 S.W.2d 199 (Ct. App. Mo. 1991)

FACTS

Two couples, Edna and Larry Brown and Mary and James Knight, formed a cable television construction business known as Knight Communications, Inc., with the four principals as directors. The Browns provided about $50,000 in capital, and the Knights operated the company. According to the signature card agreement for the corporate checking account opened in January 1986 at the Boatmen's National Bank of St. Louis and according to the understanding of the parties, each check required the signature of one of the Knights and one of the Browns. Beginning February 21, 1986, the bank began honoring checks with signatures of only one or both Knights. Between February and May 1986, 105 checks lacking a Brown signature (out of over 500 checks issued by the corporation during this time) were paid by the bank. The total of the improperly payable checks payable to the Knights was $7,696.94. One of the bank officers asserted that he had the oral permission of Mr. Brown to pay the checks but Mr. Brown later denied that he ever gave oral or written permission to the bank to honor checks without a Brown signature. The canceled checks were regularly returned to the corporation by the bank along with a periodic statement of account, but no contemporaneous objection was made to the lack of signatures by a Brown.

The Brown–Knight joint enterprise effectively ended in August 1986. At that time, Mr. Brown delivered some of the improperly paid checks to his attorney, and other canceled checks were delivered to that attorney by the Knights. In September 1988 a lawsuit was filed in the name of Knight Communications against the bank for breach of contract for unauthorized payment of the checks without the required Brown signature. This was the first time that the lack of authorization issue was raised with the bank.

ISSUE

Is the drawee bank liable to the drawer for the amount of checks it paid containing unauthorized drawer's signatures when it is notified of that fact two years after the checks were made available to the drawer?

DECISION

No. Initially, the court noted that the checks that were missing a signature of one of the Browns were "unauthorized" signatures within the meaning of the one-year statute of limitations for notifying banks of checks with unauthorized signatures. The failure of Knight Communications to discover and report the unauthorized signatures within one year from the time the bank made available to the customer a statement of account accompanied by items paid precluded the subsequent claim against the bank. The one-year time is absolute, without regard to care or lack of care of either the customer or the bank.

.... *ELECTRONIC BANKING* ....

With the development of computer technology, many banks encourage their customers to transfer funds electronically by using computers rather than paper drafts or checks. A bank customer may use a specially coded card at terminals provided by the bank to make deposits to an account, to transfer money from one checking or savings account to another, to pay bills, or to withdraw cash from an account. These new forms of transferring money have raised questions about the legal rules that apply to them, and the questions are only beginning to be resolved.

ELECTRONIC FUNDS TRANSFER ACT

The consumer who used electronic funds transfer systems (EFTs), the so-called cash machines or electronic tellers, in the early years often experienced problems in identifying and resolving mechanical errors resulting from malfunctioning EFTs. In response to these problems, Congress passed the **Electronic Funds Transfer Act** in 1978 to provide "a basic framework, establishing the rights, liabilities, and responsibilities of participants in electronic funds transfer systems" and especially to provide "individual consumer rights."

The four basic EFT systems are *automated teller machines; point-of-sale terminals,* which allow consumers to use their EFT cards like checks at retail establishments; *preauthorized payments,* such as automatic paycheck deposits or mortgage or utility payments; and *telephone transfers* between accounts or payment of specific bills by phone.

Similar to the Truth in Lending Act and the Fair Credit Billing Act (FCBA) discussed in Chapter 45, "Consumer Protection Laws," the EFT Act requires disclosure of the terms and conditions of electronic fund transfers at the time the consumer contracts for the EFT service. Among the nine disclosures required are the following: the consumer's liability for unauthorized electronic funds transfers (those resulting from loss or theft), the nature of the EFT services under the consumer's account, any pertinent dollar or frequency limitations, any charges for the right to make EFTs, the consumer's right to stop payment of a preauthorized transfer, the financial institution's liability to the consumer for failure to make or stop payments, and the consumer's right to receive documentation of transfers both at the point or time of transfer and periodically. The act also requires 21 days' notice prior to the effective date of any change in the terms or conditions of the consumer's account that pertains to the required disclosures.

The EFT Act does differ from the Fair Credit Billing Act in a number of important respects. For example, under the EFT Act, the operators of EFT systems are given a maximum of 10 working days to investigate errors or provisionally recredit the consumer's account, whereas issuers of credit cards are given a maximum of 60 days under the FCBA. The consumer's liability if an EFT card is lost or stolen also differs from his liability if a credit card is lost or stolen.

The case that follows, *Kruser v. Bank of America NT & SA,* illustrates the application of the EFT Act's provisions that require a customer to provide timely notification of any unauthorized use of his card in order to limit his liability for the unauthorized use.

KRUSER V. BANK OF AMERICA NT & SA
281 Cal. Rptr. 463 (Ct. App. Cal. 1991)

FACTS

Lawrence and Georgene Kruser maintained a joint checking account with the Bank of America, and the bank issued each of them a "Versatel" card and separate personal identification numbers that would allow access to funds in their account from automatic teller machines. The Krusers also received with their cards a "Disclosure Booklet" that provided to the Krusers a summary of consumer liability, the bank's business hours, and telephone number by which they could notify the bank in the event they believed an unauthorized transfer had been made.

The Krusers believed Mr. Kruser's card had been destroyed in September 1986. The December 1986 account statement mailed to the Krusers by the bank reflected a $20 unauthorized withdrawal of funds by someone using Mr. Kruser's card at an automatic teller machine. The Krusers reported this unauthorized transaction to the bank when they discovered it in August or September 1987.

Mrs. Kruser underwent surgery in late 1986 or early 1987 and remained hospitalized for 11 days. She then spent a period of six or seven months recuperating at home. During this time she reviewed the statements the Krusers received from the bank.

In September 1987, the Krusers received bank statements for July and August 1987 that reflected 47 unauthorized withdrawals totaling $9,020 made from an automatic teller machine, again by someone using Mr. Kruser's card. They notified the bank of these withdrawals within a few days of receiving the statements. The bank refused to credit the Krusers' account with the amount of the unauthorized withdrawals.

ISSUE

Did the failure to notify the bank in a timely fashion of the first unauthorized use of the card relieve the bank of liability for the subsequent unauthorized transfers of funds?

DECISION

Yes. If the Krusers had notified the bank of the first unauthorized transfer of $20 in a timely fashion, the subsequent unauthorized transfers some seven months later could have been prevented. The bank would have simply canceled the card, and the subsequent transfers would not have been possible. Thus, under the Electronic Funds Transfer Act, this failure on the part of the Krusers relieved the bank of liability for the subsequent unauthorized transfers. The court also found that Mrs. Kruser's illness did not excuse the failure to notify where it was undisputed that she had in fact reviewed the statement showing the transfer.

.... *QUESTIONS AND PROBLEM CASES* ....

1. What is the duty the drawee bank owes to a customer who maintains a checking account at the bank?
2. Louise Kalbe drew a check in the amount of $7,260 payable to the "order of cash" on her account at the Pulaski State Bank. The check was lost or stolen but Kalbe did not report this to the bank, nor did she attempt to stop payment on it. When the check was received by the Pulaski State Bank, Kalbe had only about $700 in her checking account. However, the bank paid the check, creating an overdraft in her account of $6,542.12. The bank then sued Kalbe to recover the amount of the overdraft. Kalbe asserted that the check was not properly payable from her account. Was the bank legally entitled to pay a check that exceeded the balance in the drawer's account and to recover the overdraft from the drawer?

3. Fitting wrote a check for $800 and gave it to the payee. She then had second thoughts about the check. She contacted the bank at which she had her checking account about the possibility of stopping payment on the check. A bank employee told her that she could not file a stop payment order until the bank opened the next morning. The next morning, Fitting did not file a stop payment order. Instead, she withdrew money from her account so that less than $800 remained in it. She believed that the bank would not pay the $800 check if there were not sufficient funds in the account to cover it. However, the bank paid the check and created an overdraft in Fitting's account. The bank then sued Fitting to recover the amount of the overdraft. Can a bank pay a customer's check even if this creates an overdraft in the customer's checking account?

4. J. E. B. Stewart received a check in the amount of $185.48 in payment of a fee from a client. Stewart presented the check, properly indorsed, to the Citizen's & Southern Bank. The bank refused to cash the check even though there were sufficient funds in the drawer's account. Stewart then sued the bank for actual damages of $185.48 for its failure to cash a valid check drawn against a solvent account in the bank. Does Stewart have a good cause of action against the bank?

5. Brenda Jones, who did business as Country Kitchen, purchased some cookware from an itinerant salesman, giving him a check in the amount of $200 for the purchase price. The salesman cashed the check at the First National Bank before noon on May 22, the day of the sale. Jones later became concerned about the lack of documentation from the salesman, thinking that the cookware might be stolen, and placed a stop-payment order with her bank, the State Bank of Conway Springs, at 3:30 that afternoon. State Bank refused to honor the check when it was presented for payment through banking channels. First National Bank, claiming to be a holder in due course, then brought suit against Jones to recover the $200 value of the check. Is the drawer of a check on which a stop-payment order was placed and honored by the bank liable to pay the check to a holder in due course?

6. *Video case.* See "Sour Grapes." Jelly Manufacturer orders some grapes by phone from Grape Grower in California on a COD basis. When the grapes arrive, Jelly Manufacturer pays for them by check before discovering that they had spoiled en route because they had been shipped in a nonrefrigerated truck. After calling Grape Grower to complain, Jelly Manufacturer calls its bank and places a stop-payment order on the check. The bank's computer fails to catch the check and the check is paid to Grape Grower. Does Jelly Manufacturer have any recourse against the bank for paying the check over the stop-payment order?

7. John Doe had a checking account at Highland National Bank in New York. Two days after John Doe died in Florida, but before Highland National knew of his death, John's sister appeared at the bank. She had a check signed by John Doe but with the amount and name of the payee left blank. She told the bank that her brother wanted to close his account. She asked how much was in the account, filled the check in for that amount, and made the check payable to herself. The bank checked her identification and verified the signature of John Doe. Then it paid the check to the sister. The executor of John Doe's estate sued Highland National Bank to recover the amount of money that was in John's account on the day he died. The executor claimed that the bank had no authority to pay checks from John Doe's account after his death. May a bank pay checks drawn on the account of a deceased customer?

8. In January of 1990, Mrs. Baker began forging her husband's checks. In June of 1991, Mr. Baker notified the bank that he had not been receiving his checking account statements. The missing statements were then personally delivered to Mr. Baker. Mr. Baker balanced his account statements in February of 1993. In March of 1993, he notified the bank that 25 of the checks that they had cashed were forgeries. Does the bank or Mr. Baker bear the liability for the forgeries?

9. In December, Whalley Company hired Nancy Cherauka as its bookkeeper. Her duties included preparing checks, taking deposits to the bank, and reconciling the monthly

checking account statements. She was not authorized to sign or cash checks. Between the following January 24 and May 31, Cherauka forged 49 checks on the Whalley account at National City Bank. Each month, National City Bank sent Whalley a statement and the canceled checks (including the forgeries) it had paid the previous month. The president of Whalley looked at the statement to see the balance in the account but he did not look at the individual checks. Then he gave the statement and checks to the bookkeeper. The January 24 forged check was sent to Whalley on February 3. In June, Whalley discovered that Cherauka was forging checks and fired her. It then brought a lawsuit against National City Bank to force it to recredit Whalley's account with the total amount of the 49 checks. Whalley claimed that the checks were not properly payable from the account. If a customer does not promptly discover and report to its bank that someone is forging checks on its account, can it require the bank to recredit its account?

10. On August 16, 1981, Frederick Ognibene went to the ATM area at a Citibank branch and activated one of the machines with his Citibank card, pressed in his personal identification code, and withdrew $20. When he approached the machine, a person was using the customer service telephone located between two ATM machines and appeared to be telling customer service that one of the machines was malfunctioning. As Ognibene was making his withdrawal the person said into the telephone, "I'll see if his card works in my machine." He then asked Ognibene if he could use his card to see if the other machine was working. Ognibene handed his card to him and saw him insert it into the adjoining machine at least two times while saying into the telephone, "Yes, it seems to be working."

When Ognibene received his Citibank statement, it showed that two withdrawals of $200 each from his account were made at 5:42 PM and 5:43 PM, respectively on August 16. His own $20 withdrawal was made at 5:41 PM. At the time, Ognibene was unaware that any withdrawals from his account were being made from the adjoining machine. Ognibene sought to have his account recredited for $400, claiming that the withdrawals had been unauthorized. Citibank had been aware for some time of a scam being perpetrated against its customers by persons who observed the customer inserting his personal identification number into an ATM and then obtaining access to the customer's ATM card in the same manner as Ognibene's card was obtained. After learning about the scam, Citibank posted signs in ATM areas containing a red circle approximately $2\frac{1}{2}$ inches in diameter in which was written "Do Not Let Your Citicard Be Used For Any Transaction But Your Own." Was Citibank required under the Electronic Funds Transfer Act to recredit Ognibene's account on the grounds that the withdrawal of the $400 was unauthorized?

PART VIII

Credit Transactions

CHAPTER 40

Introduction to Security

Many everyday transactions involve the extension of credit. For example, you might go to the dentist to have your teeth cleaned, a service for which the dentist will later send you a bill. Mark borrows $11,000 from the bank to purchase a new car with the bank taking a lien on the car until the loan is repaid. Sarah purchases a dress using her MasterCard. Rob, who is 16 years old, buys a motorcycle on a time-payment plan from a dealer who asks that Rob's father cosign the note. Mary buys a small farm on a land contract from Farmer who is retiring. Lumberyard delivers lumber to your house for use by Contractor, whom you have engaged to build a garage. Frank parks his car illegally on someone's property and she has it towed away by a local towing service; the towing service refuses to release the car to him until he pays a towing and storage charge.

These examples illustrate a number of the dimensions of credit transactions that will be discussed in this chapter, including:

- *The difference between secured and unsecured credit, and the importance of the difference to the creditor.*
- *The different ways a creditor can obtain security, including taking a lien or security interest on personal or real property and obtaining a surety or guarantor for the obligation.*
- *When common law or statutory liens are available to innkeepers, common carriers, and to artisans or tradesmen to secure the value of their services.*
- *When a mechanic's or materialman's lien on real property is available to the supplier of labor or materials.*

.... ***CREDIT*** ....

NATURE OF CREDIT

In the United States, a substantial portion of business transactions involve the extension of credit. The term *credit* has many meanings. In this chapter, **credit** will be used to mean a transaction in which money is loaned, goods are sold, or services are rendered in exchange for a promise to pay for them at some future date.

In some of these transactions, a creditor is willing to rely on the debtor's promise to pay at a later time; in others, the creditor wants some future assurance or security that the debtor will make good on his promise to pay. Various mechanisms are available to the creditor who wants to obtain security. These mechanisms include obtaining liens or security interests in personal or real property, sureties, and guarantors. Security interests in real property, sureties and guarantors, and common law liens on personal property will be covered in this chapter, and the Uniform Commercial Code rules concerning security interests in personal property will be covered in Chapter 41. Chapter 42 will deal with bankruptcy law, which may come into play when a debtor is unable to fulfill his obligation to pay his debts when they are due.

UNSECURED CREDIT

Many common transactions are based on *unsecured credit*. For example, you may have a charge account at a department store or a MasterCard account. If you buy a sweater and charge it to your charge account or your MasterCard account, unsecured credit has been extended to you. You have received goods in return for your unsecured promise to pay for them later. Similarly, if you go to a dentist to have a tooth filled and he sends you a bill payable by the end of the month, services have been rendered on the basis of unsecured credit. Consumers are not the only people who use unsecured credit. Many transactions between businesspeople utilize it. For example, a retailer buys merchandise or a manufacturer buys raw materials, promising to pay for the merchandise or materials within 30 days after receipt.

The unsecured credit transaction involves a maximum of risk to the creditor (the person who extends the credit). When goods are delivered, services rendered, or money loaned on unsecured credit, the creditor gives up all rights in the goods, services, or money. In return, the creditor gets a promise by the debtor to pay or to perform the requested act. If the debtor does not pay or keep the promise, the creditor's only course of action is to bring a lawsuit against the debtor and obtain a judgment. The creditor may then have the sheriff execute the judgment on any property owned by the debtor that is subject to execution. The creditor might also try to garnish the wages or other moneys to which the debtor is entitled. However, the debtor might be **judgment proof;** that is, the debtor might not have any property subject to execution or might not have a steady job. Under these circumstances, execution or garnishment would be of little aid to the creditor in collecting the judgment.

A businessperson may obtain credit insurance to stabilize the credit risk of doing business on an unsecured credit basis. However, the costs to the business of the insurance or of the unsecured credit losses it sustains are passed on to the consumer. The consumer pays a higher price for goods or services purchased or a higher interest rate on any money borrowed from a business that has high credit losses.

SECURED CREDIT

To minimize her credit risk, a creditor can contract for **security.** The creditor may require the debtor to convey to the creditor a **security interest** or lien on the debtor's property. Suppose you borrow $3,000 from a credit union. It might require that you put up your car as security for the loan. The creditor might also ask that some other person agree to be liable if the debtor defaults. For example, if a student who does not have a regular job goes to a bank to borrow money, the bank might ask that the student's father or mother cosign the note for the loan.

When the creditor has security for the credit he extends and the debtor defaults, the creditor can go against the security to collect the obligation. Assume that you borrow $15,000 from a bank to buy a new car and the bank takes a security interest (lien) on the car. If you fail to make your monthly payments, the bank has the right to repossess the car and have it sold so that it can recover its money. Similarly, if your father cosigned for the car loan and you default, the bank can sue your father to collect the balance due on the loan.

SURETYSHIP

SURETIES AND GUARANTORS

A **surety** is a person who is liable for the payment of another person's debt or for the performance of another person's duty. The surety joins with the person who is primarily liable in promising to make the payment or to perform the duty. For example, Kathleen, who is 17 years old, buys a used car on credit from Harry's Used Cars. She signs a promissory note, agreeing to pay $200 a month on the note until the note is paid in full. Harry's has Kathleen's father cosign the note; thus, her father is a surety. Similarly, the city of Chicago hires the B&B Construction Company to build a new sewage treatment plant. The city will probably require B&B to have a surety agreement to be liable for B&B's performance of its contract. There are insurance companies that, for a fee, will agree to be a surety for a company like B&B on its contract. If the person who is primarily liable (the principal) defaults, the surety is liable to pay or perform. Then the surety is entitled to be reimbursed by the principal.

A **guarantor** does not join in making a promise; rather, a guarantor makes a separate promise and agrees to be liable on the happening of a certain event. For example, a father tells a merchant, "I will guarantee payment of my son Richard's debt to you if he does not pay it," or "In the event that Richard becomes bankrupt, I will guarantee payment of his debt to you." A guarantor's promise must be made in writing to be enforceable under the statute of frauds.

The rights and liabilities of the surety and the guarantor are substantially the same. No distinction will be made between them in this chapter except where the distinction is of basic importance.

CREATION OF PRINCIPAL AND SURETY RELATIONSHIP

The relationship of principal and surety, or that of principal and guarantor, is created by contract. The basic rules of contract law apply in determining the existence and nature of the relationship as well as the rights and duties of the parties.

DEFENSES OF A SURETY

Suppose that Jeff's father agrees to be a surety for Jeff on his purchase of a motorcycle on credit from a dealer. If the motorcycle was defectively made and Jeff refuses to make further payments on it, the dealer might try to collect the balance due from Jeff's father. As a surety, Jeff's father can use any defenses against the dealer that Jeff has if they go to the merits of the primary contract. Thus, if Jeff has a valid defense of breach of warranty against the dealer, his father can use it as a basis for not paying the dealer.

Other defenses that go to the merits include (1) lack or failure of consideration, (2) inducement of the contract by fraud or duress, and (3) breach of contract by the other party. The personal defenses of the principal cannot be used by the surety. These personal defenses include lack of capacity, such as minority or insanity, and bankruptcy. Thus, if Jeff is only 17 years old, the fact that he is a minor cannot be used by Jeff's father to defend against the dealer. This defense of Jeff's lack of capacity to contract does not go to the merits of the contract between Jeff and the dealer and cannot be used by Jeff's father.

A surety contracts to be responsible for the performance of the principal's obligation. If the principal and the creditor change that obligation by agreement, the surety is relieved of responsibility unless the surety agrees to the change. This is because the surety's obligation cannot be changed without his consent.

For example, Fred cosigns a note that his friend Kathy has given to Credit Union to secure a loan. Suppose the note was originally for $2,500 and payable in 12 months with interest at 11 percent a year. Credit Union and Kathy later agree that Kathy will have 24 months to repay the note but that the interest will be 13 percent per year. Unless Fred consents to this change, he is discharged from his responsibility as surety. The obligation he agreed to assume was altered by the changes in the repayment period and interest rate.

The most common kind of change affecting a surety is an extension of time to perform the contract. If the creditor merely allows the principal more time without the surety's consent, this does not relieve the surety of responsibility. The surety's consent is required only where there is an agreement between the creditor and the principal as to the extension of time. In addition, the courts usually make a distinction between accommodation sureties and compensated sureties. An **accommodation surety** is a person who acts as a surety without compensation, such as a friend who cosigns a note as a favor. A **compensated surety** is a person, usually a professional such as a bonding company, who is paid for serving as a surety.

The courts are more protective of accommodation sureties than of compensated sureties. Accommodation sureties are relieved of liability unless they consent to the extension of time. Compensated sureties, on the other hand, must show that they will be harmed by an extension of time before they are relieved of responsibility because of an extension of time to which they have not consented.

CREDITOR'S DUTIES TO SURETY

The creditor is required to disclose any material facts about the risk involved to the surety. If he does not do so, the surety is relieved of liability. For example, a bank (creditor) knows that an employee, Arthur, has been guilty of criminal conduct in the past. If the bank applies to a bonding company to obtain a bond on Arthur, the bank must disclose that information to the surety. Similarly, suppose the bank has an employee, Alice, covered by a bond and discovers that Alice is embezzling money. If the bank agrees to give Alice another chance but does not report her actions to the bonding company, the bonding company is relieved of responsibility for further wrongful acts by Alice.

If the principal posts security for the performance of an obligation, the creditor must not surrender that security without the consent of the surety. If the creditor does so, the surety is relieved of liability to the extent of the value surrendered. The *Camp* case illustrates this principle.

CAMP V. FIRST FINANCIAL FEDERAL SAVINGS AND LOAN ASSOCIATION
772 S.W.2d 602 (Sup. Ct. Ark. 1989)

FACTS

Rusty Jones, a used car dealer, applied to First Financial Federal Savings and Loan Association for a $50,000 line of credit to purchase an inventory of used cars. First Financial refused to make the loan to Jones alone but agreed to do so if Worth Camp, an attorney and friend of Jones, would cosign the note. Camp agreed to cosign as an accommodation maker or surety. The expectation of the parties was that the loans cosigned by Camp would be repaid from the proceeds of the car inventory.

The original note for $25,000 was signed on August 2, 1984, and renewals were executed on January 25, 1985, September 11, 1985, and March 15, 1986, and the amount was eventually increased to $50,000. In August 1985, as Camp was considering whether to sign the September renewal note, he was advised by First Financial's loan officer that the interest on the loan had been paid. In fact, interest payments were four months delinquent. In addition, unknown to Camp, as the $50,000 credit limit was approached, First Financial began making side, or personal, loans to Jones totaling around $25,000, which were also payable out of the proceeds of the used car inventory. Camp knew nothing of these loans and thought that Jones's used car business was making payments only on the loans he had cosigned.

Jones defaulted on the $50,000 note cosigned by Camp, and First Financial brought suit against Camp on his obligation as surety on the note.

ISSUE

Was Camp relieved of his obligation as surety by First Financial's failure to disclose material facts to him?

DECISION

Yes. The court held that a surety has a defense against performance of his obligation if the creditor failed to disclose facts that materially increased the surety's risk. Here, the creditor was in possession of facts concerning the true state of Jones's payments and the secret side loans it had made. It knew that the surety, Camp, was not in possession of this information and that it was very relevant to Camp's assessment of the risk he would undertake as surety on the renewals of the note. First Financial's failure to communicate the information to Camp in a timely fashion gives him a defense to being required to perform his obligation as surety.

SUBROGATION AND CONTRIBUTION

If the surety has to perform or pay the principal's obligation, then the surety acquires all the rights that the creditor had against the principal. This is known as the surety's **right of subrogation.** The rights include the right to any collateral in the possession of the creditor, any judgment right the creditor had against the principal on the obligation, and the rights of a creditor in bankruptcy proceedings.

If the surety performs or pays the principal's obligation, she is entitled to recover her costs from the principal; this is known as the surety's **right to reimbursement.** For example, Amanda cosigns a promissory note for $250 at the credit union for her friend Anne. Anne defaults on the note, and the credit union collects $250 from Amanda on her suretyship obligation. Amanda then not only gets the credit union's rights against Anne but also the right to collect $250 from Anne.

Suppose several persons (Tom, Dick, and Harry) are cosureties of their friend Sam. When Sam defaults, Tom pays the whole obligation. Tom is entitled to collect one-third each from both Dick and Harry since he paid more than his prorated share. This is known as the cosurety's right to contribution. The relative shares of cosureties, as well as any limitations on their liability, are normally set out in the contract of suretyship.

LIENS ON PERSONAL PROPERTY

SECURITY INTERESTS IN PERSONAL PROPERTY AND FIXTURES UNDER THE UNIFORM COMMERCIAL CODE

Chapter 41 will discuss how a creditor can obtain a security interest in the personal property or fixtures of a debtor. It will also explain the rights of the creditor, the debtor, and other creditors of the debtors to the property. These security interests are covered by Article 9 of the Uniform Commercial Code, which sets out a comprehensive scheme for regulating security interests in personal property and fixtures. Article 9 does not deal with the liens that landlords, artisans, and materialmen are given by statute or with security interests in real estate. These security interests will be covered in this chapter.

COMMON LAW LIENS

Under the common—or judge-made—law, artisans, innkeepers, and common carriers (such as airlines and trucking companies) were entitled to liens to secure the reasonable value of the services they performed. An artisan such as a furniture upholsterer or an auto mechanic uses his labor and/or materials to improve personal property that belongs to someone else. The improvement becomes part of the property and belongs to the owner of the property. Therefore, the artisan who made the improvement is given a **lien** on the property until he is paid. For example, the upholsterer who recovers a sofa for you is entitled to a lien on the sofa.

The innkeeper and common carrier are in business to serve the public and are required by law to do so. Under the common law, the innkeeper was allowed to claim a lien on the guest's property brought to the hotel or inn to secure payment for the innkeeper's reasonable charges for food and lodging. Similarly, the common carrier, such as a trucking company, was allowed to claim a lien on the goods carried for the reasonable charges for the service. The justification for these liens was that because the innkeeper and common carrier were required by law to provide the service to anyone seeking it, they were entitled to the protection of a lien.

STATUTORY LIENS

While common law liens are generally recognized today, many states have incorporated this concept in statutes. Some of the state statutes have created additional liens while others have modified the common law liens to some extent. The statutes commonly provide a procedure for foreclosing the lien. **Foreclosure** is the method by which a court authorizes the sale of the personal property subject to the lien so that the creditor can obtain the money to which he is entitled.

CHARACTERISTICS OF LIENS

The common law lien and most of the statutory liens are known as **possessory liens.** They give the artisan or other lienholder the right to keep possession of the debtor's property until the reasonable charges for the service have been paid. For the lien to come into play, possession of the goods must have been entrusted to the artisan. Suppose you take a chair to an upholsterer to have it repaired. She can keep possession of it until you pay the reasonable value of the repair work. However, if the upholsterer comes to your home to make the repair, she would not have a lien on the chair because you did not give up possession of it.

The two essential elements of the lien are (1) *possession by the improver or provider of services* and (2) *a debt created by the improvement or provision of services concerning the goods.* If the artisan or other lienholder gives up the goods voluntarily, he loses the lien. For example, if you have a new engine put in your car and the mechanic gives the car back to you before you pay for the engine, the mechanic loses the lien on the car to secure your payment for the work and materials. However, if the debtor regains possession by fraud or other illegal act, the lien is not lost. Once the debt is paid, the lien is terminated, and the artisan or other lienholder no longer has the right to retain the goods. If the artisan keeps the goods after the debt has been paid, or keeps the goods without the right to a lien, he is liable for conversion or unlawful detention of goods.

FORECLOSURE OF LIEN

The right of a lienholder to possess goods does not automatically give the lienholder the right to sell the property or to claim ownership if his charges are not paid. Commonly, there is a procedure provided by statute for selling the property once it has been held for a certain period of time. The lienholder is required to give notice to the debtor and to advertise the proposed sale by posting or publishing notices. If there is no statutory procedure, the lienholder must first bring a lawsuit against the debtor. After obtaining a judgment for his charges, the lienholder can have the sheriff seize the property and have it sold at a judicial sale.

.... *SECURITY INTERESTS IN REAL PROPERTY* ....

There are three basic contract devices for using real estate as security for an obligation: (1) the real estate mortgage, (2) the deed of trust, and (3) the land contract. In

---

NATIONAL UNION V. ELAND MOTORS
651 N.E.2d 1257 (Ct. App. N.Y. 1995)

FACTS

International Automobiles, Ltd., was a company engaged in the sale and purchase of "collectors' cars." In 1975, International employed Eland Motor Car Company, a registered automotive repair shop, and its principal, Andrew Bach, to restore, repair, maintain, and store its collection of vehicles. Bach received a monthly fee of $4,000 for overseeing the collection as well as a 10 percent finder's fee for any cars he located for International and an additional 10 percent sales commission, both to be paid to Bach at the time of the sale of any such car. Over time, International ceased paying Eland and Bach for their services. In 1988, Eland asserted a garage owner's lien pursuant to New York Lien Law section 184 on the International vehicles still in its possession for the portion of the outstanding debt pertaining solely to garage services.

Section 184 of the Lien Law provides in pertinent part that a person keeping a registered motor vehicle repair shop or garage "and who in connection therewith tows, stores, maintains, keeps or repairs any motor vehicle . . . at the request or with the consent of the owner . . . has a lien upon such motor vehicle for the sum due for such [services] . . . and may detain such motor vehicle . . . at any time it may be lawfully in his possession until such sum is paid."

Eland arranged to conduct a garage keeper's lien sale in November 1988 to sell several of International's cars remaining in its possession to satisfy International's unpaid repair and storage bills. Eland duly served International with notices of the lien and sale.

National Union Fire Insurance Company had become a money judgment creditor of International's for more

(continued)

NATIONAL UNION V. ELAND MOTORS
(concluded)

than $500,000. It brought a proceeding against Eland to compel it to turn over the cars in its possession that were owned by International. Pursuant to court order Eland conducted a sale of the vehicles on June 9, 1990, and deposited the proceeds with the clerk of the court.

The trial court directed that National Union could satisfy its judgments first from the sale of the vehicles in Eland's possession, with any amount realized from the sale in excess of those judgments payable to Eland up to $139,244—the amount Eland claimed it was owed for the garage services. The court reasoned that Eland was not entitled to a priority lien because Eland and International had been engaged in a joint venture. The appellate division affirmed, holding that because the transactions between the two were more than the normal garage owner/car owner relationship, the lien law did not apply. Eland appealed.

ISSUE

Was Eland entitled to a priority garage keeper's lien on the vehicles in its possession because it had provided

repair and storage services concerning those vehicles to International?

DECISION

Yes. A bailment was undeniably established by International's voluntary relinquishment of the cars it owned to Eland for repairs, servicing, and storage. There was no evidence that Eland had any ownership interest in the vehicles or was engaged in any joint enterprise that would defeat Eland's claim that it was a bailee and entitled to recover the reasonable value of the repairs and storage it performed. No language in the statute supports the notion that the other business arrangements between Eland and International should deprive Eland of the statutory means (the lien) for recouping its reasonable compensation for the services it provided that enhanced the value of the collectible cars. Thus, Eland has the first claim on the proceeds of the sale of the cars in order to satisfy its lien.

addition, the states have enacted statutes giving mechanics, such as carpenters and plumbers, and materialmen, such as lumberyards, a right to a lien on real property into which their labor or materials are incorporated. Some states give the right to a lien only to prime contractors while other states also extend it to subcontractors.

REAL ESTATE MORTGAGE

A **mortgage** is a security interest in real property or a deed to real property that is given by the owner (the **mortgagor**) as security for a debt owed to the creditor (the **mortgagee**). Because the real estate mortgage conveys an interest in real property, it must be executed with the same formality as a deed. Unless it is executed with the required formalities, it will not be eligible for recording in the local land records. Recordation of the mortgage does not affect its validity as between the mortgagor and the mortgagee. However, if it is not recorded, it will not be effective against subsequent purchasers of the property or creditors, including other mortgagees, who have no notice of the earlier mortgage. It is important to the mortgagee that the mortgage be recorded so that the world will be on notice of the mortgagee's interest in that property. See Figure 40–1 for an example of a mortgage.

The owner (mortgagor) of property subject to a mortgage can sell the interest in the property without the consent of the mortgagee. However, the sale does not affect the mortgagee's interest in the property or claim against the mortgagor.

For example, Eric Smith owns a lot on a lake. Eric wants to build a cottage on the land, so he borrows $85,000 from First National Bank. Eric signs a note for $85,000

FIGURE 40–1   A Mortgage

MORTGAGE

THIS INDENTURE, made this 18th day of October, A.D. 2003, BETWEEN Raymond A. Dole and Deborah H. Dole, hereinafter called the Mortgagor, and First Federal Savings and Loan Association, hereinafter called the Mortgagee,

WITNESSETH, That the said Mortgagor, for and in consideration of the sum of One Dollar, to us in hand paid by the said Mortgagee, the receipt whereof is hereby acknowledged, have granted, bargained, and sold to the said Mortgagee, its heirs and assigns forever, the following described land situate, lying and being in the County of Genesee, State of Michigan, to wit:

All that certain plot, piece, or parcel of land located in the County of Genesee, State of Michigan and known and described as Lot numbered Thirty-nine (39) in William D. Green's subdivision of part of Lot numbered Twenty-two (22) in Square numbered Twelve Hundred Nineteen (1219), as per plot recorded in the Office of the Surveyor for the County of Genesee in Liber 30 at folio 32, together with the buildings and improvements thereon, and the said Mortgagor do hereby fully warrant the title to said land, and will defend the same against the lawful claims of all persons whomsoever.

PROVIDED ALWAYS, That if said Mortgagor, their heirs, legal representatives, or assigns shall pay unto the said Mortgagee, its legal representatives or assigns, a certain promissory note dated the 18th day of October, A.D. 2003, for the sum of Thirty-eight Thousand Dollars ($38,000), payable in monthly installments of Three Hundred Fifteen Dollars ($315.00) with interest at ten percent (10%) beginning on November 18, 2003, and signed by Raymond A. Dole and Deborah H. Dole and shall perform, comply with, and abide by this mortgage, and shall pay all taxes which may accrue on said land and all costs and expenses said Mortgagee may be put to in collecting said promissory note by foreclosure of this mortgage or otherwise, including a reasonable attorney's fee, then this mortgage and the estate hereby created shall cease and be null and void.

IN WITNESS WHEREOF, the said Mortgagor hereunto set their hands and seals the day and year first above written. Signed, sealed, and delivered in presence of us:

John R. Bacon   *Raymond A. Dole*

James A. Brown   *Deborah H. Dole*

ACKNOWLEDGEMENT OF MORTGAGE
State of Michigan   )
Count of Genesee)ss

I, an officer authorized to take acknowledgements according to the laws of the State of Michigan, duly qualified and acting, HEREBY CERTIFY that Raymond A. Dole and Deborah H. Dole to me personally known, this day personally appeared and acknowledged before me that they executed the foregoing Mortgage, and I further certify that I know the said persons making said acknowledgement to be the individuals described in and who executed the said Mortgage.
Susan B. Clark
Notary Public

Susan B. Clark
Susan B. Clark
Notary Public

and gives the bank an $85,000 mortgage on the land and cottage as security for his repayment of the loan. Several years later, Eric sells his land and cottage to Melinda Mason. The mortgage he gave First National might make the unpaid balance due on the mortgage payable on sale. If it does not, Eric can sell the property with the mortgage on it. If Melinda defaults on the mortgage payments, the bank can foreclose on the mortgage. If, at the foreclosure sale, the property does not bring enough money to cover the costs, interest, and balance due on the mortgage, First National is entitled to a deficiency judgment against Eric. However, some courts are reluctant to give deficiency judgments where real property is used as security for a debt and some state laws specifically disallow them where personal residential property is involved. If, on foreclosure, the property sells for more than the debt, Melinda is entitled to the surplus.

A purchaser of mortgaged property can buy it "subject to the mortgage" or may "assume the mortgage." If she buys **subject to** the mortgage and there is a default and foreclosure, the purchaser is not personally liable for any deficiency. The property is liable for the mortgage debt and can be sold to satisfy it in case of default. If the buyer **assumes** the mortgage, then she becomes personally liable for the debt and for any deficiency on default and foreclosure.

The creditor (mortgagee) may assign his interest in the mortgaged property. To do this, the mortgagee must assign the mortgage as well as the debt for which the mortgage is security.

Foreclosure is the process by which any rights of the mortgagor or the current property owner are cut off. Foreclosure proceedings are regulated by statute in the state in which the property is located. The sale commonly takes place under the supervision of a court, but in a few states no court action is required. In the latter case, the mortgagee must give notice of the proposed sale to the mortgagor and advertise to the public, with the actual sale taking place by auction. If the property is sold at a foreclosure sale and not redeemed by the owner, then the proceeds of the sale are used to pay the foreclosure costs, the interest, and the debt. Any surplus from the sale is returned to the owner of the property. Commonly, the states provide a period of time (usually six months to a year) after default on the debt during which the owner or other person with an interest in the property can **redeem** it by paying off the mortgage.

A small number of states permit what is called **strict foreclosure.** The creditor keeps the property in satisfaction of the debt, and the owner's rights are cut off. This means that the creditor has no right to a deficiency and the debtor has no right to any surplus. Strict foreclosure is normally limited to situations in which the amount of the debt exceeds the value of the property.

DEED OF TRUST

There are three parties to a **deed of trust:** (1) the owner of the property who borrows the money, (2) the trustee who holds legal title to the property put up as security, and (3) the lender who is the beneficiary of the trust. The purpose of the deed of trust is to make it easy for the security to be liquidated. However, most states treat the deed of trust like a mortgage in giving the borrower a relatively long period of time to redeem the property, thereby defeating this rationale for the arrangement.

Figure 40–2   A Deed of Trust

DEED OF TRUST

THIS DEED made this 14th day of August, 2003, by and between Harold R. Holmes, grantor, party of the first part, and Frederick B. Cannon, trustee, party of the second part, and Sarah A. Miles, party of the third part.

WITNESSETH:

The party of the first part does hereby grant unto the party of the second part, the following described property located in the District of Columbia and known as Lot numbered One Hundred Fourteen (114) in James B. Nicholson's subdivision in square numbered Twelve Hundred Forty-seven (1247), formerly Square numbered Seventy-seven (77), "Georgetown," as per plat recorded in the Office of the Surveyor for the District of Columbia in Liber Georgetown 2 at folio 34, in trust, however, to secure the balance only of the purchase price of the above described premises, evidenced by the following described obligation:

Promissory note executed by the party of the first part, payable to the party of the third part and dated August 14, 2003 in the principal sum of Sixty-four Thousand Dollars ($64,000.00) bearing interest at the rate of ten percent (10%) per annum until paid. Said principal and interest are payable in monthly installments of Seven Hundred Thirty-five Dollars ($735.00) on the 14th day of each and every month beginning September 14, 2003, and continuing every month thereafter, with the unpaid balance of said principal and interest due and payable in full on August 14, 2013.

IN WITNESS WHEREOF, the party of the first part has set his hand and seal this the day and year first above written.

Harold R. Holmes
(SEAL)

Acknowledgement
This Deed of Trust accepted this 14th day of August, 2003.

Frederick B. Cannon
Trustee

In a deed of trust transaction, the borrower deeds to the trustee the property that is to be put up as security (see Figure 40–2). The trust agreement usually gives the trustee the right to foreclose or sell the property if the borrower fails to make a required payment on the debt. Normally, the trustee does not sell the property until the lender notifies him that the borrower is in default and demands that the property be sold. The trustee then sells the property, usually at a public sale. The proceeds are applied to the costs of the foreclosure, interest, and debt. If there is a surplus, it is paid to the borrower. If there is a deficiency, the lender has to sue the borrower on the debt and recover judgment.

LAND CONTRACTS

The **land contract** is a device for securing the balance due the seller on the purchase price of real estate (see Figure 40–3). The buyer agrees to pay the purchase price over a period of time. The seller agrees to convey title to the property to the buyer when the full price is paid. Usually, the buyer takes possession of the property, pays the taxes, insures the property, and assumes the other obligations of an owner. However, the seller keeps legal title and does not turn over the deed until the pur-

FIGURE 40–3   A Land Contract

LAND CONTRACT

THIS AGREEMENT, made this 15th day of September, A.D. 2000, between Sarah A. Collins, a single woman, hereinafter designated "Vendor," and Robert H. Bowen, a single man, hereinafter designated "Vendee," in the manner following: The Vendor hereby agrees to sell and the Vendee agrees to buy all that certain piece or parcel of land being in the Township of Fenton, County of Genesee and State of Michigan, and more particularly described as follows:

Part of the Northeast $1/4$ of the Northwest $1/4$ of Section 20, Township 5 North, Range 5 East, described as follows: Beginning at a point on the North line of said Section 20, which is West along said North line, 797.72 feet from the North $1/4$ corner of said Section 20; thence continuing West along said North line, 522.72 feet; thence South 0 degrees, 18 minutes, 12 seconds East along the West $1/8$ line of said Section, 1000.0 feet; thence East parallel to the North line of said Section, 522.72 feet; thence North 0 degrees, 18 minutes, 12 seconds West parallel to said West $1/8$ line 1000.0 feet to the point of beginning, containing 12.0 acres of land, more or less, and known as 1135 Long Lake Road.

Subject to all easements, laws, ordinances, reservations, applying to this property.

For the sum of Sixty-four Thousand Nine Hundred Dollars ($64,900.00), payable as follows: Ten Thousand Dollars ($10,000), cash in hand, receipt of which is hereby acknowledged before the signing of this contract and the balance payable as follows: Three Hundred Dollars ($300.00) or more payable on the 1st day of November, 2003 and a like amount on the 1st day of each and every month thereafter until the full sum of both interest and principal has been paid in full. Interest at the rate of ten percent (10%) per annum, starting October 1, 2003, shall be deducted from each and every monthly payment and the balance applied on the principal. The entire balance, both principal and interest, to be paid in full on or before 5 years from date of closing. It is understood and agreed that the above monthly payment includes taxes and insurance that may become due and payable subsequent to the date of this contract; said amounts to be paid by Vendor and added to the principal balance.

Vendee also agrees to pay all taxes and assessments extraordinary as well as ordinary that may be levied thereon, including taxes for the year 1996, and also deferred payments on special assessments that shall become due and payable after the date thereof to be prorated to date.

The Vendee agrees to keep the buildings upon or to be placed upon the premises insured against damage by fire and wind, in such company and amount as is approved by the Vendor, for the benefit of all parties in interest; such policies shall be delivered to and held by the Vendor.

And Vendee agrees to keep the buildings and other improvements on the premises in good repair. In case the Vendee shall fail to pay taxes, effect insurance, or make necessary repairs, the Vendor may do any or all of these things and the amount paid therefore by the Vendor shall be deemed a part of the principal sum under this contract and become payable immediately with interest at the rate of ten percent (10%) per annum until paid.

The Vendor on receiving payment in full of the principal and interest, and of all other sums chargeable under the contract, agrees, at his own proper cost and expense, to execute and deliver to the Vendee, or to his assigns, upon surrender of this contract, a good and sufficient conveyance in fee simple of the above described premises, free and clear of all liens and encumbrances, except such as may have accrued thereon subsequent to the date of this contract by or through the acts or negligences of others than the Vendor, and at the option of the Vendor furnish the Vendee an abstract of title or a policy of title insurance in an amount equal to the purchase price under this contract. The Vendor hereby reserves the right to mortgage said premises at any time in an amount not in excess of the amount then due on this contract, and the Vendee agrees that the said mortgage shall be a first lien on the premises.

(continued)

---

chase price is paid. Purchases of farm property are commonly financed through the use of land contracts.

FIGURE 40-3   A Land Contract *(concluded)*

It is mutually agreed that the Vendee shall have possession of said premises from and after October 1, 2003.

If the Vendee shall fail to comply with the terms of this contract, the Vendor may take possession of the property and all the improvements on it and treat the Vendee as a tenant holding over without permission and remove him therefrom and retain any money paid hereon as stipulated damages for nonperformance of this contract. It is hereby expressly understood and declared that time is and shall be taken as of the very essence of this contract. Notice of said forfeiture may be given by depositing the notice in post office, addressed to Vendee at his last known address.

It is agreed that the stipulations contained in this contract are to apply to and bind the heirs, executors, administrators, and assigns of the respective parties to this contract.

In witness whereof, the said parties have set their hands and seals the day and year first above written.

Signed, sealed and delivered in presence of:

Walter I. Timball   *Sarah A. Collins*
                                             Sarah A. Collins

Nancy Evans Smith   *Robert H. Bowen*
                                             Robert H. Bowen

If the buyer defaults, the seller generally has the right to declare a forfeiture and take possession of the property. The buyer's rights to the property are cut off at that point. Most states give the buyer on a land contract a limited period of time to redeem his interest. Generally, the procedure for declaring a forfeiture and recovering property sold on a land contract is simpler and less time consuming than foreclosure of a mortgage. However, as is illustrated in the case that follows, *Bennett v. Galindo,* some states protect purchasers against the severity of forfeiture and either provide a

BENNETT V. GALINDO
1994 WL 613429 (D. Kan. 1994)

FACTS

Harold and Karen Galindo purchased a house from Carl Bennett and his wife, Lillian, pursuant to an installment land contract entitled "Conditional Sales Contract" and dated July 17, 1991. The contract included the following provisions: The $46,000 purchase price at a 9.5 percent fixed interest rate consisted of a down payment of $12,000 and 180 monthly installments of $355.04. The Galindos were to pay real estate taxes and insurance. They were given immediate possession of, but not legal title to, the premises. The title to the premises would not be conveyed to the Galindos until they paid the entire purchase price. The Galindos were entitled to remain in

possession unless they defaulted under the contract. The contract defined "default" as failure to pay six monthly installments, real estate taxes, or insurance premiums. If the buyers defaulted under the contract, they forfeited all money previously paid to the Bennetts and were to surrender immediate possession of the premises to the Bennetts.

On December 17, 1993, counsel for the Bennetts mailed to the Galindos a written notice to cancel based upon the buyer's failure to pay monthly installments for April through June 1993, and September through December 1993, and $234.07 in real estate taxes owed for

(continued)

BENNETT V. GALINDO
(concluded)

the last six months of 1993. Pursuant to the notice, the Galindos moved out of the property and turned over the property to the Bennetts' counsel.

On January 28, 1994, after consulting counsel concerning their rights, the Galindos filed an affidavit of equitable interest with the Register of Deeds of Crawford County, Kansas. They based their asserted equitable interest in the property upon the $19,451.34 in payments, including the down payment, that they made. A Kansas statute provides, in pertinent part, that

> In the event a default occurs in the conditions of the mortgage or most senior lien foreclosed before ⅓ of the original indebtedness has been paid, the court shall order a redemption period of six months.

The Bennetts then brought suit in federal court alleging that the Galindos have no equitable interest in the property and asking the court to remove the cloud on

their title. They argued that the Galindos' equitable redemption rights in the property lapsed, pursuant to the contract, prior to the surrender of the property.

ISSUE

Are the Galindos entitled to a six-month period to redeem the contract even though they defaulted on the contract by being in breach for more than six months?

DECISION

Yes. The $20,000 in payments made by the Galindos are substantial. Even though the installments were not always timely, forfeiture would be inequitable. The six-month equitable redemption period established by Kansas law is over and above any rights they had under the contract. Thus, the Galindos are entitled to have their equitable interest recognized and to have the six-month period provided by law to redeem the contract.

---

redemption period or require that a foreclosure procedure be used. In many states, the procedure to be followed in case of default on a land contract is specified by statute.

Ethical Implications	Suppose you have sold a farm to a young couple on a land contract that calls for them to pay off the purchase price over a 10-year period. After the couple has paid about a third of the purchase price, a serious drought damages their crop and they miss several payments, triggering your right to declare a default and reclaim possession of the property. Are there any ethical considerations involved in your taking such an action that you are otherwise legally entitled to take?

MECHANIC'S AND MATERIALMAN'S LIENS

Each state has a statute that permits persons who contract to furnish labor or materials to improve real estate to claim a lien on the property until they are paid. There are many differences among states as to exactly who can claim such a lien and the requirements that must be met to do so. In some states, the rights of all subcontractors and furnishers of materials are based on whatever rights the general contractor has and cannot exceed the amount of money due to the general contractor. In other states, subcontractors and materialmen such as lumberyards have the right to a direct lien for the full value of the work they did or the materials they furnished. The work and materials must be furnished for the improvement of a particular property or building. If they are sold generally without reference to a particular property, the provider of materials or labor is not entitled to a lien.

Type of Security Instrument	Parties	Features
Mortgage	1. Mortgagor (property owner/debtor) 2. Mortgagee (creditor)	1. Mortgagee holds a security interest (and in some states, title) in real property as security for a debt. 2. If mortgagor defaults on his obligation, mortgagee must *foreclose* on property to realize on his security interest. 3. Mortgagor has a limited time after foreclosure to *redeem* his interest.
Deed of Trust	1. Owner/Debtor 2. Lendor/Creditor 3. Trustee	1. Trustee holds legal title to the real property put up as security. 2. If debt is satisfied, the trustee conveys property back to owner/debtor. 3. If debt is not paid as agreed, creditor notifies trustee to sell the property. 4. While intended to make foreclosure easier, most states treat it like a mortgage for purposes of foreclosure.
Land Contract	1. Buyer 2. Seller	1. Seller agrees to convey title when full price is paid. 2. Buyer usually takes possession, pays property taxes and insurance, and maintains the property. 3. If buyer defaults, seller may declare a forfeiture and retake possession (most states) after buyer has limited time to redeem; some states require foreclosure.

To obtain a lien, the person who furnishes labor or materials must comply strictly with the statutory requirements that cover the form, content, and time of notice of the lien. A mechanic's or materialman's lien is foreclosed in the same manner as a court foreclosure of a real estate mortgage. Under the provisions of some statutes, the right to a mechanic's lien can be waived by the supplier in the contract to make the improvement. Before the person who is having improvements made to his property makes final payment, he may require the contractor to sign an affidavit that all materialmen and subcontractors have been paid.

In re Skyline Properties, Inc.
Century National Bank and Trust Co. v. Skyline Properties, Inc.
134 B.R. 830 (Bankr. W.D. Pa. 1992)

FACTS

In 1987 Skyline Properties commenced development of an integrated, multifaceted resort encompassing approximately 1,000 acres to be known as Hunter's Station. David Mealy was engaged to perform excavating and grading work on the project and commenced visible work on April 20, 1987. Mealy's work included bulldozing new roads, constructing parking areas, digging footers and drainage ditches, grading a basement for a new building used as a tack shop, excavating crawl spaces for new additions to an existing building subsequently used

as a sales office, grading an area for a new horse barn, and installing drains and fencing on the property. The sales office was substantially complete and opened for business on June 4, 1987, while work continued on construction of the tack shop.

On June 5, 1987, Century National Bank extended $150,000 credit to Skyline, took as collateral a mortgage on several of the parcels in the development, and recorded the mortgage on June 5, 1987. Mealy completed

(continued)

IN RE SKYLINE PROPERTIES, INC.
CENTURY NATIONAL BANK AND TRUST CO. V. SKYLINE PROPERTIES, INC.
(concluded)

his work on August 3, 1987, and filed a notice of a mechanic's lien claim on September 23, 1987. Pennsylvania law requires that claims for such liens be filed within four months after the completion of the work. A mechanic's lien for services that constitute alterations and repairs takes effect and has priority as of the date the mechanic's lien claim is filed; in the case of services constituting erection and construction, the lien of a claim takes effect and has priority "as of the date of the visible commencement upon the ground of the work of erecting or constructing the improvement."

In October 1988, the bank filed a mortgage foreclosure action against Skyline's property that it held as security for the loan. In September 1989, Mealy obtained a judgment on his claim and scheduled a sheriff's sale of the Skyline property. The sale was halted by the filing of an involuntary petition in bankruptcy. One of the issues in the bankruptcy proceeding was the relative priority of the claims of the bank and Mealy to the Skyline property.

ISSUE

Did Mealy's mechanic's lien claim have priority over the bank's mortgage?

DECISION

Yes. The court found that the work done qualified as erection and construction, not mere alteration or repair, and thus the lien took priority over the bank's mortgage because it was effective as of the date of the visible commencement of the work.

QUESTIONS AND PROBLEM CASES

1. What is the difference between purchasing real estate subject to a mortgage and assuming a mortgage?

2. Mr. and Mrs. Marshall went to Beneficial Finance to borrow money but were deemed by Beneficial's office manager, Puckett, to be bad credit risks. The Marshalls stated that their friend Garren would be willing to cosign a note for them if necessary. Puckett advised Garren not to cosign because the Marshalls were bad credit risks. This did not dissuade Garren from cosigning a note for $480, but it prompted him to ask Beneficial to take a lien or security interest in Mr. Marshall's custom-built Harley-Davidson motorcycle, then worth over $1,000. Beneficial took and perfected a security interest in the motorcycle. Marshall defaulted on the first payment. Beneficial gave notice of the default to Garren and advised him that it was looking to him for payment. Garren then discovered that Beneficial and Marshall had reached an agreement whereby Marshall would sell his motorcycle for $700; he was to receive $345 immediately, which was to be applied to the loan, and he promised to pay the balance of the loan from his pocket. Marshall paid Beneficial $89.50 and left town without giving the proceeds of the sale to Beneficial. Because Beneficial was unable to get the proceeds from Marshall, it brought suit against Garren on his obligation as surety. When Beneficial released the security for the loan (the motorcycle) without Garren's consent, was Garren relieved of his obligation as surety for repayment of the loan?

3. Wieslaw Wik was the owner of a truck tractor on which Navistar Financial Corporation held a lien to secure a purchase loan agreement. On February 21, Wik was driving his truck tractor and pulling a trailer owned by the V. Seng Teaming Company. The tractor/trailer unit overturned in a ditch. Allen's Corner Garage and Towing Service was called by the Illinois State Police. Its crew removed the cargo from the trailer and hoisted the tractor and trailer out of the ditch and onto the highway. They then took the truck, trailer, and cargo to Allen's garage for storage. The uprighting and towing of semitrailer trucks is an intricate process and involves a good deal of specialized equipment. Allen's was licensed by the Interstate Commerce Commission and the Illinois Commerce Commission as a common carrier and owned over 50 specialized trucks and

trailers for such operations. Wik defaulted on his loan agreement with Navistar and the right to possession passed to Navistar. One of its employees contacted Allen's and offered to pay the towing plus storage charges on the truck in exchange for possession of it. Allen's refused, saying it would not release the truck unless the charges for the truck, trailer, and cargo were all paid. Navistar then brought suit against Allen's to recover possession of the truck.

Subsequently, V. Seng Teaming Company paid $13,000 in towing and storage charges on the trailer and cargo and took possession of them. Navistar then reiterated its willingness to pay the towing charges but refused to pay any storage charges accruing after its initial offer. Was Allen's entitled to a common law lien for its towing and storage charges?

4. During May and June, John Shumate regularly parked his automobile on a vacant lot in downtown Philadelphia. At that time, no signs were posted prohibiting parking on the lot or indicating that vehicles parked there without authorization would be towed. On July 7, Shumate again left his car on the lot. When he returned two days later, the car was gone and the lot was posted with signs warning that parking was prohibited. Shumate learned that his car had been towed away by Ruffie's Towing Service and that the car was being held by Ruffie's at its place of business. Ruffie's refused to release the car until Shumate paid a towing fee of $44.50 plus storage charges of $4 per day. Shumate refused to pay the fee, and Ruffie's kept possession of the car. Did Ruffie's have a common law possessory lien on the car?

5. Philip and Edith Beh purchased some property from Alfred M. Gromer and his wife. Sometime earlier, the Gromers had borrowed money from City Mortgage. They had signed a note and had given City Mortgage a second deed of trust on the property. There was also a first deed of trust on the property at the time the Behs purchased it. In the contract of sale between the Behs and the Gromers, the Behs promised to "assume" the second deed of trust of approximately $5,000 at 6 percent interest. The Behs later defaulted on the first deed of trust on the property. Foreclosure was held on the first deed of trust but the proceeds of the sale left nothing

for City Mortgage on its second deed of trust. City Mortgage then brought a lawsuit against the Behs to collect the balance due on the second trust. When the Behs "assumed" the second trust, did they become personally liable for it?

6. Pope agreed to sell certain land to Pelz and retained a mortgage on the property to secure payment of the purchase price. The mortgage contained a clause providing that if Pelz defaulted, Pope had the "right to enter upon the above-described premises and sell the same at public sale" to pay the purchase price, accounting to Pelz for any surplus. What type of foreclosure does this provision contemplate: (1) strict foreclosure, (2) judicial sale, or (3) private power of sale?

7. Betty Nelson signed a promissory note payable to Family Bank in return for a loan the bank had made to her. The note was secured by a deed of trust on a duplex owned by Nelson. When the note was signed, the duplex was rented to third parties. Nelson defaulted on the note, and Family Bank filed a complaint to foreclose the trust deed. Nelson advised the bank that she and her son were occupying the duplex as their residence. Under Oregon law, a lender can obtain a deficiency judgment in connection with the foreclosure of a commercial deed of trust; however, a deficiency judgment is not available in connection with the foreclosure of a noncommercial (residential) deed of trust. If Family Bank went forward with foreclosure of the deed of trust, could it obtain a deficiency judgment against Nelson if the sale of the property produced less than the amount of the debt?

8. In October 1992, Verda Miller sold her 107-acre farm for $30,000 to Donald Kimball, who was acting on behalf of his own closely held corporation, American Wonderlands. Under the agreement, Miller retained title and Kimball was given possession pending full payment of all installments of the purchase price. The contract provided that Kimball was to pay all real estate taxes. If he did not pay them, Miller could discharge them and either add the amounts to the unpaid principal or demand immediate payment of the delinquencies plus interest. Miller also had the right to declare a

forfeiture of the contract and regain possession if the terms of the agreement were not met. In 1995, Miller had to pay the real estate taxes on the property in the amount of $672.78. She demanded payment of this amount plus interest from Kimball. She also served a notice of forfeiture on him that he had 30 days to pay. Kimball paid the taxes but refused to pay interest of $10.48. Miller made continued demands on Kimball for two months, and then filed notice of forfeiture with the county recorder in August 1995. She also advised Kimball of this. Was Miller justified in declaring a forfeiture and taking back possession of the land?

9. Albert Sharkey was the owner of a commercial building that was leased to Consolidated Freightways for more than 10 years before the lease was terminated by Consolidated on October 25, 1992. Consolidated's lease with Sharkey provided that Consolidated would leave the property in as good condition as received. Consolidated was responsible for damaging 10 overhead doors and contacted Dewco Building Systems to repair the damage. Dewco ordered new doors from Overhead.

Overhead specially ordered the doors and paid for them on delivery from the manufacturer. On March 18, 1993, Overhead submitted its bill to Dewco. Overhead was unable to collect since Dewco had gone out of business and filed for bankruptcy. Dewco had already collected $10,397 from Consolidated and owed $6,685 to Overhead. On May 10, 1993, Overhead filed a mechanic's lien against Sharkey's property and brought a lawsuit to enforce the lien. Iowa Code Section 572.2 provides that

> Every person who shall furnish any material or labor for, or perform any labor, upon any building or land for improvement, alteration or repair thereof, including those engaged in the construction or repair of any work of internal or external improvement . . . by virtue of any contract with the owner, his agent, trustee, contractor, or subcontractor shall have a lien upon such building or improvement, and land belonging to the owner on which the same is situated . . . to secure payment for material or labor furnished or labor performed.

Does Overhead have a valid claim for a mechanic's lien on Sharkey's property?

CHAPTER 41

Secured Transactions

Elaine Stanley decides that she will start a small gift shop in leased space in a shopping mall. Her personal assets are not sufficient to finance the business so she borrows some initial working capital from a bank. She purchases some display fixtures from a local supplier, making a small down payment and agreeing to pay the balance of the purchase price over the next two years. She purchases her initial inventory from several suppliers, agreeing either to pay for the goods within 60 days or to pay interest at a rate of 18 percent per year on any unpaid balance. To attract customers, she plans to offer both a layaway plan and store charge accounts.

This example illustrates a number of ways in which the extension of credit may be involved in the operation of a business. In this chapter, we will discuss:

- *How the creditors of the business, such as the bank, the supplier of the display fixtures, and the suppliers of the inventory, can obtain security for the credit they have extended.*
- *The steps the creditors must take to obtain maximum protection against the debtor–shopkeeper and against other creditors.*
- *The relative rights the creditors have vis-à-vis each other in the event the debtor–shopkeeper defaults on her obligations to them.*
- *The rights the creditors have against someone who buys the store fixtures or the goods from the debtor–shopkeeper.*
- *How the shopkeeper can protect herself when she extends credit to her customers.*

.... *INTRODUCTION* ....

ARTICLE 9 OF THE UNIFORM COMMERCIAL CODE

Today, a large portion of our economy involves the extension of credit. In many credit transactions, the creditor takes a security interest (or lien) in personal property belonging to the debtor in order to protect his investment. The law covering security interests in personal property is contained in Article 9 of the Uniform Commercial Code. Article 9, entitled "Secured Transactions," applies to situations that consumers and businesspeople commonly face, for example, the financing of an automobile, the purchase of a refrigerator on a time-payment plan, and the financing of business inventory.

If a creditor wants to obtain a security interest in the personal property of the debtor, he also wants to be sure that his interest will be superior to the claims of other creditors. To do so, the creditor must carefully comply with Article 9. Part III of this book, "Sales," pointed out that businesspersons sometimes leave out necessary terms in a contract or insert vague terms to be worked out later. Such looseness is a luxury that is not permitted when it comes to secured transactions. If a debtor gets into financial difficulties and cannot meet his obligations, it is important to the creditor that he carefully complied with Article 9. Even a minor noncompliance may result in the creditor's losing his preferred claim to the personal property of the debtor. A creditor who loses his secured interest will be only a general creditor of the debtor if the debtor is declared bankrupt. As a general creditor in bankruptcy proceedings, he may have little chance of recovering the money owed by the debtor because of the relatively low priority of such claims. This issue will be covered in detail in Chapter 42.

In 1998, the National Conference on Uniform State Laws adopted a "Revised Article 9" that has now been adopted by all 50 states with effective dates ranging from 2001 to 2002. Because Revised Article 9 is much more complex than the old Article 9 and because Article 9 has not been adopted in exactly the same form in every state, the law must be examined very carefully to determine the procedure in a particular state for obtaining a security interest and for ascertaining the rights of the creditors and debtors. However, the general concepts are the same in each state and will be the basis of our discussion in this chapter.

SECURITY INTERESTS

Basic to a discussion of secured transactions is the term **security interest.** A security interest is an interest in personal property or fixtures that a creditor obtains to secure payment or performance of an obligation (1–201[37]).[1] For example, when you borrow money from the bank to buy a new car, the bank takes a security interest in (puts a lien on)your car until the loan is repaid. If you default on the loan, the bank can repossess the car and have it sold and apply the sale price against the unpaid balance on the loan.

---

[1]The numbers in parentheses refer to the sections of the Uniform Commercial Code.

TYPES OF COLLATERAL

Goods—tangible items such as automobiles and business computers—are commonly used as collateral for loans. Article 9 of the Uniform Commercial Code also covers security interests in a much broader grouping of personal property. The Code breaks down personal property into a number of different classifications, which are important in determining how a creditor obtains an enforceable security interest in a particular kind of collateral.

The Code classifications include:

1. *Instruments.* This includes checks, notes, drafts, and certificates of deposit (9–102[a][47]).
2. *Documents of title.* This includes bills of lading, dock warrants, dock receipts, and warehouse receipts (9–102[a][30]).
3. *Accounts.* This includes the rights to payment for goods sold or leased or for services rendered that are not evidenced by instruments or chattel paper but are carried on open accounts, including lottery winnings and health care–insurance receivables. Items in the "accounts" category include such rights to payment whether or not the rights have been earned by performance (9–102[a][2]).
4. *Chattel paper.* This includes written documents that evidence both an obligation to pay money and a security interest in specific goods (9–102[a][11]). A typical example of chattel paper is what is commonly known as a *conditional sales contract.* This is the type of contract that a consumer might sign when she buys a large appliance such as a refrigerator on a time-payment plan.
5. *General intangibles.* This is a catchall category that includes, among other things, patents, copyrights, software, and franchises, (9–102[a][42]).
6. *Goods.* Goods (9–102[a][44]) are divided into several classes; the same item of collateral may fall into different classes at different times, depending on its use:
    a. *Consumer goods.* Goods used or bought primarily for personal, family, or household use, such as automobiles, furniture, and appliances (9–102[a][23]).
    b. *Equipment.* Goods used or bought for use primarily in business, including farming or a profession (9–102[a][33]).
    c. *Farm products.* Crops, livestock, or supplies used or produced in farming operations as long as they are still in the possession of a debtor who is engaged in farming (9–102[a][34]).
    d. *Inventory.* Goods held for sale or lease or to be used under contracts of service, as well as raw materials, work in process, or materials used or consumed in a business (9–102[a][48]).
    e. *Fixtures.* Goods that will be so affixed to real property that they are considered a part of the real property (9–102[a][41]).
7. *Investment property.* This includes securities such as stocks, bonds and commodity contracts (9–102[a][49]).
8. *Deposit accounts.* This includes demand, time, savings, passbook, and similar accounts maintained with a bank (9–102[a][29]).

It is important to note that an item such as a stove could in different situations be classified as inventory, equipment, or consumer goods. In the hands of the manufacturer or an appliance store, the stove is *inventory.* If it is being used in a restaurant, it *is equipment.* In a home, it is classified as *consumer goods.*

OBTAINING A SECURITY INTEREST

The goal of a creditor is to obtain a security interest in identifiable personal property that will be good against (1) the debtor, (2) other creditors of the debtor, and (3) a person who might purchase the property from the debtor. In case the debtor defaults on the debt, the creditor wants to have a better right to claim the property than anyone else. Obtaining a security interest enforceable against third parties is a two-step process consisting of **attachment** and **perfection.**

.... *ATTACHMENT OF THE SECURITY INTEREST* ....

ATTACHMENT

A security interest is not legally enforceable against a debtor until it is attached to a particular item or items of the debtor's property. The *attachment of the security interest* takes place either in a legal sense or in a physical sense. There are two basic requirements for a security interest to be attached to the goods of a debtor (9–203). First, either there must be an *agreement* by the debtor granting the creditor a security interest in particular property (*collateral*) in which the debtor has an interest or the secured party has possession of the property. Second, the creditor must give something of value to the debtor. The creditor must, for example, loan money or advance goods on credit to the debtor. Unless the debtor owes a *debt* to the creditor or an unfulfilled promise to perform, there can be no security interest. The purpose of obtaining the security interest is to secure a debt or performance.

THE SECURITY AGREEMENT

The agreement in which a debtor grants a creditor a security interest in the debtor's property generally must be *in writing* and *signed by the debtor.* A written agreement is required in all cases except where the creditor has *possession* of the collateral (9–203). Suppose you borrow $50 from a friend and give him your wristwatch as security for the loan. The agreement whereby you put up your watch as collateral does not have to be in writing to be enforceable. Because the creditor (your friend) is in possession of the collateral, an oral agreement is sufficient.

The security agreement must *clearly describe the collateral* so that it can readily be identified. For example, the year, make, and serial number of an automobile should be listed. The security agreement usually goes on to spell out the terms of the arrangement between the creditor and the debtor. Also, it normally contains a promise by the debtor to pay certain amounts of money or to perform a duty in a certain way. It will specify what events will constitute a default, for example, nonpayment by the buyer. In addition, it may contain provisions that the creditor feels are necessary to protect his security interest; for example, the debtor may be required to keep the collateral insured and/or not to move it without the creditor's consent (see Figure 41–1).

FIGURE 41-1   A Security Agreement

Mr. and Mrs.

Mrs.

BUYER Miss _Cheryl Cole_

ADDRESS _542 Oakdale_

CITY _Chicago, Il._ TEL. NO. _828-0290_

DELIVER TO: _542 Oakdale_

Account No. _C-1005_

Date

SECURITY AGREEMENT
ACE APPLIANCE

THIS AGREEMENT, executed between Ace Appliance, as Secured Party ("Seller"), and Buyer named above, as Debtor ("Buyer"): Seller agrees to sell and Buyer agrees to purchase, subject to the terms, conditions, and agreements stated in this agreement, the goods described below (the "Collateral"), Seller reserving and Buyer granting a purchase money security interest in the Collateral to secure the payment of the balance owed (Item 7) and all other present and future obligations of Buyer to Seller.

DESCRIPTION OF COLLATERAL

Quan.	Article	Unit Price		Total			TERMS	
1	Washer	425	—	425			(1) Cash Price	800⁰⁰
1	Dryer	375	—	375			(2) Down Payment	100⁰⁰
							Trade-in	
							Unpaid Principal	
							(3) Balance Owed	700⁰⁰
							(4) Finance Charge	100⁰⁰
							Time Balance	
							(5) Owed	800⁰⁰
							(6) Sales Tax	40⁰⁰
							(7) Balance Owed	840⁰⁰

Buyer agrees to pay Seller, without relief from valuation and appraisement laws, the balance owed (Item 7) of $ _840⁰⁰_

in _11_ successive ~~weekly~~ monthly installments of $ _70⁰⁰_ each and a final installment of $ _70⁰⁰_, commencing on

Jan. 1, 20_03_ and continuing thereafter on the same day of each ~~week~~ month until paid, together with all delinquent charges, costs of repossession, collection, disposition, maintenance, and other like charges, allowed by law, and reasonable attorney's fees.

This sale is made subject to the terms, conditions, and agreements stated above on the reverse side. Buyer represents that the correct name and address of Buyer is as stated above, and that all statements made by buyer as to financial condition and credit information are true.

Buyer acknowledges delivery by Seller to Buyer of a copy of this agreement.

Buyer warrants and represents that the Collateral will be kept at Buyer's address unless otherwise specified as follows: _____ ;

and will be used or is purchased for use primarily for: (check one) family or household purposes ☒; business use ☐; farming operations ☐. The Collateral will not be affixed to real estate unless checked here ☐. If the Collateral is to be affixed to real estate, a description of the real estate is as follows: _____

_____

and the name of the record owner is _____

_____

(continued)

FIGURE 41–1   A Security Agreement *(concluded)*

IN WITNESS WHEREOF, the parties have executed this agreement on this *1st* day of *Dec.*, 20*02.*
BUYER'S SIGNATURE (Ace Appliance) Seller (as Secured party) *Cheryl Cole*   By *Frank Singer*
                                                                    (as debtor)

TERMS, CONDITIONS, AND AGREEMENTS

1. The security interest of Seller shall extend to all replacements, proceeds (including tort claims and insurance), and accessories, and shall continue until full performance by Buyer of all conditions and obligations under this agreement.

2. Buyer shall maintain the Collateral in good repair, pay all taxes and other charges levied upon the Collateral when due, and shall defend the Collateral against any claims. Buyer shall not permit the Collateral to be removed from the place where kept without the prior written consent of Seller. Buyer shall give prompt written notice to Seller of any transfer, pledge, assignment, or any other process or action taken or pending, voluntary or involuntary, whereby a third party is to obtain or is attempting to obtain possession of or any interest in the Collateral. Seller shall have the right to inspect the Collateral at all reasonable times. At its option, but without obligation to Buyer and without relieving Buyer from any default, Seller may discharge any taxes, liens, or other encumbrances levied or placed upon the Collateral for which Buyer agrees to reimburse Seller upon demand.

3. If the Collateral is damaged or destroyed in any manner, the entire balance remaining unpaid under this agreement (the "Agreement Balance") shall immediately become due and payable and Buyer shall first apply any insurance or other receipts compensating for such loss to the Agreement Balance. Buyer shall fully insure the Collateral, for the benefit of both Seller and Buyer, against loss by fire, theft, and other casualties by comprehensive extended coverage insurance in an amount equal to the balance owed under this agreement.

4. Buyer shall pay all amounts payable when due at the store of Seller from which this sale is made or at Seller's principal office in *Gary*, Indiana, and upon default shall pay the maximum delinquent charges permitted by law. Upon prepayment of the Agreement Balance, Seller shall allow the minimum discount permitted by law.

5. Time is of the essence of this agreement. Buyer agrees that the following shall constitute an event of default under this Security Agreement: (*a*) the failure of Buyer to perform any condition or obligation contained in this agreement; (*b*) when any statement, representation, or warranty made by Buyer shall be found to have been untrue in any material respect when made; or (*c*) if Seller in good faith believes that the prospect of payment or performance is impaired. Upon a default, Seller, at its option and without notice or demand to Buyer, shall be entitled to declare the Agreement Balance immediately due and payable, take immediate possession of the Collateral and enter the premises at which the Collateral is located for such purpose or to render the Collateral unusable. Upon request, Buyer shall assemble and make the Collateral available to Seller at a place to be designated by Seller which is reasonably convenient to both parties. Upon repossession, Seller may retain or dispose of any or all of the Collateral in the manner prescribed by the Indiana Uniform Commercial Code and the proceeds of any such disposition shall be first applied in the following order; (*a*) to the reasonable expenses of retaking, holding, preparing for sale, selling, and the like; (*b*) to the reasonable attorney's fees and legal expenses incurred by Seller; and (*c*) to the satisfaction of the indebtedness secured by this security interest. Buyer convenants to release and hold harmless Seller from any and all claims arising out of the repossession of the Collateral. No waiver of any default or any failure or delay to exercise any right or remedy by Seller shall operate as a waiver of any other default, or of the same default in the future or as a waiver of any right or remedy with respect to the same or any other occurrence.

6. All rights and remedies of seller specified in this agreement are cumulative and are in addition to, and shall not exclude, any rights and remedies Seller may have by law.

7. Seller shall not be liable for any damages, including special or consequential damages, for failure to deliver the Collateral or for any delay in delivery of the Collateral to Buyer.

8. Buyer agrees that Seller may carry this agreement, together with any other agreements and accounts, with Buyer in one account upon its records and unless otherwise instructed in writing by Buyer, any payment of less than all amounts then due on all agreements and accounts shall be applied to any accrued delinquent charges, costs of collection and maintenance, and to the balances owing under all agreements or accounts in such order as Seller in its discretion shall determine.

9. Buyer authorizes Seller to execute and file financing statements signed only by Seller covering the Collateral described.

10. Any notice required by this agreement shall be deemed sufficient when mailed to Seller (state Seller's address), or to Buyer at the address at which the Collateral is kept.

11. Buyer shall have the benefit of manufacturers' warranties, if any; however, Seller makes no express warranties (except a warranty of title) and no implied warranties, including any warranty of MERCHANTABILITY or FITNESS. Buyer agrees that there are no promises or agreements between the parties not contained in this agreement. Any modification or rescission of this agreement shall be ineffective unless in writing and signed by both Seller and Buyer.

12. ANY HOLDER OF THIS CONSUMER CREDIT CONTRACT IS SUBJECT TO ALL CLAIMS AND DEFENSES WHICH THE DEBTOR COULD ASSERT AGAINST THE SELLER OF GOODS OR SERVICES OBTAINED WITH THE PROCEEDS HEREOF. RECOVERY HEREUNDER BY THE DEBTOR SHALL NOT EXCEED AMOUNTS PAID BY THE DEBTOR HEREUNDER.

In the case that follows, *In re Shirel*, the court found that the information contained in a credit application did not meet the requirements for a security agreement.

IN RE SHIREL
251 BR 175 (Bankr., W. D. Oklahoma 2000)

FACTS

Kevin Shirel applied for a credit card from Sight'N Sound appliance centers, Inc. The credit application, which constituted the agreement between the parties, was a barely legible, seven-page, single-spaced, small-print document. Shirel signed it on the first page. The form contained a statement that Sight'N Sound would have a "security interest" in all "merchandise" purchased with the credit card. This statement was located approximately four pages into the application.

Shirel's credit was approved, and he purchased a new refrigerator using the credit card. Several months later, Shirel filed a bankruptcy petition listing the remaining credit card debt as unsecured and the refrigerator as exempt from the claims of creditors. Subsequently, Sight'N Sound objected to the claim of exemption. It contended that Shirel had improperly listed the debt as unsecured and asserted that it held a secured interest in the refrigerator.

ISSUE

Did Sight'N Sound have a valid security interest in the refrigerator by virtue of its agreement with Shirel?

DECISION

No. The court began by noting that contracts of adhesion—such as the one in this case—are interpreted most strongly against the party preparing the form. The court went on to hold that the security agreement was not enforceable against the debtor because it did not contain an adequate description of the collateral. The phrase "all merchandise" was too imprecise and not descriptive. The description does not have to be elaborate; a sufficient one must have listed "a refrigerator."

AUTHOR'S NOTE

Although this case was decided under the 1972 version of Article 9, the same result would be expected under Revised Article 9, which places more emphasis on the nature of the description.

FUTURE ADVANCES

A security agreement may cover extensions of credit to be made in the future (9–204[c]). Such later extensions of credit are known as **future advances.** A future advance is involved where a credit union agrees to give you a line of credit of $10,000 to buy and restore an antique car but initially gives you only $1,500 to buy the car. As you draw additional money against the line of credit, you have received a future advance. The security interest that the creditor obtained earlier also covers these later advances of money to you.

By covering future advances in the security agreement, the creditor can use the collateral to protect his interest in repayment of the money advanced to the debtor at a later time. The creditor also saves transaction expense; the creditor does not need a new agreement for each future advance.

AFTER-ACQUIRED PROPERTY

A security agreement may also be drafted to grant a creditor a security interest in **after-acquired property** of the debtor, that is, property that the debtor does not currently own (or have rights in) but that he may acquire in the future. However, the security interest in the after-acquired property cannot attach to that property until the debtor obtains some property rights in the new property (9–204[a]). For example,

Dan's Diner borrows $5,000 from the bank and gives it a security interest in all the restaurant equipment it currently has as well as all that it may "hereafter acquire." If, at the time, Dan's owns only a stove, then the bank has a security interest only in the stove. However, if a month later Dan's buys a refrigerator, the bank's security interest attaches to the refrigerator at the time Dan's acquires some rights to it.

PROCEEDS

The attachment of the security interest to the collateral automatically gives the secured party a security interest in the **proceeds** on the disposal of the collateral by the debtor (9–203[f]). The term *proceeds* is defined in (9–102[a][64]). Assume that Anne buys a television set from Ace Appliance on a time-payment plan. Ace Appliance has a security interest in the television set and in any money or other proceeds that Anne obtains if she sells the set to someone else.

Similarly, if a bank loans money to a dealer to enable him to finance an inventory of new automobiles and the bank takes a security interest in the inventory, then the bank has a security interest in the cash proceeds obtained by the dealer when the automobiles are sold to customers.

ASSIGNMENT

In the past, installment sales contracts and security agreements commonly included a provision that the buyer would not assert against the assignee of a sales contract any claims or defenses that the buyer had against the seller. Such clauses made it easier for a retailer to assign its installment sales contracts (security agreements) to a financial institution such as a bank. The bank knew that it could collect from the buyer without having to worry about any claims that the buyer had against the retailer, such as for breach of warranty. The waiver clauses were usually presented to the buyer on a take-it-or-leave-it basis.

Such clauses can operate to the disadvantage of the buyer. For example, Harriet Horn agrees to buy some storm windows from Ace Home Improvement Company. She signs an installment sales contract (security agreement) promising to pay $50 a month for 24 months and giving the company a security interest in the windows. The contract contains a waiver of defenses clause. Ace assigns the contract to First Bank and goes out of business. If the storm windows were of a poorer quality than called for by the contract, Harriet would have a claim of breach of warranty against Ace. She would not have to pay Ace the full amount if it tried to collect from her. However, under these circumstances, Harriet has to pay the full amount to the bank and then can try to collect from Ace for breach of warranty. Here, Harriet might be out of luck.

Although waiver of defenses clauses in commercial contracts can generally be enforced, their use in consumer contracts has been severely restricted (9–403[d]; Official Comment). Some states have enacted legislation that abolishes the waiver of defenses clause in consumer contracts; other states have limited the use of such clauses. In addition, the Federal Trade Commission (FTC) has adopted some rules that apply to situations in which a buyer signs an installment sales contract. The FTC requires that the seller insert a specified clause in the installment sales contract and all direct loan agreements. The clause states that any assignee of the contract will be subject to any claims or defenses that the buyer–debtor could assert against the seller of the goods. (See Figure 41–1, paragraph 12. The FTC rules are discussed in Chapter 45.)

.... *PERFECTING THE SECURITY INTEREST* ....

PERFECTION

A creditor protects her security interest in collateral against other creditors of the debtor and other third persons, including some buyers of the collateral, by **perfecting** the security interest. Attachment of a security interest to collateral provided by the debtor gives the creditor rights vis-à-vis the debtor. However, a creditor is also concerned about making sure she will have a better right to the collateral than any other creditor in the event that the debtor defaults. A creditor may also be concerned about protecting her interest in the collateral if the debtor sells it to someone else. The creditor gets this protection against other creditors or purchasers of the collateral by *perfecting* her security interest.

Under the Code, there are three main ways of perfecting a security interest:

1. By filing a *public notice* of the security interest.
2. By the creditor's taking *possession or control* of the collateral.
3. In certain kinds of transactions, by mere *attachment* of the security interest (automatic perfection).

PERFECTION BY PUBLIC FILING

The most common way of perfecting a security interest is by filing a **financing statement** in the appropriate public office. The financing statement serves as constructive notice to the world that the creditor claims an interest in collateral that belongs to a certain named debtor. The financing statement usually consists of a multicopy form that is available from the Secretary of State's office (see Figure 41–2). However, the security agreement can be filed as the financing statement if it contains the required information.

To be sufficient, the financing statement must meet three basic requirements and contain certain other information. The three basic requirements are that the financing statement must (1) provide the name of the debtor, (2) provide the name of the secured party, and (3) indicate the collateral covered by the financing statement. For certain kinds of collateral, such as fixtures, timber to be cut, or oil, gas, or other minerals, additional information concerning the property on which they are located must be set forth. Figure 41–2 illustrates the kind of other information that may be required.

In addition, the financing statement must provide (1) a mailing address for the debtor, (2) a mailing address for the secured party, (3) an indication of whether the debtor is an individual or an organization, and, if the debtor is an organization, (4) the type of organization, the jurisdiction of the debtor's organization, and an organizational number for the debtor or an indication that the debtor has no organizational number.

Each state specifies where the financing statement has to be filed. In all states, a financing statement that covers fixtures must be filed in the office where a mortgage on real estate would be filed (9–501[a][1][b]). State law varies as to whether financing statements that concern commercial collateral are to be filed locally and/or in a central state file, usually in the Secretary of State's office. However, most states require central filing for collateral other than fixtures(9–502[b]). Thus, if you are a creditor taking a security interest, it is important to check the law in your state to determine where to file the financing statement (9–501).

FIGURE 41–2   A Financing Statement

UCC FINANCING STATEMENT
FOLLOW INSTRUCTIONS (front and back) CAREFULLY

A. NAME & PHONE OF CONTACT AT FILER [optional]

B. SEND ACKNOWLEDGMENT TO: (Name and Address)

THE ABOVE SPACE IS FOR FILING OFFICE USE ONLY

1. DEBTOR'S EXACT FULL LEGAL NAME - insert only one debtor name (1a or 1b) - do not abbreviate or combine names

| 1a. ORGANIZATION'S NAME | | | |

| OR | 1b. INDIVIDUAL'S LAST NAME | FIRST NAME | MIDDLE NAME | SUFFIX |

| 1c. MAILING ADDRESS | CITY | STATE | POSTAL CODE | COUNTRY |

| 1d. TAX ID #: SSN OR EIN | ADD'L INFO RE ORGANIZATION DEBTOR | 1e. TYPE OF ORGANIZATION | 1f. JURISDICTION OF ORGANIZATION | 1g. ORGANIZATIONAL ID #, if any ☐ NONE |

2. ADDITIONAL DEBTOR'S EXACT FULL LEGAL NAME - insert only one debtor name (2a or 2b) - do not abbreviate or combine names

| 2a. ORGANIZATION'S NAME | | | |

| OR | 2b. INDIVIDUAL'S LAST NAME | FIRST NAME | MIDDLE NAME | SUFFIX |

| 2c. MAILING ADDRESS | CITY | STATE | POSTAL CODE | COUNTRY |

| 2d. TAX ID #: SSN OR EIN | ADD'L INFO RE ORGANIZATION DEBTOR | 2e. TYPE OF ORGANIZATION | 2f. JURISDICTION OF ORGANIZATION | 2g. ORGANIZATIONAL ID #, if any ☐ NONE |

3. SECURED PARTY'S NAME (or NAME of TOTAL ASSIGNEE of ASSIGNOR S/P) - insert only one secured party name (3a or 3b)

| 3a. ORGANIZATION'S NAME | | | |

| OR | 3b. INDIVIDUAL'S LAST NAME | FIRST NAME | MIDDLE NAME | SUFFIX |

| 3c. MAILING ADDRESS | CITY | STATE | POSTAL CODE | COUNTRY |

4. This FINANCING STATEMENT covers the following collateral:

5. ALTERNATIVE DESIGNATION [if applicable]: ☐ LESSEE/LESSOR ☐ CONSIGNEE/CONSIGNOR ☐ BAILEE/BAILOR ☐ SELLER/BUYER ☐ AG. LIEN ☐ NON-UCC FILING

6. ☐ This FINANCING STATEMENT is to be filed [for record] (or recorded) in the REAL ESTATE RECORDS. Attach Addendum [if applicable] 7. Check to REQUEST SEARCH REPORT(S) on Debtor(s) [ADDITIONAL FEE] [optional] ☐ All Debtors ☐ Debtor 1 ☐ Debtor 2

8. OPTIONAL FILER REFERENCE DATA

FILING OFFICE COPY — NATIONAL UCC FINANCING STATEMENT (FORM UCC1) (REV. 07/29/98)

(continued)

A financing statement, generally, is valid for five years. A **continuation statement** may be filed within six months before the maturity date of a financing statement. A continuation statement is also valid for five years, unless a shorter time is specified in it (9–515). When all the debts of the debtor that are secured by a financing statement are completely satisfied, the debtor usually is entitled to a **termination statement** filed by the secured party. If the secured party does not file or furnish one to the debtor, he is liable for a fine and any damages suffered by the debtor (9–513).

FIGURE 41-2   A Financing Statement *(concluded)*

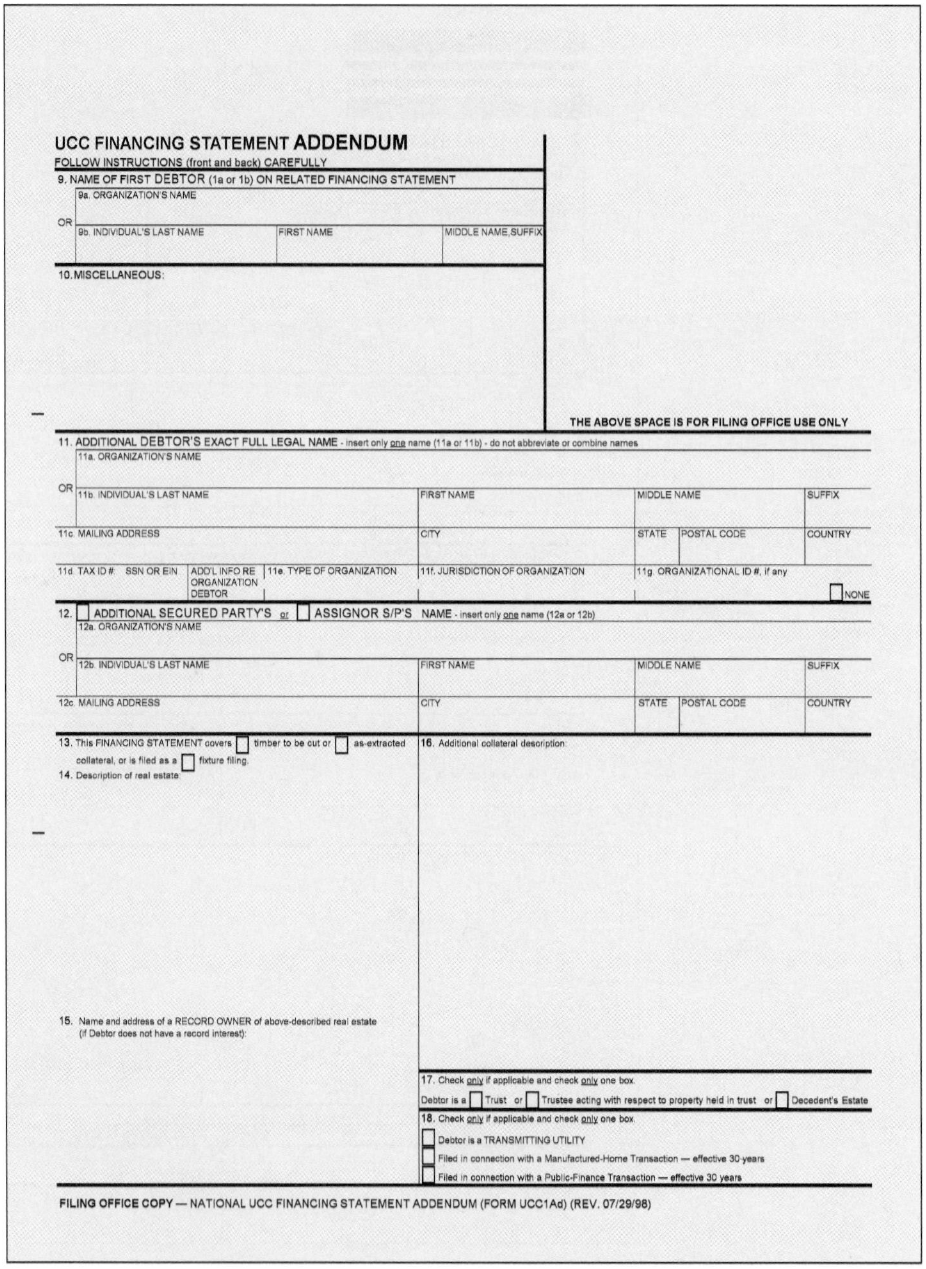

POSSESSION OR CONTROL BY SECURED PARTY AS PUBLIC NOTICE

The purpose of public filing of a security interest is to put the public on notice of the security interest. A potential creditor of the debtor or a potential buyer of the collateral can check the public records to see whether anyone else claims an interest in the debtor's property. The same objective can be reached if the debtor gives up *possession* of the collateral to the creditor or to a third person who holds the collateral for the creditor. If a debtor does not have possession of collateral he claims to own, then a potential creditor or debtor is on notice that someone else may claim an interest in it. Thus, change of possession of collateral from the debtor to the creditor/secured party, or his agent, perfects the security interest (9–313[a]).

For example, Sam borrows $50 from a pawnbroker and puts up his guitar as collateral for the loan. The pawnbroker's security interest in the guitar is perfected by virtue of his possession of the guitar.

Change of possession is not a common or convenient way for perfecting most security interests in consumer goods. It is more practicable for perfecting security interests in commercial collateral. In fact, it is the only way to perfect a security interest in money (9–312)[b][3]).

Possession of collateral by the creditor is often the best way to perfect a security interest in chattel paper and negotiable documents of title. Possession is also a possible way of perfecting a security interest in inventory. This is sometimes achieved through a **field warehousing arrangement.** For example, a finance company makes a large loan to a peanut warehouse to enable it to buy peanuts from local farmers. The finance company takes a security interest in the inventory of peanuts. It sets up a field warehousing arrangement under which a representative of the finance company takes physical control over the peanuts. This representative might actually fence off the peanut storage area and control access to it. When the peanut warehouse wants to sell part of the inventory to a food processor, it must make a payment to the finance company. Then the finance company's representative will allow the peanut warehouse to take some of the peanuts out of the fenced-off area and deliver them to the processor. In this way the finance company controls the collateral in which it has a security interest until the loan is repaid.

Possession by the creditor is usually not a practicable way of perfecting a security interest in equipment or farm products. In the case of equipment, the debtor needs to use it in the business. For example, if a creditor kept possession of a stove that was sold on credit to a restaurant, it would defeat the purpose for which the restaurant was buying the stove, that is, to use it in its business.

CONTROL

A secured party can provide a similar form of public notice by controlling the collateral (9–314). Control is the only perfection method if the collateral is a deposit account (9–312[b][1]). A secured party obtains control by one of three means: (1) the secured party is the bank with which the deposit account is maintained, (2) the debtor, secured party, and the bank have agreed that the bank will comply with the secured party's instructions regarding funds in the account, or (3) the secured party becomes the bank's customer for the deposit account.

PERFECTING BY ATTACHMENT

A creditor who sells goods to a consumer on credit or who loans money to enable a consumer to buy goods can perfect a security interest merely by attaching the security interest to the goods (9–309). A creditor under these circumstances has what is called a **purchase money security interest** in consumer goods. For example, an appliance store sells a television set to Margaret Morse on a conditional sales contract (time-payment plan). The store does not have to file its purchase money security interest in the set. The security interest is considered perfected just by virtue of its attachment to the set in the hands of the consumer.

Consumer Goods.

Perfection by attachment is not effective for three categories of consumer goods. First, if the consumer goods are motor vehicles for which the state issues certificates of title (9–302); second, if the goods are to become fixtures, the creditor can get only limited protection through perfection by attachment; to protect himself against other claimants to the real estate, he must perfect by filing a financing statement with the real estate records. The special rules that cover motor vehicles and fixtures will be discussed later in this chapter.

The third situation is the sale by a consumer debtor to another consumer debtor if the secured party did not file a financing statement (9–320[b]). If the new buyer buys from the debtor (1) without knowledge of the security interest, (2) for value, and (3) primarily for the buyer's own personal, family, or household purposes, then the new buyer takes free of the security interest. However, if the secured party filed a financing statement for the collateral, then the new buyer does not take the collateral free of the security interest.

The case that follows, *In re Rainer,* illustrates situations in which a creditor obtained perfection of its security interests merely by attachment to two vehicles that were not required to have state certificates of title.

There are also major limitations to the perfection by attachment principle. As discussed below in the "Priorities" section of this chapter, relying on attachment for perfection does not, in some instances, provide as much protection to the creditor as does public filing.

In re Rainer
In re Hovland
Horowitz v. Green Tree Financial Corp.
40 UCC Rep.2d 1123 (Bankr. W.D. N.Y. 2000)

Facts

Hovland purchased a four-wheeled off-the-road all-terrain vehicle (ATV) and Rainer purchased a Sea Doo–brand personal watercraft (PWC). In both instances the purchases were financed by the Green Tree Financial Corporation, which held a purchase money security interest (PMSI) in the ATV and the PWC. Green Tree Financial did not file financing statements because it considered them to be "consumer goods" that are not "motor vehicles" for purposes of UCC section 9–302(1).

Both Hovland and Rainer filed petitions under Chapter 7 of the Bankruptcy Code. The Bankruptcy Trustee took the position that he had priority over Green Tree Financial because it had failed to file a financing statement to perfect its security interests in the ATV and PWC. Green Tree contended that it should have priority over the Bankruptcy Trustee by virtue of its attachment of a purchase money security interest in consumer goods.

Issue

Was Green Tree Financial required to file financing statements covering the vehicles in order to prevail against another creditor (Bankruptcy Trustee)?

Decision

No. Although UCC Section 9–302(1)(d) exempts purchase money security interests in consumer goods from the requirement to file a financing statement to protect certain security interests, filing is required for interests in "motor vehicles" required to be state "registered." However, the court found, for different reasons, that the two kinds of vehicles involved in this case did not fall within the "motor vehicle" exception requiring a financing statement. In the case of the ATV, all-terrain vehicles are not explicitly excluded from the vehicle "title" requirements of state law and would at first blush seem to fall under

(continued)

> ## In re Rainer
> ## In re Hovland
> ## Horowitz v. Green Tree Financial Corp.
> ### *(concluded)*
>
> the "motor vehicle" exception. However, the court concluded that because the New York State Commissioner of Motor Vehicles had no provision for issuing titles to ATVs, they should be exempt from the UCC filing requirements. In the case of the personal watercraft, New York state law excludes from the title requirements "any vessel under 14 feet in length." Because the PWC was less than 14 feet in length, it was not subject to any state title re-
>
> quirement. In addition, the court noted that UCC Section 9–302(1)(d) makes no reference to "vessels" or "boats" and, thus, the PWC would not be within the explicit exception for "motor vehicles" requiring a title under state law. Accordingly, Green Tree Financial was not required to file a financing statement covering either the ATV or the PWC in order to have its purchase money security interest prevail against the Bankruptcy Trustee.

One potential concern for a creditor is that the use of the collateral will change from that anticipated when the security interest was obtained. For example, a computer originally purchased to be used in the home subsequently is converted to use in the business. It is important that the creditor properly perfect the security interest initially so that it will not be adversely affected by a subsequent change in use and will continue to have the benefit of its initial perfection.

MOTOR VEHICLES

If state law requires a certificate of title for motor vehicles, then a creditor who takes a security interest in a vehicle must have the security interest noted on the title (9–311[a][2][3]). Suppose a credit union loans money to Carlos to buy a new car in a state that requires certificates of title for cars. The credit union cannot rely on attachment of its security interest in the car to perfect it; rather, it must have its security interest noted on the certificate of title.

This requirement protects the would-be buyer of the car or another creditor who might extend credit based on Carlos's ownership of the car. By checking the certificate of title to Carlos's car, a potential buyer or creditor would learn about the credit union's security interest in the car. If no security interest is noted on the certificate of title, the buyer can buy—or the creditor can extend credit—with confidence that there are no undisclosed security interests.

FIXTURES

The Code also provides special rules for perfecting security interests in consumer goods that become fixtures by virtue of their attachment to or use with real property. A creditor with a security interest in consumer goods (including consumer goods that will become fixtures) obtains perfection merely by attachment of her security interest to a consumer good. However, as discussed in the "Priorities" section of this chapter, a creditor who relies on attachment for perfection will not prevail against other creditors *who hold an interest in the real estate* to which the consumer good is attached unless a special financing statement known as a *fixture filing* is filed with the real estate records to perfect the security interest (9–102; 9–334).

REMOVAL OF COLLATERAL

Debtors often move from state to state and may move collateral from state to state also. Article 9 has numerous rules that explain when the law of one jurisdiction governs the perfection and priority of security interests, how long that perfection lasts, and what happens if the debtor or the goods move to another jurisdiction. Some of these rules focus on the location of the debtor and others focus on the location of the collateral or the effectiveness of a public record, such as a certificate of title.

The general rule is that the local law of the jurisdiction in which the debtor is located governs the perfection, effect of non-perfection, and the priority of the security interest in collateral (9–301[1]; 9–307). Special rules govern particular types of collateral or nonfiling methods of perfection. For example, the law of the jurisdiction issuing a certificate of title for an automobile or truck governs perfection until (1) the certificate of title ceases to be effective or (2) the time in which the goods are subsequently covered by a certificate of title issued by another jurisdiction (9–303).

CONCEPT SUMMARY	Obtaining a Security Interest Enforceable against Third Parties	
Step	**Purpose**	**Necessary Action**
Attachment of Security Interest	To secure a debt. The debtor gives the creditor rights in the debtor's property to secure the debt owed by the creditor to the debtor.	1. Agreement by the debtor giving the creditor a security interest in specific property (collateral) in which the debtor has a legal interest or when the debtor gives possession or control to the secured parties. Agreements can include after-acquired property. Proceeds of the collateral are automatically covered. 2. The creditor must give something of value to the debtor (e.g., money or goods). Future advances are value when actually given to the debtor, normally after the first advance.
Perfection	To obtain protection against other creditors of the debtor and against purchasers of the collateral from the debtor.	1. *Public filing.* Filing a financing statement with the appropriate state or local office to put the world on notice that the creditor claims an interest in specific collateral belonging to the debtor; or in the case of a motor vehicle, noting the security interest on the certificate of title, or 2. *Possession or control by creditor.* The creditor may take possession of the collateral or gain control, thus putting other creditors and potential purchasers on notice that the creditor has an interest in the collateral (this is not practical for all kinds of collateral); or 3. *Automatic Perfection by attachment.* Limited perfection merely by attachment of the security interest is obtained where (*a*) a creditor sells consumer goods to a consumer on credit or (*b*) a creditor loans money to a consumer to enable him to buy consumer goods.

.... *PRIORITIES* ....

IMPORTANCE OF DETERMINING PRIORITY

Because several creditors may claim a security interest in the same collateral of a debtor, the Code establishes a set of rules for determining which of the conflicting security interests has priority, that is, takes precedence over other security interests or liens. Determining which creditor has priority or the best claim takes on particular importance in bankruptcy cases. Unless a creditor has perfected a secured interest in collateral that fully protects the obligation owed to him, the creditor may realize only a few cents on each dollar he is owed by the bankrupt debtor.

GENERAL PRIORITY RULES

The basic rule established by the Code is that when more than one security interest in the same collateral has been filed (or otherwise perfected), the first security interest to be filed (or perfected) has priority over any that is filed (or perfected) later (9–322[a][1]). If only one security interest has been perfected, for example, by filing, then that security interest has priority. However, if none of the conflicting security interests has been perfected, then the first security interest to be *attached* to the collateral has priority (9–322[a][3]).

Thus, if Bank A filed a financing statement covering a retailer's inventory on February 1, 2003, and Bank B filed a financing statement on March 1, 2003, covering that same inventory, Bank A would have priority over Bank B. This is true even though Bank B might have made its loan and attached its security interest to the inventory prior to the time that Bank A did so. However, if Bank A neglected to perfect its security interest by filing and Bank B did perfect, then Bank B would prevail, as it has the only perfected security interest in the inventory.

If both creditors neglected to perfect their security interest, then the first security interest that attached would have priority (9–322[a][3]). For example, if Loan Company Y has a security agreement covering a dealer's equipment dated June 1, 2003, and advances money to the dealer on that date, whereas Bank Z does not obtain a security agreement covering that equipment or advance money to the dealer until July 1, 2003, then Loan Company Y has priority over Bank Z. In connection with the last situation, it is important to note that unperfected secured creditors do not enjoy a preferred position in bankruptcy proceedings, thus giving additional importance to filing or otherwise perfecting a security interest.

PURCHASE MONEY SECURITY INTERESTS IN INVENTORY

There are several very important exceptions to the general priority rules. First, a **perfected purchase money security interest in inventory** has priority over a conflicting security interest in the same inventory *if* all four of these requirements are met. (1) the purchase money security interest is perfected at the time the debtor receives possession of the inventory, (2) the purchase money secured party gives notification in writing to the prior secured creditor before the debtor receives the inventory, (3) the holder of the competing security interest received notification within five years before the debtor receives the inventory, and (4) the notification states that the person expects to acquire a purchase money security interest in inventory of the debtor and describes the inventory (9–324[b]).

Assume that Bank A takes and perfects a security interest in" all present and after-acquired inventory" of a debtor. Then the debtor acquires some additional inventory from a wholesaler, which retains a security interest in the inventory until the debtor pays for it. The wholesaler perfects this security interest. The wholesaler has a *purchase money security interest* in inventory goods and will have priority over the prior secured creditor (Bank A) if the wholesaler has perfected the security interest by the time the collateral reaches the debtor and if the wholesaler sends notice of its purchase money security interest to Bank A before the wholesaler ships the goods. Thus, to protect itself, the wholesaler must check the public records to see whether any of the debtor's creditors are claiming an interest in the debtor's inventory. When it discovers that some are claiming an interest, it should file its own security interest and give notice of that security interest to the existing creditors (9–324[b] & [c]).

ITT COMMERCIAL FINANCE CORP. V. UNION BANK & TRUST COMPANY OF NORTH VERNON
528 N.E.2d 1149 (Ct. App. Ind. 1988)

FACTS

On October 28, 1983, Steve Gresham, doing business as Midway Cycle Sales, entered into a Wholesale Financing Agreement with ITT Commercial Finance Corporation. The agreement was to finance the purchase of new motorcycles from Suzuki Motor Corporation. ITT filed a financing statement with the Indiana Secretary of State on December 16, 1983. The description of the collateral in which ITT asserted a security interest included "all inventory, . . . replacements and proceeds." On January 9, 1984, Union Bank filed a financing statement with the Indiana Secretary of State claiming it was engaged in "floor planning of new motorcycles" for Midway Cycle Sales.

In August 1984, ITT began paying Suzuki invoices for Gresham. In July 1985, ITT sent a letter to Union Bank notifying it that it expected to acquire purchase money security interests in the inventory of Stephen Gresham d/b/a/ Midway Cycle Sales. In early 1986, Union Bank began loaning money to Gresham under its floor planning agreement with him. Actually, Gresham was "double floor planning"—that is, he was taking invoices for motorcycles that had been paid for by ITT to the Union Bank and claiming that he had paid for the motorcycles but had decided to floor plan them. When Union Bank advanced money to him, he used the money to make payments on the loans to ITT. He made no payments to Union Bank and did not pay off all of his loan to ITT.

Midway Cycle Sales went bankrupt when Union Bank repossessed 22 new Suzuki motorcycles. ITT brought suit against Union Bank, claiming that it had paid for the motorcycles and had a perfected security interest in the motorcycles that had priority over Union Bank's security interest in them. Union Bank claimed that it had a purchase money security interest in inventory that had priority over ITT's security interest.

ISSUE

Did ITT's security interest have priority over Union Bank's security interest?

DECISION

Yes. ITT had a purchase money security interest in the motorcycles that attached and was perfected before Union Bank gained a security interest in them. ITT had a purchase money security interest in the motorcycles because its money was used to acquire the motorcycles. Union Bank did not have a purchase money security interest because the money it loaned to Gresham was not used to acquire the motorcycles. Gresham already had title to them because the ITT money had been used to buy them. Union Bank's money was simply going to pay off the loan to ITT.

AUTHOR'S NOTE

This case was decided under the 1972 version of Article 9.

PURCHASE MONEY SECURITY INTERESTS IN NONINVENTORY COLLATERAL

The second exception to the general priority rule is that a *purchase money security interest in noninventory collateral* prevails over a prior perfected security interest if the purchase money security interest is perfected at the time the debtor takes possession or within 20 days afterward (9–324[a]). Assume that Bank B takes and perfects a security interest in all the present and after-acquired equipment belonging to a debtor. Then a supplier sells some equipment to the debtor, reserving a security interest in the equipment until it is paid for. If the supplier perfects the purchase money security interest by filing by the time the debtor obtains the collateral or within 20 days thereafter, it has priority over Bank B. This is because its purchase money security interest

Once a secured party has filed his security interest as a fixture filing, he has priority over purchasers or encumbrances whose interests are filed after that of the secured party (9–334[e][1]).

········ *DEFAULT AND FORECLOSURE* ········

DEFAULT

The Code does not define what constitutes default. Usually the creditor and debtor state in their agreement what events constitute a default by the buyer, subject to the Code requirement that the parties act in "good faith" in doing so. If the debtor defaults, the secured creditor has several options: (1) forget the collateral and sue the debtor on his note or promise to pay, (2) repossess the collateral and use strict foreclosure (except in some consumer goods cases) to keep collateral in satisfaction of the remaining debt (9–620), or (3) repossess and foreclose on the collateral (9–609; 9–610); then, depending on the circumstances, either sue for any deficiency or return the surplus to the debtor.

RIGHT TO POSSESSION

The agreement between the creditor and the debtor may authorize the creditor to repossess the collateral in case of default. If the debtor does default, the creditor is entitled under the Code to possession of the collateral. If the creditor can obtain

CONCEPT SUMMARY	Outcome of Priority Contests
Parties	**Outcome of Contest**
Secured Party vs. Debtor	Secured party has priority (9–201[a]; 9–203).
Secured Party vs. Secured Party (as to collateral other than fixtures)	1. *General rule for nonfixtures.* When more than one security interest in the collateral has been filed or otherwise perfected, the first security interest to be filed or perfected has priority over other security interests so long as there is no period after the filing or perfection when there is neither filing nor perfection (9–322[a]). In addition, a. a perfected security interest has priority over an unperfected security interest (9–322[a]). b. if neither conflicting security interest is perfected, then the first security interest to attach has priority over the later-attached security interest (9–322[a]) 2. *Purchase money security interest exceptions to the general rule.* Purchase money security interests are able to gain priority over other perfected security interests under some circumstances. a. *Inventory purchase.* A perfected purchase money security interest in inventory has priority over a conflicting interest in the same inventory if the purchase money security interest is perfected when the debtor receives possession of the inventory, the purchase money secured party notifies the holder of the conflicting security interest, the holder of the conflicting security interest receives the notification within five years before the debtor receives possession of the inventory, and the notification states that the sender has or expects to acquire a purchase money security interest in inventory of the debtor and describes the inventory (9–324[b]). b. *Livestock purchase money security interests.* (See 9–324[d]). c. *Collateral other than inventory and livestock.* A perfected purchase money security interest in goods other than inventory or livestock has priority over a conflicting security interest in the same goods if the purchase money security interest is perfected when the debtor receives possession of the collateral or within 20 days after the debtor receives possession of the goods (9–324[a]). *(continued)*

Outcome of Priority Contests *(concluded)*

	3. *Exceptions for possessory liens arising by operation of law.* Liens that arise under other state statutes—such as those that create liens in favor of artisans and mechanics—have priority over perfected security interests in the same collateral so long as the artisan has possession of the collateral unless the statute expressly provides that the lien does not have priority. To obtain priority, these liens must secure payment or performance of services or materials furnished by a person in the ordinary course of the person's business (9–333).

Secured Creditor vs. Creditor with Interest in Real Property on Which Fixture Is Located	1. *General rule.* Except as expressly provided in 9–334(d)–(h), a security interest in fixtures is subordinate to a conflicting interest of an encumbrancer or owner of the related real property other than the debtor (9–334[c]).
	 2. *Exceptions to the general rule.*
	   a. *Purchase money security interests.* A perfected security interest in fixtures has priority over a conflicting interest of an encumbrancer or owner of the real property if the debtor has an interest of record in or is in possession of real property, the security interest of the encumbrancer or owner arises before the goods become fixtures, and the security interest is perfected by fixture filing before the goods became fixtures or within 20 days afterward.
	   b. *Interest in special classes of fixtures.* A perfected security interest in fixtures has priority over the encumbrancer or owner of record of real property if before the goods become fixtures, (1) the security interest was perfected by any of the means permitted by the Code, (2) the fixtures are readily removable, and (3) the fixtures are one of the following types: factory or office machines, equipment that is not primarily used or leased for use in the operation of the real property, or replacements of domestic appliances (such as washing machines or dishwashers that are consumer goods (9–324[e]).

Buyers of Collateral from debtor versus Secured Creditor	1. *General rule.* A security interest in collateral continues despite the debtor's sale of the collateral to another person unless the secured party authorized the sale or disposition free of the security interest (9–315[a][1]).
	 2. *Exceptions for buyers.* There are several exceptions to the general rule. The two most common exceptions are:
	   a. *Buyers in the ordinary course of the seller's business of items in inventory.* Buyers in the ordinary course of the seller's business take free of security interests created by the seller in the favor of a secured party even if the security interest is perfected and the buyer knows of its existence. This rule applies to consumer as well as commercial buyers of inventory (9–320[a]; 1–202[9]). This rule does not cover buyers of farm products from a person engaged in farming operations.
	   b. *Exceptions for buyers of consumer goods from other consumers.* Unless the secured party perfects by possession, a consumer who buys consumer goods from another consumer takes free of a security interest even if perfected if the buyer buys without knowledge of the security interest, for value, primarily for personal, family, or household purposes, and before the secured party has filed a financing statement covering the goods (9–320[b]).

possession peaceably, he may do so (9–609[b][2]). If the collateral is in the possession of the debtor and cannot be obtained without disturbing the peace, then the creditor must take court action to repossess the collateral (9–609[b][1]). The considerations involved in determining whether there was a breach of the peace are illustrated in *Ivy v. General Motors Acceptance Corp.*

IVY V. GENERAL MOTORS ACCEPTANCE CORP.
612 So. 2d 1108 (Sup. Ct. Miss. 1992)

FACTS

Lester Ivy borrowed money from General Motors Acceptance Corp. (GMAC) to purchase a van, and GMAC acquired a security interest in the van. The security agreement contained a so-called insecurity clause that provided GMAC with the right to repossess the van immediately upon default; notice was not a prerequisite to repossession. Ivy defaulted on his obligation on the loan, and GMAC hired American Lenders Service of Jackson

(continued)

Ivy v. General Motors Acceptance Corp.
(concluded)

to repossess Ivy's van. About 6:30 AM, Dax Freeman and Jonathan Baker of American Lenders Service drove to Ivy's home. They drove on Ivy's gravel driveway, which is about a quarter-mile long, past a chicken house and the van parked near Ivy's mobile home. They quietly attempted to start the van, but their attempt failed. They then hitched the van to their tow truck and towed it away.

When Freeman and Baker reached the end of Ivy's driveway, Freeman stopped the tow truck and checked the van. At that point he saw someone running from the chicken house toward the mobile home. Ivy testified that prior to running toward the mobile home, he ran toward the tow truck "hollering and flagging for them to stop" but Freeman and Baker apparently did not see or hear Ivy at the time Freeman jumped back into the tow truck and drove off Ivy's property and onto an adjacent road. Ivy decided to chase after Freeman and Baker because he thought they were stealing his van. He jumped into a pickup truck, passed Freeman and Baker, and—according to them—pulled in front of the tow truck, and slammed on his brakes. Freeman claimed he was forced to slam on his brakes but was unable to avoid a slight collision with the rear bumper of Ivy's truck. Ivy claimed that he stopped well ahead of the tow truck, affording Freeman plenty of time to stop, but that he revved the engine and "rammed him." Ivy claimed that his head hit the rear window of the truck as a result of the collision and that he sustained a "severe vertical sprain." However, Ivy's medical bill totaled only $20 and he did not miss any work.

When Ivy exited his truck, Freeman showed him some "official looking documents," advised him that he worked for American Lenders, and stated that they were repossessing his truck at GMAC's request. There was a dispute as to whether Ivy sought to have the sheriff called concerning the accident. Freeman allowed Ivy to retrieve some personal belongings from the van and gave Ivy a telephone number to call to get his van back; at that point, they all departed the scene.

Seven months later, on October 20, Ivy filed a complaint against GMAC and American Lenders contending that the repossession of his van was invalid because there was a breach of the peace and he had been caused "personal injuries." Ivy sought actual and punitive damages. At the conclusion of a jury trial, the jury awarded Ivy $5,000 in actual damages and $100,000 in punitive damages. The trial court judge set aside the punitive damage award and both parties appealed.

Issue

Was there a "breach of the peace" in the repossession of Ivy's van, entitling him to damages?

Decision

Yes. Mississippi law authorizes a creditor or secured party to repossess collateral without judicial process if he or she can do so without breaching the peace. (Sec. 9–503)

Much of the litigation involving self-help repossession statutes involves the issue of whether a breach of peace has occurred. Disposition of this issue is not a simple task: Since physical violence will ordinarily result in a breach of peace, the secured party's right to repossession without judicial process will end if repossession evokes physical violence, either on the part of the debtor or the secured party. At the other end from physical violence, a secured party may peaceably persuade the debtor to give up the collateral so that no breach of peace occurs. Between those two extreme situations—one in which violence occurs and the other in which the debtor peaceably gives up the collateral—lies the line which divides those cases in which the secured party may exercise self-help repossession and those in which he must resort to the courts. In this instance, there was a breach of the peace, and Ivy is entitled to recover damages.

Author's Note

This case was decided under the 1972 version of Article 9, but a similar result would be expected under Revised Article 9. See Revised Section 9–609(b).

Sale of the Collateral

If the creditor has a security interest in consumer goods and the debtor has paid 60 percent or more of the purchase price or debt (and has not agreed in writing to a strict foreclosure), the creditor must sell the repossessed collateral. If less than 60 percent of the purchase price or debt has been paid, or if the collateral is other than consumer goods, the creditor may propose to the debtor that the creditor keep the collateral in satisfaction of the debt. The debtor has 20 days to object in writing. If the consumer objects, the creditor must sell the collateral. Otherwise, the creditor may keep the collateral in satisfaction of the debt.

In disposing of the collateral, the creditor must try to produce the greatest benefit both to him and to the debtor. The method of disposal must be **commercially reasonable** (9–620, 9–627). If the creditor decides to sell the collateral at a public sale such as an auction, then the creditor must give the debtor notice of the time and place of the public sale. Similarly, if the creditor proposes to make a private resale of the collateral, notice must be given to the debtor. This gives the debtor a chance to object or to otherwise protect his or her interests (9–613).

Until the collateral is actually disposed of by the creditor, the buyer has the right to **redeem** it. This means that the buyer can pay off the debt and recover reasonable expenses and fees resulting from repossession and preparation for a disposition and recover the collateral from the creditor (9–623).

DISTRIBUTION OF PROCEEDS

The Code sets out the order in which any proceeds of sale of collateral by the creditor are to be distributed. First, any expenses of repossessing the collateral, storing it, and selling it, including reasonable attorney's fees, are paid (if the security agreement provides for them). Second, the proceeds are used to satisfy the debt being foreclosed. Third, any other junior security interests or liens are paid. Finally, if any proceeds remain, the debtor is entitled to them. If the proceeds are not sufficient to satisfy the debt, then the creditor is usually entitled to a **deficiency judgment.** This means that the debtor remains personally liable for any debt remaining after the sale of the collateral (9–615[d][2]).

For example, suppose that a loan company loans Chris $5,000 to purchase a used car and takes a security interest. After making several payments and reducing the debt to $4,800, Chris defaults. The loan company pays $150 to have the car repossessed and then has it sold at an auction, incurring a sales commission of 10 percent ($450) and attorney's fees of $250. The car sells for $4,500 at the auction. From the $4,500 proceeds, the repossession charges, sales commission, and attorney's fees totaling $850 are paid first. The remaining $3,650 is applied to the $4,800 debt, leaving a balance due of $1,150. Chris remains liable to the loan company for the $1,150, unless Chris challenges the amount of the deficiency claimed (9–626[a]).

LIABILITY OF CREDITOR

A creditor who holds a security interest in collateral must be careful to comply with the provisions of Article 9 of the Code. If a creditor acts improperly in repossessing collateral or in the foreclosure and sale of it, he is liable to the parties injured. Thus, a creditor can be liable to a debtor if he acts improperly in repossessing or selling collateral (9–625).

.... *QUESTIONS AND PROBLEM CASES* ....

1. On May 19, 1990, Richard Silch purchased a camcorder at Sears Roebuck by charging it to his Sears charge account. Printed on the face of the sales ticket made at that time was the following:

This credit purchase is subject to the terms of my Sears Charge Agreement which is incorporated herein by reference and identified by the above account number. I grant Sears a security interest or lien in this merchandise, unless prohibited by law, until paid in full.

Silch's signature appeared immediately below that language on the sales ticket. The ticket also contained the brand name of the camcorder and a stock number.

Silch subsequently filed a Chapter 7 bankruptcy proceeding and was eventually discharged. Sears filed a petition to recover the camcorder from Silch, contending that it had a valid and enforceable security interest in the camcorder. Silch, in turn, contended that the sales ticket did not constitute a valid and enforceable security agreement. Does the sales ticket constitute a valid security agreement?

2. Symons, a full-time insurance salesman, bought a set of drums and cymbals from Grinnel Brothers, Inc. A security agreement was executed between them but was never filed. Symons purchased the drums to supplement his income by playing with a band. He had done this before, and his income from his two jobs was about equal. He also played several other instruments. Symons became bankrupt, and the trustee tried to acquire the drums and cymbals as part of his bankruptcy estate. Grinnel's claimed that the drums and cymbals were consumer goods and thus it had a perfected security interest merely by attachment of the security interest. Were the drums and cymbals consumer goods?

3. Nicolosi bought a diamond ring on credit from Rike-Kumber as an engagement present for his fiancèe. He signed a purchase money security agreement giving Rike-Kumber a security interest in the ring until it was paid for. Rike-Kumber did not file a financing statement covering its security interest. Nicolosi filed for bankruptcy. The bankruptcy trustee claimed that the diamond ring was part of the bankruptcy estate because Rike-Kumber did not perfect its security interest. Rike-Kumber claimed that it had a perfected security interest in the ring. Did Rike-Kumber have to file a financing statement to perfect its security interest in the diamond ring?

4. On June 10, 1994, 4-R Management, by and through its officers, Chris and Lucretia Ryan, executed a promissory note to the First Bank of Eva. The Ryans signed the note both personally and as officers of 4-R Management. The Ryans also executed a security agreement dated June 10, 1994, pledging one "book coin collection" and various other items, including a tractor, bush hog, farm products and cattle, as security for the note. The promissory note incorporated by reference this separate security agreement. The coin collection was the property of 4-R Management, and the bank took possession of the coins on June 10. In subsequent renewal notes, 4-R Management, in its corporate capacity, expressly granted the bank a security interest in the coin collection.

On November 8, 1995, 4-R Management filed a voluntary petition for relief under the Bankruptcy Code. Subsequently, the Bankruptcy Trustee sought to recover for the bankruptcy estate the coin collection being held by the bank as security. The question of whether the bank or the Bankruptcy Trustee had the better right to the coin collection turned on whether the bank had a perfected security interest in the collection. When the bank has possession of collateral pursuant to a security agreement but has not filed a financing statement on the public record, does the bank hold a perfected security interest in the collateral?

5. On November 18, Firestone and Company made a loan to Edmund Carroll, doing business as Kozy Kitchen. To secure the loan, a security agreement was executed, which listed the items of property included, and concluded as follows: "together with all property and articles now, and which may hereafter be, used or mixed with, added or attached to, and/or substituted for any of the described property." A financing statement that included all the items listed in the security agreement was filed with the town clerk on November 18, and with the Secretary of State on November 22. On November 25, National Cash Register Company delivered a cash register to Carroll on a conditional sales contract. National Cash Register filed a financing statement on the cash register with the town clerk on December 20, and with the Secretary of State on December 21. Carroll

defaulted in his payments to both Firestone and National Cash Register. Firestone repossessed all of Carroll's fixtures and equipment covered by its security agreement, including the cash register, and then sold the cash register. National Cash Register claimed that it was the title owner of the cash register and brought suit against Firestone for conversion. Did Firestone or National Cash Register have the better right to the cash register?

6. Grimes purchased a new Dodge car from Hornish, a franchised Dodge dealer. The sale was made in the ordinary course of Hornish's business. Grimes paid Hornish the purchase price of the car at the time of the sale. Hornish had borrowed money from Sterling Acceptance and had given it a perfected security interest in its inventory, including the car Grimes bought. Hornish defaulted on its loan to Sterling and Sterling then tried to recover the Dodge from Grimes. Was the car Grimes bought from Hornish still subject to Sterling Acceptance's security interest?

7. Benson purchased a new Ford Thunderbird automobile. She traded in her old automobile and financed the balance of $4,326 through the Magnavox Employees Credit Union, which took a security interest in the Thunderbird. Several months later, the Thunderbird was involved in two accidents and sustained major damage. It was taken to ACM for repairs, which took seven months and resulted in charges of $2,139.54. Benson was unable to pay the charges, and ACM claimed a garageman's lien. Does Magnavox Credit Union's lien or ACM's lien have priority?

8. In August, Norma Wade purchased a Ford Thunderbird automobile and gave Ford Motor Credit a security interest in it to secure her payment of the $7,000 balance of the purchase price. When Wade fell behind on her monthly payments, Ford engaged the Kansas Recovery Bureau to repossess the car. On the following February 10, an employee of the Recovery Bureau located the car in Wade's driveway, unlocked the door, got in, and started it. He then noticed a discrepancy between the serial number of the car and the number listed in his papers. He shut off the engine, got out, and locked the car. When Wade appeared at the door to her house, he advised her that he had been sent by Ford to repossess the car but would not do so until he had straightened out the serial number. She said that she had been making payments, that he was not going to take the car, and that she had a gun, which she would use. He suggested that Wade contact Ford to straighten out the problem. She called Ford and advised its representative that if she caught anybody on her property again trying to take her car, she would use her gun to "leave him laying right where I saw him." Wade made several more payments, but Ford again contracted to have the car repossessed. At 2:00 AM on March 5, the employee of the Kansas Recovery Bureau successfully took the car from Wade's driveway. She said that she heard a car burning rubber, looked out of her window, and saw that her car was missing. There was no confrontation between Wade and the employee since he had safely left the area before she discovered that the car had been taken. Wade then brought a lawsuit against Ford claiming, that the car had been wrongfully repossessed. She sought actual and punitive damages, plus attorney's fees. Should Ford be held liable for wrongful repossession?

9. Gibson, a collector of rare old Indian jewelry, took two of his pieces to Hagberg, a pawnbroker. The two pieces, a silver belt and a silver necklace, were worth $500 each. Hagberg loaned only $45 on the belt and $50 on the necklace. Gibson defaulted on both loans, and immediately and without notice the belt was sold for $240. A short time later, the necklace was sold for $80. At the time of their sale, Gibson owed interest on the loans of $22. Gibson sued Hagberg to recover damages for improperly disposing of the collateral. Was Gibson entitled to damages because of Hagberg's action in disposing of the collateral?

10. *Video Case.* See "TV Repair." Appliance Store acquired inventory on credit from TV Manufacturer, which retained and perfected a security interest in the TV sets until they were paid for. Appliance Store subsequently experienced financial difficulties and held a going-out-of-business sale. If TV Manufacturer had not been paid for the TV sets, would it have the legal right to recover them from individual customers who purchased them at the going-out-of-business sale?

CHAPTER 42

Bankruptcy

Individuals and businesses can, for a variety of reasons, find themselves in financial difficulty. Similarly, creditors may find that individuals and businesses to whom they have extended credit are not meeting their financial obligations. For example, Bob and Sue Brown are a young couple with two small children. Within the last three years they stretched themselves financially in the course of furnishing their home and starting their family. Recently, Bob was laid off from his job as an engineer with a telecom company. Then Sue was injured in an automobile accident and has been unable to continue substitute teaching. Bob's unemployment benefits are insufficient to provide for the ordinary family expenses, much less meet the heavy financial obligations the family has taken on. The bank has filed a notice of intent to foreclose the mortgage on their home, and other creditors have sent letters threatening to repossess their car and furnishings.

Similar problems can arise for businesses, both small and large, who get caught in economic downturns, face unanticipated competition, or make poor business decisions. Unable to meet their financial obligations as they come due, they may find themselves cut off from further credit by banks and suppliers and faced with demands and lawsuits they cannot meet.

In this chapter, you will learn about the federal Bankruptcy Act, which provides an organized procedure (1) for dealing with the problems of insolvent debtors, (2) for protecting the creditors against the debtors and against potentially unfair actions by other creditors, and (3) giving honest debtors a fresh start financially.

INTRODUCTION

When an individual, partnership, or corporation is unable to pay its debts to its creditors, a number of problems can arise. Some creditors may demand security for past debts or start court actions on their claims in an effort to protect themselves. Such actions may adversely affect other creditors by depriving them of their fair share of the debtor's assets. In addition, quick depletion of the debtor's assets may effectively prevent a debtor who needs additional time to pay off his debts from having an opportunity to do so.

At the same time, creditors need to be protected against actions to their detriment that a debtor who is in financial difficulty might be tempted to take. For example, the debtor might run off with his remaining assets or might use them to pay certain favored creditors, leaving nothing for the other creditors.

Finally, a means is needed by which a debtor can get a fresh start financially and not continue to be saddled with debts beyond his ability to pay. This chapter focuses on the laws and procedures that have been developed to deal with the competing interests that are present when a debtor is unable to pay his debts in a timely manner.

THE BANKRUPTCY ACT

The Bankruptcy Act is a federal law that provides an organized procedure under the supervision of a federal court for dealing with insolvent debtors. Debtors are considered insolvent if they are unable or fail to pay their debts as they become due. The power of Congress to enact bankruptcy legislation is provided in the Constitution. Through the years, there have been many amendments to the Bankruptcy Act. Congress completely revised it in 1978 and then passed significant amendments to it in 1984, 1986, and 1994.

The Bankruptcy Act has several major purposes. One is to ensure that the debtor's property is fairly distributed to the creditors and that some of the creditors do not obtain unfair advantage over the others. At the same time, the act is designed to protect all of the creditors against actions by the debtor that would unreasonably diminish the debtor's assets to which they are entitled. The act also provides the honest debtor with a measure of protection against the demands for payment by creditors. Under some circumstances, the debtor is given additional time to pay the creditors free of pressures that the creditors might otherwise exert. If a debtor makes a full and honest accounting of his assets and liabilities and deals fairly with the creditors, the debtor may have most, if not all, of the debts discharged and thus have a fresh start.

At one time, bankruptcy carried a strong stigma for those debtors who became involved in it. Today, this is less true. It is still desirable that a person conduct his financial affairs in a responsible manner; however, there is a greater understanding that some events such as accidents, natural disasters, illness, divorce, and severe economic dislocations are often beyond the ability of individuals to control and may lead to financial difficulty and bankruptcy.

BANKRUPTCY PROCEEDINGS

The Bankruptcy Act covers several types of bankruptcy proceedings. In this chapter our focus will be on:

1. Straight bankruptcy (liquidation).
2. Reorganizations.

3.   Family farms.
4.   Consumer debt adjustments.

The Bankruptcy Act also contains provisions that cover municipal bankruptcies, but these will not be covered in this book.

LIQUIDATIONS

A liquidation proceeding, traditionally called **straight bankruptcy,** is brought under Chapter 7 of the Bankruptcy Act. The debtor must disclose all property she owns (the bankruptcy estate) and surrender it to the **bankruptcy trustee.** The trustee separates out certain property that the debtor is permitted to keep and then administers, liquidates, and distributes the remainder of the bankrupt debtor's estate. There is a mechanism for determining the relative rights of the creditors for recovering any preferential payments made to creditors and for disallowing any preferential liens obtained by creditors. If the bankrupt person has been honest in her business transactions and in the bankruptcy proceeding, she is usually given a **discharge** (relieved) of her debts.

REORGANIZATIONS

Chapter 11 of the Bankruptcy Act provides a proceeding whereby a debtor who is engaged in business can work out a plan to try to solve financial problems under the supervision of a federal court. A reorganization plan is essentially a contract between a debtor and its creditors. The proceeding is intended for debtors, particularly businesses, whose financial problems may be solvable if they are given some time and guidance and if they are relieved of some pressure from creditors.

FAMILY FARMS

Historically, farmers have been accorded special attention in the Bankruptcy Code. Chapter 12 of the Bankruptcy Act provides a special proceeding whereby a debtor involved in a family farming operation can develop a plan to work out his financial difficulties. Generally, the debtor remains in possession of the farm and continues to operate it while the plan is developed and implemented.

CONSUMER DEBT ADJUSTMENTS

Chapter 13 of the Bankruptcy Act sets out a special procedure that enables individuals with regular income who are in financial difficulty to develop a plan under court supervision to satisfy their creditors. Chapter 13 permits compositions (reductions) of debtors and/or extensions of time to pay debts out of the debtor's future earnings.

THE BANKRUPTCY COURTS

Bankruptcy cases and proceedings are filed in federal district courts. The district courts have the authority to refer the cases and proceedings to bankruptcy judges, who are considered to be units of the district court. If a dispute falls within what is known as a **core proceeding,** the bankruptcy judge can hear and determine the controversy. Core proceedings include a broad list of matters related to the administration of a bankruptcy estate. However, if a dispute is not a core proceeding but involves a state law claim, then the bankruptcy judge can only hear the case and prepare draft findings and conclusions for review by the district court judge. Certain kinds of proceedings that will have an effect on interstate commerce have to be heard by the district court judge if any party requests that this be done. Moreover, even the district courts are precluded from deciding certain state law claims that could not normally be brought in federal court, even if those claims are related to the bankruptcy matter. Bankruptcy judges are appointed by the president for terms of 14 years.

CHAPTER 7: LIQUIDATION PROCEEDINGS

PETITIONS

All bankruptcy proceedings, including liquidation proceedings, are begun by the filing of a petition. The petition may be either a voluntary petition filed by the debtor or an involuntary petition filed by a creditor or creditors of the debtor. A **voluntary petition** in bankruptcy may be filed by an individual, a partnership, or a corporation. However, municipal, railroad, insurance, and banking corporations and savings and loan associations are not permitted to file for liquidation proceedings. It is not necessary that a person who files a voluntary petition be **insolvent,** that is, unable to pay his debts as they become due. However, the person must be able to allege that he has debts. The primary purpose for filing a voluntary petition is to obtain a discharge from some or all of the debts.

INVOLUNTARY PETITIONS

An **involuntary petition** is a petition filed by creditors of a debtor. By filing it, the creditors seek to have the debtor declared bankrupt and his assets distributed to the creditors. Involuntary petitions may be filed against many kinds of debtors; however, involuntary petitions in straight bankruptcy cannot be filed against (1) farmers, (2) ranchers, (3) nonprofit organizations, (4) municipal, railroad, insurance, and banking corporations, (5) credit unions, and (6) savings and loan associations.

If a debtor has 12 or more creditors, an involuntary petition to declare him bankrupt must be signed by at least 3 creditors. If there are fewer than 12 creditors, an involuntary petition can be filed by a single creditor. The creditor or creditors must have valid claims against the debtor that exceed by $5,000 or more the value of any security they hold. To be forced into involuntary bankruptcy, the debtor must be unable to pay his debts as they become due—or have had a custodian for his property appointed within the previous four months.

If an involuntary petition is filed against a debtor who is engaged in business, the debtor may be permitted to continue to operate the business. However, an **interim trustee** may be appointed by the court if this is necessary to preserve the bankruptcy estate or to prevent loss of the estate. A creditor who suspects that a debtor may dismantle his business or dispose of its assets at less than fair value may apply to the court for protection.

AUTOMATIC STAY PROVISIONS

The filing of a bankruptcy petition operates as an **automatic stay** of (holds in abeyance) various forms of creditor action against a debtor or his property. These actions include (1) actions to begin or continue judicial proceedings against the debtor, (2) actions to obtain possession of the debtor's property, (3) actions to create, perfect, or enforce a lien against the debtor's property, and (4) actions to set off indebtedness owed to the debtor that arose before commencement of the bankruptcy proceeding. A court may give a creditor relief from the stay if the creditor can show that the stay does not give him "adequate protection" and jeopardizes his interest in certain property. The relief to the creditor might take the form of periodic cash payments or the granting of a replacement lien or an additional lien on property.

Concerned that debtors were taking advantage of the automatic stay provisions to the substantial detriment of some creditors, such as creditors whose claims were secured by an interest in a single real estate asset, in 1994 Congress provided specific relief from the automatic stay for such creditors. Debtors must either file a plan of reorganization that has a reasonable chance of being confirmed within a reasonable time or must be making monthly payments to each such secured creditor that are in an amount equal to interest at a current fair market rate on the value of the creditor's interest in the real estate.

The 1994 amendments also specifically provide that the automatic stay provisions are not applicable to actions to establish paternity; to establish or modify orders for alimony, support, or maintenance; or for the collection of alimony maintenance or support from property that is not the property of the bankruptcy estate.

ORDER OF RELIEF

Once a bankruptcy petition has been filed, the first step is a court determination that relief should be ordered. If a voluntary petition was filed by the debtor or if the debtor does not contest an involuntary petition, this step is automatic. If the debtor contests an involuntary petition, then a trial is held on the question of whether the court should order relief. The court orders relief only if (1) the debtor is generally not paying his debts as they become due or (2) within four months of the filing of the petition, a custodian was appointed or took possession of the debtor's property. The court also appoints an interim trustee pending election of a trustee by the creditors.

MEETING OF CREDITORS AND ELECTION OF TRUSTEE

The bankrupt person is required to file a list of his assets, liabilities, and creditors, and a statement of his financial affairs. Then a meeting of creditors is called by the court. Prior to the conclusion of the meeting of creditors, the United States Trustee is required to examine the debtor to make sure he is aware of (1) the potential consequences of seeking a discharge in bankruptcy, including the effects on credit history, (2) the debtor's ability to file a petition under other chapters (such as 11, 12, or 13) of the Bankruptcy Act, (3) the effect of receiving a discharge of debts, and (4) the effect of reaffirming a debt (discussed later in this chapter).

The creditors may elect a creditors' committee. The creditors also elect a **trustee,** who, if approved by the judge, takes over administration of the bankrupt's estate. The trustee represents the creditors in handling the estate. At the meeting, the creditors have a chance to ask the debtor questions about his assets, liabilities, and financial difficulties. The questions commonly focus on whether the debtor has concealed or improperly disposed of assets.

DUTIES OF THE TRUSTEE

The trustee takes possession of the debtor's property and has it appraised. The debtor must also turn over his records to the trustee. For a time, the trustee may operate the debtor's business. The trustee also sets aside the items of property that a debtor is permitted to keep under state exemption statutes or under federal law.

FIGURE 42–1   Order and Notice of Chapter 7 Bankruptcy Filing

B16A	United States Bankruptcy court for the District of Maryland	ORDER AND NOTICE OF CHAPTER 7 BANKRUPTCY FILING, MEETING OF CREDITORS, AND FIXING OF DATES (Individual or Joint Debtor No Asset Case)

A. GENERAL INFORMATION

Name of Debtor John B. Jones D/B/A The Bath Shop	Address of Debtor 195 MAIN STREET ANNAPOLIS MD 21401

		Date Filed 01/24/03	Case Number 9060300-SD	Soc. Sec. Nos./Tax ID Nos. 050-30-4701

Addressee: WICKER PRODUCTS, INC. 2000 SMITH PIKE ALMA, MI 48030	Address of the Clerk of the Bankruptcy Court United States Bankruptcy Court 101 W. Lombard Street - Baltimore, Maryland 21201
Name and Address of Attorney for Debtor MARC A. BURNS 215 WATER STREET BALTIMORE MD 21202	Name and Address of Trustee BRUCE A. SMITH 136 S. CHARLES STREET BALTIMORE MD 21201

B. DATE, TIME AND LOCATION OF MEETING OF CREDITORS

February 28, 2003, 09:15 AM., U.S. Trustee, Fallon Federal Bldg., Rm. G-13, 31 Hopkins Plaza, Baltimore, MD 21201

C. DISCHARGE OF DEBTS

Deadline to File a Complaint Objecting to the Discharge of the Debtor or Dischargeability of a Debt: April 30, 2003

D. BANKRUPTCY INFORMATION

THERE APPEAR TO BE NO ASSETS AT THIS TIME FROM WHICH PAYMENT MAY BE MADE TO CREDITORS. DO NOT FILE A PROOF OF CLAIM UNTIL YOU RECEIVE NOTICE TO DO SO.

FILING OF A BANKRUPTCY CASE. A bankruptcy petition has been filed in this court for the person or persons named above as the debtor, and an order for relief has been entered. You will not receive notice of all documents filed in this case. All documents which are filed with the court, including lists of the debtor's property and debts, are available for inspection at the office of the clerk of the bankruptcy court.

CREDITORS MAY NOT TAKE CERTAIN ACTIONS. Anyone to whom the debtor owes money or property is a creditor. Under the bankruptcy law, the debtor is granted certain protection against creditors. Common examples of prohibited actions are contacting the debtor to demand repayment, taking action against the debtor to collect money owed to creditors or to take property of the debtor, except as specifically permitted by the bankruptcy law, and starting or continuing foreclosure actions, repossessions, or wage deductions. If unauthorized actions are taken by a creditor against a debtor, the court may punish that creditor. A creditor who is considering taking action against the debtor or the property of the debtor should review 11 U.S.C. § 362 and may wish to seek legal advice. The staff of the clerk's office is not permitted to give legal advice to anyone.

MEETING OF CREDITORS. The debtor (both husband and wife in a joint case) shall appear at the meeting of creditors at the date and place set forth above in box "B" for the purpose of being examined under oath. ATTENDANCE BY CREDITORS AT THE MEETING IS WELCOMED, BUT NOT REQUIRED. At the meeting the creditors may elect a trustee as permitted by law, elect a committee of creditors, examine the debtor, and transact such other business as may properly come before the meeting. The meeting may be continued or adjourned from time to time without further written notice to the creditors.

LIQUIDATION OF THE DEBTOR'S PROPERTY. A trustee has been appointed in this case to collect the debtor's property, if any, and turn it into money. At this time, however, it appears from the schedules of the debtor that there are no assets from which any dividend can be paid to creditors. If at a later date it appears that there are assets from which a dividend may be paid, creditors will be notified and given an opportunity to file claims.

EXEMPT PROPERTY. Under state and federal law, the debtor is permitted to keep certain money or property as exempt. If a creditor believes that an exemption of money or property is not authorized by law, the creditor may file an objection. Any objection must be filed no later than 30 days after the conclusion of the meeting of creditors.

DISCHARGE OF DEBTS. The debtor is seeking a discharge of debts. A discharge means that certain debts are made unenforceable. Creditors whose claims against the debtor are discharged may never take action to collect the discharged debts. If a creditor believes the debtor should not receive a discharge under 11 U.S.C. ß 727 or a specific debt should not be discharged under 11 U.S.C. § 523(c) for some valid reason specified in the bankruptcy law, the creditor must take action to challenge the discharge. The deadline for challenging a discharge is set forth above in box "C." Creditors considering taking such action may wish to seek legal advice.

DO NOT FILE A PROOF OF CLAIM UNLESS YOU RECEIVE A COURT NOTICE TO DO SO

For the Court: January 31, 2003	Michael Kostishak
Date	Clerk of the Bankruptcy Court

The trustee examines the claims that have been filed by various creditors and objects to those that are improper in any way. The trustee separates the unsecured property from the secured and otherwise exempt property. The trustee also sells the bankrupt's nonexempt property as soon as it is possible and consistent with the best interest of the creditors.

The trustee is required to keep an accurate account of all property and money that he receives and to promptly deposit moneys into the estate's account. At the final meeting of the creditors, the trustee presents a detailed statement of the administration of the bankruptcy estate.

See Figure 42–1 on page 818 for an example of an Order and Notice of a Chapter 7 Bankruptcy filing.

EXEMPTIONS

Even in a liquidation proceeding, the bankrupt is generally not required to give up all of his property but rather is permitted to **exempt** certain items of property. Under the Bankruptcy Act, the debtor may choose to keep *either* certain items of property that are exempted by state law *or* certain items that are exempt under federal law—unless state law specifically forbids use of the federal exemption. However, any such property that has been concealed or fraudulently transferred by the debtor may not be retained.

The debtor must elect to use either the set of exemptions provided by the state or the set provided by the federal bankruptcy law; she may not pick and choose between them. A husband and wife involved in bankruptcy proceedings must both elect either the federal or the state exemptions; where they cannot agree, the federal exemptions are deemed elected.

The **exemptions** permit the bankrupt person to retain a minimum amount of assets considered necessary to life and to his ability to continue to earn a living. They are part of the "fresh start" philosophy that is one of the purposes behind the Bankruptcy Act. The general effect of the federal exemptions is to make a minimum exemption available to debtors in all states. States that wish to be more generous to debtors can provide more liberal exemptions.

The specific items that are exempt under state statutes vary from state to state. Some states provide fairly liberal exemptions and are considered to be "debtor's havens." Items that are commonly made exempt from sale to pay debts owed to creditors include the family Bible, tools or books of the debtor's trade, life insurance policies, health aids (such as wheelchairs and hearing aids), personal and household goods and jewelry, furniture, and motor vehicles worth up to a certain amount. In the *In re Kyllogen* case that follows, a debtor sought to obtain an exemption under state law.

IN RE KYLLOGEN
264 B.R. 17 (U.S.D.C. D. Minn. 2001)

FACTS

Patricia Kyllogen owns a 5-acre lot with a home and pole barn located on it; the property has an estimated value of $350,000 and is subject to a $90,000 mortgage. She purchased the property from her parents in 1974 and built the home after she married in 1980. The couple has two daughters. She and her husband David also own an adjacent unimproved lot of approximately 5 acres located behind the lot with their home. The second lot, which is valued at $45,000, was purchased in 1988. Both

(continued)

IN RE KYLLOGEN
(concluded)

lots are heavily wooded with mature oak trees and used to be part of Patricia Kyllogens parents' family farm.

Much of the surrounding area that once had constituted the family farm has been subdivided into residential parcels of at least 2.5 acres or more; many of the parcels contain large, expensive, and upscale homes. Three or four nearby properties are occupied by individuals who have full-time outside jobs but who also grow farm crops, primarily hay, on a part-time basis.

In 1996 Kyllogen and her husband cleared one-tenth of an acre of land on the front lot and planted ginseng seeds. Ginseng is a small herbal plant harvested for its roots. The longer the root grows before it is harvested, the more valuable it is, and the earliest one can harvest ginseng root is about five to seven years after it is planted. The ginseng is planted under the shade of mature hardwood trees and, once an area is cleared and the ginseng planted, it requires relatively little care except for periodic weeding. Kyllogen was employed full-time at a Burlington Coat Factory; her husband did not have a regular full-time job, although he described himself as a ginseng farmer. In five years of operation (1996 to 2000), the ginseng farm had no income and approximately $28,000 in tax-deductible losses.

Kyllogen filed a petition in bankruptcy. She claimed her home and the 10 acres of land on which it is located as *exempt* assets of the bankruptcy estate. The Bankruptcy Trustee asserted that Kyllogen was entitled to exempt a homestead of no more than one-half of an acre of land in area with a value of no more than $200,000. Section 510.01 of the Minnesota Statutes specifically provides:

> The house owned and occupied by a debtor as the debtor's dwelling place, together with the land upon which it is situated to the amount hereinafter limited and defined shall constitute the homestead of such debtor and the debtor's family, and be exempt from seizure or sale under legal process on account of any debt not lawfully charged hereon in writing, except such as are incurred for work or materials furnished in the construction, repair or improvement of the property . . .

Section 510.02, in turn, defines the area of the homestead:

> The homestead may include any quantity of land not exceeding 160 acres and not included in the laid out or platted portion of any city. If the homestead is within the laid-out or platted portion of a city, its area must not exceed one-half of an acre. The value of the homestead exemption, whether the exemption is owned jointly or individually, must not exceed $200,000, or, if the homestead is used primarily for agricultural purposes, $500,000 . . .

ISSUE

Was Kyllogen entitled to claim the full 10 acres as her homestead on the grounds it was an agricultural operation?

DECISION

No. The court held that in this instance, Kyllogen had built a house on a sizable lot in the outer suburbs of a city and, almost as an afterthought, decided to take up small-scale hobby farming operations. Kyllogen and her husband were primarily employed off the farm, and the farming operations have never provided support for them and their family but instead have given them only healthy tax write-offs. While what they do on the one-tenth acre can be termed *farming*, it clearly is not agricultural as that term is commonly understood and it not the type of *farm* the homestead exemption was designed to protect. Kyllogen is entitled to a homestead exemption of only one-half of an acre up to $200,000.

Eleven categories of property are exempt under the federal exemption, which the debtor may elect in lieu of the state exemptions. The federal exemptions include (1) the debtor's interest (not to exceed $16,150 in value) in real property or personal property that the debtor or a dependent of the debtor uses as a residence; (2) the debtor's interest (not to exceed $2,575 in value) in one motor vehicle; (3) the debtor's interest (not to exceed $425 in value for any particular item) up to a total of $8,625 in household furnishings, household goods, wearing apparel, appliances, books, animals, crops, or musical instruments that are held primarily for the personal, family, or household use of the debtor or a dependent of the debtor; (4) the debtor's aggregate interest (not to exceed $1,075 in value) in jewelry held primarily for the personal, family, or household use of the debtor or a dependent of the debtor; (5) $850 in value of any other property of the debtor's choosing, plus up to $8,075 of unused homestead exemption; (6) the debtor's aggregate interest (not to exceed $1,675 in value) in any implements, professional books, or tools of the trade; (7) life insurance contracts; (8) interest up to $8,625 in certain dividends or interest in certain life insurance policies; (9) professionally prescribed health aids; (10) social security, disability, alimony, and other benefits reasonably necessary for the support of the debtor or his dependents; and (11) the debtor's right to receive certain insurance and liability payments. The term *value* means "fair market value as of the date of the filing of the petition." In determining the debtor's interest in property, the amount of any liens against the property must be deducted.

AVOIDANCE OF LIENS

The debtor is also permitted to **void** certain liens against exempt properties that **impair** his exemptions. The liens that can be avoided on this basis are judicial liens (other than judicial liens that secure debts to a spouse, former spouse, or child for alimony, maintenance, or support) or nonpossessory, nonpurchase money security interests in (1) household furnishings, household goods, wearing apparel, appliances, books, animals, crops, musical instruments, and jewelry that are held primarily for the personal, family, or household use of the debtor or a dependent of the debtor; (2) implements, professional books, and tools of trade of the debtor or of a dependent of the debtor; and (3) professionally prescribed health aids for the debtor or a dependent of the debtor. Debtors are also permitted to **redeem** exempt property from secured creditors by paying them the **value** of the collateral. Then the creditor is an unsecured creditor to any remaining debt owed by the debtor.

PREFERENTIAL PAYMENTS

A major purpose of the Bankruptcy Act is to ensure equal treatment for all creditors of an insolvent debtor. The act also seeks to prevent an insolvent debtor from distributing his assets to a few favored creditors to the detriment of the other creditors.

The trustee has the right to recover for the benefit of the bankruptcy estate all preferential payments made by the bankrupt person.[1] A **preferential payment** is a payment made by an insolvent debtor within 90 days of the filing of the bankruptcy petition that enables the creditor receiving the payment to obtain a greater percentage of a preexisting debt than other similar creditors of the debtor receive.

For example, Fred has $1,000 in cash and no other assets. He owes $650 to his friend Bob, $1,500 to the credit union, and $2,000 to the finance company. If Fred pays $650 to Bob and then files for bankruptcy, he has made a preferential payment to Bob. Bob has obtained his debt paid in full, whereas only $350 is left to satisfy the $3,500 owed to the credit union and the finance company. They stand to recover only 10 cents on each dollar that Fred owes to them. The trustee has the right to get the $650 back from Bob.

If the favored creditor is an "insider"—a relative of an individual debtor or an officer, director, or related party of a company—then a preferential payment made up to one year prior to the filing of the petition can be recovered.

---

[1] In the case of an individual debtor whose debts are primarily consumer debts, the trustee is not entitled to avoid preferences unless the aggregate value of the property is $600 or more.

The 1994 amendments provided that the trustee may not recover as preferential payments any bona fide payments of debts to a spouse, former spouse, or child of the debtor for alimony, maintenance, or support pursuant to a separation agreement, divorce decree, or other court order.

PREFERENTIAL LIENS

Preferential liens are treated in a similar manner. A creditor might try to obtain an advantage over other creditors by obtaining a lien on the debtor's property to secure an existing debt. The creditor might seek to get the debtor's consent to a lien or to obtain the lien by legal process. Such liens are considered *preferential* and are invalid if they are obtained on property of an insolvent debtor within 90 days of the filing of a bankruptcy petition and the lien is to secure a preexisting debt. A preferential lien obtained by an insider within one year of the bankruptcy can be avoided.

The provisions of the Bankruptcy Act that negate preferential payments and liens do not prevent a debtor from engaging in current business transactions. For example, George, a grocer, is insolvent. George's purchase of new inventory such as produce and meat for cash would not be considered a preferential payment. George's assets have not been reduced; he simply has traded money for goods to be sold in his business. Similarly, George could buy a new display counter and give the seller a security interest in the counter until he has paid for it. This is not a preferential lien. The seller of the counter has not gained an unfair advantage over other creditors, and George's assets have not been reduced by the transaction. The unfair advantage comes where an existing creditor tries to take a lien or obtain a payment of more than his share. Then the creditor has obtained a preference and it will be disallowed.

The act also permits payments of accounts in the ordinary course of business. Such payments are not considered preferential.

FRAUDULENT TRANSFERS

If a debtor transfers property or incurs an obligation with *intent to hinder, delay, or defraud creditors*, the transfer is **voidable** by the trustee. Similarly, transfers of property for less than reasonable value are voidable by the trustee. Suppose Kathleen is in financial difficulty. She "sells" her $5,000 car to her mother for $100 so that her creditors cannot claim it. Kathleen did not receive fair consideration for this transfer. It could be declared void by a trustee if it was made within a year before the filing of a bank-

---

TRUJILLO V. GRIMMETT
215 B.R. 200 (U.S. Bankr. App., 9th Cir. 1997)

FACTS

In 1991 Joseph and Toni Trujillo bought a house in Las Vegas, Nevada. Subsequently, Joseph borrowed $20,000 of his wife's savings to invest in business ventures. On November 15, 1993, the Trujillos defaulted in payment on a promissory note to Richard Hart and then entered into a stipulated agreement with him that was entered as a judgment on August 8, 1994.

In May of 1994, purportedly as security to his wife for the $20,000 loan, Joseph transferred the title to his Cadillac automobile to his son, Gilbert. Joseph instructed Gilbert to hold the title in trust until the loan was repaid. Later the Trujillos transferred to Gilbert the titles of two more vehicles, a Pontiac and a Volkswagen, purportedly to obtain a group insurance rate. No consideration was

(continued)

TRUJILLO V. GRIMMETT
(concluded)

given for the transfer of any of the vehicles, and the Trujillos retained possession and control of all three vehicles.

On August 22, 1994, the Trujillos deeded, by a quitclaim deed, their house to their daughter, Valerie Aquino. The transfer was purportedly done to obtain a loan with Aquino's credit because Joseph's outstanding debts prevented him from obtaining credit in his own name. No consideration was given to the Trujillos for the transfer of the house, and the Trujillos retained both possession and control of the house.

On May 16, 1995, within a year of transferring the vehicles and deeding the house, the Trujillos filed a petition for relief under Chapter 7 of the Bankruptcy Code. The Bankruptcy Trustee, Tom Grimmett, filed a complaint for fraudulent conveyance, requested denial of discharge against the Trujillos, and sought recovery of the fraudulently conveyed property from Gilbert and Aquino.

ISSUE

Were the transfers of the vehicles and the house fraudulent transfers that could be recovered by the trustee?

DECISION

Yes. For the trustee to be entitled to avoid a transfer as fraudulent, four elements must be satisfied: (1) the debtor must have an interest in the property, (2) the debtor must have been insolvent at the time of the transfer or become insolvent as a result of the transfer, (3) the transfer must have been made within one year of the bankruptcy filing, and (4) the debtor must have received less than a reasonably equivalent value for transfer. The four elements have been met. The Trujillos had an interest in both the house and the vehicles prior to the transfers. They quitclaimed the deed to the house to Valerie and recorded it. She now has a marketable title in the house. They transferred the title to the vehicles to Gilbert, who has title and ownership under state law. The Trujillos, by their own admission, were insolvent when the transfers were made. The transfers occurred within one year of the filing of the Chapter 7 petition. Lastly, the Trujillos received nothing for the transfers, which certainly is less than reasonably equivalent value. Thus, the trustee is entitled to recover the transfers as fraudulent.

---

ruptcy petition against Kathleen. The provisions of law concerning fraudulent transfers are designed to prevent a debtor from concealing or disposing of his or her property in fraud of creditors. Such transfers may also subject the debtor to criminal penalties and prevent discharge of the debtor's unpaid liabilities.

In the case that follows, *Trujillo v. Grimmett,* the trustee was able to avoid the transfer of three cars and a house on the grounds that the transfers were fraudulent.

CLAIMS

If creditors wish to participate in the estate of a bankrupt debtor, they must file a **proof of claim** in the estate within a certain time (usually six months) after the first meeting of creditors. Only unsecured creditors are required to file proofs of claims; secured creditors do not have to do so. However, a secured creditor whose secured claim exceeds the value of the collateral is an unsecured creditor to the extent of the deficiency. A proof of claim must be filed to support the recovery of the deficiency.

ALLOWABLE CLAIMS

The fact that a claim is provable does not ensure that a creditor can participate in the distribution of the assets of the bankruptcy estate. The claim must also be **allowed.** If the trustee has a valid defense to the claim, she can use the defense to disallow the claim or to reduce it. For example, if the claim is based on goods sold to the debtor and the seller breached a warranty, the trustee can assert the breach as a defense. All the defenses that would have been available to the bankrupt person are available to the trustee.

SECURED CLAIMS

The trustee must also determine whether a creditor has a lien or secured interest to secure an allowable claim. If the debtor's property is subject to a secured claim of a creditor, that creditor has the first claim to it. The property is available to satisfy claims of other creditors only to the extent that its value exceeds the amount of the debt secured.

PRIORITY CLAIMS

The Bankruptcy Act declares certain claims to have **priority** over other claims. The nine classes of priority claims are (1) expenses and fees incurred in administering the bankruptcy estate, (2) unsecured claims in involuntary cases that arise in the ordinary course of the debtor's business after the filing of the petition but before the appointment of a trustee or the order of relief, (3) unsecured claims for wages, salaries, or commissions of employees up to $4,300 per individual (including vacation, severance, and sick pay) earned within 90 days before the petition was filed, (4) contributions to employee benefit plans up to $4,300 per person (moreover, the claim for wages plus pension contribution is limited to $4,300 per person), (5) unsecured claims (*a*) for grain or the proceeds of grain against a debtor who owns or operates a grain storage facility or (*b*) up to $4,300 by a U.S. fisherman against a debtor who operates a fish produce storage or processing facility and who has acquired fish or fish produce from the fisherman, (6) claims of up to $1,950 each by individuals for deposits made in connection with the purchase, lease, or rental of property or the purchase of goods or services for personal use that were not delivered or provided, (7) allowed-for claims for debts to a spouse, former spouse, or child of the debtor for alimony to, maintenance for, or support of such spouse or child in connection with a separation agreement, divorce decree, or other court order (but not if assigned to someone else), (8) certain taxes owed to governmental units, and (9) allowed unsecured claims based on a commitment by the debtor to a federal depository institution regulatory agency (such as the FDIC).

DISTRIBUTION OF DEBTOR'S ESTATE

The priority claims are paid *after* secured creditors realize on their collateral or security but *before* other unsecured claims are paid. Payments are made to the nine priority classes in order to the extent there are funds available. Each class must be paid before the next class is entitled to receive anything. To the extent there are insufficient funds to satisfy all the creditors within a class, each class member receives a pro rata share of his claim.

Unsecured creditors include (1) those creditors who had not taken any collateral to secure the debt owed to them, (2) secured creditors to the extent their debt was not satisfied by the collateral they held, and (3) priority claimholders to the extent their claims exceed the limits set for priority claims. Unsecured creditors, to the extent any funds are available for them, share in proportion to their claims; they frequently receive little or nothing on their claims. Secured claims, trustee's fees, and other priority claims often consume a large part or all of the bankruptcy estate.

Special rules are set out in the Bankruptcy Act for distribution of the property of a bankrupt stockbroker or commodities broker.

CONCEPT SUMMARY   **Distribution of Debtor's Estate (Chapter 7)**

Secured creditors proceed directly against the collateral. If debt is fully satisfied, they have no further interest; if debt is only partially satisfied, they are treated as general creditors for the balance.

Debtor's Estate is Liquidated and Distributed

Priority Creditors (6 classes)

1. Costs and expenses of administration.
2. If involuntary proceeding, expenses incurred in the ordinary course of business after petition filed but before appointment of trustee.
3. Claims for wages, salaries, and commissions earned within 90 days of petition; limited to $4,000 per person.
4. Contributions to employee benefit plans arising out of services performed within 180 days of petition; limit of $4,000 (including claims for wages, salaries, and commissions) per person.
5. Unsecured claims (a) for grain or the proceeds of grain against a debtor who owns or operates a grain storage facility or (b) up to $4,000 by a United States fisherman against a debtor who operates a fish produce or processing facility and who has acquired fish or fish produce from the fisherman.
6. Claims of individuals, up to $1,800 per person, for deposits made on consumer goods or services that were not received.
7. Allowed for claims for debts to a spouse, former spouse, or child of the debtor for alimony to, maintenance for, or support of such spouse or child in connection with a separation agreement, divorce decree, or other court order (if not assigned to someone else).
8. Government claims for certain taxes.
9. Allowed unsecured claims based on a commitment by the debtor to a federal depository institution regulatory agency.

A. Distribution is made to six classes of priority claims in order.
B. Each class must be fully paid before next class receives anything.
C. If funds not sufficient to satisfy everyone in a class, then each member of the class receives same proportion of claim.

General Creditors

1. General unsecured creditors.
2. Secured creditors for the portion of their debt that was not satisfied by collateral.
3. Priority creditors for amounts beyond priority limits.

If funds are not sufficient to satisfy all general creditors, then each receive the same proportion of their claims.

Debtor

Debtor receives any remaining funds.

DISCHARGE IN BANKRUPTCY

A bankrupt person who has not been guilty of certain dishonest acts and who has fulfilled his duties as a bankrupt is entitled to a **discharge** in bankruptcy. A discharge relieves the bankrupt person of further responsibility for those debts that are dischargeable and gives the person a fresh start. A corporation is not eligible for a discharge in liquidation bankruptcy proceedings. A bankrupt person may file a written waiver of her right to a discharge. An individual may not be granted a discharge if she has obtained one within the previous six years.

OBJECTIONS TO DISCHARGE

After the bankrupt has paid all the required fees, the court gives creditors and others a chance to file objections to the discharge of the bankrupt. Objections may be filed by the trustee, a creditor, or the U.S. attorney. If objections are filed, the court holds a hearing to listen to them. At the hearing the court must determine whether the bankrupt person has committed any act that would bar discharge. If the bankrupt has not committed such an act, the court grants the discharge. If she committed an act that is a bar to discharge, the discharge is denied. It is also denied if the bankrupt fails to appear at the hearing on objections or refused earlier to submit to the questioning of the creditors.

ACTS THAT BAR DISCHARGES

Discharges in bankruptcy are intended for honest debtors. Therefore, there are a number of acts that will bar a debtor from being discharged. These acts include: (1) unjustified falsifying, concealing, or destroying of records; (2) making false statements, presenting false claims, or withholding recorded information relating to the debtor's property or financial affairs; (3) transferring, removing, or concealing property in order to hinder, delay, or defraud creditors; (4) failing to account satisfactorily

---

BYRD V. BANK OF MISSISSIPPI
207 B.R. 131 (S.D. Miss. 1997)

FACTS

In January 1990 Dr. Anthony Byrd, a dentist, applied to the Bank of Mississippi for an unsecured loan in the amount of $20,000. Prior to this time the bank had no relationship with Dr. Byrd. The bank requested and received from Dr. Byrd a 1988 individual income tax return along with a statement of his financial condition prepared by his accountant. The bank also obtained a credit report. After considering all the information, the bank granted the loan. The promissory note was renewed on a number of occasions, beginning in July 1990. On each occasion the bank requested, and was provided, a current financial statement.

The financial statement dated June 30, 1989, showed Dr. Byrd having a net worth of approximately $649,000. Listed in the financial statements was an asset consisting of 60 acres of real property with a value of $30,000. In fact, Dr. Byrd did not own the property, nor did he ever pay the property taxes on it. He later explained that he had listed it because he believed that it had passed to him on his father-in-law's death; the property was farmed by his brother-in-law. The statement also listed as an asset a residence in Covington County, Mississippi, with an appraised value of $49,800. At the time the financial statement was submitted, the property had been sold to his brother on a conditional sale contract with a purchase price of $39,000; it also was encumbered with a deed of trust securing a $39,000 note to the Bank of Simpson County. However, neither the conditional sales contract nor the note and deed of trust was mentioned in the financial statement. Dr. Byrd later explained that this was

(continued)

DISMISSAL FOR SUBSTANTIAL ABUSE

As it considered the 1984 amendments to the Bankruptcy Act, Congress was concerned that too many individuals with an ability to pay their debts over time pursuant to a Chapter 13 plan were filing petitions to obtain Chapter 7 discharges of liability. The consumer finance industry urged that Congress should preclude Chapter 7 petitions where a debtor had the prospect of future disposable income to satisfy more than 50 percent of his prepetition unsecured debts. While Congress rejected this approach, it did authorize bankruptcy courts to dismiss cases that they determined were a **substantial abuse** of the bankruptcy process. This provision appears to cover situations in which a debtor has acted in "bad faith" or in which he has the present or future ability to pay a significant portion of his current debts. The case which follows,

---

IN RE HUCKFELDT
39 F.3d 829 (8th Cir 1994)

FACTS

During their 12 years of marriage, Roger and Georgianne Huckfeldt accumulated over $250,000 in debts while Roger completed college, medical school, and six years of residency in surgery and while Georgianne completed college and law school. These debts included $166,000 in student loans to Huckfeldt and $47,000 jointly borrowed from Georgianne's parents. The Huckfeldts divorced on March 26, 1992. The divorce decree ordered Roger to pay his student loans, one-half of the debt to Georgianne's parents, and other enumerated debts totaling some $241,000. The decree also ordered Roger to hold Georgianne harmless for these debts but otherwise denied Georgianne's request for maintenance.

On June 4, 1992, six months before Roger would complete his residency, he filed a voluntary Chapter 7 petition, listing assets of $1,250 and liabilities of $546,857. After filing the petition, Roger accepted a fellowship at Oregon Health Sciences University, a one- or two-year position paying $45,000 per year, substantially less than the income he could likely earn during the pendency of his Chapter 7 proceeding. Following Roger's petition, creditors of the debts assigned to him in the divorce decree began pursuing Georgianne for repayment. She filed for bankruptcy protection in March 1993.

In September 1992, Georgianne and her parents filed a motion to dismiss Roger's Chapter 7 petition on the ground that it was filed in bad faith. They alleged that Roger had threatened to file for bankruptcy during the divorce proceeding and had commenced the bankruptcy proceeding in defiance of the divorce decree for the purpose of shifting responsibility for assigned debts to Georgianne. They also alleged that Roger had deliberately taken steps to reduce his annual income to avoid payment of his debts through the Chapter 7 liquidation.

After a hearing the bankruptcy court granted the motion to dismiss the proceeding on the grounds it was filed in bad faith, finding, among other things, that Roger could be earning $110,000 to $120,000 after expenses. The district court affirmed the decision, and Roger appealed to the court of appeals.

ISSUE

Should Roger's Chapter 7 petition be dismissed on the grounds it was filed in bad faith?

DECISION

Yes. The Bankruptcy Act incorporates a standard of good faith for the commencement, prosecution, and confirmation of bankruptcy proceedings. Here Roger filed the petition for the purpose of frustrating the divorce decree and forcing his ex-wife into bankruptcy, at a time when his financial prospects made him anything but an "honest but unfortunate debtor" needing Chapter 7 relief. After filing, he manipulated his immediate earnings to ensure that the Chapter 7 proceeding would achieve his noneconomic motives. The petition was not filed for the purpose of a just liquidation by composition with creditors but to defeat his wife from the right of the benefit she received from the divorce decree. That conduct is unworthy of bankruptcy protection, and the petition was properly dismissed.

In re Huckfeldt, illustrates a situation in which the court concluded that a petition in bankruptcy had been filed in bad faith.

CHAPTER 11: REORGANIZATIONS

RELIEF FOR BUSINESSES

Sometimes creditors benefit more from a continuation of a bankrupt debtor's business than from a liquidation of the debtor's property. Chapter 11 of the Bankruptcy Act provides a proceeding whereby the debtor's financial affairs can be reorganized rather than liquidated under the supervision of the Bankruptcy Court. Chapter 11 proceedings are available to virtually all business enterprises, including individual proprietorships, partnerships, and corporations (except banks, savings and loan associations, insurance companies, commodities brokers, and stockbrokers). In 1991, the U.S. Supreme Court in *Toibb v. Radloff* held that even though Chapter 11 was intended primarily for the use of business debtors, it is also available to individuals. Petitions for Chapter 11 reorganization proceedings can be filed either voluntarily by the debtor or involuntarily by its creditors.

ADMINISTRATION

Once a petition for a reorganization proceeding is filed and relief is ordered, the court usually appoints a committee of creditors who hold unsecured claims, a committee of equity security holders (shareholders), and a trustee. The trustee may be given the responsibility for running the debtor's business. He is usually also responsible for developing a plan for how the various claims of creditors and interests of persons (such as shareholders) are to be handled. The reorganization plan is essentially a contract between a debtor and its creditors. It may involve recapitalizing a debtor corporation and/or giving creditors some equity (shares) in the corporation in exchange for part or all of the debt owed to them. The plan must (1) divide the creditors into classes, (2) set forth how each creditor will be satisfied, (3) state which claims are impaired or adversely affected by the plan, and (4) treat all creditors in a given class the same (unless the creditors in that class consent to different treatment).

The plan is then submitted to the creditors for approval. Approval generally requires that creditors who hold two-thirds in amount and one-half in number of each class of claims impaired by the plan must accept it. Once approved, the plan goes before the court for confirmation. If the plan is confirmed, the debtor is responsible for carrying it out.

OFFICIAL COMMITTEE OF EQUITY SECURITY HOLDERS V. MABEY
832 F. 2d 299 (4th Cir. 1987)

FACTS

The A. H. Robbins Company is a publicly held company that filed a voluntary petition for relief under Chapter 11 of the Bankruptcy Code. Robbins sought refuge in Chapter 11 because of a multitude of civil actions filed against it by women who alleged they were injured by use of the Dalkon Shield intrauterine device that it manufactured and sold as a birth control device. Approximately 325,000

notices of claim against Robbins were received by the bankruptcy court.

In 1985, the court appointed the Official Committee of Security Holders to represent the interest of Robbins' public shareholders. In April 1987, Robbins filed a proposed plan of reorganization but no action was taken on the proposed plan because of a merger proposal submitted

(continued)

OFFICIAL COMMITTEE OF EQUITY SECURITY HOLDERS V. MABEY
(concluded)

by Rorer Group, Inc. Under this plan, Dalkon Shield claimants would be compensated out of a $1.75 billion fund, all other creditors would be paid in full, and the Robbins stockholders would receive stock of the merged corporation. However, it being a time of other critical activity in the bankruptcy proceeding, no revised plan incorporating the merger proposal had been filed or approved.

Earlier, in August of 1986, the court had appointed Ralph Mabey as an examiner to evaluate and suggest proposed elements of a plan of reorganization. On Mabey's suggestion, a proposed order was put before the district court supervising the proceeding that would require Robbins to establish a $15 million emergency treatment fund "for the purpose of assisting in providing tubal reconstructive surgery or in vitro fertilization to eligible Dalkon Shield claimants." The purpose of the emergency fund was to assist those claimants who asserted they had become infertile as a consequence of their use of the product. A program was proposed for administering the fund and for making the medical decisions required.

On May 21, 1987, the district court ordered that the emergency treatment fund be created. This action was challenged by the committee representing the equity security holders.

ISSUE

Was the court justified in ordering the distribution of some of the bankrupt's assets on an emergency basis before a reorganization plan was approved?

DECISION

No. The appeals court held that the district court had no authority to distribute funds to claimants prior to the allowance of claims of women who would benefit from the fund and prior to the confirmation of a plan of reorganization of Robbins. The court noted that it sympathized with the district court's concern for the Dalkon Shield claimants who desired reconstructive surgery or in vitro fertilization while they were still able to bear children, but it found that creation of the fund violated the clear language of the Bankruptcy Act, which requires a plan be confirmed before assets are distributed.

The case that follows, *Official Committee of Equity Security Holders v. Mabey,* shows that until a plan is confirmed, the bankruptcy court has no authority to distribute a portion of the bankruptcy assets to a portion of the unsecured creditors.

USE OF CHAPTER 11

During the 1980s, attempts by a number of corporations to seek refuge in Chapter 11 as a means of escaping problems they were facing received considerable public attention. Some of the most visible cases involved efforts to obtain some protection against massive product liability claims and judgments for breach of contract and to escape from collective bargaining agreements. Thus, for example, Johns-Manville Corporation filed under Chapter 11 because of the claims against it arising out of its production and sale of asbestos years earlier; A. H. Robbins Company, as illustrated in the preceding case, was concerned about a surfeit of claims arising out of its sale of the Dalkon Shield, an intrauterine birth control device. And, in 1987, Texaco, Inc., faced with a $10.3 billion judgment in favor of Pennzoil in a breach of contract action, filed a petition for reorganization under Chapter 11. Companies such as LTV and Allegheny Industries sought changes in retirement and pension plans, and other companies such as Eastern Airlines sought refuge in Chapter 11 while embroiled in labor disputes.

In the 1990s, a number of companies that were the subject of highly leveraged buyouts (LBOs), including a number of retailers and numerous real estate developers, resorted to Chapter 11 to seek restructuring and relief from their creditors. Similarly, companies such as Pan Am and TWA that were hurt by the economic slowdown and the increase in fuel prices filed Chapter 11 petitions. In 2001, Enron and K-Mart filed for reorganization under Chapter 11.

COLLECTIVE BARGAINING AGREEMENTS

Collective bargaining contracts pose special problems. Prior to the 1984 amendments, there was concern that some companies would use Chapter 11 reorganization as a vehicle for trying to avoid executed collective bargaining agreements. Congress then acted to try to prevent the misuse of bankruptcy proceedings for collective bargaining purposes.

The 1984 amendments adopt a rigorous multistep process that must be complied with in determining whether a labor contract can be rejected or modified as part of a reorganization. Among other things that must be done before a debtor or trustee can seek to avoid a collective bargaining agreement are the submission of a proposal to the employees' representative that details the "necessary" modifications to the collective bargaining agreement and assures that "all creditors, the debtor, and all affected parties are fairly treated." Then, before the bankruptcy court can authorize a rejection of the original collective bargaining agreement, it must review the proposal and find that (1) the employees' representative refused to accept it without good cause and (2) the balance of equities clearly favors the rejection of the original collective bargaining agreement.

Ethical Implications	Is it ethical for a company such as A. H. Robbins Company that is faced with significant liability for defective products it made and sold to seek the protection accorded by the bankruptcy laws? Similarly, is it ethical for a company that believes it is hampered by a labor contract under which it incurs higher labor costs than some of its competitors to try to use a Chapter 11 proceeding to get out of the labor contract?

.... CHAPTER 12: FAMILY FARMS ....

RELIEF FOR FAMILY FARMERS

Historically, farmers have been accorded special treatment in the Bankruptcy Code. In the 1978 Act, as in earlier versions, small farmers were exempted from involuntary proceedings. Thus, a small farmer who filed a voluntary Chapter 11 or 13 petition could not have the proceeding converted into a Chapter 7 liquidation over his objection so long as he complied with the act's requirements in a timely fashion. Additional protection was also accorded through the provision allowing states to opt out of the federal exemption scheme and to provide their own exemptions. A number of states used this flexibility to provide generous exemptions for farmers so they would be able to keep their tools and implements.

Despite these provisions, the serious stress on the agricultural sector in the mid-1980s led Congress in 1986 to further amend the Bankruptcy Code by adding a new Chapter 12 targeted to the financial problems of the family farm. During the 1970s and 1980s, farmland prices appreciated and many farmers borrowed heavily to expand their productive capacity, creating a large debt load in the agricultural sector. When land values subsequently dropped and excess production in the world kept farm prices low, many farmers faced extreme financial difficulty.

Chapter 12 is modeled after Chapter 13, which is discussed next. It is available only for family farmers with regular income. To qualify, a farmer and spouse must have not less than 80 percent of their total noncontingent, liquidated debt arising out of their farming operations. The aggregate debt must be less that $1.5 million, and at least 50 percent of an individual's or couple's income during the year preceding the petition must have come from the farming operation. A corporation or partnership can also qualify, provided that more than 50 percent of the stock or equity is held by one family or its relatives and they conduct the farming operation. Again, 80 percent of the debt must arise from the farming operation; the aggregate debt ceiling is $1.5 million.

The debtor is usually permitted to remain in possession to operate the farm. Although the debtor in possession has many of the rights of a Chapter 11 trustee, a trustee is appointed under Chapter 12, and the debtor is subject to his supervision. The trustee is permitted to sell unnecessary assets, including farmland and equipment, without the consent of the secured creditors and before a plan is approved. However, the secured creditor's interest attaches to the proceeds of the sale.

The debtor is required to file a plan within 90 days of the filing of the Chapter 12 petition—although the Bankruptcy Court has the discretion to extend the time. A hearing is held on the proposed plan, and it can be confirmed over the objection of creditors. The debtor may release to any secured party the collateral that secures the claim to obtain confirmation with the acceptance by that creditor.

Unsecured creditors are required to receive at least liquidation value under the Chapter 12 plan. If an unsecured creditor or the trustee objects to the plan, the court may still confirm the plan despite the objection so long as it calls for full payment of the unsecured creditor's claim or it provides that the debtor's disposable income for the duration of the plan is applied to making payments on it. A debtor who fulfills his plan or is excused from full performance because of subsequent hardship is entitled to a discharge.

.... **CHAPTER 13: CONSUMER DEBT ADJUSTMENTS** ....

RELIEF FOR INDIVIDUALS

Chapter 13 ("Adjustment of Debts for Individuals") of the Bankruptcy Act provides a way for individuals who do not want to be declared bankrupt to be given an opportunity to pay their debts in installments from future income under the protection of a federal court. Under Chapter 13, debtors have this opportunity free of problems such as garnishments and attachments of their property by creditors. Only individuals with regular incomes (including sole proprietors of businesses) who owe individually (or with their spouse) liquidated, unsecured debts of less than $250,000 and secured debts of less than $750,000 are eligible to file under Chapter 13.

PROCEDURE

Chapter 13 proceedings are initiated by the voluntary petition of a debtor filed in the Bankruptcy Court. Creditors of the debtor may *not* file an involuntary petition for a Chapter 13 proceeding. The debtor in the petition states that he is insolvent or unable to pay his debts as they mature and that he desires to effect a composition or an extension, or both, out of future earnings or income. A **composition of debts** is an arrangement whereby the amount the person owes is reduced, whereas an **extension** provides the person with a longer period of time to pay them. Commonly, the debtor files at the same time a list of his creditors as well as his assets, liabilities, and executory contracts.

Following the filing of the petition, the court calls a meeting of creditors, at which time proofs of claims are received and allowed or disallowed. The debtor is examined, and he submits a plan of payment. The plan is submitted to the secured creditors for acceptance. If they accept it and the court is satisfied that it is proposed in good faith, meets the legal requirements, and is in the interest of the creditors, the court approves the plan. The court then appoints a trustee to carry out the plan. The plan must provide for payments over a period of three years or less unless the court approves a longer period (up to five years).

No plan may be approved if the trustee or an unsecured creditor objects unless the plan provides for the objecting creditor to be paid the present value of what he is owed *or* provides for the debtor to commit all of his projected disposable income for a three-year period to pay his creditors. A critical question that the trustee and other creditors commonly focus on is whether the plan appears to have been proposed in

---

IN THE MATTER OF KELLY
217 B.R. 273 (Bankr. D. Neb. 1997)

FACTS

Paul Kelly was a graduate student at the University of Nebraska and had been working on his Ph.D. since 1991. He expected to complete it in 1999. He was also working as a clerk in a liquor store approximately 32 hours per week and earned $5.85 per hour. His monthly expenses were $743.00, and his monthly take-home pay was $761.00. Kelly borrowed money through student loans to enable him to pay tuition, fees, books, and other school-related expenses and expected to continue to do so until he finished his Ph.D.

On July 26, 1994, the U.S. District Court in Minnesota entered a judgment in the amount of $30,000 against Kelly and in favor of Capitol Indemnity Corporation. The judgment was based on a misappropriation of funds by Kelly from a bank insured by Capitol. The court's order provided that the judgment was not dischargeable in bankruptcy.

Kelly filed a Chapter 13 petition. In his Chapter 13 plan, Kelly proposed to pay a total of $7,080.00 by paying off $118.00 per month, $100.00 of which would come from student loans. In the proceeding, Kelly testified that, among other things, he was currently qualified to teach at the college or university level and could earn about $20,000 but he preferred to work part-time as a clerk while he completed graduate school. Capitol objected to the proposed plan on the grounds it was not

proposed in good faith. Capitol contended that Kelly should not be allowed to languish in graduate school, remain underemployed, and obtain the benefit of a Chapter 13 discharge. Capitol asserted that Kelly was attempting to discharge a debt that was nondischargeable under Chapter 7, proposed to make payments primarily from his student loans, and would be paying a dividend to unsecured creditors of only 8½ percent. These factors, Capitol contended, demonstrated that the plan had not been proposed in good faith and that it should not be confirmed.

ISSUE

Should confirmation of Kelly's plan be denied on the grounds it was not proposed in good faith?

DECISION

Yes. Under the proposed plan, Kelly would pay off only a small proportion of his unsecured debt. Over one-half of the debt is owed to Capitol, and this debt would be exempted from discharge in a Chapter 7 proceeding. Even though the debtor would be utilizing all of his disposable income to make the payments under the proposed plan, it is not equitable for him to remain underemployed, to obtain the benefit of an advanced college degree, and to discharge his obligations to creditors upon payment of a nominal dividend.

"good faith." The *In the Matter of Kelly* case, which follows, illustrates a situation in which the court found the plan was not proposed in good faith.

A Chapter 13 debtor must begin making the installment payment proposed in her plan within 30 days after the plan is filed. The interim payments must continue to be made until the plan is confirmed or denied. If the plan is denied, the money, less any administrative expenses, is returned to the debtor by the trustee. The interim payments give the trustee an opportunity to observe the debtor's performance and to be in a better position to make a recommendation as to whether the plan should be approved.

Once approved, a plan may be substantially modified on petition of a debtor or a creditor when there is a material change in the debtor's circumstances.

Suppose Curtis Brown has a monthly take-home pay of $1,000 and a few assets. He owes $1,500 to the credit union for the purchase of furniture, on which he is supposed to pay $75 per month. He owes $1,800 to the finance company on the purchase of a used car, which he is supposed to repay at $90 a month. He also has run up charges of $1,200 on his MasterCard account, primarily for emergency repairs to this car; he must repay this at $60 per month. His rent of $350 per month and food and other living expenses cost him another $425 per month.

Curtis was laid off from his job for a month and fell behind on his payments to his creditors. He then filed a Chapter 13 petition. In his plan he might, for example, offer to repay the credit union $50 a month, the finance company $60 a month, and MasterCard $40 a month, with the payments spread over three years rather than the shorter time for which they are currently scheduled.

DISCHARGE

When the debtor has completed her performance of the plan, the court issues an order that discharges her from the debts covered by the plan. The debtor may also be discharged even though she did not complete her payments within the three years if the court is satisfied that the failure is due to circumstances for which the debtor cannot justly be held accountable. Certain debts, such as those for restitution or certain fines in excess of $500, that are included in a sentence on a debtor's conviction of a crime are not dischargeable.

An active Chapter 13 proceeding **stays** (holds in abeyance) any straight bankruptcy proceedings and any actions by creditors to collect consumer debts. However, if the Chapter 13 proceeding is dismissed (for example, because the debtor fails to file an acceptable plan or defaults on an accepted plan), straight bankruptcy proceedings may be resumed.

ADVANTAGES OF CHAPTER 13

A debtor may choose to file under Chapter 13 to try to avoid the stigma of bankruptcy or to try to retain more of his or her property than is exempt from bankruptcy under state law. Chapter 13 can provide some financial discipline to a debtor as well as an opportunity to get some protection from her financial creditors so long as payments are made as called for by the plan. The debtor's creditors stand to benefit by possibly being able to recover a higher percentage of the debt owed to them than they would get in straight bankruptcy proceedings.

CONCEPT SUMMARY	Comparison of Major Forms of Bankruptcy Proceedings			
Purpose	**Chapter 7 Liquidation**	**Chapter 11 Reorganization**	**Chapter 12 Adjustment of Debts**	**Chapter 13 Adjustment of Debts**
Eligible Debtors	Individuals, partnerships, and corporations *except* municipal corporations, railroads, insurance companies, banks, and savings and loan associations. Farmers and ranchers are eligible only if they petition voluntarily.	Generally same as Chapter 7 except a railroad may be a debtor, and a stockbroker and commodity broker may not be a debtor under Chapter 11.	Family farmer with regular income, at least 50 percent of which comes from farming, and less than $1.5 million in debts, at least 80 percent of which is farm related.	Individuals with regular income with liquidated unsecured debts less than $250,000 and secured debts of less than $750,000.
Initiation of Proceeding	Petition by debtor (voluntary). Petition by creditors (involuntary).	Petition by debtor (voluntary). Petition by creditors (involuntary).	Petition by debtor.	Petition by debtor.
Basic Procedure	1. Appointment of trustee. 2. Debtor retains exempt property. 3. Nonexempt property is sold and proceeds distributed based on priority of claims. 4. Dischargeable debts are terminated.	1. Appointment of trustee and committees of creditors and equity security holders. 2. Debtor submits reorganization plan. 3. If plan is approved and implemented, debts are discharged.	1. Trustee is appointed but debtor usually remains in possession of farm. 2. Debtor submits a plan in which unsecured creditors must receive at least liquidation value. 3. If plan is approved and fulfilled, debtor is entitled to a discharge.	1. Debtor indicates in petition that he is seeking a composition of debts or an extension. 2. If plan is approved after submitted to creditors, then trustee is appointed. 3. If plan is approved and fulfilled, debts covered by plan are discharged.
Advantages	After liquidation and distribution of assets, most or all of debts may be discharged and debtor gets a fresh start.	Debtor remains in business and debts are liquidated through implementation of approved reorganization plan.	Debtor generally remains in possession and has opportunity to work out of financial difficulty over period of time (usually three years) through approved plan.	Debtor has opportunity to work out of financial difficulty over period of time (usually three years) through implementation of approved plan.

.... *QUESTIONS AND PROBLEM CASES* ....

1. What are the primary purposes of the Bankruptcy Act?

2. Suppose you are the creditor of a debtor who is involved in straight bankruptcy (liquidation) proceedings. Would you be best off if your claim were (1) covered by a perfected security interest in collateral of the debtor, (b) based on a claim for wages, or (c) unsecured? Explain.

3. Suppose a friend of yours is insolvent and asks for your assistance in choosing between filing for straight bankruptcy (liquidation) under Chapter 7 and filing under Chapter 13. What would you tell your friend are the major differences between the two kinds of proceedings?

4. Troy Griffin was a debtor in a Chapter 7 bankruptcy proceeding. He claimed that his 1985 Hobie Magnum sailboat was exempt from his creditors under a Texas statute that provided an exemption for "athletic and sporting" equipment. A creditor objected to the claim of exemption. Should the sailboat be considered athletic and sporting equipment and thus exempt from the claims of the debtor's creditors?

5. William Kranich, Jr., was the sole shareholder in the DuVal Financial Corporation (DFC). On November 10, 1981, Kranich filed a voluntary petition for relief under Chapter 7; on January 6, 1982, DFC also filed a voluntary petition under Chapter 7. Prior to the commencement of the Chapter 7 proceedings, Kranich conveyed his personal residence in Clearwater, Florida, to DFC. The transfer was wholly without consideration. Shortly thereafter, DFC transferred the property to William Kranich III and June Elizabeth Kranich, Kranich's son and daughter, as tenants in common. This transfer was also without consideration. The Bankruptcy Trustee brought suit to recover the property from the son and daughter on the grounds that the transfer was fraudulent. Could the trustee recover the property on the grounds that its transfer, without consideration, was fraudulent?

6. David Hott was a college graduate with a degree in business administration who was employed as an insurance agent. He and his wife graduated from college in 1986. At the time he graduated, Hott had outstanding student loans of $14,500 for which he was given a grace period before he had to repay them. Hott became unemployed. Bills began to accumulate, and a number of his outstanding bills were near the credit limits on his accounts. About that time, he received a promotional brochure by mail from Signal Consumer Discount Company, offering the opportunity to borrow several thousand dollars. The Hotts decided it appeared to be an attractive vehicle for them to use to consolidate their debts. Hott went to the Signal office and filled out a credit application. He did not list the student loan as a current debt. He later claimed that someone in the office told him he didn't have to list it if he owned an automobile but there was significant doubt about the credibility of this claim. Had he listed it, he would not have met the debt–income ratio required by Signal, and it would not have made the loan. As it was, Signal agreed to make the loan on the condition Hott pay off a car debt in order to reduce his debt–income ratio and Hott agreed to do so. On March 30, 1987, Signal loaned the Hotts $3,458.01. On June 24, 1988, the Hotts filed for bankruptcy. Signal objected to discharge of the balance remaining on its loan on the ground it had been obtained through the use of a materially false financial statement. Was discharge of the debt barred on the ground it had been obtained through the use of a materially false financial statement?

7. Brian Scholz was involved in an automobile collision with a person insured by The Travelers Insurance Company. At the time, Scholz was cited for, and plead no contest to, a criminal charge of driving under the influence of alcohol arising out of the accident. Travelers paid its insured $4,303.68 and was subrogated to the rights of its insured against Scholz. Subsequently, Travelers filed a civil action against Scholz to recover the amount it paid, and a default judgment was entered against Scholz. Eleven months later, Scholz sought relief from the bankruptcy court by filing a voluntary petition under Chapter 7. One of the questions in the bankruptcy proceeding was whether the debt owing to Travelers was nondischargeable. Is the debt dischargeable?

8. Bryant filed a Chapter 7 petition on January 7, 1984. On March 8, she filed an application to reaffirm an indebtedness owed to General Motors Acceptance Corporation (GMAC) on her 1980 Cadillac automobile. Bryant was not married, and she supported two teenage daughters. She was not currently employed, and she collected $771 a month in unemployment benefits and $150 a month in rental income from her mother. Her monthly house payments were $259. The present value of the Cadillac was $9,175; she owed $7,956.37 on it, and her monthly payments were $345.93. Bryant indicated that she wanted to keep the

vehicle because it was reliable. GMAC admitted that Bryant had been, and continued to be, current in her payments. GMAC said that the car was in no danger of being repossessed but that, absent reaffirmation, it might decide to repossess it. Under the law at the time, permission of the court was required for a reaffirmation agreement. Should the court grant Bryant's petition to reaffirm her indebtedness to GMAC?

9. John and Christine Newsom were noncommissioned officers in the U.S. Air Force who each earned $1,408 net a month. In October 1986, they filed a voluntary petition in bankruptcy under Chapter 7. At the time, they had three secured debts totaling $21,956, $21,820 of which stemmed from the purchase of a 1986 Ford Bronco and a 1985 Pontiac Trans Am. They proposed to surrender the Bronco and a secured television set to the trustee, leaving on the secured debt, $10,000, owing only the Pontiac. Their unsecured debts totaled $20,911: $6,611 from bank card use, $12,764 from retail credit, and $1,350 from credit union loans. Of the unsecured debt, $11,563 was incurred in 1986. The Newsoms filed an income and expense schedule showing that their monthly expenses totaled $2,232, including $100 for recreation and $150 for cigarettes and "walking around money." This left a surplus of $276 a month. The Bankruptcy Court, on its own motion, issued an order to the Newsoms to show why their petition should not be dismissed pursuant to the substantial abuse provision of the Bankruptcy Code. Should the Chapter 7 petition be dismissed as a substantial abuse of the provisions of the Bankruptcy Act?

10. Winifred Doersam was the borrower on three student loans made to her by First Federal Savings and Loan and guaranteed by the state of Ohio Student Loan Commission (OSLC) totaling $10,000 to finance her graduate education at the University of Dayton. Doersam also signed as the cosigner for a $5,000 student loan for her daughter, also made by First Federal and guaranteed by OSLC. With the use of the loans, she was able to obtain a position as a systems analyst with NCR Corporation, which required her to obtain a master's degree in order to retain her position at an annual salary of $24,000. Approximately six weeks before her graduation, and before the first payment on her student loans was due, Doersam filed a petition and plan under Chapter 13. In her plan, she proposed to pay $375 a month to her unsecured creditors over a 36-month period. Doersam's total unsecured debt was $18,418, 81 percent of which was comprised of the outstanding student loans. Her schedules provided for payment of rent of $300 per month and food of $400 per month. Her listed dependents included her 23-year-old daughter and her 1-year-old granddaughter. At the time, her daughter was employed in the Ohio Work Program, a program designed to help welfare recipients, for which she was paid a small salary. The OLSC objected to the plan proposed by Doersam on the grounds that it was filed in bad faith. Should the bankruptcy court refuse to confirm the plan on the grounds it was not filed in good faith?

P A R T I X

Government Regulation

CHAPTER 43

Government Regulation
of Business

Santa Ana, California, passed an ordinance prohibiting people from camping and/or storing personal possessions on public streets and other public property. The law was challenged as being a denial of equal protection because it punished people merely because of their involuntary status of being homeless. The California supreme court, using rational basis analysis rather than strict scrutiny, upheld the ordinance.[1]

- *What is equal protection? What safeguards does it offer?*
- *What is rational basis analysis? How does it differ from strict scrutiny?*
- *How do courts determine which type of constitutional analysis to use?*

---

[1]Tobe v. Santa Ana, 892 P.2d 1145 (Cal. Sup. Ct. 1995).

INTRODUCTION

The Industrial Revolution changed the nature of American society. Before the Civil War, more than 80 percent of Americans were self-employed, and the small proprietorship was the dominant form of business organization. Many forms of organization were objects of public distrust. Labor unions were treated as criminal conspiracies, and even corporations were viewed with some suspicion.

The growth of corporate power and the abusive activities of the large industrial combines and trusts after the Civil War became subjects of major public concern, producing a public outcry for federal action. Congress responded by passing the Interstate Commerce Act in 1887 and the Sherman Antitrust Act (discussed in detail in Chapter 44) in 1890.

In addition, life was becoming more complex. New forms of human activity that presented a need for regulation were (and are today) arising on an almost daily basis. Ever-expanding scientific knowledge also continued to increase our understanding of the effects of our behavior on each other and on the environment.

This tremendous growth of government regulation, while it has no doubt produced many positive social benefits, has also produced considerable public dissatisfaction. We all regularly hear complaints about government "red tape" and bureaucratic inefficiency. Some commentators argue that the costs associated with complying with government regulations are a major contributor to spiraling inflation. Others complain that operating a business is becoming more and more difficult in an environment of increasing and sometimes conflicting regulations. Regulatory agencies are criticized as being inefficient and overzealous on the one hand and "captive" tools of industry on the other.

Despite current popular disenchantment with regulation, however, it is probably fair to say that regulation is here to stay. Today we are witnessing a "deregulation" movement aimed at reducing numerous "friendly" regulations that in the past operated to shield some businesses from the forces of competition. In other areas conflicting or overlapping regulations may need to be reworked. Nonetheless, as long as the United States continues to be a highly complex and industrialized society, regulation will be an important fact of life.

STATE REGULATION OF BUSINESS

STATE POWER

State governments have very broad powers. They have the power to tax, to own and operate businesses, and to take private property for public purposes by the power of eminent domain. They also have broad "police powers" to legislate to promote the health, safety, and general welfare of their citizens.

The states retain the exclusive power to regulate **intrastate commerce**—economic activities that have no significant effect on commerce outside their own borders. Their power to regulate **interstate commerce** (commerce among the states) is limited because the Commerce Clause of the U.S. Constitution gives the federal government the power to regulate commerce "with foreign nations" and "among the several states." This, combined with the Supremacy Clause of the Constitution, which holds federal laws superior to state laws in cases of conflict, restricts the states' powers.

FEDERAL PREEMPTION

The federal government has the exclusive right to regulate all **foreign commerce** of the United States and all aspects of interstate commerce when there is an essential need for nationwide regulation. Thus, if Congress enacts valid legislation dealing with foreign or interstate commerce and state law conflicts with that legislation, the state law will be unconstitutional. In such cases, the state law is said to be **expressly preempted.** State legislation may also be preempted when Congress has demonstrated an intent to exclusively regulate an entire regulatory area. Accordingly, pervasive regulation of an activity by the federal government may prevent state regulation through **implied preemption.**

CROSBY V. NATIONAL FOREIGN TRADE COUNCIL
530 U.S. 363 (U.S. Sup.Ct. 2000)

FACTS

In response to numerous human rights violations perpetrated by the government of Burma (Myanmar), Massachusetts adopted a statute generally barring state entities from buying goods or services from any person (defined to include a business organization) identified on a restricted purchase list of those doing business with that country. The restricted list includes any business (domestic or foreign) that either is currently doing business in Burma or transacts such business at some future date. Although the state statute has no general provision for waiver or termination of its ban, it does exempt from the boycott any entities present in Burma solely to report the news or to provide international telecommunications goods or services or medical supplies. Three months later, Congress passed a statute (the Burma Act) imposing a set of mandatory and conditional sanctions on Burma. This federal law has five basic parts. First, it imposes sanctions directly on Burma. Second, it authorizes the President to impose additional sanctions subject to certain conditions. This second section makes clear that the sanctions apply only to U.S. persons or businesses and new investment in Burma; foreign businesses or U.S. companies already doing business there are exempt from its coverage. Third, the statute directs the President to work to develop a comprehensive, multilateral strategy to bring democracy to and improve human rights practices and quality of life in Burma. The fourth section requires the President to periodically report to Congress any progress toward democratization and better living conditions in Burma. Under the fifth part of the federal act, the President is authorized to waive, temporarily or permanently, any sanctions under

the law if he determines and certifies to Congress that the application of such sanction would be contrary to the national security interests of the United States. National Foreign Trade Council, a nonprofit corporation representing many companies doing business in Burma, challenged the constitutionality of the Massachusetts statute. Specifically, they argued that it was preempted by the federal Burma Act.

ISSUE

Is the Massachusetts statute preempted by the federal Burma Act?

DECISION

Yes. A fundamental principle of the Constitution is that Congress has the power to preempt state law. Even without an express provision for preemption, we have found that state law must yield to a congressional Act in at least two circumstances. When Congress intends federal law to "occupy the field," state law in that area is preempted. Even if Congress has not occupied the field, state law is naturally preempted to the extent to which it conflicts with a federal statute. We will find preemption where it is impossible for a private party to comply with both state and federal law and where, under the circumstances of the case, the challenged state law stands as an obstacle to the accomplishment and execution of the full purposes and objectives of Congress. What is a sufficient obstacle is a matter of judgment, to be informed by examining the federal statute as a whole and identifying its purpose and intended effects. Applying this standard, we see the state law as an obstacle to the accomplishment

(continued)

CROSBY V. NATIONAL FOREIGN TRADE COUNCIL
(concluded)

of Congress's full objectives under the federal Burma Act. We find that the state law undermines the intended purpose and natural effect of at least three provisions of the federal statute, that is, its delegation of effective discretion to the President to control economic sanctions against Burma, its limitation of sanctions solely to U.S. persons and new investment, and its directive to the President to proceed diplomatically in developing a comprehensive, multilateral strategy towards Burma. The federal statute places the President in a position with as much discretion to exercise economic leverage against Burma as is necessary to ensure our national security. It is just this plentitude of Executive authority that we think controls the issue of preemption here. It is simply implausible that Congress would have gone to such lengths to empower the President if it had been willing to compromise his effectiveness by deference to every provision of state statute or local ordinance that might, if enforced, blunt the consequences of discretionary Presidential action. Congress manifestly intended to limit economic pressure against the Burmese Government to a specific range. This shows that Congress calibrated its Burma policy in a deliberate effort to steer a middle path. The Massachusetts law sets a different course and conflicts with federal law at a number of points by penalizing individuals and conduct that Congress has explicitly exempted or excluded from sanctions. The state law imposes costs on most companies that do any business

in Burma. It thus penalizes businesses with preexisting investments or affiliates, all of which lie beyond the reach of the federal Act's restrictions on new investments. The state Act, moreover, imposes restrictions on foreign companies as well as domestic, whereas the federal Act limits its reach to U.S. persons. Finally, the state Act is at odds with the President's intended authority to speak for the United States among the world's nations in developing a comprehensive, multilateral strategy to bring democracy to and improve human rights practices and the quality of life in Burma. In response to the passage of the Massachusetts statute, a number of this country's trading allies and trading partners filed formal protests with the U.S. government. The European Union and Japan have gone a step further by lodging formal complaints against the U.S. in the World Trade Organization, claiming that the state Act violates certain provisions of the Agreement on Government procurement (an international treaty to which the U.S. is a party). While the Massachusetts' sanctions on Burma were adopted in pursuit of a noble goal, the restoration of democracy in Burma, these measures also risk souring our relations with key allies. This evidence in combination is more than sufficient to show that the state Act stands as an obstacle in addressing the congressional obligation to devise comprehensive, multilateral strategy. Accordingly, the state Act is preempted, and its application is unconstitutional, under the Supremacy Clause.

CONCEPT SUMMARY	The Balance between Federal and State Power
Exclusive Federal Power	Foreign commerce. Interstate commerce where there is a need for national uniformity. Interstate commerce where there is a federal statute preempting the area.

Concurrent Power	States may regulate incidental, not direct, aspects of interstate commerce if:
	   The state is furthering a legitimate local interest.
	   There is no discrimination against interstate commerce in favor of local commerce.
	   The costs to interstate commerce do not exceed the benefits to local health, safety, and welfare.

Exclusive State Power	Purely local (intrastate) functions. Recent decisions have cast great doubt on the continued viability of this restriction on federal power.

DORMANT COMMERCE CLAUSE

The Commerce Clause in the U.S. Constitution has two dimensions. First, as well be discussed in the next section, it is an affirmative grant of power to the federal government. Second, however, it has a negative sweep as well. Specifically, in what may be described as its "negative" or "dormant" aspect, the Commerce Clause limits the authority of the states to interfere with the flow of interstate commerce in two ways" (1) it prohibits discrimination directly aimed at interstate commerce and (2) it prohibits state legislation that unduly burdens interstate commerce.

Accordingly, the states are free to regulate aspects of interstate commerce that have not been preempted by the federal government as long as their efforts do not run afoul of the negative commerce clause. Four factors generally are considered in determining the validity of state legislation under this analysis. To be constitutional, the state statute must (1) further a legitimate state interest (2) not discriminate in favor of local interests and against out-of-state interests (3) allow only incidental, not direct, regulation of interstate commerce and (4) not impose costs on interstate commerce that are more excessive than necessary to bring about the state interests.

Washington v. Heckel
24 P.3d 404 (Wash. Sup.Ct. 2001)

Facts

As early as February 1996, Jason Heckel, an Oregon resident doing business as Natural Instincts, began sending unsolicited commercial e-mail, or spam, over the Internet. In 1997, Heckel developed a 46-page online booklet entitled, "How to Profit from the Internet." It described how to set up an online promotional business, acquire free e-mail accounts, and obtain software for sending bulk e-mail. Heckel marketed the booklet by sending between 100,000 and 1,000,000 unsolicited e-mail messages per week. To acquire the large volume of e-mail addresses, Heckel used the Extractor Pro software program, which harvests e-mail addresses from various online sources and enables a spammer to direct a bulk-mail message to those addresses by entering a simple command. The Extractor Pro program requires the spammer to enter a return e-mail address, a subject line, and the text of the message to be sent. The text of Heckel's message was a lengthy sale pitch that included testimonials from satisfied purchasers and culminated in an order form that the recipient could download and print. The order form included the Salem, Oregon, mailing address for Natural Instincts. The Consumer Protection Divison of the Washington State Attorney General's Office received complaints from Washington recipients of Heckel's unsolicited e-mail. They alleged that his messages contained misleading subject lines and false transmission paths. The Consumer Protection Division immediately notified Heckel that Washington State law made it illegal to use a third-party's domain name without permission, misrepresent or disguise in any other

way the message's point of origin or transmission path, or use a misleading subject line. Despite this warning, Heckel continued to send his unsolicited commercial e-mails using misleading subject lines, false or unusable return e-mail addresses, and false or misleading transmission paths. Finally, the state sued Heckel for civil damages and asked for a permanent injunction against his business practices. In response, Heckel argued that the Washington statue violated the Commerce Clause.

Issue

Does the Washington Statute unconstitutionally burden interstate commerce?

Decision

No. The Commerce Clause grants the Congress the power to regulate commerce with foreign nations and among the several states. Implicit in this affirmative grant is the negative or "dormant" Commerce Clause—the principle that the states impressibly intrude on this federal power when they enact laws that unduly burden interstate commerce. Analysis of a state law under the dormant Commerce Clause generally follows a two-step process. We first determine whether the state law openly discriminates against interstate commerce in favor of intrastate economic interest. If the law is facially neutral, applying impartially to in-state and out-of-state businesses, the analysis moves to the second step, a balancing of the local benefits against the interstate burdens. Where the state statute regulates evenhandedly

(continued)

WASHINGTON V. HECKEL
(concluded)

to effectuate legitimate local public interst, and its effects on interstate commerce are only incidental, it will be upheld unless the burden on interstate commerce is clearly excessive in relation to the putative local benefits. If a legitimate local purpose is found, then the question becomes one of degree. And the extent of the burden that will be tolerated will of course depend on the nature of the local interest involved, and whether it could be promoted with a lesser impact on interstate activities. The Washington law is not facially discriminatory. It applies evenhandedly to in-state and out-of-state spammers. Further, its local benefits surpass any alleged burden on interstate commerce. It protects the interests of three groups—Internet service providers, actual owners of forged domain names, and e-mail users. Heckel's activities, by disguising the origin of his messages, evades the service provider's filters, thereby draining the processing power of the provider's computer equipment. Further, the owners of the impermissibly used domain names and e-mail addresses suffer economic harm. For example, the registered owner of one such name alleged that his computer was shut down for three days by 7,000 responses to the bulk-mail message in which his address was forged into the spam's header. Finally, deceptive spam harms individual Internet users as well. When a spammer distorts the point of origin or transmission path of the message, e-mail recipients cannot promptly and effectively respond to the message (and thereby opt out of future mailings); their efforts to respond take time, cause frustration, and compound the problems that service providers face in delivering and storing messages.

This cost-shifting—from deceptive spammers to businesses and e-mail users—has been likened to sending junk mail with postage due. We thus recognize that the Washington statute serves the legitimate local purpose of banning the cost-shifting inherent in the sending of deceptive spam. To be weighted against the statute's local benefits, the only burden it places on spammers is the requirement of truthfulness, a requirement that does not burden commerce at all but actually facilitates it by eliminating fraud and deception. We therefore conclude that Heckel has failed to prove that the burden imposed on commerce by the state law is clearly excessive in relation to the putative local benefits. Drawing on two unsettled and poorly understood aspects of the dormant Commerce Clause analysis, Heckel contended the statute created inconsistency among the states and regulated conduct occurring wholly outside of Washington. However, this statute survives both inquiries. First, while 17 other states have passed legislation regulating electronic solicitations, the truthfulness requirements of the Washington statute do not conflict with any of the requirements in the other states' statutes, and it is inconceivable that any state would ever pass a law requiring spammers to use misleading subject lines or transmission paths. Nor does the statue violate the extraterritoriality principle in the dormant Commerce Clause analysis. Here, there is no sweeping extraterritorial effect that would outweigh the local benefits of the statute. The state law addresses the conduct of spammers in targeting Washington consumers.

FEDERAL REGULATION OF BUSINESS

Early interpretations of the Commerce Clause focused primarily on its negative power to restrict state regulation of interstate commerce. With the increase in federal regulation that followed the Civil War, the courts tended to focus on the Commerce Clause as a limitation on the federal government's power to regulate business. Federal statutes were invalidated on the ground that they were not sufficiently related to interstate commerce.

Later decisions took a broader view of the Commerce Clause, recognizing federal power to regulate activities that have a "substantial relationship" to interstate commerce. In today's highly interdependent economy, most important economic activity is within the reach of federal regulation under the current expansive view of the Commerce Clause. However, as the following case indicates, there are limits on that authority.

UNITED STATES v. MORRISON
529 U.S. 598 (U.S. Sup.Ct. 2000)

FACTS

On the evening of September 21, 1994, Christy Brzonkala and another female student met two men they know only by their first names and their status as members of the Virginia Tech football team. Within 30 minutes of first meeting Brzonkala, these two men, later identified as Antonio Morrison and James Crawford, raped her. It was not until February 1995, however, that Brzonkaly was able to identify Morrison and Crawford as the two men who had raped her. She then filed a complaint against them under Virigina Tech's Sexual Assault Policy. The Virginia Tech judicial committee found insufficient evidence to take action against Crawford but found Morrison guilty of sexual assault. He was suspended for two semesters. However, Senior Vice-President and Provost Peggy Meszaros overturned the penalty and deferred his suspension until after his graduation from Virginia Tech. As a result, Morrison was able to return to Virginia Tech on a full athletic scholarship. Brzonkala then filed suit against Morrison and Crawford, alleging that they brutally raped her because of gender animus in violation of Title III of the *Violence Against Women Act* (VAWA). That federal statute was designed to address the excalating problem of violent crime against women by establishing a right upon which a civil claim can be brought by victims of crimes of violence motivated by gender. The government, joined by Brzonkala, defended the federal statute as an appropriate exercise of Congress's power to regulate interstate commerce on the ground that violence against women is a widespread social problem with ultimate effects on the national economy. Morrison argued that the statue was beyond congressional authority and thus unconstitutional.

ISSUE

Did Congress exceed its power under the Commerce Clause when it enacted the VAWA?

DECISION

Yes. Due respect for the decisions of a coordinate branch of government demands that we invalidate a congressional enactment only upon a plain showing that Congress has exceeded its constitutional bounds. Our interpretation of the Commerce Clause, upon which this federal statute is grounded, has changed as our nation has developed. Thus, today Congress has considerably greater latitude in regulating conduct and transactions under the Commerce Clause than it did during our nation's early history. However, even under our modern, expansive interpretation of the Commerce Clause, Congress' regulatory authority is not without effective bounds. Modern Commerce Clause jurisprudence has identified three broad categories of activity that Congress may regulate under its commerce power. First, Congress may regulate the use of the channels of interstate commerce. Second, Congress is empowered to regulate and protect the instrumentalities of interstate commerce, or persons or things in interstate commerce, even though the threat may come only from intrastate activities. Finally, Congress' Commerce Clause authority includes the power to regulate those activities having a substantial relation to interstate commerce (i.e., those activities that substantially affect interstate commerce). It is not contended that this statute falls within either of the first two of these categories of Commerce Clause regulations. Instead, Brzonkala and the government seek to sustain the VAWA as a regulation of activity that substantially affects interstate commerce. To meet this standard, the federal statute mush have something to do with "commerce" or some sort of economic enterprise. Historically, our decisions have held that where economic activity substantially affects interstate commerce, federal legislation regulating that activity will be sustained. Yet, gender-motivated crimes of violence are not, in any sense of the phrase, economic activity. Further, the VAWA contains no jurisdictional element establishing that the federal cause of action is in anyway in pursuance of Congress' power to regulate interstate commerce. Instead, the statute's remedy is case over a wider, and more purely intrastate, body of violent crime. The VAWA is supported by numerous congressional findings regarding the serious impact that gender-motivated violence has on victims and their families. But the existence of congressional findings is not sufficient, by itself, to sustain the constitutionality of Commerce Clause legislation. Rather, whether particular operations affect interstate commerce sufficiently to come under the constitutional power of Congress to regulate them is ultimately a

(continued)

UNITED STATES V. MORRISON
(concluded)

judicial rather than a legislative question, and can be settled finally only by this Court. Congress found that gender-motivated violence affects interstate commerce by deterring potential victims from traveling interstate or from engaging in employment in interstate business. Yet, this type of reasoning would allow Congress to regulate any crime and thereby completely obliterate the Constitution's distinction between national and local authority. We accordingly reject the argument that Congress may regulate noneconomic, violent criminal conduct based solely on that conduct's aggregate effect on interstate commerce. The Constitution requires a distinction between what is truly national and what is truly local. In recognizing this fact we preserve one of the few principles that has been consistent since the Commerce Clause was adopted. The regulation and punishment of intrastate violence that is not directed at the instrumentalities, channels, or goods involved in interstate commerce has always been the province of the States. Brzonkala's complaint alleges that she was the victim of a brutal assault. But Congress' effort in the VAWA to provide a federal civil remedy cannot be sustained under the Commerce Clause. No civilized system of justice should fail to provide her a remedy for the conduct of Morrison. But under our federal system that remedy must be provided by Virginia, and not by the United States.

CONSTITUTIONAL CHECKS ON GOVERNMENTAL POWER

STATE ACTION

Certain constitutional checks on governmental power apply to both Congress and the states. These protections are included in the various amendments to the Constitution. However, the Constitution protects the individual only against "governmental" activity, usually called **state action.** As a result, unless such interference is prohibited by statute, private deprivation of individual liberties is permitted. In determining whether state action exists, and therefore whether the constitutional checks apply, courts examine the degree of governmental involvement in the challenged activity.

THE TAKINGS CLAUSE

The U.S. Constitution, in both the Fifth and the Fourteenth Amendments, prohibits the government (federal, state, and local) from taking real or personal property for public use without paying just compensation. This *Takings Clause* is triggered by the power of **eminent domain,** whereby the government forces private property holders to sell their land so it may be dedicated to public use. The Takings Clause has three primary components: (1) there must be a taking (2) it must be for a public purpose and (3) the private property owner is then entitled to just compensation.

Taking

Not every governmental interference with property ownership constitutes a taking. For example, the zoning ordinance enacted by many cities and counties interfere with a landowner's use of the property. However, because the interference is limited, no compensation is required. Of course, if the government physically invades the property or, in some other manner, greatly limits its value or usefulness to the owner, a taking has occurred and compensation must be paid. Anytime a landowner is denied all economically beneficial use of the property, a compensable taking has occurred.

Public Use

The government may not constitutionally take someone's property unless it is for a public purpose. These might include seizing land to build highways, water control projects, or some type of public building. The public purpose is not always so clear. For instance, in many cases cities have used their power of eminent domain in furtherance of an urban renewal project. This certainly may be a permissible public use. However, if the city turns the land over to private developers who profit fro the enterprise, the taking may well be unconstitutional.

Just Compensation

In the case of a zoning ordinance in which no taking has occurred, the government need not compensate the property owner despite the inconvenience caused by the governmental action. However, when an actual taking for public use does occur, the government must provide just compensation to the dispossessed landowner. Generally, this entails calculating the fair market value of the property involved in the taking. Of course, this does not provide complete satisfaction for many property owners. They frequently argue that the fair market value is insufficient because it fails to properly consider goodwill or future profits or that disregards peoples' emotional attachments to their land.

PHILIP MORRIS V. REILLY
267 F.3d 45 (1st Cir. 2001)

FACTS

Since the late 1970s, when consumers began demanding cigarettes with lower tar and nicotine levels, the cigarette manufacturers have increased the number of additives, other than tobacco, in their products, ostensibly to offset the lost flavor and taste. Today manufacturers report using approximately 700 additives, many of which are the focus of public health officials' concern. Each brand contains a combination of ingredients that substantially contributes to its distinctiveness and thus its competitive success. As such a formula gives a manufacturer a competitive advantage over other manufacturers who cannot, given the current state of the technology, mimic it, the manufacturers have invested many millions of dollars in creating their distinctive blends and take extensive precautions to protect the identity of the ingredients from disclosure. In 1996, Massachusetts enacted the Tobacco Ingredients and Nicotine Yield Act (the Disclosure Act), which requires each cigarette manufacturer to provide the Massachusetts Department of Public Health (DPH) with an annual report listing, for each brand, the identity of any added constituent in descending order according to weight, measure, or numerical count. It further provides that both the brand's ingredient list and nicotine yield rating shall become a public record if two conditions are met. First, the DPH must determine that there is a reasonable scientific basis for concluding that the availability of such information could reduce risks to public health. Second, the state's Attorney General must advise the DPH that the public release of the information would not constitute an unconstitutional taking of property. The Disclosure Act was enacted to enable the DPH to study the additives to determine whether they present health risks and, if the requirements for public disclosure are met, to inform consumers of such findings. Philip Morris and the other major cigarette manufacturers filed this action claiming that the Disclosure Act ran afoul of the Takings Clause. Specifically, Philip Morris complained that the ingredient-reporting provisions of the Disclosure Act would effect an uncompensated taking of its trade secrets.

(continued)

PHILIP MORRIS V. REILLY
(concluded)

ISSUE

Do the disclosure provisions of the law constitute an uncompensated taking of the manufacturer's trade secrets?

DECISION

No. There are two prongs of takings jurisprudence: *per se* (or categorical) takings and regulatory takings. Government action categorically violates the Takings Clause if it results in the permanent physical occupation of property or if it denies the owner all economically beneficial use of his property. In these instances, known as *per se* takings, just compensation is required, no matter how minor the invasion or how great the public purpose served by the regulation. In contrast, in noncategorical regulatory takings cases, courts must engage in an ad hoc, factual inquiry to determine whether the government regulation goes too far. In examining if there has been a *per se* taking, we first observe that the cases addressing land use regulations are inapposite. Landowners do not expect that the government will eliminate all economically valuable use of land without some form of compensation. This is not always the case with personal property, where owners have long recognized that new regulations may from time to time render their personal property economically worthless. An essential rationale in the *per se* takings cases is to bar the government from forcing some people alone to bear public burdens which, in all fairness and justice, should be borne by the public as a whole. Here, because the cigarette manufacturers are not asked to bear a burden that should instead be borne by Massachusetts citizens, this rationale has no relevance to the Disclosure Act. Another type of categorical taking occurs where the government denies all economically beneficial or productive use of the property. While a complete seizure of personal property may

amount to a categorical taking, we cannot conclude that the regulation of personal property which may be destructive of the value of trade secret information can be regarded as such a taking. Rather, the Disclosure Act establishes a regulatory scheme conditioning the ability to sell tobacco products in Massachusetts on the reporting for potential public disclosure of trade secret information, deemed by the legislature to serve the interest of public health. Thus, in our view, the Disclosure Act does not result in a categorical taking. We therefore turn to consideration of whether it is a regulatory taking. There are three factors to take into account in determining whether government action has gone beyond regulation and effects a taking: the character of the government action, its economic impact, and its interference with reasonable investment-backed expectations. The power of Massachusetts to regulate the marketing of tobacco products is beyond argument, particularly given that they have long been the source of public concern and the subject of government regulation. Thus, the condition that the right to continue to sell cigarettes cannot be conditioned on disclosure of trade secret information will not wash. The right of a manufacturer to maintain secrecy as to its compounds and processes must be held subject to the right of the state, in the exercise of its police power, to require that the nature of the product be fairly set forth. Such disclosure is indisputably rational where, as here, there is general concern regarding the health effects of tobacco additives. Accordingly, we conclude that the Disclosure Act, requiring manufacturers who market tobacco products in Massachusetts to report for potential public , disclosure the constituents for each brand—information the manufacturers treat as trade secrets—is a valid exercise of the police power and does not effect an unconstitutional taking.

THE DUE PROCESS CLAUSE

Historically, among the most important of the constitutional restraints on governmental power have been the Due Process Clauses of the Fifth and Fourteenth Amendments. The Fifth Amendment Due Process Clause prohibits the federal government from depriving any person "of life, liberty, or property, without due process of law." The Fourteenth Amendment applies the same standard to the states. Corporations have long been considered "persons" protected by these constitutional guaranties.

FIGURE 43–1   Procedural Due Process

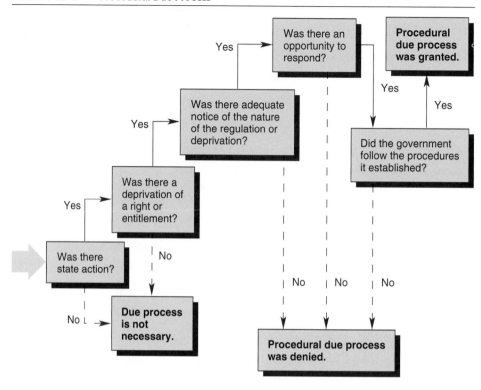

Procedural Due Process

As originally interpreted, the Due Process Clause was viewed as a guarantee of **procedural due process.** This meant that the government could accomplish its objectives only by following fair procedures. Reasonable notice, the right to a hearing before an impartial tribunal, and adherence to any established procedures were required whenever the government interfered with the rights of people. (See Figure 43–1.)

NATIONAL COUNCIL OF RESISTANCE OF IRAN v. ALBRIGHT
251 F.3d 192 (D.C. Cir. 2001)

FACTS

The National Council of Resistance of Iran (NCRI) was designated by the U.S. Secretary of State, Madeleine K. Albright, as a "foreign terrorist organization" under the Anti-Terrorism and Effective Death Penalty Act (AEDPA). Under that federal statute, the Secretary of State is empowered to make such a designation. The consequences of the designation are dire. It results in blocking any funds which the organization has on deposit with any financial institution in the United States. Representatives and certain members of the organization are barred from entry into the United States. Perhaps most importantly, all persons within or subject to the jurisdiction of the United States are forbidden from knowingly providing material support or resources to the organizaton. Despite the seriousness of consequences of the determination, the administrative process by which the Secretary makes it is a truncated one. In part, the AEDPA requires the Secretary to compile an administrative record and based upon that record to make findings. If she makes the critical findings that an entity is a foreign organization engaging in terror-

(continued)

NATIONAL COUNCIL OF RESISTANCE OF IRAN V. ALBRIGHT
(continued)

ist activities that threaten the national security of the United States, that entity then suffers the consequences listed above. However, at no point in the proceedings establishing the administrative record is the alleged terrorist organization afforded notice of the materials used against it, or a right to comment on such materials or the developing administrative record. Nothing in the statute forbids the use of third hand accounts, press stories, materials on the Internet, or other hearsay regarding the organization's activities. In fact, the Secretary may base the findings on classified material to which the organization has no access at any point during or after the proceeding to designate it as terrorist. Following the administrative designation, there is judicial review. But that review is quite limited. Review is based solely upon the administrative record. Granted, this is not in itself an unusual limitation for administrative reviews. However, under the AEDPA the aggrieved party has no opportunity to either add to or comment on the contents of that administrative record. Further, the record can, and generally does, encompass classified information used in making the designation as to which the alleged terrorist organization never has any access. After being designated as a terrorist organization, the NCRI argued that the Secretary's designation deprived it of constitutionally protected rights without due process of law.

ISSUE

Does the process for making foreign terrorist organization determinations deny the NCRI due process of law?

DECISION

Yes. We consider first the eligibility of the NCRI for constitutional protection. A foreign entity without property or presence in this country has no constitutional rights under the Due Process Clause or otherwise. However, the NCRI has entered the territory of the United States and established substantial connections with this country. Specifically, it has an overt presence within the National Press Building in Washington, D.C., and claims an interest in a bank account. Further, it has been deprived of a constitutional right. By being designated as a foreign terrorist organization, the NCRI is deprived of the previously held right to, for example, hold bank accounts and to receive material support or resources from anyone within

the jurisdiction of the United States. Thus, the most obvious rights to be impaired by the Secretary's designation is the NCRI's property rights. It is clear that a foreign organization that acquires or holds property in this country may invoke the protections of the Constitution when that property is placed in jeopardy by government intervention. This is not to say that the government cannot interfere with that and many other rights of foreign organizations present in the United States; it is only to say that when it does so it is subject to the Due Process Clause. The fundamental norm of due process clause jurisprudence requires that before the government can constitutionally deprive a person of the protected liberty or property interest, it must afford him notice and hearing. At the same time, the Supreme Court has made clear that due process, unlike some legal rules, is not a technical conception with a fixed content unrelated to time, place and circumstances. We have dispensed with *whether* the NCRI is entitled to due process; the questions remaining for use are *what* due process, and *when*. Specifically, we must determine what process is sufficient to afford the NCRI the protection of the Due Process Clause, and when—in terms of pre-deprivation or post deprivation—that process must be available. This requires the consideration of three distinct factors: (1) the private interests that will be affected by the official action; (2) the risk of an erroneous deprivation of such interest of the procedure used, and the probable value, if any, of additional or substitute procedural safeguards; and (3) the government's interest, including the function involved and the fiscal and administrative burdens that the additional or substitute procedural safeguards would entail. In considering each of these factors, the government has offered nothing that apparently weighs in favor of a post-deprivational as opposed to pre-deprivational compliance with due process requirements. While she raises foreign policy/national security concerns, she does not demonstrate how these interests will be compromised by affording organizations whatever due process they are due before their designation as foreign terrorist organizations. We therefore hold that the Secretary must afford the due process available to putative foreign terrorist organizations prior to the deprivation worked by the designating of that entity as such unless she can

(continued)

make a showing of particularized need. Clearly, the Secretary must afford the entities under consideration notice that the designation is impending. Upon adequate showing to the court, the Secretary may provide this notice after the designation whether earlier notification would impinge upon the security and other foreign policy goals of the United States. The notice must include the action sought, but need not disclose the classified information to be presented *in camera* to the court. There must then be some compliance with the hearing requirement of due process jurisprudence. While this may not necessitate a hearing closely approximating a judicial trial, it does require an opportunity to be heard at a meaningful time and in a meaningful manner.

Substantive Due Process

Even when the government provides procedural due process, the courts may find certain actions to be unconstitutional because they are substantively unfair. This notion, known as **substantive due process,** places a burden on the government to demonstrate that its actions are not arbitrary or unreasonable whenever it interferes with people's *fundamental* constitutional rights (speech, religion, privacy, right to vote, and so on). However, in instances in which the government interferes with only economic rights (property) the substantive due process analysis is largely neglected. Thus, as long as the government accords procedural due process, its actions will be constitutional.

Ethical Implications	The Due Process Clause insists that the government not deprive persons of life, liberty, or property without due process of law. This is a guaranty of certain standards of procedural and substantive fairness when dealing with governmental bodies. However, since due process is required only when there is "state action," most private employers do not owe their employees due process. Is it right to treat employees with less deference and respect than the Due Process Clause would require of state actors?

EQUAL PROTECTION CLAUSE

The Equal Protection Clause of the Fourteenth Amendment prohibits any state from arbitrarily discriminating against persons. The courts have interpreted the Fifth Amendment Due Process Clause as including a similar equal protection component. Thus, neither the states nor the federal government may unfairly discriminate. Note, however, that not all discrimination is unconstitutional—only that which is arbitrary or unfair. The courts use two types of analysis to determine whether governmental discrimination is unconstitutional under equal protection analysis.

Rational Basis Analysis

The Equal Protection Clause does not prohibit the government from imposing differential treatment as long as the discriminatory treatment bears a **rational basis** to a legitimate governmental purpose. Legislation involving nonfundamental (property) matters generally undergoes this rational basis analysis. And, for almost 60 years, the courts have consistently upheld discriminatory regulatory schemes as long as they only implicate economic matters.

Strict Scrutiny Analysis

When a statute denies people their fundamental constitutional rights (speech, religion, privacy, right to vote, and so on), the courts initially presume the governmental action to be unconstitutional. (This concept was introduced in the substantive due process material discussed earlier.) Similarly, when the government discriminates on the basis of a *suspect classification* (race, religion, sex, national origin, or color), the courts will require more than a mere rational relationship between the statutory ends and means. Instead, the legislation will be examined under **strict scrutiny.** Under this analysis, the statute will be declared unconstitutional unless the government demonstrates that it is achieving a *compelling governmental interest* in the *least intrusive manner*. (See Figure 43–2.)

The case described in the opening of this chapter implicated both due process and equal protection issues. Specifically, it was argued that the Santa Ana ordinance discriminated against poor people and interfered with their right to travel. If the court had used strict scrutiny analysis, it is conceivable the ordinance would have been declared unconstitutional. However, the court used rational basis analysis because it did not find there to be a fundamental right to travel. Further, it noted that statutes that impose burdens on the homeless do not implicate a suspect classification since they do not discriminate on the basis of race, religion, sex, national origin, or color. Thus, under rational basis analysis, the court upheld the ordinance because there was a rational relationship between the city's goal of maintaining its streets and public areas and its prohibition against camping in those streets and public areas.

FIGURE 43–2   Substantive Due Process/Equal Protection Analysis

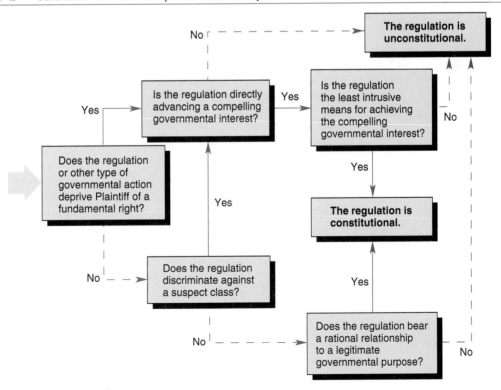

THE FIRST AMENDMENT

The First Amendment to the U.S. Constitution prohibits the government from abridging freedom of speech. Thus, speech is a fundamental right, and governmental action that limits such expression is subject to strict scrutiny analysis. However, the courts have historically distinguished between noncommercial and commercial speech when reviewing the constitutionality of governmental restrictions.

Noncommercial Speech

The courts have consistently given the highest degree of constitutional protection to **noncommercial speech** (also known as *pure* or *political speech*). Thus, governmental restrictions on noncommercial speech must undergo strict scrutiny analysis. As such, they will be upheld only if the government can show that (1) the regulation is furthering a *compelling governmental interest* and (2) the regulation is no broader than absolutely necessary (*least intrusive means*) to promote that governmental interest.

COMMERCIAL SPEECH

While constitutional safeguards have always been extended to noncommercial speech, it was long thought that **commercial speech,** such as advertising, enjoyed no First Amendment protection. However, in the mid-1970s the Supreme Court held that purely commercial speech was entitled to some constitutional protection. This protection was justified primarily by the public's interest in the free flow of accurate commercial information. Therefore, only truthful commercial speech was entitled to First Amendment protection. False, misleading, or deceptive advertising might be lawfully suppressed.

Beyond the need for commercial speech to be truthful (there is no such precondition for protection for noncommercial speech), the courts also analyze commercial speech regulations with an **intermediate scrutiny** that falls between strict scrutiny and rational basis analysis. This requires the government to establish that it has a *substantial interest* (something less than a compelling interest) and that it is *directly advancing* that interest in a manner *no more extensive than necessary* to serve that interest.

LORILLARD TOBACCO COMPANY v. REILLY
533 U.S. 525 (U.S. Sup.Ct. 2001)

FACTS

In January 1999, the Massachusetts Attorney General, Thomas E. Reilly, promulgated regulations governing the sale and advertisement of cigarettes, smokeless tobacco, and cigars. In part, the regulations place a variety of restrictions on outdoor advertising of tobacco products. They were implemented to address the incidence of tobacco use by children under legal age and to prevent access to such products by underage consumers. The regulation at issue in this case specifically prohibits tobacco advertising within a 1,000-foot radius of a school or playground. The advertising limits were challenged by a group of tobacco manufacturers and retailers. The U.S. Supreme Court ruled that the regulations, as they related to cigarette advertising, were preempted by the Federal Cigarette Labeling and Advertising Act, which prevents the states from restricting the "advertising or promotion" of cigarettes. However, because the federal statute's preemption provision does not cover smokeless tobacco or

(continued)

LORILLARD TOBACCO COMPANY V. REILLY
(continued)

cigars, the tobacco manufacturers and retailers challenged those outdoor advertising restrictions on First Amendment grounds.

ISSUE

Do the outdoor advertising restrictions violate the First Amendment?

DECISION

Yes. For over 25 years, the Court has recognized that commercial speech does not fall outside the purview of the First Amendment. Instead, the Court has afforded commercial speech a measure of First Amendment protection commensurate with its position in relation to other constitutionally guaranteed expression. In recognition of the distinction between speech proposing a commercial transaction, which occurs in an area traditionally subject to government regulation, we developed a four-part test for analyzing regulations of commercial speech. (1) At the outset, we must determine whether the expression is protected by the First Amendment. For commercial speech to come within that provision, it at least must concern lawful activity and not be misleading. (2) Next, we ask whether the asserted governmental interest is substantial. If both inquiries yield positive answers, (3) we must determine whether the regulation directly advances the governmental interest asserted, and (4) whether it is not more extensive than is necessary to serve that interest. The petitioners ask us to reject this test and apply strict scrutiny. But we see no need to break new ground. This intermediate scrutiny provides an adequate basis for our decision. Only the last two steps of the commercial speech test are at issue here. The Attorney General has stipulated that the outdoor tobacco ads are entitled to First Amendment protection. With respect to the second step, none of the petitioners contests the importance of the state's interest in preventing the use of tobacco products by minors. The third step of the commercial speech test concerns the relationship between the harm that underlies the state's interest and the means identified by the state to advance that interest. The advertising restrictions satisfy the third step as well. Our review of the record reveals that the Attorney General has provided ample documentation of the problem with underage use of smokeless tobacco and cigars. In addition, we believe there is evidence that preventing targeted campaigns and limiting youth exposure to advertising will decrease underage use of smokeless tobacco and cigars. Whatever the strength of the Attorney General's evidence to justify the outdoor advertising regulations, however, we conclude that the regulations do not satisfy the fourth step of the commercial speech analysis. This final step, the critical inquiry in this case, requires a reasonable fit between the means and ends of the regulatory scheme. These advertising limits do not meet this standard. The broad sweep of the regulations indicates that the Attorney General did not carefully calculate the costs and benefits associated with the burden on speech imposed by the regulations. By prohibiting tobacco ads within 1,000 feet of schools and playgrounds, the outdoor advertising ban would prevent advertising in 87 percent to 91 percent of the Boston area. The substantial reach of the outdoor advertising regulations is compounded by other factors. Under the regulations, "outdoor" advertising includes not only advertising located outside an establishment, but also advertising inside a store if that advertising is visible from outside the store. In some geographical areas, these regulations would constitute nearly a complete ban on the communication of truthful information about smokeless tobacco and cigars to adult consumers. The breadth and scope of the regulations, and the process by which the Attorney General adopted the regulations, do not demonstrate a careful calculation of the speech interests involved. For instance, he did not seem to consider the impact of the 1,000-foot restriction on commercial speech in metropolitan areas. Thus, the impact of the restriction on speech will vary from place to place. This demonstrates a lack of tailoring. In addition, to the extent that studies have identified particular advertising and promotion practices that appeal to youth, tailoring would involve targeting those practices while permitting others. As crafted, the regulations make no distinction among practices on this basis. The state's interest in preventing underage tobacco use is substantial, and even compelling, but it is no less true that the sale and use of tobacco products by adults is a legal activity. We must consider that tobacco retailers and manufacturers have an interest in conveying truthful information about their

(continued)

LORILLARD TOBACCO COMPANY V. REILLY
(concluded)

products to adults, and adults have a corresponding interest in receiving truthful information about tobacco products. Accordingly, we conclude that the Attorney General has failed to show that the outdoor advertising regulations for smokeless tobacco and cigars are not more extensive than necessary to advance the state's substantial interest in preventing underage tobacco use.

A careful calculation of the costs of a speech regulation does not mean that a state must demonstrate that there is no incursion on legitimate speech interests, but a speech regulation cannot unduly impinge on the speaker's ability to propose a commercial transaction and the adult listener's opportunity to obtain information about products.

ADMINISTRATIVE AGENCIES

RISE OF AGENCIES

The explosion of government regulation in this century has been accompanied, and in part aided, by another social phenomenon of great importance: the creation and widespread use of administrative agencies on both the federal and state levels. There are several reasons for this development, which some legal scholars have argued is the single most important legal development of this century. Many people who favored increased regulation of business felt that the courts and legislatures were not well suited to deal with many of the complex problems that were arising in our rapidly changing environment. They argued for the creation of specialized administrative bodies to develop a reservoir of expertise in various areas of regulation. This, it was argued, would permit the continuous and rapid development of regulatory policy without resorting to the slower, case-by-case approach followed by the courts and legislatures. Allowing such agencies to hear and judge disputes would speed up problem solving and reduce the burdens placed on our already overworked judicial system.

CHARACTERISTICS OF AGENCIES

Administrative agencies are unique in our legal system, since they are in theory part of the executive branch of government, but they also perform legislative and judicial functions. In addition to investigating and prosecuting violations of statutes and their own regulations, agencies generally have the power to issue regulations that have the force of law. They also have the power to adjudicate disputes involving alleged violations of their regulations and the statutes they are charged with enforcing.

Agency hearings are much less formal than court trials, since they never involve juries, and rules of evidence are less strictly observed. Those who are unhappy with an agency's decision must exhaust all administrative remedies before appealing the decision to a court of law. On appeal, the scope of judicial review of administrative agencies' actions is fairly limited.

LIMITS ON AGENCIES' POWERS

Agencies must conduct their affairs in accordance with basic constitutional guaranties and the various administrative procedure acts designed to restrict their actions. Due process requires that those who will be affected by agency action have advance notice of agency proceedings and the opportunity to appear at a hearing and present their views. The enabling statute that created the agency may be attacked as an unconstitutional delegation of legislative power if it does not set out adequate guidelines for agency action. In some cases, agency actions may be attached as being outside the jurisdiction of the agency as defined by the enabling statute. The courts generally do not substitute their judgment for that of an agency, even if they believe an agency's actions to be unwise. Only agency decisions that are "arbitrary and capricious" are overturned by the courts. The fact that agencies have such broad powers and are subject to such limited control is very disturbing to many people. Many people may never enter a court in their entire lifetime, but the actions of administrative agencies directly affect all our lives on a daily basis.

BREADTH OF AGENCY REGULATION

As consumers, the products we purchase, the advertising of those products, the interest rates we pay on loans, the rate we pay for utilities, and the availability and cost of public transportation are only a few of the many aspects of our lives that administrative agencies regulate. In the workplace, agencies regulate wages and hours of work, working conditions, unemployment and retirement benefits, and workers' compensation. These regulations were discussed in detail in Chapter 22. The regulation of securities by the Securities and Exchange Commission was discussed in Chapter 28.

In the marketplace, the behavior of competing firms is subject to comprehensive regulation. Chapter 44 will discuss the antitrust laws in detail. The Federal Trade Commission Act, which created one of the most active and controversial federal administrative agencies and gave it broad powers to regulate a wide variety of competitive activity, is a good example of the federal government's extensive regulation of business.

SUNDANCE ASSOCIATES V. RENO
139 F.3d 804 (10th Cir. 1998)

FACTS

Concerned about the exploitation of children by pornographers, Congress enacted the **Child Protection and Obscenity Enforcement Act,** which required producers of sexually explicit matter to maintain certain records concerning the performers that might help law enforcement agencies monitor the industry. The record-keeping requirements apply to "whoever *produces*" the material in question, and excludes from the definition of "produces" the "mere distribution or any other activity, which does not involve hiring, contracting for, managing, or otherwise arranging for the participation of the performers depicted." Pursuant to her authority to issue regulations to carry out the statutory requirements, the Attorney General issued regulations implementing the statute. Under the regulatory language, the record-keeping requirements apply to "any producer of any

book, magazine, periodical, film, videotape, or other matter that contains one or more visual depictions of actual sexually explicit conduct." The regulation includes in its definition of a "producer" any person who "produces, assembles, manufactures, publishes, duplicates, reproduces, or reissues a book, magazine, periodical, film, videotape, or other matter intended for commercial distribution that contains a visual depiction of actual sexually explicit conduct." Sundance publishes five magazines that print personal or commercial announcements by individuals seeking to contact others with similar sexual interests. The announcements typically are accompanied by pictures, most of which are sexually explicit. The pictures are submitted voluntarily to Sundance by the individuals advertising in the magazines. Sundance, therefore, does not participate in the

(continued)

SUNDANCE ASSOCIATES V. RENO
(concluded)

production of the photographs it publishes in its various magazines. Facing possible criminal liability as a "producer" under the regulation, Sundance filed a complaint alleging that the regulation's coverage was impermissibly broader than that intended by the statute.

ISSUE

Does the regulation define a "producer" more broadly than is permitted by the statute?

DECISION

Yes. When faced with a challenge to the validity of a regulation, we decide whether Congress has directly spoken to the precise question at issue. If the statute is clear and unambiguous, that is the end of the matter, for the court, as well as the agency, must give effect to the unambiguously expressed intent of Congress. The traditional deference courts pay to agency interpretation is not to be applied to alter the clearly expressed intent of Congress. If, however, the statute does not speak directly to the question at issue or is ambiguous, the court, giving considerable weight to the agency's interpretation, must decide if the agency's answer is a permissible construction of the statute. In this case, we need go no further than the initial analysis. The text and reasonable inferences from it give a clear answer against the government, and that is the end of the matter. Under the statutory scheme, the requirements do not apply to those who merely distribute or whose activity does not involve hiring, contracting for, managing, or otherwise arranging for participation of the performers depicted. The Attorney General's regulatory definition of producer fails to exclude persons from the class that the statute requires (those who have had no contact with the performers).

THE FEDERAL TRADE COMMISSION ACT

In 1914, Congress was disappointed with the efforts under the Sherman Act to control anticompetitive practices and tendencies in the American economy. One of its responses to this situation was the passage of the Federal Trade Commission Act (Congress also passed the Clayton Act, which will be discussed in the next chapter). The act created the **Federal Trade Commission** (FTC), a bipartisan administrative agency that was designed to provide expert and continuing enforcement of federal antitrust policies and to prevent unfair competitive practices in the marketplace.

Section 5 of the FTC Act gives the commission broad powers to deal with "unfair methods of competition" and "unfair or deceptive acts or practices in commerce." The FTC Act is technically not part of the antitrust laws, although restraints of trade that would violate Section 1 of the Sherman Act (discussed in the next chapter) are clearly also illegal under the FTC Act as "unfair methods of competition." The FTC Act also attacks behavior that is outside the scope of the antitrust laws. The act's prohibition of "unfair methods of competition" includes many anticompetitive practices that would not violate the letter of the antitrust laws. Under the act, the FTC has successfully attacked business practices ranging from false advertising to the exercise of coercion.

The FTC has the power to police the act by using the **cease and desist order** (an administrative order similar to an injunction). Such orders become final unless they are appealed to the courts, and their violation is punishable by fines of up to $10,000 per day. The FTC also has the power to issue **trade regulation rules,** most of which it has issued in the area of consumer protection. Violations of these rules are also punishable by fines of up to $10,000 per day. This aspect of the FTC's power will be discussed in Chapter 44.

CHAPTER 43 _Government Regulation of Business_

In addition to its responsibilities under Section 5 of the act, the FTC also has broad enforcement responsibilities under other federal statutes. It has joint jurisdiction (with the Department of Justice) over the Clayton Act. It also has jurisdiction over the Webb-Pomerene Act, the Federal Drug and Cosmetic Act, the Flammable Fabrics Act, the Lanham Trademark Act, the Fair Packaging and Labeling Act, and several consumer credit laws.

QUESTIONS AND PROBLEM CASES

1. Iowa enacted the Tobacco Use Prevention and Control Act (Control Act). The Control Act established an "initiative" to reduce the use of tobacco products. One specific provision flatly prohibited retailers from giving away cigarettes. Further, it would not permit retailers to provide free articles, gifts, or concessions in any exchange for the purchase of cigarettes. Terry K. Jones, an Iowa retailer, complained that these provisions of the Control Act hampered his business. Specifically, he contended that the prohibitions precluded him from participating in national sales promotions orchestrated by tobacco manufacturers that often involve redeeming cents-off coupons and proofs of purchase, distributing related merchandise with tobacco products (such as a free lighter with a pack of cigarettes), and offering two-for-one sales. He asserted that the giveaways and concessions foreclosed by the Control Act attract customers and generate significant sales revenue for retailers. He believed that such concessions were essential to his economic viability because federal and state regulations have severely curtailed tobacco advertising and other avenues of communicating with consumers. Further, he claimed that the Control Act particularly affects retailers situated near Iowa's borders because they face stiff competition from nearby out-of-state retailers unaffected by the Iowa statute. Accordingly, Jones filed a complaint against the state. He argued that the Control Act was unconstitutional because it was preempted by a federal statute—the Federal Cigarette Labeling and Advertising Act (FCLAA). That federal statute states: *"No requirement or prohibition based on smoking and health shall be imposed under State law with respect to the advertising or promotion of any cigarettes the packages of which are labeled in conformity with the provisions of this chapter."* Is Iowa's Control Act preempted by the federal statute?

2. On March 10, 1992, respondent, who was then a 12th-grade student, arrived at Edison High School in San Antonio, Texas, carrying a concealed .38 caliber handgun and five bullets. Acting upon an anonymous tip, school authorities confronted the respondent, who admitted that he was carrying the weapon. He was arrested and charged under Texas law with firearm possession on school premises. The next day, the state charges were dismissed after federal agents charged respondent with violating the Gun-Free School Zones Act of 1990. Under that statute, Congress made it a federal offense "for any individual knowingly to possess a firearm at a place that the individual knows, or has reasonable cause to believe, is a school zone." Respondent moved to dismiss his federal indictment on the ground that the statute was unconstitutional since it is beyond the power of Congress to legislate control over our public schools. The district court denied the motion, concluding that the statute was a constitutional exercise of Congress's well-defined power to regulate activities in and affecting commerce, and the "business" of elementary, middle, and high schools affects commerce. The court of appeals reversed, believing the statute to be beyond the power of Congress under the commerce power. Does this statute exceed Congress's authority to regulate under the Commerce Clause?

3. The Maryland Department of Human Resources revoked a child care center's license on findings that a number of preschool-age children were victims of physical and sexual abuse while in the center's care. None of the alleged victims of child abuse testified in any of the proceedings. Instead, the agency acted entirely on hearsay through the parents and

others who had spoken with the children. The child care center requested an opportunity to conduct psychological examinations of the alleged victims prior to the hearing. This request was denied. The child care center argued that the decision to revoke its license in the absence of such an examination was a denial of procedural due process. Was the decision to revoke the license a denial of procedural due process?

4. Nebraska voters adopted an article to their state constitution that prohibited nonfamily farm corporations from owning and operating Nebraska farm land. MSM Farms, a Nebraska corporation with unrelated shareholders, challenged the family farm measure on the grounds that it violated the equal protection clause of the U.S. Constitution. Specifically, MSM Farms argued that the state's prohibition of nonfamily corporate farming denied it equal protection because it was not rationally related to achieving any legitimate state purpose. Does the family farm measure discriminate in violation of the equal protection clause?

5. The domestic retail price of beer in Connecticut was consistently higher than the price of beer in the three bordering states and, as a result, Connecticut residents living in border areas frequently crossed state lines to purchase beer at lower prices. Accordingly, Connecticut enacted a statute that required out-of-state shippers of beer to affirm that their posted prices for products sold to Connecticut wholesalers were, as of the moment of posting, no higher than the prices at which those products were sold in the bordering states. A brewers' trade association and several major producers and importers of beer challenged the statute's constitutionality, contending that it violated the Commerce Clause. Is the statute unconstitutional as a violation of the Commerce Clause?

6. The Lexington School Committee decided to distribute condoms and informational packets about their proper use as a part of "safe sex' education to high school students without parental consent. This became an extremely divisive issue in the community. The local high school newspaper took a strong editorial position in favor of making condoms freely available at the school. Douglas Yeo was among the Lexington parents who opposed the new policy. He helped organize a group, LEXNET, whose stated purpose was to help inform Lexington parents about public school issues. Yeo attempted to run ads in the school newspaper encouraging students to practice abstinence and providing an address for LEXNET, but the newspaper refused to print the ad. After Yeo complained, school administrators urged the student editors to carefully reconsider their position. However, they also made it clear that they supported the students' right to decide. After the students again rejected the ad, Yeo sued on the ground that the refusal violated his constitutional right to free speech. The officials contended that Yeo's claim was without merit because there was no state action. Specifically, they asserted that the decision to reject Yeo's ad was made by the student editors and that they are not governmental actors. Was the decision to reject the ads state action?

7. A Minnesota statute banned the retail sale of milk in plastic nonreturnable containers that are not biodegradable but permitted such sales in other nonreturnable containers, such as paperboard cartons. The statute stated that the purpose of the ban was to promote resource conservation, ease solid waste disposal problems, and conserve energy. The Clover Leaf Creamery Company challenged the statute on equal protection grounds. It argued that the true purpose of the statute was to promote the interests of certain segments of the local dairy and pulpwood industries at the expense of other segments of those same industries. It also argued that paperboard containers had environmental drawbacks, that they required more energy to produce than did plastic containers, and that plastic containers took up less space at landfills and presented fewer solid waste disposal problems than did paperboard containers. Did the statute violate the Equal Protection Clause?

8. This case arises from two separate but essentially identical accidents in Georgia involving tractor-trailers. In both cases, 18-wheel tractor-trailers attempted to brake suddenly and ended up jackknifing into oncoming traffic.

Neither vehicle was equipped with an antilock braking system (ABS). In the first case, Ben Myrick was the driver of the oncoming vehicle and was left permanently paraplegic and brain damaged after being hit by a truck manufactured by Freightliner. In the second case, Grace Lindsey was killed when her vehicle collided with a tractor-trailer manufactured by Navistar. Independent suits were filed on behalf of Myrick and Lindsey against the manufacturers under state tort law, alleging that the absence of ABS was a negligent design that rendered the vehicles defective. Freightliner and Navistar argued the tort suits were pre-empted by the *National Traffic and Motor Vehicle Safety Act*. That federal statute was enacted to reduce traffic accidents as well deaths and injuries caused by traffic accidents. It requires the Secretary of Transportation to establish appropriate federal motor vehicle safety standards. The statute expressly states that whenever a federal safety standard is in effect, the states cannot establish or enforce a safety standard covering the same aspect of performance if it is not identical to the federal standard. However, the law also contained a savings clause which stated that compliance with any federal motor vehicle safety standard does not exempt any persons from liability under the common law. At the time of the accident, federal motor vehicle safety regulation addressed stopping distances or vehicle stability for trucks or trailers. Are the tort lawsuits pre-empted by the federal statute?

9. Margaret McIntyre distributed leaflets to persons attending a public meeting at the Blendon Middle School in Westerville, Ohio. At this meeting, the superintendent of schools planned to discuss an imminent referendum on a proposed school tax levy. The leaflets expressed Mrs. McIntyre's opposition to the levy. She had composed and printed the leaflet on her home computer and had paid a professional printer to make copies. Some of the handbills identified her as the author; others merely purported to express the views of "CONCERNED PARENTS AND TAX PAYERS." There is no suggestion that the text of her message was false, misleading, or libelous. While Mrs. McIntyre distributed her handbills, an official of the school district, who supported the tax proposal, advised her that the unsigned leaflets did not conform to the Ohio election laws. Undeterred, Mrs. McIntyre appeared at another meeting on the next evening and handed out more of the handbills. Later, the school official filed an official complaint with the Ohio Elections Commission charging that Mrs. McIntyre's distribution of unsigned leaflets violated the Ohio Code. The Commission agreed and imposed a fine of $100. Mrs. McIntyre challenged the constitutionality of the ban on anonymous leafletting. Does ordinance prohibiting all anonymous leafletting violate the First Amendment?

10. Coors Brewing Company applied to the Bureau of Alcohol, Tobacco and Firearms (BATF) for approval of proposed labels and advertisements that disclosed the alcohol content of its beer. BATF rejected the application on the ground that the Federal Alcohol Administration Act prohibited disclosure of the alcohol content of beer on labels or in advertising. The labeling regulations also prohibited the use of descriptive terms that suggest high alcohol content, such as "strong," "full strength," or "extra strength." Coors claimed the labeling restrictions violated its First Amendment rights. The government responded that the ban was necessary to suppress the threat of "strength wars" among brewers, who, without the regulation, would seek to compete in the marketplace based on the potency of beer. Does the labeling restriction infringe brewers' First Amendment rights?

CHAPTER 44

The Antitrust Laws

For many years, athletic footwear manufacturers have been accused of routinely pressuring retailers to sell their shoes at suggested retail prices. This benefits manufacturers by ensuring their brand image will not be tarnished by price cutting and assures retailers that rival stores will not steal customers by offering special discounts. Reebok was accused of prohibiting its retail dealers from selling shoes below designated price levels. In a 1995 consent decree with the government, Reebok, without admitting any guilt, agreed not to try to set or control retail prices and not to threaten retailers .with suspension or termination if they do not follow suggested retail prices.

- *What is price fixing? Why is it unlawful?*
- *What procedure should the courts follow in determining whether Reebok violated the antitrust laws?*
- *How might Reebok lawfully control the retail price of its athletic footwear?*

The purpose of U.S. antitrust law is to encourage and protect competition. With the growth of national markets after the Civil War, the United States witnessed an important development on the economic scene: the growth of large industrial combines and trusts. Many of these huge business entities engaged in practices aimed at destroying their competitors. This behavior led to a public outcry for legislation designed to preserve competitive market structures and prevent the accumulation of great economic power in the hands of a few firms. Congress responded by passing the **Sherman Act** in 1890, and later supplemented it with the **Clayton Act** and the **Robinson-Patman Act.**

ANTITRUST IN A GLOBAL ENVIRONMENT

The prime focus of U.S. antitrust enforcement is to protect American consumers from anticompetitive conduct. In an increasingly global environment this sometimes entails bringing antitrust actions against foreign defendants or prohibiting conduct that occurs outside of the actual territory of this country. The United States is not alone in its maintenance of domestic and international competition through the enforcement of antitrust laws. Most of the industrial nations have such legislation. International businesses must be more and more alert to the reach of these antitrust laws as they expand their operations around the world.

········ *PROCEDURAL ASPECTS OF* ········
THE SHERMAN ACT

PENALTIES

The Sherman Act makes contracts in restraint of trade and monopolization illegal. It provides **criminal** penalties for violations of its provisions (up to a $350,000 fine and/or three years in jail for individuals and up to a $10 million fine for corporate violators). It also gives the federal courts broad injunctive powers to remedy antitrust violations. The courts can order convicted defendants to divest themselves of the stock or assets of other companies or to divorce themselves from a functional level of their operations (e.g., they can order a manufacturer to sell a captive retail chain). In extreme cases, the courts can order *dissolution*—force the defendant to liquidate its assets and go out of business.

Private individuals who have been injured by antitrust violations have strong incentives to sue under the **civil** provisions of the antitrust laws. A successful antitrust plaintiff may recover **treble damages** (three times their actual losses) plus costs and attorney's fees. This can mean tremendous potential liability for antitrust defendants. Reebok, in the case that opened this chapter, agreed to a settlement without admitting any wrongdoing. Such an admission would have made it extremely vulnerable to treble damage lawsuits by retailers claiming injury.

STANDING

Private plaintiffs who seek to recover treble damages must first convince the court that they have *standing* to sue, that is, that they have suffered a direct injury as a result of the defendant's claimed antitrust violations. For instance, suppose all of the lumberyards in a city conspired to fix prices in order to ensure that lumber was not sold below some inflated figure. This is a clear violation of the antitrust laws. Builders who were forced to purchase lumber at the artificially high price would be directly injured and, accordingly, able to bring an antitrust suit. In all likelihood, however, the builders probably passed these increased costs on to home buyers in the form of higher prices for new homes. The buyers of these homes, although injured by the price-fixing, could not bring an antitrust case. They are **indirect purchasers** of the lumber and are therefore precluded from suing the lumberyards (their indirect sellers). They have no suit against the builders since it is not an antitrust violation to pass the increased costs on to the ultimate buyer.

JURISDICTION

Since the federal government's power to regulate business flows from the Commerce Clause of the U.S. Constitution, the federal antitrust laws apply only to behavior that substantially affects interstate commerce or international trade. Behavior that affects only *intrastate* (purely local) commerce is outside the scope of the federal antitrust laws and must be challenged under state antitrust statutes, some of which are not vigorously enforced.

In view of the fact that a large portion of business in the United States is conducted across state lines, it is often relatively easy to show the required impact on interstate commerce. Even behavior that takes place solely within the borders of one state can have an interstate impact in today's economy.

Extraterritorial Reach

Antitrust violations that occur within the territory of the United States (whether committed by U.S. or foreign persons) fall squarely within the jurisdictional reach of the U.S. antitrust laws. However, U.S. antitrust enforcement is not limited to conduct that occurs within U.S. borders. The Sherman Act has been interpreted to reach actions of foreign entities that have an anticompetitive effect in the United States as well as acts that limit American access to markets abroad.

Foreign Trade Antitrust Improvement Act

Seeking to clarify the confusion surrounding the extraterritorial reach of the antitrust laws, Congress enacted the Foreign Trade Antitrust Improvement Act. Specifically, this statute provides that the Sherman Act shall not apply to nonimport trade unless the conduct has a **direct, substantial, and reasonably foreseeable effect** on trade or commerce within the United States, on U.S. import trade, or on the activities of U.S. exporters.

SECTION 1 OF THE SHERMAN ACT

Section 1 of the Sherman Act provides:

> Every contract, combination in the form of trust or otherwise, or conspiracy, in restraint of trade or commerce among the several states, or with foreign nations is declared to be illegal.

A *contract* is any agreement, express or implied, between two or more persons to restrain competition; a *combination* is a continuing partnership in restraint of trade; and a *conspiracy* occurs when two or more persons join together for the purpose of restraining trade.

JOINT ACTION

From the language of the statute, it is apparent that the purpose of Section 1 is to attack joint action in restraint of trade. Accordingly, unilateral actions, even if they have an anticompetitive effect, do not violate Section 1. For instance, a wholesaler may "suggest" that a retail outlet sell an item at a certain price. As long as the two businesses did not *agree* that the goods would be sold at that price, Section 1 has not been violated. Further, a manufacturer may terminate a dealer who has failed to follow a "suggested marketing practice" (e.g., selling below the suggested resale price or failing to provide a service department) even though such a practice may tend to raise prices and lower competition. Such a unilateral refusal to deal is not joint action and therefore cannot be prohibited by Section 1.

Determining when a court will infer an agreement from the actions of the defendants is a constant problem for businesses. Some areas are fairly clear cut. For example, it has long been held that a corporation cannot conspire with itself or with its employees. And the Supreme Court has ruled that a corporation could not conspire with a wholly owned subsidiary. Consignments have also been held to be unilateral action. A consignment agreement is one in which the owner of goods delivers them to another who is to act as the owner's agent in selling the goods. If a manufacturer delivers all goods to its dealers on a consignment basis, it can lawfully fix the price of those goods since the goods remain its property and are not the property of the dealers. (The dealer is the agent of the manufacturer and, like the employee situation above, cannot conspire with its principal/employer.) Courts appear more likely to infer joint action if the defendants are both competitors (as opposed to dealings between a supplier and a distributor) and/or if the dealings involve the discussion of price.

BLOMKEST FERTILIZER v. POTASH CORPORATION OF SASKATCHEWAN
203 F.3d 1028 (8th Cir. 2000)

FACTS

Potash is a mineral which is an essential ingredient in fertilizer. Because potash is an essential ingredient, the demand for potash is "inelastic," meaning that people will continue to buy it even if the price goes up and they will not buy much more even if the price goes down. The effect of this inelastic demand is that low prices are bad for producers because the low price does not result in more sales except insofar as one producer can take sales away from other producers. Conversely, producers benefit from high prices because they can sell about as much potash and keep the extra money. Furthermore, the North American potash industry is an oligopoly. Prices in oligopolies tend to be higher than those in purely competitive markets and will fluctuate independently of supply and demand. Price uniformity is normal in such a market because all producers in an oligopoly must charge roughly the same price or risk losing market share. The Canadian province of Saskatchewan is the source of most potash consumed in the United States. That province originally founded Potash Corporation of Saskatchewan (PCS), which holds 38 percent of the North American potash production capacity. However, as a governmental company, PCS suffered huge losses as it mined potash in quantities that far outstripped global demand. Finally, in 1986, after the company was privatized, it appointed new management who significantly reduced its output and raised its prices. During that same year, a U.S. potash producer complained that the Canadian producers were dumping their product (selling below fair market value) in the United States. The U.S. Department of Commerce negotiated a Suspension Agreement with the Canadian producers that raised the price of potash by setting a minimum price at which each Canadian producer could sell in the United States.

(continued)

BLOMKEST FERTILIZER V. POTASH CORPORATION OF SASKATCHEWAN
(continued)

Immediately after entering into this agreement, PCS announced that it was raising its prices by $18 per ton, and the other Canadian producers quickly followed suit. Blomkest Fertilizer, a potash consumer, now alleges that between 1987 and 1994, the Canadian producers, led by PCS, have colluded to increase the price of potash. It has sued them under Section 1 of the Sherman Act. The producers, in turn, maintain that any price increases were the product of the interdependent nature of the industry. In short, they claim that Section 1 does not apply because they have acted independently rather than jointly. Blomkest's proof of joint action is primarily circumstantial, consisting of economic evidence of supracompetitive pricing and evidence of price discussions among competitors. The potash producers moved for summary judgment on the ground that the plaintiffs had not produced any evidence that showed that the defendants had conspired rather than setting their prices individually taking into account their competitors' probable responses.

ISSUES

Should the court dismiss the claim as a matter of law because there is no proof of joint action?

DECISION

Yes. Section 1 prohibits only *joint* action by two or more parties in restraint of trade. Thus, in conspiracy cases, the only difference between legal and illegal conduct is the existence of an agreement to do the same thing the parties could have done legally without an agreement. Because it is important to punish only the forbidden conduct and to avoid deterring legal economic activity, a submissible antitrust conspiracy case must include some evidence that tends to exclude the possibility of independent action by the alleged conspirators. Applied in this case, the standard requires that if it is as reasonable to infer from the evidence a price-fixing conspiracy as it is to infer independent activity, the plaintiff's claim, without more, fails on summary judgment. The plaintiff's price-fixing claim is based on a theory of conscious parallelism. *Conscious parallelism* is the process not in itself unlawful, by which firms in a concentrated market might in effect share monopoly power, setting their prices at a profit-maximizing, supracompetitive level by recognizing

their economic interests. The plaintiff's point out that the producers' prices were roughly equivalent during the alleged conspiracy, despite differing production costs. It further points out that price changes by one producer were quickly met by the others. This establishes only that the producers consciously paralleled each other's prices. Evidence that a business consciously met the pricing of its competitors does not prove a violation of Section 1 because it does not prove the existence of an agreement (joint action). An agreement is properly inferred from conscious parallelism only when certain "plus factors" exist. A plus factor refers to the additional facts or factors required to be proved as a prerequisite to finding that parallel behavior amounts to a conspiracy. However, even if one or more plus factors are shown, a court must still find, based upon all the evidence, that the plaintiff's evidence tends to exclude the possibility of independent action. Blomkest asserts that it has established the existence of two plus factors: (1) interfirm communications among the producers and (2) the producers' acts against self-interest. Courts have held that a high level of communications among competitors can constitute plus factors which, when combined with parallel behavior, supports an inference of conspiracy. Clearly, the plaintiff has presented evidence that there have been roughly three dozen instances of price verifications between employees of the competing producers. However, these price verification communications concerned charges on only particular completed sales, not future market prices. There is no evidence to support the inference that the verifications had an impact on price increases. While the other producers' prices did increase immediately after the price increase by PCS, this should be expected in an oligopolistic market. Common sense dictates that a conspiracy to fix a price would involve one company communicating with another company before a price quotation to the customer. Here, however, these sporadic communications consisted solely of verifications on a price of a completed sale. Evidence that defendants have acted against economic interest can also constitute a plus factor. However, where there is an independent business justification for the defendant's behavior, no inference of conspiracy can be drawn. The only evidence of actions against interest that the plaintiff

(continued)

BLOMKEST FERTILIZER V. POTASH CORPORATION OF SASKATCHEWAN
(concluded)

has identified is the producer's uniform participation in the Suspension Agreement. Blomkest argues that those producers with low dumping margins could have undercut the other producers' prices and gained market share while still maintaining prices at profitable levels. However, great uncertainty always accompanies a dumping investigation. Therefore, the producers, by uniformly taking part in the Suspension Agreement and following PCS

price leadership, obtained both certainty and a higher price for potash sold in the United States. The plaintiff has thus failed to carry its burden to rebut the producers' independent business justification for their actions. Because Blomkest has failed to present evidence of joint action among the producers, its claim under Section 1 of the Sherman Act must be dismissed.

Ethical Implications	An agreement between a manufacturer and a retailer fixing the retail price at which the manufacturer's products would be sold to the public would be illegal joint action. However, because of the express language in Section 1, a suggestion by the manufacturer (which was complied with by the retailer) would be perfectly legitimate since it would be unilateral action. Yet if the suggestion was strongly worded, the ultimate effect would be the same—the retailer would comply with the manufacturer's wishes. Is it ethical to circumvent Section 1 through such verbal gymnastics?

SECTION 1 ANALYSIS

After a finding of joint action, the court must examine the nature of the alleged violation to determine its legal status. Such joint action will be treated as either a per se or a rule of reason violation. Per se activities are automatically illegal, while the legality of a rule of reason action can be determined only after examining the behavior's ultimate effect on competition.

PER SE RESTRAINTS

When faced with the difficult problem of deciding what kinds of joint action amounted to a restraint of trade, the courts concluded that some kinds of behavior always have a negative effect on competition that can never be excused or justified. These kinds of acts are classed as **per se** illegal; they are conclusively presumed to be illegal. While per se rules have been criticized as shortcuts that sometimes oversimplify economic realities, they do speed up lengthy trials and provide sure guidelines for business.

Price-Fixing

The essential characteristic of a free market is that the price of goods and services is determined by the play of forces in the marketplace. Attempts by competitors to interfere with the market and control prices are called **horizontal price-fixing** and are illegal per se under Section 1. Price-fixing may take the form of direct agreements among competitors about what price they will sell a product for or what price they will offer for a product. It may also be accomplished by agreements on the quantities to be produced, offered for sale, or bought. Whether done directly or indirectly, horizontal price-fixing is always illegal and can never be legally justified.

Attempts by manufacturers to control the resale price of their products are also within the scope of Section 1. This kind of behavior is called **vertical price-fixing** or *resale price maintenance*. As was discussed above, manufacturers can lawfully state a "suggested retail price" for their products, since this does not involve joint action. If the manufacturer gets the retailer to agree to follow the suggested price, however, such an agreement is joint action in restraint of trade and may be illegal per se under Section 1.

For years all contracts, combinations, or conspiracies to fix prices were per se illegal. However, in 1997 the U.S. Supreme Court reversed over 30 years of antitrust precedent by holding that vertical, maximum price-fixing agreements should be scrutinized under the rule of reason, rather than per se, analysis. As you read this landmark case, *State Oil Company v. Khan*, consider the reasons the court changed its approach to vertical price fixing.

STATE OIL COMPANY V. KHAN
522 U.S. 3 (U.S. Sup. Ct. 1997)

FACTS

Barkat U. Khan entered into an agreement with State Oil Company to lease and operate a gas station and convenience store owned by State Oil. The agreement provided that Khan would obtain the station's gasoline supply from State Oil at a price equal to a suggested retail price set by State Oil, less a margin of 3.25 cents per gallon. Under the agreement, Khan could charge any amount for gasoline sold to the station's customers, but if the price charged was higher than State Oil's suggested retail price, the excess was to be rebated to State Oil. Khan could sell gasoline for less than State Oil's suggested retail price, but any such decrease would reduce his 3.25 cents-per-gallon margin. After Khan fell behind in lease payments, State Oil gave notice of its intent to terminate the agreement. At State Oil's request, the state court appointed a receiver to operate the gas station. The receiver operated the station for several months without being subject to the price restraints in Khan's agreement with State Oil. This permitted the receiver to obtain an overall profit margin in excess of 3.25 cents per gallon by lowering the price of regular-grade gasoline and raising the price of premium grades. Khan sued State Oil, alleging that State Oil had engaged in price fixing in violation of Section 1 of the Sherman Act by preventing him from raising or lowering retail gas prices. According to the complaint, but for the agreement with State Oil, Khan could have charged different prices based on the grades of gasoline, in the same way that the receiver had, thereby achieving increased sales and profits. Khan claimed that his allegations stated a per se violation of the Sherman Act.

ISSUE

Did State Oil's conduct constitute a per se violation of the Sherman Act?

DECISION

No. Although the Sherman Act, by its terms, prohibits every agreement "in restraint of trade," this Court has long recognized that Congress intended to outlaw only unreasonable restraints. As a consequence, most antitrust claims are analyzed under a "rule of reason," according to which the finder of fact must decide whether the questioned practice imposes any unreasonable restraint on competition, taking into account a variety of factors, including specific information about the relevant business, its condition before and after the restraint was imposed, and the restraint's history, nature, and effect. Some types of restraints, however, have such predictable and pernicious anticompetitive effect, and such limited potential for procompetitive benefit, that they are deemed unlawful per se. This per se treatment is appropriate once experience with a particular kind of restraint enables the Court to predict with confidence that the rule of reason will condemn it. Thus, we have expressed reluctance to adopt per se rules with regard to restraints imposed in the context of business relationships where the economic impact of certain practices is not immediately obvious. For

(continued)

STATE OIL COMPANY V. KHAN
(concluded)

almost 30 years, this Court has applied per se analysis to all price-fixing agreements, including arrangements that fix the maximum resale price of goods. We acknowledged that maximum and minimum price fixing may have different consequences in many situations, but nonetheless we condemned maximum price fixing for substituting the perhaps erroneous judgment of a seller for the forces of the competitive market. However, today we overrule the line of cases holding that vertical maximum price fixing is per se unlawful. Our reconsideration is informed by several of our decisions, as well as a considerable body of scholarship discussing the effects of vertical restraints. Our analysis is also guided by our general view that the primary purpose of the antitrust laws is to protect interbrand competition. Low prices benefit consumers regardless of how those prices are set, and so

long as they are above predatory levels, they do not threaten competition. Our interpretation of the Sherman Act also incorporates the notion that condemnation of practices resulting in lower prices to consumers is especially costly because cutting prices in order to increase business is the very essence of competition. So informed, we find it difficult to maintain that vertically-imposed maximum prices could harm consumers or competition to the extent necessary to justify their per se invalidation. We of course do not hold that all vertical maximum price fixing is per se lawful. Instead, vertical maximum price fixing, like the majority of commercial arrangements subject to the antitrust laws, should be evaluated under rule of reason. In our view, rule-of-reason analysis will effectively identify those situations in which vertical maximum price fixing amounts to anticompetitive conduct.

Group Boycotts and Concerted Refusals to Deal

A single firm can lawfully refuse to deal with certain firms or agree to deal only on certain terms. However, any such agreement by two or more firms to boycott or terminate another is a per se violation of Section 1. Thus, if a distributor persuades a manufacturer to refuse to deal with a rival distributor, the two conspiring parties would have committed a per se violation of Section 1.

Division of Markets

Any agreement among competing firms to divide up the available market by assigning each other exclusive territories is a horizontal division of markets and is illegal per se. The idea is that each firm is given a monopoly in its assigned territory.

RULE OF REASON VIOLATIONS

Any behavior that has not been classified as a per se violation is judged under rule of reason analysis. A rule of reason trial involves a complex, often lengthy attempt by the court to balance the anticompetitive effects of the defendants' acts against any competitive justifications for their behavior. If the court concludes that the defendants' acts had a significant anticompetitive effect that was not offset by any positive impact on competition, their behavior is held illegal. Recent antitrust decisions indicate that the Supreme Court is moving away from per se rules in favor of rule of reason treatment for many kinds of economic activity. This trend is consistent with the Court's increased willingness to consider new economic theories seeking to justify behavior previously declared illegal per se.

Actually, the per se rules might be viewed merely as special applications of the rule of reason for certain types of restraints that experience shows will always or almost always fail rule of reason. Rule of reason itself has been broken into two categories: full rule of reason analysis and abbreviated rule of reason analysis.

Full rule of reason analysis applies to a broader category of restraints in which the competitive reasonableness cannot be ascertained without a thorough examination of their pernicious and beneficial effects in the relevant product and geographic markets. Restraints of this type may ultimately be found anticompetitive and illegal, but, unlike per se restraints, they are not facially so. Their legality cannot be determined until after a court conducts a full market analysis.

Abbreviated rule of reason analysis is utilized for restraints that have an obvious adverse impact on competition; however, they do not deserve per se treatment because their overall reasonableness cannot be ascertained without a preliminary assessment of their procompetitive effects. This "quick look" form of rule of reason analysis skips the inquiry into anticompetitve effects because they are obvious from the general nature of the restraint. In these types of cases, the judicial analysis focuses solely on any procompetitive justifications offered in support of the activity. Consider the following case in which the court employs an abbreviated rule of reason analysis to find the defendant liable for violating Section 1 of the Sherman Act.

CONTINENTAL AIRLINES, INC. V. UNITED AIR LINES, INC.
2002 U.S. App. LEXIS 637 (4th Cir. 2002)

FACTS

Many airline passengers prefer to avoid checking baggage and, instead, to carry their bags onto aircraft. However, in the 1990s, a healthy economy, among other causes, contributed to a significant increase in air travel so that by the middle of the decade, many aircraft did not have sufficient under-seat or overhead storage bin space to stow securely the number and size of bags brought onboard by the increasing number of passengers. The competitive market compelled carriers, including Continental and United, to address this issue. Some explored the feasibility of installing carry-on baggage "templates" at airports to screen "oversized" bags. Continental experimented with such a template but ultimately rejected it because customer feedback showed that it irritated customers. Instead, Continental chose to increase aircraft carry-on storage capacity and to relax its carry-on baggage policy. Specifically, at the cost of over $12.4 million, it retrofitted its entire fleet. As a result, Continental received numerous industrywide accolades for customer satisfaction among frequent fliers. Continental believes that its approach distinguishes it from other carriers and gives it a competitive advantage. United responded differently. Despite customer dissatisfaction, United imposed strict limits on the size and number of bags its passengers were allowed to carry onto its aircraft. This dispute arose when, over Continental's objectives, United convinced AMC, the managing authority at

Dulles Airport, to install carry-on baggage templates at its two security checkpoints. AMC, an unincorporated association of the 29 air carriers that use Dulles airport, considers and resolves airport operational issues that involve more than one carrier. At Dulles passengers must pass through common security checkpoints in the main terminal before proceeding to a departure gate. Both of Dulles's checkpoints lead to one common "sterile" area, where passengers board shuttles that take them to midfield concourses where the individual gates are located. Because all passengers departing from Dulles must pass through one of the two security checkpoints to reach their departure gates, the installation of the templates effectively restricts the size of carry-on bags for the passengers of all carriers at Dulles, including Continental. One week after the carry-on baggage templates were installed at Dulles, Continental sued United and AMC for violation of Section 1 of the Sherman Act. Specifically, Continental argued that the agreement to restrict the size of carry-on baggage at Dulles was a naked restriction on nonprice competition among air carriers that injured Continental by eliminating any competitive advantage the airline has by virtue of its expanded aircraft storage bins and its liberal carry-on baggage policies and practices. The federal district court, using the "quick look" rule of reason analysis, granted a summary judgment in favor of Continental.

(continued)

CONTINENTAL AIRLINES, INC. V. UNITED AIR LINES, INC.

(concluded)

ISSUE

Should the court grant Continental a summary judgment under "quick look" analysis?

DECISION

No. Section 1 of the Sherman Act prohibits every combination in restraint of trade. The Supreme Court, however, long ago established that Section 1 outlaws only restraints that are "unreasonably restrictive of competitive conditions." Thus, to prevail on a claim that a horizontal restraint violates Section 1, a plaintiff must prove that the restraint is unreasonable. A plaintiff cannot prove the unreasonableness of a restraint merely by showing that it caused economic injury. Rather, because the antitrust laws were enacted for the protection of competition, not competitors, a plaintiff must show that the net effect of a challenged restraint is harmful to competition. In determining whether a horizontal agreement violates Section 1, the Supreme Court has authorized three methods of analysis: (1) *per se* analysis, for obviously anticompetitive restraints, (2) quick-look analysis, for those with some procompetitive justification, and (3) the full "rule of reason," for restraints whose net impact on competition is particularly difficult to determine. The boundaries between these levels of analysis are fluid; there is generally no categorical line to be drawn between restraints that give rise to an intuitively obvious inference of anticompetitive effect and those that call for more detailed treatment. Instead, the three methods are best viewed as a continuum on which the amount and range of information needed to evaluate, a restraint varies depending on how highly suspicious and how unique the restraint is. The first approach, *per se* analysis, permits courts to make categorical judgments that certain practices, including horizontal price fixing and horizontal output restraints, have such predictable and pernicious anticompetitive effect, and such limited potential for procompetitive benefit, that they are deemed unlawful without any need to conduct a detailed study of the markets on which the restraints operate or the actual effect of those restraints on competition. At the other end of the spectrum, if the reasonableness of a restraint cannot be determined without a thorough analysis of its net effects on competition in the relevant market, courts must apply a full rule-of-reason analysis. The required analysis varies by case and may extend to a plenary market examination covering the facts peculiar to the business, the history of the restraint, and the reasons why it was imposed, as well as the availability of reasonable, less restrictive alternatives. Sometimes, the anticompetitive impact of a restraint is clear from a quick look, as in a *per se* case, but procompetitive justifications for it also exist. Such intermediate cases may involve an industry in which horizontal restraints on competition are essential if the product is to be available at all, or in which a horizontal restraint otherwise plausibly increases economic efficiency and renders markets more, rather than less, competitive. In quick-look cases involving plausible procompetitive justifications, a full record may often be necessary. Certainly courts have been wary of summary judgment in the context of quick-look analysis. In fact, we have not found a single case in which the Supreme Court has approved a quick-look analysis in which the parties received less than a full evidentiary hearing. Applying these principles to the case at hand, it seems clear that the summary judgment should be vacated since the district court performed too quick an analysis on an insufficiently developed factual record. For instance, while the lower court properly rejected *per se* analysis because airlines must cooperate to share airports, it failed to recognize the extent to which Dulles's indisputably unique architectural configuration requires careful consideration of the template program's competitive effect. Beyond the general need for greater cooperation at Dulles than at other airports, United and Continental each make a more specific claim, related to Dulles's Unique configuration, as to why their respective preferred outcomes benefit competition. On remand, the district court ultimately may have to choose between two procompetitive claims; either outcome would both help and hurt competition, and which helps competition more than the other may be far from plain. Thus, a fuller examination is necessary. In addition, the district court must conduct a hearing so it can fully consider the plausibility of any justifications that United might offer on behalf of the template program. For these reasons, we vacate the judgment of the district court granting summary judgment and remand the case for further proceedings. We leave to the district court the question whether on remand it can effectively assess the alleged restraint by a modified quick-look analysis or whether it must undertake a more extensive rule-of-reason analysis.

Vertical Nonprice Restraints on Distribution

A manufacturer can lawfully, as a matter of business policy, "unilaterally" assign exclusive dealerships to its dealers or limit the number of dealerships it grants in any geographic area. (Since there is no joint action, there is no violation of Section 1.) However, manufacturers may run afoul of Section 1 if they require their dealers to "agree" to refrain from selling to customers outside their assigned territories or to unfranchised dealers inside their assigned territories. Such vertical, nonprice restraints are analyzed under the rule of reason.

Joint Ventures and Strategic Alliances

Joint ventures (or strategic alliances) are arrangements in which two or more entities collaborate with respect to research, development, production, marketing, or distribution. Because they generally involve cooperation between actual or potential competitors, joint ventures could possibly violate Section 1 of the Sherman Act. Recognizing the tremendous competitive advantages that the United States might gain from joint research and development, and joint production, Congress enacted the National Cooperative Research and Production Act, which mandates that U.S. courts examine research and development joint ventures as well as joint production ventures under rule of reason analysis. Further, if the venture partners have complied with the act's notification requirements, they are liable for only actual (rather than treble) damages in any civil suits that successfully challenge the arrangement.

While marketing and distribution joint ventures do not fall within the statute Act, the Department of Justice recommends that they also be scrutinized under rule of reason analysis. However, courts will not employ rule of reason analysis unless the joint arrangement truly constitutes some form of economic integration. If the cooperation actually is no more than a "sham" joint venture designed to restrict output or maintain prices, it will be treated as a per se violation of Section 1.

Licensing Arrangements

A firm frequently will attempt to exploit the market by licensing its intellectual property (e.g., patents, copyrights, trade secrets, and know-how) to manufacturers or distributors. These licenses give the licensee the right to use the licensor's technology (generally for a limited period of time) for certain purposes. They permit the licensor to combine its intellectual property with the manufacturing or distribution skills of the licensee in order to more efficiently exploit its special technology. However, licensing arrangements often raise antitrust issues because they generally involve restraints on the competitive activities of the licensor and/or licensee. (For example, an exclusive license means that no one other than the licensee can manufacture or sell the product in a designated territory.)

Despite their restrictive potential, licensing arrangements can maximize consumer welfare by ensuring that new technology reaches the marketplace in the quickest and most efficient manner. Further, by guaranteeing that new ideas realize their maximum return, they encourage the development of new technology. For these reasons, the Justice Department has recommended that licensing agreements undergo rule of reason analysis.

SECTION 2 OF THE SHERMAN ACT

When a firm acquires monopoly power—the power to fix prices or exclude competitors—in a particular market, the antitrust laws' objective of promoting competitive market structures has been defeated. Monopolists have the power to fix price unilaterally, since they have no effective competition. Section 2 of the Sherman Act was designed to attack monopolies. It provides:

> Every person who shall monopolize, or attempt to monopolize, or combine or conspire with any other person or persons to monopolize any part of trade or commerce among the several states, or with foreign nations shall be deemed guilty of a felony.

The first thing a student should note about the language of Section 2 is that it does not outlaw monopolies. It outlaws the act of "monopolizing." In order to show a violation of Section 2, the government or a private plaintiff must show not only that the defendant firm has monopoly power but also that there is an intent to monopolize on the defendant's part. Secondly, joint action is not necessary in order to violate Section 2; a single firm can be guilty of *monopolizing* or *attempting to monopolize*.

INTENT TO MONOPOLIZE

Courts look at how the defendant acquired monopoly power. If the defendant intentionally acquired monopoly power or attempted to maintain it after having acquired

CONCEPT SUMMARY   **Section 1 of the Sherman Act**

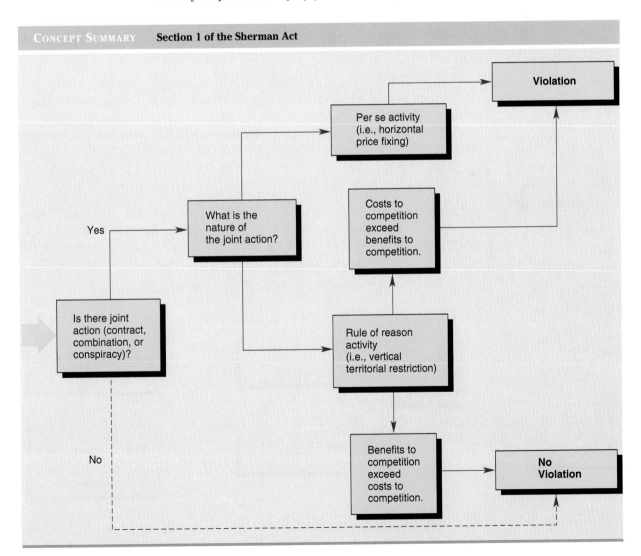

it, intent to monopolize has been shown. However, if the defendant acquires a dominant market position through superior products and service or other demonstrations of business acumen, the intent to monopolize will not be found.

So, the defendant must convince the court that its monopoly power simply happened and is not the result of a conscious attempt to acquire or maintain it. If the defendant has monopoly power because it "built a better mousetrap," made wise decisions when other competitors did not, or simply was the first entrant or only survivor in a market that can support only one firm of its kind (e.g., the only newspaper in a small town), no violation of Section 2 exists.

MONOPOLY POWER

Monopoly power exists when a firm controls a very high percentage share of the relevant market. The decided cases in this area indicate that a firm must have captured approximately 70 percent or more of the relevant market to have monopoly power. In order to determine the defendant's market share, the court in a Section 2 case must define the relevant market. This is a crucial part of the proceedings, since the broader the relevant market is drawn, the smaller the defendant's market share will be. There are two components to a relevant market determination: the geographic market and the product market.

Geographic Market

The relevant geographic market is determined by economic realities. Where do the sellers of the goods or services in question customarily compete? Transportation cost is often a critical factor that limits geographic market size. Thus, the relevant geographic market may be a small area for cement but the whole nation for transistors.

Product Market

The relevant product market is composed of those products that are "reasonably interchangeable by consumers for the same purposes" (the **functional interchangeability test**). The idea here is that a firm's power to fix price is limited by the availability of competing products that buyers find acceptable. (See Figure 44–1.)

FIGURE 44–1   Monopolization

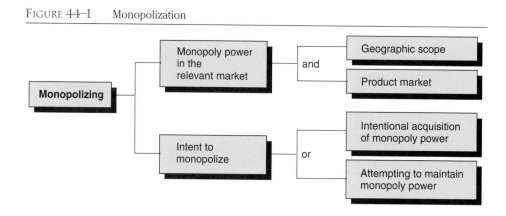

UNITED STATES V. MICROSOFT CORPORATION
253 F.3d 34 (D.C. Cir. 2001)

FACTS

The United States and a group of states bought a civil antitrust actions against Microsoft Corporation. The plaintiffs charged, in essence, that Microsoft had waged an unlawful campaign in defense of its monopoly position in the market for operating systems designed to run on Intel-compatible personal computers (PCs). Relying almost exclusively on Microsoft's varied efforts to unseat Netscape Navigator as the preeminent internet browser, the plaintiffs claimed that Microsoft violated Section 2 of the Sherman Act by engaging in monopolization through a series of exclusionary, anticompetitive, and predatory acts designed to maintain its monopoly power.

ISSUE

Has Microsoft violated Section 2 of the Sherman Act?

DECISION

Yes. Just over six years have passed since Mircrosoft engaged in the first conduct that plaintiffs alleged to be anticompetitive. Six years seems like an eternity in the computer industry. By the time a court can assess liability, firms, products, and the marketplace are likely to have changed dramatically. This threatens enormous practical difficulties for courts considering the appropriate measure of relief. How does a court go about restoring competition to a dramatically changed, and constantly changing, marketplace? Further, we decide this case against a backdrop of significant debate amongst academics and practitioners over the extent to which "old economy" Section 2 monopolization doctrines should apply to firms competing in dynamic technological markets characterized by network effects. In such markets, one product or standard tends toward dominance, because the utility that a user derives from consumption of the good increases with the number of other agents consuming the good. Competition in such industries is "for the field" rather than "within the field." Section 2 of the Sherman Act makes it unlawful for a firm to monopolize. The offense of monopolization has two elements: (1) the possession of monopoly power in the relevant market and (2) the willful acquisition or maintenance of that power as distinguished from growth or development as a consequence of a superior product, business acumen, or historic accident. While merely possessing monopoly power is not itself an antitrust violation, it is a necessary element of a monopolization charge. More precisely, a firm is a monopolist if it can profitably raise prices substantially above the competitive level. Because direct proof of such ability is rarely available, courts more typically examine market structure in search of circumstantial evidence of monopoly power. Under this structural approach, monopoly power may be inferred from a firm's possession of a dominant share of a relevant market that is protected by entry barriers. Entry barriers are factors that prevent new rivals from timely responding to an increase in price above the competitive level. Because the ability of consumers to turn to other suppliers restrains a firm from raising prices above the competitive level, the relevant market must include all products reasonably interchangeable by consumers for the same purpose. Here, the relevant market is the licensing of all Intel-compatible PC operating systems worldwide because there are currently no products, and there are not likely to be any in the near future, that a significant percentage of computer users worldwide could substitute for these operating systems without incurring substantial costs. Having thus properly defined the relevant market, we find that Microsoft's Windows accounts for a greater than 95 percent share. Of course, a predominant market share does not by itself indicate monopoly power because of the possibility of competition from new entrants. However, a certain structural barrier protects Microsoft's future market position. That barrier—the applications barrier to entry—stems from two characteristics of the software market: (1) most consumers prefer operating systems for which a large number of applications have already been written; and (2) most developers prefer to write for operating systems that already have a substantial consumer base. This "chicken-and-egg" situation ensures that applications will continue to be written for the already dominant Windows, which in turn ensures that consumers will continue to prefer it over other operating systems. As discussed above, having a monopoly does not by itself

(continued)

UNITED STATES v. MICROSOFT CORPORATION
(concluded)

violate Section 2. A firm violates Section 2 only when it acquires or maintains, or attempts to acquire or maintain, a monopoly by engaging in exclusionary conduct. Microsoft has engaged in such predatory conduct to maintain its monopoly position by deliberately engaging in conduct designed to prevent the effective distribution and use of Netscape Navigator as an Internet browser. For instance, Microsoft's agreements licensing Windows to equipment manufacturers were designed to prevent them from distributing browsers other than Microsoft's Internet Explorer. Further, because Microsoft's executives did not believe the licensing restrictions alone would be sufficient to reverse the direction of Netscape Navigator's usage share, Microsoft set out to bind its Internet Explorer more tightly to Windows as a technical matter. This both prevented the original equipment manufacturers from pre-installing Navigator and deterred consumers from using it. Microsoft also extended valuable promotional treatment to the 10 most powerful Internet access providers in exchange for their commitment to promote and distribute Internet Explorer and to exile

Navigator from the desktop. For instance, Microsoft put an America Online (AOL) icon in the Online Service folder on the Windows desktop. In return, AOL would not promote any non-Microsoft browser, nor provide software using any non-Microsoft browser except at the customer's request. Even then AOL promised to not supply more than 15 percent of its subscribers with a browser other than Internet Explorer. Further, during a period when Apple's business was in steep decline, Microsoft threatened to stop developing the popular "Office" software for Apple computers unless Apple agreed to install Internet Explorer and refrain from installing Navigator on its computers during the default installation. Finally, Microsoft viewed Java as a potential threat to Windows' position as the only widely used platform for software development. Accordingly, it coerced Intel to stop aiding Sun Microsystems in improving Java technologies. Each of these activities by Microsoft constitute the use of anticompetitive means to maintain a monopoly in violation of Section 2 of the Sherman Act.

THE CLAYTON ACT

The Clayton Act was passed in 1914 to supplement the Sherman Act by attacking specific practices that monopolists had historically followed to gain monopoly power. The idea was to "nip monopolies in the bud" before a full-blown restraint of trade or monopoly power was achieved. The Clayton Act was intended to be "preventive" in nature, and in most cases only the **probability** of a significant anticompetitive effect must be shown to establish a violation.

Since the Clayton Act deals with probable harms to competition, there is no criminal liability for Clayton Act violations. Treble damages are available to private plaintiffs, however, and the Federal Trade Commission has the power to enforce the act through the use of cease and desist orders.

SECTION 3

Section 3 of the Clayton Act was basically designed to attack three kinds of anticompetitive behavior: tie-in (or tying) contracts, exclusive dealing contracts, and requirements contracts. Section 3 makes it illegal to lease or sell commodities or to fix a price for commodities on the condition or agreement that the buyer or lessee will not deal in the commodities of the competitors of the seller or lessor if doing so may "substantially lessen competition or tend to create a monopoly in any line of commerce."

Section 3 applies only to **commodities** (goods), so tie-in, exclusive dealing, and requirements contracts that involve services must be attacked under Section 1 of the

Sherman Act. Section 3 does not apply to cases in which a manufacturer has entered true consignment arrangements with its distributors, since no sale or lease occurs in such cases. No formal agreement is required for a violation of Section 3; any use by the seller of economic power to stop buyers from dealing with the seller's competitors is enough to satisfy the statute.

Tie-In Contracts

Tie-in contracts (tying contracts) occur when a seller refuses to sell a product (the tying product) to a buyer unless the buyer also purchases another product (the tied product) from the seller. So, if Acme Seeds, Inc., refuses to sell its seeds (the tying product) to farmers unless they also agree to buy fertilizer (the tied product) from Acme, this is a tie-in contract; the sale of fertilizer is tied to the sale of seeds.

The economic harm from such contracts is that Acme's competitors in the sale of fertilizer are foreclosed from competing for sales to Acme's buyers, since Acme has used its power in the seed market to force its buyers to buy its fertilizer. There is no legitimate reason why Acme's buyers would ever want to enter tie-in contracts, and therefore the courts have treated such agreements harshly. Tie-in contracts are illegal under Section 3 if (1) the seller has monopoly power in the tie-in product or (2) the seller has foreclosed competitors from a substantial volume of commerce in the tied product. So, if Acme has monopoly power in its seeds or has managed to tie in a substantial dollar volume in fertilizer sales, its tie-in contracts violate Section 3. (See Figure 44–2.)

Tie-in contracts may also violate Section 1 of the Sherman Act. For example, in the *Microsoft* case, the government also complained that Microsoft illegally tied its Internet Explorer Web browser (the tied product) to its Windows operating system (the

---

FIGURE 44–2   A Tie-In Case under Section 3 of the Clayton Act

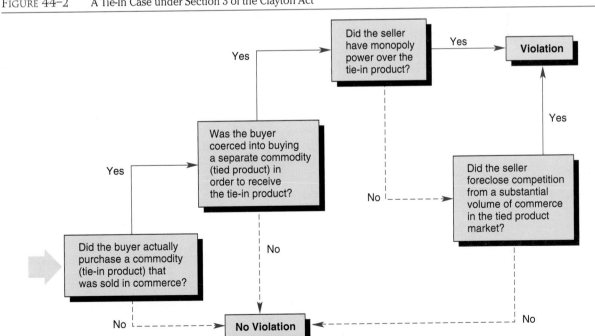

tying product). However, in that case, the appellate court reversed the district court's conclusion that Microsoft's tying behavior was per se illegal. The appellate court believed that rule of reason analysis was more appropriate because per se analysis is reserved for those instances where courts have considerable experience with the business relationships. In *Microsoft*, on the other hand, the appellate court felt the case was providing the judiciary with its first up-close look at the technological integration of added functionality into software that serves as a platform for third-party applications. Ultimately, the Department of Justice decided to drop tying claim.

Exclusive Dealing and Requirements Contracts

An *exclusive dealing contract* is created when a buyer agrees to sell only the product lines of his seller. For example, a lawn and garden store agrees to sell only Brand A lawn mowers. A *requirements contract* is created when a buyer agrees to purchase all of its needs in a certain item from one seller, for example, a candy manufacturer that agrees to buy all the sugar it requires from one sugar refiner. The economic harm of such contracts is that the competitors of the seller are foreclosed from competing for sales to the buyer for the duration of the contract.

These contracts were initially treated like tie-in contracts, with the courts looking at the dollar amount of commerce foreclosed from competition to determine their legality. However, courts today recognize that, unlike tie-in contracts, exclusive dealing and requirements contracts can benefit both the buyer and the seller by reducing selling costs and assuring buyers of a supply of needed items. Therefore, in determining the legality of an exclusive dealing or requirements contract, courts today look at the percentage share of the relevant market foreclosed to competition by the contract.

Section 7

Section 7 of the Clayton Act was designed to provide a tool for attacking **mergers**—a term broadly used in this section to refer to the acquisition of one company by another. It prohibits any corporation engaged in commerce from acquiring all or part of the stock or assets of any other corporation engaged in commerce, except for investment purposes only, when the effect of the acquisition may be to "substantially lessen competition" or "tend to create a monopoly" in "any line of commerce in any section of the country."

The "line of commerce" and "section of the country" concepts in Section 7 are similar to the relevant product and geographic market concepts in Section 2 of the Sherman Act, but they may be more loosely applied due to the preventive nature of Section 7. Similarly, Section 7 invalidates mergers that involve a probable anticompetitive effect at the time of the merger.

Horizontal Mergers

A court seeking to determine the legality of a *horizontal* merger (between competitors) under Section 7 considers the market share of the resulting firm. In recent years, the Supreme Court has been less willing to presume that anticompetitive effects result whenever a horizontal merger produces a firm with a large market share. Instead, the Court has been insisting on a higher level of proof that a contested merger is likely to have a negative effect on competition.

Vertical Mergers

A *vertical* merger is a supplier–customer merger. Vertical mergers occur when a firm acquires a captive market for its products or a captive supplier of a product it regularly buys, thereby becoming a vertically integrated operation (operating on more than one competitive level). The anticompetitive effect of vertical integration is that a share of the relevant market is foreclosed to competition. The competitors of a manufacturer that acquires a chain of retail stores are no longer able to compete for sales to the acquired stores. The competitors of a supplier acquired by a larger buyer are no longer able to compete for sales to that buyer. (Analysis of vertical mergers is very similar to the analysis accorded exclusive dealing arrangements.)

Conglomerate Mergers

Conglomerate mergers are neither horizontal nor vertical. A conglomerate (a large firm that controls numerous other firms in diverse industries) may acquire a firm in a new product market or a firm in the same product market as one of its captive firms but in a different geographic market.

CONCEPT SUMMARY	Types of Mergers	
Category	**Description**	**Example**
Horizontal	Between competitors	One automobile manufacturer merges with another automobile manufacturer.
Vertical	Between a supplier and its customer	An oil producer merges with an oil refiner.
Conglomerate	Between two largely unrelated businesses	A candy company merges with a greeting cards company.

Conglomerate mergers that create a potential for reciprocal dealing have been successfully challenged under Section 7. If a conglomerate purchases a firm that produces a product that another member of the conglomerate regularly buys, or buys a product that another member firm regularly sells, the potential for reciprocal buying is obvious. A conglomerate may also acquire a firm that produces products that the conglomerate's suppliers regularly purchase. Suppliers that are eager to continue selling to the conglomerate may therefore be induced to purchase their requirements from the acquired firm.

Sometimes a conglomerate merger can have an adverse effect on competition by eliminating a potential entrant in the product market. This would occur if a manufacturer of detergents merged with a producer of bleach. Arguably, the detergent manufacturer, since its product line is so closely related to bleach, imposes a competitive check on the bleach industry by the very fact that it might independently enter the market if bleach producers begin reaping monopoly profits.

Hart-Scott-Rodino Antitrust Improvements Act

Proposed mergers or acquisitions affecting U.S. commerce that exceed certain size thresholds must be reported to the Federal Trade Commission and the Department of Justice. Then under the terms of the Hart-Scott-Rodino Antitrust Improvements Act, there is a prescribed waiting period before the transaction can be completed. This waiting period can be extended if the government requests additional information regarding the proposed deal.

THE ROBINSON-PATMAN ACT

DIRECT PRICE DISCRIMINATION

Section 2(a) of the Robinson-Patman Act prohibits discrimination in price between different purchasers of "commodities of like grade and quality" when the effect of the price discrimination may be to "substantially lessen competition or tend to create a monopoly" in any relevant market, or to "injure, destroy, or prevent competition with any person who either grants or knowingly receives the benefits of such discrimination, or with the customers of either of them." To violate Section 2(a), the discriminatory sales must occur roughly within the same period of time and involve goods of like grade and quality. Some substantial physical difference is necessary to justify a different price to competing buyers. So, a manufacturer that sells "house brand" products to a chain store for less than it sells its own brand name products to the chain's competitors has violated Section 2(a) if the only difference between the products is their label. The Robinson-Patman Act, like the Clayton Act, requires only that price discrimination have a probable anticompetitive effect.

DEFENSES TO DIRECT PRICE DISCRIMINATION

A seller who can **cost justify** discriminatory prices by showing that the difference in price is solely the product of actual cost savings, such as lower transportation or production costs, has a defense under Section 2(a). Sellers can also lawfully discriminate in price when doing so reflects **changing conditions** in the marketplace that affect the marketability of goods, such as their deterioration or obsolescence. Finally, Section 2(b) allows sellers to **meet competition** in good faith by granting a discriminatory price in order to retain a customer who has been offered a lawful, lower price by one of the seller's competitors.

HOOVER COLOR CORPORATION V. BAYER CORPORATION
199 F.3d 160 (4th Cir. 1999)

FACTS

Hoover Color Corporation is one of several primary distributors of Bayferrox, a synthetic iron oxide pigment used to color paint, plastics, and building and concrete products. It alleges that Bayer Corporation, its supplier, discriminated in favor of Bayer's larger distributors of Bayferrox by implementing a volume-based incentive discount pricing system. Under this system, the price each distributor paid for Bayferrox depended on the total amount of the product it purchased. Hoover, which purchased substantially smaller quantities of Bayferrox than either of its two competitors (Rockwood Industries and Landers-Segal Company), paid significantly more for the product than they did. Bayer began its system of

volume-based incentive discounts in 1980. At that time, Bayer was building a large manufacturing plant which had high fixed costs. Hoover maintains that Bayer pursued its volume-based pricing strategy in order to obtain the bulk orders necessary to make the new plant profitable. After it began losing sales to Rockwood and Landers-Segal, Hoover brought suit against Bayer for price discrimination in violation of the Robinson-Patman Act. Bayer did not deny that its volume-based pricing strategy discriminated against low-volume purchasers. However, it claimed that it offered the lower prices to Rockwood and Landers-Segal out of a good faith competitive necessity to meet competition for their business.

(continued)

HOOVER COLOR CORPORATION V. BAYER CORPORATION
(concluded)

Hoover responded by arguing that the meeting competition defense requires proof not just to general competition in the marketplace but also to the equally low price of a competitor.

ISSUE

Is Bayer's motive of meeting general competition in the marketplace sufficient to trigger the meeting competition defense?

DECISION

No. Congress enacted the Robinson-Patman Act to prevent a large buyer from securing a competitive advantage over a small buyer solely because of the large buyer's quantity purchasing ability. The Act thus seeks to increase competition by regulating large buyers' economic power. When one or a few large buyers dominate a market in which many suppliers compete for sales, these buyers can, if unrestrained, force the suppliers to sell at such low prices as to prevent new buyers from entering the market. However, to ensure that the statute confines its ban on price discrimination to those situations in which the desire for increased competition would justify legal constraints, Congress also provided sellers with the meeting competition affirmative defense. The Robinson-Patman Act has not enjoyed wide approval. Indeed, professional and academic opinion has almost uniformly condemned the statute. We must nevertheless attempt to interpret and apply the law, whatever its faults, as written and intended by Congress. To establish a prima facie case of price discrimination, the plaintiff must prove (1) a seller sold the same product at different prices to different purchasers and (2) such differences in price reasonably may cause an injury to competition. The plaintiff may prove the first element—price difference—through evidence of volume-based discounts that are theoretically, but not functionally, available to all buyers. The second element—possible injury to competition—so obviously follows from the first that it is established prima facie by proof of substantial price discrimination between competing purchasers over time. It a buyer makes out a prima facie case of price discrimination, a seller can nonetheless avoid liability under the Robinson-Patman Act if it can demonstrate that it set is prices in a good faith attempt to meet an equally low price of a competitor. This affirmative

defense requires more than a showing of facts that would have led a reasonable person to believe that a lower price was available to the favored purchaser from a competitor. Rather, to establish the defense, a seller must also prove that the lower price was made in good faith to meet the competitor's low price. Documenting competition in the market and the threat of reduced sales as a result of that competition is not enough to trigger the defense. Most markets are competitive and pricing is therefore almost always driven by considerations of competitive pressures. Therefore, if the Robinson-Patman Act provided a defense to every seller who could document a good faith attempt to meet general competition in the market place, the meeting competition defense would virtually obliterate the protection Congress sought to provide buyers. Thus, the statute provides no defense from the ban on discriminatory pricing when that pricing is based on general competition in the market but affords a seller an absolute affirmative defense when its prices are set in good faith to meet an equally low price of a competitor. Hence, this defense places emphasis on individual competitive situations, rather than upon a general system of competition. In this case there is strong evidence that Bayer did not institute the volume discounts to meet an equally low price offered by a competitor. First, one reason for the volume discounts was to maintain a high volume of business for Bayer's new production facility so it would be cost effective. A seller's attempt to set prices to satisfy the high volume necessary to operate its plant successfully certainly does not establish that the prices were set to meet a specific competitor's prices, and Bayer must prove the latter. Further, Bayer's agreements with Rockwood and Landers-Segal lend additional support to the conclusion that Bayer did not create the volume-based discount pricing system to match the offers of a competitor. These agreements contain, in addition to the provision for volume discounts, a separate express agreement that provides Bayer the opportunity to match any lower price offer before the buyers accepted such an offer. Thus, wholly apart from the volume-based discounts, the contracts provide an explicit mechanism for Bayer to receive and match competing offers. Given this evidence, it is reasonable to assume that Bayer did not need or intend the volume discounts to match competing offers.

INDIRECT PRICE DISCRIMINATION

In passing the Robinson-Patman Act, Congress recognized that sellers could indirectly discriminate among competing buyers by making discriminatory payments to them or by furnishing them with certain services that were not available to their competitors. Section 2(d) prohibits sellers from making discriminatory payments to competing customers for services (such as advertising or promotional activities) or facilities (such as shelf space furnished by the customers in connection with the marketing of the goods). Section 2(e) prohibits sellers from discriminating in the services they furnish to competing customers. Thus, a seller would violate this provision if he provided a favored customer with a display case or a demonstration kit.

Sellers may lawfully provide such payments or services only if these are made available to competing customers on proportionately equal terms. This means notifying customers of the availability of such services and distributing them according to some rational basis, such as the quantity of goods the customer purchases. The seller must devise a flexible plan that enables various classes of buyers, large chains or small independents, to participate. (See Figure 44–3.)

Ethical Implications   Is it ethical for a buyer to lie to her seller, claiming that she received a lower bid from one of the seller's competitors?

FIGURE 44–3   Price Discrimination

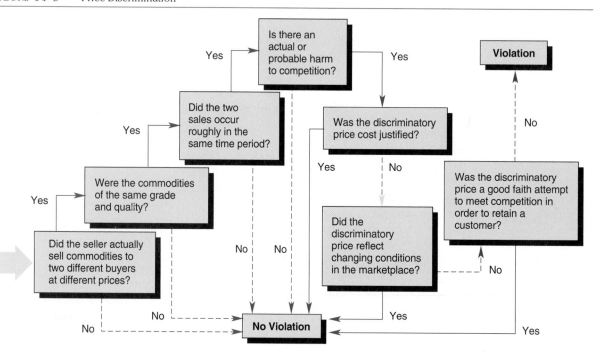

.... **LIMITS ON ANTITRUST** ....

THE PARKER DOCTRINE

The Parker Doctrine, often referred to as the **state action exemption**, exempts many anticompetitive acts from the antitrust laws. This exemption embraces the actions of state officials under the authority of state law and the actions of private firms or individuals under the supervision of authorized state officials. Thus, many of the licensing schemes limiting entry into the various professions are permissible, notwithstanding their anticompetitive effects, because they are shielded from antitrust by the state action exemption.

THE NOERR DOCTRINE

The Noerr Doctrine allows people and businesses to join together and lobby governmental officials for various ends even though the desired action may harm their competitors or otherwise limit competition. This exception was based on the right of petition recognized by the Constitution and the policy of ensuring that governmental officials have an adequate supply of information.

A.D. BEDELL WHOLESALE COMPANY V. PHILIP MORRIS INCORPORATED
263 F.3d 239 (3d Cir. 2001)

FACTS

In the mid-1990s, numerous states commenced lawsuits against the four major tobacco companies (Majors) to recoup healthcare costs and reduce smoking by minors. The states alleged a wide range of deceptive and fraudulent practices by the tobacco companies over decades of sales. The Majors are responsible for 98 percent of cigarette sales in the United States. On November 23, 1998, the Majors and the State Attorneys General executed the Multistate Settlement Agreement (Agreement). Afterwards, 20 other tobacco companies, representing 2 percent of the market, joined the settlement as Subsequent Participating Manufacturers (SPMs). The addition of the SPMs meant that nearly all of the cigarette producers in the domestic market had signed the Agreement. Their addition was significant. The Majors allegedly feared that any Non-Participating Manufacturers (NPMs), cigarette manufacturers left out of a settlement, would be free to expand market share or could enter the market with lower prices, drastically altering the Majors' future profits and their ability to increase prices to pay for the settlement. A.D. Bedell, a cigarette wholesaler, brought an antitrust lawsuit challenging sections of the Agreement allegedly designed to maintain market share and restrict entry. One section, the Renegade

Clause, allegedly was designed to prevent current cigarette manufacturers from decreasing prices to increase market share and to bar new entrants from the market. One part of the Renegade Clause creates strong disincentives for SPMs to increase their production and market share. The mechanism, which forces SPMs to pay additional penalties into the settlement fund if they exceed their historic market share, allegedly discourages the SPMs from underpricing the Majors to increase market share, even if they could efficiently do so. Another part of the Renegade Clause requires that if NPMs gain market share, the Majors may decrease their principal payments to the settlement fund at a rate greater than their actual loss of market share. Finally, the Agreement encouraged the states to enact a model Qualifying Statute that would impose additional taxes on NPMs. Further, the Majors financed an enforcement fund that the states could use to investigate and sue NPMs. These provisions largely coerced tobacco companies to join the Agreement. At the same time, they allegedly create severe obstacles to market entry, or to increasing production and market share. This is not accidental. The Agreement explicitly proclaims its purpose to reduce the ability of NPMs to seize market share because of

(continued)

A.D. BEDELL WHOLESALE COMPANY V. PHILIP MORRIS INCORPORATED
(concluded)

competitive advantage accruing from not contributing to the settlement. It is these barriers to entry and increased production that A.D. Bedell claims form an output cartel that violates Section 1 of the Sherman Act. Because output is restricted and because of inelastic demand for cigarettes, in part due to their addictive nature, the Agreement allegedly permitted the Majors to raise their prices to near monopoly levels—levels allegedly above those necessary to fund the settlement payments. Rapid price increases of this magnitude would ordinarily permit competitors to maintain or reduce prices or prompt new competitors to enter the market. But the plaintiff asserted that neither occurred because the barriers erected by the Agreement effectively barred entry and discouraged tobacco companies from maintaining a lower price because of the penalties for increased production. Philip Morris and the other majors argued that, even if the Agreement does violate the antitrust laws, they are immune from liability under the Noerr doctrine, which protects petitioning activity.

ISSUE

Are the Majors immune from antitrust prosecution under the Noerr doctrine?

DECISION

Yes. Under the Noerr doctrine, a party who petitions the government for redress generally is immune from antitrust liability. This doctrine is rooted in the First Amendment and fears about the threat of liability chilling political speech. The immunity reaches not only to petitioning the legislative and executive branches of government but also to the right to petition extends to all departments of government, including the judiciary. The Noerr immunity applies to actions which might otherwise violate the Sherman Act because the federal antitrust laws do not regulate the conduct of private individuals in seeking anticompetitive action from the government. The antitrust laws are designed for the business world and are not at all appropriate for application in the political arena. Under the Noerr doctrine, private parties may be immunized against liability stemming from antitrust injuries flowing from valid petitioning. This includes two distinct types of actions. A petitioner may be immune from the antitrust injuries which result from the petitioning itself. Also, and particularly relevant here, parties are immune from liability arising from the antitrust injuries caused by government action which results from petitioning. Here, it is clear that, in negotiating the Multistate Settlement Agreement, the defendants engaged in petitioning activity with sovereign states and are immune from antitrust liability under the Noerr doctrine. The fact that the motivating purpose behind the Agreement may have been to create a cartel guaranteeing the tobacco companies supracompetitive profits does not alter this conclusion. The parties' motives are generally irrelevant and carry no legal significance. At the same time, it bears noting that the petitioning here invoked the States' traditional powers to regulate the health and welfare of its citizens.

INTERNATIONAL TRADE LIMITATIONS

Sovereign Immunity

When foreign governments are involved in commercial activities affecting U.S. competitors, our antitrust policy may be at odds with our foreign policy. Accordingly, the Foreign Sovereign Immunities Act of 1976 (FSIA) provides that the governmental actions of foreign sovereigns and their agents are exempt from antitrust liability. The commercial activities of foreign sovereigns, however, are not included within this **sovereign immunity** doctrine. Significant international controversy exists over the proper criteria for determining when a governmental activity is commercial.

Sovereign Compulsion

Closely related to the act of state doctrine is the foreign **sovereign compulsion** defense. Under this doctrine, private parties may be excused from complying with our antitrust laws when their anticompetitive conduct has been directed or compelled by a foreign government. The defense is not available unless the foreign government has actually compelled, rather than merely permitted or encouraged, the anticompetitive activity. Further, it will not apply if the anticompetitive conduct has occurred primarily within the territory of the United States.

Act of State Doctrine

The **act of state doctrine** provides that a U.S. court cannot adjudicate a politically sensitive dispute that would require the court to determine the legality of a sovereign act by a foreign nation. Similar to sovereign immunity, the act of state doctrine recognizes the importance of respecting the sovereignty of other nations.

Export Trading Company Act

As the U.S. trade balance worsened and its imports began to exceed its exports, the importance of facilitating exports was recognized. One response to this was the passage of the Export Trading Company Act of 1982. This act allows exporters whose goods or services will not be resold in the United States to apply to the Department of Commerce for a "certificate of review." If the Commerce Department finds that the exporter's activities will not unduly restrain trade or affect domestic prices or unfairly compete against other U.S. exporters, the Commerce Department, with the concurrence of the Justice Department, will issue the certificate.

The export trade certificate imparts a presumption of legality on the certified conduct of the export trading company and, even if an injured party can prove that a violation has occurred, it can receive only actual (rather than treble) damages. The Commerce Department may modify or revoke an export trade certificate if it determines that the trading company no longer is complying with the terms of the certificate.

.... *QUESTIONS AND PROBLEM CASES* ....

1. In 1984, an antitrust consent decree took AT&T out of the local telephone service business and left AT&T a long-distance telephone service provider competing with firms such as MCI and Sprint. The decree transformed AT&T's formerly owned local telephone companies into independent firms. At the same time, the decree insisted that those local firms help ensure competitive long-distance service by guaranteeing long-distance companies physical access to their systems and to their local customers. To guarantee that physical access, some local telephone firms had to install new call-switching equipment; and to do this, they often had to remove old call-switching equipment. Discon sold the removal services used by New York Telephone Company, a firm supplying local telephone services. New York Telephone Company is a subsidiary of NYNEX Corporation, which owns Material Enterprises Company, a purchasing entity that bought removal services for New York Telephone. Discon claimed that Material Enterprises had switched its purchases from Discon to Discon's competitor, AT&T Technologies, as part of an attempt to defraud local telephone services customers by hoodwinking regulators. According to Discon, Material Enterprises would pay AT&T Technologies more than Discon would have charged for similar removal services. It did so because it could pass the higher prices on to New York Telephone, which in turn could pass those prices on to telephone consumers in the form of higher regulatory-agency-approved telephone service charges. At the end of the year, Material Enterprises would receive a special rebate from AT&T Technologies, which Material Enterprises would share with its corporate parent, NYNEX. Discon added that it refused to participate in this

fraudulent scheme, with the result that Material Enterprises would not buy from Discon, and Discon went out of business. Discon claimed that Material Enterprise's decision not to buy from Discon constituted a group boycott which was per se illegal. Has Material Enterprises committed a group boycott which is per se unlawful?

2. USA Petroleum claimed that Atlantic Richfield (ARCO) violated Section 1 of the Sherman Act by conspiring with its retail service station dealers to fix retail prices at below-market levels. USA asserted that ARCO's strategy was to eliminate the independent dealers by fixing and subsidizing below-market prices and siphoning off the independents' volumes and profits. ARCO claimed that USA did not have standing to sue because ARCO's maximum resale price maintenance scheme increased rather than decreased competition. It argued that maximum resale price maintenance brings prices lower, not higher. Thus, if competitors failed, it was because they were not able to match the low prices charged by ARCO's dealers. Is USA Petroleum entitled to antitrust damages due to ARCO's resale price maintenance scheme?

3. Blaine was licensed to operate a Meineke discount muffler shop in Hartford, Connecticut. In the franchise agreement, Meineke agreed not to license or operate another muffler shop within a three-mile area of Blaine's franchise. This dispute arose when Blaine alleged that Meineke licensed other franchises within his territory. He also claimed that Meineke wrongfully refused his request to operate another Meineke franchise in another community. Blaine sued Meineke and the other franchisees, claiming that they violated his franchise agreement and ignored his request for a new franchise in furtherance of a combination or conspiracy to monopolize the Hartford area. Did Meineke violate Section 2 of the Sherman Act?

4. Roland, a substantial dealer in construction equipment, was for many years the area's exclusive distributor of International Harvester construction equipment. After buying Harvester's construction equipment division, Dresser signed a dealership agreement with Roland. The agreement was terminable at will by either party on 90 days' notice. It did not contain an exclusive dealing clause. Eight months later, Roland signed a similar agreement with Komatsu. Several months after discovering this fact, Dresser gave notice to Roland of its intention to terminate its dealership. Roland argued that Dresser's decision to terminate the dealership demonstrated the existence of an implied exclusive dealing contract in violation of Section 3 of the Clayton Act. Did Dresser and Roland have an illegal exclusive dealing contract?

5. For many years Spray-Rite Service Corporation, a wholesale distributor of agricultural chemicals, sold herbicides manufactured by Monsanto. Spray-Rite was a discount operation, buying in large quantities and selling at low margins. Monsanto then announced that it would appoint distributors on a yearly basis and renew distributorships according to whether the distributor could be expected "to exploit fully" the market in its geographic area of primary responsibility. After receiving numerous complaints from other distributors about Spray-Rite's pricing policies, Monsanto refused to renew Spray-Rite's distributorship on the grounds that Spray-Rite had failed to hire trained salesmen and to promote sales to dealers adequately. Spray-Rite filed suit against Monsanto, arguing that Monsanto had terminated Spray-Rite's distributorship as a part of a conspiracy with the complaining distributors. Does the fact that Monsanto terminated Spray-Rite in response to complaints from its other distributors make the termination illegal?

6. PepsiCo complains of Coca-Cola's behavior in a market described as "sales of fountain-dispensed soft drinks distributed through food service distributors throughout the United States. This market allegedly consists of an increasing number of restaurant chains, movie theater chains, and other "on-premise" accounts that purchase most of their supplies, including fountain soft drink products, through food service distributors. Food service distributors are independent companies that distribute a broad variety of food products, paper products,

and other supplies, including fountain-dispensed soft drinks, in consolidated deliveries to restaurant chains, movie theater chains and other customers. These distributors carry thousands of items and supply all of a customer's needs at once. Because food service distributors offer a form of one-stop shopping, their customers take delivery of all of the customer's supplies from only one distributor at each of the customer's locations. Virtually all of the soft drink volume of these accounts is in fountain-dispensed products and the cost of switching a fountain business to bottles and cans would be prohibitive. According to PepsiCo, other modes of delivery also fail to present an adequate alternative to distribution through food service distributors. PepsiCo alleges that Coca-Cola dominates the market described above because virtually every major food service distributor in America today has an agreement to distribute only Coca-Cola products. PepsiCo claims that when it began to emerge as a threat to Coca-Cola's market dominance, Coca-Cola embarked on a strategy to use its market power to perpetuate its monopoly by threatening food service distributors with the loss of Coke if they dared carry Pepsi and actually cutting off any distributors who decided to carry Pepsi anyway. PepsiCo maintains that Coca-Cola's strategy threatens to freeze PepsiCo out of the market and leave customers who require delivery through food service distributors with no alternative to Coke. PepsiCo alleges that Coca-Cola is guilty of actual or attempted unlawful monopolization of the relevant market in violation of Section 2 of the Sherman Act. Coca-Cola moved to dismiss on the ground that PepsiCo's complaint failed to establish either (1) a valid relevant market or (2) prohibited anticompetitive conduct. Has PepsiCo stated a valid claim for relief under Section 2 of the Sherman Act?

7. George Haug was an authorized parts and service dealer of Rolls Royce automobiles. Rolls Royce Motorcars is an importer and wholesaler of Rolls Royce automobiles as well as the parts distributor. It controlled the market for parts with respect to its automobiles. According to Haug's complaint, Rolls Royce officials were paid commercial bribes to discriminate in favor of Carriage House, one of Haug's competitors. The complaint alleged that Rolls Royce gave preferences to Carriage House consisting of more favorable credit and price terms with respect to parts; payment of the rent of Carriage House; allowing Carriage House a price differential; and enabling Carriage House to offer customers free work paid for by Rolls Royce while requiring Haug to charge similarly situated customers. Rolls Royce claimed that the allegation that Haug was harmed by price differentials given to Carriage House was insufficient in law as a basis for a Robinson-Patman claim in the absence of some allegation of a threat thereby to competition as a whole. Should the court dismiss Haug's Robinson-Patman claim against Rolls Royce?

8. Sylvania, in an attempt to increase its share of the national television sales market, adopted a franchise plan that limited the number of Sylvania franchises granted in a given area and allowed Sylvania's franchisees to sell only from specified store locations. Continental T.V., a Sylvania franchisee, became dissatisfied when Sylvania appointed one of Continental's competitors in the San Francisco area as a Sylvania franchisee and Continental was then denied permission to sell Sylvania television sets in Sacramento. Continental sued, claiming that Sylvania's location restrictions were a per se violation of Section 1 of the Sherman Act. Is Continental correct? Explain.

9. Northwest Wholesale Stationers is a purchasing cooperative made up of approximately 100 office supply retailers. It acts as the primary wholesalers for its member retailers. While nonmembers also may buy supplies from Northwest, members effectively buy supplies at substantially lower prices than nonmembers. Pacific Stationery, a member of Northwest, sold office supplies at both the wholesale and retail level. Pacific continued doing this even after Northwest amended its bylaws to prohibit members from engaging in sales at both levels. (A grandfather clause in the amendment permitted Pacific to continue its membership rights.) However, later and without explanation, Northwest's membership voted to expel Pacific from the cooperative venture. Pacific brought

an antitrust suit, claiming that its expulsion amounted to a per se illegal group boycott. Has Northwest committed a per se violation of the Sherman Act?

10. The Ivy League universities and MIT formed an Overlap Group that compared proposed financial aid packages for more than 10,000 common admittees. In most cases it eliminated any financial aid variances so that a family's expenses would be the same wherever a student enrolled. After a two-year investigation, the Justice Department brought antitrust charges against the Ivy League schools and MIT for illegally fixing the amounts of financial aid given to prospective students. All of the schools except MIT agreed to settle the antitrust charges by promising not to collude in the future on financial aid, tuition levels, or faculty salaries. After a trial, a federal district court found that the Overlap Agreement constituted price fixing. Due to the nonprofit status and educational mission of the alleged conspirators, the court declined to apply *per se* illegality. However, faced with what it believed was a plainly anticompetitive agreement, it applied an abbreviated rule of reason and took only a "quick look" to determine whether MIT presented any plausible procompetitive defenses that justified the Overlap Agreement. It dismissed MIT's argument that the program widened the pool of applicants, increased consumer choice, and opened the doors of the nation's most elite universities to diversely gifted students of varied socioeconomic backgrounds. The district court deemed these explanations to be social welfare justifications and flatly rejected the contention that the elimination of competition may be justified by noneconomic considerations. Should the court have considered MIT's defenses under a rule of reason analysis?

CHAPTER 45

Consumer Protection Laws

Fischl applied to General Motors Acceptance Corporation (GMAC) for financing to buy a BMW. GMAC turned him down after receiving a report from a credit agency that erroneously listed his current job as past employment. The letter rejecting his application stated that his credit references were insufficient.

- *Is Fischl entitled to a better explanation of why his credit application was rejected?*
- *Can Fischl get the erroneous information corrected?*
- *Can Fischl sue for any damages he suffered?*

.... *INTRODUCTION*

For many years, consumers dealt with merchants and providers of services on the basis of *caveat emptor* (let the buyer beware). Buyers were expected to look out for and protect their own interests. In addition, much of the law concerning the sales of goods and the extension of credit was structured to protect business interests rather than consumer interests. Beginning in the mid-1960s, at about the same time that the law of product liability was changing, many consumers recognized that these sales and credit laws put them at a disadvantage in trying to protect what they thought were their rights. Consumer groups lobbied Congress, state legislatures, and city halls to pass statutes or ordinances changing this body of law to make it more favorable to consumers.

Many everyday consumer problems are addressed by these laws. For example, have you, like Fischl, ever been denied credit without getting an adequate explanation from the creditor? Have you ever had a department store or charge card company credit your payment to the wrong account or refuse to correct an error in your bill? Have you ever been harassed by a debt collector for a bill you do not owe or one you have already paid? The laws covering these situations will be discussed in this chapter.

FEDERAL TRADE COMMISSION ACT

The Federal Trade Commission Act, which is the grandfather of "consumer protection" legislation, was passed in 1914. Under the act, the five-member Federal Trade Commission (FTC) has authority to decide whether specific marketing and sales practices are unfair or deceptive, and whether those practices may be harmful to competition among manufacturers, distributors, and sellers. After making such a decision, the FTC may order the company that is engaged in the unlawful conduct to cease and to take corrective action. It may also ask a federal court to award redress, such as giving refunds or damages to injured consumers. The FTC has the power to establish rules that govern conduct in certain industries. It also enforces most of the federal consumer protection laws and regulations that are discussed in this chapter, as well as many others. (See Table 45–1.)

.... *CONSUMER CREDIT LAWS*

Because of the widespread use of credit by consumers, the federal government and the states have enacted a series of statutes and regulations to govern credit transactions. These credit laws are designed to increase consumers' knowledge before they enter into credit transactions and to give consumers certain rights. The laws are also intended to ensure that consumers are treated fairly and without discrimination throughout the course of a credit transaction.

TRUTH IN LENDING ACT

In 1969, Congress gave consumers the right to be advised of all terms of their credit transactions (purchases on credit) at or before the time they sign the credit contract. The **Truth in Lending Act (TILA)** is intended to furnish the consumer with a better opportunity to shop for credit among merchants, finance companies, credit unions, and banks. Another purpose is to enable the consumer to understand all the charges made in connection with credit. The TILA requires that the interest rate be stated

TABLE 45–1   Some of the Major Acts Enforced by the FTC

Regulation of Economic Competition

FTC Act Section 5 (including Sherman Act standards)—discussed in this chapter and in Chapter 44

Clayton Act—discussed in Chapter 44

Robinson-Patman Act—also discussed in Chapter 44

Hart-Scott-Rodino Antitrust Improvements Act of 1976—requires that certain companies planning mergers notify and provide information to the FTC and the Justice Department

Magnuson-Moss Warranty Act—discussed in Chapter 17

Consumer Protection Measures Discussed in This Chapter

FTC Act Section 5

Truth in Lending Act (including 1988 Fair Credit and Charge Card Disclosure Act and Home Equity Loan Consumer Protection Act)

Consumer Leasing Act

Fair Credit Billing Act

Fair Credit Reporting Act

Equal Credit Opportunity Act

Fair Debt Collection Practices Act

Telemarketing and Consumer Fraud and Abuse Prevention Act

FTC Holder in Due Course Rule

Other Measures

Export Trade Act—empowers FTC to supervise registration and operation of associations of U.S. exporters engaged in export trade

Fair Packaging and Labeling Act—regulates packaging and labeling of consumer products to ensure accurate quality and value comparisons

Flammable Fabrics Act—FTC has some enforcement powers under act regulating manufacture, sale, and importation of flammable fabrics

Fur Products Labeling Act—regulates labeling, other identification, and advertising of fur products

Hobby Protection Act—regulates certain imitations of political campaign materials and certain imitation coins and paper money

Lanham Act—empowers FTC to petition for the cancellation of certain trademarks

Smokeless Tobacco Act—empowers FTC to approve manufacturers' plans for rotation and display of statements on smokeless tobacco packages and ads

Textile Fiber Products Identification Act—regulates labeling and other identification of textile fiber products

Wool Products Labeling Act—regulates labeling and other identification of wool products

Source: 1993 United States Government Manual and various statutes.

clearly in terms of an annual percentage rate. The contract or disclosure form must also show the dollar costs of credit as the finance charge. The term *finance charge* includes all costs related to the extension of credit. These costs may include loan fees and fees for credit reports. Charges for life, health, or accident insurance written in connection with the purchase on credit may also be part of the finance charge if the insurance is required for the extension of credit. The act does not fix or limit interest rates or other credit charges. However, state laws may set limits on the interest rates that can be charged in a credit transaction.

One of the act's most significant protections is the buyer's (debtor's) right to cancel the contract. The act provides a cancellation right, technically called a "right of rescission," for three business days after the purchase on credit or after such time as the creditor makes the required disclosure. The right is limited to cases in which the debtor's home is used as collateral but does not apply to first mortgages that finance the purchase or construction of a home. The creditor must give the purchaser written notice of the right to cancel. If the purchaser cancels, he also must give notice in writing. A typical example of the kind of transaction in which the debtor has the right to cancel is major home repair or remodeling on credit. Consumers who purchase a furnace or carpeting for their home have the same right if the lender takes a security interest or lien on the home. The cancellation right can be waived under certain circumstances.

The act also requires disclosure of all credit terms in advertising if the advertiser mentions one or more of the credit terms. An advertisement that states "$10 down payment" or "12 percent interest" or "$99 per month" must also include all of the relevant terms. These include the annual percentage rate, the down payment, and the terms of repayment. This requirement helps the consumer put the advertised terms into perspective. The act also regulates advertising about *home equity loans* and the information that must be revealed on the application form for such a loan, the terms of the home equity loan, and the actions the creditor can take pursuant to it. For example, the creditor cannot unilaterally terminate the plan and require immediate payment.

The TILA contains many terms regulating credit card plans. One of the most important is the rule limiting a cardholder's liability for unauthorized use of a credit card to a maximum of $50. *Unauthorized use* is defined as use by a person who lacks express, implied, or apparent authority to use the card. Thus, charges on a stolen credit card that exceed $50 would generally not have to be paid by the cardholder. The $50 limit has also been extended to debit cards if the loss is reported within two days.

SMITH V. CASH STORE MANAGEMENT INC.
195 F.3d 325 (7th Cir. 1999)

FACTS

Cash Store Management (SCM) made "payday loans." In such loans, the borrower writes a check and post-dates it to the end of the loan period, which is typically for two weeks. The loans have high annual percentage rates—in Smith's case, 521 percent. At the end of the two weeks, the borrower can renew the loan for another two weeks by paying the interest. When the loan was given or renewed, CSM stapled to the top of the loan agreement a receipt that labeled the finance charge as either a deferred deposit check fee or deferred deposit extension fee. CSM stapled the receipt to the upper left-hand corner of the loan agreements, physically covering up some of the required TILA disclosures, and failed to use the

term "finance charge" that is used in the federal disclosure box on the loan agreement. Smith sued for CSM's failure to follow the Act.

ISSUE

If proved, do CSM's actions violate the Truth in Lending Act?

DECISION

Yes. The sufficiency of TILA-required disclosures is to be viewed from the standpoint of the "ordinary consumer," not the viewpoint of a federal judge or an English professor. It is a valid legal claim that CSM printed confusing or misleading terms on the receipt and stapled the receipt in such a way as to obscure the required disclosures.

CONSUMER LEASING ACT

An amendment to the TILA, the **Consumer Leasing Act,** requires the creditor to disclose the aggregate costs of leasing consumer goods. It also requires that the lease agreement define the consumer's liability at the end of the lease. The act applies to leases of consumer goods if the leases are for more than four months and the total contractual obligation does not exceed $25,000. Lessors who violate the act's requirements are subject to the same penalties as those prescribed under the TILA.

FAIR CREDIT BILLING ACT

In 1974, Congress supplemented the Truth-in-Lending Act with the **Fair Credit Billing Act (FCBA).** The FCBA provides certain protections for users of credit cards. It prescribes the procedures to be followed both by the holder of the credit card and by the issuer of the card. If the credit card holder thinks that the card issuer has made an error on the statement, such as not crediting a payment or showing a charge that was not made by the customer, he has 60 days from the time the statement was mailed to report, in writing, the error. The card issuer then has 30 days to tell the cardholder that his report has been received. In no more than 90 days, or two billing cycles, the card issuer must either correct the account or, after investigating the bill, explain why it believes the original bill or statement was accurate.

The FCBA also limits the card issuer's freedom to report items the consumer disputes as late payments (delinquencies) to credit reporting agencies such as credit bureaus until the investigation is complete and the cardholder has had the opportunity to pay the charge. In such cases, the card issuer must inform the cardholder of the persons or companies to which the card issuer sends its report. The card issuer who fails to comply with the act forfeits the right to collect up to $50 from the cardholder. The act also permits the seller to offer discounts if the buyer pays cash for a purchase rather than using a credit card.

FAIR CREDIT REPORTING ACT

The principal purpose of the **Fair Credit Reporting Act (FCRA)** is to ensure that information concerning a person's credit background supplied by her creditors is both up-to-date and accurate. It covers credit information supplied to potential creditors, insurers, or employers of that person. Accuracy has become even more important as employers increase their use of credit agency reports to screen applicants. A secondary goal of the act is to guard against disclosure of such confidential information to persons who request it for purposes other than those specified in the act. The act does not apply when an individual applies for commercial, rather than consumer, credit or insurance.

The FCRA offers special protection to persons who have been denied credit, insurance, or employment, such as Fischl, the consumer in the introductory case. A consumer who is denied credit by the person who received a credit report is entitled to disclosure of the name and address of the credit reporting agency (credit bureau) that made the report. The consumer may require the credit reporting agency (as the provider of the information) to reinvestigate information disputed by the consumer and to delete any inaccurate or obsolete information from the file. If the dispute is not resolved at that point (for example, if the consumer still objects to the accuracy of the information), the consumer may file a brief statement of her version of the dispute for the credit file. The credit reporting agency is then required by the act to state that the consumer disputes the information when it gives out the information in the consumer's file. If inaccurate or unverifiable information is deleted from the consumer's file, the consumer may request the reporting agency to contact any person who had been given the deleted information. Recipients who obtained the credit report for *credit* or *insurance purposes* within six months prior to deletion must be advised of the deletion. If the request for credit information was for *employment purposes* and was made within two years of the deletion, then the requestor must be notified of the deletion of the inaccurate or unverifiable information.

Employers who obtain credit information about a job applicant must notify the applicant if he was not hired at least in part on the basis of a credit report. Several states have also enacted laws that require such disclosure as well as limit the kinds of information employers can obtain from applicants' credit reports.

The act offers several additional protections to consumers. First, a consumer has the right to have a consumer report withheld from anyone who under the law does not have a legitimate business need for the information. Second, the consumer can sue for damages for negligent violation of the act and for the collection of attorney's fees and court costs if the suit is successful. If the violation of the act is found to be willful, punitive damages may also be awarded. Third, the credit reporting agency may not report most adverse information more than seven years old. However, the fact that the consumer was declared bankrupt can be reported for 10 years after the bankruptcy. Fourth, the FCRA imposes a duty of disclosure on people who deny credit or increase its cost to the consumer because of information obtained from a person *other than a consumer reporting agency* if the consumer so requests.

Because of the increasing reliance of companies, employers, insurers, and others on credit reports, it is important for individuals to regularly check their credit information. This is especially true because of the growing problem of identity theft. The following Supreme Court case underlines the importance of a timely check.

TRW Inc. v. Andrews
122 S. Ct. 441 (2001)

FACTS

In 1993, Adelaide Andrews filled out a form at her doctor's office in Santa Monica, California. She listed her name, Social Security number, and other information. The receptionist, Andrea Andrews, copied the data and moved to Las Vegas where, in 1994, she opened credit accounts using Adelaide's Social Security number and her own last name and address. TRW furnished copies of Adelaide's credit report to companies to which Andrea had applied for credit. Adelaide did not find out about it until 1995, when she sought to refinance her home and in the process received a copy of her credit report. The report showed Andrea's activities. Seventeen months later Adelaide sued TRW for failing to follow procedures under the Act. It released the information even though several things in the request form did not match the record including the first name, birth date and address.

TRW defended by arguing that the two-year statute of limitations had run. Adelaide argued that the limitations period should not begin to run until after discovery of the problem.

ISSUE

Should the statutory two-year limitation period begin when the consumer discovers the problem?

DECISION

No. Congress enacted the FCRA in 1970 to promote efficiency in the Nation's banking system and to protect consumer privacy. The Act requires credit reporting agencies to maintain "reasonable procedures" designed "to assure maximum possible accuracy of the information" contained in credit reports, and to limit the furnishing of

(continued)

TRW Inc. v. Andrews
(concluded)

such reports only to certain parties spelled out in the Act. It also spells out a two-year statute of limitations for most claims brought under the Act. A discovery rule is generally applied at the federal level when the statute is silent on the limitations period. Here there is a spe- cific two-year period except when disclosure is willfully inaccurate. This shows Congress' intent to preclude judi- cial implication of a discovery rule. We are not at liberty to make general Congress' explicit desegnation of the two-year rule.

EQUAL CREDIT OPPORTUNITY ACT

The **Equal Credit Opportunity Act (ECOA)** prohibits discrimination in credit trans- actions on grounds of sex, marital status, race, color, religion, national origin, and age. For example, the ECOA protects the 63-year-old applicant for a mortgage who plans to work 5 to 7 years longer and seeks a 15-year mortgage. The lender cannot turn down the application solely because of the applicant's age. The act also assists the widow or divorced woman who may not have a credit history in her own name as well as the young applicant so long as she is old enough to enter into a valid contract. The act applies to banks, finance companies, retail stores, credit card issuers (such as gasoline companies or Diner's Club), and other firms that regularly extend credit.

The protections afforded by the ECOA cover all phases of the credit transaction. The creditor may not do any of the following: discourage the application for credit, refuse to grant a separate account to a married woman if she is a credit applicant, or ask about the applicant's marital status if a separate account is requested. There are two exceptions to the prohibition against asking about marital status. The creditor may do so if security is required for the account or if state laws (such as community property laws) require otherwise.

The creditor must either accept or reject a credit application within 30 days. If the creditor denies a credit application, it must provide the specific reasons for that de- nial within a reasonable time or tell the consumer that he or she has the right to spe- cific reasons. Such statements as "You didn't meet our minimum standards" or "You didn't receive enough points on our credit scoring system" do not comply with the ECOA.

The consumer is also entitled to have creditors report to credit reporting agencies in the names of both spouses the credit history of any account shared by a married couple. In other words, if Mrs. Ray Hughes shares an account in her husband's name, she may ask the credit agency to retroactively report that account in her name as well as her husband's. The credit experience concerning all accounts that both spouses may use and on which both are liable must be reported by creditors in both names. The ECOA also prohibits a creditor from using unfavorable information about an ac- count that an applicant shared with a spouse or former spouse. To trigger this prohi- bition, the applicant must show that the bad credit rating does not accurately reflect his or her willingness or ability to pay.

The ECOA does not guarantee credit or unlimited credit to any person. Creditors may still set standards on which they will grant credit. They may not set standards that have the effect of denying credit to a protected class (such as women or the elderly), and they may not apply their standards on a discriminatory basis.

FAIR DEBT COLLECTION PRACTICES ACT

Public concern about harassment by debt collectors, including late-night phone calls and threats of violence, led Congress in 1977 to pass the **Fair Debt Collection Practices Act (FDCPA).** Most states also have laws aimed at abuses by debt collectors. The federal act allows exemptions for states with similar laws as long as there are adequate provisions for enforcement. The federal act affects only the practices of debt collection agencies that collect consumer bills for creditors other than themselves. It does not cover retail stores, banks, or businesses that collect their own debts in their own name.

Actions prohibited in the FDCPA are listed in the Consumer Credit Laws Concept Summary shown later in this chapter. The act is enforced by the Federal Trade Commission. The consumer may sue for violations of the act; however, there are limits on the damages and penalties that the consumer may recover from the collection agency. The consumer may recover attorney's fees if she wins the suit. If a debt collector brings a suit that is found to be harassing, the winning consumer defendant may also collect attorney's fees.

GAMMON V. GC SERVICES LIMITED PARTNERSHIP
27 F.3d 1254 (7th Cir. 1994)

FACTS

GC sent a letter to Gammon in an effort to collect a debt Gammon owed. The letter stated, in part, "We provide the systems used by a major branch of the federal government and various state governments to collect delinquent taxes. . . . You must surely know the problems you will face later if you do not pay." In judging whether these statements were misleading, the trial court used a "least sophisticated" consumer standard. This standard was challenged on appeal.

ISSUE

Is the "least sophisticated" consumer the appropriate test to use to determine whether a practice is misleading under the FDCPA?

DECISION

No. The FDCPA prohibits debt collectors from using "any false, deceptive, or misleading representation" including implying that the collector is vouched for or affiliated with the U.S. government or any state. The standard to use to judge whether GC's letter violated the act is not the "least sophisticated" consumer. It is virtually impossible to analyze a debt collection letter based on this standard. Literally, the person is not merely below average, but is on the very last rung on the sophistication ladder—he is the single most unsophisticated consumer who exists. Even assuming he would be willing to do so, such a consumer would likely not be able to read a collection notice with care (or at all), let alone interpret it in a reasonable fashion. A better standard to protect the consumer of below-average sophistication or intelligence is simply "unsophisticated." This standard protects the consumer who is uninformed, naive, or trusting, yet it allows an objective element of reasonableness. The reasonableness element shields complying debt collectors from liability for unrealistic or peculiar interpretations of collection letters. Using this standard, the unsophisticated consumer reasonably could interpret GC's letter as implying that the government bodies mentioned vouch for or are affiliated with the collection agency. The language in the letter appears to be cleverly drafted to insinuate what obviously cannot be stated directly. It is hard to imagine what the agency intended other than to intimidate the unsophisticated consumer with the power of having the tax collecting units of the federal and state governments in its corner, or at least at its disposal.

TELEMARKETING AND CONSUMER FRAUD AND ABUSE PREVENTION ACT

Under the **Telemarketing and Consumer Fraud and Abuse Prevention Act** (Telemarketing Act), the FTC established the Telemarketing Sales Rules in 1995 to prevent deceptive and abusive telemarketing practices. The rules require that telemarketers disclose to customers the total cost of the goods or services offered, any material restrictions or conditions on the use or purchase of the goods or services, and the terms of any refund or exchange policies mentioned in the solicitation. These disclosures must be made before the customer pays for the goods or services. Other disclosures must be made if the solicitation pertains to a prize promotion.

In an effort to protect consumers from harassing solicitations, the rules prohibit telemarketers from engaging in abusive practices including causing the phone to ring or engaging in phone conversations repeatedly with the intent to harass, abuse, or annoy the person called, or calling a person who previously said that she does not want to get calls from the seller. Calls cannot be made after 9:00 PM or before 8:00 AM local time. In addition, the telemarketer must clearly disclose the seller, the sales purpose of the call, what is being sold, and the fact that no purchase or payment is necessary to win a prize or participate in a prize promotion.

FTC HOLDER IN DUE COURSE RULE

Consumers who have purchased defective goods or services on credit have frequently been frustrated when the seller assigns the right to payment (the debt) to a third party. The consumer may face demands for payment from the third party, while at the same time she finds that the seller is unwilling to correct the defects or has disappeared. In fact, the consumer might be obligated to pay the third party even though there is no likelihood that the defective performance will be remedied. This could happen if (1) the consumer signed a negotiable instrument that had been negotiated to a holder in due course (see Chapter 37), or (2) the consumer signed an installment sales contract containing a waiver of defenses clause whereby the consumer agreed to assert any defenses she had on the contract against the seller only and not against any assignee of the sales contract.

For example, Harold agrees to pay Ace Improvement $2,500 to put aluminum siding on his house. He signs a promissory note agreeing to pay the note in 24 monthly installments. Ace negotiates the note to a finance company and goes out of business after completing only part of the work on Harold's house. If the finance company can qualify as a holder in due course of the note, it may be able to enforce payment against Harold even though he will not get what he bargained for from Ace Improvement. This results from the basic principle of negotiable instruments law that a holder in due course takes the instrument free of personal defenses (e.g., misrepresentation, nondelivery, nonperformance, or breach of warranty) between the original parties to the instrument.

In 1975, The Federal Trade Commission took action to deal with such situations and adopted the **Holder in Due Course** rule. The rule is designed to preserve for consumers in most purchase money credit transactions the right to use claims and defenses against a holder in due course. It makes it an unfair trade practice for a seller, in the course of financing a consumer purchase or certain leases of goods or services, to use procedures to separate the consumer's duty to pay from the seller's duty to perform.

When the buyer executes a sales contract that includes a promissory note, or signs an installment sales contract that includes a waiver of defenses clause, the following statement (titled "Notice") must be included in bold type:

NOTICE

ANY HOLDER OF THIS CONSUMER CREDIT CONTRACT IS SUBJECT TO ALL CLAIMS AND DEFENSES WHICH THE DEBTOR COULD ASSERT AGAINST THE SELLER OF GOODS OR SERVICES OBTAINED PURSUANT HERETO OR WITH THE PROCEEDS HEREOF. RECOVERY HEREUNDER BY THE DEBTOR SHALL NOT EXCEED AMOUNTS PAID BY THE DEBTOR HEREUNDER.

If the seller arranges with a third-party lender for a direct loan to finance the buyer's purchase, the seller may not accept the proceeds of the loan unless the consumer credit contract between the buyer and the lender contains the following statement in bold type:

NOTICE

ANY HOLDER OF THIS CONSUMER CREDIT CONTRACT IS SUBJECT TO ALL CLAIMS AND DEFENSES WHICH THE DEBTOR COULD ASSERT AGAINST THE SELLER OF GOODS OR SERVICES OBTAINED WITH THE PROCEEDS HEREOF. RECOVERY HEREUNDER BY THE DEBTOR SHALL NOT EXCEED AMOUNTS PAID BY THE DEBTOR HEREUNDER.

CONCEPT SUMMARY	**Consumer Credit Laws**	
Truth-in-Lending Act	Provides the consumer with important credit information (including credit advertising).	Requires: 1. The interest rate to be clearly stated as an annual percentage rate. 2. Disclosure of the *finance* charge (all costs of the credit). 3. The debtor be allowed to rescind for three business days when the home is used for collateral.
Fair Credit Reporting Act	Designed to ensure timely and accurate reporting about a person's credit background and to control disclosure in consumer credit situations.	Requires: 1. A person denied credit be allowed to challenge the information supplied. 2. The credit reporting agency to investigate information claimed wrong. 3. Correction of outdated or wrong information and notification of credit information recipients. 4. Information not be disclosed to those without a legitimate business need for it.
Consumer Leasing Act	Provides the consumer with important credit information involving leases of consumer goods for more than four months.	Requires: 1. Disclosure of aggregate cost of leasing goods. 2. Disclosure of consumer's liability at the end of the lease.
Equal Credit Opportunity Act	Prohibits discrimination in credit transactions on the grounds of sex, marital status, race, color, religion, national origin, or age.	Requires: 1. Creditor to accept or reject application within 30 days. 2. If rejected, creditor must specify reasons. 3. Applicant cannot be asked about marital status when asking for a separate account, and a married woman cannot be refused a separate account on that basis. 4. Creditor not to discourage the application for credit.

(continued)

CONCEPT SUMMARY	**Consumer Credit Laws** *(concluded)*	
Fair Debt Collection Practices Act	Prohibits debt collection agencies from using certain harassing techniques when collecting another's debt.	Actions prohibited: 1. Debt collectors may not contact a consumer at unusual or inconvenient times, or at all if the consumer is represented by an attorney. 2. Debt collectors may not contact a consumer where he or she works if the employer objects. 3. Debt collectors may not use harassing or intimidating tactics or abusive language against *any* person, including the debtor. 4. Debt collectors may not use false or misleading tactics, such as posing as lawyers or police officers. 5. Debt collectors may not contact third parties other than the consumer's attorney, the creditor, the attorney of the creditor, the attorney of the debt collector, or a consumer reporting agency if otherwise permitted by the law, about payment of a debt, unless authorized. 6. Debt collectors cannot communicate again with the consumer, after receiving the consumer's written refusal to pay the debts except to inform the consumer of actions that the collector may take. 7. Debt collectors may not deposit a postdated check prior to the date on it.
Telemarketing and Consumer Fraud and Abuse Prevention Act	Prevents deceptive and abusive telemarketing practices.	Requires: 1. Disclosure of who is calling, what is being sold, the total cost, restrictions, and rules about prizes. Prohibits: 1. Calling between 9:00 PM and 8:00 AM. 2. Harassing or abusive calls.
Holder in Due Course Rule	Preserves the right of consumers to use claims and defenses against a holder in due course of their credit contract.	Requires: 1. Bold type notices in the consumer's credit contract and the lender's contract. 2. All defenses available to the purchaser against the seller can also be available against the holder in due course.

The required statement provides that all defenses available to the purchaser against the seller of the merchandise are also available against the holder in due course. It does this *only* when the consumer's credit contract (promissory note or installment sales contract) contains the required provision. The provision is treated in the same manner as other written terms and conditions in the agreement. It must appear without qualification. A consumer credit contract that includes the required statement in conjunction with other clauses that limit or restrict its application does not satisfy the requirement that the contract "contain the notice."

The FTC rule does not eliminate any rights that the consumer may have as a matter of federal, state, or local law. It creates no new claims or defenses. For example, the rule does not create a warranty claim or defense where the product is sold "as is." The rule also does not alter statutes of limitations or other state-created limitations on the consumer's enforcement of claims and defenses. Finally, the claims or defenses relied on must relate to the sale transaction that is financed; for example, the consumer cannot sue on the grounds of the seller's negligent maintenance of business premises that caused the buyer to break her leg while waiting for warranty service.

Failure to comply with the regulation exposes the seller to a possible fine of $10,000 per violation in a civil action brought by the FTC.

######### *CONSUMER PRODUCT SAFETY ACT*

BACKGROUND

The large number of injuries caused by defective consumer products led Congress to pass the **Consumer Product Safety Act (CPSA)** in 1972. In order to advance Congress's goal of promoting product safety, the act established the Consumer Product Safety Commission (CPSC), an independent regulatory agency composed of five presidentially appointed commissioners, each serving a seven-year term. The CPSC is the main federal agency concerned with product safety. Its authority is basically limited to *consumer products*. Not within the commission's domain, however, are certain products regulated by other agencies, including motor vehicles and equipment, firearms, aircraft, boats, drugs, cosmetics, and food products.

STANDARDS

The CPSC is empowered to issue *product safety standards*. These may (1) involve the performance of consumer products or (2) require product warnings or instructions. A product safety standard should be issued only when the product in question presents an *unreasonable* risk of injury and the standard is *reasonably necessary* to prevent or reduce that risk. The commission may also issue rules *banning* certain "hazardous" products. Such rules are permissible when, in addition to presenting an unreasonable risk of injury, the product is so dangerous that no feasible product safety standard would protect the public from the risks it poses.

REMEDIES

In addition, the CPSC can bring suit in federal district court to eliminate the dangers presented by *imminently hazardous* consumer products. These are products that pose an immediate and unreasonable risk of death, serious illness, or severe personal injury. Finally, manufacturers, distributors, and retailers are required to notify the CPSC if they have reason to know that their products present a *substantial product hazard*. Such a hazard exists when the product creates a substantial risk of injury to the public, either because it violates a CPSC safety rule or for other reasons. In such cases, the commission may, among other things, order the private party to give notice of the problem to those affected by it, repair or replace the product, or submit its own corrective action plan.

    The CPSA provides a host of other remedies and enforcement devices in addition to those already discussed. The commission and the U.S. attorney general may sue for *injunctive relief* or the *seizure* of products to enforce various provisions of the act. *Civil penalties* against those who knowingly violate various CPSA provisions and CPSC rules are also possible. *Criminal penalties* may be imposed on those who knowingly and willfully violate such provisions and rules after CPSC notification of their failure to comply. In addition, any *private party* may sue for an *injunction* to enforce any CPSC rule or order, after giving proper notice, if at the time of the suit the commission or the attorney general has not begun an action based on the alleged violation. Finally, those injured because of a knowing and willful violation of a CPSC rule or order may sue for *damages* if the amount in controversy exceeds $10,000.

######### *LEMON LAWS*

Next to homes, vehicles are the most expensive purchase most consumers make. Unfortunately for many, the vehicles came with significant problems that the consumers

FIGURE 45–1   Typical Lemon Law Coverage

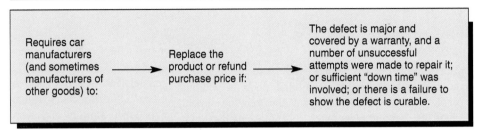

were unable to get their dealers to fix. By 1981, complaints about auto dealers were first on the list of consumer complaints received by the FTC. While the UCC provided some remedies for the consumer, these often proved inadequate or difficult to pursue. In response, a majority of states have now passed **"lemon laws"** that are designed to provide more appropriate relief.

While the laws vary from state to state, they tend to have the same structure. If a car under warranty has a significant defect affecting the car's use or value, and the seller does not fix that defect in a specified number of times or the car is out of commission for a specified period of time, the consumer is entitled to a remedy. Remedies generally include return of the purchase price or a new car. For example, assume Jill's car has a defective seal that allows significant amounts of water to leak in when it rains. Jill has taken it back to the dealer four times; each time, she is assured that it is fixed but it still leaks. If the statute in Jill's state says that the dealer is allowed four attempts to fix the defect, Jill would now be entitled to pursue the remedies established by the statute. (See Figure 45–1.)

Most statutes require that disputes arising under them be arbitrated. The arbitration, which is usually binding on the manufacturer but not on the consumer, is handled by panels set up by the car companies. Because of the practice of "lemon laundering" (reselling cars that manufacturers have been forced to take back without telling the new owners about the car's problem history), some states have expanded their statutes. Under these statutes, manufacturers are required to fully disclose to the subsequent buyer the car's problems, and in some cases, physically brand it as a lemon.

FORD MOTOR CO. v. BARRETT
800 P.2d 367 (Sup. Ct. Wash. 1990)

FACTS

Barrett bought a new 1985 Ford Thunderbird from Mossy Ford. It soon developed a steering problem that caused the car to "pull" to the left. The dealer was unable to correct the problem despite several attempts to do so. Barrett filed a claim under the Washington "lemon law" and the claim proceeded to arbitration. The three-person arbitration panel ordered Ford to repurchase the car. Ford sought review of the arbitral decision in the trial court, and, in addition, challenged the statute's provisions that

require a manufacturer that loses its appeal to pay the consumer's attorney's fees and costs, and $25 per day for all days beyond 40 days following the decision in which it did not provide the consumer with the free use of a comparable loaner car. Ford alleged these fees, which in Barrett's case amounted to $8,750, were unconstitutional because they denied it equal protection.

ISSUE

Is the lemon law constitutional?

(continued)

FORD MOTOR CO. V. BARRETT
(concluded)

DECISION

Yes. Ford alleges it is denied equal protection because consumers may appeal an arbitral decision without penalty but dealers who appeal and lose the appeal must pay fees and costs of the consumer. The presumption of constitutionality of a statute is especially strong when it pertains to purely business and economic activity. The legislature, in passing the law, recognized that a new motor vehicle is a major consumer purchase and that a defective motor vehicle is likely to create a hardship for the consumer. The law was designed to give a manufacturer sufficient incentive to provide good quality control and better warranty service. A consumer has a general lack of economic resources compared to the manufacturer's access to skillful legal counsel and experience with warranty disputes. The consumer needs protection from frivolous appeals, and the manufacturers need incentives to comply with arbitration decisions. Providing for attorney's fees and a loaner car or a fee for the failure to provide it rationally protects the consumer's interests when the manufacturer appeals and loses. Thus, the statute is constitutional.

In addition to the lemon laws, other laws regulate consumer car transactions. For example, the Federal Trade Commission requires used car dealers to display a *Buyer's Guide* on each car that tells whether the car is covered by a warranty and, if it is, the type and duration of the warranty as well as the name of the person to contact if a problem arises. If the sale is conducted in Spanish, the guide must be in Spanish. For problems with new cars, the National Highway Traffic Safety Administration requires manufacturers to tell new-car buyers about a hotline they should call, in addition to their dealer, if they suspect their vehicle has a safety defect.

Computers are quickly gaining the status of a necessity in consumers' lives. Like cars, some may be lemons. Several states are now considering computer lemon laws that would set relatively short time periods in which the computer must be fixed and allow the manufacturer only two or three chances to fix it. If is it not fixed, the consumer must be given the choice of a new computer of equal or greater value, or a refund.

.... *QUESTIONS AND PROBLEM CASES* ....

1. Describe some of the main protections that consumers gain under the Fair Credit Reporting Act.
2. What is the main idea behind the Holder in Due Course rule?
3. Describe the typical terms of a lemon law.
4. Grolier, Inc., sold encyclopedias and other reference publications door to door and through the mail. It engaged in a number of false, deceptive, and misleading trade practices, and used many deceptive recruiting techniques to attract salespeople, for example, ads listing "management trainee" positions that did not exist. It used fraudulent methods to develop sales leads such as false surveys and contests, and it instructed its salespeople to use deception to gain entrance into homes, to misrepresent prices, and to produce false and misleading endorsement letters. The FTC issued a cease and desist order and ordered Grolier to take specific action to correct these practices. Grolier appealed, arguing that the FTC exceeded its power by issuing orders that infringed on First Amendment free speech rights. Is this correct?
5. In 1979, Gloria established a Visa account at the Walker Bank. On her request, cards were issued in her and her husband's name. Soon thereafter, the couple separated, and Gloria notified the bank that she either wanted the account closed or the bank to deny further extensions of credit to her husband. The bank required the cards to

be returned to it in order to close the account. Gloria did not return the cards until three months later, after her husband had charged several things. When Gloria refused to pay for those charges, the bank sued. Is Gloria's liability limited to $50, or must she pay for all the charges?

6. Beach obtained a loan using his home as collateral in 1986. When the bank began foreclosure in 1992, Beach alleged that the bank had failed to make the disclosures required by the TILA and that therefore he could rescind the mortgage agreement and thereby reduce the amount he owed. Can a borrower rescind a loan after three years have passed if the lender has not made the requisite TILA disclosures?

7. Miller, a married woman, wanted to buy love seats. The furniture store offered to arrange financing through the Public Industrial Loan Company. Public later refused to extend credit unless Miller's husband cosigned for the loan because Public had received an unfavorable credit report on Miller from a credit agency. Did Public violate the Equal Credit Opportunity Act?

8. Trans Union Corp. (TUC) and TRW, credit reporting agencies, had credit reports on Philbin that contained false information such as that he was subject to a $9,500 tax lien and had delinquent accounts. Some of the false

information pertained to Philbin's father. In 1990, the companies were notified to correct the information. Philbin was denied credit six times between 1990 and 1993. After he obtained TUC and TRW credit reports from one of the lenders who rejected him for a loan, he saw that the reports again contained erroneous information. Philbin sued, alleging violations of the FCRA. Is he correct?

9. Juras took out several student loans while attending Montana State University (MSU). He defaulted on the loans, and MSU assigned his notes to the Aman Collection Service for collection. Aman sent Juras a letter stating that it was in possession of his grade transcript and it would not release it until he paid his debt. A subsequent letter stated that he would not get his transcript even if the debt were discharged in bankruptcy and it cited a case as authority. It also asserted that withholding the transcript was required by federal law. Most of this was false. Does Juras have a case under the FDCPA?

10. A bank is trying to increase its portfolio of car loans, so it solicits referrals of loan customers from a local auto dealer. The dealer suggests a special one-day promotion during which the bank's customers would receive a $200 discount from the sticker price if they finance their purchases through the bank. What do the dealer and the bank have to do to comply with the FTC's Holder in Due Course rule?

CHAPTER 46

Environmental Regulation

A chemical plant sits on the banks of a river. Black smoke belches from its smokestacks, a smelly haze drifts over the plant, and multicolored liquids ooze from pipes into the river. Behind the plant is a brackish green pond where waste materials from the plant have been deposited. On the loading dock, barrels containing new products for sale are mixed in with almost empty barrels returned by customers. A fenced enclosure shields a huge pile of cardboard, rags soaked with various chemicals, leftover paint, and discarded chemical containers and other trash awaiting transit to the local landfill.

This scene, common in this country 35 years ago and still found in many places in the world, were once viewed as a sign of a successful community. Such a plant meant jobs and economic vitality. Today, we realize that unchecked pollution can impose unacceptable economic and environmental costs. Thus, the operator of a facility such as a chemical plant must, among other things, be concerned with:

- *Controls on the emission of the products of combustion and of toxic chemicals to the atmosphere.*
- *Limits on the sewage and industrial effluents that can be discharged into a river or to the local sewage treatment plant.*
- *Controls on the storage, transportation, treatment, or disposal of hazardous wastes, including the need to segregate different kinds of wastes that may be subject to different limitations on disposal.*
- *The need to consider the potential impact on the environment of the product and its packaging not only during their intended use but also after their useful life.*

.... *INTRODUCTION* ....

Today's businessperson must be concerned with not only competing effectively against competitors but also complying with a myriad of regulatory requirements. For many businesses, particularly those that manufacture goods or that generate wastes, the environmental laws and regulations loom large in terms of the requirements and costs they impose. They can have a significant effect on the way businesses have to be conducted as well as on their profitability. This area of the law has expanded dramatically over the last three decades, and environmental issues are a concern of people and governments around the world. This chapter briefly discusses the development of environmental law and outlines the major federal statutes that have been enacted to control pollution of air, water, and land.

HISTORICAL PERSPECTIVE

Historically, people assumed that the air, water, and land around them would absorb their waste products. In recent times, however, it has become clear that nature's capacity to assimilate people's wastes is not infinite. Burgeoning population, economic growth, affluence, and the products of our industrial society pose risks to human health and the environment. Indeed, one of the challenges of our time is how to achieve "sustainable development"—that is, the level and kind of economic development that do not unreasonably trade off long-term sustainability for the sake of short-term benefits.

Concern about the environment is not a recent phenomenon. In medieval England, Parliament passed "smoke control" acts making it illegal to burn soft coal at certain times of the year. Where the owner or operator of a piece of property is using it in such a manner as to unreasonably interfere with another owner's (or the public's) health or enjoyment of his property, the courts have long entertained suits to abate the nuisance. Nuisance actions, which are discussed in Chapter 32, are frequently not ideal vehicles for dealing with widespread pollution problems. Rather than a hit-or-miss approach, a comprehensive across-the-board approach may be required.

Realizing this, the federal government, as well as many state and local governments, had passed laws to abate air and water pollution by the late 1950s and 1960s. As the 1970s began, concern over the quality and future of the environment produced new laws and fresh public demands for action. During the 1980s, these laws were refined and, in some cases, their coverage was extended. Today, environmental concerns continue to be in evidence around the globe, and many countries, both individually and collectively, continue to take steps to address those concerns. Accordingly, it is important that the businessperson be cognizant of the legal requirements and the public's environmental concerns in operating a business.

THE ENVIRONMENTAL PROTECTION AGENCY

In 1970, the Environmental Protection Agency (EPA) was created to consolidate the federal government's environmental responsibilities. Over the decade of the 1970s, Congress passed comprehensive new legislation covering, among other things, air and water pollution, pesticides, ocean dumping, and waste disposal. Among the factors prompting these laws were protection of human health, aesthetics, economic costs of continued pollution, and protection of natural systems.

The initial efforts were aimed at pollution problems that could largely be seen, smelled, or tasted. As control requirements have been put in place, implemented by industry and government, and progress has been noted in the form of cleaner air and water, attention has focused increasingly on problems that are somewhat less visible but potentially more threatening—the problems posed by toxic substances. These problems have come into more prominence as scientific research has disclosed the risks posed by some substances, as the development of new technology has facilitated the detection of the suspect substances in ever more minute quantities, and increased monitoring and testing are carried out.

Other changes are evolving in the tools and approaches being used by the government to deal with environmental problems. Much of the initial effort to address such problems involved what is known as command and control regulation, an approach that is heavily prescriptive and relies on an intensive enforcement presence to ensure the regulations are followed. In recent years, however, the government has looked to supplement—or to replace in part—the command and control system with the use of economic incentives and voluntary approaches to try to bring about the desired results.

THE NATIONAL ENVIRONMENTAL POLICY ACT

The National Environmental Policy Act (NEPA) was signed into law on January 1, 1970. In addition to creating the Council of Environmental Quality in the Executive Office of the President, the act required that an **environmental impact statement** be prepared for every recommendation or report on legislation and for every *major federal action significantly affecting the quality of the environment*. The environmental impact statement must (1) describe the environmental impact of the proposed action, (2) discuss impacts that cannot be avoided, (3) discuss the alternatives to the proposed action, (4) indicate differences between short- and long-term impacts, and (5) detail any irreversible commitments of resources.

NEPA requires a federal agency to consider the environmental impact of a project before the project is undertaken. Other federal, state, and local agencies, as well as interested citizens, have an opportunity to comment on the environmental impact of the project before the agency can proceed. Where the process is not followed, citizens can and have gone to court to force compliance with NEPA. A number of states and local governments have passed their own environmental impact laws requiring NEPA-type statements for major public and private developments.

While the federal and state laws requiring the preparation of environmental impact statements appear directed at government actions, it is important to note that the government actions covered often include the granting of permits to private parties. Thus, businesspeople may readily find themselves involved in the preparation of an environmental impact statement—for example, in connection with a marina to be built in navigable waters or a resort development that will impact wetlands, both of which require permits from the U.S. Army Corps of Engineers. Similarly, a developer seeking a local zoning change so she can build a major commercial or residential development may find that she is asked to finance a study of the potential environmental impact of her proposed project.

·········· *AIR POLLUTION* ··········

BACKGROUND

Fuel combustion, industrial processes, and solid waste disposal are the major contributors to air pollution. People's initial concern with air pollution related to what they could see—visible or smoke pollution. In the 1880s, Chicago and Cincinnati enacted smoke control ordinances. As the technology became available to deal with smoke and particulate emissions, attention was given as well to other, less visible gases that could adversely affect human health and vegetation and that could lead to increased acidity of lakes, thus making them unsuitable for fish.

CLEAN AIR ACT

The Clear Air Act—enacted in 1970—provides the basis for our present approach to air pollution control. In 1977, Congress made some modifications to the 1970 Clean Air Act and added provisions designed to prevent deterioration of the air in areas where its quality currently exceeds that required by federal law. Thirteen years then passed before Congress, in 1990, enacted a major revision to the act to deal with acid rain, hazardous air pollutants, and smog problems that were not satisfactorily dealt with under the existing legislation.

AMBIENT AIR CONTROL STANDARDS

The Clean Air Act established a comprehensive approach for dealing with air pollution. EPA is required to set **national ambient air quality standards** for the major pollutants that have an adverse impact on human health—that is, to set the amount of a given pollutant that can be present in the air around us. The ambient air quality standards are to be set at two levels: (1) **primary standards,** which are designed to protect the public's health from harm and (2) **secondary standards,** which are designed to protect vegetation, materials, climate, visibility, and economic values. Pursuant to this statutory mandate, EPA has set ambient air quality standards for carbon monoxide, nitrogen oxide, sulfur oxide, ozone, lead, and particulate matter.

Each state is required to develop—and to obtain EPA approval for—a **state implementation plan** for meeting the national ambient air quality standards. This necessitates an inventory of the various sources of air pollution and their contribution to the total air pollution in the air quality region. The major emitters of pollutants are then required to reduce their emissions to a level that ensures that overall air quality will meet the national standards.

For example, a factory may be required to limit its emissions of volatile organic compounds (a contributor to ozone or smog) to a certain amount per unit of production or hour of operation; similarly, a power plant might have its emissions of sulfur oxides and nitrogen oxides limited to so many pounds per Btu of energy produced. The states have the responsibility for deciding which activities must be regulated or curtailed so that emissions will not exceed the national standards.

Because by the late 1980s many of the nation's major urban areas were still not in compliance with the health-based standards for ozone and carbon monoxide, Congress in its 1990 amendments imposed an additional set of requirements on the areas that were not in compliance. Thus, citizens living in the areas and existing businesses, as well as prospective businesses seeking to locate in the designated areas, face increasingly stringent control measures designed to bring the areas into alignment with the national standards. These new requirements mean that businesses such as bakeries that are generally not thought of as major polluters of the air must further control their emissions and that paints and other products that contain solvents may have to be reformulated. In addition, businesses seeking to build new facilities, modify existing facilities, or increase production may have to "offset" any increased emissions by decreasing emissions or by buying pollution emission rights from others in the area.

Acid Rain Controls

Responding to the 1970 Clean Air Act, which sought to protect the air in the area near sources of air pollution, many electric-generating facilities built tall smokestacks so that emissions were dispersed over a broader area. Unwittingly, this contributed to long-range transport of some of the pollutants, which changed chemically enroute and fell to earth many miles away in the form of acid rain, snow, fog, or dry deposition. For a number of years, a considerable debate ensued over acid rain, in particular as to whether it was a problem, what kind of damage it caused, whether anything should be done about it, and who should pay for the cost of limiting it.

The 1990 amendments addressed acid deposition by among other things placing a cap on the overall emissions of the contributors to it (the oxides of sulfur and nitrogen) and requiring electric utilities to reduce their emissions to specified levels in two steps by 2000. This requires most electric-generating facilities in the country to install large control devices known as *scrubbers*, to switch to lower-sulfur coal, or to install so-called clean coal technologies. The 1990 amendments also provided an innovative system whereby companies whose emissions are cleaner than required by law can sell their rights to emit more sulfur oxide to other companies that may be finding it more difficult to meet the standards.

Control of Air Toxics

The Clean Air Act also requires EPA to regulate the emission of **toxic air pollutants.** Under this authority, EPA has set standards for asbestos, beryllium, mercury, vinyl chloride, benzene, and radionuclides. Unhappy with the slow pace of regulation of toxic air pollutants, Congress in 1990 specified a list of chemicals for which EPA is required to issue regulations requiring the installation of the *maximum available control technology*. The regulations are to be developed and the control technology installed by industry in phases. Thus, while many toxic emissions largely went unregulated, that situation has changed. In addition, a number of companies are voluntarily reducing their emissions of toxic chemicals to levels below those they are required to meet by law.

The case that follows, *United States v. Midwest Suspension and Brake*, involves the enforcement of an EPA regulation that controls the management and disposal of asbestos and asbestos-containing materials.

United States v. Midwest Suspension and Brake
49 F.3d 197 (6th Cir. 1994)

FACTS

Midwest Suspension and Brake is in the business of supplying parts for heavy-duty truck suspensions, steering systems, and brakes. One of the operations it performs concerning brake systems involves the collection and rehabilitation of used brake shoes for resale. During the rehabilitation process, brake shoes are disassembled, and parts, which may contain asbestos, are discarded. Some brake shoes are delined, a procedure performed by removing rivets that hold the brake lining to the brake table and then cleaning, sandblasting, painting, and relining the table with a new brake block. Old brake blocks and brake linings, which contain asbestos, are discarded.

During an EPA inspection of the Midwest facility, numerous emissions of asbestos were documented and the shop floor yielded detectable amounts of asbestos. As a result, EPA issued a "finding of violation" of the "no visible emission" requirement of the National Emission

(continued)

UNITED STATES V. MIDWEST SUSPENSION AND BRAKE
(concluded)

Standard for Hazardous Air Pollutants (NESHAP) for asbestos. To resolve the matter, Midwest agreed to the issuance of an Administrative Order (AO) that required that Midwest comply with the Clean Air Act and the asbestos NESHAP, including the no visible emission requirement.

As a preventative measure, the AO specified waste management requirements for Midwest operations including the following: (1) that delining wastes fall into a sturdy cardboard box, instead of falling to the ground; (2) that the box be securely closed and wrapped so that it would not leak when discarded; and (3) that the box bear a warning label. The AO also required that the floor of the delining area be vacuumed, not swept, and that the vacuum residue be tightly sealed before disposal. Finally, the AO required that asbestos waste be segregated and separately disposed of, without compacting, at a landfill.

Subsequent EPA inspections of the Midwest facility found numerous violations of the AO—as did inspections by the Wayne County (Michigan) Health Department. Asbestos wastes were being compacted, resulting in visible emissions. Vacuum residue was not tightly sealed, and boxes of delining wastes were improperly taped, resulting in visible emissions during landfill disposal. Asbestos-containing materials were being dropped on the shop floor and the floor was being broom cleaned rather than vacuumed.

When efforts to have Midwest comply with the AO were unsuccessful, EPA filed suit against it in federal court. EPA sought injunctive relief as well as civil penalties of up to $25,000 per day for each violation. The federal district court found that Midwest had violated the Clean Air Act and ordered it to pay a $50,000 civil penalty. Midwest appealed, contending among other things that it did not fall under the Clean Air Act or the asbestos NESHAP because it did not fabricate friction products containing asbestos within the meaning of the act.

ISSUE

Is Midwest a fabricator of asbestos friction products containing asbestos and thus subject to the requirements of the Clean Air Act?

DECISION

Yes. Under the act, the Asbestos NESHAP standards apply in part to operations that "fabricate friction products containing commercial asbestos." Fabricating is defined as "the processing of a manufactured product that contains commercial asbestos." Midwest's brake refurbishing operations clearly fall within this definition of processing. Midwest fabricates brake shoes by cutting and altering used brake shoes by removing their linings, which may contain asbestos, and by assembling refurbished brake cores with new linings, which may contain asbestos, for sale as rebuilt shoes. The entire rebuilding operation is a process of fabrication. Thus, Midwest is required to comply with the provisions of the act.

NEW SOURCE CONTROLS

The act requires that **new stationary sources,** such as factories and power plants, install the **best available technology** for reducing air pollution. EPA is required to establish the standards to be met by new stationary sources and has done so for the major types of stationary sources of air pollution. This means that a new facility covered by the regulations must install state-of-the-art control technology, even if it is locating in an area where the air quality is better than that required by law.

PERMITS

In the 1990 amendments to the Clean Air Act, Congress established a permit system whereby major sources of air pollution—particularly those subject to the NSPS, air toxics, nonattainment, and acid rain provisions of the act—as well as certain other sources have to obtain permits that will specify the limits on emissions from the sources. The permits also contain monitoring and reporting requirements. Once a state permitting program is approved by EPA, the permits are issued by the state. A controversial issue in the permitting regulations is when a source has to seek a modification of the permit because of process or operational changes that might increase emissions. This can greatly complicate the timely execution of business plans.

ENFORCEMENT

The primary responsibility for enforcing the air quality standards lies with the states, but the federal government has the right to enforce the standards if the states fail to do so. The Clean Air Act also provides for suits by citizens to force the industry or the government to fully comply with the act's provisions.

AUTOMOBILE POLLUTION

The Clean Air Act provides specifically for air pollution controls on transportation sources such as automobiles. The major pollutants from automobiles are carbon monoxide, hydrocarbons, and nitrogen oxides. Carbon monoxide is a colorless, odorless gas that can dull mental performance and even cause death when inhaled in large quantities. Hydrocarbons, in the form of unburned fuel, are part of a category of air pollutants known as volatile organic compounds (VOCs). VOCs combine with nitrogen oxides under the influence of sunlight to become ozone. We sometimes know it as *smog*.

The 1970 Clean Air Act required a reduction by 1975 of 90 percent in the amount of the carbon monoxide and hydrocarbons emitted by automobiles and by 1976 of 90 percent in the amount of the nitrogen oxides emitted. At the time, these requirements were "technology forcing"; that is, the manufacturers could not rely on already existing technology to meet the standards but had to develop new technology. Ultimately, most manufacturers had to go beyond simply making changes in engine design and utilize pollution control devices known as *catalytic converters*.

Subsequently, Congress addressed the question of setting even more stringent limits on automobile emissions while requiring that the new automobiles get better gas mileage. The 1990 amendments require further limitations on emissions from tailpipes, the development of so-called clean-fueled vehicles for use in cities with dirty air, and the availability of oxygenated fuels (which are cleaner burning) in specified areas of the country that are having difficulty meeting the air quality limits at least part of the year. These new requirements have had significant ramifications for the oil and automobile industries. In the case of the oil industry, it has had to "reformulate" some of the gasoline it sells.

Under the Clean Air Act, no manufacturer may sell vehicles subject to emission standards without prior certification from EPA that the vehicles meet the required standards. The tests are performed on prototype vehicles, and if they pass, a certificate of conformity covering that type of engine and vehicle is issued. EPA subsequently can test vehicles on the assembly line to make sure that the production vehicles are meeting the standards. The manufacturers are required to warrant that the vehicle, if properly maintained, will comply with the emission standards for its useful life. If EPA discovers that vehicles in actual use exceed the emission standards, it may order the manufacturer to recall and repair the defective models; this is a power that EPA has exercised on a number of occasions.

The act also provides for the regulation and registration of fuel additives such as lead. In the 1980s, lead was largely phased out of use as an octane enhancer in gasoline. As indicated previously, the 1990 amendments provide for the availability of alternative fuels based on ethanol and methanol.

INTERNATIONAL AIR PROBLEMS

During the late 1970s and 1980s, concern developed that the release of chlorine-containing substances such as chlorofluorocarbons (CFCs) used in air conditioning, refrigeration, and certain foam products was depleting the stratospheric ozone layer. This could lead to more ultraviolet radiation reaching the earth and, in turn, more skin cancer. Subsequently, a number of nations, acting under the aegis of the United Nations, signed a treaty agreeing first to limit any increases in production of CFCs and ultimately to phase out their use. The 1990 amendments to the Clean Air Act implement the obligations of the United States under the treaty and provide for the phasedown and phaseout of a number of chlorofluorocarbons; accordingly, many businesses have developed or located substitutes for those chemicals that are henceforth available only in reduced quantities, if at all.

Other air pollution issued with international dimensions that may result in multi-national control efforts are acid rain and global warming/climate change resulting, in part, from increased emissions of carbon dioxide to the atmosphere.

Ethical Implications

Suppose a manufacturing facility emits into the air a chemical that it has reason to believe is inadequately regulated by EPA and that poses a significant threat to nearby residents even at levels lower than permitted by EPA. As manager of the facility, would you be satisfied to meet the EPA required level or would you install the additional controls you believe necessary to achieve a reasonably safe level?

INDOOR AIR POLLUTION

As we increased the insulation in our buildings and tightened them up to conserve energy, we generally reduced the air exchange and increased the concentrations of pollutants in our homes and workplaces. In recent years, attention has been focused on a number of indoor air problems. These include indoor radon gas, asbestos, the products of combustion from fireplaces and stoves, molds and pollens, formaldehyde, cigarette smoke, pesticides, and cleaning products. Some of these problems are being dealt with on a problem-by-problem, or product-by-product, basis under various laws. Others are being dealt with by providing information to consumers so that they can take appropriate action to protect themselves. And, in some cases, Congress and other legislative bodies have required that steps be taken, such as the federal requirement for schools to inspect for asbestos and to remove it where certain unsafe conditions are found.

RADIATION CONTROL

For many years, there has been concern about radioactivity, particularly radioactivity from nuclear-fueled power plants. Some of these concerns were accentuated by the accident at Chernobyl in the former U.S.S.R. and the one at Three Mile Island in the United States. Citizens are specifically concerned about the release of radioactivity into the environment during normal operation of the nuclear reactors, possible accidents through human error or mechanical failure, and disposal of the radioactive wastes generated by the reactors. There is concern that the discharge of heated water used to cool the reactor—thermal pollution—may cause damage to the environment.

Currently, the problems of reactor safety are under the jurisdiction of the Nuclear Regulatory Commission, which exercises licensing authority over nuclear power plants. The Environmental Protection Agency is responsible for setting standards for radioactivity in the overall environment and for dealing with the problem of disposal of some radioactive waste. The thermal pollution problem is handled by EPA pursuant to its water pollution control authorities. In addition, EPA has the responsibility for regulating emissions from a variety of other sources, such as uranium mill tailing piles and uranium mines.

WATER POLLUTION

BACKGROUND

History is replete with plagues and epidemics brought on by poor sanitation and polluted water. Indeed, preventing waterborne disease has, through time, been the major reason for combating water pollution. In the early 1970s, fishing and swimming were prohibited in many bodies of water, game fish could no longer survive in some waters where they had formerly thrived, and Lake Erie was becoming choked with algae and was considered to be dying. The nation recognized that water pollution could affect public health, recreation, commercial fishing, agriculture, water supplies, and aesthetics. During the 1970s, Congress enacted three major statutes to deal with protecting our water resources: the Clean Water Act; the Marine Protection, Research, and Sanctuaries Act; and the Safe Drinking Water Act.

EARLY FEDERAL LEGISLATION

Federal water pollution legislation dates back to the 19th century when Congress enacted the River and Harbor Act of 1886. The act provided that in order to deposit or discharge "refuse" into a navigable waterway, a discharge permit had to be obtained from the Army Corps of Engineers. Under some contemporary court decisions, even hot water discharged from nuclear power plants has been considered "refuse." The permit system established pursuant to the "Refuse Act" was replaced in 1972 by a more comprehensive permit system administered by EPA.

The initial Federal Water Pollution Control Act (FWPCA) was passed in 1948. Amendments to the FWPCA in 1956, 1965, 1966, and 1970 increased the federal government's role in water pollution abatement and strengthened its enforcement powers.

CLEAN WATER ACT

The 1972 amendments to the FWPCA—known as the *Clean Water Act*—were as comprehensive in the water pollution field as the 1970 Clean Air Act was in the air pollution field. They proclaimed two general goals for this country: (1) to achieve wherever possible by July 1, 1983, water clean enough for swimming and other recreational uses and clean enough for the protection and propagation of fish, shellfish, and wildlife and (2) by 1985 to have no discharges of pollutants into the nation's waters. The goals reflected a national frustration with the lack of progress in dealing with water pollution and a commitment to end such pollution. The new law set out a series of specific actions that federal, state, and local governments and industry were to take by certain dates and provided strong enforcement provisions to back up the deadlines. In 1977, and again in 1987, Congress enacted some modifications to the 1972 act that adjusted some of the deadlines and otherwise fine-tuned the act.

Under the Clean Water Act, the states have the primary responsibility for preventing, reducing, and eliminating water pollution, but the states have to do this within a national framework with EPA empowered to move in if the states do not fulfill their responsibilities.

CONTROLS ON INDUSTRIAL WASTES

The law set a number of deadlines to control water pollution from industrial sources. Industries discharging wastes into the nation's waterways were required to install the "best available" water pollution control technology, and new sources of industrial pollution must use the "best available demonstrated control technology." In each instance, EPA is responsible for issuing guidelines as to the "best available" technologies. Industries that discharge their wastes into municipal systems are required to pretreat the wastes so that they will not interfere with the biological operation of the plant or pass through the plant without treatment.

WATER QUALITY STANDARDS

The act continued and expanded the previously established system of setting **water quality standards** that define the uses of specific bodies of water such as recreational water supply, public water supply, propagation of fish and wildlife, and agricultural and industrial water supply. Then, the maximum daily loads of various kinds of pollutants are set so that the water will be suitable for the designated type of use. The final step is to establish limits on the dischargers' pollutants so that the standards should be met.

DISCHARGE PERMITS

The act requires all *municipal and industrial dischargers* to obtain **permits** that spell out the amounts and types of pollutants that the permit holder will be allowed to discharge and any steps that it must take to reduce its present or anticipated discharge.

ENFORCEMENT

Dischargers are also required to keep records, install and maintain monitoring equipment, and sample their discharges. Penalties for violating the law range from a minimum of $2,500 for a first offense up to $50,000 per day and two years in prison for subsequent violations. In *United States v. Hopkins*, which follows, a corporate vice president was convicted and sentenced to prison for his role in knowingly violating the Clean Water Act.

UNITED STATES V. HOPKINS
53 F. 3d 533 (2nd Cir. 1995)

FACTS

Spirol International Corporation is a manufacturer of metal shims and fasteners and is located in northeastern Connecticut. Spirol's manufacturing operation involves a zinc-based plating process that generates substantial amounts of wastewater containing zinc and other toxic materials; this wastewater is discharged into the nearby Five Mile River. The U.S. Environmental Protection Agency (EPA) has delegated to the State of Connecticut's Department of Environmental Protection (DEP) the authority to administer the Clean Water Act provisions applicable to Spirol's discharges into the river. In 1987, Spirol entered into a consent order with DEP requiring Spirol to pay a $30,000 fine for past violations and to comply in the future with discharge limitations specified in the order. In February 1989, DEP issued a modified "wastewater discharge permit" imposing more restrictive limits on the quantity of zinc and other substances that Spirol was permitted to release into the river.

From 1987 through September 6, 1990, Robert Hopkins was Spirol's vice president for manufacturing. Hopkins signed the 1987 consent decree on behalf of Spirol and had the corporate responsibility for ensuring compliance with the order and the DEP permit. The DEP permit required Spirol each week to collect a sample of its wastewater and send it to an independent laboratory by Friday morning of that week. Spirol was required to report the laboratory results to DEP in a discharge monitoring report once a month. Under the DEP permit, the concentrations of zinc in Spirol's wastewater were not to exceed 2.0 milligrams per liter in any weekly sample nor to average more that 1.0 milligram per liter in any month.

During the period March 1989 to September 1990, Spirol began its weekly sampling process on Monday. A composite sample was taken and analyzed in house. If it contained less than 1.0 milligram of zinc, it was sent to the independent laboratory with a "chain of custody" record signed by Hopkins. However, if it exceeded 1.0 milligram of zinc, it was discarded and another sample taken and tested the following day. In 54 of the 78 weeks, the samples were sent to the laboratory later than Tuesday. If the Wednesday sample also failed the in-house test, Hopkins would sometimes order that it be discarded and another taken on Thursday, but more often he instructed his subordinates doing the testing to dilute

the sample with tap water or to reduce the zinc concentration using an ordinary coffee filter. Any Friday sample that failed the in-house test was always diluted or filtered so that a good sample could be sent to the laboratory by the Friday deadline. In some samples sent to the laboratory there was more tap water than wastewater.

During this period Hopkins filed with DEP monthly discharge monitoring reports consolidating the weekly tests from the independent laboratory. The reports showed no zinc concentrations above 1.0 milligram per liter. On each report, Hopkins signed the following certification:

> I certify under penalty of law that this document and all attachments were prepared under my direction or supervision in accordance with a system designed to assure that qualified personnel properly gather and evaluate the information submitted. Based on my inquiry of the person or persons who administer the system, or those persons directly responsible for gathering the information, the information is, to the best of my knowledge and belief, true, accurate and complete. I am aware that there are significant penalties for submitting false information, including the possibility of fine and imprisonment for knowing violations.

Contrary to Hopkins's certifications, his subordinates testified that he had caused the samples to be tampered with about 40 percent of the time. On some 25–30 occasions when he had been told that a satisfactory sample had finally been obtained by means of dilution or filtration, Hopkins responded, "I know nothing, I hear nothing." Hopkins was told that the testing procedures were improper, yet he continued to sign the certifications and Spirol continued its discharges into the river.

In December 1993, Hopkins was charged in a three-count indictment alleging (1) that he had knowingly falsified or tampered with Spirol's discharge sampling methods, (2) that he had knowingly violated the conditions of the permit, and (3) that he had conspired to commit those offenses. Hopkins was convicted following a jury trial and sentenced to 21 months in prison, with two years probation following that, and a $7,500 fine. Hopkins appealed, arguing that the government should have been required to prove that he intended to violate the law and that he had specific knowledge of the particular statutory, regulatory, or permit requirements

(continued)

UNITED STATES V. HOPKINS
(concluded)

imposed under the Clean Water Act. The government contended that it was enough to prove that he had acted voluntarily or intentionally to falsify, tamper with, or render inaccurate a monitoring method—or to violate the permit—and that he did not do so by mistake, accident, or other innocent reason.

ISSUE

Could Hopkins be convicted of a knowing violation where it was shown he had acted intentionally to falsify the monitoring information and to violate the permit?

DECISION

Yes. A knowing violation of the Clean Water Act can be established by the intentional doing of certain acts, even though the actor is not aware of the precise proscription set out in the law.

Any citizen or group of citizens whose interests are adversely affected has the right to bring a court action against anyone violating an effluent standard or limitation or an order issued by EPA or a state. Citizens also have the right to take court action against EPA if it fails to carry out mandatory provisions of the law.

WETLANDS

Another aspect of the Clean Water Act that has the potential to affect businesses as well as individual property owners involves the provisions concerning wetlands. Generally, wetlands are transition zones between land and open water. Under section 404 of the act, any dredging or filling activity in a wetland that is part of the navigable waters of the United States requires a permit before the activity can be commenced. The permit program is administered by the Army Corps of Engineers with involvement of the Environmental Protection Agency.

As can be seen in *Bersani v. U.S. Environmental Protection Agency*, the permit requirement can limit a landowner's use of his property where the fill activity is viewed as injurious to the values protected by the act.

BERSANI V. U.S. ENVIRONMENTAL PROTECTION AGENCY
674 F. Supp. 405 (N.D.N.Y. 1987)

FACTS

Pyramid Companies was an association of partnerships in the business of developing, constructing, and operating shopping centers; John Bersani was a principal in one of the partnerships. In 1983, Pyramid became interested in developing a shopping mall in the Attleboro, Massachusetts, area and focused its attention on an 82-acre site located on an interstate highway in South Attleboro known as "Sweeden's Swamp."

The project contemplated altering or filling some 32 acres of the 49.6 acres of wetlands on the property. At the same time, Pyramid planned to excavate 9 acres of uplands (nonwetlands) to create new wetlands and to alter some 13 acres of existing wetlands to enhance their value for fish and wildlife.

In 1984, Pyramid applied to the U.S. Army Corps of Engineers for a permit under section 404 of the Clean

(continued)

BERSANI V. U.S. ENVIRONMENTAL PROTECTION AGENCY
(concluded)

Water Act to do the dredge and fill work in the wetlands. As part of its application, it was required to submit information on practicable alternative sites for its shopping mall. One site that subsequently was focused on by the Corps and the Environmental Protection Agency was about three miles north in North Attleboro. Pyramid relied on several factors in claiming that the site was not a practicable alternative to its proposed site; namely, the site lacked sufficient traffic volume and access from local roads, potential department store tenants had expressed doubts about the feasibility of the site, and previous attempts to develop the site had met with strong resistance from the surrounding community. However, subsequent to the time Pyramid examined the site, another major developer of shopping centers had taken an option to acquire the property.

The New England Division Engineer of the Corps recommended that the permit be denied because a practicable alternative with a less adverse effect on the environment existed. The Chief of Engineers directed that the permit be issued, noting that the alternative site was not available to Pyramid since it was owned by a competitor and that even if it was considered available, Pyramid had made a convincing case that the site would not fulfill its objectives for a successful project. EPA then exercised its prerogative under the Clean Water Act to veto the permit on the grounds that filling Sweeden's Swamp to build the shopping mall would have an unacceptable adverse effect on the environment. In its view, another less environmentally damaging site had been available to Pyramid at the time it made its site selection and thus any adverse effects on Sweeden's Swamp were avoidable. Bersani and Pyramid then brought suit challenging the denial of its permit application.

ISSUE

Should Pyramid be permitted to drain and fill a wetland if another less environmentally damaging site was available for the construction of a shopping center?

DECISION

No. The court noted that a shopping center is not water dependent and does not need to be located with access or proximity to a wetland or other aquatic body. Accordingly, practicable alternatives are presumed to be available that do not require the filling of a wetland. In order to overcome the presumption, an applicant must prove that no such alternative exists. Here, it was reasonable for EPA to find that there was an alternative site available in the area for the construction of a shopping center and thus to deny Pyramid a permit to fill a wetland to construct its proposed shopping center.

OCEAN DUMPING

The Marine Protection, Research, and Sanctuaries Act of 1972 set up a **permit system** regulating the dumping of all types of materials into ocean waters. EPA has the responsibility for designating disposal sites and for establishing the rules governing ocean disposal. The Ocean Dumping Ban Act of 1987 required that all ocean dumping of municipal sludge and industrial wastes be terminated by the end of 1991. Thus, the remaining questions of ocean dumping concern the disposal of dredge spoils to keep harbors open.

DRINKING WATER

In 1974 Congress passed, and in 1986 and again in 1996 it amended, the Safe Drinking Water Act, which was designed to protect and enhance the quality of our drinking water. Under the act, EPA sets **primary drinking water standards,** which provide minimum levels of quality for water to be used for human consumption. The act also establishes a program governing the injection of wastes into wells. The primary responsibility for complying with the federally established standards lies with the states. Where the states fail to enforce the drinking water standards, the federal government has the right to enforce them.

WASTE DISPOSAL

BACKGROUND

Historically, concern about the environment focused on air and water pollution as well as the protection of natural resources and wildlife. Relatively little attention was paid to the disposal of wastes on land. When EPA was formed, much of the solid and hazardous waste generated was being disposed of in open dumps and landfills. While some of the waste we produce can be disposed of without presenting significant health or environmental problems, some industrial, agricultural, and mining wastes, and even some household wastes, are hazardous and can present serious problems. Unless wastes are properly disposed of, they can cause air, water, and land pollution as well as contamination of the underground aquifers from which much of our drinking water is drawn. Once aquifers have been contaminated, it can take them a very long time to cleanse themselves of pollutants.

In the 1970s, the discovery of abandoned dump sites such as Love Canal in New York and the "Valley of the Drums" in Kentucky heightened public concern about the disposal of toxic and hazardous wastes. Congress has enacted several laws regulating the generation and disposal of hazardous waste. The Resource Conservation and Recovery Act is aimed at the proper management and disposal of wastes that are being generated currently. The Comprehensive Environmental Response, Compensation, and Liability Act focuses on the cleanup of past disposal sites that threaten public health and the environment.

THE RESOURCE, CONSERVATION AND RECOVERY ACT

The Resource Conservation and Recovery Act (RCRA) was originally enacted in 1976 and significantly amended in 1984. It provides the federal government and the states with the authority to regulate facilities that *generate, treat, store, and dispose of hazardous waste*. Most of the wastes defined as *hazardous* are subject to a "cradle to the grave" tracking system and must be handled and disposed of in defined ways.

RCRA requires persons who generate, treat, store, or transport specified quantities of hazardous waste to notify EPA of that fact, to obtain an ID number that must be placed on a manifest that accompanies all shipments, to meet certain standards, and to follow specified procedures in the handling of the wastes, and to keep records. Those who treat, store, or dispose of hazardous wastes must obtain permits. See Figure 46–1 for a sample of the form that must accompany all shipments of hazardous waste from point of generation until its final treatment or disposal.

In addition, operators of land disposal facilities must meet financial responsibility requirements and monitor groundwater quality. EPA determines whether certain kinds of wastes should be banned entirely from land disposal unless treated first.

UNDERGROUND STORAGE TANKS

In 1984, Congress directed that EPA also regulate underground product storage tanks such as gasoline tanks to prevent and respond to leaks from them that might contaminate underground water. Subsequently, owners of tanks have had to upgrade or replace them with tanks that are corrosion resistant and have the capacity to be monitored for leaks.

FIGURE 46–1　　　Sample Uniform Hazardous Waste Manifest Form*

SAMPLE "UNIFORM HAZARDOUS WASTE MANIFEST" FORM

Please Print or type　　(Form designed for use on elite (12-pitch) typewriter)　　Form Approved OMB 2000-0404 Expires 7-31-99

UNIFORM HAZARDOUS WASTE MANIFEST	1. Generator's US EPA ID No. V A D 0 0 1 2 3 4 5 6 7 0 0 0 0 7	2. Page 1 of	Information in the shaded areas is not required by federal law

3. Generator's Name and Mailing Address
GENERAL METAL PROCESSING CO.
501 MAIN ST
SMALLTOWN, VA 23000

A. State Manifest Document Number

4. Generator's Phone No. (804) 555-0509

B. State Generator's ID

5. Transporter 1 Company Name
SAFETY HAULER
6. US EPA ID Number V A D 0 0 8 9 1 2 3 4 5

C. State Transporter's ID

D. Transporter's Phone

7. Transporter 2 Company Name
8. US EPA ID Number

E. State Transporter's ID

F. Transporter's Phone

9. Designated Facility Name and Site Address
DISPOS-ALL, INC
1800 NORTH AVE.
FRIENDLY TOWN, VA 2300
10. US EPA ID Number V A D 0 0 6 F 8 9 1 2 3

G. State Facility's ID

H. Facility's Phone

11. US DOT Description (Including Proper Shipping Name, Hazard Class, and ID Number)	12. Containers No.	Type	13. Total Quantity	13. Unit Wt/Vol	I. Waste No.
a. HAZARDOUS WASTE, LIQUID OR SOLID, NOS ORM-E NA9189	0 0 2	D M	0 0 1 1 1 0	GAL	
b. WASTE CYANIDE SOLUTION, NOS UN1935	0 0 1	D M	0 0 0 5 5	GAL	
c. WASTE FLAMMABLE SOLUTION, NOS UN1993	0 0 1	D M	0 0 0 5 5	GAL	
d.					

J. Additional Descriptions for Materials Listed Above

K. Handling Codes for Wastes Listed Above

15. Special Handling Instructions and Additional Information

16. Generator's Certification: I hereby declare that the contents of this consignment are fully and accurately described above by proper shipping name and classified, packed, marked, labeled, and are in all respects in proper condition for transport by highway according to applicable international and national regulations.

Unless I am a small quantity generator who has been exempted by statute or regulation from the duty to make a waste minimization certification under Section 3002(b) of RCRA, I also certify that I have a program in place to reduce the volume and toxicity of waste generated to the degree I have determined to be economically practicable and I have selected the method of treatment, storage, or disposal currently available to me which minimizes the present and future threat to human health and the environment.

Printed/ Typed Name JOSEPHINE K. DOE	Signature *Josephine K. Doe*	Month Day Year 0 8 3 0 0 2

17. Transporter 1 Acknowledgement of Receipt of Materials

Printed/Typed Name	Signature	

18. Transporter 2 Acknowledgement of Receipt of Materials

Printed/Typed Name	Signature	Month Day Year

19. Discrepancy Indication Space

20. Facility Owner or Operator: Certification of receipt of hazardous materials covered by this manifest except as noted in Item 19.

Printed/Typed Name	Signature	Month Day Year

EPA Form 8700-22 (Rev. 4-85) Previous Edition is obsolete.

Information in the shaded areas is not required by federal law, but this or other additional information may be required by your state.

.... **STATE RESPONSIBILITIES** ....

EPA sets minimum requirements for a state RCRA program and then delegates the responsibility for conducting the program to the states when they have the legal ability and interest to administer it. Until a state assumes partial or complete responsibility for an RCRA program, the federal government administers the program.

ENFORCEMENT

Failure to comply with the hazardous waste regulations promulgated under RCRA can subject the violator to civil and criminal penalties. In *United States v. Dean*, which follows, an employee of a company that disposed of hazardous waste without an RCRA permit was held criminally liable.

UNITED STATES V. DEAN
969 F.2d 187 (6th Cir. 1992)

FACTS

General Metal Fabricators, Inc. (GMF), owned and operated a facility in Erwin, Tennessee, which was engaged in metal stamping, plating, and painting. The facility utilized hazardous chemicals and generated hazardous waste but did not have an RCRA permit, nor did it maintain the required records of the treatment, storage, and disposal of hazardous substances. The hazardous waste disposal practices at GMF were discovered by chance by state waste-management authorities whose attention was caught, while they were driving to an appointment at another facility, by two 55-gallon drums abandoned among weeds on GMF's property.

The owners of GMF, Joseph and Jean Sanchez, as well as Clyde Griffith, the plant manager, and Gale Dean, the production manager, were indicted for conspiracy to violate RCRA, and, individually, for violations of various sections of RCRA. At his request, Dean's trial was severed from that of the other defendants.

As production manager, Dean had day-to-day supervision of GMF's production process and employees. Among his duties was the instruction of employees on hazardous waste handling and disposal. Numerous practices at GMF violated RCRA. GMF's plating operations utilized rinse baths, contaminated with hazardous chemicals, which were drained through a pipe into an earthen lagoon outside the facility. In addition, Dean instructed employees to shovel various kinds of solid wastes from the tanks into 55-gallon drums. Dean ordered the construction of a pit, concealed behind the facility, into which 38 drums of such hazardous waste had been tossed. The contents spilled onto the soil from open or corroded drums. Chemical analyses of soil and solid wastes revealed that the pit and the lagoon were contaminated with chromium. In addition, the pit was contaminated with toluene and xylene solvents. All of these substances are considered hazardous under RCRA. Drums of spent chromic acid solution were also illegally stored on the premises.

Dean was familiar with the chemicals used in each of the tanks on the production line and with the manner in which the contents of the rinse tanks were deposited in the lagoon. Material Safety Data Sheets (MSDS) provided to GMF by the chemical manufacturer clearly stated that the various chemicals in use at GMF were hazardous and were subject to federal pollution control laws. Dean was familiar with the MSDS and knowledgeable about their contents. The MSDS delivered with the chromic acid made specific reference to RCRA and to related EPA regulations. Dean told investigators that he "had read this RCRA waste code but thought it was a bunch of bullshit."

Dean was convicted of conspiracy to violate RCRA as well as of (1) failure to file documentation of hazardous waste generation, storage, and disposal, (2) storage of spent chromic acid without a permit, (3) disposal of chromic acid rinse water and sludges in a lagoon without a permit, and (4) disposal of paint sludge and solvent wastes in a pit without a permit, all in violation of RCRA. Dean appealed his conviction.

(continued)

UNITED STATES V. DEAN
(concluded)

ISSUE	**DECISION**
Can an employee of a company required by RCRA to have a permit to dispose of hazardous waste be held criminally liable for disposal of wastes in violation of RCRA?	Yes. The statute penalizes "any person" who "knowingly treats, stores or disposes of any hazardous waste . . . without a permit." The language of the statute is unambiguous, and Dean clearly was a "person" who committed the act proscribed by the statute.

SOLID WASTE

Mining, commercial, and household activity generates a large volume of waste material that can present problems if it is not disposed of properly. As population density has increased, also increasing the total volume of waste, it has become more difficult to find places where the waste material can be disposed of on land or incinerated. RCRA authorized EPA to set minimum standards for such disposal, but states and local government bear the primary responsibility for the siting and regulation of such activity.

As the cost and difficulty of disposing of wastes increases, attention is focused on reducing the amount of waste to be disposed of, on looking for opportunities to recycle some of the material in the waste stream, and on changing the characteristics of the material that must ultimately be disposed of so that it poses fewer environmental problems. One of the significant challenges faced by tomorrow's businessperson will be in designing products, packaging, and production processes so as to minimize the waste products that result.

A significant problem for both government and industry is the difficulty in trying to site new waste facilities. The NIMBY, or not-in-my-backyard syndrome, is pervasive as people almost universally desire to have the wastes from their everyday lives and from the economic activity in their community disposed of in someone else's neighborhood—any place but their own. As governments try to cope with the reality of finding places to dispose of wastes in an environmentally safe manner and at the same time cope with public opposition to siting new facilities, the temptation is strong to try to bar wastes from other areas from being disposed of in local facilities.

In the landmark case of *City of Philadelphia v. New Jersey*, the U.S. Supreme Court struck down an attempt by the state of New Jersey to prohibit the importation of most solid waste originating outside the state on the grounds that it violated the Commerce Clause of the United States Constitution. An ironic twist is that more than a decade later, we find a number of other eastern and midwestern states trying to find ways to block the importation of wastes from New Jersey into their states. In recent years the Supreme Court has had the occasion to reiterate its holding in *City of Philadelphia v. New Jersey* in a series of new cases involving efforts by states to block or limit the flow of solid and hazardous waste from outside their state to disposal sites within the state. One of the cases in this series of cases, *Fort Gratiot Sanitary Landfill, Inc. v. Michigan Department of Natural Resources*, follows.

FORT GRATIOT SANITARY LANDFILL, INC. V. MICHIGAN DEPARTMENT OF NATURAL RESOURCES
112 S.Ct. 2019 (1992)

FACTS

In 1978 Michigan enacted its Solid Waste Management Act (SWMA), which required every Michigan county to estimate the amount of solid waste that would be generated in the county in the next 20 years and to adopt a plan providing for its disposal at facilities that comply with state health standards. After holding public hearings, the St. Clair County Board of Commissioners adopted a solid waste plan for St. Clair County. In 1987, the Michigan Department of Natural Resources issued a permit to Fort Gratiot Sanitary Landfill, Inc., to operate a sanitary landfill as a solid waste disposal area in the county. In December 1988, the Michigan legislature amended the SWMA by adopting two provisions concerning the "acceptance of waste or ash generated outside the county of disposal area." The new provisions, which were effective immediately, prohibited the acceptance of out-of-county wastes unless the acceptance of such waste was explicitly authorized in the approved county solid waste management plan.

In February 1989, Fort Gratiot submitted an application to the St. Clair County Solid Waste Planning Committee for authority to accept up to 1,750 tons per day of out-of-state waste at its landfill. In the application Fort Gratiot promised to reserve sufficient capacity to dispose of all solid waste generated in the county in the next 20 years. The planning committee denied the application. Because the county's management plan did not authorize the acceptance of any out-of-county waste, Fort Gratiot was effectively prevented from receiving any solid waste that did not originate in St. Clair County.

Fort Gratiot then brought a lawsuit seeking a judgment declaring that the waste import restrictions violated the Commerce Clause of the U.S. Constitution and thus were unconstitutional, and enjoining their enforcement. Fort Gratiot contended that requiring a private landfill operator to limit its business to the acceptance of local waste constituted impermissible discrimination against interstate commerce. The district court dismissed the lawsuit. It concluded, first, that the statute did not discriminate against interstate commerce because the limitation applied equally to Michigan counties outside the county as well as to out-of-state waste. It also noted that each county had discretion to accept out-of-state waste and that any incidental burden on interstate commerce was not excessive in relation to the public health and environmental benefits derived by Michigan from the statute. The court of appeals affirmed the ruling, and Fort Gratiot appealed to the U.S. Supreme Court.

ISSUE

Did the Michigan waste import restrictions violate the U.S. Constitution's Commerce Clause by discriminating against interstate commerce?

DECISION

Yes. The Supreme Court noted that any state statute that discriminates against interstate commerce is unconstitutional unless the discrimination is justified by a valid factor unrelated to economic protectionism. It went on to state that solid waste was a protected item of interstate commerce and that in 1978 it had held that a New Jersey law prohibiting the import of most solid or liquid waste that originated or was collected outside the limits of the state violated the Commerce Clause. In this case, the purported discrimination in favor of county waste and the fact that some Michigan counties accepted out-of-county or out-of-state waste did not obviate the discriminatory effect. The Supreme Court went on to hold that the state had not met its burden of showing that waste import restrictions furthered health and safety concerns that could not be adequately served by nondiscriminatory alternatives.

SUPERFUND

In 1980, Congress passed the Comprehensive Environmental Response Compensation and Liability Act (CERCLA), commonly known as "Superfund," to deal with the problem of *uncontrolled or abandoned hazardous waste sites*. In 1986, it strengthened and expanded the law. Under the Superfund law, EPA is required to identify and assess the sites in the United States where hazardous wastes had been spilled, stored, or abandoned.

EPA has now identified more than 30,000 such sites. The sites are ranked on the basis of the type, quantity, and toxicity of the wastes; the number of people potentially exposed to the wastes; the different ways (e.g., air or drinking water) in which they might be exposed; the risks to contamination of aquifers; and other factors. The sites with the highest ranking are placed on the National Priority List to receive priority federal and/or state attention for cleanup. These sites are subjected to a careful scientific and engineering study to determine the most appropriate cleanup plan. Once a site has been cleaned up, the state is responsible for managing it to prevent future environmental problems. EPA also has the authority to quickly initiate actions at hazardous waste sites—whether or not the site is on the priority list—to address *imminent hazards* such as the risk of fire, explosion, or contamination of drinking water.

The cleanup activity is financed by a tax on chemicals and feedstocks. However, EPA has the authority to require that a site be cleaned up by those persons who were responsible for it, either as the owner or operator of the site, a transporter of wastes to the site, or the owner of wastes deposited at the site. Where EPA expends money to clean up a site, it has the legal authority to recover its costs from those who were responsible for the problem. The courts have held that such persons are "*jointly and severally responsible for the cost of cleanup.*" The concept of joint liability is discussed in Chapter 5. The *Chem-Dyne* case that follows involves a challenge to the concept of joint and several liability by the contributors to a major hazardous waste site. Of concern to many businesspeople is the fact that this stringent and potentially very expensive liability can in some instances be imposed on a current owner who had nothing to do with the contamination, such as a subsequent purchaser of the property.

UNITED STATES v. CHEM-DYNE CORP.
572 F. Supp. 802 (S.D. Ohio 1983)

FACTS

The United States brought a lawsuit under the Comprehensive Environmental Response, Compensation, and Liability Act (CERCLA) against 24 defendants who had allegedly generated or transported some of the hazardous substances located at the Chem-Dyne treatment facility in Ohio. The government sought to be reimbursed for money that it had spent in cleaning up hazardous wastes at the facility and asserted that each defendant was jointly and severally liable for the entire cost of the cleanup. The defendants contested the claim that they were jointly and severally liable and moved for summary judgment in their favor on this issue.

ISSUE

Under the Superfund law, are persons who contributed hazardous wastes to a particular facility jointly and severally liable for the cost of cleanup if they cannot establish their divisible share of the cleanup costs?

DECISION

Yes. While the Superfund law does not explicitly provide for joint and several liability, it adopts the liability rules developed under the common law. Under the common law, when two or more persons acting independently cause a distinct or single harm for which there is a reasonable basis for division according to the contribution of each, each is subject to liability only for the portion of the total harm that he has himself caused. But where two or more persons cause a single and indivisible harm, each is subject to liability for the entire harm. The court also held that where the conduct of two or more persons liable under CERCLA has combined to

(continued)

UNITED STATES V. CHEM-DYNE CORP.
(concluded)

violate the statute, and one or more of the defendants seek to limit their liability on the ground that the entire harm is capable of apportionment, the burden of proof as to apportionment is on each defendant.

Here, the question of whether the defendants are jointly or severally liable for the cleanup costs turns on a fairly complex factual determination. The Chem-Dyne facility contains a variety of hazardous wastes from 289 generators or transporters, consisting of about 608,000 pounds of material. Some of the wastes have been commingled, and the identities of the sources of these wastes remain unascertained. The fact of the mixing of the wastes raises an issue as to the divisibility of the harm. Further, a dispute exists over which of the wastes have contaminated the groundwater, the degree of their migration, and the concomitant health hazard. Finally, the volume of waste of a particular generator is not an accurate predictor of the risk associated with the waste because the toxicity or migratory potential of a particular hazardous substance generally varies independently with the volume of the waste. Because the divisibility of the harm and the resulting cost could not be established, all the contributors are jointly and severally liable.

COMMUNITY RIGHT TO KNOW AND EMERGENCY CLEANUP

As part of its 1986 amendments to Superfund, Congress enacted a series of requirements for emergency planning, notification of spills and accidents involving hazardous materials, disclosure by industry to the community of the presence of certain listed chemicals, and notification of the amounts of various chemicals being routinely released into the environment in the area of a facility. This legislation was in response to the accident at Bhopal, India, in 1984 and to several industrial accidents in the United States.

Firms subject to the requirements have to carefully plan how they will communicate with the surrounding community what chemicals are being regularly released and what precautions the facility has taken to protect the community from regular or accidental releases. Mindful of the difficulty of explaining to a community why large emissions of hazardous substances are taking place, a significant number of companies have undertaken to reduce those emissions below levels they are currently required to meet by law.

REGULATION OF CHEMICALS

BACKGROUND

More than 60,000 chemical substances are manufactured in the United States, and they are used in a wide variety of products. While these chemicals contribute much to the standard of living we enjoy, some of them are toxic or have the potential to cause cancer, birth defects, reproductive failure, and other health-related problems. These risks may be posed in the manufacturing process, during the use of a product, or as a result of the manner of disposal of the chemical or product.

EPA has two statutory authorities that give it the ability to prevent or restrict the manufacture and use of new and existing chemicals to remove unreasonable risks to human health or the environment. These authorities are the Federal Insecticide, Fungicide, and Rodenticide Act and the Toxic Substances Control Act.

REGULATION OF AGRICULTURAL CHEMICALS

The vast increase in the American farmer's productivity over the past few decades has been in large measure attributable to the farmer's use of chemicals to kill the insects, pests, and weeds that have historically competed with the farmer for his crops. Some of the chemicals, such as pesticides and herbicides, have been a mixed blessing. They have enabled people to dramatically increase productivity and to conquer disease. On the other hand, dead fish and birds have provided evidence that the chemicals were building up in the food chain and proving fatal to some species. Unless such chemicals are carefully used and disposed of, they can present a danger to the applicator and to the consumer of food and water. Gradually, people have realized the need to focus on the effects of using such chemicals.

EPA enforces the Federal Insecticide, Fungicide, and Rodenticide Act (FIFRA). This act gives EPA the authority to *register pesticides* before they can be sold, to provide for the certification of applicators or pesticides designated for "restrictive" use, to set limits on the amounts of pesticide residue permitted on crops that provide food for people or animals, and to register and inspect pesticide-manufacturing establishments.

When the EPA administrator has reason to believe that continued use of a particular pesticide poses an "imminent hazard," he may **suspend** its registration and remove it from the market. When the administrator believes that there is a less than imminent hazard but that the environmental risks of continuing to use a pesticide outweigh its benefits, the administrator may initiate a *cancellation of registration proceeding*. This proceeding affords all interested persons—manufacturers, distributors, users, environmentalists, and scientists—an opportunity to present evidence on the proposed cancellation. Cancellation of the registration occurs when the administrator finds that the product will cause "unreasonable adverse effects on the environment." In 1989, Congress amended the law to accelerate EPA's review of products approved under older, less-restrictive standards and to increase the speed at which unreasonably dangerous products can be removed from the market.

Those involved in the food production and distribution processes must keep a close watch on regulatory developments at EPA concerning the registration, cancellation, and suspension of products as well as actions EPA takes concerning the possible residues on food products. During the 1980s, the agency took highly publicized actions concerning the use of ethylene dibromide (EDB), a fumigant, on citrus and grain products, the use of sulfites on table grapes, the use of Alar on apples, and the use of chlordane as a treatment against termite infestation. In each instance, the economic well-being of many businesses was at risk if they did not adequately anticipate and/or deal with the EPA's actions and the publicity that resulted from those actions.

The case that follows, *King v. E. I. Du Pont de Nemours & Co.*, involves the question of whether registration of a product under FIFRA, including approval of its proposed label, preempts any subsequent state law claims based on an asserted failure to warn of dangers associated with use of the registered product.

KING V. E. I. DU PONT DE NEMOURS & CO.
35 E.R.C. 1925 (U.S.D.C. Me. 1993)

FACTS

Ernest King and Edward Higgins were employed by the Maine Department of Transportation (MDOT). As part of their employment duties, King and Higgins seasonally sprayed one or more herbicides manufactured by E. I. Du Pont de Nemours and Company (Du Pont), the Dow Chemical Company (Dow), Velsicol Chemical Company (Velsicol) and Sandoz Corporation (Sandoz). As a result of their exposure to the herbicides they claimed to have experienced nausea, headaches, loss of appetite, irritability, loss of concentration, muscle pains, joint pain and moodiness, memory loss, and continued deterioration of vision; in addition, Higgins claims to suffer from numbness in his extremities.

King and Higgins brought suit against Du Pont, Dow, Velsicol, and Sandoz seeking to impose liability for damages under state tort law theories of negligence and strict liability. They claimed that the chemical companies had failed to warn them about the safe and proper use of the herbicides as well as about the harm and danger of exposure to these products. The chemical companies moved for summary judgment in their favor. One of the key questions was whether the Federal Insecticide, Fungicide, and Rodenticide Act (FIFRA) preempted state tort claims based on failure to warn or inadequate warnings relating to products subject to the act's labeling requirements. The parties stipulated that all of the product labels in question were submitted to and approved by the EPA in accordance with FIFRA.

Under FIFRA, the EPA cannot approve an herbicide unless it complies with the requirements established in FIFRA and the EPA labeling regulations promulgated to implement the act. The EPA regulations detail how warning labels are to be presented and provide specific requirements for the content, placement, type, size, and promotion of the warnings. "Label" is defined under FIFRA to include "the written, printed, or graphic matter on, or attached to, the pesticide or device or any of its containers or wrappers." Required warnings are specified according to the degree to which ingestion or contact with an herbicide is toxic, and these warnings must include precautionary statements about risks posed to humans. The regulations also specify necessary directions on how to use each chemical.

The procedure for registration under FIFRA requires that each applicant file a statement with the administrator of the EPA that includes the name of the chemical, a statement of all claims to be made for the product, any directions for the product's use, and a full description of the tests made and the results thereof upon which the claims are based.

The 1972 amendments to FIFRA added a section expressly setting forth the states' authority to regulate pesticides. This section states in relevant part:

(a) In general. A state may regulate the sale or use of any federally registered pesticide or device in the state, but only if and to the extent the regulation does not permit any sale or use prohibited by the [act].

(b) Uniformity. Such state shall not impose or continue in effect any requirements for labeling or packaging different from those required under this [act].

ISSUE

Are tort claims under state law based on failure to warn preempted by FIFRA?

DECISION

Yes. The statute's language, by itself, is a powerful limit on state power over labeling. Moreover, the legislative history also indicates that this was Congress's intent. Congress recognized that while the intent of the provision was to leave to the states the authority to impose stricter regulation on pesticide use than that required under the act, subsection (b) preempted any state labeling or packaging requirements differing from such requirements under the act. The contention that the chemical companies failed to adequately warn the plaintiffs of the dangers inherent in their products is expressly preempted under subsection (b) because, if successful, such claims would constitute state-imposed "requirements for labeling or packaging in addition to or different from those required [under FIFRA]."

TOXIC SUBSTANCES CONTROL ACT

The other major statute regulating chemical use focuses on other toxic substances—such as asbestos and PCBs—and on the new chemical compounds that are developed each year. The Toxic Substances Control Act, which was enacted in 1976, requires that chemicals be tested by manufacturers or processors to determine their effect on human health or the environment before the chemicals are introduced into commerce. The act also gives EPA the authority to regulate chemical substances or mixtures that present an *unreasonable risk of injury to health or the environment* and to take action against any such substances or mixtures that pose an imminent hazard.

This legislation was enacted in response to the concern that thousands of new substances are released into the environment each year, sometimes without adequate consideration of their potential for harm, and that it is not until damage from a substance occurs that its manufacture or use is properly regulated. At the same time, a goal of the act is not to unduly impede or create unnecessary economic barriers to technological innovation.

BIOTECHNOLOGY

The development of techniques to genetically manipulate organisms, often referred to generally as *biotechnology*, offers considerable promise to provide food and health care and to generate a range of new products and production processes. At the same time, biotechnology raises concerns about the potential to adversely affect human health or the environment. Responsibility for regulating research and use of biotechnology is shared in the federal government among the Food and Drug Administration, the Department of Agriculture, the Environmental Protection Agency, and the

CONCEPT SUMMARY	Major Environmental Laws
Act	**Focus**
Clean Air Act	Protects quality of ambient (outdoor) air through national ambient air quality standards, state implementation plans, control of air toxics, new source performance standards, and controls on automobiles and fuels.
Clean Water Act	Protects and enhances quality of surface waters by setting water quality standards and limiting discharges by industry and municipalities to those waters through permit system; also regulates dredging and filling of wetlands.
Marine Protection, Research, and Sanctuaries Act	Regulates dumping of all types of material into ocean waters.
Safe Drinking Water Act	Protects and enhances quality of our drinking water. Also regulates disposal of wastes in wells.
Resource Conservation and Recovery Act (RCRA)	Establishes a cradle-to-the-grave regulatory system for handling and disposal of hazardous wastes; also deals with solid waste.
Comprehensive Environmental Response Compensation and Liability Act (Superfund)	Provides a program to deal with hazardous waste that was inadequately disposed of in the past; financed in part by tax on chemicals and feedstocks.
Federal Insecticide, Fungicide, and Rodenticide Act (FIFRA)	Regulates the sale and use of chemicals to be used as pesticides and herbicides, including residues permitted on crops intended for use as food.
Toxic Substances Control Act (TSCA)	Requires preclearance of new chemicals and provides for regulation of existing chemicals that pose an unreasonable risk to health or the environment.

National Institutes of Health. Generally, a review of such activity is required before it takes place. This process is of considerable import to companies that are developing genetically engineered organisms for commercial purposes; it can affect both the speed at which they are able to get the products to market and the public's confidence that release of the organisms does not pose an unreasonable risk.

Ethical Implications

Suppose that a multinational chemical company with its primary manufacturing facilities in the United States plans to build a manufacturing facility in a developing country where there are few, if any, real state-imposed environmental regulations. Is it sufficient for the company to simply meet the environmental requirements of the host country? Is there any ethical obligation to do more—for example, to build the facility to meet the requirements it would have to meet in this country?

.... *QUESTIONS AND PROBLEM CASES* ....

1. What are the major requirements a person who generates, treats, stores, or transports significant quantities of hazardous waste must meet?

2. The Interstate Commerce Commission has the power to approve or set the tariff rates that railroads charge shippers. As a result of past ICC approvals, the railroad tariffs call for higher shipping charges to carry scrap metals and paper than to carry virgin materials. This disparity operates as an economic discrimination against recycled goods. A group of law students have formed an organization known as SCRAP (Students Challenging Regulatory Agency Procedures). SCRAP is concerned that the ICC-approved rate structure discourages the environmentally desirable user of recycled goods. The ICC approved a 2.5 percent across-the-board surcharge in railroad shipping rates and indicated that no environmental impact statement was necessary because there was "no environmental impact." SCRAP is concerned that the increase will further the discrimination against used materials and files suit against the ICC to require that an environmental impact statement be prepared. Should the court decide that an environmental impact statement is required?

3. In August 1986, Tzavah Urban Renewal Corporation purchased from the city of Newark a building formerly known as the Old Military Park Hotel. While the buyer was given an opportunity to inspect the building, it was not informed by the city that the building was

permeated with asbestos-containing material. At the time of the purchase, the building was in great disrepair and had been uninhabited for many years. Its proposed renovation was to be a major urban renewal project. In June 1987, Tzavah contracted with Greer Industrial Corporation to "gut" the building. While the work was going on, an EPA inspector visited the site and concluded that the hotel was contaminated with asbestos. He observed Greer employees throwing asbestos-laced objects out of the windows of the building and noted an uncovered refuse pile next to the hotel that contained asbestos. The workers were not wetting the debris before heaving it out the windows, and the refuse pile was also dry. As a result, asbestos dust was being released into the air. Although the hotel was located in a commercial district, there were private homes nearby. Renovation of buildings contaminated with asbestos is regulated under the Clean Air Act. The EPA regulations require building owners or operators to notify EPA before commencing renovation or demolition and prescribe various procedures for storage and removal of the asbestos. Tzavah failed to provide the required notice or to comply with procedures required. After being notified by EPA of the violation of the law, Tzavah stopped the demolition work, left the building unsecured, and left the waste piles dry and uncovered. EPA tried informally to get Tzavah to complete the work in accordance with the asbestos regulations; when Tzavah did not take action, EPA brought a lawsuit against Tzavah to do so. Should the court issue an injunction requiring Tzavah to abate the hazard posed by the dry asbestos remaining in the hotel?

4. In July 1984 Vanguard Corporation began operating a metal furniture manufacturing plant in Brooklyn, New York. The plant is located in an area that has not attained the national ambient air quality standards for ozone. The plant is a major stationary source (i.e., has the potential to emit more than 100 tons a year) of volatile organic compounds that contribute to the formation of ozone in the atmosphere. The New York State implementation plan (SIP) requires that metal-coating facilities use paint that contains less than 3 pounds of organic solvent (minus water) per gallon at the time of coating. On August 24, 1984, EPA notified Vanguard that it was not in compliance with the SIP provision concerning coatings and issued it a notice of violation. Vanguard sought to defend against the notice of violation on the grounds that it had used its best faith efforts to comply but that it was technologically and economically infeasible. It indicated that it wanted 18 more months to come into compliance. Should Vanguard be held to be in violation of the Clean Air Act?

5. Charles Hanson owned land abutting Keith Lake, a freshwater lake that was subject to some tidal flooding as a result of its connection with tidal waters. In order to minimize the detrimental effects from the tidal activities and consequent flooding, Hanson deposited a large quantity of dirt, rock, bricks, sheet metal, and other debris along the shoreline of his property. He did so without obtaining a permit from the U.S. Army Corps of Engineers under section 404 of the Clean Water Act, which controls dumping and filling activities in navigable waters of the United States. Under the law, discharges of pollutants into navigable waters without a permit are forbidden. The term *pollutant* is defined to include "dredged spoil, solid waste, incinerator residue, sewage, garbage, sewage sludge, munitions, chemical wastes, biological materials, radioactive materials, heat, wrecked or discarded equipment, rock, sand, cellar dirt, and industrial, municipal and agricultural waste

discharged into water." EPA brought an enforcement action against Hanson claiming he had violated the Clean Water Act. Should the court find that Hanson violated the act?

6. Mall Properties, Inc., was an organization that for many years had sought to develop a shopping mall in the town of North Haven, Connecticut, a suburb of New Haven. Because the proposed development would require the filling of some wetlands, Mall Properties was required to obtain a permit from the Corps of Engineers pursuant to Section 404 of the Clean Water Act. The city of New Haven opposed development of the mall—and the granting of the permit—on the grounds it would jeopardize the fragile economy of New Haven. The Corps of Engineers found the net loss of wetlands would be substantially compensated for by a proposed on-site wetland creation. Relying primarily on the socioeconomic concerns of the city of New Haven, the District Engineer rejected the proposed permit. Mall Properties then brought suit against the Corps of Engineers, claiming that the decision was arbitrary and capricious. Should the District Engineer have relied on socioeconomic factors unrelated to the project's environmental impacts in making a decision on the permit?

7. Johnson & Towers, Inc., is in the business of overhauling large motor vehicles. It uses degreasers and other industrial chemicals that contain chemicals classified as "hazardous wastes" under the Resource Conservation and Recovery Act (RCRA), such as methylene chloride and trichloroethylene. For some period of time, waste chemicals from cleaning operations were drained into a holding tank and, when the tank was full, pumped into a trench. The trench flowed from the plant property into Parker's Creek, a tributary of the Delaware River. Under RCRA, generators of such wastes must obtain a permit for disposal from the Environmental Protection Agency (EPA). EPA had neither issued, nor received an application for, a permit for the Johnson & Towers operations. Over a three-day period, federal agents saw workers pump waste from the tank into the trench, and on the third day toxic chemicals flowed into the creek. The company and two of its employees, Jack

Hopkins, a foreman, and Peter Angel, the service manager, were indicted for unlawfully disposing of hazardous wastes. The company pled guilty. The federal district court dismissed the criminal charges against the two individuals, holding that RDRA's criminal penalty provisions imposing fines and imprisonment did not apply to employees. The government appealed. Can employees of a corporation be held criminally liable if their actions on behalf of the corporation violate the federal hazardous waste law?

8. In 1979, Anne Arundel County, Maryland, enacted two related ordinances. One absolutely prohibited the disposal in and the transportation through Anne Arundel County of various hazardous wastes not originating in that county. Another ordinance required a license to dispose of hazardous waste in the county; it also required a license to transport hazardous wastes through the county. Browning-Ferris, Inc. (BFI), is the owner and operator of a landfill located in Anne Arundel County that is licensed by the state of Maryland to receive hazardous wastes; BFI is also a hauler of hazardous wastes within the county. The county notified BFI that it expected BFI to comply with the new regulations, and BFI filed a lawsuit challenging the ordinances and seeking to have them enjoined. How should the court rule?

9. The Royal McBee Corporation manufactured typewriters at a factory in Springfield, Missouri. As a part of the manufacturing process, Royal McBee generated cyanide-based electroplating wastes, sludge from the bottom of electroplating tanks, and spent plating bath solution. As a part of their duties, Royal McBee employees dumped the wastes onto the surface of the soil on a vacant lot adjoining the factory. This took place between 1959 and 1962. Over time, the waste materials migrated outward and downward from the original dumping site, contaminating a large area. In 1970, the manufacturing facility and lot were sold to General Electric, which operated the plant but did not engage in any dumping of wastes on the vacant lot. In the mid-1980s, General Electric was required by EPA and the state of Missouri, under the authority of the federal Superfund law, to clean up the contamination at the site. General Electric then brought a lawsuit against the successor corporation of Royal McBee's typewriter business, Litton Business Systems, to recover for the costs it incurred in cleaning up the site. Under the Superfund law, "any person who at the time of disposal of any hazardous substance owned or operated any facilities at which such hazardous substances were disposed of, shall be liable for any other necessary costs of response incurred by any other person" consistent with the Superfund law and regulations. Is General Electric entitled to recover its cleanup costs from Litton?

10. Chemlawn sells pesticide products for use on residential lawns. The active ingredients in Chemlawn's products are registered with the Environmental Protection Agency pursuant to the Federal Insecticide, Fungicide, and Rodenticide Act (FIFRA). Deborah Ryan brought a lawsuit against Chemlawn seeking damages for injuries she claimed that she and her son Kevin sustained from the use of Chemlawn products. Ryan claims that the products are unsafe for commercial use and that they have been inadequately tested by EPA. Chemlawn contends that Ryan should take her complaints to EPA, which has the responsibility for determining whether the products are safe to be sold. How should the court decide?

CHAPTER 47

International Law

For seven years Borden, Inc., licensed Meiji Milk Products Co. of Tokyo to make and sell margarine products in Japan under Borden's trademarks. Just as the agreement was about to expire, Borden discovered that Meiji was intending to substitute its own margarine products on the shelves of retail outlets throughout Japan using packaging confusingly similar to Borden's. Borden filed a suit in a federal district court in New York seeking to enjoin Meiji from distributing or marketing the products.[1]

- *What is a licensing agreement? What are its risks? Is it the best method of structuring operations to take advantage of international opportunities?*
- *How do multinational businesses reduce the risk of doing business in the international environment?*
- *What laws govern international transactions?*

---

[1] *The Wall Street Journal*, September 4, 1990, p. B4.

SOURCES OF INTERNATIONAL LAW

When a U.S. firm considers an international undertaking, it may face a very different environment from the one it confronted in its domestic operations. The parties to international transactions are much less likely to know each other well because they are separated by great distances. Further, it is more difficult to pursue remedies when multiple legal systems are involved. Finally, currency differences and the multitude of restrictions that may constrain a company's right to remove funds from a particular country increase the complexity involved in carrying out international operations. The answers to the legal questions raised by international transactions come from a mix of the laws of our own country, those of the other country or countries involved, and certain doctrines of international law.

INTERNATIONAL REGULATION OF SALES AGREEMENTS

Countries have attempted to address some of the problems raised by international transactions through the drafting of compacts or codes that apply across national boundaries. Typically, countries will agree to be bound by them, and then adjust their internal laws, if necessary, so they are in compliance with the laws laid out in the compact or code. While such codes have existed since the early part of this century, it has been only in the last half of this century that they have gained many signatories. As the pace of international trade has increased, so has support for such agreements.

CONVENTION ON CONTRACTS FOR THE INTERNATIONAL SALE OF GOODS

The wide variety of national approaches to contract law greatly impeded global trade. Business lawyers were required to spend a great deal of time researching the different legal schemes in order to draft agreements that would protect the parties' expectations throughout the world. Transactions often were delayed or otherwise burdened by disagreements between the parties over the selection of a particular choice of law provision within the contract. In an attempt to overcome these problems, the **United Nations Convention on Contracts for the International Sale of Goods (CISG)** was created. The fundamental goal of the CISG is to unify and codify an international law of sales.

    The CISG was designed to unify and codify an international law of sales in much the same way that the Uniform Commercial Code provides uniformity and stability for transactions among contracting parties from different states in the United States. It provides rules governing the formation of international contracts and regulates the transfer of goods under those contracts.

Comparing the CISG with the UCC

Despite many similarities to the Uniform Commercial Code (UCC), the CISG does differ in several respects. First, the CISG applies only to commercial sales of goods while the UCC governs both consumer and commercial transactions. Second, while the UCC has some provisions holding merchants to higher standards than those imposed on nonmerchants, the CISG does not. (This is because all parties must be merchants under the CISG since it applies only to commercial sales.) Third, the UCC (with some exceptions) requires contracts for the sale of goods in excess of $500 to be in writing. The CISG has no writing requirement unless the contract contains a written provision requiring that modifications or terminations be in writing. Finally, the CISG generally requires that acceptance be a mirror image of the offer while the UCC's "battle of the

Table 47–1　CISG versus UCC

	CISG	UCC
Application	*International commercial* sales of goods	*Any* sale of goods
Parties	Applies only to merchants	Applies to any party (merchants often held to higher standards)
Acceptance	"Mirror image" rule (certain terms considered material)	"Battle of forms" rule (nonmaterial terms may vary)
Consideration	None needed to modify contract	None needed to modify contract
Writing	No writing needed	Sale of goods in excess of $500 requires a writing

forms" provision permits the acceptance to vary from the terms of the offer. (See Table 47–1.)

THE CHOICE-OF-LAW CONVENTION

The Hague Convention on the Law Applicable to Contracts for the International Sale of Goods (Choice-of-Law Convention) resulted from an attempt to harmonize choice-of-law rules with the CISG. It provides courts in the signatory countries with rules for determining which law applies to contracts for the sales of goods when those contracts involve parties from different countries. It allows contracting parties to specify which country's laws will apply to their transaction but also provides a way for the court to decide if the parties have not so chosen.

If both parties to a contract reside in countries that have adopted the CISG, those terms automatically will control the transaction unless the agreement contains a provision specifically rejecting its applicability. If the buyer and seller are not from countries that have adopted the CISG, it will not govern unless their contract specifically calls for its application. Otherwise, the governing law, when not specified in the contract, will be the law of the country in which the seller's place of business is located.

PRIVATE INTERNATIONAL LAW

The conventions discussed above are only two of several that can apply to international transactions. Combined, they provide the framework for handling many of the problems that would arise in international contracts. However, many of the countries whose businesses routinely engage in international dealings are not signatories of the conventions; thus, they do not apply to a major portion of international transactions. In such situations, the parties either must shape their dealings in light of the uncertainties traditionally inherent in the international legal arena or establish through their contractual negotiations the body of rules that will govern their transaction.

Choice-of-Law and Forum Selection Clauses

To the extent that there is a difference between the contract law of the seller's nation and that of the buyer's country, courts typically will respect the choice of the parties as to which law applies if the parties, as is usual, have included a **choice-of-law** clause in the agreement. Selecting the appropriate body of rules to govern the transaction is not enough, however. The parties frequently will wish to decide in advance on a suitable forum in which the dispute resolution should occur. Often this may be a neutral location that offers no special advantage to either of the parties. Such provisions are likely to be honored by the courts if they are freely negotiated, not contrary to any public policy, and not severely inconvenient for either party. Thus, the parties may agree that their contract is to be governed by the CISG (choice of law) with disputes to be resolved in the courts of the United States (forum selection). In the case that opened this chapter, Borden and Meiji had previously agreed that their disputes would be governed by the laws and courts of New York.

MARRA V. PAPANDREOU
216 F.3d 1119 (D.C. Cir. 2000)

FACTS

In 1994, the Greek Ministry of Tourism announced an international tender for licenses to operate 10 casinos in specified locations throughout Greece. Marrecon Enterprises submitted the highest bid for a license to operate a casino just outside of Athens. Thus, the then-minister of tourism issued an official resolution granting the license to Marrecon. The license gave Marrecon the right to construct and operate a luxury casino complex in partnership with the Greek government. The license also contained a forum-selection clause which provided: *"Any dispute or disagreement between the State and Marrecon Enterprises arising from the application of this license, the interpretation or performance of its terms, the extent of the rights and obligations of the State and the holder of this license, and in general any matter that may occur concerning the license, shall be settled by the Greek courts."* Shortly after Marrecon secured the license, local political opposition against the construction of the casino developed. As a result, the Greek tourism minister resigned and the government and Marrecon began negotiations to relocate at a different site near Athens. However, for reasons that are not clear, the government became unfavorably disposed to Marrecon's project and began exploring avenues for "recalling" the license. Ultimately, the government issued a resolution identifying legal defects in the licensing process and, accordingly, revoked the license from the time it came into effect. Rosemarie Marra, with a 9 percent interest in Marrecon, sued the Greek government in a U.S. district court for breach of contract. The Greek government moved to dismiss Marra's complaint on the grounds that her lawsuit in the United States was barred by the license's forum-selection clause. In response, she argued that the Greek government's action in officially revoking the contract as a whole barred it from relying on the forum-selection provision.

ISSUE

Did the action by the Greek government invalidate the forum selection clause?

DECISION

No. Federal courts must establish their jurisdiction to hear cases before adjudicating their merits. A forum-selection clause is understood not merely as a contract provision but also as a distinct contract in and of itself—that is, an agreement between the parties to settle disputes in a particular forum—that is separate from the obligations the parties owe each other under the remainder of the contract. It is clear to us that this forum-selection clause, if enforceable, requires Marra to file her suit in Greece. The clause is broadly written, encompassing "any dispute or disagreement" between the parties "arising from the application of this license." This brings us to the more difficult issue of the clause's enforceability. U.S. courts long ago jettisoned the longstanding American judicial hostility to forum-selection clauses as founded in the parochial concept that all disputes must be resolved under our laws and in our courts. Further, Marra does not point to factors typically relied upon by litigants seeking to avoid enforcement of forum-selection clauses—for instance, that the clause is the product of fraud or that its enforcement would contravene a strong public policy of the forum in which the suit is brought.

(continued)

MARRA V. PAPANDREOU
(concluded)

Rather, she argues that the Greek government should be prevented from availing itself of a forum-selection clause that is part of a contract that it professes to have "revoked." Each party's position produces an anomaly. Marra notes that the Greek government's resolution revoking her license was retroactive in effect, legally extinguishing the license as of the date it was issued. If that is so, she asks, how can the Greek government now seek refuge in a provision of a nonexistent license? The Greek government responds that it is no less logical to allow someone to sue under a contract while at the same time claiming not to be bound by a provision within that contract. Moreover, in the Greek government's view, Marra is trapped in a lose–lose situation in her attempt to pursue litigation in the United States: Either the license was indeed lawfully revoked and she has no cause of action, or the license is valid and she is bound by the license's terms to pursue her case in the Greek courts. While there is no entirely satisfactory answer to this conundrum, we think that the Greek government has the stronger position. Marra's argument relies heavily on the implications that flow, under well-settled principles of contract law, from a party's "repudiation" of a contract. (Once a party repudiates a contract, it has no right to demand perfor-

mance from the nonrepudiating party.) The repudiation shoe does not quite fit here, for two reasons. First, adherence to the forum is not an obligation owed by Marra to the Greek government, but a condition precedent to suit under the contract, binding equally on both parties. Second, the rule urged by Marra is contrary to the conceptual understanding, noted above, of a forum-selection clause from the contract in which it is contained. Therefore, while the Greek government's denial of its contractual obligations to Marra relieves her of her duty to perform her side of the contract's terms (for instance, she is no longer obligated to pay her annual license fee), that action does work a repudiation of the forum-selection clause unless it is specifically directed at the clause itself. We might have reached a different conclusion had there been a dispute as to whether the license had been voluntarily agreed to by the parties. Then it could be argued—even if once accepts, as we do, the position that a forum-selection clause is severable from the contract containing it—that if the parties never entered into the contract in the first place, they by definition did not agree to the forum selection clause. However, Marra offers no challenge to the making of the agreement between the parties to adjudicate their disputes in Greece.

Arbitration

The increasing volume of international trade, coupled with the complex nature of many of these relationships, has led to greater and greater reliance on arbitration to resolve contractual disputes. This settlement of disputes by a nonjudicial third party is increasingly called for in international contracts because it is cheaper, quicker, and more private than resolving disputes through litigation. Equally important, however, is the fact that it can take place in a neutral location. The increase in trade with countries such as China, Japan, and Korea, where mediation rather than litigation of disputes is traditional, has given added impetus to this trend.

The growing attractiveness of arbitration has resulted in the establishment of arbitration centers in world capitals such as London, Paris, Cairo, Hong Kong, and

CONCEPT SUMMARY	**Advantages of Arbitration**
	1. May be faster and cheaper than litigation.
	2. May continue business relationship while arbitration is occurring.
	3. May select an arbiter with special knowledge of industry.
	4. May keep subject matter confidential.

Stockholm, and major cities such as Geneva and New York. Recognition and enforcement of international arbitration agreements and awards is generally controlled through multilateral treaties including the Foreign Arbitral Awards Convention. An outgrowth of this trend has been the emergence of several major arbitral institutions that have conducted their own sets of rules and procedures. However, the parties to a contract are free to opt for a more informal or ad hoc arbitration arrangement based on their own set of guidelines. Such agreements are legally enforceable as long as the parties have agreed to abide by the arbitrator's decision.

The United States and most of its trading partners are signatories to the 1958 New York Convention. This agreement places the burden on the party opposing the enforcement of an arbitral award. This convention broadly construes the authority of arbitral panels and severely limits the power of the party to overturn an arbitral award. However, the United States will recognize the enforceability of an award only where the nation of the other party has ratified the convention and only where the dispute is commercial in nature.

INTERNATIONAL PAPER V SCHWABEDISSEN MASCHINEN & ANLAGEN
206 F.3d 411 (4th Cir. 2000)

FACTS

International Paper Company sought to purchase an industrial saw manufactured by Schwabedissen Maschinen & Anlagen GMBH, a German corporation. Accordingly, International Paper sent to Wood Systems Incorporated, a U.S. distributor of Schwabedissen saws, a non-binding letter of intent to purchase a new double trim saw. International Paper's personnel then visited Schwabedissen's facility in Germany to observe its production process. Upon their return, in a purchase order from International Paper to Wood dated May 17, 1991, International Paper agreed to buy and Wood agreed to sell the Schwabedissen saw, in accordance with a performance guarantee and certain specifications. On June 6, 1991, Schwabedissen sent Wood an "Order Confirmation/Contract" for the saw International Paper sought to purchase. This contract included the terms of an additional document that contained an arbitration clause providing that *"any dispute arising out of the Contract shall be finally settled, in accordance with the Rules of Conciliation and Arbitration of the International Chamber of Commerce."* On June 12, 1991, Wood sent a purchase order for the saw to Schwabedissen, together with specifications from International Paper's purchase order. In response, Schwabedissen arranged for delivery of the saw, which was installed at International Paper's plant in late December 1991. According to International Paper, the saw completely failed to operate after it was installed. No written contract ever existed between International Paper and Schwabedissen, but International Paper maintains that when difficulty arose as to the saw's operation, Schwabedissen orally agreed to repair the saw but failed to do so. On July 9, 1993, after Wood declared bankruptcy, International Paper filed a complaint against Schwabedissen in a U.S. federal district court, alleging breach of contract and breach of warranties based on the May 17, 1991, purchase order with Wood. International Paper alleged that Wood acted as an agent for Schwabedissen and therefore Schwabedissen was liable under that purchase order. At the district court hearing, International Paper contended that it had no knowledge of, and so could not be bound by, the arbitration clause that was part of the Wood–Schwabedissen contract. However, the court rejected this argument, reasoning that because International Paper sought to take advantage of certain commitments that were made by Schwabedissen to Wood in the Wood–Schwabedissen contract, it was bound by all commitments in that contract, including the arbitration provision.

ISSUE

Should International Paper be required to submit this dispute to arbitration?

(continued)

INTERNATIONAL PAPER V SCHWABEDISSEN MASCHINEN & ANLAGEN
(concluded)

DECISION

Yes. International Paper's principal contention is that the arbitration clause in the Wood–Schwabedissen contract cannot be enforced against International Paper because it is a nonsignatory to that agreement. Generally, arbitration is a matter of contract and a party cannot be required to submit to arbitration any dispute which he has not agreed so to submit. While a contract cannot bind parties to arbitrate disputes they have not agreed to arbitrate, it does not follow that an obligation to arbitrate attaches only to one who has personally signed the written arbitration provision. Rather, a party can agree to submit to arbitration by means other than personally signing a contract containing an arbitration clause. Well-established common law principles dictate that in an appropriate case, a nonsignatory can enforce, or be bound by, an arbitration provision within a contract executed by other parties. This could be by (1) assumption, (2) agency, (3) veil piercing/alter ego, or (4) estoppel. We believe the doctrine of equitable estoppel applies here. Equitable estoppel precludes a party from asserting rights he otherwise would have had against another when his own conduct renders assertion of those rights contrary to equity. In the arbitration context, the doctrine recognizes that a party may be estopped from asserting that the lack of his signature on a written contract precludes enforcement of the contract's arbitration clause when he has consistently maintained that other provisions of the same contract should be enforced to benefit him. To allow a plaintiff to claim the benefit of the contract and simultaneously avoid its burdens would both disregard equity and contravene the purposes underlying enactment of the Arbitration Act. Applying these principles here we can only conclude that International Paper is estopped from refusing to arbitrate its dispute with Schwabedissen The Wood–Schwabedissen contract provides part of the factual foundation for every claim asserted by International Paper against Schwabedissen. It specifically alleges that Schwabedissen failed to honor the warranties in the Wood–Schwabedissen contract and it seeks damages in accordance with that contract. International Paper's entire case hinges on its asserted rights under the Wood–Schwabedissen contract; it cannot seek to enforce those contractual rights and avoid the contract's requirement that "any dispute arising out of" the contract be arbitrated.

SALES ABROAD OF DOMESTICALLY MANUFACTURED PRODUCTS

The export of a product manufactured at home is the most common form of international transaction engaged in by U.S. firms. A firm may make direct sales to customers abroad, or it may appoint one or more distributors for a particular country or region that purchase the product from the U.S. firm and resell it to customers in their territory. These two methods of exploiting the world market can involve different legal problems.

DIRECT SALES TO CUSTOMERS ABROAD

A direct sale to a customer abroad based simply on the customer's contractual promise to pay when the goods arrive frequently does not provide the seller with sufficient assurance of payment. The U.S. seller may not know its overseas customer well enough to determine the customer's financial condition or any tendency of the customer to refuse payment by quibbling over the conformity of the goods with the contract if the customer no longer wants the goods when they arrive. If payment is not forthcoming for either of these reasons, the seller will find it difficult and expensive to pursue its legal rights under the contract. Even if the seller feels assured that the buyer will pay for the goods on arrival, the time required for shipping the goods will often mean that payment will not be received until months after shipment.

Documentary Exchanges

To solve these problems, the seller frequently insists on structuring the sale as a **documentary irrevocable letter of credit transaction.** The transaction usually has two parties in addition to the U.S. seller and its foreign customer: an **issuing bank** located in the customer's country, with which the customer typically has close banking relations, and a **confirming bank** located in the United States that is well known to the seller. In this type of transaction, the issuing bank, under an agreement with the buyer, issues a **letter of credit** agreeing to pay a stated amount when it is presented with a **bill of lading** and any other documents called for in the letter. The bill of lading is a document issued by a carrier acknowledging that the seller has delivered particular goods to it—for example, eight tractors of a certain model—and entitling the holder to receive these goods at the place of destination. The confirming bank promises to pay the seller on the letter of credit. The confirmation thus performs a function similar to that performed by the endorsement of a note. The confirmation is needed because the seller, unlike the confirming bank, may not know any more about the financial integrity of the issuing bank than it knows about that of the buyer.

The first step in this type of transaction is a simple sales contract between the seller and the buyer that conditions shipment of the goods by the seller on the seller's receipt of a letter of credit and its confirmation. If everything works as planned, the seller delivers the goods to the carrier and is issued a bill of lading, which it presents to the confirming bank in return for payment. The confirming bank sends the bill of lading to the issuing bank for reimbursement. The issuing bank, which by that time will have received payment from the customer (unless the issuing bank and the buyer have entered into special credit arrangements between themselves), will deliver the bill of lading to the customer for use in obtaining the goods on their arrival.

This arrangement solves the various problems confronting sellers in direct sales to customers abroad. The seller has a promise of immediate payment from an entity it knows to be financially solvent (the confirming bank). Since payment is made to the seller well before the goods arrive, the buyer cannot claim that the goods are defective and refuse to accept delivery and pay for them, leaving the seller with the burden of suing. (Of course, if the goods are truly defective on arrival, the customer can commence an action for damages against the seller based on their original sales contract.)

The laws governing letters of credit generally insist that the promises made by the issuing and confirming banks are independent of the underlying sales contract between the seller and the customer. The confirming bank's only responsibility is to make sure that the bill of lading covers the goods identified in the letter of credit and that any other documents called for in the letter strictly conform to its requirements. If so, the confirming bank is required to pay the seller. It is no defense that the customer has refused to pay the issuing bank or even, generally, that the customer claims to know that the goods are defective. (See Figure 47–1.)

FIGURE 47–1   Documentary Credit

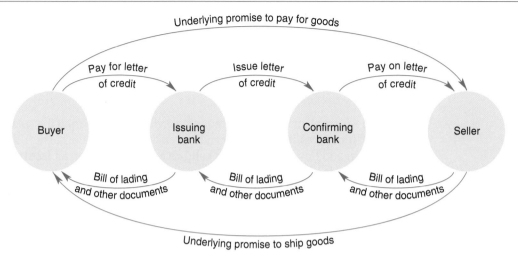

245 F.3d 82 (2nd Cir. 2001)

FACTS

On June 11, 1996, Sky Industries obtained a $1.5 million letter of credit from Hamilton Bank for the benefit of Sung-Jin Trading Company in connection with Sky's planned purchase of leather sport shoes from Sung-Jin. In reality, neither Sky nor Hamilton intended the credit would be negotiated. Instead Sky used the letter of credit to demonstrate that it had a business relationship with various Asian companies to which Sky sought to send exports. The contract between Sky and Hamilton provided that in order to obtain payment on the letter of credit, the beneficiary must provide an authenticated telex from Hamilton and that Hamilton would not send the telex unless Sky previously had deposited the full value of the letter of credit with Hamilton. Thus, Hamilton believed itself to be protected against negligent or fraudulent negotiation of the credit. Specifically, the terms of the letter of credit provided that drafts could be negotiated "at 180 days after transport document date" upon presentation of the credit along with a bill of lading, an original and three copies of a commercial invoice and packing list, and "copy of authenticated telex from issue bank to advising bank, indicating quantity to be shipped, destination, and nominating transporting company." The credit also specified that it was issued pursuant to the Uniform Customs and Practice for Documentary Credits (UCP). Later in June, Sung-Jin attempted to negotiate the letter of credit to Kookmin Bank; however, the bank repeatedly stated that it would not accept the credit without an authenticated telex. However, on July 13, Kookmin paid on the letter of credit after one of its employees was persuaded by Sung-Jin that the authenticated telex requirement had been eliminated. On July 22, Kookmin presented the letter of credit, draft, and shipping documents in order to obtain payment. Hamilton returned the documents to Kookmin by courier on July 24, along with a letter stating that Hamilton would not honor the letter of credit because presentment was "not in compliance with the terms and conditions of the credit." Kookmin received the documents on July 27, and presented them to Hamilton again on August 6. Hamilton rejected the presentation a second time. On that date, Kookmin received a telecommunication from Hamilton explaining that Hamilton had rejected the presentation because it lacked an authenticated telex. After Kookmin was unsuccessful in recouping its loss from Sung-Jin, it filed a lawsuit to recover damages for Hamilton's refusal to honor its letter of credit. Specifically, Kookmin argued that Hamilton must honor the credit because of its failure to make a timely and specific disclaimer.

(continued)

HAMILTON BANK v. KOOKMIN BANK
(concluded)

ISSUE

Will Hamilton, the issuing bank, be required to honor the letter of credit?

DECISION

Yes. Article 14 of the UCP allows an issuing bank to refuse to pay on a letter of credit if it determines that the documents on their face are not in compliance with the terms and conditions of the credit. However, the issuing bank must give notice of its refusal by telecommunication or, if that is not possible, by other expeditious means, without delay but no later than the seventh banking day following the day of receipt of the documents. Further, that notice must state all discrepancies in respect of which the bank refuses the documents. Failure to comply with Article 14's notice provisions precludes the issuing bank from claiming that the documents are not in compliance with the terms and conditions of the credit. Hamilton did not comply with Article 14 in two respects: Its first and only timely disclaimer was not sent by telecommunication and it failed to specify the grounds for disclaimer. Nevertheless, Hamilton seeks to avoid preclusion by arguing that Kookmin negligently or knowingly forwarded non-complying documents by submitting the letter of credit without the required authenticated telex. We agree that a reasonable person could find that Kookmin knew or should have known an authenticated telex was required, but we find that this issue of fact is not material. Hamilton relies on Article 13 of the UCP, which states that banks must examine all documents stipulated in the credit with reasonable care to ascertain whether or not they appear on their face to be in compliance with the terms and conditions of the credit. Hamilton contends that Kookmin's failure to comply with Article 13 prevents it from relying on Article 14. However, nothing in Article 14 requires that the negotiating bank comply with Article 13 in order to rely on Article 14's preclusion provision, and the preclusion language is mandatory and admits of no exception.

Countertrade

With global demand for credit on the increase and many banks hesitant to finance international sales, more and more exporters are forced to resort to less desirable options. Countertrade is one such option. In general, it involves the linking of two or more trade obligations using some form of product-for-product exchange. Thus, the seller, in order to secure a contract with the buyer, may agree to purchase goods designated by the buyer. In reality, there is no single form of countertrade transaction; instead the parties usually will individualize their contract by combining different types of countertrading techniques. And while numerous nations themselves practice countertrade, there is no uniform national or international legislation governing its use. In fact, in 1979 the United Nations Commission on International Trade Law (UNCITRAL) adopted the position that countertrade took too many different forms to be fit for uniform international regulation.

The risks accompanying a countertrade arrangement extend well beyond those associated with normal commercial transactions. With countertrade there may be three or more interrelated agreements involving as many or more different parties. Not only must the parties concern themselves with the content of each contract for the purchase of goods, but also they must carefully define the linkages between each set of agreements.

SALES ABROAD THROUGH A DISTRIBUTOR

If a U.S. firm believes that there is a substantial market for its product in some area abroad, it may find that appointing a distributor located in that country is a more effective and efficient way to exploit the market than selling directly to customers. If so, it will sign a distribution agreement—a contract between the seller and the distributor that sets forth a wide range of conditions of the distributorship. The interpretation and enforceability of most of these terms—such as price, method of payment, currency of payment, product warranties, guaranties of supply availability, and guaranties of minimum purchases—primarily involve contract law.

International Franchising

There are several advantages that a U.S. firm may derive from establishing a franchise system for distributing its products in the world market beyond those inherent in the basic concept of franchising.[2] First, when the franchisee is a native of the target country, the operation will not be troubled by as many problems stemming from language or cultural differences. Second, the franchisee will be more likely to understand local regulations affecting the business. Third, through the use of a foreign-owned franchise, the U.S. company may be able to avoid local restrictions on foreign investment. Finally, the local franchisee may be less threatened by political instability (e.g., the threat of expropriation) than would a foreign company.

The effectiveness of the franchise relationship often will turn on the ability of the parties to reach a comprehensive franchise agreement. In the absence of an agree-

---

CONCEPT SUMMARY   The Documentary Credit

1. The buyer and seller enter into the underlying contract.
2. Buyer applies for a letter of credit from issuing bank. (Buyer may pay for the letter now or later, depending on its credit standing.)
3. Issuing bank instructs confirming bank to pay seller on the letter of credit on seller's presentation of required documents to confirming bank.
4. Confirming bank pays seller and sends documents to issuing bank.
5. Issuing bank presents documents to buyer.
6. Buyer presents documents (bill of lading) to shipper in exchange for goods.

---

ment to the contrary, the laws of the franchisee's country generally will govern the relationship. And in some matters—patents, trademarks, and antitrust—those laws will apply regardless of the agreement. Many countries will not permit franchise agreements to stand unless the parties agree to the jurisdiction of the local courts. Accordingly, the political stability of the target country is vitally important in the long-term success of a franchising relationship. (See Table 47–2.)

. . . . LICENSING TECHNOLOGY TO . . . . MANUFACTURERS ABROAD

A U.S. firm can exploit the world market by licensing its technology to a foreign manufacturer. The technology may be embodied in the product (a **product innovation**), giving it superior features, or it may be used in the manufacture of the product (a **process innovation**), lowering the cost of production and permitting a more competitive price for the product. The chapter opener involved Borden licensing its trademark to Meiji, a Japanese manufacturer and distributor. While this initially

---

[2]By licensing its name or ideas to a franchisee, the franchisor can avoid the need to invest great amounts of capital into its distribution network. Franchising was discussed in more detail in Chapter 23.

Table 47–2   Advantages of International Franchising

1. Franchisee has advantage of franchisor's expertise on numerous matters intimately related to the goods or services
2. Franchisor does not need vast sums of capital to establish distribution network
3. Local management better acquainted with language and culture
4. Local franchisees more in tune with laws of foreign government
5. Franchisee less threatened by political bias against foreigners
6. Avoids the need for detailed supervision of distributors who are many miles away

opened the Japanese market to Borden products, eventually it allowed Meiji to become one of Borden's competitors.

PATENTS

Some of the technology that a firm develops is patentable. If a firm acquires a valid patent in a particular country based on a process innovation, it can prohibit the use of the technology in that country in the manufacture of any product other than its own. If the patent is based on a product innovation, sales in that country of a product other than the firm's own product, wherever manufactured, are prohibited as well. It is not difficult for a firm to acquire **parallel patents** in each of the major countries maintaining a patent system. Many such countries are parties to the International Convention for the Protection of Industrial Property Rights. This results in a certain degree of uniformity in their patent laws and in a recognition of the date of the first filing in any of the countries as the filing date for all. Once having established such a worldwide position, a U.S. firm can, in return for an agreement to pay royalties, license a manufacturer abroad to manufacture and, if a product innovation is involved, to sell the product within a particular territory.

TRADE SECRETS

Other technology may not be patented either because it is not patentable or because a firm makes a business decision not to patent it. If the technology is a process innovation, the firm that developed it may still be able to control its use abroad by keeping it a secret. The firm can license the know-how to a particular manufacturer for use in a defined territory in return for promises to pay royalties and to keep the know-how confidential. Such an arrangement is more likely to be workable where considerable technical assistance from the licensor (in the form of plant design or employee skill training) is necessary in order to transfer the technology to the licensee.

LEGAL PROBLEMS WITH LICENSING ARRANGEMENTS

Antitrust Concerns

International licensing of technology, if done on an exclusive basis, can give rise to the same kinds of antitrust questions under the laws of the foreign country or countries constituting the territory as do exclusive distributorships. An exclusive license of a product innovation means that no one other than the licensee, not even the licensor, can manufacture or sell the product in the designated territory. Thus, competition among products using the same technology is limited.

Gray Market Goods

A domestic manufacturer may transfer its trademark rights to a foreign company to use overseas pursuant to a licensing arrangement. One risk of such a transfer is that the goods that are legally manufactured overseas may find their way back into this country in competition with the holder of the U.S. trademark. This phenomenon is known as the *gray market*. A **gray market good** is a genuine product bearing a valid U.S. trademark that is bought outside the United States and then resold in this country by unauthorized importers and distributors. U.S. trademark holders may challenge the importation of gray market goods on trademark infringement grounds where there is the likelihood of confusion to consumers. Further, the U.S. trademark holder may attempt to have U.S. Customs prohibit importation of the gray market goods.

QUALITY KING DISTRIBUTORS V. L'ANZA RESEARCH INTERNATIONAL
118 S. Ct. 1125 (U.S. Sup. Ct. 1998)

FACTS

L'anza Research International is a California corporation engaged in the business of manufacturing and selling shampoos, conditioners, and other hair care products. It has copyrighted the labels that are affixed to those products. In the United States, L'anza sells exclusively to domestic distributors who have agreed to resell within limited geographic areas and then only to authorized retailers such as barber shops, beauty salons, and professional hair care colleges. L'anza has found that the American public is generally unwilling to pay the price charged for high-quality products, such as L'anza's products, when they are sold along with the less expensive lower-quality products that are generally carried by supermarkets and drug stores. L'anza promotes the domestic sales of its products with extensive advertising in various trade magazines and at point of sale, and by providing special training to authorized retailers. L'anza also sells its products in foreign markets. In those markets, however, it does not engage in comparable advertising or promotion; its prices to foreign distributors are 35 percent to 40 percent lower than the prices charged to domestic distributors. Three shipments of L'anza products with copyrighted labels affixed were sold to a distributor in Malta. Those goods then found their way back to the United States without the permission of L'anza and were sold in California by unauthorized retailers who had purchased them at discounted prices from Quality King

Distributors. L'anza brought suit against Quality King, alleging that the importation and subsequent distribution of those products bearing copyrighted labels violated L'anza's exclusive rights under the copyright laws to reproduce and distribute copyrighted material in the United States. Quality King responded that its actions were authorized by the "first sale" doctrine.

ISSUE

Has Quality King violated L'anza's rights under the copyright laws?

DECISION

No. This is an unusual copyright case because L'anza does not claim that anyone has made unauthorized copies of its copyrighted labels. Instead, L'anza is primarily interested in protecting the integrity of its method of marketing the products to which the labels are affixed. Courts have long held that the exclusive statutory right to sell applies only to the first sale of a copyrighted work. Congress subsequently codified this holding. In this case, L'anza relies on the terms of its contracts with its domestic distributors to limit their sales to authorized retail outlets. However, it does not, and could not, claim that the copyright statute would enable L'anza to treat unauthorized resales by its domestic distributors as an infringement of its exclusive right to distribute copies of

(continued)

QUALITY KING DISTRIBUTORS V. L'ANZA RESEARCH INTERNATIONAL
(concluded)

its labels. L'anza does claim, however, that contractual provisions are inadequate to protect it from the actions of foreign distributors who may resell L'anza products to American vendors unable to buy from L'anza's domestic distributors, and that the Copyright Act, properly construed, prohibits such unauthorized competition. The most relevant portion of the statute provides: "Importation into the United States, without the authority of the owner of the copyright . . . of copies . . . of a work that . . . [has] been acquired outside the United States is an infringement of the exclusive right to distribute copies." It is significant that this provision does not categorically prohibit the unauthorized importation of copyrighted materials. Instead, it provides that such importation is an infringement of the exclusive right to distribute copies under the statute. However, the exclusive right to distribute is a limited right. One of those limitations is the "first sale" doctrine which permits the owner of a lawfully made copy to sell that copy. After the first sale of a copyrighted item that is lawfully made, any subsequent purchaser, whether from a domestic or a foreign reseller, is obviously an owner of that item. Read literally, the Copyright Act unambiguously states that such an owner "is

entitled, without the authority of the copyright owner, to sell" that item. The whole point of the first sale doctrine is that once the copyright owner places a copyrighted item in the stream of commerce by selling it, he has exhausted his exclusive statutory right to control its distribution. The parties have debated at length the wisdom or unwisdom of governmental restraints on what is sometimes described as either the "gray market" or the practice of "parallel importing." In previous cases, we have used those terms to refer to the importation of foreign-manufactured goods bearing a valid United States trademark without the consent of the trademark holder. We are not at all sure that those terms appropriately describe the consequences of an American manufacturer's decision to limit its promotional efforts to the domestic market and to sell its products abroad at discounted prices that are so low that its foreign distributors can compete in the domestic market. But even if they do, whether or not we think it would be wise policy to provide statutory protection for such price discrimination is not a matter that is relevant to our duty to interpret the text of the Copyright Act.

INVESTMENT TO ESTABLISH A MANUFACTURING OPERATION ABROAD

Before a U.S. firm decides to establish a manufacturing operation abroad, a wide variety of legal issues must be examined. Many of them are peculiar to the particular country that is being considered as the location of the facility. Labor laws may be very different from our own and may impose long-term obligations on the employer. Import license requirements and high tariffs may force the firm to use local sources of supplies and raw materials and to manufacture locally a certain percentage by value of the parts used in assembling the final product. Some countries generally prohibit foreigners from having a majority equity interest in any operation within their borders, and many manufacturing activities may require licenses from governmental authorities.

Three problems of a more general nature will be examined here: (1) liability of a U.S. corporation for the contracts and torts of its foreign subsidiary; (2) investment repatriation; and (3) expropriation.

PARENT LIABILITY FOR THE ACTIVITIES OF FOREIGN SUBSIDIARIES

A U.S. corporation may form a subsidiary corporation to carry out its overseas operations. One reason for such a strategy is to limit the parent corporation's financial risk to the amount of capital that it has invested in its subsidiary. (Limited liability is discussed in Chapter 23.) Recent years, however, have witnessed a growing trend toward holding parent corporations liable for the activities of their foreign subsidiaries. More and more, courts may impose this special duty on parents when the subsidiary is dealing with hazardous technology, particularly when the subsidiary is doing business in a less-developed country lacking in the technology needed to protect against the potential harm.

REPATRIATION OF EARNINGS AND INVESTMENT

Many countries, particularly those in the developing world, have regulations concerning the conversion of their currency into a foreign currency such as dollars and the remittance of those funds to another country. When a U.S. firm wishes to repatriate some of the earnings from an operation in a country with such regulations by causing its subsidiary to pay a dividend, permission must be obtained from the currency exchange authorities. These authorities operate under rules that are intended to encourage foreign firms to reinvest their earnings in the country rather than send them home. Some countries place an absolute limit, stated in terms of a set percentage of the amount that a firm has invested (the original amount and any reinvestment of retained earnings), on the amount of earnings that may be repatriated each year. Other countries place a substantial "income withholding tax" on repatriated earnings, which increases in percentage with the amount repatriated. If a U.S. firm wants to sell or liquidate its operations, all proceeds in excess of the original investment are usually considered dividends, and their repatriation may be either prohibited or taxed at a very high rate. The existence of such regulations in a country means that a U.S. firm should normally not consider a major investment in that country unless it is prepared to make a long-term commitment.

EXPROPRIATION

One of the biggest fears of a U.S. firm investing in a politically unstable country is **expropriation**—the taking of its facilities by the host government—without adequate compensation. If the property of a U.S. firm in a foreign country is taken by the host government and the U.S. firm does not receive adequate compensation after exhausting the legal remedies available to it in that country, the firm's only legal option is to try to find property located outside the country that belongs to the host government and to seek compensation from the proceeds of the sale of that property. This requires finding a legally recognized forum (a court of another nation or an international arbitral tribunal) that is willing to listen, establishing before the forum a claim that the taking without compensation has damaged the firm in violation of international law, and convincing the authority having jurisdiction over the host government's property that the property should be used to satisfy the claim. This is a very difficult course of action and there is a high probability that the firm will be frustrated at some step and be left without compensation.

Insurance

The best protection against the risk of expropriation is insurance. In order to encourage U.S. private investment in developing countries, the U.S. government established the Overseas Private Investment Corporation (OPIC). OPIC offers low-cost expropriation insurance for certain kinds of investment projects in designated countries. If an

UNITED STATES-IMPORT PROHIBITION OF CERTAIN SHRIMP AND SHRIMP PRODUCTS
RECOURSE TO ARTICLE 21.5 OF THE DSU BY MALAYSIA
(concluded)

by new legislation that had three major thrusts: (1) it required the U.S. Secretary of State to negotiate with foreign nations for the development of bilateral and multilateral treaties for the protection of sea turtles; (2) it prohibited the importation of shrimp or shrimp products that were harvested by commercial methods that threatened sea turtles; and (3) it provided an exception from this embargo in cases where the President certified that the government of the harvesting nation had adopted a regulatory program comparable to that of the United States. Malaysia and other shrimp exporters who did not receive this presidential certification challenged the U.S. embargo under the World Trade Organization (WTO) dispute resolution process. Specifically, they complained that the U.S. measure constituted an illegal quantitative restriction. In response, the U.S. argued that the embargo fell within Article XX of the GATT, which permits restrictions that are necessary to protect human, animal, or plant life or health, or that are relating to the conservation of exhaustible natural resources. Initially, a WTO Appellate Body agreed that the sea turtles were an exhaustible resource and that the U.S. embargo related to conservation. However, it concluded that the U.S. measure was a form of unjustifiable discrimination because in its application it had an intended and actual coercive effect on the specific policy decisions made by foreign governments. It was condemned as rigid and unbending since it required nations to TED-programs, such as the United States, regardless of the fact that they may have other methods of safeguarding sea turtles when harvesting shrimp. It criticized the United States for failing to pursue comprehensive negotiations with all of the shrimp-exporting nations. (The United States had negotiated a multilateral treaty with exporters in the Caribbean/Western Atlantic region, but nowhere else.) The Appellate Body stressed that the unilateral and non-consensual approach followed by the United States was not the only course available to protect sea turtles, stressing that import prohibitions should be weapons of last resort. In response to this decision, the United States revised the manner in which it granted certification for import eligibility. Instead of insisting that exporting nations

require the use of TEDs, it granted certification if the country could show that it required a "comparably effective" regulatory program. The United States also engaged in efforts to negotiate an agreement with the governments of the Indian Ocean and South-East Asia region (including Malaysia) and had offered and was providing technical assistance on the design, construction, installation, and operation of TEDs. Despite these efforts, Malaysia again brought an action before the WTO, asserting that the steps taken by the U.S. did not remove the elements of "arbitrary and unjustifiable discrimination."

ISSUE

Has the U.S. response brought it in compliance with the WTO Appellate Body decision?

DECISION

Yes. Malaysia asserted that the United States should have negotiated and *concluded* an international agreement on the protection and conservation of sea turtles before imposing an import prohibition. In response, the United States argued that it was sufficient that it had in fact made serious, good faith efforts to negotiate and conclude such an agreement. Malaysia is incorrect. The efforts made by the United States to negotiate a multilateral treaty for the protection of sea turtles in the Indian Ocean and South-East Asia region are comparable to those that led to the conclusion of the treaty with the nations of the Caribbean/Western Atlantic region. Therefore, in view of the serious, good faith efforts made by the United States to negotiate an international agreement, its application of the shrimp import certification program no longer constitutes a means of unjustifiable or arbitrary discrimination. Likewise, it is not illegal for the United States to condition market access on an exporting country's adoption of a program comparable in effectiveness to the specific program required in the United States. This gives sufficient latitude to the exporting country to adopt a regulatory program that is suitable to the specific conditions prevailing in its territory. We find that the U.S. measure is now applied in a manner that meets the requirements of Article XX of the GATT.

.... *THE EUROPEAN UNION* ....

The European Union (EU) embraces 15 countries with a combined population of more than 350 million people.[3] As originally planned, the European Community was to become an integrated trade bloc, uniting the economies of its member states. At its simplest, this involved eliminating tariffs among its members and establishing common tariffs for outside countries. This was followed by the removal of most barriers to the free movement of goods, service, capital, and persons. The steady dismantling of these obstacles to economic union has bred greater expectations among many powerful interests within the European Union. With the recent launching of an EU currency, the Euro, it is now plausible that the European Union also will achieve a monetary and political union that may culminate in a European superstate that stretches from the Mediterranean Sea to the Arctic Ocean.

CONCEPT SUMMARY	Single European Market
Physical Barriers	• Customs posts at intra-EU national borders removed. • Immigrations and customs controls removed.
Technical Barriers	• Restrictions on cross-border movement of laborers removed. • Compatibility problems in telecommunications removed. • Strict enforcement of EU antitrust laws. • Uniform EU building code. • National preferences for government procurement removed. • Uniform health and safety regulations. • Harmonized packaging and labeling standards.
Fiscal Barriers	• Uniform tax treatment of intramember and intermember transactions by all member states. • Harmonized excise duties by member states. • Creation of a single currency.

Removal of Barriers

Creating a "Single Europe" required removing the physical, technical, and fiscal barriers to an internal market. Removal of the physical barriers entailed abolition of the immigration and customs formalities that once sealed the borders of the member states. Removal of the technical barriers required effectively harmonizing the patchwork of national health and safety regulations and product standards that once pervaded the continent. Finally, removing fiscal barriers required the elimination of the different rates of taxation among the member states and the collection of tariffs at the national borders.

Implications for U.S. Businesses

An integrated Europe is a fact of life. For the most part, all of the regulations essential to the creation of a single market for goods and services have been implemented. Still, there will continue to be variations among the 15 member states that will complicate the economic environment for U.S. businesses. Further, elimination of internal

---

[3]Austria, Belgium, Denmark, Finland, France, Germany, Greece, Ireland, Italy, Luxembourg, the Netherlands, Portugal, Spain, Sweden, and the United Kingdom are members of the European Union.

barriers will not automatically translate into a breakdown of external barriers. Burdensome testing and certification requirements and other forms of discriminatory regulations pose serious technical barriers to non-European traders, perhaps ultimately threatening the erection of a "Fortress Europe."

U.S. businesses must carefully monitor the economic and legal situation in the various member states if they hope to overcome these potential barriers. Despite the Single Europe movement, there still are wide variations among the national governments in their implementation and enforcement of internal market directives. Likewise, the many languages and diverse cultures represented on the European continent often result in marked differences in consumer preferences from one region to another. For these reasons, it is more important than ever that U.S. business managers understand the workings of the European Union and establish an effective European presence if they hope to take full advantage of the Single European movement.

THE NORTH AMERICAN FREE TRADE AGREEMENT

Partially in response to the rise of a Single Europe, the United States proposed an **Enterprise for the Americas Initiative** designed to promote regional economic integration in the Western Hemisphere. The program rests on three pillars: (1) stimulation of market-oriented investment reforms; (2) reduction of the debt obligations of the Latin American and Caribbean nations; and (3) elimination of barriers to trade. The centerpiece of the initiative was the creation of a hemispheric free trade area stretching from the Arctic to the southern tip of South America.

Because of the tremendous disparities in political and economic development among the nations, initial efforts have focused on the creation of a North American Free Trade Agreement **(NAFTA)** involving Canada, Mexico, and the United States. Only after the economies of the other nations mature will they be granted membership into this core group.

General Principles

Encompassing a market of more than 360 million people and a combined output of more than $6 trillion, NAFTA seeks to eliminate barriers to the free flow of goods, services, and investment over a 15-year period. Because of political pressures within each nation, the treaty envisions a phased removal of these obstacles with the length of transition period varying from industry to industry.

A fundamental goal of the NAFTA negotiations was the elimination of barriers to trade in goods and services among the three members. The treaty carries out these objectives in two important ways. First, each participant agrees to accord **national treatment** to goods imported from either of the other two nations. This means that the NAFTA countries will ensure that none of their national or local laws discriminate against the goods of the other members. Second, the treaty is designed to secure greater market access for each member state within the borders of the other two. Some of these measures provide for the elimination of tariffs and a reduction in import and export restrictions. However, certain country of origin labeling requirements remain in effect.

Ethical Implications	Is it ethical for U.S. manufacturers to move their operations to Mexico in order to take advantage of less stringent environmental standards? Is it ethical to move to Mexico in order to lower wage costs?

Dispute Resolution

NAFTA has established a mechanism for resolving trade disputes through the use of binational panels. The treaty provides elaborate provisions for settling two distinct types of disputes: (1) antidumping and countervailing duty matters and (2) conflicts over a country's interpretation or application of the treaty. The dispute settlement procedures are subject to strict time limits designed to prevent the lengthy delays that characterize many international dispute mechanisms.

IN THE MATTER OF CROSS-BORDER TRUCKING SERVICES
File No. USA-MEX-98-2008-01
Final Report of the Panel, February 6, 2001

FACTS

In 1980, Canada allowed reciprocal access for U.S. trucking operators in its domestic market, but Mexico did not offer such reciprocal access. In 1982, the United States imposed a moratorium against the issuance of new motor carrier operating authority to foreign carriers. This provision applied to Canada and Mexico, however; with respect to Canada, the moratorium was immediately lifted in response to Canada's confirmation that U.S. carriers would have continued access to the Canadian market. In contrast, with respect to Mexico, the moratorium was not lifted because the United States believed that U.S. trucks were largely precluded from providing service into Mexico. However, Mexican trucking companies that already were licensed to provide service in the United States were exempted from the moratorium under a "grandfather clause." That moratorium has continued in effect. The purpose of the moratorium was to encourage Mexico and Canada to lift their restrictions on market access for U.S. firms. Although the moratorium has continued in place with regard to Mexico, there were some exceptions allowed to facilitate cross-border trade. These included exceptions for U.S.-owned Mexican trucks. Mexican carriers have been permitted to operate in the commercial zones associated with municipalities along the United States–Mexico border since before 1982. Throughout the border zone transport, goods that are transshipped through the border zone generally remain in the same trailer. The trailer is transferred between long-haul and drayage tractors, and then back to a domestic long-haul tractor, as it crosses into the border zone. The Mexican trailer then is kept on the U.S. tractor during the transport throughout the United States, attached to different U.S. tractors. NAFTA came into force on January 1, 1994. It obligated the parties to phase out certain reservations to the national treatment and most favored nation treatment principles. With respect to cross-border trucking service, NAFTA stipulated that a Mexican national will be permitted to obtain operating authority to provide cross-boundary trucking services in border states by December 18, 1995. Further, it stated that a Mexican national will be permitted to obtain operating authority to provide cross-border trucking service throughout the United States by January 1, 2000. Starting before the enforcement of NAFTA and since, the governments of Mexico and the United States actively worked to improve the coordination on the regulation of motor carriers. Despite the efforts by the three nations to harmonize and coordinate their truck safety regulations prior to the 1995 deadline, significant difference existed between the Mexican and U.S. regulatory systems on that date. Accordingly, the United States continued its moratorium on Mexican trucks after the 1995 deadline. While the United States began accepting applications from Mexican motor carriers, it stated that their final disposition would be delayed until after consultations between the United States and Mexico to further improve their motor carrier safety and security regimes. Both countries agree that the Mexican regulatory system is not identical to that of the United States and Canada. Their disagreement is therefore whether the differences in their respective domestic regulatory systems justify the U.S. ban on Mexican trucks entering U.S. territory. Specifically, the United States contends that these regulatory system differences justify exclusion of Mexican trucks, while Mexico contends that internal regulatory systems are irrelevant to the operating authority of individual carriers in the United States.

ISSUE

Has the United States violated its NAFTA obligations by excluding Mexican trucks from U.S. territory?

(continued)

IN THE MATTER OF CROSS-BORDER TRUCKING SERVICES
(concluded)

DECISION

Yes. The U.S. blanket refusal to review and consider for approval any Mexican-owned carrier applications for authority to provide cross-border trucking services was and remains a breach of the U.S. obligations under NAFTA's national treatment and most favored treatment obligations. The inadequacies of the Mexican regulatory system provide an insufficient legal basis for the United States to maintain a moratorium on the consideration of applications by Mexican trucking firms. However, it is important to note what the Panel is not making a determination that the parties to NAFTA may not set the level of protection that they consider appropriate in pursuit of legitimate regulatory objectives. It is not disagreeing that the safety of trucking services is a legitimate regulatory objective. Nor is the panel imposing a limitation on the application of safety standards properly established and applied pursuant to the applicable obligations of the Parties under NAFTA. The Panel recommends that the United States take appropriate steps to bring its practices with respect to cross-border trucking services and investment into compliance with its obligations under the applicable provisions of NAFTA. It notes that such compliance would not necessarily require providing favorable consideration to all or to any specific number of applications from Mexican-owned trucking firms,

when it is evident that a particular applicant or applicants may be unable to comply with U.S. trucking regulations when operating in the United States. Nor does it require that all Mexican-domiciled firms currently providing trucking services in the United States be allowed to continue to do so, if and when they fail to comply with U.S. safety regulations. The United States may not be required to treat applications from Mexican trucking firms in exactly the same manner as applications from U.S. or Canadian firms, as long as they are reviewed on a case-by-case basis. Similarly, it may not be unreasonable for a NAFTA Party to conclude that to ensure compliance with its own local standards from another NAFTA country, it may be necessary to implement different procedures with respect to such service providers. Thus, to the extent that the inspection and licensing requirements for Mexican trucks and drivers wishing to operate in the United States may not be "like" those in place in the United States, different methods of ensuring compliance with the U.S. regulatory regime may be justifiable. However, if the United States does impose requirements on Mexican carriers that differ from those imposed on U.S. or Canadian carriers, any such decision must (a) be made in good faith with respect to a legitimate safety concern and (b) implement differing requirements that fully conform with all relevant NAFTA provisions.

FREE TRADE AGREEMENT VERSUS COMMON MARKET

NAFTA is a free trade agreement while the European Union is a common market. A free trade agreement confines itself to the regulation and harmonization of trade and investment among its members. Accordingly, each of the NAFTA partners will maintain its own tariff rates for countries that don't belong to the free trade agreement. As a common market, the European Union establishes a common economic policy for trade and investment within the community as well as a common external tariff. Further, the European Union has expressed a long-range interest in creating a common monetary policy and a common foreign policy. The NAFTA members have not indicated any similar desires.

THE FOREIGN CORRUPT PRACTICES ACT

BACKGROUND

The Foreign Corrupt Practices Act (FCPA) makes it a crime for any American firm to offer, promise, or make payments or gifts of anything of value to foreign officials and certain others. It also establishes record-keeping and internal control requirements for firms subject to the Securities Exchange Act of 1934.

THE PAYMENTS PROHIBITION

Payments are prohibited if the person making the foreign payment knows or should know that some or all of it will be used for the purpose of influencing a governmental decision. An offer to make a prohibited payment or a promise to do so is a violation, even if the offer is not accepted or the promise is not carried out. Payments of kickbacks to foreign businesses and their officials are not prohibited, unless it is known or should be known that these payments will be passed on to government officials or other illegal recipients.

Some payments to government officials (called "grease" payments) are not illegal as long as the recipient has no discretion in carrying out a governmental function. For example, suppose a corporation applies for a radio license in Italy and makes a payment to the government official who issues the licenses. If the official grants licenses to every applicant and the payment merely speeds up the processing of the application, the FCPA is not violated. On the other hand, if only a few applicants are granted licenses and the payment is made to ensure that the corporation will obtain a license, the payment is illegal.

RECORD-KEEPING AND INTERNAL CONTROLS REQUIREMENTS

The FCPA also imposes record-keeping and internal controls requirements. The purpose of such controls is to prevent unauthorized payments and transactions as well as unauthorized access to company assets. This section requires companies to keep records that accurately reflect all of their transactions. It also requires the establishment and maintenance of a system of internal accounting controls. This system must provide "reasonable assurances" that unauthorized transactions are not taking place. Each company must maintain its records in a fashion that will permit it to prepare financial statements that conform to generally accepted accounting principles. Furthermore, at reasonable intervals, management must compare the records with the actual assets available to see if they are accurate. If they are not, it must find out why.

.... *QUESTIONS AND PROBLEM CASES* ....

1. MCC-Marble Ceramic Center (MCC) is a Florida corporation engaged in the retail sale of tiles, and Ceramic Nuova d'Agostino S.p.A. (D'Agostino) is an Italian corporation engaged in the manufacture of ceramic tiles. MCC's president, Juan Carlos Monzon, met representatives of D'Agostino at a trade fair in Bologna, Italy, and negotiated an agreement to purchase ceramic tiles from D'Agostino based on samples he examined at the trade fair. Monzon, who spoke no Italian, communicated with Gianni Silingardi, then D'Agostino's commercial director, through a translator, Gianfranco Copelli, who was himself an agent of D'Agostino. The parties apparently arrived at an oral agreement on the crucial terms of price, quality, quantity, delivery, and payment. They then recorded these terms on one of D'Agostino's standard, preprinted order forms, and Monzon signed the contract on MCC's behalf. The parties also entered into a requirements contract, subject to which D'Agostino agreed to supply MCC with high grade ceramic tile at specific discounts as long as MCC purchased sufficient quantities of tile. MCC completed a number of additional order forms requesting tile deliveries pursuant to that agreement. MCC brought suit against D'Agostino claiming a breach of the requirements contract when D'Agostino failed to satisfy certain orders. D'Agostino responded that it was under no obligation to fill MCC's orders because MCC had defaulted on payment for previous shipments. In support of its position, D'Agostino relied on the preprinted terms of the contracts that MCC had executed.

The executed forms were printed in Italian and contained terms and conditions on both the front and reverse. On the front of the order form directly beneath Monzon's signature was the statement: *"The buyer hereby states that he is aware of the sales conditions stated on the reverse and that he expressly approves of them."* One such term on the back of the form states: *"Default or delay in payment within the time agreed upon gives D'Agostino the right to suspend or cancel the contract itself and to cancel possible other pending contracts and the buyer does not have the right to indemnification or damages."* MCC responded that the tile it had received was of a lower quality than contracted for and that, pursuant to the *Convention for the International Sale of Goods* (CISG), it was entitled to reduce payment in proportion to the defects. D'Agostino, however, noted that clause 4 on the reverse of the order form states: *"Possible complaints for defects of merchandise must be made in writing by means of a certified letter within and not later than 10 days after receipt of the merchandise."* Although MCC had complained about the quality of the deliveries it received, it never submitted any written complaints. However, MCC argued that the parties never intended the terms and conditions printed on the reverse side of the order form to apply to their agreements. As evidence for this assertion, MCC submitted affidavits from Monzon, Silingardi, and Copelli, which supported its claim that the parties subjectively intended not to be bound by the terms on the reverse side of the order form. D'Agostino responded that affidavits alleging the subjective intent of the parties contradicted the terms of the subsequent written agreement and, as such, were barred by the parole evidence rule. Does the parole evidence rule bar evidence of the parties' subjective intent?

2. Texpor and Oxford entered into a sales contract in which Texpor was to sell high-quality cotton sweatshirts to Oxford. In connection with the purchase orders, Oxford arranged for Trust Company Bank to issue an irrevocable letter of credit in favor of Texpor in the amount of $242,000. The parties later amended this letter of credit in order to accommodate Texpor's delay in delivering the first two shipments. On January 20 Texpor made the first shipment and, upon presentation of the shipping documents, received payment under the letter of credit. After receiving the shipment, Oxford discovered that most of the sweatshirts were defective. On February 3 Texpor made the second shipment and again presented identical documents to Trust Company Bank. On this occasion the bank refused to honor the credit, claiming that the documents did not conform to the requirements of the letter of credit. Among the discrepancies were a missing room number, a misdescription of the address on the invoice, and an omission of the word "Oxford" as it appeared on the letter of credit. In a suit against the bank for wrongful dishonor, Texpor claimed that the documents were satisfactory since there was no possibility that they would mislead the bank. Did the issuing bank wrongfully dishonor the letter of credit?

3. Bacchus Associates, a New York partnership that distributes fruit at wholesale, contracted with Galaxie Negoce, S.A., a Moroccan fruit supplier. Bacchus bought a shipload of fruit from Galaxie and chartered a ship to transport it from Morocco to Massachusetts. The ship was the *M/V Sky Reefer*, a refrigerated cargo ship owned by M. H. Martima, S.A., a Panamanian company, and time chartered to Nichiro Gyogyo Kaisha, Ltd., a Japanese company. Stevedores hired by Galaxie loaded and stowed the cargo. As is customary in these types of transactions, when it received the cargo from Galaxie, Nichiro as carrier issued a form bill of lading to Galaxie as shipper and consignee. Once the ship set sail from Morocco, Galaxie tendered the bill of lading to Bacchus according to the terms of a letter of credit posted in Galaxie's favor. Among the rights and responsibilities set out in the bill of lading were arbitration and choice-of-law clauses. These stated that the contract was to be governed by Japanese law and that any dispute was to be referred to arbitration in Tokyo by the Tokyo Maritime Arbitration Commission of the The Japan Shipping Exchange. When the vessel's hatches were opened for discharge in Massachusetts, Bacchus discovered that thousands of boxes of oranges had shifted in the cargo holds, resulting in more than $1 million in damages. Bacchus

received $733,442.90 in compensation from Vimar Seguros y Reaseguros, Bacchus' marine cargo insurer. Vimar and Bacchus then brought suit against Martima and *M/V Sky Reefer* in a federal district court in Massachusetts. The defendants moved to stay the action and compel arbitration in Tokyo under the arbitration clause in the bill of lading. Bacchus and Vimar argued that the foreign arbitration clause in the bill of lading was invalid under the *Carriage of Goods by Sea Act* (COGSA) because it lessens liability in a sense that COGSA prohibits. Specifically, they claimed that the arbitration clause lessens COGSA liability because it increases the transaction costs of obtaining relief and puts a hurdle in the way of enforcing liability. They asserted that the arbitration clause gives carriers an effective means to secure settlements lower than if cargo owners could sue in a convenient forum. Should the court enforce the arbitration of clause in the bill of lading?

4. Tennessee Imports, a U.S. corporation with its principal place of business in Tennessee, contracted with Prix Italia, an Italian corporation doing business in Venice, Italy. Under the terms of their agreement, Tennessee Imports was given the exclusive sales rights over Prix Italia's pricing and labeling machines in the United States. The contract, which was drafted by Prix Italia, contained an arbitration clause requiring that all contractual disputes be settled by the Arbitration Court of the Chamber of Commerce in Venice, Italy. When a dispute arose, Tennessee Imports filed suit against Prix Italia in a U.S. district court. Prix Italia, citing the arbitration clause, petitioned the U.S. court to dismiss on the grounds of improper venue. Tennessee Imports claimed that the arbitration clause was not enforceable because the bargaining power between the two parties was unequal. In essence, it argued that since the machines manufactured by Prix Italia were unavailable from any other source, it was forced to accept the terms of Prix Italia's contract. Should the U.S. court enforce the parties' agreement to arbitrate in Italy?

5. McDonnell Douglas Corporation (MDC) contracted to supply Iran with military aircraft parts. Because of the political turmoil that erupted in Iran in the latter part of 1978, MDC became concerned for the safety of its employees in Iran and subsequently ordered their evacuation. Further, the U.S. Air Force ordered that no further foreign military sales items be released for shipment. Following these events, MDC suspended all work in progress under its Basic Ordering Agreement with Iran. The Iranian government sued MDC on the grounds that it breached the contract and claimed that the trial should be conducted in Iran because the agreement between the parties contained a forum-selection clause stating that disputes "should be settled through the Iranian Courts." MDC argued that the forum-selection clause should not be enforced because (1) the agreement providing that disputes "should" be settled by Iranian courts was not binding and (2) the current Iranian legal system was ill disposed to fairly adjudicate the dispute. Should the court uphold the forum selection clause?

6. Alaska Textile is a New York-based textile company that exports fabric from India. Lloyd Williams Fashions, a manufacturer of women's clothing, contracted with Alaska to buy several thousand yards of Indian silk which were to be delivered to Lloyd's facility in Hong Kong. To make payment, Lloyd arranged for Chase Manhattan Bank to issue two letters of credit in favor of Alaska for $82,500 and $47,141.25 respectively. The silk was shipped from India to Hong Kong on April 2, but Alaska, the shipper, did not forward the necessary documents to the collecting bank, Merchants Bank of New York, until April 26. Merchant's letter of credit examiner, known as Junior, reviewed Alaska's documents and noted three discrepancies: (1) the documents were stale (presented more than 21 days after the goods had been shipped); (2) the description of the goods did not strictly conform to the credits; and (3) the airway bill lacked a "notify party" designation. Junior informed Alaska of these discrepancies, at least one of which, late presentation, was incurable. Undeterred, Alaska directed Merchants to present the discrepant documents to Chase anyway "as is, with discrepancies." Merchants presented the documents and a form collection letter to Chase the very next

day. Under a space on the form denominated "SPECIAL INSTRUCTIONS," Merchant typed, "Documents are presented on an approval basis." Chase examined the documents on the third and fourth banking days following presentment. Chase noted discrepancies in the documents that justified dishonor, promptly advised Lloyd of the discrepancies, and asked whether it would waive them. Alaska then tried to persuade Lloyd to authorize payment under the credits. Over the next two weeks, Alaska and Lloyd, both in desperate financial condition, continued to negotiate over payment for the silk. On May 9 (eight banking days after presentment), Chase told Junior that there were discrepancies which justified dishonor, but that Lloyd had not yet decided whether to waive them. When Chase asked Junior how to proceed, he essentially instructed Chase to sit on the documents, pending Lloyd's decision. Finally, in September, Alaska sued Chase for wrongful dishonor of the letters of credit. Alaska argued that because Chase had violated "timely notice" provisions of the *Uniform Customs and Practices for Documentary Credits* (UCP), it was precluded from asserting that the documents were discrepant. Did the bank wrongfully dishonor the letters of credit?

7. Once almost the exclusive province of military and governmental bodies, cryptography is now increasingly available to businesses and private individuals wishing to keep their communications confidential. To do so, users encrypt and decrypt communications, records, and other data. Through encryption, users seek to prevent the unauthorized interception, viewing, tampering, and forging of such data. Without encryption, information sent by a computer is unsecured. Without encryption those other than the intended recipient may view sensitive information. Today, computers and electronic devices have largely replaced mechanical encryption. In using electronic devices, encryption can be done with dedicated hardware (such as a telephone scrambler's electronic circuitry) or with computer software. Encryption software carries out a cryptographic "algorithm," which is a set of instructions that directs computer hardware to encrypt plaintext into an encoded

ciphertext. Mathematical functions or equations usually make up the instructions. Like all software, encryption programs can take two general forms: object code and source code. Source code is a series of instructions to a computer in programming languages such as BASIC, PERL, or FORTRAN. Object code is the same set of instructions translated into binary digits (1s and 0s). While source code is not directly executable by a computer, the computer can easily convert it into executable object code with "compiler" or "interpreter" software. In 1996, President Clinton issued an executive order that found that the export of encryption software must be controlled because of such software's function capacity, rather than because of any possible informational value of such software. Subsequent export regulations controlling the "export" of certain software, defined "export" of controlled encryption source code and object code software as "downloading, or causing the downloading of, such software to locations … outside the United States … unless the person making the software available takes precautions adequate to prevent unauthorized transfer of such code outside the United States." Posting software on the Internet is an export. However, it is nearly impossible for most Internet users to carry out or verify the precautions. Because of the difficulty of the precautions, almost any posting of software on the Internet is an export. Peter Junger, a law professor who teaches computer law at Case Western Reserve University Law School, wishes to post to his website various encryption programs that he has written to show how computers work. Such a posting is an export under the Export Regulations. Encryption source code in printed form is not subject to the Export Regulations and, thus, is outside the scope of the licensing requirement. Junger sought a Commerce Department determination whether it restricted his materials from export. While deciding that Junger's printed textbook containing encryption code could be exported, the Commerce Department said that export of a software program itself would need a license. Junger claims the Export Administration Regulations violated rights protected by the

First Amendment. Do the export controls on encryption software violate rights protected by the First Amendment?

8. Rewe-Zentral AG, an importer, applied to the German Federal Monopoly for Spirits for licenses to import spirits to be sold in Germany. Included in the list of alcoholic beverages Rewe wished to import was Cassis de Dijon, a French liqueur containing an alcohol content of between 15 and 20 percent. The German authorities denied Rewe's request, citing German regulations that prohibited the importation and sale of spirits containing less than 32 percent alcohol content. Is the German regulation an unlawful barrier to the free movement of goods?

9. Canada enacted regulations prohibiting the export of unprocessed salmon and herring. Responding to complaints by the United States, a GATT panel found the Canadian laws to violate GATT. After informing the United States that it would abide by the GATT decision, Canada revoked the offending legislation. However, several months later the Canadian government enacted new laws that required salmon and herring to be landed in Canada before they could be exported to the United States for processing. The United States called for the formation of a binational panel, arguing that the new regulations were a trade barrier that discriminated against U.S. processors. Canada defended on the grounds that its landing requirement fell within an exception for measures relating to the conservation of an exhaustible natural resource. Should the binational panel find the landing requirement to be a trade barrier that violates NAFTA?

10. The West German government, under various regional development programs, provided low-interest loans and investment subsidies in the form of cash grants and tax credits to West German float glass manufacturers. U.S. competitors petitioned for a countervailing duty on West German float glass imported into this country on the grounds that the benefits were bounties or grants within the countervailing duty law. West Germany advised the U.S. Treasury Department that the benefits were designed to offset the disadvantages that would discourage companies from moving to and expanding in less prosperous regions of the country. In addition, the recipients of the benefits sold the preponderance of their glass in West Germany. The percentage of subsidized products that was exported to the United States was very small and that amount of the subsidy was less than 2 percent of the value of the float glass. Should the Treasury Department assess a countervailing duty to offset the subsidy given the West German manufacturers?

CHAPTER 48

Internet Law

New York passed a law making it a felony to distribute to children under age 17, over a computer communications system, material of a sexual nature that is harmful to minors. However, a federal district court struck down the law as an undue burden on interstate commerce. The court felt that the laudable benefits derived from the statute are inconsequential in relation to the severe burdens it imposes on interstate commerce. According to the court "the unique nature of cyberspace necessitates uniform national treatment and bars the states from enacting inconsistent regulatory schemes."[1]

- *What is the Internet?*
- *What legal problems are likely to arise in connection with use of the Internet?*
- *Are the traditional legal rules applicable to conduct occurring on the Internet?*

---

[1]*American Library Association v. Pataki*, 969 F. Supp. 160 (S.D.N.Y. 1997).

INTRODUCTION

The *Internet* has been described as a global communications medium that links people and all types of institutions throughout the world. It was first created as a research network for scientists and academics. However, with the advent of the World Wide Web in the 1990s, businesses and consumers discovered its many advantages, and its growth soared. It has been estimated that no more than 300 computers were linked to the Internet in 1981. Fifteen years later, almost 10 million computers were linked.

In reality, the Internet is a decentralized system of links among computers and computer networks. The information available through these links is as diverse as the millions of computer users, and it may be transmitted almost simultaneously, and often anonymously, throughout the world. No entity controls the Internet. In fact, its decentralized and chaotic nature seems to preclude effective control in many instances.

Yet, as the chapter opener indicates, there are growing demands for the government to regulate the Internet to curb the most flagrant abuses and bring some semblance of order to the system. This chapter explores the governmental response to these demands and investigates the areas of law most commonly implicated by Internet use. These include jurisdiction, free speech, torts, privacy, criminal law, intellectual property, and contracts. The chapter examines the extent to which traditional legal doctrines are transferable to the Internet and provides the reader with a better understanding of how to predict the form and substance of future regulatory efforts.

JURISDICTION

A court may not decide a legal dispute unless it has **personal jurisdiction** over the defendant. Personal jurisdiction generally does not exist unless the defendant has some close connection with the territory where the suit is brought.

MINIMUM CONTACTS

There seldom is a personal jurisdiction problem if the defendant is a resident of the territory where the court is located. Similarly, personal jurisdiction is likely to exist if a nonresident defendant is physically present in that territory. However, the situation is more uncertain in cases where a lawsuit is filed against a nonresident who was not physically present in the territory served by the court. In those instances, the court is unlikely to have personal jurisdiction unless it can be shown that the nonresident defendant has certain *minimum contacts* (close connection) with the territory where the suit is brought. The minimum contacts requirement generally is met if the defendant intentionally conducts business in the territory or was served process (notification of the suit) while physically present in the territory.

JURISDICTION OVER ON-LINE ACTIVITIES

Legal rules against online misconduct are difficult to enforce without the assistance of the courts. However, courts cannot hear cases unless they have personal jurisdiction over the defendant. Thus, it is important to understand when a court has jurisdiction over a nonresident computer user.

Courts have developed a three-part test to determine whether they have jurisdiction over nonresident defendants. First, the nonresident defendant must do some act or consummate some transaction within the territory or perform some act by which she purposefully avails herself of the privilege of conducting activities within the territory. Second, the claim that is the basis of the lawsuit must be one which arises out of or results from the nonresident defendant's territory-related activities. Third, the exercise of jurisdiction must be reasonable. Using this test, courts have never held that an Internet advertisement alone is sufficient to subject an advertiser to jurisdiction in the plaintiff's home state. They require that the nonresident defendant have purposefully availed himself of business in the forum state. Consider the following case.

COMPUSERVE V. PATTERSON
89 F.3d 1257 (6th Cir. 1996)

FACTS

CompuServe is a computer information service headquartered in Ohio. It contracts with individual subscribers to provide access to computing information services via the Internet. It also operates an electronic mail conduit to provide its subscribers computer software products, which may originate from CompuServe itself or from other parties. Software generated and distributed in this manner is often referred to as "shareware." Shareware makes money only through the voluntary compliance of the "end user," who pays the voluntary fee directly to CompuServe. In this case, Richard Patterson, a resident of Texas, placed items of shareware on the CompuServe system for others to use and purchase. CompuServe compensated Patterson by paying him 85 percent of the voluntary fees it collected from shareware users. When he became a shareware provider, Patterson signed a shareware registration agreement provided by CompuServe. This agreement expressly provided that it was entered into in Ohio and was to be governed by Ohio law. Patterson's assent to the terms of the agreement was first manifested at his own computer in Texas and then transmitted to the CompuServe computer system in Ohio. When a dispute arose over Patterson's software product, CompuServe filed suit against him in the federal district court for the Southern District of Ohio.

ISSUE

Did the Ohio court have personal jurisdiction over Patterson?

DECISION

Yes. Patterson's contacts with Ohio, which have been almost entirely electronic in nature, are sufficient to support the district court's exercise of personal jurisdiction

over him. Breakthroughs in the communications and transportation industries have led to the relaxation of the limits on courts' jurisdiction because all but the most remote forums are easily accessible. The Internet represents perhaps the latest and greatest manifestation of these globe-shrinking trends. It enables anyone with the right equipment and knowledge to operate an international business cheaply, and from a desktop. To determine whether personal jurisdiction exists over a defendant, federal courts apply the law of the forum state. Ohio law allows the state to exercise personal jurisdiction over nonresidents on claims arising from the nonresident's transacting any business in Ohio. This jurisdictional requirement must comport with federal constitutional law, which requires that Patterson has had sufficient contacts with Ohio that the exercise of jurisdiction is fair. The court employs three criteria to make this determination. First, the defendant must purposefully avail himself of the privilege of acting in Ohio. Second, the lawsuit must arise from his activities there. Third, the acts of Patterson or the consequences he causes must have a substantial enough connection with Ohio to make the exercise of jurisdiction over him reasonable. There can be no doubt that Patterson purposefully transacted business in Ohio. Moreover, this was a relationship intended to be ongoing in nature. Because Patterson entered into a contract with CompuServe, an Ohio company, and injected his software into the stream of commerce, he has ample contacts with the state. Further, CompuServe's claims arise out of Patterson's activities in Ohio. Finally, this exercise of jurisdiction is reasonable in light of the state's strong interest in resolving a dispute involving an Ohio company and Patterson's voluntary participation in the company's shareware registration agreement.

FIRST AMENDMENT ISSUES

The First Amendment and its protection of the freedom of expression may provide the most important source of legal rights on the Internet. After all, the World Wide Web permits people and organizations to instantaneously communicate with one another on any number of topics through electronic mail (e-mail), mailing list services (listservs), newsgroups, and chat rooms. In fact, the Web may be likened to a vast library containing millions of indexed publications that are readily available to readers. Simultaneously, it offers a worldwide shopping mall offering access to a wide variety of goods and services. For these reasons, attempts to regulate on-line activities are bound to implicate First Amendment issues.

CONSTITUTIONAL SAFEGUARDS FOR SPEECH

Our freedom of expression (discussed in Chapter 43) is not absolute. First, the First Amendment protects against only governmental interference with speech. Thus, private on-line companies may place any number of restrictions on the exchange of information by their members without violating the First Amendment.

GOVERNMENT REGULATION OF COMMERCIAL SPEECH

On-line advertising is a form of commercial speech. As such, it is entitled to less First Amendment protection than is noncommercial speech. For example, false, misleading, or deceptive advertisements are entitled to no First Amendment protection at all. And, in order to regulate even truthful advertisements, the government need show only that it is pursuing a substantial interest. (Commercial speech analysis is described in Chapter 43.)

On-Line Advertising

Electronic bulletin boards and websites permit computer users to interact with businesses around the world without ever leaving their homes or workplaces. This promises to revolutionize the ways in which businesses advertise their goods and services. In particular, this technology opens the door for more creative ways to customize advertisements to the wants and needs of individual consumers.

Computer Junk Mail

As more and more people have moved on-line, there has been a corresponding rise in the number of complaints about computer junk mail. Mass advertisers have developed automated programs that compile the e-mail addresses of Internet users. They then bombard the networks with millions of ads to e-mail users. Private on-line companies complain that these mass e-mailings, known as **spam,** overload their servers and threaten to severely disrupt the Internet.

Several remedies short of demanding government regulation are available to deal with spam. First, the on-line companies may take private action to block mass mailings from access to the system. Second, a variety of computer makers are now marketing software that will automatically eliminate all advertising from Web pages. Finally, the on-line companies may sue advertisers who make unauthorized mass e-mailings for trespass. This remedy is discussed later in this chapter in *America Online v. IMS.*

In recent years, the states have begun passing legislation aimed at combating the increasing amounts of spam that clutter the Internet. However, such legislation by the states is open to criticism as undue interference with interstate commerce. For instance, in the opener to this chapter, the federal district court struck down New York's prohibition of electronic messages harmful to minors because it feared the threat of inconsistent state regulations that could ultimately paralyze development of the Internet altogether. On the other hand, recent decisions in various state courts have permitted antispam legislation to stand when it is properly limited to minimize the adverse effects on out-of-state interests. One such case, *Washington v. Heckel*, appears in Chapter 43. Consider the following case in which a California appellate court upholds a statute regulating spam.

FERGUSON V FRIENDFINDERS
2002 Cal. App. LEXIS 2 (Cal. 1st App.Ct. 2002)

FACTS

A California statute regulates conduct by persons or entities doing business in the state who transmit unsolicited advertising materials, including e-mail documents. The statute defines unsolicited e-mail documents as any e-mailed document consisting of advertising materials when the documents (a) are addressed to recipients who do not have existing business or personal relationships with the initiator and (b) were not sent at the request of or with the consent of the recipient. It requires any person or entity conducting business in California who causes unsolicited e-mail documents to be sent to (1) establish a toll-free telephone number or valid sender-operated return e-mail address that recipients may use to notify the sender not to e-mail further unsolicited documents; (2) include as the first text in the e-mailed document a statement notifying the recipient of that number or address; (3) not send any further unsolicited material to anyone who has made such a request; and (4) include in the subject line of each e-mail message "ADV:" as the first four characters or "ADV:ADLT" as the first nine characters if the advertisement pertains to adult material. The statute specifically applies to such unsolicited e-mailed documents that are delivered to a California resident via an electronic mail service provider's service or equipment located in California. When Ferguson, a California resident, sued Friendfinders for violating this statute, the defendant argued that the state law violated the Commerce Clause.

ISSUE

Does the California statute violate the Commerce Clause?

DECISION

No. The Commerce Clause encompasses an implicit or dormant limitation on the authority of the states to enact legislation affecting interstate commerce. To determine if state laws violate this restriction, the Supreme Court has articulated two primary lines of inquiry: first, whether the statute discriminates against interstate commerce and, second, whether it imposes a burden on interstate commerce that is clearly excessive in relation to the putative local benefits. With respect to the first inquiry, regulations that discriminate against out-of-state actors are subject to rigorous scrutiny. In this case there is no such discrimination; the California statute applies equally to in-state and out-of-state actors. Still, the defendant argues that this inquiry also is applicable to state laws that directly regulate interstate commerce. It contends that any regulation of the Internet is a regulation of interstate commerce since the Internet knows no geographic boundaries. However, this argument is flawed because the statute limits is reach to those who do business in California and transmit spam to California residents via equipment located in California. Thus, this statute must undergo the second line of inquiry, which is a balancing test that requires a court to uphold state legislation that serves an important public interest unless the benefits of that legislation are outweighed by the burden imposed on interstate commerce. Like traditional paper "junk" mail, spam can be annoying and waste time. Further, it causes additional problems because it is easy and inexpensive to create but difficult and costly to eliminate. It can be and usually is sent to many recipients at one time

(continued)

FERGUSON V FRIENDFINDERS
(concluded)

at little or no cost to the sender. Studies indicate that 10 to 30 percent of all e-mail sent on a given day consists of spam. Because of this volume, Internet Service Providers incur significant business-related costs accommodating bulk e-mail advertising and dealing with the problems it creates. The financial harms caused by the proliferation of spam have been exacerbated by the use of deceptive tactics which are used to disguise the identity of the sender and the nature of the message. Such tactics increase the already significant costs that spam imposes on Internet users. We agree that protecting a state's citizens from the economic damage caused by deceptive spam constitutes a legitimate local purpose. As importantly, to the extent that California requires truthfulness in advertising, it does not burden interstate commerce at all but actually facilitates it by eliminating fraud and deception. Nor do the statute's affirmative disclosure requirements impose any appreciable burden on senders of spam. We conclude, therefore, that the burdens imposed by the statute are minimal and do not outweigh its benefits.

GOVERNMENT REGULATION OF NONCOMMERCIAL SPEECH

Governmental regulation of on-line expression is permitted when it meets certain constitutional standards. For instance, the government may not regulate the content of noncommercial messages unless the restriction (1) is furthering a compelling governmental interest and (2) interferes with the expression no more than is necessary to advance the government's interest. Consider the following case.

AMERICAN CIVIL LIBERTIES UNION V. ZELL
977 F. Supp. 1228 (N.D. Ga. 1997)

FACTS

Georgia passed a law making it a crime for any person to knowingly "transmit any data through a computer network for the purpose of setting up, maintaining, operating, or exchanging data with an electronic mailbox . . . [or] home page . . . if such data uses any individual name . . . to falsely identify the person." A variety of Internet users challenged the constitutionality of the statute. They argued that it has tremendous implications for Internet users, many of whom "falsely identify" themselves on a regular basis for the purposes of communicating about sensitive topics without subjecting themselves to ostracism or embarrassment.

ISSUE

Is the regulation constitutional?

DECISION

No. Enforcement of the statute should be enjoined because it imposes content-based restrictions which are not narrowly tailored to achieve the state's purported compelling interest. Because the identity of the speaker is no different from other components of a document's contents that the author is free to include or exclude, the statute's prohibition of Internet transmissions which "falsely identify" the sender constitutes a presumptively invalid content-based restriction. The state may impose content-based restrictions only to promote a "compelling state interest" and only through the use of "the least restrictive means" to further the articulated interest. The statute's asserted purpose, fraud prevention, is a compelling interest. However, the statute is not narrowly tailored to achieve that end and instead sweeps innocent, protected speech within its scope. Specifically, by its plain language the criminal prohibition applies regardless of whether a speaker has any intent to deceive or whether deception actually occurs. Therefore, it could apply to a wide range of transmissions which "falsely identify" the sender, but are not "fraudulent" within the specific meaning of the criminal code.

REGULATION OF ON-LINE OBSCENITY

Congress and the state legislatures are regularly bombarded with complaints over the dissemination of obscene material over the Internet. Under current constitutional analysis, obscene expression is not entitled to any First Amendment protection. Thus, those who transmit such material over the Internet may be subject to criminal punishment.

The U.S. Supreme Court has developed a three-part test for determining whether expression is obscene: (1) whether the average person applying contemporary community standards would find the work, taken as a whole, appeals to the prurient interest; (2) whether the work depicts or describes, in a patently offensive way, sexual conduct specifically prohibited by local law; (3) whether the work, taken as a whole, lacks serious literary, artistic, political, or scientific value.

The obscenity test provides special problems for Internet users because sexually explicit transmission may be simultaneously downloaded in numerous communities throughout the country. Because each community is free to develop its own obscenity determination, material that is legally permitted in the locale of the sender may be prohibited in the community of one or more recipients. However, courts do not seem to be troubled by this fact. As the following case indicates, they permit prosecution to occur in either the district of dissemination or the district of downloading. Further, obscenity is determined by the standards of the community where the trial takes place.

UNITED STATES V. THOMAS
74 F. 3d 701 (6th Cir. 1996)

FACTS

Robert and Carleen Thomas operated the Amateur Action Computer Bulletin Board System (AABBS) from their home in Milpitas, California. Its features included e-mail, chat lines, public messages, and files that members could access, transfer, and download to their own computers and printers. The AABBS contained approximately 14,000 files depicting images of bestiality, oral sex, incest, sadomasochistic abuse, and sex scenes involving urination. Actual access to the files, however, was limited to members who were given a password after they paid a membership fee and submitted a signed application form that Robert reviewed. A U.S. postal inspector purchased a membership under an assumed name. He then dialed the AABBS telephone number, logged on and, using his computer/modem in Memphis, Tennessee, downloaded several files. Afterwards, Robert and Carleen were charged in Tennessee with violating federal obscenity laws and knowingly using and causing to be used a combined computer/telephone system for the purpose of transporting obscene, computer-generated materials in interstate commerce. Ultimately, Robert and Carleen were sentenced to 37 and 30 months of incar-

ceration, respectively. In determining their guilt, the court used the community standards of obscenity in Tennessee rather than in California.

ISSUE

Should the community standards of Tennessee govern this case?

DECISION

Yes. Under the first prong of the obscenity test, the jury is to apply "contemporary community standards." In cases involving on-line distribution of obscene material, juries are properly instructed to apply community standards of the geographic area where the materials are sent. The computer-generated images were electronically transferred from the Thomas's home in California to Tennessee. Established law allows that the Thomas's may be prosecuted for transmitting materials which are obscene under Tennessee community standards, though they may be tolerated by the community standards of California. Prosecution may be brought either in the district of dispatch or the district of receipt, and obscenity is

(continued)

UNITED STATES V. THOMAS
(concluded)

determined by the standards of the community where the trial takes place. This is not a situation where the bulletin board operators had no knowledge or control over the jurisdictions where materials were distributed for downloading or printing. They had in place methods to limit user access in jurisdictions where the risk of a finding of obscenity was greater than that of California.

REGULATION OF CHILD PORNOGRAPHY

Congress enacted the Child Pornography Prevention Act of 1996 (CPPA) in recognition of the fact that computer technology permits the alteration of innocent pictures of children to create depictions of those same children in various sexual poses. The legislation is based on the assumption that such computer-generated images are just as dangerous to the welfare of minors as pornographic material using actual children. Congress concluded that child pornography endangers more than children actually used in photographs. It believed that child pornography also stimulates sexual appetites, thereby encouraging the activities of child molesters and pedophiles. Thus, the CPPA prevents the use of computer technology to create the illusion that children were actually used in sexually explicit photographs or images.

Most governmental restrictions of on-line child pornography are likely to be upheld by the courts since, like obscenity, child pornography does not receive any First Amendment protection. Further, material that might not otherwise be classified as obscene may be prohibited if it illustrates children engaging in sexual conduct.

During 1999, the 9th Circuit Court of Appeals ruled that the CPPA was both overly broad and vague and, therefore, unconstitutional. However, earlier that same year the Court of Appeals for the 1st Circuit found no such infirmities and held that the CPPA fully satisfied the First Amendment requirements. Ultimately, to reconcile these differences between the two circuits, the U.S. Supreme Court granted certiorari during 2001 to examine the legislation. It is highly likely that the Supreme Court will uphold the CPPA in light of its strong deference generally accorded to the interest of protecting the well-being of minors.

REGULATION OF INDECENT EXPRESSION

Sexually explicit material may be neither obscenity nor child pornography. Instead, it is indecent. The government may not entirely prohibit indecent expression unless the law is furthering a compelling governmental interest in the least intrusive manner. And, although the courts have permitted the broad regulation of indecent materials on the radio or television, they have not been eager to embrace such regulation on the Internet. This is because indecency on the Internet does not seem to pose the same threats as it does on radio and television. Internet users are unlikely to encounter indecent materials accidentally. Further, there are systems available that permit parents to control the materials that may be available on a home computer. Consider the following case where a public library attempted to use filtering software to block access to objectionable materials.

MAINSTREAM LOUDOUN V. BOARD OF TRUSTEES
1998 U.S. Dist. LEXIS 4725 (E.D. Va. 1998)

FACTS

The library board for the Loudoun County public libraries adopted a policy that requires that site-blocking software be installed on all library computers so as to block child pornography, obscene material, and material deemed harmful to juveniles. A group of library patrons allege that the policy impermissibly blocks their access to protected speech because the filtering software chosen by the library restricts many publications which are not obscene or pornographic, including materials unrelated to sex altogether. The library contends that, even if the First Amendment limits its discretion to remove materials, it has an unblocking procedure that ensures the constitutionality of the policy because it allows library staff to make certain that only constitutionally unprotected materials are blocked. Under the unblocking policy, library patrons who have been denied access to a site may submit a written request which must include their name, telephone number, and a detailed explanation of why they desire access to the blocked site. The patrons argue that the unblocking procedure constitutes an unconstitutional burden on the right of library patrons to access protected speech.

ISSUE

Does the library policy violate the First Amendment rights of library patrons?

DECISION

Yes. The First Amendment applies to, and limits, the discretion of a public library to place content-based restrictions on access to constitutionally protected materials within its collection. Consistent with the mandate of the First Amendment, a public library, like other enterprises run by the state, may not be run in such a manner as to prescribe what shall be orthodox in politics, nationalism, religion, or other matters of opinion. The factors which justify giving high school libraries broad discretion to remove materials are not present in this case. The plaintiffs in the case are adults rather than children. Children, whose minds and values are still developing, have traditionally been afforded less First Amendment protection, particularly within the context of public high schools. In contrast, adults are deemed to have acquired the maturity needed to participate fully in democratic society, and their right to speak and receive speech is entitled to full First Amendment protection. This holding does not obligate public libraries to act as unwilling conduits of information, because the library board need not provide access to the Internet at all. Having chosen to provide access, however, the library board may not thereafter selectively restrict certain categories of Internet speech because it disfavors their content. The library's unblocking policy does not remedy the First Amendment problems inherent in the site-blocking policy. The unblocking policy forces adult patrons to petition the government for access to otherwise protected speech. Indeed, the Loudoun County unblocking policy is a chilling regulation because it grants library staff standardless discretion to refuse access to protected speech.

MISCONDUCT IN CYBERSPACE

Law enforcement officials are now actively policing cyberspace to deter and punish misconduct by computer users. Of course, not all people are happy with this turn of events. In fact, many Internet users complain that this extension of traditional rules and regulations to cyberspace is unwarranted. However, rising levels of computer crime and tortious behavior have spurred legislators at both the state and federal levels to insist on a greater governmental presence in cyberspace.

DEFAMATION

Under traditional tort law, one who publishes untrue statements that injure the reputation or character of another may be liable for defamation. Perhaps because of the spontaneity and frontier spirit that seem so prevalent in cyberspace, incidents of defamation seem particularly frequent on the Internet. Because such messages may reach millions of people throughout the world in a matter of seconds, malicious statements may have a tremendous capacity to injure innocent victims.

Efforts to prevent defamatory statements on the Internet have been thwarted to some degree by the ability of computer users to operate under an alias. However, some on-line service companies have been willing to reveal an author's true identity when confronted by a court subpeona. One potential remedy, suing the on-line service companies that operate the bulletin boards where the defamatory statement appears, is no longer available to injured plaintiffs. As the following case makes clear, the Communications Decency Act immunizes service providers from liability for messages that originated with third parties.

PATENTWIZARD V. KINKO'S
163 F.Supp.2d 1069 (D.C. S.D. 2001)

FACTS

Michael Neustel is a patent lawyer with a national reputation. Besides his law practice, Neustel owns and operates a PatentWizard, a firm that markets software aimed at people who want to patent their inventions. Kinko's provides Internet access by renting computers to individual users. It does not keep a record of the identities of the persons who rent its computers and does not give a unique Internet Protocol address to each of its rented computers. These omissions make it possible for a Kinko's user to log onto the Internet under a pseudonym, without fear that other Internet users will be able to trace his online statements back to him in the real world, or even to a particular Kinko's computer. On My 9, 2000, Neustel hosted a chat room session about software that had been recently released by PatentWizard. One of several participants in the chat room was a user with the screen name "Jimmy" who logged on from a Kinko's computer. During the session, Jimmy made numerous disparaging statements about Neustel and PatentWizard which Neustel claims defamed him and interfered with his prospective business relationships. Due to the configuration of the Kinko's computer network, Neustel has been unable to locate and pursue remedies against Jimmy. Thus, in lieu of suing Jimmy, Neustel brought an action against Kinko's for negligent failure to monitor its computer network and aiding and abetting defamation. Kinko's moved to dismiss the claims, arguing they are prohibited by federal law.

ISSUE

Does federal law prohibit this lawsuit against Kinko's?

DECISION

Yes. The Communications Decency Act limits lawsuits against those who provide access to the Internet. Specifically, §230 of this federal statute states: *"No provider or user of an interactive computer service shall be treated as the publisher or speaker of any information provided by another information content provider."* This statute prevents a plaintiff from bringing such cases under either federal or state law. Both parties agree that Kinko's is a provider of an "interactive computer service" as defined by the Act and that Jimmy was an "information content provider." The question in this case, then, is whether the claims in Neustel's complaint seek to treat Kinko's as a publisher or speaker of information that Jimmy posted on the Internet. Kinko's is a publisher for purposes of §230. Previous decisions have made clear that the common law of defamation applies both to publishers and distributors and have lumped both under the term "publisher." In enacting §230, Congress meant to insulate distributors as well as publishers from liability for defamation. Neustel's Complaint treats Kinko's as a publisher in two ways. First, it seeks to treat Kinko's as a distributor by imposing liability upon Kinko's for its conduct in disseminating Jimmy's statements. This is itself prohibited by §230. Second, the Complaint seeks to place Kinko's in Jimmy's shoes, by holding Kinko's responsible for defamatory matter that was published by Jimmy. Yet the plain language of §230 creates a federal immunity to any cause of action that would make service providers liable for information originating with a

(continued)

PATENTWIZARD V. KINKO'S
(concluded)

third-party user of the servers. That federal immunity extends to Kinko's and bars Neustel's claims in this case. Clearly, this case implicates some important issues of policy. On the one hand, the ability of individual users to log onto the Internet anonymously, undeterred by traditional social and legal restraints, tends to promote the kind of unrestrained, robust communication that many people view as the Internet's most important contribution to society. On the other hand, the ability of members of the public to link an individual's online identity to his physical self is essential to preventing the Internet's exchange of ideas from causing harm in the real world. The legislative resolution of these issues will, indirectly, shape the content of communication over the Internet. For now, §230 of the Communications Decency Act errs on the side of robust communication, and prevents Neustel from moving forward with his claims.

CYBER-TORTS

Defamation is not the only intentional tort for which computer users might be found liable for damages in a civil action. Internet service providers are beginning to bring trespass actions against spam distributors who flood the Internet with unsolicited advertisements. This practice of mailing unsolicited bulk e-mail causes serious problems for the service providers. Because many of the bulk e-mail lists are outdated and contain a large percentage of invalid or nonexistent e-mail addresses, they severely increase the load on servers, as the servers first attempt to deliver the message and then, if unsuccessful, return the undelivered message to the sender. Additional strain is placed on the server when the sender falsifies the origin of e-mail with a false address because the server will unsuccessfully try for hours and sometimes days to return the undelivered e-mail to the invalid sender. Consider the following case where an on-line service company convinces the court that a spam distributor has committed the intentional tort of trespass.

AMERICA ONLINE V. IMS
1998 U.S. Dist. LEXIS 20645 (E.D. Va. 1998)

FACTS

America Online is an Internet service provider. Joseph Melle, Jr., is the creator and operator of TSF Marketing and TSF Industries (collectively "TSF"). AOL alleges that Melle and TSF improperly sent unauthorized bulk e-mail advertisements (spam) to AOL subscribers. Specifically, AOL claims that Melle sent over 60 million e-mail messages over the course of 10 months; that he continued to send unauthorized bulk e-mail after he was notified in writing by AOL to cease and desist these activities; that his activities caused AOL to spend technical resources and staff time to "defend" its computer system and its membership against this spam; and that Melle's messages damaged AOL's goodwill among its members and generated more than 50,000 member complaints. AOL sued Melle and TSF under trespass to chattels.

ISSUE

Should AOL prevail in its trespass suit against Melle?

DECISION

Yes. The undisputed facts establish that Melle committed a trespass to chattels. A trespass to chattels occurs when one party intentionally uses or intermeddles with personal property in rightful possession of another without authorization. One who commits a trespass to chattels is liable to its rightful possessor for actual damages

(continued)

AMERICA ONLINE V. IMS
(concluded)

suffered by reason of loss of its use. Courts have begun to recognize that the unauthorized mailing of unsolicited bulk e-mail may constitute a trespass to chattels under state law. Melle sent unsolicited e-mail advertising to hundreds of thousands of Internet users, many of whom were subscribers to AOL's Internet services. He further concealed the origin of the messages by forging header information. Melle's conduct fully satisfies all of the ele-

ments of AOL's claim of trespass to chattels. It is undisputed that Melle intentionally caused contact with AOL's computer network by sending bulk e-mail messages, Melle's contact with AOL's computer network was unauthorized, and Melle's contact with AOL's computer network injured AOL's business goodwill and diminished the value of its possessory interest in its computer network. AOL is entitled to summary judgment.

COMPUTERS AND PRIVACY

Privacy issues are a matter of growing concern among government and business leaders as they seek to expand electronic commerce. At present, there are few privacy guarantees on the Internet. Many employees do not realize that the e-mail messages they receive on their employers' computers may belong to the employer and, as such, may be read by the employer.

The privacy concerns arise in other areas as well. For instance, it is now quite common to read news stories reporting incidents of computer hackers infiltrating e-mail files and accessing confidential information. Further, sometimes the simple act of visiting a website may result in private information about the users being sold to marketers. It has been quite common for websites to give out users names, addresses, and social security numbers to interested merchants.

Ethical Implications	Netscape's browser contained a feature, called "cookie," which permitted merchants to discover precisely what users were looking for in their websites. (The company now permits users to deactivate the cookies feature.) Is it ethical to distribute such information without the knowledge and the consent of the user?

CYBER-CRIME

Legislation currently exists at both the state and federal levels prohibiting unauthorized access to, or use of, a computer. It also is a crime for people to access the services of commercial service providers without paying their fees. And it is illegal to for computer hackers to alter or destroy data stored in another person's computer. In fact, there exist numerous criminal statutes outlawing a range of online activities such as theft, distribution of obscene materials, destruction of property, and trespass.

Two specific federal statutes that are concerned with protecting privacy in the electronic environment are worth brief mention. They are the *Electronic Communications Privacy Act* (ECPA) and the *Computer Fraud and Abuse Act* (CFAA).

The Electronic Communications Privacy Act

The ECPA broadly imposes privacy obligations on those who process and handle electronic communications as well as on those who intercept such messages. It is a derivative of the original federal wiretap law enacted in 1968. Congress believed an update was necessary in light of the dramatic changes in computer and telecommunications technologies in recent years. The ECPA actually contains two major provisions: (1) its Wiretap Act protects against unauthorized interception of electronic communications and (2) its Stored Communication Act protects against unauthorized access and disclosure of electronic communication while it is in electronic storage.

The Wiretap provisions make it unlawful for an electronics communication provider to intentionally disclose or use the contents of electronics communications. However, there are exceptions to these proscriptions. For instance, it would be permissible to intercept, use, or disclose such communications if such action were necessary to protect the provider's property rights or if the actions were taken in cooperation with law enforcement or intelligence officials as part of a government-authorized surveillance.

Electronically stored data is protected by the Stored Communication provisions. This part of the statute prohibits access to and disclosure of such information by third parties both when they had no authority and when they have exceeded their authority. However, this specific application of the ECPA applies only to third parties; senders and recipients of stored communications are not covered. Further, while public service communications providers generally are prohibited from disclosing the contents of stored communications, the Act does not reach private storage systems.

The Computer Fraud and Abuse Act

The CFAA civilly and criminally prohibits certain access to computers. Specifically, it bars a person without authorization from knowingly transmitting a program, information, code, or command with the intent of causing damage to a computer which is used in interstate or foreign commerce or communications. The *Shurgard Storage Centers* case, which appears in Chapter 21, examines what is meant by "authorized access" to a protected computer. Other provisions in the statute prohibit interference with computers used by, or for the benefit of, the government or financial institutions.

In general, the CFAA seeks to protect the privacy of information and communications as well as the national security of the United States. Simultaneously, it prohibits acts of sabotage or vandalism to protected computers or networks. Consider the following case, which orders a preliminary injunction because it believes the CFAA probably has been violated.

EF CULTURAL TRAVEL BV v. EXPLORICA
274 F.3d 577 (1st Cir. 2001)

FACTS

EF Cultural Tours, which has been in business for more than 35 years, is the world's largest private student travel organization. Early in 2000, after several key employees left EF, they were employed by Explorica, and that company began to compete in the field of global tours for high school students. Explorica's vice president, Philip Gormley, who was a former vice president of information strategy at EF, envisioned that Explorica could gain a substantial advantage over all other student tour companies, and especially EF, by undercutting EF's already competitive prices on student tours. Gormley considered several ways to obtain and utilize EF's prices: by manually keying in the information from EF's brochures and other printed materials; by using a scanner to record that same

(continued)

EF Cultural Travel BV v. Explorica
(continued)

information; or by manually searching for each tour offered through EF's website. Ultimately, Gormley engaged Zefer, Explorica's Internet consultant, to design a computer program called a "scraper" to glean all of the necessary information from EF's website. Zefer designed the program in three days. The scraper has been likened to a "robot," a tool that is extensively used on the Internet. Robots are used to gather information for countless purposes, ranging from compiling results for search engines such as Yahoo! to filtering for inappropriate content. The widespread deployment of robots enables global Internet users to find comprehensive information quickly and almost effortlessly. Like a robot, the scraper sought information through the Internet. Unlike other robots, however, the scraper focused solely on EF's website, using information that other robots would not have. Specifically, Zefer utilized tour codes whose significance was not readily understandable to the public. With the tour codes, the scraper accessed EF's website repeatedly and easily obtained pricing information for those specific tours. The scraper sent more than 30,000 inquiries to EF's website and recorded the pricing information into a spreadsheet. Zefer ran the scraper program twice, first to retrieve the 2000 tour prices and then the 2001 prices. All told, the scraper downloaded 60,000 lines of data, the equivalent of eight telephone directories of information. Once Zefer scraped all of the prices, it sent a spreadsheet containing EF's pricing information to Explorica, which then systematically undercut EF's prices. Explorica thereafter printed its own brochures and began competing in EF's tour market. After the development and use of the scraper came to light, EF filed an action, alleging violations of the *Computer Fraud and Abuse Act* (CFAA). It sought a preliminary injunction barring Explorica and Zefer from using the scraper program and demanded the return of all materials generated through use of the scraper.

Issue

Should the court issue a preliminary injunction prohibiting use of the scraper program?

Decision

Yes. A court should issue a preliminary injunction only upon considering the likelihood of success on the merits. Thus, unless we believe that EF is likely to succeed on the merits of its CFAA claim, the preliminary injunction

should not be issued. EF has argued that it is likely to succeed under a portion of the CFAA which holds: "*[Whoever] knowingly and with intent to defraud, accesses a protected computer without authorization, or exceeds authorized access, and by means of such conduct furthers the intended fraud and obtains anything of value . . . shall be punished.*" EF alleges that Explorica and Zefer knowingly and with intent to defraud, accessed the server hosting EF's website more than 30,000 times to obtain proprietary pricing and tour information and confidential information about EF's technical abilities. At the heart of this dispute is whether the defendants' actions either were "without authorization" or "exceeded authorized access" as defined by the CFAA. We conclude that because of the broad confidentiality agreement between EF and its former employee, Gormley, use of scraper exceeded authorized access. Thus, we do not reach the more general arguments about whether use of a scraper alone renders access unauthorized. While he still was employed by EF, Gormley signed a confidentiality agreement in which he agreed "to maintain in strict confidence and not to disclose to any third party . . . any confidential or proprietary information." Yet, the record contains at least two communications from Gormley to Zefer seeming to rely on information about EF to which he was privy only because of his employment there. They point to Gormley's heavy involvement in the conception of the scraper program. Furthermore, the voluminous spreadsheet containing all of the scraped information includes the tour codes, which EF claims are proprietary information. Each page of the spreadsheet produced by Zefer includes the tour and gateway codes, the date of travel, and the price of the tour. An uninformed reader would disregard the tour codes as nothing but gibberish. Although the codes can be correlated to the actual tours and destination points, the codes standing alone need to be translated to be meaningful. Here, there is ample evidence that Gormley provided Explorica proprietary information about the structure of the website and the tour codes. To be sure, gathering manually the various codes through repeated searching and deciphering of the URLs theoretically may be possible. Practically speaking, however, if proven, Explorica's wholesale use of EF's travel codes to facilitate gathering EF's prices from its website reeks of use—and,

(continued)

EF Cultural Travel BV v. Explorica
(concluded)

indeed, abuse—of proprietary information that goes beyond any authorized use of EF's website. If EF's allegations are proven, it will likely prove that whatever authorization Explorica had to navigate around EF's site (even in a competitive vein), it exceeded that authorization by providing proprietary information and know-how to Zefer to create the scraper. Since EF is likely to succeed on the merits of its CFAA claim, a preliminary injunction is ordered.

BALANCING PRIVACY AND LAW ENFORCEMENT

Obviously, technological breakthroughs are increasing our capabilities at a tremendous rate. Unfortunately, however, they also are providing new and more complex ways for law breakers to commit crimes. The task for the government, particularly its law enforcement officials, has been to simultaneously develop advanced methods of detecting cyber-crimes. In the aftermath of the terrorist attacks of September 11, 2001, Congress enacted the *USA Patriot Act*. This legislation lowers the standards for governmental surveillance of foreign nationals. It also permits the government to gather information about e-mail messages both sent and received by individuals. The law dispenses with the probable cause standard that normally is required before authorities can search a suspect's person or property. Further, it now considers certain computer crimes to constitute acts of terrorism.

It is too early to determine the effect that such legislation will have on both law enforcement or individual liberties. However, more than ever it stresses the importance of having a judiciary that can adequately consider the proper balance between law enforcement and our constitutional rights in a computerized environment. The following case provides an example of this interplay between privacy and crime prevention.

UNITED STATES V. SCARFO
2001 U.S. Dist. LEXIS 21561 (D.C. N.J. 2001)

FACTS

Acting pursuant to federal search warrants, the FBI entered Nicodemo Scarfo's business office to search for evidence of an illegal gambling and loansharking operation. During their search of the business, the FBI came across a personal computer and attempted to access its various files. In particular, agents were unable to gain entry to an encrypted file named "Factors." Suspecting that the Factors file contained evidence of an illegal gambling and loansharking operation, the FBI returned to the location and, pursuant to two search warrants, installed what is known as a "Key Logger System" (KLS) on the computer to decipher the passphrase to the encrypted file, thereby gaining entry to the file. The KLS records the keystrokes an individual enters on a personal computer's keyboard. The government used the KLS in order to "catch" Scarfo's passphrases to the encrypted file while he was entering them onto his keyboard. Scarfo's personal computer features a modem for communication over telephone lines, and he possesses an America Online account. The FBI obtained the passphrase to the Factors file and retrieved what is alleged to be incriminating evidence. Scarfo filed a motion to suppress the evidence recovered from his computer. Specifically, he argued that the FBI search was too broad and that the KLS may have operated during periods when Scarfo (or any other user of the computer) was communicating via modem over telephone lines, thereby unlawfully intercepting wire communications

(continued)

UNITED STATES V. SCARFO
(concluded)

without having applied for a wiretap pursuant to federal statute.

ISSUE

Should the evidence from the encrypted file be suppressed?

DECISION

No. In this day and age, it appears that on a daily basis we are overwhelmed with new and exciting, technologically advanced gadgetry. Indeed, the amazing capabilities bestowed upon us by science are at times mind-boggling. As a result, we must be ever vigilant against the evisceration of constitutional rights at the hands of modern technology. Yet, at the same time, it is likewise true that modern-day criminals have also embraced technological advances and used them to further their felonious purposes. Each day, advanced computer technologies and the increased accessibility to the Internet mean that criminal behavior is becoming more sophisticated and complex. This includes the ability to find new ways to commit old crimes, as well as new crimes beyond the comprehension of courts. As a result of this surge in so-called cyber crime, law enforcement's ability to vigorously pursue such rogues cannot be hindered where all constitutional limitations are scrupulously observed. This case presents an interesting issue of first impression dealing with the ever-present tension between individual privacy and liberty rights and law enforcement's use of new and advanced technology to vigorously investigate criminal activity. It appears that no district court in the country has addressed a similar issue. Of course, the matter takes on added importance in light of the events of September 11, 2001, and potential national security implications. Scarfo's first argument is that since the government had the ability to capture and record only those keystrokes relevant to the passphrase to the encrypted file, and because it received an unnecessary overcollection of data, the search was unlawful. This claim is without merit. The Fourth Amendment contains a particularity requirement that constrains law enforcement personnel from undertaking a boundless and exploratory rummaging through one's personal property. Here, however, the encrypted file could not be accessed via traditional investigative means. Thus, the warrants specifically authorized the officers to install and leave behind software, firmware, and/or hardware equipment which will monitor the inputted data entered on the computer so the FBI can capture the password necessary to decrypt computer files by recording the key related information as it is entered. That the KLS recorded keystrokes typed into Scarfo's keyboard other than the searched-for passphrase is of no consequence. During many lawful searches, police officers may not know the exact nature of the incriminating evidence sought until they stumble upon it. Scarfo also contends that the KLS intercepted wire communications in violation of the federal wiretap statute by recording keystrokes of e-mail or other communications made over a telephone or cable line while the modem operated. These are the only conceivable wire communications which might emanate from Scarfo's computer and potentially fall under the wiretap statute. However, we reject this argument because there is no evidence that the KLS technique utilized in deciphering the passphrase intercepted any wire communications. As part of the investigation into Scarfo's computer, the FBI did not install and operate any component which would search for and record data entering or exiting the computer from the transmission pathway through the modem attached to the computer. Neither did the FBI install or operate any KLS component which would search for or record any fixed data stored within the computer. Recognizing that Scarfo's computer had a modem and thus was capable of transmitting electronic communications via the modem, the FBI configured the KLS to avoid intercepting electronic communications typed on the keyboard and simultaneously transmitted in real time via the communication ports. Hence, when the modem was operating, the KLS did not record keystrokes. Accordingly, the motion to suppress the evidence is denied.

.... *INTELLECTUAL PROPERTY RIGHTS* ....

Intellectual property law governs the ownership of text, photographs, and other original materials. Because computer technology permits people to transform such material into digital form so that it can be transmitted and downloaded into its original form, on-line communications sometimes trigger intellectual property analysis. The areas where intellectual property questions in cyberspace most often occur seem to be copyrights, trademarks, and domain names.

COPYRIGHTS IN CYBERSPACE

Copyright owners possess the exclusive right to (1) reproduce the copyrighted work, (2) prepare adaptations based on the original copyrighted material, (3) sell or otherwise transfer copies of the copyrighted material, and (4) publicly display the copyrighted material. Nobody else is permitted to exercise these rights without the consent of the copyright owner.

Copyright Infringement

A person will not succeed in a copyright infringement lawsuit unless she proves two things. First, she must establish her ownership of a valid copyright. Second, she must show that the defendant copied constituent elements of her protected works. If these two steps are met, the copyright owner will succeed in her infringement suit if she proves that the defendant exercised any of the ownership rights listed in the previous paragraph.

The Fair Use Doctrine

A defendant in an on-line copyright infringement suit may avoid liability if he can establish that his use of copyrighted material fell within the **fair use** doctrine. Courts look at four factors when deciding whether this defense applies: (1) if the copyrighted material is used for noncommercial purposes, (2) if the copyrighted material is informational rather than creative, (3) if there are substantial differences between the copyrighted work and the derivative work, and (4) if the use does not diminish the value or marketability of the original copyrighted work.

A&M RECORDS v. NAPSTER
239 F.3d 1004 (9th Cir. 2001)

FACTS

Digital MP3 files are created through a process called "ripping." Ripping software allows a computer owner to copy an audio compact disk (audio CD) directly onto a computer's hard drive by compressing the audio information on the CD into the MP3 format. The MP3's compressed format allows for rapid transmission of digital audio files from one computer to another by electronic mail or any other file transfer protocol. Napster facilitates the transmission of MP3 files between and among users. Through a process commonly called "peer-to-peer" file sharing, Napster allows its users to (1) make MP3 music files stored on individual computer hard drives available for copying by other Napster users, (2) search for MP3 music files stored on other users' computers, and (3) transfer exact copies of the contents of other users'

MP3 files from one computer to another via the Internet. These functions are made possible by Napster's Music-Share software, available free of charge from Naptser's Internet site, and Napster's network servers and server-side software. Napster provides technical support for the indexing and searching of MP3 files, as well as for its other functions, including a "chat room," where users can meet to discuss music, and a directory where participating artists can provide information about their music. In order to copy MP3 files through the Napster system, a user must first access Napster's Internet site and download the MusicShare software to his individual computer. Once the software is installed, the user can access the Napster system. A&M and other plaintiffs engaged in the commercial recording, distribution, and sale of

(continued)

A&M Records v. Napster
(concluded)

copyrighted musical compositions and sound recordings allege that Napster is a contributory copyright infringer. Accordingly, they have asked the court to enjoin Napster from engaging, or facilitating others, in copying, downloading, uploading, transmitting, or distributing their copyrighted musical compositions and sound recordings.

Issue

Should the court enjoin Napster's activities?

Decision

Yes. Preliminary injunctive relief is available to a party who demonstrates either (1) a combination of probable success on the merits and the possibility of irreparable harm or (2) that serious questions are raised and the balance of hardships tips in its favor. These two formulations represent two points on a sliding scale in which the required degree of irreparable harm increases as the probability of success decreases. A&M must satisfy two requirements to present a prima facie case of direct infringement: (1) they must show ownership of the allegedly infringed material and (2) they must demonstrate that the alleged infringers violate at least one exclusive right granted to copyright holders under federal law. It has sufficiently demonstrated ownership. As much as 87 percent of the files available on Napster are copyrighted and more than 70 percent of those are owned by A&M or the other plaintiffs. Further, A&M's exclusive rights were violated since a majority of Napster's users employ the service to download and upload copyrighted music. And doing that constitutes direct infringement of A&M's musical compositions. Thus, Napster users infringe at least two of the copyright holders' exclusive rights: the rights of reproduction and distribution. Napster asserted an affirmative defense—it contends that its users do not directly infringe A&M's copyrights because the users are engaged in fair use of the material. The factors which guide a court's fair use determination are (1) the purpose and character of the use, (2) the nature of the copyrighted work, (3) the amount and substantiality of the portion used in relation to the work as a whole, and (4) the effect of the use upon the potential market for the work or the value of the work. However, after considering each of these factors, we conclude that Napster's users are not fair users. The repeated and exploitive copying of these works, even if the copies are not offered for sale, may constitute a commercial use. Further, works like these—that are creative in nature—are closer to the core of intended copyright protection than are more fact-based works. In addition, the copying at issue here was wholesale copying of the entire work. Finally, Napster has harmed the market in two ways: it reduces audio CD sales among college students and it raises barriers to A&M's entry into the market for digital downloading of music. We reject Napster's arguments that its users merely download MP3 files to "sample" the music in order to decide whether to purchase the recording. Sampling remains a commercial use even if some users eventually purchase the music. This is because free promotional downloads are highly regulated by the record companies and they collect royalties for song samples available on retail Internet sites. An injunction should be issued because Napster is likely to be found liable for contributory copyright infringement. Traditionally, one who, with knowledge of the infringing activity, induces, causes, or materially contributes to the infringing conduct of another, may be held liable as a contributory infringer. Put differently, liability exists if the defendant engages in personal conduct that encourages or assists the infringement. Napster, by its conduct, knowingly encourages and assists the infringement of A&M's copyrights. If a computer system operator learns of specific infringing material available on its system and fails to purge such material from the system, the operator knows of and contributes to direct infringement. Further, Napster materially contributes to the infringing activity. It provides the site and facilities for direct infringement.

Trademarks in Cyberspace

Any word, name, symbol, device, or combination thereof used by a manufacturer or seller to identify its products and to distinguish them from the products of its competitors is a **trademark.** Similar words or devices used to identify and distinguish services are called **service marks.** The Lanham Act provides trademark and service mark owners with legal protection against users in order to help purchasers properly identify favored products or services. Further, sellers and manufacturers would have less incentive to innovate and strive for quality if their products and services could be easily confused with those of their competitors.

Because trademark and service mark protection was primarily designed to protect against confusion, the Lanham Act traditionally permitted more than one business to use the same mark if they did not compete in the same area or line of business. However, in recent years **trademark dilution** laws have been used to protect "distinctive" or "famous" marks from unauthorized use even when confusion was unlikely. Instead of focusing on consumer protection, the trademark dilution laws are designed to protect the investment of trademark owners.

DOMAIN NAMES

Web site addresses on the Internet are based on a **domain name** system. The domain name identifies the person, business, or other organization that owns a website. They are important because they assist consumers or other interested persons in quickly locating a particular website. Naturally, a business generally would prefer to use its trademark or service mark as its domain name because of the consumer recognition that accompanies such marks. Problems arise because frequently more than one business may own the trademark or service mark, yet only one of them may register that mark as its domain name.

In recent years, courts have been confronting more and more cases involving *cyber-squatters*. These are people who register another's trademark or service mark as their own domain name and then attempt to sell it to the mark's original owner. As the following case indicates, courts sometimes use trademark infringement or dilution laws to punish cyber-squatters.

PANAVISION INTERNATIONAL L.P. v. TOEPPEN
1998 U.S. App. LEXIS 7557 (9th Cir. 1998)

FACTS

Panavision holds registered trademarks to the names "Panavision" and "Panaflex" in connection with motion picture camera equipment. It promotes the trademarks through motion picture and television credits and other media advertising. Panavision attempted to register a website on the Internet with the domain name. It could not do that, however, because Dennis Toeppen had already established a website using Panavision's trademark as his domain name. Toeppen's Web page for this site displayed photographs of the City of Pana, Illinois. Toeppen offered to "settle the matter" if Panavision would pay him $13,000 in exchange for the domain name. Additionally, he stated that if Panavision agreed to his offer, he would not "acquire any other Internet addresses which are alleged by Panavision Corporation to be its property." After Panavision refused Toeppen's demand, he registered Panavision's other trademark as a domain name. Toeppen's Web page at that site simply displays the word "Hello." Toeppen has registered domain names for various other companies including Delta Airlines, Neiman Marcus, Eddie Bauer, Lufthansa, and over 100 other marks. He has attempted to sell domain names for other trademarks for prices ranging from $10,000 to $15,000. Panavision filed an action against Toeppen for trademark dilution. It claims that Toeppen is in the business of stealing trademarks, registering them as domain names, and then selling them to the rightful trademark owners.

(continued)

PANAVISION INTERNATIONAL L.P. v. TOEPPEN
(concluded)

ISSUE

Is Toeppen liable for trademark dilution?

DECISION

Yes. In order to prove a violation of the Federal Trademark Dilution Act a plaintiff must show that (1) the mark is famous; (2) the defendant is making a commercial use of the mark in commerce; (3) the defendant's use began after the mark became famous; and (4) the defendant's use of the mark dilutes the quality of the mark by diminishing the capacity of the mark to identify and distinguish goods and services. Toeppen does not dispute that Panavision's trademark is famous, that his use began after the mark became famous, or that the use was in commerce. However, he does argue that his use was not commercial and that his use did not cause dilution in the quality of the trademark. First, he asserts that a domain name is simply an address and cannot constitute a commercial use. This argument misstates his use of the Panavision mark. Toeppen's "business" is to register trademarks as domain names and then sell them to the rightful trademark owners. He acts as a "spoiler," preventing Panavision and others from doing business on the Internet under their trademarked names unless they pay his

fee. This is a commercial use. Toeppen made a commercial use of Panavision's trademarks. It does not matter that he did not attach the marks to a product. Toeppen's commercial use was his attempt to sell the trademarks themselves. "Dilution" is defined as "the lessening of the capacity of a famous mark to identify and distinguish goods or services, regardless of the presence or absence of (1) competition between the owner of the famous mark and other parties, or (2) likelihood of confusion, mistake, or deception." A significant purpose of a domain name is to identify the entity that owns the Web site. A customer who is unsure about a company's domain name will often guess that the domain name is the company's name. Using a company's name or trademark as a domain name is also the easiest way to locate that company's Web site. Use of "search engine" can turn up hundreds of web sites, and there is nothing equivalent to a phone book or directory assistance for the Internet. Moreover, potential customers of Panavision will be discouraged if they cannot find its Web page by typing in "<Panavision.com>," but instead are forced to wade through hundreds of Web sites. This dilutes the value of Panavision's trademark.

CYBER-CONTRACTS

Electronic contracting is becoming more and more commonplace. More and more people are purchasing goods and services they find advertised on websites, and agreements frequently are made through an exchange of e-mail messages. In large part, most electronic contracting issues may be resolved through a familiarity with traditional contract rules. Further, an Article 2B of the Uniform Commercial Code is being drafted that will adapt the traditional Uniform Commercial Code rules to cyberspace.

GENERAL CONTRACT RULES

Websites, like newspaper advertisements, generally will be treated as invitations to buyers to make an offer rather than as offers themselves. Thus, when a computer user orders goods or services he finds advertised on a website, the user is offering to buy the goods or services at the advertised terms. The website owner is then free to accept or reject this offer. However, the timing of the acceptance is likely to differ from traditional contract law. Rather than having an authorized acceptance taking effect upon dispatch, courts are likely to hold that an electronic acceptance is not effective until it is actually received by the offeror.

Writing issues are not likely to be serious impediments to on-line contracting. Most oral contracts are enforceable. Further, even when a writing is required by contract law, this requirement should be easy to satisfy since most electronic messages can be printed out into a tangible form.

Legislative Reforms

Legislation has been enacted at both the federal and state levels to facilitate electronic contracting without the need to revise traditional contract rules and without favoring any particular technology. During 2001, a new federal statute—the *Electronic Signatures in Global and National Commerce Act* (E-SIGN)—became effective. Specifically, this new law prevents the courts from denying legal effect to a contracting party's signature because it is communicated electronically. Simultaneously, it stipulates that contracting parties cannot be required to contract electronically. In fact, E-SIGN sets precise rules that businesses must follow when seeking consumer consent to electronic contracts. These include gaining a consumer's "affirmative consent" to receive contractual information electronically, making clear when consent is for more than a single transaction, and spelling out the procedures and price for withdrawing consent in the future. E-businesses must not only make clear to consumers the system's requirements for receiving electronic data but also refrain from imposing consent withdrawal fees if the consumer, at some future date, can longer receive electronic information because the business has upgraded its system.

By 2001, at least 37 states had enacted the *Uniform Electronic Transactions Act* (UETA). Like E-SIGN, UETA precludes courts from rejecting contracts merely because they are in electronic form while also making clear that parties cannot be compelled to use the electronic form. Unlike E-SIGN, however, UETA does not offer specific rules governing when consent has been given electronically.

Shrinkwrap Contracts

Legal controversies frequently flow from the use of **shrinkwrap** terms by the sellers of computer software. Buyers generally receive the software in packages that contain a disk or a CD. The outside of the package is likely to contain language stating that the buyer agrees to accept the additional terms that are contained inside the shrinkwrap package.

Article 2B of the Uniform Commercial Code recommends that these shrinkwrap terms should be enforceable if they meet three conditions. First, the purchaser must have some opportunity to review the terms. Second, the purchaser must be clearly informed of what she must do to accept the terms. Finally, the terms should not be enforceable unless the purchaser voluntarily accepted them. Consider the following case.

Hill v. Gateway 2000
105 F.3d 1147 (7th Cir. 1997)

Facts

Rich and Enza Hill ordered a Gateway 2000 computer system by telephone. They paid by giving their credit card number during the telephone conversation. The computer arrived in a box which also contained a list of terms said to govern the contract unless the Hills returned the computer within 30 days. One of the terms in the box containing the computer was an arbitration clause. Rich and Enza Hill kept the computer for more than 30 days before complaining about its components and performance. When they ultimately filed suite Gateway asked the court to enforce the arbitration clause. In response, the Hills claimed that the arbitration clause

(continued)

HILL v. GATEWAY 2000
(concluded)

did not stand out. They conceded that they noticed the statement of terms but denied reading it closely enough to discover the agreement to arbitrate. Accordingly, they argued that they should be permitted to go to court.

ISSUE

Should the court enforce the arbitration clause?

DECISION

Yes. A contract need not be read to be effective; people who accept take the risk that the unread terms may in retrospect prove unwelcome. Practical considerations support allowing vendors to enclose the full legal terms with their products. If the staff at the other end of the telephone for direct-sales operations such as Gateway's had to read the four-page statement before taking the buyer's credit card number, the droning voice would anesthetize rather than enlighten many potential buyers. Others would hang up in rage over the waste of their time. Customers as a group are better off when vendors skip costly and ineffectual steps such as telephonic

recitation, and use instead a simple approve-or-return device. Competent adults are bound by such documents, read or unread. Perhaps the Hills would have had a better argument if they had been first alerted to the bundling of hardware and legal-ware after opening the box and wanted to return the computer in order to avoid disagreeable terms, but were dissuaded by the expense of shipping. This raises an interesting question, but one that need not detain us because the Hills knew before they ordered the computer that the carton would include *some* important terms, and they did not seek to discover these in advance. Shoppers have three principal ways to discover these things. First, they can ask the vendor to send a copy before deciding whether to buy. Second, shoppers can consult public sources (computer magazines, the websites of vendors) that may contain this information. Third, they may inspect the documents after the product's delivery. The Hills took the third option. By keeping the computer beyond 30 days, the Hills accepted Gateway's offer, including the arbitration clause.

QUESTIONS AND PROBLEM CASES

1. The Communications Decency Act of 1996 contains two provisions that have direct application to the Internet. First, the "indecent transmission" provision prohibits the knowing transmission of obscene or indecent messages to any recipient under 18 years of age. Second, the "patently offensive display" provision prohibits the knowing sending or displaying of patently offensive messages in a manner that is available to a person under 18 years of age. The breadth of these two prohibitions is qualified by two affirmative defenses. One covers those who take "good faith, reasonable, effective, and appropriate actions" to restrict access by minors to the prohibited communications. The other encompasses those who restrict access to covered material by requiring certain designated forms of age proof, such as a verified credit card or an adult identification number or code. Do the "indecent

transmission" and "patently offensive display" provisions violate the First Amendment?

2. CompuServe operates a computer communication service through a proprietary nationwide computer network. In addition to allowing access to the extensive content available within its own proprietary network, CompuServe also provides its subscribers with a link to the much larger resources of the Internet. This allows its subscribers to send and receive electronic messages, known as "e-mail," by the Internet. Cyber Promotions is in the business of sending unsolicited e-mail advertisements on behalf of itself and its clients to hundreds of thousands of Internet users, many of whom are CompuServe subscribers. CompuServe ordered Cyber to stop using CompuServe's computer equipment to process and store the unsolicited e-mail. Instead, Cyber sent an increasing volume of e-mail

APPENDIXES

A

The Constitution of the United States of America

B

Glossary of Legal Terms and Definitions

C

Spanish-English Equivalents for Important Legal Terms

APPENDIX A

The Constitution of the United States of America

PREAMBLE

We the People of the United States, in Order to form a more perfect Union, establish Justice, insure domestic Tranquility, provide for the common defense, promote the general Welfare, and secure the Blessings of Liberty to ourselves and our Posterity, do ordain and establish this Constitution for the United States of America.

ARTICLE I

Section 1

All legislative Powers herein granted shall be vested in a Congress of the United States, which shall consist of a Senate and House of Representatives.

Section 2

The House of Representatives shall be composed of Members chosen every second Year by the People of the several States, and the Electors in each State shall have the Qualifications requisite for Electors of the most numerous Branch of the State Legislature.

No Person shall be a Representative who shall not have attained to the age of twenty five Years, and been seven Years a Citizen of the United States, and who shall not, when elected, be an Inhabitant of that State in which he shall be chosen.

Representatives and direct Taxes shall be apportioned among the several States which may be included within this Union, according to their respective Numbers, which shall be determined by adding to the whole Number of free Persons, including those bound to Service for a Term of Years, and excluding Indians not taxed, three fifths of all other Persons.[1] The actual Enumeration shall be made within three Years after the first Meeting of the Congress of the United States, and within every subsequent Term of ten Years, in such Manner as they shall by Law direct. The Number of Representatives shall not exceed one for every thirty Thousand, but each State shall have at Least one Representative, and un-til such enumeration shall be made, the State of New Hampshire shall be entitled to choose three, Massachusetts eight, Rhode-Island and Providence Plantations one, Connecticut five, New York six, New Jersey four, Pennsylvania eight, Delaware one, Maryland six, Virginia ten, North Carolina five, South Carolina five, and Georgia three.

When vacancies happen in the Representation from any State, the Executive Authority thereof shall issue Writs of Election to fill such Vacancies.

The House of Representatives shall choose their Speaker and other Officers; and shall have the sole Power of Impeachment.

Section 3

The Senate of the United States shall be composed of two Senators from each State, chosen by the Legislature thereof,[2] for six Years; and each Senator shall have one Vote.

Immediately after they shall be assembled in Consequence of the first Election, they shall be divided as equally as may be into three Classes. The Seats of the Senators of the first Class shall be vacated at the Expiration of the second Year, of the second Class at the Expiration of the fourth Year, and of the third Class at the Expiration of the sixth Year, so that one third may be chosen every second Year; and if Vacancies happen by Resignation, or otherwise, during the Recess of the Legislature of any State, the Executive thereof may make temporary Appointments until the next Meeting of the Legislature, which shall then fill such Vacancies.[3]

No Person shall be a Senator who shall not have attained to the Age of thirty Years, and been nine Years a Citizen of the United States, and who shall not, when elected, be an Inhabitant of that State for which he shall be chosen.

---

[1]Changed by the Fourteenth Amendment.

[2]Changed by the Seventeenth Amendment.
[3]Changed by the Seventeenth Amendment.

The Vice President of the United States shall be President of the Senate, but shall have no Vote, unless they be equally divided.

The Senate shall chuse their other Officers, and also a President pro tempore, in the Absence of the Vice President, or when he shall exercise the Office of President of the United States.

The Senate shall have the sole Power to try all Impeachments. When sitting for that Purpose, they shall be on Oath or Affirmation. When the President of the United States is tried, the Chief Justice shall preside: And no Person shall be convicted without the Concurrence of two thirds of the Members present.

Judgment in Cases of Impeachment shall not extend further than to removal from Office, and disqualification to hold and enjoy any Office of honor, Trust or Profit under the United States: but the Party convicted shall nevertheless be liable and subject to Indictment, Trial, Judgment and Punishment, according to Law.

Section 4
The Times, Places and Manner of holding Elections for Senators and Representatives, shall be prescribed in each State by the Legislature thereof; but the Congress may at any time by Law make or alter such Regulations, except as to the Places of chusing Senators.

The Congress shall assemble at least once in every Year, and such Meeting shall be on the first Monday in December, unless they shall by Law appoint a different Day.[4]

Section 5
Each House shall be the Judge of the Elections, Returns and Qualifications of its own Members, and a Majority of each shall constitute a Quorum to do Business; but a smaller Number may adjourn from day to day, and may be authorized to compel the Attendance of absent Members, in such Manner, and under such Penalties as each House may provide.

Each House may determine the Rules of its Proceedings, punish its Members for disorderly Behaviour, and with the Concurrence of two thirds, expel a Member.

Each House shall keep a Journal of its Proceedings, and from time to time publish the same, ex-

cepting such Parts as may in their Judgment require Secrecy; and the Yeas and Nays of the Members of either House on any question shall, at the Desire of one fifth of those Present, be entered on the Journal.

Neither House, during the Session of Congress, shall, without the consent of the other, adjourn for more than three days, nor to any other Place than that in which the two Houses shall be sitting.

Section 6
The Senators and Representatives shall receive a Compensation for their Services, to be ascertained by Law, and paid out of the Treasury of the United States. They shall in all Cases, except Treason, Felony and Breach of the Peace, be privileged from Arrest during their Attendance at the Session of their respective Houses, and in going to and returning from the same; and for any Speech or Debate in either House, they shall not be questioned in any other Place.

No Senator or Representative shall, during the Time for which he was elected, be appointed to any civil Office under the Authority of the United States, which shall have been created, or the Emoluments whereof shall have been increased during such time; and no Person holding any Office under the United States, shall be a Member of either House during his Continuance in Office.

Section 7
All Bills for raising Revenue shall originate in the House of Representatives; but the Senate may propose or concur with Amendments as on other Bills.

Every Bill which shall have passed the House of Representatives and the Senate, shall, before it becomes a Law, be presented to the President of the United States; If he approves he shall sign it, but if not he shall return it, with his Objections to that House in which it shall have originated, who shall enter the Objections at large on their Journal, and proceed to reconsider it. If after such Reconsideration two thirds of that House shall agree to pass the Bill, it shall be sent, together with the Objections, to the other House, by which it shall likewise be reconsidered, and if approved by two thirds of that House, it shall become a Law. But in all such Cases the Votes of both Houses shall be determined by Yeas and Nays, and the Names of the Persons voting for and against the Bill shall be entered on the Journal of each House respectively. If any Bill shall not be

---

[4]Changed by the Twentieth Amendment.

returned by the President within ten Days (Sundays excepted) after it shall have been presented to him, the Same shall be a Law, in like Manner as if he had signed it, unless the Congress by their Adjournment prevent its Return, in which Case it shall not be a Law.

Every Order, Resolution, or Vote to which the concurrence of the Senate and House of Representatives may be necessary (except on a question of Adjournment) shall be presented to the President of the United States; and before the Same shall take Effect, shall be approved by him, or being disapproved by him, shall be repassed by two thirds of the Senate and House of Representatives, according to the Rules and limitations prescribed in the Case of a Bill.

Section 8

Congress shall have Power To lay and collect Taxes, Duties, Imposts and Excises, to pay the Debts and provide for the common Defence and general Welfare of the United States; but all Duties, Imposts and Excises shall be uniform throughout the United States.

To borrow Money on the credit of the United States;

To regulate Commerce with foreign Nations, and among the several States, and with the Indian Tribes;

To establish an uniform Rule of Naturalization, and uniform Laws on the subject of Bankruptcies throughout the United States;

To coin Money, regulate the Value thereof, and of foreign Coin, and fix the Standard of Weights and Measures;

To provide for the Punishment of counterfeiting the Securities and current Coin of the United States;

To establish Post Offices and post Roads;

To promote the Progress of Science and useful Arts, by securing for limited Times to Authors and Inventors the exclusive Right to their respective Writings and Discoveries;

To constitute Tribunals inferior to the supreme Court;

To define and punish Piracies and Felonies committed on the high Seas, and Offences against the Law of Nations;

To declare War, grant Letters of Marque and Reprisal, and make Rules concerning Captures on Land and Water;

To raise and support Armies, but no Appropriation of Money to that Use shall be for a longer Term than two Years;

To provide and maintain a Navy;

To make Rules for the government and Regulation of the land and naval Forces;

To provide for calling forth the Militia to execute the Laws of the Union, suppress Insurrections and repel Invasions;

To provide for organizing, arming, and disciplining, the Militia, and for governing such Part of them as may be employed in the Service of the United States, reserving to the States respectively, the Appointment of the Officers, and the Authority of training the Militia according to the discipline prescribed by Congress;

To exercise exclusive Legislation in all Cases whatsoever, over such District (not exceeding ten Miles square) as may, by Cession of particular States, and the Acceptance of Congress, become the Seat of the Government of the United States, and to exercise like Authority over all Places purchased by the Consent of the Legislature of the State in which the Same shall be, for the Erection of Forts, Magazines, Arsenals, dock-Yards, and other needful Buildings;—And

To make all Laws which shall be necessary and proper for carrying into Execution the foregoing Powers, and all other Powers vested by this Constitution in the Government of the United States, or in any Department or Officer thereof.

Section 9

The Migration or Importation of such Persons as any of the States now existing shall think proper to admit, shall not be prohibited by the Congress prior to the Year one thousand eight hundred and eight, but a Tax or duty may be imposed on such Importation, not exceeding ten dollars for each Person.

The Privilege of the Writ of Habeas Corpus shall not be suspended, unless when in Cases of Rebellion or Invasion the public Safety may require it.

No Bill of Attainder or ex post facto Law shall be passed.

No Capitation, or other direct, Tax shall be laid, unless in Proportion to the Census of Enumeration herein before directed to be taken.[5]

No Tax or Duty shall be laid on Articles exported from any State.

---

[5]Changed by the Sixteenth Amendment.

No Preference shall be given by any Regulation of Commerce or Revenue to the Ports of one State over those of another: nor shall Vessels bound to, or from, one State, be obliged to enter, clear, or pay Duties in another.

No Money shall be drawn from the Treasury, but in Consequence of Appropriations made by Law; and a regular Statement and Account of the Receipts and Expenditures of all public Money shall be published from time to time.

No Title of Nobility shall be granted by the United States: And no Person holding any Office of Profit or Trust under them, shall, without the Consent of the Congress, accept of any present, Emolument, Office, or Title, of any kind whatever, from any King, Prince, or foreign State.

Section 10

No State shall enter into any Treaty, Alliance, or Confederation; grant Letters of Marque and Reprisal; coin Money; emit Bills of Credit; make any Thing but gold and silver coin a Tender in Payment of Debts; pass any Bill of Attainder, ex post facto Law, or Law impairing the Obligation of Contracts, or grant any Title of Nobility.

No State shall, without the consent of the Congress, lay any Imposts or Duties on Imports or Exports, except what may be absolutely necessary for executing its inspection Laws: and the net Produce of all Duties and Imposts, laid by any State on Imports or Exports, shall be for the Use of the Treasury of the United States; and all such Laws shall be subject to the Revision and Controul of the Congress.

No State shall, without the consent of Congress, lay any Duty of Tonnage, keep Troops, or Ships of War in time of Peace, enter into any Agreement or Compact with another State, or with a foreign Power, or engage in War, unless actually invaded, or in such imminent Danger as will not admit of delay.

ARTICLE II
Section 1

The executive Power shall be vested in a President of the United States of America. He shall hold his Office during the Term of four Years, and, together with the Vice President, chosen for the same Term, be elected, as follows

Each state shall appoint, in such Manner as the Legislature thereof may direct, a Number of Electors, equal to the whole Number of Senators and Repre-

sentatives to which the State may be entitled in Congress: but no Senator or Representative, or Person holding an Office of Trust or Profit under the United States, shall be appointed an Elector.

The Electors shall meet in their respective States, and vote by Ballot for two Persons, of whom one at least shall not be an inhabitant of the same State with themselves. And they shall make a List of all the Persons voted for, and of the Number of Votes for each; which List they shall sign and certify, and transmit sealed to the Seat of the Government of the United States, directed to the President of the Senate. The President of the Senate shall, in the Presence of the Senate and House of Representatives, open all the Certificates, and the Votes shall then be counted. The Person having the greatest Number of Votes shall be the President, if such Number be a Majority of the whole Number of Electors appointed; and if there be more than one who have such Majority, and have an equal Number of Votes, then the House of Representatives shall immediately chuse by Ballot one of them for President; and if no Person have a Majority, then from the five highest on the List the said House shall in like Manner chuse the President. But in chusing the President, the Votes shall be taken by States, the Representation from each State having one Vote; A quorum for this purpose shall consist of a Member or Members from two thirds of the States, and a Majority of all the States shall be necessary to a Choice. In every Case, after the Choice of the President, the Person having the greatest Number of Votes of the Electors shall be the Vice President. But if there should remain two or more who have equal Votes, the Senate shall chuse from them by Ballot the Vice President.[6]

The Congress may determine the Time of chusing the Electors, and the Day on which they shall give their Votes; which Day shall be the same throughout the United States.

No Person except a natural born Citizen, or a Citizen of the United States, at the time of the Adoption of this Constitution, shall be eligible to the Office of President; neither shall any Person be eligible to that Office who shall not have attained to the Age of thirty five Years, and been fourteen Years a Resident within the United States.

In Case of the Removal of the President from Office, or of his Death, Resignation, or Inability to

---

[6]Changed by the Twelfth Amendment.

discharge the Powers and Duties of the said Office, the Same shall devolve on the Vice President, and the Congress may by Law provide for the Case of Removal, Death, Resignation or Inability, both of the President and Vice President, declaring what Officer shall then act as President, and such Officer shall act accordingly, until the Disability be removed, or a President shall be elected.[7]

The President shall, at stated Times, receive for his Services, a Compensation, which shall neither be encreased nor diminished during the Period for which he shall have been elected, and he shall not receive within that Period any other Emolument from the United States, or any of them.

Before he enters on the Execution of his Office, he shall take the following Oath or Affirmation:—"I do solemnly swear (or affirm) that I will faithfully execute the Office of President of the United States, and will to the best of my Ability, preserve, protect, and defend the Constitution of the United States."

Section 2
The President shall be Commander in Chief of the Army and Navy of the United States, and of the Militia of the several States, when called into the actual Service of the United States; he may require the Opinion, in writing, of the principal Officer in each of the executive Departments, upon any Subject relating to the Duties of their respective Offices, and he shall have Power to grant Reprieves and Pardons for Offences against the United States, except in Cases of Impeachment.

He shall have Power, by and with the Advice and Consent of the Senate, to make Treaties, provided two thirds of the Senators present concur; and he shall nominate, and by and with the Advice and Consent of the Senate, shall appoint Ambassadors, other public Ministers and Consuls, Judges of the supreme Court, and all other Officers of the United States, whose Appointments are not herein otherwise provided for, and which shall be established by Law; but the Congress may by Law vest the Appointment of such inferior Officers, as they think proper, in the President alone, in the Courts of Law, or in the Heads of Departments.

The President shall have Power to fill up all Vacancies that may happen during the Recess of the Senate, by granting Commissions which shall expire at the End of their next Session.

Section 3
He shall from time to time give to the Congress Information of the State of the Union, and recommend to their Consideration such Measures as he shall judge necessary and expedient; he may, on extraordinary Occasions, convene both Houses, or either of them, and in Case of Disagreement between them, with Respect to the Time of Adjournment, he may adjourn them to such Time as he shall think proper; he shall receive Ambassadors and other public Ministers; he shall take Care that the Laws be faithfully executed, and shall Commission all the Officers of the United States.

Section 4
The President, Vice President and all civil Officers of the United States, shall be removed from Office on Impeachment for, and Conviction of, Treason, Bribery, or other high Crimes and Misdemeanors.

ARTICLE III
Section 1
The judicial Power of the United States, shall be vested in one supreme Court, and in such inferior Courts as the Congress may from time to time ordain and establish. The Judges, both of the supreme and inferior Courts, shall hold their Offices during good Behaviour, and shall, at stated Times, receive for their Services, a Compensation, which shall not be diminished during their Continuance in Office.

Section 2
The judicial Power shall extend to all Cases, in Law and Equity, arising under this Constitution, the Laws of the United States, and Treaties made, or which shall be made, under their Authority;—to all Cases affecting Ambassadors, other public Ministers and Consuls;—to all Cases of admiralty and maritime Jurisdiction;—to Controversies to which the United States shall be a party;—to Controversies between two or more States;—between a State and Citizens of another State,[8]—between Citizens of different States;—between Citizens of the same State claiming Lands under Grants of different States, and between

[7]Changed by the Twenty-fifth Amendment.

[8]Changed by the Eleventh Amendment.

a State, or the Citizens thereof, and foreign States, Citizens or Subjects.

In all Cases affecting Ambassadors, other public Ministers and Consuls, and those in which a State shall be Party, the supreme Court shall have original Jurisdiction. In all the other Cases before mentioned, the supreme Court shall have appellate Jurisdiction, both as to Law and Fact, with such Exceptions, and under such Regulations as the Congress shall make.

The Trial of all Crimes, except in Cases of Impeachment, shall be by Jury: and such Trial shall be held in the State where the said Crimes shall have been committed; but when not committed within any State, the Trial shall be at such Place or Places as the Congress may by Law have directed.

Section 3

Treason against the United States, shall consist only in levying War against them, or in adhering to their Enemies, giving them Aid and Comfort. No Person shall be convicted of Treason unless on the Testimony of two Witnesses to the same overt Act, or on Confession in open Court.

The Congress shall have Power to declare the Punishment of Treason, but no Attainder of Treason shall work Corruption of Blood, or Forfeiture except during the Life of the Person attained.

ARTICLE IV
Section 1

Full Faith and Credit shall be given in each State to the public Acts, Records, and judicial Proceedings of every other State. And the Congress may by general Laws prescribe the Manner in which such Acts, Records and Proceedings shall be proved, and the Effect thereof.

Section 2

The Citizens of each State shall be entitled to all Privileges and Immunities of Citizens in the several States.

A Person charged in any State with Treason, Felony, or other Crime, who shall flee from Justice, and be found in another State, shall on Demand of the executive Authority of the State from which he fled, be delivered up, to be removed to the State having Jurisdiction of the Crime.

No Person held to Service or Labour in one State, under the Laws thereof, escaping into another, shall,

in consequence of any Law or Regulation therein, be discharged from such Service or Labour, but shall be delivered up on Claim of the Party to whom such Service or Labour may be due.[9]

Section 3

New States may be admitted by the Congress into this Union; but no new State shall be formed or erected within the Jurisdiction of any other State; nor any State be formed by the Junction of two or more States, or Parts of States, without the Consent of the Legislatures of the States concerned as well as of the Congress.

The Congress shall have Power to dispose of and make all needful Rules and Regulations respecting the Territory or other Property belonging to the United States; and nothing in this Constitution shall be so construed as to Prejudice any Claims of the United States, or of any particular State.

Section 4

The United States shall guarantee to every State in this Union a Republican Forum of Government, and shall protect each of them against Invasion; and on Application of the Legislature, or of the Executive (when the Legislature cannot be convened) against domestic Violence.

ARTICLE V

The Congress, whenever two thirds of both Houses shall deem it necessary, shall propose Amendments to this Constitution, or, on the Application of the Legislatures of two thirds of the several States, shall call a Convention for proposing Amendments, which in either Case, shall be valid to all Intents and Purposes, as Part of this Constitution, when ratified by the legislatures of three fourths of the several States, or by Conventions in three fourths thereof, as the one or the other Mode of Ratification may be proposed by the Congress; Provided that no Amendment which may be made prior to the Year One thousand eight hundred and eight shall in any Manner affect the first and fourth Clauses in the Ninth Section of the first Article; and that no State, without its consent, shall be deprived of its equal Suffrage in the Senate.

---

[9]Changed by the Thirteenth Amendment.

ARTICLE VI

All Debts contracted and Engagements entered into, before the Adoption of this Constitution, shall be as valid against the United States under this constitution, as under the Confederation.

The Constitution, and the Laws of the United States which shall be made in Pursuance thereof; and all Treaties made, or which shall be made, under the Authority of the United States, shall be the supreme Law of the Land; and the Judges in every State shall be bound thereby, any Thing in the Constitution or Laws of any State to the Contrary notwithstanding.

The Senators and Representatives before mentioned, and the Members of the several State Legislatures, and all executive and judicial Officers, both of the United States and of the several States, shall be bound by Oath or Affirmation, to support this Constitution; but no religious Test shall ever be required as a Qualification to any Office or public Trust under the United States.

ARTICLE VII

The Ratification of the Conventions of nine States, shall be sufficient for the Establishment of this Constitution between the States so ratifying the Same.

Done in Convention by the Unanimous Consent of the States present the Seventeenth Day of September in the Year of our Lord one thousand seven hundred and eighty seven and of the Independence of the United States of America the Twelfth. In witness whereof We have hereunto subscribed our Names.

AMENDMENTS

[The first 10 amendments are known as the "Bill of Rights."]

Amendment 1   (Ratified 1791)

Congress shall make no law respecting an establishment of religion, or prohibiting the free exercise thereof; or abridging the freedom of speech, or of the press; or the right of the people peaceably to assemble, and to petition the Government for a redress of grievances.

Amendment 2   (Ratified 1791)

A well regulated Militia, being necessary to the security of a free State, the right of the people to keep and bear Arms, shall not be infringed.

Amendment 3   (Ratified 1791)

No Soldier shall, in time of peace be quartered in any house, without the consent of the Owner, nor in time of war, but in a manner to be prescribed by law.

Amendment 4   (Ratified 1791)

The right of the people to be secure in their persons, houses, papers, and effects, against unreasonable searches and seizures, shall not be violated, and no Warrants shall issue, but upon probable cause, supported by Oath or affirmation, and particularly describing the place to be searched, and the persons or things to be seized.

Amendment 5   (Ratified 1791)

No person shall be held to answer for a capital, or otherwise infamous crime, unless on a presentment or indictment of a Grand Jury, except in cases arising in the land or naval forces, or in the Militia, when in actual service in time of War or public danger; nor shall any person be subject for the same offence to be twice put in jeopardy of life or limb; nor shall be compelled in any criminal case to be a witness against himself, nor be deprived of life, liberty, or property, without due process of law; nor shall private property be taken for public use, without just compensation.

Amendment 6   (Ratified 1791)

In all criminal prosecutions, the accused shall enjoy the right to a speedy and public trial, by an impartial jury of the State and district wherein the crime shall have been committed, which district shall have been previously ascertained by law, and to be informed of the nature and cause of the accusation; to be confronted with the witnesses against him; to have compulsory process for obtaining Witnesses in his favor, and to have assistance of counsel for his defence.

Amendment 7   (Ratified 1791)

In Suits at common law, where the value in controversy shall exceed twenty dollars, the right of trial by jury shall be preserved, and no fact tried by a jury, shall be otherwise re-examined in any Court of the United States, than according to the rules of the common law.

Amendment 8   (Ratified 1791)

Excessive bail shall not be required, nor excessive fines imposed, nor cruel and unusual punishments inflicted.

Amendment 9   (Ratified 1791)

The enumeration in the Constitution, of certain rights, shall not be construed to deny or disparage others retained by the people.

Amendment 10   (Ratified 1791)

The powers not delegated to the United States by the Constitution, nor prohibited by it to the States, are reserved to the States respectively, or to the people.

Amendment 11   (Ratified 1795)

The Judicial power of the United States shall not be construed to extend to any suit in law or equity, commenced or prosecuted against one of the United States by Citizens of another State, or by Citizens or Subjects of any Foreign State.

Amendment 12   (Ratified 1804)

The Electors shall meet in their respective states, and vote by ballot for President and Vice-President, one of whom, at least, shall not be an inhabitant of the same state with themselves; they shall name in their ballots the person voted for as President, and in distinct ballots the person voted for as Vice-President, and they shall make distinct lists of all persons voted for as President, and of all persons voted for as Vice-President, and of the number of votes for each, which lists they shall sign and certify, and transmit sealed to the seat of the government of the United States, directed to the President of the Senate;—The President of the Senate shall, in the presence of the Senate and House of Representatives, open all the certificates and the votes shall then be counted;— The person having the greatest number of votes for President, shall be the President, if such number be a majority of the whole number of Electors appointed; and if no person have such majority, then from the persons having the highest numbers not exceeding three on the list of those voted for as President, the House of Representatives shall choose immediately, by ballot, the President. But in choosing the President, the votes shall be taken by states, the representation from each state having one vote; a quorum for this purpose shall consist of a member or members from two-thirds of the states, and a ma-

jority of all the states shall be necessary to a choice. And if the House of Representatives shall not choose a President whenever the right of choice shall devolve upon them, before the fourth day of March next following, then the Vice-President shall act as president, as in the case of the death or other constitutional disability of the President.[10]—The person having the greatest number of votes as Vice-President, shall be the Vice-President, if such number be a majority of the whole number of Electors appointed, and if no person have a majority, then from the two highest numbers on the list, the Senate shall choose the Vice-President; a quorum for the purpose shall consist of two-thirds of the whole number of Senators, and a majority of the whole number shall be necessary to a choice. But no person constitutionally ineligible to the office of President shall be eligible to that of Vice-President of the United States.

Amendment 13   (Ratified 1865)
Section 1

Neither slavery nor involuntary servitude, except as a punishment for crime whereof the party shall have been duly convicted, shall exist within the United States, or any place subject to their jurisdiction.

Section 2

Congress shall have power to enforce this article by appropriate legislation.

Amendment 14   (Ratified 1868)
Section 1

All persons born or naturalized in the United States, and subject to the jurisdiction thereof, are citizens of the United States and of the State wherein they reside. No State shall make or enforce any law which shall abridge the privileges or immunities of citizens of the United States; nor shall any State deprive any person of life, liberty, or property, without due process of law; nor deny to any person within its jurisdiction the equal protection of the laws.

Section 2

Representatives shall be apportioned among the several States according to their respective numbers, counting the whole number of persons in each State, excluding Indians not taxed. But when the

---

[10]Changed by the Twentieth Amendment.

right to vote at any election for the choice of electors for President and Vice President of the United States, Representatives in Congress, the Executive and Judicial officers of a State, or the members of the Legislature thereof, is denied to any of the male inhabitants of such State, being twenty-one[11] years of age, and citizens of the United States, or in any way abridged except for participation in rebellion, or other crime, the basis of representation therein shall be reduced in the proportion which the number of such male citizens shall bear to the whole number of male citizens twenty-one years of age in such State.

Section 3

No person shall be a Senator or Representative in Congress, or elector of President and Vice President, or hold any office, civil or military, under the United States, or under any State, who, having previously taken an oath, as a member of Congress, or as an officer of the United States, or as a member of any State legislature, or as an executive or judicial officer of any State, to support the Constitution of the United States, shall have engaged in insurrection or rebellion against the same, or given aid or comfort to the enemies thereof. But congress may by a vote of two-thirds of each House, remove such disability.

Section 4

The validity of the public debt of the United States, authorized by law, including debts incurred for payment of pensions and bounties for services in suppressing insurrection or rebellion, shall not be questioned. But neither the United States nor any State shall assume or pay any debt or obligation incurred in aid of insurrection or rebellion against the United States, or any claim for the loss or emancipation of any slave; but all such debts, obligations and claims shall be held illegal and void.

Section 5

The Congress shall have power to enforce, by appropriate legislation, the provisions of this article.

Amendment 15   (Ratified 1870)
Section 1

The right of citizens of the United States to vote shall not be denied or abridged by the United States or by

---

[11]Changed by the Twenty-sixth Amendment.

any State on account of race, color, or previous condition of servitude.

Section 2

The Congress shall have power to enforce this article by appropriate legislation.

Amendment 16   (Ratified 1913)

The Congress shall have power to lay and collect taxes on incomes, from whatever source derived, without apportionment among the several States, and without regard to any census or enumeration.

Amendment 17   (Ratified 1913)

The Senate of the United States shall be composed of two Senators from each State, elected by the people thereof, for six years; and each Senator shall have one vote. The electors in each State shall have the qualifications requisite for electors of the most numerous branch of the State legislatures.

When vacancies happen in the representation of any State in the Senate, the executive authority of such State shall issue writs of election to fill such vacancies: *Provided*, That the legislature of any State may empower the executive thereof to make temporary appointments until the people fill the vacancies by election as the legislature may direct.

This amendment shall not be so construed as to affect the election or term of any Senator chosen before it becomes valid as part of the Constitution.

Amendment 18   (Ratified 1919; Repealed 1933)
Section 1

After one year from the ratification of this article the manufacture, sale, or transportation of intoxicating liquors within, the importation thereof into, or the exportation thereof from the United States and all territory subject to the jurisdiction thereof for beverage purposes is hereby prohibited.

Section 2

The Congress and the several States shall have concurrent power to enforce this article by appropriate legislation.

Section 3

This article shall be inoperative unless it shall have been ratified as an amendment to the Constitution by the legislatures of the several States, as provided in the Constitution, within seven years from the date of the submission hereof to the States by the Congress.[12]

Amendment 19   (Ratified 1920)

The right of citizens of the United States to vote shall not be denied or abridged by the United States or by any State on account of sex.

Congress shall have power to enforce this article by appropriate legislation.

Amendment 20   (Ratified 1933)
Section 1

The terms of the President and Vice President shall end at noon on the 20th day of January, and the terms of Senators and Representatives at noon on the 3d day of January, of the years in which such terms would have ended if this article had not been ratified; and the terms of their successors shall then begin.

Section 2

The Congress shall assemble at least once in every year, and such meeting shall begin at noon on the 3rd day of January, unless they shall by law appoint a different day.

Section 3

If, at the time fixed for the beginning of the term of the President, the President elect shall have died, the Vice President elect shall become President. If a President shall not have been chosen before the time fixed for the beginning of his term, or if the President elect shall have failed to qualify, then the Vice President elect shall act as President until a President shall have qualified; and the Congress may by law provide for the case wherein neither a President elect nor a Vice President elect shall have qualified, declaring who shall then act as President, or the manner in which one who is to act shall be selected, and such person shall act accordingly until a President or Vice President shall have qualified.

Section 4

The Congress may by law provide for the case of the death of any of the persons from whom the House of Representatives may choose a President whenever the right of choice shall have devolved upon them, and for the case of the death of any of the persons from whom the Senate may choose a Vice President whenever the right of choice shall have devolved upon them.

Section 5

Sections 1 and 2 shall take effect on the 15th day of October following the ratification of this article.

Section 6

This article shall be inoperative unless it shall have been ratified as an amendment to the Constitution by the legislatures of three-fourths of the several States within seven years from the date of its submission.

Amendment 21   (Ratified 1933)
Section 1

The eighteenth article of amendment to the Constitution of the United States is hereby repealed.

Section 2

The transportation or importation into any State, Territory, or possession of the United States for delivery or use therein of intoxicating liquors, in violation of the laws thereof, is hereby prohibited.

Section 3

This article shall be inoperative unless it shall have been ratified as an amendment to the constitution by conventions in the several States, as provided in the Constitution, within seven years from the date of the submission hereof to the States by the Congress.

Amendment 22   (Ratified 1951)
Section 1

No person shall be elected to the office of the President more than twice, and no person who has held the office of President, or acted as President, for more than two years of a term to which some other person was elected President shall be elected to the office of the President more than once. But this Article shall not apply to any person holding the office of President when this Article was proposed by the Congress, and shall not prevent any person who may be holding the office of President, or acting as President, during the term within which this Article becomes operative from holding the office of President

---

[12]Repealed by the Twenty-first Amendment.

or acting as President during the remainder of such term.

Section 2

This Article shall be inoperative unless it shall have been ratified as an amendment to the Constitution by the legislatures of three-fourths of the several States within seven years from the date of its submission to the States by the Congress.

Amendment 23   (Ratified 1961)
Section 1

The District constituting the seat of Government of the United States shall appoint in such manner as the Congress may direct:

A number of electors of President and Vice President equal to the whole number of Senators and Representatives in Congress to which the District would be entitled if it were a State, but in no event more than the least populous State; they shall be in addition to those appointed by the States, but they shall be considered, for the purposes of the election of President and Vice President, to be electors appointed by a State; and they shall meet in the District and perform such duties as provided by the twelfth article of amendment.

Section 2

The Congress shall have power to enforce this article by appropriate legislation.

Amendment 24   (Ratified 1964)
Section 1

The right of citizens of the United States to vote in any primary or other election for President or Vice President, for electors for President or Vice President, or for Senator or Representative in Congress, shall not be denied or abridged by the United States or any State by reason of failure to pay any poll tax or other tax.

Section 2

The Congress shall have power to enforce this article by appropriate legislation.

Amendment 25   (Ratified 1967)
Section 1

In case of the removal of the President from office or of his death or resignation, the Vice President shall become President.

Section 2

Whenever there is a vacancy in the office of the Vice President, the President shall nominate a Vice President who shall take office upon confirmation by a majority vote of both Houses of Congress.

Section 3

Whenever the President transmits to the President pro tempore of the Senate and the Speaker of the House of Representatives his written declaration that he is unable to discharge the powers and duties of his office, and until he transmits to them a written declaration to the contrary, such powers and duties shall be discharged by the Vice President as Acting President.

Section 4

Whenever the Vice President and a majority of either the principal officers of the executive departments or of such other body as Congress may by law provide, transmit to the President pro tempore of the Senate and the Speaker of the House of Representatives their written declaration that the President is unable to discharge the powers and duties of his office, the Vice President shall immediately assume the powers and duties of the office as Acting President.

Thereafter, when the President transmits to the President pro tempore of the Senate and the Speaker of the House of Representatives his written declaration that no inability exists, he shall resume the powers and duties of his office unless the Vice President and a majority of either the principal officers of the executive department or of such other body as Congress may by law provide, transmit within four days to the President pro tempore of the Senate and the Speaker of the House of Representatives their written declaration that the President is unable to discharge the powers and duties of his office. Thereupon Congress shall decide the issue, assembling within forty-eight hours for that purpose if not in session. If the Congress, within twenty-one days after receipt of the latter written declaration, or, if Congress is not in session, within twenty-one days after Congress is required to assemble, determines by two-thirds vote of both Houses that the President is unable to discharge the powers and duties of his office, the Vice President shall continue to discharge the same as Acting President; otherwise, the

President shall resume the powers and duties of his office.

Amendment 26   (Ratified 1971)
Section 1
The right of citizens of the United States, who are eighteen years of age or older, to vote shall not be denied or abridged by the United States or by any State on account of age.

Section 2
The Congress shall have power to enforce this article by appropriate legislation.

Amendment 27   (Ratified 1992)
No law, varying the compensation for the services of the Senators and Representatives, shall take effect, until an election of Representatives shall have intervened.

Appendix B

Glossary of Legal Terms and Definitions

Abatement of Nuisance Removal of a nuisance by court action.

Ab Initio From the beginning. A contract that is void ab initio is void from its inception.

Absque Injuria Without violation of a legal right.

Abstract of Title A summary of the conveyances, transfers, and other facts relied on as evidence of title, together with all such facts appearing of record that may impair its validity. It should contain a brief but complete history of the title.

Abutting Owners Those owners whose lands touch.

Acceleration The shortening of the time for the performance of a contract or the payment of a note by the operation of some provision in the contract or note itself.

Acceptance The actual or implied receipt and retention of that which is tendered or offered. The acceptance of an offer is the assent to an offer that is requisite to the formation of a contract. It is either express or evidenced by circumstances from which such assent may be implied.

Accession In it legal meaning, it is generally used to signify the acquisition of property by its incorporation or union with other property.

Accommodation Paper A negotiable instrument signed without consideration by a party as acceptor, drawer, or indorser for the purpose of enabling the payee to obtain credit.

Accord and Satisfaction The adjustment of a disagreement as to what is due from one person to another, and the payment of the agreed amount.

Account Stated An account that has been rendered by one to another and that purports to state the true balance due, which balance is either expressly or impliedly admitted to be due by the debtor.

Acknowledgment A form for authenticating instruments conveying property or otherwise conferring rights. It is a public declaration by the grantor that the act evidenced by the instrument is his act and deed. Also an admission or confirmation.

Acquit To set free or judicially to discharge from an accusation; to release from a debt, duty, obligation, charge, or suspicion of guilt.

Actionable Remedial by an action at law.

Action ex Contractu An action arising out of the breach of a contract.

Action ex Delicto An action arising out of the violation of a duty or obligation created by positive law independent of contract. An action in tort.

Act of God An occurrence resulting exclusively from natural forces that could not have been prevented or whose effects could not have been avoided by care or foresight.

Act of State An act done by the sovereign power of a country. It cannot be questioned by a court of law.

Adjudge To give judgment; to decide; to sentence.

Adjudicate To adjudge; to settle by judicial decree; to hear or try and determine, as a court.

Ad Litem During the pendency of the action or proceeding.

Administrator A man appointed by a probate court to settle the estate of a deceased person. His duties are customarily defined by statute. If a woman is appointed, she is called the administratrix.

Adverse Possession Open and notorious possession of real property over a given length of time that denies ownership in any other claimant.

Advisement When a court takes a case under advisement, it delays its decision until it has examined and considered the questions involved.

Affidavit A statement or declaration reduced to writing and sworn or affirmed to before an officer who has authority to administer an oath or affirmation.

Affirm To confirm a former judgment or order of a court. Also, to declare solemnly instead of making a sworn statement.

Affirmative Action Preferential hiring or promotion on the basis of minority status or gender.

After-Acquire Property Property of the debtor that is obtained after a security interest in the debtor's property has been created.

Agent An agent is the substitute or representative of his principal and derives his authority from him.

Aggrieved   One whose legal rights have been invaded by the act of another is said to be aggrieved. Also, one whose pecuniary interest is directly affected by a judgment, or whose right of property may be divested thereby, is to be considered a party aggrieved.

Alienation   The voluntary act or acts by which one person transfers his or her own property to another.

Aliquot   Strictly, forming an exact proper divisor, but treated as meaning fractional when applied to trusts, and so on.

Allegation   A declaration, a formal averment or statement of a party to an action in a declaration or pleading of what the party intends to prove.

Allege   To make a statement of fact; to plead.

Alternative Dispute Resolution (ADR)   A general name applied to the many nonjudicial means of settling private disputes.

Amortize   In modern usage, the word means to provide for the payment of a debt by creating a sinking fund or paying in installments.

Ancillary   Auxiliary to. An ancillary receiver is a receiver who has been appointed in aid of, and in subordination to, the primary receiver.

Answer   The pleading of a defendant in which he or she may deny any or all the facts set out in the plaintiff's declaration or complaint.

Anticipatory Breach   The doctrine of the law of contracts that when the promisor has repudiated the contract before the time of performance has arrived, the promisee may sue forthwith.

Apparent Authority   When in absence of actual authority, a principal knowingly permits an agent to hold himself out as possessing authority to enter a contract on behalf of the principal.

Appearance   The first act of the defendant in court.

Appellant   A person who files an appeal.

Appellate Jurisdiction   Jurisdiction to revise or correct the work of a subordinate court.

Appellee   A party against whom a cause is appealed from a lower court to a higher court, called the "respondent" in some jurisdictions.

Applicant   A petitioner; one who files a petition or application.

Appurtenance   An accessory; something that belongs to another thing; for example, buildings are appurtenant to the land and a bar would be appurtenant to a tavern.

Arbitrate   To submit some disputed matter to selected persons and to accept their decision or award as a substitute for the decision of a judicial tribunal.

Argument   The discussion by counsel for the respective parties of their contentions on the law and the facts of the case being tried in order to aid the jury in arriving at a correct and just conclusion.

Articles of Incorporation   A document that must be filed with a secretary of state to create a corporation. Usually, it includes the basic rights and responsibilities of the corporation and the shareholders.

Assent   To give or express one's concurrence or approval of something done. Assent does not include consent.

Assignable   Capable of being lawfully assigned or transferred; transferable; negotiable. Also, capable of being specified or pointed out as an assignable error.

Assignee   A person to whom an assignment is made.

Assignment   A transfer or setting over of property or some right or interest therein, from one person to another. In its ordinary application, the word is limited to the transfer of choices in action; for example, the assignment of a contract.

Assignor   The maker of an assignment.

Assumpsit   An action at common law to recover damages for breach of contract.

Assurance   To provide confidence or to inform positively.

Attachment   Taking property into the legal custody of an officer by virtue of the directions contained in a writ of attachment. A seizure under a writ of a debtor's property.

Attest   To bear witness to; to affirm; to be true or genuine.

Attorney-in-fact   A person who is authorized by his principal, either for some particular purpose, or to do a particular act, not of a legal character.

Authentication   Such official attestation of a written instrument as will render it legally admissible in evidence.

Authority   Judicial or legislative precedent; delegated power; warrant.

Averment   A positive statement of fact made in a pleading.

Avoidable   Capable of being nullified or made void.

Bad Faith   The term imports a person's actual intent to mislead or deceive another; an intent to take an unfair and unethical advantage of another.

Bailee   The person to whom a bailment is made.

Bailment   A delivery of personal property by one person to another in trust for a specific purpose, with a contract, express or implied, that the trust shall be faithfully executed and the property returned or duly accounted for when the special purpose is accomplished, or kept until the bailor reclaims it.

Bailor   The maker of a bailment; one who delivers personal property to another to be held in bailment.

Bankruptcy   The state of a person who is unable to pay his or her debts without respect to time; one whose liabilities exceeds his or her assets.

Bar   As a collective noun, it is used to include those persons who are admitted to practice law, members of the bar. The court itself. A plea or peremptory exception of a defendant sufficient to destroy the plaintiff's action.

Barratry   The habitual stirring up of quarrels and suits; a single act would not constitute the offense.

Bearer   The designation of the bearer as the payee of a negotiable instrument signifies that the instrument is payable to the person who seems to be the holder.

Bench   A court; the judges of a court; the seat on which the judges of a court are accustomed to sit while the court is in session.

Beneficiary   The person for whose benefit an insurance policy, trust, will, or contract is established but not the promisee. In the case of a contract, the beneficiary is called a third-party beneficiary. A donee beneficiary is one who is not a party to a contract but who receives the promised performance as a gift. A creditor beneficiary is one who is not a party to a contract but receives the performance in discharge of a debt owed by the promisee to him.

Bequeath   Commonly used to denote a testamentary gift of real estate; synonymous with "to devise."

Bid   To make an offer at an auction or at a judicial sale. As a noun, it means an offer.

Bilateral Contract   A contract in which the promise of one of the parties forms the consideration for the promise of the other; a contract formed by an offer requiring a reciprocal promise.

Bill of Exchange   An unconditional order in writing by one person to another, signed by the person giving it, requiring the person to whom it is addressed to pay on demand or at a fixed or determinable future time a sum certain in money to order or to bearer.

Bill of Lading   A written acknowledgment of the receipt of goods to be transported to a designated place and delivery to a named person or to his or her order.

Bill of Sale   A written agreement by which one person assigns or transfers interests or rights in personal property to another.

Binder   Also called a binding slip—brief memorandum or agreement issued by an issuer as a temporary policy for the convenience of all the parties, constituting a present insurance in the amount specified, to continue in force until the execution of a formal policy.

"Blue Sky" Laws   A popular name for statutes regulating the sale of securities and intended to protect investors against fraudulent and visionary schemes.

Board Initiative   The board of directors' act of proposing a matter. This is required in any fundamental corporate change.

Bona Fide   Good faith.

Bond   A promise under seal to pay money.

Breaking Bulk   The division or separation of the contents of a package or container.

Brief   A statement of a party's case; usually an abridgement of either the plaintiff's or defendant's case prepared by his or her attorneys for use of counsel in a trial at law. Also, an abridgment of a reported case.

Broker   An agent who bargains or carries on negotiations in behalf of the principal as an intermediary between the latter and third persons in transacting business relative to the acquisition of contractual rights, or to the sale or purchase of property the custody of which is not intrusted to him or her for the purpose of discharging the agency.

Bulk Transfer   The sale or transfer of a major part of the stock of goods of a merchant at one time and not in the ordinary course of business.

Burden of Proof   The necessity or obligation of affirmatively proving the fact or facts in dispute on an issue raised in a suit in court.

Buyout   The purchase of a corporation.

Buyer in Ordinary Course of Business   A person who, in good faith and without knowledge that the sale to him is in violation of a third party's ownership rights or security interest in the goods, buys in ordinary course from a person who is in the business of selling goods of that kind.

Bylaw   A rule or law of a corporation for its government. It includes all self-made regulations of a corporation affecting its business and members that do not operate on third persons, or in any way affect their rights.

Call   A notice of a meeting to be held by the stockholders or board of directors of a corporation. Also, a demand for payment. In securities trading, a negotiable option contract granting the bearer the right to buy a certain quantity of a particular security at the agreed price on or before the agreed date.

Cancellation   The act of crossing out a writing. The operation of destroying a written instrument.

Capacity   The ability to incur legal obligations and acquire legal rights.

Caption   The heading or title of a document.

Carte Blanche A signed blank instrument intended by the signer to be filled in and used by another person without restriction.

Case Law The law extracted from decided cases.

Cashier's Check A bill of exchange, drawn by a bank on itself, and accepted by the act of issuance.

Cause of Action A right to action at law arises from the existence of a primary right in the plaintiff, and an invasion of that right by some civil wrong on the part of the defendant; the facts that establish the existence of that right and that civil wrong constitute the cause of action.

Caveat Emptor Let the buyer beware. This maxim expresses the general idea that the buyer purchases at his peril, and that there are no warranties, either express or implied, made by the seller.

Caveat Venditor Let the seller beware. It is not accepted as a rule of law in the law of sales.

Cease and Desist Order An administrative order prohibiting a party from doing something.

Certification The return of a writ; a formal attestation of a matter of fact; the appropriate marking of a certified check.

Certified Check A check that has been "accepted" by the drawee bank and has been so marked or certified that it indicates such acceptance.

Cestui Que Trust The person for whose benefit property is held in trust by a trustee.

Champerty The purchase of an interest in a matter in dispute so as to take part in the litigation.

Chancellor A judgment of a court of chancery.

Chancery Equity or a court of equity.

Charge To charge a jury is to instruct the jury as to the essential law of the case. The first step in the prosecution of a crime is to formally accuse the offender or charge him with the crime.

Charter An instrument or authority from the sovereign power bestowing the right or power to do business under the corporate form of organization. Also the organic law of a city or town, and representing a portion of the statute law of the state.

Chattel An article of tangible property other than land.

Chattel Mortgage An instrument whereby the owner of chattels transfers the title to such property to another as security for the performance of an obligation subject to be defeated on the performance of the obligation. Under the UCC, called merely a security interest.

Chattel Real Interests in real estate less than a freehold, such as an estate for years.

Check A written order on a bank or banker payable on demand to the person named or his order or bearer and drawn by virtue of credits due the drawer from the bank created by money deposited with the bank.

Choice-of-Law The law a court decides to use based on the agreement between parties or location of events or parties.

Chose in Action A personal right not reduced to possession but recoverable by a suit at law.

C.I.F. An abbreviation for cost, freight, and insurance, used in mercantile transactions, especially in import transactions.

Citation A writ issued out of a court of competent jurisdiction, commanding the person therein named to appear on a day named to do something therein mentioned.

Citation of Authorities The reference to legal authorities such as reported cases or treatises to support propositions advanced.

Civil Action An action brought to enforce a civil right; in contrast to a criminal action.

Class Action An action brought on behalf of the plaintiff and others similarly situated.

Close Corporation A corporation in which directors and officers, rather than the shareholders, have the right to fill vacancies occurring in their ranks. Also used to refer to any corporation whose stock is not freely traded and whose shareholders are personally known to each other.

C.O.D. "Cash on Delivery" When goods are delivered to a carrier for a cash on delivery shipment, the carrier must not deliver without receiving payment of the amount due.

Code A system of law; a systematic and complete body of law.

Codicil Some addition to or qualification of one's last will and testament.

Cognovit To acknowledge an action. A cognovit note is a promissory note that contains an acknowledgment clause.

Collateral Property put up to secure the performance of a promise, so that if the promisor fails to perform as promised, the creditor may look to the property to make him whole.

Collateral Attack An attempt to impeach a decree, a judgment, or other official act in a proceeding that has not been instituted for the express purpose of correcting or annulling or modifying the decree, judgment, or official act.

Collateral Contract A contract in which one person agrees to pay the debt of another if the principal debtor fails to pay. See *Guaranty*.

Comaker A person who with another or others signs a negotiable instrument on its face and thereby becomes primarily liable for its payment.

that it had been previously dishonored, if such was the fact; (3) that he took it in good faith and for value; (4) that at the time it was negotiated to him he had no notice of any infirmity in the instrument or defect in the title of the person negotiating it.

Holding Company   A corporation whose purpose or function is to own or otherwise hold the shares of other corporations either for investment or control.

Homestead   In a legal sense, the word means the real estate occupied as a home and also the right to have it exempt from levy and forced sale. It is the land, not exceeding the prescribed amount, on which the dwelling house, or residence, or habitation, or abode of the owner thereof and his family resides, and includes the dwelling house as an indispensable part.

Illusory   Deceiving or intending to deceive, as by false appearances; fallacious. An illusory promise is a promise that appears to be binding but that in fact does not bind the promisor.

Immunity   A personal favor granted by law, contrary to the general rule.

Impanel   To place the names of the jurors on a panel; to make a list of the names of those persons who have been selected for jury duty; to go through the process of selecting a jury that is to try a cause.

Implied Warranty   An implied warranty arises by operation of law and exists without any intention of the seller to create it. It is a conclusion or inference of law, pronounced by the court, on facts admitted or proved before the jury.

Inalienable   Incapable of being alienated, transferred, or conveyed; nontransferable.

in Camera   In the judge's chambers; in private.

Incapacity   In its legal meaning, it applies to one's legal disability, such as infancy, want of authority, or other personal incapacity to alter a legal relationship.

Inception   Initial stage. The word does not refer to a state of actual existence but to a condition of things or circumstances from which the thing may develop; as the beginning of work on a building.

Inchoate   Imperfect; incipient; not completely formed.

Indemnify   To hold harmless against loss or damage.

Indemnity   An obligation or duty resting on one person to make good any loss or damage another has incurred while acting at his request or for his benefit. By a contract of indemnity one may agree to saving another from a legal consequence of the conduct of one of the parties or of some other person.

Indenture   Indentures were deeds that originally were made in two parts, formed by cutting or tearing a single sheet across the middle in a jagged or indented line, so that the two parts might be subsequently matched; and they were executed by both grantor and grantee. Later, the indenting of the deed was discontinued, yet the term came to be applied to all deeds that were executed by both parties.

Independent Contractor   One who, exercising an independent employment, contracts to do a piece of work according to his or her own methods, and without being subject to the control of the employer except as to result. The legal effect is to insulate the employing party from liability for the misconduct of the independent contractor and his employees.

Indictment   An accusation founded on legal testimony of a direct and positive character, and the concurring judgment of at least 12 of the grand jurors that on the evidence presented to them the defendant is guilty.

Indorsement   Writing on the back of an instrument; the contract whereby the holder of a bill or note transfers to another person his right to such instrument and incurs the liabilities incident to the transfer.

Infant   See Minor.

Information   A written accusation of crime brought by a public prosecuting officer to a court without the intervention of a grand jury.

Injunction   A restraining order issued by a court of equity; a prohibitory writ restraining a person from committing or doing an act, other than a criminal act, that appears to be against equity and conscience. There is also the mandatory injunction that commands an act to be done or undone and compels the performance of some affirmative act.

in Pari Delicto   Equally at fault in tort or crime; in equal fault or guilt.

in Personam   Against the person.

in re   In the matter; in the transaction.

in rem   Against a thing and not against a person; concerning the condition or status of a thing.

Inside Information   Confidential information possessed by a person due to his relationship with a business.

Insolvency   The word has two distinct meanings. It may be used to denote the insufficiency of the entire property and assets of an individual to pay his or her debts, which is its general meaning and its meaning as used in the Bankruptcy Act; but in a more restricted sense, it expresses the inability of a party to pay his debts as they become due in the regular course of his business, and it is so used when traders and merchants are said to be insolvent.

in Statu Quo   In the existing state of things.

Instrument   In its broadest sense, the term includes formal or legal documents in writing, such as contracts, deeds, wills, bonds, leases, and mortgages. In the law of evidence, it has still a wider meaning and includes not merely documents but witnesses and things animate and inanimate that may be presented for inspection.

Insurable Interest   Any interest in property the owner of which interest derives a benefit from the existence of the property or would suffer a loss from its destruction. It is not necessary, to constitute an insurable interest, that the interest is such that the event insured against would necessarily subject the insured to loss; it is sufficient that it might do so.

Inter Alia   Among other things or matters.

Interlocutory   Something not final but deciding only some subsidiary matter raised while a lawsuit is pending.

Interpleader   An equitable remedy applicable where one fears injury from conflicting claims. Where a person does not know which of two or more persons claiming certain property held by him or her has a right to it, filing a bill of interpleader forces the claimants to litigate the title between themselves.

Inter Se   Among themselves.

Intervention   A proceeding by which one not originally made a party to an action or suit is permitted, on his own application, to appear therein and join one of the original parties in maintaining his cause of action or defense, or to assert some cause of action against some or all of the parties to the proceeding as originally instituted.

Intestate   A person who has died without leaving a valid will disposing of his or her property and estate.

in Toto   In the whole, altogether, wholly.

in Transitu   On the journey. Goods are as a rule considered as in transitu while they are in the possession of a carrier, whether by land or water, until they arrive at the ultimate place of their destination and are delivered into the actual possession of the buyer, whether or not the carrier has been named or designated by the buyer.

Ipso Facto   By the fact itself; by the very fact; by the act itself.

Joint Bank Account   A bank account of two persons so fixed that they shall be joint owners thereof during their mutual lives, and the survivor shall take the whole on the death of the other.

Jointly   Acting together or in concert or cooperating; holding in common or interdependently, not separately. Persons are "jointly bound" in a bond or note when both or all must be sued in one action for its enforcement, not either one at the election of the creditor.

Jointly and Severally   Persons who find themselves "jointly and severally" in a bond or note may all be sued together for its enforcement, or the creditor may select any one or more as the object of his suit.

Joint Tenancy   An estate held by two or more jointly, with an equal right in all to share in the enjoyments of the land during their lives. Four requisites must exist to constitute a joint tenancy: the tenants must have one and the same interest; the interest must accrue by one and the same conveyance; they must commence at one and the same time; and the property must be held by one and the same undivided possession. If any one of these four elements is lacking, the estate will not be one of joint tenancy. An incident of joint tenancy is the right of survivorship.

Judgment   The sentence of the law on the record; the application of the law to the facts and pleadings. The last word in the judicial controversy; the final consideration and determination of a court of competent jurisdiction on matters submitted to it in an action or proceeding.

Judgment Lien   The statutory lien on the real property of a judgment debtor that is created by the judgment itself. At common law a judgment imposes no lien on the real property of the judgment debtor, and to subject the property of the debtor to the judgment it was necessary to take out a writ called an elegit.

Judgment N.O.V. (judgment non obstante veredicto)   Judgment notwithstanding the verdict. Under certain circumstances, the judge has the power to enter a judgment that is contrary to the verdict of the jury. Such a judgment is a judgment non obstante veredicto.

Jurisdiction   The right to adjudicate concerning the subject matter in a given case. The modern tendency is to make the word include not only the power to hear and determine but also the power to render the particular judgment in the particular case.

Jury   A body of lay persons, selected by lot, or by some other fair and impartial means, to ascertain, under the guidance of the judge, the truth in questions of fact arising either in civil litigation or a criminal process.

Kite   To secure the temporary use of money by issuing or negotiating worthless paper and then redeeming such paper with the proceeds of similar paper. The word is also used as a noun, meaning the worthless paper thus employed.

Laches   The established doctrine of equity that, apart from any question of statutory limitation, its courts will discourage delay and sloth in the enforcement of rights. Equity demands conscience, good faith, and reasonable diligence.

Law Merchant   The custom of merchants, or lex mercatorio, that grew out of the necessity and convenience of business, and that, although different from the general rules of the common law, was engrafted into it and became part of it. It was founded on the custom and usage of merchants.

Leading Case A case often referred to by the courts and by counsel as having settled and determined a point of law.

Leading Questions Those questions that suggest to the witness the answer desired, assume a fact to be proved that is not proved, or, embodying a material fact, admit of an answer by a simple negative or affirmative.

Lease A contract for the possession and use of land on one side, and a recompense of rent or other income on the other, a conveyance to a person for life, or years, or at will in consideration of a return of rent or other recompense.

Legacy A bequest; a testamentary gift of personal property. Sometimes incorrectly applied to a testamentary gift of real property.

Legal According to the principles of law; according to the method required by statute; by means of judicial proceedings; not equitable.

Legitimacy A person's status embracing his right to inherit from his ancestors, to be inherited from, and to bear the name and enjoy the support of his father.

Lemon Law A type of state consumer protection law.

Letter of Credit An instrument containing a request (general or special) to pay to the bearer or person named money, or sell him or her some commodity on credit or give something of value and look to the drawer of the letter for recompense.

Levy At common law, a levy on goods consisted of an officer's entering the premises where they were and either leaving an assistant in charge of them or removing them after taking an inventory. Today, courts differ as to what is a valid levy, but by the weight of authority there must be an actual or constructive seizure of the goods. In most states, a levy on land must be made by some unequivocal act of the officer indicating the intention of singling out certain real estate for the satisfaction of the debt.

License A personal privilege to do some act or series of acts on the land of another, without possessing any estate therein. A permit or authorization to do what, without a license, would be unlawful.

Lien In its most extensive meaning, it is a charge on property for the payment or discharge of a debt or duty; a qualified right; a proprietary interest that, in a given case, may be exercised over the property of another.

Life Estate See Estate for Life.

Limited Liability Company A form of organization that is neither corporation nor partnership, but has elements of both.

Limited Partnership A form of business organization that has one or more general partners who manage the business and have unlimited liability for the obligations of the business and one or more limited partners who do not manage and have limited liability.

Lis Pendens A pending suit. As applied to the doctrine of lis pendens, it is the jurisdiction, power, or control that courts acquire over property involved in a suit, pending the continuance of the action, and until its final judgment therein.

Listing Contract A so-called contract whereby an owner of real property employs a broker to procure a purchaser without giving the broker an exclusive right to sell. Under such an agreement, it is generally held that the employment may be terminated by the owner at will, and that a sale of the property by the owner terminates the employment.

Litigant A party to a lawsuit.

Long Arm Statute A statute subjecting a foreign corporation to jurisdiction although it may have committed only a single act within the state.

Magistrate A word commonly applied to lower judicial officers such as justices of the peace, police judges, town recorders, and other local judicial functionaries. In a broader sense, a magistrate is a public civil officer invested with some part of the legislative, executive, or judicial power given by the Constitution. The President of the United States is the chief magistrate of the nation.

Maker A person who makes or executes an instrument, the signer of an instrument.

Mala Fides Bad faith.

Malfeasance The doing of an act that a person ought not to do at all. It is to be distinguished from misfeasance, which is the improper doing of an act that a person might lawfully do.

Malicious Prosecution An intentional tort designed to protect against the wrongful initiation of criminal proceedings.

Malum in Se Evil in and of itself. An offense or act that is naturally evil as adjudged by the senses of a civilized community. Acts malum in se are usually criminal acts but not necessarily so.

Malum Prohibitum An act that is wrong because it is made so by statute.

Mandamus We command. It is a command issuing from a competent jurisdiction, in the name of the state or sovereign, directed to some inferior court, officer, corporation, or person, requiring the performance of a particular duty therein specified, which duty results from the official station of the party to whom it is directed, or from operation of law.

Margin A deposit by a buyer in stocks with a seller or a stockbroker, as security to cover fluctuations in the market in reference to stocks that the buyer has purchased but for which he has not paid. Commodities are also traded on margin.

Marshals   Ministerial officers belonging to the executive department of the federal government, who with their deputies have the same powers of executing the laws of the United States in each state as the sheriffs and their deputies in such state may have in executing the laws of that state.

Material   Important. In securities law, a fact is material if a reasonable person would consider it important in his decision to purchase shares or to vote shares.

Mechanic's Lien   A claim created by law for the purpose of securing a priority of payment of the price of value of work performed and materials furnished in erecting or repairing a building or other structure; as such, it attaches to the land as well as to the buildings erected therein.

Mediation   A form of dispute resolution in which the disputing parties resolve their dispute with the help of a third party, the mediator.

Mens Rea   A guilty mind, criminal intent.

Merchant   Under the Uniform Commercial Code, one who regularly deals in goods of the kind sold in the contract at issue, or holds himself out as having special knowledge or skill relevant to such goods, or who makes the sale through an agent who regularly deals in such goods or claims such knowledge or skill.

Merchantable   Of good quality and salable, but not necessarily the best. As applied to articles sold, the word requires that the article shall be such as is usually sold in the market, of medium quality, and bringing the average price.

Merger   In corporation law, traditionally, a transaction by which one corporation acquires another corporation, with the acquiring corporation being owned by the shareholders of both corporations and the acquired corporation going out of existence. Today, loosely applied to any negotiated acquisition of one corporation by another.

Minitrial   A form of dispute resolution in which the disputants voluntarily hear a shortened version of their cases presented by their lawyers, then try to negotiate a settlement.

Minor   A person who has not reached the age at which the law recognizes a general contractual capacity (called majority), formerly 21 years; recently changed to 18 in many states.

Misdemeanor   Any crime that is punishable neither by death nor by imprisonment in a state prison.

Mistrial   An invalid trial due to lack of jurisdiction, error in selection of jurors, or some other fundamental requirement.

Mitigation of Damages   A reduction in the amount of damages due to extenuating circumstances.

Moiety   One half.

Mortgage   A conveyance of property to secure the performance of some obligation, the conveyance to be void on the due performance thereof.

Motive   The cause or reason that induced a person to commit a crime.

Movables   A word derived from the civil law and usually understood to signify the utensils that are to furnish or ornament a house, but it would seem to comprehend personal property generally.

Mutuality   Reciprocal obligations of the parties required to make a contract binding on either party.

Necessaries   With reference to a minor, the word includes whatever is reasonably necessary for his or her proper and suitable maintenance, in view of the income level and social position of the minor's family.

Negligence   The word has been defined as the omission to do something that a reasonable person, guided by those considerations that ordinarily regulate human affairs, would do, or doing something that a prudent and reasonable person would not do.

Negotiable   Capable of being transferred by indorsement or delivery so as to give the holder a right to sue in his or her own name and to avoid certain defenses against the payee.

Negotiable Instrument   An instrument that may be transferred or negotiated, so that the holder may maintain an action thereon in his own name.

No Arrival, No Sale   A sale of goods "to arrive" or "on arrival," per or ex a certain ship, has been construed to be a sale subject to a double condition precedent, namely, that the ship arrives in port and that when it arrives the goods are on board, and if either of these conditions fails, the contract becomes nugatory.

Nolo Contendere   A plea in a criminal action that has the same effect as a guilty plea except that it does not bind the defendant in a civil suit on the same wrong.

Nominal Damages   See Damages.

Non Compos Mentis   Totally and positively incompetent. The term denotes a person entirely destitute or bereft of his memory or understanding.

Nonfeasance   In the law of agency, it is the total omission or failure of an agent to enter on the performance of some distinct duty or undertaking that he or she has agreed with the principal to do.

Non Obstante Veredicto   See Judgment Non Obstante Veredicto.

Nonsuit   A judgment given against a plaintiff who is unable to prove a case, or when the plaintiff refuses or neglects to proceed to trial.

No Par Value Stock   Stock of a corporation having no face or par value.

Notice   A person has notice of a fact if she knows it, has reason to know it, or has been given proper notification of it.

Noting Protest   The act of making a memorandum on a bill or note at the time of, and embracing the principal facts attending, its dishonor. The object is to have a record from which the instrument of protest may be written, so that a notary need not rely on his memory for the fact.

Novation   A mutual agreement, between all parties concerned, for the discharge of a valid obligation on the part of the debtor or another, or a like agreement for the discharge of a debtor to his creditor by the substitution of a new creditor.

Nudum Pactum   A naked promise, a promise for which there is no consideration.

Nuisance   In legal parlance, the word extends to everything that endangers life or health, gives offense to the senses, violates the laws of decency, or obstructs the reasonable and comfortable use of property.

Oath   Any form of attestation by which a person signifies that he is bound in conscience to perform an act faithfully and truthfully. It involves the idea of calling on God to witness what is averred as truth, and it is supposed to be accompanied with an invocation of His vengeance, or a renunciation of His favor, in the event of falsehood.

Obiter Dictum   That which is said in passing; a rule of law set forth in a court's opinion, but not necessary to decide the case.

Objection   In the trial of a case, it is the formal remonstrance made by counsel to something that has been said or done, in order to obtain the court's ruling thereon; and when the court has rules, the alleged error is preserved by the objector's exception to the ruling, which exception is noted in the record.

Obligee   A person to whom another is bound by a promise or other obligation; a promisee.

Obligor   A person who is bound by a promise or other obligation; a promisor.

Offer   A proposal by one person to another that is intended of itself to create legal relations on acceptance by the person to whom it is made.

Offeree   A person to whom an offer is made.

Offeror   A person who makes an offer.

Opinion   The opinion of the court represents merely the reasons for its judgment, while the decision of the court is the judgment itself.

Option   A contract whereby the owner of property agrees with another person that such person shall have the right to buy the property at a fixed price within a certain time. There are two independent elements in an option contract: First, the offer to sell, which does not become a contract until accepted; second, the completed contract to leave the offer open for a specified time.

Order   A court decree.

Ordinance   A legislative enactment of a county or an incorporated city or town.

Ostensible Authority   Such authority as a principal, either intentionally or by want or ordinary care, causes or allows a third person to believe the agent to possess.

Ostensible Partners   Members of a partnership whose names are made known and appear to the world as partners.

Overdraft   The withdrawal from a bank by a depositor of money in excess of the amount of money he or she has on deposit there.

Overplus   That which remains; a balance left over.

Owner's Risk   A term employed by common carriers in bills of lading and shipping receipts to signify that the carrier does not assume responsibility for the safety of the goods.

Par   Par means equal, and par value means a value equal to the face of a bond or a stock certificate.

Parol   Oral; verbal; by word of mouth; spoken as opposed to written.

Parties   All persons who are interested in the subject matter of an action and who have a right to make defense, control the proceedings, examine and cross-examine witnesses, and appeal from the judgment.

Partition   A proceeding the object of which is to enable those who own property as joint tenants or tenants in common to put an end to the tenancy so as to vest in each a sole estate in specific property or an allotment of the lands and tenements. If a division of the estate is impracticable, the estate ought to be sold and the proceeds divided.

Partners   Those persons who contribute property, money, or services to carry on a joint business for their common benefit, and who own and share the profits thereof in certain proportions; the members of a partnership.

Partnership   A form of business organization; specifically, an association of two or more persons to carry on as co-owners of a business for profit.

Patent   A patent for land is a conveyance of title to government lands by the government; a patent of an invention is the right of monopoly secured by statute to those who invent or discover new and useful devices and processes.

Pawn A pledge; a bailment of personal property as security for some debt or engagement, redeemable on certain terms, and with an implied power of sale on default.

Payee A person to whom a payment is made or is made payable.

Pecuniary Financial; pertaining or relating to money; capable of being estimated, computed, or measured by money value.

Pendente Lite During the litigation.

Per Curiam By the court; by the court as a whole.

Peremptory Challenge A challenge to a proposed juror that a defendant in a criminal case may make as an absolute right, and that cannot be questioned by either opposing counsel or the court.

Perfection The process or method by which a secured party obtains a priority in certain collateral belonging to a debtor against creditors or claimants of a debtor; it usually entails giving notice of the security interest, such as by taking possession or filing a financial statement.

Performance As the word implies, it is such a thorough fulfillment of a duty as puts an end to obligations by leaving nothing to be done. The chief requisite of performance is that it shall be exact.

Perjury The willful and corrupt false swearing or affirming, after an oath lawfully administered, in the course of a judicial or quasi-judicial proceeding as to some matter material to the issue or point in question.

Per Se The expression means by or through itself; simply; as such; in its own relations.

Petition In equity pleading, a petition is in the nature of a pleading (at least when filed by a stranger to the suit) and forms a basis for independent action.

Plaintiff A person who brings a suit, action, bill, or complaint.

Plaintiff in Error The unsuccessful part to the action who prosecutes a writ of error in a higher court.

Plea A plea is an answer to a declaration or complaint or any material allegation of fact therein that, if untrue, would defeat the action. In criminal procedure, a plea is the matter that the accused, on his arraignment, alleges in answer to the charge against him.

Pledge A pawn; a bailment of personal property as security for some debt or engagement, redeemable on certain terms, and with an implied power of sale on default.

Pledgee A person to whom personal property is pledged by a pledgor.

Pledgor A person who makes a pledge of personal property to a pledgee.

Polygraph A mechanical test used to help determine whether someone is telling the truth.

Positive Law Laws actually and specifically enacted or adopted by proper authority of the government of a jural society, as distinguished from principles of morality or laws of honor.

Possession Respecting real property, possession involves exclusive dominion and control such as owners of like property usually exercise over it. Manual control of personal property either as owner or as one having a qualified right in it.

Power of Attorney A written authorization to an agent to perform specified acts on behalf of his or her principal. The writing by which the authority is evidenced is termed a letter of attorney and is dictated by the convenience and certainty of business.

Precedent A previous decision relied on as authority.

Preemption A state or local law is stricken when federal legislation dealing with interstate commerce regulates the same activity (expressly) or when Congress has shown an intent to reserve such regulatory power (impliedly).

Preference The act of a debtor in paying or securing one or more of his creditors in a manner more favorable to them than to other creditors or to the exclusion of such other creditors. In the absence of statute, a preference is perfectly good, but to be legal it must be bona fide and not a mere subterfuge of the debtor to secure a future benefit to himself or to prevent the application of his property to his debts.

Prerogative A special power, privilege, or immunity, usually used in reference to an official or his office.

Presumption A term used to signify that which may be assumed without proof, or taken for granted. It is asserted as a self-evident result of human reason and experience.

Prima Facie At first sight; a fact that is presumed to be true unless disproved by contrary evidence.

Principal In agency law, one under whose direction an agent acts and for whose benefit that agent acts.

Priority Having precedence or the better right.

Privilege A right peculiar to an individual or body.

Privity A mutual or successive relationship as, for example, between the parties to a contract.

Probate A term used to include all matters of which probate courts have jurisdiction, which in many states are the estates of deceased persons and of persons under guardianship.

Proceeds Whatever is received on the sale, exchange, collection, or other disposition of collateral.

Process In law, generally the summons or notice of beginning of suit.

Proffer To offer for acceptance or to make a tender of.

Promisee The person to whom a promise is made.

Promisor   A person who makes a promise to another; a person who promises.

Promissory Estoppel   An estoppel arising on account of a promise that the promisor should expect to and which does induce an action or forbearance of a substantial nature.

Promoters   The persons who bring about the incorporation and organization of a corporation.

Pro Rata   According to the rate, proportion, or allowance.

Prospectus   An introductory proposal for a contract in which the representations may or may not form the basis of the contract actually made; it may contain promises that are to be treated as a sort of floating obligation to take effect when appropriated by persons to whom they are addressed, and amount to a contract when assented to by any person who invests his money on the faith of them.

Pro Tanto   For so much; to such an extent.

Proximate Cause   That cause of an injury that, in natural and continuous sequence, unbroken by any efficient intervening cause, produces the injury, and without which the injury would not have occurred.

Qualified Acceptance   A conditional or modified acceptance. In order to create a contract, an acceptance must accept the offer substantially as made; hence, a qualified acceptance is no acceptance at all, is treated by the courts as a rejection of the offer made, and is in effect an offer by the offeree, which the offeror may, if he chooses, accept and thus create a contract.

Quantum Meruit   As much as is deserved. A part of a common law action in assumpsit for the value of services rendered.

Quash   To vacate or make void.

Quasi Contract   An obligation arising not from an agreement between the parties but from the voluntary act of one of them or some relation between them that will be enforced by a court.

Quasi-Judicial   Acts of public officers involving investigation of facts and drawing conclusions from them as a basis of official action.

Quid Pro Quo   Something for something. The term is used in employment law to describe a form of sexual harassment in which a job benefit is conditioned on sexual favors.

Quiet Enjoyment   A tenant's right to use the leasehold in peace and without disturbance.

Quiet Title, Action to   An action to establish a claimant's title in land by requiring adverse claimants to come into court to prove their claim or to be barred from asserting it later.

Quitclaim Deed   A deed conveying only the right, title, and interest of the grantor in the property described, as distinguished from a deed conveying the property itself.

Quorum   That number of persons, shares represented, or officers who may lawfully transact the business of a meeting called for that purpose.

Quo Warranto   By what authority. The name of a writ (and also of the whole pleading) by which the government commences an action to recover an office or franchise from the person or corporation in possession of it.

Ratification   The adoption or affirmance by a person of a prior act that did not bind him.

Rebuttal   Testimony addressed to evidence produced by the opposite party; rebutting evidence.

Receiver   One appointed by a court to take charge of a business or the property of another during litigation to preserve it and/or to dispose of it as directed by the court.

Recognizance   At common law, an obligation entered into before some court of record or magistrate duly authorized, with a condition to do some particular act, usually to appear and answer to a criminal accusation. Being taken in open court and entered on the order book, it was valid without the signature or seal of any of the obligors.

Recorder   A public officer of a town or county charged with the duty of keeping the record books required by law to be kept in his or her office and of receiving and causing to be copied in such books such instruments as by law are entitled to be recorded.

Redemption   The buying back of one's property after it has been sold. The right to redeem property sold under an order or decree of court is purely a privilege conferred by, and does not exist independently of, statute.

Redress   Remedy; indemnity; reparation.

Release   The giving up or abandoning of a claim or right to a person against whom the claim exists or the right is to be enforced or exercised. It is the discharge of a debt by the act of the party, in distinction from an extinguishment that is a discharge by operation of law.

Remainderman   One who is entitled to the remainder of the estate after a particular estate carved out of it has expired.

Remand   An action of an appellate court returning a case to the trial court to take further action.

Remedy   The appropriate legal form of relief by which a remediable right may be enforced.

Remittitur   The certificate of reversal issued by an appellate court on reversing the order or judgment appealed from.

Replevin   A common law action by which the owner recovers possession of his own goods.

Repudiation   Indicating to another party to a contract that the party does not intend to perform his obligations.

Res   The thing; the subject matter of a suit; the property involved in the litigation; a matter; property; the business; the affair; the transaction.

Res Adjudicata   A matter that has been adjudicated; that which is definitely settled by a judicial decision.

Rescind   As the word is applied to contracts, to rescind in some cases means to terminate the contract as to future transactions, while in others it means to annul the contract from the beginning.

Residue   All that portion of the estate of a testator of which no effectual disposition has been made by his will otherwise than in the residuary clause.

Respondent   The defendant in an action; a party adverse to an appellant in an action that is appealed to a higher court. The person against whom a bill in equity was exhibited.

Restitution   Indemnification.

Reversion   The residue of a fee simple remaining in the grantor, to commence in possession after the determination of some particular estate granted out by him. The estate of a landlord during the existence of the outstanding leasehold estate.

Reversioner   A person who is entitled to a reversion.

Right   When we speak of a person having a right, we must necessarily refer to a civil right, as distinguished from the elemental idea of a right absolute. We must have in mind a right given and protected by law, and a person's enjoyment thereof is regulated entirely by the law that creates it.

Riparian   Pertaining to or situated on the bank of a river. The word has reference to the bank and not to the bed of the stream.

Sale of Goods   The transfer of ownership to tangible personal property in exchange for money, other goods, or the performance of service.

Sanction   The penalty that will be incurred by a wrongdoer for the breach of law.

Satisfaction   A performance of the terms of an accord. If such terms require a payment of a sum of money, then "satisfaction" means that such payment has been made.

Scienter   In cases of fraud and deceit, the word means knowledge on the part of the person making the representations, at the time when they are made, that they are false. In an action for deceit, it is generally held that scienter must be proved.

Seal   At common law, a seal is an impression on wax or some other tenacious material, but in modern practice the letters "l.s." (locus sigilli) or the word "seal" enclosed in a scroll, either written or printed, and acknowledged in

the body of the instrument to be a seal, are often used as substitutes.

Security   That which makes the enforcement of a promise more certain than the mere personal obligation of the debtor or promisor, whatever may be his possessions or financial standing. It may be a pledge of property or an additional personal obligation, but it means more than the mere promise of the debtor with property liable to general execution.

Security Agreement   An agreement that creates or provides a security interest or lien on personal property. A term used in the UCC including a wide range of transactions in the nature of chattel mortgages, conditional sales, and so on.

Security Interest   A lien given by a debtor to his creditor to secure payment or performance of a debt or obligation.

Seizin   In a legal sense, the word means possession of premises with the intention of asserting a claim to a freehold estate therein; it is practically the same thing as ownership; it is a possession of a freehold estate, such as by the common law is created by livery of seizin.

Sequester   To keep jurors under court supervision, day and night, until the end of a case.

Service   As applied to a process of courts, the word ordinarily implies something in the nature of an act or proceeding adverse to the party served, or of a notice to him.

Setoff   A setoff both at law and in equity is that right that exists between two parties, each of whom, under an independent contract, owes an ascertained amount to the other, to set off their respective debts by way of mutual deduction, so that, in any action brought for the larger debt, the residue only, after such deduction, shall be recovered.

Severable Contract   A contract that is not entire or indivisible. If the consideration is single, the contract is entire; but if it is expressly or by necessary implication apportioned, the contract is severable. The question is ordinarily determined by inquiring whether the contract embraces one or more subject matters, whether the obligation is due at the same time to the same person, and whether the consideration is entire or apportioned.

Shareholder   It is generally held that one who holds shares on the books of the corporation is a shareholder and that one who merely holds a stock certificate is not. Shareholders may become such either by original subscription, by direct purchase from the corporation, or by subsequent transfer from the original holder.

Share of Stock   The right that its owner has in the management, profits, and ultimate assets of the corporation. The tangible property of a corporation and the shares of stock therein are separate and distinct kinds of property and belong to different owners, the first being the property of an artificial person—the corporation; the latter the property of the individual owner.

Sight   A term signifying the date of the acceptance or that of protest for the nonacceptance of a bill of exchange; for example, 10 days after sight.

Sinking Fund   A fund accumulated by an issuer to redeem corporate securities.

Situs   Location; local position; the place where a person or thing is, is his situs. Intangible property has no actual situs, but it may have a legal situs and for the purpose of taxation its legal situs is at the place where it is owned and not at the place where it is owed.

Sole Proprietorship   A form of business under which one person owns and controls the business.

Sovereign Immunity   Generally, the idea that the sovereign (or state) may not be used unless it consents to such a suit.

Specific Performance   Performance of a contract precisely as agreed on; the remedy that arose in equity law to compel the defendant to do what he agreed to do.

Stare Decisis   The doctrine or principle that the decisions of the court should stand as precedents for future guidance.

Stated Capital   Defined specifically in the Model Business Corporation Act; generally, the amount received by a corporation on issuance of its shares except that assigned to capital surplus.

Status Quo   The existing state of things.

Statute of Limitations   A statute that requires that certain classes of lawsuits must be brought within defined limits of time after the right to begin them accrued or the right to bring the lawsuit is lost.

Stay   To hold an order or decree in abeyance.

Stipulation   An agreement between opposing counsel in a pending action, usually required to be made in open court and entered on the minutes of the court, or else to be in writing and filed in the action, ordinarily entered into for the purpose of avoiding delay, trouble, or expense in the conduct of the action.

Stockholder   See Shareholder.

Stoppage in Transitu   A right that the vendor of goods on credit has to recall them, or retake them, on the discovery of the insolvency of the vendee. It continues so long as the carrier remains in the possession and control of the goods or until there has been an actual or constructive delivery to the vendee, or some third person has acquired a bona fide right in them.

Strict Liability   Legal responsibility placed on an individual for the results of his actions irrespective of whether he was culpable or at fault.

Sub Judice   Before a court.

Sub Nom   Under the name.

Subpoena   A process the purpose of which is to compel the attendance of a person whom it is desired to use as a witness.

Subrogation   The substitution of one person in the place of another with reference to a lawful claim or right, frequently referred to as the doctrine of substitution. It is a device adopted or invented by equity to compel the ultimate discharge of a debt or obligation by the person who in good conscience ought to pay it.

Sui Generis   Of its own kind; peculiar to itself.

Summary Judgment   A decision of a trial court without hearing evidence.

Summary Proceedings   Proceedings, usually statutory, in the course of which many formalities are dispensed with. But such proceedings are not concluded without proper investigation of the facts, or without notice, or an opportunity to be heard by the person alleged to have committed the act, or whose property is sought to be affected.

Summons   A writ or process issued and served on a defendant in a civil action for the purpose of securing his appearance in the action.

Supra   Above; above mentioned; in addition to.

Surety   One who by accessory agreement, called a contract of suretyship, binds himself with another, called the principal, for the performance of an obligation in respect to which such other person is already bound and primarily liable for such performance.

T/A   Trading as, indicating the use of a trade name.

Tacking   The adding together of successive periods of adverse possession of persons in privity with each other, in order to constitute one continuous adverse possession for the time required by the statute, to establish title.

Tangible   Capable of being possessed or realized; readily apprehensible by the mind; real; substantial; evident.

Tariff   A custom or duty imposed on foreign merchandise imported into a country.

Tenancy   A tenancy exists when one has let real estate to another to hold of him as landlord. When duly created and the tenant put into possession, he is the owner of an estate for the time being, and has all the usual rights and remedies to defend his possession.

Tender   An unconditional offer of payment, consisting in the actual production in money or legal tender of a sum not less than the amount due.

Tender Offer   An offer to security holders to acquire their securities in exchange for money or other securities.

Tenement   A word commonly used in deeds that passes not only lands and other inheritances but also offices, rents, commons, and profits arising from lands. Usually it is applied exclusively to land, or what is ordinarily denominated real property.

Tenor The tenor of an instrument is an exact copy of the instrument. Under the rule that an indictment for forgery must set out in the instrument according to its "tenor," the word means an exact copy that the instrument is set forth in the very words and figures.

Tenure The manner of holding or occupying lands or offices. The most common estate in land is tenure in "fee simple." With respect to offices, tenure imports time, for example, "tenure for life" or "during good behavior."

Testament A last will and testament is the disposition of one's property to take effect after death.

Testator A deceased person who died leaving a will.

Testatrix Feminine of testator.

Testimony In some context, the word bears the same import as the word "evidence," but in most connections it has a much narrower meaning. Testimony is the words heard from the witness in court, and evidence is what the jury considers it worth.

Title Legal ownership; also, a document evidencing legal rights to real or personal property.

Time is of the Essence A contract clause which allows a court to deem late performance a material breach unless the penalty on the promisor would be unjust. A court may imply time of the essence if late performance would be of little or no value to the promisee.

Tippee A person who is given information by insiders in breach of trust.

Tort An injury or wrong committed, either with or without force, to the person or property of another. Such injury may arise by nonfeasance, or by the malfeasance or the misfeasance of the wrongdoer.

Tort-Feasor A person who commits a tort; a wrongdoer.

Tortious Partaking of the nature of a tort; wrongful; injurious.

Trade Fixtures Articles of personal property that have been annexed to the freehold and that are necessary to the carrying on of a trade.

Trade Secret A secret formula, pattern, process, program, device, method, technique, or compilation of information that is used in its owner's business and affords that owner a competitive advantage. Trade secrets are protected by state law.

Transcript A copy of a writing.

Transferee A person to whom a transfer is made.

Transferor A person who makes a transfer.

Treasury Shares Shares of stock of a corporation that have been issued as fully paid to shareholders and subsequently acquired by the corporation.

Treble Damages Three times provable damages, as may be granted to private parties bringing an action under the antitrust laws.

Trespass Every unauthorized entry on another's property is a trespass and any person who makes such an entry is a trespasser. In its widest signification, trespass means any violation of law. In its most restricted sense, it signifies an injury intentionally inflicted by force either on the person or property of another.

Trial An examination before a competent tribunal, according to the law of the land, of the facts or law put in issue in a cause, for the purpose of determining such issue. When the court hears and determines any issue of fact or law for the purpose of determining the rights of the parties, it may be considered a trial.

Trover A common law action for damages due to a conversion of personal property.

Trust A confidence reposed in one person, who is termed trustee, for the benefit of another, who is called the cestui que trust, respecting property that is held by the trustee for the benefit of the cestui que trust. As the word is used in the law pertaining to unlawful combinations and monopolies, a trust in its original and typical form is a combination formed by an agreement among the shareholders in a number of competing corporations to transfer their shares to an unincorporated board of trustees, and to receive in exchange trust certificates in some agreed proportion to their shareholdings.

Trustee A person in whom property is vested in trust for another.

Trustee in Bankruptcy The federal bankruptcy act defines the term as an officer, and she is an officer of the courts in a certain restricted sense but not in any such sense as a receiver. She takes the legal title to the property of the bankrupt and in respect to suits stands in the same general position as a trustee of an express trust or an executor. Her duties are fixed by statute. She is to collect and reduce to money the property of the estate of the bankrupt.

Ultra Vires Act An act of a corporation that is beyond the powers conferred on the corporation.

Unilateral Contract A contract formed by an offer or a promise on one side for an act to be done on the other, and a doing of the act by the other by way of acceptance of the offer or promise; that is, a contract wherein the only acceptance of the offer that is necessary is the performance of the act.

plea   alegato
polygraph   aparato para detector mentiras
positive law   ley positive
post dated check   cheque posfechado
Power of Attorney   poder actual
precedent   precedente
privity   relacion juridical o contractual
probate   validacion de testamento
promise   a quien se promete
promisor   prometedor
promissory estoppel   impedimento promisorio
promoters   promotores
prospectus   prospecto
proximate cause   causa immediata
quasi contract   cuasicontracto
ratification   ratificacion
rebuttal   refutación
recorder   registrador, grabador
redemption   redención
remand   devolver
remedy   remedio
res   asunto
respondent   respondiente
satisfaction   satisfaction
scienter   a sabiendas
security agreement   accuerdo de seguridad
shareholder   accionista
sovereign immunity   inmunidad soberana
specific performance   ejecucion de lo
   estipulado en un contrato
State Capital   dicha capital
stare decisis   acaturse a los precedentas
   judiciales

status quo   el estado de las cosas en un momento
   dado
stockholder   accionista
subpoena   citacion
summary judgment   sentencia sumaria
summons   emplazamiento
testimony   testimonio
tort   daño legal
tortious   dañoso
trial   jucio
transcript   transcripción
treble damages   danos triplcados
trustee in bankruptcy   sindico concursal
unliquidated debt   deuda no liquidado
ultra vires act   acta fuera de la facultead de una
   corporacion
usury   usura
venue   lugar de jurisdicción
verdict   verdicto
versus   contra
void   nulo
voidable   anulable
waive   renunciar
waiver   renuncia
warranty   garantia
whistleblowing   un empleado que informa sobre
   actividades ilicitas en su empresa
writ   orden judicial
writ of certiorari   auto de avocación
writ of executional (or garnishment)
   ejecutoria, mandamiento de ejecución

SUBJECT INDEX